Grilliot's Introduction to Law and the Legal System

Grilliot's Introduction to Law and the Legal System

Sixth Edition

Frank A. Schubert

NORTHEASTERN UNIVERSITY

Houghton Mifflin Company   Boston   Toronto

Geneva, Illinois   Palo Alto

Princeton, New Jersey

Editor-in-Chief: Bonnie Binkert
Editorial Assistant: Joan Horan
Editorial Production Manager: Nancy Doherty Schmitt
Editorial Assistant: Kate Burden
Senior Production/Design Coordinator: Sarah Ambrose
Senior Manufacturing Coordinator: Marie Barnes
Marketing Manager: Michael Mercier

Cover Designer: Len Massiglia, LMA Communications
Cover Image: Steve Dunwell/The Image Bank

Printed in the U.S.A.

Library of Congress catalog number: 95–76945

ISBN: 0–395–746663
Examination Copy ISBN: 0–395–764955

23456789–QM–99 98 97 96

To Glendon Schubert, my father, to honor his fifty years of college teaching.

—F.A.S.

Contents

Preface   xxiii

I INTRODUCTION   1

WHAT IS LAW?   1
Law as Power   1
Natural Law   2
Historical Jurisprudence   2
Utilitarian Law   3
Analytical Positivism   4
Legal Realism   5
Sociological Jurisprudence and Legal Sociology   5

OBJECTIVES OF LAW   6
Continuity and Stability   6
Adaptability   7
Justice, Speed, and Economy   7
Determining Desirable Public Policy   8

ORIGIN OF LAW IN THE UNITED STATES   9
The Origins of English Common Law   9
The Norman Invasion   10

The Development of the Common Law   11

The Origin of the English Equitable Court   13

READING CASES   15
  E.I. Du Pont de Nemours & Co., Inc. v. Christopher   15

CASE ANALYSIS   19

Sample Brief   21

CONSTITUTIONAL POLICYMAKING   23
  Cruzan v. Director, Missouri Dept. of Health   23

DUE PROCESS   30

Substantive Due Process   31

Substantive Due Process and Economic and Social Regulation   32

The Scope of Substantive Due Process   33
  Kolender, Chief of Police of San Diego, v. Lawson   33

Procedural Due Process   37
  Goss v. Lopez   38

CRIMINAL AND CIVIL LAW   42
  Katko v. Briney   44

TORT AND CONTRACT LAW   49

Torts   49

Contracts   49
  Suggs v. Norris   50

Chapter Questions   53
Notes   56

II THE JUDICIAL SYSTEM   59

COURTS   59

Trial Courts   60

Appellate Courts   61

STATE COURT SYSTEMS   62

JURISDICTION   62

Subject Matter Jurisdiction in State Court   63
  *In the Matter of the Application of Arthur Hyde RICE to Register and
  Confirm Title to Land Situated in Kailua, District of Koolaupoko, Oahu,
  City and County of Honolulu, State of Hawaii*   64

Jurisdiction Over the Person   65

Long-Arm Statutes   66

In Personam Jurisdiction Over Corporations   67

Jurisdiction Over Property—*In Rem* Jurisdiction   69

Procedural Due Process Requirements   69
   Calder v. Jones   69

Venue   72
   In re Union Carbide Corporation Gas Plant Disaster at Bhopal, India, in December 1984   73

THE FEDERAL COURT SYSTEM   77

THE U.S. DISTRICT COURTS   77

Subject Matter Jurisdiction   77

The Plaintiff's Choice of Forum   79
   Ramírez de Arellano v. Eastern Airlines, Inc.   79

In Rem or *In Personam* Jurisdiction   83

Venue in Federal Courts   83

Removal from State to Federal Courts (Removal Jurisdiction)   83
   Gatch v. Hennepin Broadcasting Associates, Inc.   84

The *Erie* Doctrine   85
   Carson v. National Bank   86

THE 13 U.S. COURTS OF APPEALS   88

THE U.S. SUPREME COURT   89

Chapter Questions   92
Notes   95

III CIVIL PROCEDURE   96

A PROCEDURAL PRIMER   97

PROCEEDINGS BEFORE A CIVIL TRIAL—A CLOSER LOOK   100

Hiring a Lawyer   100
   Fracasse v. Brent   101

The Pleadings   105

Methods of Service   107
   Dorsey v. Gregg   109

Pretrial Motions   110
   Meyers v. Ramada Hotel and Operating Co., Inc.   111

Discovery and Pretrial Conference   114
   Downey v. Dixon   *115*

CIVIL TRIALS   117

Selection of the Jury   117

Opening Statements and Examination of Witnesses   119
   Alexander v. Chapman   *121*

RULES OF EVIDENCE   125

Relevance and Materiality   125

Competency   125

The Best Evidence Rule   126

The Hearsay Rule   126

Privileges   126
   Cline v. William H. Friedman & Assoc.   *127*

Trial Motions   129

Jury Verdict and Posttrial Motions   130
   Cody v. Atkins   *130*

Judgment and Execution   134
   Newhouse v. Farmers National Bank   *134*

Chapter Questions   *136*
Notes   *140*

IV INSTITUTIONAL SOURCES OF AMERICAN LAW   141

COMMON LAW AND CIVIL LAW LEGAL SYSTEMS   141

CONSTITUTIONS   142

LEGISLATION   142

The Power to Legislate   144

Federal Government   144

State Government   145

Federal Supremacy   145

Constitutionality of Statutes   146

Ex Post Facto Laws   147

Statutory Construction   148

ADMINISTRATIVE AGENCIES   149

JUDICIAL DECISION MAKING   149

Following Precedent   150

The Holding and Rule of the Case   151
  State v. Butler   *152*

Requirements for a Precedent   155

The Retroactive Versus Prospective Application Question   155
  Adkins v. Sky Blue, Inc.,   *155*

Absence of Precedent   160
  Strunk v. Strunk   *161*

RECOGNIZING LAWS OF OTHER STATES AND COUNTRIES   165

Conflict of Laws   165

Tort Cases   166
  Hubbard Manufacturing Co., Inc., v. Greeson   *166*

Contract Cases   168

Full Faith and Credit   169
  GNLV Corporation v. Jackson   *170*

Comity   171
  Somportex Limited v. Philadelphia Chewing Gum Corporation   *171*

Chapter Questions   *174*
Notes   *177*

V LIMITATIONS IN SEEKING RELIEF   178

CASE OR CONTROVERSY   178
  American Postal Workers Union v. Frank   *179*

MOOTNESS   182
  DeFunis v. Odegaard   *183*

POLITICAL QUESTIONS   186
  Belk v. United States   *186*

THE ACT OF STATE DOCTRINE   189

STATUTE OF LIMITATIONS   189
  Marybeth Atkins v. Jiminy Peak, Inc.   *192*

RES JUDICATA   195
  Caporino v. Lacasse   *196*

IMMUNITY FROM LEGAL ACTION   198

Sovereign Immunity   198

Immunity of Government Officials   199
    Forrester v. White   *200*

Charitable Immunity   203
    Thompson v. Mercy Hospital   *204*

Immunity Among Family Members   205
    Hurst v. Capitell   *206*

Immunity Through Contract   208
    Gimpel v. Host Enterprises, Inc.   *208*

Chapter Questions   *210*

VI JUDICIAL REMEDIES   214

COMMON LAW REMEDIES   214

Compensatory Damages   216
    Macomber v. Dillman   *217*

Punitive Damages   222
    Volz v. Coleman Co., Inc.   *223*

Nominal Damages   226

Liquidated Damages   226
    Lakewood Creative Costumers v. Sharp   *227*

EQUITABLE REMEDIES   229

Injunctions   229
    Gano v. School District No. 411 of Twin Falls County, Idaho   *230*

Reformation and Rescission   232
    Department of Transportation v. Ronlee, Inc.   *233*

Court of Conscience   236
    Campbell Soup Company v. Wentz   *237*

Equitable Maxims   239
    New York Football Giants v. Los Angeles Chargers Football Club   *240*

Specific Performance   242
    Bloch v. Hillel Torah North Suburban Day School   *244*

Restitution   245
    Iacomini v. Liberty Mutual Insurance Company   *246*

Declaratory Judgment   248

Jury Trial   249
    State v. Yelsen Land Company   *249*

Chapter Questions   *251*
Notes   *255*

VII CRIMINAL LAW AND PROCEDURE 256

CRIMINAL LAW 256

Sources of American Criminal Law 257

Classification of Crimes 257

Constitutional Limitations on Criminalization 258
  Loving v. Commonwealth of Virginia 259

The Imposition of Punishment 263

THE BASIC COMPONENTS OF A CRIMINAL OFFENSE 263

The Wrongful Act 263
  People v. Shaughnessy 264

Special Rules 266

Status Crimes 267

The Criminal State of Mind 267
  State v. Gordon 268

Strict Liability 273

Vicarious Liability 273

Causation 274
  Commonwealth v. Berggren 274

Inchoate Crime 276

The Racketeer Influenced and Corrupt Organization Act 277

Defenses 277
  United States v. Scott 278

CRIMINAL PROCEDURE 282

PROCEEDINGS PRIOR TO TRIAL 282

Arrest 283
  Draper v. United States 283

Investigatory Detentions (Stop and Frisk) 288
  Adams v. Williams 288

Custodial Interrogation 291

Searches and Seizures 292
  New Jersey v. T.L.O. 293

Bail 298
  United States v. Salerno 299

The Right to an Attorney 304

Line-ups 305

Preliminary Hearing and Grand Jury 305

Arraignment   306

THE CRIMINAL TRIAL   306
  Sullivan v. Louisiana   *309*

Trial by Jury   311

Fair and Public Trial   312

Right to a Speedy Trial and Cross Examination   312

The Prosecutor's Role   312

Sentencing   312

Appeal   313

Habeas Corpus   313

Chapter Questions   *314*
Notes   *318*

VIII FAMILY LAW   320

INTRODUCTION   320
  Wisconsin v. Yoder   *321*

THE FAMILY   330

What Is a Family?   330
  Moore v. City of East Cleveland, Ohio   *331*

CREATING FAMILY RELATIONSHIPS   337

Marriage   337
  Zablocki v. Redhail   *338*

Marriage Solemnization Ceremonies   342

Common Law Marriages   342

Adoption   342

Matching   343
  Adoption of Tammy   *346*

Voluntary/Involuntary Adoption   350

The Adoption Petition   351
  Lehr v. Robertson   *351*

Interim Orders   356

Foster Care   356

FAMILY RELATIONS IN ONGOING FAMILIES   357

Spousal Considerations   357

Decision Making Within Traditional Families 358

Evidentiary Privileges 359

The Parent-Child Relationship 359
State ex rel. Hermesmann v. Seyer 359

Child Support 363
Nash v. Mulle 364

Noneconomic Obligations 370

Parental Immunity from Suit by Child 370

ENDING SPOUSAL RELATIONSHIPS 370

Annulment 370

Legal Separations 371

Divorce/Dissolution 371

Jurisdictional and Procedural Considerations 374

Jurisdiction 374

Procedure 374

Allocation of Financial Obligations 375

Court-ordered Alimony 375

Child Custody and Child Support 376
In re Marriage of Riddle 377

Preferred Custody Statutes 379

Child Support 380

Property Division 380

Common Law/Equitable Distribution Approach 381
O'Brien v. O'Brien 381

Determining Fairness 387

Community Property Approach 387

Conclusion 388

Chapter Questions 388
Notes 391

IX CONTRACTS 395

A BRIEF HISTORY OF AMERICAN CONTRACT LAW 395

NATURE AND CLASSIFICATION OF CONTRACTS 397

Valid, Void, Voidable, and Unenforceable Contracts 397

Bilateral and Unilateral Contracts 398

AGREEMENT   398

Offer   399

Termination of an Offer   399

Acceptance   400
   Pluhacek v. Nebraska Lutheran Outdoor Ministries, Inc.   401

REALITY OF CONSENT   403

Duress   404

Undue Influence   404

Fraud   405

Misrepresentation   406

Mistake   406
   Carter v. Matthews   406

CONSIDERATION   408
   Modern Laundry and Dry Cleaning v. Farrer   410

CAPACITY   413

Minors   413

Transactions a Minor Cannot Avoid   413

Disaffirmance of Contract   414

Insane People   415

ILLEGALITY   416

Contracts Against Public Policy   417
   Principal Casualty Insurance Company v. Blair   417

Agreements to Commit Crimes   419

Agreements to Commit Civil Wrongs   419
   Diaz v. Indian Head, Inc.   420

WRITING   422

Agreement by Executor or Administrator   423

Agreement in Consideration of Marriage   423

Agreement to Answer for the Debt of Another   423

Agreements Not to Be Performed in One Year   424

Agreement Conveying an Interest in Real Property   424
   Mulford v. Borg-Warner Acceptance Corp.   425

Sale of Goods   426

Parol Evidence Rule   426
   Jinright v. Russell   427

ASPECTS OF CONTRACT PERFORMANCE   428

Accord and Satisfaction   428

Anticipatory Repudiation   429

Warranties   429

Discharge, Rescission, and Novation   429

Transfers of Duties and Rights   430
    Macke Company v. Pizza of Gaithersburg, Inc.   431

Contracts for the Benefit of Third Parties   433
    Castorino v. Unifast Bldg. Products   433

The Duty to Perform and Breach of Contract   435
    Clarkson v. Orkin Exterminating Co., Inc.   436

REMEDIES FOR BREACH OF CONTRACT   438

Common Law Remedies   438
    Anuszewski v. Jurevic   438

Punitive Damages   440
    Hibschman Pontiac, Inc. v. Batchelor   440

Equitable Remedies   443

UCC Remedies for Breach of Contract for the Sale of Goods   444

Chapter Questions   *444*
Notes   *448*

X PROPERTY   449

HISTORICAL DEVELOPMENT OF THE REGULATION OF
REAL PROPERTY   449

CLASSIFICATIONS OF PROPERTY   451
    Far West Modular Home Sales, Inc. v. Proaps   452

Property Ownership   454

Title   455

GOVERNMENT'S RIGHT TO REGULATE AND TAKE
PRIVATE PROPERTY   455

Zoning   456

Eminent Domain   456
    Dolan v. City of Tigard   458

Taxation   469

Nuisance   469
    Feeley v. Borough of Ridley Park   470

REAL PROPERTY   472

Estates in Land   472

Easements   473

Licenses   473

Covenants   473
    Sherwood Estates Homes Association, Inc. v. McConnell   474

Adverse Possession   476

The Recording System   477

PERSONAL PROPERTY   477

Purchase   477

Creation   477

Capture   478

Accession   478

Finding   478
    Favorite v. Miller   478

Confusion   481

Gift   481

Inheritance   482

BAILMENTS   482
    York v. Jones   483

Chapter Questions   486
Notes   489

XI   THE LAW OF TORTS   491

HISTORICAL EVOLUTION OF AMERICAN TORT LAW   491

FUNCTIONS OF TORT LAW   492

INTENTIONAL TORTS   492

Assault   492

Battery   492
    Estate of Berthiaume v. Pratt, M.D.   493

Conversion   496

Trespass   496
  Ivancic v. Olmstead   *497*

Malicious Prosecution   499

False Imprisonment   499
  Hainz v. Shopko Stores, Inc.   *499*

Defamation   502

Interference with Contract Relations   503

Infliction of Mental Distress   503

Invasion of Privacy   504
  Carson v. Here's Johnny Portable Toilets, Inc.   *504*

NEGLIGENCE   508

Malpractice   509
  Gilhooley v. Star Market Co., Inc.   *510*

Duty of Care   512
  Weirum v. RKO General, Inc.   *513*

Liability Rules for Specialized Activities   516
  Wright v. Webb   *518*

Proximate Cause   520
  Anglin v. Florida Department of Transportation   *521*

Contributory Negligence and Assumption of Risk Defenses   525

Comparative Negligence   526
  Stein v. Langer   *526*

Negligence and Product Liability   528
  Laaperi v. Sears Roebuck & Co., Inc.   *529*

Imputed Negligence   533
  Dumas v. Lloyd   *534*

No-Fault Liability Statutes   537

STRICT LIABILITY   537

Abnormally Dangerous Activities   537
  Westberry v. Blackwell   *538*

Strict Liability and Product Liability   540
  Leichtamer v. American Motors Corp.   *541*

Tort Reform   545

Joint and Several Liability   546

Caps on Noneconomic Damages   546

Limiting Punitive Damages   546

Statutes of Limitations   547

Court Annexed Alternative Dispute Resolution (ADR)   547

Collateral Source Rule   547

Chapter Questions   547
Notes   551

XII ADMINISTRATIVE LAW AND ADMINISTRATIVE AGENCIES   553

THE RISE OF ADMINISTRATIVE AGENCIES   553

ORGANIZATION AND CLASSIFICATION OF FEDERAL AGENCIES   555

Functions of Administrative Agencies   555
  Askildson v. Commissioner of Public Safety   558

ADMINISTRATIVE AGENCY POWERS   561

Rule-making Power   562
  Chip Steak Company v. Hardin   562

Investigative Power   565
  Dow Chemical Company v. United States   566

Adjudicative Power   570

JUDICIAL REVIEW   570

Timing of Review   571

Recognition of Administrative Competence and Scope of Review   571
  Arndt v. Department of Licensing and Regulation   572

ADMINISTRATIVE AGENCIES AND THE REGULATION OF BUSINESSES   575

Occupational Safety and Health Administration   575
  Whirlpool Corp. v. Marshall   576

Federal Trade Commission and Consumer Credit Protection   579

Environmental Protection Agency   581

History of Pollution Control   582

Air Pollution   582

Water Pollution   583
  Southern Pines Associates v. United States   583

Pesticide Control   586

Hazardous Wastes Disposal   586

Enforcement of Environmental Laws   587

Chapter Questions   587
Notes   591

XIII   EMPLOYMENT AND DISCRIMINATION   593

THE CONCEPT OF EQUALITY   593

HISTORY OF EMPLOYMENT REGULATION   594

State Judicial Remedies   595

State Wrongful Termination Legislation   596

TITLE VII OF THE CIVIL RIGHTS ACT OF 1964   596

Title VII Discrimination Theories   597

Employer Defenses   598
    Sarni Original Dry Cleaners, Inc., v. Cooke   598

Title VII Remedies   601

Affirmative Action   602
    Adarand Constructors, Inc., v. Pena   603

The Equal Employment Opportunity Commission   611
    Jones v. Western Geophysical Co.   611

Gender-based Discrimination   614
    EEOC v. Red Baron Steak Houses   614

Religion   619
    EEOC v. Ithaca Industries, Inc.   619

ADDITIONAL PROTECTION AGAINST DISCRIMINATION   622

Discrimination Against Disabled People   622
    Stutts v. Freeman   623

Age Discrimination in Employment Act   625
    EEOC v. El Paso Natural Gas Co.   627

Employment Discrimination and Sexual Preference   631
    DeSantis v. Pacific Tel. & Tel. Co., Inc.   631

EMPLOYMENT DISCRIMINATION AND THE UNION MOVEMENT   634
    Textile Workers v. Darlington Manufacturing Company   634

National Labor Relations Board   638
    Teamsters, Local 456 and J.R. Stevenson Corporation   639

Labor-Management Reporting and Disclosure Act   643

Chapter Questions   643
Notes   646

XIV ALTERNATIVE DISPUTE RESOLUTION   649

VOLUNTARY ADR   650

COURT-ANNEXED ADR   651
   Pittsburgh Corning Corp. v. Bradley   652

ADR TECHNIQUES   655

Settlement Conferences   655
   Kothe v. Smith   656

Arbitration   658
   Gilmer v. Interstate/Johnson Lane Corp.   658

Voluntary Arbitration   664

Judicial Enforcement of Arbitration Awards   665
   Mastrobuono v. Shearson Lehman Hutton, Inc.   665

Court-Annexed Arbitration   668
   Gilling v. Eastern Airlines, Inc.   669

JOINTLY USED ADR METHODS   672

Mediation   672
   Rhea v. Massey-Ferguson, Inc.   673

MINI-TRIALS   674

Summary Jury Trials   675
   Arabian American Oil Co. v. Scarfone   676

Private Trials   678

Chapter Questions   678
Notes   681

THE CONSTITUTION OF THE UNITED STATES   683

GLOSSARY OF SELECTED TERMS FROM THE LAW
DICTIONARY   701

CASE INDEX   723

SUBJECT INDEX   725

Preface

This book provides an introduction to a topic every educated citizen should know about—law and the American legal system. It gives students an interesting and exciting means of developing an understanding of the strengths and weaknesses of law. A basic understanding of law's philosophical, historical, and cultural antecedents and its fundamentals promotes a better understanding of the role law plays in a complex modern society. From this understanding, students can decide for themselves whether the lawmaking institutions—the legislative, judicial, and administrative agencies—are dealing adequately with society's many problems.

This text is designed to stimulate students to exercise their powers of reasoning. Students read case reports of real-world problems along with textual and appellate court discussions of alternative approaches and theories to resolving the underlying disputes. Case analysis helps students to develop an understanding of legal method and legal reasoning.

This course is designed for basic law courses offered in any graduate or undergraduate program. It is a survey of the American legal system that can be used in courses such as Survey of Law, Introduction to Law and the Legal System, Legal Environment of Business, and Legal Process. This course could be an integral part of a business, political science, criminal justice, interdisciplinary, paralegal, or any other similar program in an institution of higher education.

New to the Sixth Edition

The Sixth Edition includes a new chapter on family law that was added to reflect the tremendous interest that has been shown in this topic in recent years. Concerns about the legal definition of what constitutes a family, the duties and obligations of family members, and the role of law in divorce and adoption proceedings are issues about which students have personal experience, strong beliefs, and much curiosity. Family-related topics lend themselves to spirited class participation and create a vehicle for talking about broader and fundamental issues of substantive and procedural public policy.

The importance of legislation as a source of American law has been emphasized and integrated with the previously existing discussion of judicial lawmaking in a chapter entitled Institutional Sources of American Law. Throughout the text, new cases which have proven to be more effective teaching tools in the classroom have replaced previous choices. The discussions of civil procedure and alternative dispute resolution have been significantly rewritten to improve clarity. A discussion of the important topic of tort reform has also been added.

Instructors will probably differ as to whether the Civil Procedure chapter should precede Institutional Sources of American Law. I prefer the current sequencing because it has been my experience in teaching this subject for twenty years that students have an easier time reading and understanding case reports after they have studied civil procedure. However, instructors can easily assign the chapters to suit their own preferences.

Most case footnotes have been deleted. When footnotes were retained, original numbers have been used. Many citations have similarly been omitted, as well as less important portions of majority opinions. Ellipses have been inserted to indicate such omissions.

Teaching and Learning Aids

Law, like other disciplines, has a language of its own. A glossary of selected terms from *The Law Dictionary (Cochran's Law Lexicon,* 6th Edition) is included at the end of the book to help students. The Constitution of the United States is also reprinted there.

Grilliot's Introduction to Law and the Legal System is accompanied by a *Study Guide* and an *Instructor's Resource Manual.* The *Study Guide* provides students with case summaries and a series of review exercises to test comprehension. Case summaries and case questions appear in the *Instructor's Resource Manual,* followed by a section of test items for each chapter, including completion, true-false, multiple choice, and essay questions.

Acknowledgments

This revision would not have been possible without the valuable contributions of several people. The following reviewers were instrumental in shaping the Sixth Edition:

Kay Y. Rute, Washburn University of Topeka
James C. Foster, Oregon State University
Leonard Mandelbaum, Seattle University

Lee Weinberg, University of Pittsburgh
Darel F. Swenson, North Hennepin Community College

The manuscript for the Sixth Edition was also significantly improved by the dedicated professionals at Houghton Mifflin. Special thanks are extended to Denise Clinton, Bonnie Binkert, Kelly Faughnan, Joan Horan, Nancy Doherty Schmitt, and Kate Burden.

Finally, I'd like to thank my wife, Barbara; my daughter, Tracy Lea; and my son, Andy for their continuing support, patience, and understanding throughout the duration of this project. This edition is dedicated to my father, Professor Glendon A. Schubert of the University of Hawaii, to honor his fifty years of college teaching and to thank him for kindling my interest in law.

F.A.S.

Grilliot's
Introduction to Law
and the Legal System

I

Introduction

WHAT IS LAW?

The study of legal philosophy is called *jurisprudence*. Many of the world's greatest philosophers have theorized about the nature and meaning of law. Jurisprudential philosophers ask questions such as: "What is law?" "Is bad law, law?" "Is custom law?" "Is law what it says in the statute books or what really happens in practice?" Philosophers have debated the essential nature of law for centuries, yet there is no single commonly accepted definition. This chapter begins by summarizing some of the schools of legal philosophy in order to introduce students to different ways of answering this fundamental question: "What is law?"[1]

Law as Power

Some philosophers argued that laws are nothing more than the will of those who hold power. In totalitarian regimes, military power often controls governmental institutions, and laws are essentially edicts. In a democracy, political majorities control legislative bodies and determine who exercises executive authority, and appellate court majorities determine legal precedents.

According to this view, the validity of a law does not depend on whether it is socially good or bad. It is apparent, for example, that tyrannies, monarchies, and democracies have produced socially beneficial laws. They have also produced laws that are unjust and "wrongful." What these different forms of government have in common is that each is based on power and that possessing the power to enforce its laws is central to each government's existence. This philosophy can be criticized for ignoring arbitrariness, abuses of power, and tyranny and for producing bad law.

1

Natural Law

Natural law philosophers argued that law is that which reflects, or is based on, the built-in sense of right and wrong that exists within every person at birth. Some believed that this sense was God-given; others believed it was an intrinsic part of human nature.[2] Natural law philosophers argued that society does not create law because true law is self-evident and describes ethical, or "right," behavior. Thus, even though during apartheid, the all-white, South African government may have had the power to enact racially discriminatory statutes, such statutes were not truly "law" because they were morally abhorrent.

This natural law philosophy was very influential in seventeenth- and eighteenth-century Europe. Revolutionaries who sought to overthrow established monarchies were attracted to natural law because it established a philosophical foundation for political reform.

Natural law thinking has greatly influenced American law as well. American civil rights advocates currently use time-tested natural law arguments that were used thirty and forty years ago to oppose racial discrimination. They argue that discriminatory statutes should not be respected as law because they are so blatantly unfair. Constitutional provisions that require government to treat all persons fairly and impartially (the due process and equal protection clauses) are other examples.

Our tort system is also a reflection of natural law thinking. It is "right" that people who intend no harm but who carelessly cause injury to other people should have to pay compensation for the damages. Similarly, if two people voluntarily enter into a contract, it is "right" that the parties comply with its terms or pay damages for the breach. (However, our law confers power in our judges to refuse to enforce contractual provisions that are too one-sided.) Finally, it is "right" to punish persons who commit crimes for those acts.

When there is no consensus in society about what is right and wrong, however, the notion of natural law falters. Current examples of this problem include issues such as abortion and capital punishment.

Historical Jurisprudence

Historical jurisprudence evolved in response to the natural law philosophy. Aristocrats were attracted to this school because it provided a justification for preserving the status quo and the preferential treatment of powerful elites that was deeply rooted in cultural tradition. The historical philosophy of law integrated the notion that law is the will of the sovereign with the idea of the "spirit of the people."[3] That is, law is only valid to the extent that the will of the sovereign is compatible with long-standing social practices, customs, and values. Law, according to this view, could not be arbitrarily imposed by legislators whose legal source was "right" reasoning. Instead, the historical school insisted that only practices that have withstood the test of time could be thought of as law.[4] Further, these philosophers believed that law changes slowly and invisibly as human conduct changes.

A major advantage of historical jurisprudence is that it promotes stability in law. In fact, much law is largely grounded in judicially approved custom. Our contemporary American real estate law,[5] property law,[6] and contract law[7] are some of the areas in which long-standing practices continue to be recognized as law. Custom has also played an important role in determining the meaning of the Constitution. Appellate courts such as the United States Supreme Court trace provisions of the Bill of Rights to their historical statutory and case law antecedents. They do this because they recognize that some beliefs, practices, procedures, and relationships between people and the state have become fundamental to our culture.

Occasionally a sovereign will enact legislation that significantly contravenes long-standing custom. A few years ago the Massachusetts legislature enacted a mandatory seat belt law. Many citizens believed that the state was infringing on a matter of personal choice. They insisted that the matter be placed on the ballot, and the law was repealed in a statewide referendum.[8]

A major problem with historical jurisprudence is determining at what point a practice has become a custom. How long must a practice have been followed and how widespread must it be accepted to be recognized as customary?

Utilitarian Law

The utilitarian school of law concentrated on the social usefulness of legislation rather than on metaphysical notions of goodness and justice.[9] Utilitarians thought that government was responsible for enacting laws that promote the general public's happiness. They believed that the desire to maximize pleasure and minimize pain is what motivates people, and that legislatures were responsible for inducing people to act in socially desirable ways through a legislated system of incentives and disincentives.[10] For example, if the pain imposed by a criminal sentence exceeds the gain realized by an offender in committing the offense, future criminal actions will be deterred. Additionally, they thought that law should focus on providing people with security and equality of opportunity. They maintained that property rights should be protected because security of property is crucial to attaining happiness. People, they thought, should perform their contracts because increased commercial activity and economic growth produce socially beneficial increases in employment.

Utilitarians also favored the simplification of legal procedures. They opposed checks and balances, legal technicalities, and complex procedures. They believed that these "formalities" increased the costs and length of the judicial process and made the justice system ineffective and unresponsive to the needs of large numbers of average people. Instead, utilitarians would favor small claims courts, with their simplified pleading requirements, informality, low cost, and the optional use of lawyers.

Utilitarian influence can be found in legislative enactments that require the nation's broadcasters to operate "in the public interest," in "lemon laws" and other consumer protection legislation. A major problem with utilitarianism is that everyone does not agree about what is pleasurable and what is painful. And many, if not most, political scientists would dispute that legislators actually make decisions according to the pleasure-pain principle.

Analytical Positivism

Analytical positivists asserted that law was a self-sufficient system of legal rules that the sovereign issues in the form of commands to the governed. These commands do not depend for legitimacy on extraneous considerations such as reason, ethics, morals, or even social consequences.[11] However, the sovereign's will was law only if it was developed according to duly established procedures, such as the enactments of a national legislature.

Thus the apartheid laws passed by the previously all-white South African legislature were "the law" of that country at that time to the same extent that civil rights legislation enacted by the United States Congress was the law of this country. Each of these lawmaking bodies was exercising sovereign power in accordance with provisions of a national constitution. Individuals and governmental officials would have no right to disobey laws with which they personally disagree due to moral, ethical, or policy objections. Positivists would also maintain that trial jurors have a legal obligation to apply the law according to the judge's instructions, even if that means disregarding strongly held personal beliefs about the wisdom of the law or its application in a particular factual dispute.

Members of this philosophical school would view disputes about the goodness or badness of legal rules as extra-legal.[12] They would maintain that such issues do not relate to the law *as it is*. This approach promotes stability and security. It also legitimizes governmental line drawing (such as laws that specify the age at which people can lawfully drink and vote, or those that determine automobile speed limits).

In the United States, people often disagree with governmental decisions about foreign policy as well as about such issues as housing, the financing of public education, health care, abortion, environmental protection, and the licensing of nuclear power plants. Many contend that governmental officials are pursuing wrongful, and sometimes immoral, objectives. Such concerns, however, are generally unpersuasive in our courts. If governmental officials are authorized to make decisions, act within constitutional limitations, and follow established procedures, even decisions that are unpopular with some segments of society are nevertheless law.

But is law really just a closed system of rules and the product of a sovereign? Doesn't international law exist despite the absence of a sovereign? Don't contracting parties routinely create their own rules without any sovereign involvement unless a dispute arises that results in litigation? And is law really morally neutral? Shouldn't the positivist approach be criticized if it protects governmental officials who act unfairly?

Legal Realism

The legal realists were concerned with the behavior of judges and juries rather than focusing solely on legal rules.[13] They were convinced that legal rules do not primarily determine who wins and loses in the courtroom.[14] Rules, they pointed out, do not adequately account for witness perjury and bias, nor do they compensate for the differing levels of ability, knowledge, and prejudice in individual lawyers, judges, and jurors. Realists believe that deciding the facts of a case is a unique process that does not lend itself to rationalization. Because legal realists were nonempirical in their methodology, they were unable to answer their own questions—they did, however, point the way to others who empirically examined such issues.

Sociological Jurisprudence and Legal Sociology

Many early sociologists were interested in examining jurisprudence from a social scientific perspective. Their methodology was empirical, and they focused on what they called the living law—not the law declared by legislature and courts, but the informal rules that actually influence social behavior.

The sociological school maintains that law can only be understood when the formal system of rules are considered in conjunction with social realities (or facts). In this sense, they are similar to the historical school. However, the historical school approached time in terms of centuries, whereas the sociological school focused on ten or twenty year segments. Sociological jurisprudes would note that during the last thirty years, for example, the courts and legislatures have made many attempts to eliminate racial discrimination in voting, housing, employment, and education. It is clear that the law on the books has significantly changed. It is equally clear from scholarly studies based on empirically collected data, however, that discrimination continues. The written law provides for equal opportunity, and on the surface, racial discrimination is not as obvious as it once was. But the social facts continue to reveal various subtle forms of racism that law has not been able to legislate or adjudicate away. Similarly, employment discrimination against women, older workers, and the disabled continues despite the enactment of federal and state legislation that legally puts an end to such practices. Informally enforced social norms that condone bigotry and inflict personal indignities and economic inequities on targeted segments of society are not easily legislated away.

Although this approach effectively points out the discrepancies between the promise and the reality of enacted law, it often fails to produce practical solutions to the problems. Should judges be encouraged to consider social consequences in addition to legal rules in reaching decisions? If so, might this not result in arbitrary, discretionary decisions that reflect only the personal preferences of one particular jurist or group of jurists?

Legal sociologists such as Donald Black have gone beyond the legal realists. Using quantitative methodological tools, they examine such factors as the financial standing, race, social class, respectability, and cultural differences of those involved in disputes.[15] In addition, they evaluate the social facts of the lawyers and judges working on the case as well as those of the parties. In theory, legal outcomes should not be affected by differences in the socio-economic status of the litigants, because all are "equal" before the law. Individual plaintiffs, for example, should be able to win when suing multinational corporations. But legal sociologists claim that the facts do not support this theory.[16] The rule of law is a myth, they say, because legal rules fail to take into account the impact of social diversity on litigation. Discrimination is a fact of modern life, and different combinations of social factors will produce disparate legal outcomes.[17] Donald Black points out that disputes between friends, neighbors, and family members are rarely litigated because "law varies directly with relational distance."[18] It can be persuasively argued that well-trained lawyers should decide whether to settle a case or go to trial, whether to try a case to a judge or a jury, and whether to appeal only after carefully considering the relevant social factors and relationships.[19]

Legal sociologists raise issues that challenge fundamental postulates of our society. If people become convinced that legal outcomes are largely a function of sociological considerations, rather than the application of impartial rules, the integrity of the judicial process itself will be undermined as will the legitimacy of government. If research, however, can reveal more precisely how various combinations of sociological factors influence legal outcomes, this information could be used either to eliminate the bias or to develop alternative mechanisms for resolving particular types of disputes.

OBJECTIVES OF LAW

One of the foundations of our society is the belief that ours is a nation committed to the rule of law. No person is above the law. Our shared legal heritage binds us together as Americans. We use law to regulate people in their relationships with each other, and in their relationships with government. Law reflects our societal aspirations, our culture, and our political and economic beliefs. It provides mechanisms for resolving disputes and for controlling government officials. Private law includes property, family, tort, probate, and corporate law. Public law includes constitutional, criminal, and administrative law. Common to both, however, are certain legal objectives.

Continuity and Stability

It is important that established laws change gradually. Litigants have greater confidence that justice has been done when preexisting rules are used to determine legal outcomes. Laws work best when people become aware of them and learn how they work and why they are necessary. Stable laws are also more likely to be applied uniformly and consistently throughout a jurisdiction, and will be better understood by those charged with enforcement.

Stable laws are also very important to creating and maintaining a healthy economy because they are predictable and serve as a guide for conduct. Businesspeople, for example, are not likely to incur risk in a volatile legal and political environment. They are likely to feel more comfortable in making investments and taking economic risks where it appears likely that the future will resemble the present and the recent past. This stability is threatened by society's appetite for producing rules. Various state and federal legislative and administrative rule-making bodies are currently promulgating so many regulations that it is difficult, if not impossible, for affected citizens to stay current.

Adaptability

In one sense it would be desirable if society could create a great big "legal cookbook" that contained a prescribed law or rule for every conceivable situation. We would then only have to look in the cookbook for definitive answers to all legal problems. In reality, there is no such cookbook. Legislators produce statutes that have a broad scope and are designed to promote the public health, safety, welfare, and morals. Judges make law in conjunction with resolving disputes that have been properly brought before the court. Experience has shown that legislative enactments and judicial opinions produce imperfect law. Lawmakers cannot anticipate every factual possibility. Courts, in particular, often feel compelled to recognize exceptions to general rules in order to provide justice in individual cases. Judges often find that there are gaps in the law that have to be filled in order to decide a case, or that a long-standing rule no longer makes any sense, given current circumstances and societal values. In this way law adapts to social, environmental, and political changes within our evolving society.

Justice, Speed, and Economy

Although most people would agree with the preamble to the United States Constitution that it is the role of the government "to establish justice," there is no consensus about what that means. Some see justice as a natural law type settlement, which means each party to a dispute receives what he or she is due. To other people justice means that a specified process was followed by governmental institutions. In some situations, justice requires the elimination of discretion so that law is applied more equally. In other situations, justice requires the inclusion of discretion (equity) in order that the law not be applied too mechanically. In this respect, it is helpful to look at recent history. Our current notions of justice with respect to race, gender, and class differ from the views of many of our forebears. Posterity will probably have a concept of justice that differs from our own.

Rule 1 of the Federal Rules of Civil Procedure provides that procedural rules should be construed "to secure the just, speedy and inexpensive determination of every action." Although it would be desirable if our judicial systems could satisfy all three of these objectives, they are often in conflict. As a society, we continually have to make choices about how much justice we desire and can afford.

Consider a society dedicated to achieving the highest possible levels of justice in its judicial system. Elaborate measures would be required to ensure that all relevant evidence has been located and all possible witnesses identified and permitted to testify. In such a society, all litigants would be entitled to the services of investigators, thorough pretrial discovery procedures, and qualified and experienced trial attorneys. Great care would have to be taken to ensure that jurors were truly unbiased and competent to render a fair verdict. Only highly probative evidence would be permitted as proof, and various levels of appellate review would be required to carefully consider whether significant substantive or procedural errors were made at trial. Obviously, such a process would be very slow and very expensive. Denying deserving plaintiffs a recovery until it had run its course could itself be unfair because a recovery would be denied for several years.

Instead, some judicial systems build in cost-cutting measures such as six-person juries instead of twelve-person juries. They also make it easier for juries to reach decisions by permitting less-than-unanimous verdicts. Although each cost-cutting step risks more error in the system, there are limits to how much justice society is willing to provide. People have a multitude of needs including medical care, housing, education, and defense, as well as a limited interest in paying taxes. These competing needs have to be prioritized. In recent years, governmental funding of poverty lawyers has been greatly reduced. This has occurred at a time when the costs of litigating average cases have risen substantially. As the costs of using the legal system increase, fewer persons will be able to afford to use litigation to resolve their disputes. Some private attorneys will decline to represent a potential client if the likely recovery in the case will not produce an acceptable profit.

An example of how law balances the desire for justice with a concern for cost is seen in this chapter in the case of *Goss v. Lopez*. In that case the United States Supreme Court determined that public school administrators only have to provide rudimentary procedural due process to students who face short suspensions. The Supreme Court explained that requiring schools to provide students with extensive trial-type procedures would make the disciplinary process too expensive. In Chapter 14 we will examine alternative lower-cost methods for resolving disputes.

Determining Desirable Public Policy

Historically, law is used to determine desirable public policy. It has been used to establish and then abolish discrimination on the basis of race, gender, age, and sexual preference. Law has been used to promote environmental protection and to permit resource exploitation. Through law, society determines whether capital punishment is permissible and whether women have the right to obtain abortions.

ORIGIN OF LAW IN THE UNITED STATES

The British victory over the French in the French and Indian War and the signing of the Treaty of Paris (1763) concluded the competition between the two nations for domination of North America. A French victory might well have resulted in the establishment of the civil law system of France in the colonies along the Atlantic seaboard. The British victory, however, preserved the English common law system for what would become the United States. The following discussion highlights some of the important milestones in the development of the common law.

The Origins of English Common Law

Anglo-Saxon kings ruled England prior to 1066. During the reign of Edward the Confessor (1042–1066), wealthy landowners and noblemen, called earls, gained power over local affairs. There was no central legislature or national judicial court. Instead, the country was organized into communal units, based on population. Each was called the hundred, and was headed by an official called the reeve. The primary function of the hundred was judicial; it held court once each month and dealt with routine civil and criminal matters. Local freemen resolved these cases in accordance with local custom.[20]

The hundreds were grouped into units called shires (counties) that had in earlier times often been Anglo-Saxon kingdoms. The shire was of much greater importance than the hundred. The king used it for military, administrative, and judicial purposes. The king administered the shires through the person of the shire reeve (sheriff). Royal sheriffs existed in each of the shires throughout the country. The sheriff was the king's principal judicial and administrative officer at the local level. Sheriffs collected taxes, urged support of the king's administrative and military policies, and performed limited judicial functions.[21] The shire court, composed of all the freemen in the county, was held twice a year and was presided over by the bishop and the sheriff.[22] It handled criminal, civil, and religious matters that were too serious or difficult for the hundred court as well as disputes about land ownership.[23] The freemen in attendance used local custom as the basis for making decisions, even in religious matters, resulting in a variety of regional practices throughout the country. Anglo-Saxon law did not permit a person to approach the king to appeal the decisions of these communal courts.[24]

The Anglo-Saxon king had a number of functions. He raised armies and a navy for the defense of the kingdom. He issued writs, which were administrative letters containing the royal seal.[25] The writs were used to order courts to convene, the sheriffs to do justice, and to award grants of land and privileges.[26] The king administered the country with the assistance of the royal household, an early form of king's council.[27] He also declared law (called dooms),[28] sometimes after consulting with the Witan, a national assembly of important nobles.[29]

When Edward the Confessor died childless in 1066, the candidates to succeed him were his brother-in-law Harold, the Earl of Wessex, and his cousin, William, Duke of Normandy (a French duchy). Harold was English and the most powerful baron in the country. William was French. Each claimed that Edward had selected him as the next king. William also claimed that Harold had agreed to support William's claim to the throne.[30] Harold, however, was elected king by the Witan and was crowned. William's response was to assemble an army, cross the English Channel, and invade England.

The Norman Invasion

In 1066, Duke William of Normandy with 5,000 soldiers and 2,500 horses defeated the Anglo-Saxons and killed King Harold at the Battle of Hastings.[31] William became King of England and the Normans assumed control of the country. Although the Anglo-Saxons had implemented a type of feudalism before the invasion, the Normans developed and refined it. *Feudalism* was a military, political, and social structure that ordered relationships between people. Under feudalism, a series of duties and obligations existed between a lord and his vassals. In England, the Normans merged feudalism with the Anglo-Saxon institution of the national king. William insisted, for example, that all land in England belonged ultimately to the king, and in 1086 he required all landholders to swear allegiance to him.[32] In this way, all his barons and lords and their vassals were personally obligated to him by feudal law. At his coronation, King William decreed that Englishmen could keep the customary laws that had been in force during the reign of the Anglo-Saxon King Edward the Confessor. This meant that the communal, hundred, and shire courts could continue to resolve disputes between the English as they had in the past.[33] William did, however, make one significant change in the jurisdiction of the communal courts: he rejected the Anglo-Saxon practice of allowing church officials to use the communal courts to decide religious matters. Instead, he mandated that the church should establish its own courts and that religious matters should be decided according to canon (church) law, rather than customary law.[34] William also declared that the Normans would settle their disputes in the courts of the lords and barons in agreement with feudal law.

England at that time consisted of two societies, one French and the other English.[35] French was the language spoken by the victorious Normans, as well as by the king, the upper classes, the clergy, and scholars.[36] English was only spoken by the lower classes following the invasion, and it did not achieve prominence and become the language of the courts and the "common law" until 1362.[37] The French legacy can be seen in many words used by lawyers today. *Acquit, en banc, voir dire, demurrer, embezzle,* and *detainer* are some examples of "English" words that were borrowed from the French. Although the Normans spoke French, formal written documents were written in Latin. This may help to explain why students reading law in the 1990s encounter

Latin words such as *certiorari, subpoena, mens rea, actus reus, in camera, mandamus, capias,* and *pro se.*

The Development of the Common Law

Over time, marriages between Norman and English families blurred the old class system. William's son Henry (who became Henry I), for example, married a descendant of the Anglo-Saxon royal house.[38] It was not until after 1453, when the French drove the English out of France (except for Calais), however, that the Normans and English were unified as one nation.

William died in 1100. The most important of his successors—in terms of the development of the common law—were Henry I and Henry's grandson, Henry II. After the death of the very unpopular William II, the nobles elected Henry I as king. Henry I had promised the nobles that if elected he would issue a charter in which he pledged to respect the rights of the nobles.[39] He also promised to be a fair ruler in the manner of William I. This charter is significant because it was a model for the most famous of all charters, *Magna Carta.*[40]

Henry I ruled during a prosperous period and strengthened the king's powers while making peace with the church and feudal barons. He also strengthened the judiciary by requiring members of his council, the Curia Regis, to ride circuit occasionally throughout the country listening to pleas and supervising the local courts. During this period, the communal courts, the religious courts, and the feudal courts of the barons were still meeting and there was much confusion over jurisdiction.[41] Henry I encouraged people who distrusted the local courts to turn to the king for justice.

Henry II was the king most involved in the development of the central judiciary and the common law.[42] He created a professional royal court to hear civil litigation between ordinary parties (common pleas) and staffed this court with barons who had learned how to judge from working as members of the *Curia Regis.*[43] The king had some of his judges sit with him at Westminster (in London), and others traveled throughout the country listening to pleas and supervising local courts.[44] These royal judges applied the same law in each of the jurisdictions in which they held court.[45] They did not treat each case as if it were a case of first impression, or apply the customary law of the particular region. Decisions were not based on abstract principles and theories. The royal judges decided disputes in a consistent manner throughout the country, based on slowly evolving legal rules adopted by the members of the court.[46]

There were important procedural incentives for bringing suit in the court of common pleas rather than in local courts. One was that the losing party in a communal or feudal court could have the decision reviewed by common pleas. Another was that the king enforced royal court judgments. Lastly, royal courts used juries instead of trials by battle and ordeal.[47]

One problem that was often brought to the king involved land disputes between neighboring nobles. One noble would claim part of his neighbor's land and seize it without bringing the matter to the attention of any court. Henry II's response was to allow victims to petition him for issuance of a *writ of right*. This writ was purchased from the king and directed the communal courts to do full justice without delay or to appear in a royal court and give an explanation.[48] The development of the writ of right resulted in a law making it illegal to dispossess someone of land without a trial conducted according to a royal writ.

The Normans became very creative in the way they used writs. Under the Norman kings, suitors had to obtain writs in order to litigate any claim. As the demand for writs increased, the responsibility for issuing them was transferred from the king to the chancellor,[49] and in later years to the courts themselves. Each writ conferred jurisdiction on a designated court to resolve a particular dispute. It also specified many of the procedures to be followed since there was no general code of civil procedure to regulate the conduct of litigation.[50] A writ, for example, would often be addressed to the sheriff and would require him to summons in the defendant and convene a jury. In Henry I's era, there were very few writs. By Henry III's reign, many writs existed including entry, debt, detinue, account, replevin, covenant, and novel disseisin (wrongful ejection).[51] A few master registers of writs were developed to form a primitive "law library."

By roughly 1200 the principal components of the common law system were in place. National law had replaced local and regional customs of the shire and hundred. A body of royal judges applied a common law throughout the nation, a tradition of respecting precedent was established, and the writ system was functioning.[52]

The development of legal literature was important to the development and improvement of the common law.[53] Henry Bracton, a thirteenth-century English lawyer, wrote commentaries on the writs of the day during the reign of Henry III (Henry II's grandson) and collected cases from the preceding twenty years.[54] During the fourteenth and fifteenth centuries, lawyers and law students began a series of "Year Books," a collection of the cases that had been heard in the most important courts for each year. The Year Books were discontinued in 1535 and were replaced by case reports, informal collections by various authors. Some of these authors, such as Chief Justice Edward Coke (pronounced "cook"), were well known and highly respected.[55] Coke published thirteen volumes of cases between 1572 and 1616. The reports established a process that in 1865 resulted in the publication of official law reports. In 1765, Sir William Blackstone, an Oxford professor, published a collection of his lectures in a book entitled *Commentaries on the Laws of England,* which was immensely popular in the American colonies. The first American judicial reports were published in 1789, and James Kent's influential *Commentaries on American Law* was published between 1826 and 1830.[56]

The common law came to what is now the United States as a result of Britain's colonization policies. In the early 1600s British monarchs began awarding charters to merchants and proprietors who would establish colonies along the Atlantic coast of North America. Over the next 150 years, a steady flow of immigrants, most of whom were British, crossed the Atlantic, bringing the English language, culture, law books, and the English legal tradition. The common law was one major component of that tradition; another was the court of equity.

The Origin of the English Equitable Court

Until the fourteenth century, the common law courts were willing to consider arguments based on conscience as well as law. The judges were concerned with equity (fairness and mercy), as well as legality. By the fifteenth century, however, the common law courts were sometimes less concerned with justice than with technicalities. Common law pleading was complex and jury tampering was common.[57] The courts often refused to allow parties to testify, and there were no procedures for discovering an opponent's evidence. Although the common law courts were able to act against land and would award money judgments, they refused to grant injunctive relief (court orders directing individuals to perform or refrain from engaging in certain acts).[58] Unusual situations arose for which there was no common law relief, or where the relief available was inadequate as a remedy. In addition, the law courts were often slow, and litigation was very costly. Increasingly, dissatisfied parties began to petition the king and his council to intervene in the name of justice. As the number of petitions rose, the king and council forwarded the petitions to the chancellor.[59]

The *chancellor*, originally a high-ranking member of the clergy, was part of the royal household. He was the king's leading advisor in political matters and was a professional administrator. The chancellor's staff included people with judicial experience who issued the writs that enabled suitors to litigate in the common law courts.[60] Because they were ecclesiastics, the early chancellors were not trained as common law lawyers. They were well educated,[61] however, and were familiar with the canon law of the Roman Catholic Church.[62] As a result, the chancellors were often more receptive to arguments based on morality than to arguments based exclusively on legality.

As chancellors began to hear petitions, the *court of chancery*, or equity court, came into being. It granted relief based on broad principles of right and justice in cases in which the restrictions of the common law prevented it. Chancellors began to use the *writ of subpoena* to speed up their hearings and the *writ of summons* to require people to appear in the chancery.[63] Chancery trials were conducted before a single judge who sat without a jury. The chancellor, who exercised discretion and did not rely on precedent in granting relief, would only act where extraordinary relief was required, because no writ applied to the wrong from which the petitioner sought relief. One such area was specific performance of contracts. Although a suit for what we would call breach of contract could be maintained in a common law court, that court could not require a contracting party to perform his bargain. The chancellor, however, could issue such an order directed to the nonperforming person and could enforce it with the contempt power.

The equity court became very popular and was very busy by the middle 1500s. For centuries, common law and equity were administered in England by these two separate courts. Each court applied its own system of jurisprudence and followed its own judicial rules and remedies. Much of traditional equity is based on concepts such as adequacy, practicality, clean hands, and hardship (matters we will discuss in Chapter 6). The equity court's workload continued to grow, as did the chancellor's staff. By the seventeenth century, the most important of the chancellor's staff clerks were called masters in chancery. The chief master was called the Master of the Rolls. Masters in chancery helped the chancellor conduct the equity court, particularly while the chancellor was performing nonjudicial duties for the king.

Initially, despite their differing aims, the common law courts and the equity court cooperated with each other. Starting with Henry VIII's reign, common law lawyers rather than ecclesiastics were named chancellor, which improved relations between law and equity.[64] Sir Thomas More, as chancellor, invited the common law judges to incorporate the notion of conscience into the common law, but the judges declined, preferring to stand behind the decisions of the juries. Gradually, however, this dual-court system created a competition for business, and the common law courts became more flexible by borrowing from equity. The equitable courts were also changing, and chancellors began to identify jurisdictional boundaries between the equitable and common law courts. Equity, for example, agreed to furnish a remedy only when the common law procedure was deficient or the remedy at common law was inadequate.[65]

Beginning in 1649, the decisions of the chancellors were sporadically collected and published, a process that led to the establishment of equitable precedent.[66] Eventually, equitable precedent made the equity courts as formalistic and rigid as the common law courts had been in equity's early days.[67] This dual-court system continued in England until the passage by Parliament of the Judicature Acts of 1873 and 1875 which merged the equitable and common law courts into a unified court.

The North American colonies along the Atlantic coast differed from British precedent when it came to the establishment of equity courts. Massachusetts never established an equity court, and its trial courts were not permitted to exercise the equitable powers of the chancellor until 1870. Maryland, New York, New Jersey, Delaware, North Carolina, and South Carolina established separate courts for common law and equity. However, by 1900 common law and equity had merged into a single judicial system in most states.

As you read the cases that follow, you will notice that plaintiffs often request legal and equitable relief in the same complaint. A plaintiff may demand money damages (common law relief), a declaratory judgment (equitable relief), and an injunction (equitable relief) in the complaint. This creates no problem for the courts. The legal issues will be tried by a jury (unless the parties prefer a bench trial) and the equitable issues will be decided by the judge sitting as a chancellor according to the rules of equity. In Chapter 6 we will look more closely at the differences between the common law and equitable remedies.

READING CASES

The application of law to factual situations is necessary when there is a controversy between two or more people or when parties seek guidance concerning the consequences of their conduct or proposed conduct. The court cases in this text involve disputes that the parties were unable to resolve by themselves and that were brought to the trial and appellate courts for a decision. Most disputes, however, are settled by the parties outside court based on professional predictions of what a court would do.

Students learn to understand the legal process and the relationship between judicial theories and practical legal problems by analyzing actual court cases. The cases in this text illustrate particular points of law. They also convey current legal theory. These cases should serve as points of departure for discussions about the legal response to current social problems. It is important to understand the strengths and weaknesses of law as an instrument of social change.

The case decisions are official explanations of the judge's decision-making process as they apply legal principles to factual situations and test these applications in terms of their potential consequences. Thus, in analyzing each case decision, students should focus attention on the underlying factual situation, the law that the court applied, whether the decision was just, and the future impact of the decision when it is used as precedent.

The first case concerns private law and shows how law affects business morality. Note how the court has to balance competing social values in reaching its decision. Commercial morality has become a vital interest of society because of the size and power of modern business organizations.

One last tip is in order before reading the first case. Students in their first law course should expect to use the glossary or a legal dictionary frequently. Law has its own language, and understanding legal jargon is essential to understanding the cases.

E.I. Du Pont de Nemours & Co., Inc. v. Christopher
431 F.2d 1012
U.S. Court of Appeals, Fifth Circuit
August 25, 1970

Goldberg, Justice

This is a case of industrial espionage in which an airplane is the cloak and a camera the dagger. The defendants-appellants, Rolfe and Gary Christopher, are photographers in Beaumont, Texas. The Christophers were hired by an unknown third party to take aerial photographs of new construction at the Beaumont plant of E.I. Du Pont de Nemours & Company, Inc. Sixteen photographs of the Du Pont facility were taken from the air on March 19, 1969, and these photographs were later developed and delivered to the third party.

Du Pont employees apparently noticed the airplane on March 19 and immediately began an investigation to determine why the craft was circling over the plant. By that afternoon the investigation had disclosed that the craft was involved in a photographic expedition and that the

Christophers were the photographers. Du Pont contacted the Christophers that same afternoon and asked them to reveal the name of the person or corporation requesting the photographs. The Christophers refused to disclose this information, giving as their reason the client's desire to remain anonymous.

Having reached a dead end in the investigation, Du Pont subsequently filed suit against the Christophers, alleging that the Christophers had wrongfully obtained photographs revealing Du Pont's trade secrets which they then sold to the undisclosed third party. Du Pont contended that it had developed a highly secret but unpatented process for producing methanol, a process that gave Du Pont a competitive advantage over other producers. This process, Du Pont alleged, was a trade secret developed after much expensive and time-consuming research, and a secret that the company had taken special precautions to safeguard. The area photographed by the Christophers was the plant designed to produce methanol by this secret process, and because the plant was still under construction parts of the process were exposed to view from directly above the construction area. Photographs of that area, Du Pont alleged, would enable a skilled person to deduce the secret process for making methanol. Du Pont thus contended that the Christophers had wrongfully appropriated Du Pont trade secrets by taking the photographs and delivering them to the undisclosed third party. In its suit Du Pont asked for damages to cover the loss it had already sustained as a result of the wrongful disclosure of the trade secret and sought temporary and permanent injunctions prohibiting any further circulation of the photographs already taken and prohibiting any additional photographing of the methanol plant.

The Christophers answered with . . . [a motion] to dismiss for lack of jurisdiction and failure to state a claim upon which relief could be granted. Depositions were taken during which the Christophers again refused to disclose the name of the person to whom they had delivered the photographs. Du Pont then filed a motion to compel an answer to this question and all related questions.

On June 5, 1969, the trial court held a hearing on the pending motions . . . [and] granted Du Pont's motion to compel the Christophers to divulge the name of their client. . . . Agreeing with the trial court's determination that Du Pont had stated a valid claim, we affirm the decision of that court.

This is a case of first impression, for the Texas courts have not faced this precise factual issue, and sitting as a diversity court we must sensitize our *Erie* antennae to decide what the Texas courts would do if such a situation were presented to them. The only question involved in this interlocutory appeal is whether Du Pont has asserted a claim upon which relief can be granted. The Christophers argued both at trial and before this court that they committed no "actionable wrong" in photographing the Du Pont facility and passing these photographs on to their client because they conducted all of their activities in public airspace, violated no government aviation standard, did not breach any confidential relation, and did not engage in any fraudulent or illegal conduct. In short, the Christophers argue that for an appropriation of trade secrets to be wrong there must be a trespass, other illegal conduct, or breach of a confidential relationship. We disagree.

It is true, as the Christophers assert, that the previous trade secret cases have contained one or more of these elements.

However, we do not think that the Texas courts would limit the trade secret protection exclusively to these elements. On the contrary, in *Hyde Corporation v. Huffines*, 1958, 314 S.W.2d 763, the Texas Supreme Court specifically adopted the rule found in the Restatements of Torts which provides:

> "One who discloses or uses another's trade secret, without a privilege to do so, is liable to the other if
> "a. he discovered the secret by improper means, or
> "b. his disclosure or use constitutes a breach of confidence reposed in him by the other in disclosing the secret to him." . . .

Thus, although the previous cases have dealt with a breach of a confidential relationship, a trespass, or other illegal conduct, the rule is much broader than the cases heretofore encountered. Not limiting itself to specific wrongs, Texas adopted subsection (a) of the Restatement which recognizes a cause of action for the discovery of a trade secret by any "improper" means. . . .

The question remaining, therefore, is whether aerial photography of plant construction is an improper means of obtaining another's trade secret. We conclude that it is and that the Texas courts would so hold. The Supreme Court of that state had declared that "the undoubted tendency of the law has been to recognize and enforce higher standards of commercial morality in the business world." *Hyde Corporation v. Huffines*, at 773. That court has quoted with approval articles indicating that the *proper* means of gaining possession of a competitor's secret process is "through inspection and analysis" of the product in order to create a duplicate. Later another Texas court explained:

> "The means by which the discovery is made may be obvious, and the experi-

mentation leading from known factors to presently unknown results may be simple and lying in the public domain. But these facts do not destroy the value of the discovery and will not advantage a competitor who by unfair means obtains the knowledge *without paying the price expended by the discoverer.*" (*Brown v. Fowler*, 316 S.W.2nd 111.)

We think, therefore, that the Texas rule is clear. One may use his competitor's secret process if he discovers the process by reverse engineering applied to the finished product; one may use a competitor's process if he discovers it by his own independent research; but one may not avoid these labors by taking the process from the discoverer without his permission at a time when he is taking reasonable precautions to maintain its secrecy. To obtain knowledge of a process without spending the time and money to discover it independently is *improper* unless the holder voluntarily discloses it or fails to take reasonable precautions to ensure its secrecy.

In the instant case the Christophers deliberately flew over the Du Pont plant to get pictures of a process which Du Pont had attempted to keep secret. The Christophers delivered their pictures to a third party who was certainly aware of the means by which they had been acquired and who may be planning to use the information contained therein to manufacture methanol by the Du Pont process. The third party has a right to use this process only if he obtains this knowledge through his own research efforts; but thus far all information indicates that the third party has gained this knowledge solely by taking it from Du Pont at a time when Du Pont was making reasonable efforts to preserve its secrecy. In such a situation Du Pont has a valid cause of action to prohibit the Christophers from improperly discovering its trade secret and to prohibit the undisclosed third party from using the improperly obtained information.

We note that this view is in perfect accord with the position taken by the authors of the Restatement. In commenting on improper means of discovery, the savants of the Restatement said:

> "f. *Improper Means of Discovery*. The discovery of another's trade secret by improper means subjects the actor to liability independently of the harm to the interest in the secret. Thus, if one uses physical force to take a secret formula from another's pocket, or breaks into another's office to steal the formula, his conduct is wrongful and subjects him to liability apart from the rule stated in this Section. Such conduct is also an improper means of procuring the secret under this rule. But means may be improper under this rule even though they do not cause any other harm than that to the interest in the trade secret. Examples of such are fraudulent misrepresentations to induce disclosure, tapping of telephone wires, eavesdropping or other espionage. A complete catalogue of improper means is not possible. In general they are means which fall below the general accepted standards of commercial morality and reasonable conduct."

In taking this position, we realize that industrial espionage of the sort here perpetrated has become a popular sport in some segments of our industrial community. However, our devotion to free-wheeling industrial competition must not force us into accepting the law of the jungle as the standard of morality expected in our commercial relations. Our tolerance of the espionage game must cease when the protections required to prevent another's spying cost so much that the spirit of inventiveness is dampened. Commercial privacy must be protected from espionage that could not have been reasonably anticipated or prevented.

We do not mean to imply, however, that everything not in plain view is within the protected vale, nor that all information obtained through every extra optical extension is forbidden. Indeed, for our industrial competition to remain healthy there must be breathing room for observing a competing industrialist. A competitor can and must shop his competition for pricing and examine his products for quality, components, and methods of manufacture. Perhaps ordinary fences and roofs must be built to shut out incursive eyes; but we need not require the discoverer of a trade secret to guard against the unanticipated, the undetectable, or the unpreventable methods of espionage now available.

In the instant case Du Pont was in the midst of constructing a plant. Although after construction the finished plant would have protected much of the process from view, during the period of construction the trade secret was exposed to view from the air. To require Du Pont to put a roof over the unfinished plant to guard its secret would impose an enormous expense to prevent nothing more than a schoolboy's trick. We introduce here no new or radical ethic, since our ethos has never given moral sanction to piracy. The marketplace must not deviate far from our mores. We should not require a person or corporation to take unreasonable precautions to prevent another from doing that which he ought not to do in the first place. Reasonable precautions against predatory eyes we may require; but an impenetrable fortress is an unreasonable requirement, and we are not disposed to burden industrial inventors with such a duty in order to protect the fruits of their efforts. "Improper" will always be a word of many nuances, determined by time, place, and circumstances. We therefore need not proclaim a catalogue of commercial improprieties. Clearly, however, one of its commandments does say, "Thou shalt not appropriate a trade secret through deviousness under circumstances in which countervailing defenses are not reasonably available."

Having concluded that aerial photography, from whatever altitude, is an improper method of discovering the trade secrets exposed during construction of the Du Pont plant, we need not worry about whether the flight pattern chosen by the Christophers violated any federal aviation regulations. Regardless of whether the flight was legal or illegal in that sense, the espionage was an improper means of discovering Du Pont's trade secret.

The decision of the trial courts is affirmed and the case remanded to that court for proceedings on the merits.

Case Questions

1. The court in *Hyde Corporation v. Huffines,* cited in the *Du Pont* opinion, stated that the law has tended to "recognize and enforce higher standards of commercial morality." Should the law perform that function?
2. Which philosophies of law does the court appear to rely upon in determining the outcome of this case? Which does it reject?
3. Most disputes are settled outside of court by the parties to the dispute based on a prediction of what the court would do if the case went before it. Would a lawyer be able to predict the result of the *Du Pont* case with a high degree of certainty?
4. Explain the extent to which the objectives of law were addressed in the *Du Pont* case.

CASE ANALYSIS

Since the *Du Pont* case is the first reported judicial decision of this book, a brief analysis of it is appropriate. The heading consists of four items. The first line contains the names of the parties to the suit. E.I. Du Pont de Nemours & Company, Inc., the party that brought the suit, is the *plaintiff*. Rolfe and Gary Christopher are the *defendants*. When there is more than one plaintiff or defendant, it is appropriate to include only one name. This is why the heading reads "Christopher" rather than "Christophers." The Christophers are the *appellants*, the parties who appealed to a higher court from the decision of a lower court. The other party to an appeal is called the *appellee*.

The next item in the heading describes the volume and page where the case can be found. The *Du Pont* case is reported in volume 431 of the second series of the *Federal Reporter*, on page 1012. The name of the court that decided the dispute is next in the heading, followed by the date the decision was reached. The first item in the body of the court opinion is the name of the judge who wrote the court opinion. Usually only one judge is selected to write the majority opinion, even though several judges may have participated in reaching the decision.

In the suit, Du Pont asked for *damages* (money to cover the loss sustained as a result of the defendant's action) and for an *injunction* (an order by the court prohibiting the action of the defendants). What the plaintiff really wanted was to know for whom the defendants were taking the pictures. The defendants asked that the court dismiss the complaint against them for the plaintiff's failure to state a claim, meaning that there was no legal basis for granting relief. The court denied the motion. Since the case was on *appeal*, a judicial review of a decision rendered by a lower court, the appellate court could have affirmed, remanded, reversed, or dismissed the appeal. The court rejected the motion to dismiss and chose to affirm and remand the case. By *affirming*, the appellate court rules that the lower court's decision is valid and reasserts the judgment. To render a judgment of *reversal* is to vacate and set aside the lower court's judgment. Note that reversals can be in part. When a case is *remanded*, it is returned to the lower court, generally with instructions, so that further proceedings may be taken.

The *issue* that the court had to decide in this case was whether aerial photography of plant construction is an improper means of obtaining another's trade secret. This was a case of *first impression*, meaning that no decision in Texas had been reached on the point at issue. The federal court tried to determine the law for the state of Texas. The court searched for factual situations in previously decided Texas cases comparable to the factual situation of the case before it. The court extracted from the previously decided comparable cases the principle on which those cases were decided and applied those principles of law to the case at hand.

In order to reap the benefits of the case study method, one must read each case accurately and pay close attention to detail. After reading a case, one should have not merely a general sense or the gist of what the case says, but a precise understanding of what the court did. Careful attention should be given to the *holding* of the case—what the court decided on the facts of the case.

Opinions are often discursive. Judges often discuss issues they need not decide. Their statements on these issues are labeled *dicta*. Although these statements may be important, they lack the authority of the case's holding.

Most students find it helpful to *brief* a case. After careful reading and analysis of a case, one should be able to write a brief without referring to the case again. Briefing with the case aside provides a check on understanding as well as an incentive to careful reading. A brief should contain the parts of the case selected as important, organized for the purpose at hand rather than in the haphazard order in which they may be reported.

The following brief of the *Du Pont* case illustrates one way of briefing. The elements in the example are usually found in most briefs though writing style is often a matter of individual preference. It is usually desirable to keep copying from the text of the case to a minimum; briefs are not exercises in stenography. This brief was written to help students who have not previously read a case report. It is intended to help these students understand what is important in the material they have read.

Sample Brief

E.I. Du Pont de Nemours & Co., Inc. v. Christopher
431 F.2d 1012 (1970)

Parties:
Appellee (plaintiff below) Du Pont
Appellant (defendant below) Rolfe Christopher et al.

Facts:
Du Pont had developed a highly secret but as-yet-unpatented process for producing methanol that would give it a competitive advantage in the methanol-producing market. Du Pont had taken special precautions to safeguard disclosure of this secret process which was developed after much expensive and time-consuming research. Du Pont had also designed a plant, which was under construction, where the methanol would be produced by the secret process. Because the plant was still under construction, part of the process was exposed to view from above the construction area. A skilled person would have been able to determine the nature of the trade secret from aerial photographs of the construction area.

Rolfe and Gary Christopher were photographers who were hired by an undisclosed third party to take aerial photographs of the Du Pont plant. The Christophers took photographs from the air, developed them, and delivered them to the third party.

Prior Proceedings:
This case was originally brought before the United States District Court for the Eastern District of Texas. The Christophers brought pretrial motions arguing that Du Pont did not have a claim and therefore there was no need to go through a full trial. The court denied the Christophers' motion (meaning that it believed that Du Pont had stated a legal claim under the law of the state of Texas). The Christophers then made a motion for immediate appellate review of that determination (this is called an interlocutory appeal) pursuant to a federal statute [28 U.S.C.A. 1292 (b)].

The Christophers argued that the district court's decision (that Du Pont had stated a legal claim) was clearly erroneous.

Issues Presented or Questions of Law:
Did Du Pont state a claim upon which relief could be granted under Texas law?

Was the taking of aerial photographs of the Du Pont plant an improper method of discovering a trade secret?

Arguments or Objectives of the Parties:

Du Pont argued that it had designed a plant to produce methanol by a highly secret process. The plant was under construction and was without a roof, exposing various aspects of the process. The process was a trade secret that would be discernible by a skilled person through the examination of photographs of the exposed areas. The Christophers had, Du Pont argued, by taking aerial photographs of the plant, illegally obtained their trade secret for producing methanol.

Du Pont sued for a sum of money (damages) to make up for the losses it had suffered from the disclosure of its trade secret. It also asked the court to prohibit the Christophers, by means of injunctions, from circulating the photographs any further and to prohibit any more photographing of the methanol plant.

The Christophers argued that they did nothing wrong by taking aerial photographs of the Du Pont plant. They further argued that they had not wrongfully appropriated any trade secret because they were in public airspace and therefore had not trespassed on Du Pont's property. They were not employees or agents of Du Pont and therefore no confidential relationship existed and the taking of photographs was not illegal conduct. Because their conduct was not wrongful, and no prior cases had been decided in Texas prohibiting their conduct, the Christophers argued that Du Pont was not stating a claim that would entitle it to compensation.

Disposition or Order by the Court:

The Court of Appeals found that the district court's decision (that Du Pont had stated a claim) was correct and affirmed the decision. The court sent the case back to district court for a full trial on Du Pont's claim requesting damages and injunctions for the wrongful taking of its trade secrets by the Christophers.

Holding/Rule of Law:

The taking of aerial photographs to obtain knowledge of a trade secret without spending the time and money to discover it independently is improper.

Rationale:

(A) Texas courts have never previously decided this issue. Previous Texas cases on trade secrets have only addressed situations in which parties have trespassed on another's property to obtain a trade secret, or have performed some illegal conduct, or have violated a confidential relationship. These three conditions should not be viewed, however, as an exhaustive listing of improper methods of obtaining trade secrets.

(B) The rule that provides that a party is liable for trade secrets discovered by improper means was adopted in *Hyde v. Huffines*.

(C) "Proper means" involves paying the price for the information by either spending time and money or obtaining permission from the discoverer.

The only exceptions to this rule are when the discoverer gives the information voluntarily or fails to take reasonable precautions to prevent its disclosure.

(D) Although our society encourages competition in industry, this must be weighed against the standards of morality and ethics expected in commercial relations. Industrial espionage tactics must stop when the cost of guarding against them is so high as to prevent or deter inventiveness. Simply because an espionage tactic could not have been reasonably anticipated or prevented does not mean that it should be tolerated or that the party victimized should bear the cost.

(E) Requiring Du Pont to put a roof over the unfinished plant would be unreasonable.

CONSTITUTIONAL POLICYMAKING

The second case illustrates the difficult policymaking role of the judiciary in a case involving public law. This case involves the balancing of interests: those of the state in protecting life and the constitutionally protected "liberty" rights of the individual (whether presently competent or incompetent) to refuse death-prolonging procedures.

Here, the devoted parents of an incompetent person in a persistent vegetative state sought to stop her life-support systems. They sought and obtained judicial authorization at the trial court level for termination. The Missouri Supreme Court reversed the decision of the trial court. It interpreted state law as requiring in substituted judgment cases that the parents of an incompetent clearly and convincingly prove that the incompetent would have wanted the life-support systems withdrawn under such circumstances. The United States Supreme Court was asked to decide whether Missouri's requirement of clear and convincing evidence of the incompetent's wishes violated the U.S. Constitution. The Supreme Court also had to decide whether the U.S. Constitution requires states, in cases such as this, to accept the substituted judgment of close family members.

Cruzan v. Director, Missouri Dept. of Health
110 S.Ct. 2841
U.S. Supreme Court
June 25, 1990

Chief Justice Rehnquist delivered the opinion of the Court.

Petitioner Nancy Beth Cruzan was rendered incompetent as a result of severe injuries sustained during an automobile accident. Co-petitioners Lester and Joyce Cruzan, Nancy's parents and co-guardians, sought a court order directing the withdrawal of their daughter's artificial feeding and hydration equipment after it became apparent that she had virtually no chance of recovering her cognitive faculties. The Supreme Court of Missouri held that because there was no clear and convincing evidence of Nancy's desire to have life-sustaining treatment withdrawn under such circumstances, her parents lacked authority to effectuate such a request. We granted certiorari, . . . and now affirm.

On the night of January 11, 1983, Nancy Cruzan lost control of her car as she traveled down Elm Road in Jasper County, Missouri. The vehicle overturned, and Cruzan was discovered lying face down in a ditch without detectable respiratory or cardiac function. Paramedics were able to restore her breathing and heartbeat at the accident site, and she was transported to a hospital in an unconscious state. An attending neurosurgeon diagnosed her as having sustained probable cerebral contusions compounded by significant anoxia (lack of oxygen). The Missouri trial court in this case found that permanent brain damage generally results after 6 minutes in an anoxic state; it was estimated that Cruzan was deprived of oxygen from 12 to 14 minutes. She remained in a coma for approximately three weeks and then progressed to an unconscious state in which she was able to orally ingest some nutrition. In order to ease feeding and further the recovery, surgeons implanted a gastrostomy feeding and hydration tube in Cruzan with the consent of her then husband. Subsequent rehabilitative efforts proved unavailing. She now lies in a Missouri state hospital in what is commonly referred to as a persistent vegetative state: generally, a condition in which a person exhibits motor reflexes but evinces no indications of significant cognitive function. The State of Missouri is bearing the cost of her care.

After it had become apparent that Nancy Cruzan had virtually no chance of regaining her mental faculties her parents asked hospital employees to terminate the artificial nutrition and hydration procedures. All agree that such a removal would cause her death. The employees refused to honor the request without court approval. The parents then sought and received authorization from the state trial court for termination. The court found that a person in Nancy's condition had a fundamental right under the State and Federal Constitutions to refuse or direct the withdrawal of "death prolonging procedures." The court also found that Nancy's "expressed thoughts at age twenty-five in somewhat serious conversation with a housemate friend that if sick or injured she would not wish to continue her life unless she could live at least halfway normally suggests that given her present condition she would not wish to continue on with her nutrition and hydration."

The Supreme Court of Missouri reversed by a divided vote. . . .

We granted certiorari to consider the question of whether Cruzan has a right under the United States Constitution which would require the hospital to withdraw life-sustaining treatment from her under these circumstances.

At common law, even the touching of one person by another without consent and without legal justification was a battery. . . .

This notion of bodily integrity has been embodied in the requirement that informed consent is generally required for medical treatment. Justice Cardozo, while on the Court of Appeals of New York, aptly described this doctrine: "Every human being of adult years and sound mind has a right to determine what shall be done with his own body; and a surgeon who performs an operation without his patient's consent commits an assault, for which he is liable in damages." . . .

The logical corollary of the doctrine of informed consent is that the patient generally possesses the right not to consent, that is, to refuse treatment. Until about 15 years ago and the seminal decision in *In re Quinlan*, . . . the number of right-to-refuse-treatment decisions were relatively few. . . . More recently, however, with the advance of medical technology capable of sustaining life well past the point where natural forces would have brought certain death in earlier times, cases involving the right to refuse life-sustaining treatment have burgeoned. . . .

In the *Quinlan* case, young Karen Quinlan suffered severe brain damage as the result of anoxia, and entered a persistent vegetative state. Karen's father sought judicial approval to disconnect his daughter's respirator. The New Jersey Supreme Court granted the relief, holding that Karen had a right of privacy grounded in the Federal Constitution to terminate treatment. . . . The court . . . concluded that the "only practical way" to prevent the loss of Karen's privacy right due to her incompetence was to allow her guardian and family to decide "whether she would exercise it in these circumstances."

After *Quinlan*, however, most courts have based a right to refuse treatment either solely on the common law right to informed consent or on both the common law right and a constitutional privacy right. . . .

As these cases demonstrate, the common-law doctrine of informed consent is viewed as generally encompassing the right of a competent individual to refuse medical treatment. Beyond that, these decisions demonstrate both similarity and diversity in their approach to decision of what all agree is a perplexing question with unusually strong moral and ethical overtones. State courts have available to them for decision a number of sources—state constitutions, statutes, and common law—which are not available to us. In this Court, the question is simply and starkly whether the United States Constitution prohibits Missouri from choosing the rule of decision which it did. This is the first case in which we have been squarely presented with the issue of whether the United States Constitution grants what is in common parlance referred to as a "right to die." . . .

The Fourteenth Amendment provides that no State shall "deprive any person of life, liberty, or property, without due process of law." The principle that a competent person has a constitutionally protected liberty interest in refusing unwanted medical treatment may be inferred from our prior decisions. . . .

But determining that a person has a "liberty interest" under the Due Process Clause does not end the inquiry; "whether respondent's constitutional rights have been violated must be determined by balancing his liberty interests against the relevant state interests." . . .

Petitioners insist that under the general holdings of our cases, the forced administration of life-sustaining medical treatment, and even of artificially-delivered food and water essential to life, would implicate a competent person's liberty interest. . . .

Petitioners go on to assert that an incompetent person should possess the same right in this respect as is possessed by a competent person. . . .

The difficulty with petitioners' claim is that in a sense it begs the question: an incompetent person is not able to make an informed and voluntary choice to exercise a hypothetical right to refuse treatment or any other right. Such a "right" must be exercised for her, if at all, by some sort of surrogate. Here, Missouri has in effect recognized that under certain circumstances a surrogate may act for the patient in electing to have hydration and nutrition withdrawn in such a way as to cause death, but it has established a procedural safeguard to assure that the action of the surrogate conforms as best it may to the wishes expressed by the patient while competent. Missouri requires that evidence of the incompetent's wishes as to the withdrawal of treatment be proved by clear and convincing evidence. The question, then, is whether the United States Constitution forbids the establishment of this procedural requirement by the State. We hold that it does not.

Whether or not Missouri's clear and convincing evidence requirement comports with the United States Constitution depends in part on what interests the State may properly seek to protect in this situation. Missouri relies on its interest in the protection and preservation of human life, and there can be no gainsaying this interest. As a general matter, the States—indeed, all civilized nations—demonstrate their commitment to life by treating homicide as [a] serious crime. Moreover, the majority of States in this country have laws imposing criminal penalties on one who assists another to commit suicide. We do not think a State is required to remain neutral in the face of an informed and voluntary decision by a physically-able adult to starve to death.

But in the context presented here, a State has more particular interests at stake. The choice between life and death is a deeply personal decision of obvious and overwhelming finality. We believe Missouri may legitimately seek to safeguard the personal element of this choice through the imposition of heightened evidentiary requirements. It cannot be disputed that the Due Process Clause protects an interest in life as well as an interest in refusing life-sustaining medical treatment. Not all incompetent patients

will have loved ones available to serve as surrogate decisionmakers. . . .

A State is entitled to guard against potential abuses in such situations. Similarly, a State is entitled to consider that a judicial proceeding to make a determination regarding an incompetent's wishes may very well not be an adversarial one, with the added guarantee of accurate factfinding that the adversary process brings with it. Finally, we think a State may properly decline to make judgments about the "quality" of life that a particular individual may enjoy, and simply assert an unqualified interest in the preservation of human life to be weighed against the constitutionally protected interests of the individual.

In our view, Missouri has permissibly sought to advance these interests through the adoption of a "clear and convincing" standard of proof to govern such proceedings. . . .

We believe that Missouri may permissibly place an increased risk of an erroneous decision on those seeking to terminate an incompetent individual's life-sustaining treatment. An erroneous decision not to terminate results in a maintenance of the status quo; the possibility of subsequent developments such as advancements in medical science, the discovery of new evidence regarding the patient's intent, changes in the law, or simply the unexpected death of the patient despite the administration of life-sustaining treatment, at least create the potential that a wrong decision will eventually be corrected or its impact mitigated. An erroneous decision to withdraw life-sustaining treatment, however, is not susceptible of correction. . . .

In sum, we conclude that a State may apply a clear and convincing evidence standard in proceedings where a guardian seeks to discontinue nutrition and hydration of a person diagnosed to be in a persistent vegetative state. . . .

The Supreme Court of Missouri held that in this case the testimony adduced at trial did not amount to clear and convincing proof of the patient's desire to have hydration and nutrition withdrawn. In so doing, it reversed a decision of the Missouri trial court which had found that the evidence "suggest[ed]" Nancy Cruzan would not have desired to continue such measures, but which had not adopted the standard of "clear and convincing evidence" enunciated by the Supreme Court. The testimony adduced at trial consisted primarily of Nancy Cruzan's statements made to a housemate about a year before her accident that she would not want to live should she face life as a "vegetable," and other observations to the same effect. The observations did not deal in terms with withdrawal of medical treatment or of hydration and nutrition. We cannot say that the Supreme Court of Missouri committed constitutional error in reaching the conclusion that it did.

Petitioners alternatively contend that Missouri must accept the "substituted judgment" of close family members even in the absence of substantial proof that their views reflect the views of the patient. . . .

No doubt is engendered by anything in this record but that Nancy Cruzan's mother and father are loving and caring parents. If the State were required by the United States Constitution to repose a right of "substituted judgment" with anyone, the Cruzans would surely qualify. But we do not think the Due Process Clause requires the State to repose judgment on these matters with anyone but the patient herself. Close family members may have a strong feeling—a feeling not at all ignoble or unworthy, but not entirely disinterested, either—that they do

not wish to witness the continuation of the life of a loved one which they regard as hopeless, meaningless, and even degrading. But there is no automatic assurance that the view of close family members will necessarily be the same as the patient's would have been had she been confronted with the prospect of her situation while competent. All of the reasons previously discussed for allowing Missouri to require clear and convincing evidence of the patient's wishes lead us to conclude that the State may choose to defer only to those wishes, rather than confide the decision to close family members.

The judgment of the Supreme Court of Missouri is

Affirmed.

Justice Brennan, with whom Justice Marshall and Justice Blackmun join, dissenting

> "Medical technology has effectively created a twilight zone of suspended animation where death commences while life, in some form, continues. Some patients, however, want no part of a life sustained only by medical technology. Instead they prefer a plan of medical treatment that allows nature to take its course and permits them to die with dignity."

Nancy Cruzan has dwelt in that twilight zone for six years. She is oblivious to her surroundings and will remain so. . . . Her body twitches only reflexively, without consciousness. The areas of her brain that once thought, felt, and experienced sensations have degenerated badly and are continuing to do so. The cavities remaining are filling with cerebrospinal fluid. The "cerebral cortical atrophy is irreversible, permanent, progressive and ongoing." . . . "Nancy will never interact meaningfully with her environment again. She will remain in a persistent vegetative state until her death." Because she cannot swallow, her nutrition and hydration are delivered through a tube surgically implanted in her stomach.

A grown woman at the time of the accident, Nancy had previously expressed her wish to forgo continuing medical care under circumstances such as these. Her family and her friends are convinced that this is what she would want. A guardian ad litem appointed by the trial court is also convinced that this is what Nancy would want. Yet the Missouri Supreme Court, alone among state courts deciding such a question, has determined that an irreversibly vegetative patient will remain a passive prisoner of medical technology —for Nancy, perhaps for the next 30 years.

Today the Court, while tentatively accepting that there is some degree of constitutionally protected liberty interest in avoiding unwanted medical treatment, including life-sustaining medical treatment such as artificial nutrition and hydration, affirms the decision of the Missouri Supreme Court. The majority opinion, as I read it, would affirm that decision on the ground that a State may require "clear and convincing" evidence of Nancy Cruzan's prior decision to forgo life-sustaining treatment under circumstances such as hers in order to ensure that her actual wishes are honored. Because I believe that Nancy Cruzan has a fundamental right to be free of unwanted artificial nutrition and hydration, which right is not outweighed by any interests of the State, and because I find that the improperly biased procedural obstacles imposed by the Missouri Supreme Court impermissibly burden that right, I respectfully dissent. Nancy Cruzan is entitled to choose to die with dignity. . . .

II
A

The right to be free from unwanted medical attention is a right to evaluate the potential benefit of treatment and its possible consequences according to one's own values and to make a personal decision whether to subject oneself to the intrusion. For a patient like Nancy Cruzan, the sole benefit of medical treatment is being kept metabolically alive. Neither artificial nutrition nor any other form of medical treatment available today can cure or in any way ameliorate her condition. Irreversibly vegetative patients are devoid of thought, emotion and sensation; they are permanently and completely unconscious. . . .

There are also affirmative reasons why someone like Nancy might choose to forgo artificial nutrition and hydration under these circumstances. Dying is personal. And it is profound. For many, the thought of an ignoble end, steeped in decay, is abhorrent. A quiet, proud death, bodily integrity intact, is a matter of extreme consequence. . . .

Such conditions are, for many, humiliating to contemplate, as is visiting a prolonged and anguished vigil on one's parents, spouse, and children. A long, drawn-out death can have a debilitating effect on family members. For some, the idea of being remembered in their persistent vegetative states rather than as they were before their illness or accident may be very disturbing. . . .

B

Although the right to be free of unwanted medical intervention, like other constitutionally protected interests, may not be absolute, no State interest could outweigh the rights of an individual in Nancy Cruzan's position. Whatever a

State's possible interests in mandating life-support treatment under other circumstances, there is no good to be obtained here by Missouri's insistence that Nancy Cruzan remain on life-support systems if it is indeed her wish not to do so. Missouri does not claim, nor could it, that society as a whole will be benefited by Nancy's receiving medical treatment. No third party's situation will be improved and no harm to others will be averted....

III
D

A State's inability to discern an incompetent patient's choice still need not mean that a State is rendered powerless to protect that choice. But I would find that the Due Process Clause prohibits a State from doing more than that. A State may ensure that the person who makes the decision on the patient's behalf is the one whom the patient himself would have selected to make that choice for him. And a State may exclude from consideration anyone having improper motives. But a State generally must either repose the choice with the person whom the patient himself would most likely have chosen as proxy or leave the decision to the patient's family.

IV

As many as 10,000 patients are being maintained in persistent vegetative states in the United States, and the number is expected to increase significantly in the near future. Medical technology, developed over the past 20 or so years, is often capable of resuscitating people after they have stopped breathing or their hearts have stopped beating. Some of those people are brought fully back to life. Two decades ago, those who were not and could not swallow and digest food, died. Intravenous solutions could not provide sufficient calories to maintain people for more than a short time. Today, various forms of artificial feeding have been developed that are able to keep people metabolically alive for years, even decades....

The 80% of Americans who die in hospitals are "likely to meet their end ... 'in a sedated or comatose state; betubed nasally, abdominally and intravenously; and far more like manipulated objects than like moral subjects.'" A fifth of all adults surviving to age 80 will suffer a progressive dementing disorder prior to death....

The new medical technology can reclaim those who would have been irretrievably lost a few decades ago and restore them to active lives. For Nancy Cruzan, it failed, and for others with wasting incurable disease it may be doomed to failure. In these unfortunate situations, the bodies and preferences and memories of the victims do not escheat to the State; nor does our Constitution permit the State or any other government to commandeer them. . . . Yet Missouri and this Court have displaced Nancy's own assessment of the processes associated with dying. They have discarded evidence of her will, ignored her values, and deprived her of the right to a decision as closely approximating her own choice as humanly possible. They have done so disingenuously in her name, and openly in Missouri's own. That Missouri and this Court may truly be motivated only by concern for incompetent patients makes no matter. As one of our most prominent jurists warned us decades ago: "Experience should teach us to be most on our guard to protect liberty when the government's purposes are beneficent.... The greatest dangers to liberty lurk in insidious encroachment by men of zeal, well meaning but without understanding." *Olmstead v. United States*, 277 U.S. 438, 479 (1928) (Brandeis, J., dissenting). I respectfully dissent.[1]

[1] Editor's Note: Following the U.S. Supreme Court's decision in the *Cruzan* case, her parents asked the County Probate Court Judge for a second hearing. They claimed to have new evidence that would prove that Nancy would not have wanted to live in a vegetative state. The hearing was held on November 1, 1990. At that time, three of Nancy's former coworkers testified as did her doctor. The state of Missouri did not participate in this hearing, having established the legal standard before the U.S. Supreme Court. On December 14, 1990, the judge ruled that clear and convincing evidence of Nancy's intentions had been shown and that the feeding tube could be removed. Nancy Cruzan died on December 26, 1990.

Case Questions

1. Why do you think that the state of Missouri opposed the parents' efforts to disconnect the life-support systems?
2. Does the U.S. Supreme Court majority believe that an incompetent person possesses the same rights as a competent person to refuse food and water?
3. What might competent persons do who wish to avoid the problems encountered by the Cruzans?
4. Why do justices Brennan, Marshall, and Blackmun dissent?
5. Was justice done in this case?

DUE PROCESS

The due process clauses of the Fifth and Fourteenth Amendments to the U.S. Constitution provide that no person shall be "deprived of life, liberty or property without due process of law." These clauses are deeply embedded in Anglo-American legal history, tracing their lineage to 1215. In June of that year, English barons decided that King John had been acting arbitrarily and in violation of their rights. They sought protection from the king in the Magna Carta, a charter containing 63 chapters that limited the king's powers.[68] Chapter 39 of the Magna Carta is the predecessor of our due process clauses. It provided that

> "no man shall be captured or imprisoned or disseised or outlawed or exiled or in any way destroyed, nor will we go against him or send against him, except by the lawful judgment of his peers or by the law of the land."[69]

The barons amassed an army, confronted the king, and forced him to agree to Magna Carta. Subsequent monarchs reissued Magna Carta many times over the next two centuries.[70] In 1354 the words "by the law of the land" (which were initially written in Latin) were translated into English to mean "by due process of the law."[71] In the seventeenth century these words were interpreted to include the customary rights and liberties of Englishmen.[72] English legal commentators further expanded the scope of due process by arguing that it included what philosopher John Locke called each individual's natural right to "life, liberty, and property."[73]

Magna Carta's influence in this country is apparent in the 1776 constitutions of Maryland and North Carolina, which contain verbatim due process language taken from Magna Carta. In 1787 the due process clause was included in the Fifth Amendment to the U.S. Constitution. Every person in our society has an inherent right to due process of law, which protects him or her from arbitrary, oppressive, and unjust governmental actions. If a proceeding results in the denial of fundamental fairness and shocks the conscience of a court, a violation of due process has occurred. In addition, under both the Fifth and Fourteenth Amendments, a corporation, as well as a partnership or unincorporated association, is a person to whom that protection applies.

Due process of the law focuses on life, liberty, and property. "Life" can be defined as all personal rights that are judicially protected. "Liberty," as will be further explained below, covers a vast scope of rights. It infers the absence of arbitrary and unreasonable governmental restraint on an individual conducting business or using property. "Property" is everything that may be subject to ownership, including real and personal property, obligations, rights, and other intangibles.

Determining what due process means in a given factual situation has been a matter for the judiciary. In this, the courts are influenced by modes of proceeding that were well established under English common law prior to the enactment of our Constitution. They are also influenced by contemporary events, values, and political and economic conditions.

The due process guarantee protects people from unfairness in the operation of both substantive and procedural law. Substantive law refers to the law that creates, defines, and regulates rights. It defines the legal relationship between the individual and the state and among individuals themselves and is the primary responsibility of the legislative branch of the government. Procedural law prescribes the method used to enforce legal rights. It provides the machinery by which individuals can enforce their rights or obtain redress for the invasion of such rights.

Substantive Due Process

The Fifth Amendment guarantee of due process of law was included in the Bill of Rights in order to place limits on the federal government. It was intended to control the Congress and prior to the Civil War, it was primarily used to protect property rights from governmental regulation. The due process clause was also interpreted by the Supreme Court to overrule those parts of the Missouri Compromise that prohibited slavery. In the *Dred Scott* case (60 U.S. 393 [1856]), the Supreme Court ruled that slaves were property and, thus, the due process clause prohibited Congress from making slavery illegal. This is a historical irony, given the role due process has played in promoting civil rights in recent decades. Even during the Civil War era, many abolitionists interpreted due process differently and identified this Fifth Amendment clause as the basis for their convictions, maintaining that states had no right to deny slaves, or any other person, the right to life, liberty, or property without due process of law.

The addition of the Fourteenth Amendment to the Constitution in 1868 reflected the abolitionists' position. From that point forward, state governments were constitutionally required to provide due process of law and equal protection of the law to *all* people.

Substantive Due Process and Economic and Social Regulation

In the years following the enactment of the Fourteenth Amendment, the U.S. Supreme Court began a slow process of expanding the substantive meaning of due process. One area of concern to the Court involved state legislative efforts to regulate the economy.

The Court was asked to use the due process clause to strike down state laws affecting the freedom of contract. In the early cases, the states usually won if they were legislating to protect the public's health, welfare, safety, and morals. Gradually, however, justices began to consider whether the individual's liberty interests were being infringed by state attempts to provide protection to workers in the employer-employee relationship. In the 1890s the Court began to strike down state laws that established minimum wages for women, and that limited the number of hours bakers could work each day and week. The Court concluded that these laws exceeded the state's legislative power because they infringed upon the individual's due process right to liberty. The individual had the right to determine how many hours he or she wanted to work—at least in nonhazardous occupations, they maintained. And a legislative attempt to set minimum wages for women hospital workers was viewed by the Court as "price fixing." The Court was, in effect, sitting in judgment on legislative policies. The due process clause was the instrument it used to strike down economic legislation with which it disagreed.

The depression of the 1930s resulted in New Deal legislative initiatives that were intended to stimulate the economy. Congress created numerous agencies and programs in order to benefit industry, labor, savers and investors, farmers, and the needy. However, the Supreme Court struck down many of these New Deal laws between 1934 and 1936. This made the Court very unpopular in the "court" of public opinion and the president responded by proposing that Congress increase the size of the Court, presumably so that he could nominate people for the new seats who were sympathetic to New Deal legislation. In 1936, the Supreme Court began to reverse itself and uphold New Deal legislation. In addition, federal and state legislation setting minimum wages and maximum hours of work were sustained. The Court had decided that the due process right to liberty included protecting the community health, welfare, and safety. In addition, it abandoned its efforts to determine whether legislation was in the public welfare, leaving such matters to legislative bodies.

The Scope of Substantive Due Process

In the 1920s the Supreme Court had begun to recognize that an individual's liberty rights included more than just property rights. Individual "liberty" also required the constitutional protection of certain kinds of conduct. The justices of the U.S. Supreme Court differed, however, about whether such rights could be "found" within the meaning of due process. Although various justices on the Court proposed limits on the scope of substantive due process, the majority on the court adopted what is called the selective incorporation approach. This approach recognizes that *all* rights that the Court deems to be fundamental are included in the concept of due process.

Fundamental rights include those that have historically been part of the common law tradition, such as the First Amendment freedoms. Other fundamental rights include intimate decisions relating to marriage, procreation, contraception, family relations, child rearing, and education. The determination of whether a right is fundamental is made on a case-by-case basis.

It is important to emphasize that the Fifth and Fourteenth Amendment due process clauses operate only as restraints on government. One of the consequences of this limitation is that private schools have considerably more procedural latitude than public schools. Private elementary and secondary schools can regulate what students wear, substantially restrict student expression and behavior, enforce a common moral code, and enforce rules that are so vague that they would not be constitutionally acceptable in a public school. If private schools contract with their students to provide due process, or if they violate public policy, commit torts, or act inequitably, courts have been increasingly willing to intervene. Over the years there has been an expansion of the concept of "state action" and a closer relationship between private schools and government in the form of grants, scholarships, and research funds to institutions of higher education. Courts are beginning to require procedural due process in actions of those private colleges and universities that have such governmental involvement.

The next case in this chapter, *Kolender v. Lawson*, illustrates another aspect of substantive due process. Here, the Supreme Court has invoked the due process clause to overturn legislation that is either too vague or overly broad. Vague or overly broad statutes fail to provide citizens with fair notice of what is prohibited, and more important, according to the Court, they permit police officers to act arbitrarily.

Kolender, Chief of Police of San Diego, v. Lawson

461 U.S. 352
U.S. Supreme Court
May 2, 1983

Justice O'Connor delivered the opinion of the Court.

This appeal presents a facial challenge to a criminal statute that requires persons who loiter or wander on the streets to provide a "credible and reliable" identification and to account for their presence when requested by a peace officer under circumstances that would justify a stop under the standards of *Terry v. Ohio*, 392 U.S. 1 (1968).[1] We conclude that the statute as it has been construed is unconstitutionally vague within the meaning of the Due Process Clause of the Fourteenth Amendment by failing to clarify what is contemplated by the requirement that a suspect provide a "credible and reliable" identification. Accordingly, we affirm the judgment of the court below.

I

Appellee Edward Lawson was detained or arrested on approximately 15 occasions between March 1975 and January 1977 pursuant to Cal. Penal Code Ann. § 647(e) (West 1970).[2] Lawson was prosecuted only twice, and was convicted once. The second charge was dismissed.

Lawson then brought a civil action in the District Court for the Southern District of California seeking a declaratory judgment that § 647(e) is unconstitutional, a mandatory injunction to restrain enforcement of the statute, and compensatory and punitive damages against the various officers who detained him. The District Court found that § 647(e) was overbroad because "a person who is stopped on less than probable cause cannot be punished for failing to identify himself." The District Court enjoined enforcement of the statute, but held that Lawson could not recover damages because the officers involved acted in the good-faith belief that each detention or arrest was lawful.

. . . Lawson cross-appealed, arguing that he was entitled to a jury trial on the issue of damages against the officers. The Court of Appeals affirms the District Court determination as to the unconstitutionality of § 647(e). [T]he Court of Appeals reversed the District Court as to its holding that Lawson was not entitled to a jury trial to determine the good faith of the officers in his damages action against them, and remanded the case to the District Court for trial.

The officers appealed to this Court from that portion of the judgment of the Court of Appeals which declared § 647(e) unconstitutional and which enjoined its enforcement. . . .

II

In the courts below, Lawson mounted an attack on the facial validity of § 647(e). "In evaluating a facial challenge to a state law, a federal court must, of course, consider any limiting construction that a state court or enforcement agency has proffered." . . . . As construed by the California Court of Appeals, § 647(e) requires that an individual provide "credible and reliable" identification when

---

[1] California Penal Code Ann. § 647(e) (West 1970) provides: "Every person who commits any of the following acts is guilty of disorderly conduct, a misdemeanor. . . . (e) Who loiters or wanders upon the streets or from place to place without apparent reason or business and who refuses to identify himself and to account for his presence when requested by any peace officer so to do, if the surrounding circumstances are such as to indicate to a reasonable man that the public safety demands such identification."

[2] The District Court failed to find facts concerning the particular occasions on which Lawson was detained or arrested under § 647(e). However, the trial transcript contains numerous descriptions of the stops given both by Lawson and by the police officers who detained him. For example, one police officer testified that he stopped Lawson while walking on an otherwise vacant street because it was late at night, the area was isolated, and the area was located close to a high crime area. Tr. 266–267. Another officer testified that he detained Lawson, who was walking at a late hour in a business area where some businesses were still open, and asked for identification because burglaries had been committed by unknown persons in the general area. *Id.*, at 207. The appellee states that he has never been stopped by police for any reason apart from his detentions under § 647(e).

requested by a police officer who has reasonable suspicion of criminal activity sufficient to justify a *Terry* detention. . . . "Credible and reliable" identification is defined by the State Court of Appeals as identification "carrying reasonable assurance that the identification is authentic and providing means for later getting in touch with the person who has identified himself." . . . In addition, a suspect may be required to *account for his presence . . .* to the extent that it assists in producing credible and reliable identification. . . ." Under the terms of the statute, failure of the individual to provide "credible and reliable" identification permits the arrest.

III

Our Constitution is designed to maximize individual freedoms within a framework of ordered liberty. Statutory limitations on those freedoms are examined for substantive authority and content as well as for definiteness or certainty of expression. . . .

As generally stated, the void-for-vagueness doctrine requires that a penal statute define the criminal offense with sufficient definiteness that ordinary people can understand what conduct is prohibited and in a manner that does not encourage arbitrary and discriminatory enforcement. . . . Although the doctrine focuses both on actual notice to citizens and arbitrary enforcement, we have recognized recently that the more important aspect of the vagueness doctrine "is not actual notice, but the other principal element of the doctrine—the requirement that a legislature establish minimal guidelines to govern law enforcement." . . . Where the legislature fails to provide such minimal guidelines, a criminal statute may permit "a standardless sweep [that] allows policemen, prosecutors, and juries to pursue their personal predilections." . . .

Section 647(e), as presently drafted and as construed by the state courts, contains no standard for determining what the suspect has to do in order to satisfy the requirement to provide a "credible and reliable" identification. As such, the statute vests virtually complete discretion in the hands of the police to determine whether the suspect has satisfied the statute and must be permitted to go on his way in the absence of probable cause to arrest. An individual, whom police may think is suspicious but do not have probable cause to believe has committed a crime, is entitled to continue to walk the public streets "only at the whim of any police officer" who happens to stop that individual under § 647(e). . . . Our concern here is based upon the "potential for arbitrarily suppressing First Amendment liberties. . . ." In addition, 647(e) implicates consideration of the constitutional right to freedom of movement. . . .

Section 647(e) is not simply a "stop-and-identify" statute. Rather, the statute requires that the individual provide a "credible and reliable" identification that carries a "reasonable assurance" of its authenticity, and that provides "means for later getting in touch with the person who has identified himself." . . . In addition, the suspect may also have to account for his presence "to the extent it assists in producing credible and reliable identification." . . .

At oral argument, the appellants confirmed that a suspect violated § 647(e) unless "the officer [is] satisfied that the identification is reliable". . . . In giving examples of how suspects would satisfy the requirement, appellants explained that a jogger, who was not carrying identification, could, depending on the particular officer, be required to answer a series of questions concerning the route that he followed to arrive at the place where the officers detained him,[9] or could satisfy the identification requirement simply by reciting his name and address. . . .

It is clear that the full discretion accorded to the police to determine whether the suspect has provided a "credible and reliable" identification necessarily "entrust[s] law-making 'to the moment-to-moment judgment of the policeman on his beat.'" . . . Section 647(e) "furnishes a convenient tool for 'harsh and discriminatory enforcement by local prosecuting officials, against particular groups deemed to merit their displeasure,'" . . . and "confers on police a virtually unrestrained power to arrest and charge persons with a violation." . . . In providing that a detention under § 647(e) may occur only where there is the level of suspicion sufficient to justify a *Terry* stop, the State ensures the existence of "neutral limitations on the conduct of individual officers." . . . Although the initial detention is justified, the State fails to establish standards by which the officers may determine whether the suspect has complied with the subsequent identification requirement.

Appellants stress the need for strengthened law enforcement tools to combat the epidemic of crime that plagues our Nation. The concern of our citizens with curbing criminal activity is certainly a matter requiring the attention of all branches of government. As weighty as this concern is, however, it cannot justify legislation that would otherwise fail to meet constitutional standards for definiteness and clarity. . . . Section 647(e), as presently construed, requires that "suspicious" persons satisfy some undefined identification requirement, or face criminal punishment. Although due process does not require "impossible standards" of clarity, this is not a case where further precision in the statutory language is either impossible or impractical.

IV

We conclude § 647(e) is unconstitutionally vague on its face because it encourages arbitrary enforcement by failing to describe with sufficient particularity what a suspect must do in order to satisfy the statute.[10] Accordingly, the judgment of the Court of Appeals is affirmed, and the case is remanded for further proceedings consistent with this opinion.

It is so ordered.

[9] To the extent that § 647(e) criminalizes a suspect's failure to answer such questions put to him by police officers, Fifth Amendment concerns are implicated. It is a "settled principle that while the police have the right to request citizens to answer voluntarily questions concerning unsolved crimes they have no right to compel them to answer." *Davis v. Mississippi*, 394 U.S. 721, 727, n. 6 (1969).

[10] Because we affirm the judgment of the court below on this ground, we find it unnecessary to decide the other questions raised by the parties because our resolution of these other issues would decide constitutional questions in advance of the necessity of doing so. . . . The remaining issues raised by the parties include whether § 647(e) implicated Fourth Amendment concerns, whether the individual has a legitimate expectation of privacy in his identity when he is detained lawfully under *Terry*, whether the requirement that an individual identify himself during a *Terry* stop violates the Fifth Amendment protection against compelled testimony, and whether inclusion of the *Terry* standard as part of a criminal statute creates other vagueness problems. The appellee also argues that section 647(e) permits arrests on less than probable cause.

Case Questions

1. When the U.S. Supreme Court determined whether the California Statute was unconstitutionally void for vagueness, what standards of evaluation did the Court use?

f the two principal elements of the vagueness doctrine is more
t?

uldn't police officers be entrusted by law with the discretion to
whether an individual has provided credible and reliable
ation?

ellants argued that law enforcement tools need to be powerful in
combat crime. What considerations did the court find even more
ng?

aw is very much concerned with procedure. The underlying prem-
ustice is more likely to result when correct procedures have been
followed. All states and the federal government have extensive rules that
govern criminal and civil litigation; these are subject to modification by federal
and state legislative and judicial bodies. Although some rules are essentially
arbitrary—for instance, one that requires a defendant to file an answer within
twenty days of being served with a summons and complaint—other procedures are thought to be essential to due process and have been given constitutional protection. This latter category of rules promotes accurate fact-finding
and fairness and is used in all jurisdictions in every case.

Procedural due process rules play a major role in criminal cases, placing
limits on police investigative techniques and prosecutorial behavior, and
outlining how criminal trials should be conducted.

Even when the Supreme Court has interpreted the due process clause of the
Fourteenth Amendment to require a procedural right, however, it sometimes
permits states to deviate from practices followed in federal courts. Procedural
due process, for example, guarantees criminal defendants who are subject to
more than six months' incarceration upon conviction the right to a jury trial.
A defendant who stands trial in a state court, however, may not receive the
same type of jury trial as in a federal court. Due process has been interpreted
to permit states to accept nonunanimous jury verdicts in criminal cases where
a unanimous verdict would be required in a federal court. Similarly, states are
not constitutionally mandated to provide twelve-member juries even though
twelve jurors are required in federal court.

In civil cases, due process rules are less extensive. They ensure that the
court has jurisdiction over the parties, that proper notice has been given to
defendants, and that the parties have an equal opportunity to present evidence
and argument to the decision maker. In both types of litigation, procedural
due process rules help ensure that decisions are made in a fair and reasonable manner.

As mentioned earlier, however, accuracy and fairness are not the only
considerations. Elaborate procedural requirements are costly in terms of time,
money, and utility. When the Supreme Court decides that a procedural right

is fundamental to due process, there are often financial costs imposed on government, society, and individual litigants. Due process requirements can also lengthen the time it takes to conclude litigation, adding to the existing backlogs in many jurisdictions. Courts, therefore, generally try to balance accuracy against its cost on a case-by-case basis. In criminal cases the need for accurate decision making is paramount, and the requirements of due process are quite extensive.

As we will see in the following case of *Goss v. Lopez*, however, the requirements of due process are much less stringent when a public school board proposes to suspend a student for disciplinary infractions of school rules. The justices of the U.S. Supreme Court have differed on which procedural rights are constitutionally required and when they should be applied. In *Goss v. Lopez* four justices did not believe that the due process clause required public school boards to hold hearings in conjunction with minor school suspensions.

Goss v. Lopez
419 U.S. 565
U.S. Supreme Court
January 22, 1975

White, Justice

This appeal by various administrators of the Columbus, Ohio, Public School System (CPSS) challenges the judgment of a three-judge federal court, declaring that appellees—various high school students in the CPSS—were denied due process of law contrary to the command of the Fourteenth Amendment in that they were temporarily suspended from their high schools without a hearing either prior to suspension or within a reasonable time thereafter, and enjoining the administrators to remove all references to such suspensions from the students' records.

Ohio law, Rev. Code Ann. §3313.64 (1972), provides for free education to all children between the ages of 6 and 21. Section §3313.66 of the Code empowers the principal of an Ohio public school to suspend a pupil for misconduct for up to 10 days or to expel him. In either case, he must notify the student's parents within 24 hours and state the reasons for his

action. A pupil who is expelled, or his parents, may appeal the decision to the Board of Education and in connection therewith shall be permitted to be heard at the board meeting. The Board may reinstate the pupil following the hearing. No similar procedure is provided in §3313.66 or any other provision of state law for a suspended student. Aside from a regulation tracking the statute, at the time of the imposition of the suspensions in this case the CPSS itself had not issued any written procedure applicable to suspensions. Nor, so far as the record reflects, had any of the individual high schools involved in this case. Each, however, had formally or informally described the conduct for which suspension could be imposed.

The nine named appellees, each of whom alleged that he or she had been suspended from public high school in Columbus for up to 10 days without a hearing pursuant to Section 3316.66, filed an action under 42 U.S.C. § 1983 against the Columbus Board of Education and various administrators of the CPSS. The complaint sought a declaration that Section 3313.66 was unconstitutional in that it permitted public school administrators to deprive plaintiffs of their rights to an education without a hearing of any kind, in violation of the procedural due process component of the Fourteenth Amendment. It also sought to enjoin the public school officials from issuing future suspensions pursuant to Section 3313.66 and to require them to remove references to the past suspensions from the records of the students in question.

The proof below established that the suspensions arose out of a period of widespread student unrest in the CPSS during February and March 1971. . . . Two named plaintiffs, Dwight Lopez and Betty Crome, were students at the Central High School and McGuffey Junior High School, respectively. The former was suspended in connection with a disturbance in the lunchroom which involved some physical damage to school property. Lopez testified that at least 75 other students were suspended from his school on the same day. He also testified below that he was not a party to the destructive conduct but was instead an innocent bystander. Because no one from the school testified with regard to this incident, there is no evidence in the record indicating the official basis for concluding otherwise. Lopez never had a hearing.

Betty Crome was present at a demonstration at a high school other than the one she was attending. There she was arrested together with others, taken to the police station, and released without being formally charged. Before she went to school on the following day, she was notified that she had been suspended for a 10-day period. Because no one from the school testified with respect to this incident, the record does not disclose how the McGuffey Junior High School principal went about making the decision to suspend Crome, nor does it disclose on what information the decision was based. It is clear from the record that no hearing was ever held. . . .

At the outset, appellants contend that because there is no constitutional right to an education at public expense, the Due Process Clause does not protect against expulsions from the public school system. This position misconceives the nature of the issue and is refuted by prior decisions. The Fourteenth Amendment forbids the State to deprive any person of life, liberty, or property without due process of law. Protected interests in property are normally "not created by the Constitution. Rather, they are created and their dimensions are defined" by an independent source such as state statutes or rules entitling the citizen to certain benefits. . . .

Although Ohio may not be constitutionally obligated to establish and maintain a public school system, it has nevertheless done so and has required its children to attend. Those young people do not "shed their constitutional rights" at the schoolhouse door. . . . "The Fourteenth Amendment, as now applied to the States, protects the citizen against the State itself and all of its creatures—Boards of Education not excepted." The authority possessed by the State to prescribe and enforce standards of conduct in its schools, although concededly very broad, must be exercised consistently with constitutional safeguards. Among other things, the State is constrained to recognize a student's legitimate entitlement to a public education as a property interest which is protected by the Due Process Clause and which may not be taken away for misconduct without adherence to the minimum procedures required by that clause.

The Due Process Clause also forbids arbitrary deprivations of liberty. "Where a person's good name, reputation, honor, or integrity is at stake because of what the government is doing to him," the minimal requirements of the Clause must be satisfied. School authorities here suspended appellees from school for periods of up to 10 days based on charges of misconduct. If sustained and recorded, those charges could seriously damage the students' standing with their fellow pupils and their teachers as well as interfere with later opportunities for higher education and employment. It is apparent that the claimed right of the State to determine unilaterally and without due process whether that misconduct has occurred immediately collides with the requirements of the Constitution. . . .

A short suspension is, of course, a far milder deprivation than expulsion. But "education is perhaps the most important function of state and local governments," . . . and the total exclusion from the educational process for more than a trivial period, and certainly if the suspension is for 10 days, is a serious event in the life of the suspended child. Neither the property interest in educational benefits temporarily denied nor the liberty interest in reputation, which is also implicated, is so insubstantial that suspensions may constitutionally be imposed by any procedure the school chooses, no matter how arbitrary. . . .

At the very minimum, therefore, students facing suspension and the consequent interference with a protected property interest must be given *some* kind of notice and afforded *some* kind of hearing. "Parties whose rights are to be affected are entitled to be heard; and in order that they may enjoy that right, they must first be notified." . . .

The prospect of imposing elaborate hearing requirements in every suspension case is viewed with great concern, and many school authorities may well prefer the untrammeled power to act unilater-

ally, unhampered by rules about notice and hearing. But it would be a strange disciplinary system in an educational institution if no communication was sought by the disciplinarian with the student in an effort to inform him of his dereliction and to let him tell his side of the story in order to make sure that an injustice is not done. "Fairness can rarely be obtained by secret, one-sided determination of facts decisive of rights. . . ." "Secrecy is not congenial to truth-seeking and self-righteousness gives too slender an assurance of rightness. No better instrument has been devised for arriving at truth than to give a person in jeopardy of serious loss notice of the case against him and opportunity to meet it." . . .

Students facing temporary suspension have interests qualifying for protection of the Due Process Clause, and due process requires, in connection with a suspension of 10 days or less, that the student be given oral or written notice of the charges against him and, if he denies them, an explanation of the evidence the authorities have and an opportunity to present his side of the story. The Clause requires at least these rudimentary precautions against unfair or mistaken findings of misconduct and arbitrary exclusion from school. . . .

We stop short of construing the Due Process Clause to require, countrywide, that hearings in connection with short suspensions must afford the student the opportunity to secure counsel, to confront and cross-examine witnesses supporting the charge, or to call his own witnesses to verify his version of the incident. Brief disciplinary suspensions are almost countless. To impose in each such case even truncated trial-type procedures might well overwhelm administrative facilities in many places and, by diverting resources, cost more than it would save in educational effectiveness. Moreover, further formalizing the suspension process and escalating its formality and adversary nature may not only make it too costly as a regular disciplinary tool but also destroy its effectiveness as part of the teaching process.

On the other hand, requiring effective notice and informal hearing permitting the student to give his version of the events will provide a meaningful hedge against erroneous action. At least the disciplinarian will be alerted to the existence of disputes about facts and arguments about cause and effect. He may then determine himself to summon the accuser, permit cross-examination, and allow the student to present his own witnesses. In more difficult cases, he may permit counsel. In any event, his discretion will be more informed and we think the risk of error substantially reduced. . . .

We should also make it clear that we have addressed ourselves solely to the short suspension, not exceeding 10 days. Longer suspensions or expulsions for the remainder of the school term, or permanently, may require more formal procedures. Nor do we put aside the possibility that in unusual situations, although involving only a short suspension, something more than the rudimentary procedures will be required.

The District Court found each of the suspensions involved here to have occurred without a hearing, either before or after the suspension, and that each suspension was therefore invalid and the statute unconstitutional insofar as it permits such suspensions without notice or hearing. Accordingly, the judgment is
Affirmed.

Justice Powell, with whom the Chief Justice, Justice Blackmun, and Justice Rehnquist join, dissenting

The Court today invalidates an Ohio statute that permits student suspensions from school without a hearing "for not more than ten days." . . .

The Court's decision rests on the premise that, under Ohio law, education is a property interest protected by the Fourteenth Amendment's Due Process Clause and therefore that any suspension requires notice and a hearing. In my view, a student's interest in education is not infringed by a suspension within the limited period prescribed by Ohio law. Moreover, to the extent that there may be some arguable infringement, it is too speculative, transitory, and insubstantial to justify imposition of a *constitutional* rule. . . .

The Court thus disregards the basic structure of Ohio law in posturing this case as if Ohio had conferred an unqualified right to education, thereby compelling the school authorities to conform to due process procedures in imposing the most routine discipline. . . .

The Ohio suspension statute allows no serious or significant infringement of education. It authorizes only a maximum suspension of eight school days, less than 5% of the normal 180-day school year. Absences of such limited duration will rarely affect a pupil's opportunity to learn or his scholastic performance. Indeed, the record in this case reflects no educational injury to appellees. Each completed the semester in which the suspension occurred and performed at least as well as he or she had in previous years. Despite the Court's unsupported speculation that a suspended student could be "seriously damaged," there is no factual showing of any such damage to appellees. . . .

Today's opinion . . . holds in effect that government infringement of any interest to which a person is entitled, no matter what the interest or how inconsequential the infringement, requires *con-stitutional* protection. As it is difficult to think of any less consequential infringement than suspension of a junior high school student for a single day, it is equally difficult to perceive any principled limit to the new reach of procedural due process.

Case Questions

1. Do students in a public or private institution have only a *privilege* to continue their education in that institution, or do they have a *right* to do so?
2. What minimum standards of procedure do you think should be mandatory in the review of student discipline?
3. How does the Court provide for exceptions to this rule?
4. What does the Court hope to accomplish with such minimal procedural protections?

CRIMINAL AND CIVIL LAW

The distinction between criminal and civil law is a very important concept in our legal system (see Figure 1–1). This text deals primarily with civil law. A civil suit involves a dispute between private individuals involving either a breach of an agreement or a breach of a duty imposed by law. A criminal action is brought by the government against an individual who has allegedly committed a crime. Crimes are classified as treason, felonies, and misdemeanors, depending on the punishment attached to the crime. *Treason* is a crime defined only by the Constitution, article III, section 3, clause 1. To commit treason—levying war against the United States, or adhering to or giving aid or comfort to its enemies—there must be an overt act and the intent to commit treason. A *felony* is a crime that is classified by statute of the place in which it is committed. That is, the severity of the punishment for a felony varies from place to place. A felony is generally regarded as being any criminal offense for which a defendant may be imprisoned for more than one year, or executed. One determines whether a crime is a felony according to the sentence that might lawfully be imposed, not according to the sentence actually ordered. Felonies do not include *misdemeanors*, which are offenses that are generally punishable by a maximum term of imprisonment of less than one year.

In a civil suit, the court attempts to remedy the dispute between individuals by determining their legal rights, awarding money damages to the injured party, or directing one party to perform or refrain from performing a specific act. Since a crime is an act against society, the criminal court punishes a guilty defendant by imposing a fine or imprisonment or both.

In a criminal prosecution, the rules of court procedure differ. In order to meet the burden of proof to find a person guilty of a crime, guilt must be

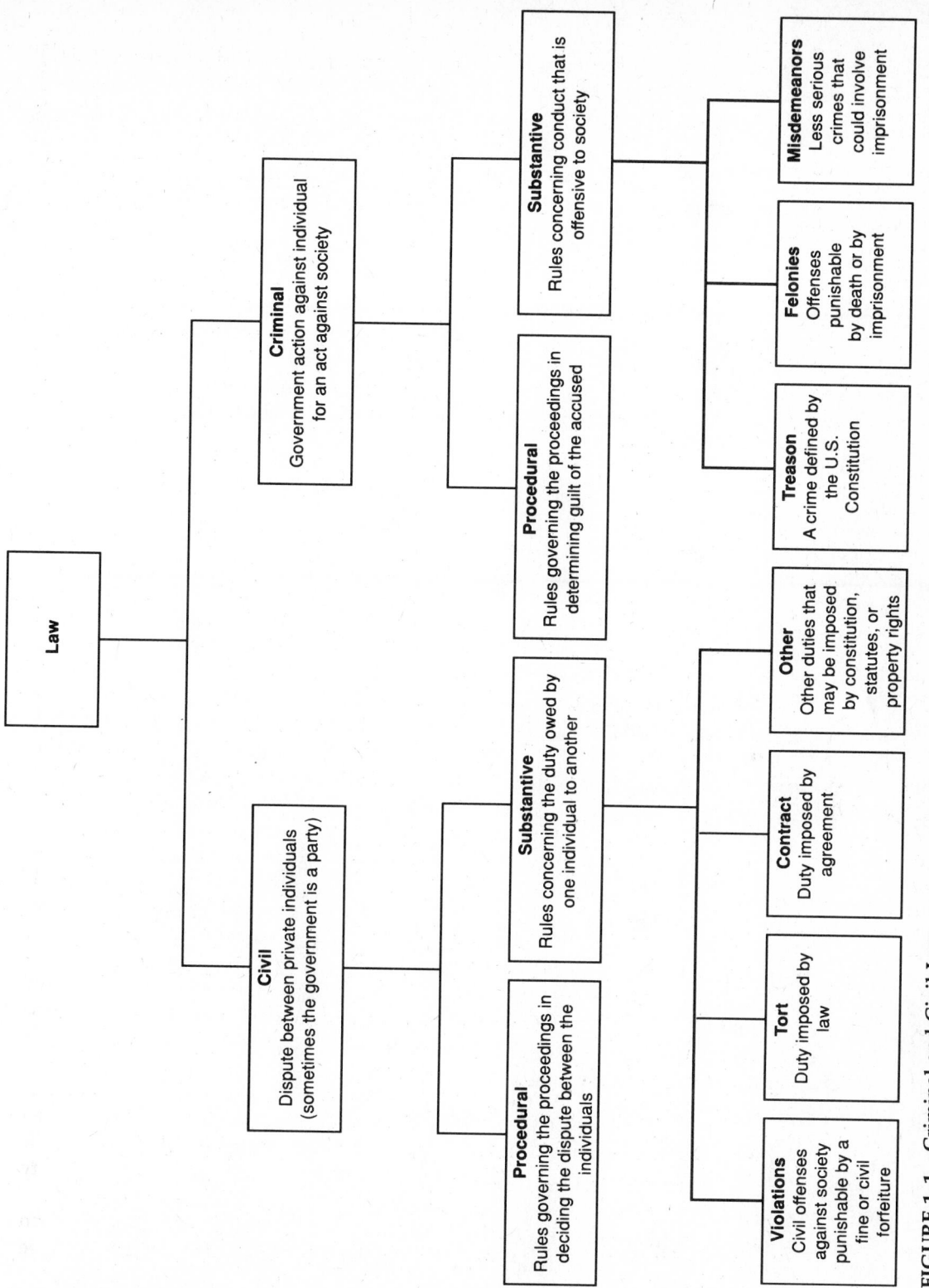

FIGURE 1-1   Criminal and Civil Law

proved beyond a reasonable doubt, a stricter standard than the preponderance of evidence usually required in a civil case.

As we will see in the next case, when the same act gives rise to both a criminal proceeding and a civil suit, the actions are completely independent of each other. *Katko v. Briney* involves a civil suit for damages brought against the victim of a criminal larceny, by the person convicted of committing the crime.

Katko v. Briney
183 N.W.2d 657
Supreme Court of Iowa
February 9, 1971

Moore, Chief Justice

The primary issue presented here is whether an owner may protect personal property in an unoccupied boarded-up farmhouse against trespassers and thieves by a spring gun capable of inflicting death or serious injury.

We are not here concerned with a man's right to protect his home and members of his family. Defendants' home was several miles from the scene of the incident to which we refer *infra*.

Plaintiff's action is for damages resulting from serious injury caused by a shot from a 20-gauge spring shotgun set by defendants in a bedroom of an old farmhouse which had been uninhabited for several years. Plaintiff and his companion, Marvin McDonough, had broken and entered the house to find and steal old bottles and dated fruit jars which they considered antiques.

At defendants' request, plaintiff's action was tried to a jury consisting of residents of the community where defendants' property was located. The jury returned a verdict for plaintiff and against defendants for $20,000 actual and $10,000 punitive damages.

After careful consideration of defendants' motions for judgment notwith-standing the verdict and for new trial, the experienced and capable trial judge overruled them and entered judgment on the verdict. Thus we have this appeal by defendants. . . .

Most of the facts are not disputed. In 1957 defendant Bertha L. Briney inherited her parents' farmland in Mahaska and Monroe Counties. For about ten years, 1957 to 1967, there occurred a series of trespassing and housebreaking events with loss of some household items, the breaking of windows, and "messing up of the property in general." The latest occurred June 8, 1967, prior to the event on July 16, 1967, herein involved.

Defendants through the years boarded up the windows and doors in an attempt to stop the intrusions. They had posted "no trespass" signs on the land several years before 1967. The nearest one was 35 feet from the house. On June 11, 1967, defendants set a "shotgun trap" in the north bedroom. After Mr. Briney cleaned and oiled his 20-gauge shotgun, the power of which he was well aware, defendants took it to the old house where they secured it to an iron bed with the barrel pointed at the bedroom door. It was rigged with wire from the doorknob to the gun's trigger so that it would fire when the door was opened. Briney first pointed the gun so an intruder would be hit in the stomach but at Mrs. Briney's suggestion it was lowered to hit the legs. He admitted he did so "because I was mad and tired of being tormented" but "he did not intend to injure anyone." He gave no explanation of why he used a loaded shell and set it to hit a person already in the house. Tin was nailed over the bedroom window. The spring gun could not be seen from the outside. No warning of its presence was posted.

Plaintiff lived with his wife and worked regularly as a gasoline station attendant in Eddyville, seven miles from the old house. He had observed it for several years while hunting in the area and considered it as being abandoned. He knew it had long been uninhabited. In 1967 the area around the house was covered with high weeds. Prior to July 16, 1967 plaintiff and McDonough had been to the premises and found several old bottles and fruit jars which they took and added to their collection of antiques. On the latter date about 9:30 P.M. they made a second trip to the Briney property. They entered the old house by removing a board from a porch window which was without glass. While McDonough was looking around the kitchen area, plaintiff went to another part of the house. As he started to open the north bedroom door the shotgun went off, striking him in the right leg above the ankle bone. Much of his leg, including part of the tibia, was blown away. Only by McDonough's assistance was plaintiff able to get out of the house and after crawling some distance, he was put in his vehicle and rushed to a doctor and then to a hospital. He remained in the hospital 40 days.

Plaintiff's doctor testified he seriously considered amputation but eventually the healing process was successful. Some weeks after his release from the hospital plaintiff returned to work on crutches. He was required to keep the injured leg in a cast for approximately a year and wear a special brace for another year.

He continued to suffer pain during this period.

There was undenied medical testimony plaintiff had a permanent deformity, a loss of tissue, and a shortening of the leg.

The record discloses plaintiff to trial time had incurred $710 medical expense, $2056.85 for hospital service, $61.80 for orthopedic service and $750 as loss of earnings. In addition thereto the trial court submitted to the jury the question of damages for pain and suffering and for future disability.

Plaintiff testified he knew he had no right to break and enter the house with intent to steal bottles and fruit jars therefrom. He further testified he had entered a plea of guilty to larceny in the nighttime of property of less than $20 value from a private building. He stated he had been fined $50 and costs and paroled during good behavior from a 60-day jail sentence. Other than minor traffic charges, this was plaintiff's first brush with the law. On this civil case appeal, it is not our prerogative to review the disposition made of the criminal charge against him.

The main thrust of defendants' defense in the trial court and on this appeal is that "the law permits use of a spring gun in a dwelling or warehouse for the purpose of preventing the unlawful entry of a burglar or thief." . . . [T]he court referred to the early case history of the use of spring guns and stated under the law their use was prohibited except to prevent the commission of felonies of violence and where human life is in danger. The instruction included a statement breaking and entering is not a felony of violence.

Instruction 5 stated: "You are hereby instructed that one may use reasonable force in the protection of his property, but such right is subject to the qualification that one may not use such means of force as will take human life or inflict great bodily injury. Such is the rule even though the injured party is a trespasser and is in violation of the law himself."

Instruction 6 stated: "An owner of premises is prohibited from willfully or intentionally injuring a trespasser by means of force that either takes life or inflicts great bodily injury; and therefore a person owning a premise is prohibited from setting out 'spring guns' and like dangerous devices which will likely take life or inflict great bodily injury, for the purpose of harming trespassers. The fact that the trespasser may be acting in violation of the law does not change the rule. The only time when such conduct of setting a 'spring gun' or a like dangerous device is justified would be when the trespasser was committing a felony of violence or a felony punishable by death, or where the trespasser was endangering human life by his act."

Instruction 7, to which defendants made no objection or exception, stated:

> "To entitle the plaintiff to recover for compensatory damages, the burden of proof is upon him to establish by a preponderance of the evidence each and all of the following propositions:

> "1. That defendants erected a shotgun trap in a vacant house on land owned by defendant, Bertha L. Briney, on or about June 11, 1967, which fact was known only by them, to protect household goods from trespassers and thieves.
> "2. That the force used by defendants was in excess of that force reasonably necessary and which persons are entitled to use in the protection of their property.
> "3. That plaintiff was injured and damaged and the amount thereof.

> "4. That plaintiff's injuries and damages resulted directly from the discharge of the shotgun trap which was set and used by defendants."

The overwhelming weight of authority, both textbook and case law, supports the trial court's statement of the applicable principles of law.

Prosser on Torts, third edition, pages 116–118, states that:

> "the law has always placed a higher value upon human safety than upon mere rights in property[. I]t is the accepted rule that there is no privilege to use any force calculated to cause death or serious bodily injury to repel the threat to land or chattels, unless there is also such a threat to the defendant's personal safety as to justify a self-defense. . . . [S]pring guns and other man-killing devices are not justifiable against a mere trespasser, or even a petty thief. They are privileged only against those upon whom the landowner, if he were present in person, would be free to inflict injury of the same kind."

Restatement of Torts, §85, page 180, states that:

> "the value of human life and limbs, not only to the individual concerned but also to society, so outweighs the interest of a possessor of land in excluding from it those whom he is not willing to admit thereto that a possessor of land has, as is stated in §79, no privilege to use force intended or likely to cause death or serious harm against another whom the possessor sees about to enter his premises or meddle with his chattel, unless the intrusion threatens death or serious bodily harm to the occupiers or users of the premises. . . . A possessor of land cannot do indirectly and by a mechanical device that which, were he present, he could not do immediately and in person. Therefore, he cannot gain a

privilege to install, for the purpose of protecting his land from intrusions harmless to the lives and limbs of the occupiers or users of it, a mechanical device whose only purpose is to inflict death or serious harm upon such as may intrude, by giving notice of his intention to inflict, by mechanical means and indirectly, harm which he could not, even after request, inflict directly were he present." . . .

In *Hooker v. Miller*, 37 Iowa 613, we held defendant vineyard owner liable for damages resulting from a spring gun shot although plaintiff was a trespasser and there to steal grapes. At pages 614, 615, this statement is made: "This court has held that a mere trespass against property other than a dwelling is not a sufficient justification to authorize the use of a deadly weapon by the owner in its defense; and that if death results in such a case it will be murder, though the killing be actually necessary to prevent the trespass. . . ." At page 617 this court said: "[T]respassers and other inconsiderable violators of the law are not to be visited by barbarous punishments or prevented by inhuman inflictions of bodily injuries."

The facts in *Allison v. Fiscus*, 156 Ohio 120, decided in 1951, are very similar to the case at bar. There plaintiff's right to damages was recognized for injuries received when he feloniously broke a door latch and started to enter defendant's warehouse with intent to steal. As he entered, a trap of two sticks of dynamite buried under the doorway by defendant owner was set off and plaintiff seriously injured. The court held the question whether a particular trap was justified as a use of reasonable and necessary force against a trespasser engaged in the commission of a felony should have been submitted to the jury. The Ohio Supreme Court recognized the plaintiff's right to

recover punitive or exemplary damages in addition to compensatory damages. . . .

In *United Zinc & Chemical Co. v. Britt*, 258 U.S. 268, 275, the Court states: "The liability for spring guns and mantraps arises from the fact that the defendant has . . . expected the trespasser and prepared an injury that is no more justified than if he had held the gun and fired it."

In addition to civil liability many jurisdictions hold a landowner criminally liable for serious injuries or homicide caused by spring guns or other set devices. . . .

In Wisconsin, Oregon and England the use of spring guns and similar devices is specifically made unlawful by statute. . . .

The legal principles stated by the trial court in instructions 2, 5 and 6 are well established and supported by the authorities cited and quoted *supra*. There is no merit in defendants' objections and exceptions thereto. Defendants' various motions based on the same reasons stated in exceptions to instructions were properly overruled.

Plaintiff's claim and the jury's allowance of punitive damages, under the trial court's instructions relating thereto, were not at any time or in any manner challenged by defendants in the trial court as not allowable. We therefore are not presented with the problem of whether the $10,000 award should be allowed to stand.

We express no opinion as to whether punitive damages are allowable in this type of case. If defendants' attorneys wanted that issue decided, it was their duty to raise it in the trial court.

The rule is well established that we will not consider a contention not raised in the trial court. In other words, we are a court of review and will not consider a contention raised for the first time in this court. . . .

Under our law punitive damages are not allowed as a matter of right. When malice is shown or when a defendant acted with wanton and reckless disregard of the rights of others, punitive damages may be allowed as punishment to the defendant and as a deterrent to others. Although not meant to compensate a plaintiff, the result is to increase his recovery. He is the fortuitous beneficiary of such an award simply because there is no one else to receive it.

The jury's findings of fact including a finding that defendants acted with malice and with wanton and reckless disregard, as required for an allowance of punitive or exemplary damages, are supported by substantial evidence. We are bound thereby.

This opinion is not to be taken or construed as authority that the allowance of punitive damages is or is not proper under circumstances such as exist here. We hold only that a question of law not having been properly raised cannot in this case be resolved.

Study and careful consideration of defendants' contentions on appeal reveal no reversible error.

Affirmed.

Larson, Justice, dissenting

I respectfully dissent, first because the majority wrongfully assumes that by installing a spring gun in the bedroom of their unoccupied house the defendants intended to shoot any intruder who attempted to enter the room. Under the record presented here, that was a fact question. Unless it is held that these property owners are liable for any injury to an intruder from such a device regardless of the intent with which it is installed, liability under these pleadings must rest on two definite issues of fact, i.e., did the defendants intend to shoot the invader, and if so, did they employ unnecessary and unreasonable force against him?

It is my feeling that the majority oversimplifies the impact of this case on the law, not only in this but other jurisdictions, and that it has not thought through all the ramifications of this holding.

There being no statutory provisions governing the right of an owner to defend his property by the use of a spring gun or other like device, or of a criminal invader to recover punitive damages when injured by such an instrumentality while breaking into the building of another, our interest and attention are directed to what should be the court determination of public policy in these matters. On both issues we are faced with a case of first impression. We should accept the task and clearly establish the law in this jurisdiction hereafter. I would hold there is no absolute liability for injury to a criminal intruder by setting up such a device on his property, and unless done with an intent to kill or seriously injure the intruder, I would absolve the owner from liability other than for negligence. I would also hold the court had no jurisdiction to allow punitive damages when the intruder was engaged in a serious criminal offense such as breaking and entering with intent to steal. . . .

Case Questions

1. Suppose that, instead of a spring gun, the Brineys had unleashed on the premises a vicious watchdog that severely injured Katko's leg. Would the result have been different? What if the watchdog were properly chained?

2. When may one set a spring gun and not be subject to liability? What can one legally do to protect property or life?
3. What do you think the consequences would be if the dissenting judge's suggestions had become law?
4. A case involving breaking and entering and shooting a gun might appear to be a criminal matter. What factors make this a civil lawsuit?

TORT AND CONTRACT LAW

A person has a right to bring civil action against another for a wrongful act or omission that causes injury to him or her. The basis of the suit is a violation of some duty owed to the injured person. This duty arises either from an agreement of the persons or by operation of the law.

Torts

Tort law establishes standards of conduct that all citizens must meet. A plaintiff sues in tort to recover money damages for injuries to his or her person, reputation, property, or business caused by a breach of a legal duty.

A tort is any wrongful act, not involving a breach of an agreement, for which such a civil action may be maintained. The wrongful act can be intentional or unintentional. Intentional torts are based on the defendant's willful misconduct or intentional wrongdoing. This does not necessarily mean the defendant had a hostile intent, only that he or she had a belief that a particular harmful result was substantially likely to follow. *Katko v. Briney* was such a case. When Briney rigged the spring gun, he did so believing that serious bodily injury was very likely to occur to any intruder who opened the door. Briney was civilly found to have violated the standard of care owed by a property owner to a trespasser such as Katko under the circumstances of that case. A person who commits an intentional tort may also be committing a criminal act, for which the government may bring criminal charges. As we saw in *Katko v. Briney*, the tort and criminal actions would be independent of each other.

An unintentional tort occurs when a person acts negligently. That is, he or she unintentionally fails to live up to the community's ideal of reasonable care. Every person has a legal duty to act toward other people as a reasonable and prudent person would have acted under the circumstances. Torts will be discussed more fully in Chapter 11.

Contracts

A contract is a promissory agreement between two or more people that creates, modifies, or destroys a legally enforceable obligation. People voluntarily enter into a contract in order to create private duties for mutual advantage. Thus, under ordinary conditions, contractual terms are not imposed by law. There are exceptions to this rule; however, the essence of contract law is the enforcement of a promise voluntarily made.

Although contract law is more thoroughly discussed in Chapter 9, it will be helpful to introduce it here. In the legal sense, the term contract does not mean the tangible document that contains evidence of an agreement. Rather, a contract is the legally enforceable agreement itself. There are three parts to every contract: *offer, acceptance,* and *consideration.* An offer is a communication of a promise, with a statement of what is expected in return. An offer is made with the intention of creating an enforceable legal obligation. Acceptance is the evidence of assent to the terms of the offer. Consideration is the inducement each party has to enter into an agreement. Only legally enforceable obligations are called contracts.

A person who fails to perform a contractual obligation has breached the contract. The plaintiff brings a suit in contract to obtain legal relief from the breaching party. The normal remedy for a breach of contract is monetary damages, although in appropriate circumstances, the breaching party may be ordered to perform his or her agreement.

Contracts may be oral, written, express (explicit terms), implied in fact (inferred from the person's actions), or implied in law. In *Suggs v. Norris,* which follows, the trial court permitted the jury to find an implied-in-law agreement from the facts of the case, even though there was no oral or written document evidencing a contract.

Suggs v. Norris
364 S.E.2d 159
Court of Appeals of North Carolina
February 2, 1988

Wells, Judge

The overriding question presented by this appeal is whether public policy forbids the recovery by a plaintiff partner to an unmarried but cohabiting or meretricious relationship, from the other partner's estate, for services rendered to or benefits conferred upon the other partner through the plaintiff's work in the operation of a joint business when the business proceeds were utilized to enrich the estate of the deceased partner.

Defendant argues under her first three assignments of error that any agreement between plaintiff and the decedent providing compensation to plaintiff for her efforts in the raising and harvesting of produce was void as against public policy because it arose out of the couple's illegal cohabitation. While it is well-settled that no recovery can be had under either a contractual or restitutionary (*quantum meruit*) theory arising out of a contract or circumstances which violate public policy, . . . defendant's application of the rule to the present case is misplaced.

This Court has made it clear that we do not approve of or endorse adulterous meretricious affairs, *Collins v. Davis,* 68 N.C.App. 588. . . . We made it clear in *Collins,* however, that cohabiting but unmarried individuals are capable of "entering into enforceable express or implied contracts for the purchase and improvement of houses, or for the loan and repayment of money." . . . Judge Phillips, writing for the majority, in *Collins* was careful to point out that if illicit sexual intercourse had provided the consideration for the contract or implied agreement, all claims arising therefrom, having been founded on illegal consideration, would then be unenforceable.

While our research has disclosed no other North Carolina cases which address this specific issue, we do find considerable guidance in the decisional law of other states. Most notable is Justice Tobriner's landmark decision in *Marvin v. Marvin*, 18 Cal.3d 660, . . . (1976) which held that express contracts between unmarried cohabiting individuals are enforceable unless the same are based solely on sexual services. . . .

The *Marvin* Court also held that an unmarried couple may, by words and conduct, create an implied-in-fact agreement regarding the disposition of their mutual properties and money as well as an implied agreement of partnership or joint venture. . . . Finally, the court endorsed the use of constructive trusts wherever appropriate and recovery in *quantum meruit* where the plaintiff can show that the services were rendered with an expectation of monetary compensation. . . .

Other jurisdictions have fashioned and adhered to similar rules. In *Kinkenon v. Hue*, 207 Neb. 698 . . . (1981), the Nebraska Supreme Court confirmed an earlier rule that while bargains made in whole or in part for consideration of sexual intercourse are illegal, any agreements not resting on such consideration, regardless of the marital status of the two individuals, are enforceable. . . .

Likewise, the New Jersey Supreme Court held as enforceable an oral agreement between two adult unmarried partners where the agreement was not based "explicitly or inseparably" on sexual services. *Kozlowski v. Kozlowski*, 80 N.J. 378 . . .

(1979). In *Fernandez v. Garza*, 88 Ariz. 214, (1960), the Arizona Supreme Court held that plaintiff's meretricious or unmarried cohabitation with decedent did not bar the enforcement of a partnership agreement wherein the parties agreed to share their property and profits equally and where such was not based upon sexual services as consideration. . . .

We now make clear and adopt the rule that agreements regarding the finances and property of an unmarried but cohabiting couple, whether express or implied, are enforceable as long as sexual services or promises thereof do not provide the consideration for such agreements. . . .

In the present case, the question is before this Court on an appeal of the trial court's denial of defendant's Motion for Judgment Notwithstanding the Verdict; therefore, our standard of review is whether the evidence viewed in the light most favorable to plaintiff is sufficient to support the jury verdict. *Wallace v. Evans*, 60 N.C.App. 145, . . . (1982). Applying the foregoing standard, we find that plaintiff's evidence that she began work for the decedent in his produce business several years before she began cohabiting with him and that at the time she began work she believed the two of them were "partners" in the business, was sufficient evidence for the jury to have inferred that plaintiff's work comprised a business relationship with decedent which was separate and independent from and of their cohabiting relationship. Therefore, the jury may have inferred that sexual services did not provide the consideration for plaintiff's claim. We therefore hold that plaintiff's claim for a *quantum meruit* recovery was not barred as being against public policy. Defendant's first three assignments of error are overruled.

Defendant next argues under assignments of error 4 and 5 that the trial court erred in submitting a *quantum meruit* recovery issue to the jury because any services rendered by plaintiff were either gratuitous or incidental to an illegal relationship. As we have already addressed the issue of illegality we are concerned here only with the question of whether there existed sufficient evidence to submit the issue of recovery in *quantum meruit* to the jury.

The trial court placed the following issue regarding a quasi-contract or *quantum meruit* recovery before the jury:

> *Issue Four:*
> 4. Did DARLENE SUGGS render services to JUNIOR EARL NORRIS involving the raising, harvesting and sale of produce under such circumstances that the Estate of JUNIOR EARL NORRIS should be required to pay for them?
> ANSWER: Yes

Recovery on *quantum meruit* requires the establishment of an implied contract. . . . The contract may be one implied-in-fact where the conduct of the parties clearly indicates their intention to create a contract or it may be implied-in-law based on the restitutionary theory of quasi-contract which operates to prevent unjust enrichment. . . . An implied-in-law theory required the plaintiff to establish that services were rendered and accepted between the two parties with the mutual understanding that plaintiff was to be compensated for her efforts. . . . Moreover, plaintiff's efforts must not have been gratuitous as is generally presumed where services are rendered between family or spousal members. . . .

In the present case, the evidence clearly showed that the plaintiff had from 1973 until the death of the decedent in 1983 operated a produce route for and with the decedent. According to several witnesses' testimony, plaintiff had worked decedent's farm, disced and cultivated the soil, and harvested and marketed the produce. Plaintiff, working primarily without the decedent's aid, drove the produce to various markets over a 60 mile route. She handled all finances and deposited them in the couple's joint banking account. Finally, the evidence showed that the decedent, an alcoholic, depended almost entirely on plaintiff's work in the produce business and as well her care of him while he was ill. Because of plaintiff's efforts the couple had amassed seven vehicles valued at $20,000; some farm equipment valued at $4,000; $8,000 in cash in the account, and all debts which had attached to the farm when plaintiff began working with decedent in 1973 were paid—all due to plaintiff's efforts. Additionally, plaintiff testified that when she began work with the decedent in 1973 she believed they were partners and that she was entitled to share in one-half the profits.

The foregoing evidence clearly establishes a set of facts sufficient to have submitted a quasi-contractual issue to the jury and from which the jury could have inferred a mutual understanding between plaintiff and the decedent that she would be remunerated for her services. Plaintiff's efforts conferred many years of benefits on the decedent and the decedent, by all accounts, willingly accepted those benefits.

Because the evidence viewed in the light most favorable to plaintiff was clearly sufficient to permit the jury to find a mutual understanding between plaintiff and decedent that plaintiff's work in the produce business was not free of charge and because plaintiff's work in the produce business was not of the character usually found to be performed gratuitously, . . .

| defendant's Motions for Directed Verdict and Judgment Notwithstanding the Ver- | dict were properly denied. No Error. |

Case Questions

1. Darlene Suggs' suit against the estate of Junior E. Norris was based on what legal theories?
2. Under what circumstances does the court indicate the contracts between unmarried but cohabiting persons would not be enforceable?
3. Why should a court be able to create a contract after a dispute arises for parties who never signed a binding contract?

Chapter Questions

1. Define the following terms:

affirm
analytical positivism
appeal
appellant
appellee
canon law
case of first impression
chancellor
civil suit
common law
contract
criminal law
Curia Regis
damages
defendant
dicta
due process clause
equity
court of equity
express contract
felony
feudalism
hearing
holding
historical jurisprudence
hundred
implied contract

injunction
legal realism
Magna Carta
misdemeanor
money damages
natural law
plaintiff
procedural due process
public policy
quantum meruit
quasi-contract
remand
reeve
reverse
shire
sociological jurisprudence
substantive due process
tort
trade secret
trespass
trial court instructions
unjust enrichment
utilitarian law
void-for-vagueness doctrine
writ
writ of right
Year Books

2. A Cincinnati, Ohio, ordinance makes it a criminal offense for "three or more persons to assemble, except at a public meeting of citizens, on any of the sidewalks, street corners, vacant lots, or mouths of alleys, and there conduct themselves in a manner annoying to persons passing by, or occupants of adjacent buildings." Coates, a student involved in a demonstration, was arrested and convicted for the violation of this ordinance. His argument on appeal was that the ordinance on its face violated the Fourteenth Amendment. Is this a valid contention?
   Coates v. City of Cincinnati, 402 U.S. 611 (1971)

3. Fuentes purchased a stove and stereo from Firestone Tire and Rubber Company. Payment was to be made in monthly installments over a period of time. After two-thirds of the payments were made, Fuentes defaulted. Firestone filed an action for repossession and at the same time instructed the sheriff to seize the property pursuant to state law. The sheriff seized the property before Fuentes even knew of Firestone's suit for repossession. Fuentes claims that she was deprived of due process because her property was taken without notice or a hearing. What should the result be?
   Fuentes v. Shervin, 407 U.S. 67 (1972)

4. Plaintiff brought a class action on behalf of all female welfare recipients residing in Connecticut and wishing divorces. She alleged that such class was prevented from bringing divorce suits by Connecticut statutes that require payment of court fees and costs of service of process as a condition precedent to access to the courts. Plaintiff contended that such statutes violate basic due process considerations. Is her argument valid?
   Boddie v. Connecticut, 401 U.S. 371 (1970)

5. Like many other states, Connecticut requires nonresidents of the state who are enrolled in the state university system to pay tuition and other fees at higher rates than residents of the state who are so enrolled. A Connecticut statute defined as a nonresident any unmarried student if his or her "legal address for any part of the one-year period immediately prior to his application for admission . . . was outside of Connecticut," or any married student if his or her "legal address at the time of his application for admission . . . was outside of Connecticut." The statute also provided that the "status of a student, as established at the time of his application for admission . . . shall be his status for the entire period of his attendance." Two University of Connecticut students who claimed to be residents of Connecticut were by the statute classified as nonresidents for tuition purposes. They claimed that the due process clause does not permit Connecticut to deny an individual the opportunity to present evidence that he or she is a *bona fide* resident entitled to state rates and that they are being deprived of property without due process. Is this a valid argument?
   Vlandis v. Kline, 412 U.S. 441 (1973)

6. Pursuant to an Ohio law that authorizes mayors to sit as judges in cases of ordinance violations and certain traffic offenses, the mayor of

Monroeville, Ohio, convicted Clarence Ward for violation of two local ordinances and fined him $50 for each offense. The defendant was convicted under Monroeville ordinance 47–12, sections 2 and 29, which are, respectively, failure to comply with a lawful order of a police officer and failure to produce a driver's license on request of a police officer. The mayor of Monroeville has wide executive powers and general supervision of all village affairs, as well as being judge and chief conservator of the peace. A large part of the village income is derived from fines, forfeitures, costs, and fees imposed by the mayor's court—about 40% of the village revenues in the past year. Ward alleges that his right to due process of law has been violated. He contends on appeal that the mayor's court is not an impartial tribunal as required by the Fourteenth Amendment, even though he has a right to a whole new trial in the county court if he wishes. Is Ward correct? Is this a violation of substantive or procedural due process? Why?

Ward v. Village of Monroeville, Ohio, 409 U.S. 57 (1972)

7. Steve was driving home from his college classes one fine winter day when he saw a snowball coming toward his car. The snowball turned out to be a rock covered with snow, and the impact caused a dent in Steve's orange Volkswagen. Steve stopped his car, and after examining the damage, walked toward Greg, the person he thought threw the snowball. Steve asked to see Greg's gloves. Since Greg's gloves were wet, Steve assumed that Greg was the guilty party and punched him in the mouth. Jay, who was standing about ten feet away behind a tree, was the person who actually threw the snowball. List and explain the various suits that could result from this happening.

8. Defendant set a spring gun in his barn opposite a stall used as a hen roost in order to protect his chickens from thieves. The hen roost contained only a few chickens. Deceased was killed when he trespassed on the property and caused the gun to be discharged by disturbing a wire that was attached to the gun and stretched across the passageway in front of the roost. Is there a possible criminal suit against the defendant? Is there a possible civil suit against the defendant?

State v. Plumlee, 177 La. 687, 149 So. 425 (1933)

9. On June 1, 1975, Ralph's car and Walt's car collided. Each was driving his own car. Walt admitted liability. Ralph and Walt were both covered by the same insurance company, XYZ Mutual. XYZ told Ralph that it would pay for his repairs. Ralph believed the company and did not bring legal action against Walt. XYZ failed to send Ralph a check and kept ignoring his inquiries. On June 1, 1977, Ralph received notice that the repairs would not be paid for. By then the statute of limitations had run out, so Ralph had no recourse against Walt. The state in which Ralph lives imposes a duty on insurance companies to act in good faith toward clients. Ralph brings action against XYZ. Is the action in tort or contract? Explain.

See Escambia Treating Co. v. Aetna Casualty & Surety Co., 421 F.Supp. 1367 (1976)

10. The Automatic Canteen Company of America purported to sell a particular vending machine route to the Continental Lake Vendors Corporation. Continental Lake was to supply all machines and foodstuffs, while Automatic Canteen assigned its supply contracts with customers to Continental Lake. Continental Lake defaulted on its payments to Automatic, and Automatic sued Continental Lake under local personal property law for the debt owed it by Continental Lake. Continental Lake contended that no property ever exchanged hands. Is Continental Lake's contention correct? *Automatic Canteen Co. of America v. Wharton, 358 F.2d 587 (2d Cir., 1966)*

Notes

1. Special recognition goes to Bruce D. Fisher and Edgar Bodenheimer. Students seeking more extensive treatment of this material, see Fisher, *Introduction to the Legal System* (St. Paul, MN: West Publishing Co., 1977); and Bodenheimer, *Jurisprudence* (Cambridge, MA: Harvard University Press, 1967).

2. Murphy and Coleman, *An Introduction to Jurisprudence* (Totowa, NJ: Rowman and Allenheld Publishers, 1984), p. 13.

3. Bodenheimer, p. 71; and Fisher, p. 7.

4. Bodenheimer, p. 72.

5. For example, adverse possession, delivery of a deed, the concept of escheat, estate, and the covenant of seisin, and the rule against restraints on alienation.

6. Property law addresses the notion that property equals rights, the rights of a finder vis-à-vis everyone but the true owner, the importance of delivery in the making of a gift, or the right of survivorship in joint tenancies.

7. The concept of consideration, silence as acceptance, and the Statute of Frauds are addressed by contract law.

8. The Massachusetts legislature has again enacted a mandatory seat belt law. An attempt to repeal this statute was unsuccessful.

9. G. Sabine, *A History of Political Theory*, 3rd Ed. (New York: Holt, Rinehart and Winston, 1961), pp. 681–684; and Bodenheimer, p. 85.

10. Bodenheimer, p. 84; and B. H. Levy, *Anglo-American Philosophy of Law* (New Brunswick, NJ: Transaction Publishers, 1991), pp. 19–23.

11. Bodenheimer, pp. 94, 99; and Levy, pp. 29–36.

12. Bodenheimer, p. 96; and Fisher, p. 11.

13. Bodenheimer, p. 116; and Fisher, p. 19.

14. D. Black, *Sociological Justice* (New York: Oxford University Press, 1989), p. 5; and Fisher, p. 19.

15. Black, p. 21.

16. Black, pp. 24–25 and Chapter 2 "Sociological Litigation."

17. Black, pp. 9–13, 21–22.

18. Black, p. 12.

19. Black, pp. 24–25, 95–96.

20. F. Marcham, *A History of England* (New York: Macmillan Co., 1937), p. 62.

21. G. Keeton, *The Norman Conquest and the Common Law* (London: Ernest Benn Limited, 1966), p. 14.

22. Keeton, p. 128; and Marcham, pp. 60–61.

23. T.F.F. Plucknett, *A Concise History of the Common Law* (Little, Brown and Co., 1956), p. 102.

24. Marcham, p. 62; and Plucknett, p. 144.

25. Keeton, p. 23.

26. Barlow, p. 51; Loyn, p. 78; and Brooke, p. 78.

27. Plucknett, p. 139.

28. A.K.R. Kiralfy, *Potter's Historical Introduction to English Law,* 4th Ed. (London: Sweet and Maxwell Ltd., 1962), p. 11.

29. Plucknett, p. 141; and Keeton, p. 13.

30. Marcham, p. 80.

31. Plucknett, p. 11; and Barlow, p. 81.

32. Marcham, p. 83.

33. Ibid., p. 86.

34. Ibid., p. 90; and Plucknett, p. 12.

35. Marcham, pp. 110–111.

36. Keeton, p. 160.

37. A.C. Baugh and T. Cable, *A History of the English Language,* 3rd Ed. (Englewood Cliffs, NJ: Prentice Hall, 1978), pp. 145, 148–149.

38. Brooke, pp. 160, 192.

39. Ibid., p. 156; and Plucknett, p. 14.

40. Marcham, p. 118; and Plucknett, p. 22.

41. Plucknett, p. 15.

42. Brooke, pp. 182–185; and Loyn, p. 128.

43. Marcham, pp. 156–157.

44. Plucknett, p. 103.

45. Keeton, p. 125.

46. Ibid., p. 201.

47. Loyn, p. 139.

48. Marcham, p. 131; and Plucknett, p. 355.

49. Marcham, p. 295.

50. Plucknett, p. 408; and Potter, p. 21.

51. Plucknett, p. 357.

52. R. Walsh, *A History of Anglo-American Law* (Indianapolis: Bobbs-Merrill Co., 1932), p. 65.

53. P.H. Winfield, *Chief Sources of English Legal History* (Cambridge: Harvard University Press, 1925).

54. Plucknett, p. 259.

55. Ibid., pp. 280–281.

56. M. Grossberg, *Governing the Hearth* (Chapel Hill: University of North Carolina Press, 1985), p. 15

57. Marcham, p. 295.

58. Plucknett, p. 178.

59. Ibid., p. 180.

60. Ibid., p. 280; and Marcham, p. 295.

61. Cardinal Wolsey was educated at Oxford, and Becket was educated at the Universities of Paris and Bologna (Brooke, p. 64).

62. Brooke, p. 64.

63. D. Roebuck, *The Background of the Common Law,* 2nd Ed. (Oxford University Press, 1990), p. 64; and Marcham, p. 295.

64. Plucknett, p. 688.

65. Ibid., p. 689; and Potter, pp. 581–584.

66. Potter, p. 280; and Plucknett, pp. 693–694.

67. Roebuck, p. 68.

68. Loyn, p. 141; and Brooke, pp. 220–223.

69. Marcham, p. 143; and Brooke, p. 221.

70. Brooke, p. 223.

71. C.A. Miller, "The Forest of Due Process of Law: The American Constitutional Tradition," in Pennock and Chapman, *Due Process* (New York: New York University Press, 1977), p. 6.

72. Ibid.

73. Ibid., p. 9.

II

The Judicial System

COURTS

A court is a governmental body that is empowered to resolve disputes according to law. Courts are reactive institutions. They do not undertake to adjudicate disputes by themselves, and can only act when someone files suit.

Courts are created in accordance with constitutional provisions and legislative acts. The legislative branch of the government usually has the right to establish and change courts, to regulate many of their procedures, and to limit their jurisdiction.

In the United States, we have a separate judicial system for each of the states and the federal government. These systems vary in size and complexity, although they usually have hierarchical structures as illustrated in Figure 2–1 (see page 63). Since federal and state judicial systems function simultaneously throughout the nation, conflicts can arise with respect to jurisdictional issues, substantive law, supremacy, and the finality of decisions.

Although each of the states has developed its own unique structure, substantive law, rules, and procedures, there is an underlying common law heritage. In our nation's formative years we were greatly influenced by English structures, procedures, and substantive law. Yet from the earliest days, the states modified the old structures to meet contemporary needs. They modified or replaced both substantive law and legal structures when necessary, and created new ones. Each of the various states was independently charged with dispensing justice in its courts. Each system had the capacity to adapt, reform, and experiment. From those early days down to the present, the states have borrowed from each other in order to improve the administration of justice.

Even though fifty-one judicial systems are available to resolve disputes, very few cases actually go to trial. Disputes are usually settled outside the

59

courtroom on the basis of the lawyer's predictions of what would happen if the case were tried. Litigation is very expensive and time consuming, which encourages litigants to settle cases without a trial.

Trial Courts

Courts are classified by function: there are trial courts and appellate courts. A trial court hears and decides controversies by determining facts and applying appropriate rules. The opposing parties to a dispute establish their positions by introducing evidence of the facts and by presenting arguments on the law.

The right of a trial by jury provides litigants with a choice of trying the case to a single judge or to a jury of peers. When a case is litigated before a judge instead of a jury, it is called a *bench trial*. The judge controls the entire trial and determines the outcome. In a jury trial, the decision-making functions are divided between the judge and the jury, which provides a safeguard of checks and balances. The judge rules on the admissibility of evidence, decides questions of law, and instructs the jury. The jury listens to the testimony, evaluates the evidence, and decides what facts have been proven. In many instances, the testimony of witnesses is contradictory. In such cases, the jury can determine the facts only after deciding which witnesses should be believed. It then applies the law to those facts in accordance with the judge's instructions. The judge supervises the entire litigation. This includes ruling on pretrial motions, supervising discovery, and conducting the trial, matters that will be addressed in Chapter 3.

When the jury's verdict is submitted, the jury decides who wins and what the recovery will be. Over half of the states permit a less-than-unanimous verdict in civil cases. The usual requirement in such states is five jurors in agreement out of six. Unless the parties stipulate otherwise, the rule in federal civil trials is that the jury verdict must be unanimous.

The law may authorize the jury to use a *special verdict*. This means that the jury answers specific questions related to certain factual issues in the case. A special verdict is used to focus the jury's attention on the evidence and the factual disputes in the case. It discourages jurors from determining the case's outcome by deciding which party they would like to see win the lawsuit. When the jury returns a special verdict, the judge applies the law to the jury's answers and reaches a final judgment.

It is often said that questions of fact are for the jury and questions of law are for the judge. A factual issue is presented when reasonable people could arrive at different results in deciding what happened in an actual event. When an inference is so certain that all reasonable people must draw the same conclusion, it becomes a question of law for the judge. It is often difficult to make a distinction between questions of fact and questions of law.

There is no need for a trial (either to a jury or to the court) unless there is a factual dispute between the parties. If the parties agree about the facts, but disagree about the law, the judge can determine the applicable law and dispose of the case by *motion for summary judgment*.

A jury was traditionally composed of twelve people. Today, many jurisdictions have authorized six-person juries. Jurors are chosen from the community, and their qualifications are reviewed before they are seated. At trial, they make their decision in private.

Although federal and state constitutions guarantee the right to a trial by jury, there is some dispute about the effectiveness of the jury system. Jury trials take more time to conduct than bench trials and contribute to the congestion of court dockets. Jury trials also are expensive. Because jurors do not know how to evaluate evidence, rules of evidence and trial procedures have been developed so that they are exposed only to competent evidence and permissible argument. In a bench trial, many of these procedures and rules can be eliminated or relaxed.

In addition, juries are known to be very unpredictable, sometimes arbitrary, and add uncertainty to the adjudication process. Lawyers deal with this uncertainty by attempting to discover jurors' hidden tendencies, biases, and attitudes. More and more trial attorneys employ jury research firms in big cases to help them select the jury and prepare and present their clients' cases. Attorneys who try such cases develop special skills and strategies that they would be unlikely to use in a bench trial before an experienced judge.

One of the most important benefits of the jury system is that it allows citizens to participate in the legal process. A jury is supposed to represent a cross section of the public, whereas a judge does not. Despite the weaknesses of the jury system, it is not likely that the right to a trial by jury will be eliminated in the near future.

Appellate Courts

Appellate courts review the decisions of trial courts. Usually, an appeal can only be taken from a lower court's judgment. In the case of *Du Pont v. Christopher*, however, we saw that some jurisdictions permit a limited interlocutory appeal to be made prior to a trial in some circumstances. That is, appellate review may determine a controlling question of law before the case itself is decided. In a civil action, any dissatisfied party generally may appeal to a higher court. In criminal cases, the defendant usually may appeal, but the prosecution generally may not.

The appellate court reviews the proceedings of the trial court and decides whether the trial court acted in accordance with the law, and whether the appellant properly preserved the error. This means that an attorney cannot observe error occurring in a trial court and do nothing. The attorney must inform the judge of the error and request specific relief. Failure to object results in a waiver of the right to subsequently raise the matter on appeal.

An appellate court bases its decision solely on the theories argued and evidence presented in the lower court. There are no witnesses or jury at the appellate level. The appellate court does not retry the facts of the case, and no new arguments or proof are permitted. The appellate court reaches its decision by using only the record of the proceedings in the lower court, the written briefs filed by both parties to the appeal, and the parties' oral arguments given before the appellate judges. The record of the proceedings in the lower court includes the pleadings, pretrial papers, depositions, and a transcript of the trial proceedings and testimony.

STATE COURT SYSTEMS

The power to create courts is an attribute of every sovereignty. The various states of the United States have exercised this power either by constitutional provisions or by statutory enactments. The power to create courts includes the authority to organize them, including the establishment of judgeships, and to regulate their procedure and jurisdiction.

Although judicial systems vary considerably from state to state, a state court system usually consists of probate courts, a large number of courts with limited jurisdiction, courts with residual jurisdiction, and appellate courts, as illustrated in Figure 2–1.

Courts of limited jurisdiction—inferior courts—are limited as to subject matter and territory. For example, the justice of the peace court administers justice in minor matters at the local level such as civil cases involving small sums of money and minor criminal matters. A state judicial system also usually includes a probate court to handle deceased persons' estates. The jurisdiction of local courts, such as municipal, city, and county courts, is limited to a specified territory. The jurisdiction of small claims and municipal courts is also limited to relatively low maximum amounts of damages that may be awarded. In small claims proceedings, representation by attorney and ordinary court procedure may be dispensed with.

Trial courts of residual jurisdiction in the state court system may bear the name of common pleas, district, superior, circuit, or even—in New York State —supreme court. These courts have the power to hear all types of cases. The primary function of trial courts is to exercise original jurisdiction. (Original jurisdiction is the power to take note of a suit at its beginning, try it, and pass judgment on the law and the facts of the controversy.) Generally, they also exercise appellate jurisdiction over decisions of courts of limited jurisdiction.

A state's judicial system may provide an intermediate appellate court analogous to the court of appeals in the federal system. Not all states provide this intermediate step. A final appellate court, analogous to the U.S. Supreme Court, serves as the highest court in the state. It reviews appeals of major questions emanating from the lower state courts, and at the state level its decision is final.

JURISDICTION

Jurisdiction is the power or authority of a court to determine the merits of a dispute and to grant relief. A court has jurisdiction when it has this power both over the subject matter of the case and over the persons of the plaintiff

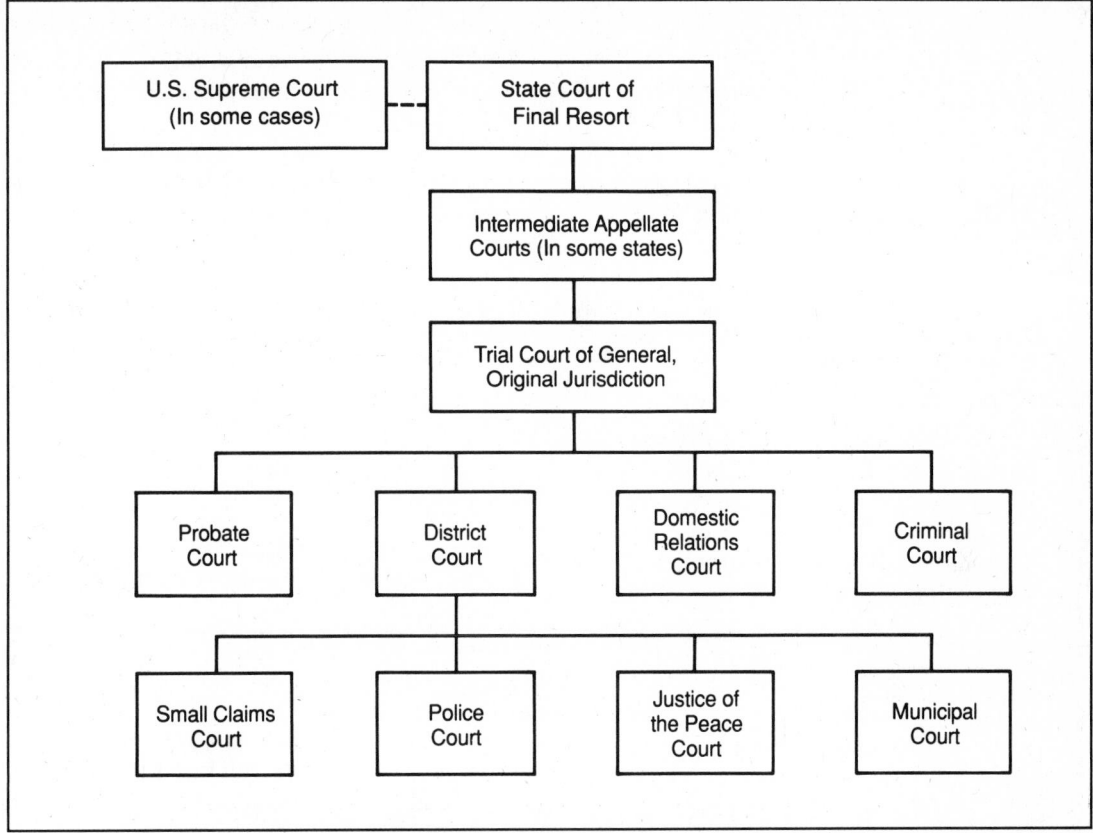

FIGURE 2–1   A State Court System

Source: Adapted from Arnold J. Goldman and William D. Sigismond, *Business Law: Principles & Practices*, 2nd Ed. Copyright © 1988 by Houghton Mifflin Company. Used with permission.

and defendant or the property that is in dispute. The court itself must determine whether it has jurisdiction over a controversy presented before it. This is true even if neither party questions the court's jurisdiction. Once a court has acquired jurisdiction, it keeps it throughout the case, even if a party changes domicile or removes property from the state. When more than one court has a basis for jurisdiction, the first to exercise it has exclusive jurisdiction until the case is concluded. Questions about jurisdiction should be resolved before the court concerns itself with other matters involved in the case.

Subject Matter Jurisdiction in State Court

Legislatures, in accordance with state constitutions, have the right to allocate the workload throughout the state's judicial system. This means that the legislature usually determines each court's subject matter jurisdiction (the types of controversies that can be litigated in that court). The parties to a lawsuit cannot by consent confer subject matter jurisdiction on a court.

Courts of general jurisdiction are authorized to handle most types of controversies. Other judicial systems are structured around courts of specialized jurisdiction, for example, housing courts, juvenile courts, probate courts, and land courts. Occasionally, subject matter jurisdiction is determined by the dollar amount involved in the controversy, such as in small claims courts and municipal courts.

In the following case, a petitioner attempts to litigate two breach of contract claims in a court that only has subject matter jurisdiction over land.

In the Matter of the Application of Arthur Hyde RICE to Register and Confirm Title to Land Situated in Kailua, District of Koolaupoko, Oahu, City and County of Honolulu, State of Hawaii
713 P.2d 426
Supreme Court of Hawaii
February 3, 1986

Wakatsuki, Justice

Appellees Richard A. Breton and Margaret Mary Breton, as Sellers, filed a petition in the land court against Appellant Central Pacific Supply Corporation (hereinafter "CPS"), as Buyer, seeking to cancel the Agreement of Sale of a leasehold interest and for damages. The Bretons alleged that CPS had breached the Agreement by defaulting on the payment due thereon and by vacating the premises. CPS timely answered the complaint and counterclaimed against the Bretons for the breach of the Agreement and sought a rescission of the Agreement and damages. The land court, after trial, found in favor of the Bretons against CPS on both the complaint and the counterclaim. Thereafter, CPS filed a motion to set aside the findings of fact, conclusions of law and judgment, and to set the matter for a jury trial. The land court denied the motion, and CPS filed timely notices of appeal.

I.

In answer to the Breton's petition to cancel Agreement of Sale, one of CPS's defenses was that the land court lacked jurisdiction over the subject matter of the petition. The land court, after trial, concluded that it had "jurisdiction of the parties and this cause of action."

Although the issue of jurisdiction of the land court over the subject matter was not questioned at the trial level nor raised in this appeal, we hold, *sua sponte*, that the land court lacked jurisdiction over the subject matter of the Breton's petition.

"The lack of jurisdiction over the subject matter cannot be waived by the parties." . . . If the parties do not raise the issue, "a court *sua sponte* will, for unless jurisdiction of the court over the subject matter exists, any judgment rendered is invalid." . . . "Such a question is in order at any stage of the case, and though a lower court is found to have lacked jurisdiction, we have jurisdiction here on appeal, not of the merits, but for the purpose of correcting an error in jurisdiction." . . .

II.

The land court derives its jurisdiction from section 501–1 of the Hawaii Revised

Statutes (HRS).[1] "The land court is a court of limited jurisdiction, created for a special purpose, that of carrying into effect what is known as the Torrens title scheme, derives all of its power from the statutes

[1]HRS § 501-1 in relevant part reads: A court is established, called the land court, which shall have exclusive original jurisdiction of all applications for the registration of title to land and easements or rights in land held and possessed in fee simple within the State, with power to hear and determine all questions arising upon such applications, *and also have jurisdiction over such other questions as may come before it under this chapter,* subject to the rights of appeal under this chapter. The proceedings upon the applications shall be proceedings in rem against the land, and the decrees shall operate directly on the land and vest and establish title thereto. (Emphasis added.)

relating to it, and can exercise no power not found within those statutes." . . .

The Bretons' petition to cancel the Agreement of Sales and for damages and CPS's counterclaim for rescission of the Agreement and for damages are both causes of action arising out of alleged breaches of the Agreement. Both are breach of contract actions over which the land court does not have jurisdiction under any of the provisions of chapter 501 of the Hawaii Revised Statutes, as amended.

The judgment of the land court is void for lack of jurisdiction. This appeal is dismissed.

Case Questions

1. Why is subject matter jurisdiction so crucial that any court, including the Hawaii Supreme Court, should raise such an issue on its own initiative when the parties failed to make it an issue at trial or on appeal?
2. Why was the land court unable to render a judgment with respect to the breach of contract actions?

Jurisdiction over the Person

In every lawsuit, the plaintiff consents to personal jurisdiction (*in personam* jurisdiction) when he or she files the action with a clerk of court in the forum state. To issue a judgment affecting the rights of the defendant, however, the forum court must also have personal jurisdiction over the defendant. For example, assume that the plaintiff has won a lawsuit and the court has determined that the plaintiff is entitled to collect money damages. If the court has personal jurisdiction over the defendant, it can issue a judgment requiring the defendant (now called a *judgment debtor*), to pay money damages to the plaintiff (called a *judgment creditor*). If the judgment debtor doesn't pay, the judgment creditor will be entitled to take the judgment to any state in which the judgment debtor owns property and there have it enforced. The U.S. Supreme Court has ruled, however, that due process prohibits a court from exercising personal jurisdiction over a party unless that person has sufficient minimum contacts with the state in which that court is located (called the *forum state*). The minimum contacts requirement is satisfied if the defendant's actions and connections with the forum state are such that he or she should reasonably expect to be subject to jurisdiction. The Supreme Court established the minimum contacts rule in order to protect "traditional notions of fair play and substantial justice." For example, due process would be violated if a defendant who had no contacts of any sort with Alabama could be subject to the jurisdiction of Alabama courts. As we will see in a discussion of *full faith and credit*, in Chapter 4, judgments rendered without proper jurisdiction are unenforceable in other states.

The sufficiency of the defendant's contacts with the forum state is determined by looking at the particular facts of each case. Sufficient minimum contacts, for example, exist in the state in which the defendant is domiciled. A person's *domicile* is the state in which the defendant has established his or her permanent home and to which the defendant returns after temporary absences. Factors such as where a person is licensed to drive, votes, and is employed are considered in determining domicile. Other traditional ways of establishing personal jurisdiction include serving the defendant with a summons (see Figure 2–2) within the boundaries of the forum state,[1] service at the defendant's residence, or by the defendant's voluntary consent to the court's jurisdiction. Consent takes different forms and occurs when:

1. The defendant makes a *general appearance* in a case. In many jurisdictions, if defendants wish to challenge the court's jurisdiction over their persons, a *special appearance* must be entered for that purpose. If the defendants make a general appearance by arguing the facts of the case, they are by implication consenting to personal jurisdiction. Notice how the defendant in the next case, *Calder v. Jones*, made a special appearance to challenge personal jurisdiction.

2. A nonresident is alleged to have committed a tortious act within the forum state. We will see in *Calder v. Jones* how the forum state's summons can be served on the defendant in some other state under these circumstances.

3. A nonresident drives a motor vehicle on the roads of the forum state and becomes involved in a collision. Under the laws of most states, the motorist impliedly appoints an official of the forum state to be his agent for receiving service of the plaintiff's summons arising from the accident.

Long-Arm Statutes

Every state has enacted what are called *long-arm statutes* (see Figure 2–3) that permit the exercise of personal jurisdiction over nonresident defendants who have had sufficient minimum contacts with the forum state. A long-arm statute allows the plaintiff to serve the forum state's summons on the defendant in some other state. When a plaintiff successfully uses the long-arm statute, the defendant can be required to return to the forum state and defend the lawsuit. If the defendant fails to do so, he or she risks the entry of a default judgment.

```
STATE OF WISCONSIN          _____ Court      _____ County

_____, Plaintiff

        v.                              Summons File No.  _____

_____, Defendant

The State of Wisconsin

To each person named above as a defendant:

    You are hereby notified that the plaintiff named above has filed a
lawsuit or other legal action against you. The complaint, which is at-
tached, states the nature and basis of the legal action.
    Within 20 days of receiving this summons, you must respond with a
written answer, as that term is used in chapter 802 of the Wisconsin
Statutes, to the complaint. The court may reject or disregard an answer
that does not follow the requirements of the statutes. The answer must
be sent or delivered to the court, whose address is . . . . , and to . . . . ,
plaintiff's attorney, whose address is . . . . . You may have an attorney
help or represent you.
    If you do not provide a proper answer within 20 days, the court may
grant judgment against you for the award of money or other legal action
requested in the complaint, and you may lose your right to object to
anything that is or may be incorrect in the complaint. A judgment may be
enforced as provided by law. A judgment awarding money may become
a lien against any real estate you own now or in the future, and may also
be enforced by garnishment or seizure of property.

Dated: . . . . . . , 19 . . .

                                    [signed]  _____
                                              Attorney for Plaintiff

                                    Address:  _____
```

FIGURE 2–2   State of Wisconsin Statutory Form of Summons [Sec. 801.095]

In Personam Jurisdiction over Corporations

Every corporation has been incorporated by one of the fifty states and is
therefore subject to *in personam* jurisdiction in that state's courts. A corpora
tion may also consent to *in personam* jurisdiction in other states. Generally a

§ 3. Transactions or conduct for personal jurisdiction

A court may exercise personal jurisdiction over a person, who acts directly or by an agent, as to a cause of action in law or equity arising from the person's

(a) transacting any business in this commonwealth;

(b) contracting to supply services or things in this commonwealth;

(c) causing tortious injury by an act or omission in this commonwealth;

(d) causing tortious injury in this commonwealth by an act or omission outside this commonwealth if he regularly does or solicits business, or engages in any other persistent course of conduct, or derives substantial revenue from goods used or consumed or services rendered, in this commonwealth;

(e) having an interest in, using or possessing real property in this commonwealth;

(f) contracting to insure any person, property or risk located within this commonwealth at the time of contracting; or

(g) living as one of the parties to a duly and legally executed marriage contract, with the marital domicile of both parties having been within the commonwealth for at least one year within the two years immediately preceding the commencement of the action, notwithstanding the subsequent departure of the defendant in said action from the commonwealth, said action being valid as to all obligations or modifications of alimony, custody, child support or property settlement orders relating to said marriage or former marriage, if the plaintiff continues to reside within the commonwealth.

FIGURE 2–3 Massachusetts Long-Arm Statute [Massachusetts General Laws Annotated Chapter 223A]

state will require that all corporations doing business within its borders register with it and appoint a state government official as its agent. This official will be authorized to receive service of process relating to litigation arising in the wake of its presence and its business activities conducted within that state. Soliciting orders, writing orders, and entering into contracts would establish a corporate presence that would be sufficient for *in personam* jurisdiction. The mere presence of corporate officers within the forum state or the occasional shipping of orders into the forum state is not sufficient for personal jurisdiction.

Jurisdiction over Property—*In Rem* Jurisdiction

A state court has jurisdiction over property located within the state. The property may be real (land and buildings) or personal (clothes, cars, televisions, checking accounts, antique clocks, etc.). This is called *in rem* jurisdiction, or jurisdiction over things. An *in personam* decision, however, imposes liability on a person and is personally binding. A decision *in rem* is directed against the property itself and resolves disputes about property rights. A court can determine the rights to property that is physically located within the forum state regardless of whether the court has personal jurisdiction over all interested individuals. For example, if two parties—one of whom is from out of state—dispute the ownership of a piece of land in Montana, the courts of Montana can determine ownership because it relates to property located in that state.

Procedural Due Process Requirements

In addition to establishing a basis for jurisdiction over the person or the property that is in dispute, a court must give proper notice to a defendant. The statutes of each jurisdiction often make distinctions between the type of notice required for *in personam* actions and *in rem* actions. This subject is covered in more detail in Chapter 3.

The following case of *Calder v. Jones* addresses several of the issues just discussed. Notice how Shirley Jones, the plaintiff, established *in personam* jurisdiction over the defendants.

Calder v. Jones
465 U.S. 783
U.S. Supreme Court
March 20, 1984

Justice Rehnquist delivered the opinion of the Court.

Respondent Shirley Jones brought suit in California Superior Court claiming that she had been libeled in an article written and edited by petitioners in Florida. The article was published in a national magazine with a large circulation in California. Petitioners were served with process by mail in Florida and caused special appearances to be entered on their behalf, mov-ing to quash the service of process for lack of personal jurisdiction. The Superior Court granted the motion on the ground that First Amendment concerns weighed against an assertion of jurisdiction otherwise proper under the Due Process Clause. The California Court of Appeals reversed, rejecting the suggestion that First Amendment considerations enter into the jurisdictional analysis. We now affirm.

Respondent lives and works in California. She and her husband brought this suit against the National Enquirer, Inc., its local distributing company, and petitioners for libel, invasion of privacy, and intentional infliction of emotional harm. The Enquirer is a Florida corporation with its principal place of business in Florida. It publishes a national weekly newspaper with a total circulation of over 5 million. About 600,000 of those copies, almost twice the level of the next highest state, are sold in California. Respondent's and her husband's claims were based on an article that appeared in the Enquirer's October 9, 1979, issue. Both the Enquirer and the distributing company answered the complaint and made no objection to the jurisdiction of the California court.

Petitioner South is a reporter employed by the Enquirer. He is a resident of Florida, though he frequently travels to California on business. South wrote the first draft of the challenged article, and his byline appeared on it. He did most of his research in Florida, relying on phone calls to sources in California for the information contained in the article. Shortly before publication, South called respondent's home and read to her husband a draft of the article so as to elicit his comments upon it. Aside from his frequent trips and phone calls, South has no other relevant contacts with California.

Petitioner Calder is also a Florida resident. He has been to California only twice—once, on a pleasure trip, prior to the publication of the article and once after to testify in an unrelated trial. Calder is president and editor of the Enquirer. He "oversee[s] just about every function of the Enquirer." . . . He reviewed and approved the initial evaluation of the subject of the article and edited it in its final form. He also declined to print a retraction requested by respondent. Calder has no other relevant contacts with California.

In considering petitioners' motion to quash service of process, the Superior Court surmised that the actions of peti-

tioners in Florida, causing injury to respondent in California, would ordinarily be sufficient to support an assertion of jurisdiction over them in California.[5] But the court felt that special solicitude was necessary because of the potential "chilling effect" on reporters and editors which would result from requiring them to appear in remote jurisdictions to answer for the content of articles upon which they worked. The court also noted that respondent's rights could be "fully satisfied" in her suit against the publisher without requiring petitioners to appear as parties. The Superior Court, therefore, granted the motion.

The California Court of Appeals reversed. . . . The court agreed that neither petitioner's contacts with California would be sufficient for an assertion of jurisdiction on a cause of action unrelated to those contacts. . . . But the court concluded that a valid basis for jurisdiction existed on the theory that petitioners intended to, and did, cause tortious injury to respondent in California. The fact that the actions causing the effects in California were performed outside the State did not prevent the State from asserting jurisdiction over a cause of action arising out of those effects. The court rejected the Superior Court's conclusion that First Amendment considerations must be weighed in the scale against jurisdiction.

A timely petition for hearing was denied by the Supreme Court of California. . . . On petitioners' appeal to this Court, probable jurisdiction was postponed. . . . Treating the jurisdictional state-

---

[5] California's "long-arm" statute permits an assertion of jurisdiction over a nonresident defendant whenever permitted by the State and Federal Constitutions. California Civ. Proc. Code Ann. § 410.10 (West 1973) provides: "A court of this state may exercise jurisdiction on any basis not inconsistent with the Constitution of this state or of the United States."

ment as a petition for writ of certiorari, as we are authorized to do, . . . we hereby grant the petition.

The Due Process Clause of the Fourteenth Amendment to the United States Constitution permits personal jurisdiction over a defendant in any State with which the defendant has "certain minimum contacts . . . such that the maintenance of the suit does not offend 'traditional notions of fair play and substantial justice.' . . . In judging minimum contacts, a court properly focuses on "the relationship among the defendant, the forum, and the litigation." . . .

The allegedly libelous story concerned the California activities of a California resident. It impugned the professionalism of an entertainer whose television career was centered in California.[9] The article was drawn from California sources, and the brunt of the harm, in terms both of the respondent's emotional distress and the injury to her professional reputation, was suffered in California. In sum, California is the focal point both of the story and of the harm suffered. Jurisdiction over petitioners is therefore proper in California based on the "effects" of their Florida conduct in California. . . .

Petitioners argue that they are not responsible for the circulation of the article in California. A reporter and an editor, they claim, have no direct economic stake in their employer's sales in a distant State. Nor are ordinary employees able to control their employer's marketing activity. The mere fact that they can "foresee" that the article will be circulated and have an effect in California is not sufficient for an assertion of jurisdiction. . . . They do not "in effect appoint the [article their] agent for service of process." . . . Petitioners liken themselves to a welder employed in Florida who works on a boiler which subsequently explodes in California. Cases which hold that jurisdiction will be proper over the manufacturer, . . . should not be applied to the welder who has no control over and derives no direct benefit from his employer's sales in that distant State.

Petitioners' analogy does not wash. Whatever the status of their hypothetical welder, petitioners are not charged with mere untargeted negligence. Rather, their intentional, and allegedly tortious, actions were expressly aimed at California. Petitioner South wrote and petitioner Calder edited an article that they knew would have a potentially devastating impact upon respondent. And they knew that the brunt of that injury would be felt by respondent in the State in which she lives and works and in which the National Enquirer has its largest circulation. Under the circumstances, petitioners must "reasonably anticipate being haled into court there" to answer for the truth of the statements made in their article. . . . An individual injured in California need not go to Florida to seek redress from persons who, though remaining in Florida, knowingly cause the injury in California.

Petitioners are correct that their contacts with California are not to be judged according to their employer's activities there. On the other hand, their status as employees does not somehow insulate them from jurisdiction. Each defendant's contact with the forum State must be assessed individually. . . . In this case, petitioners are primary participants in an alleged wrongdoing intentionally directed at a California resident, and jurisdiction over them is proper on that basis.

We also reject the suggestion that First Amendment concerns enter into the juris-

[9] The article alleged that respondent drank so heavily as to prevent her from fulfilling her professional obligations.

dictional analysis. The infusion of such considerations would needlessly complicate an already imprecise inquiry. . . . Moreover, the potential chill on protected First Amendment activity stemming from libel and defamation actions is already taken into account in the constitutional limitations on the substantive law governing such suits. . . . To reintroduce those concerns at the jurisdictional stage would be a form of double counting. We have already declined in other contexts to grant special procedural protections to defendants in libel and defamation actions in addition to the constitutional protections embodied in the substantive laws. . . .

We hold that jurisdiction over petitioners in California is proper because of their intentional conduct in Florida calculated to cause injury to respondent in California. The judgment of the California Court of Appeals is Affirmed.

Case Questions

1. Why should the U.S. Supreme Court require that a defendant have minimum contacts with the forum state?
2. What should a court examine in deciding if the minimum contacts rule has been satisfied?
3. What does the Court find to be the specific actions that constitute the basis for the minimum contacts in this case?

Venue

Venue requirements determine the place where judicial authority should be exercised. Once personal jurisdiction has been established, a plaintiff has to litigate in a court that has subject matter jurisdiction over the controversy and in a place that the legislature says is a permissible venue.

State legislatures enact venue statutes to distribute the judicial workload throughout the system. They often provide for venue in the county or district where the cause of action arose, the county or district in which the defendant resides, and the county or district in which the plaintiff resides. In cases where the venue requirements can be satisfied in more than one district, the plaintiff's choice will usually prevail.

Parties wishing to challenge venue must assert their objections promptly, or they may be waived. In both civil and criminal cases venue may be considered improper for several reasons. A court may decline to hear a case for fear of local prejudice, for the convenience of litigants and witnesses, or in the interests of justice.

In a civil case, the most common reason given for a court to decline to exercise jurisdiction is that it believes the case can proceed more conveniently in another court. This is known as the *doctrine of forum non conveniens*. The doctrine is applied with discretion and caution. One frequent ground for applying the doctrine occurs when the event that gave rise to the suit took place somewhere other than in the forum state. The difficulties of securing the attendance of out-of-state witnesses and applying foreign law may make decision making inconvenient. The court balances the conveniences between the forum court and another court and weighs the obstacles to a fair proceeding and advantage.

The plaintiff's choice of forum is not changed except for very good reason, as is illustrated in the following case.

In re **Union Carbide Corporation Gas Plant Disaster at Bhopal, India, in December 1984**
809 F.2d 1987
U.S. Court of Appeals, Second Circuit
January 14, 1987

Mansfield, Circuit Judge

This appeal raises the question of whether thousands of claims by citizens of India and the Government of India arising out of the most devastating industrial disaster in history—the deaths of over 2,000 persons and injuries of over 200,000 caused by lethal gas known as methyl isocyanate which was released from a chemical plant operated by Union Carbide India Limited (UCIL) in Bhopal, India—should be tried in the United States or in India. The Southern District of New York, John F. Keenan, *Judge*, granted a motion of Union Carbide Corporation (UCC), a defendant in some 145 actions commenced in federal courts in the United States, to dismiss these actions on grounds of *forum non conveniens* so that the claims may be tried in India, subject to certain conditions. The individual plaintiffs appeal from the order
. . .

The accident occurred on the night of December 2–3, 1984 when winds blew the deadly gas from the plant operated by UCIL into densely occupied parts of the city of Bhopal. UCIL is incorporated under the laws of India. Fifty and nine-tenths percent of its stock is owned by UCC, 22% is owned or controlled by the government of India, and the balance is held by approximately 23,500 Indian citizens. The stock is publicly traded on the Bombay Stock Exchange. The company is engaged in the manufacture of a variety of products, including chemicals, plastics, fertilizers and insecticides, at 14 plants in India and employs over 9,000 Indian citizens. It is managed and operated entirely by Indians in India.

. . . On March 29, 1985, India enacted the Bhopal Gas Leak Disaster (Processing of Claims) Act, granting to its government, the UOI, the exclusive right to represent the victims in India or elsewhere. Thereupon the UOI, purporting to act in the capacity of *parens patriae*, and with retainers executed by many of the victims, on April 8, 1985, filed a complaint in the Southern District of New York on behalf of all victims of the Bhopal disaster. . . . The UOI's decision to bring suit in the United States was attributed to the fact that, although numerous lawsuits (by now, some 6,500) had been instituted by victims in India against UCIL, the Indian courts did not have jurisdiction over UCC, the parent company, which is a defendant in the United States actions. . . .

In its opinion dismissing the actions the district court analyzed the *forum non conveniens* issues, applying the standards and weighing the factors suggested by the

Supreme Court. . . . At the outset Judge Keenan concluded . . . that, since the plaintiffs were not residents of the United States but of a foreign country, their choice of the United States as a forum would not be given the deference to which it would be entitled if this country were their home. . . . [T]he district court declined to compare the advantages and disadvantages to the respective parties of American versus Indian Laws or to determine the impact upon plaintiffs' claims of the laws of India, where UCC had acknowledged that it would make itself amenable to process, except to ascertain whether India provided an adequate alternative forum, as distinguished from no remedy at all. Judge Keenan reviewed thoroughly the affidavits of experts on India's law and legal system, which described in detail its procedural and substantive aspects, and concluded that, despite some of the Indian system's disadvantages, it afforded an adequate alternative forum for the enforcement of plaintiffs' claims.

The Indian judiciary was found by the court to be a developed, independent and progressive one. . . .

The tort law of India, which is derived from common law and British precedent, was found to be suitable for resolution of legal issues arising in cases involving highly complex technology. Moreover, Indian courts would be in a superior position to construe and apply applicable Indian laws and standards than would courts of the United States. . . . Judge Keenan further found that the absence of juries and contingent fee arrangements in India would not deprive the claimants of an adequate remedy. . . .

As the district court found, the record shows that the private interests of the respective parties weigh heavily in favor of dismissal on grounds of *forum non conveniens*. The many witnesses and sources of proof are almost entirely located in India, where the accident occurred, and could not be compelled to appear for trial in the United States. The Bhopal plant at the time of the accident was operated by some 193 Indian nationals, including the managers of seven operating units employed by the Agricultural Products Division of UCIL, who reported to Indian Works Managers in Bhopal. The plant was maintained by seven functional departments employing over 200 more Indian nationals. UCIL kept at the plant daily, weekly and monthly records of plant operations and records of maintenance as well as records of the plant's Quality Control, Purchasing and Stores branches, all operated by Indian employees. The great majority of documents bearing on the design, safety, start-up and operation of the plant, as well as the safety training of the plant's employees, is located in India. Proof to be offered at trial would be derived from interviews of these witnesses in India and study of the records located there to determine whether the accident was caused by negligence on the part of the management or employees in the operation of the plant, by fault in its design, or by sabotage. In short, India has greater ease of access to the proof than does the United States.

The plaintiffs seek to prove that the accident was caused by negligence on the part of UCC in originally contributing to the design of the plant and its provision for storage of excessive amounts of the gas at the plant. . . .

The vital parts of the Bhopal plant, including its storage tank, monitoring instrumentation, and vent gas scrubber, were manufactured by Indians in India. Although some 40 UCIL employees were given some safety training at UCC's plant in West Virginia, they represented a small fraction of the Bhopal plant's employees. The vast majority of plant employees were selected and trained by UCIL in Bhopal. The manual for start-up of the Bhopal plant was prepared by Indians employed by UCIL.

In short, the plant has been constructed and managed by Indians in India. No Americans were employed at the plant at the time of the accident. . . . No Americans visited the plant for more than one year prior to the accident, and during the 5-year period before the accident the communications between the plant and the United States were almost nonexistent.

The vast majority of material witnesses and documentary proof bearing on causation of and liability for the accident is located in India, not the United States, and would be more accessible to an Indian court than to a United States court. The records are almost entirely in Hindi or other Indian languages, understandable to an Indian court without translation. The witnesses for the most part do not speak English but Indian languages understood by an Indian court but not by an American court. These witnesses could be required to appear in an Indian court but not in a court of the United States. Although witnesses in the United States could not be subpoenaed to appear in India, they are comparatively few in number and most are employed by UCC which, as a party, would produce them in India, with lower overall transportation costs than if the parties were to attempt to bring hundreds of Indian witnesses to the United States. Lastly, Judge Keenan properly concluded that an Indian court would be in a better position to direct and supervise a viewing of the Bhopal plant, which was sealed after the accident. Such a viewing could be of help to a court in determining liability issues.

After a thorough review, the district court concluded that the public interest concerns, like the private ones, also weigh heavily in favor of India as the situs for trial and disposition of the cases. The accident and all relevant events occurred in India. The victims, over 200,000 in number, are citizens of India and located there. The witnesses are almost entirely Indian citizens. The Union of India has a greater interest than does the United States in facilitating the trial and adjudication of the victims' claims. . . .

India's interest is increased by the fact that it has for years treated UCIL as an Indian national, subjecting it to intensive regulations and governmental supervision of the construction, development and operation of the Bhopal plant, its emissions, water and air pollution, and safety precautions. Numerous Indian government officials have regularly conducted on-site inspections of the plant and approved its machinery and equipment, including its facilities for storage of the lethal methyl isocyanate gas that escaped and caused the disaster giving rise to the claims. Thus India has considered the plant to be an Indian one and the disaster to be an Indian problem. It therefore has a deep interest in ensuring compliance with its safety standards. Moreover, plaintiffs have conceded that in view of India's strong interest and its greater contacts with the plant, its operations, its employees, and the victims of the accident, the law of India, as the place where the tort occurred, will undoubtedly govern. In contrast, the American interests are relatively minor. Indeed, a long trial of the 145 cases here would unduly burden an already overburdened court, involving both jury hardship and heavy expense. It would face the court with numerous practical difficulties, including the almost impossible task of attempting to understand extensive relevant Indian regulations published in a foreign language and the slow process of receiving testimony of scores of witnesses through interpreters.

Having made the foregoing findings, Judge Keenan dismissed the actions against UCC on the grounds of *forum non conveniens*. . . .

Discussion

The standard to be applied in reviewing the district court's *forum non conveniens* dismissal was clearly expressed by the Supreme Court . . . as follows:

> "The *forum non conveniens* determination is committed to the sound discretion of the trial court. It may be reversed only when there has been a clear abuse of discretion; where the court has considered all relevant public and private interest factors, and where its balancing of these factors is reasonable, its decision deserves substantial deference."

Having reviewed Judge Keenan's detailed decision, in which he thoroughly considered the comparative adequacy of the forums and the public and private interests involved, we are satisfied that there was no abuse of discretion in his granting dismissal of the action. On the contrary, it might reasonably be concluded that it would have been an abuse of discretion to deny a *forum non conveniens* dismissal. . . . Practically all relevant factors demonstrate that transfer of the cases to India for trial and adjudication is both fair and just to the parties.

Plaintiffs' principal contentions in favor of retention of the cases by the district court are that deference to the plaintiffs' choice of forum has been inadequate, that the Indian courts are insufficiently equipped for the task, that UCC has its principal place of business here, that the most probative evidence regarding negligence and causation is to be found here, that federal courts are much better equipped through experience and procedures to handle such complex actions efficiently than Indian courts, and that a transfer of the cases to India will jeopardize a $350 million settlement being negotiated by plaintiffs' counsel. All of these arguments, however, must be rejected.

Little or no deference can be paid to the plaintiffs' choice of a United States forum when all but a few of the 200,000 plaintiffs are Indian citizens located in India who, according to the UOI, have revoked the authorization of American counsel to represent them here and have substituted the UOI, which now prefers Indian courts. The finding of our district court, after exhaustive analysis of the evidence, that the Indian courts provide a reasonably adequate alternative forum cannot be labelled clearly erroneous or an abuse of discretion.

The emphasis placed by plaintiffs on UCC's having its domicile here, where personal jurisdiction over it exists, is robbed of significance by its consent to Indian jurisdiction. Plaintiffs' contention that the most crucial and probative evidence is located in the United States is simply not in accord with the record or the district court's findings. . . .

As so modified the district court's order is affirmed.

Case Questions

1. If the plaintiffs choose to file their lawsuit in the United States instead of India, why shouldn't this choice of forum be honored? Why do you think the plaintiffs filed their case in New York instead of India?

2. What interests should a court weigh in determining whether to decline jurisdiction under the doctrine of *forum non conveniens*?
3. Can you think of any "objectives of law" that played a role in the determination of this case?

THE FEDERAL COURT SYSTEM

Article III, section 1, of the U.S. Constitution is the basis of our federal court system. It provides that "the judicial power of the United States shall be vested in one supreme court, and in such inferior courts as Congress may, from time to time, ordain and establish." Congress first exercised this power by passing the Judiciary Act of 1789 which has been amended and supplemented many times in order to establish the various federal courts as well as their jurisdiction and procedures.

The federal court system consists of the district courts, exercising original federal jurisdiction; courts of appeals, exercising intermediate federal jurisdiction; and the U.S. Supreme Court, sitting as the highest court for both federal and state cases involving federal questions. Alongside these courts of general jurisdiction, there are the U.S. Claims Court, which decides nontort claims filed against the United States; the U.S. Tax Court, which reviews decisions of the Secretary of the Treasury with respect to certain provisions of the Internal Revenue Code; the U.S. Court of International Trade, which has jurisdiction over civil actions relating to embargoes on imports, customs duties, and revenues from imports or tonnage; the Federal Bankruptcy Court, which hears bankruptcy cases; and the Court of Military Appeals, which is a court of final appeal involving military criminal matters. (See Figure 2–4.)

THE U.S. DISTRICT COURTS

There are 94 federal district courts, at least one in each state and territory in the United States. They are the courts of original jurisdiction and serve as the trial court in the federal court system. The federal district courts are given limited subject matter jurisdiction by the Constitution and by Congress. Article III provides that federal courts have jurisdiction over "all cases . . . arising under . . . the laws of the United States."

Subject Matter Jurisdiction

The district courts have original jurisdiction in federal criminal cases. Because there are no federal common law crimes, all federal criminal actions must be based on federal statutes.

In civil actions, the district courts have subject matter jurisdiction over two categories of cases:

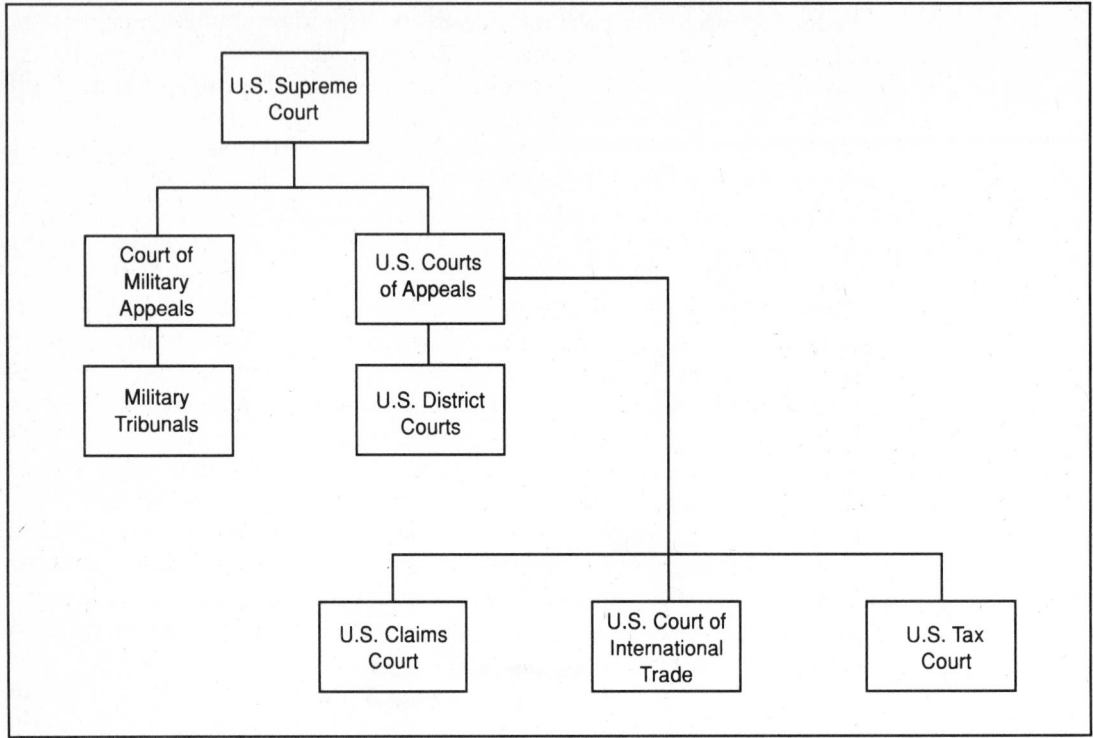

FIGURE 2–4   The Federal Court System

Source: Adapted from Arnold J. Goldman and William D. Sigismond, *Business Law: Principles & Practices*, 2nd Ed. Copyright © 1988 by Houghton Mifflin Company. Used with permission.

1. *Federal question jurisdiction* exists where the case involves claims based on the Constitution, laws, or treaties of the United States. Such claims would include suits by the United States and civil rights, patent, copyright, trademark, unfair competition, and admiralty suits.

2. *Diversity of citizenship jurisdiction* exists if a suit is between citizens of different states or between a citizen of a state and an alien, and if the amount in controversy exceeds $50,000 (the *jurisdictional amount*). Diversity jurisdiction provides qualifying plaintiffs with a choice of a federal or state forum for many types of civil actions. However, federal courts have traditionally declined to exercise diversity jurisdiction in divorce actions, child custody cases, and probate matters.

State citizenship is a key concept in diversity cases. For natural citizens, state citizenship is closely related to the establishment of a principal residence· (domicile). Thus a person who presently makes her home in Texas is a citizen of Texas. If she spends the summer working in Colorado and plans to return to Texas in September, she would still be a citizen of Texas.

Federal diversity jurisdiction requires that the diversity of citizenship be complete. This means that in a multiple-party suit, no one plaintiff and one defendant can be citizens of the same state. Thus, if a citizen of New York brings suit against two defendants, one a citizen of Wisconsin and one a citizen of Michigan, there would be total diversity of citizenship. A federal district court would have jurisdiction over the subject matter if the plaintiff is suing in good faith for over $50,000. If, however, one of the defendants was a citizen of New York, there would not be complete diversity of citizenship necessary for jurisdiction.

Congress has provided special citizenship rules for corporations. A corporation is considered a citizen in the state where it is incorporated as well as in the state of its principal place of business. For example, a corporation incorporated in Delaware with its principal place of business in New York cannot sue or be sued by citizens of either of the two states in a diversity case in a federal district court.

Diversity jurisdiction avoids exposing the defendant to possible prejudice in the plaintiff's state court. There are many who argue against diversity jurisdiction, however, claiming that the fear of possible prejudice does not justify the expense of the huge diversity caseload in federal courts. See Figure 2–5 for data regarding the number of and types of cases commenced and pending in U.S. district courts.

The Plaintiff's Choice of Forum

There are various factors that influence plaintiffs in their choice of a federal or state forum. One forum may be more attractive than another because it is closer and more convenient for the plaintiff. The plaintiff's attorney may be influenced by the reputation of the county or court in terms of the size of verdicts awarded there, by whether the forum is rural or urban, and by the reputations of the plaintiff and defendant within the forum. Plaintiffs may also be influenced to file in a federal forum if the federal procedural rules are more liberal than the corresponding state rules.

In the following case, a plaintiff files a diversity suit in federal district court, but fails to satisfy the jurisdictional amount requirement. Please note that prior to May 19, 1989, the jurisdictional amount requirement was $10,000, and not the current $50,000.

Ramírez de Arellano v. Eastern Airlines, Inc.
629 F. Supp. 189
U.S. District Court (District of Puerto Rico)
December 12, 1985

Gierbolini, District Judge

Plaintiffs have brought the present action against defendant Eastern Airlines, Inc. (Eastern) for damages as a result of an incident which occurred onboard a plane bound from Miami, Florida to San Juan, Puerto Rico. Defendant's conduct is alleged to constitute a violation of 49 U.S.C.

Type of Case	Cases Commenced				Cases Pending			
	1980	1990	1991	1992	1980	1990	1991	1992
Cases total	168,789	217,879	207,690	226,895	186,113	244,570	237,040	224,302
Contract actions[1]	49,052	46,039	42,396	51,246	40,521	42,497	41,588	42,170
Recovery of overpayments[2]	15,588	10,878	7,932	17,475	6,696	4,686	4,663	6,368
Real property actions	11,067	9,505	9,795	10,143	15,436	8,743	7,657	7,893
Tort actions	32,539	43,759	37,287	36,469	41,062	77,998	69,734	47,744
Personal injury	27,517	40,593	34,007	33,147	34,994	74,141	65,792	43,819
Personal injury product liability[1]	(NA)	18,679	12,399	10,769	9,118	47,288	39,264	17,038
Asbestos	(NA)	13,687	7,142	4,673	(NA)	38,849	31,218	8,843
Other personal injury	27,517	21,914	21,608	22,378	25,876	26,853	26,528	26,781
Personal property damage	5,022	3,166	3,280	3,322	6,068	3,857	3,942	3,925
Actions under statutes[1]	75,574	118,465	118,085	128,921	88,534	114,853	117,538	125,934
Civil rights[1]	12,944	18,793	19,337	23,419	18,819	23,791	24,009	27,220
Employment	5,017	8,413	8,144	10,275	8,893	11,490	11,156	12,738
Bankruptcy suits	1,688	5,056	5,013	5,243	1,443	3,941	4,083	4,379
Commerce (ICC rates, etc.)	1,105	2,401	1,556	2,475	6,194	1,441	1,189	1,306
Environmental matters	557	958	1,075	1,252	751	1,538	1,719	1,988
Prisoner petitions	23,287	42,630	42,476	46,452	18,008	35,793	37,259	40,894
Forfeiture and penalty	3,019	6,193	5,581	5,492	2,282	4,886	4,967	4,951
Labor laws	8,640	13,841	14,684	15,800	9,045	12,112	12,778	13,446
Protected property rights[3]	3,783	5,700	5,231	5,670	4,014	5,448	5,296	5,497
Securities commodities and exchanges	1,694	2,629	2,245	1,998	3,255	4,636	4,555	4,137
Social Security laws	9,043	7,439	7,695	8,415	13,154	8,068	8,154	8,739
Tax suits	3,262	2,604	2,639	2,305	3,075	2,850	2,713	2,429
Freedom of information	627	407	363	439	617	451	465	548

NA Not available. [1]Includes other types not shown separately. [2]Includes enforcement of judgments in student loan cases, and overpayments of veterans benefits. [3]Includes copyright, patent, and trademark rights.

FIGURE 2–5 U.S. District Courts—Civil Cases Commenced and Pending: 1980 to 1992

Source: Administrative Office of the U.S. Courts, *Annual Report of the Director,* 1993.

§ 1374(b). Jurisdiction is invoked pursuant to 28 U.S.C. §§ 1331, 1332 and 1337.[1]

The complaint alleges that on May 22, 1983, co-plaintiff Alfred Ramírez de Arellano (Ramírez) and his daughter Esther Ramírez de Arellano (Esther Ramírez) boarded Eastern Flight 967 with a first class ticket and a boarding pass. Approximately twenty minutes after boarding the plane and while plaintiffs were seated in their respective seats, employees of defendant required co-plaintiff Ramírez to move from the first class seat to a seat in the coach section of the plane. Ramírez alleges that the captain of the flight treated him in an "unruly and menacing manner" and used "abusive language" in forcing him to relinquish his seat. As a result of the captain's attitude, Ramírez claims that he suffered intense mental anguish and humiliation which caused damages estimated at $60,000.00. He also requests punitive damages in the amount of $200,000.00. In addition, Ramírez also requests $100.00 for the difference between the first class service he allegedly contracted for and the class of service he actually received. Co-plaintiff Esther Ramírez alleges that she suffered intense mental anguish and humiliation in witnessing the incident suffered by her father and estimates her damages in the sum of $15,000.00.

Eastern has filed a motion to dismiss on the grounds that the amount in controversy in the present case does not reach the required jurisdictional amount.

[1] 28 U.S.C. Sec. 1331 is a federal statute that provides for federal question jurisdiction. 28 U.S.C. Sec. 1332 provides for federal jurisdiction in diversity of citizenship cases. 28 U.S.C. Sec. 1337 provides federal jurisdiction over civil actions that arise under an Act of Congress regulating Commerce or protecting trade and commerce. 49 U.S.C. Sec. 1374(b) prohibited airlines from unreasonably showing preference to or unreasonably discriminating against any particular person.—*Ed.*

Defendant further alleges that there is no cause of action under § 1374(b). Depositions have been filed in support of Eastern's motion.

In addition to the presence of diversity of citizenship, a prerequisite for jurisdiction under 28 U.S.C. § 1332 is that "the matter in controversy exceed the sum or value of $10,000 exclusive of interest and costs. . . ."

In *Saint Paul Mercury Indemnity Co. v. Red Cab Co.*, 303 U.S. 283, 288–89 . . . (1938), the Supreme Court formulated the controlling principles for determining whether or not an action meets the jurisdictional amount:

> "The rule governing dismissal for want of jurisdiction in cases brought in the federal court is that, unless the law gives a different rule, the sum claimed by the plaintiff controls if the claim is apparently made in good faith. It must appear to a legal certainty that the claim is really for less than the jurisdictional amount to justify dismissal."

The Court also noted that the party invoking the court's jurisdiction bears the burden of alleging with sufficient particularity the facts creating jurisdiction and of supporting the allegation if challenged. . . . Plaintiffs have not met this burden. Plaintiffs' assertions of mental anguish and humiliation are conclusory at best and cannot by any stretch of the imagination justify a damage claim of $10,000.00. The present case does not involve physical injuries of any kind, no hospitalization, no loss of income nor is there any evidence that plaintiffs have consulted any medical personnel for purposes of diagnosis or treatment as a result of the emotional upset suffered. . . .

During his deposition, Ramírez testified that after the alleged incident he returned home, went to work on the following day and no changes were made in his work schedule as a consequence of the same. He did not consult any type of professional, medical or otherwise, regarding his physical and mental condition.

When questioned as to the nature of his damages, Ramírez claimed that he had the impression that he was being ridiculed and humiliated and that he was being pointed out as a troublemaker. He also stated that there were probably many people in the aircraft who knew him although he did not know who they were; plaintiff believed they probably knew him because he had been related to show business. When asked if he had knowledge as to the reactions of people in the vicinity of the incident, Ramírez stated he had no such knowledge since he did not observe their reactions, but that he had "an awareness."

In response to the question concerning the effect of the incident on his life, Ramírez answered that his life had not been profoundly affected by the incident. Ramírez also stated that he supposed that the effects of the humiliation would wear off in a period of time.

Regarding the damages suffered by co-plaintiff Esther Ramírez, she testified at the deposition that she felt very uncomfortable and nervous during the trip and suffered a bad period ("mal rato") as a result of the incident involving her father. Ms. Ramírez did not consult any type of professional, medical or otherwise, in relation to this alleged incident.

Clearly, there is a significant lack of proof that defendant's conduct caused anything more than momentary embarrassment. In *Jiménez-Puig v. Avis Rent-A-Car System*, 574 F.2d 37 (1st Cir.1978) the First Circuit Court of Appeals held that the jurisdictional amount was not met by a claim of brief embarrassment and some residual anger resulting from a car-rental clerk's public destruction of plaintiff's credit card and an announcement that plaintiff's credit was canceled because he did not pay his bills. . . .

Finally, Ramírez alleges that the conduct of Eastern constituted unjust discrimination and subjected him to unreasonable prejudice or disadvantage in respect to other passengers, all in violation of Title 49 U.S.C. 1374(b). . . . Since the incident which gives rise to the alleged federal discrimination claim occurred on May 23, 1983, plaintiffs' federal statutory action is . . . nonexistent as a matter of law. . . .

Section 1374(b) of Title 49 has definitely been eliminated as of January 1, 1983. Notwithstanding, plaintiffs argue that the relationship between a passenger and an airline is governed by federal law and such common law principles as have been assimilated to federal law, and that under federal common law punitive damages may be awarded.

However, state law determines the nature and extent of the right to be enforced in a diversity case. . . . Differently stated, a federal court sitting in diversity must apply the choice of law rules of the forum state. . . . Therefore, Puerto Rico law applies in this case.

Although Puerto Rico law provides for broad recovery for all damage caused through fault or negligence, . . . it does not allow punitive damages. . . . Thus, plaintiffs' claim for punitive damages must be disallowed.

In view of all of the foregoing, we conclude that to a legal certainty any damages plaintiffs may have suffered fall far short of the required jurisdictional amount of over $10,000.00; that the damages claimed in the complaint are without any factual basis, were not claimed in good faith, and were made solely for the purpose of obtaining federal jurisdiction. Therefore, this court has no jurisdiction under 28 U.S.C. § 1332 or under § 1331. Moreover, since the present action does not arise under any federal statute, there is no jurisdiction under 28 U.S.C. § 1337.

Wherefore, defendant's motion for summary judgment is hereby granted and the present action is dismissed.

The clerk shall enter the judgment accordingly.

So ordered.

Case Questions

1. What are the controlling principles for determining if an action satisfies the jurisdictional amount requirement?
2. What conclusion does the court reach after applying the controlling principles to the plaintiff's assertions in this case?

In Rem or *In Personam* Jurisdiction

In order for a district court to hear a civil case, it must have, in addition to jurisdiction over the subject matter, jurisdiction over the property in an *in rem* proceeding or over the person of the defendant in an *in personam* proceeding. Jurisdiction over the person is normally acquired by serving a summons within the territory. In an ordinary civil action, the summons may be properly served anywhere within the territorial limits of the state in which the district court is located. A federal summons may also be served anywhere that a state summons could be served pursuant to the state's long-arm statute.

Venue in Federal Courts[2]

Congress has provided that venue generally exists in the federal district where any defendant resides, if all defendants reside in the same state. Or it exists where the claim arose or the property is located.

If neither of the above choices is appropriate, in a diversity case, venue will exist in the federal district in which the defendant is subject to personal jurisdiction at the time the action is filed. In federal question cases, the alternative venue is the federal district in which any defendant can be found.

A corporation-defendant is subject to suit in any federal district in which it is subject to personal jurisdiction when the suit is filed.

Removal from State to Federal Courts (Removal Jurisdiction)

Except in those areas in which federal courts have exclusive jurisdiction, a suit does not have to be brought in a federal district court just because that court could exercise jurisdiction over the subject matter and over the person or property. A plaintiff may bring a dispute in any state or federal court that has jurisdiction.

A defendant sued in a state court may have a right to have the case removed to the federal courts. Any civil action brought in a state court may be moved by the defendant to a federal district court if the district court has jurisdiction. In other words, if the suit is one that could have been initiated in a district court, it is removable. When any of the defendants to a suit are citizens of the state in which the action is brought, the suit is not removable unless it is a claim arising under the Constitution, treaties, or laws of the United States. For example, if a citizen of New York sues a citizen of Ohio in a state court in Ohio for breach of contract or tort, the defendant could not have the case removed. The defendant could have the case removed if the suit were brought in any other state. Where the basis of jurisdiction is diversity of citizenship, that basis must exist at the time of filing the original suit and also at the time of petitioning for removal.

In the following case, a state court defendant petitions to remove a case from a state to a federal court. However, he neither establishes diversity jurisdiction nor raises a federal question.

Gatch v. Hennepin Broadcasting Associates, Inc.

349 F. Supp. 1180
U.S. District Court, D. Minnesota
October 7, 1972

Neville, District Judge

This case comes before the court by way of removal from the Minnesota district court of Hennepin County. Plaintiff alleges in his complaint that he is a radio broadcaster conducting a "personality talk-radio-host and commentator show" in the Twin Cities area; that he has a contract to do so with Arrow Broadcasting Company, Inc., which in turn has purchased under a contract certain broadcasting time from the defendant radio station KTCR and KTCR-FM, a duly licensed radio station in Hennepin County, Minnesota; that while both contracts were in full force and effect he was cut off the air on several occasions without justification or excuse and was not allowed to broadcast. Plaintiff himself has no direct contract with the defendant radio station but sues it in tort for alleged "illegal and unwarranted interference with defendant's contractual relation" with Arrow Broadcasting Company, Inc. The latter is not a party-defendant in this lawsuit. The complaint does not purport to and does not allege the presence of any federal question as such, does not assert the violation of any federal statute, and refers only quite incidentally to rules and regulations of the Federal Communications Commission with which he alleges full compliance.

The defendant has filed a one-page answer in the form of a general denial. At the hearing on the motion, however, its counsel orally asserted the defenses (1) that Arrow Broadcasting Company was and is delinquent in the amount of some $7000 to $8000 in its contract payments due defendant; . . . (2) that plaintiff's program was entitled "smut-talk" and engendered certain sex-oriented responses and caused unfavorable and unsavory publicity for the radio station possibly putting its Federal Communications license in jeopardy if obscene talk and conversations were permitted to be broadcast over its station. This is the only alleged Federal question raised, and this is not in fact asserted in either pleading.

The court having considered the matter does not believe it has removal jurisdiction in this case and so has remanded the same to the Minnesota state court. There is no diversity of citizenship here. Even though the jurisdiction limit of $10,000 is alleged, removal jurisdiction would have to depend solely on whether a Federal question is involved.

It is well established by a long line of authority in removal proceedings that Federal jurisdiction must be disclosed "upon the face of the complaint, unaided

by the answer or by the petition for removal." . . . It has been held that a suit may be removed where the real nature of the claim asserted in the complaint is Federal, irrespective of whether it is so characterized. . . . [I]n this case neither the complaint, nor, for that matter, the answer disclose any real Federal question. Collateral federal issues even if asserted by way of answer are not grounds for removal to federal court. . . . In sum, plaintiff here does not seek relief arising under the laws or the Constitution of the United States, but merely asserts a tort action arising out of alleged unlawful interference by a third party with a contractual relationship. No Federal question is in any sense alleged to be an essential part of plaintiff's cause of action.

Case Questions

1. Since the federal court refused to permit removal of the case to federal court, where must the action be entertained?
2. Why might a party prefer to litigate in a federal rather than a state court?
3. When must a plaintiff assert a federal question if such plaintiff wants to try the case in federal court? What can a defendant do if a plaintiff brings a case in a state court, but raises a federal question?

The *Erie* Doctrine

In adjudicating state matters, a federal court is guided by a judicial policy known as the *Erie* doctrine. In the 1938 landmark case of *Erie Railroad Company v. Tompkins*, 304 U.S. 64, the U.S. Supreme Court decided that federal questions are governed by federal law. In other cases, however, the substantive law that should generally be applied in federal courts is the law of the state. The law of the state was defined as including judicial decisions as well as statutory law. In addition, there is no federal general common law governing state matters. A federal district court is bound by the statutes and precedents of the state in which it sits.

This restriction prevents a federal court and a state court from reaching different results on the same issue of state law. You will recall that the federal judge in our first case, *Du Pont v. Christopher*, tried to determine what the Texas state courts would do if that case had been litigated in a state court. The court "applied" Texas substantive law because the question of whether aerial photography is an improper method of discovering a trade secret is a matter of state tort law. It does not raise any federal constitutional or statutory issues.

The *Erie* doctrine, which went to the heart of relations between the state and federal courts, is one of the most important judicial policies ever adopted by the U.S. Supreme Court. Many of the civil cases brought subsequent to this landmark case have been affected by the decision.

Where state and federal procedural rules differ, the *Erie* doctrine does not generally require that federal courts apply state procedural rules. Instead, the Federal Rules of Civil Procedure apply in federal courts unless they would: significantly affect a litigant's substantive rights, encourage forum shopping, or promote a discriminatory application of the law. The Federal Rules of Civil Procedure were not designed to have any effect upon the rules of decision.

In the following case, the district court relied on the *Erie* doctrine in deciding whether the plaintiff had stated a claim upon which relief could be granted.

Carson v. National Bank
501 F.2d 1082
U.S. Court of Appeals, Eighth Circuit
July 30, 1974

Per Curiam[1]

This case is before the Court upon appeal . . . from an order granting . . . judgment in favor of defendants on the first count of a two-count complaint.

The count which was dismissed was based on diversity of citizenship and alleged that defendants, in advertising a travel tour, used the name and image of the plaintiff without his permission, thereby damaging him. The District Court . . . dismissed the count on the ground that, under Nebraska law, it failed to state a claim upon which relief could be granted.

The facts are undisputed. Defendants, a bank and its wholly owned subsidiary travel agency, placed an advertisement bearing the name and picture of Mr. Car-

son, the well-known television personality and nightclub performer, in several newspapers and in a pamphlet distributed to bank customers. The advertisement concerned a travel tour to Las Vegas organized by defendant Travel Unlimited, Inc., which was called "Nebraskan Johnny Carson's Tour of Las Vegas." Mr. Carson was to be performing at a Las Vegas nightclub during the time scheduled for the tour, and tickets to his show were included in the tour package. Mr. Carson did not approve the use of his name and photograph, nor was he connected in any way with the travel venture.

. . . [T]he federal courts must apply the law of the state wherein the United States District Court is located. Here, the applicable principles must, therefore, be determined from an examination of the law of the state of Nebraska. The District Court, after examining that law, determined that Count I of the complaint failed to state a claim upon which relief could be granted. The only issue on appeal is

---

[1]An opinion written by the entire court rather than by just one judge. —*Ed.*

whether the trial court was correct in that interpretation of Nebraska law. . . .

We therefore have undertaken our own review of Nebraska law, and particularly the case of *Brunson v. Ranks Army Store*, 161 Neb. 519, 73 N.W.2d 803 (1955). This case . . . formed the basis for the District Court's conclusion that plaintiff's first cause of action did not state a claim upon which relief could be granted.

Plaintiff Brunson was an actor who was hired by Ranks Army Store to reenact the Brinks armed robbery as a publicity device. The Store failed to warn the local police of the planned re-enactment, and Mr. Brunson was arrested and jailed during the staged robbery. Thereafter, the Store ran advertisements setting forth the story of Brunson's arrest and incarceration, using Brunson's name and picture. Brunson sued the Store, charging in one count that his right to privacy, which he had not waived, was violated by the use of the picture and story without his consent and he had thereby been subjected to ridicule, embarrassment, and humiliation. The Nebraska Supreme Court affirmed the lower court's dismissal of the action, stating:

> "Our research develops no Nebraska case holding that this court has in any form or manner adopted the doctrine of the right of privacy, and there is no precedent in this state establishing the doctrine. Nor has the Legislature of this state conferred such a right of action by statute. . . . We therefore hold that the action of the trial court in sustaining the defendant's demurrer to plaintiff's action based on the right of privacy was correct and needs no further comment."

Brunson, argues plaintiff here, sought damages not for his loss of the opportunity to sell his name for commercial purposes, but for the mental suffering he underwent as a result of the revelation of an embarrassing incident. . . . All these actions stem from the initial recognition of a right to control the use of one's own name and image, which the Nebraska Supreme Court explicitly rejected in *Brunson*. Plaintiff's characterization of his action as one seeking damages for "misappropriation" cannot serve as a means to escape the rule of the *Brunson* case. If the Nebraska court had intended to recognize an action for "misappropriation," *Brunson* would certainly have been an appropriate place for some indication of such intention, since Brunson, like Carson, alleged that his picture and name had been used without his permission in an advertising scheme. (Brunson had agreed that his picture could be used in connection with the re-enactment of the robbery, but had not contracted for the use of his name and picture in connection with his actual arrest and incarceration.)

Such a result might seem anomalous today where the vast majority of states have recognized a "right to privacy" by court decision or statute, and where the plaintiff's first cause of action, in most jurisdictions, would clearly state a claim upon which relief could be granted. However, the fact that Nebraska has followed a different course from that of other states is not reason for this court to determine that Nebraska would now wish to judicially change its law. This court must look to Nebraska law as it is and not as one might believe it ought to be.

Plaintiff argues that we need not slavishly adhere to the last ruling of the Nebraska Supreme Court in a similar case, but should determine what the present Supreme Court would do if faced with this case now. We have done so, but we believe that the best method of ascertaining what the Nebraska court would do with this case is to examine what it has done with similar cases in the past.

The *Brunson* case has not been overruled, nor has any subsequent case we have found cast any doubt on its continuing authority. . . . [T]he learned District Judge, familiar with the law of Nebraska, has concluded that *Brunson* states the current law of Nebraska. We conclude that his interpretation was, and is, correct.

Affirmed.

Case Questions

1. Why did the federal district court have jurisdiction in this case?
2. Since the case was heard in federal court, why didn't the judge apply the law as generally applied in the nation, rather than the law of Nebraska?
3. Since the *Brunson* case was decided so long ago (1955), and most other states have recognized a "right to privacy," why didn't the federal court overturn Nebraska's "outdated" substantive tort law regarding these types of cases?

THE 13 U.S. COURTS OF APPEALS

The United States has been divided by Congress into eleven circuits (clusters of states), and a court of appeals has been assigned to each circuit. A court of appeals has also been established for the District of Columbia. In 1982, Congress created a new court of appeals with broad territorial jurisdiction and with very specialized subject matter jurisdiction. This court is called the Court of Appeals for the Federal Circuit. Its job is to review appeals from the U.S. district courts throughout the nation in such areas as patent, trademark, and copyright cases; cases in which the United States is the defendant; and cases appealed from the U.S. Court of International Trade and the U.S. Claims Court. Figure 2–6 shows the boundaries of the 13 circuits.

These appellate courts hear appeals on questions of law from decisions of the federal district courts in their circuits and review findings of federal administrative agencies. For most litigants, they are the ultimate appellate tribunals of the federal system. Appeal to these courts is a matter of right, not discretion, so long as proper procedures are followed.

When attorneys wish to appeal decisions of lower tribunals, they must follow such procedures to get the cases before a court of appeals. Notice of appeal must be filed within thirty days from the entry of judgment, sixty days when the United States or an officer or agent thereof is a party. A cost bond (in civil cases) may be required to ensure payment of the costs of the appeal. Both the record on appeal and a brief must be filed.

Attorneys must then persuade the judges that the lower tribunals committed errors that resulted in injustices to their clients. On appeal, the court of appeals does not substitute its judgment for that of the lower tribunal's finding of fact. It does reverse the lower court's decision if that decision

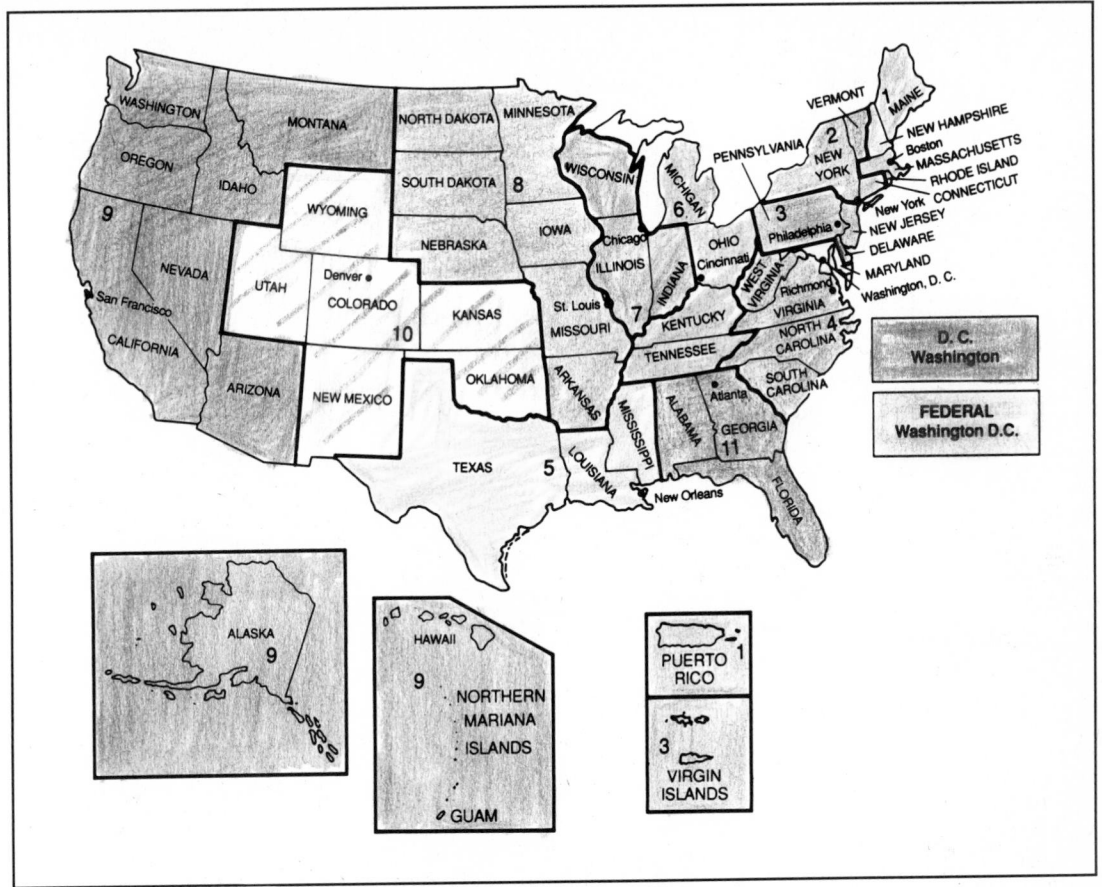

FIGURE 2–6 **The Thirteen Federal Judicial Circuits**

was clearly erroneous. See Figure 2–7 for statistical information regarding the types and number of cases decided by U.S. Courts of Appeals between 1980 and 1992.

THE U.S. SUPREME COURT

The U.S. Supreme Court has existed since 1789. Today the Court consists of a chief justice and eight associate justices. It exercises both appellate and original jurisdiction. Its chief function is to act as the last and final court of review over all cases in the federal system and some cases in the state system.

Supreme Court review is not a matter of right. A party wishing to have its case reviewed by the Supreme Court (called a *petitioner*) is required by statute to file a petition for a *writ of certiorari* with the Court. The other party, called the *respondent*, will have the right to oppose the granting of the writ. The Court grants *certiorari* only where there are special and important reasons

Item	1980	1984	1985	1986	1987	1988	1989	1990	1991	1992
Cases commenced[1]	**23,200**	**31,490**	**33,360**	**34,292**	**38,176**	**37,524**	**39,734**	**40,898**	**42,033**	**46,032**
Criminal	4,405	4,881	4,989	5,134	5,260	6,012	8,020	9,493	9,949	10,956
U.S. civil	4,654	6,259	6,744	6,415	6,292	6,210	6,349	6,626	6,663	7,113
Private civil	10,200	15,466	16,827	17,876	19,246	20,464	20,626	20,490	20,798	22,862
Administrative appeals	2,950	3,045	3,179	3,187	2,723	3,043	2,965	2,578	2,764	3,052
Cases terminated[1]	**20,887**	**31,185**	**31,387**	**33,774**	**34,444**	**35,888**	**37,372**	**38,520**	**41,414**	**42,933**
Criminal	3,993	4,876	4,892	5,134	5,039	5,284	6,297	7,509	9,198	9,830
U.S. civil	4,346	6,074	6,363	6,535	6,227	6,386	6,127	6,379	6,579	6,797
Private civil	8,942	15,309	15,743	17,276	18,338	19,798	20,313	20,369	20,698	21,628
Administrative appeals	2,643	3,212	2,760	3,235	3,237	2,625	2,914	2,582	3,148	2,801
Cases disposed of[2]	**10,607**	**14,327**	**16,369**	**18,199**	**18,502**	**19,178**	**19,322**	**21,006**	**22,707**	**23,162**
Affirmed or granted	8,017	10,961	12,286	13,398	13,681	14,953	15,240	16,629	17,988	18,463
Reversed or denied	1,845	2,382	2,770	3,249	2,924	2,664	2,617	2,565	2,503	2,681
Other	745	984	1,313	1,552	1,897	1,561	1,465	1,812	2,216	2,018
Median months[3]	8.9	8.3	10.3	10.3	10.3	10.1	10.3	10.1	10.2	10.5

[1] Includes original proceedings and bankruptcy appeals not shown separately. [2] Terminated on the merits after hearing or submission. [3] Prior to 1985, the figure is from filing of complete record to final disposition; beginning 1985, figure is from filing notice of appeal to final disposition.

FIGURE 2-7 U.S. Courts of Appeals—Cases Commenced and Disposition: 1980 to 1992

Source: Administrative Office of U.S. Courts, *Annual Report of the Director,* 1993.

Action	1980	1983	1984	1985	1986	1987	1988	1989	1990	1991
Total cases on docket	**5,144**	**5,100**	**5,006**	**5,158**	**5,123**	**5,268**	**5,657**	**5,746**	**6,316**	**6,770**
Appellate cases on docket	2,749	2,688	2,575	2,571	2,547	2,577	2,587	2,416	2,351	2,451
From prior term	527	520	539	400	476	440	446	384	365	365
Docketed during present term	2,222	2,168	2,036	2,171	2,071	2,137	2,141	2,032	1,986	2,086
Cases acted upon[1]	2,324	2,220	2,253	2,185	2,189	2,224	2,271	2,096	2,042	2,124
Granted review	167	140	167	166	152	157	130	103	114	103
Denied, dismissed, or withdrawn	1,999	1,902	1,953	1,863	1,876	1,919	1,973	1,881	1,802	1,913
Summarily decided	90	71	59	78	71	66	75	44	81	52
Cases not acted upon	425	468	322	386	358	353	316	320	309	327
Pauper cases on docket	2,371	2,394	2,416	2,577	2,564	2,675	3,056	3,316	3,951	4,307
Cases acted upon	2,027	1,992	2,087	2,189	2,250	2,263	2,638	2,891	3,436	3,768
Granted review	17	9	18	20	15	23	17	19	27	17
Denied, dismissed, or withdrawn	1,968	1,968	2,050	2,136	2,186	2,210	2,577	2,824	3,369	3,716
Summarily decided	32	10	14	24	38	21	32	35	28	22
Cases not acted upon	344	402	329	388	314	412	418	425	515	539
Original cases on docket	24	18	15	10	12	16	14	14	14	12
Cases disposed of during term	7	7	8	2	1	5	2	2	3	1
Total cases available for argument	**264**	**269**	**271**	**276**	**270**	**280**	**254**	**204**	**201**	**196**
Cases disposed of	162	189	184	175	179	175	173	147	131	130
Cases argued	154	184	175	171	175	167	170	146	125	127
Cases dismissed or remanded without argument	8	5	9	4	4	8	3	1	6	2
Cases remaining	102	80	87	101	91	105	81	57	70	66
Cases decided by signed opinion	144	174	159	161	164	151	156	143	121	120
Cases decided by per curiam opinion	8	6	11	10	10	9	12	3	4	4
Number of signed opinions	123	151	139	146	145	139	133	129	112	107

[1]Includes cases granted review and carried over to next term, not shown separately.

FIGURE 2–8 U.S. Supreme Court—Cases Filed and Disposition: 1980 to 1991

Source: Office of the Clerk, Supreme Court of the United States, unpublished data.

for so doing. If four or more justices are in favor of granting the petition, the writ issues and the case is accepted. The Court thus controls its docket, reserving its time and efforts for the cases that seem to the justices to deserve consideration. Figure 2–8 illustrates the number of cases the Supreme Court addressed between 1980 and 1991.

The U.S. Supreme Court is the only court specifically created in the Constitution. All other federal courts are statutorily created by the Congress. The Constitution provides for the Court's original jurisdiction. Original jurisdiction is the power to take note of a suit at its beginning, try it, and pass judgment on the law and the facts of the controversy. The Constitution has given the Court the power to perform the function of trial court in cases affecting ambassadors, public ministers, and consuls, and in controversies in which a state is a party. Usually the power is not exclusive, nor is the Court required to hear all cases over which it has original jurisdiction.

Article III authorizes Congress to determine the Court's appellate jurisdiction. A history-making example occurred in 1983 when Congress enacted the Military Justice Act. This act conferred jurisdiction on the Supreme Court to directly review designated categories of appeals from the Court of Military Appeals. These appeals are brought to the Court pursuant to the writ of certiorari procedure. This marked the first time in the history of the United States that any Article III court was authorized to review the decisions of military courts.

Chapter Questions

1. Define the following terms:

bench trial	jurisdictional amount
doctrine of *forum non conveniens*	limited jurisdiction
domicile	long-arm statutes
diversity of citizenship jurisdiction	minimum contacts requirement
Erie doctrine	motion for summary judgment
federal question jurisdiction	original jurisdiction
forum state	quash
general appearance	residual jurisdiction
general jurisdiction	removal jurisdiction
intermediate appellate court	special appearance
in personam jurisdiction	special verdict
in rem jurisdiction	subject matter jurisdiction
judgment creditor	summons (also called process)
judgment debtor	venue
jurisdiction	writ of *certiorari*

2. A man and a woman, both married to others, had been engaged in meretricious relations for some years. The man was a resident of New York and never lived in Florida. She pleaded with him to come to Florida to see

her, since her husband had died. She wrote him a letter at his office address telling him that her mother was sick in Ireland and asking him to come to Miami to advise her on her recent state of affairs, hinting that she would arrange accommodations for them. He told her exactly when he would arrive. He arrived at 6 o'clock in the morning at the Miami Airport and saw her standing some 75 feet away. As he approached her, a deputy sheriff stopped him and asked his name. When he replied, the deputy handed him a summons. A suit was brought by her for $500,000 for money loaned to him and for seduction under promise of marriage. Does the Florida court have jurisdiction over him? Can it render an effective *in personam* judgment against him if he leaves and disregards the complaint? What if he had come to Miami on ordinary business?

Wyman v. Newhouse, 93 F.2d 313 (2d Cir. 1937)

3. Miller sold a gas cooking stove to Nelson at Miller's place of business in Wisconsin. Miller sent one of his employees to deliver the stove to Nelson's home in Illinois. At the request of the employee, Nelson assisted in unloading the stove from the truck. In the course of this operation, the employee negligently pushed the stove so that it severed one finger on Nelson's right hand and injured another. Could Nelson effectively sue Miller in a state court in Illinois?

Nelson v. Miller, 11 Ill.2d 378, 143 N.E.2d 673 (1957)

4. Mr. and Mrs. Woodson instituted a product liability action in an Oklahoma state court to recover for personal injuries sustained in Oklahoma in an accident involving a car that they had bought in New York while they were New York residents. The Woodsons were driving the car through Oklahoma at the time of the accident. The defendants were the car retailer and its wholesaler, both New York corporations, who did no business in Oklahoma. The defendants entered a special appearance, claiming that the Oklahoma state court did not have personal jurisdiction. Would there be enough "minimum contacts" between the defendants and the forum state for the forum state to have personal jurisdiction over the defendants?

World-Wide Volkswagen Corp. v. Woodson, 444 U.S. 286 (1980)

5. Mr. and Mrs. Mottley were injured while riding a passenger train on the Short Line Railroad in Kentucky about 20 years ago. As compensation for their injuries, Short Line agreed to issue a lifetime free travel pass to the Mottleys. A year ago, Congress passed a law forbidding railroads to issue free passes. Short Line promptly canceled the Mottleys' pass, in compliance with the law. The Mottleys filed a complaint in federal court in Kentucky alleging that Short Line made a contract with them 20 years ago to issue them a free pass for life and that the railroad had canceled it last year. The complaint further alleged that the reason for this cancellation was the law against free passes; and that unless the law is construed as not requiring the cancellation of the Mottleys' pass, it deprived the Mottleys of their property without due process, in violation of the Fifth

Amendment. Why did the Mottleys' complaint fail to confer jurisdiction of the case on the U.S. District Court in Kentucky, as presenting a federal question?

Louisville & Nashville R.R. v. Mottley, 211 U.S. 149 (1908)

6. In this hypothetical diversity of citizenship case, federal law requires complete diversity of citizenship between plaintiffs and defendants and an amount in controversy greater than $50,000 in order for federal courts to entertain jurisdiction of an action. Tom Jones and Leonard Woodrock were deep-shaft coal miners in West Virginia, although Leonard lived across the border in Kentucky. Tom purchased a new Corsair, a National Motors car, from Pappy's Auto Sales, a local firm. National Motors Corporation is a large auto manufacturer with its main factory in South Bend, Indiana, and incorporated in Kentucky. When Tom was driving Leonard home from the mine, the Corsair's steering wheel inexplicably locked. The car hurtled down a 100-foot embankment and came to rest against a tree. The Corsair, which cost $2,100, was a total loss. Tom and Leonard suffered damages of $48,000 apiece for personal injuries. Can Tom sue National Motors for damages in a federal court? Why? Can Leonard? Can Leonard and Tom join their claims and sue National Motors in federal court?

7. Several Arizona citizens brought a diversity suit in a federal district court against Harsh Building Company, an Oregon corporation. All parties involved in the suit stipulated that the defendant had its principal place of business in Oregon. During the trial, evidence showed that the only real business activity of Harsh Building Co. was owning and operating the Phoenix apartment complex, which was the subject of the suit. The plaintiffs lost the suit. On appeal, they claimed that the district court did not have jurisdiction because of lack of diversity of citizenship. Did the plaintiffs waive their right to challenge jurisdiction?

Bialac v. Harsh Building Co., 463 F.2d 1185 (9th Cir. 1972)

8. National Mutual Insurance Company is a District of Columbia corporation. It brought a diversity action in the U.S. District Court of Maryland against Tidewater Transfer Company, a Virginia corporation doing business in Maryland. National Mutual contends that, for diversity purposes, a D.C. resident may file suit against the resident of a state. Tidewater Transfer disagrees. What should be taken into consideration in deciding whether the District of Columbia can, for diversity purposes, be regarded as a state?

National Mutual Insurance v. Tidewater Transfer Co., 337 U.S. 582 (1949)

9. A check was drawn on the U.S. Treasury through the Federal Reserve Bank of Philadelphia, Pennsylvania, to the order of Paul Friendly for $324.20, to cover services rendered in his government job. The check was mailed to Friendly's address in Butler, Pennsylvania, but for some reason it never reached him. An unknown person presented the check to the J.C. Penney store in Clearfield, Pennsylvania, endorsed it, and presented

identification. Penney's cashed the check and endorsed it to the Clearfield Trust Company for payment. Clearfield endorsed it to the Federal Reserve Bank, guaranteeing all previous endorsements as genuine. When Friendly notified the government that he had not received his check, the forgery was discovered. The Treasury Department waited more than six months before notifying Clearfield Trust and J.C. Penney of the forgery. The United States then sued Clearfield Trust for the $324.20. Clearfield defended on the ground that the government waited too long before giving notice of the forgery. Under Pennsylvania law, the trust company wins. Under federal common law, the United States wins. Which law governs? *Based on Clearfield Trust Co. v. United States, 318 U.S. 363 (1943)*

10. Alsie H. Parks, a black woman, was demoted from her position as high school counselor and offered a job as a teacher. Parks refused to accept the teaching position. Instead, she filed a civil rights action in federal court, alleging that the school board's action was racially motivated and thus invalid. She asked for reinstatement as high school counselor. At trial, evidence was introduced on both sides of the question. The school board's action was sustained on a finding that Parks was professionally incompetent. Parks appealed the decision of the district court on the racial motivation issue. In addition, for the first time, she alleged that she was denied due process, since no hearing was held prior to her dismissal. Can the court of appeals consider Parks' complaint of lack of a hearing? Why? How should the court go about evaluating whether Parks' dismissal was based on the fact that she is black?
Board of Education v. Parks, 469 F.2d 1315 (5th Cir. 1972)

11. John Popovici is a citizen of Rumania. As Rumania's vice consul in the United States, he lived in Cleveland, Ohio, where he met and married his wife. Now Helen Popovici wants to sue him for divorce in an Ohio state court. Popovici, however, wants the suit brought in a federal district court, since federal district courts have original jurisdiction over "suits against . . . consuls or vice consuls." Consider the nature of the suit and the criteria for federal jurisdiction. Can Mrs. Popovici sue her husband for divorce in federal court?
Popovici v. Angler, 280 U.S. 379 (1930)

Notes

1. *Burnham v. Superior Court,* 495 U.S. 604 (1990).
2. 28 U.S.C 1391.

III

Civil Procedure

As a passive adjudicator of disputes, courts neither initiate nor encourage litigation. The court system does nothing until one of the parties has called on it through appropriate procedures. Procedural rules create the process that is used to decide the merits of a dispute. At the beginning of the process, these rules explain what a plaintiff must do to start a lawsuit and how the plaintiff can assert a legal claim against a defendant. Defendants are similarly told how to raise defenses and claims once they have been notified of suit. Procedural rules govern what documents must be prepared, what each must contain, and how they should be presented to the court and the defendant. Once the lawsuit has been initiated, procedures govern how the parties discover relevant information and evidence, especially when it is in the possession of one's opponent. Rules also govern the conduct of trials, any enforcement procedures necessary after trial, the conduct of appeals, and the imposition of sanctions on rule violators. The principal objective of procedural law is to give the parties to a dispute an equal and fair opportunity to present their cases to a nonprejudiced and convenient tribunal. If procedural rules are correctly drafted and implemented, both parties to the dispute should feel that they have been fairly treated.

Although all procedures must satisfy constitutional due process requirements, the state and federal governments have promulgated separate rules of civil procedure that govern the litigation process in their respective forums. Parties litigating in the state courts of Oregon follow the *Oregon Rules of Civil Procedure*. In federal courts, however, the *Federal Rules of Civil Procedure* (FRCP), and supplementing local rules or orders developed by each federal district court also apply. Recently, Congress and the U.S. Supreme Court have been encouraging district courts to experiment with procedural reforms. Several reforms have been implemented with little difficulty. The new discovery rules requiring mandatory, cooperative self-disclosure, however, have proven to be very controversial and have encountered considerable opposition at the district court level. Congress will consider the results of the ongoing experiments and decide whether further changes are required.

The purpose of this chapter is to explain the procedures that govern a civil suit from the time a litigant decides to sue until final court judgment. Indispensable to an understanding of these systems is a familiarity with the various stages and terms that are encountered in a civil proceeding.

A PROCEDURAL PRIMER

The following highly simplified overview of litigation is intended to give you a sense of the big picture before we examine each stage of the process in more detail. Like a trial attorney's opening statement in a jury trial, it is intended to help you to see how the various procedural stages fit together. Obviously, this abbreviated treatment omits many of the details and is intentionally very limited in scope.

Every lawsuit is based on some event that causes a person to feel that he or she has been legally injured in some manner by another (see Figure 3–1). The injured party will often contact an attorney to discuss the matter. The attorney will listen to the facts, make a determination about whether the client has a case, and present the client with a range of options for pursuing a claim. These options will often include informal attempts to settle the claim, alternative dispute resolution methods such as those discussed in Chapter 14, and filing suit in court. After weighing the costs and benefits of each option and listening to the advice of the attorney, the client will make a decision as to how to proceed. If the decision is made to file suit, the lawyer will draft a document called a *complaint* and a *writ of summons*, and serve them on the defendant in accordance with the law. The complaint will explain the plaintiff's claims and requested relief. The summons will inform the defendant to serve a document called an *answer* on the plaintiff's attorney by a statutorily determined date. If the defendant's attorney finds any legal defects in jurisdiction, venue, form, or substance in either the summons or the complaint, he or she can make motions seeking modification or dismissal of the action. Assuming that the motions are denied and any defects are corrected, the defendant will then draft and serve a timely answer to prevent the plaintiff from winning the case by default due to the defendant's inaction.

Once the complaint has been properly served and filed with the court, the *discovery* phase begins. This is where each party learns as much as possible about the case. Virtually all relevant information can be obtained from sources who are friendly, neutral, or adverse, such as the opposing party. Obviously, some information is not discoverable, such as an attorney's trial strategy, research notes (work product), and other material that is classified as privileged. Later in the chapter, we will learn specific techniques lawyers use during the discovery phase.

After the facts have been sufficiently investigated, one or both parties will frequently request the court to dispose of the case and award a *judgment* (the

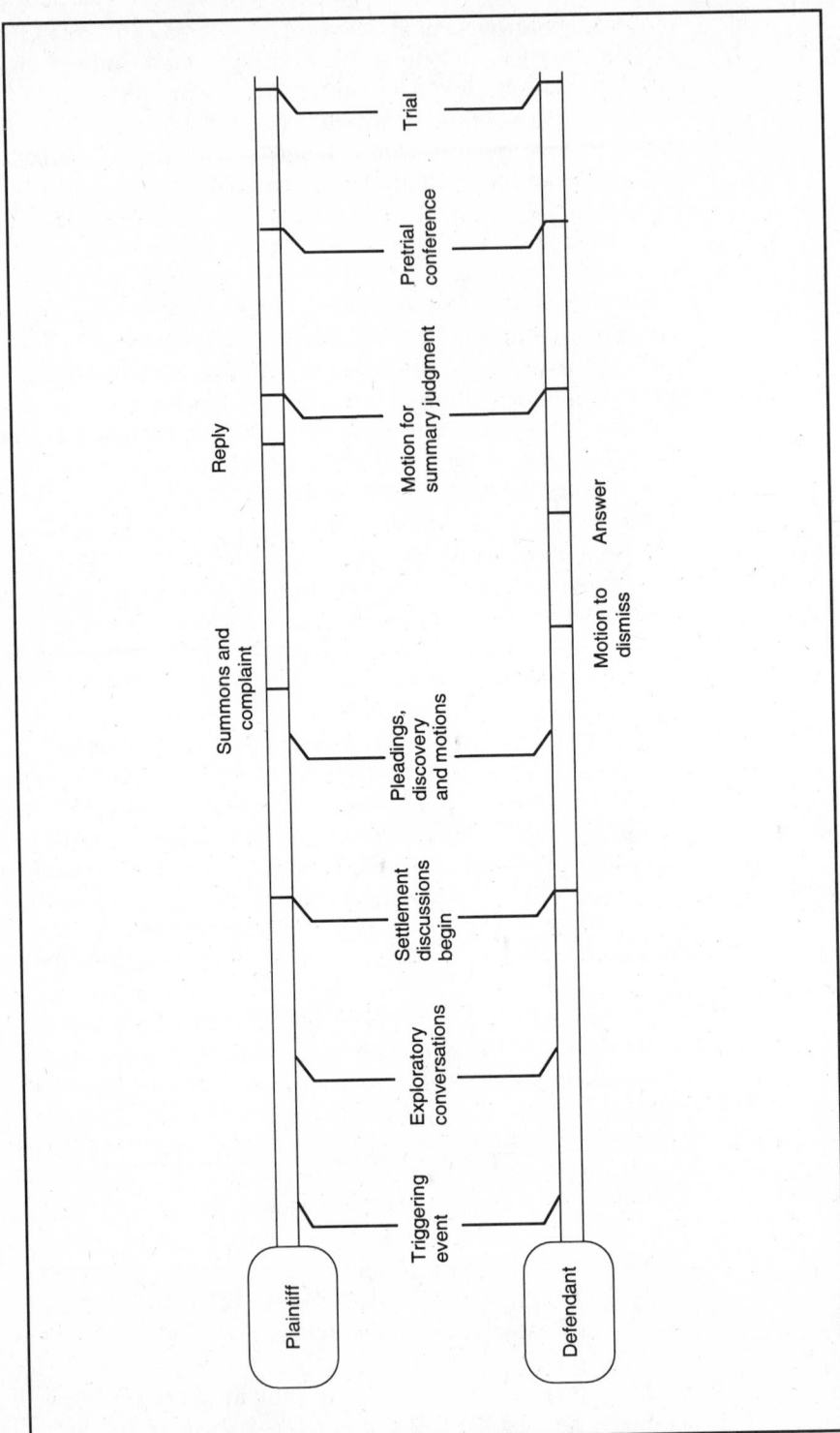

FIGURE 3–1   Proceedings Before a Civil Trial

court's final decision in a case), rather than proceeding to trial. This request, called a *motion for summary judgment*, is properly granted when the plaintiff and defendant substantially agree about the important facts in the case. If there is no dispute about the significant facts, there is no reason to conduct a trial. In that situation, the judge can resolve any dispute about what legal rule applies to this particular set of facts and award a judgment to the deserving party.

It is important to note that informal discussions between the attorneys often take place at all stages of the process, up to and even during the course of the trial, in an effort to settle the case. These discussions usually intensify once motions for summary judgment have been denied and it appears that the case will be tried. Assuming that summary judgment is denied and there is no negotiated settlement, what usually follows is the pretrial conference.

At a pretrial conference, the court and the attorneys will meet to define the issues, prepare for the trial, and discuss the possibility of settlement. At this meeting the parties can indicate how many days they believe it will take to try the case, try to resolve evidentiary and discovery problems, and schedule any necessary pretrial hearings. After the meeting, a pretrial order will be signed by the judge which records the decisions that were made at the conference.

Before proceeding to trial, many jurisdictions will require or encourage the litigating parties to participate in *alternative dispute resolution* (ADR). The majority of state legislatures have approved some form of ADR, and over one-third of the federal courts participate to some degree.[1]

Alternative dispute resolution is an umbrella concept for a variety of procedures designed to assist parties resolve their disputes without trials. Jurisdictions participate in ADR to differing degrees. Some mandate cooperation, and others make participation optional. In Chapter 14 we explain such ADR techniques as mediation, arbitration, summary jury trials, and mini-trials, but we emphasize that any party dissatisfied with the ADR process can insist on proceeding to trial. There is a continuing dispute as to whether ADR is living up to its proponents' claims and producing faster, less expensive, and higher quality justice than litigation.[2]

Only 3 to 4 percent of all lawsuits filed actually are decided at trial.[3] Non-jury trials, where a judge decides the factual issues (also known as *bench trials*), are conducted differently from trials in which juries render a verdict. In bench trials, for example, there are no jurors to select, the attorneys generally do not make opening statements, the rules of evidence are often relaxed, and there are no jury instructions to prepare and deliver. The judge will consider the evidence presented by each party and determine whether the plaintiff has satisfied the burden of proof. At the end of a bench trial, the judge will announce findings of fact, state conclusions of law, and award a judgment.

Additional procedures are necessary for jury trials. The jurors have to be carefully selected, and in major trials the lawyers may seek help from trial consultants. Because jurors generally know little about rules of evidence and the applicable law, the lawyers do not present their cases as they would in a bench trial. Judges must keep the lawyers in check and ensure that the jury is exposed only to evidence that is relevant, material, and legally adequate (competent). After each side has had the opportunity to present evidence and cross-examine opposing witnesses, the attorneys will conclude by arguing their case to the jury. After the closing arguments, the judge instructs the jury on the law and sends it out to deliberate. The jury deliberates until it reaches a verdict, which it reports to the court. After deciding any postverdict motions, the court will enter a judgment in favor of one of the parties and award relief accordingly. Normally, any party dissatisfied with the judgment will have a specified number of days after the entry of judgment in which to make an appeal.

PROCEEDINGS BEFORE A CIVIL TRIAL—A CLOSER LOOK

With the preceding overview in mind, we will now proceed to a closer look at the pretrial phases of civil litigation. The first step involves a triggering event that injures the plaintiff or damages his or her property. The next step usually involves the plaintiff selecting an attorney.

It is important to understand that in general, each party pays for his/her attorney's fee irrespective of who ultimately prevails in the substantive dispute. This is subject to exceptions where statutory law provides otherwise and where common law judicial doctrines permit the court to order the loser to pay the winner's attorney fees.

Hiring a Lawyer

The period between the event that gives rise to the suit (the triggering event) and the filing of a complaint is known as the *informal discovery* period. The court has neither knowledge of nor interest in the plaintiff's cause of action against the defendant.

During this time, the plaintiff contacts an attorney and describes the circumstances that led to the injury. The attorney discusses in general terms the legal alternatives available and usually asks for an opportunity to conduct an independent investigation to assess the value of the claim. This meeting is known as an exploratory conversation. At this point, the plaintiff and the attorney are not contractually bound to each other.

After the exploratory conversation and further investigation, the plaintiff meets once again with the attorney to determine which course of action should be taken. The attorney presents an evaluation of the case in terms of the remedies available, the probability of achieving a favorable verdict, and the nature and probability of the award likely to be granted. At this point, the plaintiff retains the attorney as a representative in the judicial proceedings that are likely to follow.

Attorney's fees may be determined in several ways. They may charge the client by the hour. They may take a percentage of the damages collected (*contingent fee*), in which case they receive nothing if the client loses. They may be on a retainer, in which case they are paid a certain sum per year to handle all their client's legal problems. Or they may charge a flat rate for their services.

When the plaintiff's lawyer has been officially retained, the defendant is so informed. This information puts the defendant on notice that the plaintiff is preparing to seek an adjudicative settlement of the claim. If the defendant has not already retained an attorney, this is the time to do so. The attorneys meet, with or without their clients, to discuss a reasonable settlement. These discussions are referred to as *settlement conferences.* If they prove unsuccessful, the judicial machinery is set in motion.

Clients retain the power to discharge their lawyers at any time. In the following case, the Supreme Court of California weighs this right against the rule of damages.

Fracasse v. Brent
6 Cal.3d 784, 494 P.2d 9
Supreme Court of California
March 10, 1972

Burke, Associate Justice

In this case we are asked to reconsider the rule of damages which allows an attorney who has been discharged without cause by his client to recover as damages the full fee specified in the contract of employment, regardless of the reasonable value of his services or the extent of work performed under that contract. For the reasons hereinafter stated, we have concluded that this rule is inconsistent with the strong policy, expressed both judicially and legislatively, in favor of the client's absolute right to discharge his attorney at any time, and that the attorney should be limited to a *quantum meruit* recovery for the reasonable value of his services, upon the occurrence of any contingency contemplated by his contract.

Plaintiff, George Fracasse, is a duly licensed attorney at law, who was retained by defendant Ray Raka Brent to prosecute a claim for personal injuries in her behalf. On or about March 12, 1969, Fracasse and Brent entered into a written contingent fee agreement, under which

Brent agreed that Fracasse's compensation would be 33 ⅓ percent of any settlement made at least 30 days prior to the original trial date and 40 percent of any recovery obtained thereafter, whether by settlement or judgment.

Sometime thereafter, but before any recovery had been obtained in the personal injury suit, Brent informed Fracasse that she wished to discharge him and retain another attorney. She did so and, on January 16, 1970, Fracasse filed the instant action, entitled "Complaint for Declaratory Relief." Alleging that his discharge was without cause, and that Brent had breached her contract and had refused to give Fracasse the fee to which he would have been entitled thereunder, Fracasse prayed for a declaration that the contract was valid and that he had a one-third interest in any monies ultimately recovered in the personal injury action. . . . The trial court . . . held that the complaint did not state a cause of action. . . . This appeal followed. . . .

"It is recognized as a part of the ethical rules governing the legal profession that an attorney will not sue a client for a fee except to prevent injustice, imposition, or fraud. . . . The relation of attorney and client is one of special confidence and trust and the dignity and integrity of the legal profession demand that the interests of the client be fully protected. . . . Without public confidence in the members of the legal profession which is dependent upon absolute fairness in the dealings between attorney and client, courts cannot function in the proper administration of justice. And inherent in the relationship between attorney and client is the fact that the client must rely almost entirely upon the good faith of the attorney who alone can make an informed estimate of the value of the client's legal right and of the expense and effort necessary to enforce it. These considerations have given rise to the generally accepted rule that a client may discharge his attorney at any time with or without cause. But that is not enough. The right to discharge is of little value if the client must risk paying the full contract price for services rendered upon a determination by a court that the discharge was without legal cause. The client may frequently be forced to choose between continuing the employment of an attorney in whom he had lost faith, or risking the payment of double contingent fees equal to the greater portion of any amount eventually recovered. . . ."

It has long been recognized in this state that the client's power to discharge an attorney, with or without cause, is absolute. . . . In discussing the unique relationship between attorney and client, this court stated that "the interest of the client in the successful prosecution or defense of the action is superior to that of the attorney, and he has the right to employ such attorney as will in his opinion best subserve his interest. The relation between them is such that the client is justified in seeking to dissolve that relation whenever he ceases to have absolute confidence in either the integrity or the judgment or the capacity of the attorney.

. . . The fact that the attorney has rendered valuable services under his employment, or that the client is indebted to him therefor, or for the moneys advanced in the prosecution or defense of the action, does not deprive the client of this right. . . ."

We have concluded that a client should have both the power and the right at any time to discharge his attorney with or without cause. Such a discharge does not constitute a breach of contract for the reason that it is a basic term of the contract, implied by law into it by reason of the special relationship between the contracting parties, that the client may terminate that contract at will. It would be anomalous and unjust to hold the client liable in damages for exercising that basic implied right. . . .

Amicus contends that there will be substantial difficulty in ascertaining the amount of recovery under a *quantum meruit* theory. The same difficulty—if such it be—is also present, however, in cases in which an attorney has been discharged with "cause" and yet such difficulty does not appear to have been insurmountable. . . . Nor do we believe that abandonment of the present rule will lead to a wholesale discharging of attorneys by clients motivated solely by a desire to save attorneys' fees. To the extent that such discharge is followed by the retention of another attorney, the client will in any event be required, out of any recovery, to pay the former attorney for the reasonable value of his services. Such payment, in addition to the fee charged by the second attorney, should certainly operate as a self-limiting factor on the number of attorneys so discharged. To the extent that such discharge occurs "on the courthouse steps," where the client executes a settlement obtained after much work by the attorney, the factors involved in a determination of reasonableness would certainly justify a finding that the entire fee was the reasonable value of the attorney's services.

In short, we find no injustice in a rule awarding a discharged attorney the reasonable value of the services he has rendered up to the time of discharge. In doing so, we preserve the client's right to discharge his attorney without undue restriction, and yet acknowledge the attorney's right to fair compensation for work performed. . . .

One of the significant factors in determining the reasonableness of an attorney's fee is "the amount involved and the result obtained." . . . It is apparent that any determination of the "result obtained" is impossible, and any determination of the "amount involved" is, at best, highly speculative . . . until the matter has finally been resolved. Second, and perhaps more significantly, we believe it would be improper to burden the client with an absolute obligation to pay his former attorney regardless of the outcome of the litigation. The client may and often is very likely to be a person of limited means for whom the contingent fee arrangement offers the only realistic hope of establishing a legal claim. Having determined that he no longer has the trust and confidence in his attorney necessary to sustain that unique relationship, he should not be held to have incurred an absolute obligation to compensate his former attorney. Rather, since the attorney agreed initially to take his chances on recovering any fee whatever, we believe that the fact that the success of the litigation is no longer under his control is insufficient to justify imposing a new and more onerous burden on the client. Hence, we believe that the attorney's action for reasonable compensation accrues only when the contingency stated in the original agreement has

occurred—i.e., the client has had a recovery by settlement or judgment. It follows that the attorney will be denied compensation in the event such recovery is not obtained.

In summary, we hold that an attorney discharged with or without cause is entitled to recover the reasonable value of his services rendered to the time of discharge. . . . We further hold that the cause of action to recover compensation for services rendered under a contingent fee contract does not accrue until the occurrence of the stated contingency. In light of these rules, it seems clear that there is no present controversy such as would justify the courts in exercising its discretion to entertain an action for declaratory relief. . . .

The judgment of the trial court is affirmed.

Sullivan, Justice, dissenting

. . . We are confronted here with two questions: First, whether an attorney at law who has been discharged without cause by his client may bring a declaratory relief action to obtain a determination of his rights under a written contingency fee contract; and second, what may be the extent of his recovery under such circumstances.

The majority hold (1) that the action for declaratory relief is premature because the amount of any possible award cannot be determined before disposition of the client's underlying claim; and (2) that the client's discharge of the attorney without cause does not constitute a breach of the contingency fee contract so as to make the client liable for damages on the contract because he had "both the power and the right at any time to discharge his attorney with or without cause." . . . Neither logic, traditional principles of contract law, nor the weight of precedent supports either holding. . . . The court held that since the attorney's damages could not be assessed until his former client recovered a specific amount, the attorney's action was premature. . . .

Here, plaintiff is not seeking damages for breach, but merely a *declaratory judgment* determining that defendant is *conditionally* liable under the contract and applying the established rule for calculating the amount of liability. . . . [T]he relief sought here by plaintiff does not require the court to predict whether and to what extent defendant will recover in his underlying personal injury suit. . . . [P]laintiff prays only for the court's recognition of his contractual right to receive a fixed percentage of any amount eventually recovered by defendant. . . . The fact that no judgment has been rendered . . . furnishes no reason for denying the former equitable relief under the declaratory relief procedure. . . .

The majority, however, do not stop at this point but, fashioning new rules as to the measure of damages in respect to attorney-client contracts, conclude that the action should be dismissed on this basis also. I cannot accept these new rules which are arrived at only after a wholesale uprooting of settled principles of contract law and an omnibus overturning of precedent. I now turn to this aspect of the case.

I start with an established rule of general contract law long recognized and adhered to by California courts. "One who has been injured by a breach of contract has an election to pursue any of three remedies. He may treat the contract as rescinded and may recover upon a *quantum meruit* so far as he has performed; or he may keep the contract alive, for the benefit of both parties, being at all times ready and able to perform; or, third, he may treat the repudiation as putting an end to the contract for all purposes of performance, and sue for the profits he would have realized if he had not been prevented from performing." . . . This rule applies as to contracts between principal and agent and to contracts for services. . . . Until today there has been nothing in the development of California law which has qualified or restricted the above rule when applied to agreements between an attorney and his client. Although such contracts are subject to the usual precepts governing persons standing in a confidential relationship, no statute, decision or rule of professional conduct has declared that they are not subject to general contract law. No authority has ever so jettisoned respected contract principles to decree, as do the majority today, that a solemn, valid agreement between attorney and client may be dissolved into thin air at the mere whim of the client. . . .

Case Questions

1. What is the difference between contracts between attorneys and their clients and other contracts?
2. List the pros and cons of contingent fees.
3. Should a court uphold a contingent fee contract between attorney and client that prohibits a settlement by the client?

4. If an attorney's client decides not to prosecute the claim, should the attorney be allowed to continue to prosecute the cause, to secure the contingent fee?

5. A criminal defendant is accorded the right to have a court-appointed attorney. Should civil litigants be accorded a similar right to court-appointed counsel? Are prepaid legal services—for example, group insurance coverage for litigation expenses—the solution? Are legal services such as public defender systems and legal aid societies the solution?

6. Should an attorney who fits the description of an "ambulance chaser" be disbarred? What if the attorney solicits professional employment by advertising?

The Pleadings

The pleading stage begins after the client has chosen a lawyer and decides to bring suit. The role of pleadings in Anglo-American law goes back to the earliest days of the English common law system and writ system.[4] In the twelfth century, persons wishing to litigate in the royal courts had to purchase an original writ (such as the Writ of Right) from the king or chancellor in order to establish the court's jurisdiction. Each writ specified the procedures and substantive law to be followed in deciding the dispute.[5] The writ would often require the plaintiff to make an oral recitation (a pleading) in which the claims would be stated, after which the defendant would be entitled to respond orally. In this way the parties would inform the court of the nature of the dispute.[6] In time, the practice of oral pleadings was replaced with written documents, and the common law and equitable pleading process became very complex, overly technical, cumbersome, and long.

In 1848, New York merged the common law and equity courts and replaced its writ system with a newly enacted Code of Civil Procedure. Thus began a reform movement that swept the country and produced modern code pleading at the state level. The popularity of code pleading convinced Congress to enact the Rules Enabling Act in 1934 which led to the development and adoption in 1938 of the Federal Rules of Civil Procedure.

Modern pleadings are much less complex than in earlier times and are somewhat less important because of liberal discovery rules. They continue, however, to establish the basis for jurisdiction, briefly state facts giving rise to the complaint, aid in the formulation of the issues, and indicate the relief sought. Today, the pleadings consist of the plaintiff's complaint, the defendant's *answer*, and, rarely, the plaintiff's reply.

The *complaint* is a written document in which the plaintiff alleges jurisdiction, sets forth facts that he or she claims entitle the plaintiff to relief from the defendant, and demands relief. Figure 3–2 provides a sample of a federal complaint.

The complaint is the first pleading. It is filed with the court and served on the defendant with a *writ of summons*.[7] The writ of summons warns the

UNITED STATES DISTRICT COURT
. . . . District of . . . .

:
. . . . Plaintiff :
                 v.   :
. . . . Defendant :
:

Civil Action No. . . . .
COMPLAINT

JURY TRIAL DEMANDED

This is a civil action seeking damages under the laws of the State of . . . . . . for injuries to the person of the plaintiff, and to her automobile, caused by the defendant's negligent and/or willful, wanton, or reckless conduct.

1. The court has jurisdiction of this matter by virtue of the fact that the plaintiff is a citizen of the State of . . . . . , and the defendant, ... , is a citizen of the State of . . . . . , and the amount in controversy exceeds $50,000 exclusive of interest and costs.

2. This suit is brought purusant to Section . . . . . . of the Revised Statutes.

3. The plaintiff, ... , is, and at all times material to this action was, a resident of the City of . . . . . . , State of . . . . . .

4. The defendant, ... , is, and at all time material to this action was, a resident of the City of . . . . . . , State of . . . . . .

5. At all times hereinafter mentioned, plaintiff was in the exercise of all due care and caution for her own safety and the safety of others.

6. On . . . . . . , 199 . . . . at or about . . . . P.M., plaintiff, ... , was operating her automobile in a northerly direction along United States Route . . . . at or about . . . . miles north of . . . .

7. On . . . . . . , 199 . . . . at or about . . . . P.M., defendant, ... , was operating her motor automobile in a southerly direction along United States Route . . . . at or about . . . . miles north of . . . .

8. At that date and time, defendant, ... , negligently operated her vehicle in one or more of the following ways:

    a. Improperly failed to give a signal of her intention to make a turn.

    b. Negligently made an improper left-handed turn, without yielding the right-of-way to traffic coming in the opposite direction.

    c. Negligently failed to yield the right-of-way.

    d. Operated her vehicle on the wrong side of the road.

    e. Negligently failed to keep said vehicle under proper control.

    f. Operated her vehicle in a negligent manner.

    g. Negligently failed to stop her vehicle when danger to the plaintiff was imminent.

9. As a result of one or more of the acts or omissions complained of, the vehicle driven by . . . . . . was caused violently to collide with the vehicle driven by . . . . . .

10. As a direct and proximate result thereof, the plaintiff suffered painful, severe and permanent injuries, loss of income, and has incurred, and will continue to incur, expenses for medical care and further, ... was caused to expend the sum of $ . . . . to repair the damages to her automobile caused by the accident.

    WHEREFORE, plaintiff, ... , prays for judgment against the defendant, ... , in the sum of . . . . dollars ($ . . . .) plus costs.

    Plaintiff requests a jury trial.

. . . .
Attorney for Plaintiff
Office and P.O. Address

. . . .

FIGURE 3–2 Complaint

defendant that a default judgment can be awarded to the plaintiff unless the defendant responds with a pleading called an *answer* (see Figure 3–3) within a stated period of time (usually 20 days).

Methods of Service

The *summons* (see Figure 2–2) must be served to the defendant in time for the person to take action in defense. This right is constitutionally guaranteed by the *due process clauses*. There are several methods to serve the summons which can be found in the statute books of each state. These requirements must be precisely followed and may differ from *in personam* and *in rem* actions. Clearly the most desirable method is to deliver personally the summons to the defendant. Some jurisdictions require that the summons be served within a specified period of time. The Federal Rules of Civil Procedure, for example, requires service within 120 days of the filing of the complaint. The summons, sometimes called *process*, is generally served by a process server or sheriff.

As previously mentioned, the recently amended federal rules provide incentives that encourage defendants to waive voluntarily their right to be formally served with process. For defendants in federal court who agree to waive, the benefit is the right to take 60 days to respond to the complaint rather than the normal 20 days. The benefit to plaintiffs is in not having to pay someone to serve the summons and complaint. Defendants who refuse to honor a requested waiver of service can be required to pay the service costs unless they can show good cause for the refusal.

In addition to having the summons personally served on a defendant, many states permit service by certified or registered mail, return receipt requested. This method is increasingly preferred because it is inexpensive and generally effective. You may recall that this method of service was used in the case of *Calder v. Jones* in Chapter 2.

Where personal service of a summons and the complaint to a defendant is not possible, the law often permits what is called *substituted* or *alternative service*. This method involves mailing the summons and complaint to the defendant by certified mail and leaving these documents at the defendant's home with a person who resides there and who is of "suitable age and discretion." Traditionally, this means someone fourteen or over. If the plaintiff is suing a corporation, the statutes usually authorize the use of substituted service on a designated agent or even a state official such as the secretary of state or the commissioner of insurance. The agent or official then would send a copy of the documents to the corporation. In some circumstances, the statutes provide for *constructive service*, which means publishing the notice of summons in the legal announcements section of newspapers. Traditionally, the law required that the summons be published for three weeks.

The answer is a responsive written document in which the defendant makes admissions or denials, asserts legal defenses, and raises counterclaims. An *admission* means that there is no need to prove that fact during the trial. A

UNITED STATES DISTRICT COURT
. . . . . . .District of . . . .

. . . . .Plaintiff   :

             :   Civil Action No. . . . .

    v.   :   ANSWER

. . . . Defendant :

             :   JURY TRIAL DEMANDED

Now comes the defendant in the above-captioned action and gives the following answers to the plaintiff's complaint:

   1. Denies the allegations of paragraphs 1 and 2 of the complaint.
   2. Admits the allegations of paragraphs 3 and 4 of the complaint.
   3. Denies the allegations of paragraphs 5 through 10 of the complaint.

FIRST AFFIRMATIVE DEFENSE

This court lacks subject matter jurisdiction as the amount in controversy does not exceed $50,000, exclusive of interest and cost.

SECOND AFFIRMATIVE DEFENSE

Plaintiff was guilty of negligence which was a contributing cause of the accident in that the plaintiff was negligently operating her automobile at the time that same collided with defendant's automobile. The plaintiff is therefore barred from recovery.

WHEREFORE, the defendant demands that the plaintiff's complaint be dismissed and that the costs of this action be awarded the defendant.

Defendant claims a trial by jury.

                . . . .
                Attorney for Defendant
                Office and P.O. Address
                . . . .
                . . . .

FIGURE 3–3   Answer

denial creates a factual issue to be proved. Facts that may bar the plaintiff from recovery constitute a *defense*. The defendant may also make a claim for relief against the plaintiff by raising a *counterclaim* in the answer. A counterclaim is appropriate when the defendant has a cause of action against a plaintiff arising out of essentially the same set of events that gave rise to the plaintiff's claim. For example, assume that *P* observes *D* fishing without permission on *P*'s land and tells *D* to vacate. If *P* kicks *D* in the back as *D* leaves the property, *P* is committing a battery against *D*. *P* could bring suit against *D* for trespass, and *D* could counterclaim against *P* for the battery. *P* could file a *reply* to the defendant's answer. In this reply, the plaintiff may admit, deny, or defend against the factual allegations contained in the answer.

A defendant who has been properly served with a summons and complaint defaults by failing to file a written answer in a timely manner. The court can then award judgment to the plaintiff for the award of money or other legal relief that was demanded in the complaint. In a default judgment, the defendant loses the right to object to anything that is incorrect in the complaint.

In the following case, the plaintiff was awarded a default judgment against the defendant. The defendant in *Dorsey v. Gregg* sought to vacate the default judgment because the trial court lacked jurisdiction over his person due to the inadequacy of the service.

Dorsey v. Gregg
784 P.2nd 154
Court of Appeals of Oregon
January 13, 1988

Richardson, Presiding Judge

Defendant seeks vacation of a default judgment, contending that the trial court lacked jurisdiction over him. We reverse.

Plaintiff's complaint was filed on December 5, 1985. Defendant, a student of the University of Oregon, lived in Eugene. He was a member of a fraternity but did not reside at the fraternity house. Personal service was attempted at the fraternity house from December 29 through February 19, 1986. No attempt was made to serve defendant at his residence even though his address was available from the university. On March 4, the trial court granted plaintiff's motion for alternative service. The motion was supported by the affidavit of Hoyt, which states:

> "I am an employee of Barristers' Aid, Inc., a civil process service corporation engaged in delivery of documents among attorneys and in serving civil process in the Lane County area. From on or about

December 29, 1985, [to] February 18, 1986, I have made numerous attempts to serve the Defendant, Joseph Gregg, at his fraternity. On various occasions I would call in advance and find that his vehicle was there, or that they expected him to eat dinner at the fraternity that evening. However, upon arriving there in the evening for purposes of serving Mr. Gregg, various individuals there would profess that he no longer resides at the fraternity, nor that he ever eats at the facility nor visits.

> "It has become apparent to me and other individuals in our office who have attempted service upon Mr. Gregg, that the members of the fraternity are 'covering' for him, and are not cooperating in allowing us to learn his whereabouts at any given time.

> "It is my opinion that, if service was made upon a member of the fraternity, due notice of that would be conveyed to Mr. Gregg from earlier statements of members that he remained in the Eugene-Springfield area, and attended fraternity house functions."

The trial court authorized service "upon a person in charge or other resident member present" at the fraternity and by certified mail, return receipt requested, addressed to defendant's father at a Beaverton address.

Defendant first contends that the trial court erred in ordering the alternative service, because Hoyt's supporting affidavit was insufficient under ORCP 7D(6)(a). That rule provides, in relevant part:

> "On motion upon *a showing by affidavit that service cannot be made by any method otherwise specified in these rules* or other rule or statute, the court, at its discretion, may order service by any method or combination of methods which under the circumstances is most reasonably calculated to apprise the defendant of the existence and pendency of the action, including but not limited to: publication of summons; mailing without publication to a specified post office address of defendant, return receipt requested, deliver to addressee only; or posting at specified locations." (Emphasis supplied.)

In *Dhulst and Dhulst*, 657 P.2d 231 (1983), the trial court ordered alternative service on the husband by publication and registered mail. The supporting affidavit addressed the reasons why the husband could not be personally served, but it was silent about the other types of service authorized by ORCP 7D(3)(a)(i). We held that, because the affidavit was insufficient to support alternative service under ORCP 7D(6)(a), "the trial court [had] erred in ordering [the alternative service]. Because [the alternative service] was improper, the trial court lacked personal jurisdiction over [the] husband." The default decree against the husband was therefore set aside.

Here, Hoyt's affidavit makes no mention of any attempt to locate and serve defendant at his "dwelling house or usual place of abode." ORCP 7D(3)(a)(i). It only details attempts to serve defendant at the fraternity house where he had not resided for at least a year before the filing of this action. . . . The affidavit fails to comply with the requirement of ORCP 7D(6)(a), and the trial court erred in ordering alternative service. The alternative service was therefore invalid, and the trial court lacked personal jurisdiction over defendant.

Reversed and remanded with instruction to vacate the judgment.

Case Questions

1. Why is the law so concerned with proper service of process?
2. Why did the Oregon Court of Appeals rule that the alternative service of process was invalid?
3. If the circumstances allow a court in the plaintiff's state to assert jurisdiction over an out-of-state defendant, what is the proper method of serving process?

Pretrial Motions

The second stage of the litigation process involves decisions about whether motions are filed prior to trial. Sometimes a defendant's lawyer, after receiving the plaintiff's complaint, will decide to challenge the complaint due to legal insufficiency. For example, the complaint might be poorly drafted and so vague that the defendant can't understand what is being alleged, whether the venue might be wrong, or whether there might be some problem with service. In such situations the attorney may choose to file a *motion to dismiss* (sometimes also called a *demurrer* or a "12(b) motion" in some jurisdictions), prior to preparing the answer. In *Du Pont v. Christopher*, we saw a *motion to dismiss* made by the defendant on the grounds that the plaintiff's complaint failed to state a claim upon which relief could be granted under Texas law. The motion to dismiss is decided by a judge, and jurisdictions differ about permitting the attorneys to argue orally the merits of the motion. If the judge grants the motion, the plaintiff will often try to cure any defect by amending the complaint. If the judge denies the motion, the defendant will normally submit an answer. Alleged defects in the answer and reply can also be raised through a motion to dismiss or an equivalent motion used for that purpose in a particular jurisdiction.

The *motion for summary judgment* can be made by either or both parties. It is intended to dispose of controversies when no genuine issues of material fact exist, or where the facts necessary to prove the other party's case are not provable or are not true. The motion is supported with proof in the form of affidavits and depositions. This proof is used to illustrate that there is no need to conduct a trial because there is no factual dispute between the parties. The party opposing the motion will present affidavits and depositions to prove the existence of contested issues of fact. Such proof may also be used to show the impossibility of certain facts alleged by an opposing party. For example, a complaint might accuse a defendant of various counts of negligence in operating a car. However, if the defendant was in jail that day, it could be proved that he or she could not possibly have committed the acts in question. The defendant in this instance would move for a summary judgment. Motions for summary judgment are disfavored by courts because, when granted, a party is denied a trial.

Summary judgment should not be granted if there is a genuine issue of material fact because it would deprive the parties of their right to a trial. In the following opinion, we see a case in which an appellate court ruled that the trial court improperly granted the motion for summary judgment.

Meyers v. Ramada Hotel and Operating Co., Inc.
833 F.2d 1521
U.S. Court of Appeals, Eleventh Circuit
December 15, 1987

Per Curiam

The district court ruled that the appellant failed to show a genuine issue of material fact on the issue of whether her attack at a hotel was foreseeable. Finding that a genuine issue of material fact was shown, we reverse for a jury trial.

Cathleen Meyers, the appellant, and a friend rented a room at the Ramada Inn at Ft. Walton Beach, Florida. Meyers had previously stayed at the hotel on several occasions and considered it the place to go because of its popularity with young people. The room was on the fifth floor of a six story building, known as the tower, which consisted of 194 rooms.

On August 20, 1983, at about 2:00 A.M., Meyers took an elevator from the ground floor up to the fifth floor to the hotel room to retrieve her driver's license, while her friend waited in an automobile in the parking garage. In the elevator on the way up, a man asked Meyers if he could use her restroom; she said, "No!" When the elevator doors opened on the fifth floor, Meyers went toward her room. The man initially walked in the opposite direction, but then turned around and just as Meyers was opening her door, forced his way into the room. He raped her. After a time, the man left the room. Meyers went to another room where the occupants called security and accompanied Meyers back to her room.

The Ramada Inn had employed security guards for about ten years, mainly to control noise and keep trespassers from using the pool. During the time period of this incident (2 A.M.), three security guards were on duty. One guard, Lieutenant Ashmore, patrolled the main hotel building (tower) and the pool; the other two guards patrolled the remainder of the premises. Ashmore routinely checked the building every thirty to forty minutes by riding the elevator to the top of the building, walking down each hall, then taking the stairs down to the next floor until the entire building had been patrolled. When Ashmore received notice of this attack, he had just completed a check of the building and had walked around to the back of the building to the boardwalk area. Upon receiving a call from the motel's front desk reporting this incident, Ashmore went to the fifth floor, spoke with Meyers about the attack, and stationed the other two guards around the outside of the

tower to watch for anyone who might run out. Although Ashmore again went through the building checking each floor and its stairwells, the assailant was never located or identified.

Tolbert Enterprises owned the hotel and operated it as a Ramada Inn under a franchise agreement with Ramada Inns, Inc.

Meyers sued Ramada Hotel Operating Company, Inc., et al. (Ramada), for negligence for allowing her to be criminally attacked as she entered her room. The district court granted Ramada's motion for summary judgment on the grounds that it owed no duty to Meyers because the attack was unforeseeable.

In order to establish foreseeability and duty, Meyers produced evidence that the hotel night clerk had been robbed in 1969; within the seventeen months preceding the attack on Meyers, law enforcement officers charged a person on the premises with resisting arrest with force; and law enforcement officers also arrested five men for the attempted sale of 2.2 pounds of cocaine for $58,000 (one of the men carried a loaded .38 caliber revolver). Records from law enforcement agencies showed several arrests in the hotel for trespassing and drug possession. Two miles from the Ramada Inn, at another hotel, and within seventeen months of this incident, a man had kidnapped a woman at knife point and committed sexual battery against her. Records also showed numerous arrests for drug and alcohol related offenses (none involving physical violence) at a park immediately adjacent to the Ramada Inn. Arrests had also been made for lewd conduct by an adult towards a minor female child and between males, all within a couple of miles of the Ramada Inn.

The hotel contained three bars with live bands, including one bar and discotheque on the top floor, one floor above Meyers's room. The bars attracted outsiders to the hotel, and the top-floor bar required use of the elevators or stair wells, each of which allowed access to all floors of the hotel. Fred Tolbert, the franchise owner, had received reports that some of the cocktail waitresses believed a man was hanging around the bar at closing time and that the waitresses were afraid.

Discussion

Meyers contends the district court erred in granting summary judgment because the evidence, particularly of crimes in and around the Ramada Inn, raised a genuine issue of material fact as to the foreseeability of the attack. This contention constitutes the sole issue in this case.

On this appeal of the district court's entry of summary judgment, we take the facts in the light most favorable to the non-moving party, Meyers. . . .

Meyers was a business invitee to whom Ramada owed a duty to guard against dangers of which it should have been aware. . . . This duty extends to reasonably foreseeable criminal acts against the business invitee. . . . Evidence relevant to foreseeability includes the general likelihood of harm to the invitee, criminal activity in the vicinity, and security measures taken by the owner of the premises. . . .

The evidence Meyers presented of criminal conduct in the vicinity of the Ramada Inn is, to an extent, relevant to the determination of foreseeability . . . (statistical evidence of high crime rate within one mile of post office where a rape took place held admissible). Other evidence relative to foreseeability include compliance of the premises with industry standards, the presence of suspicious individuals around the premises, and the peculiar security problems associated with the hotel, such as the number of bars and the fact that stairwells were apparently not restricted to emergency use only. . . . The landowner's provision of security services may itself serve as evidence of foreseeability of harm. . . .

The evidence introduced by Meyers raises a genuine issue of material fact as to the foreseeability of a criminal attack on business invitees of the Ramada Inn. The question of foreseeability is a prerequisite to the determination of duty and causation.

Ramada relies upon *Doe v. United States*, 718 F.2d 1039 (1983). In *Doe*, this court held that where in a two year period preceding the rape of a woman in a post office lobby "the only incidents reported at the post office with criminal overtones did not involve actual or threatened injury to invitees." . . . The plaintiff in *Doe* introduced evidence of serious crimes committed within a mile of the post office over a two year period. That evidence included 19 rapes, 8 homicides, 176 robberies, and about 560 assaults. The evidence of incidents with criminal overtones occurring on the postal premises included three incidents of juveniles breaking into postal boxes to steal mail, breaking of windows with rocks and BB guns, a juvenile's attempt to steal a bicycle, and the attempted theft of a battery from a postal vehicle.

In *Doe*, this court also considered it significant that in the nineteen-year history of the post office, never had a crime been perpetrated against a person, such as an assault, committed on the postal premises or in its immediate vicinity. . . .

In this case, within the seventeen months preceding the assault on Meyers, one man was charged with resisting arrest with force. In another arrest for the attempted sale of 2.2 pounds of cocaine for $58,000, one of the men arrested had a loaded .38 caliber revolver on his person. The evidence also showed that the hotel's night manager had been robbed in 1969. This evidence of criminal incidents involving threats to the safety of persons on the premises is stronger than in *Doe*. . . . Also factors which distinguish this case from *Doe* include the fact that sexual and other personal attacks are more likely in a hotel room than in a post office lobby, that alcoholic beverages were served over an extended period of time, and large numbers of people, strangers to each other and to management, were encouraged to congregate in the early morning hours. Therefore, we reverse the district court and remand the case for trial. We note, however, that the district court properly marshalled controlling precedent, but concluded that no duty was shown, as a matter of law. We disagree; on the facts of this case, Meyers created a material fact issue on foreseeability, which determines duty. A jury trial is necessary.

Reversed and remanded.

Case Questions

1. What purpose is the summary judgment motion expected to serve?
2. According to the court, when is a summary judgment motion properly granted?
3. Why was summary judgment improper under the facts of this case?

Discovery and Pretrial Conference

To prevent surprise at the trial, each party is provided with tools of *discovery* before trial in order to identify the relevant facts concerning the case. Discovery is based on the premise that prior to a civil action each party is entitled to information in the possession of others. This includes the identity and location of persons; the existence and location of documents; known facts; and opinions of experts.

There is a distinction between the right to obtain discovery and the right to use in court the statements or information that are the product of discovery. The restrictions that are made concerning the admissibility in court of the product of discovery will be discussed later in the chapter. The requirements for discovery are as follows: the information sought cannot be privileged, it must be relevant, it cannot be the "work product" of an attorney, and good cause must be shown to require a physical or mental examination.

The tools of discovery are depositions, written interrogatories to parties, production of documents, physical and mental examinations, and requests for admissions. In an *oral deposition* a witness is examined under oath outside court before an official of the court. The party wishing the deposition must give notice to the opposing party to the suit so that that person may be present to cross-examine the witness. The questioning of the witness at an oral deposition is thus much the same as it would be in a courtroom. Alternatively, an attorney may prepare a list of questions to be answered by a witness in writing. This report is called a *written deposition. Written interrogatories to the parties* are similar to written depositions in that both are lists of questions that must be answered in writing and under oath. Interrogatories are simpler, however, and can be submitted only to the parties to the case, not to witnesses. One party to the suit may compel the *production of documents* or things in the possession of the other party for inspection. When the mental or physical condition of a party is at issue, a court may order the party to submit to an examination by a physician. Finally, one party may send to the other party a *request for admissions or denials* to certain specified facts or to the genuineness of certain documents. If no reply is made to such a request, the matters are considered admitted for the purpose of the suit.

All discovery except for physical examinations can be done without a court order. In case of noncompliance, the discovering party may request a court order to compel compliance. Failure to comply with the court order results in sanctions provided in the discovery statute.

Discovery may begin after the filing of the complaint, but usually commences after the answer is filed and continues until trial. In addition, a pretrial conference may be called by the judge in order to discuss the issues of the case. A judge and the two opposing lawyers discuss and evaluate the controversy informally. They consider the simplification and sharpening of the issues, admissions and disclosure of facts, possible amendments to the pleadings, the limitation of the number of witnesses, the possibility of reaching an out-of-court settlement, and any other matters that may aid in the speedy and just disposition of the action.

The following case, *Downey v. Dixon*, addresses the failure of a defendant to answer interrogatories or to attend his deposition.

Downey v. Dixon
362 S.E.2d 317
Court of Appeals of South Carolina
November 9, 1987

Sanders, Chief Judge

The single issue presented by this appeal is whether the Circuit Court erred in ruling on the motion of appellant Verneva W. Downey that sanctions be imposed against respondent William M. Dixon for his failure to answer interrogatories or attend his deposition as required by the South Carolina Rules of Civil Procedure,

effective July 1, 1985. We reverse and remand the case for a new trial.

Ms. Downey sued Mr. Dixon and respondent Lonnie M. Starnes, alleging that Mr. Dixon had caused a motor vehicle accident in which she had been seriously injured. (Her claim against Mr. Starnes was based on the allegation that Mr. Dixon had been acting as his "employee, agent and/or servant.") Ms. Downey prayed for a judgment in the amount of $250,000 actual damages, as well as punitive damages in an unspecified amount.

Mr. Dixon and Mr. Starnes answered, alleging that the accident had been caused by the acts of Ms. Downey, asserting the defense of contributory negligence based on her acts, but not alleging any specific acts of Ms. Downey as having caused the accident or having contributed to its cause.

Ms. Downey served interrogatories on counsel for Mr. Dixon and Mr. Starnes asking that they state what acts of hers they were relying on to support the allegations contained in their answer. Mr. Dixon and Mr. Starnes did not respond to her interrogatories.

Ms. Downey then served notice on counsel for Mr. Dixon and Mr. Starnes of the taking of the deposition of Mr. Dixon. Mr. Dixon failed to attend the deposition, and Ms. Downey moved for an order striking his answer or, in the alternative, for an order refusing to allow him to testify at the trial of the case.

Counsel for Mr. Dixon and Mr. Starnes did not offer any excuse for their failure to respond to the interrogatories of Ms. Downey or for the failure of Mr. Dixon to attend the deposition except to say that he had "never been able to get with the respondent, William M. Dixon."

The Circuit Court did not impose either of the sanctions sought by Ms. Downey but instead fined Mr. Dixon $50. The case thereafter proceeded to trial, which resulted in a jury verdict being returned for Mr. Dixon and Mr. Starnes and judgment being entered based on the verdict.

Ms. Downey contends that the Circuit Court erred in not imposing the sanctions which she sought.

The imposition of sanctions is generally entrusted to the sound discretion of the Circuit Court. . . . Nevertheless, whatever sanction is imposed should serve to protect the rights of discovery provided by the Rules. . . .

The sanction imposed in the instant case did no more than minimally enrich the county tax coffers. The rights of discovery provided by the Rules were not protected in any way. Neither was Ms. Downey accorded the rights of discovery provided by the Rules, nor was the sanction imposed against Mr. Dixon a meaningful deterrent to those who might fail to submit to discovery in the future. (It is perfectly obvious that few, if any, litigants would willingly submit to the discovery provided by the Rules if the alternative were simply paying $50.)

We reject the argument that the judgment should not be reversed because it does not appear Ms. Downey was surprised by the fact Mr. Dixon testified at trial. Of course, Ms. Downey could have anticipated that Mr. Dixon was going to testify at trial. (This was undoubtedly why she propounded the interrogatories and sought to take his deposition.) However, there is no indication she knew what he was going to say when he testified. An abiding maxim of the successful trial lawyer, like the motto of the Boy Scouts, is "Be Prepared." . . . The rights of discovery provided by the Rules give the trial lawyer the means to be prepared for trial. Where these rights are not accorded, prejudice must be presumed and, unless the party who has failed to submit to discovery can show a lack of prejudice, reversal is required.

For these reasons, the judgment for Mr. Dixon and Mr. Starnes is reversed and the case is remanded for a new trial.

Reversed and remanded.

Case
Questions

1. What should a party do when an opponent fails to follow the rules of civil procedure with respect to discovery?
2. The media often depicts courtroom lawyers using surprise witnesses and evidence. In reality, thorough discovery usually destroys any possibility of surprise. Is this good or bad? Exhaustive discovery is very expensive. One party will frequently be able to afford more discovery than his or her opponent. Does that change your mind about the value of discovery?
3. What sanction was imposed by the trial court in this case?
4. Why did the court of appeals reverse?

CIVIL TRIALS

A trial is a legal procedure that is available to parties who have been otherwise unwilling or unable to resolve their differences through negotiations, settlement offers, and even mediation attempts. Trials involve the staging of a confrontation between the plaintiff and the defendant as contradicting witnesses and arguments collide in a courtroom in accordance with procedural and evidentiary rules. The trial process may, as a result of appeals and / or new trials, take many years, but it will ultimately result in a dismissal of the complaint or in a judgment.

In some cases, parties with a right to present their evidence to a jury prefer instead to try their case to a judge. This is called a bench trial. Bench trials can be scheduled more quickly, and they take less time to conclude because the procedures associated with the jury are eliminated. Bench trials also cost the parties less money than would the same case tried to a jury.

The right to a federal jury trial is provided by the Seventh Amendment to the U.S. Constitution to parties involved in a common law civil action. The right to a jury trial in the state judicial system is determined by state law, and may not exist for some types of actions such as equitable claims and small claims cases.

The judge is responsible for making sure that (1) the jury is properly selected in a jury trial; (2) due process requirements for a fair trial are satisfied; (3) proper rulings are made with respect to the admissibility of evidence; (4) the rules of procedure are followed by the parties; and (5) the judgment is awarded in accordance with law.

Selection of the Jury

The procedure discussed here applies only to jury trials (see Figure 3–4). Jurors are selected at random from a fair cross section of the community, usually from a list of registered voters, and summoned to the courthouse for jury duty. After a case has been assigned to a courtroom, the judge calls in a group of prospective jurors, who take their seats in the jury box. A *voir dire* (literally, "to speak the truth") examination is conducted to determine each juror's qualifications for duty under the appropriate statute, and any grounds for a challenge for cause, or information on which to base a peremptory challenge. A challenge for cause may be based on prejudice or bias. A juror's relationship, business involvement, or other close connection with one of the parties or attorneys may also be considered cause for replacing a juror. Attorneys for both sides may make as many challenges for cause as they wish, and it is within the judge's sound discretion to replace a juror for cause. In

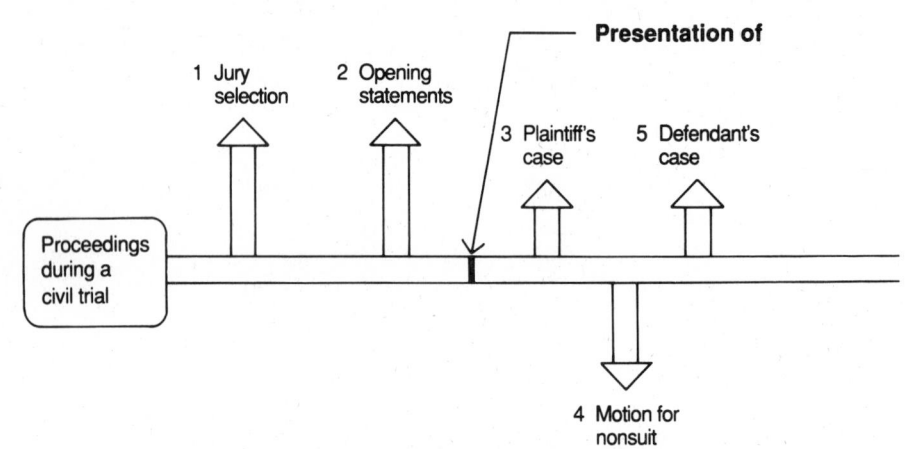

1   Prospective jurors are questioned by attorneys and judge. A prospective juror is dismissed if an attorney successfully makes a challenge for cause or exercises a peremptory challenge.

2   Attorneys explain facts of case in general to judge and jury. Plaintiff's attorney's opening argument usually precedes defendant's.

3   Plaintiff's attorney presents witnesses, documents, and other evidence to substantiate allegations in complaint.

4   Defendant's attorney moves for an involuntary dismissal (motion for nonsuit) if it is felt that plaintiff failed to prove allegations. If judge agrees, motion is granted and plaintiff loses. If judge disagrees, motion is denied and trial continues.

5   Defendant's attorney presents witnesses, documents, and other evidence to rebut plaintiff's case.

6   Plaintiff's attorney presents evidence to rebut evidence brought out during presentation of defendant's case.

7   Defendant's attorney presents evidence to rebut any new matters brought out during plaintiff's rebuttal.

8   After both parties rest their case, either or both parties may move for a directed verdict. If judge feels that reasonable persons could not disagree that the moving party should win, judge grants motion. If motion is granted, moving party wins and trial is over. If motion is denied, trial continues.

FIGURE 3–4   Proceedings During a Civil Trial

addition to the challenges for cause, each party is given a limited number of peremptory challenges that may be exercised at will, where no reason for the challenge need be given.

Opening Statements and Examination of Witnesses

After a jury has been selected and sworn, the trial begins with an opening statement by the plaintiff's attorney. The opening statement explains the case in general, including the attorney's legal theories and what he or she intends

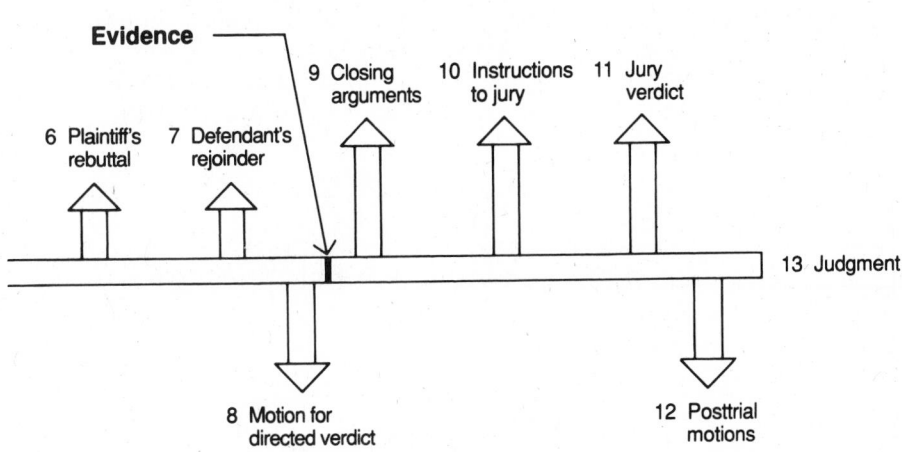

9   Both attorneys sum up evidence for jury. They suggest how the jury should resolve specific disputed items. Plaintiff's attorney argues first, but may reserve time to rebut defendant's attorney's closing argument.

10 Judge explains substantive law to jury, and tells how it should be applied to facts. Both attorneys may suggest specific instructions to judge, but final instructions are left to judge's discretion.

11 After deliberation, jury returns either a general or special verdict or both. A general verdict is simply a declaration of winner and amount of recovery. A special verdict is answer to specific factual questions requested by judge.

12 After jury returns its verdict, either or both parties may move to have verdict set aside by filing a motion for a new trial or a motion for a judgment notwithstanding verdict of jury or relief from judgment. If the judge grants the motion, judge renders judgment in accordance with jury verdict.

13 By rendering judgment, judge declares who prevailed at trial and amount of recovery. If losing party does not voluntarily pay prescribed amount, winning party can force payment by obtaining an order of execution.

to prove. The defendant's lawyer may also present an opening statement introducing legal theories of the case and the facts the defense intends to prove.

In order for the plaintiff to win the case, the disputed allegations of the complaint must be proved by presenting evidence. Witnesses and exhibits are produced by both parties to the suit. If witnesses do not voluntarily appear to testify, they may be ordered by means of a *subpoena* (see Figure 3-5) to appear in court. A *subpoena duces tecum* issued by the court commands a witness to produce a document that is in his or her possession. If witnesses refuse to appear, to testify, or to produce required documents, or if they perform any act that disrupts the judicial proceedings, they may be punished for contempt of court.

Judges have much discretion with respect to the order of production of evidence. Normally, a plaintiff's attorney presents the plaintiff's case first. The attorney presents witnesses, documents, and other evidence, and rests the case when he or she decides that enough evidence has been produced to substan-

---

**UNITED STATES DISTRICT COURT
FOR THE ..... DISTRICT OF .....
.... DIVISION**

....
     Plaintiff,

        v.   **Civil Action No. ....**

....
     Defendant.

To: .... *[name and address of witness]*
    You are commanded to appear in the United States District Court for the .... District of ...., at .... in the City of ....,
State of ..... on the ..... day of ....., 19..... at ..... o'clock
.....M. to testify on behalf of ..... in the above pending action.
Dated ....., 19......
[Name and address of attorney]

                                              [Signature and title of clerk]

[Seal]

FIGURE 3–5 Subpoena—For Attendance of Witness [FRCP 45(a)]

tiate the allegations. Defendant's lawyer then presents the defendant's case in the same manner. When the defense is finished, the plaintiff's attorney may introduce additional witnesses and exhibits in rebuttal of the defense's case. If new matters are brought out by the rebuttal, the defendant may introduce evidence in rejoinder, limited to answering the new matters.

Both attorneys introduce their own witnesses and question them. This is called *direct examination.* The opposing attorney *cross-examines* the witnesses after the direct examination is completed. Attorneys may conduct *redirect examinations* of their own witnesses following the cross-examinations. Attorneys generally may not ask their own witnesses leading questions (except for preliminary questions to introduce a witness or questions to a hostile witness). A leading question is one that suggests the answer to the witness. For instance, if an attorney asks, "You've never seen this gun before, have you?" the witness is almost told to answer no. Leading questions are permissible on cross-examination because they promote the purpose of cross-examination: testing the credibility of witnesses. Upon cross-examination, for example, an attorney could ask a witness the following question: "Isn't it true, Mr. Smith, that you are a firearms expert?" The following case illustrates what can happen when the use of leading questions gets out of hand.

Alexander v. Chapman
711 S.W.2d 765
Supreme Court of Arkansas
June 16, 1986

Hickman, Justice

This is a medical malpractice case. John Alexander was 53 years old when he died on October 1, 1979, from a heart attack. Dr. Jerry Chapman and the clinic with which he was then associated, Crestview Family Clinic, treated Alexander several times for symptoms that could have been heart related. On July 14 and 24, 1979, he was hospitalized and treated by Chapman and his associates. He was seen thereafter on August 1, 16 and 19, and September 26. Dr. Chapman was telephoned September 28 because Alexander was weak and had chest pains. He died three days later. Alexander's widow and son sued, claiming that the appellees failed to diagnose and treat Alexander's illness and, thus, failed to prevent his death. The trial lasted

seven days, and the jury returned a verdict for the appellees.

The question on appeal is whether the trial court abused its discretion in failing to deal with the trial tactics of the appellees' attorney. Among the allegations are that counsel repeatedly and continually led witnesses and violated a pretrial order that prohibited the mentioning of certain matters. . . .

This case, . . . presents the unique situation where counsel was repeatedly admonished and the court repeatedly sustained objections to the leading questions, was even presented with a motion to strike the testimony, yet counsel's conduct was not stopped. The trial court decided that striking the testimony was too severe a sanction, yet was unable to stop the leading. Counsel also violated pretrial orders. After the trial, a motion for a new trial was filed, citing violations of the pretrial order, comments by appellees' counsel, and counsel's conduct in examination of the witnesses. Now we must decide whether the trial court's decisions at the trial and in denying the new trial were an abuse of discretion. In doing so we must necessarily decide whether conduct of counsel, ordinarily a matter which lies within the court's sound discretion, can go so far that some sanction must be taken. There are limits to everything and when counsel cannot or will not abide by the rules of evidence and of the trial court, and the trial court cannot stop the violations, we have to. The contention on appeal is that although no one instance of counsel's conduct would be cause for reversal, all of the violations combined to deny the appellants a fair trial. We have to agree and the only acceptable course is to reverse the trial court.

Before trial, appellants moved that the appellees be prohibited from mentioning certain matters during voir dire, arguments or any part of the trial. In a pretrial order the trial court granted the motion in the following instances relevant to this appeal: (1) there was to be no suggestion that a verdict for the appellants would be tantamount to a "conviction" of the appellees; (2) there was to be no suggestion of any "credibility enhancing" items such as religious activities; and (3) no suggestion that a verdict for the appellants would have a damaging effect on medical services.

The order was clearly violated in closing argument when appellees' counsel said, "you see, even $1.00 *convicts* my client of malpractice, doesn't it?" (Italics supplied.) Upon objection, the trial court asked counsel to rephrase the statement.

During opening and closing arguments, appellees' counsel stated that next to God, his family and his patients, the lawsuit was the most important thing in the doctor's life. No objection was made beyond the motion in limine and in the motion for a new trial. This was not a flagrant violation of the pretrial order.

In closing appellees' counsel also said, "A judge once said, we've got to be careful in these cases not to make doctors guarantors of good results or a cure." Appellants' counsel objected that what another judge said is not the law. The trial court essentially overruled the objection and then appellees' counsel said, "And we must, therefore, be careful lest we find very few, if any, who would accept the responsibility of being a doctor, you see." The appellants contended in their motion for a new trial and argue on appeal that this violated the pretrial order prohibiting any suggestion that a verdict for the appellants would have a damaging effect on medical services. Again the statement is not a clear and undisputable violation of the pretrial order, but it does touch on a subject that was ruled prohibited. When these violations are considered along with the continued leading of witnesses during the trial, the errors become more significant.

Leading questions were continually used in the examination of appellees' experts. During direct examination of the appellees' expert witnesses, there were 28 objections to leading questions. Once the court admonished counsel without being prompted by an objection. Fourteen objections were sustained. Three times there was no ruling. Twice the question was withdrawn by appellees' counsel. The appellants' objections were overruled nine times.

Before appellants' counsel asked for the sanction that appellees' counsel be prohibited from continuing to inquire after leading, the court admonished appellees' counsel five times, four times of which were of the court's own volition. For instance, once the court said, "[appellees' counsel], it is [leading], sir. I would appreciate it if you would ask questions rather than making statements and asking is that true." Another time the court said, "Yes, and I think that was pretty blatant leading that last time, [appellees' counsel]. Please sir, let's please confine your questions to this gentleman to be questions." Finally appellants' counsel requested that if appellees' counsel continued to lead, that he be prohibited from inquiring further into the subject. The court responded to the request by admonishing appellees' counsel. . . .

After that there were five more objections to leading questions until appellants' counsel asked that the responses be stricken. The trial court refused but admonished appellees' counsel to "please confine your questions to questions." There were seven objections to leading questions after that. At one time appellants' counsel renewed their motion and the following colloquy occurred:

> [Appellants' counsel]: Secondly, I despair of what to do with respect to leading questions. If I continue to object, I'm going to not only alienate the jury, but it's my impression that the defense counsel is trying to beat the Court down on leading questions. And not only do I run the risk of alienating the jury, but if the Judge overrules me when they're leading, then that makes my other objections look bad. *So I move to strike the testimony of all of the defense witnesses* on the grounds that their testimony has been warped completely out of kilter by suggestive, leading questions. (Italics supplied.)

> The Court: *Well, of course I'm not going to do that.* I don't think it's that serious. I think there is a constant problem with leading questions, [appellees' counsel]. And I don't know what to do about it either. I certainly don't want to strike your witnesses, but there are a lot of

comments. . . . I'm getting sensitive to it now because I expect [appellants' counsel] to jump up every time there's a leading question and say, oop, here we go again. And I'm getting sensitive to it and I'm getting overreactive to it in the sense I'm waiting for it each time because I'm waiting for [appellants' counsel] to jump up. . . .

> [Appellants' counsel]: That's the very importance of it right there, Your Honor. I know the jury is getting irritated with me for making what is a proper objection.

> The Court: I don't think they are frankly. . . . I don't think any great damage is being done to be honest with you, [appellant's counsel]. I don't think this is turning the case around and it's a situation in which the questions would not have been answered the same way if they'd been asked properly. It's not a situation where these witnesses are being led down the path. I know it's annoying to you and [appellants' counsel] and I know it's bothering the devil out of you and I'm getting to be bothered now because I'm sensitive to you all jumping up, and properly so, and I'm getting sensitive to the whole thing myself. I don't think it's determining the outcome of this case by any way, mean, shape or form. It's just an annoying thing that's bothering you and it's beginning to bother me.

> So I'm not going to strike the testimony. I'm going to caution [appellees' counsel] once again to watch that and avoid any sidebar comments and to quit leading his witnesses. And we'll note your objection for the record.

The motion was renewed one other time, and the trial court instructed the witness not to answer the leading question. Appellants' counsel asked that a continued objection be noted, which it was.

Improper leading includes improper suggestion and improper ratification. . . .

Suggestion occurs when a question indicates the answer desired and ratification occurs when a question is suggestive, contains factual detail which could and should originate with the witness and the witness adopts the detail and the form in which it is expressed. . . .

Following are examples where counsel improperly suggested the desired answers from his expert witnesses:

> Q. All right. In your experience, does the computer overread or underread EKGs?
> A. The computer tended to overread EKGs.
> Q. And that's the way it should be don't you agree?
> A. I would prefer it that way.
> Q. So that all doubt is resolved on behalf of the patient to try to give patient help if he needs it?
> A. Every benefit of the doubt.
>   . . .

Some of the sanctions for leading questions . . . are: striking the improper question and permitting a proper one, admonishment at the bench or before the jury, striking the improper question and refusing to allow counsel to reask, contempt, and mistrial. . . .

Here counsel repeatedly ignored the trial court's warnings concerning leading questions. The court conceded it could not or would not take action beyond admonishment. Only once did it instruct the witness not to respond. If counsel will not comply with the trial court's requests, then some sanction, with teeth, must be used against him. We are certain the leading would have stopped had the trial court granted appellants' motion to preclude further inquiry. The appellants were entitled to have the leading stopped.

Trial courts by necessity are granted great power and discretion to preserve the order of their courtrooms. They have at their command numerous sanctions to see that rules are followed. Because the sanctions exist they are usually not necessary, but sometimes they must be used. Some sanctions should have been used in this case. The appellants were entitled to have the case presented to the jury in the words of witnesses, not counsel. In finding an abuse of discretion in not employing those sanctions, we emphasize that our decision is necessarily limited to the facts this record presents.

The appellees urge us to find no error because the appellants failed to move for a mistrial, to object during closing argument, or to demonstrate prejudice. In this case, as counsel for the appellants pointed out, it would have been to the appellees' benefit to have a mistrial declared since it is they who are seeking to preserve the status quo. Repeated objections were made and timely motions made giving the trial judge an opportunity to stop the tactics. The trial judge essentially conceded he could not stop counsel. The impression left with the jury could not help but prejudice the appellants' case.

While the responsibility for the conduct of the trial falls on the trial court, experienced counsel should not go too far in testing the patience of the system. Besides continued leading and violating the pretrial order, appellees' counsel asked an expert whether he believed Dr. Chapman to be negligent. Counsel knew full well that the answer was an impermissible opinion on the ultimate issue and withdrew the question upon objection. There should be no attempt to elicit such evidence on retrial. . . .

Reversed and remanded.

Case   1. Why are leading questions objectionable on direct examination?
Questions   2. What steps can a judge take to control an attorney who repeatedly refuses
                   to comply with the rules of civil procedure, which prohibit the use of
                   leading questions on direct examination?

RULES OF EVIDENCE

Certain rules governing the admissibility of evidence must be followed in examining witnesses and in producing documents. Federal trials are conducted according to the Federal Rules of Evidence and each of the fifty states has its own rules of evidence which regulate state trials. These rules apply both to jury and nonjury trials, although they are applied less strictly in the latter. Many are actually policy statements and trial judges have considerable discretion in their application. The court's decisions on admissibility are generally upheld on appeal unless there has been a clear abuse of discretion. The judge may instruct the jury to disregard evidence that has been improperly presented before it, but it is difficult to evaluate the effect that this excluded evidence has on the jurors' decision-making process. Once jurors have heard testimony, they may not be able simply to forget it. Thus, if the judge concludes that significant prejudice has occurred and that instructing the jury is an inadequate remedy, a mistrial will be declared.

Relevance and Materiality

Evidence, whether it be testimony, demonstrative evidence (such as photographs, charts, and graphs), or physical evidence is admissible only if it is relevant. That is, it must logically tend to prove or disprove some issue of consequence that is in dispute at the trial. Irrelevant evidence confuses the jury, wastes court time, and is often prejudicial. Relevancy is sometimes confused with materiality which has to do with the probative value of evidence. Probative evidence tends to prove something of importance to the case. Relevant evidence that has little probative value is immaterial. Evidence that is either immaterial or irrelevant should be excluded.

Competency

Evidence must be competent (legally adequate) to be admissible. Competency is a broad concept. To be competent, witnesses have to take an oath or affirm that they will testify truthfully. A nonexpert witness is limited to testimony about what he or she has heard or seen firsthand; the opinions and conclusions of such a witness are "incompetent."

As fact-finder, the jury must draw its own conclusions from the evidence. However, where special expertise is required to evaluate a fact situation, a jury may not be competent to form an opinion. In that case, a person with special training, knowledge, or expertise may be called to testify as an expert witness. Doctors, for example, are frequently called as expert witnesses in personal injury cases. The qualifications and expertise of such witnesses must be established to the court's satisfaction before an expert witness's opinion is admissible.

The Best Evidence Rule

The best evidence rule requires that, unless they are unobtainable, original documents rather than copies be introduced into evidence. Even when the original writing is unobtainable, secondary evidence of the contents is admissible only if the unavailability is not the fault of the party seeking to introduce the evidence. In this situation, the best available alternative proof must be presented. For example, a carbon copy of a writing is preferred over oral testimony as to its contents.

The Hearsay Rule

The hearsay evidence rule excludes evidence proceeding not from the personal knowledge of the witness but from the repetition of what was said or written outside court by another person, and which is offered for the purpose of establishing the truth of what was said or written. The person who made the out-of-court statement may have been lying, joking, or speaking carelessly. The witness reporting the statement in court may have a poor memory. This exclusionary rule guarantees the opportunity to cross-examine the person who made the out-of-court statement and prevents highly unreliable evidence from being considered.

The hearsay rule contains many exceptions. The *res gestae* (spontaneous exclamations) exception permits courts to admit in court spontaneous declarations uttered simultaneously with the occurrence of an act. The basis for the admission is the belief that a statement made instinctively at the time of an event, without the opportunity for formulation of a statement favorable to one's own cause, is likely to be truthful.

Privileges

Evidence may also be excluded because a privilege exists. Witnesses cannot be forced to give testimony that might expose them to a criminal prosecution. Confidential communications between husband and wife are often privileged in judicial proceedings, as well as information given by a patient to a doctor for the purpose of treatment. All jurisdictions recognize the attorney-client privilege in order to encourage informed legal services. The privilege applies to all communications from a client to a lawyer in the course of professional consultation. In addition, the attorney's work product, including all matters considered to be part of the preparation of a case, is privileged. These privileges may be waived by the witness for whose protection they are intended.

The following case involves the physician-patient privilege. This privilege permits a patient to prevent his or her physician from disclosing confidential medical information the patient has revealed to the doctor while receiving professional services.

Cline v. William H. Friedman & Assoc.
862 S.W.2d 754 (Mo.App.E.D. 1994)
Missouri Court of Appeals, Eastern District
Aug. 30, 1994

Carl R. Gaertner, Judge

Defendant, William H. Friedman & Associates, Inc., d/b/a Park Central Institute, appeals from a judgment in favor of plaintiff, Peggy Cline, in the amount of $536,750 in a medical malpractice action. We reverse and remand. . . .

On February 1, 1988, plaintiff consulted with William H. Friedman at the Park Central Institute about her desire for corrective eyelid surgery. Plaintiff was concerned that her eyelids were sagging, making her look old and tired. After conducting a physical examination, Dr. Friedman recommended that plaintiff undergo bilateral blepharoplasty, a surgical procedure in which excess skin, tissue and fat is removed from both the upper and lower eyelids. Plaintiff consented, and Dr. Friedman scheduled the surgery for February 15, 1988. Dr. Friedman claims he also explained to the plaintiff that blepharoplasty involves the risks of blindness, infections, allergic reactions to anesthesia, and temporary lagophthalmus . . . [a condition in which the eye cannot be completely closed]. . . . Plaintiff, however, testified that the doctor did not inform her of the risk of lagophthalmus.

Dr. Friedman performed the blepharoplasty without any complications. After a brief stay in the recovery room, plaintiff returned home. Later that evening, plaintiff discovered that she could not completely close her eyelids and that her upper lids would spasm when she attempted to close them, forcing her to tape shut the lids in order to sleep.

Plaintiff returned the next day for a follow-up visit. She claims she told Dr. Friedman she could not completely close her eyelids. Dr. Friedman, however, testified that plaintiff never expressed a complaint and that he noted no problems after examining her. Dr. Friedman again examined plaintiff on February 22, 1988, and noted no problems. Plaintiff, however, testified that she complained she still could not close her eyes and her vision was blurred. On February 29, 1988, an ophthalmologist examined plaintiff and prescribed a lubricating ointment to treat her symptoms. On March 7, 1988, plaintiff returned to see Dr. Friedman and expressed a number of complaints, including an inability to close her eyelids, blurred vision, eye dryness, near blindness and depression. The doctor examined her, noted that her eyes were inflamed and diagnosed plaintiff as having bilateral lagophthalmus. Concerned that she might have corneal exposure, he referred plaintiff to an ophthalmologist, Dr. Frank O'Donnell.

Plaintiff went to O'Donnell's office, and Dr. Byron Santos examined her. He recommended that she continue patching her eyes at night and that she apply lubricating drops and a prescribed lubricating ointment on her eyes. Plaintiff went to another ophthalmologist, Dr. Michael Beatty, on March 10, 1988. Beatty examined plaintiff, concurred with Santos' recommendations and also advised that she massage coca butter on her upper eyelids.

Dr. Friedman examined plaintiff for the last time on March 14, 1988. During this visit, plaintiff complained of retro-orbital pain, blurred vision, and scratchiness in her eyes. When plaintiff attempted to close her eyes, the upper lids would flutter. The doctor noted that her eyelids appeared to be healing properly, her eyes were tearing properly, she could achieve almost total eyelid closure, and he could achieve total closure by exerting gentle pressure on her brow.

From March 15, 1988, until January 1993, plaintiff was examined by a number of eye specialists. These specialists did not change her treatment, and they all observed varying degrees of lagophthalmus and corneal exposure in the lower portion of plaintiff's corneas.

After a five-day jury trial, the jury returned a verdict in favor of plaintiff for $674,750. The trial court remitted $138,000 as being in excess of the maximum recovery allowable for non-economic damages in a medical malpractice case, § 538.215 RSMo. 1986, and denied defendant's motions for new trial, for judgment notwithstanding the verdict and for further remittitur. This appeal followed. . . .

III. *Plaintiff's Mental Condition*

In its third point, defendant argues the trial court erroneously prohibited it from gathering and introducing evidence concerning plaintiff's mental condition. Defendant's point centers on the court's refusal to permit it to depose plaintiff's psychiatrist, Dr. Robert Brookes, and the court's exclusion of Brookes' testimony and records.

The admission or exclusion of evidence is within the sound discretion of the trial court. We will not disturb the court's determination on this issue absent substantial or glaring injustice. . . .

Plaintiff initially placed her mental and emotional condition in issue by seeking damages for "mental anguish." During discovery, plaintiff revealed to defendant that Brookes had treated her, released Brookes' medical records concerning plaintiff to defendant, and permitted defendant to depose Brookes.

Defendant later learned that plaintiff sought additional treatment from Brookes for depression and insomnia. Plaintiff released to defendant Brookes' most recent medical records, prompting defendant to subpoena Brookes for a discovery deposition. On the day of the scheduled deposition, however, plaintiff invoked her patient-physician privilege and filed a motion for a protective order to quash the deposition.

The trial court granted plaintiff's motion but ordered her to strike "mental anguish" from her damages allegations. Plaintiff complied with the order and later filed a motion in limine to prevent defendant from referring to her mental condition. The trial court ruled that defendant could introduce evidence concerning any medications plaintiff used but precluded any mention of her mental condition.

Defendant argues that plaintiff waived her patient-physician privilege by placing her mental condition at issue and divulging the privileged communications. Defendant planned to use this evidence to corroborate its own testimony that plaintiff's injuries were caused by hysterical blepharospasm, a condition associated with depression and psychiatric illness.

Section 491.060(5) RSMo Supp. 1993 prevents a physician from disclosing by testimony in court or formal discovery confidential medical information acquired while attending a patient in a professional manner. The physician-patient privilege includes medical records, . . . and it applies to psychiatrists. . . . The policy supporting the statute is "to protect the patient by allowing him to make full disclosure without fear that the information will be used against him." . . .

The physician-patient privilege belongs to the patient, and only he can waive it. . . . The privilege may be waived in numerous ways. Once a party places the matter of his physical or mental condition in issue under the pleadings, the party waives the privilege with respect to any information bearing on the issue. . . . Furthermore, a party can impliedly waive the privilege through an act showing a clear, unequivocal purpose to divulge the confidential information. . . .

It is beyond question that plaintiff initially waived her physician-patient privilege by placing her mental condition in issue in an attempt to recover for "mental anguish." Consistent with this position, plaintiff disclosed the confidential information by permitting defendant to review Brookes' records and depose him. The only issue that remains is whether plaintiff can revoke her waiver of the privilege.

The Missouri Supreme Court has squarely addressed this issue, declaring that: "the medical privilege only covers matters that are confidential. Once there is a disclosure of the information in any form, it is no longer confidential and therefore no longer privileged." . . . Plaintiff clearly waived the privilege and invited defendant to act upon that waiver prior to her revocation of the waiver. The trial court, therefore, erred in prohibiting defendant from deposing Brookes and from entering his records and testimony into evidence.

Additional points asserted by defendant on appeal need not be addressed. For the reasons set forth, the judgment of the trial court is reversed, and the cause is remanded for a new trial.

Grimm, P.J., and Ahrens, J., concur.

Case Questions

1. According to the appeals court, when did the plaintiff waive the physician-patient privilege in this case?
2. The appeals court ruled that the trial court committed reversible error. What was the nature of the error?
3. What legal principle controls this case?

Trial Motions

If, after the plaintiff's attorney presents plaintiff's case, the defendant's attorney believes that the plaintiff was unable to substantiate the essential allegations adequately, the defendant may make a *motion for nonsuit*. The judge grants the motion only if a reasonable person could not find in favor of the plaintiff after considering the evidence most favorable to the plaintiff. If the motion is granted, the case is over and the plaintiff loses.

If the motion for a nonsuit is denied or not made at all, the defendant's lawyer then presents the defendant's case and tries to disprove the plaintiff's evidence or substantiate the defendant's arguments. Witnesses and exhibits are presented, following the same procedure as the plaintiff's—direct examination followed by cross-examination. After the defendant rests his or her case, the plaintiff then may produce evidence to rebut the defendant's evidence.

At the end of the presentation of evidence—but before the issues are submitted to the jury—either or both parties may make a motion for a directed verdict. The motion is granted for the party making the motion if the judge decides that the case is perfectly clear and that reasonable people could not disagree on the result. If the motion is granted, the moving party wins the dispute without the jury deciding the case. If no motion for a directed verdict is made, or if made and denied, the case is submitted to the jury.

Jury Verdict and Posttrial Motions

Both attorneys have an opportunity to make oral arguments to the jury summarizing their cases. The judge then instructs the members of the jury as to how they should proceed. Although jury deliberations are secret, certain restrictions must be observed to avoid possible grounds for setting aside the verdict. These include prohibitions on juror misconduct, such as drunkenness; the use of unauthorized evidence, such as secretly visiting the scene of an accident; or disregarding the judge's instructions, such as discussing the merits of the case over lunch with a friend.

After the verdict has been rendered, a party not satisfied with it may move for judgment notwithstanding the verdict, a new trial, or relief from judgment. A motion for *judgment notwithstanding the verdict* (j.n.o.v.) is granted when the judge decides that reasonable people could not have reached the verdict that the jury has reached. A *new trial* before another jury may be granted by a judge for a variety of reasons, including excessive or grossly inadequate damages, newly discovered evidence, questionable jury verdict, errors in the production of evidence, or simply the interest of justice. A motion for *relief from judgment* is granted if the judge finds a clerical error in the judgment, newly discovered evidence, or fraud that induced the judgment.

The appellant in the following case made a motion for directed verdict at the close of all the evidence. She also made post-verdict motions for j.n.o.v. and a new trial. She appealed from the court's denial of all three motions.

Cody v. Atkins
658 P.2d 59
Supreme Court of Wyoming
February 4, 1983

Raper, Justice

This appeal arose from a negligence action brought by Lois M. Cody (appellant) against Alfred Atkins (appellee) for injuries she allegedly sustained in an automobile collision between her car and appellee's pickup. Appellant appeals from the judgment on a jury verdict entered by the district court in favor of appellee. . . .

At about 7:00 o'clock A.M. on the morning of November 13, 1980, appellant's car was struck from behind by a pickup driven by appellee. At the time of the accident appellant was stopped for a red light in the right-hand, west-bound lane of 16th Street at the intersection of 16th Street and Snyder Avenue in Cheyenne, Wyoming. The right front corner of appellee's vehicle struck the left rear corner of appellant's car. In the words of a police officer who investigated the accident, the lane of traffic in which the accident occurred was ice covered and "very slick." It was overcast and snowing lightly at the time the accident occurred but visibility was not impaired. Neither party complained of injuries when questioned by the investigating officer at the accident scene; however, later that day appellant complained of injuries and was taken to the emergency room at Memorial Hospital where she was examined and released. Appellant was subsequently hospitalized and treated for numerous physical complaints that she alleged resulted from the accident.

Appellant brought suit June 5, 1981, complaining that appellee's negligent operation of his vehicle had caused harm to her. On March 1, 1982, appellant filed an amended complaint against appellee. Appellee answered the complaints by admitting that his pickup collided with appellant's car but denying appellant's remaining allegations of negligence, etc.; there were no counterclaims made nor affirmative defenses asserted by appellee. The matter was tried before a six-person jury May 10 and 11, 1982, in the district court in Cheyenne. At the close of appel-

lee's case, appellant made a motion for directed verdict. . . . The district court denied the motion. The jury then, after receiving its instructions and deliberating on the matter, returned a verdict in favor of appellee. Following the trial, appellant made timely motions for a new trial . . . and for a judgment notwithstanding the verdict. . . . The district court denied both motions; this appeal followed.

I

The first issue appellant raises for our consideration is the propriety of the district court's denial of his motion for a directed verdict. . . . We . . . have held that since a directed verdict deprives the parties of a determination of the facts by a jury, such motion should be cautiously and sparingly granted. . . .

In the majority of our decisions in which directed verdicts are at issue, we have dealt with directed verdicts sought by the defendant; here we are faced with the opposite situation of a plaintiff seeking a directed verdict. In general, the standard in directing a verdict for a plaintiff is similar to the standard used to direct one against him. . . . It is proper to direct a verdict for the plaintiff in those rare cases where there are no genuine issues of fact to be submitted to a jury. . . . In a negligence action a verdict may be directed for the plaintiff when there is no evidence that would justify a jury verdict for the defendant. . . . A directed verdict for the plaintiff is proper when there is no dispute as to a material fact, and when reasonable jurors cannot draw any other inferences from the facts than that propounded by the plaintiff. . . . In a negligence action, then, we need only determine that there was sufficient evidence to permit a reasonable jury to find that the defendant acted without negligence to hold that appellant's motion was properly denied. We so hold.

In this case appellee presented evidence that the roadway he was traveling on was slippery due to snow and ice; that he had been attempting to slow down and to stop to avoid a collision for some 400 feet prior to impact; that he had slowed from 20 m.p.h. to 5 m.p.h. in the 400 feet prior to impact; that he had attempted to drive to the left and avoid the collision; that his ability to stop was further complicated because he was traveling downhill; and that he was in control of his vehicle at all times prior to the collision. Although we were unable to find where appellee had testified in so many words that he had not been negligent, the jury could have properly inferred as much from the evidence we have outlined. Although appellant contends otherwise, the concept of an automobile accident occurring without a finding of negligence is not novel in our jurisprudence. . . . The district court could not have, in the face of appellee's evidence showing an absence of negligence, directed a verdict for appellant. Therefore, we hold the district court properly denied appellant's motion for directed verdict.

II

Appellant next argues that the district court erred in denying her motion for a judgment notwithstanding the verdict (J.N.O.V.). . . . As previously noted, appellant had sought and had been denied a directed verdict at the close of the evidence; therefore, we reach this issue. Before deciding the issue, however, we first set out the standard of review we shall employ. . . .

J.N.O.V. can only be granted where there is an absence of any substantial evidence to support the verdict entered. . . . The test then for granting a J.N.O.V. is virtually the same as that employed in determining whether a motion for directed verdict should be granted or denied. . . .

The logic behind similar standards of review is that it allows the district court another opportunity to determine the legal question of sufficiency of the evidence raised by the motion after the jury has reached a verdict. . . . In close cases the J.N.O.V. procedure promotes judicial economy. When a J.N.O.V. is reversed, for example, an appellate court can remand for reinstatement of the original verdict, where a new trial is generally required when a directed verdict is reversed. . . .

In the case before us, we have, in ruling on the directed verdict question, already held that there was sufficient evidence presented to create a question of fact for the jury to determine on the issue of appellee's negligence. For those same reasons we must also hold that the district court correctly denied appellant's motion for a J.N.O.V.

III

We next reach appellant's final argument that the district court erred in denying her motion for a new trial. . . . Appellant's motion set forth the following grounds for obtaining a new trial:

> "1. That the Verdict is not Sustained by sufficient Evidence and is Contrary to Law.
> "2. That Errors of Law were Committed at the Trial."

Appellant then centers her argument around the first ground. The position appellant takes is that she was entitled to a new trial because the jury's verdict was not consistent with the evidence. We disagree. . . .

A court's exercise of the power to grant a new trial is not a derogation of the right of a jury trial but is one of that right's historic safeguards. . . . The power to grant a new trial gives the trial court the power to prevent a miscarriage of justice. . . . Trial courts should grant new trials whenever, in their judgment, the jury's verdict fails to administer substantial justice to the parties. . . .

> "The right of trial by jury includes the right to have the jury pass upon questions of fact by determining the credibility of witnesses and the weight of conflicting evidence. The findings of fact, however, are subject to review by the trial judge who, like the jury, has had the benefit of observing the demeanor and deportment of the witnesses. If he concludes that the evidence is insufficient to support the verdict, he should grant a new trial. . . ."

This court has acknowledged that when a court could have properly granted a J.N.O.V. for insufficient evidence, it was not error to grant a motion for a new trial. . . . That does not mean, however, that the same standards apply for granting a new trial and a J.N.O.V.; the standard must be more lenient for exercising the power to grant new trials to preserve that power's historic role as a safety valve in our system of justice. . . .

> "When the evidence is wholly insufficient to support a verdict, it is the duty of the trial court to direct a verdict or enter a judgment n.o.v., and the court has no discretion in that respect. But, the granting of a new trial involves an element of discretion which goes further than the mere sufficiency of the evidence. It embraces all the reasons which inhere in the integrity of the jury system itself. . . ."

It is well settled in Wyoming that trial courts are vested with broad discretion when ruling on a motion for new trial, and that on review we will not overturn the trial court's decision except for an abuse of that discretion. . . .

In this case, appellant argues there was not sufficient evidence before the jury to entitle them to find in favor of appellee. As we pointed out in our discussion of appellant's first issue, appellee presented sufficient evidence to permit the jury to reach the issue of negligence. Also, as we said earlier, the mere fact that the collision occurred does not in itself indicate negligence. Therefore, after hearing the testimony of the witnesses and observing their demeanor, the district court exercised its discretion and denied appellant's motion for a new trial. The district court thereby indicated its belief that under the circumstances of the case no substantial injustice would occur in upholding the jury's verdict. Appellant has presented no convincing argument that would persuade us that the district court abused its discretion. Therefore, we hold that the district court did not err when it denied appellant's motion for a new trial.

Affirmed.

Case Questions

1. Does granting a new trial because the jury awarded excessive damages infringe the plaintiff's constitutional right to a jury trial?
2. Does a reduction of the amount of damages by the court as a condition for denying a new trial invade the province of the jury?

3. When is it proper for a judge to grant a directed verdict motion?
4. What is the purpose of the motion for judgment notwithstanding the verdict (j.n.o.v.)?

Judgment and Execution

A judgment is awarded by the judge after the jury reaches its verdict. Judgment follows an unsuccessful motion to set aside the verdict, and states the court's final decision in the case. Either party may appeal the court's judgment to an appellate court if dissatisfied. If the judgment awards money damages to the plaintiff and the defendant (now called a judgment debtor) does not voluntarily pay the prescribed amount, on application of the winning party, the court clerk issues an *execution* addressed to the sheriff. The sheriff seizes the defendant's property and sells it to pay for the judgment. The statute authorizing judicial sale includes safeguards to prevent abuse of defendant's rights. Alternatively, the plaintiff (who is now called a judgment creditor) may have a *lien* placed against the judgment debtor's property. A lien is a legal claim against property and is created when the clerk of courts dockets the judgment. The judgment debtor's property cannot be transferred until the lien is satisfied. This often means that when the property is sold, part of the proceeds are paid to the judgment creditor to satisfy the lien.

The following case involves the purchase of property at a sheriff's sale. The purchaser appealed the trial court's decision to set aside the sale.

Newhouse v. Farmers National Bank
532 N.E.2d 26
Court of Appeals of Indiana, First District
January 5, 1989

Ratliff, Chief Judge

Statement of the Case

James and Carol Newhouse appeal from the Hancock Superior Court's grant of summary judgment in favor of the Farmers National Bank of Shelbyville. We reverse.

Facts

The facts as viewed most favorably to James and Carol Newhouse, the non-movants, reveal that the Farmers National Bank of Shelbyville (hereinafter Bank)

obtained a foreclosure judgment against Gary and Carole Miller on certain real estate located in Rush County. Pursuant to the foreclosure decree, the Bank's attorney, John Murphy, prepared a notice of foreclosure sale of the property. The notice provided that the sale would be held at the Rush County Sheriff's office on March 5, 1987, between the hours of 10:00 a.m. and 1:00 p.m. Murphy hand-delivered the notice of sale to the Rushville Republican, a local newspaper, which published the notice on January 23, 20, and February 6 of 1987.

On March 5, 1987, the Newhouses were present at the Rush County Sheriff's office between the hours published for the sale, and placed a bid of Three Thousand Dollars ($3,000). At 1:00 p.m. the sheriff accepted the Newhouses' bid as the highest and only bid, sold the property to the Newhouses, and ended the sale. At approximately 1:35 p.m. Murphy arrived at the sheriff's office and attempted to tender the Bank's bid of Thirty-four Thousand Two Hundred Dollars ($34,200) on the property. The sheriff refused the bid and stated that the property had been sold to the Newhouses. Murphy then attempted to persuade the Newhouses to sell their interest in the property. The Newhouses refused. Murphy promised that the Bank would challenge the sale.

On March 6, 1987, a Sheriff's Deed was executed and delivered to the Newhouses. The deed was recorded at 3:00 p.m. the same day. After the Newhouses received title to the property, they received a copy of the Bank's Verified Motion to Set Aside the Sheriff's Sale which was filed on March 6, 1987, and received by the sheriff on March 9, 1987. The motion cited mistake on the part of Murphy, who believed that the time of the sale was between 10:00 a.m. and 3:00 p.m. as was the practice in Shelby County. The motion also stated that the price was inadequate and requested that the trial court set aside the sheriff's sale.

In April of 1987, the Bank filed a Motion for Summary Judgment accompanied by an affidavit. The affidavit indicated that Murphy had been at a cook-out with friends in Rush County prior to 1:00 p.m. on the date of the sale. The affidavit also indicated that Murphy believed that the sale would be held between the hours of 10:00 a.m. and 4:00 p.m. The Newhouses opposed the Motion for Summary Judgment and requested a change of venue which was granted on July 10, 1987. Venue was changed to the Superior Court of Hancock County on July 23, 1987. On December 11, 1987, the Hancock Superior Court granted the Bank's Motion for Summary Judgment. The Newhouses appeal from this judgment.

Issue

While the Newhouses presented two (2) issues in their brief, we rephrase them into the following issue:

Whether the trial court improperly vacated the sheriff's sales by granting the Bank's Motion for Summary Judgment?

Discussion and Decision

In Indiana a trial court may set aside a sheriff's sale in the exercise of its sound discretion. *Smith v. Federal Land Bank of Louisville* (1985), Ind.App., 472 N.E.2d 1298, 1302. As stated in *Smith*,

> "It appears that generally the law allows the trial court to take a common sense approach in deciding whether or not to vacate a bid. The court takes into consideration all circumstances, such as the inadequacy of the price, the effect of procedural irregularities, inequitable conduct, evidence of mistake or misapprehension, and problems with title."
> . . .

As indicated in *Smith*, inadequacy of price is generally only a factor to be considered by the trial court. However, mere inadequacy of price alone may be sufficient to justify, but not compel, setting aside a sale if the disparity between the value of the property sold and the price paid is so great as to "shock the sense of justice and right."

Generally a trial court's decision to vacate a sheriff's sale will be reached after an evidentiary hearing and after an evaluation of the weight and credibility of the evidence. When a decision is reached under these circumstances we will not reverse absent an abuse of discretion. . . .

The trial court improperly granted summary judgment in the present case for two reasons. First, the trial court mistakenly found that no genuine issue of material fact exists. The trial court properly found that no genuine issue exists as to the fact that the scheduled time of the sheriff's sale differed from the scheduled times in Murphy's home county, or as to the fact that Murphy did not tender a timely bid. However, other evidence and the inferences to be drawn therefrom does conflict as to the reason Murphy was late. The evidence indicates that Murphy gave several reasons for being late, including: (1) the difference in the scheduled sale time and the practice in his home county, (2) his personal problems involving a sick relative, and (3) his attendance at a cookout. This evidence could raise an inference of mistake. However, the evidence indicates also that Murphy not only prepared and delivered the notice of the sheriff's sale but also that the notice was published. Thus, the evidence also could raise an inference of negligence. While a common sense approach to the question of whether to set aside a sheriff's sale might provide relief for mistake, the equities of a case involving negligence should not provide relief. . . . Therefore, since a genuine issue exists as to the inferences to be drawn from the evidence, summary judgment was inappropriate.

In the present case, the evidence of the inadequate price and mistake would permit, not compel, the vacation of the sheriff's sale. Therefore, the trial court improperly granted summary judgment.

Reversed.

Case Questions

1. Why did the court of appeals reverse the trial court?
2. When can a court set aside an execution sale of real estate on the grounds of inadequacy of price?
3. What will happen in this case after this decision?

Chapter Questions

1. Define the following terms:

alternative dispute resolution	directed verdict
alternative service	discovery
answer	execution
bench trial	general verdict
complaint	hearsay
contingent fee	judgment
counterclaim	judgment notwithstanding the
constructive service	verdict (j.n.o.v.)
default	lien
deposition	motion for directed verdict
direct examination	motion for summary judgment

motion for new trial
motion for nonsuit
motion for relief from judgment
motion to dismiss
oral deposition
personal service
petition
pleading
pretrial conference
privilege
process

production of documents
reply
request for admissions
request for waiver of service
settlement conference
substituted service
voir dire
writ of summons
written deposition
written interrogatories

2. Robert Wilkinson was a resident of California and an officer of the now defunct St. Paul Transportation Company. In June, Wilkinson was served in California with a criminal summons from a Minnesota court for a misdemeanor allegedly committed when Wilkinson was in Minnesota. The arraignment for the misdemeanor charge was scheduled for September 25. Wilkinson flew to Minnesota to attend the arraignment. As he ascended the courthouse steps, a U.S. marshal approached him and handed him a summons to appear in a civil action brought against him by the Interstate Commerce Commission (ICC) for activities involving the St. Paul Transportation Company. Consider policy questions arising from Wilkinson's appearance in response to the criminal summons. Was the service of summons and complaint on Wilkinson sufficient to give the Minnesota court jurisdiction in the civil action?
Interstate Commerce Commission v. St. Paul Transportation Co., 39 F.R.D. 309 (D.C. Minn. 1966)

3. A car driven by James Murphy struck a boy, Thomas Ball, and injured him. Immediately after the accident, according to Thomas Ball's mother, Murphy "told me that he was sorry, that he hoped my son wasn't hurt. He had to call on a customer and was in a bit of a hurry to get home." At trial, Murphy denied telling Ball that he was involved in his employment at the time of the accident. It was shown, however, that part of his normal duties for his employer, Murphy Auto Parts Company, included making calls on customers in his car. Can Ball have the statement admitted in court as a spontaneous exclamation?
Murphy Auto Parts Co. v. Ball, 249 F.2d 508 (1957)

4. On June 30, 1961, Trans World Airlines, Inc. (TWA), filed a complaint against Toolco in federal court alleging that Toolco was guilty of various antitrust violations arising from the period when Toolco controlled TWA's management decisions. Jurisdiction over Toolco was properly obtained, and plaintiff commenced discovery proceedings. Howard Hughes had at all times been the sole owner of Toolco and the guiding light in all transactions between Toolco and TWA. On February 7, 1963, the court ordered a deposition to be taken from Howard Hughes on February 11, 1963, under the Federal Rules of Civil Procedure. Toolco and Hughes advised the court

that they had made a decision not to attend the deposition. Hughes did not attend the deposition, and a default judgment for $145 million was rendered against Hughes and Toolco, including treble damages under the Antitrust Act. Would such a drastic remedy be proper?

Trans World Airlines v. Hughes Tool Co., 308 F. Supp. 679 (S.D.N.Y. 1969), aff'd, 449 F.2d 51 (2d Cir. 1971)

5. James Duke filed a suit against Pacific Telephone & Telegraph Company (PT&T) and two of its employees for invasion of privacy through unauthorized wiretapping. Duke claimed that defendant's employees installed an interception device on his telephone line without his knowledge or consent for the sole purpose of eavesdropping. Through the use of the bugging devices, defendants acquired information that they communicated to the police department, resulting in his arrest. Although the charges were dismissed, he was discharged from his job. As part of the plaintiff's discovery, oral depositions were taken of the employees. The defendants refused to answer (1) questions relating to the procedure used in making unauthorized tapes of phone conversations (training of personnel, equipment, authority among employees), (2) questions relating to the deponent's knowledge of the illegality of unauthorized monitoring, (3) questions relating to a possible working relationship between the police and PT&T, and (4) questions relating to the monitoring of telephone conversations of subscribers other than the plaintiff. The defendants claimed that these questions were irrelevant to the litigation and therefore not proper matters for discovery. Do you agree?

Pacific Telephone & Telegraph Co. v. Superior Court, 2 Cal.3d 161, 465 P.2d 854, 84 Cal. Rptr. 718 (1970)

6. A doctor testified in a personal injury case that the plaintiff had become 20% disabled as a result of a back injury. However, during jury deliberations, one of the jurors said that it had been his experience that employers are very reluctant to hire people with a history of back trouble, and that therefore the plaintiff might never get a job at all. Should a juror be permitted to make such statements to fellow jurors during their deliberations?

Texas Employers' Insurance Association v. Price, 336 S.W.2d 304 (Texas 1960)

7. W. R. Reeves filed suit under the Federal Employers Liability Act against his employer, Central of Georgia Railway Company, seeking damages he allegedly suffered when the train on which he was working derailed near Griffin, Georgia. The liability of the defendant railroad was established at trial, and the issue of damages remained to be fixed. Several physicians testified regarding the injuries received by Reeves. Reeves also testified. On the witness stand, he said that an examining physician had told him that he would be unable to work because of a weakness in his right arm, a dead place on his arm, stiffness in his neck, and nerve trouble in his back. Why did admission of this testimony into evidence constitute reversible error?

Central of Georgia Ry. Co. v. Reeves, 257 So.2d 839 (Ga. 1972)

8. On December 10, 1962, Rosch obtained a judgment against Kelly in the superior court of Orange County, California. The California Code permits execution of a judgment only within ten years after entry of a judgment. If this is not done, the judgment may be enforced only by leave of court, after notice to the judgment debtors, accompanied by an affidavit setting forth the reasons for the failure to proceed earlier. The plaintiff made no attempt to enforce the judgment in California before Kelly moved to Texas in 1970. On February 15, 1974, the plaintiff attempted to execute on the California judgment in Texas. Does the Texas court have to allow execution under the full-faith-and-credit clause?
   Rosch v. Kelly, 527 F.2d 871 (5th Cir. 1976)

9. Lemmie Branch sued Ben Bullock for negligence after a metal sign affixed to the front of Bullock's store broke loose and fell on Branch as he walked down the sidewalk. Evidence was introduced, and the lawyers went into their final argument. Before a jury, Branch's attorney argued, "What would I have to pay to inflict a half-inch cut into your skull, to render you unconscious, to put you home in bed for a week, to force you to use a cane or crutches for the balance of your life with your walk affected, with your speech affected, with your handwriting affected? What do you think it's worth? The older you grow, the more precious and sweeter life becomes. How much would you sell me a year of your life for?" Was this argument improper? Why? Is Bullock entitled to a new trial?
   Bullock v. Branch, 130 So.2d 74 (Fla. 1961)

10. Smith brought a suit against Bryant for trespassing on her property and for maliciously cutting down growing crops. Bryant's lawyer filed an answer to the complaint, but withdrew from the case on the day set for trial, because of nonpayment of his fee. The judge granted a continuance until the next morning. In the morning following the day her counsel resigned, Bryant defended her case without the assistance of a lawyer, and lost the dispute. Was Bryant's lawyer at liberty to abandon her case? Is Bryant entitled to a new trial?
    Smith v. Bryant, 264 N.C. 208, 141 S.E.2d 303 (1965)

11. William Cothey was driving west on Brookpark Road at a speed of 25 to 35 mph in a 35-mph zone. A truck driven by an employee of the Jones-Lemley Trucking Company started to turn left across the road into the driveway of the Clifton Concrete Company, and the right front of Cothey's car struck the right side of the Jones-Lemley truck. The point of impact was on Cothey's side of the road, 7 feet north of the double yellow line and 15 feet south of the north curb line and driveway entrance. Cothey is suing Jones-Lemley on a negligence theory for injuries sustained in the collision. Ohio law imposes a duty on a motorist to operate his vehicle as would a reasonably prudent person under the circumstances. At the close of plaintiff's evidence, as summarized above, should the court grant Jones-Lemley's motion for nonsuit on the ground that it was not negligent?
    Cothey v. Jones-Lemley Trucking Co., 176 Ohio St. 342 (1964)

Notes

1. M.L. Shaw, *Courts Point Justice in a New Direction,* The National Law Journal C1 (April 11, 1994).

2. J.D. Rosenberg, *Court Studies Confirm That Mandatory Mediation Works,* The National Law Journal C7 (April 11, 1994); D.R. Hensler, *Does ADR Really Save Money? The Jury's Still Out,* The National Law Journal C2–5 (April 11, 1994); W.R. Wilson, *Only Voluntary ADR Programs Ensure Constitutional Rights,* The National Law Journal C6 (April 11, 1994).

3. Shaw, p. C1.

4. T.F.F. Plucknett, *A Concise History of the Common Law,* 5th Ed. (Boston: Little, Brown and Co., 1956), p. 408.

5. Ibid., pp. 408–409.

6. Ibid., p. 400.

7. The recent amendments to the Federal Rules of Civil Procedure have significantly altered the service requirement in federal court. Rule 4(d) requires plaintiffs to send a copy of the complaint and a request for waiver of service to the defendant. A defendant who signs the waiver of service is allowed 60 days from the date of the notice to file an answer. If the defendant fails to sign the waiver and has no good cause for such refusal, the defendant can be required to pay for the service costs and the plaintiff's costs in going to court to obtain enforcement.

IV

Institutional Sources of American Law

It is important to understand that the rules constituting American law derive from several authoritative sources. The most important of these are the federal and state constitutions; legislation produced at the federal, state, and local levels of government; decisions of federal and state courts; and the regulations and adjudicatory rulings of federal, state, and local administrative agencies. In this chapter we shall preview each of these major sources of law and focus on the legislative and judicial branches of government.

COMMON LAW AND CIVIL LAW LEGAL SYSTEMS

From your reading of Chapter 1, you have already seen how the English common law system developed over many centuries.[1] You know that as judges decided cases, rules slowly evolved and became recognized as judicial precedents, which began to be written down and followed. These practices made it possible for cases raising a particular issue to be decided in essentially the same way throughout England. With its emphasis on judge-made law, this approach differs markedly from the legal systems found in France, Germany, and Italy. Those countries follow a different approach, often referred to as the civil law system.[2]

Civil law systems are based upon detailed legislative codes rather than judicial precedents. Such a code is a comprehensive, authoritative collection of rules covering all the principal subjects of law. Civil law codes are often developed by academicians and then enacted by legislative bodies. They are based on philosophy, theory, and abstract principles. Civil law systems usually reject the use of precedent, dispense with juries in civil cases, and avoid complex rules of evidence. In civil law countries, judges are expected to base their decisions on the appropriate provisions of the relevant code, and they do not treat the decisions of other judges as authoritative sources.

The civil law tradition traces its roots to historically famous codes of law such as those of ancient Rome (*Corpus Juris Civilis*) and the *Code Napoleon*. At present, Europe, Central and South America, the Province of Quebec, the former French colonies of Africa, and the State of Louisiana have adopted the civil law system.

Although the common law system has had much more impact on American law, the civil law system has been of increasing influence. For example, early 19th century American legislatures wanted to replace the complex and ponderous system of common law pleading, and reformers campaigned in favor of replacing the traditional approach with legislated codes. Today, codes of civil procedure regulate litigation in all federal and state courts. Many states have taken a similar approach with respect to probate law, criminal law, and commercial law. State legislatures in forty-nine states, for example, have adopted the Uniform Commercial Code to replace the common law with respect to the sale of goods.

CONSTITUTIONS

Each of the fifty states and the federal government are sovereignties. Each is a complete government with a legislative, an executive, and a judicial branch, and each has a written constitution. The written constitution is the fundamental source of the rule of law within each jurisdiction. It creates a framework for the exercise of governmental power and allocates responsibility among the branches of government. It authorizes and restrains the exercise of governmental authority, protects fundamental rights, and provides an orderly vehicle for legal change. Laws and governmental actions that violate its terms are unconstitutional.

The Federal Constitution grants certain powers to the federal government in Article I, such as the rights to regulate interstate commerce, operate post offices, declare war, and coin money. The states, however, retain many important powers and can implement significant change by enacting statutes and by amending their state constitutions. One strength of our federal form of government is that states can innovate and experiment without having to obtain permission from other states. Nebraska's constitution, for example, provides for a unicameral legislature (the only state to do so), and Louisiana is unique in that it does not confer common law powers on its judges. States constitutions can even provide greater protections for individual liberties than are required under the United States Constitution.

LEGISLATION

To maintain social harmony, society needs uniformly operating rules of conduct. The responsibility for determining the rules lies primarily with legislative bodies. The legislative branch creates law by enacting statutes. An examination of legislation reveals the problems and moods of the nation. Legislatures write history through the legislative process. There have been legislative reactions to almost all political, social, and business problems that have faced society. Laws have been passed in response to wars, depressions, civil rights problems, crime, and concern for cities and the environment. Checks and balances have been built into the system in order to prevent overreaction by the legislature and to promote wise and timely legislation.

The process of enacting statutes is lengthy and complex. At the federal level, it is a procedure that involves 535 persons in the House and Senate who represent the interests of their constituents, themselves, and the country. A proposed bill may encounter numerous obstacles. Mere approval by the legislative bodies does not ensure passage, for at both federal and state levels the executive branch has the power to veto a bill. Another check on legislation can come once a bill becomes law. At that point, the constitutionality of the legislative act may be challenged in court.

With the exception of bills for raising revenue, which must originate in the House (article I, section 7 of the Constitution), it makes no difference in which body a bill is introduced, because a statute must be approved by both houses of the legislature. However, the legislative process varies slightly between the Senate and House. If differences exist between the House and Senate versions of a bill, a joint conference committee meets to reconcile the conflicts and draft a compromise bill.

After a bill has been approved by both houses and certain formalities have been completed, it must be approved and signed by the president of the United States to become effective. If the president vetoes a bill—which rarely occurs—it does not become law unless the veto is overridden by a two-thirds vote of both houses.

Defeat of a bill is far more common than passage. More than 95 percent of all legislation introduced is defeated at some point. Still, much legislation *is* signed into law each year. Legislative death can result at any stage of the process, and from many sources. For legislation to be successful in passing, assignment to the proper committee is crucial. However, committees can be cruel. They may refuse to hold hearings. They may alter a bill completely. Or they may kill it outright. If a proposed statute survives the committee stage, the House Rules Committee or the Senate majority leaders determine the bill's destiny. Once a bill reaches the floor of the House or Senate, irrelevant proposals—known as *riders*—may be added to it. Or drastic amendments can so alter it that it is defeated. The possibilities are almost endless.

The need for certainty and uniformity in the laws among the states is reflected in federal legislation and uniform state laws. A great degree of uniformity has been accomplished among the states on a number of matters. An important example is the Uniform Commercial Code. With increased interstate business operations, business firms pressured for uniform laws dealing with commercial transactions among states. Judges, law professors, and leading members of the bar drafted the Uniform Commercial Code for adoption by the individual states. The UCC was first adopted by the Pennsylvania legislature in 1953, and has now been adopted at least partially in all fifty states. The UCC covers sales, commercial paper, bank collection processes, letters of credit, bulk transfers, warehouse receipts, bills of lading, other documents of title, investment securities, and secured transactions.

The Power to Legislate

Legislative bodies are organized in accordance with the provisions of the U.S. and state constitutions. They are governmental institutions with wide ranging responsibilities. The power to enact bills, to raise taxes, to conduct investigations and hold hearings, and to direct how public money will be appropriated gives legislatures a major voice in determining public policy. It is widely understood today, however, that legislative bodies actually share policy making duties with three other major governmental institutions—the president/governor, the administrative agencies, and the judiciary. These institutions, to differing degrees, have a tendency to compete with each other for political and public support. It is out of this process of institutional conflict and compromise that public policy emerges. Because the legislature is composed of persons directly elected by the people, it is a branch of government that in some instances is too responsive to public demands and insufficiently sensitive to the requirements of the constitution.

Federal Government

Legislative power is the power to establish rules of law for the government and regulation of the people. The people are the source of all legislative authority. The U.S. Constitution enumerates the powers granted by the people to the federal government. The U.S. government is based on delegated and enumerated powers. It cannot exercise any authority that is not granted to it by the Constitution, either expressly or by implication. Whenever the federal government's right to exercise authority is in question, recourse must be made to the Constitution to determine the government's authority, either in express words or by implication. The powers that the Constitution delegates to the U.S. government are comprehensive and complete. They are without limitations other than those in the Constitution.

Article I, section 8, of the Constitution is an important source of federal regulatory laws. The powers to tax and regulate interstate commerce are just two of these expressly delegated powers. The Constitution declares in article I, section 8, clause 18, that Congress is specifically empowered to enact all laws necessary and proper to carry into effect the powers expressly granted to it. This legislative authority has been broadly exercised. Yet any legislation enacted under this provision has had a basis in the enumerated powers of article I, section 8. State powers have been restricted by the necessary-and-proper clause, especially in the area of commerce.

Constitutional amendments are also sources of congressional legislative authority. For example, the Fourteenth, Nineteenth, and Twenty-third amendments are such sources. Congress may also delegate its legislative power. This power is the source of regulatory agencies' power to establish rules in selected fields.

State Government

The authority that resides in every sovereignty to pass laws for its internal regulation and government is called *police power*. It is the power inherent in the state to pass reasonable laws necessary to preserve the public health, safety, morals, and welfare. Police power of the states is not a grant derived from a written constitution; the federal Constitution assumes the preexistence of the police power. The Tenth Amendment to the Constitution reserves to the states any power not delegated to the federal government. Police power exists without any reservation in the Constitution, although both federal and state constitutions set limits in the exercise of this power.

The basis of the police power is the state's obligation to protect its citizens and provide for the safety and order of society. This yields a broad, comprehensive authority. The definition of crimes and the regulating of trades and professions are examples of this vast scope of power. A mandatory precondition to the exercise of police power is the existence of an ascertainable public need for a particular statute, and the statute must bear a real and substantial relation to the end that is sought. The possession and enjoyment of all rights may be limited under the police power, provided that it is reasonably exercised.

Limitations on the police power have never been drawn with exactness or determined by a general formula. The power may not be exercised for private purposes or for the exclusive benefit of a few. Its scope has been declared to be greater in emergency situations. Otherwise its exercise must be in the public interest, must be reasonable, and may not be repugnant to the rights implied or secured in the Constitution.

Powers delegated by the federal government and individual state constitutions also serve as a basis for state legislation. Any activity solely attributable to the sovereignty of the state may not be restrained by Congress.

Federal Supremacy

The U.S. Constitution divides powers between the federal government and the states. Certain powers are delegated to the federal government alone. Others are reserved to the states. Still others are exercised concurrently by both. The Tenth Amendment to the Constitution specifies that the "powers not delegated to the United States by the Constitution . . . are reserved to the states . . . or to the people." Unlike the federal power, which is granted, the state already has its power, unless expressly or implicitly denied by the state or federal constitutions. Each state has the power to govern its own affairs, except where the Constitution has withdrawn that power.

The powers of both the federal and state governments are to be exercised so as not to interfere with each other's exercise of power. Whenever there is a conflict, state laws must yield to federal acts to the extent of the conflict. This requirement is expressed by the supremacy clause in article VI of the Constitution.

Under the supremacy clause, Congress can enact legislation that may supersede state authority and pre-empt state regulations. The pre-emption doctrine is based on the supremacy clause. Hence state laws that frustrate or are contrary to congressional objectives in a specific area are invalid. In considering state law, one takes into account the nature of the subject matter, any vital national interests that may be involved, or perhaps the need for uniformity between state and federal laws, and the expressed or implied intent of Congress. It is necessary to determine whether Congress has sought to occupy a particular field to the exclusion of the states. All interests, both state and federal, must be examined.

Constitutionality of Statutes

The power to declare legislative acts unconstitutional is the province and the duty of the judiciary, even though there is no express constitutional grant of the power. It is generally presumed that all statutes are constitutional and that a statute will not be invalidated unless the party challenging it clearly shows that it is offensive to either a state or federal constitution. When a court encounters legislation that it believes to be unconstitutional, it first tries to interpret the statute in a narrow way with what is called a limiting construction. An act of the legislature is declared invalid only as a last resort if it is clearly incompatible with a constitutional provision.

The right and power of the courts to declare whether the legislature has exceeded the constitutional limitations is one of the highest functions of the judiciary. The Supreme Court declared in *Marbury v. Madison*, 5 U.S. (1 Cranch) 137 (1803) that the judicial branch has the power to declare void an act of the legislature that conflicts with the Constitution. The issue of the supremacy of the U.S. Constitution, and the right of individuals to claim protection thereunder whenever they were aggrieved by application of a contrary statute, was decided in *Marbury*. Chief Justice John Marshall wrote the opinion for the Court, stating in part:

> The question, whether an act, repugnant to the Constitution, can become the law of the land, is a question deeply interesting to the United States; but, happily, not of an intricacy proportioned to its interest. It seems only necessary to recognize certain principles, supposed to have been long and well established, to decide it.
>
> That the people have an original right to establish, for their future government, such principles as, in their opinion, shall most conduce to their own happiness, is the basis on which the whole American fabric has been erected. The

exercise of this original right is a very great exertion; nor can it, nor ought it, to be frequently repeated. The principles, therefore, so established, are deemed fundamental. And as the authority from which they proceed is supreme, and can seldom act, they are designated to be permanent.

. . . It is a proposition too plain to be contested, that the Constitution controls any legislative act repugnant to it; or that the legislature may alter the Constitution by an ordinary act.

Between these alternatives there is no middle ground. The Constitution is either a superior paramount law, unchangeable by ordinary means, or it is on a level with ordinary legislative acts, and, like other acts, is alterable when the legislature shall please to alter it.

If the former part of the alternative be true, then a legislative act, contrary to the Constitution, is not law; if the latter part be true, then written constitutions are absurd attempts, on the part of the people, to limit a power, in its own nature illimitable. . . .

It is, emphatically, the province and duty of the judicial department to say what the law is. Those who apply the rule to particular cases must of necessity expound and interpret that rule. If two laws conflict with each other, the courts must decide on the operation of each.

So, if a law be in opposition to the Constitution; if both the law and the Constitution apply to a particular case, so that the court must either decide that case, conformable to the law, disregarding the Constitution, or conformable to the Constitution, disregarding the law; the court must determine which of the conflicting rules governs the case. This is of the very essence of judicial duty.

If, then, the courts are to regard the Constitution—and the Constitution is superior to any ordinary act of the legislature—the Constitution, and not such ordinary act, must govern the case to which they both apply.

Ex Post Facto Laws

Article I, section 9, of the federal Constitution prohibits Congress from enacting *ex post facto* laws or bills of attainder. The state legislatures are likewise prohibited by article I, section 10.

An *ex post facto* law is a law that makes acts criminal that were not criminal at the time they were committed. Statutes that make a crime greater than when committed, impose greater punishment, or make proof of guilt easier have also been held to be unconstitutional *ex post facto* laws. Laws are unconstitutional when they alter the definition of a penal offense or its consequence to people who commit that offense, to their disadvantage. An accused is deprived of a substantial right provided by the law that was in force at the time when the offense was committed.

The *ex post facto* clause restricts legislative power and does not apply to the judicial function. The doctrine applies exclusively to criminal or penal statutes. The impact of *ex post facto* may not be avoided by disguising criminal punishment in a civil form. When a law imposes punishment for certain activity of the past and future, even though it is void for the punishment of past activity, it is valid insofar as the law acts prospectively. A law is not *ex post facto* if it "mitigates the rigor" of the law or simply reenacts the law in force when the crime was done.

To determine if a legislative act unconstitutionally punishes past activity, courts examine the intent of the legislature. The court, after examining the text of the law and its legislative history, makes a determination as to whether an act that imposes a present disqualification is, in fact, merely the imposition of a punishment for a past event. The principle governing the inquiry is whether the aim of the legislature was to punish an individual for past activity, or whether a restriction on a person is merely incident to a valid regulation of a present situation, such as the appropriate qualifications for a profession.

A constitutionally prohibited bill of attainder involves the singling out of an individual or group for punishment. Bills of attainder are acts of a legislature that apply either to named individuals or to easily ascertainable members of a group in such a way as to impose punishments on them without a trial. For example, an act of Congress that made it a crime for a member of the Communist party to serve as an officer of a labor union was held unconstitutional as a bill of attainder (*United States v. Brown*, 381 U.S. 437, 1965).

Statutory Construction

To declare what the law shall be is a legislative power; to declare what the law *is* is a judicial power. The courts are the appropriate body for construing acts of the legislature. Since courts decide only real controversies and not abstract or moot questions, a court does not construe statutory provisions unless required for the resolution of a case before it. A statute is open to construction only when the language used in the act is ambiguous and requires interpretation. Where the statutory language conveys a clear and definite meaning, there is no occasion to use rules of statutory interpretation.

Courts have developed rules of statutory construction to determine the meaning of legislative acts. For interpreting statutes, the legislative will is the all-important and controlling factor. In theory, the sole object of all rules for interpreting statutes is to discover the legislative intent; every other rule of construction is secondary.

It is the duty of the judiciary in construing criminal statutes to determine whether particular conduct falls within the intended prohibition of the statute. Criminal statutes are enforced by the court if worded so that they clearly convey the nature of the proscribed behavior. Legislation must be appropriately tailored to meet its objectives. Therefore it cannot be arbitrary, unreasonable, or capricious. A court holds a statute void for vagueness if it does not give a person of ordinary intelligence fair notice that some contemplated conduct is forbidden by the act. The enforcement of a vague statute would encourage arbitrary and erratic arrests and convictions.

Penal statutes impose punishment for offenses committed against the state. They include all statutes that command or prohibit certain acts and establish penalties for their violation. Penal statutes are enacted for the benefit of the public. They should receive a fair and reasonable construction. The words used should be given the meaning commonly attributed to them. Criminal statutes are to be strictly construed, and doubts are to be resolved in favor of the accused. *Strict construction* means that the statute should not be enlarged by implication beyond the fair meaning of the language used. However, the statute should not be construed so as to defeat the obvious intention of the legislature.

A literal interpretation of statutory language can lead to unreasonable, unjust, or even absurd consequences. In such a case, a court is justified in adopting a construction that sustains the validity of the legislative act, rather than one that defeats it.

Courts do not have legislative authority and should avoid "judicial legislation." To depart from the meaning expressed by the words of the statute so as to alter it is not construction—it is legislative alteration. A statute should not be construed more broadly or given greater effect than its terms require. Nothing should be read into a statute that was not intended by the legislature. Courts, however, don't always adhere to the principle.

Statutes are to be read in the light of conditions at the time of their enactment. A new meaning is sometimes given to the words of an old statute because of changed conditions. The scope of a statute may appear to include conduct that did not exist when the statute was enacted—for example, certain activity related to technological progress. Such a case does not preclude the application of the statute thereto.

ADMINISTRATIVE AGENCIES

As we will see in more detail in Chapter 12, legislative bodies often delegate some of their authority to governmental entities called agencies, boards, authorities, and commissions. Legislatures do this when they lack expertise in an area requiring constant oversight and specialized knowledge. Agencies such as the Environmental Protection Agency; the Securities and Exchange Commission; the boards that license doctors, attorneys, and barbers; and public housing authorities are other examples.

Legislative bodies often permit the agencies to exercise investigative and rule-making powers. Administrative rules, if promulgated according to law, have the same force as statutes. Some agencies also are delegated authority to conduct adjudicatory hearings before administrative law judges who will determine whether agency rules have been violated.

JUDICIAL DECISION MAKING

Our society is not able to legislate laws that address every societal problem. Sometimes a court encounters a case that presents a problem that has not been previously litigated within the jurisdiction. In such a case, the court will try to base its decision on a statute, ordinance, or administrative regulation. If none can be found, it will base its decision on general principles of the common law (principles that have been judicially recognized as precedent in previous cases). This judge-made law has an effect similar to a statute in such situations. Legislatures can modify or replace judge-made law either by passing legislation or through constitutional amendment.

In this portion of the chapter we will learn about the use of common law precedents and how judges determine which body of substantive law to apply when the facts of a case involve the laws of more than one state or country.

One of the most fundamental principles of the common law is the *doctrine of stare decisis*. A doctrine is a policy, in this case a judicial policy, that guides courts in making decisions. The doctrine normally requires lower-level courts to follow the legal precedents that have been established by higher-level courts. Following precedent helps to promote uniformity and predictability in judicial decision making. All judges within a jurisdiction are expected to apply a rule of law the same way until that rule is overturned by a higher court.

Following Precedent

Literally, *stare decisis* means that a court will "stand by its decisions" or those of a higher court. This doctrine originated in England and was used in the colonies as the basis of their judicial decisions.

A decision on an issue of law by a court is followed in that jurisdiction by the same court or by a lower court in a future case presenting the same—or substantially the same—issue of law. A court is not bound by decisions of courts of other states, although such decisions may be considered in the decision-making process. A decision of the U.S. Supreme Court on a federal question is absolutely binding on state courts as well as on lower federal courts. Similarly, a decision of a state court of final appeal on an issue of state law is followed by lower state courts and federal courts in the state dealing with that issue.

The doctrine of *stare decisis* promotes continuity, stability, justice, speed, economy, and adaptability within the law. It helps our legal system to furnish guidelines so that people can anticipate legal consequences when they decide how to conduct their affairs. It promotes justice by establishing rules that enable many legal disputes to be concluded fairly. It eliminates the need for every proposition in every case to be subject to endless relitigation. Public faith in the judiciary is increased where legal rules are consistently applied and are the product of impersonal and reasoned judgment. In addition, the quality of the law decided on is improved, as more careful and thorough consideration is given to the legal questions than would be the case if the determinations affected only the case before the court.

Stare decisis is not a binding rule, and a court need not feel absolutely bound to follow previous cases. However, courts are not inclined to deviate from it, especially when the precedents have been treated as authoritative law for a long time. The number of decisions announced on a rule of law also has some bearing on the weight of the precedent. When a principle of law established by precedent is no longer appropriate because of changing economic, political, and social conditions, however, courts should recognize this decay and overrule the precedent to reflect what is best for society.

The Holding and Rule of the Case

Under the doctrine of *stare decisis*, only a point of law necessarily decided in a reported judicial opinion is binding on other courts as precedent. A question of fact determined by a court has no binding effect on a subsequent case involving similar questions of fact. The facts of each case are recognized as being unique.

Those points of law decided by a court to resolve a legal controversy constitute the *holding* of the case. In other words, the court holds that a certain rule of law applies to the given factual situation of the case and renders its decision accordingly. The rule of law as applied to the facts of the case expresses the *rule of the case*. Under *stare decisis*, the rule of the case is applied to future cases with the same or closely analogous factual situations. The rule of the case as expressed in a court's holding becomes a precedent that guides courts in their decisions and is generally considered to be the law.

Sometimes, in their opinions, courts make comments that are not necessary to support the decision. These extraneous judicial expressions are referred to as *dictum*. They have no value as precedent because they do not fit the facts of the case. The reason for drawing a distinction between holding and *dictum* is that only the issues before the court have been argued and fully considered. Even though *dictum* is not binding under the doctrine of *stare decisis*, it is often considered persuasive. Other judges and lawyers can determine what the decision makers are thinking and gain an indication of how the problem may be handled in the future.

It is the task of the lawyer and judge to find the decision or decisions that set the precedent for a particular factual situation. In court, lawyers argue about whether a prior case should or should not be recognized as controlling in a subsequent case.

The Ohio Supreme Court had to make such a decision in the following 1969 case. Did the prosecution violate Butler's federal due process rights when it used his voluntary, in-custody statement (that was obtained without prior *Miranda* warnings) to *impeach* his trial testimony? The U.S. Supreme Court had ruled in a 1954 case (*Walder v. United States*) that prosecutors could impeach a testifying defendant with illegally obtained evidence once the defendant had "opened the door" with false testimony. The U.S. Supreme Court's *Miranda v. Arizona* (1966) opinion seemed to suggest that constitutional due process prevented the government from using such statements for any purpose. In *Miranda*, however, the prosecution had used the defendant's statement to prove guilt, not to impeach the defendant's testimony. Butler's lawyer argued to the Ohio Supreme Court that (1) the language contained in *Miranda* applied to impeachment uses, (2) *Miranda* should be recognized as controlling, and (3) Butler's statement was inadmissible. The lawyers for the State of Ohio disagreed. They argued (1) *Miranda* was not controlling, because Butler's facts were distinguishable from the facts in *Miranda*, (2) the *Walder* case was controlling, and (3) Butler's statement was admissible for purposes of impeachment.

State v. Butler
19 Ohio St. 2d 55, 249 N.E.2d 818
Supreme Court of Ohio
July 9, 1969

Schneider, Justice

. . . The offense for which appellant was indicted, tried, and convicted occurred on August 30, 1964. He struck Annie Ruth Sullivan with a jack handle, causing an injury which resulted in loss of sight of her left eye. Appellant was apprehended and arrested by the Cincinnati police, and while in custody he was interrogated by police officers. Prior to the questioning, the police gave no explanation to appellant as to his rights to remain silent and have an attorney present. The interrogation was recorded and reduced to writing. Over objection by appellant's counsel, these questions and answers were repeated by the prosecutor at trial to impeach statements made by appellant during cross-examination.

Appellant appeared before the municipal court of Hamilton County on November 22, 1965. Probable cause was found and appellant was bound over to the Hamilton County grand jury. Bond was set at $500, which appellant posted. The grand jury returned an indictment for the offense of "maiming." Appellant was arraigned and pleaded not guilty, after which the court appointed counsel. Trial was set. A jury was waived and appellant was found guilty by the court of the lesser included offense of aggravated assault. The court of appeals affirmed the judgment of conviction.

Appellant raises [the question in this appeal as to] whether, in cross-examination of a defendant the prosecutor may use prior inconsistent statements of the defendant, made to police without *Miranda* warnings, in order to impeach his credibility. . . .

Appellant's . . . contention is that the prosecution violated his Fifth Amendment right against self-incrimination by using statements of his which were made to police during in-custody interrogation with no warning of his right to silence or to counsel. . . . The United States Supreme Court . . . in *Miranda v. Arizona* [1966], . . . held there that the prosecution's use of statements of an accused, made to police without prior warnings of his rights to remain silent, to counsel and appointed counsel if indigent, was a violation of the accused's Fourteenth and Fifth Amendment right against self-incrimination. . . .

The appellant took the stand and, on cross-examination by the prosecution, he made assertions as to the facts surrounding the crime. A recorded statement appellant made to a detective after arrest was then read to him to show a prior inconsistent statement. Counsel objected, but the court allowed the statement to be used as evidence to impeach the witness's credibility. Appellant contends that this use of the statements, made without cautionary warnings, violated his Fifth Amendment rights as defined by *Miranda v. Arizona, supra.* . . .

We cannot agree. First, the statements used by the prosecution were not offered by the state as part of its direct case against appellant, but were offered on the issue of his credibility after he had been sworn and testified in his own defense. Second, the statements used by the prosecution were voluntary, no claim to the contrary having been made.

The distinction between admissibility of wrongfully obtained evidence to prove the state's case in chief and its use to impeach the credibility of a defendant who takes the stand was expressed in *Walder v.*

United States [1954] . . . "It is one thing to say that the government cannot make an affirmative use of evidence unlawfully obtained. It is quite another to say that the defendant can turn the illegal method by which evidence in the Government's possession was obtained to his own advantage, and provide himself with a shield against contradiction of his untruths. . . ."

Those words of Justice Frankfurter were uttered in regard to evidence inadmissible under the Fourth Amendment exclusionary rule. In the case of the Fifth Amendment, even greater reason exists to distinguish between statements of an accused used in the prosecution's direct case and used for impeachment in cross-examining the accused when he takes the stand. We must not lose sight of the words of the Fifth Amendment: ". . . nor shall be compelled to be a witness against himself. . . ." This is a privilege accorded an accused not to be compelled to testify, nor to have any prior statements used by the prosecution to prove his guilt. We cannot translate those words into a privilege to lie with impunity once he elects to take the stand to testify. . . .

We do not believe that . . . *Miranda* . . . dictates a conclusion contrary to ours. In *Miranda*, the court indicated that statements of a defendant used to impeach his testimony at trial may not be used unless they were taken with full warnings and effective waiver. However, we note that in all four of the convictions reversed by the decision, statements of the accused, taken without cautionary warnings, were used by the prosecution as direct evidence of guilt in the case in chief.

We believe that the words of Chief Justice Marshall regarding the difference between holding and *dictum* are applicable here. "It is a maxim not to be disregarded, that general expressions, in every opinion, are to be taken in connection with the case in which those expressions are used. If they go beyond the case, they may be respected, but ought not to control the judgment in a subsequent suit when the very point is presented for decision. The reason of this maxim is obvious. The question actually before the court is investigated with care, and considered in its full extent. Other principles which may serve to illustrate it are considered in their relation to the case decided, but their possible bearing on all other cases is seldom completely investigated." . . .

The court, in *Miranda*, was not faced with the facts of this case. Thus, we do not consider ourselves bound by the *dictum* of *Miranda*.

The "linch pin" (as Mr. Justice Harlan put it . . .) of *Miranda* is that police interrogation is destructive of human dignity and disrespectful of the inviolability of the human personality. In the instant case, the use of the interrogation to impeach the voluntary testimony of the accused is neither an assault on his dignity nor disrespectful of his personality. He elected to testify, and cannot complain that the state seeks to demonstrate the lack of truth in his testimony.

Finally, we emphasize that the statements used by the prosecution were voluntarily made. The decision in *Miranda* did not discard the distinction between voluntary and involuntary statements made by an accused and used by the prosecution. . . . Lack of cautionary warnings is one of the factors to consider in determining whether statements are voluntary or not. However, appellant here has never claimed that the statements used to impeach were involuntary. Thus, we assume they were voluntary, and hold that voluntary statements of an accused made to police without cautionary warnings are admissible on the issue of credibility after defendant has been sworn and testifies in his own defense. . . .

Judgment affirmed.[1]

Duncan, Justice, dissenting

. . . The use of statements made by the defendant for impeachment without the warnings set forth in *Miranda v. Arizona* . . . having been given, is reversible error.

In *Miranda*, Chief Justice Warren stated . . .

> "The warnings required and the waiver necessary in accordance with our opinion today are, in the absence of a fully effective equivalent, prerequisites to the admissibility of *any statement made by a defendant.* No distinction can be drawn between statements which are direct confessions and statements which amount to 'admissions' of part or all of an offense. The privilege against self-incrimination protects the individual from being compelled to incriminate himself in any manner; it does not distinguish degrees of incrimination. Similarly, for precisely the same reason, *no distinction may be drawn between inculpatory statements and statements alleged to be merely 'exculpatory.'* If a statement made

> were in fact truly exculpatory, it would, of course, never be used by the prosecution. *In fact, statements merely intended to be exculpatory by the defendant are often used to impeach his testimony at trial or to demonstrate untruths in the statement given under interrogation and thus to prove guilt by implication.* These statements are incriminating in any meaningful sense of the word and may not be used without the full warnings and effective waiver required for any other statement." . . . [Emphasis supplied.]

This *specific* reference to impeachment, I believe, forecloses the use of defendant's in-custody statement in the instant case.

The United States Court of Appeals for the Second Circuit . . . arrived at a decision contrary to that arrived at by the majority in this case. Judge Bryan . . . stated:

> "These pronouncements by the Supreme Court may be technically *dictum.* But it is abundantly plain that the court intended to lay down a firm general rule with respect to the use of statements unconstitutionally obtained from a defendant in violation of *Miranda* standards. The rule prohibits the use of such statements whether inculpatory or exculpatory, whether bearing directly on guilt or on collateral matters only, and whether used on direct examination or for impeachment." . . .

I would reverse.

[1]The U.S. Supreme Court addressed this issue in a 1971 case, *Harris v. New York* (401 U.S. 222). The Court declared that the *Miranda* rule did not require suppression. Due process permitted the prosecution's use of a defendant's voluntary, in-custody statement (obtained without prior *Miranda* warnings) to impeach a testifying defendant's credibility.

Case Questions

1. Explain the difference between holding and *dictum.*
2. Can the holding of a case be broader than the precedent relied on?
3. Why should *dictum* not be considered binding under the doctrine of *stare decisis*?
4. Was *Miranda* properly relied on by the majority in the *Butler* case?
5. If this same case had been decided by the United States Court of Appeals for the Second Circuit, would the decision have been different or the same? Why?

Requirements for a Precedent

Only a judicial opinion of the majority of a court on a point of law can have *stare decisis* effect. A dissent has no precedential value, nor does the fact that an appellate court is split make the majority's decision less of a precedent. When judges are equally divided as to the outcome of a particular case, no precedent is created by that court. This is true even though the decision affirms the decision of the next-lower court.

In addition, in order to create precedent, the opinion must be reported. A decision by a court without a reported opinion does not have *stare decisis* effect. In the great majority of cases, no opinion is written. Appellate courts are responsible for practically all the reported opinions, although occasionally a trial judge will issue a written opinion relating to a case tried to the court. Trial judges do not write opinions in jury cases. There are over three million reported U.S. judicial decisions.

Once a reported judicial precedent-setting opinion is found, the effective date of that decision has to be determined. For this purpose, the date of the court decision, not the date of the events that gave rise to the suit, is crucial.

The Retroactive Versus Prospective Application Question

A court has the power to declare in its opinion whether a precedent-setting decision should have retroactive or prospective application. *Retroactive effect* means that the decision controls the legal consequences of causes of action arising before the announcement of the decision. *Prospective effect* means that the new rule will apply to all questions subsequently coming before that court and the lower courts of the jurisdiction. In general, unless the precedent-setting court has expressly indicated otherwise, or unless special circumstances warrant the denial of retroactive application, the decision is entitled to retroactive as well as prospective effect to all actions that are neither *res judicata* nor barred by a *statute of limitations* as of the date of the precedent-setting decision.

The next case illustrates how courts make this decision. The court examines three factors in determining whether to grant retroactive application: (1) the degree of reliance on the rule of law being overruled, (2) the extent to which prospective application would advance or retard the purpose of the new rule, and (3) the extent to which retroactivity would be substantially inequitable. Courts decide this issue on a case-by-case basis.

Adkins v. Sky Blue, Inc.
702 P.2d 549
Supreme Court of Wyoming
May 24, 1985

Cardine, Justice

During the evening of May 4, 1982, Christopher Kennedy became intoxicated as a result of drinking liquor at a bar known as "The Lounge." On leaving "The Lounge" that evening he purchased and consumed more liquor before departing

Casper, Wyoming. Approximately twenty miles north of Medicine Bow, Wyoming, the automobile being driven by Christopher Kennedy struck plaintiff Leland Adkins's vehicle head-on in Mr. Adkins's lane of travel. Christopher Kennedy was killed, as were his two passengers. Leland Adkins and his passenger suffered personal injuries in the accident resulting in Adkins being left a quadriplegic. Some time after the accident a blood sample, taken from the body of Christopher Kennedy, determined his blood alcohol level to be .11%. Leland Adkins filed suit in the United States District Court for the District of Wyoming against "The Lounge," its owners and employee to recover damages for the personal injuries suffered by him.

The United States District Court found that Adkins's case involved a question of law of the State of Wyoming which might be determinative of the action and that there was no clear and controlling precedent in the decisions of the Supreme Court of the State of Wyoming; it therefore certified for instruction, pursuant to § 1–13–106, W.S.1977, the following question.

> "Do third persons injured by an intoxicated patron of a liquor vendor state a claim for relief against the liquor vendor for causes of action that arose prior to *McClellan v. Tottenhoff,* . . . (Wyo.1983)?"

We answer the certified question in the negative.

In *Parsons v. Jow,* . . . the bar owner sold intoxicating liquor to McCall, a minor, who became drunk and crashed his car into a building. Plaintiff, a passenger in the car at the time, sued the bar owner to recover damages resulting from his personal injuries. The trial court dismissed plaintiff's complaint for failure to state a claim upon which relief could be granted. We affirmed stating that

> " . . . it cannot be denied there was no cause of action at common law against a vendor of liquor in favor of one injured by a vendee who becomes intoxicated—this for the reason that the proximate cause of injury was deemed to be the patron's consumption of liquor and not its sale. . . .
>
> "Statutes, in a number of states, have changed the common law rule and subjected a tavern keeper to liability to a third party, where injury results from the furnishing of intoxicating liquor. The statutes are called civil damage or dramshop acts.

* * * * * *

> "The legislature of Wyoming has not seen fit to change the common law rule as it applies in this case. Whether legislation in the nature of a dramshop act or a civil damage statute should be included as part of our liquor control code is within the province of the legislature." . . .

Thus, the Wyoming Supreme Court issued a clear pronouncement that it would not undertake to adopt a dramshop law by judicial decision but would leave that to the legislature. When the question of liability for sale of liquor to an intoxicated person was next considered in *Snyder v. West Rawlins Properties, Inc.* . . . (D.Wyo.1982), the United States District Court, relying upon the pronouncements of the Wyoming Supreme Court stated:

> "The general rule is that in the absence of a civil damage or dramshop act enacted by the state legislature, the common law provided that no remedy existed against a tavern owner or vendor of liquor for injuries to a [third] party. Wyoming does not have a civil damages or dramshop act."

Thus, as late as February 1982, there was no reason for anyone to suspect that the Wyoming Supreme Court would, at the next opportunity, impose liability upon the vendors of liquor by an over-ruling decision rather than leaving the matter to the legislature.

McClellan v. Tottenhoff, decided June 28, 1983, involved the sale of alcoholic beverage to a minor who became intoxi-cated and drove a car so as to fatally in-jure the plaintiff. Without prior warning or suggestion of what was to occur, the court in *McClellan v. Tottenhoff,* supra, stated:

> "The rule that there is no cause of action when a vendor sells liquor to a consumer who injures a third party was created by the courts. We see no reason to wait any longer for the legislature to abrogate it, Common law created by the judiciary can be abrogated by the judiciary." . . .

The common law has served us well because it is flexible, able to grow and meet the requirements of changing condi-tions and a different society. There are times when change is necessary; but the doctrine of *stare decisis* is also important in an organized society. Change, therefore, should occur slowly, deliberately after much experience, and if possible so as not to affect vested rights or things in the past. Thus, it is said that:

> "[T]he courts may apply or effectuate common law principles in the light of altered or new conditions, and when the circumstances and conditions are differ-ent, in that the common law principles are unsuitable to new circumstances or conditions, the needs of society, or in conflict with public policy, the courts may make such changes or modifications as the situation requires." (Footnotes omitted.) 15A C.J.S. Common Law § 13. . . .

Acknowledging that there ought to be an extreme reluctance to change the common law and recognizing the obvious benefits of the doctrine of *stare decisis,* yet on occasion it does become eminently clear that society has long passed beyond the point where an ancient doctrine remains viable. This court believed it had arrived at that place in deciding *McClellan v. Tottenhoff,* supra—now the law of this state—and in stating:

> "We hereby overrule *Parsons v. Jow,* supra.
>
> * * * * * *
>
> "*Henceforth,* cases involving vendors of liquor and injured third parties will be approached in the same manner as other negligence cases.
>
> * * * * * *
>
> "We hold that a vendor of liquor owes a duty to exercise the degree of care re-quired of a reasonable person in light of all the circumstances." (Emphasis added.) . . .

The rule of *McClellan v. Tottenhoff,* supra, became effective with the issuance of the court's opinion on June 28, 1983. The accident in which plaintiff was in-volved and which is the subject of this case, occurred May 5, 1982, more than a year prior to the court's pronouncement in *McClellan v. Tottenhoff.* If the rule an-nounced in *McClellan v. Tottenhoff,* supra, applies prospectively only—that is in the future, *henceforth* and from now on—then plaintiff's case is subject to the common-law rule of nonliability for sellers of intoxicating liquor as stated in *Parsons v. Jow.* And, as was held in *Parsons v. Jow,* it must be dismissed.

Initially it was held that a court issuing an overruling decision had merely discovered and announced existing law; since the overruling case did not create new law, but merely recognized what had always been the law, such law would operate both retrospectively and prospectively:

" '[B]ut the modern decisions, taking a more pragmatic view of the judicial function, have recognized the power of a court to hold that an overruling decision is operative prospectively only and is not even operative upon the rights of the parties to the overruling case. As a matter of constitutional law, retroactive operation of an overruling decision is neither required nor prohibited.' "

Where an overruling decision announces a change in the common law, some guidelines are set forth in *Chevron Oil Company v. Huson*, 404 U.S. 97 (1971), for whether its operation should be retrospective or prospective only:

"In our cases dealing with the nonretroactivity question, we have generally considered three separate factors. First, the decision to be applied nonretroactively must establish a new principle of law, either by overruling clear past precedent on which litigants may have relied, . . . or by deciding an issue of first impression whose resolution was not clearly foreshadowed. . . . Second, it has been stressed that 'we must . . . weigh the merits and demerits in each case by looking to the prior history of the rule in question, its purpose and effect, and whether retrospective operation will further or retard its operation.' . . . Finally, we have weighed the inequity imposed by retroactive application, for '[w]here a decision of this Court could produce substantial inequitable results if applied retroactively, there is ample basis in our cases for avoiding the "injustice or hardship" by a holding of nonretroactivity.' " Id., 92 S.Ct. at 355.

This court has on several occasions considered whether a change in law should operate retrospectively or prospectively. In *Nehring v. Russell*, . . . (1978), we stated that

" . . . the determination is ours to make, [and] we conclude that in consideration of all the factors and any prior reliances involved, our holding should be applied prospectively only, i.e., to this action and all causes of action accruing after 30 days following the date of this decision."
. . .

It has been repeatedly stated that where a decision might produce substantial inequitable results if applied retroactively, it is appropriate to avoid such hardship or injustice by providing for prospective operation only. *Chevron Oil Company v. Huson*, supra. Vendors of liquor in this state had no reason to suspect that this court would adopt a dramshop-type law placing liability on vendors of liquor. There were no cases following *Parsons v. Jow*, supra, suggesting an imminent change in the law. The court had given its firm assurance in *Parsons v. Jow*, . . . that this was a matter for the legislature. As late as 1982, in *Snyder v. West Rawlins Properties, Inc.*, . . . the United States District Court, District of Wyoming, reaffirmed the rule of *Parsons v. Jow*, . . . which provided nonliability to third persons injured by an intoxicated patron of a liquor vendor. Liquor vendors had no reason to obtain insurance or otherwise protect themselves against liability that did not exist. Insuring against this kind of broad liability is expensive, and they surely were justified in relying upon the pronouncement of this court in not purchasing insurance coverage.

The public policy of *McClellan v. Tottenhoff* and the purpose to be served by imposing civil liability upon vendors of liquor are to cause them (a) to exercise care in dispensing liquor, (b) to refuse liquor to intoxicated persons or refuse to sell in violation of law; and (c) to provide financial responsibility for negligence. Those purposes are not served or affected by retroactive operation of the law, for the incident complained of had already occurred—nothing could be done to change it. The stated public policy would not be promoted by holding the vendor retroactively liable for damages. We note here also that the legislature, at its 1985 general session, was concerned about this area of the law and enacted legislation on this subject.

It is suggested that the case for prospective operation of the rule of *McClellan v. Tottenhoff* is weak because vendors of alcoholic beverage cannot seriously and in good conscience contend that they violated the liquor laws relying upon *Parsons v. Jow* to escape civil liability. We do not suggest they violated the law relying upon *Parsons v. Jow*. We do suggest they may not have purchased expensive insurance or otherwise obtained financial protection against this newly-created liability in reliance upon *Parsons v. Jow*. That is the reliance of which we speak. With respect to the violation of the liquor laws in reliance upon *Parsons v. Jow*, that is not likely, for severe criminal sanctions are imposed as are procedures resulting in the loss of a liquor license whether by revocation or refusal to renew.

There was no series of cases following *Parsons v. Jow* that suggested or even intimated that the court might overrule *Parsons v. Jow*. The vendors of liquor justifiably relied upon the law as we stated it to be. To hold now that a vendor of liquor, not liable for damages under the law existing at the time of the accident involved nevertheless, a year later, became liable because of a change in the law by an overruling case would be manifestly unfair.

We find comfort in the language of the court in *McClellan v. Tottenhoff* wherein we stated that *"henceforth"* this type of case would be determined upon ordinary negligence principles. It is held that such terms as "hereafter," "thereafter," and "shall be" speak to prospective operation. 82 C.J.S. Statutes § 413. Henceforth is in the same category. It is defined as:

> "A word of futurity, which, as employed in legal documents, statutes, and the like, always imports a continuity of action or condition from the present time forward, but excludes all the past." Black's Law Dictionary (5th ed. 1979).

We, therefore, hold that the rule of *McClellan v. Tottenhoff*, supra, applies prospectively only, to claims or causes of action that accrue after the date of its publication, to wit, June 28, 1983.

Brown, Justice, dissenting

In holding that *McClellan v. Tottenhoff*, . . . (1983), has only prospective application, the majority bases its decision on language in the *McClellan* case, and the notion that vendors of liquor relied on *Parsons v. Jow*, . . . (1971) to insulate them from civil liability in the illegal sale of liquor. . . .

There is no clear prohibition in *McClellan* against retrospective application nor is there a clear mandate requiring only prospective application. The general rule is that, in civil cases, decisions are to be applied retroactively. . . .

In *Malan v. Lewis*, . . . (1984), the court stated:

> "The *general rule* from time immemorial is that the ruling of a court is deemed to state the true nature of the law both retrospectively and prospectively. In civil cases, at least, constitutional law neither requires nor prohibits retroactive operation of an overruling decision, [Citations] but in the vast majority of cases a decision is effective both prospectively and retrospectively, even an overruling decision. [Citations.] Whether the *general rule* should be departed from

depends on whether a substantial injustice would otherwise occur. [Citation.]" (Emphasis added.) . . .

These cases, of course, are not without exception:

"Although there is a traditional general rule in favor of giving retroactive effect to an overruling decision, it has become recognized that this rule is subject to various exceptions, for example, where there has been justifiable reliance on decisions which are subsequently overruled and those who have so relied may be substantially harmed if retroactive effect is given to the overruling decision. . . ." Annot., 10 A.L.R.3d 1384 (1966).

The case before us, however, is the weakest case imaginable for an exception from the general rule. How can vendors of alcoholic beverages seriously and in good conscience contend that they violated the liquor laws, relying on *Parsons v. Jow* to escape civil liability? . . .

Brannigan v. Raybuck, . . . (1983), has elements of both the case before us and the *McClellan* case. In *Brannigan*, the surviving parents of minor passengers and the driver killed in an automobile accident brought a wrongful death action against tavern operators for negligently furnishing liquor to the decedents. The court en banc held, among other things, that where violation of a statute pertaining to furnishing liquor to those who are underage or who are already intoxicated is shown, negligence exists as a matter of law and the rule may be retroactively and prospectively applied. . . .

Both the majority and this dissent strive mightily albeit circuitously to arrive at divergent views. Both argue that logic, precedent, and justice support their position. Both avoid the real basis of how the decision was made or, from the dissent's view, should have been made.

"... [M]ost courts now treat the question of how an overruling decision should operate as one of judicial policy rather than of judicial power, and recognize that varying results may be reached, depending on the particular circumstances presented and the particular rule affected." Annot., 10 A.L.R.3d 1378 (1966).

I would hold that *McClellan* should be applied retroactively as well as prospectively.

Case Questions

1. Why should there be a strong presumption in favor of retroactivity in civil cases?
2. Why did the Wyoming Supreme Court apply the three tests established in the *Chevron* case?
3. Why did the Wyoming Supreme Court conclude that the *McClellan* precedent should apply only prospectively?

Absence of Precedent

When judges are confronted by a novel fact situation, they must rely on their own sense of justice and philosophy of law. The public interest, tradition, prevailing customs, business usage, and moral standards are important considerations in the decision-making process. Judges encountering a case of first impression first look for guidance within the forum state (as was done by the court in the *Du Pont* case in Chapter 1). When precedent is lacking in the forum state, decisions of other state and federal courts, as well as English decisions, may be considered persuasive on the legal point at issue.

The trial court in the following case encountered a problem that was unique. The trial and appellate courts were required to make decisions without being able to benefit from the experience of others as reflected in statutory law and common law opinions. They had to create new law when life and death were at stake. Note that three of the seven members of the appellate court dissented.

Strunk v. Strunk
445 S.W.2d 145
Court of Appeals of Kentucky
September 26, 1969

Osborne, Judge

The specific question involved upon this appeal is: Does a court of equity[1] have power to permit a kidney to be removed from an incompetent ward of the state upon petition of his committee, who is also his mother, for the purpose of being transplanted into the body of his brother, who is dying of a fatal kidney disease? We are of the opinion it does.

The facts of the case are as follows: Arthur L. Strunk, 54 years of age, and Ava Strunk, 52 years of age, of Williamstown, Kentucky, are the parents of two sons. Tommy Strunk is 28 years of age, married, an employee of the Penn State Railroad and a part-time student at the University of Cincinnati. Tommy is now suffering from chronic glomerus nephritis, a fatal kidney disease. He is now being kept alive by frequent treatment on an artificial kidney, a procedure that cannot be continued much longer.

Jerry Strunk is 27 years of age, incompetent, and through proper legal proceed-

[1] Equity is discussed in Chapters 1 and 6—*Ed.*

ings has been committed to the Frankfort State Hospital and School, which is a state institution maintained for the feeble-minded. He has an IQ of approximately 35, which corresponds with the mental age of approximately six years. He is further handicapped by a speech defect, which makes it difficult for him to communicate with persons who are not well acquainted with him. When it was determined that Tommy, in order to survive, would have to have a kidney, the doctors considered the possibility of using a kidney from a cadaver if and when one became available, or one from a live donor if this could be made available. The entire family, his mother, father, and a number of collateral relatives, were tested. Because of incompatibility of blood type or tissue, none was medically acceptable as a live donor. As a last resort, Jerry was tested and found to be highly acceptable. This immediately presented the legal problem as to what, if anything, could be done by the family, especially the mother and the father, to procure a transplant from Jerry to Tommy. The mother as a committee petitioned the county court for authority to proceed with the operation. The court found that the operation was necessary, that under the peculiar circumstances of this case, it would not only be beneficial to Tommy but also beneficial to Jerry because Jerry was greatly dependent on Tommy, emotionally and psychologically, and that his well-being would be jeopardized more severely by the loss of his brother than by the removal of a kidney.

Appeal was taken to the Franklin Circuit Court where the chancellor reviewed the record, examined the testimony of the witnesses, and adopted the findings of the county court.

A psychiatrist, in attendance to Jerry, who testified in the case, stated in his opinion the death of Tommy under these circumstances would have "an extremely traumatic effect upon him [Jerry]."

The Department of Mental Health of this commonwealth has entered the case as *amicus curiae* and on the basis of its evaluation of the seriousness of the operation as opposed to the traumatic effect on Jerry as a result of the loss of Tommy, recommended to the court that Jerry be permitted to undergo the surgery. Its recommendations are as follows: "It is difficult for the mental defective to establish a firm sense of identity with another person. The acquisition of this necessary identity is dependent on a person whom one can conveniently accept as a model and who at the same time is sufficiently flexible to allow the defective to detach himself with reassurances of continuity. His need to be social is not so much the necessity of a formal and mechanical contact with other human beings as it is the necessity of a close intimacy with other men, the desirability of a real community of feeling, an urgent need for a unity of understanding. Purely mechanical and formal contact with other men does not offer any treatment for the behavior of a mental defective; only those who are able to communicate intimately are of value to hospital treatment in these cases. And this generally is a member of the family.

"In view of this knowledge, we now have particular interest in this case. Jerry Strunk, a mental defective, has emotions and reactions on a scale comparable to that of a normal person. He identifies with his brother Tom. Tom is his model, his tie with his family. Tom's life is vital to the continuity of Jerry's improvement at Frankfort State Hospital and School. The testimony of the hospital representative reflected the importance to Jerry of his visits with his family and the constant inquiries Jerry made about Tom's coming to see him. Jerry is aware he plays a role in the relief of this tension. We the Department of Mental Health must take all possible steps to prevent the occurrence of any guilt feelings Jerry would have if Tom were to die.

"The necessity of Tom's life to Jerry's treatment and eventual rehabilitation is clearer in view of the fact that Tom is his only living sibling and at the death of their parents, now in their fifties, Jerry will have no concerned, intimate communication so necessary to his stability and optimal functioning.

"The evidence shows that at the present level of medical knowledge, it is quite remote that Tom would be able to survive several cadaver transplants. Tom has a much better chance of survival if the kidney transplant from Jerry takes place."

Upon this appeal, we are faced with the fact that all members of the immediate family have recommended the transplant. The Department of Mental Health has likewise made its recommendation. The county court has given its approval. The circuit court has found that it would be to the best interest of the ward of the state that the procedure be carried out. Throughout the legal proceedings, Jerry has been represented by a guardian *ad litem*, who has continually questioned the power of the state to authorize the removal of an organ from the body of an incompetent who is a ward of the state. We are fully cognizant of the fact that the question before us is unique. Insofar as we have been able to learn, no similar set of facts has come before the highest court of any of the states of this nation or the federal courts. The English courts have apparently taken a broad view of the inherent power of the equity courts with regard to incompetents. *Ex parte White-bread* (1816), . . . holds that courts of equity have the inherent power to make provisions for a needy brother out of the estate of an incompetent. . . . The inherent rule in these cases is that the chancellor has the power to deal with the estate of the incompetent in the same manner as the incompetent would if he had his faculties. This rule has been extended to cover not only matters of property but also to cover the personal affairs of the incompetent. . . .

The right to act for the incompetent in all cases has become recognized in this country as the doctrine of substituted judgment and is broad enough not only to cover property but also to cover all matters touching on the well-being of the ward. . . .

The medical practice of transferring tissue from one part of the human body to another (autografting) and from one human being to another (homografting) is rapidly becoming a common clinical practice. In many cases, the transplants take as well when the tissue is dead as when it is alive. This has made practicable the establishment of tissue banks where such material can be stored for future use. Vascularized grafts of lungs, kidneys, and hearts are becoming increasingly common. These grafts must be of functioning, living cells with blood vessels remaining anatomically intact. The chance of success in the transfer of these organs is greatly increased when the donor and the donee are genetically related. It is recognized by all legal and medical authorities that several legal problems can arise as a result of the operative techniques of the transplant procedure. . . .

The renal transplant is becoming the most common of the organ transplants. This is because the normal body has two functioning kidneys, one of which it can reasonably do without, thereby making it possible for one person to donate a kidney to another. Testimony in this record shows that there have been over 2500 kidney transplants performed in the United States up to this date. The process can be effected under present techniques with minimal danger to both the donor and the donee. . . .

Review of our case law leads us to believe that the power given to a committee under KRS 387.230 would not extend so far as to allow a committee to subject his ward to the serious surgical techniques here under consideration unless the life of his ward be in jeopardy. Nor do we believe the powers delegated to the county court by virtue of the above statutes would reach so far as to permit the procedure which we [are] dealing with here.

We are of the opinion that a chancery court does have sufficient inherent power to authorize the operation. The circuit court having found that the operative procedures are to the best interest of Jerry Strunk and this finding having been based on substantial evidence, we are of the opinion the judgment should be affirmed. We do not deem it significant that this case reached the circuit court by way of an appeal as opposed to a direct proceeding in that court.

Judgment affirmed.

Hill, C.J., Milliken, and Reed, JJ., concur.

Neikirk, Palmore, and Steinfeld, JJ., dissent.

Steinfeld, Judge, dissenting

Apparently because of my indelible recollection of a government which, to the everlasting shame of its citizens, embarked on a program of genocide and experimentation with human bodies, I have been more troubled in reaching a decision in this case than in any other. My sympathies and emotions are torn between a compassion to aid an ailing young man and a duty to fully protect unfortunate members of society.

The opinion of the majority is predicated on the authority of an equity court to speak for one who cannot speak for himself. However, it is my opinion that in considering such right in this instance, we must first look to the power and authority vested in the committee, the appellee herein. KRS 387.060 and KRS 387.230 do nothing more than give the committee the power to take custody of the incompetent and the possession, care, and management of his property. Courts have restricted the activities of the committee to that which is for the best interest of the incompetent. . . . The authority and duty have been to protect and maintain the ward, to secure that to which he is entitled and preserve that which he has. . . .

The wishes of the members of the family or the desires of the guardian to be helpful to the apparent objects of the ward's bounty have not been a criterion. "A curator or guardian cannot dispose of his ward's property by donation, even though authorized to do so by the court on advice of a family meeting, unless a gift by the guardian is authorized by statute." . . .

Two Kentucky cases decided many years ago reveal judicial policy. In *W.T. Sistrunk & Co. v. Navarra's Committee,* . . .

105 S.W.2d 1039 (1937), this court held that a committee was without right to continue a business which the incompetent had operated prior to his having been declared a person of unsound mind. More analogous is *Baker v. Thomas,* . . . 114 S.W.2d 1113 (1938), in which a man and woman had lived together out of wedlock. Two children were born to them. After the man was judged incompetent, his committee, acting for him, together with his paramour, instituted proceedings to adopt the two children. In rejecting the application and refusing to speak for the incompetent, the opinion stated: "The statute does not contemplate that the committee of a lunatic may exercise any other power than to have the possession, care, and management of the lunatic's or incompetent's estate." . . .

The majority opinion is predicated on the finding of the circuit court that there will be psychological benefits to the ward but points out that the incompetent has the mentality of a six-year-old child. It is common knowledge beyond dispute that the loss of a close relative or a friend to a six-year-old child is not of major impact. Opinions concerning psychological trauma are at best most nebulous. Furthermore, there are no guarantees that the transplant will become a surgical success, it being well known that body rejection of transplanted organs is frequent. The life of the incompetent is not in danger, but the surgical procedure advocated creates some peril.

It is written in *Prince v. Massachusetts,* 321 U.S. 158 (1944), that "Parents may be free to become martyrs themselves. But it does not follow they are free, in identical circumstances, to make martyrs of their children before they have reached the age of full and legal distinction when they can make the choice for themselves." The ability to fully understand and consent is a prerequisite to the donation of a part of the human body. . . .

Unquestionably, the attitudes and attempts of the committee and members of the family of the two young men whose critical problems now confront us are commendable, natural, and beyond reproach. However, they refer us to nothing indicating that they are privileged to authorize the removal of one of the kidneys of the incompetent for the purpose of donation, and they cite no statutory or other authority vesting such right in the courts. The proof shows that less compatible donors are available and that the kidney of a cadaver could be used, although the odds of operational success are not as great in such cases as they would be with the fully compatible donor brother.

I am unwilling to hold that the gates should be open to permit the removal of an organ from an incompetent for transplant, at least until such time as it is conclusively demonstrated that it will be of significant benefit to the incompetent. The evidence here does not rise to that pinnacle. To hold that committees, guardians, or courts have such awesome power, even in the persuasive case before us, could establish legal precedent, the dire result of which we cannot fathom. Regretfully I must say no.

Neikirk and Palmore, JJ., join with me in this dissent.

Case Questions

1. The Court of Appeals of Kentucky is the court of last resort in that state. The *Strunk* decision is now Kentucky law. Does the decision make mental institutions a storehouse of human bodies available for distribution to the more productive members of society whenever the state decides that someone's need outweighs the danger to the incompetent?
2. The justice who wrote the dissenting opinion says he was influenced by his background. To what recent history was he referring?
3. Which opinion, the majority or dissent, was more persuasive?
4. Where no legal cases have a direct bearing on the issue of a case, should the court turn to other disciplines for authority?

RECOGNIZING LAWS OF OTHER STATES AND COUNTRIES

Conflict of Laws

Every person within the territorial limits of a government is bound by its laws. However, it is well recognized that law does not of its own force have any effect outside the territory of the sovereignty from which its authority is derived. Since each of the fifty states is an individual sovereignty that creates its own common and statutory law, there are often inconsistencies among the laws of the various states. When the facts of a case under consideration have occurred in more than one state or country, and a court must make a choice between the laws of different states or nations, a conflict case is presented. For example, in *Calder v. Jones* (Chapter 2), a plaintiff from California filed suit in her local court against a newspaper editor and author who allegedly libeled her from Florida. The California trial court in that case had to decide whether the tort law of California or some other state should be applied.

Another type of conflict-of-laws case involves a situation in which an event occurred in one state and the suit is brought in another state. For example, a driver from Michigan might bring suit in Kentucky regarding an automobile collision in Ohio involving a driver from Kentucky. In this situation, the court must decide whether to apply its own substantive law, the law of the state in which the events occurred, or possibly the law of some other state.

Conflict-of-laws rules have been developed by each state to assist its courts in determining whether and when foreign substantive law should be given effect within the territory of the forum. (Remember that a state court follows that state's procedural law.) The rules afford some assurance that a case will be treated in the same way under the appropriate substantive law, no matter where the suit is brought. Foreign law may be enforced or given effect when the conflict-of-laws rule determining such enforcement or recognition is part of the law of the local jurisdiction.

It is important to remember that the *Erie* doctrine (see *Carson* case in Chapter 2) applies to conflict cases. Federal judges will follow the conflict-of-laws rules that would be applied in the courts of the state in which the federal court is located.

Tort Cases

The traditional approach in tort cases is to apply the law of the place where the wrong was committed—*lex loci delicti commissi*. The place of the wrong is where the last event necessary to make the actor liable takes place or where the person or thing harmed is situated at the time of the wrong. The following case exemplifies a trend that had been occurring in recent years. The Indiana Supreme Court used the *Hubbard* case to replace the traditional *lex loci delicti commissi* rule with the *significant relationship rule*. The significant relationship approach is more flexible than a rigid *lex loci* approach. A court following the significant relationship rule can apply the law of the place that has the most significant contacts with the incident or event in dispute.

Hubbard Manufacturing Co., Inc., v. Greeson
515 N.E.2d 1071
Supreme Court of Indiana
December 1, 1987

Shepard, Chief Justice

The question is whether an Indiana court should apply Indiana tort law when both parties are residents of Indiana and the injury occurred in Illinois.

Plaintiff Elizabeth Greeson, an Indiana resident, filed a wrongful death action in

Indiana against defendant Hubbard Manufacturing Co., Inc., an Indiana corporation. The defendant corporation built lift units for use in cleaning, repairing, and replacing streetlights.

On October 29, 1979, Donald Greeson, plaintiff's husband and also a resident of Indiana, happened to be working in Illinois maintaining street lights. He died that day while using a lift unit manufactured by Hubbard in Indiana.

Elizabeth Greeson's suit alleged that defective manufacture of Hubbard's lift unit caused her husband's death. When she raised the possibility that Illinois products liability law should be applied to this case, Hubbard moved the trial court for a determination of the applicable law. The trial court found that Indiana had more significant contacts with the litigation but felt constrained to apply Illinois substantive law because the decedent's injury had been sustained there. The Court of Appeals expressed the opinion that Indiana law should apply but concluded that existing precedent required use of Illinois law. . . .

We grant transfer to decide whether Indiana or Illinois law applies.

Greeson's complaint alleged two bases for her claim: "the defective and unreasonably dangerous condition of a lift type vehicle sold . . . by the defendant" and "the negligence of the defendant." Both theories state a cause for liability based on Hubbard's manufacture of the vehicle in Indiana.

The differences in Indiana law and Illinois law are considerable. First, in Indiana a finding that the product represented an open and obvious danger would preclude recovery on the product liability claim. . . . to impress liability on manufacturers the defect must be hidden and not normally observable. Under Illinois law, the trier of fact may find product liability even if the danger is open and obvious. . . . Second, under Indiana law misuse would bar recovery. . . . In Illinois misuse merely reduces a plaintiff's award. . . . These differences are important enough to affect the outcome of the litigation.

Choosing the applicable substantive law for a given case is a decision made by the courts of the state in which the lawsuit is pending. An early basis for choosing law applicable to events transversing several states was to use the substantive law of the state "where the wrong is committed" regardless of where the plaintiff took his complaint seeking relief. . . .

The historical choice-of-law rule for torts, . . . was *lex loci delicti commissi*, which applied the substantive law where the tort was committed. *Burns v. Grand Rapids and Indiana Railroad Co.* (1888). . . . The tort is said to have been committed in the state where the last event necessary to make an actor liable for the alleged wrong takes place.

Rigid application of the traditional rule to this case, however, would lead to an anomalous result. Had plaintiff Elizabeth Greeson filed suit in any bordering state the only forum which would not have applied the substantive law of Indiana is Indiana. . . . To avoid this inappropriate result, we look elsewhere for guidance.

Choice-of-law rules are fundamentally judge-made and designed to ensure the appropriate substantive law applies. In a large number of cases, the place of the tort will be significant and the place with the most contacts. . . . In such cases, the traditional rule serves well. A court should be allowed to evaluate other factors when the place of the tort is an insignificant contact. In those instances where the place of the tort bears little connection to the legal action, this Court will permit the consideration of other factors such as:

1. the place where the conduct causing the injury occurred;
2. the residence or place of business of the parties; and
3. the place where the relationship is centered.

Restatement (Second) of Conflicts of Laws § 145(2) (1971). These factors should be evaluated according to their relative importance to the particular issues being litigated.

The first step in applying this rule in the present case is to consider whether the place of the tort "bears little connection" to this legal action. The last event necessary to make Hubbard liable for the alleged tort took place in Illinois. The decedent was working in Illinois at the time of his death and the vehicle involved in the fatal injuries was in Illinois. The coroner's inquest was held in Illinois, and the decedent's wife and son are receiving benefits under the Illinois Workmen's Compensation Laws. None of these facts relates to the wrongful death action filed against

Hubbard. The place of the tort is insignificant to this suit.

After having determined that the place of the tort bears little connection to the legal action, the second step is to apply the additional factors. Applying these factors to this wrongful death action leads us to the same conclusion that the trial court drew: Indiana has the more significant relationship and contacts. The plaintiff's two theories of recovery relate to the manufacture of the lift in Indiana. Both parties are from Indiana; plaintiff Elizabeth Greeson is a resident of Indiana and defendant Hubbard is an Indiana corporation with its principal place of business in Indiana. The relationship between the deceased and Hubbard centered in Indiana. The deceased frequently visited defendant's plant in Indiana to discuss the repair and maintenance of the lift. Indiana law applies.

The Court of Appeals decision is vacated and the cause remanded to the trial court with instructions to apply Indiana law.

Case Questions

1. Under *lex loci delicti commissi*, how should a court determine where a tort was committed?
2. Why did the Indiana Supreme Court decide to replace the traditional *lex loci delicti commissi* approach?
3. What contacts were evaluated by the court in determining which state had a more significant relationship with the occurrence and with the parties?

Contract Cases

All states have developed their own conflict-of-laws rules for contractual disputes, which differ from the rules that apply to tort cases. In contractual disputes, depending on the facts involved and jurisdictional preferences, courts have historically applied the law of place in any of the following ways: (1) where the action was instituted (*lex fori*), (2) where the contract was to be performed (*lex loci solutionis*), (3) which law the parties intended to govern their agreement, (4) the law of the state where the last act necessary to complete the contract was done and which created a legal obligation (*lex loci contractus*), and (5) the law of the state that has the greatest concern with the event and the parties (significant relationship rule). A court may choose to follow its own substantive law of contracts and will do so if the application of the foreign law would offend its public policy.

Courts often honor the law intended by the parties to be controlling. The state chosen usually has a substantial connection with the contract, but courts have held that no such connection is necessary if the parties intended that that state's laws govern the agreement. For example, automobile and house insurance contracts generally included a choice-of-law clause, usually a forum selected by the lawyers for the insurance company, and "agreed to" by the insured. If a contract fails to include a choice-of-law clause, courts may still determine the parties' intent by examining the facts surrounding the contract.

One of the important developments in contract law has been the enactment by all states of at least some provisions of the Uniform Commercial Code (UCC). This code was created in order to enhance the uniformity of state laws regulating certain commercial transactions. The UCC does not apply to all types of contracts. It does not apply, for example, to employment contracts, services, or to the sale of real property. With respect to conflicts of law, the UCC basically follows the significant relationship rule when parties to contracts have not specified a choice of law.

Full Faith and Credit

Since each state in the United States is a distinct sovereignty, this implies that each of the states is entitled to disregard the constitutions, statutes, records, and judgments of other states. Thus, the refusal of some states to recognize and enforce the judgments issued by other states would deny justice to those who had taken their disputes to court. Judgment debtors could flee to a state that refuses to recognize and enforce judgments from the issuing state, undermining public confidence in the law.

The authors of the U.S. Constitution anticipated this problem and addressed it in Article IV, section 1, which provides that "full faith and credit shall be given in each state to the public acts, records, and judicial proceedings of every other state." Thus, the Constitution requires the states to cooperate with each other and binds them together into one nation. Since final judgments of each state are enforceable in every other state, irrespective of differences in substantive law and public policy, the full faith and credit requirement also helps to preserve the legal differences that exist from state to state.

Another important benefit of the full faith and credit requirement is that it puts teeth into the doctrine of *res judicata*. Once a valid judgment has been rendered in one state, the claims adjudicated in that lawsuit cannot be relitigated by the same parties in some other state.

A state can justifiably refuse to grant full faith and credit to another state's judgment under limited circumstances, for example, when the issuing court has failed to follow the mandates of the federal Constitution regarding due process of law. Full faith and credit can be denied where the issuing court did not have minimum contacts with the person of the judgment debtor, or where the judicial proceedings denied the judgment debtor the constitutionally required elements of notice and an opportunity for a hearing.

Article IV, section 1, only requires that the states provide full faith and credit to other states. The federal Full Faith and Credit Act (28 USC Section 1738), however, requires all federal courts to afford full faith and credit to state court judgments.

Although a properly authenticated judgment of an issuing state is presumptively valid and binding in all other states, it is not self implementing. A judgment creditor who has to go to some other state to enforce a judgment will have to begin an action against the judgment debtor in the nonissuing state. The courts of the nonissuing state will then have to enforce the foreign judgment in the same manner as it would one of its own judgments, even if enforcing the judgment would contravene the enforcing state's public policy. In the following case, the public policies of Nevada and Texas differ regarding the enforcement and recognition of gambling debts.

GNLV Corporation v. Jackson
736 S.W.2d 893
Court of Appeals of Texas—Waco
August 27, 1987

Thomas, Justice

The court permanently enjoined GNLV Corp., a Nevada corporation, from enforcing a Nevada judgment against Gene Jackson, a Texas resident, because the judgment would offend Texas public policy against enforcing a gambling debt. A state cannot deny full faith and credit to another state's judgment solely on the ground that it offends the public policy of the state where it is sought to be enforced. . . . Therefore, the judgment will be reversed.

GNLV, a Nevada corporation, obtained a $58,202.36 judgment against Gene Jackson in Nevada, and then filed an authenticated copy of the judgment with the district clerk of Johnson County, Texas, under the Uniform Enforcement of Foreign Judgments Act. . . . Jackson filed a motion to enjoin enforcement of the judgment on the ground that it would violate Texas public policy against enforcing a gambling debt. The parties stipulated that the Nevada judgment was based on a gambling debt, that the Nevada court had jurisdiction of the subject matter and of Jackson, and that the judgment was final. The court permanently enjoined GNLV from enforcing the Nevada judgment on the ground that it violated Texas public policy.

Texas has a well-established public policy of not recognizing or enforcing rights arising from gambling transactions. . . . However, Texas cannot deny full faith and credit to the Nevada judgment because it offends this public policy. . . . Thus, the court erred when it permanently enjoined GNLV from enforcing the Nevada judgment on the ground of Texas public policy. The judgment is reversed and the cause is remanded for further proceedings.

Case
Questions

1. How did the lower Texas court commit error?
2. Can you think of a situation in which the lower Texas court would not have been in error for refusing to enforce the Nevada judgment?

Comity

No mandate in international law requires one nation to give effect to the laws of another country. *Comity* is the recognition that one sovereignty allows to the legislative, executive, or judicial acts of another as a matter of courtesy or respect. Each jurisdiction determines for itself the extent to which comity is applied. Generally, courts give effect to the laws and judicial decisions of another sovereignty unless to do so would be repugnant to its public policy or prejudicial to its interests or to the interest of its citizens. The following case involves a British judgment creditor (the party that won the judgment at trial) who sought comity in a U.S. court.

Somportex Limited v. Philadelphia Chewing Gum Corporation

453 F.2d 435
U.S. Court of Appeals, Third Circuit
December 20, 1971

Aldisert, Circuit Judge

Several interesting questions are presented in this appeal from the district court's order . . . granting summary judgment to enforce a default judgment entered by an English court. To resolve them, a complete recitation of the procedural history of this case is necessary.

This case has its genesis in a transaction between appellant, Philadelphia Chewing Gum Corporation, and Somportex Limited, a British corporation, which was to merchandise appellant's wares in Great Britain under the trade name "Tarzan Bubble Gum." . . . For reasons not relevant to our limited inquiry, the transaction never reached fruition.

Somportex filed an action against Philadelphia for breach of contract in the Queen's Bench Division of the High Court of England. Notice of the issuance of a Writ of Summons was served, in accordance with the rules and with the leave of the High Court, upon Philadelphia at its registered address in Havertown, Pennsylvania, on May 15, 1967. The extraterritorial service was based on the English version of long-arm statutes utilized by many American states. Philadelphia then consulted a firm of English solicitors, who, by letter of July 14, 1967, advised its Pennsylvania lawyers:

> "I have arranged with the Solicitors for Somportex Limited that they will let me have a copy of their Affidavit and exhibits to that Affidavit which supported their application to serve out of the Jurisdiction. Subject to the contents of the Affidavit, and any further information that can be provided by Philadelphia Chewing Gum Corporation after we have had the opportunity of seeing the Affidavit, it may be possible to make an application to the Court for an Order setting the Writ aside. But for such an

application to be successful we will have to show that on the facts the matter does not fall within the provision of . . . the long-arm statute. . . .

"In the meantime we will enter a conditional Appearance to the Writ on behalf of Philadelphia Chewing Gum Corporation in order to preserve the status quo."

On August 9, 1967, the English solicitors entered a conditional appearance to the Writ and filed a motion to set aside the Writ of Summons. At a hearing before a Master on November 13, 1967, the solicitors appeared and disclosed that Philadelphia had elected not to proceed with the summons or to contest the jurisdiction of the English court, but instead intended to obtain leave of court to withdraw appearance of counsel. The Master then dismissed Philadelphia's summons to set aside Plaintiff's Writ of Summons. Four days later, the solicitors sought to withdraw their appearance as counsel for Philadelphia, contending that it was a conditional appearance only. On November 28, 1967, after a Master granted the motion, Somportex appealed. The appeal was denied after hearing before a single judge, but the Court of Appeal, reversing the decision of the Master, held that the appearance was unconditional and that the submission to the jurisdiction by Philadelphia was, therefore, effective. But the court let stand "the original order which was made by the Master on November 13 dismissing the application to set aside. The Writ therefore will stand. On the other hand, if the American company would wish to appeal from the order of November 13, I see no reason why the time should not be extended, and they can argue that matter out at a later stage if they should so wish."

Thereafter, Philadelphia made a calculated decision: it decided to do nothing.

It neither asked for an extension of time nor attempted in any way to proceed with an appeal from the Master's order dismissing its application to set aside the Writ. Instead, it directed its English solicitors to withdraw from the case. There being no appeal, the Master's order became final.

Somportex then filed a Statement of Claim which was duly served in accordance with English Court rules. In addition, by separate letter, it informed Philadelphia of the significance and effect of the pleading, the procedural posture of the case, and its intended course of action.

Philadelphia persisted in its course of inaction; it failed to file a defense. Somportex obtained a default judgment against it in the Queen's Bench Division of the High Court of Justice in England for the sum of £39,562.10.10 (approximately $94,000). The award reflected some $45,000 for loss of profit, $46,000 for loss of good will, and $2500 for costs, including attorneys' fees.

Thereafter, Somportex filed a diversity action in the court below, seeking to enforce the foreign judgment, and attached to the complaint a certified transcript of the English proceeding. The district court . . . granted plaintiff's motion for summary judgment. . . .

Appellant presents a cluster of contentions supporting its major thesis that we should not extend hospitality to the English judgment. First, it contends, and we agree, that because our jurisdiction is based solely on diversity, "the law to be applied . . . is the law of the state," in this case, Pennsylvania law. . . . Pennsylvania distinguishes between judgments obtained in the courts of her sister states, which are entitled to full faith and credit, and those of foreign courts, which are subject to principles of comity. . . .

Comity is a recognition which one nation extends within its own territory to the legislative, executive, or judicial acts of another. It is not a rule of law, but one of practice, convenience, and expediency. Although more than mere courtesy and accommodation, comity does not achieve the force of an imperative or obligation. Rather, it is a nation's expression of understanding which demonstrates due regard both to international duty and convenience and to the rights of persons protected by its own laws. Comity should be withheld only when its acceptance would be contrary or prejudicial to the interest of the nation called upon to give it effect. . . .

"When an action is brought in a court of this country by a citizen of a foreign country against one of our own citizens . . . and the foreign judgment appears to have been rendered by a competent court, having jurisdiction of the cause and of the parties and upon due allegations and proofs, the opportunity to defend against them, and its proceedings are according to the course of a civilized jurisprudence, and are stated in a clear and formal record, the judgment is *prima facie* evidence, at least, of the truth of the matter adjudged; and it should be held conclusive upon the merits tried in the foreign court, unless some special ground is shown for impeaching the judgment, as by showing that it was affected by fraud or prejudice, or that by the principles of international law, and by the comity of our own country, it should not be given full credit and effect." . . .

Appellant's contention that the district court failed to make an independent examination of the factual and legal basis of the jurisdiction of the English Court at once argues too much and says too little. The reality is that the court did examine the legal basis of asserted jurisdiction and decided the issue adversely to appellant. . . .

Thus, we will not disturb the English court's Adjudication. That the English judgment was obtained by appellant's default instead of through an adversary proceeding does not dilute its efficacy. In the absence of fraud or collusion, a default judgment is as conclusive an adjudication between the parties as when rendered after answer and complete contest in the open courtroom. . . .

English law permits recovery, as compensatory damages in breach of contract, of items reflecting loss of good will and costs, including attorneys' fees. These two items formed substantial portions of the English judgment. Because they are not recoverable under Pennsylvania law, appellant would have the foreign judgment declared unenforceable because it constitutes an ". . . action on the foreign claim [which] could not have been maintained because [it was] contrary to the public policy of the forum." . . . We are satisfied with the district court's disposition of this argument:

> "The Court finds that . . . while Pennsylvania may not agree that these elements should be included in damages for breach of contract, the variance with Pennsylvania law is not such that the enforcement 'tends clearly to injure the public health, the public morals, the public confidence in the purity of the administration of the law, or to undermine that sense of security for individual rights, whether of personal liberty or of private property, which any citizen ought to feel, is against public policy.'" . . .

For the reasons heretofore rehearsed, we will not disturb the English Court's adjudication of jurisdiction; we have deemed as irrelevant the default nature of the judgment; we have concluded that the English compensatory damage items do not offend Pennsylvania public policy;

and [we] hold that the English procedure comports with our standards of due process. . . .

We are not persuaded that appellant met its burden of showing that the British "decree is so palpably tainted by fraud or prejudice as to outrage our sense of justice, or [that] the process of the foreign tribunal was invoked to achieve a result contrary to our laws of public policy or to circumvent our laws or public policy."

. . .

The judgment of the district court will be affirmed.

Case Questions

1. Is it likely that there will ever be a "full faith and credit" clause applying to all nations of the world?
2. What effect should be given to a foreign judgment when it comes up for recognition in the courts of another country? Should it make any difference if the foreign forum had applied the other country's laws? Suppose the foreign judgment was handed down under the foreign forum's own law in an effort to promote a racist policy of that government. Should that judgment be enforceable in the United States?
3. Can you think of any nations whose judicial decisions would not be accorded comity by any state in the United States under any circumstances?

Chapter Questions

1. Define the following terms:

comity
common law
conflict of laws
dictum
doctrine of substituted judgment
ex post facto
foreign law
forum
full faith and credit
guardian *ad litem*
holding
impeach

lex fori
lex loci contractus
lex loci delicti commissi
lex loci solutionis
police power
prima facie evidence
prospective effect
retroactive effect
significant relationship rule
sovereignty
stare decisis
supremacy clause

2. On May 20, Evans crashed into a train owned and operated by the Pennsylvania Railroad Co. at its crossing in Nassau, Sussex County. As a matter of law, the court found that the "Nassau crossing is extremely hazardous." On December 1 of that same year, Edna and George Wyatt

ran into a Pennsylvania Railroad train at the same crossing while George was driving them home from a party. Does the doctrine of *stare decisis* require that the court in *Wyatt* accept the conclusion announced in the *Evans* case?

Wyatt v. Pennsylvania Railroad Co., 158 F. Supp. 502 (D. Del. 1958)

3. Constable Dunn received a radio report that Arthur and Spencer Parker had left a beer garden in Cheatham County, Tennessee, without paying for their beer, a possible misdemeanor. When the Parkers' car passed Dunn's cruiser at high speed, Dunn switched on his siren and began chasing them. As they raced into Davidson County, Dunn fired his gun several times at the fleeing car. The bullets punctured the Parker car's tires, overturning the vehicle and killing Spencer Parker. According to Tennessee law, a police officer has no right to use deadly force to stop a fleeing misdemeanant, but the question arose whether the constable's surety was liable on his bond. The Tennessee Supreme Court has ruled several times that a surety was not liable to an injured party when the damage was done under mere color of office. In this situation, since the constable committed an act that he was not permitted to do (shooting at Parker's car), the surety would not be liable for the damages because the act was done under mere color of office. However, since the last ruling of the state supreme court on the subject, the Tennessee legislature passed a law holding sureties liable even when the act was done under mere color of office. The case is before an appellate court after being dismissed in trial court. Must the appellate court follow the state supreme court rulings as controlling precedents, or should it follow the recent statute?

State v. Dunn, 282 S.W.2d 203 (Tenn. 1943)

4. While en route to jury duty, Evans sustained a personal injury as a result of carelessness on the part of the county commissioners in permitting the concrete steps at the El Paso County Courthouse to deteriorate. The lower court dismissed the complaint under the doctrine of governmental immunity. On appeal, the Supreme Court of Colorado, in its opinion dated March 22, 1971, decided to abolish governmental immunity for that state. The courts stated, "Except as to the parties in this proceeding the ruling here shall be prospective only and shall be effective only as to causes of action arising after June 30, 1972." Why might a court make its decision effective as a precedent some 15 months after the date of its decision?

Evans v. Board of County Commissioners, 174 Colo. 97, 482 P.2d 968 (1971)

5. S. P. Whitney, a West Virginia contractor, was under contract with the state of West Virginia to construct State Route 2 near East Steubenville, just across the border from Steubenville, Ohio. Since the area was very hilly, Whitney used high explosives, such as dynamite and nitroglycerin, to clear the way for the road. One particularly large blast damaged a storeroom of the Steubenville Plate and Window Glass Company, located across the border in Ohio. The damage was extensive, and most of the

stored glass was broken and unusable. Keeping in mind that the blasting was done in West Virginia and the damage occurred in Ohio, which state's law will govern the action brought in a West Virginia court by Steubenville Plate Glass against Whitney?

Dallas v. Whitney, 118 W. Va. 106 (1936)

6. ABC, Inc., entered into a contract with XYZ, Inc., whereby ABC was to build a building for XYZ in Detroit, Michigan, at the price of $1 million. ABC was incorporated in Ohio with its principal place of business in Chicago, Illinois. XYZ is a Delaware corporation with its home office in New York. The contract was negotiated primarily in Chicago but became effective when it was signed at XYZ's home office. There was a dispute concerning the agreement, and XYZ sued ABC in a federal district court in Ohio. Which state law would govern the dispute if the court follows (1) the *lex fori* approach, (2) the *lex loci contractus* approach, or (3) the *lex loci solutionis* approach?

7. Mr. and Mrs. Barzda bought a motel located in Georgia from William Stagina. Thereafter, they sought a transfer to themselves of Stagina's franchise to operate as a Quality Courts Motel. The franchise agreement had been signed by Stagina in Florida and provided that Florida law should be applied to govern interpretation of the contract. When complications developed regarding the transfer of the franchise, the Barzdas sued Quality Courts Motel, Inc., to force transfer. Under Florida law, the Barzdas had no standing to sue, being merely incidental beneficiaries of the franchise agreement between Stagina and Quality Courts Motel, Inc. However, under Georgia law, the Barzdas had standing and could compel transfer of the franchise. Should the court in Georgia apply its own law or Florida law to settle the dispute between Quality Courts and the Barzdas?

Barzda v. Quality Courts Motel, Inc., 386 F.2d 417 (5th Cir. 1967)

8. Charles and Nora Overcash moved from Missouri to Kansas so that Charles could work for the Yellow Cab Company in Kansas. The contract for employment was signed in Kansas, but Overcash did much of the work in Missouri. Charles suffered injuries in the regular course of his employment, which led to his death. His widow employed counsel and filed a claim under Kansas Workmen's Compensation Law. A stipulation was entered into by his widow and Yellow Cab to pay the maximum amount available under Kansas law. Before the final hearing, Nora Overcash, after consulting a Missouri lawyer, decided to pursue her claim under the Missouri Workmen's Compensation Act, which allowed significantly higher awards. Nora Overcash appeared at the final Kansas hearing and through her Missouri counsel asked that the stipulation be withdrawn. This motion was denied and the award entered according to the Kansas stipulation. Meanwhile, Yellow Cab filed a suit in federal court asking the court to enjoin the Missouri action to avoid multiplicity of suits. Does full faith and credit require that the previous Kansas award be given

precedence over a Missouri Workmen's Compensation award, and that the Missouri proceedings be enjoined? Note that the Kansas award is the equivalent of a court settlement.

Yellow Cab Transit v. Overcash, 133 F.2d 228 (8th Cir. 1942)

9. Mr. and Mrs. Stewart had been married for five years and were residents of the state of Wyoming until their divorce two years ago. Mr. Stewart initiated divorce proceedings after the couple had become estranged and won a decree of absolute divorce from his wife. The divorce decree of the Wyoming court awarded custody of the children to their mother. After the divorce became final, Mrs. Stewart took the children and moved to Buffalo, New York. Mr. Stewart came to New York a month ago and obtained a writ of *habeas corpus*, asking for the custody of his children. In his petition, Mr. Stewart alleged that his former wife was incapable of properly raising the children. Consider the nature of the decree, the relief prayed for by Mr. Stewart, and the issues of public policy involved. Must the New York court accord full faith and credit to the Wyoming decree awarding custody of the children to the mother, or may it make an independent inquiry into the facts?

Ex parte Stewart, 137 N.Y. Supp. 202, 77 Misc. 524 (1912)

10. Thome, a resident of the state of Oregon, brought an action in superior court in California charging that Macken, while in the state of Oregon, "did alienate and destroy the affections of the plaintiff's wife, and did entice and abduct her from said plaintiff, thereby depriving him of the assistance, comfort, and society of his wife to his damage in the sum of $25,000." Macken defended on the ground that California law had abolished the cause of action for alienation of affections. Under the doctrine of comity, must the California court entertain an action abolished by statute in California, but permitted in Oregon where the cause of action originally arose?

Thome v. Macken, 136 P.2d 116 (Cal. 1943)

Notes

1. You might want to refresh your memory and review this material in conjunction with your current reading.
2. L. Fuller, *Anatomy of the Law* (New York: Praeger, 1968), p. 85.

V

Limitations in Seeking Relief

Public courts are one means to resolve legal disputes. (Some other alternatives are discussed in Chapter 14.) However, potential litigants are not free to bring any matter they want resolved before any court. This chapter describes various common law, constitutional, and statutory requirements that limit access to the public courts.

The court that entertains a suit must have jurisdiction (discussed in Chapter 2). In addition, there must be a genuine dispute between the parties, because courts generally do not give advice or answer theoretical questions. Courts may also refuse to decide disputes that are inappropriate for judicial determination, or that have not been brought within a specified time. Courts also will refuse to relitigate cases that have already been judicially resolved.

In certain circumstances, the public interest requires that an entity, person, or classification of people receive special protection from lawsuits. Such protection is called immunity. Historically, varying degrees of immunity are granted to governments, certain public officials, and charitable institutions. The law also regulates the extent to which family members can sue one another.

CASE OR CONTROVERSY

It is the duty of courts to adjudicate actual controversies between parties with adverse interests and conflicting claims. The adversary system assumes that the best way to find truth and do justice is to require disputing parties to use their full faculties against each other in court. Where the parties are of one interest and want the same relief, a judicial tribunal does not ordinarily entertain the action. A friendly, arranged suit without adverse interests is not permitted. *Collusion* exists when one party is financing and controlling both sides of the litigation. Courts refuse to hear collusive cases.

A court will decline to decide an abstract, theoretical, or *moot* proposition. A controversy appropriate for judicial determination exists only when there is a definite and real dispute. A controversy also must be *ripe* for judicial determination. Ripeness exists when the subject of a controversy or a government act has a direct adverse effect on the party making the challenge. A court does not decide a question that may arise in the future or set rules to guide litigants in their future conduct.

In addition, the person bringing a court action must have *standing*, that is, a legally sufficient personal interest in the dispute to be entitled to bring suit. The person suing must be adversely affected by the defendant's conduct. With a few notable exceptions (such as for the parents of minor children and guardians of incompetents), one person cannot sue to recover for another person who has been legally injured. Most persons who have sustained legal injuries refuse to bring suit. They make this decision because the persons who have caused them harm are their friends, relatives, neighbors, and acquaintances. The standing requirement ensures that the injured person is in control of the decision to sue, prevents undesired and unnecessary suits, and prevents people who have marginal or derivative interests from filing multiple suits.

To be within the federal judicial power, a matter must be a "case" or "controversy" as required by Article III, section 2, of the U.S. Constitution. The U.S. Supreme Court has always construed the *case or controversy* requirement as precluding the federal courts from advising the other branches of the government or anyone else. However, in some states where the constitution imposes this duty, the courts issue *advisory opinions* to government officials concerning certain matters of law. In this capacity, the court acts only as an adviser; its opinion does not have the effect of a judicial decision.

Many state constitutions follow the U.S. Constitution and do not provide for the rendering of advisory opinions. The executive and legislative branches may seek advice from the attorney general when the constitution does not provide for judicial advisory opinions or when the question is outside the scope of authorization. Generally, courts do not have the power to decide questions that do not affect the rights of the litigants before them.

In the following case, the Postal Workers Union brought suit against the U.S. Postal Service to stop the USPS from requiring job applicants to undergo drug testing.

American Postal Workers Union v. Frank

968 P.2d 1373

United States Court of Appeals, First Circuit

July 6, 1992

Frank M. Coffin, Senior Circuit Judge

The American Postal Workers Union seeks declaratory and injunctive relief requiring the United States Postal Service to stop mandatory drug testing of applicants for employment. Because we find that the Union lacks standing, we are constrained to dismiss this case without reaching the sensitive constitutional issue at the heart of the litigation.

I. Background

This lawsuit challenges, as violative of Fourth Amendment privacy rights, the Postal Service's policy of requiring job applicants to submit to urinalysis drug testing. The Union represents individuals who presently are postal service employees. Some of those employees underwent drug testing before they were hired, but this lawsuit does not request damages for the asserted violation of their rights. Rather, the Union seeks a declaration that the policy is unconstitutional, and an injunction barring future testing of applicants. The Union thus pursues remedies that will benefit only would-be Union members.

The district court, in a ruling from the bench, granted summary judgment for the Postal Service. Although the court referred to "a problem with standing," it nevertheless reached the merits to conclude that the balance of interests weighed in favor of the Postal Service's need to exclude drug-using individuals from employment. Accordingly, the court held that the Postal Service's pre-employment drug testing is a reasonable search under the Fourth Amendment. . . .

II. Discussion

A. Principles of Standing

Case or Controversy

Article III of the Constitution confines federal courts to deciding only actual cases and controversies. *Allen v. Wright*, 468 U.S. 737 (1984). This limitation on federal jurisdiction underlies the standing doctrine, which is designed to assure that issues are presented to the court "in the context of a specific live grievance." . . .

Standing is thus a threshold question in every federal case, requiring the court to determine "whether the plaintiff has 'alleged such a personal stake in the outcome of the controversy' as to warrant *his* invocation of federal-court jurisdiction and to justify exercise of the court's remedial powers on his behalf." . . .

The standing inquiry has three elements. A litigant must [1] "'show that he personally has suffered some actual or threatened injury as a result of the putatively illegal conduct of the defendant' and [2] that the injury 'fairly can be traced to the challenged action' and [3] 'is likely to be redressed by a favorable decision.'" . . .

The personal injury prong of the inquiry has triggered the most Supreme Court scrutiny and a substantial body of precedent devoted to defining the nature of the requisite harm. . . . The alleged injury, for example, must be real and immediate rather than abstract or conjectural. A mere interest in a situation—no matter how deeply felt, or how important the issue—will not substitute for actual injury. . . . The Court has noted that

> "the decision to seek review must be placed 'in the hands of those who have a direct stake in the outcome.' *Sierra Club v. Morton*, 405 U.S. 727. . . . (1972). It is not to be placed in the hands of 'concerned bystanders,' who will use it simply as a 'vehicle for the vindication of value interests.'" . . .

The less visited second and third components of the standing inquiry—"traceability" and "redressability"—denote two forms of causation. "[T]he former examines the causal connection between the assertedly unlawful conduct and the alleged injury, whereas the latter examines the causal connection between the alleged injury and the judicial relief requested." . . .

When a litigant has met all three requirements, it can fairly be assumed that a case or controversy has been established, and that "the particular plaintiff is entitled to an adjudication of the particular claims asserted." . . .

Associational Standing

The Union does not contend that it has suffered any "personal" injury from the drug testing. Instead, it invokes the doctrine of "associational," or "representational," standing, which permits organizations, in certain circumstances, to premise standing entirely upon injuries suffered by their members. . . .

This doctrine does not eliminate the constitutional requirement of a live case or controversy between the parties, but it recognizes that injury to an organization's members may satisfy Article III and allow the organization to litigate in federal court on their behalf. . . .

The test for associational standing is—like the basic standing inquiry—tripartite. The plaintiff association must show that (a) at least one of its members possesses standing to sue in his or her own right—i.e., that the member can satisfy the three requirements of injury, traceability *and redressability*; (b) the interests the suit seeks to vindicate are germane to its purpose; and (c) neither the claim asserted nor the relief requested requires the participation of individual members in the lawsuit. . . .

To establish its right to bring the instant action, the Union must demonstrate compliance with these prerequisites. As we discuss in Section B below, it cannot do so. Because the Union members are unable to meet the redressability prong of the basic standing inquiry, they lack standing. As a result, the Union is unable to fulfill the first condition for associational standing—that at least one member possess standing to sue as an individual. In light of this deficiency, we do not consider whether the Union could satisfy the other two prongs of the associational standing test.

B. Union Members' Standing

If the question at this juncture were simply whether any of the Union's members could allege harm from the disputed policy, we might well resolve the standing issue in its favor. Among the Union's present membership are individuals who submitted to the drug test. These members have a concrete claim of injury— that they were subjected to an unreasonable search in violation of the Fourth Amendment.

Supreme Court caselaw teaches, however, that while the past injury suffered by these members would give them standing to bring actions for damages, it is an insufficient predicate for equitable relief. In *Los Angeles v. Lyons*, 461 U.S. 95, (1983), the Court reaffirmed the principle that past exposure to harm will not, in and of itself, confer standing upon a litigant to obtain equitable relief "[a]bsent a sufficient likelihood that he will again be wronged in a similar way." . . .

The *Lyons* holding derives from the third prong of the standing inquiry, conditioning justiciability on whether the plaintiff's injury is likely to be redressed by the requested relief. It is based on the obvious proposition that a prospective remedy will provide no relief for an injury that is, and likely will remain, entirely in the past. . . .

Because the drug testing policy is applied only to job applicants, no Union member faces a realistic risk of future exposure to it. Consequently, the declaratory and injunctive relief sought by the

Union will not alleviate its members' injuries. Like Lyons, the Union members have live claims for damages. The presence of viable damages claims, however, does not establish a "present case or controversy regarding [equitable] relief." . . . For such relief, therefore, the Union's members, and thus the Union, lack standing. . . .

The Union argues that this case differs in a significant respect from *Lyons* and other cases in which plaintiffs sought equitable relief based on past injury. The focus in those cases, according to the Union, was on the unlikely recurrence of the challenged conduct. Here, however, because the Postal Service continues to perform pre-employment drug testing on a daily basis, there is "a very real and substantial conflict for which the issuance of declaratory relief would be particularly appropriate." . . .

That the Postal Service consistently imposes the drug test on applicants demonstrates that a live dispute exists, but it does not demonstrate that the Union has a direct stake in the dispute. The Union does not explain how its members—all of whom, by definition, are postal service employees, rather than applicants—are

hurt by the continuing use of the test on non-member job applicants. Nothing in the relevant caselaw suggests that guaranteed repetition of the injury to *someone* lessens the need for a particularized dispute between the plaintiff and defendant.

We recognize that the Union has a serious claim of constitutional magnitude. Even an important substantive issue cannot be brought to federal court, however, if a plaintiff fails to satisfy Article III's requirements. . . .

While the concept of standing defies precise definition or mechanical application . . . , the court made it quite clear in *Lyons* that the baseline requirements are unyielding. A plaintiff must demonstrate a concrete injury caused by the defendant and remediable by the requested relief to satisfy Article III. Measuring the facts of this case against those well-established foundational criteria requires us to conclude that the Union lacks standing.

Accordingly, the judgment of the district court granting summary judgment for defendants is vacated, and the cause is remanded with instructions to dismiss the complaint for lack of jurisdiction.

Case Questions

1. What does the court say is required for standing in this case?
2. What does the standing requirement seek to prevent?
3. Are you satisfied with the court's rationale for finding against the plaintiff?

MOOTNESS

Moot cases are outside the judicial power because there is no case or controversy. Mootness is an aspect of ripeness, in that there is no reason to try a case unless there has been some direct adverse effect on some party. Deciding when a case is moot is sometimes difficult. An actual controversy must not only exist at the date the action was filed, but it also must exist at the appellate stage. Courts recognize an exception to the mootness rule when the issue is capable of repetition. If a defendant is "free to return to his or her old ways," the public interest in determining the legality of the practices will prevent mootness. In the following case, the passage of time made a case "moot" in the eyes of the U.S. Supreme Court.

DeFunis v. Odegaard
416 U.S. 312
U.S. Supreme Court
April 23, 1974

Per Curiam

In 1971 the petitioner Marco DeFunis, Jr., applied for admission as a first-year student at the University of Washington Law School, a state-operated institution. The size of the incoming first-year class was to be limited to 150 persons, and the Law School received some 1600 applications for these 150 places. DeFunis was eventually notified that he had been denied admission. He thereupon commenced this suit in a Washington trial court, contending that the procedures and criteria employed by the Law School Admissions Committee invidiously discriminated against him on account of his race in violation of the equal protection clause of the Fourteenth Amendment to the United States Constitution.

DeFunis brought the suit on behalf of himself alone, and not as the representative of any class, against the various respondents, who are officers, faculty members, and members of the Board of Regents of the University of Washington. He asked the trial court to issue a mandatory injunction commanding the respondents to admit him as a member of the first-year class entering in September 1971, on the grounds that the Law School admissions policy had resulted in the unconstitutional denial of his application for admission.

The trial court agreed with his claim and granted the requested relief. DeFunis was, accordingly, admitted to the Law School and began his legal studies there in the fall of 1971. On appeal, the Washington Supreme Court reversed the judgment of the trial court and held that the Law School admissions policy did not violate the Constitution. By this time, DeFunis was in his second year at the Law School.

He then petitioned this Court for a writ of certiorari, and Mr. Justice Douglas, as Circuit Justice, stayed the judgment of the Washington Supreme Court pending the "final disposition of the case by this Court." By virtue of this stay, DeFunis has remained in law school, and was in the first term of his third and final year when this Court first considered his . . . petition in the fall of 1973. Because of our concern that DeFunis' third-year standing in the Law School might have rendered this case moot, we requested the parties to brief the question of mootness before we acted on the petition. In response, both sides contended that the case was not moot. The respondents indicated that, if the decision of the Washington Supreme Court were permitted to stand, the petitioner could complete the term for which he was then enrolled, but would have to apply to the faculty for permission to continue in the school before he could register for another term.

We granted the petition for certiorari on November 19, 1973. . . . The case was orally argued on February 26, 1974. . . .

The starting point for analysis is the familiar proposition that "federal courts are without power to decide questions that cannot affect the rights of litigants in the case before them." . . . The inability of the federal judiciary "to review moot cases derives from the requirement of Art. III of the Constitution under which the exercise of judicial power depends on the existence of a case or controversy." . . . Although as a matter of Washington state law, it appears that this case would be saved from mootness by "the great public interest in the continuing issues raised by this appeal," the fact remains that under Art. III, "[e]ven in cases arising in the state courts, the question of mootness is a federal one which a federal court must resolve before it assumes jurisdiction." . . .

The respondents have represented that, without regard to the ultimate resolution of the issues in this case, DeFunis will remain a student in the law school for the duration of any term in which he has already enrolled. Since he has now registered for his final term, it is evident that he will be given an opportunity to complete all academic and other requirements for graduation and, if he does so, he will receive his diploma regardless of any decision this Court might reach on the merits of this case. . . . The controversy between the parties has thus clearly ceased to be "definite and concrete" and no longer "touch[es] the legal relations of parties having adverse legal interests." . . .

There is a line of decisions in this Court standing for the proposition that the "voluntary cessation of allegedly illegal conduct does not deprive the tribunal of power to hear and determine the case, i.e., does not make the case moot." . . . These decisions and the doctrine they reflect would be quite relevant if the question of mootness here had arisen by reason of unilateral change in the *admissions procedures* of the Law School. For it was the admissions procedures that were the target of this litigation, and a voluntary cessation of the admissions practices complained of could make this case moot only if it could be said with assurance "that 'there is no reasonable expectation that the wrong will be repeated.'" . . . But mootness in the present case depends not at all upon a "voluntary cessation" of the admissions practices that were the subject of this litigation. It depends, instead, upon the simple fact that DeFunis is now in the final quarter of the final year of his course of study, and the settled and unchallenged policy of the Law School to permit him to complete the term for which he is now enrolled.

It might also be suggested that this case presents a question that is "capable of repetition" . . . and is thus amenable to federal adjudication even though it might otherwise be considered moot. But DeFunis will never again be required to run the gauntlet of the Law School's admission process, and so the question is certainly not "capable of repetition" so far as he is concerned. . . .

Because the petitioner will complete his law school studies at the end of the term for which he has now registered regardless of any decision this Court might reach on the merits of this litigation, we conclude that the Court cannot, consistently with the limitations of Art. III of the Constitution, consider the substantive constitutional issues tendered by the parties. Accordingly, the judgment of the Supreme Court of Washington is vacated, and the cause is remanded for such proceedings as by the Court may be deemed appropriate.

It is so ordered. . . .

Mr. Justice Brennan, with whom Mr. Justice Douglas, Mr. Justice White, and Mr. Justice Marshall concur, dissenting

I respectfully dissent. Many weeks of the school term remain, and petitioner may not receive his degree despite respondents' assurances that petitioner will be allowed to complete this term's schooling regardless of our decision. Any number of unexpected events—illness, economic necessity, even academic failure—might prevent his graduation at the end of the term. Were that misfortune to befall, and were petitioner required to register for yet another term, the prospect that he would again face the hurdle of the admissions policy is real, not fanciful; for respondents warn that "Mr. DeFunis would have to take some appropriate action to request continued admission for the remainder of his law school education, and *some discretionary action by the university on such request would have to be taken.*" . . . [P]etitioner might once again have to run the gauntlet of the University's allegedly unlawful admissions policy. The Court therefore proceeds on an erroneous premise in resting its mootness holding on a supposed inability to render any judgment that may affect one way or the other petitioner's completion of his law studies. For surely if we were to reverse the Washington Supreme Court, we could insure that, if for some reason petitioner did not graduate this spring, he would be entitled to re-enrollment at a later time on the same basis as others who have not faced the hurdle of the University's allegedly unlawful admissions policy.

In these circumstances, and because the University's position implies no concession that its admissions policy is unlawful, this controversy falls squarely within the Court's long line of decisions holding that the "[m]ere voluntary cessation of allegedly illegal conduct does not moot a case." . . . Since respondents' voluntary representation to this Court is only that they will permit petitioner to complete this term's studies, respondents have not borne the "heavy burden," . . . of demonstrating that there was not even a "mere possibility" that petitioner would once again be subject to the challenged admissions policy. On the contrary, respondents have positioned themselves so as to be "free to return to [their] old ways." . . .

Moreover, in endeavoring to dispose of this case as moot, the Court clearly disserves the public interest. The constitutional issues that are avoided today concern vast numbers of people, organizations, and colleges and universities, as evidenced by the filing of twenty-six *amicus curiae* briefs. Few constitutional questions in recent history have stirred as much debate, and they will not disappear. They must inevitably return to the federal courts and ultimately again to this Court. . . . Although the Court should, of course, avoid unnecessary decisions of constitutional questions, we should not transform principles of avoidance of constitutional decisions into devices for sidestepping resolution of difficult cases.

On what appears in this case, I would find that there is an extant controversy and decide the merits of the very important constitutional questions presented.

Case Questions   1. If the plaintiff had been in his second-to-last term of law school when the Supreme Court heard the case, would its decision have been different?

2. The dissenting justices feel that the majority disserved the public interest. Why? Do you agree?
3. In the first paragraph of the decision, the court notes that the University of Washington Law School is a state-operated institution. Why is this an important fact?
4. Did the U.S. Supreme Court decide the merits of this case?

POLITICAL QUESTIONS

The courts can also decline to decide cases that raise *political questions*. The federal Constitution allocates separate governmental power to the legislative, executive, and judicial branches. As members of the judicial branch of government, the courts exercise judicial powers. As the political departments, the executive and legislative branches are entrusted with certain functions, such as conducting foreign relations, making treaties, or submitting our country to the jurisdiction of international courts. Such issues fall outside the jurisdiction of the courts. Courts classify an issue as justiciable or as a nonjusticiable political question on a case-by-case basis.

In the following case, Americans formerly held hostage by Iran filed suit against the United States, claiming that provisions of the agreement President Carter negotiated with Iran infringed on their property rights. The hostages argued that the U.S. government had taken their property rights when it agreed to extinguish the hostages' claims against their Iranian captors. The U.S. Court of Appeals affirmed the U.S. Claims Court's application of the political questions doctrine.

Belk v. United States
858 F.2d 706
U.S. Court of Appeals, Federal Circuit
September 22, 1988

Friedman, Circuit Judge

This is an appeal from a judgment of the United States Claims Court granting summary judgment dismissing a complaint by former hostages held in the United States Embassy in Tehran, Iran. The appellants seek just compensation for the alleged taking by the United States of their property right to sue Iran for injuries sustained while held hostage—a right the United States extinguished in connection with obtaining the release of the hostages. The Claims Court dismissed the complaint on alternative grounds: (1) that the government's action did not constitute a taking, and (2) that the complaint would require the resolution of political questions, which the court could not do. . . .

I

The appellants are 15 United States citizens, 13 of whom were held hostage in the United States Embassy in Tehran from November 4, 1979 to January 20, 1981, and the wives of two of the hostages. The United States had attempted unsuccessfully to obtain the release of the hostages in various ways. . . . The hostages finally were released by agreements arranged through the government of Algeria.

The United States signed these agreements (commonly referred to as the Algiers Accords) on January 19, 1981. . . .

The relevant provision of the Algiers Accords prohibits United States nationals from prosecuting claims related to the seizure of the hostages, their detention, and injuries to them or their properties that arose out of events that occurred before the date of the Accords. . . . The day after the United States signed the Algiers Accords, the hostages were released.

Following the appellants' release, they filed the present suit against the United States in the Claims Court. The complaint alleged that the appellants had "valid and valuable causes of action against the Islamic Republic of Iran, its officials, agents, instruments, and employees" resulting from the mistreatment the appellants suffered while being held hostage; that before the Accords were executed, the appellants "were entitled to prosecute their valid and valuable causes of action and to collect upon their claims" in the "federal district courts of the United States" and "in Iran itself"; and that by executing the Accords the United States "barred plaintiffs from prosecuting any and all of their existing and potential causes of action against Iran in any court or forum anywhere in the world" and thereby "extinguished plaintiffs' valid causes of action."

According to the complaint, these causes of action "constituted valuable private property rights," which the United States has "taken for public use without just compensation." The complaint asserted that the appellants are entitled to recover from the United States just compensation "equivalent to the damages they could have recovered from Iran had defendant not extinguished their claims."

The United States moved for summary judgment. The Claims Court granted the motion, and dismissed the complaint. . . . The court held that the complaint raised a political question because "[t]his case involves a policy decision made by the President during a crisis situation." . . . The court noted that " '[a] judicial inquiry into whether the President could have extracted a more generous settlement from another country would seriously interfere with his ability to carry on diplomatic relations.' " . . . The court concluded that the President's extinguishment of the plaintiffs' claim could not ground a cause of action for a taking "because such an action is not susceptible to judicial review." . . .

III

On the undisputed facts, the Claims Court correctly held that the appellants have not stated a valid or judicially cognizable claim for a taking of private property for a public use, for which the United States is required to pay just compensation.

A

Assuming without deciding that the appellants' claims against Iran constituted "property" under the Fifth Amendment's takings clause, the extinguishment of those claims pursuant to the Algiers Accords did not constitute a taking of that property. . . . Although the Algiers Accords did not provide any alternative forum in which the hostages could assert their claims, that fact is not sufficient to establish a taking.

The President's action in implementing the Algiers Accords was primarily designed to benefit the hostages. It followed their imprisonment for 14 months and various unsuccessful attempts by the United States to obtain their release. The day after the Accords were signed, the hostages were released. The President's authority to extinguish the kind of claims against Iran that the appellants seek to assert is no more novel, done as it was "in return for" the hostages' freedom and perhaps their very lives. As the Claims Court pointed out in its ruling from the bench following argument in which it granted summary judgment for the government: "there's no doubt that if the question was put by the President in some hypothetical world that you want to be released from Iran as of today or would you want to go on indefinitely preserving your right to sue Iran at some late date, there wouldn't have been a millionth of a second pause on the part of the hostages or their spouses, as to which way to go on that.". . .

B

We also agree with the Claims Court's alternative holding that adjudication of the appellants' taking claim would involve the court in the resolution of a political question. The President is "the sole organ of the federal government in the field of international relations." . . . Issues involving foreign relations frequently present questions not meet for judicial determination. In *Baker v. Carr*, 369 U.S. 186, . . . the Court explained:

> "Prominent on the surface of any case held to involve a political question is found a textually demonstrable constitutional commitment of the issue to a coordinate political department; or a lack

of judicially discoverable and manageable standards for resolving it; or the impossibility of deciding without an initial policy determination of a kind clearly for nonjudicial discretion; or the impossibility of a court's undertaking independent resolution without expressing lack of the respect due coordinate branches of government; or an unusual need for unquestioning adherence to a political decision already made; or the potentiality of embarrassment from multifarious pronouncements by various departments on one question."

Most, if not all, of those concerns are present in this case. It involves a policy decision made by the President during a time of crisis. The appellants apparently contend that the President should not have entered into the Algiers Accords because he could have obtained better terms, and that the Accords themselves were illegal because the President was coerced into agreeing to them. The determination whether and upon what terms to settle the dispute with Iran over its holding of the hostages and obtain their release, necessarily was for the President to make in his foreign relations role. That determination was "of a kind clearly for nonjudicial discretion," and there are no "judicially discoverable and manageable standards" for reviewing such a Presidential decision. A judicial inquiry into whether the President could have extracted a more favorable settlement would seriously interfere with the President's ability to conduct foreign relations. . . .

C

Although the appellants underwent an agonizing experience, they have not stated a valid claim for a taking by the United States of their causes of action against Iran that, as they frame their case, is appropriate for judicial resolution. If there is to be any compensation of the appellants for the mistreatment and suffering they underwent during their captivity as hostages in Iran, it must be provided by one of the other "coordinate branches of government."

Conclusion

The judgment of the United States Claims Court granting summary judgment dismissing the complaint is
Affirmed.

Case Questions

1. What might have been the ramifications if the *Belk* court decided the merits of this case?
2. A cause of action (or a right to sue) is a property right under the due process clause of the Fifth Amendment. What are some other property rights?

THE ACT OF STATE DOCTRINE

The judicially created Act of State doctrine can be traced back to England in 1674. It provides that American courts should not determine the validity of public acts committed by a foreign sovereign within its own territory. The doctrine is grounded in pragmatism: it prevents our courts from making pronouncements about matters over which they have no power. Judicial rulings about such matters could significantly interfere with the conduct of foreign policy—a matter which the Constitution assigns to the political branches of government. The Constitution does not require the Act of State doctrine; it is based on the relationships among the three branches of the federal government.

Assume, for example, that a foreign dictator confiscates a warehouse containing merchandise belonging to an American corporation. The American corporation subsequently files suit in an American court to challenge the foreign nation's laws and procedures, alleging that the dictator did not have a valid right to confiscate the merchandise. The American court can apply the Act of State doctrine and refuse to make any pronouncements about the foreign nation's laws or procedures. The law presumes the public acts of a foreign sovereign within its own territory to be valid.

STATUTE OF LIMITATIONS

There is a time period, established by the legislature, within which an action must be brought upon claims or rights to be enforced. This law is known as the *statute of limitations* (see Figure 5–1). The statute of limitations compels the

	Contract				Negligence			Tort — Intentional Torts								
	Breach of Sales Contract	Breach of Warranty	Oral	Written	Personal Injury	Wrongful Death	Medical Malpractice	Assault and Battery	Fraud and Deceit	Libel	Slander	Trespass	Damage to Personal Property	Conversion	False Imprisonment	Malicious Prosecution
Alabama	4	4	6	6	1	2	2	6	2	1	1	6	1	6	6	1
Alaska	4	4	6	6	2	2	2	2	2	2	2	6	6	6	2	2
Arizona	4	4	3	6	2	2	2	2	3	1	1	2	2	2	1	1
Arkansas	4	4	3	5	3	3	2	1	5	3	1	3	3	3	1	5
California	4	4	2	4	1	1	3	1	3	1	1	3	3	3	1	1
Colorado	4	4	3	3	2	2	2	1	1	1	1	2	2	3	1	2
Connecticut	4	4	3	6	2	2	2	3	3	2	2	3	3	3	3	3
Delaware	4	4	3	3	2	2	2	2	3	2	2	3	2	3	2	2
District of Columbia	4	4	3	3	3	1	3	1	3	1	1	3	3	3	1	1
Florida	4	4	4	5	4	2	2	4	4	2	2	4	4	4	4	4
Georgia	4	4	4	6	2	2	2	2	4	1	1	4	4	4	2	2
Hawaii	4	4	6	6	2	2	2	2	6	2	2	2	2	6	6	6
Idaho	4	4	4	5	2	2	2	2	3	2	2	3	3	3	2	4
Illinois	4	4	5	10	2	2	2	2	5	1	1	5	5	5	2	2
Indiana	4	4	6	10	2	2	2	2	6	2	2	6	2	6	2	2
Iowa	5	5	5	10	2	2	2	2	5	2	2	5	5	5	2	2
Kansas	4	4	3	5	2	2	2	1	2	1	1	2	2	2	1	1
Kentucky	4	4	5	15	1	1	1	1	5	1	1	5	2	2	1	1
Louisiana	10	1	10	10	1	1	1	1	1	1	1	1	1	1	1	1
Maine	4	4	6	6	6	2	2	2	6	2	2	6	6	6	2	6
Maryland	4	4	3	3	3	3	3	1	3	1	1	3	3	3	3	3
Massachusetts	4	4	6	6	3	3	3	3	3	3	3	3	3	3	3	3
Michigan	4	4	6	6	3	3	2	2	6	1	1	3	3	3	2	2
Minnesota	4	4	6	6	6	3	2	2	6	2	2	6	6	6	2	2
Mississippi	6	6	3	6	6	2	2	1	6	1	1	6	6	6	1	1
Missouri	4	4	5	10	5	3	2	2	5	2	2	5	5	5	2	5
Montana	4	4	5	8	3	3	3	2	2	2	2	2	2	2	2	5
Nebraska	4	4	4	5	4	2	2	1	4	1	1	4	4	4	1	1
Nevada	4	4	4	6	2	2	2	2	3	2	2	3	3	3	2	2
New Hampshire	4	4	3	3	3	3	2	3	3	3	3	3	3	3	3	3
New Jersey	4	4	6	6	2	2	2	2	6	1	1	6	6	6	2	2
New Mexico	4	4	4	6	3	3	3	3	4	3	3	4	4	4	3	3
New York	4	4	6	6	3	2	2½	1	6	1	1	3	3	3	1	1

FIGURE 5–1   Statutes of Limitations for Civil Actions (in Years)

| | Contract | | | | Tort | | | | | | | | | | | |
| | | | | | Negligence | | | Intentional Torts | | | | | | | | |
	Breach of Sales Contract	Breach of Warranty	Oral	Written	Personal Injury	Wrongful Death	Medical Malpractice	Assault and Battery	Fraud and Deceit	Libel	Slander	Trespass	Damage to Personal Property	Conversion	False Imprisonment	Malicious Prosecution
North Carolina	4	4	3	3	3	2	3	1	3	1	1	3	3	3	1	3
North Dakota	4	4	6	6	6	2	2	2	6	2	2	6	6	6	2	6
Ohio	4	4	6	15	2	2	1	1	4	1	1	4	2	4	1	1
Oklahoma	5	5	3	5	2	2	2	1	2	1	1	2	2	2	1	1
Oregon	4	4	6	6	2	3	2	2	2	1	1	6	6	6	2	2
Pennsylvania	4	4	4	4	2	2	2	2	2	1	1	2	2	2	2	2
Rhode Island	4	4	10	10	3	2	3	10	10	10	1	10	10	10	3	10
South Carolina	6	6	6	6	6	6	3	2	6	2	2	6	6	6	2	6
South Dakota	4	4	6	6	3	3	2	2	6	2	2	6	6	6	2	6
Tennessee	4	4	6	6	1	1	1	1	3	1	½	3	3	3	1	1
Texas	4	4	2	4	2	2	2	2	2	1	1	2	2	2	2	1
Utah	4	4	4	6	4	2	2	1	3	1	1	3	3	3	1	1
Vermont	4	4	6	6	3	2	3	3	6	3	3	6	3	6	3	3
Virginia	4	4	3	5	2	2	2	2	1	1	1	5	5	5	2	1
Washington	4	4	3	6	3	3	3	2	3	2	2	3	3	3	2	3
West Virginia	4	4	5	10	2	2	2	2	2	1	1	2	2	2	1	1
Wisconsin	6	6	6	6	3	3	3	2	6	2	2	6	6	6	2	6
Wyoming	4	4	8	10	4	2	2	1	4	1	1	4	4	4	1	1

FIGURE 5–1 Statutes of Limitations for Civil Actions (in Years) *continued*

exercise of a right of action within a reasonable time, so that the opposing party has a fair opportunity to defend and will not be surprised by the assertion of a stale claim after evidence has been lost or destroyed. With the lapse of time, memories fade and witnesses may die or move. The prospects for impartial and comprehensive fact-finding diminish.

The statutory time period begins to run immediately on the accrual of the cause of action, that is, when the plaintiff's right to institute a suit arises. If the plaintiff brings the suit after the statutory period has run, the defendant may plead the statute of limitations as a defense. Although jurisdictions have differing definitions, a cause of action can be generally said to exist when the defendant breaches some legally recognized duty owed to the plaintiff and thereby causes some type of legally recognized injury to the plaintiff.

Generally, once the statute of limitations begins to run, it continues to run until the time period is exhausted. However, many statutes of limitation contain a "saving clause," listing conditions and events that "toll" or suspend the running of the statute. The occurrence of one of these conditions may also extend the limitations period for a prescribed period of time. In personal injury cases, for example, the statute may start to run from the date of the injury or from the date when the injury is discoverable, depending on the jurisdiction. Conditions that may serve to toll the running of the statute or extend the time period include infancy, insanity, imprisonment, court orders, war, and fraudulent concealment of a cause of action by a trustee or other fiduciary. The commencement of an action almost universally tolls the running of the statute of limitations. Thus, once an action is commenced on a claim within the statutory time period, it does not matter if judgment is ultimately rendered after the period of limitations has expired.

In the following case the interests of consumers were pitted against the economic welfare of an important industry (and a major regional employer) within the state. The state legislature used the statute of limitations and a 90-day notification requirement to further the economic interests of the state's ski industry at the expense of consumers.

This decision has utilitarian underpinnings, because the ski industry is critical to the economic welfare of the entire western part of the state. The legislature feared that the industry might fail without this protection.

Marybeth Atkins v. Jiminy Peak, Inc.
514 N.E.2d 850
Massachusetts Supreme Judicial Court
November 5, 1987

O'Connor, Justice

This case presents the question whether an action by an injured skier against a ski area operator is governed by the one-year limitation of actions provision of G.L.c. 143, § 71P, where the plaintiff's theories of recovery are negligence and breach of warranty, as well as breach of contract, in the renting of defective ski equipment.

In her original complaint, filed on December 5, 1984, the plaintiff alleged that on March 20, 1982, she sustained serious injuries while skiing at the defendant's ski resort, and that those injuries were caused by defective ski equipment she had rented from the rental facility on the premises. She further alleged that the defendant had not inspected or adjusted the equipment, and this failure amounted to negligence and breach of contract. In an amended complaint filed on February 14, 1986, the plaintiff added counts alleging that the defendant had breached warranties of merchantability and fitness for a particular purpose.

The defendant moved for summary judgment on the ground that the plaintiff's action was barred by the statute of limitations. A judge of the Superior Court granted the motion, and the plaintiff appealed. We transferred the case to this court on our own motion, and now affirm.

The statute we must interpret, G.L.c. 143, § 71P, imposes a one-year limitation on actions "against a ski area operator for injury to a skier." There is no contention that the defendant is not a "ski area operator," or that this action is not "for injury to a skier." The text of the statute, then, seems fully to support the decision of the Superior Court judge. The plaintiff argues, however, that the statute should be construed as governing only actions based on a defendant ski area operator's violation of those duties prescribed by G.L.c.143, § 71N. Section 71N requires that ski areas be maintained and operated in a reasonably safe manner, and prescribes methods by which skiers must be warned about the presence of equipment and vehicles on slopes and trails. The plaintiff thus contends that the statute does not bar her lawsuit because her action does not assert a violation of § 71N but rather was brought against the defendant solely in its capacity as a lessor of ski equipment. We do not interpret the statute in this limited way. Rather, we conclude that the one-year limitation in § 71P applies to all personal injury actions brought by skiers against ski area operators arising out of skiing injuries.

If the Legislature had intended that the one-year limitation apply only to actions alleging breach of a ski area operator's duties under § 71N, it easily could have employed language to that effect instead of the sweeping terms contained in the statute. Nothing in § 71P suggests that its reach is so limited.

The plaintiff contends that there is no sound basis for applying the one-year limitation to her action, because if she "had rented skis from an independently operated ski rental shop which leased space in the Defendant's base lodge, such an independent rental shop could not defend against the Plaintiff's action by relying upon Section 71P." Hence, she argues, it makes no sense to afford special protection to lessors of ski equipment who happen also to be ski operators. We

assume for purposes of this case that the plaintiff's assertion that § 71P would not apply to an independent ski rental shop is correct. But we cannot say that, in enacting § 71P, the Legislature could not reasonably have decided that ski area operators require more protection than do other sectors of the ski industry. "Personal injury claims by skiers . . . may be myriad in number, run a whole range of harm, and constitute a constant drain on the ski industry." . . . The Legislature appears to have concluded that, in view of this perceived threat to the economic stability of owners and operators of ski areas, not shared by those who simply rent ski equipment, a short period for the commencement of skiers' personal injury actions against ski operators, regardless of the fault alleged, is in the public interest. . . .

Because § 71P applies to the plaintiff's action, the Superior Court judge correctly concluded that the plaintiff's action was time barred.

Judgment affirmed.

Liacos, J. (dissenting, with whom Wilkins and Abrams, JJ., join)

I respectfully dissent. The court's interpretation of G.L.c. 143, § 71P (1986 ed.), is too broad. The general purpose of G.L.c. 143, § § 71H–71S (1986 ed.), is to set the terms of responsibility for ski area operators and skiers in a sport which has inherent risks of injury or even death. This legislative intent to protect ski area operators was designed, as the court indicates, not only to decrease the economic threat to the ski industry, but also to enhance the safety of skiers.

An examination of the whole statutory scheme reveals, however, that the Legislature did not intend to protect the ski area operators from claims for all harm which occurs in connection with skiing accidents, regardless of where the negligence that caused the harm takes place. Indeed, this court decided not long ago that G.L.c. 143, § 71P, on which it relies to rule adversely on this plaintiff's claim, did not apply to wrongful death actions arising from injuries on the ski slope. *Grass v. Catamount Dev. Corp.*, 390 Mass. 551 (1983) (O'Connor, J.). The court now ignores the wisdom of its own words in *Grass*, supra at 553: "Had the Legislature intended that G.L.c. 143, § 71P, should apply to claims for wrongful death as well as to claims for injuries not resulting in death, we believe it would have done so expressly. . . ." Here, however, the court extends the protective provisions of § 71P to ordinary commercial activity simply because it occurred at the base of a ski area and was conducted by the operator of the ski slope. No such intent can be perceived in this statute. To the contrary, the statute clearly manifests an intent to promote safety on ski slopes by regulating, through the creation of a recreational tramway board and otherwise, the operation of tramways, chair lifts, "J bars," "T bars," and the like (§ § 71H–71M). The statute defines the duties both of ski area operators and skiers (§ § 71K–71O).

In § 71O, liability of ski area operators for ski slope accidents is sharply limited: "A skier skiing down hill shall have the duty to avoid any collision with any other skier, person or object on the hill below him, and, except as otherwise provided in this chapter, the responsibility for collisions by any skier *with any other skier or person shall be solely that of the skier or person involved and not that of the operator,* and the responsibility for the collision with an obstruction, man-made or otherwise, shall be solely that of the skier and not that of the operator, provided that such obstruction is properly marked

pursuant to the regulations promulgated by the board" (emphasis supplied). Clearly, then, the statutory scheme is designed not only to enhance the safety of skiers, but also to limit the liability of a ski area operator for his negligent activities which cause injuries (but not deaths, see *Grass*, supra) on the ski slopes. It is in this context that the court ought to consider the additional protection of a ninety-day notice requirement, as well as the short statute of limitations of one year found in § 71P.

General Laws c. 143, § 71P, imposes a ninety-day notice requirement and a one-year statute of limitations on a party who brings suit against a ski area operator. The imposition in § 71P of the ninety-day notice requirement as a condition precedent to recovery confirms, I think, my view that this statute is designed only to protect the ski area operator as to claims arising from conditions on the ski slope. But there is an even stronger argument against the court's position—that is in the very language of the statute. A "[s]ki area operator" is defined in G.L.c. 143, § 71I(6), as "the owner or operator of a ski area." In the same subsection, a "[s]ki area" is defined as: "[A]ll of the slopes and trails under the control of the ski area operator, including cross-country ski areas, slopes and trails, and any recreational tramway in operation on any such slopes or trails administered or operated as a single enterprise *but shall not include base lodges, motor vehicle parking lots and other portions of ski areas used by skiers when not actually engaged in the sport of skiing*" (emphasis supplied).

The alleged negligence and breach of warranty that occurred in this case happened in the rental shop in the base lodge area. It was there that the defendant rented allegedly defective equipment to the plaintiff and failed to check and to adjust that equipment. The injury was not due to ungroomed snow or exposed rocks or any condition on the slopes or trails under the control of the ski area operator. Rather, the injury allegedly was the result of a transaction in the rental shop, not of a defect on the slope. The rental shop is an area excluded from the purview of G.L.c. 143, § 71P, and thus the ninety-day notice requirement and the one-year statute of limitations do not apply.

The Legislature intended to separate the many functions of a ski area operator so as to focus on the business of operating ski slopes and trails. The statute does not apply where the alleged negligent behavior occurs when the ski area operator is acting as a restauranteur, barkeeper, parking lot owner, souvenir vendor, or, as is the case here, rental agent. For this reason, I would reverse the judgment of the Superior Court.

Case Questions

1. Marybeth Atkins severely broke her leg while using skis and ski bindings rented from a shop at a ski resort. The shop was owned and operated by the owners of the resort. What argument did Atkins make to the court in an effort to avoid the one-year statute of limitations?
2. Why did the state legislature require a 90-day notice as well as a one-year statute of limitations of potential plaintiffs?
3. Do you agree with the dissenters, who feel that the negligent action that caused the harm occurred in the rental shop (an area not covered by the statute), or with the majority, who feel that the accident occurred on the slopes (an area covered by the statute)?

RES JUDICATA

Res judicata literally means that the matter has been already decided. A final decision by a competent court on a lawsuit's merits concludes the litigation of the parties and constitutes a bar (puts an end to) a new suit. When a plaintiff wins his or her lawsuit, the claims that he or she made (and could have made, but didn't) merge into the judgment and are extinguished. Thus no subsequent suit can be maintained against the same defendant based on the same claim. This is known as the principle of bar and merger. Once a claim has been judicially decided it is finally decided. The loser may not bring a new suit against the winner for the same claim in any court. The loser's remedy is to appeal the decision of the lower court to a higher court.

The *res judicata* doctrine reduces litigation and prevents harassment of or hardship on an individual who otherwise could be sued twice for the same cause of action. In addition, if the parties realize that they have only one chance to win, they will make their best effort.

For *res judicata* to apply, two conditions must be met. First, there must be an identity of parties. Identity means that parties to a successive lawsuit are the same as, or in privity with, the parties to the original suit. Privity exists where there is a relationship between two people that allows one not directly involved in the case to take the place of the one who is a party. Thus, if a person dies during litigation, the executor of the estate may take the deceased person's place in the lawsuit. Privity exists between the person who dies and the executor, so that as far as this litigation is concerned, they are the same person.

Second, there must be an identity of claims. In other words, for *res judicata* to bar the suit, the claim—or cause of action—in the first case must be the same the second time the litigation is attempted. For instance, if A sues B for breach of contract and loses, *res judicata* prohibits any further action on that same contract by A and B (except for appeal). A could, however, sue B for the breach of a different contract, because that would be a different cause of action.

The principle of bar and merger is illustrated in the following case. In this case, the plaintiff attempted to relitigate a claim that had been previously adjudicated in order to obtain additional compensatory damages.

Caporino v. Lacasse
511 A.2d 445
Supreme Judicial Court of Maine
June 20, 1986

Glassman, Justice

The plaintiff, Karen Caporino, appeals from the judgment of the Superior Court, York County, affirming the summary judgment rendered by the District Court, Biddeford, in favor of the defendant, Leo Lacasse. She contends on appeal that her instant suit is not barred by the judgment in her favor in a prior small claims proceeding. We hold that the District Court properly granted summary judgment for the defendant and affirm the judgment.

I

In February, 1984, Caporino filed a small claims action against Lacasse. After hearing, the court in April, 1984, ordered judgment for Caporino in the amount of $163.95. In July, 1984, Caporino filed a complaint in District Court, alleging that she had sustained bodily injuries caused by Lacasse's failure to inspect and maintain his premises. In a subsequently filed memorandum Caporino stated:

> "Plaintiff's small claims action and this pending action involve circumstances and events relating to a personal injury she suffered on premises owned by the Defendant, and subsequent damages suffered by Plaintiff."

Lacasse moved for summary judgment on the ground that the identical cause of action had been litigated in the small claims proceeding and that the instant suit was therefore barred by the doctrine of *res judicata*. The District Court rendered summary judgment in favor of Lacasse, and Caporino's successive appeals to the Superior Court and this court ensued.

II

Caporino contends on appeal that the statutory small claims proceeding . . . is not an appropriate forum for personal injury litigation and points to the unavailability of discovery procedures and the jurisdictional limitations on damages. . . . We note preliminarily that Caporino chose the small claims forum and thus by her choice secured its advantages and subjected herself to its limitations. . . .

More specifically, Caporino contends that under 14 M.R.S.A. § 7485 the doctrine of *res judicata* applies only to the amount recovered in the small claims proceeding and does not foreclose her from seeking subsequent and additional damages in an alternative forum. We disagree.

The instant case involves the branch of *res judicata* usually called bar and merger. The doctrine of bar and merger prohibits relitigation of a cause of action between the same parties or their privies, once a valid final judgment has been rendered in an earlier suit on the same cause of action. . . . The doctrine is justified by concerns for judicial economy, the stability of final judgments, and fairness to litigants. . . . In order to apply the doctrine of bar and merger, the court must determine that 1) the same parties or their privies are involved; 2) a valid final judgment was entered in the prior action; and 3) the matters presented for decision were or might have been litigated in the prior action. . . .

Once these determinations are made, the court must further determine whether the matters presented for decision in the instant suit *should* have been litigated in the prior action, that is, whether the instant suit presents the same cause of action. . . .

Section 7485 states the effect of a valid final judgment in a small claims proceeding. Our examination of this provision leads us to conclude that the doctrine of bar and merger applies to the instant case.

Pursuant to the first sentence of section 7485, facts found or issues adjudicated in a small claims proceeding may not be deemed found or adjudicated for the purpose of a proceeding based on "any other cause of action." This sentence does not prevent application of bar and merger to the instant case that represents the identical cause of action for the claimed negligence of Lacasse as did the prior small claims proceeding.

The second sentence provides that the small claims judgment "shall be res judicata as to the amount in controversy." By its very terms this sentence bars the instant suit. The same parties are involved as in the earlier action, and a valid final judgment was entered in the prior action. Caporino admits that the prior and the instant actions involve the same set of circumstances and events. Thus the facts of the two actions are "related in time, space, [and] origin" and "their treatment as a unit conforms to the parties' expectations." . . . The essential duty Lacasse is alleged to have breached is the same in each case: the duty to maintain his premises in a safe condition. . . . Thus the operative facts of the two actions constitute the same transaction and should be treated as an identical cause of action. . . . Caporino has sought monetary relief in each suit, and the relief she obtained in the prior suit became "res judicata as to the amount in controversy." We hold therefore that the District Court properly determined that the doctrine of *res judicata* barred Caporino's instant suit against Lacasse.

The entry is:

Judgment affirmed.

All concurring.

Case
Questions

1. What policy reasons exist for the doctrine of *res judicata*?
2. What factors must be shown for bar and merger to apply?
3. Assume that the parties in each of two lawsuits are identical. Assume further, that most of the factual issues in each suit are also identical, but that the causes of action are different. Should the second lawsuit be barred?

IMMUNITY FROM LEGAL ACTION

The law provides immunity from tort liability where to do so is thought to be in the best interest of the public. Immunities are an exception to the general rule that a remedy must be provided for every wrong and they are not favored by courts. They make the right of the individual to redress a private wrong subservient to what the law recognizes as a greater public good. Immunity does not mean that the conduct is not tortious in character, but only that for policy reasons the law denies liability resulting from the tort. Today, many courts are willing to abolish or limit immunities when it becomes apparent that the public is not actually deriving any benefit from their existence.

Sovereign Immunity

It is a basic principle of common law that no sovereign may be sued without its express consent. When a person sues the government, the person is actually suing the taxpayers and themselves, because any judgment is paid for out of public revenues. The payment of judgments would require the expenditure of funds raised to provide services to the public.

The doctrine of governmental immunity from liability originated in the English notion that "the king can do no wrong." (Ironically, although most U.S. courts have retained the doctrine, England has repudiated it.) Congress consented to be sued in contract cases in the 1887 Tucker Act. In 1946 the federal government passed the Federal Tort Claims Act in which the U.S. government waived its immunity from tort liability. It permitted suits against the federal government in federal courts for negligence or wrongful acts committed by its employees within the scope of their employment. Liability is based on the applicable local tort law. Thus, the government may be sued in its capacity as a landlord and as an invitor (a term explained in Chapter 9), as well as for negligent acts and omissions (concepts explained in Chapter 10). Immunity was not waived for all acts of federal employees, however. Acts within the discretionary function of a federal employee or acts of military and naval forces in time of war are examples of situations in which immunity has not been waived. In addition, members of the armed forces who have suffered a service-related injury due to governmental negligence are denied the right to sue. Permitting such suits has been thought to undermine military discipline. State governments also enjoy sovereign immunity.

Courts have made a distinction between governmental and *proprietary functions*. When a public entity is involved in a governmental function, it is generally immune from tort liability. When the government engages in activity that is usually carried out by private individuals or that is commercial in character, it is involved in a proprietary function, and the cloak of immunity is lost. For example, a state is not immune when it provides a service that a corporation may perform, such as providing electricity.

Courts currently favor limiting or abolishing sovereign immunity. Their rationale is the availability of liability insurance and the perceived inequity of denying relief to a deserving claimant. Many jurisdictions have replaced blanket sovereign immunity with tort claims acts that limit governmental liability. For example, they can reduce exposure to suit by restricting recoveries to the limits of insurance policies or by establishing ceilings on maximum recoveries (often ranging from $25,000 to $100,000). Many states continue to immunize discretionary functions and acts.

Immunity of Government Officials

As described in the previous section, executive, legislative, and judicial officers are afforded immunity when they act within the scope of their authority and in the discharge of their official duties. Immunity increases the likelihood that government officials will act impartially and fearlessly in carrying out their public duties. Thus, it is in the public interest to shield responsible government officers from harassment or ill-founded damage suits based on acts they committed in the exercise of their official responsibility. Prosecutors, for example, enjoy immunity when they decide for the public who should be criminally prosecuted. Public defenders are not immunized, however, because their clients are private citizens, and not the general public.

This immunity applies only when public officers are performing discretionary acts, in conjunction with official functions. Officials are not immune from liability for tortious conduct when they transcend their lawful authority and invade the constitutional rights of others. They are legally responsible for their personal torts.

Some argue that granting immunity to officials does not protect individual citizens from damage caused by oppressive or malicious conduct on the part of public officers. Government officials may in some jurisdictions lose their immunity if they act maliciously or for an improper purpose rather than honestly or in good faith.

High-level executive, legislative, and judicial officials with discretionary functions enjoy more immunity than lower-level officials. Judges, for example, are absolutely immune when they exercise judicial powers, regardless of their motives or good faith, whereas police officers enjoy a more limited privilege. The following case demonstrates, however, that judges can be sued for actions not involving the exercise of judicial functions.

Forrester v. White
108 S.Ct. 538
U.S. Supreme Court
January 12, 1988

Justice O'Connor delivered the opinion of the Court.

This case requires us to decide whether a state-court judge has absolute immunity from a suit for damages under 42 U.S.C. § 1983 for his decision to dismiss a subordinate court employee. The employee, who had been a probation officer, alleged that she was demoted and discharged on account of her sex, in violation of the Equal Protection Clause of the Fourteenth Amendment. We conclude that the judge's decisions were not judicial acts for which he should be held absolutely immune.

I

Respondent Howard Lee White served as Circuit Judge of the Seventh Judicial Circuit of the State of Illinois and Presiding Judge of the Circuit Court in Jersey County. Under Illinois law, Judge White had the authority to hire adult probation officers, who were removable in his discretion. . . . In addition, as designee of the Chief Judge of the Seventh Judicial Circuit, Judge White had the authority to appoint juvenile probation officers to serve at his pleasure. . . .

In April 1977, Judge White hired petitioner Cynthia A. Forrester as an adult and juvenile probation officer. Forrester prepared presentence reports for Judge White in adult offender cases, and recommendations for disposition and placement in juvenile cases. She also supervised persons on probation and recommended revocation when necessary. In July 1979, Judge White appointed Forrester as Project Supervisor of the Jersey County Juvenile Court Intake and Referral Services Project, a position that carried increased supervisory responsibilities. Judge White demoted Forrester to a nonsupervisory position in the summer of 1980. He discharged her on October 1, 1980.

Forrester filed this lawsuit in the United States District Court for the Southern District of Illinois in July 1982. . . . A jury found that Judge White had discriminated against Forrester on account of her sex, in violation of the Equal Protection Clause of the Fourteenth Amendment. The jury awarded her $81,818.80 in compensatory damages under § 1983. Forrester's other claims were dismissed in the course of the lawsuit.

After Judge White's motion for judgment notwithstanding the verdict was denied, he moved for a new trial. The District Court granted this motion, holding that the jury verdict was against the weight of the evidence. Judge White then moved for summary judgment on the ground that he was entitled to "judicial immunity" from a civil damages suit. This motion, too, was granted. Forrester appealed.

A divided panel of the Court of Appeals for the Seventh Circuit affirmed the grant of summary judgment. The majority reasoned that judges are immune for activities implicating the substance of their decisions in the cases before them, although they are not shielded "from the trials of life generally." . . . Some members of a judge's staff aid in the performance of adjudicative functions, and the threat of suits by such persons could make a judge reluctant to replace them even after losing confidence in their work. This could distort the judge's decision-making and thereby indirectly affect the rights of litigants. Here, Forrester performed functions that were "inextricably tied to discretionary decisions that have consistently been considered judicial acts." . . . Unless Judge White felt free to replace Forrester, the majority thought, the quality of his own decisions might decline. The Court of Appeals therefore held that Judge White was absolutely immune from Forrester's civil damages suit. . . .

II

Suits for monetary damages are meant to compensate the victims of wrongful actions and to discourage conduct that may result in liability. Special problems arise, however, when government officials are exposed to liability for damages. To the extent that the threat of liability encourages these officials to carry out their duties in a lawful and appropriate manner, and to pay their victims when they do not, it accomplishes exactly what it should. By its nature, however, the threat of liability can create perverse incentives that operate to *inhibit* officials in the proper performance of their duties. In many contexts, government officials are expected to make decisions that are impartial or imaginative, and that above all are informed by considerations other than the personal interests of the decision-maker. Because government officials are engaged by definition in governing, their decisions will often have adverse effects on other persons. When officials are threatened with personal liability for acts taken pursuant to their official duties, they may well be induced to act with an excess of caution or otherwise to skew their decisions in ways that result in less than full fidelity to the objective and independent criteria that ought to guide their conduct. In this way, exposing government officials to the same legal hazards faced by other citizens may

detract from the rule of law instead of contributing to it.

Such considerations have led to the creation of various forms of immunity from suit for certain government officials. Aware of the salutary effects that the threat of liability can have, however, as well as the undeniable tension between official immunities and the ideal of the rule of law, this Court has been cautious in recognizing claims that government officials should be free of the obligation to answer for their acts in court. Running through our cases, with fair consistency, is a "functional" approach to immunity questions other than those that have been decided by express constitutional or statutory enactment. Under that approach, we examine the nature of the functions with which a particular official or class of officials has been lawfully entrusted, and we seek to evaluate the effect that exposure to particular forms of liability would likely have on the appropriate exercise of those functions. Officials who seek exemption from personal liability have the burden of showing that such an exemption is justified by overriding considerations of public policy, and the Court has recognized a category of "qualified" immunity that avoids unnecessarily extending the scope of the traditional concept of absolute immunity. . . .

This Court has generally been quite sparing in its recognition of claims to absolute official immunity. . . .

III

As a class, judges have long enjoyed a comparatively sweeping form of immunity, though one not perfectly well-defined. Judicial immunity apparently originated, in medieval times, as a device for discouraging collateral attacks and thereby helping to establish appellate procedures as the standard system for correcting judicial error. . . . More recently, this Court found that judicial immunity was "the settled doctrine of the English courts for many centuries, and has never been denied, that we are aware of, in the courts of this country." . . .

The purposes served by judicial immunity from liability in damages have been variously described. In *Bradley v. Fisher*, . . . the Court emphasized that the nature of the adjudicative function requires a judge frequently to disappoint some of the most intense and ungovernable desires that people can have. If judges were personally liable for erroneous decisions, the resulting avalanche of suits, most of them frivolous but vexatious, would provide powerful incentives for judges to avoid rendering decisions likely to provoke such suits. . . . The resulting timidity would be hard to detect or control, and it would manifestly detract from independent and impartial adjudication. Nor are suits against judges the only available means through which litigants can protect themselves from the consequences of judicial error. Most judicial mistakes or wrongs are open to correction through ordinary mechanisms of review, which are largely free of the harmful side-effects inevitably associated with exposing judges to personal liability. . . .

This Court has never undertaken to articulate a precise and general definition of the class of acts entitled to immunity. The decided cases, however, suggest an intelligible distinction between judicial acts and the administrative, legislative, or executive functions that judges may on occasion be assigned by law to perform. . . .

IV

In the case before us, we think it clear that Judge White was acting in an admini-

strative capacity when he demoted and discharged Forrester. Those acts—like many others involved in supervising court employees and overseeing the efficient operation of a court—may have been quite important in providing the necessary conditions of a sound adjudicative system. The decisions at issue, however, were not themselves judicial or adjudicative. . . .

The majority below thought that the threat of vexatious lawsuits by disgruntled ex-employees could interfere with the quality of a judge's decisions:

> "The evil to be avoided is the following: A judge loses confidence in his probation officer, but hesitates to fire him because of the threat of litigation. He then retains the officer, in which case the parties appearing before the court are the victims, because the quality of the judge's decision-making will decline." . . .

There is considerable force in this analysis, but it in no way serves to distinguish judges from other public officials who hire and fire subordinates. Indeed, to the extent that a judge is less free than most executive branch officials to delegate decisionmaking authority to subordinates, there may be somewhat less reason to cloak judges with absolute immunity from such suits than there would be to protect such other officials. . . . Absolute immunity, however, is "strong medicine, justified only when the danger of [officials' being] deflect[ed from the effective performance of their duties] is very great." . . . (Posner, J., dissenting). The danger here is not great enough. Nor do we think it significant that, under Illinois law, only a judge can hire or fire probation officers. To conclude that, because a judge acts within the scope of his authority, such employment decisions are brought within the court's "jurisdiction," or converted into "judicial acts," would lift form above substance. . . .

We conclude that Judge White was not entitled to absolute immunity for his decisions to demote and discharge Forrester. In so holding, we do not decide whether Judge White is entitled to a new trial, or whether he may be able to claim a qualified immunity for the acts complained of in Forrester's suit. The judgment of the Court of Appeals is reversed and the case is remanded for further proceedings consistent with this opinion.

It is so ordered.

Case Questions

1. When are judges immune and when not immune from tort liability?
2. How effective would government officials be if they were subject to personal liability suit for official acts made within the scope of their authority?
3. What factors did the Supreme Court have to balance in reaching its decision in this case?

Charitable Immunity

The judicial doctrine that excuses charitable institutions from tort liability was created in England in 1846 and was recognized in this country in the 1870s. In the late 1800s and early 1900s, when many of the charitable immunity precedents were established, charitable institutions were often financially weak. The courts feared that they would not financially survive if people who accepted charity were permitted to sue in tort the institutions that provided them with care. They feared that donors would refuse to make donations if funds intended to be used to provide care were used to pay tort claims. Others argued that people who accepted charity had assumed the risk of negligent care from the charitable institution.

The most important argument against charitable immunity is that it is unjust to victims. Indigents, who are least able to assume the risk, are made to assume all the costs resulting from the charitable institution's negligence. In addition, the doctrine of charitable immunity helps to perpetuate the delivery of inferior care to the poor. It is argued that if the doctrine were abolished, such institutions would be forced to take greater precautions to avoid judgments and that the quality of care provided to indigents would significantly improve. In addition, injured victims would be able to obtain compensation for their injuries.

In the following case, a hospital invoked the charitable immunity defense, despite receiving less than one percent of its annual revenues in the form of charitable donations.

Thompson v. Mercy Hospital

483 A.2d 706

Supreme Judicial Court of Maine

October 29, 1984

Nichols, Justice

The narrow issue presented in this appeal is whether a hospital which derives less than one percent of its annual revenue from charitable sources is entitled in a tort action to the defense of charitable immunity. We conclude that it is not.

On February 22, 1982, the Plaintiff, Dorothy A. Thompson, entered a complaint against the Defendant, Mercy Hospital, in Superior Court, Cumberland County; the complaint alleged that the Plaintiff was mentally retarded and that the Defendant had negligently given her inadequate training and supervision in the operation of a pressing machine in its Portland facility. It was further alleged that the Plaintiff's left hand was drawn into the machine and sustained "partial permanent impairment." The Plaintiff sought damages for medical expenses and for pain and suffering.

The Defendant filed a motion to dismiss, invoking the defense of charitable immunity. Hearing on this motion was continued to allow the Plaintiff to conduct discovery limited to the issue of whether the Defendant was a charitable institution for purposes of immunity from tort liability. Following a hearing on the Plaintiff's motion to compel, it was determined that the Plaintiff could discover the sources of the Defendant's revenue by percentages but not by amounts. The Plaintiff drafted its interrogatories accordingly, and the Defendant answered them on December 6, 1982.

These answers revealed that unrestricted gifts and bequests comprised .6%, .5% and .1%, respectively, of the Defen-

dant's annual revenues in the fiscal years 1980, 1981, and 1982, while specific donations constituted .3%, .1% and .1%, respectively, of its revenues for these same years.

. . . After the hearing, the Superior Court granted the motion. . . .

On appeal, the Plaintiff argues that the Superior Court erred in applying the doctrine of charitable immunity to the Defendant. . . .

The doctrine of charitable immunity is a creation of our common law. Except for one significant restriction imposed by statute, its applicability in Maine is controlled entirely by the precedents of this Court. Under the leading cases, in order to qualify for charitable immunity, an institution must, *inter alia*, derive its funds "mainly from public and private charity." . . . This requirement is one of the "constituent elements" of charitable institutions for tort immunity purposes. . . . In its absence, charitable immunity is not available. . . .

We have recognized two rationales for this immunity: "(1) that funds donated for charitable purposes are held in trust to be used exclusively for those purposes, and (2) that to permit the invasion of these funds to satisfy tort claims would destroy the sources of charitable support upon which the enterprise depends." . . . Neither rationale justifies extending immunity to an organization which derives only a modicum of its financial support from charitable sources. The small fraction of the Defendant's revenues donated for charitable purposes need not be depleted to satisfy tort claims. Even where its insurance coverage may be insufficient to satisfy such claims fully, the Defendant can draw exclusively upon its noncharitable revenues. The second rationale is inapplicable because the Defendant's survival does not depend on its sources of charitable support.

The Defendant proposes an additional justification for charitable immunity: "that to permit tort actions against an uninsured nonprofit hospital would have a serious and dramatic effect upon the quality of that facility's health care." We have never approved this rationale, and we decline to do so now. It is based on unfounded supposition.

The defense of charitable immunity is unavailable to an institution in the Defendant's financial position. We decline to extend the scope of this much criticized doctrine to shield the Defendant in the tort case before us. . . .

The entry, therefore, must be:

Appeal sustained.

Judgment vacated.

Remanded for entry of a summary judgment for the Plaintiff against the Defendant on the defense of charitable immunity and further proceedings consistent with the opinion herein.

All concurring.

Case Questions

1. What does it mean when the court states, "The doctrine of charitable immunity is a creation of our common law," and why is this fact significant?
2. What problem arises where immunity is granted to a hospital providing critical medical care on a nonprofit basis?
3. Did the Supreme Judicial Court of Maine find the defendant guilty of negligence?

Immunity Among Family Members

American courts have traditionally recognized two types of immunities among family members. *Interspousal immunity* prevented suits in tort between husbands and wives, and *parental immunity* severely limited the types of suits children could bring against their parents.

Traditionally, husbands and wives have been immune from liability for torts committed against their spouses. It was argued that personal tort actions between husband and wife would disrupt the peace and harmony of the home. In old common law doctrine, husband and wife were considered as one person. Today, of course, they are considered to be separate legal entities. The courts have developed exceptions to the common law immunity, and many states have done away with it entirely.

Parental immunity was created by U.S. courts in 1891. Many courts thought it in society's interest to prohibit unemancipated minor children from maintaining actions for negligence or intentional torts against their parents. At common law, children remained minors until they reached the age of twenty-one. Today, legislation has reduced this age to eighteen. A child is unemancipated until the parents surrender the right of care, custody, and earnings of such child, and renounce their parental duties. Many courts believed that subjecting the parent to suit by the child might interfere with domestic harmony, deplete family funds at the expense of the other family members, encourage fraud or collusion, and interfere with the discipline and control of children. However, unemancipated minor children have always been able to enforce contracts or property rights against their parents. The parental immunity doctrine has been significantly eroded in the United States.

The following case demonstrates the reluctance of courts to immunize parental conduct where there is no necessity for the immunity. Here, the court created an exception to the doctrine of parental immunity so that children can sue their parents for sexual abuse.

Hurst v. Capitell
539 So.2d 264
Supreme Court of Alabama
January 15, 1989

Per Curiam

Melissa Hurst, a minor, through her grandmother, sued her stepfather, Alfred Capitell, for damages based upon claims of sexual abuse. She also sued her natural mother, Mary Jane Capitell, claiming damages based upon her alleged aiding and abetting in Mr. Capitell's sexual abuse and based upon Mrs. Capitell's alleged willful and wanton conduct and negligent performance of her duties as a mother, all of which allegedly allowed the abuse to occur. The trial court dismissed the action as to Mrs. Capitell and granted summary judgment in favor of Mr. Capitell, based upon the parental immunity doctrine because of his *in loco parentis* status. Melissa appeals from those rulings and asks us to reconsider the philosophy supporting the parental immunity doctrine and to abolish it.

The parental immunity doctrine had its genesis in the United States in *Hewellette v. George*, 68 Miss. 703, 9 So. 885 (1891), in which a minor daughter was precluded from suing her deceased mother's estate for damages resulting from mental suffering and injury to her character incurred during her confinement in an asylum for 11 days caused by her mother. The court gave this reason for its holding:

> "The peace of society, and of the families composing society, and a sound public policy, designed to subserve the repose of families and the best interests of society, forbid to the minor child a right to appear in court in the assertion of a claim to civil redress for personal injuries suffered at the hands of the parent. The state, through its criminal laws, will give the minor child protection from parental violence and wrongdoing, and this is all the child can be heard to demand."

The parental immunity doctrine was not based upon English common law, statutes, or previous cases; rather, it was judicially created by the Mississippi Supreme Court. In fact, even the *Hewellette* opinion recognized the limitation on the application of parental immunity to those cases involving unemancipated children:

> "If . . . the relation of parent and child had been finally dissolved, insofar as that relationship imposed the duty upon the parent to protect and care for and control, and the child to aid and comfort

and obey, *then it may be the child could successfully maintain an action against the parent for personal injuries.* But so long as the parent is under obligation to care for, guide, and control, and the child is under reciprocal obligation to aid and comfort and obey, no such action as this can be maintained."

The first Alabama case addressing the issue of parental immunity, . . . quoted from a New Hampshire case that states a similar reason for the rule: . . .

"the 'disability of a child to sue the parent for an injury negligently inflicted by the latter upon the former while a minor *is not absolute, but is imposed for the protection of family control and harmony, and exists only where the suit, or the prospect of a suit, might disturb the family relations.'"* . . .

Because the doctrine was judicially created, it is not exclusively a legislative issue and it may be judicially qualified. Since our decision . . . to defer to the Legislature on this issue, the Legislature has declined to act in regard to the doctrine, while the incidents of sexual abuse involving children have continued to occur. To leave children who are victims of such wrongful, intentional, heinous acts without a right to redress those wrongs in a civil action is unconscionable, especially where the harm to the family fabric has already occurred through that abuse. Because we see no reason to adhere to the doctrine of parental immunity when the purpose for that immunity is no longer served, as in Melissa's case, we are today creating an exception to the doctrine, limited to sexual abuse cases only.

In creating this exception for sexual abuse cases, we believe it is unnecessary to spell out a separate body of procedural and substantive rules to govern such cases. Traditional rules of tort law relating to intentional infliction of personal injury are generally sufficient for the governance of such claims and the defenses asserted thereto. . . .

In creating this exception to the parental immunity doctrine, we make no distinction between natural or adoptive parents or stepparents; the plethora of such cases as Melissa's indicates that sexual abuse is not a respecter of parental status. Thus, civil suits by children against parents for sexual abuse are not confined to a particular category of "parent." Therefore, the trial court's dismissal in favor of Mary Jane Capitell and its summary judgment for Alfred Capitell are both reversed and the case is remanded for trial.

Reversed and remanded.

Case Questions

1. The court in *Hewellette v. George*, cited in the *Capitell* opinion, explained why children should not be permitted to maintain civil lawsuits against their parents. Do you think this philosophy (which was developed in 1891) should still guide our courts today? Why?
2. Why did the court feel it could create this exception?
3. What did Melissa Hurst win?

Immunity Through Contract

In addition to the immunities imposed by law, parties can create their own immunities by agreeing not to sue. Because policy favors freedom of contract, the agreement may be enforced in a court of law. However, courts are often reluctant to do so. An immunity provision in a contract is construed against the party asserting the contract and is held invalid if the contract is against public policy or is a result of unfair negotiations. Factors that the court considers in determining whether to enforce the agreement are the subject matter involved, the clause itself, the relation of the parties, and the relative bargaining power of the parties.

A basic tenet of freedom of contract is that both parties are free to negotiate the terms of the contract. As a result, the contract should reflect a real and voluntary meeting of the minds. Therefore the equality of bargaining power is an important consideration for courts in determining unfair negotiations. Different courts may accord different degrees of importance to such elements as superior bargaining power, a lack of meaningful choice by one party, take-it-or-leave-it propositions, or exploitation by one party of another's known weaknesses.

The trial court in the following case enforced a bicycle rental agreement that contained an exculpatory clause. The plaintiff signed the agreement without carefully reading its terms. The defendant, who allegedly rented a bicycle with defective brakes to the plaintiff, was granted summary judgment.

Gimpel v. Host Enterprises, Inc.

640 F.Supp. 972

U.S. District Court, Eastern District of Pa.

July 24, 1986

Memorandum and Order

Troutman, Senior District Judge

On August 25, 1985, plaintiff Reuben Gimpel was injured when he fell from a bicycle rented at the Host Enterprises, Inc., resort in Lancaster, Pennsylvania. Gimpel was allegedly unable to stop the bicycle because of a malfunction of its brakes due to Host's failure to properly maintain and inspect it.

Defendant Host has moved for summary judgment, contending that the rental agreement which Gimpel signed contains an exculpatory clause releasing Host from any liability arising from the rental and use of the bicycle. . . .

Turning to the merits of the motion for summary judgment, we look first to the law of Pennsylvania to determine the effect of exculpatory clauses in general before examining the clause at issue here.

In *Employers Liability Assurance Corp., Ltd. v. Greenville Business Men's Association,* . . . 224 A.2d 620 (1966), the Pennsylvania Supreme Court set forth the conditions under which such clauses are valid and enforceable:

"Generally speaking, an exculpatory clause is valid if: (a) 'it does not contravene any policy of the law, that is, if it is not a matter of interest to the public or State; . . .' (b) 'the contract is between persons relating entirely to their own private affairs'; . . . (c) 'each party is a free bargaining agent' and the clause is not in effect 'a mere contract of adhesion, whereby [one party] simply adheres to a document which he is powerless to alter having no alternative other than to reject the transaction entirely.' . . .

"Assuming, *arguendo*, that the instant exculpatory clause satisfies all three conditions and is valid, our case law requires that, even if valid, an exculpatory clause must meet certain standards [to be enforceable]. . . .

"Such standards are: (1) contracts providing for immunity from liability for negligence must be construed strictly since they are not favorites of the law; . . . (2) such contracts 'must spell out the intentions of the parties with the greatest of particularity'; . . . and show the intent to release from liability 'beyond doubt by express stipulation' and '[n]o inference from words of general import can establish it'; . . . (3) such contracts must be construed with every intendment against the party who seeks the immunity from liability; . . . (4) the burden to establish immunity from liability is upon the party who asserts such immunity." . . .

As noted, the exculpatory clause at issue here was contained in the rental agreement for the bicycle, called the "Ride Charge Agreement," and reads as follows:

"User agrees to return said item in the same condition as when received, ordinary wear and tear excepted. *User agrees to indemnify and hold Host free and harmless from all injuries to person or persons, including death, damages to property, loss of time, and/or any and all other loss or damages, whether caused or occasioned by the negligence of Host, its employees or servants, or any other person whatsoever, arising or flowing from the use, operation or rental of the said item by User.* User agrees to pay or reimburse Host for all charges incidental to all breakages, shortages, damages, or losses other than such ordinary wear to said item caused by User."

In the case of *Zimmer v. Mitchell and Ness*, . . . 385 A.2d 437 (1978), the court considered and found valid and enforceable a very similar exculpatory clause. There, as here, the plaintiff was injured when sports equipment which he had rented at a resort allegedly malfunctioned.

Despite Gimpel's efforts to distinguish *Zimmer* on the basis of the nature of the resort, we are not persuaded that the Superior Court was responding to a need for heightened protection for ski resorts as compared to other kinds of resorts when it upheld the exculpatory clause at issue in that case. Rather, we believe that guests at all types of resorts are in essentially the same position when they seek to rent equipment. Thus, we conclude, as did the Pennsylvania Superior Court, that the contract at issue here, which concerns a preprinted rental agreement containing the exculpatory clause, contravenes no policy of the law, was between private parties and that each party was a free bargaining agent. Consequently, the clause is valid.

Next, we consider whether the clause expressly provides for Host's immunity from liability and whether Host has borne its burden of proof in the matter. It is clear that the language of the clause is both detailed and unequivocal in releasing Host from liability for negligence in connection with the rental of the bicycle. Moreover, Host has produced the "Ride Charge Agreement" which Gimpel identified at his deposition as the agreement he signed before he obtained the bicycle. . . . Therefore, we conclude that the exculpatory clause is enforceable against the plaintiff. . . .

We find no merit in Gimpel's argument that he "couldn't" read the contract before he signed it. Although he did not have his reading glasses with him when he arrived at the rental office, he could have requested that either the friend who accompanied him or Host's employee read the agreement to him before he signed it. Having already concluded that he was a free bargaining agent, we can find no basis for Gimpel's argument that Host's employee was obliged to call his attention to the exculpatory clause and its implications.

In summary, we conclude that the exculpatory clause at issue here meets the conditions set forth by the Pennsylvania Supreme Court for both validity and enforceability. Moreover, we reject plaintiff's attempt to engraft additional conditions onto the plain requirements of Pennsylvania law. For the foregoing reasons, we will grant Host's motion for summary judgment.

Case Questions

1. What three conditions are necessary for exculpatory clauses to be valid under Pennsylvania law?
2. What conditions are necessary for valid exculpatory clauses to be enforceable?

Chapter Questions

1. Define the following terms:

Act of State doctrine
advisory opinion
cases and controversies
collusion
insurance
moot
political question
property right

privity
public policy
res judicata
small claims action
sovereign immunity
Speech or Debate Clause
statute of limitations
standing

2. Vanderbuilt, owner of the Benign Manor Apartments, was dismayed by the building commissioner's decision to place her housing complex into a lower rent bracket under the city's rent control ordinance. The older tenants were worried that units might be rented to persons of lower economic and social status, and Vanderbuilt was afraid that she might lack funds. Darrow, Vanderbuilt's attorney, assured her that the rent control ordinance was patently unconstitutional. After considering Darrow's advice, Vanderbuilt decided not to lower the rent and to finance a lawsuit by Smith, an elderly tenant, against herself as landlord. Smith's suit would ask that the rent be lowered and Vanderbuilt could defend on the ground

that the rent control ordinance was unconstitutional. Does this lawsuit meet the case-or-controversy requirement? Why?

United States v. Johnson, 319 U.S. 302 (1943)

3. After conducting lengthy hearings, the commissioner of the Food and Drug Administration (FDA) published a regulation in the *Federal Register*, requiring drug manufacturers to label each of their products with its generic name every time the proprietary or trade name is used, including in the drug's advertising. The Pharmaceutical Manufacturers Association fears that profits on drug sales will plunge because the regulation makes consumers aware that certain brand name drugs can be obtained at a significant savings under their generic names. Although the regulation does not become enforceable for 90 days, the PMA has filed an action seeking (1) a declaratory judgment that the regulation is beyond the powers of the commissioner and (2) an injunction against enforcement of the regulation. Consider whether the case poses concrete issues sufficient to satisfy the case-or-controversy requirements. For purposes of judicial review, is the case "green," "ripe," or "rotten"? Would your answer be different if the PMA sought judicial review after the regulation becomes enforceable?

Abbott Laboratories v. Gardner, 378 U.S. 136 (1967)

4. According to a collective bargaining agreement between the Miami Longshoremen's Union and Bilgeway Fisheries, Inc., the longshoremen agreed to spend June and July of the next two summers working at the Bilgeway cannery on Grand Bahama Island. About half the union's members were native Bahamians living in Miami as resident aliens and hoping to become naturalized citizens. In February, the director of immigration informed the union that the Immigration Act provided that any alien seeking to enter the United States from the Bahamas would be treated as an alien entering the United States for the first time. The union and its alien members sued the director of immigration to enjoin him from interpreting the law so as to include the resident Bahamian longshoremen, claiming that, if so construed, the law is unconstitutional. Is this case appropriate for adjudication as a "case or controversy"?

International Longshoremen's Union v. Boyd, 347 U.S. 222 (1954)

5. On February 1, 1974, John Smith bought a car for $1,000. He paid $200 down and signed a promissory note for $800, due in one year. Assume that the note was never paid and the applicable statute of limitations is five years. The plaintiff could wait until what date to bring a civil suit for nonpayment of the note?

6. Armco Recreational Products, Inc., allegedly discriminated against Ernest McKinney on October 6, 1972. Ernest was 19 years old at the time. On July 1, 1973, the age of majority was changed from 21 to 18. McKinney turned 21 on May 5, 1974. McKinney filed a claim under the Civil Rights Act on February 18, 1976. There is a two-year statute of limitations on the Civil

Rights Act. Will the court hear McKinney's claim, or will it be barred by the statute of limitations?

McKinney v. Armco Recreational Products, Inc., 419 F.Supp. 464 (1976)

7. Zweily insured his car with Nationwide Insurance Company for $100 deductible property damage. His car collided with a truck driven by Steigerwalt. The damage to Zweily's car was extensive. Pursuant to a subrogation agreement in the policy, Nationwide paid Zweily $2,105 for damage to his car, and became subrogated for such amount to Zweily's claim against Steigerwalt. Zweily sued Steigerwalt for personal injuries and the $100 deductible portion of his property damage, alleging that Steigerwalt was negligent in driving his truck. Later, Nationwide also sued Steigerwalt for the $2,105 it paid to Zweily. Although Steigerwalt was aware of the two cases against him, he made no motion to join the claims or even to suggest they be joined. In the Zweily case, the jury returned a verdict for defendant, thus finding no negligence on Steigerwalt's part. In Nationwide's action against him, Steigerwalt asserted that the issue of his negligence had been decided in the previous action and that Nationwide, being in privity with Zweily, was barred from trying that issue again. What is your answer to this question? Refer back to the *Whitehead* case, 254 N.E.2d 10.

8. The S.S. *Santo Domingo* was seized by rebels while in port in the city of Santo Domingo in the Dominican Republic. The rebels directed small arms and automatic weapon fire from the ship on an element of the U.S. Army, which had occupied parts of the city to protect U.S. nationals. The U.S. Army returned the fire and sank the ship. The owner of the ship brought an action against the United States, claiming that the sinking of the ship was taking of private property for public use without just compensation. Should the owner of the ship be entitled to compensation from the United States?

American Manufacturers Mutual Insurance Co. v. United States, 453 F.2d 1380, 197 Ct. Cl. 99 (1972)

9. Judge Stump of a circuit court in Indiana, a court of general jurisdiction, approved a mother's petition to have her "somewhat retarded" 15-year-old daughter sterilized. The judge approved the mother's petition the same day, without a hearing and without notice to the daughter or appointment of a guardian *ad litem*. The operation was performed on Linda Sparkman, but she was told that she was having her appendix removed. A few years later, after Sparkman married and discovered that she had been sterilized, she and her husband brought suit against Judge Stump. Should Judge Stump be immune under the circumstances?

Stump v. Sparkman, 435 U.S. 349 (1978)

10. Peter Constantino was a public defender assigned to defend Mary Spring. Prior to Mary's trial, Peter told the judge he thought Mary was crazy. Bail was set and Mary was placed in a mental institution. Peter failed to tell

Mary how she could arrange bail. Claiming that her prolonged stay in the mental institution was caused by Peter's negligence, Mary sued Peter for malpractice. Peter claims that his position as an officer of the court gives him the defense of judicial immunity. Who wins? Why?

Spring v. Constantino, 362 A.2d 871 (1975)

11. St. Joseph's, a large church maintaining a grade school and involved in much community work, conducted bingo games every Friday night to raise funds for the school and for other projects. The games became very popular and attendance was open to the public. Blankenship, not a church member, who enjoyed playing bingo, walked into the church basement, paid $1 admission, and received two bingo cards. As she sat down on a metal chair, the chair collapsed and Blankenship fell to the floor, seriously injuring her spine. She is suing the church for personal injuries. Keeping in mind the fact that the church is a charitable institution and that all the proceeds of the bingo games go to charity, will the doctrine of charitable immunity prevent Blankenship's recovery?

Blankenship v. Alter, 171 Ohio St. 65 (1960)

12. Ella O'Callaghan, a tenant in an apartment building, was injured when she fell while crossing the paved courtyard on her way from the garage to her apartment. She instituted an action to recover for her injuries, alleging that they were caused by defective pavement in the courtyard. Before the case was tried, O'Callaghan died and her administrator was substituted as plaintiff. The jury returned a verdict in the sum of $14,000. The defendant landlord appealed, contending that the action should have been barred by virtue of an exculpatory clause in the lease. The administrator contended that the exculpatory clause should be invalidated as against public policy, and pointed to the fact that there was a housing shortage, which caused a disparity of bargaining power. Write an opinion for the appellate court's holding.

O'Callaghan v. Waller & Beckwith Realty Co., 15 Ill. 2d 436, 155 N.E.2d 545 (1959)

VI

Judicial Remedies

Once a person has established a substantive right through judicial procedures, the court will award relief. Judicial relief can assume many different forms, called remedies. The most common remedies include (1) awarding money damages (compensatory and punitive damages), (2) requiring someone to do or refrain from doing something (injunctive relief), (3) restoring a person to a previous position to prevent unjust enrichment (restitution), (4) judicially determining the parties' rights (declaratory judgment), and (5) judicially rewriting a written instrument to reflect the real agreement of the parties (reformation). In U.S. jurisprudence, the remedies are classified either as common law remedies or as equitable remedies. Figure 6–1 illustrates the interrelationships of judicial remedies.

COMMON LAW REMEDIES[1]

Common law remedies are generally limited to the court's determination of some legal right and the award of money damages. There are some exceptions. For example, when parties want the court's opinion concerning their legal rights, without seeking damages or injunctive relief, they seek a declaratory judgment. In addition, both the common law remedies of ejectment and replevin seek restitution. An *ejectment* occurs when a trespasser secures full possession of the land and the owner brings an action to regain possession as well as damages for the unlawful detention of possession. Usually, this process involves a title dispute between plaintiff and defendant, and the ejectment action settles this dispute. *Replevin* is an action used to recover possession of personal property wrongfully taken. Once the action is brought, the goods are seized from defendant after proper notice has been given.

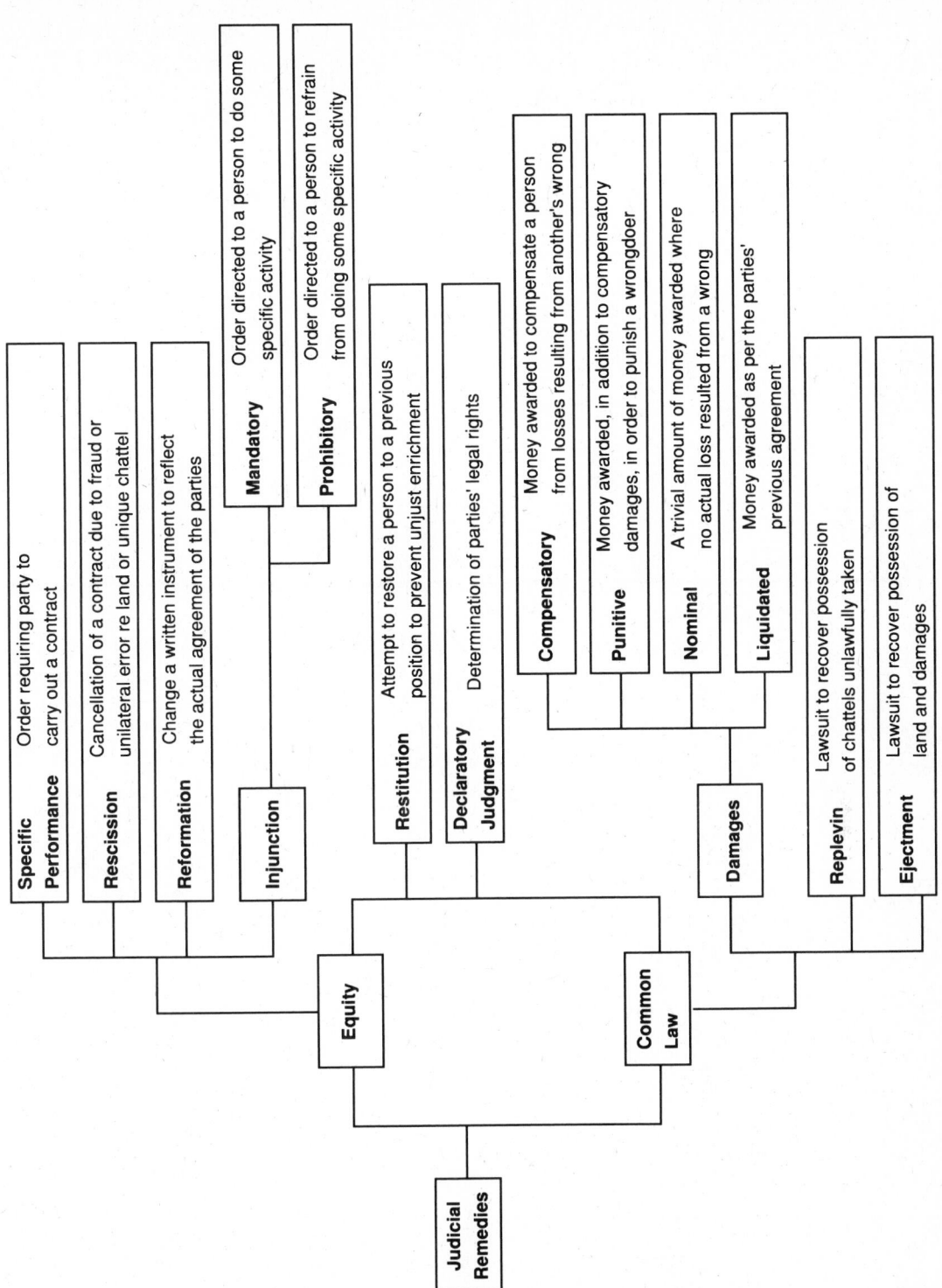

FIGURE 6-1 Judicial Remedies

Usually, however, a common law court grants relief in the form of damages, a sum of money awarded as compensation for an injury sustained as the consequence of either a tortious act or a breach of a legal obligation. Damages are classified as compensatory, punitive, nominal, and liquidated.

Compensatory Damages

Compensatory damages are awarded to compensate the plaintiff for pecuniary losses that resulted from the defendant's tortious conduct or breach of contract. They may be awarded for loss of time or money, bodily pain and suffering, permanent disabilities or disfigurement, injury to reputation, and mental anguish. Future losses are also recoverable; however, recovery is not allowed for consequences that are remote, indirect, or speculative.

Damages are usually limited to those reasonably foreseeable by the defendant as a result of the breach. Assume two plaintiffs have a contract to buy some equipment needed in order to open their new business, and a defendant breaches by nondelivery. If the plaintiffs sue for lost profits from the delay in opening because they have to procure alternative goods, they would probably not recover, because the defendant could not have foreseen this, not knowing that the opening depended on the delivery. Also, future profits are very difficult to measure with any degree of certainty.

In awarding compensatory damages, the court's objective is to put the plaintiff in the same financial position as existed before the commission of the tort, or, in a contract case, in the financial position that would have resulted had the promise been fulfilled. In the absence of circumstances giving rise to an allowance of punitive damages, the law will not put the injured party in a better position than the person would have been in had the wrong not been done.

A person who is injured must use whatever means are reasonable in order to avoid or minimize damages. This rule is called the *avoidable harm doctrine*. It prevents recovery for damages that could have been foreseen and avoided by reasonable effort without undue risk, expense, or humiliation. For example, P sues to recover the loss of a crop, because D removed some rails from P's fence, and as a result, cattle escaped and destroyed the crop. Since P, knowing the rails were missing, did not repair the fence, only the cost of repairing the fence is recoverable, because the loss of the crop could have been avoided.

When the defendant's misconduct causes damages, but also operates directly to confer some benefit on the plaintiff, then the plaintiff's damage claim may be diminished by the amount of the benefit conferred. This policy is called the *benefit rule*. For example, a trespasser digs on plaintiff's land, but the digging works to drain swampy areas and improves the value. The plaintiff may recover for the trespass and any damage it caused, but the defendant gets a credit for the value of the benefit conferred. However, this credit exists only for clear benefits and not for those that are remote and uncertain. Problems arise in deciding what is a benefit and by what standard to measure it.

Compensatory damages may be categorized as either general or special. This distinction is very important to lawyers because general damages do not have to be specifically pleaded, whereas special damages must be listed in the pleadings. *General damages* are those that are the natural and necessary result of the wrongful act or omission, and thus, can normally be expected to accompany the injury. Pain and suffering, mental anguish, and the loss of enjoyment of life are damages that occur so frequently in the tort of battery that they do not have to be specifically pleaded. *Special damages* are awarded for injuries that arise from special circumstances of the wrong. A plaintiff in a battery case, for example, would have to specifically plead such special damages as medical and hospital expenses, loss of earnings, and a diminished ability to work.

Putting a dollar value on the plaintiff's loss for the purpose of compensation often becomes a difficult task. Because the amount of damages is a factual question and decisions on factual issues do not create precedent, previous case decisions are not binding. The amount of damages is decided by a jury, unless a jury trial has been waived.

The next case involves a plaintiff who seeks to recover a variety of damages for medical malpractice. The court rules that the state's public policy prohibits her from recovering for all that she claims. The concurrence contains a discussion of the benefits rule and the rule requiring the mitigation of damages.

Macomber v. Dillman
505 A.2d 810
Supreme Judicial Court of Maine
February 27, 1986

Glassman, Justice

I

In April of 1984, the plaintiffs, Roxanne and Steven Macomber, filed a complaint against the defendants, Carter F. Dillman and the Webber Hospital Association. The complaint alleged, *inter alia*, that as a proximate result of the defendants' negligent and careless failure to comply with the standard of care of medical practice in the performance of a tubal ligation on Roxanne for the purpose of permanent sterilization, Roxanne was not permanently sterilized and had conceived and given birth to a child, Mazie. Although the plaintiffs did not allege in their complaint that Mazie is a healthy, normal child, they did not allege otherwise, and the parties have agreed to these facts. Plaintiffs sought damages from defendants "including, but not limited to, the cost of raising and educating Mazie May Macomber, the medical and other expenses of the pregnancy and childbirth, the medical and other expenses of a subsequent hysterectomy for purposes of sterilization, lost wages, loss of consortium, the medical and other expenses of the unsuccessful tubal ligation, permanent physical impairment to Roxanne Macomber resulting from bearing Mazie May, her sixth child, and physical and mental pain and suffering resulting [therefrom]."

Defendants filed motions for dismissal or summary judgment on the grounds that the plaintiffs by their complaint failed to state a claim for which relief could be granted and could not recover damages for the cost of rearing and educating a healthy, normal child. After hearing, the Superior Court entered its order denying the defendants' motions and adopting the analysis that should the plaintiffs prevail they would be entitled to recover "all reasonable, foreseeable, and proximately caused damages, including the expenses of child rearing." The court refused to rule on whether damages so recoverable by plaintiffs "should be offset by benefits" of parenthood.

On a joint motion of the parties, the Superior Court reported the case to this court thereby posing the following questions of law: (1) Did the Superior Court by its order properly deny the defendants' motion to dismiss the plaintiff's complaint for failure to state a claim against the defendants for which relief can be granted? (2) Did the Superior Court by its order properly set forth the damages that the plaintiffs could recover should they prevail in their action against the defendants?

II

We first address the question of whether the plaintiffs have by their complaint stated a claim against the defendants. Contrary to the defendants' contention, the plaintiffs' action does not represent a new cause of action in the state of Maine. "Since the early days of the common law a cause of action in tort has been recognized to exist when the negligence of one person is the proximate cause of damage to another person." . . . When a plaintiff claims he has suffered a personal injury as the result of medical mistreatment, his remedy lies in a complaint for negligence. . . . The necessary elements of a cause of

action for negligence are a duty owed, a breach of that duty proximately causing the plaintiff's injuries and resulting damages. . . . Applying these principles to the allegations in the plaintiffs' complaint, it is clear that the necessary elements of a cause of action in negligence have been set forth against the defendants.

III

We next consider whether the Superior Court correctly established the scope of recoverable damages. We are aware that the courts which have considered this type of case have not reached a consensus as to damages, if any, that may be recoverable. . . .

We hold for reasons of public policy that a parent cannot be said to have been damaged or injured by the birth and rearing of a healthy, normal child. Accordingly, we limit the recovery of damages, where applicable, to the hospital and medical expenses incurred for the sterilization procedures and pregnancy, the pain and suffering connected with the pregnancy and the loss of earnings by the mother during that time. Our ruling today is limited to the facts of this case, involving a failed sterilization procedure resulting in the birth of a healthy, normal child.

We also must address whether the plaintiff, Steven Macomber, may recover for loss of consortium of his wife, Roxanne. For centuries courts have recognized a husband's right to recover damages for the loss of consortium when a tortious injury to his wife detrimentally affects the spousal relationship. . . . Because his wife's cause of action is for negligence, Steven Macomber may recover proven damages for loss of consortium.

The entry is:

The order of the Superior Court is modified to limit the scope of recoverable damages, and as so modified, affirmed. Remanded to the Superior Court for further proceedings consistent with the opinion herein.

McKusik, Nichols, and Roberts, J.J., concurring.

Scolnik, Justice, concurring in part and dissenting in part

Although I concur that a cause of action exists for medical malpractice in the performance of a tubal ligation, I am unable to agree with the Court's judicially imposed limitation on the damages that are recoverable. The Court reasons that in no circumstances can a parent be said to have been damaged by the birth and rearing of a healthy, normal child. This rationale, however, is not only plainly inconsistent with the Court's recognition of a cause of action but also totally ignores the fact that many individuals undergo sterilization for the very purpose of avoiding such a birth. Moreover, the Court's opinion is an unwarranted departure from the fundamental principle of tort law that once a breach of duty has been established, the tortfeasor is liable for all foreseeable damages that proximately result from his acts. I dissent because, in my view, the jury should be permitted to consider awarding damages for child rearing costs.

By finding that a parent is not harmed by the birth of a healthy child, the Court's opinion is logically inconsistent. In the first part of its opinion, the Court applies traditional tort principles to recognize a cause of action for negligence resulting in an unwanted conception and subsequent birth of a normal, healthy child. Although the opinion is noticeably silent as to what the required harm is to support the cause of action, . . . the Court has in effect concluded that the birth of a normal child is recognized as an injury that is directly attributable to the health-care provider's negligence. In the second part of its opinion, however, the Court states that based on unarticulated reasons of public policy, the birth of a normal, healthy child cannot be said to constitute an injury to the parents. As a result, the Court limits the damages that a parent can recover to the hospital and medical expenses incurred for the sterilization procedure and the pregnancy, the pain and suffering connected with the pregnancy and the loss of earnings sustained by the mother during that time. If, however, the birth of a child does not constitute an injury, no basis exists for any award of damages. Damages for "pain and suffering" and medical expenses incidental to child birth cannot be recoverable if the birth itself is not an injury. Similarly, if the parent is to be compensated for the loss of earnings that result from the pregnancy, should she not equally be compensated for the identical loss following the birth of the child? The Court's opinion fails to reconcile these obvious inconsistencies.

Not only is the Court's opinion internally inconsistent, but its stated rationale to support an artificial limitation on the scope of recoverable damages ignores reality. To hold that a parent cannot be said to have been damaged or injured by the birth and rearing of a normal, healthy child is plainly to overlook the fact that many married couples, such as the plaintiffs, engage in contraceptive practices and undergo sterilization operations for the very purpose of avoiding the birth of [a] child. Many of these couples resort to such conception avoidance measures because, in their particular circumstances, the physical or financial hardships in raising another child are too burdensome. Far from supporting the view that the birth of a child is in all situations a benefit, the social reality is that, for many, an unplanned and unwanted child can be a clear detriment. . . . "[W]hen a couple has chosen not to have children, or not to have any more children, the suggestion arises that for them, at least, the birth of a child would not be a net benefit." . . . This is not to say that there are not many benefits associated with the raising of a child. The point is that it is unrealistic universally to proclaim that the joy and the companionship a parent receives from a healthy child always outweigh the costs and difficulties of rearing that child. As one judge explained:

> "A couple privileged to be bringing home the combined income of a dual professional household may well be able to sustain and cherish an unexpected child. But I am not sure the child's smile would be the most memorable character-istic to an indigent couple, where the husband underwent a vasectomy or the wife underwent a sterilization proce-dure, not because they did not desire a child, but rather because they faced the stark realization that they could not afford to feed an additional person, much less clothe, educate and support a child when that couple had trouble supporting one another. The choice is not always giving up personal amenities in order to buy a gift for the baby; the choice may only be to stretch necessities beyond the breaking point to provide for a child that the couple had purposely set out to avoid having." . . .

I know of no instance where we have strayed from the common law principle that a tortfeasor is liable for every foresee-able injury proximately caused by his negligent act and we should avoid doing so here. The Court states that public policy dictates the result it reaches with-out explaining the source from which it was derived or the foundation on which it rests. This is not a case where change is required in the common law, without leg-islative help, because of a conflict between an outdated judicially crafted policy and contemporary legal philosophy. . . . In fact, I am sure that the Court realizes that substantial disagreement exists among the courts as to whether a parent is harmed by the birth of an unexpected child. This fact coupled with the empirical reality that many individuals choose to forego parenthood for economic or other reasons demonstrates that the Court's unexpli-cated judicial declaration of public policy is unwarranted. . . .

In my view, it is the duty of this Court to follow public policy, not to for-mulate it, absent a clear expression of public opinion. Moreover, it has always been the public policy of this State to provide relief to those injured by tort-feasors and to allow for compensation for damages caused by their acts. To deprive the plaintiffs in this case of the opportu-nity to recover compensation for all their damages contravenes this basic policy. Any limitation on the scope of recoverable damages in such cases is best left to the Legislature where the opportunity for wide ranging debate and public partici-pation is far greater than in the Law Court. . . .

Rather than to rely on unstated no-tions of public policy, the better approach to determine what damages may be re-coverable is to apply traditional common-law rules. It is certainly foreseeable that a medical health professional's failure properly to perform a tubal ligation will result in the birth of an unplanned child. As a result of the tortfeasor's act, the parents, who had chosen not to have a child, find themselves unexpectedly bur-dened both physically and financially. They seek damages not because they do not love and desire to keep the child, but because the direct and foreseeable consequences of the health-care provider's negligence has forced burdens on them that they sought and had a right to avoid.

In assessing damages for child rearing costs, I would follow those jurisdictions that have adopted the "benefit rule" of the Restatement (Second) of Torts § 920 (1979). . . . The benefit rule recognizes that various tangible and intangible benefits accrue to the parents of the unplanned child and therefore to prevent unjust enrichment, their benefits should be weighed by the factfinder in determining damages associated with the raising of the unexpected child. The rule provides that "[w]hen the defendant's tortious conduct has caused harm to the plaintiff or to his property and in so doing has conferred a special benefit to the interest of the plaintiff that was harmed, the value of the benefit conferred is considered in mitigation of damages, to the extent that this is equitable." . . . The assessment of damages, if any, should focus on the specific interests of the parents that were actually impaired by the physician's negligence. An important factor in making that determination would be the reason that sterilization was sought, whether it was economic, genetic, therapeutic or otherwise. . . . The advantages of this approach were succinctly stated by the Arizona Supreme Court.

> "By allowing the jury to consider the future costs, both pecuniary and non-pecuniary, of rearing and educating the child, we permit it to consider all the elements of damage on which the parents may present evidence. By permitting the jury to consider the reason for the procedure and to assess and offset the pecuniary and non-pecuniary benefits which will inure to the parents by reason of their relationship to the child, we allow the jury to discount those damages, thus reducing speculation and permitting the verdict to be based upon

the facts as they actually exist in each of the unforeseeable variety of situations which may come before the court. We think this by far the better rule. The blindfold on the figure of justice is a shield from partiality, not from reality."
. . .

Although the benefit rule approach requires the jury to mitigate primarily economic damages by weighing them against primarily noneconomic factors, I reject the view that such a process is "an exercise in prophecy, an undertaking not within the specialty of our factfinders." . . . The calculation of the benefits a parent could expect to receive from the child is no more difficult than similar computations of damages in wrongful death actions, for extended loss of consortium or for pain and suffering. . . .

As a final note, the parents should not be forced to mitigate their damages by resorting to abortion or to adoption. A doctrine of mitigation of damages known as the avoidable consequences rule requires only that reasonable measures be taken. . . . Most courts that have considered the matter have held, as a matter of law, neither course of action would be reasonable. . . . I agree. The tortfeasor takes the injured party as he finds him and has no right to insist that the victims of his negligence have the emotional and mental make-up of a woman who is willing to undergo an abortion or offer her child for adoption. Moreover, the parents should not be precluded from recovering damages because they select the most desirable alternative and raise the child. Accordingly, the avoidable consequences rule is not relevant to the issue of the recovery of child rearing expenses.

Damages recoverable under the cause of action recognized today by this Court should not be limited by unstated notions of public policy so as arbitrarily to limit recovery of proximately caused and foreseeable damages. I recognize that this is an extremely difficult case but I find no public policy declaring that physicians should be partially immunized from the consequences of a negligently performed sterilization operation nor declaring that the birth of a healthy child is in all circumstances a blessing to the parents. Accordingly, I see no justification for supporting a departure from the traditional rules that apply to tort damages.

I would affirm, without modification, the order of the Superior Court and permit the recovery of the potential costs of rearing the child.

Case Questions

1. Why does the court majority hold that the parents could recover damages for hospital and medical expenses, pain and suffering connected with the unwanted pregnancy, the loss of earnings by the mother during the pregnancy, and loss of consortium but denies a recovery for the cost of rearing and educating a healthy, normal child?
2. The dissenting justice argues that the majority opinion is inconsistent. Explain the inconsistencies.
3. After carefully reading the majority and dissenting opinions, how would you rule?

Punitive Damages

Damages can also be awarded to punish defendants for their conduct and to deter others from similar conduct. These are called *punitive* or *exemplary* damages, and are awarded to the plaintiff beyond the compensatory amount. They are additional damages for a civil wrong and are not imposed as a substitute for criminal punishment. An award of punitive damages also may include an award of attorneys' fees. We will see in the next case, *Volz v. Coleman,* that any type of negligence, even gross or extreme, is insufficient to award punitive damages. Such an award is appropriate only when a defendant has engaged in aggravated, wanton, reckless, malicious, or oppressive conduct. This includes all acts done with an evil disposition, or a wrong and unlawful motive, or the willful doing of an injurious act without a lawful excuse. Punitive damages are generally available only for intentional torts, and for some statutory wrongs.

Some of the actions that may result in punitive damage awards are: copyright and trademark infringement, corporate crimes such as antitrust violations, insurers not paying off on their policies, wrongful discharge by an employer, libel and slander, wrongful death, trespass, conversion, battery, and securities fraud. Traditionally, punitive damages have not been awarded in contract cases, even in situations in which there has been a malicious breach.

Some jurisdictions have modified this rule in some situations. If a breach of contract is accompanied by a malicious tort, exemplary damages will be awarded for the tort.

In *Volz v. Coleman*, the appellate court reviewed a trial jury's $1.06 million punitive damages award. The court had to decide whether reasonable jurors, as a matter of law, could have found Coleman's actions to have been malicious, spiteful, outrageous, oppressive, or intolerable.

Volz v. Coleman Co., Inc.
748 P.2d 1191
Supreme Court of Arizona
December 17, 1987

Cameron, Justice

I. Jurisdiction

This is a petition for review, filed by The Coleman Co., Inc. (Coleman), of an opinion of the court of appeals which affirmed a trial court judgment and award in favor of the respondents Sharon Volz and Valley National Bank, co-conservators of the Plaintiff, Shannon Haddix. . . .

II. Question Presented

We granted the petition for review to consider whether punitive damages were properly awarded. . . .

III. Facts

On 15 August 1983, while camping with her family, five-year-old Shannon Haddix (plaintiff) was severely burned by ignited gasoline. Her stepfather, Ron Volz, was pumping the fuel tank on his Coleman stove when, according to his testimony, a stream of fuel, without warning, ejected through the filler cap, crossed the campfire, ignited, and landed on Shannon, some 10–12 feet away. Volz testified that, after refueling the tank, he had screwed the cap on tightly before pressurizing the tank for the morning meal. He added that

he did not pour any more fuel into the tank for the evening meal, and that he had checked the cap to make sure that it was tight before pumping the tank in the evening. Volz testified that because the pump was "pretty stiff" after only three to six pumps, he knew that the tank had retained pressure from the morning use.

The plaintiff presented expert testimony concerning the design of the cap and alternative cap designs that Coleman could have utilized. John B. Sevart, an engineer with a private consulting practice and with two engineering companies, testified that, in his opinion, the design of a gas tank using a cap with a vent-hole is defective with respect to safety. Kenneth John Saczalski, a professor of engineering at Northern Arizona University and the owner of a private consulting company, testified that there were alternative cap designs that Coleman could have utilized to accomplish ventilation of the tank without the cap having any of the vent-hole characteristics.

Coleman has manufactured camp stoves for over forty-five years. During this time, Coleman has introduced 25–50 million stoves into the marketplace. From the early 1940s through 1963, Coleman equipped its camp stoves with a vent-hole filler cap used in this case. This same cap was used on fuel-burning lanterns also manufactured by Coleman.

In using the Coleman stove, the fuel must be pressurized so that it will flow from the tank to the burner. Pressurization is accomplished by pumping the sealed tank until the plunger handle becomes resistant. To refuel a Coleman tank, the cap on the end of the tank opposite the plunger handle is unscrewed and removed. The cap, however, needs to have some type of ventilation capacity in order to equalize the interior pressure of the tank with that of the exterior atmosphere as the cap is removed. If the cap is removed without a ventilation feature, then removal of the cap will create a sudden pressure surge causing a discharge of fuel in a stream-like manner.

In 1963, the vent-hole filler cap for use in the stove was discontinued by Coleman and was replaced with a cap referred to as the "Plamann patent." The Plamann patent cap, because it is internally broached, directs any type of pressurized discharge from the tank in a downward direction, rather than in an outward direction as in the vent-hole filler cap. In 1963, however, several hundred thousand stoves were already in the marketplace equipped with the vent-hole filler cap. The Volz's received the stove in question as a Christmas gift in 1982. The stove, however, contained the old cap and not the newer "Plamann Patent" cap. Coleman never issued warnings to users about the old caps nor did it recall any of the stoves or lanterns containing these caps.

A 1963 internal Coleman document and a 1967 patent application were introduced into evidence that discussed the defects in the vent-hole filler cap and improvements that would be gained by redesigning the venting system. However, Coleman employees, both engineers and management-level, repeatedly testified that no warning on the use of Coleman fuel in the tank and stove was necessary because "common sense" would indicate to a person that the "hazardous sub-stance" of the Coleman fuel should not be used in such a way that a stream would be emitted from the tank. Those employees also testified that Coleman redesigned the original cap into the "Plamann patent" cap because it was more functional to use and economical to produce, and *not* because of safety reasons. Indeed, testimony was introduced at trial indicating that there was no safety advantage to the "Plamann patent" cap when compared to the vent-hole filler cap.

The 1963 Coleman internal memorandum stated: "[b]ecause, under many circumstances the gasoline . . . tends to foam when the pressure is relieved, . . . [such] gasoline froth [can blow] out through this vent hole." Furthermore, the memo stated that it was not possible to control the direction in which the stream traveled.

Additionally, the testimony of Coleman employees Randy May, director of technical services, William Marsh, director of design engineering for the outgoing products division, Jerry Koontz, national service manager, and William Townsend, a technical research engineer, indicated that Coleman had notice since 1960 of the tendency of the cap to spray fuel. However, Coleman's head of outgoing products division, Elwood Little, did not believe it was hazardous to loosen the cap and believed the instructions were clear that the tank needed to be kept level. Koontz testified that fuel sprayed only if the tank was not level and the cap was loose. He also testified that if the stove were operated in the proper manner a person could not "pump enough pressure into it to shoot fuel 12 feet."

Despite Coleman's knowledge of the possibility of fuel spraying through the vent hole of the filler cap, no warnings were issued advising the user not to open the cap except when the tank was level and not near a flame. Coleman's design project manager, Frank Schmidt, testified that there were no instructions on how to relieve pressure from the tank. Relieving pressure would prevent the possibility of fuel spraying out if the tank were not level or if the cap were loose. Testimony of other Coleman employees emphasized that Coleman only had notice of fuel spraying when the cap was unscrewed. In the present case, Volz testified that he had not unscrewed the cap and that the fuel was released "spontaneously."

The jury awarded plaintiff $6.8 million in compensatory damages and $1.06 million in punitive damages. The defendant appealed and the court of appeals affirmed the awards. Defendant petitioned this court for review. We granted the petition only on the issue of punitive damages.

IV. Punitive Damages

In both its motion for a new trial and on appeal, Coleman contends that it was error for the trial court to give a punitive damages instruction. We agree.

Punitive damages are awarded in order to punish the wrongdoer and deter others from emulating the same conduct. . . . The focus is on the wrongdoer's attitude and conduct. . . . The punitive damages standard in Arizona requires "something more" than gross negligence. . . . The "something more" is the evil mind, which is satisfied by evidence "that defendant's wrongful conduct was motivated by spite, actual malice, or intent to defraud" or defendant's "conscious and deliberate disregard of the interest and rights of others." . . .

To obtain punitive damages, a plaintiff must prove that "defendant's evil hand was guided by an evil mind." . . . This "evil mind" element may be shown by either (1) evil actions; (2) spiteful motives; or (3) outrageous, oppressive or intolerable conduct that creates substantial risk of tremendous harm to others. . . . The fact that a manufacturer continues to market a product is not in itself enough to show the evil mind necessary for punitive damages. . . .

This court has expressly rejected awarding punitive damages based on gross negligence or mere reckless disregard of the circumstances. . . . We have stated that such terms as "gross," "reckless," and "wanton conduct" convey little and fail to focus the jury's attention on the important question—the defendant's motives. . . .

As one court has noted:

> "It is quite clear, we think, from the evidence, that the jury could well have found negligence or even gross negligence on the part of this defendant. But negligent conduct, no matter how gross or wanton, cannot be equated with the conduct required for punitive damages. We hold, therefore, that plaintiff's evidence in this case was insufficient as a matter of law to demonstrate that type of "outrageous conduct" on which an award of punitive damages must depend. *Thomas v. American Cytoscope Makers, Inc.*, 414 F.Supp. 255, 267 (E.D.Pa. 1976) (applying Pennsylvania law in a products liability action)."

This is a case of negligence, or even gross negligence, and the jury so found in awarding compensatory damages. It is not, however, a case of punitive damages or the "something more" than gross negligence. . . .

V. Disposition

The award of punitive damages is reversed and set aside. The judgment as amended is affirmed.

Case
Questions

1. What must be present to justify an award of punitive damages?
2. What public policy is promoted by punitive damages?
3. What kinds of activities did the court indicate plaintiffs should offer to prove that the defendant's "evil hand was guided by an evil mind?"

Nominal Damages

If a defendant breaches a legal duty owed to the plaintiff and injures that person, compensatory damages may be awarded. The compensatory damages are measured by the amount of the loss. *Nominal damages* are awarded when there has been a breach of an agreement or an invasion of a right, but there is no evidence of any specific harm. This occurs, for example, if a person trespasses on your land, but causes no actual harm. In such a situation, the plaintiff would only be entitled to a judgment for a trivial amount, such as one dollar or fifty dollars. The judge awards this token sum to vindicate the plaintiff's claim or to establish a legal right. Nominal damages also are awarded when a plaintiff proves breach of duty and harm, but neglects to prove the value of the loss. They are also allowable when the defendant's invasion of the plaintiff's rights produces a benefit.

Courts award nominal damages because a judgment for money damages is the only way a common law court can establish the validity of the plaintiff's claim. Students should be careful not to confuse nominal charges with small compensatory damage awards, which are awarded where the actual loss was minor.

Liquidated Damages

Parties may agree, in advance, about the amount to be paid as compensation for loss in the event of a breach of contract. *Liquidated damages* are the stipulated sum contained in such an agreement. An example of this can be seen in the *Campbell Soup* case (page 237), where Campbells' contract with the Wentz brothers included a provision for damages of $50 per acre if the contract was breached. If the court determines that the amount stipulated in the agreement is a punishment used to prevent a breach, rather than an estimate of actual damages, it will deem that sum a penalty and refuse to enforce it. Traditionally, the court upholds a liquidated damage clause only when (1) the damages in case of breach are uncertain or difficult to compute, (2) the parties have agreed in advance to liquidate the damages, and (3) the amount agreed on is reasonable and not disproportionate to the probable loss. Another form of liquidated damages results when money is deposited to guarantee against future damages.

Occasionally, a plaintiff who has suffered no actual damages can recover substantial liquidated damages; however, this occurs only rarely. Some courts require plaintiffs to prove some actual loss before the liquidated damage clause is triggered.

In the following case, the liquidated damages are disproportionate to the loss sustained.

Lakewood Creative Costumers v. Sharp
509 N.E.2d 77
Court of Appeals of Ohio, Cuyahoga County
March 24, 1986

Parrino, Chief Justice

Defendant Angel Sharp appeals the trial court's judgment in favor of plaintiff Lakewood Creative Costumers. For the reasons discussed below, the trial court's judgment is modified and as modified is affirmed.

I

The facts giving rise to the instant appeal are as follows.

On October 27, 1984, Angel Sharp rented a Halloween costume from Lakewood Creative Costumers. The agreement signed by Sharp provided that the costume was to be returned by November 1, 1984. The fee for the rental was $20.

The defendant failed to return the costume by November 1, 1984. Sharp testified before a referee that she had attempted to return the costume once, but that the store was closed. She then put the costume in her closet and forgot about it. Sharp eventually returned the costume on January 20, 1985.

On January 11, 1985, Lakewood Creative Costumers filed suit against Sharp in Lakewood Municipal Court, Small Claims Division. The complaint alleged that Sharp had breached her contract. The plaintiff sought to enforce a liquidated

damages clause in the contract which provided that "an amount equal to one-half the rental fee will be charged for each day the costume is returned late." Under that clause, the plaintiff would have been entitled to $790 in liquidated damages from Sharp.[1] In its complaint, however, the plaintiff only sought $500 in damages.

At a hearing before a referee, a representative of Lakewood Creative Costumers testified that he definitely lost one rental of the costume, and that the costume cost $20 to make.

The referee applied the aforementioned clause, and noted that based on the language of the contract, Lakewood Creative Costumers was entitled to $790. However, since the plaintiff only sought $500, the referee recommended a judgment in that amount.

Angel Sharp filed objections to the referee's report arguing, *inter alia*, that the liquidated damages clause was in the nature of a penalty and, therefore, should not be enforced under Ohio law. In an entry filed with the clerk of courts on March 28, 1985, the trial court overruled the defendant's objections, and rendered judgment against Angel Sharp in the amount of $400.

The defendant filed a timely appeal, raising a single assignment of error.

---

[1] The costume was returned seventy-nine days late. One half the rental fee was $10. Therefore, under the liquidated damages clause the amount due was seventy-nine times ten, or $790.

II

Assignment of error.

> "A provision in a costume-rental contract providing for payment of one-half the rental fee for each day the costume is returned late is void and unenforceable as a penalty where the rental fee is $20.00, the replacement cost of the costume is $20.00, the costume would have been rented at most for one day during the period the customer was late in returning it, and the customer would have at most been liable for the replacement cost of the costume had it been returned in a damaged condition."

A clause in a contract providing for liquidated damages in the event of a breach is valid and enforceable where the sum stipulated is in reasonable proportion to the loss actually sustained; the actual damages incurred by the breach are uncertain or difficult to ascertain; and the contract is consistent with the conclusion that it was the intention of the parties that damages in the amount stated should follow the breach thereof. . . .

The liquidated damages clause in the instant case clearly fails under the aforementioned test. First, the sum stipulated is not reasonably proportionate to the loss sustained. The only evidence of damage by the appellee was the loss of a single rental, a twenty dollar value.[2] Under the

[2] We are assuming that the value of the lost rental is equal to the cost of the appellant's rental of the same costume.

liquidated damages clause, however, the appellant could ultimately have been held liable for $790. A liquidated damages clause which provides for an amount nearly forty times the actual damages is not reasonably proportionate to the loss sustained, and thus is invalid. . . .

Second, the actual damages incurred by the breach are not uncertain or difficult to ascertain. The actual damages incurred are relatively easy to ascertain. They simply consist of any lost rental sales, together with the cost of getting the costume returned. Liquidated damages are appropriate only where actual damages are uncertain or difficult to ascertain. . . . Therefore, the clause in the case at bar is void.

Accordingly, the appellant's assignment of error is sustained.

III

The liquidated damages clause which provided that "an amount equal to one-half the rental fee will be charged for each day the costume is returned late" is hereby found to be void and unenforceable. The trial court's judgment is therefore reduced to the amount of actual damages proven, twenty dollars from the loss of a single rental, plus the court costs. The trial court's judgment is affirmed as modified.

Judgment affirmed as modified.

Nahra and Krupansky, JJ., concur.

Case Questions

1. What policy prevents a court from enforcing a liquidated damage clause that is designed to deter a party from breaching a contract and to harshly punish the party in the event of a breach?
2. Why did the appellate court decide that the liquidated damages clause in the rental agreement was unenforceable?

3. According to the court, what is required for a liquidated damage clause to be valid and enforceable?

EQUITABLE REMEDIES

An equitable remedy would have been dealt with by a court of equity before the merger of equity and the common law courts. Today, most courts in the United States are empowered to grant both equitable and legal relief as required to achieve justice. However, the availability of equitable remedies is a matter for judges and not juries. Traditionally, courts only grant equitable remedies when the common law remedies are inadequate.

Injunctions

An injunction is an equitable remedy in the form of a judicial order directing the defendant to act or refrain from acting in a specified way. An order compelling one to do an act is called a *mandatory injunction*, whereas one prohibiting an act is called a *prohibitory injunction*. An injunction may be enforced by the contempt power of a court, and a defendant may be fined, sent to jail, or deprived of the right to litigate issues, if he or she disobeys an injunction. This order must be obeyed until it is reversed, even if it is issued erroneously or the court lacks jurisdiction.

Injunctions may be divided into three classes: (1) permanent, (2) preliminary or interlocutory, and (3) temporary restraining orders. A permanent injunction is a decree issued after a full opportunity to present evidence. It is permanent only in the sense that it is supposed to be a final solution to a dispute. It may still be modified or dissolved later. A preliminary or interlocutory injunction is granted as an emergency measure before a full hearing is held. There must be notice to the defendant and a hearing, usually informal. This remedy is generally limited to situations in which there is a serious need to preserve the status quo until the parties' rights have finally been decided. Thus a preliminary injunction continues only until a further order of the court is issued.

The temporary restraining order, known as a TRO, is an *ex parte* injunction. This means that it is granted without notice to the defendant. The trial judge has heard only the plaintiff's side of the case. Because of the potential for abuse, certain procedures protect a defendant. A TRO may not be granted unless irreparable harm would result and there is no time for notice and a hearing. There must be clear evidence on the merits of the case. The court should look at any damage to defendant that would be noncompensable in money if plaintiff's relief is later shown to be improper. This consideration must be balanced with plaintiff's harm if the TRO is not granted. Factors weigh more heavily against the plaintiff, since there is no notice to defendant.

Certain classes of cases are not considered proper subject matter for injunctions. In general, an injunction is not issued to stop a criminal prosecution or to prevent crimes. However, this law has been modified in recent years by regulatory statutes or civil rights statutes. Injunctions are usually not proper in defamation cases, because they would intrude on the defendant's constitutional right of free speech and would be considered prior restraint.

The following case illustrates how a judge deciding an equity case makes a decision to grant or deny injunctive relief. The judge's balancing of the interests and the harm is a hallmark of equity.

Gano v. School District No. 411 of Twin Falls County, Idaho
674 F.Supp. 796
U.S. District Court for the District of Idaho
November 5, 1987

Memorandum Decision

Callister, Chief Judge

The Court has before it the plaintiff's motion for preliminary injunction. The Court held an evidentiary hearing on October 30, 1987, and ruled from the bench that the motion would be denied. This memorandum decision will constitute the Court's written findings pursuant to Fed.R.Civ.P. 52(a).

The plaintiff, Rod Gano, Twin Falls High School student, was requested by members of the senior class to draw a caricature of three administrators: (1) Twin Falls High School Principal Frank Charlton; (2) Vice-Principal Norman Thomas; and (3) Dean of Men Richard Baun. The plaintiff drew the caricature and it was transferred to T-shirts to be sold to other students during homecoming week.

One of those T-shirts was made a part of the record in this case. It shows the three administrators sitting against a fence labeled "Bruin Stadium, Home of the Bruins." Each administrator is holding a different alcoholic beverage and is acting drunk. While one administrator holds aloft a beer mug, another holds a wine cooler, while the third grasps a bottle of whiskey. A case of "light beer" sits nearby. A phrase, "It doesn't get any better than this," not coincidentally lifted from a television beer commercial, appears just below the caricature.

When the administrators discovered the T-shirts, and the plan to sell them to the students, they suspended the plaintiff. The suspension lasted two days, October 5 and 6, 1987, and the plaintiff returned to school on October 7, 1987. The unrebutted affidavits of the administrators establish that this disciplinary action has been removed from the plaintiff's file. For attendance purposes, the plaintiff was not cited for being absent on October 5 and 6, 1987. He is noted as being absent during second period on October 8, 1987. On that date he wore the T-shirt to school, and was told to go home and change shirts during second period. He wore the T-shirt again on October 15, 1987, and was sent home to change it. Although he was free to return to school without the T-shirt, he failed to return on October 16, 1987, and is listed as being absent on that date. If the plaintiff continues to wear the T-shirt, he will be sent home to change it. For the purposes of this case, there are no other absences or disciplinary actions at issue.

On October 16, 1987, the plaintiff filed this action along with a motion for preliminary injunction. The motion seeks to enjoin defendants "from suspending or interfering with the plaintiff's attendance at Twin Falls High School for wearing a T-shirt with the caricature on it until such time as those matters alleged by way of the verified complaint filed herein have been litigated or otherwise resolved." . . .

There are two alternative tests, one of which must be met in order to grant a preliminary injunction. The first test requires that the Court find (1) the moving party will suffer irreparable injury if the injunctive relief is not granted; (2) there is a substantial likelihood that the moving party will succeed on the merits; (3) in balancing the equities the nonmoving party will not be harmed more than the moving party is helped; and (4) granting injunctive relief is in the public interest.

The second test requires the moving party to demonstrate either (1) a combination of probable success on the merits and the possibility of irreparable harm; or (2) that serious questions are raised and the balance of hardship tips sharply in his favor. These two tests are not separate; they are the outer reaches of a single continuum. . . .

The Court will employ the second test, and will examine first the plaintiff's chance for success on the merits. The plaintiff argues that his First Amendment freedom of speech right will be abridged if he is disciplined for wearing the T-shirt. Unfortunately, neither the plaintiff, nor plaintiff's counsel, was able to articulate the expression which was in danger of suppression. Did the T-shirt represent a political protest? Was it a criticism of administration policies? Testimony and argument from the plaintiff, his counsel, and other witnesses, indicated that the T-shirts were not intended to criticize or be disrespectful to the administrators. What message is conveyed by the T-shirts?

The T-shirt portrays the three administrators with alcoholic beverages on school property during a homecoming activity. It is a misdemeanor to consume alcoholic beverages on school property at any school activity. . . . There is no evidence in the record that the three administrators have ever so imbibed. The plaintiff's T-shirt thus falsely accuses the three administrators of committing a misdemeanor. For this expression, the plaintiff demands protection. Is he so entitled? The United States Supreme Court has stated that students cannot be disciplined for wearing black armbands to protest the Vietnam War, but can be disciplined for making sexually explicit speeches at school assemblies. . . . *Bethel School Dist. No. 403 v. Fraser.* . . . To understand these cases, one must first understand that discipline and debate are equally effective teaching tools. A robust exchange of ideas can only occur effectively within a civilized context. The school is actively engaged in teaching when it sets the bounds for proper conduct. As the United States Supreme Court stated in the *Bethel* case:

> "The process of educating our youth for citizenship in public schools is not confined to books, the curriculum, and the civics class; school must teach by example the shared values of a civilized social order. Consciously or otherwise, teachers—and indeed the older students—demonstrate the appropriate form of civil discourse and political expression by their conduct and deportment in and out of class. Inescapably, like parents, they are role models. The schools, as instruments of the state, may determine that the essential lessons of civil, mature conduct cannot be conveyed in a school that tolerates lewd, indecent, or offensive speech and conduct such as that indulged in [here]."

In the present case, the school has determined that the T-shirt—which is clearly offensive—cannot be tolerated. In this state, the schools are statutorily charged with teaching about the "effects of alcohol." . . . When the school disciplines the plaintiff for wearing a T-shirt falsely depicting the administrators in an alcoholic stupor, it is engaged in its statutory duty. It is teaching the students that falsely accusing one of being drunk is not acceptable. The administrators are role models, as stated by the United States Supreme Court, and their position would be severely compromised if this T-shirt was circulated among the students. This case appears to clearly fall within the *Bethel* precedent, and thus the Court finds that the plaintiff has only a minuscule chance of success on the merits.

With regard to the balance of harm, the plaintiff would be effectively prevented from falsely accusing the administrators of being drunks. The Court cannot find that the plaintiff suffers much harm by being so prevented. When this case is examined in its entirety, the plaintiff has so little success on the merits and would suffer so little harm that the Court finds that a preliminary injunction is not warranted. The Court will therefore deny the motion for preliminary injunction.

Case Questions

1. Why did the court deny the plaintiff's claim for injunctive relief?
2. What basis did the court give for rejecting the plaintiff's First Amendment freedom-of-speech claims?
3. How was the public interest protected by the court's denial of the plaintiff's claim for injunctive relief?
4. What type of injunctive relief was requested and granted in the *Gano* case?

Reformation and Rescission

The equitable remedy of reformation is granted when a written agreement fails to express accurately the parties' agreement because of mistake, fraud, or the drafter's ambiguous language. Its purpose is to rectify or reform a written instrument in order that it may express the real agreement or intention of the parties.

The equitable remedy of rescission is granted when one of the parties' consent to a contract is obtained through duress, undue influence, fraud, innocent misrepresentation, or when either or both of the parties made a mistake concerning the contract. Rescission means the court cancels the agreement. If a court orders rescission, each party normally has to return any property or money received from the other party in performance of the agreement (*restitution*). This topic, with an illustrative case (*Carter v. Matthews*), is addressed in Chapter 9.

The following case involves a contractor who was the successful bidder on a public construction contract. The contractor made a unilateral error in computing his bid. It then brought suit seeking the equitable remedy of reformation. The appellate court majority ruled that the plaintiff was not entitled to reformation. The dissenting judge disagreed on the basis of the defendant's inequitable conduct. The majority opinion also discusses the equitable remedy of rescission and explains why the plaintiff has waived any claim to that remedy.

Department of Transportation v. Ronlee, Inc.
518 So.2d 1326
District Court of Appeal of Florida,
Third District
December 22, 1987

Per Curiam

The threshold question presented is whether the successful bidder for a government road construction contract is entitled to reformation of the contract to increase the price by $317,463 based on a unilateral mistake, after the competing bids are all opened, where the new contract price would still be lower than the second lowest bid.

The Department of Transportation (DOT) solicited bids pursuant to section 337.11, Florida Statutes (1985), for the construction of an interchange at the intersection of State Road 826 and Interstate 75 in Hialeah. On December 7, 1983, DOT declared Ronlee, Inc. the apparent low bidder with a bid of $15,799,197.90. The second lowest bid exceeded Ronlee's bid by $610,148.

On February 13, 1984, DOT entered into a contract with Ronlee to construct the project based on the bid, and on March 7, 1984, gave Ronlee notice to proceed with the project. Five days later, Ronlee advised DOT that the bid contained a "stupid mistake" in the amount of $317,463. The letter alleged an error with respect to the unit price for concrete culverts which occurred when an em-

ployee of Ronlee erroneously transcribed a phone quote of $525 for each culvert as $5.25 each. By letter dated March 21, 1984, DOT informed Ronlee that it was aware of the apparently unbalanced unit price for the concrete culverts, but that it was unable, as a matter of state policy, to permit an increase in the contract price.

Nevertheless, on March 22, 1984, having made no effort to withdraw the bid, Ronlee began construction of the project. Twenty-one months later, with the project seventy-five percent completed, Ronlee filed suit against DOT seeking reformation of the contract. Both sides moved for a summary judgment, agreeing that the material facts were not in dispute. Ronlee's motion for summary judgment was granted, the trial court holding that DOT's silence about Ronlee's apparent error in price calculations constituted inequitable conduct and that reformation of the contract would not undermine the competitive bidding process. In addition to the $317,463, the court awarded Ronlee $60,000 in prejudgment interest and costs. We reverse.

Where a contractor makes a unilateral error in formulating his bid for a public contract, the remedy is rescission of the contract. . . . Florida courts have permitted a contractor to *withdraw* a bid on a public contract, subject to certain equitable conditions. In *State Board of Control v. Clutter Construction Corp.,* . . . a contractor was permitted to withdraw a bid on a showing of the following equitable factors: (1) the bidder acted in good faith in submitting the bid; (2) in preparing the bid there was an error of such magnitude that enforcement of the bid would work severe hardship upon the bidder; (3) the error was not a result of gross negligence or willful inattention; (4) the error was discovered and communicated to the public body, *along with a request for permission to withdraw the bid*, before acceptance.

No reported Florida decision has permitted reformation by belated request of a bid contract for a public project in order to make it profitable to the contractor. *Graham v. Clyde*, . . . is the only case presented by the parties where reformation was even sought as relief for a mistaken bid. There a building contractor was low bidder on a proposal to construct a public school building and was awarded the contract. The following day he notified public officials that he had made a mistake of $5,000 in computing items in his bid and asked to be relieved of his obligation to perform according to the contract terms. He offered to perform the contract for $5,000 more, which was still less than the next low bidder. The circuit court did not grant a reformation but did rescind the contract and enjoined the school board from attempting to enforce it.

The Florida Supreme Court, citing a number of cases from other jurisdictions, reversed, holding that unilateral errors are not generally relieved and that there was no equitable basis for relief. In an opinion by Justice Terrell the court stated the reason for the firm rule:

> "If errors of this nature can be relieved in equity, our system of competitive bidding on such contracts would in effect be placed in jeopardy and there would be no stability whatever to it. It would encourage careless, slipshod bidding in some cases and would afford a pretext for the dishonest bidder to prey on the public. . . . After the bid is accepted, the bidder is bound by his error and is expected to bear the consequence of it.". . .

The prevailing view is that reformation is not the appropriate form of relief for unilateral mistakes in public contract bids where the bidder is negligent. . . . The reason for not permitting reformation of bid contracts for public projects based on unilateral mistake is the same in other jurisdictions—to prevent collusive schemes between bidders, or between bidders and awarding officials, or multiple claims from contractors asserting mistake and claiming inequity at taxpayers' expense. . . .

A written instrument may be reformed where it fails to express the intention of the parties as a result of mutual mistake, or unilateral mistake accompanied by inequitable conduct by the other party. . . . Because the mistake in this instance was admittedly unilateral, in order to obtain reformation of the contract, Ronlee was obligated to show by clear and convincing evidence that DOT's conduct in not calling Ronlee's attention to a possible error in the bid tabulations was fraudulent or otherwise inequitable. . . . That burden was not carried. The Department's failure to call Ronlee's attention to the error in calculation was of no consequence since Ronlee discovered its own error shortly after the Department learned of the miscalculation.

Competitive bidding statutes are enacted to protect the public and should be construed to avoid circumvention. . . . A government unit is not required to act for the protection of a contractor's interest; it is entitled to the bargain obtained in accepting the lowest responsible bid and is under no obligation to examine bids to ascertain errors and to inform bidders accordingly. . . . Absent an obligation to do so, failure of the government in this case to call the bidder's attention to a relatively minor two percent error in its calculations, after the bids were opened, was not such fraud or imposition as would entitle the bidder to reformation of the contract.

Further, Ronlee forfeited any right it may have had to reformation or rescission. It had knowledge of its own mistake at least ten days before commencement of construction. Ronlee's conduct in performing according to the terms of the agreement for twenty-one months instead of seeking to withdraw the bid, after DOT had advised that it could not administratively correct the error, effected a waiver of rights. *See Farnham v. Blount,* . . . (any unreasonable or unnecessary delay by a party seeking to cancel an instrument based on fraud or other sufficient cause will be construed as a waiver or ratification). . . .

Reversed and remanded with instructions to enter judgment for the Department of Transportation.

Hendry and Ferguson, JJ., concur.

Schwartz, Chief Judge, dissenting

With respect, I must dissent. The majority does not say that the record shows and the trial judge found just the inequitable conduct by the DOT which, under principles it acknowledges, renders reformation an entirely appropriate remedy; although the DOT was aware of the mistake when the bids were opened and well before construction commenced, it deliberately failed to inform the contractor of this fact. The final judgment under review contains, among others, the following, essentially undisputed determinations:

"(e) The Defendant acknowledged receipt of notice, *prior* to commencement of construction, of the existence of the error and further acknowledged that the

Plaintiff's bid 'error was unintentional' and 'resulted from inexperienced personnel' generating a simple mathematical error by misplacing a decimal point and 'not comprehending the reasonableness of the money figures being used.' (Exhibit 'D' to Plaintiff's Motion).

"(f) Indeed, the Defendant even admitted that *prior* to the Plaintiff's March 12, 1984 notification to the Defendant, the Defendant had already been 'aware of the apparent unbalanced unit price of the item of Class II Concrete Culverts' (Exhibits 'D' and 'C' to Plaintiff's Motion; Plaintiff's Motion at 5–6, 9). Exhibit 'C', a December 19, 1983 computer printout (entitled 'summary of bids') produced by Defendant during discovery, demonstrates that the 'apparent unbalanced unit price' with respect to the bids 'opened at Tallahassee, Florida on December 7, 1983' was known to Defendant promptly upon examination of the bids.

"3. The Court is therefore of the view that plaintiff has proved inequitable conduct by the Defendant by clear and convincing proof. Clearly, the Defendant was aware, or certainly should have been aware, that the unit item bid price for 400–2–1 Class II Concrete Culverts was one hundred (100) times less than the nearest unit price for the same item. However, the Defendant chose wrongfully to remain silent as to the existence of this error and, further, refused to act equitably after the Plaintiff had discovered the error and promptly acted to notify the Defendant of the error."

On this basis, the trial court held:

"4. While the Court is not unmindful of the fact that competitive bidding statutes should be construed to avoid circumvention, under the unique facts of the case *sub judice,* the integrity of the competitive bidding process will not be undermined with the granting of contract reformation. Where, as here, the differential between the mistaken bid and the second lowest bid exceeds the amount of the error sought to be reformed, no frustration or harm to beneficial purpose can fairly be demonstrated."

I entirely agree.

It is undisputed that, through a simple mistake in decimal point transcription, Ronlee was out and the DOT was in over $300,000 in material expenses. Short of reliance on the well-known playground maxim about keepers and weepers, there is no reason why the state should be entitled to retain this found money. Under ordinary reformation law, the combination of a unilateral mistake and inequitable conduct fully justifies that relief, . . . and no bases exist or are advanced for the application of a different rule merely because a process of competitive bidding is involved. Since the correction of the mistake would still bring the appellee under the next highest bid, no administratively difficult process of rebidding would be required and none of the purported horribles—"collusive schemes between bidders, or between bidders and awarding officials, or multiple claims from contractors asserting mistake and claiming inequity at taxpayers' expense," . . . are even arguably implicated. . . . I would not refuse to reach a just result here because of the mechanical application of an unsupportable rule or out of a necessarily unjustified fear that someone may in the future misapply our holding in a materially different situation.

The very salutary Florida rule of unilateral mistake—which represents a minority view on the question, . . .—is that the courts will relieve one of the consequences of such an error and the opposite party should be deprived of any consequent windfall whenever there is neither a detrimental reliance upon the mistake nor an inexcusable lack of due care which led to its commission. . . . Neither is present in this case. While the law of our state says otherwise, the majority has permitted DOT successfully to play "gotcha" with Ronlee's money. The state, perhaps even more and certainly no less than a private party, should not be permitted to do so. . . . I would affirm.

Case Questions

1. Why did the trial court grant the plaintiff's summary judgment motion and order reformation in this case?
2. What is the difference between reformation and rescission of a contract?
3. Could Ronlee have rescinded the contract?

Court of Conscience

In equity's early period, chancellors were almost always members of the clergy attempting to attain justice between parties to a dispute. A court of equity has always been considered to be a court of conscience in which natural justice and moral rights take priority over precedent. For example, a chancellor may decline to grant a plaintiff relief because of the plaintiff's wrongdoing in connection with the dispute. A chancellor may also decline to enforce a contract clause that is too unfair or one-sided. Such a clause would be declared to be unconscionable. To enforce it by granting equitable remedies would "shock the conscience of the court."

In the two cases that follow, the plaintiffs/appellants acted inequitably. Why did the courts in these cases decide that equitable relief is inappropriate?

Campbell Soup Company v. Wentz
172 F.2d 80
U.S. Court of Appeals, Third Circuit
December 23, 1948

Goodrich, Circuit Judge

These are appeals from judgments of the District Court denying equitable relief to the buyer under a contract for the sale of carrots. . . .

The transactions which raise the issues may be briefly summarized. On June 21, 1947, Campbell Soup Company (Campbell), a New Jersey corporation, entered into a written contract with George B. Wentz and Harry T. Wentz, who are Pennsylvania farmers, for delivery by the Wentzes to Campbell of *all* the Chantenay red-cored carrots to be grown on fifteen acres of the Wentz farm during the 1947 season. . . . The contract provides . . . for delivery of the carrots at the Campbell plant in Camden, New Jersey. The prices specified in the contract ranged from $23 to $30 per ton according to the time of delivery. The contract price for January 1948 was $30 a ton.

The Wentzes harvested approximately 100 tons of carrots from the fifteen acres covered by the contract. Early in January, 1948, they told a Campbell representative that they would not deliver their carrots at the contract price. The market price at that time was at least $90 per ton, and Chantenay red-cored carrots were virtually unobtainable.

On January 9, 1948, Campbell, suspecting that [defendant] was selling it[s] "contract carrots," refused to purchase any more, and instituted these suits against the Wentz brothers . . . to enjoin further sale of the contract carrots to others, and to compel specific performance of the contract. The trial court denied equitable relief. We agree with the result reached, but on a different ground from that relied upon by the District Court. . . . A party may have specific performance of a contract for the sale of chattels if the legal remedy is inadequate. Inadequacy of the legal remedy is necessarily a matter to be determined by an examination of the facts in each particular instance.

We think that on the question of adequacy of the legal remedy the case is one appropriate for specific performance. It was expressly found that at the time of the trial it was "virtually impossible to obtain Chantenay carrots in the open market." This Chantenay carrot is one which the plaintiff uses in large quantities, furnishing the seed to the growers with whom it makes contracts. It was not claimed that in nutritive value it is any better than other types of carrots. Its blunt shape makes it easier to handle in processing. And its color and texture differ from other varieties. The color is brighter than other carrots. . . . It did appear that the plaintiff uses carrots in fifteen of its twenty-one soups. It also appeared that it uses these Chantenay carrots diced in some of them and that the appearance is uniform. The preservation of uniformity in appearance in a food article marketed throughout the country and sold under the manufacturer's name is a matter of considerable commercial significance and one which is properly considered in determining whether a substitute ingredient is just as good as the original.

The trial court concluded that the plaintiff had failed to establish that the carrots, "judged by objective standards," are unique goods. This we think is not a pure fact conclusion like a finding that Chantenay carrots are of uniform color. It is either a conclusion of law or of mixed fact and law and we are bound to exercise our independent judgment upon it. That the test for specific performance is not necessarily "objective" is shown by the many cases in which equity has given it to enforce contracts for articles—family heirlooms and the like—the value of which was personal to the plaintiff.

Judged by the general standards applicable to determining the adequacy of the legal remedy we think that on this point the case is a proper one for equitable relief. There is considerable authority, old and new, showing liberality in the granting of an equitable remedy. We see no reason why a court should be reluctant to grant specific relief when it can be given without supervision of the court or other time-consuming processes against one who has deliberately broken his agreement. Here the goods of the special type contracted for were unavailable on the open market, the plaintiff had contracted for them long ahead in anticipation of its needs, and had built up a general reputation for its products as part of which reputation uniform appearance was important. We think if this were all that was involved in the case, specific performance should have been granted.

The reason that we shall affirm instead of reversing with an order for specific performance is found in the contract itself. We think it is too hard a bargain and too one-sided an agreement to entitle the plaintiff to relief in a court of con-

science. For each individual grower the agreement is made by filling in names and quantity and price on a printed form furnished by the buyer. This form has quite obviously been drawn by skillful draftsmen with the buyer's interests in mind.

Paragraph 2 provides for the manner of delivery. Carrots are to have their stalks cut off and be in clean sanitary bags or other containers approved by Campbell. This paragraph concludes with a statement that Campbell's determination of conformance with specifications shall be conclusive.

The defendants attack this provision as unconscionable. We do not think that it is, standing by itself. We think that the provision is comparable to the promise to perform to the satisfaction of another and that Campbell would be held liable if it refused carrots which did in fact conform to the specifications.

The next paragraph allows Campbell to refuse carrots in excess of twelve tons to the acre. The next contains a covenant by the grower that he will not sell carrots to anyone else except the carrots rejected by Campbell nor will he permit anyone else to grow carrots on his land. Paragraph 10 provides liquidated damages to the extent of $50 per acre for any breach by the grower. There is no provision for liquidated or any other damages for breach of contract by Campbell.

The provision of the contract which we think is the hardest is paragraph 9. . . . It will be noted that Campbell is excused from accepting carrots under certain circumstances. But even under such circumstances, the grower, while he cannot say Campbell is liable for failure to take the carrots, is not permitted to sell them elsewhere unless Campbell agrees. This is the kind of provision which the late Francis H. Bohlen would call "carrying a good joke too far." What the grower may do with his product under the circumstances set out is not clear. He has covenanted not to store it anywhere except on his own farm and also not to sell to anybody else.

We are not suggesting that the contract is illegal. Nor are we suggesting any excuse for the grower in this case who has deliberately broken an agreement entered into with Campbell. We do think, however, that a party who has offered and succeeded in getting an agreement as tough as this one is, should not come to a chancellor and ask court help in the enforcement of its terms. That equity does not enforce unconscionable bargains is too well-established to require elaborate citation.

The plaintiff argues that the provisions of the contract are separable. We agree that they are, but do not think that decisions separating out certain provisions from illegal contracts are in point here. As already said, we do not suggest that this contract is illegal. All we say is that the sum total of its provisions drives too hard a bargain for a court of conscience to assist. . . .

The judgments will be affirmed.

Case Questions

1. If the plaintiff had sued for damages, would the result of the suit have been different?
2. Campbell Soup Company lost this case in its attempt to get equitable relief. May it now sue for money damages?
3. If the contract between Campbell Soup Company and Wentz were not unconscionable, would specific performance of the contract be an appropriate remedy? What is necessary before specific performance will be granted?
4. Why did the court hold the contract to be unconscionable and therefore unenforceable in equity?

Equitable Maxims

Instead of using rules of law in reaching decisions, courts of equity used *equitable maxims*, which are short statements that contain the gist of much equity law. These maxims were developed over the years (with no agreement as to the number or order) and today are used as guides in the decision-making process in disputes in equity. The following are some of the equitable maxims:

Equity does not suffer a wrong to be without a remedy.

Equity regards substance rather than form.

Equality is equity.

Equity regards as done that which should be done.

Equity follows the law.

Equity acts *in personam* rather than *in rem*.

Whoever seeks equity must do equity.

Whoever comes into equity must do so with clean hands.

Delay resulting in a prejudicial change defeats equity (*laches*).

New York Football Giants v. Los Angeles Chargers Football Club
291 F.2d 471
U.S. Court of Appeals, Fifth Circuit
June 14, 1961

Tuttle, Chief Judge

In the case of *Detroit Football Company v. Robinson*, 186 F.Supp. 933, 934, Judge Wright, of the District Court for the Eastern District of Louisiana, said: "This case is but another round in the sordid fight for football players, a fight which begins before these athletes enter college and follows them through their professional careers. It is a fight characterized by deception, double dealing, campus jumping, secret alumni subsidization, semi-professionalism and professionalism. It is a fight which has produced as part of its harvest this current rash of contract jumping suits. It is a fight which so conditions the minds and hearts of these athletes that one day they can agree to play football for a stated amount for one group, only to repudiate that agreement the following day or whenever a better offer comes along. . . ."

We have read cases cited in Judge Wright's opinion and we share his disgust at the sordid picture too often presented in this kind of litigation. So much so, in fact, that we conclude that in an appropriate case, the federal equity court, which is the tribunal usually appealed to for a decree of specific performance of injunction, must decline to lend its aid to either party to a transaction that in its inception offends concepts of decency and honest dealing, such as the case before us.

In the fall of 1959, Flowers was an outstanding football player on the University of Mississippi team. His team was to play a post-season game on January 1, 1960, at the Sugar Bowl in New Orleans against a traditional rival, Louisiana State University.

The well-understood rules of the Southeastern Conference (SEC) and the National Collegiate Athletic Association (NCAA) made ineligible from further participation in intercollegiate games any player who had signed a contract to play with a professional team. Flowers wanted above all else to play in the Sugar Bowl game. On a trip to New York City for other purposes he was invited by the Giants' official Mara to come to his office where he was urged to sign a contract to play two seasons, beginning in 1960, with the Giants. He told Mara he wanted to retain his eligibility to play in the Sugar Bowl game. . . .

Following such a proposal by Mara, Flowers signed the standard form of contract of the National Football League, and received checks totaling $3500 as a sign-on bonus, and then returned to Mississippi. One of the terms of the contract was that: "This agreement shall become valid and binding upon each party hereto only when, as and if it shall be approved by the

Commissioner." Part of the deceit agreed to between the parties was an agreement that Mara would not submit the contract to the Commissioner until after January 1. Flowers later made some effort by telephone on or about December 5th to withdraw from the contract. Thereafter, the Giants promptly filed the contract with the Commissioner, and he "approved" it on December 15. However, at Mara's request, he withheld announcement of his approval until after January 1st. On December 29th Flowers had negotiations with the Los Angeles Chargers, as a result of which he was offered a better contract, but which was not formally executed until after the Sugar Bowl game on January 1st. He wrote a letter to the Giants on December 29th, stating that he was withdrawing from his agreement with them. He returned the uncashed checks for the bonus money. Flowers played in the game, all his fans presumably thinking that he was still an eligible player, thanks to the deception proposed by the Giants and entered into by him.

The trial court held that until the "contract" was approved by the Commissioner, it was not binding. . . . It held, therefore, that when Mara, contrary to his agreement not to submit the contract to the Commissioner until after January 1st, did so, the approval by the Commissioner was not effective to make it binding and that Flowers still had the legal right to cancel until January 1st. The trial court, therefore, entered judgment for both defendants.

Without considering the legal issues on the merits, we affirm the judgment of the trial court. We do so by application of the age-old, but sometimes overlooked, doctrine that "he who comes into equity must come with clean hands." . . . This equitable maxim is far more than a mere banality. It is a self-imposed ordinance that closes the doors of a court of equity to one tainted with the inequitableness or bad faith relative to the matter in which he seeks relief, however improper may have been the behavior of defendant. That doctrine is rooted in the historical concept of court of equity as a vehicle for affirmatively enforcing the requirements of conscience and good faith. This presupposes a refusal on its part to be the "abettor of iniquity." Thus while "equity does not demand that its suitors shall have led blameless lives" . . . as to other matters, it does require that they shall have acted fairly and without fraud or deceit as to the controversy in issue. . . .

"This maxim necessarily gives wide range to the equity court's use of discretion in refusing to aid the unclean litigant. It is 'not bound by formula or restrained by any limitation that tends to trammel the free and just exercise of discretion.' . . . Accordingly, one's misconduct need not necessarily have been of such a nature as to be punishable as a crime or as to justify legal proceedings of any character. Any willful act concerning the cause of action which rightfully can be said to transgress equitable standards of conduct is sufficient cause for the invocation of the maxim by the chancellor.

"Moreover, where a suit in equity concerns the public interest as well as the private interests of the litigants this doctrine assumes even wider and more significant proportions. For if an equity court properly uses the maxim to withhold its assistance in such a case it not only prevents a wrongdoer from enjoying the fruits of his transgression but averts an injury to the public. The determination of when the maxim should be applied to bar this type of suit thus becomes of vital significance. . . .

". . . A court of equity acts only when and as conscience commands, and if the conduct of the plaintiff be offensive to the dictates of natural justice, then, whatever may be the rights he possesses and whatever use he may make of them in a court of law, he will be held remedyless in a court of equity."

Here the plaintiff's whole difficulty arises because it admittedly took from Flowers what it claims to be a binding contract, but which it agreed with Flowers that it would, in effect, represent was not in existence in order to deceive others who had a very material and important interest in the subject matter. If there had been a straightforward execution of the document, followed by its filing with the Commissioner, none of the legal problems now presented to this court to untangle would exist. We think no party has the right thus to create problems by its devious and deceitful conduct and then approach a court of equity with a plea that the pretended status which it has foisted on the public be ignored and its rights be declared as if it had acted in good faith throughout.

When it became apparent from uncontradicted testimony of Mara that this deceit was practiced in order to bring into being the "contract" sued upon, the trial court should have dismissed the suit without more on the basis of the "clean-hands" doctrine.

To the extent that the final judgment of the trial court dismissed the complaint as amended, with costs adjudged against the plaintiff, the said judgment is affirmed. To the extent that the judgment proceeded to a legal determination as to the validity of the contracts between the parties, we conclude that, in the view we take of the equitable principles applicable, these judgments should not have been reached. . . .

As thus modified the judgment is affirmed.

Case Questions

1. What is the equitable maxim used here, and how was it violated?
2. What approach or role should the court use in a situation in which both parties have done wrong?
3. Did the court appear to have any personal feelings about this case or its subject matter? Should the court allow such feelings to be evident?

Specific Performance

Specific performance is an equitable remedy that is identified with breaches of contract. The plaintiff brings suit to obtain a court order that requires the defendant to fulfill his or her contractual obligations. Specific performance will only be granted where there is a valid contract.[2] It is enforced through the use of the contempt power.

Like all equitable relief, specific performance is limited to situations in which there is no adequate remedy at common law. This means that under the particular circumstances of the case, the plaintiff can establish that a breach of contract action for money damages is inadequate. We saw an example of this in the *Campbell* case. Campbell wanted the court to order the Wentz brothers to live up to their contractual obligations to deliver Chantenay carrots to Campbell. Campbell argued that requiring the Wentz brothers to pay Campbell $50 per acre in liquidated damages for breach of contract was an inadequate remedy. Campbell contended that it couldn't go out on the open market and purchase Chantenay carrots from another seller. There was no alternative source of supply.

Specific performance is usually applied in situations involving contracts for the sale of land and unique goods. Common law relief is often inadequate for unique goods, because one cannot take money damages and go out and purchase the same item. A similar item might be purchased, but that is not what the parties had bargained. The buyer had an agreement to purchase a particular, unique property item. Thus, if a seller and buyer have contracted for the sale of land, a painting, sculpture, an antique car, or a baseball card collection, money damages are just not a substitute for the item. The Chantenay carrot was unique for Campbell soup. It was the only carrot that would work in the machinery. Consumers of Campbell soups were accustomed to that particular carrot's firmness, consistency, color, and taste.

A plaintiff must have substantially performed, or be ready to perform, his or her obligations under the contract in order to be entitled to specific performance. This is referred to as a condition precedent for specific performance.

In addition, equity courts are concerned with practicality. For example, an equitable court generally will not order one person to fulfill a personal service contract and perform work for another. Such a decree would be tantamount to involuntary servitude. It is also impractical for a court to require one person to work for another. Such an order could involve the court in a never-ending series of employer-employee spats.

A defendant can assert various equitable defenses in response to a plaintiff's claim for specific performance. These include (1) unclean hands (see page 241), (2) hardship, and (3) *laches*. Hardship involves sharp practices where the contractual terms are entirely one-sided and where there is a gross inadequacy of consideration. Hardship exists because one party is attempting to take unfair advantage of the other party. *Laches* is an equitable defense that is used to deny equitable relief where a plaintiff's unreasonable delay in bringing the action has caused prejudicial harm to the defendant. This defense is similar to the common law defense of statute of limitations. The equitable defense of *laches* does not involve any specific period of time.

Contracts for the sale of goods are governed by the Uniform Commercial Code (UCC).[3] The UCC provides buyers with a right to specific performance in 2-716, and sellers with an equivalent remedy in 2-709.

The court in the following case explains why specific performance is not granted where a contract calls for the performance of personal services.

Bloch v. Hillel Torah North Suburban Day School
426 N.E.2d 976
Appellate Court of Illinois,
First District, Third Division
September 9, 1981

McNamara, Justice

Plaintiffs appeal from an order of the trial court granting summary judgment in favor of defendant Hillel Torah North Suburban Day School. Helen Bloch is a grade school child who was expelled from defendant, a private Jewish school, at mid-year in 1980. Her parents brought this action seeking to enjoin expulsion and for specific performance of defendant's contract to educate Helen.

The complaint alleged that defendant arbitrarily and in bad faith breached its contract, and that Helen's expulsion was motivated by defendant's disapproval of plaintiff's leadership role in combatting an epidemic of head lice at the school. The complaint also alleged that the school uniquely corresponded exactly to the religious commitments desired by plaintiffs. Defendant's answer stated that Helen was expelled, pursuant to school regulations, for excessive tardiness and absences. The parties also disputed the duration of the contractual obligation to educate. Defendant contended that the contract was to endure only for a school year since tuition for only that period of time was accepted by it. Plaintiffs maintained that the contract, as implied by custom and usage, was to endure for eight years, the first year's tuition creating irrevocable option contracts for the subsequent school years, provided that Helen conformed to defendant's rules.

After the trial court denied plaintiff's request for a preliminary injunction, both sides moved for summary judgment. The trial court denied plaintiff's motion and granted the motion of the defendant. In the same order, the trial court gave plaintiffs leave to file an amended complaint for money damages.

Whether a court will exercise its jurisdiction to order specific performance of a valid contract is a matter within the sound discretion of the court and dependent upon the facts of each case. . . . Where the contract is one which establishes a personal relationship calling for the rendition of personal services, the proper remedy for a breach is generally not specific performance but rather an action for money damages. . . . The reasons for denying specific performance in such a case are as follows: the remedy at law is adequate; enforcement and supervision of the order of specific performance may be problematic and could result in protracted litigation; and the concept of compelling the continuance of a personal relationship to which one of the parties is resistant is repugnant as a form of involuntary servitude. . . .

Applying these principles to the present case, we believe that the trial court properly granted summary judgment in favor of defendant. It is beyond dispute that the relationship between a grade school and a student is one highly personal in nature. Similarly, it is apparent that performance of such a contract requires a rendition of a variety of personal services. Although we are cognizant of the difficulties in duplicating the personal services offered by one school, particularly one like defendant, we are even more aware of the difficulties pervasive in compelling the continuation of a relationship between a young child and a private school which openly resists that relationship. In such a case, we believe the trial court exercises sound judgment in ruling that plaintiffs are best left to their remedy for damages. . . .

Illinois law recognizes the availability of a remedy for monetary damages for a private school's wrongful expulsion of a student in violation of its contract. . . . And especially, where, as here, the issue involves a personal relationship between a grade school and a young child, we believe plaintiffs are best left to a remedy for damages for breach of contract.

For the reasons stated, the judgment of the circuit court of Cook County is affirmed, and the cause is remanded for further proceedings permitting plaintiffs to file an amended complaint for money damages.

Affirmed and remanded.

Rizzi, P. J., and McGillicuddy, J., concur.

Case Questions

1. What problems might have been encountered in court-ordered specific performance?
2. In what types of cases would specific performance be granted?

Restitution

The remedy of restitution is in some situations an equitable remedy and in other cases a common law remedy. *Restitution* means restoration to the plaintiff of property in the possession of the defendant. The purpose of restitution is to prevent unjust enrichment, which means that a person should not be allowed to profit or be enriched inequitably at another's expense. Thus a person is permitted recovery when another has received a benefit and retention of it would be unjust.

The restoration may be *in specie*, in which a specific item is recovered by the plaintiff from the defendant. In many situations, an *in specie* recovery is impossible or impractical. In such instances, the remedy might have to be "substitutionary," whereby the defendant is ordered to return to the plaintiff as restitution the dollar value of any benefit he or she has received. If so, the amount is determined by the defendant's gain, not by the plaintiff's loss, as in the case of money damages. So if D takes P's car, worth $4,000, and sells it to someone else at $8,000, D may be liable to make restitution to P for the full amount of $8,000. P never had $8,000, only a car worth half as much, but is still entitled to the total amount. If there was cash in the glove compartment, P would be entitled to recover that also.

The following case discusses restitution in both the common law and equitable contexts. The court first determines whether the plaintiff was entitled to a statutory mechanics lien or a common law lien. It is only after ruling the plaintiff ineligible for a lien under the common law that the court turns to equity. The balancing of interests and harm to produce a just result is clearly evidenced here. Observe how damages are computed in an unjust enrichment case. The court said the mechanic's recovery would be limited to the difference in a vehicle's value before and after it was repaired and he would not receive damages reflecting his hourly rate.

Iacomini v. Liberty Mutual Insurance Company
497 A.2d 854
Supreme Court of New Hampshire
August 7, 1985

Douglas, Justice

The issue presented in this case is whether a party may subject an owner's interest in an automobile to a lien for repair and storage charges, without the owner's knowledge, acquiescence, or consent. We hold that no common law or statutory lien may be created under such circumstances but that equitable relief for unjust enrichment may be appropriate.

On August 10, 1983, the plaintiff, Richard Iacomini, d/b/a Motor Craft of Raymond, contracted with one Theodore Zadlo for the towing, storage, and repair of a 1977 Mercedes Benz 450-SL. Mr. Zadlo represented himself to be the owner of the car and presented the plaintiff with a New Hampshire registration certificate for the car bearing Zadlo's name. In fact, the car did not belong to Mr. Zadlo but had been stolen in 1981 from a car lot in New Jersey. The defendant, Liberty Mutual Insurance Company, had earlier fulfilled its policy obligations by reimbursing the owner of the stolen car $22,000. It thereby had gained title to the vehicle.

Extensive damage was done to the car after its theft, and Zadlo brought the car to Mr. Iacomini for the purpose of repairing this damage. The plaintiff kept the car at his garage, where he disassembled it in order to give a repair estimate. He apparently never fully reassembled it. Mr. Zadlo periodically returned to the plaintiff's garage to check the status of the repair work.

In October 1983, the Raymond Police Department notified the plaintiff that the Mercedes was a stolen car and also notified Liberty Mutual of the location of the car. Mr. Iacomini at that point moved the vehicle from the lot to the inside of his garage where it remained for the next several months. Liberty Mutual contacted the plaintiff soon after it learned of the vehicle's location to arrange its pick-up. The plaintiff refused to relinquish the car until he had been reimbursed for repair and storage fees.

. . . Liberty Mutual instituted a replevin action . . . seeking return of the car. . . . On the basis of facts presented at a hearing . . . in the replevin action, the Court . . . found that the plaintiff (defendant in that action) did not have a valid statutory lien since the vehicle was brought to the plaintiff by one other than the owner. The court then ordered Mr. Iacomini to make the vehicle available forthwith to Liberty Mutual with the proviso that Liberty Mutual retain the vehicle in its possession and ownership for a period of at least ninety days in order to allow Mr. Iacomini the opportunity to file an action against Liberty Mutual relating to repairs.

The plaintiff petitioned for an *ex parte* attachment, . . . claiming approximately $10,000, most of which was for storage fees. . . . [T]he same court entered judgment in Liberty Mutual's favor finding that "the plaintiff was not authorized or instructed by the legal or equitable owner of the automobile to perform any repair work on the vehicle." On either the day before, or the day of, the hearing, . . . the plaintiff filed a Motion to Specify Claim to include an action for unjust enrichment. Liberty Mutual objected to the plaintiff's attempt to amend his cause of action at that date, and the court denied the motion. It also denied the plaintiff's requests for findings that the value of the car had been enhanced by the plaintiff and that denial of the plaintiff's claim would result in unjust enrichment. This appeal followed.

The law generally recognizes three types of liens: statutory, common law, and equitable. . . . The statutes provide as follows:

> For Storage. "Any person who maintains a public garage, public or private airport or hangar, or trailer court for the parking, storage or care of motor vehicles or aircraft or house trailers brought to his premises or placed in his care *by or with the consent of the legal or equitable owner* shall have a lien upon said motor vehicle or aircraft or house trailer, so long as the same shall remain in his possession, for proper charges due him for the parking, storage or care of the same." . . .

> For Labor. "Any person who shall, by himself or others, perform labor, furnish materials, or expend money, in repairing, refitting or equipping any motor vehicle or aircraft, *under a contract expressed or implied with the legal or equitable owner*, shall have a lien upon such motor vehicle or aircraft, so long as the same shall remain in his possession, until the charges for such repairs, materials, or accessories, or money so used or expended have been paid." . . .

"[I]n the case of a statutory lien, the specified requisites must be strictly observed." . . . By the language of the statute, no lien may be created on an automobile as to the owner without the owner's knowledge, acquiescence, or consent.

Under the present circumstances, where the repairman contracted with the possessor of a stolen vehicle for the repair of the car, it is difficult to imagine how the owner could have consented to, or acquiesced in, the repair of the vehicle. The owner in this case had no idea even where the car was located. Whether the plaintiff was reasonable in believing Mr. Zadlo to be the true owner is irrelevant to whether a contract existed between him and Liberty Mutual.

Prior to the passage of a statute on the subject of mechanics' liens, . . . "there existed here and elsewhere a lien at common law in favor of anyone who upon request expended labor and materials upon another's property." . . . The statutory lien does not supplant, but supplements, the common law mechanics lien, so that we must also look to the rights of the plaintiff under the common law. . . .

As with the statutory liens, common law liens on property for repair costs could be created only by the owner or by a person authorized by him. "By common law, every person, who employs labor and skill upon the goods of another, *at the request of the owner*, without a special contract, is entitled to retain the goods until a proper recompense is made." . . . New Hampshire common law is consistent with the common law of other jurisdictions which also require the owner's consent or acquiescence before a lien may be established on the property of the owner. . . .

The necessity of the owner's consent is consistent with the contractual relationship between the lienor and the lienee which underlies the establishment of a lien. . . . As discussed previously, no such contractual relationship may be inferred where a possessor of a stolen vehicle turns it over to a garageman for repairs; accordingly, no lien is created against the owner. This is the correct result under the common law even though hardships may result to a good faith repairman. "There are many hard cases . . . of honest and innocent persons, who have been obliged to surrender goods to the true owners without remedy. . . . But these are hazards to which persons in business are continually exposed." . . . Of course, the repairman would always have a cause of action against the third party who contracted with him for repairs without the owner's consent.

Although the facts of this case do not establish either a statutory or common law lien, the plaintiff may be entitled to restitution under principles of equity. An equitable lien may be imposed to prevent unjust enrichment in an owner whose

property was improved, for the increased value of the property. . . . "In the absence of a contractual agreement, a trial court may require an individual to make restitution for unjust enrichment if he has received a benefit which would be unconscionable to retain." . . . The trial court must determine whether the facts and equities of a particular case warrant such a remedy. . . .

We here note that "when a court assesses damages in an unjust enrichment case, the focus is not upon the cost to the plaintiff, but rather it is upon the value of what was actually received by the defendants." . . . In this case, the damages would thus be the difference between the value of the vehicle before and after the plaintiff worked on it, regardless of its worth when stolen.

Reversed and remanded.

Case Questions

1. Why should the defendant insurance company be required to pay the plaintiff repairman for services that the plaintiff performed without the defendant's knowledge or consent?
2. What is an equitable lien? How does it work?
3. How does a judge determine the amount of an award in an unjust enrichment case?

Declaratory Judgment

When someone seeks a judicial determination of the rights and obligations of the parties, that person is seeking the remedy of *declaratory judgment*. The court determines what the law is, or the constitutionality or the meaning of the law. For example, if a legislative body passes a statute making your business activity illegal, you could continue to operate the business and be arrested. You could also try to prevent the enforcement of the law by seeking a declaratory judgment. This action asks a court to determine whether the statute in question is constitutional. Because a judge granting declaratory judgment does not issue any orders telling anyone to act or refrain from acting, people who are seeking declaratory relief often ask for injunctive relief as well.

Declaratory judgment is considered by some courts to be an equitable remedy and by other courts to be a legal remedy.

Jury Trial

Cases are set for a jury trial only if a right to jury trial exists and one or both of the parties properly asserts this right. For the most part, trial by jury is a constitutional right. The Seventh Amendment to the U.S. Constitution guarantees litigants in federal court a jury trial in suits at common law, and most state constitutions make similar provisions. However, there is no constitutional right to a jury trial in equity cases because jury trials were not a part of chancery procedure.

Parties in most U.S. courts may join common law and equitable remedies in the same action, without giving up their right to a jury trial. A jury decides the legal issues, and the judge decides the equitable issues. In the following case the appellant objected when the trial court classified the action as exclusively in equity.

State v. Yelsen Land Company
257 S.C. 401, 185 S.E.2d 897
Supreme Court of South Carolina
January 5, 1972

Littlejohn, Justice

This action was commenced by the State of South Carolina to settle a dispute concerning ownership and control of certain tidelands, submerged lands, and waters adjacent to Morris Island in Charleston Harbor. The State seeks to enjoin the defendants from trespassing upon the property involved, and seeks confirmation of title to the land in the State.

By way of answer and counterclaim, defendants assert title to the area in question, and allege that the State has trespassed upon it. They seek judgment confirming title in themselves, and seek monetary damages for wrongful taking, forbidden by the constitution. They also seek attorney fees and an injunction against the State. Their claim of title to the

area stems from grants by the state of South Carolina to their predecessors in title.

After the case had been placed on the calendar for a jury trial, and the case reached for trial on the roster, the judge, on his own motion and over the objection of the State, referred all issues for trial to the Master in Equity for Charleston County. The State duly excepted to this order of reference and has appealed.

The sole question raised on this appeal is whether the judge erred in ordering the issues tried by the master instead of a jury.

The complaint in this action asserts that "Plaintiff has no adequate remedy at law and therefore brings this action in equity. . . ." Defendants Yelsen Land Company, Inc. and Dajon Realty Company likewise assert in their answer and counterclaim that "Defendants have no adequate remedy at law to prevent further trespass. . . ." Defendants contend that all parties have alleged this to be a matter in equity, and that a trial by jury has therefore been waived.

The State's assertion that it "has no adequate remedy at law" was, perhaps, unfortunate. Obviously, it referred to the injunctive relief sought, which is purely equitable. But the character of an action is not necessarily determined by such recitations in the pleadings. Rather, it is the nature of the issues and the remedies which are sought that is determinative.

A great many actions are of a hybrid nature. They involve not only issues normally tried by a jury, but also issues normally tried in equity without a jury. This court noted . . .

> "Under our Code practice legal and equitable issues and rights may be asserted in the same complaint, and legal and equitable remedies and relief afforded in the same action. In such event the legal issues are for determination by the jury, and the equitable issues for the judge sitting as a chancellor. The legal and equitable issues should be separated and each tried by the appropriate branch of the court." . . .

Both the State and the defendants seek injunctive relief in this action. An action for such relief is equitable. . . .

But both the State and the defendants assert title to the tidelands here in question. And when an issue of title to real estate is raised, such issue is generally triable by jury. . . .

Bryan v. Freeman . . . was a suit to remove a cloud on and quiet title to land. The complaint alleged that plaintiffs had title to land. Defendants, by answers, asserted paramount title. The issue there was whether the action should have been referred to a master. In holding that the trial court acted properly in refusing to refer the action to a master, we said:

> "An action to remove a cloud on and quiet title to land is one in equity. . . . However, when the defendant's answer raises an issue of paramount title to land, such as would, if established, defeat plaintiff's action, it is the duty of the court to submit to a jury the issue of title as raised by the pleadings." . . .

The facts before us require the same holding as the *Bryan* case. All parties seek equitable relief, and all parties seek relief triable at law. We do not think that the allegation in the complaint that this is an action in equity warrants the conclusion, as argued by defendants, that the plaintiff waived its right to a jury trial. To hold that the State voluntarily relinquished its right to a jury trial of the law issues involved would require a strained construction of the allegation in the complaint. It was the duty of the lower court to submit the law issues to a jury.

Reversed.

Case Questions

1. What was the common law part of the case? What was the equity part of the case?
2. Who will decide the equity claims? Who will decide the common law claims?
3. Suppose a party has a single claim of relief, but demands various remedies, some available at law and some available only in equity. Will the case be tried before a jury?

4. What determined the character of the action in the instant case—the nature of the issues or the recitations in the pleadings?

Chapter Questions

1. Define the following terms:

avoidable harm doctrine	liquidated damages
benefit rule	maxims
common law lien	nominal damages
compensatory damages	punitive damages
declaratory judgment	reformation
ejectment	remedy
equitable remedy	replevin
equitable lien	rescission
ex parte	restitution
exemplary damages	special damages
general damages	specific performance
injunctive relief	statutory lien
in specie	unjust enrichment
jurisprudence	waiver
laches	

2. Since 1950, Harris-Walsh, Inc., has been engaged in the removal of anthracite coal, by strip mining within the limits of the Borough of Dickson City, Pennsylvania. On June 28, 1963, the borough adopted an ordinance requiring that strip mine operators furnish bonds sufficient to reclaim stripped land in all future mining operations. The Dickson City ordinance also provides for certain criminal penalties for violation of the above ordinance. Since Harris-Walsh has been mining the area for many years, it feels it should be able to continue to mine in its old fashion. Can Harris-Walsh invoke the jurisdiction of a court of equity?
   Harris-Walsh, Inc. v. Dickson City, 216 A.2d 329 (Pa. 1966)

3. Pet Ponderosa Memorial Gardens leased 10 acres of land from Memory Gardens to be used as a pet cemetery. This land was adjacent to Memory Gardens' human cemetery. As part of the lease, the pet cemetery was allowed to use all available water each evening for two hours to develop and maintain its landscaping. Then Memory Gardens abruptly cut off the water supply, and as a result, the grass and other plantings died. The pet cemetery tried to renegotiate the lease without success. It found that hiring a water truck to haul in water was too expensive. Other water supplies could not be obtained. The pet cemetery instituted a suit and sought a preliminary injunction. Should this relief be granted?
   Memory Gardens of Las Vegas v. Pet Ponderosa M.G., 492 P.2d 123 (Nev. 1972)

4. For a number of years, a gambling establishment and saloon, called the Sycamore Cafe, was conducted on Central Avenue in Louisville, Kentucky, in an industrial and residential district. The proprietors, the Goose brothers, had been arrested numerous times for gambling, disorderly conduct, malicious assault, and other crimes. Records show that these charges were "filed away," or stooges were employed to "take the rap." The record of the Goose brothers and the Sycamore Cafe is a sordid one of flagrant violations of the law occurring at all times of the day and night. Can the commonwealth's attorney enjoin the continuation of these activities at the Sycamore Cafe by invoking the jurisdiction of a court of equity for injunctive purposes?

   Goose v. Commonwealth, 305 Ky 644, 205 S.W.2d 326 (1947)

5. During the summer of 1961, Harry Kapchuk and other stockholders reorganized the capital structure of Seashore Food Products, Inc., by creating an issue of no-par common stock with voting rights. The Kapchuk group retained 15% of this issue for themselves on the basis of three shares for every dollar of contributed capital. In August 1962, Seashore Food Products became heavily indebted to Seymour Friend and other creditors, some being close affiliates of the corporation. The debts were so large that the corporation faced bankruptcy. Acting as officers of the corporation, the Kapchuk group explained the situation to Friend and the creditors' group, and proposed that bankruptcy could be averted if the creditors would accept corporate stock in payment of their claims against the corporation. This was agreed to, and the transfer of stock to the creditors was made on the basis of one share of stock for every three dollars of corporate debt. Primarily because of the Kapchuk's skillful management, the corporation regained its solvency and began to prosper. In February 1966, Friend and other creditors filed suit, asking that a constructive trust be imposed on the stock acquired by Kapchuk during corporate reorganization because Kapchuk failed to disclose during the 1962 negotiations that he obtained this stock at three shares for one dollar. What equitable doctrine bars such relief to Friend and the creditors' group? Why?

   Friend v. Kapchuk, 216 So.2d 783 (Fla. 1968)

6. The owner of a professional basketball club, the Carolina Cougars, sued to enjoin William Cunningham, a professional basketball player, from performing services as a player for any other basketball club. The trial court denied the relief because the Cougars had unclean hands. The Cougars had contacted Cunningham while he was under contract with the Philadelphia 76ers and agreed to pay him $80,000 for sitting out the 1970–71 season, thereby repudiating the option on his services. Cunningham, while under contract with the 76ers, signed a three-year contract with the Cougars, commencing with the 1971–72 season, which was after the term of his contract with the 76ers. Cunningham refused to perform for the Cougars because he received a higher offer from the 76ers. In your

opinion, should the equitable relief sought have been denied under the clean-hands doctrine?

Munchak Corp. v. Cunningham, 457 F.2d 721 (4th Cir. 1972)

7. Archie Sparrow, a cowboy experienced in training horses, met a rancher and fellow rodeo rider, Chip Morris, at a rodeo in Florida. After comparing notes on various rodeos, Morris offered Sparrow a job for sixteen weeks working on Morris's ranch in Arkansas. Sparrow accepted, and as compensation, Morris agreed to give Sparrow $400 and a brown horse named Kerro. When Sparrow first came to Morris's ranch, Kerro was practically unbroken. However, Sparrow worked with the horse during his spare time, and by the time his sixteen weeks were up, Kerro was well on his way to becoming a first-class riding horse. Morris returned at the end of the sixteen weeks and gave Sparrow a check for $400, but refused to deliver the horse. Is Sparrow entitled to specific performance on the contract to deliver the horse? Why or why not?

Morris v. Sparrow, 287 S.W.2d 583 (Ark. 1956)

8. Inez Vacarro, who had had two miscarriages, received injections of a hormone to prevent miscarriages throughout the third pregnancy. A child was born with severe birth defects. The child's deformity was the result of the ingestion of the drug Delalutin, manufactured and sold by Squibb Corporation to prevent miscarriages. In a suit against Squibb, should the father, mother, and/or child be allowed recovery for emotional distress?

Vacarro v. Squibb Corp., 71 A.D.2d 270, 422 N.Y.2d 679 (1979)

9. Blummer Waddell Lamm's husband died on August 3. She employed Edward Shingleton, an undertaker, to conduct the funeral and purchased from him a casket and vault. Shingleton represented the vault as watertight, and warranted that it would protect the body from water for years. On the Wednesday before Thanksgiving, Lamm discovered that the vault had risen six inches above the ground during the preceding period of rainy weather. She reported this immediately to Shingleton. On the following Saturday, employees of Shingleton and the cemetery met at the grave to move the vault into a freshly prepared adjoining grave. When the vault was raised it was discovered that mud and water had entered it and the casket was wet. Lamm testified that this caused her considerable shock and she became a nervous wreck. She also testified that while the men were discussing getting the mud out of the vault, Shingleton loudly said he was not going to clean it out and "To hell with the whole damned business, it's no concern of mine." This language made Lamm so nervous that she could hardly stand. Lamm is suing Shingleton and the cemetery for failure to perform their contractual duties in a reasonable and workmanlike manner. Consider the nature of the contract. Can Lamm recover for mental anguish as part of her compensatory damages?

Lamm v. Shingleton, 231 N.C. 10, 55 S.E.2d 810 (1949)

10. In January, Evergreen Amusement Corporation entered into a contract with Milstead for the construction of a drive-in theater on land it had recently purchased. Work was to be completed by June 1 so that Evergreen could operate its theater during the peak summer months. Because unforeseen difficulties arose due to a faulty survey, thousands of dollars of extra fill dirt was needed, and work was not completed until the middle of August. Evergreen refused to pay Milstead for the extra work, and Milstead sued Evergreen for the cost of the extra fill, labor, and other materials. Evergreen counterclaimed for $12,500 profits allegedly lost during the period from June 1 to the middle of August. Evergreen sought to introduce a local drive-in owner and marketing consultant as a witness. The witness was prepared to testify that (1) a market survey showed a need for a drive-in theater in the area; (2) profits for the months in question could be estimated accurately by examining the theater's profits during the corresponding months of its second year of operation; and (3) weather, population, and competition were approximately the same in both years. However, the court refused to hear such testimony and in effect disallowed Evergreen's counterclaim for lost profits. Loss of profits is a well-recognized element of damages. Why did the court refuse to consider the issue?

    Evergreen Amusement Corp. v. Milstead, 112 A.2d 901 (Md. 1955)

11. Prisoners sued their jailers for money damages for cruel and unusual punishment by the state prison authorities in violation of their constitutional rights. Included among these practices were the imposition of a bread-and-water diet; arbitrary use of tear gas; taping, chaining, or handcuffing of inmates to cell bars; extended periods of confinement in solitary confinement cells; placing prisoners naked in a hot, roach-infested cell; and arbitrary removal of good conduct time, thereby extending a man's compulsory prison term by months, and in the case of one of the plaintiffs, by years. Is the computation of damages possible?

    Landman v. Royster, 354 F.Supp. 1302 (E.D. Va. 1973)

12. Florence Allman and her husband were the owners of a 150-horsepower ski boat, which they kept at the Lake of the Ozarks in Missouri. On August 9, Florence decided to go water-skiing and asked Jesse Bird, a fellow skier, to drive the towboat. They went out on the lake accompanied by Florence's son Johnny. The boat was stopped in the middle of the lake, and Florence jumped into the water and began to adjust her skis. As she was taking up the slack in the towline, Bird suddenly slammed the boat into forward gear and took off, catching Florence's hand and arm in the tangled towline. Johnny shouted for Bird to stop, but Bird kept accelerating. Finally, Johnny's shouts induced Bird to stop the boat. Florence's hand and arm were severely and permanently injured. As Bird knew, it is customary for drivers to take the slack out of the line and signal the skier when they are ready to start. Florence Allman is suing

Jesse Bird for her personal injuries. Can she recover punitive damages on the above facts? What legal language characterizes the nature of Bird's action of starting the boat without regard for Florence's safety?

Allman v. Bird, 353 P.2d 216 (Kan. 1960)

13. Younce went for a drive one summer's day with her infant daughter Gloria. When they stopped for a stop sign, their car was struck from the rear by a car driven by Baker. Younce and her daughter sued Baker for personal injuries sustained as a result of the collision. Baker admitted that his negligence was the proximate cause of the collision, but denied that the plaintiffs suffered injury or damage as a result thereof. The court instructed the jury to find whether the plaintiff suffered any injury as a result of the collision, and, if so, the dollar amount of the damage. The jury returned its verdict of no injuries and no damages. Are the plaintiffs still entitled to nominal damages, since the defendant admitted that he negligently caused the collision?

Younce v. Baker, 9 Ohio App.2d 259, 224 N.E.2d 144 (1966)

14. On July 17, 1944, the Tally brothers, owners of the Glenn Ranch, a summer resort in the San Bernardino mountains, leased the ranch and its hotel and tourist facilities to Mr. and Mrs. McCarthy. The lease was for ten years, and rental was $10,000 per year. The McCarthys moved in on August 31, 1944, and operated the resort business and paid the rent until October 31, 1950. On November 28, 1950, the Tallys served the McCarthys a notice to pay rent or vacate the premises. On December 1, 1950, McCarthy notified the Tally brothers that he surrendered the premises. A receiver was appointed, and the Tallys sued the McCarthys for damages. The lease provided, *inter alia*, that if the lessee abandoned the property within 10 years, lessees would be liable to lessors for actual damages plus liquidated damages of $10,000 for injury to the goodwill and trade name of the business. At the time of the breach in November, the Glenn Ranch was closed for the season and no tourists were permitted to occupy the premises. May the Tallys recover the liquidated damages?

McCarthy v. Tally, 297 P.2d 981 (Cal. 1956)

Notes

1. Students should review the discussion in Chapter 1 with respect to the historical development of equity and the common law.

2. You can learn about the requirements of a valid contract by reading Chapter 9. In general, a valid contract must be clear, the terms must be reasonably certain, and there must have been an agreement between competent parties supported by consideration, which does not contravene principles of law and which in some circumstances must be in writing.

3. Please see the discussion on the Uniform Commercial Code in Chapter 9 and in the glossary.

VII

Criminal Law and Procedure

This chapter introduces students to some of the fundamental principles of criminal law and criminal procedure. Each of these subjects could be a course in itself; in one chapter it is only possible to examine the major issues associated with each topic.

CRIMINAL LAW

William Blackstone, an English judge and author of *Commentaries on the Laws of England* (1765–1769), defined a crime as a wrong committed against the public,[1] a definition that is still widely recognized as appropriate. Defining a wrong against the public is a responsibility of government. In a democracy, this necessarily involves a balancing of interests: society needs to protect itself and its citizens from harm, but society also must protect the rights of individuals to be free from undue governmental interference. Various provisions of the U.S. Constitution provide the federal government with jurisdiction to enact penal laws with respect to federal matters. These include crimes involving interstate commerce, federal tax laws, crimes that are committed against federal property or federal officials or that intrude on federal governmental activities, and crimes that protect citizenship rights. At the same time, the Fourteenth Amendment and the Bill of Rights guarantee individual liberties and protection from government. As limited sovereigns, the state governments and their political subdivisions have primary responsibility within each state to provide for the public health, public safety, public welfare, and public morals. Like the U.S. Constitution, however, state constitutions also protect individual liberties, and may provide privacy rights that exceed the protections guaranteed by their federal counterpart.

Sources of American Criminal Law

You will recall from the discussion in Chapter 1 that the colonists along the eastern seaboard of North America were very influenced by the English common law, which defined offenses both judicially and legislatively. While the influence of common law was diminished following the American Revolution because of public opposition to things English,[2] many of the states that abolished common law crimes converted most of them into statutes.[3] Although these "American" statutes deviated in some respects from the common law, they retained significant aspects of that heritage. In addition, some states continued to recognize common law crimes without statutes and judges with common law authority could use this to augment the criminal statutes. They also could rely on well-established legal principles to define new offenses in the absence of precedent.

In the twentieth century, the legislative branch has replaced the judiciary as the dominant criminal law policymaker. The inventions of the automobile, fax machine, copying machines, airplanes, and computers, and the growth of sophisticated banking / finance companies and the securities industry produced as a by-product new and previously unforeseen criminal opportunities. Legislative bodies responded by enacting prodigious numbers of new criminal laws. Some of these laws were well thought out; others were enacted on a piecemeal basis to appease voters without sufficient attention to detail or to appropriate constitutional limitations such as vagueness and overbreadth.

The complexities of modern society and the common law's imprecision led reformers, among them the drafters of the influential Model Penal Code, to call for its abolishment. Today, most states define criminal offenses only through statutes, an approach that is consistent with federal law. In 1812, the U.S. Supreme Court decided that article I, section 8, of the U.S. Constitution does not include among the enumerated powers the power to adopt the common law. Thus, all federal crimes had to be statutory. Both the federal and state courts, however, turn to common law definitions for help in statutory construction.

Classification of Crimes

The common law classified crimes as either *mala in se* or *mala prohibita*. *Mala in se* crimes were offenses that were intrinsically bad, such as murder, rape, arson, and theft. Acts that were criminal only because the law defined them as such were classified as *mala prohibita*. A second way of categorizing crime is in terms of the harm they cause to society. Today, state statutes are often organized so that crimes of a particular type are clustered, for example, crimes against persons (rape, kidnapping, battery, murder, etc.), crimes against property (larceny, robbery, burglary, arson, etc.), and crimes against government (contempt, perjury, bribery, etc.).

Crimes can also be classified as felonies and misdemeanors and the distinction between the two is essentially a decision of each state's legislature. In some states, felonies are crimes that are served in state prisons and misdemeanors are offenses served in county jails. Other jurisdictions provide that crimes authorizing a sentence of incarceration of over one year are felonies, while those authorizing sentences of one year or less are misdemeanors. The distinction between misdemeanor and felonious theft is usually based on the value of the stolen article. Felony thresholds in theft cases range from $20 in South Carolina to $2000 in Pennsylvania. In recent years, other classification schemes have gained popularity, for example, white-collar crime (tax evasion, insider trading, kickbacks, defrauding governmental agencies, etc.) and victimless crimes (smoking marijuana, loitering, homosexuality, etc.). Other crimes have been reclassified: driving while intoxicated, a misdemeanor twenty years ago, is today a felony.

Constitutional Limitations on Criminalization

The Constitution limits the imposition of criminal liability and criminal punishments. A criminal statute, for example, must be reasonably precise, since one that is too vague or overly broad violates substantive due process. In *Kolender v. Lawson*, for example, the U.S. Supreme Court ruled that a California statute was too vague, explaining that due process requires that a penal statute define the criminal offense "with sufficient definiteness that ordinary people can understand what conduct is prohibited and in a manner that does not encourage arbitrary and discriminatory enforcement." A statute suffers from overbreadth if its terms are so general that it could be used to arrest a person engaged in activities protected by the First Amendment.

Article I, sections 9 and 10, of the Constitution prohibit federal and state legislative bodies from enacting *ex post facto* laws—laws that make acts criminal that were not criminal at the time they were committed. Statutes that make a crime greater than when committed, impose greater punishment, or make proof of guilt easier have also been held to be unconstitutional *ex post facto* laws. Laws also are unconstitutional if they alter the definition of a penal offense or its consequence to the disadvantage of people who have committed that offense. A law is not *ex post facto* if it "mitigates the rigor" of the law or simply reenacts the law in force when the crime was done. The *ex post facto* clause restricts only legislative power and does not apply to the judiciary. In addition, the doctrine applies exclusively to penal statutes, whether civil or criminal in form (see *Hiss v. Hampton*, 338 F.Supp. 1141 (1972)).

The Constitution also prohibits bills of attainder—acts of a legislature that apply either to named individuals or to easily ascertainable members of a group in such a way as to impose punishments on them without a trial. In *United States v. Brown*, 381 U.S. 437 (1965), for example, an act of Congress that made it a crime for a member of the Communist party to serve as an officer of a labor union was held unconstitutional as a bill of attainder by the Supreme Court.

Although no specific provision in the federal Constitution guarantees a general right of personal privacy, the U.S. Supreme Court has recognized that a limited privacy right is implicit in the due process guarantees of life, liberty, and property in the Fourth and Fifth amendments, and in the First, Ninth, and Fourteenth amendments. The Court also has recognized that certain fundamental liberties are inherent in the concept of ordered liberty as reflected in our nation's history and tradition and has selected them for special protection. These rights include personal intimacies relating to the family, marriage, motherhood, procreation, and child rearing. The Court has also recognized that a person's home is entitled to special privacy protection. For example, it has prevented the enforcement of state obscenity laws within the home where the conduct in question involved protected First Amendment rights.

The limited constitutionally recognized right of privacy is not absolute and is subject to limitations when the government's interest in protecting society becomes dominant. However, a statute affecting a fundamental constitutional right will be subjected to strict and exacting scrutiny, and the statute will fail to pass constitutional muster unless the state proves a compelling need for the law and shows that its goals cannot be accomplished by less restrictive means. If a challenged statute does *not* affect a fundamental constitutional right, the law will be upheld if it is neither arbitrary nor discriminatory, and if it bears a rational relation to a legitimate legislative purpose—protecting the public health, welfare, safety, or morals. A state can satisfy this rational basis test if it can show that there is some conceivable basis for finding such a rational relationship.

The Equal Protection Clause of the Fourteenth Amendment to the Constitution also limits legislatures in defining crimes. Originally intended to secure freedom to black people, this clause prohibits state legislative classification schemes that have the effect of denying to any race, class, or individual the equal protection of the law. Classifications based on race, religion, or alienage are inherently suspect, as are classifications that trammel upon fundamental personal rights. Suspect classifications are subject to strict scrutiny and can be justified only by a ''compelling'' state interest. Classifications that are not suspect need only be rationally related to a legitimate state interest to justify discriminatory treatment.

The boundaries of the protection afforded by the Equal Protection Clause have not been precisely defined. For example, the Supreme Court's treatment of gender-based classifications is not yet clear. There is some evidence that gender-based classifications (rape laws focused only on males or draft laws favoring females) will be measured by a third test that is in between the strict scrutiny and rational basis tests.

The case of *Loving v. Virginia* illustrates the constitutional limitations imposed by the Fourteenth Amendment Due Process and Equal Protection clauses on the state's right to criminalize conduct.

Loving v. Commonwealth of Virginia *388 U.S. 1* *U.S. Supreme Court*	*June 12, 1967* **Mr. Chief Justice Warren delivered the opinion of the Court.**

This case presents a constitutional question never addressed by this Court: whether a statutory scheme adopted by the State of Virginia to prevent marriages between persons solely on the basis of racial classifications violates the Equal Protection and Due Process Clauses of the Fourteenth Amendment. For reasons which seem to us to reflect the central meaning of those constitutional commands, we conclude that these statutes cannot stand consistently with the Fourteenth Amendment.

In June 1958, two residents of Virginia, Mildred Jeter, a Negro woman, and Richard Loving, a white man, were married in the District of Columbia pursuant to its laws. Shortly after their marriage, the Lovings returned to Virginia and established their marital abode in Caroline County. At the October Term, 1958, of the Circuit Court of Caroline County, a grand jury issued an indictment charging the Lovings with violating Virginia's ban on interracial marriages. On January 6, 1959, the Lovings pleaded guilty to the charge and were sentenced to one year in jail; however, the trial judge suspended the sentence for a period of 25 years on the condition that the Lovings leave the State and not return to Virginia together for 25 years. He stated in an opinion that:

"Almighty God created the races white, black, yellow, malay and red, and he placed them on separate continents. And but for the interference with his arrangement there would be no cause for such marriages. The fact that he separated the races shows that he did not intend for the races to mix."

After their convictions, the Lovings took up residence in the District of Columbia. On November 6, 1963, they filed a motion in the state trial court to vacate the judgment and set aside the sentence on the ground that the statutes which they had violated were repugnant to the Fourteenth Amendment. The motion not having been decided by October 28, 1964, the Lovings instituted a class action in the United States District Court for the Eastern District of Virginia requesting that a three-judge court be convened to declare the Virginia antimiscegenation statutes unconstitutional and to enjoin state officials from enforcing their convictions. On January 22, 1965, the state trial judge denied the motion to vacate the sentences, and the Lovings perfected an appeal to the Supreme Court of Appeals of Virginia. On February 11, 1965, the three-judge District Court continued the case to allow the Lovings to present their constitutional claims to the highest state court.

The Supreme Court of Appeals upheld the constitutionality of the antimiscegenation statutes and, after modifying the sentence, affirmed the conviction. The Lovings appealed this decision. . . .

The two statutes under which appellants were convicted and sentenced are part of a comprehensive statutory scheme aimed at prohibiting and punishing interracial marriages. The Lovings were convicted of violating § 20–58 of the Virginia Code:

"*Leaving State to evade law.*—If any white person and colored person shall go out of this State, for the purpose of being married, and with the intention of returning, and be married out of it, and afterwards return to and reside in it, cohabiting as man and wife, they shall be punished as provided in § 20–59."

Section 20–59, which defines the penalty for miscegenation, provides:

"*Punishment for marriage.*—If any white person intermarry with a colored person, or any colored person intermarry with a white person, he shall be guilty of a felony and shall be punished by confinement in the penitentiary for not less than one nor more than five years."

. . .

The Lovings have never disputed in the course of this litigation that Mrs. Loving is a "colored person" or that Mr. Loving is a "white person" within the meanings given those terms by the Virginia statutes.

Virginia is now one of 16 States which prohibit and punish marriages on the basis of racial classifications. Penalties for miscegenation arose as an incident to slavery and have been common in Virginia since the colonial period. The present statutory scheme dates from the adoption of the Racial Integrity Act of 1924, passed during the period of extreme nativism which followed the end of the First World War. The central features of this Act, and current Virginia law, are the absolute prohibition of a "white person" marrying other than another "white person," a prohibition against issuing marriage licenses until the issuing official is satisfied that the applicants' statements as to their race are correct, certificates of "racial composition" to be kept by both local and state registrars, and the carrying forward of earlier prohibitions against racial intermarriage.

I.

In upholding the constitutionality of these provisions in the decision below, the Supreme Court of Appeals of Virginia referred to its 1955 decision in *Naim v. Naim*, . . . as stating the reasons supporting the validity of these laws. In *Naim*, the state court concluded that the State's legitimate purposes were "to preserve the racial integrity of its citizens," and to prevent "the corruption of blood," "a mongrel breed of citizens," and "the obliteration of racial pride," obviously an endorsement of the doctrine of White Supremacy. . . . The court also reasoned that marriage has traditionally been subject to state regulation without federal intervention, and, consequently, the regulation of marriage should be left to exclusive state control by the Tenth Amendment.

While the state court is no doubt correct in asserting that marriage is a social relation subject to the State's police power, . . . the State does not contend in its argument before this Court that its powers to regulate marriage are unlimited notwithstanding the commands of the Fourteenth Amendment. . . . Instead, the State argues that the meaning of the Equal Protection Clause, as illuminated by the statements of the Framers, is only that state penal laws containing an interracial element as part of the definition of the offense must apply equally to whites and Negroes in the sense that members of each race are punished to the same degree. Thus, the State contends that, because its miscegenation statutes punish equally both the white and the Negro participants in an interracial marriage, these statutes, despite their reliance on racial classifications, do not constitute an invidious discrimination based upon race. The second argument advanced by the State assumes the validity of its equal application theory. The argument is that, if the Equal Protection Clause does not outlaw miscegenation statutes because of their reliance on racial classifications, the question of constitutionality would thus become whether there was any rational basis for a State to treat interracial marriages differently from other marriages. On this question, the State argues, the scientific evidence is substantially in doubt and, consequently, this Court should defer to the wisdom of the state legislature in adopting its policy of discouraging interracial marriages.

Because we reject the notion that the mere "equal application" of a statute containing racial classifications is enough to remove the classifications from the Fourteenth Amendment's proscription of all invidious racial discriminations, we do not accept the State's contention that these statutes should be upheld if there is any possible basis for concluding that they serve a rational purpose. . . . In the case at bar, we deal with statutes containing racial classifications, and the fact of equal application does not immunize the statute from the very heavy burden of justification which the Fourteenth Amendment has traditionally required of state statutes drawn according to race. . . .

There can be no question but that Virginia's miscegenation statutes rest solely upon distinctions drawn according to race. The statutes proscribe generally accepted conduct if engaged in by members of different races. Over the years, this Court has consistently repudiated "[d]istinctions between citizens solely because of their ancestry" as being "odious to a free people whose institutions are founded upon the doctrine of equality." . . . At the very least, the Equal Protection Clause demands that racial classifications, especially suspect in criminal statutes, be subjected to the "most rigid scrutiny," . . . and, if they are ever to be upheld, they must be shown to be necessary to the accomplishment of some permissible state objective, independent of the racial discrimination which it was the object of the Fourteenth Amendment to eliminate. Indeed, two members of this Court have already stated that they "cannot conceive of a valid legislative purpose . . . which makes the color of a person's skin the test of whether his conduct is a criminal offense." . . .

There is patently no legitimate overriding purpose independent of invidious racial discrimination which justifies this classification. The fact that Virginia prohibits only interracial marriages involving white persons demonstrates that the racial classifications must stand on their own justification, as measures designed to maintain White Supremacy. We have consistently denied the constitutionality of measures which restrict the rights of citizens on account of race. There can be no doubt that restricting the freedom to marry solely because of racial classifications violates the central meaning of the Equal Protection Clause.

These statutes also deprive the Lovings of liberty without due process of law in violation of the Due Process Clause of the Fourteenth Amendment. The freedom to marry has long been recognized as one of the vital personal rights essential to the orderly pursuit of happiness by free men.

Marriage is one of the "basic civil rights of man," fundamental to our very existence and survival. . . . To deny this fundamental freedom on so unsupportable a basis as the racial classifications embodied in these statutes, classifications so directly subversive of the principle of equality at the heart of the Fourteenth Amendment, is surely to deprive all the State's citizens of liberty without due process of law. The Fourteenth Amendment requires that the freedom of choice to marry not be restricted by invidious racial discriminations. Under our Constitution, the freedom to marry or not marry a person of another race resides with the individual and cannot be infringed by the State.

These convictions must be reversed. It is so ordered.

Reversed.

Case
Questions

1. Virginia argued to the Supreme Court that its miscegenation statute did not constitute an invidious classification scheme based on race. What was the basis for this position?
2. What response did the Supreme Court make to Virginia's restrictions on an individual's right to decide whether to marry a person of another race?

The Imposition of Punishment

It is a principle of U.S. law that people convicted of crimes receive only punishments that have been provided by law. Also, legislative bodies are limited in the types of sentences they can provide by the Eighth Amendment's protection against the imposition of cruel and unusual punishments. The Supreme Court has interpreted this provision as preventing the use of "barbaric punishments as well as sentences that are disproportionate to the crime committed." The meaning of "barbaric punishment" has been the subject of much recent discussion in debate over capital punishment. The majority of the Supreme Court has consistently rejected arguments that imposition of capital punishment is barbaric, emphasizing that capital punishment was known to the common law and was accepted in this country at the time the Eighth Amendment was adopted. They also point out that at least thirty-five states have enacted statutes providing for the death penalty, citing this as evidence that society continues to view capital punishment as appropriate and necessary.

The Eighth Amendment's proportionality requirement can be traced to the Virginia Declaration of Rights (1775), the English Bill of Rights (1689), the Statute of Westminster (1275), and even Magna Carta (1215). The Supreme Court has used this principle to strike down sentences imposed pursuant to (1) a statute authorizing a jail sentence for drug addiction (because it is cruel and unusual punishment to incarcerate a person for being ill), (2) a statute authorizing the death penalty for rapists, and (3) a statute authorizing a sentence of life imprisonment without parole for a recidivist who wrote a one-hundred-dollar check on a nonexisting account.

THE BASIC COMPONENTS
OF A CRIMINAL OFFENSE

A criminal offense includes the following components: (1) the wrongful act, (2) the guilty mind, (3) concurrence, and in some crimes, (4) causation. Proof of each element is required beyond a reasonable doubt for a conviction.

The Wrongful Act

The wrongful act, or *actus reus*, is most easily defined by example. The wrongful act of larceny includes an unlawful taking and carrying away of another person's property. The wrongful act in a battery is the unjustified, offensive, or harmful touching of another person. The law makes a distinction between acts that are classified as voluntary, and those that result from reflexive acts, epileptic seizures, or hypnotic suggestion (see the Model Penal Code in Figure 7–1). A voluntary act occurs when the accused causes his or her body to move in a manner that produces prohibited conduct. The following case illustrates the requirement that criminal acts be voluntary.

People v. Shaughnessy
319 N.Y.S.2d 626
District Court, Nassau County, Third District
March 16, 1971

Lockman, Judge

On October 9th, 1970, shortly before 10:05 p.m., the Defendant in the company of her boy friend and two other youngsters proceeded by automobile to the vicinity of the St. Ignatius Retreat Home, Searingtown Road, Incorporated Village of North Hills, Nassau County, New York. The Defendant was a passenger and understood that she was headed for the Christopher Morley Park which is located across the street from the St. Ignatius Retreat Home and has a large illuminated sign, with letters approximately 8 inches high, which identifies the park. As indicated, on the other side of the street the St. Ignatius Retreat Home has two pillars at its entrance with a bronze sign on each pillar with 4 to 5 inch letters. The sign is not illuminated. The vehicle in which the Defendant was riding proceeded into the grounds of the Retreat House and was stopped by a watchman and the occupants including the Defendant waited approximately 20 minutes for a Policeman to arrive. The Defendant never left the automobile.

The Defendant is charged with violating Section 1 of the Ordinance prohibiting entry upon private property of the Incor-

porated Village of North Hills, which provides: "No person shall enter upon any privately owned piece, parcel or lot of real property in the Village of North Hills without the permission of the owner, lessee or occupant thereof. The failure of the person, so entering upon, or found to be on, such private property, to produce upon demand, the written permission of the owner, lessee or occupant to enter upon, or to be on, such real property, shall be and shall constitute presumptive evidence of the violation of this Ordinance."

The Defendant at the conclusion of the trial moves to dismiss on the grounds that the statute is unconstitutional. Since the Ordinance is Malum Prohibitum, in all likelihood the Ordinance is constitutional. . . . However, it is unnecessary to pass upon the constitutionality of the Ordinance since there is another basis for dismissal.

The problem presented by the facts in this case brings up for review the primary elements that are required for criminal accountability and responsibility. It is only from an accused's voluntary overt acts that criminal responsibility can attach. An overt act or a specific omission to act must occur in order for the establishment of a criminal offense.

The physical element required has been designated as the *Actus Reus*. The mental element is of course better known as the *Mens Rea*. While the mental element

MODEL PENAL CODE*
Official Draft, 1985

Copyright 1985 by The American Law Institute.
Reprinted with the permission of The American Law Institute.

Section 2.01. Requirement of Voluntary Act; Omission as Basis of Liability; Possession as an Act

(1) A person is not guilty of an offense unless his liability is based on conduct which includes a voluntary act or the omission to perform an act of which he is physically capable.

(2) The following are not voluntary acts within the meaning of this Section:

(a) a reflex or convulsion;

(b) a bodily movement during unconsciousness or sleep;

(c) conduct during hypnosis or resulting from hypnotic suggestion;

(d) a bodily movement that otherwise is not a product of the effort or determination of the actor, either conscious or habitual.

(3) Liability for the commission of an offense may not be based on an omission unaccompanied by action unless:

(a) the omission is expressly made sufficient by the law defining the offense; or

(b) a duty to perform the omitted act is otherwise imposed by law.

(4) Possession is an act, within the meaning of this Section, if the possessor knowingly procured or received the thing possessed or was aware of his control thereof for a sufficient period to have been able to terminate his possession.

*A collection of suggestions for reforming American criminal law, the Model Penal Code was prepared by a private association of professors, lawyers, and judges called the American Law Institute. Over two-thirds of the states have adopted at least some of its provisions and hundreds of courts have been influenced by its suggestions.

FIGURE 7–1   Model Penal Code Section 2.01

may under certain circumstances not be required as in crimes that are designated *Malum Prohibitum,* the *Actus Reus* is always necessary. It certainly can not be held to be the intent of the legislature to punish involuntary acts.

The principle which requires a voluntary act or omission to act had been codified . . . and reads as follows in part: "The minimal requirement for criminal liability is the performance by a person of conduct which includes a *voluntary act or the omission to perform an act* which he is physically capable of performing. . . ."

The legislature may prescribe that an act is criminal without regard to the doer's intent or knowledge, but an involuntary act is not criminal (with certain exceptions such as involuntary acts resulting from voluntary intoxication).

In the case at bar, the People have failed to establish any act on the part of the Defendant. She merely was a passenger in a vehicle. Any action taken by the vehicle was caused and guided by the driver thereof and not by the Defendant. If the Defendant were to be held guilty under these circumstances, it would dictate that she would be guilty if she had been unconscious or asleep at the time or even if she had been a prisoner in the automobile. There are many situations which can be envisioned and in which the trespass statute in question would be improperly applied to an involuntary act. One might conceive of a driver losing control of a vehicle through mechanical failure and the vehicle proceeding onto private property which is the subject of a trespass.

Although the Court need not pass on the question, it might very well be proper to hold the driver responsible for his act even though he was under the mistaken belief that he was on his way to Christopher Morley Park. The legislature has provided statutes which make mistakes of fact or lack of knowledge no excuse in a criminal action. However, if the driver had been a Defendant, the People could have established an act on the part of the Defendant driver, to wit, turning his vehicle into the private property.

In the case of the Defendant now before the Court, however, the very first and essential element in criminal responsibility is missing, an overt voluntary act or omission to act and, accordingly, the Defendant is found not guilty.

Case Questions

1. Judge Lockman's opinion explains that a voluntary act is normally necessary for criminal liability. What would be an example of an involuntary act?
2. Under what conditions should people be criminally liable for having omitted to act?

Special Rules

When the law recognizes the existence of a legal duty, the failure to act is equivalent to a criminal act. The duty to act can be imposed by statute (filing income tax returns, registering with selective service, registering firearms), by contract (such as that between parents and a day care center), as a result of one's status (parent-child, husband-wife), or because one has assumed a responsibility (voluntarily assuming responsibility for providing food to a person under disability).

Another exception to the requirement of a physical act is recognized in possession offenses in which the law treats the fact of possession as the equivalent of a wrongful act. For example, a person found with a controlled substance in his jacket pocket is not actually engaging in any physical act. Possession can be actual, as when the accused is found with the contraband on his or her person, or constructive, as when the contraband is not on the suspect's person, but is under the suspect's dominion and control.

Status Crimes

The Supreme Court has emphasized the importance of the wrongful act requirement in its decisions relating to status crimes, ruling that legislatures cannot make the status of "being without visible means of support" or "being ill as a result of narcotic addiction" into crimes. Selling a controlled substance can be made criminal because it involves a voluntary act. The condition of being an addict, however, is a status.

The Criminal State of Mind

The second requirement of a criminal offense (subject to a few exceptions) is that an alleged criminal offender possess a criminal state of mind (*mens rea*) at the time of the commission of the wrongful act. This is called a concurrence of a wrongful act with a wrongful state of mind. Concurrence is required because some people who commit wrongful acts do not have a wrongful state of mind. For example, if the student sitting next to you mistakenly picks up your copy of a textbook, instead of her copy, and leaves the classroom, there has been a wrongful act but no wrongful intent. While it is easy to theoretically make this distinction between accidental and criminal acts, it is often difficult to prove that a person acted with *mens rea*, and prosecutors often have to prove *mens rea* indirectly and circumstantially. In addition, judges routinely instruct jurors that the law permits them to find that a defendant intended the natural and probable consequences of his or her deliberate acts. This instruction is based on human experience: most people go about their daily affairs intending to do the things they choose to do.

In the United States, *mala in se* offenses require proof of criminal intent. *Mala prohibita* offenses may require criminal intent (in possession of a controlled substance, for instance), or they may involve no proof of intent at all (as in traffic offenses or sales of illegal intoxicating beverages to minors).

There are two major approaches to *mens rea*, one formed by the traditional common law approach, the other by the Model Penal Code. The common law approach recognizes three categories of intent: general intent, specific intent, and criminal negligence. *General intent* crimes include serious offenses such as rape and arson and less serious offenses such as trespass and simple battery. For conviction of a general intent crime, the prosecution has to prove that the accused intended to commit the *actus reus*, that is, intended the consequences of his or her voluntary acts. The common law permitted the trier of fact to infer a wrongful state of mind from proof that the actor voluntarily did a wrongful act. Thus, a person who punches another person in anger (without any lawful justification or excuse) may be found to have possessed general criminal intent.

A *specific intent* crime requires proof of the commission of an *actus reus*, plus a specified level of knowledge or an additional intent, such as an intent to commit a felony. A person who possesses a controlled substance (the *actus reus*) and who at the time of the possession has an intent to sell (an additional specified level of intent beyond the commission of the *actus reus*) has committed a specific intent crime.

Criminal negligence results from unconscious risk creation. For example, a driver who unconsciously takes his or her eyes off the road to take care of a crying infant is in fact creating risks for other drivers and pedestrians. Thus the driver's unreasonable conduct created substantial and unjustifiable risks. If the driver is unaware of the risk creation, he or she is acting negligently.

The defendant in the following case was charged and convicted of the specific intent crime of robbery. He appealed his conviction on the ground that he did not have specific intent—the intent to permanently deprive the true owner of his property.

State v. Gordon
321 A.2d 352
Supreme Judicial Court of Maine
June 17, 1974

Wernick, Justice

An indictment returned (on June 27, 1972) by a Cumberland County Grand Jury to the Superior Court charged defendant, Richard John Gordon, with having committed the crime of "armed robbery" in violation of 17 M.R.S.A. § 3401–A. A separate indictment accused defendant of having, with intention to kill, assaulted a police officer, one Harold Stultz. Defendant was arraigned and pleaded not guilty to each charge. Upon motion by the State, and over defendant's objection, the residing Justice ordered a single trial on the two indictments. The trial was before a jury. On the "assault" the jury was unable to reach a verdict and as to that charge a mistrial was declared. The jury found defendant guilty of "armed robbery." From the judgment of conviction entered on the verdict defendant has appealed, assigning ten claims of error.

We deny the appeal.

The jury was justified in finding the following facts.

One Edwin Strode and defendant had escaped in Vermont from the custody of the authorities who had been holding them on a misdemeanor charge. In the escape defendant and Strode had acquired two hand guns and also a blue station wagon in which they had fled from Vermont through New Hampshire into Maine. Near Standish, Maine, the station wagon showed signs of engine trouble, and defendant and Strode began to look for another vehicle. They came to the yard of one Franklin Prout. In the yard was Prout's 1966 maroon Chevelle and defendant, who was operating the station wagon, drove it parallel to the Prout Chevelle. Observing that the keys were in the Chevelle, Strode left the station wagon and entered the Chevelle. At this time Prout came out of his house into the yard. Strode pointed a gun at him, and the defendant and Strode then told Prout that they needed his automobile, were going to take it but they "would take care of it and see he [Prout] got it back as soon as possible." With defendant operating the station wagon and Strode the Chevelle, defendant and Strode left the yard and proceeded in the direction of Westbrook. Subsequently, the station wagon was abandoned in a sand pit, and defendant and Strode continued their flight in the Chevelle. A spectacular series of events followed—including the alleged assault (with intent to kill) upon Westbrook police officer, Stultz, a shoot-out on Main Street in Westbrook, and a high speed police chase, during which the Chevelle was driven off the road in the vicinity of the Maine Medical Center in Portland where it was abandoned, Strode and defendant having commandeered another automobile to resume their flight. Ultimately, both the defendant and Strode were apprehended, defendant having been arrested on the day following the police chase in the vicinity of the State Police Barracks in Scarborough. . . .

[D]efendant maintains that the evidence clearly established that (1) defendant and Strode had told Prout that they "would take care of . . . [the automobile] and see [that] he [Prout] got it back as soon as possible" and (2) defendant intended only a temporary use of Prout's Chevelle. Defendant argues that the evidence thus fails to warrant a conclusion beyond a reasonable doubt that defendant had the specific intent requisite for "robbery." (Hereinafter, reference to the "specific intent" necessary for "robbery" signifies the "specific intent" incorporated into "robbery" as embracing "larceny.")

Although defendant is correct that robbery is a crime requiring a particular specific intent, . . . defendant wrongly apprehends its substantive content.

A summarizing statement appearing in defendant's brief most clearly exposes his misconception of the law. Acknowledging that on all of the evidence the jury could properly

". . . have inferred . . . that [defendant and Strode] . . . intended to get away from the authorities by going to New York or elsewhere *where they would abandon* the car . . .", (emphasis supplied)

defendant concludes that, nevertheless, the State had failed to prove the necessary specific intent because it is

". . . entirely irrational to conclude . . . that the defendant himself intended at the time he and Strode took the car, *to keep the car in their possession for any length of time.*" (emphasis supplied)

Here, defendant reveals that he conceives as an essential element of the specific intent requisite for "robbery" that the wrongdoer must intend: (1) an advantageous relationship between himself and the property wrongfully taken, and (2) that such relationship be permanent rather than temporary.

Defendant's view is erroneous. The law evaluates the "animus furandi" of "robbery" in terms of the detriment projected to the legally protected interests of the owner rather than the benefits intended to accrue to the wrongdoer from his invasion of the rights of the owner. . . .

[M]any of the earlier decisions reveal language disagreements, as well as conflicts as to substance, concerning whether a defendant can be guilty of "robbery" without specifically intending a gain to himself (whether permanent or temporary), so-called "lucri causa." In the more recent cases, there is overwhelming consensus that "lucri causa" is not necessary. . . .

We now decide, in confirmatory clarification of the law of Maine, that "lucri causa" is not an essential element of the "animus furandi" of "robbery." . . . [T]he specific intent requisite for "robbery" is defined solely in terms of the injury projected to the interests of the property owner:—specific intent "to deprive permanently the owner of his property." . . .

The instant question thus becomes: on the hypothesis, arguendo, that defendant here actually intended to use the Prout automobile "only temporarily" (as he would need it to achieve a successful flight from the authorities), is defendant correct in his fundamental contention that this, *in itself*, negates, *as a matter of law*, specific intent of defendant to deprive permanently the owner of his property? We answer that defendant's claim is erroneous.

Concretely illustrative of the point that a wrongdoer may intend to use wrongfully taken property "only temporarily" and yet, without contradiction, intend that the owner be deprived of his property permanently is the case of a defendant who proposes to use the property only for a short time and then to destroy it. At the opposite pole, and excluding (as a matter of law) specific intent to deprive permanently the owner of his property, is the case of a defendant who intends to make a temporary use of the property and then by his own act to return the property to its owner. Between these two extremes can lie various situations in which the legal characterization of the wrongdoer's intention, as assessed by the criterion of whether it is a specific intent to deprive permanently the owner of his property, will be more or less clear and raise legal problems of varying difficulty.

In these intermediate situations a general guiding principle may be developed through recognition that a "taking" of property is *by definition* "temporary" only if the possession, or control, effected by the taking is relinquished. Hence, measured by the correct criterion of the impact upon the interests of the owner, the wrongdoer's "animus furandi" is fully explored for its true legal significance only if the investigation of the wrongdoer's state of mind extends beyond his anticipated *retention* of possession and includes an inquiry into his contemplated manner of *relinquishing* possession, or control, of the property wrongfully taken.

On this approach, it has been held that when a defendant takes the tools of another person with intent to use them temporarily and then to leave them wherever it may be that he finishes with his work, the fact-finder is justified in the conclusion that defendant had specific intent to deprive the owner permanently of his property. . . .

Similarly, it has been decided that a defendant who wrongfully takes the property of another intending to use it for a short time and then to relinquish possession, or control, in a manner leaving to chance whether the owner recovers his property is correctly held specifically to intend that the owner be deprived permanently of his property.

The rationale underlying these decisions is that to negate, as a matter of law, the existence of specific intent to deprive permanently the owner of his property, a wrongful taker of the property of another must have in mind not only that his retention of possession, or control, will be "temporary" but also that when he will relinquish the possession, or control, he will do it in some manner (whatever, particularly, it will be) he regards as having affirmative tendency toward getting the property returned to its owner. In the absence of such thinking by the defendant, his state of mind is fairly characterized as *indifference* should the owner *never* recover his property; and such indifference by a wrongdoer who is the moving force separating an owner from his property is appropriately regarded as his "willingness" that the owner *never* regain his property. In this sense, the wrongdoer may appropriately be held to entertain specific intent that the deprivation to the owner be permanent. . . .

On this basis, the evidence in the present case clearly presented a jury question as to defendant's specific intent. Although defendant may have stated to the owner, Prout, that defendant

> "would take care of . . . [the automobile] and see [that] . . . [Prout] got it back as soon as possible,"

defendant himself testified that

> "[i]n my mind it was just to get out of the area. . . . Just get out of the area and leave the car and get under cover somewhere."

This idea to "leave the car" and "get under cover somewhere" existed in defendant's mind as part of an uncertainty about where it would happen. Because defendant was ". . . sort of desperate dur-

ing the whole day," he had not "really formulated any plans about destination."

Such testimony of defendant, together with other evidence that defendant had already utterly abandoned another vehicle (the station wagon) in desperation, plainly warranted a jury conclusion that defendant's facilely uttered statements to Prout were empty words, and it was defendant's true state of mind to use Prout's Chevelle and abandon it in whatever manner might happen to meet the circumstantial exigencies of defendant's predicament—without defendant's having any thought that the relinquishment of the possession was to be in a manner having some affirmative tendency to help in the owner's recovery of his property. On this finding the jury was warranted in a conclusion that defendant was indifferent should the owner, Prout, *never* have back his automobile and, therefore, had specific intent that the owner be deprived permanently of his property.

Appeal denied.

Case Questions

1. What must a wrongful taker of property do to avoid legal responsibility for having specific intent to deprive the owner permanently of his property?
2. Does a wrongful taker of property have specific intent if the taker does not intend to keep the property for any particular period of time?

The Model Penal Code recognizes four categories of intent. To be criminally culpable, a person must act purposely, knowingly, recklessly, or negligently (see Figure 7–2).

A person acts *purposely* when he or she has a conscious desire to produce a prohibited result or harm, such as when one person strikes another in order to injure the other person.

A person acts *knowingly* when he or she is aware that a prohibited result or harm is very likely to occur, but nevertheless does not consciously intend

MODEL PENAL CODE
Official Draft, 1985

Section 2.02 General Requirements of Culpability

*   *   *

(2) Kinds of Culpability Defined.

(a) *Purposely.*

A person acts purposely with respect to a material element of an offense when:

(i)   if the element involves the nature of his conduct or a result thereof, it is his conscious object to engage in conduct of that nature or to cause such a result; and

(ii) if the element involves the attendant circumstances, he is aware of the existence of such circumstances or he believes or hopes that they exist.

(b) *Knowingly.*

A person acts knowingly with respect to a material element of an offense when:

(i)   If the element involves the nature of his conduct or the attendant circumstances, he is aware that his conduct is of that nature or that such circumstances exist; and

(ii) if the element involves a result of his conduct, he is aware that it is practically certain that his conduct will cause such a result.

(c) *Recklessly.*

A person acts recklessly with respect to a material element of an offense when he consciously disregards a substantial and unjustifiable risk that the material element exists or will result from his conduct. The risk must be of such a nature and degree that, considering the nature and purpose of the actor's conduct and the circumstances known to him, its disregard involves a gross deviation from the standard of conduct that a law-abiding person would observe in the actor's situation.

(d) *Negligently.*

A person acts negligently with respect to a material element of an offense when he should be aware of a substantial and unjustifiable risk that the material element exists or will result from his conduct. The risk must be of such a nature and degree that the actor's failure to perceive it, considering the nature and purpose of his conduct and the circumstances known to him, involves a gross deviation from the standard of care that a reasonable person would observe in the actor's situation.

FIGURE 7–2   Model Penal Code Section 2.02

the specific consequences that result from the act. If a person sets a building on fire, the person may be aware that it is very likely that people inside will be injured, and yet hopes that the people escape and that only the building is burned.

A person acts *recklessly* when he or she consciously disregards the welfare of others and creates a significant and unjustifiable risk. The risk has to be one that no law-abiding person would have consciously undertaken or created. A driver acts recklessly if he or she consciously takes his or her eyes off the road to take care of a crying infant, is aware that this conduct creates risks for other drivers and pedestrians, and is willing to expose others to jeopardy.

As seen in the common law approach, negligence involves unconscious risk creation. A driver acts *negligently* if he or she unconsciously takes his or her eyes off the road to take care of a crying infant, is unaware that this conduct creates substantial and unjustifiable risks for other drivers and pedestrians, and yet has not acted reasonably while operating a motor vehicle.

Strict Liability

A *strict liability* offense represents a major exception to the requirement that there be a concurrence between the criminal act and criminal intent. In such offenses, the offender poses a generalized threat to society at large. Examples include a speeding driver, a manufacturer who fails to comply with pure food and drug rules, or a liquor store owner who sells alcohol to minors. With respect to such *mala prohibita* offenses, the legislature may provide that the offender is strictly liable. The prosecution need only prove the *actus reus* to convict the accused; there is no intent element.

Vicarious Liability

Criminal law recognizes two conditions under which individuals and groups can be held criminally liable for actions committed by other people. Employers can be held responsible for the acts of their employees that occur within the course and scope of employment. For example, if a bartender illegally sells to minors, the bartender's employer (as well as the bartender) can be prosecuted. *Vicarious liability* helps to impress on employers the importance of insisting that employees comply with legal requirements. However, an employer can be held vicariously liable only for strict liability offenses. In addition, people convicted vicariously can only be subject to a fine or forfeiture.

Corporations can also be held vicariously liable for criminal acts, if employees authorized to act for the corporation commit criminal acts to enhance corporate profits. Such crimes might include price fixing, stock misrepresentation, theft, violations of environmental laws or the National Pure Food and Drug Act, and fraud. Corporations have even been indicted for murder. The punishment options for corporations are limited, however. The law permits the imposition of fines, but these are often inadequate in size, and it is obvious that corporations cannot go to jail.

Causation

There are some criminal offenses that require proof that the defendant's conduct caused a given result. In a homicide case, for example, the prosecution must prove that the defendant's conduct caused death. To be convicted of an assault, the defendant's actions must have caused the victim to fear an impending battery. In a battery, the defendant's conduct must have caused a harmful or offensive touching. In contrast, offenses such as perjury, reckless driving, larceny, and burglary criminalize conduct irrespective of whether any actual harm results.

The prosecution must establish *causation* beyond a reasonable doubt whenever it is an element of a crime. A key to establishing causation is the legal concept of "proximate cause." Criminal liability only attaches to conduct that is determined to be the proximate or legal cause of the harmful result. This includes both direct and indirect causation. Often the legal cause is the direct cause of harm. If the defendant strikes the victim with his fist and injures him, the defendant is the direct cause of the injury. If the defendant sets in motion a chain of events that eventually results in harm, the defendant may be the indirect cause of the harm.

Proximate cause is a flexible concept. It permits fact-finders to sort through various factual causes and determine whom should be found to be legally responsible for the result. In addition, an accused is only responsible for the reasonably foreseeable consequences that follow from his or her acts. The law provides, for example, that an accused is not responsible for consequences that follow the intervention of a new, and independent, causal force. The next case, *Commonwealth v. Berggren*, illustrates the legal principle that an accused is only responsible for consequences that are reasonably foreseeable.

Commonwealth v. Berggren
496 N.E.2d 660
Supreme Judicial Court of Massachusetts
August 26, 1986

Lynch, Justice

The defendant is awaiting trial before a jury of six in the Barnstable Division of the District Court on a complaint charging him with motor vehicle homicide by negligent operation of a motor vehicle so as to endanger public safety (G.L. c. 90, § 24G(*b*) [1984 ed.]). The District Court judge granted the joint motion to "report an issue" to the Appeals Court pursuant to Mass.R. Crim.P. 34, 378 Mass. 905 (1979). We transferred the report here on our own motion.

We summarize the stipulated facts. On March 29, 1983, about 8:28 P.M., Patrolman Michael Aselton of the Barnstable police department was on radar duty at Old Stage Road in Centerville. He saw the defendant's motorcycle speed by him and commenced pursuit in a marked police cruiser with activated warning devices. The defendant "realized a cruiser was behind him but did not stop because he was 'in fear of his license.' " The pursuit lasted roughly six miles through residential, commercial and rural areas. At one point, the defendant had gained a 100-

yard lead and crossed an intersection, continuing north. The patrolman's cruiser approached the intersection at about "76 m.p.h. minimal" and passed over a crown in the roadway which caused the patrolman to brake. The wheels locked and the cruiser slid 170 yards, hitting a tree. Patrolman Aselton died as a result of the impact. The defendant had no idea of the accident which had occurred behind him. "No other vehicles were in any way involved in the causation of the accident." The stipulation further states that the decision to terminate a high speed chase "is to be made by the officer's commanding officer." No such decision to terminate the pursuit had been made at the time of the accident. The Barnstable police department determined that patrolman Aselton died in the line of duty.

We understand the report to raise the question whether the stipulated facts would be sufficient to support a conviction of motor vehicle homicide by negligent operation under G.L. c. 90, § 24G(*b*). We hold that it is.

A finding of ordinary negligence suffices to establish a violation of § 24G.

The Appeals Court has observed: "It would seem to follow that if the jury's task is to find ordinary negligence, then the appropriate principles of causation to apply are those which have been explicated in a large body of decisions and texts treating the subject in the context of the law of torts." . . .

The defendant argues, however, that the "causation theory properly applied in criminal cases is not that of proximate cause." . . . If this theory has any application in this Commonwealth, . . . it does not apply to a charge of negligent vehicular homicide. We adopt instead the suggestion of the Appeals Court and conclude

that the appropriate standard of causation to be applied in a negligent vehicular homicide case under § 24G is that employed in tort law.

The defendant essentially contends that since he was one hundred yards ahead of the patrolman's cruiser and was unaware of the accident, his conduct cannot be viewed as directly traceable to the resulting death of the patrolman. The defendant, however, was speeding on a motorcycle at night on roads which his attorney at oral argument before this court characterized as "winding" and "narrow." He knew the patrolman was following him, but intentionally did not stop and continued on at high speed for six miles. From the fact that the defendant was "in fear of his license," it may reasonably be inferred that he was aware that he had committed at least one motor vehicle violation. Under these circumstances, the defendant's acts were hardly a remote link in the chain of events leading to the patrolman's death. . . . The officer's pursuit was certainly foreseeable, as was, tragically, the likelihood of serious injury or death to the defendant himself, to the patrolman, or to some third party. The patrolman's death resulted from the "natural and continuous sequence" of events caused by the defendant's actions. . . .

We conclude that the proper standard of causation for this offense is the standard of proximate cause enunciated in the law of torts. We further conclude that, should the jury find the facts as stipulated in the instant case, and should the only contested element of the offense of motor vehicle homicide by negligent operation be that of causation, these facts would support a conviction under G.L. c. 90, § 24G(*b*).

Report answered.

Case
Questions

1. Explain the difference between factual and legal causation, based on the facts of this case.
2. Why should the defendant be legally responsible for a result that he didn't even know had occurred?

Inchoate Crime

The criminal law recognizes society's need to protect itself from dangerous people who have not yet completed their intended criminal acts. Thus the law defines the preparatory activities of solicitation, attempt, and conspiracy as criminal offenses called inchoate crimes.

Solicitation is a specific intent crime committed by a person who asks, hires, or encourages another to commit a crime. It makes no difference whether the solicited person accepts the offer or not; the solicitation itself constitutes the *actus reus* for this offense. All jurisdictions treat solicitations to commit a felony as a crime, and some jurisdictions also criminalize solicitations to commit a misdemeanor.

The crime of *attempt* is committed by a person who has the intent to commit a substantive criminal offense and does an act that tends to corroborate the intent, under circumstances that do not result in the completion of the substantive crime. For example, assume that person Y intends to commit armed robbery of a bank. Y dresses in clothing that disguises his appearance, wears a police scanner on his belt, carries a revolver in his coat pocket, wears gloves, and drives to a bank. Y approaches the front door with one hand in his pocket and the other over his face. When he attempts to open the front door he discovers that the door is locked and that it is just after the bank's closing time. Y quickly returns to his car, leaves the bank, and is subsequently apprehended by police. Y had specific intent to rob the bank, and took many substantial steps to realize that intent; however, he was unable to complete the crime because of his poor timing. Y has committed the crime of attempted robbery.

The crime of *conspiracy* is committed when two or more people combine to commit a criminal act. The essential *actus reus* of conspiracy is the agreement to commit a criminal act, coupled with the commission of some overt act by one or more of the co-conspirators that tends to implement the agreement. The prosecution can prove the existence of an unlawful agreement either expressly or inferentially. The crime of conspiracy is designed to protect society from group criminality. Organized groups bent on criminal activity pose a greater threat to the public than do the isolated acts of individuals. Conspiracy is a separate crime, and unlike attempt, does not merge into the completed substantive offense. Thus a person can be prosecuted both for murder and conspiracy to murder. If a member of the conspiracy wants to abandon the joint enterprise, he or she must notify every other co-conspirator. Conspiracy is a powerful prosecutorial weapon.

The Racketeer Influenced and Corrupt Organization Act

In 1970, the federal government enacted a criminal statute called the Racketeer Influenced and Corrupt Organization Act (RICO). This statute and its state counterparts have been very important weapons in combatting organized criminal activity such as drug trafficking, the theft and fencing of property, syndicated gambling, and extortion. A very broad statute, RICO applies to all people and organizations, whether public or private. It focuses on patterns of racketeering activity, the use of money obtained from racketeering to acquire legitimate businesses, and the collection of unlawful debt. The act defines racketeering activity as involving eight state crimes and twenty-four federal offenses called the predicate acts. A person who has committed two or more of the predicate acts within a ten-year period has engaged in a pattern of racketeering activity. People convicted under RICO can be punished by the forfeiture of real and personal property acquired with money obtained through racketeering, fines, and up to twenty years' incarceration. Civil penalties, including the award of treble damages, can also be recovered.

Defenses

The law recognizes that special circumstances may exist that should mitigate or eliminate criminal responsibility. Jurisdictions differ as to the availability of particular defenses and their definitions. These include insanity, intoxication, entrapment, defense of persons and property, and duress.

Insanity is one of the infrequently used and most controversial of the defenses. A defendant who claims insanity admits having committed the act, but denies criminal responsibility for that act. Because insanity is a legal and not a medical term, jurisdictions use different tests to define insanity. The *M'Naghten Rule* specifies that a defendant is not guilty if he or she had a diseased mind at the time of the act and was unable to distinguish right from wrong or was unaware of the nature and quality of his or her act due to a diseased mind. The *Irresistible Impulse Test* specifies that a defendant is not guilty if he or she knows that an act is wrong and is aware of the nature and quality of the act, but cannot refrain from committing the act. The Model Penal Code specifies that a defendant is not criminally responsible for his or her conduct due to either mental disease or defect and if the defendant lacked substantial capacity to understand its criminality or comply with legal requirements.

Intoxication is recognized as a defense in limited circumstances. Most jurisdictions distinguish voluntary intoxication, which is generally not a defense, from involuntary intoxication. A person who commits a crime while voluntarily intoxicated will only have a defense if the intoxication is quite severe. A defendant cannot be convicted of a specific intent crime if the intoxication was so severe that the person was incapable of forming specific intent. Some states have broadened that rule to recognize the intoxication defense as applicable in any crime requiring *mens rea* for conviction. Involuntary intoxication, such as when a person inadvertently ingests incompatible medicines, relieves the defendant of criminal responsibility if he or she was rendered incapable of distinguishing right from wrong.

The defense of *entrapment* was created to deter police officers from inducing innocent people to commit crimes. If an officer provides a person who is previously disposed to commit a criminal act with the opportunity to do so, that is not entrapment. If, however, an officer placed the notion of criminal wrongdoing in the defendant's mind, and that person was previously undisposed to commit the act, entrapment has occurred and the charges will be dismissed. In entrapment cases, the defendant admits having done a criminal act, but the law relieves him or her of criminal responsibility.

The law also recognizes an individual's right to defend his or her person and property and others. A person is entitled to use reasonable force to defend himself or herself from death or serious bodily harm. Obviously, the amount of force that can be used in defense depends upon the type of force being used by the attacker. An attack that threatens neither death nor serious bodily harm does not warrant the use of deadly force in defense. When the attack has been repelled, the defender does not have the right to continue using force to obtain revenge. Although the common law required one to "retreat to the wall" before using deadly force in self-defense, the modern rule permits a person to remain on his or her property and to use reasonable force (including the reasonable use of deadly force) in self-defense. A person also has a right to use necessary and reasonable force to defend another person from attack if the other person is entitled to act in self-defense. However, as we saw in *Katko v. Briney*, in Chapter 1, it is never justifiable to use force that could cause death or serious bodily injury solely in defense of property.

A person who commits a crime only because he or she was presently being threatened with death or serious bodily injury may assert the defense called *duress* or *coercion*. This defense is based on the theory that the person who committed the *actus reus* was not exercising free will. Most states do not allow the use of this defense in murder cases. In addition, coercion is difficult to establish. It fails, as we see in the next case, if there was a reasonable alternative to committing the crime, such as running away or contacting the police.

United States v. Scott
901 F.2d 871
U.S. Court of Appeals, Tenth Circuit
April 20, 1990

Seay, District Judge

Appellant, Bill Lee Scott, was found guilty by a jury and convicted of one count of conspiracy to manufacture metham- phetamine in violation of 21 U.S.C. § 2, and one count of manufacturing methamphetamine in violation of 21 U.S.C. § 841(a)(1), and 18 U.S.C. § 2. Scott appeals his convictions contending that he was denied a fair trial when the district court refused to instruct the jury on the defense of coercion. We disagree, and therefore affirm the judgment of the district court.

I.

Between the middle of August 1987, and the early part of January 1988, Scott made approximately six trips to Scientific Chemical, a chemical supply company in Humble, Texas. Scott made these trips at the request of codefendant Mark Morrow. These trips resulted in Scott purchasing various quantities of precursor chemicals and laboratory paraphernalia from Scientific Chemical. Some trips resulted in Scott taking possession of the items purchased, other trips resulted in the items being shipped to designated points to be picked up and delivered at a future date. These chemicals and laboratory items were purchased to supply methamphetamine laboratories operated by Morrow in New Mexico with the assistance of Silas Rivera and codefendants George Tannehill, Jerry Stokes, and Robert Stokes.

Scott first became acquainted with Morrow when Morrow helped him move from Portales, New Mexico, to Truth or Consequences, New Mexico, in late July or early August 1987. . . . Shortly thereafter, Morrow became aware that Scott was going to Houston, Texas, to sell some mercury and Morrow asked Scott if he could pick up some items from Scientific Chemical. . . . Scott made the trip to Scientific Chemical and purchased the items Morrow requested. . . . Scott subsequently made approximately five other trips to Scientific Chemical at Morrow's request to purchase various quantities of precursor chemicals and assorted labware. . . . During the course of one trip on August 31, 1987, Scott was stopped by Drug Enforcement Administration agents after he had purchased chemicals from Scientific Chemical. . . . The agents seized the chemicals Scott had purchased as well as $10,800 in U.S. currency and a fully loaded .38 Smith and Wesson. . . . Scott was not arrested at that time. . . . Scott, however, was subsequently indicted along with the codefendants after the seizure of large quantities of methamphetamine and precursor chemicals from a laboratory site in Portales in January 1988.

At trial Scott claimed that his purchase of the chemicals and labware on behalf of Morrow was the result of a well-established fear that Morrow would kill him or members of his family if he did not act as Morrow had directed. Scott further claimed that he did not have any reasonable opportunity to escape the harm threatened by Morrow. To support this defense of coercion Scott testified on his own behalf as to the nature and circumstances of the threats. Scott testified that approximately one month after the August 31, 1987, trip Morrow called him at his home in Truth or Consequences and talked him into a meeting in Houston to "get that straightened out." It was Scott's contention that Morrow might not have believed that the money and chemicals had been seized and that Morrow might have thought that he had merely kept the money. . . .

After the trip to Houston and Scientific Chemical to confirm Scott's story about the seizure of the chemicals and cash, Morrow contacted Scott at Scott's daughter's house in Portales to have Scott make another trip to Scientific Chemical to make another purchase. . . . After Scott declined to make another trip, Morrow responded by stating that Scott would not want something to happen to his daughter or her house. . . . Scott thereafter made the trip for Morrow. . . .

Approximately one week later, Morrow again came by Scott's daughter's house and wanted Scott to make another trip. . . . At some point during this discussion they decided to go for a ride in separate vehicles. . . . After travelling some distance, they both stopped their vehicles and pulled off to the side of the road. . . . Morrow pulled out a machine gun and two banana clips and emptied the clips at bottles and rocks. . . . Morrow stated "you wouldn't want to be in front of that thing would you?" and "you wouldn't want any of your family in front of that, would you?" . . . Scott responded negatively to Morrow's statements and thereafter made another trip to Scientific Chemical for Morrow. . . . On another occasion, Scott testified that Morrow threatened him by stating that he had better haul the chemicals if he knew what was good for him. . . .

Scott testified that Morrow not only knew his adult daughter living in Portales, but that he knew his wife and another daughter who were living in Truth or Consequences and that Morrow had been to the residence in Truth or Consequences. . . . Scott testified that he made these trips for Morrow because he feared for the safety of his family in light of the confrontations he had with Morrow. . . . Scott stated he had no doubt that Morrow would have carried out his threats. . . . Scott was aware of information linking Morrow to various murders. . . . Scott further testified that he did not go to the police with any of this information concerning Morrow because he had gone to them before on other matters and they did nothing. . . . Further, Scott believed that Morrow had been paying a DEA agent in Lubbock, Texas, for information regarding investigations. . . .

On cross-examination Scott testified that all of Morrow's threats were verbal, . . . that he saw Morrow only a few times between August 1987 and January 1988, . . . that he had an acquaintance by the name of Bill King who was a retired California Highway Patrolman living in Truth or Consequences, . . . and that he could have found a law enforcement official to whom he could have reported the actions of Morrow. . . .

II.

A coercion or duress defense requires the establishment of three elements: (1) an immediate threat of death or serious bodily injury, (2) a well-grounded fear that the threat will be carried out, and (3) no reasonable opportunity to escape the threatened harm. . . .

Scott proffered a coercion instruction to the district court in conformity with the above elements. Scott . . . contended that the testimony before the court concerning coercion was sufficient to raise an issue for the jury and that a coercion instruction should be given. The district court found that Scott had failed to meet his threshold burden as to all three elements of a coercion defense. Accordingly, the district court refused to give an instruction on the defense of coercion.

Scott contends that the district court committed reversible error by substituting its judgment as to the weight of his coercion defense rather than allowing the jury to decide the issue. Scott maintains that he presented sufficient evidence to place in issue the defense of coercion and that it was error for the district court to usurp the role of the jury in weighing the evidence. We disagree and find that the district court acted properly in requiring Scott to satisfy a threshold showing of a coercion defense, and in finding the evidence insufficient to warrant the giving of a coercion instruction. In doing so, we find the evidence clearly lacking as to the third element for a coercion defense— absence of any reasonable opportunity to escape the threatened harm.

Only after a defendant has properly raised a coercion defense is he entitled to an instruction requiring the prosecution to prove beyond a reasonable doubt that he was not acting under coercion when he performed the act or acts charged. . . .

The evidence introduced must be sufficient as to *all* elements of the coercion defense before the court will instruct the jury as to such defense. . . . If the evidence is lacking as to any element of the coercion defense the trial court may properly disallow the defense as a matter of law and refuse to instruct the jury as to coercion. . . . Consequently, a defendant who fails to present sufficient evidence to raise a triable issue of fact concerning the absence of any reasonable opportunity to escape the threatened harm is not entitled to an instruction on the defense of coercion. . . .

The evidence in this case as to Scott's ability to escape the threatened harm wholly failed to approach the level necessary for the giving of a coercion instruction. Scott's involvement with Morrow covered a period of time in excess of one hundred twenty-five days. Scott's personal contact with Morrow was extremely limited during this time. Scott had countless opportunities to contact law enforcement authorities or escape the perceived threats by Morrow during this time. Scott made no attempt to contact law enforcement officials regarding Morrow's activities. In fact, Scott even failed to take advantage of his acquaintance, King, a retired law enforcement official, to seek his assistance in connection with Morrow's threats and activities. Scott's failure to avail himself of the readily accessible alternative of contacting law enforcement officials is persuasive evidence of the hollow nature of Scott's claimed coercion defense. . . . Clearly, the record establishes that Scott had at his disposal a reasonable legal alternative to undertaking the acts on behalf of Morrow. . . .

Morrow did not accompany Scott when he made the purchases nor was there any evidence that Scott was under surveillance by Morrow. In fact, Scott's contact with Morrow was limited and he admitted he saw Morrow only a few times during the course of his involvement on behalf of Morrow between August 1987 and January 1988. Based on all of these circumstances, the district court was correct in finding that Scott had failed to establish that he had no reasonable opportunity to escape the threatened harm by Morrow.

III.

In conclusion, we find that Scott failed to present sufficient evidence to establish that he had no reasonable opportunity to escape the harm threatened by Morrow. Accordingly, the district court properly refused to instruct the jury as to the defense of coercion. We affirm the judgment of the district court.

Case Questions

1. What must a defendant do to be entitled to a jury instruction on the defense of coercion?
2. Given the facts of this case, why did the trial court refuse to give the instruction?

CRIMINAL PROCEDURE

Criminal procedure is that area of the law that deals with the administration of criminal justice, from the initial investigation of a crime and the arrest of a suspect through trial, sentence, and release.

The goal of criminal justice is to protect society from antisocial activity without sacrificing individual rights, justice, and fair play. The procedures used to apprehend and prosecute alleged criminal offenders must comply with the requirements of the law. One objective of using the adversary system involving prosecutors and defense attorneys is to ensure that procedural justice is accorded the defendant. The judge umpires the confrontation between the litigants and tries to ensure that both parties receive a fair trial—one that accords with the requirements of the substantive and procedural law. The judge or jury determines the guilt or innocence of the accused by properly evaluating the facts presented in open court. Ideally, the truth emerges from adversarial proceedings conducted in a manner consistent with constitutional guarantees. (See Figure 7–3.)

The constitutional limitations on the way governmental officials procedurally go about investigating criminal offenses and prosecuting alleged criminal offenders are primarily contained in the very general statements of the Fourth, Fifth, Sixth, Eighth, and Fourteenth amendments to the U.S. Constitution. The U.S. Supreme Court as well as the other federal and state courts have played a significant role in determining what these amendments actually mean in practice. Does the Constitution mandate that arrested persons who are indigent be provided a court-appointed attorney? Does the Constitution require that twelve-person juries be convened in criminal cases, or are six-person juries sufficient? Do defendants have a constitutional right to be convicted beyond a reasonable doubt by a unanimous jury, or can a guilty verdict be received that is supported by nine out of twelve jurors?

PROCEEDINGS PRIOR TO TRIAL

A criminal trial occurs only after several preliminary stages have been completed. Although there are some jurisdictional variations in the way these stages occur, some generalizations can be made. The "typical" criminal prosecution originates with a police investigation of a crime that has been either reported to officers or that officers have discovered through their own initiatives. This investigation establishes if there really was a crime committed, and if so, determines the identity and whereabouts of the offender. In their investigations, officers are limited by federal and state constitutional and statutory law: (1) They are only permitted to make arrests if they have sufficient evidence to constitute probable cause; (2) they are similarly limited in undertaking searches and seizures; and (3) they are limited in the way they conduct custodial interrogations and line-ups. The failure to follow correct procedures in the preliminary stages of a criminal case can result in the suppression of evidence and the dismissal of the charges filed against the accused. Violations of a defendant's constitutional rights can also result in a civil and / or criminal lawsuit against the responsible police officers.

Arrest

An arrest occurs when an officer takes someone into custody for the purpose of holding the person to answer a criminal charge. The arrest must be made in a reasonable manner and the force employed must be reasonable in proportion to the circumstances and conduct of the party being arrested. The officer need not be an eyewitness to the crime, so long as *probable cause* exists. This means that the officer has a well-grounded belief that the individual being arrested has committed, or is committing, an offense.

If police officers intend to make a routine felony arrest in the suspect's home, the U.S. Supreme Court requires that they first obtain an arrest warrant. An arrest warrant is an order issued by a judge, magistrate, or other judicial officer commanding the arresting officer to take an individual into custody and to bring the person before the court to answer criminal charges. Before the court will issue a warrant, a written complaint containing the name of the accused, or a description of the accused, must be filed. The complaint must be supported by affidavits and contain a description of the offense and the surrounding circumstances. A *warrant* is then issued if the court magistrate decides that (1) the evidence supports the belief that (2) probable cause exists to believe that (3) a crime has been committed and (4) the suspect is the probable culprit. Many times, the complaining party does not have firsthand information and is relying on hearsay. The warrant may still be issued if the court believes that there is substantial basis for crediting it.

Some policing agencies, such as the FBI, make a large number of arrests based on warrants. Most arrests, however, are made without a warrant, as illustrated in the following *Draper* case. This case also explains what constitutes probable cause to arrest.

Draper v. United States
358 U.S. 307
U.S. Supreme Court
January 26, 1959

Mr. Justice Whittaker delivered the opinion of the Court.

The evidence offered at the hearing on the motion to suppress was not substantially disputed. It established that one Marsh, a federal narcotic agent with 29 years' experience, was stationed at Denver; that one Hereford had been engaged as a "special employee" of the Bureau of Narcotics at Denver for about six months, and from time to time gave information to Marsh regarding violations of the narcotic laws, for which Hereford was paid small sums of money, and that Marsh had always found the information given by Hereford to be accurate and reliable. On September 3, 1956, Hereford told Marsh that James Draper (petitioner) recently had taken up abode at a stated address in Denver and "was peddling narcotics to several addicts" in that city. Four days later, on

Police   **Prosecution**   **Courts**

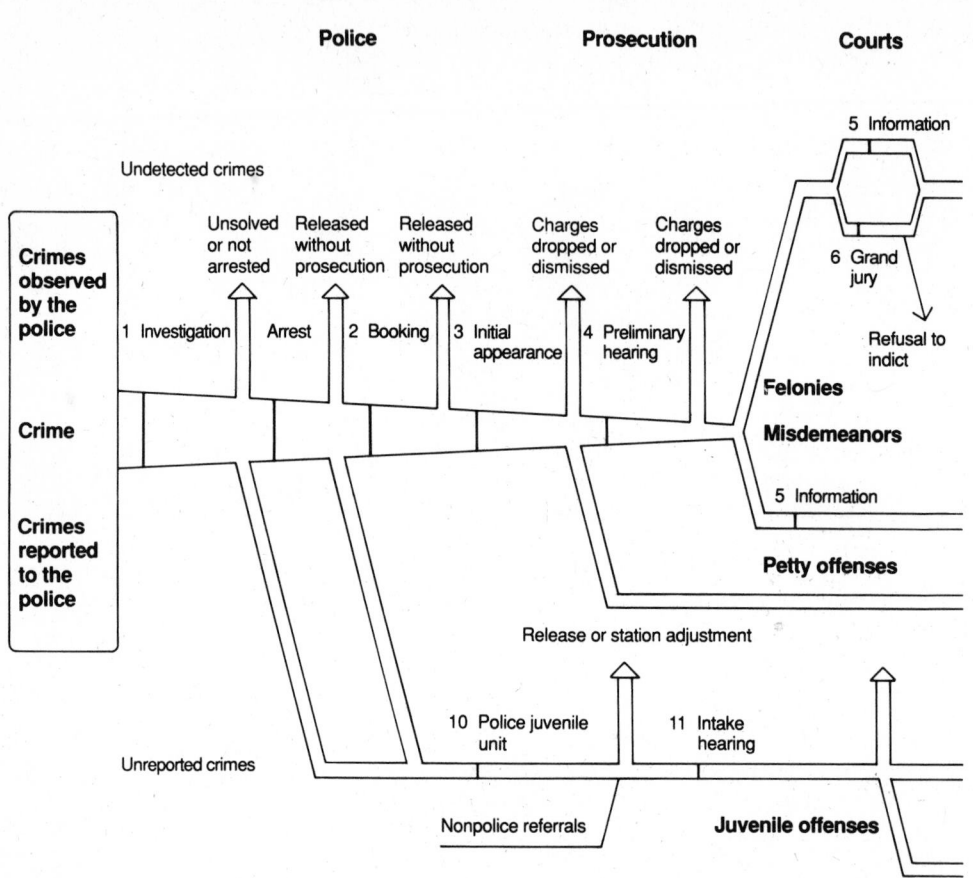

1 May continue until trial.

2 Administrative record of arrest. First step of which, temporary release on bail, may be available.

3 Before magistrate, commissioner, or justice of peace. Formal notice of charge, advice of rights. Bail set. Summary trials for petty offenses usually conducted here without further processing.

4 Preliminary testing of evidence against defendant. Charge may be reduced. No separate preliminary hearing for misdemeanors in some systems.

5 Charge filed by prosecutor on basis of information submitted by police or citizens. Alternative to grand jury indictment; often used in felonies, almost always in misdemeanors.

A simple yet comprehensive view of the movement of cases through the criminal justice system. Procedures in individual jurisdictions may vary from pattern shown here. Differing widths of lines indicate relative volumes of cases disposed of at various points in system, but these are only suggestive, since no nationwide data of the sort exist.

FIGURE 7–3 General View of the Criminal Justice System

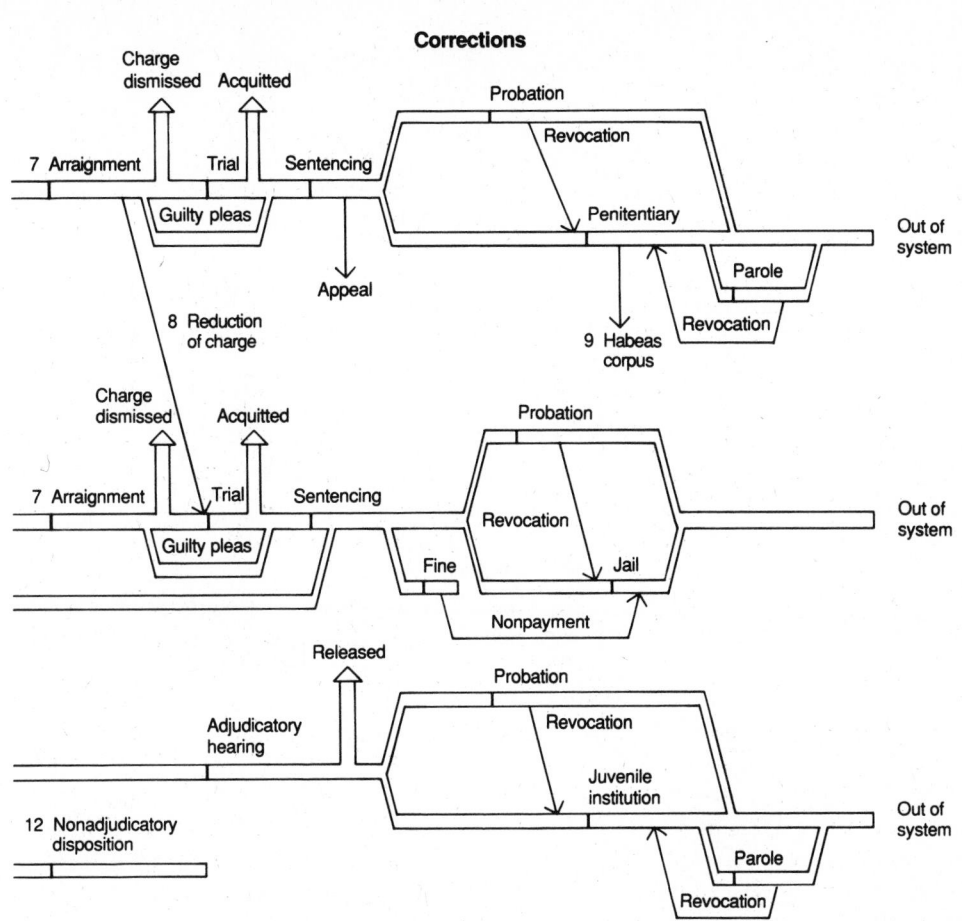

Corrections

6 Reviews whether government evidence is sufficient to justify trial. Some states have no
grand jury system; others seldom use it.

7 Appearance for plea: defendant elects trial by
judge or jury (if available); counsel for
indigent usually appointed here in felonies.
Often not at all in other cases.

8 Charge may be reduced at any time before trial
in return for guilty plea or for other reasons.

9 Challenge on constitutional grounds to legality
of detection. May be sought at any point in
process.

10 Police often hold informal hearings and
dismiss or adjust many cases without further
processing.

11 Probation officer decides desirability of further
court action.

12 Welfare agency, social services, counseling,
medical care, etc. for cases where adjudicatory
handling not needed.

Source: The Challenge of Crime in a Free Society, The President's Commission on Law Enforcement and Administration of Justice (Washington, D.C., 1967).

September 7, Hereford told Marsh "that Draper had gone to Chicago the day before [September 6] by train [and] that he was going to bring back three ounces of heroin [and] that he would return to Denver either on the morning of the 8th of September or the morning of the 9th of September also by train." Hereford also gave Marsh a detailed physical description of Draper and of the clothing he was wearing, and said that he would be carrying "a tan zipper bag" and habitually "walked real fast."

On the morning of September 8, Marsh and a Denver police officer went to the Denver Union Station and kept watch over all incoming trains from Chicago, but they did not see anyone fitting the description that Hereford had given. Repeating the process on the morning of September 9, they saw a person, having the exact physical attributes and wearing the precise clothing described by Hereford, alight from an incoming Chicago train and start walking "fast" toward the exit. He was carrying a tan zipper bag in his right hand and the left was thrust in his raincoat pocket. Marsh, accompanied by the police officer, overtook, stopped and arrested him. They then searched him and found the two "envelopes containing heroin" clutched in his left hand in his raincoat pocket, and found the syringe in the tan zipper bag. Marsh then took him (petitioner) into custody. Hereford died four days after the arrest and therefore did not testify at the hearing on the motion. . . . [T]he Narcotic Control Act of 1956 . . . provides in pertinent part:

> "The Commissioner . . . and agents, of the Bureau of Narcotics . . . may— . . .
> "(2) Make arrests without warrant for violations of any law of the United States relating to narcotic drugs . . . where the violation is committed in the presence of the person making the arrest

or where such person had reasonable grounds to believe that the person to be arrested has committed or is committing such a violation."

The crucial question for us then is whether knowledge of the related facts and circumstances gave Marsh "probable cause" within the meaning of the Fourth Amendment, and "reasonable grounds" . . . to believe that petitioner had committed or was committing a violation of the narcotic laws. If it did, the arrest, though without warrant, was lawful. . . .

Petitioner . . . contends (1) that the information given by Hereford to Marsh was "hearsay" and, because hearsay is not legally competent evidence in a criminal trial, could not legally have been considered, but should have been put out of mind, by Marsh in assessing whether he had "probable cause" and "reasonable grounds" to arrest petitioner without a warrant, and (2) that, even if hearsay could lawfully have been considered, Marsh's information should be held insufficient to show "probable cause" and "reasonable grounds" to believe that petitioner had violated or was violating the narcotic laws and to justify his arrest without a warrant.

Considering the first contention, we find petitioner entirely in error. *Brinegar v. United States*, 338 U.S. 160, . . . has settled the question the other way. There, in a similar situation, the convict contended "that the factors relating to inadmissibility of the evidence [for] *purposes of proving guilt at the trial*, deprive[d] the evidence as a whole of sufficiency to show probable cause for the search. . . ." But this Court, rejecting that contention, said: "[T]he so-called distinction places a wholly unwarranted emphasis upon the criterion of admissibility in evidence, to prove the accused's guilt, of facts relied upon to show probable cause. The emphasis, we think, goes much too far in confusing and disregarding the difference between what is required to prove guilt in a criminal case and what is required to show probable cause for arrest or search. It approaches requiring (if it does not in practical effect require) proof sufficient to establish guilt in order to substantiate the existence of probable cause. There is a large difference between the two things to be proved [guilt and probable cause], as well as between the tribunals which determine them, and therefore a like difference in the *quanta* and modes of proof required to establish them." . . .

Nor can we agree with petitioner's second contention that Marsh's information was insufficient to show probable cause and reasonable grounds to believe that petitioner had violated or was violating the narcotic laws and to justify his arrest without a warrant. The information given to narcotic agent Marsh by "special employee" Hereford may have been hearsay to Marsh, but coming from one employed for that purpose and whose information had always been found accurate and reliable, it is clear that Marsh would have been derelict in his duties had he not pursued it. And when, in pursuing that information, he saw a man, having the exact physical attributes and wearing the precise clothing and carrying the tan zipper bag that Hereford had described, alight from one of the very trains from the very place stated by Hereford and start to walk at a "fast" pace toward the station exit, Marsh had personally verified every facet of the information given him by Hereford except whether the petitioner

had accomplished his mission and had the three ounces of heroin on his person or in his bag. And surely, with every other bit of Hereford's information being thus personally verified, Marsh had "reasonable grounds" to believe that the remaining unverified bit of Hereford's information—that Draper would have the heroin with him—was likewise true.

"In dealing with probable cause . . . as the very name implies, we deal with probabilities. These are not technical; they are the factual and practical considerations of everyday life on which reasonable and prudent men, not legal technicians, act." *Brinegar v. United States.* Probable cause exists where "the facts and circumstances within . . . [the arresting officer's] knowledge and of which they had reasonably trustworthy information [are] sufficient in themselves to warrant a man of reasonable caution in the belief that" an offense has been or is being committed. . . .

We believe that, under the facts and circumstances here, Marsh had probable cause and reasonable grounds to believe that petitioner was committing a violation of the laws of the United States relating to narcotic drugs at the time he arrested him. The arrest was therefore lawful, and the subsequent search and seizure, having been made incident to that lawful arrest, were likewise valid. It follows that petitioner's motion to suppress was properly denied and that the seized heroin was competent evidence lawfully received at the trial.

Affirmed.

Case Questions

1. Why did the Supreme Court allow hearsay evidence to be used to establish probable cause, when it would have been inadmissible at trial?

2. Do you believe that an officer who has time to obtain an arrest warrant should have to do so in lieu of making a warrantless arrest in a public place?

Investigatory Detentions (Stop and Frisk)

The requirement that police officers have probable cause to arrest makes it difficult for them to investigate individuals whose conduct aroused their suspicions. The Supreme Court was asked in 1968 to balance police investigative needs against citizen privacy rights in the famous case of *Terry v. Ohio*. In *Terry*, the Supreme Court ruled that it was reasonable under the Fourth Amendment for police officers to make brief seizures of individuals based on reasonable suspicion. The court interpreted the Fourth Amendment as permitting officers to detain suspiciously acting individuals so that their identity could be determined and so that officers could question them about their behavior. However, police officers must be able to articulate the specific facts and circumstances that created a reasonable suspicion in their minds that criminal activity has been, is being, or is about to be committed.

Further, the Supreme Court has ruled that officers who can articulate facts and circumstances that suggest the stopped individual is armed have a right to make a "frisk." The frisk is less than a full search and consists of the patdown of the outer clothing of a stopped individual in order to locate weapons that might be used against the officer. If an officer, while conducting the patdown, feels an object that could be a weapon, the officer is entitled to reach inside the clothing and take the object. If a seized object or weapon is lawfully possessed, it must be returned upon the conclusion of the *investigatory detention*. If the weapon is unlawfully possessed, it can be seized and used in a criminal prosecution.

Stop and frisk is a very controversial technique in many communities. Police are frequently accused of making stops of individuals based on factors such as race, age, and choice of friends, rather than on actual evidence of impending criminal activity. Officers are also accused of making investigative stops and frisks for the purpose of conducting exploratory searches for evidence. The Supreme Court emphasized in the following case, *Adams v. Williams*, that the purpose of the frisk is to protect the officer, and not a pretext for an exploratory search for criminal evidence.

Adams v. Williams
407 U.S. 143
U.S. Supreme Court
June 12, 1972

Mr. Justice Rehnquist delivered the opinion of the Court.

Respondent Robert Williams was convicted in a Connecticut state court of illegal possession of a handgun found during a "stop and frisk," as well as of possession of heroin that was found during a full search incident to his weapons arrest. After respondent's conviction was affirmed by the Supreme Court of Connecticut, . . . this Court denied certiorari. . . . Williams' petition for federal habeas corpus relief was denied by the District Court and by a divided panel of the Second Circuit, . . . but on rehearing *en banc* the Court of Appeals granted relief. . . . That court held that evidence introduced at Williams' trial had been obtained by an unlawful search of his person and car, and thus the state court judgments of conviction should be set aside. Since we conclude that the policeman's actions here conformed to the standards this Court laid down in *Terry v. Ohio*, 392 U.S. 1 (1968), we reverse.

Police Sgt. John Connolly was alone early in the morning on car patrol duty in a high-crime area of Bridgeport, Connecticut. At approximately 2:15 a.m. a person known to Sgt. Connolly approached his cruiser and informed him that an individual seated in a nearby vehicle was carrying narcotics and had a gun at his waist.

After calling for assistance on his car radio, Sgt. Connolly approached the vehicle to investigate the informant's report. Connolly tapped on the car window and asked the occupant, Robert Williams, to open the door. When Williams rolled down the window instead, the sergeant reached into the car and removed a fully loaded revolver from Williams' waistband. The gun had not been visible to Connolly from outside the car, but it was in precisely the place indicated by the informant. Williams was then arrested by Connolly for unlawful possession of the pistol. A search incident to that arrest was conducted after other officers arrived. They found substantial quantities of heroin on Williams' person and in the car, and they found a machete and a second revolver hidden in the automobile.

Respondent contends that the initial seizure of his pistol, upon which rested the later search and seizure of other weapons and narcotics, was not justified by the informant's tip to Sgt. Connolly. He claims the policeman's action were unreasonable under the standards set forth in *Terry v. Ohio*. . . .

In *Terry* this Court recognized that "a police officer may in appropriate circumstances and in an appropriate manner approach a person for purposes of investigating possibly criminal behavior even though there is no probable cause to make an arrest." . . . The Fourth Amendment does not require a policeman who lacks the precise level of information necessary for probable cause to arrest to simply shrug his shoulders and allow a crime to occur or a criminal to escape. On the contrary, *Terry* recognizes that it may be the essence of good police work to adopt an intermediate response. . . . A brief stop of a suspicious individual, in order to determine his identity or to maintain the status quo momentarily while obtaining more information, may be most reasonable in light of the facts known to the officer at the time. . . .

The Court recognized in *Terry* that the policeman making a reasonable investigatory stop should not be denied the opportunity to protect himself from attack by a hostile suspect. "When an officer is justified in believing that the individual whose suspicious behavior he is investigating at close range is armed and presently dangerous to the officer or to others," he may conduct a limited protective search for concealed weapons. . . . The purpose of this limited search is not to discover evidence of crime, but to allow the officer to pursue his investigation without fear of violence, and thus the frisk for weapons might be equally necessary and reasonable, whether or not carrying a concealed weapon violated any applicable state law. So long as the officer is entitled to make a forcible stop, and has reason to believe that the suspect is armed and dangerous, he may conduct a weapons search limited in scope to this protective purpose. . . .

Applying these principles to the present case, we believe that Sgt. Connolly acted justifiably in responding to his informant's tip. The informant was known to him personally and had provided him with information in the past. This is a stronger case than obtains in the case of an anonymous telephone tip. The informant here came forward personally to give information that was immediately verifiable at the scene. Indeed, under Connecticut law, the informant might have been subject to immediate arrest for making a false complaint had Sgt. Connolly's investigation proved the tip incorrect. Thus, while the Court's decisions indicate that this informant's unverified tip may have been insufficient for a narcotics arrest or search warrant . . . the information carried enough indicia of reliability to justify the officer's forcible stop of Williams.

In reaching this conclusion, we reject respondent's argument that reasonable cause for a stop and frisk can only be based on the officer's personal observation, rather than on information supplied by another person. Informants' tips, like all other clues and evidence coming to a policeman on the scene, may vary greatly in their value and reliability. One simple rule will not cover every situation. Some tips, completely lacking in indicia of reliability, would either warrant no police response or require further investigation before a forcible stop of a suspect would be authorized. But in some situations—for example, when the victim of a street crime seeks immediate police aid and gives a description of his assailant, or when a credible informant warns of a specific impending crime—the subtleties of the hearsay rule should not thwart an appropriate police response.

While properly investigating the activity of a person who was reported to be carrying narcotics and a concealed weapon and who was sitting alone in a car in a high-crime area at 2:15 in the morning, Sgt. Connolly had ample reason to fear for his safety. When Williams rolled down his window, rather than complying with the policeman's request to step out of the car so that his movements could more easily be seen, the revolver allegedly at Williams' waist became an even greater threat. Under these circumstances the policeman's action in reaching to the spot where the gun was thought to be hidden constituted a limited intrusion designed to insure his safety, and we conclude that it was reasonable. The loaded gun seized as a result of this intrusion was therefore admissible at Williams' trial. . . .

Once Sgt. Connolly had found the gun precisely where the informant had predicted, probable cause existed to arrest Williams for unlawful possession of the weapon. Probable cause to arrest depends "upon whether, at the moment the arrest was made . . . the facts and circumstances within [the arresting officers'] knowledge and of which they had reasonably trustworthy information were sufficient to warrant a prudent man in believing that the [suspect] had committed or was committing an offense." . . . In the present case the policeman found Williams in possession of a gun in precisely the place predicted by the informant. This tended to corroborate the reliability of the informant's further report of narcotics and, together with the surrounding circumstances, certainly suggested no lawful explanation for possession of the gun.

Probable cause does not require the same type of specific evidence of each element of the offense as would be needed to support a conviction. . . . Rather, the court will evaluate generally the circumstances at the time of the arrest to decide if the officer had probable cause for his action. . . .

Under the circumstances surrounding Williams' possession of the gun seized by Sgt. Connolly, the arrest on the weapons charge was supported by probable cause, and the search of his person and of the car incident to that arrest was lawful. . . . The fruits of the search were therefore properly admitted at Williams' trial, and the Court of Appeals erred in reaching a contrary conclusion.

Reversed.

Case Questions

1. What facts and circumstances provided the reasonable suspicion for Sgt. Connolly's actions?
2. Why did the Supreme Court majority reject the defendant's argument that *Terry* stops should be based only on an officer's personal observations?

Custodial Interrogation

Part of the criminal investigative procedure involves questioning suspects with the aim of obtaining confessions and disclosures of crimes.

The privilege against self-incrimination applies to this questioning done outside the courtroom as well as at the trial. In general, only statements that are voluntarily made by a suspect are admissible. That is, statements must be the product of free and rational choice. The statements cannot be the result of promises, threats, inducements, or physical abuse. However, the U.S. Supreme Court has ruled that confessions that are neither voluntary nor intelligently made can in some instances be admissible if the coercion amounts to "harmless error."

In the case of *Miranda v. Arizona*, 384 U.S. 436 (1966), the Supreme Court required that people being interrogated while in police custody must first be informed in clear and unequivocal language that they have the right to remain silent, that anything they say can and will be used against them in court, that they have the right to consult with a lawyer and to have a lawyer with them during interrogation, and that they have the right to an appointed lawyer to represent them if they are indigent. If police officers conduct a custodial interrogation without giving these warnings they violate an accused's Fifth Amendment privilege against self-incrimination. In such a situation, a court may suppress the prosecution's use of the accused's statement at trial to prove his or her guilt. Such statements may, however, be admissible at trial to impeach the credibility of a testifying defendant.

The protections afforded by the *Miranda* warnings may be waived in certain circumstances. The standard is whether a defendant in fact knowingly and voluntarily waived his or her rights.

Searches and Seizures

Examinations of a person or premises are conducted by officers of the law in order to find stolen property or other evidence of guilt to be used by the prosecutor in a criminal action. With some exceptions, a warrant must be obtained by an officer before making a search. (See Figure 7–4.)

As in the case of an arrest warrant, the Fourth Amendment requires probable cause for searches and seizures. Probable cause is usually determined by the magistrate from a written complaint supported by oath or affirmation, filed by someone who has personal information concerning items to be seized. A warrant must be specific and sufficiently descriptive. In addition, the officer conducting the search cannot go outside the limits set by the warrant. Officers normally must give notice of the search before entering by force, although exceptions are made where the announcement could endanger the officer's safety or could result in the destruction of evidence (such as drugs being flushed down the toilet).

All searches and seizures do not require warrants, however. It is possible for a person to waive his or her Fourth Amendment rights and consent to a search that would otherwise be unconstitutional. Police officers may also conduct warrantless searches under the following circumstances: incident to a custodial arrest (to protect the police officer, prevent escape, and prevent the destruction of evidence), when in hot pursuit of an armed and fleeing felon (exigent circumstances), and at national borders (to prevent smuggling).

In 1914, the U.S. Supreme Court ruled that the Fourth Amendment prevented the use of evidence obtained from an illegal search and seizure in federal prosecutions. This *exclusionary rule* remedy was incorporated into the Fourteenth Amendment's due process clause and made binding on the states in the 1961 case of *Mapp v. Ohio* (367 U.S. 643). While illegally obtained evidence may not be used by the government to prove the defendant's guilt, such evidence *may* be used to contradict (impeach) a defendant's trial testimony, thus showing that the defendant's testimony may be untruthful.

The exclusionary rule has not been applied in a rigid manner, and various exceptions have been recognized by the U.S. Supreme Court. Where a recognized exception applies, the evidence can still be admitted as evidence of guilt, despite the violation of the Fourth Amendment. Examples are the independent source exception—where an untainted source of evidence is known to exist that is wholly unrelated to the illegal search and seizure—and the good faith exception—which applies if the police acted reasonably and relied on what subsequently turned out to be a defective warrant in obtaining evidence.

In the following case, the Supreme Court was asked to decide whether the exclusionary rule remedy should apply to a search conducted by school officials of a high school student's purse.

SEARCH WARRANT

To .... *[specify official or officials authorized to execute warrant]:*
   Affidavit having been made before me by .... *[affiant]* that he has reason to believe that on the ..... [person of *or* premises known as] .... *[state name of suspect or specify exact address, including apartment or room number, if any, and give description of premises]*, in the City of .... , State of .... , in the .... District of .... , there is now being concealed certain property, namely, ... *[specify, such as:* certain dies, hubs, molds and plates, fitted and intended to be used for the manufacture of counterfeit coins of the United States, in violation of .... *(cite statute)]*, and as I am satisfied that there is probable cause to believe that the property so described is being concealed on the .... [person *or* premises] above .... [named *or* described], and that grounds for issuance of a search warrent exist,
   You are hereby commanded to search within .... [ten] days from this date the .... [person *or* place] named for the property specified, serving this warrant and making the search .... [in the daytime *or* at any time in the day or night], and if the property be found there to seize it, leaving a copy of this warrant and a receipt for the property taken, and prepare a written inventory of the property seized, and promptly return this warrant and bring the property before me, as required by law.
   Dated .... , 19.....

[Signature and title]

FIGURE 7–4   Sample Search Warrant [FRCrP 41(c)]

New Jersey v. T. L. O.
469 U.S. 325
U.S. Supreme Court
January 15, 1985

Justice White delivered the opinion of the Court.

I

On March 7, 1980, a teacher at Piscataway High School in Middlesex County, N.J. discovered two girls smoking in a lavatory. One of the two girls was the respondent T. L. O., who at that time was a 14-year-old high school freshman. Because smoking in the lavatory was a violation of a school rule, the teacher took the two girls to the Principal's office, where they met with Assistant Vice Principal Theodore Choplick. In response to questioning by Mr. Choplick, T. L. O.'s companion admitted that she had violated the rule. T. L. O., however, denied that she had been smoking in the lavatory and claimed that she did not smoke at all.

Mr. Choplick asked T. L. O. to come into his private office and demanded to see her purse. Opening the purse, he found a pack of cigarettes, which he removed from the purse and held before T. L. O. as he accused her of having lied to him. As he reached into the purse for the cigarettes, Mr. Choplick also noticed a package of cigarette rolling papers. In his experience, possession of rolling papers by high school students was closely associated with the use of marihuana. Suspecting that a closer examination of the purse might yield further evidence of drug use, Mr. Choplick proceeded to search the purse thoroughly. The search revealed a small amount of marihuana, a pipe, a number of empty plastic bags, a substantial quantity of money in one-dollar bills, an index card that appeared to be a list of students who owed T. L. O. money, and two letters that implicated T. L. O. in marihuana dealing.

Mr. Choplick notified T. L. O.'s mother and the police, and turned the evidence of drug dealing over to the police. At the request of the police, T. L. O.'s mother took her daughter to police headquarters, where T. L. O. confessed that she had been selling marihuana at the high school. On the basis of the confession and the evidence seized by Mr. Choplick, the State brought delinquency charges against T. L. O. in the Juvenile and Domestic Relations Court of Middlesex County. Contending that Mr. Choplick's search of her purse violated the Fourth Amendment, T. L. O. moved to suppress the evidence found in her purse as well as her confession, which, she argued, was tainted by the allegedly unlawful search. The Juvenile Court denied the motion to suppress. . . .

. . . Having denied the motion to suppress, the court . . . found T. L. O. to be a delinquent and sentenced her to a year's probation.

On appeal, . . . a divided Appellate Division affirmed the trial court's finding that there had been no Fourth Amendment violation. . . . T. L. O. appealed the Fourth Amendment ruling, and the Supreme Court of New Jersey reversed the judgment of the Appellate Division and ordered the suppression of the evidence found in T. L. O.'s purse.

. . . We granted the State of New Jersey's petition for certiorari.

II

In determining whether the search at issue in this case violated the Fourth Amendment, we are faced initially with the question whether that Amendment's prohibition on unreasonable searches and seizures applies to searches conducted by public school officials. We hold that it does.

It is now beyond dispute that "the Federal Constitution, by virtue of the Fourteenth Amendment, prohibits unreasonable searches and seizures by state officers." . . . Equally indisputable is the proposition that the Fourteenth Amendment protects the rights of students against encroachment by public school officials. . . .

Because the individual's interest in privacy and personal security "suffers whether the government's motivation is to investigate violations of criminal laws or breaches of other statutory or regulatory standards," . . . it would be anomalous to say that the individual and his private property are fully protected by the Fourth Amendment only when the individual is suspected of criminal behavior."

We have held school officials subject to the commands of the First Amendment . . . and the Due Process Clause of the Fourteenth Amendment. . . . If school authorities are state actors for purposes of the constitutional guarantees of freedom of expression and due process, it is difficult to understand why they should be deemed to be exercising parental rather than public authority when conducting searches of their students. More generally, the Court has recognized that "the concept of parental delegation" as a source of school authority is not entirely "consonant with compulsory education laws." . . . Today's public school officials do not merely exercise authority voluntarily conferred on them by individual parents; rather, they act in furtherance of publicly mandated educational and disciplinary policies. . . . In carrying out searches and other disciplinary functions pursuant to such policies, school officials act as representatives of the State, not merely as surrogates for the parents, and they cannot claim the parents' immunity from the strictures of the Fourth Amendment.

III

To hold that the Fourth Amendment applies to searches conducted by school authorities is only to begin the inquiry into the standards governing such searches. Although the underlying command of the Fourth Amendment is always that searches and seizures be reasonable, what is reasonable depends on the context within which a search takes place. The determination of the standard of reasonableness governing any specific class of searches requires "balancing the need to search against the invasion which the search entails." . . . On one side of the balance are arrayed the individual's legitimate expectations of privacy and personal security; on the other, the government's need for effective methods to deal with breaches of public order.

We have recognized that even a limited search of the person is a substantial invasion of privacy. . . . We have also recognized that searches of closed items of personal luggage are intrusions on protected privacy interests, for "the Fourth Amendment provides protection to the owner of every container that conceals its contents from plain view." . . . A search of a child's person or of a closed purse or other bag carried on her person,[5] no less than a similar search carried out on an adult, is undoubtedly a severe violation of subjective expectations of privacy. . . .

Nor does the State's suggestion that children have no legitimate need to bring personal property into the schools seem well anchored in reality. Students at a minimum must bring to school not only the supplies needed for their studies, but also keys, money, and the necessaries of personal hygiene and grooming. In addition, students may carry on their persons or in purses or wallets such nondisruptive yet highly personal items as photographs, letters, and diaries. Finally, students may have perfectly legitimate reasons to carry with them articles of property needed in connection with extra-curricular or recreational activities. In short, schoolchildren may find it necessary to carry with them a variety of legitimate, noncontraband items, and there is no reason to conclude

[5] We do not address the question, not presented by this case, whether a schoolchild has a legitimate expectation of privacy in lockers, desks, or other school property provided for the storage of school supplies. Nor do we express any opinion on the standards (if any) governing searches of such areas by school officials or by other public authorities acting at the request of school officials. . . .

that they have necessarily waived all rights to privacy in such items merely by bringing them onto school grounds.

Against the child's interest in privacy must be set the substantial interest of teachers and administrators in maintaining discipline in the classroom and on school grounds. Maintaining order in the classroom has never been easy, but in recent years, school disorder has often taken particularly ugly forms: drug use and violent crime in the schools have become major social problems. . . . Even in schools that have been spared the most severe disciplinary problems, the preservation of order and a proper educational environment requires close supervision of schoolchildren, as well as the enforcement of rules against conduct that would be perfectly permissible if undertaken by an adult. . . . Accordingly, we have recognized that maintaining security and order in schools requires a certain degree of flexibility in school disciplinary procedures, and we have respected the value of preserving the informality of the student-teacher relationship. . . .

How, then, should we strike the balance between the schoolchild's legitimate expectations of privacy and the school's equally legitimate need to maintain an environment in which learning can take place? It is evident that the school setting requires some easing of the restrictions to which searches by public authorities are ordinarily subject. The warrant requirement, in particular, is unsuited to the school environment: requiring a teacher to obtain a warrant before searching a child suspected of an infraction of school rules (or of the criminal law) would unduly interfere with the maintenance of the swift and informal disciplinary procedures needed in the schools. Just as we have in other cases dispensed with the warrant requirement when "the burden of obtaining a warrant is likely to frustrate the governmental purpose behind the search," we hold today that school officials need not obtain a warrant before searching a student who is under their authority. . . .

We join the majority of courts that have examined this issue in concluding that the accommodation of the privacy interests of schoolchildren with the substantial need of teachers and administrators for freedom to maintain order in the schools does not require strict adherence to the requirement that searches be based on probable cause to believe that the subject of the search has violated or is violating the law. Rather, the legality of a search of a student should depend simply on the reasonableness, under all the circumstances, of the search. Determining the reasonableness of any search involves a twofold inquiry: first, one must consider "whether the . . . action was justified at its inception," . . . second, one must determine whether the search as actually conducted "was reasonably related in scope to the circumstances which justified the interference in the first place." . . . Under ordinary circumstances, a search of a student by a teacher or other school official will be "justified at its inception" when there are reasonable grounds for suspecting that the search will turn up evidence that the student has violated or is violating either the law or the rules of the school. Such a search will be permissible in its scope when the measures adopted are reasonably related to the objectives of the search and not excessively intrusive in light of the age and sex of the student and the nature of the infraction.

This standard will, we trust, neither unduly burden the efforts of school authorities to maintain order in their schools nor authorize unrestrained intrusions upon the privacy of schoolchildren. By focusing attention on the question of reasonableness, the standard will spare teachers and school administrators the necessity of schooling themselves in the niceties of probable cause and permit them to regulate their conduct according to the dictates of reason and common sense. At the same time, the reasonableness standard should ensure that the interests of students will be invaded no more than is necessary to achieve the legitimate end of preserving order in the schools.

IV

There remains the question of the legality of the search in this case. . . .

The incident that gave rise to this case actually involved two separate searches, with the first—the search for cigarettes—providing the suspicion that gave rise to the second—the search for marihuana. Although it is the fruits of the second search that are at issue here, the validity of the search for marihuana must depend on the reasonableness of the initial search for cigarettes, as there would have been no reason to suspect that T. L. O. possessed marihuana had the first search not taken place. T. L. O. had been accused of smoking, and had denied the accusation in the strongest possible terms when she stated that she did not smoke at all. Surely it cannot be said that under these circumstances, T. L. O.'s possession of cigarettes would be irrelevant to the charges against her or to her response to those charges. T. L. O.'s possession of cigarettes, once it was discovered, would both corroborate the report that she had been smoking and undermine the credibility of her defense to the charge of smoking. . . .

Of course, the New Jersey Supreme Court . . . held that Mr. Choplick had no reasonable suspicion that the purse would contain cigarettes. This conclusion is puzzling. A teacher had reported that T. L. O. was smoking in the lavatory. Certainly this report gave Mr. Choplick reason to suspect that T. L. O. was carrying cigarettes with her; and if she did have cigarettes, her purse was the obvious place in which to find them. Mr. Choplick's suspicion that there were cigarettes in the purse was . . . the sort of "common-sense conclusio[n] about human behavior" upon which "practical people"—including government officials—are entitled to rely. . . .

Our conclusion that Mr. Choplick's decision to open T. L. O.'s purse was reasonable brings us to the question of the further search for marihuana once the pack of cigarettes was located. The suspicion upon which the search for marihuana was founded was provided when Mr. Choplick observed a package of rolling papers in the purse as he removed the pack of cigarettes. Although T. L. O. does not dispute the reasonableness of Mr. Choplick's belief that the rolling papers indicated the presence of marihuana, she does contend that the scope of the search Mr. Choplick conducted exceeded permissible bounds when he seized and read certain letters that implicated T. L. O. in drug dealing. This argument, too, is unpersuasive. The discovery of the rolling papers concededly gave rise to a reasonable suspicion that T. L. O. was carrying marihuana as well as cigarettes in her purse. This suspicion justified further exploration of T. L. O.'s purse, which turned up more evidence of drug-related activities: a pipe, a number of plastic bags of the type commonly used to store marihuana, a small quantity of marihuana, and a fairly substantial amount of money. Under these circumstances, it was not unreasonable to extend the search to a separate zippered compartment of the purse; and when a search of that compartment revealed an index card containing a list of "people who owe me money" as well as two letters, the inference that T. L. O. was involved in marihuana trafficking was substantial enough to justify Mr. Choplick in examining the letters to determine whether they contained any further evidence. In short, we cannot conclude that the search for marihuana was unreasonable in any respect.

Because the search resulting in the discovery of the evidence of marihuana dealing by T. L. O. was reasonable, the New Jersey Supreme Court's decision to exclude that evidence from T. L. O.'s juvenile delinquency proceedings on Fourth Amendment grounds was erroneous. Accordingly, the judgment of the Supreme Court of New Jersey is

Reversed.

Case Questions

1. Under what circumstances can public school teachers and administrators conduct a warrantless search of a student's wallet, purse, or book bag?
2. Can state courts interpret state statutes and constitutions so that they provide greater privacy rights than are required by the federal Constitution?

Bail

Although the U.S. Constitution does not guarantee criminal defendants the right to *bail*, at the present time, bail is authorized for all criminally accused persons except those charged with capital offenses (crimes for which punishment may be death). There is also much constitutional debate about whether legislatures can classify certain other noncapital offenses as nonbailable.

Under the traditional money bail system, the judge sets bail to ensure the defendant's attendance in court and obedience to the court's orders and judgment. The accused is released after he or she deposits with a clerk cash, a bond, or a secured pledge in the amount of bail set by the judge. In 1951 the U.S. Supreme Court declared that the Eighth Amendment prevents federal judges and magistrates from setting bail at a figure higher than an amount reasonably calculated to assure the defendant's appearance at trial. However, the Eighth Amendment's prohibition against excessive bail has been interpreted to apply only to the federal government, and has not been incorporated into the Fourteenth Amendment. Thus, it is not binding on the states.

During the early 1960s there was considerable dissatisfaction with the money bail system in this country because it discriminated against low-income people. Reform legislation was enacted in many states. The bail reform statutes made it easier for criminally accused people to obtain their release, since judges were required to use the least restrictive option that would ensure that the accused appeared for trial. In appropriate cases, a defendant could be released on his or her own recognizance (an unsecured promise to appear when required), upon the execution of an unsecured appearance bond, or upon the execution of a secured appearance bond. A judge or magistrate could impose appropriate limitations on the accused's right to travel as well as his or her contacts with other people. The judge's decision was based on the defendant's offense, family roots, and employment history. The court was empowered to revoke bail if the accused was found in possession of a firearm, failed to maintain employment, or disregarded the limitations.

Public fear about crimes committed by individuals out on bail resulted in the enactment of legislation authorizing preventive detention in the Federal Bail Act of 1984. Under these laws, people thought to be dangerous, who were accused of serious crimes, could be denied bail. The targeted crimes included violent crimes, offenses punishable by life imprisonment, and drug-related crimes punishable by a term of incarceration exceeding ten years. At a hearing a court would determine if the accused was likely to flee and if judicially imposed bail conditions would reasonably protect the public safety. In appropriate cases the court was authorized to deny bail and detain the accused until trial. The constitutionality of preventive detention was addressed by the U.S. Supreme Court in the following case.

United States v. Salerno
481 U.S. 739
U.S. Supreme Court
May 26, 1987

Chief Justice Rehnquist delivered the opinion of the Court.

The Bail Reform Act of 1984 allows a federal court to detain an arrestee pending trial if the Government demonstrates by clear and convincing evidence after an adversary hearing that no release conditions "will reasonably assure . . . the safety of any other person and the community." The United States Court of Appeals for the Second Circuit struck down this provision of the Act as facially unconstitutional, because, in that court's words, this type of pretrial detention violates "substantive due process."

I

Responding to "the alarming problem of crimes committed by persons on release,"

. . . Congress formulated the Bail Reform Act of 1984, . . . as the solution to a bail crisis in the federal courts. The Act represents the National Legislature's considered response to numerous perceived deficiencies in the federal bail process. By providing for sweeping changes in both the way federal courts consider bail applications and the circumstances under which bail is granted, Congress hoped [to] "give the courts adequate authority to make release decisions that give appropriate recognition to the danger a person may pose to others if released." . . .

To this end, § 3141(a) of the Act requires a judicial officer to determine whether an arrestee shall be detained. Section 3142(e) provides that "[i]f, after a hearing pursuant to the provisions of subsection (f), the judicial officer finds that no condition or combination of conditions will reasonably assure the appearance of the person as required and the safety of any other person and the community, he shall order the detention of the person prior to trial." Section 3142(f) provides the arrestee with a number of procedural safeguards. He may request the presence of counsel at the detention hearing, he may testify and present witnesses in his behalf, as well as proffer evidence, and he may cross-examine other witnesses appearing at the hearing. If the judicial officer finds that no conditions of pretrial release can reasonably assure the safety of other persons and the community, he must state his findings of fact in writing, . . . and support his conclusion with "clear and convincing evidence." . . .

The judicial officer is not given unbridled discretion in making the detention determination. Congress has specified the considerations relevant to that decision. These factors include the nature and seriousness of the charges, the substantiality of the Government's evidence against the arrestee, the arrestee's background and characteristics, and the nature and seriousness of the danger posed by the suspect's release. . . . Should a judicial officer order detention, the detainee is entitled to expedited appellate review of the detention order. . . .

Respondents Anthony Salerno and Vincent Cafaro were arrested on March 21, 1986, after being charged in a 29-count indictment alleging various Racketeer Influenced and Corrupt Organizations Act (RICO) violations, mail and wire fraud offenses, extortion, and various criminal gambling violations. The RICO count alleged 35 acts of racketeering activity, including fraud, extortion, gambling, and conspiracy to commit murder. At respondents' arraignment, the Government moved to have Salerno and Cafaro detained pursuant to § 3142(e), on the ground that no condition of release would assure the safety of the community or any person. The District Court held a hearing

at which the Government made a detailed proffer of evidence. The Government's case showed that Salerno was the "boss" of the Genovese Crime Family of La Cosa Nostra and that Cafaro was a "captain" in the Genovese Family. According to the Government's proffer, based in large part on conversations intercepted by a court-ordered wiretap, the two respondents had participated in wide-ranging conspiracies to aid their illegitimate enterprises through violent means. The Government also offered the testimony of two of its trial witnesses, who would assert that Salerno personally participated in two murder conspiracies. Salerno opposed the motion for detention, challenging the credibility of the Government's witnesses. He offered the testimony of several character witnesses as well as a letter from his doctor stating that he was suffering from a serious medical condition. Cafaro presented no evidence at the hearing, but instead characterized the wiretap conversations as merely "tough talk."

The District Court granted the Government's detention motion, concluding that the Government had established by clear and convincing evidence that no condition or combination of conditions of release would ensure the safety of the community or any person.

. . . Respondents appealed, contending that to the extent that the Bail Reform Act permits pretrial detention on the ground that the arrestee is likely to commit future crimes, it is unconstitutional on its face. Over a dissent, the United States Court of Appeals for the Second Circuit agreed. . . . The court concluded that the Government could not, consistent with due process, detain persons who had not been accused of any crime merely because they were thought to present a danger to the community. . . . It reasoned that our criminal law system holds persons accountable for past actions, not anticipated future actions. Although a court could detain an arrestee who threatened to flee before trial, such detention would be permissible because it would serve the basic objective of a criminal system—bringing the accused to trial.

II

. . . Respondents present two grounds for invalidating the Bail Reform Act's provisions permitting pretrial detention on the basis of future dangerousness. First, they rely upon the Court of Appeals' conclusion that the Act exceeds the limitations placed upon the Federal Government by the Due Process Clause of the Fifth Amendment. Second, they contend that the Act contravenes the Eighth Amendment's proscription against excessive bail. We treat these contentions in turn.

A

. . . Respondents first argue that the Act violates substantive due process because the pretrial detention it authorizes constitutes impermissible punishment before trial. . . .

As an initial matter, the mere fact that a person is detained does not inexorably lead to the conclusion that the government has imposed punishment. . . . To determine whether a restriction on liberty constitutes impermissible punishment or permissible regulation, we first look to legislative intent. . . .

The legislative history of the Bail Reform Act clearly indicates that Congress did not formulate the pretrial detention provisions as punishment for dangerous individuals. . . . Congress instead perceived pretrial detention as a potential solution to a pressing societal problem. . . . There is no doubt that preventing danger to the community is a legitimate regulatory goal. . . .

Nor are the incidents of pretrial detention excessive in relation to the regulatory goal Congress sought to achieve. The Bail Reform Act carefully limits the circumstances under which detention may be sought to the most serious of crimes. . . . The arrestee is entitled to a prompt detention hearing . . . and the maximum length of pretrial detention is limited by the stringent time limitations of the Speedy Trial Act. . . . Moreover, . . . the conditions of confinement envisioned by the Act "appear to reflect the regulatory purposes relied upon by the" Government. . . . [T]he statute at issue here requires that detainees be housed in a "facility separate, to the extent practicable, from persons awaiting or serving sentences or being held in custody pending appeal." . . . We conclude, therefore, that the pretrial detention contemplated by the Bail Reform Act is regulatory in nature, and does not constitute punishment before trial in violation of the Due Process Clause. . . .

The government's interest in preventing crime by arrestees is both legitimate and compelling. . . . The Bail Reform Act . . . narrowly focuses on a particularly acute problem in which the Government interests are overwhelming. The Act operates only on individuals who have been arrested for a specific category of extremely serious offenses. . . . Congress specifically found that these individuals are far more likely to be responsible for dangerous acts in the community after arrest. . . . Nor is the Act by any means a scattershot attempt to incapacitate those who are merely suspected of these serious crimes. . . . In a fullblown adversary hearing, the Government must convince a neutral decisionmaker by clear and convincing evidence that no conditions of release can reasonably assure the safety of the community or any person. . . . While the Government's general interest in preventing crime is compelling, even this interest is heightened when the Government musters convincing proof that the arrestee, already indicted or held to answer for a serious crime, presents a demonstrable danger to the community. Under these narrow circumstances, society's interest in crime prevention is at its greatest.

On the other side of the scale, of course, is the individual's strong interest in liberty. We do not minimize the importance and fundamental nature of this right. But, as our cases hold, this right may, in circumstances where the government's interest is sufficiently weighty, be subordinated to the greater needs of society. We think that Congress' careful delineation of the circumstances under which detention will be permitted satisfies this standard. When the Government proves by clear and convincing evidence that an arrestee presents an identified and articulable threat to an individual or the community, we believe that, consistent with the Due Process Clause, a court may disable the arrestee from executing that threat.

B

Respondents also contend that the Bail Reform Act violates the Excessive Bail Clause of the Eighth Amendment. . . .

The Eighth Amendment addresses pretrial release by providing merely that "[e]xcessive bail shall not be required." This Clause, of course, says nothing about whether bail shall be available at all. Respondents nevertheless contend that this Clause grants them a right to bail calculated solely upon considerations of flight. . . . Respondents concede that the right to bail they have discovered in the

Eighth Amendment is not absolute. A court may, for example, refuse bail in capital cases. And . . . a court may refuse bail when the defendant presents a threat to the judicial process by intimidating witnesses. . . .

While we agree that a primary function of bail is to safeguard the courts' role in adjudicating the guilt or innocence of defendants, we reject the proposition that the Eighth Amendment categorically prohibits the government from pursuing other admittedly compelling interests through regulation of pretrial release. . . . Even if we were to conclude that the Eighth Amendment imposes some substantive limitations on the National Legislature's powers in this area, we would still hold that the Bail Reform Act is valid. Nothing in the text of the Bail Clause limits permissible government considerations solely to questions of flight. The only arguable substantive limitation of the Bail Clause is that the government's proposed conditions of release or detention not be "excessive" in light of the perceived evil. Of course, to determine whether the government's response is excessive, we must compare that response against the interest the government seeks to protect by means of that response. Thus, when the government has admitted that its only interest is in preventing flight, bail must be set by a court at a sum designed to ensure that goal, and no more. . . . We believe that when Congress has mandated detention on the basis of a compelling interest other than prevention off light, as it has here, the Eighth Amendment does not require release on bail.

III

In our society liberty is the norm, and detention prior to trial or without trial is the carefully limited exception. We hold that the provisions for pretrial detention in the Bail Reform Act of 1984 fall within that carefully limited exception. The Act authorizes the detention prior to trial of arrestees charged with serious felonies who are found after an adversary hearing to pose a threat to the safety of individuals or to the community which no condition of release can dispel. . . . [N]umerous procedural safeguards . . . must attend this adversary hearing. We are unwilling to say that this congressional determination, based as it is upon that primary concern of every government—a concern for the safety and indeed the lives of its citizens—on its face violates either the Due Process Clause of the Fifth Amendment or the Excessive Bail Clause of the Eighth Amendment.

The judgment of the Court of Appeals is therefore

Reversed.

Justice Marshall, with whom Justice Brennan joins, dissenting

This case brings before the Court for the first time a statute in which Congress declares that a person innocent of any crime may be jailed indefinitely, pending the trial of allegations which are legally presumed to be untrue, if the Government shows to the satisfaction of a judge that the accused is likely to commit crimes, unrelated to the pending charges, at any time in the future. Such statutes, consistent with the usages of tyranny and the excesses of what bitter experience teaches us to call the police state, have long been thought incompatible with the fundamental human rights protected by our Constitution. Today a majority of this Court holds otherwise. Its decision disregards basic principles of justice established centuries ago and enshrined beyond the reach of governmental interference in the Bill of Rights.

. . .

II

The majority approaches respondents' challenge to the Act by dividing the discussion into two sections, one concerned with the substantive guarantees implicit in the Due Process Clause, and the other concerned with the protection afforded by the Excessive Bail Clause of the Eighth Amendment. This is a sterile formalism, which divides a unitary argument into two independent parts and then professes to demonstrate that the parts are individually inadequate.

On the due process side of this false dichotomy appears an argument concerning the distinction between regulatory and punitive legislation. The majority concludes that the Act is a regulatory rather than a punitive measure. . . . The majority finds that "Congress did not formulate the pretrial detention provisions as punishment for dangerous individuals," but instead was pursuing the "legitimate regulatory goal" of "preventing danger to the community." . . . Concluding that pretrial detention is not an excessive solution to the problem of preventing danger to the community, the majority thus finds that no substantive element of the guarantee of due process invalidates the statute.

This argument does not demonstrate the conclusion it purports to justify. Let us apply the majority's reasoning to a similar, hypothetical case. After investigation, Congress determines (not unrealistically) that a large proportion of violent crime is perpetrated by persons who are unemployed. It also determines, equally reasonably, that much violent crime is committed at night. From amongst the panoply of "potential solutions," Congress chooses a statute which permits, after judicial proceedings, the imposition of a dusk-to-dawn curfew on anyone who is unemployed. Since this is not a measure enacted for the purpose of punishing the unemployed, and since the majority finds that preventing danger to the community is a legitimate regulatory goal, the curfew statute would, according to the majority's analysis, be a mere "regulatory" detention statute, entirely compatible with the substantive components of the Due Process Clause. . . .

The majority proceeds as though the only substantive right protected by the Due Process Clause is a right to be free from punishment before conviction. The majority's technique for infringing this right is simple: merely redefine any measure which is claimed to be punishment as "regulation," and, magically, the Constitution no longer prohibits its imposition. Because . . . the Due Process Clause protects other substantive rights which are infringed by this legislation, the majority's argument is merely an exercise in obfuscation.

IV

. . . Honoring the presumption of innocence is often difficult; sometimes we must pay substantial social costs as a result of our commitment to the values we espouse. But at the end of the day the presumption of innocence protects the innocent; the shortcuts we take with those whom we believe to be guilty injure only those wrongfully accused and, ultimately, ourselves.

Throughout the world today there are men, women, and children interned indefinitely, awaiting trials which may never come or which may be a mockery of the word, because their governments believe them to be "dangerous." Our Constitution, whose construction began two centuries ago, can shelter us forever from the evils of such unchecked power. Over 200 years it has slowly, through our efforts, grown more durable, more expansive, and more just. But it cannot protect us if we lack the courage, and the self-restraint, to protect ourselves. Today a majority of the Court applies itself to an ominous exercise in demolition. Theirs is truly a decision which will go forth without authority, and come back without respect.

I dissent.

Case Questions

1. According to the Bail Reform Act of 1984, what factors must a judicial officer consider in making the decision to require that an accused person be denied bail?
2. What arguments were raised by the defendants against the Bail Reform Act?
3. Why did justices Marshall and Brennan dissent?

The Right to an Attorney

As said earlier, a defendant has an unqualified right to the assistance of retained counsel at all formal stages of a criminal case. An indigent defendant is entitled to a court-appointed attorney under much more limited circumstances. An indigent who is subjected to custodial interrogation by the police is entitled to an appointed attorney in order to protect the Fifth Amendment privilege against self-incrimination. His or her Sixth Amendment right to counsel does not arise until after adversarial judicial proceedings have begun, when the government has formally initiated criminal proceedings against a defendant—usually, after the defendant's initial appearance before a court.

The Supreme Court has ruled that an indigent defendant cannot be sentenced to a term of incarceration for a criminal offense unless appointed counsel was afforded to the defendant at all "critical stages" of a prosecution. Postindictment line-ups for identification purposes, initial appearances, and preliminary hearings, as well as trials and sentencing hearings, are examples of such critical stages. Finally, the Court has recognized that indigents convicted of criminal offenses who want to appeal the trial court's judgment only have a Fourteenth Amendment right to appointed counsel for purposes of a first appeal.

Line-ups

The police conduct *line-ups* before witnesses for the purpose of identifying a suspect. When formal charges are pending, an accused may not be in a line-up before witnesses for identification unless the accused and accused's counsel have been notified in advance. In addition, the line-up may not be conducted unless counsel is present, so that the defendant's counsel is not deprived of the right to effectively challenge the line-up procedures and any identifications that result. It is interesting to note that the U.S. Supreme Court has not required the presence of an attorney where an array of photographs is used in lieu of an actual line-up. Unlike a line-up, a photo array is not a trial-like confrontation that requires the presence of the accused.

Preliminary Hearing and Grand Jury

In order to weed out groundless or unsupported criminal charges before trial, a preliminary hearing is conducted or a grand jury is convened. In an informal *preliminary hearing*, the magistrate examines the facts superficially to determine whether there is a strong enough case to hold the arrestee for further proceedings. The prosecution presents evidence before the magistrate, without a jury, in order to determine if there is probable cause. The accused has a right to be present at the preliminary hearing and to present evidence. If there is no chance of conviction because of lack of evidence, the magistrate dismisses the charges.

A *grand jury*, composed of people selected at random from the list of registered voters, decides whether there is reason to believe an accused has committed an offense, not whether the person is guilty or innocent. Thus they determine whether a person should be brought to trial. The decision is based on evidence heard during a secret criminal investigation attended by representatives of the state and witnesses. The grand jury has the right to *subpoena* witnesses and documents for their investigation. The accused has no right to be present at the proceedings. A grand jury returns an *indictment* (an accusation in writing) to the court if it believes that the evidence warrants a conviction. (See Figure 7–5.)

For prosecutions involving crimes against the United States, the Fifth Amendment provides that all prosecution for *infamous crimes* (an offense carrying a term of imprisonment in excess of one year) must be commenced by a grand jury indictment. Virtually all states provide for a preliminary hearing for charges involving a felony. Approximately half of the states require a grand jury indictment, while the remainder use a bill of information (a formal charging document prepared by the prosecutor and filed with the court).

Arraignment

An arraignment follows a grand jury indictment or the judge's finding of probable cause at a preliminary hearing. At *arraignments*, accused people are advised of the formal charges against them as required by the Sixth Amendment. The description of the charges must be sufficiently clear so that the defendant may be able to enter an intelligent plea. The accused are also asked whether they understand the charges and whether they have an attorney. The court appoints counsel if the accused cannot afford an attorney. Finally, a trial date is set at the arraignment. Defendants and their counsel must be given adequate opportunity to prepare for trial.

The defendant is called on to enter a plea at the arraignment. This plea may be guilty, *nolo contendere*, or not guilty. The plea of *guilty* is entered in the great majority of situations; it is simply a confession of guilt. The plea of *nolo contendere* is the same as a guilty plea, except that it cannot be used later against the accused as an admission. It is a confession only for the purposes of the criminal prosecution and does not bind the defendant in a civil suit for the same wrong. When the defendant pleads *not guilty*, the prosecution has the burden of proving him or her guilty beyond a reasonable doubt at the trial.

Plea bargaining is the process by which the accused agrees to enter a plea of guilty, often to a lesser offense, in exchange for a promise by the prosecuting attorney to recommend either a relatively light sentence or a dismissal of part of the charges. The judge does not have to accept the prosecutor's recommendations and will explain this to the defendant before accepting a negotiated plea.

THE CRIMINAL TRIAL

Every person who is charged with a crime has a constitutional right to a trial. In this way a defendant has the opportunity to confront and cross-examine the

```
            UNITED STATES DISTRICT COURT
         FOR THE ...... DISTRICT OF ......
                ....... DIVISION

United States of America,
        Plaintiff,                 Crim. No. ..............
            v.                     (.....–USC § ........
_____)
        Defendant.


                    INDICTMENT

    The grand jury charges:
    On or about the ...... day of ......, 19......, in the ......
District of ......, ....... [defendant] ....... [state essential facts
constituting offense charged], in violation of ....... USC § ........
Dated ......., 19.....


                    A True Bill.


                                      [Signature],
                                       Foreman


.......,
United States Attorney.
```

FIGURE 7–5 Sample Indictment [FRCrP 7(c)]

witnesses against him or her, testify and present evidence and arguments as a defense against the charges, have the assistance of an attorney in most cases, and take full advantage of the rights and protections afforded all people accused of crimes under the Constitution. Trial procedures are essentially the same in criminal and civil trials. The prosecution is the plaintiff and must initially present legally sufficient evidence of the defendant's criminal culpability with respect to each element of the crime or the judge will dismiss the charges and terminate the trial. A criminal defendant, unlike a civil defendant, has a constitutional right not to testify at trial. This privilege is often waived be defendants, however, because they wish to explain their version of the facts to the jury or to the judge in a bench trial. Every criminal defendant (and juvenile charged with a criminal offense) is additionally protected by the constitutional due process requirement that the prosecution prove guilt beyond a reasonable doubt in order to be entitled to a judgment of conviction.[4]

Before we read the case of *Sullivan v. Louisiana*, it is necessary to discuss two preliminary matters. In *Sullivan*, the trial judge's jury instruction defining reasonable doubt was almost identical to an instruction given in a previous case, *Cage v. Louisiana*.[5] Read the *Cage* instruction that follows and see whether you can identify any constitutional problems:[6]

> If you entertain a reasonable doubt as to any fact or element necessary to constitute the defendant's guilt, it is your duty to give him the benefit of that doubt and return a verdict of not guilty. Even where the evidence demonstrates a probability of guilt, if it does not establish such guilt beyond a reasonable doubt, you must acquit the accused. This doubt, however, must be a reasonable one; that is one that is founded upon a real tangible substantial basis and not upon mere caprice and conjecture. It must be such a doubt as would give rise to a grave uncertainty, raised in your mind by reasons of the unsatisfactory character of the evidence or lack thereof. A reasonable doubt is not a mere possible doubt. It is an actual substantial doubt. It is a doubt that a reasonable man can seriously entertain. What is required is not an absolute or mathematical certainty, but a moral certainty.

The U.S. Supreme Court in *Cage* determined that this instruction was unconstitutional. The Court noted that the trial court did at one point instruct the jury to convict only if guilt is proven beyond a reasonable doubt, "but it then equated a reasonable doubt with a 'grave uncertainty' and an 'actual substantial doubt' and stated that what was required was a 'moral certainty' that the defendant was guilty." The Court concluded, "It is plain to us that the words 'substantial' and 'grave,' as they are commonly understood, suggest a higher degree of doubt than is required for acquittal under the reasonable doubt standard. When those statements are then considered with the reference to 'moral certainty,' rather than evidentiary certainty, it becomes clear that a reasonable juror could have interpreted the instruction to allow a finding of guilt based on a degree of proof below that required by the Due Process Clause."[7]

In *Sullivan v. Louisiana*, the constitutionally erroneous *Cage* instruction was again given by the trial court. The defendant, relying on the *Cage* precedent, appealed to the Louisiana Supreme Court arguing that his murder conviction should be reversed. That court agreed that a constitutional error had occurred, but it refused to reverse Sullivan's conviction because, in its opinion, the error was harmless beyond a reasonable doubt.

According to the U.S. Supreme Court, a defendant's conviction need not be automatically reversed just because it has been proved that constitutional error occurred during the trial. In most instances, the Court has ruled there should be no reversal where the quantity and quality of the factual evidence introduced at trial is consistent with the jury's verdict and is so strong that appellate courts can conclude beyond a reasonable doubt that the constitutional error "did not contribute to the jury's verdict."[8]

In *Sullivan*, the U.S. Supreme Court granted *certiorari* to determine whether the giving of a constitutionally deficient instruction on the meaning of reasonable doubt can amount to harmless error.

Sullivan v. Louisiana
113 S.Ct. 2078
U.S. Supreme Court
June 1, 1993

Justice Scalia delivered the opinion of the Court.

The question presented is whether a constitutionally deficient reasonable-doubt instruction may be harmless error.

I

Petitioner was charged with first-degree murder in the course of committing an armed robbery at a New Orleans bar. His alleged accomplice in the crime, a convicted felon named Michael Hillhouse, testifying at the trial pursuant to a grant of immunity, identified petitioner as the murderer. Although several other people were in the bar at the time of the robbery, only one testified at trial. This witness, who had been unable to identify either Hillhouse or petitioner at a physical line-up, testified that they committed the robbery, and that she saw petitioner hold a gun to the victim's head. There was other circumstantial evidence supporting the conclusion that petitioner was the triggerman. . . . In closing argument, defense counsel argued that there was reasonable doubt as to both the identity of the murderer and his intent.

In his instructions to the jury, the trial judge gave a definition of "reasonable doubt" that was, as the State conceded below, essentially identical to the one held unconstitutional in *Cage v. Louisiana*, 498 U.S. 39, . . . (1990) (*per curiam*).

The jury found petitioner guilty of first-degree murder and subsequently recommended tha the be sentenced to death. The trial court agreed. On direct appeal, the Supreme Court of Louisiana held . . . that the erroneous instruction was harmless beyond a reasonable doubt. It therefore upheld the conviction, though remanding for a new sentencing hearing because of ineffectiveness of counsel in the sentencing phase. We granted certiorari. . . .

II

The Sixth Amendment provides that "[i]n all criminal prosecutions, the accused shall enjoy the right to a speedy and public trial, by an impartial jury. . . ." In *Duncan v. Louisiana*, 391 U.S. 145, 149, (1968), we found this right to trial by jury in serious criminal cases to be "fundamental to the American scheme of justice," and therefore applicable in state proceedings. The right includes, of course, as its most important element, the right to have the jury, rather than the judge, reach the requisite finding of "guilty." Thus, although a judge may direct a verdict for the defendant if the evidence is legally insufficient to establish guilt, he may not direct a verdict for the State, no matter how overwhelming the evidence.

What the factfinder must determine to return a verdict of guilty is prescribed by the Due Process Clause. The prosecution bears the burden of proving all elements of the offense charged, . . . and must persuade the factfinder "beyond a reasonable doubt" of the facts necessary to establish each of those elements. . . .

This beyond-a-reasonable-doubt requirement, which was adhered to by virtually all common-law jurisdictions, applies in state as well as federal proceedings.

It is self-evident, we think, that the Fifth Amendment requirement of proof beyond a reasonable doubt and the Sixth

Amendment requirement of a jury verdict are interrelated. It would not satisfy the Sixth Amendment to have a jury determine that the defendant is *probably* guilty, and then leave it up to the judge to determine . . . whether he is guilty beyond a reasonable doubt. In other words, the jury verdict required by the Sixth Amendment is a jury verdict of guilty beyond a reasonable doubt. Our opinion in *Cage* . . . held that an instruction of the sort given here does not produce such a verdict. Petitioner's Sixth Amendment right to jury trial was therefore denied.

III

In *Chapman v. California*, 386 U.S. 18, . . . (1967), we rejected the view that all federal constitutional errors in the course of a criminal trial require reversal. We held that the Fifth Amendment violation of prosecutorial comment upon the defendant's failure to testify would not require reversal of the conviction if the State could show "beyond a reasonable doubt that the error complained of did not contribute to the verdict obtained." . . . The *Chapman* standard recognizes that "certain constitutional errors, no less than other errors, may have been 'harmless' in terms of their effect on the factfinding process at trial." . . . Although most constitutional errors have been held amenable to harmless-error analysis, see *Arizona v. Fulminante*, 111 S.Ct. 1246, 1252, . . . some will always invalidate the conviction. *Gideon v. Wainwright*, 372 U.S. 335, . . . (1963) (total deprivation of the right to counsel); *Tumey v. Ohio*, 273 U.S. 510, . . . (1927) (trial by a biased judge); *McKaskle v. Wiggins*, 465 U.S. 168, . . . (1984) (right to self-representation). The question in the present case is to which category the present error belongs.

Chapman itself suggests the answer. Consistent with the jury-trial guarantee, the question it instructs the reviewing court to consider is not what effect the constitutional error might generally be expected to have upon a reasonable jury, but rather what effect it had upon the guilty verdict in the case at hand. . . . Harmless-error review looks, we have said, to the basis on which "the jury *actually rested* its verdict." *Yates v. Eatt*, 111 S.Ct. 1884, . . . (1991) (emphasis added). The inquiry, in other words, is not whether, in a trial that occurred without the error, a guilty verdict would surely have been rendered, but whether the guilty verdict actually rendered in *this* trial was surely unattributable to the error. That must be so, because to hypothesize a guilty verdict that was never in fact rendered—no matter how inescapable the findings to support that verdict might be—would violate the jury-trial guarantee.

Since, for the reasons described above, there has been no jury verdict within the meaning of the Sixth Amendment, the entire premise of *Chapman* review is simply absent. There being no jury verdict of guilty-beyond-a-reasonable-doubt, the question whether the *same* verdict of guilty-beyond-a-reasonable-doubt would have been rendered absent the constitutional error is utterly meaningless. There is no *object*, so to speak, upon which harmless-error scrutiny can operate. The most an appellate court can conclude is that a jury *would surely have found* petitioner guilty beyond a reasonable doubt— not that the jury's actual finding of guilty beyond a reasonable doubt *would surely not have been different* absent the constitutional error. That is not enough. . . . The Sixth Amendment requires more than appellate speculation about a hypothetical jury's action, or else directed verdicts for the State would be sustainable on appeal; it requires an actual jury finding of guilty.

Denial of the right to a jury verdict of guilt beyond a reasonable doubt is certainly an error of the former sort, the jury guarantee being a "basic protectio[n]" whose precise effects are unmeasurable, but without which a criminal trial cannot reliably serve its function. . . . The right to trial by jury reflects, we have said, "a profound judgment about the way in which law should be enforced and justice administered." *Duncan v. Louisiana*, 391 U.S., at 155. . . . The deprivation of that right, with consequences that are necessarily unquantifiable and indeterminate, unquestionably qualifies as "structural error."

The judgment of the Supreme Court of Louisiana is reversed, and the case is remanded for proceedings not inconsistent with this opinion.

It is so ordered.

Case Questions

1. What is the essence of the harmless-error doctrine?
2. How does harmless error relate to the right to a jury trial?
3. Why does the U.S. Supreme Court reject application of harmless-error analysis where the reasonable doubt instruction is constitutionally defective?
4. What policy arguments can you make for and against the use of harmless-error analysis?

The Sixth and Fourteenth Amendments guarantee accused people many important rights including notice of the charges, trial by jury, a speedy and public trial, and representation by counsel. Also protected by these amendments are the right to present witnesses and evidence and to cross-examine opposing witnesses.

Trial by Jury

Accused people have a constitutional right to have their guilt or innocence decided by a jury composed of people representing a cross section of their community (this right to a jury trial does not extend to offenses traditionally characterized as petty offenses). The jury trial right is a safeguard against arbitrary and highhanded actions of judges.

Unless a jury trial is waived, the jury is selected at the beginning of the trial. The number of jurors ranges from six to twelve, depending on state law. A unanimous decision is not required for conviction in all states. However, twelve jurors are required in federal criminal courts, and a unanimous decision is necessary for a conviction. If a jury cannot agree on a verdict, it is called a *hung jury* and the judge dismisses the charges. In this situation, the prosecutor may retry the defendant before a new jury.

If a defendant pleads guilty, there are no questions of fact for a jury to decide, and the judge will proceed to the sentencing phase.

Fair and Public Trial

The right to be confronted by their accusers in an adversary proceeding protects accused people from being convicted by testimony given in their absence without the opportunity of cross-examination. The defendant also has a right to a public trial. This constitutional right prevents courts from becoming instruments of persecution through secret action. The right is not unlimited, however. It is subject to the judge's broad power and duty to preserve order and decorum in the courtroom. Judges may limit the number of spectators in order to prevent overcrowding or to prevent disturbances. Judges also have the power to impose sanctions on participants and observers for acts that hinder or obstruct the court in administering justice.

Right to a Speedy Trial and Cross Examination

The accused's right to a speedy trial is interpreted as meaning that the trial should take place as soon as possible without depriving the parties of a reasonable period of time for preparation. This right, applicable to both the state and federal courts, protects an accused from prolonged imprisonment prior to trial, prevents long delay that could impair the defense of an accused person through the loss of evidence, and prevents or minimizes public suspicion and anxiety connected with an accused who is yet untried.

The right to speedy trial attaches when the prosecution begins, either by indictment or by the actual restraints imposed by arrest. How much time must elapse to result in an unconstitutional delay varies with the circumstances. The accused has the burden of showing that the delay was the fault of the state and that it resulted in prejudice.

The Prosecutor's Role

The sovereignty has the duty of prosecuting those who commit crimes; its attorney for this purpose is the prosecutor. As trial lawyer for the sovereignty, the prosecutor has extensive resources for investigation and preparation. The prosecutor is not at liberty to distort or misuse this information, and must disclose information that tends to relieve the accused of guilt. Any conduct of a prosecutor or judge that hinders the fairness of a trial to the extent that the outcome is adversely affected violates the defendant's right to due process.

Sentencing

Following jury conviction or a guilty plea, judges decide the punishment based on broad legislative guidelines. In reaching their decisions, they may consider unsworn or out-of-court information relevant to the circumstances of the crime and to the convicted person's life or prior record. Judges may spend days hearing testimony during a criminal trial, yet spend very little time deciding on a sentence. Their decisions may range from the maximum allowed by law to a suspended sentence. Parties found guilty may challenge the constitutionality of their sentences. They may argue that a sentence is "cruel and unusual" in violation of the Eighth Amendment, or that it violates the Equal Protection Clause of the Fourteenth Amendment.

Appeal

The federal and state constitutions guarantee defendants a fair trial, but not an error-free trial. In the federal and state judicial systems appellate courts determine if significant errors that warrant correction were committed by lower courts. The federal Constitution does not require states to provide for appellate review, although all defendants who enter a plea of not guilty are granted at least one appeal. The states differ in the number of discretionary appeals that are made available. A defendant who appeals has to exhaust all appellate opportunities at the state level and raise a federal question before petitioning the U.S. Supreme Court for a writ of *certiorari*. A person convicted of a crime in a federal district court can obtain review in the U.S. Court of Appeals, and then petition the U.S. Supreme Court for *certiorari*.

The prosecution is prohibited by the Fifth Amendment's double jeopardy clause, and by due process, from appealing a court's entry of a judgment of acquittal based on a jury verdict or on the insufficiency of the evidence. Statutes, however, may permit the prosecution to appeal: (1) pretrial court orders suppressing evidence, (2) a trial judge's refusal to enter judgment on the jury's guilty verdict and the entry instead of judgment for the defendant (J.N.O.V.), (3) where the sentencing judge abused his or her discretion and imposed an "inadequate" sentence, and (4) from a judgment of acquittal for the sole purpose of clarifying the law.

Habeas Corpus

The writ of *habeas corpus* (Latin for "you have the body") is used to question the legality of the detention of a prisoner; its sole function is to release petitioners from unlawful imprisonment. The writ of *habeas corpus* was recognized in Article I, section 9, of the U.S. Constitution. In 1789 Congress enacted statutes extending *habeas corpus* to federal prisoners and in 1867 included state prisoners in the writ's protection.

Federal *habeas corpus* has much strategic importance because it permits many convicted people to seek collateral review of their sentences in a federal court. While the odds are overwhelmingly against a convicted person obtaining a writ of *certiorari* from the U.S. Supreme Court, a prisoner may be able to attack the conviction in a federal district court through *habeas corpus*. The writ is granted when prisoners are able to show through arguments in a full hearing that their incarceration violates their legal rights. An unlimited number of petitions for a writ of *habeas corpus* is allowed to one who is incarcerated; however, very few *habeas corpus* proceedings succeed.

The substantive scope of *habeas corpus* has been left to the judiciary and was expanded by the U.S. Supreme Court during the 1960s and 1970s. The Court made it easier for state prisoners to challenge their state convictions by asking for *habeas corpus* review in a U.S. district court. Such prisoners would allege that their convictions were tainted by violations of their federally protected constitutional rights. Since the middle 1970s, however, the Court's personnel has significantly changed and the trend has been to limit the scope of federal *habeas corpus* review. For example, prisoners who unsuccessfully raised Fourth Amendment search and seizure issues in state courts are generally barred from having these issues reviewed by way of federal *habeas corpus*.

Chapter Questions

1. Define the following terms:

actus reus
arraignment
arrest
attempt
bail
bill of attainder
causation
conspiracy
cruel and unusual punishment
custodial interrogation
due process
duress
entrapment
Equal Protection Clause
exclusionary rule
ex post facto
felony
fundamental liberties
grand jury
habeas corpus
harmless-error doctrine
inchoate crime
indictment
insanity
intoxication
investigatory detentions (stop and frisk)
knowingly

larceny
line-ups
mala in se
mala prohibita
mens rea
misdemeanor
negligently
nolo contendere
pardon
parole
plea bargaining
preliminary hearing
preventive detention
probable cause
prosecutor
proximate cause
purposely
reasonable suspicion
recklessly
recognizance
solicitation
status crimes
strict liability
suspect classification
vicarious liability
warrant
writ

2. Viven Harris was charged on two counts of selling heroin to an under-cover police officer. At trial, Harris admitted knowing the undercover police officer, but denied that he had made one of the sales charged, and claimed that the contents of the two bags delivered to the officer was baking powder, not heroin. On cross-examination, the prosecution questioned Harris concerning statements he had made immediately following arrest that partially contradicted his direct testimony. Harris responded that he could not remember any of the questions or answers of the police interrogation recited by the prosecutor. Although Harris did not claim that the statements made to the police were coerced or involuntary, the prosecution conceded that the statements were inadmissible for the purpose of establishing Harris's guilt because of the absence of the *Miranda* warnings. The trial judge instructed the jury that the statements could be used only in determining the defendant's credibility. Was it proper to admit the statements for purposes of discrediting Harris's testimony?
   Harris v. New York, 401 U.S. 222 (1971)

3. Beckwith, a taxpayer, made certain statements to Internal Revenue agents. These statements were made during the course of a noncustodial interview in a criminal tax investigation. The interview was conducted in Beckwith's home after he voluntarily allowed the agents to enter. Beckwith was later tried for criminal tax fraud and—although he had not been given *Miranda* warnings before making the statements—his statements were admitted and used against him. What would be the court's reasoning in permitting these incriminating statements to be used?
   Beckwith v. United States, 425 U.S. 341 (1976)

4. Defendant Butler moved to suppress evidence of his incriminating statements at his trial. These statements were made to a federal agent during custodial interrogation without counsel present. The agent testified that Butler had been advised of his rights at the time of his arrest and then taken to a local FBI office for interrogation. Butler had an eleventh-grade education. He was given an advice-of-rights form, which he read, and he stated that he understood his rights. However, Butler refused to sign a waiver provision at the bottom. After being told that he need not talk or sign anything, Butler stated that he would talk, but not sign anything. He said nothing when advised of his right to counsel. He never requested counsel or attempted to terminate the questioning. Did Butler effectively waive his rights under *Miranda*?
   North Carolina v. Butler, 441 U.S. 369 (1979)

5. Roosevelt Harris was convicted of possessing liquor on which no tax had been paid, in violation of federal law. The federal tax investigator's affidavit supporting the search warrant, the execution of which resulted in the discovery of the illicit liquor, stated that (1) Harris had a reputation with the investigator for over four years as being a trafficker in illicit distilled spirits. (2) During that time the local constable had located illicit whiskey

in an abandoned house under Harris's control. (3) On the date of the affidavit, the affiant (tax investigator) had received sworn oral information from a person whom the affiant found to be a prudent person, and who feared for his life should his name be revealed, that the informant had purchased illicit whiskey from the residence described. Is the affidavit sufficient to establish probable cause for issuing a search warrant?

United States v. Harris, 403 U.S. 573 (1971)

6. Police officers, armed with an arrest warrant but not a search warrant, were admitted to Chimel's home by his wife. They waited until Chimel arrived and served him with the warrant. Although he denied the officers' request to "look around," they conducted a search of the entire house "as incident to the lawful arrest." Are items taken from Chimel's home admissible at trial?

Chimel v. California, 395 U.S. 752 (1969)

7. Murphy voluntarily came to the police station in connection with the strangulation death of his wife. At that time he had not been arrested, although there was probable cause to believe that he had committed the murder. Shortly after Murphy's arrival at the station (where he was met by retained counsel), the police noticed a dark spot on his finger. Suspecting that the spot might be dried blood and knowing the evidence of strangulation is often found under the assailant's fingernails, the police asked him if they could take a sample of scrapings from his fingernails. He refused. Under protest and without a warrant, the police proceeded to take the samples, which turned out to contain traces of skin and blood cells and fabric from the victim's nightgown. This incriminating evidence was admitted at his trial, which ended in a conviction. Murphy appealed the conviction, claiming that the fingernail scrapings were the product of a search prohibited by the Fourth Amendment. Is this a valid argument?

Cupp v. Murphy, 412 U.S. 291 (1973)

8. A complaint charges the defendant with breaking and entering. The defendant has an honorable discharge from the Army, a family living in the community, and is unemployed. It appears that a drug addiction was a motivation. What must the judge consider in determining bail under the Federal Bail Reform Act?

18 U.S.C. § 3141

9. An Illinois statute provides that accused persons can secure pretrial release: (1) on personal recognizance; (2) by execution of a bail bond, with a deposit of 10 percent of the bail, all but 10 percent of which (amounting to 1 percent of the bail) is returned on performance of the bond conditions; and (3) by execution of a bail bond, secured by a full amount deposit in cash, authorized securities, or certain real estate, all of which is returned on performance of the bond conditions. John Schilb, charged with two traffic offenses, secured pretrial release after depositing 10 percent of

the bail fixed. He was convicted of one offense and acquitted of the other. After he paid his fine, all but 1 percent of the bail (amounting to $7.50) was refunded. In a class action, he challenged the Illinois system on due process and equal protection grounds, claiming that the 1 percent retention charge is imposed on only one segment of the class gaining pretrial release, and on the poor, but not the rich; and that its imposition on an accused who is found innocent constitutes a court cost against the non-guilty. Do his arguments have merit?
Schilb v. Kuebel, 404 U.S. 357 (1971)

10. Defendant's trial on a North Carolina criminal trespass indictment ended with a declaration of a mistrial when the jury failed to reach a verdict. After the case had been postponed for two terms, the defendant filed a motion in which he petitioned the court to ascertain when the state intended to bring him to trial. While this motion was being considered, the state's prosecutor moved for permission to take a *"nolle prosequi* with leave," a procedural device whereby the accused is discharged from custody but remains subject to prosecution at any time in the future at the discretion of the prosecutor. Would entry of the *nolle prosequi* order violate the defendant's right to a speedy trial?
Klopfer v. North Carolina, 386 U.S. 213 (1967)

11. Florida law provides for a six-person jury in noncapital cases. Defendant Williams, charged with robbery, makes a pretrial motion to impanel a twelve-person jury instead of a six-person jury, claiming that a six-person jury violates his Sixth Amendment right to a "trial by jury." Rule on the motion.
Williams v. Florida, 399 U.S. 78 (1970)

12. Somerville was indicted for theft on March 19, 1965. His case was called for trial in November of that year, and a jury was impaneled and sworn. On the following day, the prosecuting attorney realized that the indictment was deficient because it did not allege that Somerville intended to deprive the owner of his property permanently. The Illinois Constitution prohibits amendment of indictments except for formal errors. The trial court decided that it was useless to proceed with the trial and granted the state's motion for a mistrial. Somerville was reindicted, tried, and found guilty. Was this double jeopardy?
Illinois v. Somerville, 410 U.S. 458 (1973)

13. William Allen was indicted by an Illinois grand jury for armed robbery, a crime carrying a sentence of up to thirty years in prison. At the pretrial stage, Allen refused court-appointed counsel and insisted on conducting his own defense. When it was time to examine prospective jurors, Allen asked insulting and repetitive questions. After a warning by the trial judge, Allen used vile language in addressing the judge and repeatedly berated the jury. When Allen tore up the file of his advisory counsel and threw it on the courtroom floor, the trial judge ordered Allen removed

from the courtroom. Periodically Allen was returned to the courtroom, only to resume his obscene outbursts. The Sixth Amendment to the Constitution provides that the accused has a right to be present at trial and confront the accusers. Did the trial judge violate Allen's rights by removing him from the courtroom? What alternative sanctions were available?

Illinois v. Allen, 397 U.S. 337 (1970)

14. Defendant's wife was bludgeoned to death. From the outset, officials focused suspicion on the defendant, who was arrested and charged with murder. During the entire pretrial period, virulent and incriminating publicity about the defendant and the murder made the case notorious, and the news media frequently aired charges besides those for which the defendant was tried. During the trial, news reporters were allowed to take over almost the entire courtroom. The movement of the reporters in the courtroom caused frequent confusion and disrupted the trial. Before the jurors began deliberations, they were not sequestered and had access to all news media. The petitioner filed a *habeas corpus* petition, contending that he did not receive a fair trial. How do you believe the U.S. Supreme Court ruled with respect to the *habeas corpus* petition?

Sheppard v. Maxwell, 384 U.S. 333 (1966)

15. A California statute makes it a misdemeanor punishable by imprisonment for any person "to be addicted to the use of narcotics." Thus the statute makes the "status" of narcotic addiction a criminal offense for which offenders may be prosecuted at any time before they reform, even though they have never used or possessed any narcotics within the state and have not been guilty of any antisocial behavior there. If someone has been sentenced to prison under this statute, what issue should be raised on appeal?

Robinson v. California, 370 U.S. 660 (1962)

16. Willie Francis was convicted of murder in a state court and sentenced to be electrocuted. A warrant for his execution was duly issued. He was prepared for electrocution, placed in the electric chair, and subjected to a shock that was intended to cause his death but failed to do so, presumably because of some mechanical difficulty. He was removed from the chair and returned to prison. Another warrant for his execution at a later date was issued. Was this a violation of the cruel and unusual clause?

Louisiana ex rel. Francis v. Resweber, 329 U.S. 459 (1947)

Notes

1. G. Jones, *The Sovereignty of the Law* (Toronto: University of Toronto Press, 1973), pp. 189–191.

2. D. Schwartz, *The Law in America* (New York: McGraw-Hill, 1974), p. 9.

3. Schwartz, pp. 12–18, 72, 73.
4. *In re Winship*, 379 U.S. 358 (1970).
5. *Cage v. Louisiana*, 498 U.S. 38 (1990).
6. Ibid., p. 41.
7. Ibid.
8. See Chief Justice Rehnquist's concurrence in *Sullivan*.

VIII

Family Law

INTRODUCTION

The concept of what constitutes a family in the 1990s differs greatly from that of earlier times. The seventeenth-century family had many more responsibilities. It was expected to provide members with food and shelter; to supply education, religious instruction, and discipline; and to nurse the injured and ill and care for the elderly.[1]

In contemporary America, many of these traditional family responsibilities are performed outside the family unit by public and private institutions such as schools, churches, prisons, hospitals, and nursing homes. The number of children under eighteen years of age living with a single parent has increased from 15 percent in 1970 to 29 percent in 1992.[2] Many of these families face enormous economic difficulties. They must struggle to meet even the most basic needs of their immediate members and have little ability to provide care for elders.[3] As children grow into adolescence, they become more mobile and independent than in the past, and parents often find themselves having less ability to exercise influence and control.[4]

These changes in families have been accompanied by changes in society's legal expectations about family life.[5] Family law, also called domestic relations law, has been recognized as a legal subfield only since the early 1900s.[6] Despite the rather recent formal recognition of family law, legal institutions have long been concerned with the rights and responsibilities of family members.

One of the most enduring features of the Western legal tradition is the deference shown by the law to family self-governance, also called family autonomy.[7] This deference was recognized in Roman law[8] and was subsequently incorporated into Anglo-Saxon law,[9] canon law (the law applied in the English ecclesiastical courts, the courts that historically handled domestic relations cases),[10] and the common law.[11]

From *Chapman v. Mitchell*, 44 A2d 392, 393 (1945)

" . . . the plaintiff [husband] is the master of his household. He is the managing head, with control and power to preserve the family relation, to protect its members and to guide their conduct. He has the obligation and responsibility of supporting, maintaining, and protecting the family and the correlative right to exclude intruders and unwanted visitors from the home despite the whims of the wife."

FIGURE 8–1   The Role of the Father—An Old-Fashioned View

Also dating from the time of the Roman emperors, however, is the legal recognition that society, through government, has a legitimate right to prevent the maltreatment and abuse of family members.[12]

These two legal principles accompanied the English immigrants who settled the eastern seaboard of North America and were widely accepted, although they were modified to meet the particular needs of each colony.[13]

In colonial America, the family was the most important unit of society. It was essential to preserving public order and producing economic stability.[14] After the Revolutionary War, the structure of the family was weakened by the ready availability of land, the shortage of labor, and the ease with which individuals could migrate.[15] Independence also brought a greater appreciation for the rights of individuals within the family and a corresponding decline in the outmoded view of a father's traditional rights that is reflected in Figure 8–1.[16] This trend has continued to the present time, and today mothers and fathers have equal rights and responsibilities.

The United States Supreme Court has reinforced family autonomy by ruling that married couples have the right to make decisions regarding the use of birth control[17] and whether they will become parents. If they do, it is they who will decide how many children they will have and how those children will be raised.[18] This right to raise children includes decisions about the nature and extent of their education and their religious upbringing.

In the following case, Amish parents were prosecuted for violating a state-mandated compulsory school-attendance law by withdrawing their children from school after completion of the eight grade. The parents appealed their convictions and claimed the law infringed on their constitutionally protected right to determine the religious development of their children.

Wisconsin v. Yoder
406 U.S. 205
U.S. Supreme Court

May 15, 1972
Mr. Chief Justice Burger delivered the opinion of the Court.

On petition of the State of Wisconsin, we granted the writ of certiorari in this case to review a decision of the Wisconsin Supreme Court holding that respondents' convictions for violating the State's compulsory school-attendance law were invalid under the Free Exercise Clause of the First Amendment to the United States Constitution made applicable to the States by the Fourteenth Amendment. For the reasons hereafter stated we affirm the judgment of the Supreme Court of Wisconsin.

Respondents Jonas Yoder and Wallace Miller are members of the Old Order Amish religion, and respondent Adin Yutzy is a member of the Conservative Amish Mennonite Church. They and their families are residents of Green County, Wisconsin. Wisconsin's compulsory school-attendance law required them to cause their children to attend public or private school until reaching age 16 but the respondents declined to send their children, ages 14 and 15, to public school after they complete the eight grade. The children were not enrolled in any private school, or within any recognized exception to the compulsory-attendance law, and they are conceded to be subject to the Wisconsin statute.

On complaint of the school district administrator for the public schools, respondents were charged, tried, and convicted of violating the compulsory-attendance law in Green County Court and were fined the sum of $5 each. Respondents defended on the ground that the application of the compulsory-attendance law violated their rights under the First and Fourteenth Amendments. The trial testimony showed that respondents believed, in accordance with the tenets of Old Order Amish communities generally, that their children's attendance at high school, public or private, was contrary to the Amish religion and way of life. They believed that by sending their children to high school, they would not only expose themselves to the danger of the censure of the church community, but, as found by the county court, also endanger their own salvation and that of their children.

They object to the high school, and higher education generally, because the values they teach are in marked variance with Amish values and the Amish way of life; they view secondary school education as an impermissible exposure of their children to a "worldly" influence in conflict with their beliefs. The high school tends to emphasize intellectual and scientific accomplishments, self-distinction, competitiveness, worldly success, and social life with other students. Amish society emphasizes informal learning-through-doing; a life of "goodness, "rather than a life of intellect; wisdom, rather than technical knowledge; community welfare, rather than competition; and separation from, rather than integration with, contemporary worldly society.

Formal high school education beyond the eighth grade is contrary to Amish beliefs, not only because it places Amish children in an environment hostile to Amish beliefs with increasing emphasis on competition in class work and sports and with pressure to conform to the styles, manners, and ways of the peer group, but also because it takes them away from their community, physically and emotionally, during the crucial and formative adolescent period of life. During this period, the children must acquire Amish attitudes favoring manual work and self-reliance and the specific skills needed to perform the adult role of an Amish farmer or housewife. They must learn to enjoy physical labor. Once a child has learned basic reading, writing, and elementary mathematics, these traits, skills, and attitudes admittedly fall within the category of those best learned through example and "doing" rather than in a classroom. And, at this time in life, the Amish child must also grow in his faith and his relationship to the Amish community if he is to be prepared to accept the heavy obligations imposed by adult baptism. In short, high school attendance with teachers who are not of the Amish faith—and may even be hostile to it—interposes a serious barrier to the integration of the Amish child into the Amish religious community. . . .

The Amish do not object to elementary education through the first eight grades as a general proposition because they agree that their children must have basic skills in the "three R's" in order to read the Bible, to be good farmers and citizens, and to be able to deal with non-Amish people when necessary in the course of daily affairs. They view such a basic education as acceptable because it does not significantly expose their children to worldly values or interfere with their development in the Amish community during the crucial adolescent period. While Amish accept compulsory elementary education generally, wherever possible they have established their own elementary schools in many respects like the small local schools of the past. In the Amish belief higher learning tends to develop values they reject as influences that alienate man from God. . . .

Although the trial court in its careful findings determined that the Wisconsin compulsory school-attendance law "does interfere with the freedom of the Defendants to act in accordance with their sincere religious belief" it also concluded that the requirement of high school attendance until age 16 was a "reasonable and constitutional" exercise of governmental power, and therefore denied the motion to dismiss the charges. The Wisconsin Circuit Court affirmed the convictions. The Wisconsin Supreme Court, however, sustained respondents' claim under the Free Exercise Clause of the First Amendment and reversed the convictions. . . .

I

There is no doubt as to the power of a State, having a high responsibility for education of its citizens, to impose reasonable regulations for the control and duration of basic education. See, *e.g.,* Pierce v. Society of Sisters, 268 U.S. 510 (1925). Providing public schools ranks at the very apex of the function of a State. Yet even this paramount responsibility was, in *Pierce,* made to yield to the right of parents to provide all equivalent education in a privately operated system. . . .

II

We come then to the quality of the claims of the respondents concerning the alleged encroachment of Wisconsin's compulsory school-attendance statute on their rights and the rights of their children to the free exercise of the religious beliefs they and their forbears have adhered to for almost three centuries.

. . . [T]he values of parental direction of the religious upbringing and education of their children in their early and formative years have a high place in our society. Thus, a State's interest in universal education, however highly we rank it, is not totally free from a balancing process when it impinges on fundamental rights and interests, such as those specifically protected by the Free Exercise Clause of the First Amendment, and the traditional interest of parents with respect to the religious upbringing of their children. . . .

It follows that in order for Wisconsin to compel school attendance beyond the eighth grade against a claim that such attendance interferes with the practice of a legitimate religious belief, it must appear either that the State does not deny the free exercise of religious belief by its requirement, or that there is a state interest of sufficient magnitude to override the interest claiming protection under the Free Exercise Clause. . . .

As the society around the Amish has become more populous, urban, industrialized, and complex, particularly in this century, government regulation of human affairs has correspondingly become more detailed and pervasive. The Amish mode of life has thus come into conflict increasingly with requirements of contemporary society exerting a hydraulic insistence on conformity to majoritarian standards. So long as compulsory education laws were confined to eight grades of elementary basic education imparted in a nearby rural schoolhouse, with a large proportion of students of the Amish faith, the Old Order Amish had little basis to fear that school attendance would expose their children to the worldly influence they reject. . . . The conclusion is inescapable that secondary schooling, by exposing Amish children to worldly influences in terms of attitudes, goals, and values contrary to beliefs, and by substantially interfering with the religious development of the Amish child and his integration into the way of life of the Amish faith community at the crucial adolescent stage of development, contravenes the basic religious tenets and practice of the Amish faith, both as to the parent and the child.
. . .

In sum, the unchallenged testimony of acknowledged experts in education and religious history, almost 300 years of consistent practice, and strong evidence of a sustained faith pervading and regulating respondents' entire mode of life support the claim that enforcement of the State's requirement of compulsory formal education after the eighth grade would gravely endanger if not destroy the free exercise of respondents' religious beliefs.

III

Neither the findings of the trial court nor the Amish claims as to the nature of their faith are challenged in this Court by the State of Wisconsin. Its position is that the State's interest in universal compulsory formal secondary education to age 16 is so great that it is paramount to the undisputed claims of respondents that their mode of preparing their youth for Amish life, after the traditional elementary education, is an essential part of their religious belief and practice. Nor does the State undertake to meet the claim that the Amish mode of life and education is inseparable from and a part of the basic tenets of their religion—indeed, as much a part of their religious belief and practices as baptism, the confessional, or a sabbath may be for others.

Wisconsin concedes that under the Religion Clauses religious beliefs are absolutely free from the State's control, but it argues that "actions," even though religiously grounded, are outside the protection of the First Amendment. But our decisions have rejected the idea that religiously grounded conduct is always outside the protection of the Free Exercise Clause. It is true that activities of individuals, even when religiously based, are often subject to regulation by the States in the exercise of their undoubted power to promote the health, safety, and general welfare, or the Federal Government in the exercise of its delegated powers. . . .

But to agree that religiously grounded conduct must often be subject to the broad police power of the State is not to deny that there are areas of conduct protected by the Free Exercise Clause of the First Amendment and thus beyond the power of the State to control, even under regulations of general applicability. . . .

This case, therefore, does not become easier because respondents were convicted for their "actions" in refusing to send their children to the public high school; in this context belief and action cannot be neatly confined in logic-tight compartments.

. . . Nor can this case be disposed of on the grounds that Wisconsin's requirement for school attendance to age 16 applies uniformly to all citizens of the State and does not, on its face, discriminate against religions or a particular religion, or that it is motivated by legitimate secular concerns. A regulation neutral on its face may, in its application, nonetheless offend the constitutional requirement for governmental neutrality if it unduly burdens the free exercise of religion. . . .

The State advances two primary arguments in support of its system of compulsory education. It notes, as Thomas Jefferson pointed out early in our history, that some degree of education is necessary to prepare citizens to participate effectively and intelligently in our open political system if we are to preserve freedom and independence. Further, education prepares individuals to be self-reliant and self-sufficient participants in society. We accept these propositions.

However, the evidence adduced by the Amish in this case is persuasively to the effect that an additional one or two years of formal high school for Amish children in place of their long-established program of informal vocational education would do little to serve those interests. Respondents' experts testified at trial, without challenge, that the value of all education must be assessed in terms of its capacity to prepare the child for life. It is one thing to say that compulsory education for a year or two beyond the eighth grade may be necessary when its goal is the preparation of the child for life in modern society as the majority live, but it is quite another if the goal of education be viewed as the preparation of the child for life in the separated agrarian community that is the keystone of the Amish faith.

The State attacks respondents' position as one fostering "ignorance" from which the child must be protected by the State. No one can question the State's duty to protect children from ignorance but this argument does not square with the facts disclosed in the record. Whatever their idiosyncrasies as seen by the majority, this record strongly shows that the Amish community has been a highly successful social unit within our society, even if apart from the conventional "mainstream." Its members are productive and very law-abiding members of society; they reject public welfare in any of its usual modern forms. The Congress itself recognized their self-sufficiency by authorizing exemption of such groups as the Amish from the obligation to pay social security taxes.

It is neither fair nor correct to suggest that the Amish are opposed to education beyond the eighth grade level. What this record shows is that they are opposed to conventional formal education of the type provided by a certified high school because it comes at the child's crucial adolescent period of religious development. . . .

The State, however, supports its interest in providing an additional one or two years of compulsory high school education to Amish children because of the possibility that some such children will choose to leave the Amish community, and that if this occurs they will be ill-equipped for life. The State argues that if Amish children leave their church they should not be in a position of making their way in the world without the education available in the one or two additional years the State requires. However, on this record, that argument is highly speculative. There is no specific evidence of the loss of Amish adherents by attrition, nor is there any showing that upon leaving the Amish community Amish children, with their practical agricultural training and habits of industry and self-reliance, would become burdens on society because of educational shortcomings. . . .

The independence and successful social functioning of the Amish community for a period approaching almost three centuries and more than 200 years in this country are strong evidence that there is at best a speculative gain, in terms of meeting the duties of citizenship, from an additional one or two years of compulsory formal education. Against this background it would require a more particularized showing from the State on this point to justify the severe interference with religious freedom such additional compulsory attendance would entail.

. . . Wisconsin's interests in compelling the school attendance of Amish children to age 16 emerges as somewhat less substantial than requiring such attendance for children generally. For, while agricultural employment is not totally outside the legitimate concerns of the child labor laws, employment of children under parental guidance and on the family farm from age 14 to age 16 is an ancient tradition that lies at the periphery of the objectives of such laws. There is no intimation that the Amish employment of their children on family farms is in any way deleterious to their health or that Amish parents exploit children at tender years. Any such inference would be contrary to the record before us. Moreover, employment of Amish children on the family farm does not present the undesirable economic aspects of eliminating jobs that might otherwise be held by adults. . . .

IV

Finally, the State, on authority of Prince v. Massachusetts, argues that a decision exempting Amish children from the State's requirement fails to recognize the substantive right of the Amish child to a secondary education, and fails to give due regard to the power of the State as *parens patriae* to extend the benefit of secondary education to children regardless of the wishes of their parents. Taken at its broadest sweep, the Court's language in *Prince*, might be read to give support to the State's position.

This case, of course, is not one in which any harm to the physical or mental health of the child or to the public safety, peace, order, or welfare has been demonstrated or may be properly inferred.

. . . [O]ur holding today in no degree depends on the assertion of the religious interest of the child as contrasted with that of the parents. It is the parents who are subject to prosecution here for failing to cause their children to attend school, and it is their right of free exercise, not that of their children, that must determine Wisconsin's power to impose criminal penalties on the parent. The dissent argues that a child who expresses a desire to attend public high school in conflict with the wishes of his parents should not be prevented from doing so. There is no reason for the Court to consider that point since it is not an issue in the case. The children are not parties to this litigation. The State has at no point tried this case on the theory that respondents were preventing their children from attending school against their expressed desires, and indeed the record is to the contrary. The State's position from the outset has been that it is empowered to apply its compulsory-attendance law to Amish parents in the same manner as to other parents—that is, without regard to the wishes of the child. That is the claim we reject today.

Our holding in no way determines the proper resolution of possible competing interests of parents, children, and the State in an appropriate state court proceeding in which the power of the State is asserted on the theory that Amish parents are preventing their minor children from attending high school despite their expressed desires to the contrary. Recognition of the claim of the State in such a proceeding would, of course, call into question traditional concepts of parental control over the religious upbringing and education of their minor children recognized in this Court's past decisions. It is clear that such an intrusion by a State into family decisions in the area of religious training would give rise to grave questions of religious freedom comparable to those raised here and those presented in Pierce v. Society of Sisters. . . . On this record we neither reach nor decide those issues. . . .

Indeed it seems clear that if the State is empowered, as *parens patriae*, to "save"

a child from himself or his Amish parents by requiring an additional two years of compulsory formal high school education, the State will in large measure influence, if not determine, the religious future of the child. Even more markedly than in *Prince*, therefore, this case involves the fundamental interest of parents, as contrasted with that of the State, to guide the religious future and education of their children. The history and culture of Western civilization reflect a strong tradition of parental concern for the nurture and upbringing of their children. This primary role of the parents in the upbringing of their children is now established beyond debate as an enduring American tradition.

. . . Where nothing more than the general interest of the parent in the nurture and education of his children is involved, it is beyond dispute that the State acts "reasonably" and constitutionally in requiring education to age 16 in some public or private school meeting the standards prescribed by the State.

However read, the Court's holding in *Pierce* stands as a charter of the rights of parents to direct the religious upbringing of their children. And, when the interests of parenthood are combined with a free exercise claim of the nature revealed by this record, more than merely a "reasonable relation to some purpose within the competency of the State" is required to sustain the validity of the State's requirement under the First Amendment. To be sure, the power of the parent, even when linked to a free exercise claim, may be subject to limitation . . . if it appears that parental decisions will jeopardize the health or safety of the child, or have a potential for significant social burdens. But in this case, the Amish have introduced persuasive evidence undermining the arguments the State has advanced to support its claims in terms of the welfare of the child and society as a whole. . . .

V

For the reasons stated we hold, with the Supreme Court of Wisconsin, that the First and Fourteenth Amendments prevent the State from compelling respondents to cause their children to attend formal high school to age 16. . . .

It cannot be overemphasized that we are not dealing with a way of life and mode of education by a group claiming to have recently discovered some "progressive" or more enlightened process for rearing children for modern life.

Aided by a history of three centuries as an identifiable religious sect and a long history as a successful and self-sufficient segment of American society, the Amish in this case have convincingly demonstrated the sincerity of their religious beliefs, the interrelationship of belief with their mode of life, the vital role that belief and daily conduct play in the continued survival of Old Order Amish communities and their religious organization, and the hazards presented by the State's enforcement of a statute generally valid as to others. . . .

Nothing we hold is intended to undermine the general applicability of the State's compulsory school-attendance statutes or to limit the power of the State to promulgate reasonable standards that, while not impairing the free exercise of religion, provide for continuing agricultural vocational education under parental and church guidance by the Old Order Amish or others similarly situated. The States have had a long history of amicable and effective relationships with church-sponsored schools, and there is no basis for assuming that, in this related context,

reasonable standards cannot be established concerning the content of the continuing vocational education of Amish children under parental guidance, provided always that state regulations are not inconsistent with what we have said in this opinion.

Affirmed.

Mr. Justice Douglas, dissenting in part

I

I agree with the Court that the religious scruples of the Amish are opposed to the education of their children beyond the grade schools, yet I disagree with the Court's conclusion that the matter is within the dispensation of parents alone. The Court's analysis assumes that the only interests at stake in the case are those of the Amish parents on the one hand, and those of the State on the other. The difficulty with this approach is that, despite the Court's claim, the parents are seeking to vindicate not only their own free exercise claims, but also those of their high-school-age children.

If the parents in this case are allowed a religious exemption, the inevitable effect is to impose the parents' notions of religious duty upon their children. Where the child is mature enough to express potentially conflicting desires, it would be an invasion of the child's rights to permit such an imposition without canvassing his views.

And, if an Amish child desires to attend high school, and is mature enough to have that desire respected, the State may well be able to override the parent's religiously motivated objections.

Religion is an individual experience. It is not necessary, nor even appropriate, for every Amish child to express his views on the subject in a prosecution of a single adult. Crucial, however, are the views of the child whose parent is the subject of the suit. Frieda Yoder has in fact testified that her own religious views are opposed to high-school education. I therefore join the judgment of the Court as to respondent Jonas Yoder. But Frieda Yoder's views may not be those of Vernon Yutzy or Barbara Miller. I must dissent, therefore, as to respondents Adin Yutzy and Wallace Miller as their motion to dismiss also raised the question of their children's religious liberty.

II

This issue has never been squarely presented before today. Our opinions are full of talk about the power of the parents over the child's education.

. . . [W]e have in the past analyzed similar conflicts between parent and State with little regard for the views of the child. See Prince v. Massachusetts, *supra.* Recent cases, however, have clearly held that the children themselves have constitutionally protectible interests.

These children are "persons" within the meaning of the Bill of Rights. We have so held over and over again.

On this important and vital matter of education, I think the children should be entitled to be heard. While the parents, absent dissent, normally speak for the entire family, the education of the child is a matter on which the child will often have decided views. He may want to be a pianist or an astronaut or an oceanographer. To do so he will have to break from the Amish tradition.

It is the future of the student, not the future of the parents, that is imperiled by today's decision. If a parent keeps his child out of school beyond the grade school, then the child will be forever barred from entry into the new and amazing world of diversity that we have today. The child may decide that that is the preferred course, or he may rebel. It is the student's judgment, not his parents', that is essential if we are to give full meaning to what we have said about the Bill of Rights and of the right of students to be masters of their own destiny. If he is harnessed to the Amish way of life by those in authority over him and if his education is truncated, his entire life may be stunted and deformed. The child, therefore, should be given an opportunity to be heard before the State gives the exemption which we honor today.

The views of the two children in question were not canvassed by the Wisconsin courts. The matter should be explicitly reserved so that the new hearings can be held on remand of the case.

Case Questions

1. On what grounds did Wisconsin require school attendance until a child reaches sixteen years of age?
2. Why did respondents Yoder, Miller, and Yutzy refuse to allow their fourteen- and fifteen-year-old children to attend school?
3. What did the Supreme Court justices decide in this case, and why did they decide it this way?
4. Do you agree with Justice Douglas's dissent?

THE FAMILY

Although the law defers to parental choice in many contexts, we saw in the *Yoder* case that government has a mandate to intervene whenever parental authority presents "harm to the physical or mental health of the child. . . ."[19] Laws exist in every state to protect children from abuse and neglect.

Given the complexity of family law and the limitations of available space, this chapter can provide only an introductory overview of the topic. It will discuss how families are created, the nature of the rights and responsibilities of family members, how family relationships are terminated, and emerging issues such as the evolving dispute about the nature of the family.[20]

What Is a Family?

Although it is apparent that a *family* always includes people in a relationship, major disagreements exist about the precise meaning of the term. Traditionally, families have been based on kinship and defined as the "customary legal relationship established by birth, marriage, or adoption."[21] This definition has been challenged recently on the ground that it is too rigid. Critics argue that even if they are unmarried, "two adult lifetime partners whose relationship is long term and characterized by an emotional and financial commitment and interdependence"[22] should receive the same rights and benefits as those who have been married. Anthropologists such as Collier, Rosaldo, and Yanagisako have favored such a functional approach. They think of families as "spheres of human relationships" that "hold property, provide care and welfare, and attend particularly to the young—a sphere conceptualized as a realm of love and intimacy," as contrasted with other more "impersonal" relationships.[23]

The legal definition of family becomes important because special rights, benefits, and privileges favor family membership. Some of these benefits are intangible, such as the societal approval that accompanies birth, marriage, and to some extent adoption. Another example is the sense of identity that family members have as to who they are and how they fit into the larger society.[24] Many other benefits are more tangible. Federal law, for example, favors married taxpayers who file jointly, and it provides social security benefits to family members in some circumstances. State legislatures also provide economic and noneconomic benefits favoring family members. Although states differ greatly as to the nature and scope of the benefits provided, they often include housing rights, homestead acts that protect some family property from creditors, statutory provisions that determine inheritance rights in the event a family member dies without leaving a will, mutual spousal support obligations, evidentiary privileges that prohibit adverse spousal testimony and that protect private spousal communications, and limited tort immunities. Many employers also favor families. Employee fringe benefit packages frequently provide family members with health and life insurance programs, as well as family leave and educational benefits.

Strong families perform essential tasks and help to create social and economic stability.[25] The family unit is expected to produce and care for the needs of the young. This includes raising children who will grow into responsible, well-adjusted adults. Family members are expected to care for each other from "cradle to grave," especially in times of crisis. When families do not or cannot meet the most basic responsibilities, they have to be met at public expense.

In the following case, the City of East Cleveland sought to enforce a housing ordinance that restricted the occupancy of a dwelling unit to a single family. The ordinance defined "family" so restrictively that it was criminal for a grandmother to live under the same roof with one of her grandsons (see Figure 8–2). As written, the law prohibited a grandmother, her adult son and his child, Dale, Jr., and another grandson, John (who was a first cousin of Dale, Jr.), from living as a family. John had moved to his grandmother's house after the death of his mother. The grandmother, Inez Moore, was criminally convicted of the crime and sentenced to serve a jail term of five days and to pay a twenty-five-dollar fine. Mrs. Moore appealed her conviction, because she believed the statute violated her rights under the due process clause of the Fourteenth Amendment. Notice the Supreme Court's sympathy for the concept of the extended family, as well as the roles played by race, culture, and economics in defining the nature of a family.

Moore v. City of East Cleveland, Ohio
431 U.S. 494
U.S. Supreme Court
May 31, 1977

Mr. Justice Powell announced the judgment of the Court, and delivered an opinion in which Mr. Justice Brennan, Mr. Justice Marshall, and Mr. Justice Blackmun joined.

East Cleveland's housing ordinance, like many throughout the country, limits occupancy of a dwelling unit to members of a single family. . . . But the ordinance contains an unusual and complicated definitional section that recognizes as a "family" only a few categories of related individuals. . . . Because her family, living together in her home, fits none of those categories, appellants stand convicted of a criminal offense. The question in this case is whether the ordinance violates the Due Process Clause of the Fourteenth Amendment.

I

Appellant, Mrs. Inez Moore, lives in her East Cleveland home together with her son, Dale Moore Sr., and her two grandsons, Dale, Jr., and John Moore, Jr. The two boys are first cousins rather than brothers; we are told that John came to live with his grandmother and with the elder and younger Dale Moores after his mother's death.

In early 1973, Mrs. Moore received a notice of violation from the city, stating that John was an "illegal occupant" and directing her to comply with the ordinance. When she failed to remove him from her home, the city filed a criminal charge. Mrs. Moore moved to dismiss, claiming that the ordinance was constitutionally invalid on its face. Her motion was overruled, and upon conviction she was sentenced to five days in jail and a $25 fine. The Ohio Court of Appeals affirmed after giving full consideration to

Living Arrangement	1970 Total	1980 Total	1990 Total	1992			
				Total[1]	White	Black	Hispanic Origin[2]
Grandchild of householder under 18 years (1,000)	**2,214**	**2,306**	**3,155**	**3,253**	**1,887**	**1,208**	**458**
Percent of all children under 18 years	3.2	3.6	4.9	4.9	3.6	11.6	6.0
With both parents present (1,000)	363	310	467	502	428	25	118
With mother only present (1,000)	817	922	1,563	1,740	957	719	220
With father only present (1,000)	78	86	191	144	96	40	23
With neither parent present (1,000)	957	988	935	867	407	424	97
Total, percent distribution	**100.0**	**100.0**	**100.0**	**100.0**	**100.0**	**100.0**	**100.0**
With both parents present	16	13	15	15	23	2	26
With mother only present	37	40	50	53	51	60	48
With father only present	4	4	6	4	5	3	5
With neither parent present	43	43	30	27	22	35	21

Excludes children whose parent(s) maintain the home, even though grandparents are living with them. [1] Includes other races not shown separately. [2] Persons of Hispanic origin may be of any race.

FIGURE 8–2 Children Living in the Home of Their Grandparents, by Presence of Parents, Race, and Hispanic Origin: 1970–1992

Sources: U.S. Bureau of the Census, Current Population Reports, P20-468, and earlier reports.

her constitutional claims, and the Ohio Supreme Court denied review. . . .

II

The city argues that our decision in *Village of Belle Terre v. Boraas*, 416 U.S. 1, 94 (1974), requires us to sustain the ordinance attacked here.

But one overriding factor sets this case apart from *Belle Terre*. The ordinance there affected only *unrelated* individuals. It expressly allowed all who were related by "blood, adoption, or marriage" to live together, and in sustaining the ordinance we were careful to note that it promoted "family needs" and "family values." . . . East Cleveland, in contrast, has chosen to regulate the occupancy of its housing by slicing deeply into the family itself. This is no mere incidental result of the ordinance. On its face it selects certain categories of relatives who may live together and declares that others may not. In particular, it makes a crime of a grandmother's choice to live with her grandson in circumstances like those presented here.

When a city undertakes such intrusive regulation of the family, . . . the usual judicial deference to the legislature is inappropriate. "This Court has long recognized that freedom of personal choice in matters of marriage and family life is one of the liberties protected by the Due Process Clause of the Fourteenth Amendment." *Cleveland Board of Education v. LaFleur.* 414 U.S. 632, . . . (1974). . . . But when the government intrudes on choices concerning family living arrangements, this Court must examine carefully the importance of the governmental interests advanced and the extent to which they are served by the challenged regulation. . . .

When thus examined, this ordinance cannot survive. The city seeks to justify it as a means of preventing overcrowding, minimizing traffic and parking congestion, and avoiding an undue financial burden on East Cleveland's school system. Although these are legitimate goals, the ordinance before us serves them marginally, at best. For example, the ordinance permits any family consisting only of husband, wife, and unmarried children to live together, even if the family contains a half dozen licensed drivers, each with his or her own car. At the same time it forbids an adult brother and sister to share a household, even if both faithfully use public transportation. The ordinance would permit a grandmother to live with a single dependent son and children, even if his school-age children number a dozen, yet it forces Mrs. Moore to find another dwelling for her grandson John, simply because of the presence of his uncle and cousin in the same household. We need not labor the point. Section 1341.08 has but a tenuous relation to alleviation of the conditions mentioned by the city.

III

The city would distinguish the cases based on *Meyer* and *Pierce*. It points out that none of them "gives grandmothers any fundamental rights with respect to grandsons," . . . and suggests that any constitutional right to live together as a family extends only to the nuclear family —essentially a couple and their dependent children.

To be sure, these cases did not expressly consider the family relationship presented here. They were immediately concerned with freedom of choice with respect to childbearing, *e.g.*, *LaFleur, Roe v. Wade, Griswold, supra,* or with the rights of parents to the custody and companionship of their own children, *Stanley v. Illinois, supra,* or traditional parental authority in matters of child rearing and education. *Yoder, Ginsberg, Pierce, Meyer, supra.* But unless we close our eyes to the basic reasons why certain rights associated with the family have been accorded shelter under the Fourteenth Amendment's Due Process Clause, we cannot avoid applying the force and rationale of these precedents to the family choice involved in this case. . . .

Appropriate limits on substantive due process come not from drawing arbitrary lines but rather from careful "respect for the teachings of history [and], solid recognition of the basic values that underlie our society."

Our decisions establish that the Constitution protects the sanctity of the family precisely because the institution of the family is deeply rooted in this Nation's history and tradition. It is through the family that we inculcate and pass down many of our most cherished values, moral and cultural.

Ours is by no means a tradition limited to respect for the bonds uniting the members of the nuclear family. The tradition of uncles, aunts, cousins, and especially grandparents sharing a household along with parents and children has roots equally venerable and equally deserving of constitutional recognition. Over the years millions of our citizens have grown up in just such an environment, and most, surely, have profited from it. Even if conditions of modern society have brought about a decline in extended family households, they have not erased the accumulated wisdom of civilization, gained over the centuries and honored throughout our history, that supports a larger conception of the family. Out of choice, necessity, or a sense of family responsibility, it has been common for close relatives to draw together and participate in the duties and the satisfactions of a common home. Deci-

sions concerning child rearing, which *Yoder, Meyer, Pierce* and other cases have recognized as entitled to constitutional protection, long have been shared with grandparents or other relatives who occupy the same household—indeed who may take on major responsibility for the rearing of the children. Especially in times of adversity, such as the death of a spouse or economic need, the broader family has tended to come together for mutual sustenance and to maintain or rebuild a secure home life. This is apparently what happened here.

Whether or not such a household is established because of personal tragedy, the choice of relatives in this degree of kinship to live together may not lightly be denied by the State. *Pierce* struck down an Oregon law requiring all children to attend the State's public schools, holding that the Constitution "excludes any general power of the State to standardize its children by forcing them to accept instruction from public teachers only." . . . By the same token the Constitution prevents East Cleveland from standardizing its children—and its adults—by forcing all to live in certain narrowly defined family patterns.

Reversed.

Mr. Justice Brennan, with whom Mr. Justice Marshall joins, concurring

I join the plurality's opinion. I agree that the Constitution is not powerless to prevent East Cleveland from prosecuting as a criminal and jailing a 63-year-old grandmother for refusing to expel from her home her now 10-year-old grandson who has lived with her and been brought up by her since his mother's death when he was less than a year old. I do not question that a municipality may constitutionally zone to alleviate noise and traffic congestion and to prevent overcrowded and unsafe living conditions, in short to enact reasonable land-use restrictions in furtherance of the legitimate objectives East Cleveland claims for its ordinance. But the zoning power is not a license for local communities to enact senseless and arbitrary restrictions which cut deeply into private areas of protected family life. East Cleveland may not constitutionally define "family" as essentially confined to parents and the parents' own children. The plurality's opinion conclusively demonstrates that classifying family patterns in this eccentric way is not a rational means of achieving the ends East Cleveland claims for its ordinance, and further that the ordinance unconstitutionally abridges the "freedom of personal choice in matters of . . . family life [that] is one of the liberties protected by the Due Process Clause of the Fourteenth Amendment." . . . I write only to underscore the cultural myopia of the arbitrary boundary drawn by the East Cleveland ordinance in the light of the tradition of the American home that has been a feature of our society since our beginning as a Nation—the "tradition" in the plurality's words, "of uncles, aunts, cousins, and especially grandparents sharing a household along with parents and children. . . ."

. . . The line drawn by this ordinance displays a depressing insensitivity toward the economic and emotional needs of a very large part of our society.

In today's America, the "nuclear family" is the pattern so often found in much of white suburbia. . . .

The Constitution cannot be interpreted, however to tolerate the imposition by government upon the rest of us of white suburbia's preference in patterns of family living. The "extended family" that provided generations of early Americans with social services and economic and emotional support in times of hardship, and was the beachhead for successive waves of immigrants who populated our cities, remains not merely still a pervasive living pattern, but under the goad of brutal economic necessity, a prominent pattern—virtually a means of survival— for large numbers of the poor and deprived minorities of our society. For them compelled pooling of scant resources requires compelled sharing of a household.

The "extended" form is especially familiar among black families. We may suppose that this reflects the truism that black citizens, like generations of white immigrants before them, have been victims of economic and other disadvantages that would worsen if they were compelled to abandon extended, for nuclear, living patterns. . . .

I do not wish to be understood as implying that East Cleveland's enforcement of its ordinance is motivated by a racially discriminatory purpose: The record of this case would not support that implication. But the prominence of other than nuclear families among ethnic and racial minority groups, including our black citizens, surely demonstrates that the "extended family" pattern remains a vital tenet of our society. It suffices that in prohibiting this pattern of family living as a means of achieving its objectives, appellee city has chosen a device that deeply intrudes into family associational rights that historically have been central, and today remain central, to a large proportion of our population. . . . Indeed, *Village of Belle Terre v. Boraas*, 416 U.S. 1 . . . (1974), the case primarily relied upon by the appellee, actually supports the Court's decision. The Belle Terre ordinance barred only unrelated individuals from constituting a family in a single-family zone. The village took special care in its brief to emphasize that its ordinance did not in any manner inhibit the choice of *related* individuals to constitute a family, whether in the "nuclear" or "extended" form. This was because the village perceived that choice as one it was constitutionally powerless to inhibit. Its brief stated: "Whether it be the extended family of a more leisurely age or the nuclear family of today the role of the family in raising and training successive generations of the species makes it more important, we dare say, than any other social or legal institution. . . . *If any freedom not specifically mentioned in the Bill of Rights enjoys a 'preferred position' in the law it is most certainly the family.*" . . . The cited decisions recognized, as the plurality recognizes today, that the choice of the "extended family" pattern is within the "freedom of personal choice in matters of . . . family life [that] is one of the liberties protected by the Due Process Clause of the Fourteenth Amendment." . . .

Mr. Justice Stevens, concurring in the judgment

In my judgment the critical question presented by this case is whether East Cleve-land's housing ordinance is a permissible restriction on appellant's right to use her own property as she sees fit. . . .

There appears to be no precedent for an ordinance which excludes any of an owner's relatives from the group of persons who may occupy his residence on a permanent basis. Nor does there appear to be any justification for such a restriction on an owner's use of his property. The city has failed totally to explain the need for a rule which would allow a homeowner to have two children live with her if they are brothers, but not if they are cousins. Since this ordinance has not been shown to have any "substantial relation to the public health, safety, morals, or general welfare" of the city of East Cleveland, and since it cuts so deeply into a fundamental right normally associated with the ownership of residential property—that of an owner to decide who may reside on his or her property . . . East Cleveland's unprecedented ordinance constitutes a taking of property without due process and without just compensation.

For these reasons, I concur in the Court's judgment.

Case Questions

1. What is the Supreme Court plurality's underlying criticism of the City of East Cleveland ordinance?
2. This case involves due process, a concept discussed in Chapter 1. How does due process apply in this instance?
3. Why does Justice Stevens write a concurring opinion?

Although most courts reject the functional definition of family, New York's highest court accepted it in 1989 in an eviction case brought under New York City's Rent and Eviction Regulations.[26] In eviction proceedings, said the court, "a more realistic, and certainly equally valid view of a family includes two adult lifetime partners whose relationship is long term and characterized by an emotional and financial commitment and interdependence."[27]

Several municipal governments have recognized, by ordinance or executive order, the "domestic partnership" status so that an employee's domestic partner could be treated in a manner equivalent to the treatment of a spouse for purposes of medical and bereavement leaves.[28]

CREATING FAMILY RELATIONSHIPS

An individual's family relationships are primarily created through marriage, parenthood, birth or adoption, and (to a much lesser extent) foster care placements. Each of these relationships will be examined in turn.

Marriage

When two people decide to marry, they are voluntarily seeking to enter into a number of relationships involving personal, economic, social, religious, and legal considerations. It is often said that marriage is a contract, and to an extent that is true, but it is unlike other civil contracts because of the extent of governmental regulation. In 1888 the United States Supreme Court noted that "[other] contracts may be modified, restricted, or enlarged, or entirely released upon the consent of the parties. Not so with marriage. The relation once formed, the law steps in and holds the parties to various obligations and liabilities. It is an institution, in the maintenance of which in its purity the public is deeply interested, for it is the foundation of the family and of society, without which there would be neither civilization nor progress."[29]

Marriage is regulated by the states, and each state determines who may marry, the duties and obligations of marriage, and how marriages are terminated. Although eligibility requirements for marriage differ from state to state, they generally include minimum age thresholds, prohibitions on marriage between close relatives, monogamy (it is illegal to marry someone who is already married), and competency (neither party can be mentally incompetent). Furthermore, the parties must not be of the same sex, and both must be entering the marriage voluntarily. The parties indicate their consent to the marriage by jointly applying for a license. Issuance of the license certifies that the applicants have complied with the relevant marriage eligibility requirements.

Although states have broad rights to regulate marriage, there are constitutional limitations on this power. This was demonstrated in 1967 in a case argued before the U.S. Supreme Court involving a Virginia criminal statute prohibiting interracial marriages. In the case of *Loving v. Virginia*, the Supreme Court was asked to determine whether such a statute was constitutionally permissible under the Fourteenth Amendment's Due Process and Equal Protection Clauses. The justices ruled that the "freedom to marry or not marry a person of another race resides with the individual and cannot be infringed by the state." You can find the *Loving* case in Chapter 7 on page 260. The following case offers another example of constitutional limitations. This case involves a 1978 constitutional challenge to a Wisconsin statute that prohibited persons who were behind on their child support payments from getting married.

Zablocki v. Redhail
434 U.S. 374
U.S. Supreme Court
January 18, 1978

Mr. Justice Marshall delivered the opinion of the Court.

At issue in this case is the constitutionality of a Wisconsin statute, Wis.Stat. §§ 245.10(1), (4), (5) (1973), which provides that members of a certain class of Wisconsin residents may not marry, within the State or elsewhere, without first obtaining a court order granting permission to marry. The class is defined by the statute to include any "Wisconsin resident having minor issue not in his custody and which he is under obligation to support by any court order or judgment." The statute specifies that court permission cannot be granted unless the marriage applicant submits proof of compliance with the support obligation and, in addition, demonstrates that the children covered by the support order "are not then and are not likely thereafter to become public charges." No marriage license may lawfully be issued in Wisconsin to a person covered by the statute, except upon court order; any marriage entered into without compliance with § 245.10 is declared void; and persons acquiring marriage licenses in violation of the section are subject to criminal penalties. . . .

I

Appellee Redhail is a Wisconsin resident who, under the terms of § 245.10, is unable to enter into a lawful marriage in Wisconsin or elsewhere so long as he maintains his Wisconsin residency. The facts, according to the stipulation filed by the parties in the District Court, are as follows. In January 1972, when appellee was a minor and a high school student, a paternity action was instituted against him in Milwaukee County Court, alleging that he was the father of a baby girl born out of wedlock on July 5, 1971. After he appeared and admitted that he was the child's father, the court entered an order on May 12, 1972, adjudging appellee the father and ordering him to pay $109 per month as support for the child until she reached 18 years of age. From May 1972 until August 1974, appellee was unemployed and indigent, and consequently was unable to make any support payments.

On September 27, 1974, appellee filed an application for a marriage license with appellant Zablocki, the County Clerk of Milwaukee County, and a few days later the application was denied on the sole ground that appellee had not obtained a court order granting him permission to marry, as required by § 245.10. . . .

II

In evaluating §§ 245.10(1), (4), (5) under the Equal Protection Clause, "we must first determine what burden of justification the classification created thereby must meet, by looking to the nature of the classification and the individual interests affected." . . . Since our past decisions make clear that the right to marry is of fundamental importance, and since the classification at issue here significantly interferes with the exercise of that right, we believe that "critical examination" of the state interests advanced in support of the classification is required. . . .

The leading decision of this Court on the right to marry is *Loving v. Virginia*, 388 U.S. 1, (1967). In that case, an interracial couple who had been convicted of violating Virginia's miscegenation laws challenged the statutory scheme on both equal protection and due process grounds. The Court's opinion could have rested solely on the ground that the statutes discriminated on the basis of race in violation of the Equal Protection Clause. . . . But the Court went on to hold that the laws arbitrarily deprived the couple of a fundamental liberty protected by the Due Process Clause, the freedom to marry. The Court's language on the latter point bears repeating:

> "The freedom to marry has long been recognized as one of the vital personal rights essential to the orderly pursuit of happiness by free men.
> "Marriage is one of the 'basic civil rights of man,' fundamental to our very existence and survival."

Although *Loving* arose in the context of racial discrimination, prior and subsequent decisions of this Court confirm that the right to marry is of fundamental importance for all individuals. Long ago, in *Maynard v. Hill*, 125 U.S. 190, . . . (1888), the Court characterized marriage as "the most important relation in life," . . . and as "the foundation of the family and of society, without which there would be neither civilization nor progress." . . . In *Meyer v. Nebraska*, 262 U.S. 390, . . . (1923), the Court recognized that the right "to marry, establish a home and bring up children" is a central part of the liberty protected by the Due Process Clause, . . .

and in *Skinner v. Oklahoma* . . . 316 U.S. 535, . . . (1942), marriage was described as "fundamental to the very existence and survival of the race." . . .

More recent decisions have established that the right to marry is part of the fundamental "right of privacy" implicit in the Fourteenth Amendment's Due Process Clause. In *Griswold v. Connecticut*, 381 U.S. 479, . . . (1965), the Court observed:

> "We deal with a right of privacy older than the Bill of Rights—older than our political parties, older than our school system. Marriage is a coming together for better or for worse, hopefully enduring, and intimate to the degree of being sacred. It is an association that promotes a way of life, not causes; a harmony in living, not political faiths; a bilateral loyalty, not commercial or social projects. Yet it is an association for as noble a purpose as any involved in our prior decisions." . . .

It is not surprising that the decision to marry has been placed on the same level of importance as decisions relating to procreation, childbirth, child rearing, and family relationships. As the facts of this case illustrate, it would make little sense to recognize a right of privacy with respect to other matters of family life and not with respect to the decision to enter the relationship that is the foundation of the family in our society. The woman whom appellee desired to marry had a fundamental right to seek an abortion of their expected child, see *Roe v. Wade*, or to bring the child into life to suffer the myriad social, if not economic, disabilities that the status of illegitimacy brings. . . .

Surely, a decision to marry and raise the child in a traditional family setting must receive equivalent protection. And, if appellee's right to procreate means anything at all, it must imply some right to enter the only relationship in which the State of Wisconsin allows sexual relations legally to take place.

By reaffirming the fundamental character of the right to marry, we do not mean to suggest that every state regulation which relates in any way to the incidents of or prerequisites for marriage must be subjected to rigorous scrutiny. To the contrary, reasonable regulations that do not significantly interfere with decisions to enter into the marital relationship may legitimately be imposed. . . .

The statutory classification at issue here, however, clearly does interfere directly and substantially with the right to marry.

Under the challenged statute, no Wisconsin resident in the affected class may marry in Wisconsin or elsewhere without a court order, and marriages contracted in violation of the statute are both void and punishable as criminal offenses. Some of those in the affected class, like appellee, will never be able to obtain the necessary court order, because they either lack the financial means to meet their support obligations or cannot prove that their children will not become public charges. These persons are absolutely prevented from getting married. Many others, able in theory to satisfy the statute's requirements, will be sufficiently burdened by having to do so that they will in effect be coerced into forgoing their right to marry. And even those who can be persuaded to meet the statute's requirements suffer a serious intrusion into their freedom of choice in an area in which we have held such freedom to be fundamental.

III

When a statutory classification significantly interferes with the exercise of a fundamental right, it cannot be upheld unless it is supported by sufficiently important state interests and is closely tailored to effectuate only those interests. . . .

Appellant asserts that two interests are served by the challenged statute: the permission-to-marry proceeding furnishes an opportunity to counsel the applicant as to the necessity of fulfilling his prior support obligations; and the welfare of the out-of-custody children is protected. We may accept for present purposes that these are legitimate and substantial interests, but, since the means selected by the State for achieving these interests unnecessarily impinge on the right to marry the statute cannot be sustained. . . .

First, with respect to individuals who are unable to meet the statutory requirements, the statute merely prevents the applicant from getting married, without delivering any money at all into the hands of the applicant's prior children. More importantly, regardless of the applicant's ability or willingness to meet the statutory requirements, the State already has numerous other means for exacting compliance with support obligations, means that are at least as effective as the instant statute's and yet do not impinge upon the right to marry. Under Wisconsin law, whether the children are from a prior marriage or were born out of wedlock, court-determined support obligations may be enforced directly via wage assignments, civil contempt proceedings, and criminal penalties. And, if the State believes that parents of children out of their custody should be responsible for ensuring that those children do not become public charges, this interest can be achieved by adjusting the criteria used for determining the amounts to be paid under their support orders.

There is also some suggestion that § 245.10 protects the ability of marriage applicants to meet support obligations to prior children by preventing the applicants from incurring new support obligations. But the challenged provisions of § 245.10 are grossly underinclusive with respect to this purpose, since they do not limit in any way new financial commitments by the applicants other than those arising out of the contemplated marriage. The statutory classification is substantially overinclusive as well: Given the possibility that the new spouse will actually better the applicant's financial situation, by contributing income from a job or otherwise, the statute in many cases may prevent affected individuals from improving their ability to satisfy their prior support obligations. And, although it is true that the applicant will incur support obligations to any children born during the contemplated marriage, preventing the marriage may only result in the children being born out of wedlock, as in fact occurred in appellee's case. Since the support obligation is the same whether the child is born in or out of wedlock, the net result of preventing the marriage is simply more illegitimate children.

The statutory classification created by §§ 245.10(1), (4), (5) thus cannot be justified by the interests advanced in support of it. The judgment of the District Court is, accordingly,

Affirmed.

Mr. Justice Stewart, concurring in the judgment

I cannot join the opinion of the Court. To hold, as the Court does, that the Wisconsin statute violates the Equal Protection Clause seems to me to misconceive the meaning of that constitutional guarantee. The Equal Protection Clause deals not with substantive rights or freedoms but with invidiously discriminatory classifications. . . .

Like almost any law, the Wisconsin statute now before us affects some people and does not affect others. But to say that it thereby creates "classifications" in the equal protection sense strikes me as little short of fantasy. The problem in this case is not one of discriminatory classifications, but of unwarranted encroachment upon a constitutionally protected freedom. I think that the Wisconsin statute is unconstitutional because it exceeds the bounds of permissible state regulation of marriage, and invades the sphere of liberty protected by the Due Process Clause of the Fourteenth Amendment.

I

I do not agree with the Court that there is a "right to marry" in the constitutional sense. That right, or more accurately that privilege, is under our federal system peculiarly one to be defined and limited by state law. . . . A State may not only "significantly interfere with decisions to enter into marital relationship," but may in many circumstances absolutely prohibit it. Surely, for example, a State may legitimately say that no one can marry his or her sibling, that no one can marry who is not at least 14 years old, that no one can marry without first passing an examination for venereal disease, or that no one can marry who has a living husband or wife. But, just as surely, in regulating the intimate human relationship of marriage there is a limit beyond which a State may not constitutionally go. . . .

II

. . . Although the Court purports to examine the bases for legislative classifications and to compare the treatment of legislatively defined groups, it actually erects substantive limitations on what States may do. Thus, the effect of the Court's decision in this case is not to require Wisconsin to draw its legislative classifications with greater precision or to afford similar treatment to similarly situated persons. Rather, the message of the Court's opinion is that Wisconsin may not use its control over marriage to achieve the objectives of the state statute. Such restrictions on basic governmental power are at the heart of substantive due process.

Case Questions

1. The Supreme Court majority ruled that a statute preventing persons under support orders from marrying without judicial approval is a classification that significantly interfered with the exercise of a fundamental privacy right. What is significant about classifying a right as *fundamental*?
2. Why does Justice Stewart agree with the majority on the judgment in this case, but disagree with the rationale?

Marriage Solemnization Ceremonies

States generally require that persons intending to marry solemnize their union with either a civil or a religious ceremony. The solemnization ceremony provides tangible and public evidence that a marriage has occurred. It demonstrates that the parties mutually desire to marry and are legally qualified.[30]

Common Law Marriages

Some states recognize privately created, informal marriages by agreement that dispense with licenses and solemnization ceremonies. There are called *common law marriages*. Although each state that recognizes common law marriages has its own particular requirements, states generally require the parties to be of age and unmarried. Most important, the parties must have established the relationship of husband and wife, live together as a married couple, and present themselves to the world as being married. Living together, jointly owning property, and having a child are insufficient acts, in themselves, to establish a common law marriage. Some states have statutes protecting the validity of such marriages, others recognize their validity by court decisions, and many refuse to recognize them at all. Nevertheless, the courts of a state that does not permit common law marriage will recognize persons as married who were parties to a valid common law marriage in some other state.

Adoption

Informal adoptions existed in this country from its earliest days, and into the 1860s orphans were often apprenticed to masters so that they could pay for their room and board.[31] Since adoption was unknown to the common law, adoption law in the United States is traced to 1851 when Massachusetts enacted the first statute.[32]

Although modern statutes permit the adoption of adults, subject to some exceptions,[33] most adoptions involve children. Adoption is primarily a social and a legal process by which the rights and duties accompanying the parent-child relationship are transferred from birth parents to adoptive parents. State adoption statutes were originally intended primarily to help qualified childless couples "normalize" their marriages,[34] but today the statutes provide families for many abandoned, abused, deserted, neglected, or unwanted children, who might otherwise need to be supported at public expense.

Adoptions can be classified as either independent or agency placements. In *agency adoptions*, the birth parents consent to the termination of their parental rights and surrender the child to an adoption agency to select the adoptive parent(s) and place the child. An *independent adoption* takes place when the birth parent(s) themselves interview prospective adoptive parents and make a selection without agency involvement. Some states prohibit independent adoptions and require that agencies participate in the process.

Becoming an adoptive parent is highly regulated and the procedures vary by state and by the type of adoption. It often makes a difference whether the adoption involves an agency or is independent, is between relatives, or is of an adult. In adoptions between related persons, for example, where a stepparent wishes to adopt his or her spouse's child, the investigative process is often simplified or eliminated. In an independent adoption, the nature and scope of any investigation is left up to the birth parent(s). They interview prospective adoptive parents and place the child without agency participation. When a public or private agency licensed by the state places a child for adoption, the law usually requires close scrutiny. Adoptive parents who are unrelated to an adoptive child are carefully investigated to determine whether the placement is suitable and in the best interests of the child. This investigation is often very detailed and probes most areas of an applicant's life. The probe results in a report that includes information on the applicant's race, age, marital status, and financial condition, the "adequacy of the home environment," and information about very personal matters such as religious preferences, current romantic interests, and sexuality.[35]

Matching

The investigative process makes it possible for agencies to rank prospective adoptive parents in terms of how closely they match the agency's conception of the ideal family for the child. Those who most closely fit the profile are often matched with the most "desirable" adoptees.[36] Married petitioners generally rank higher than unmarrieds, younger higher than older, able bodied higher than disabled, and heterosexuals higher than homosexuals.[37]

Agency placement decisions that hinge on considerations of race, religion, and sexual orientation have been challenged in the courts. Judicial bodies have struggled with the question of whether to support or oppose laws and policies prohibiting or disfavoring interracial adoptions. Although the U.S. Supreme Court decided in 1984 that race should not be used as the decisive factor in resolving child custody disputes,[38] it has made no comparable decision directly involving adoptions. Lower courts have declared as unconstitutional state statutes that prohibit interracial adoptions[39] and permit the consideration of race only as a "relevant but not a decisive factor," but this standard has not been generally implemented.[40] Race is still commonly considered in placement decisions.[41] Some states have responded to the constitutional ambiguity by enacting preference laws that favor adoptive parents who share the same ethnic or racial background of the adoptee (see Figure 8–3). Reports persist that agencies continue the practice of making transracial placements only as a last resort.[42]

Interracial adoption is a topic heavily laden with emotion, most of the fury arising where whites seek to adopt nonwhite children. Questions are frequently raised about whether white adoptive parents have the ability to fully develop a nonwhite adoptive child's racial identity and appreciation for the richness of his or her culture.[43]

Congress enacted legislation (the Multiethnic Placement Act of 1994) containing language that prohibits adoption agencies from discriminating against adoptive parents solely on the basis of race, color, or national origin. However, this statute also contains language that allows agencies to consider a child's racial identity and cultural needs in making placement decisions. Thus, agencies can routinely prevent white adoptive parents from adopting nonwhite children by carefully justifying the decision on the basis of the child's cultural needs. The parents then have the burden of proving that this justification is merely a pretext for invidious discrimination. Because most children in need of placement in the 1990s are nonwhite, and because most of those seeking to adopt are white, it is likely that Congress and the courts in the 1990s will clarify the extent to which race is a permissible consideration in adoption placement decisions.

State statutes often express a preference that adoptive parents be of the same religion as the adoptee or birth parent(s).[44] Should adoptive parents who are of mixed religions, who adhere to obscure faiths, or who are atheists be legally disadvantaged in placement decisions?[45] Should adoptive parents have the right to choose the religion of their adoptive child, or must they raise the child in the faith chosen by the birth parents? Does it matter whether the adoptive child's religion differs from that of the other members of the adoptive family?[46] Questions like these are easy to ask, but they raise policy issues that are difficult to resolve.

You will recall from reading *Wisconsin v. Yoder* that the U.S. Supreme Court has strongly indicated that government should remain neutral in religious matters, and we saw the Court support parental choice regarding the religious upbringing of children. But the Court has not attempted to answer, as a general proposition, whether religious matching is in the best interest of adoptive children.

Civ.Code, § 222.35

Whenever a child is being considered for adoption, the following order of placement preferences regarding racial background or ethnic identification shall be used, subject to the provisions of this section, in determining the adoptive setting in which the child should be placed:

(a) In the home of a relative.

(b) If a relative is not available, or if placement with available relatives is not in the child's best interest, with an adoptive family with the same racial background or ethnic identification as the child. If the child has a mixed racial or ethnic background, placement shall be made with a family of the racial or ethnic group with which the child has the more significant contacts.

(c) If placement cannot be made under the rules set forth in this section within 90 days from the time the child is relinquished for adoption or has been declared free from parental custody or control, the child is free for adoption with a family of a different racial background or ethnic identification where there is evidence of sensitivity to the child's race, ethnicity, and culture. The child's religious background shall also be considered in determining an appropriate placement. A child may not be free for adoption with a family of a different racial background or ethnic identification pursuant to this subdivision however, unless it can be documented that a diligent search meeting the requirements of [Civil Code] Section 222.37 for a family meeting the placement criteria has been accomplished.

Civ.Code, § 222.36

A determination of good cause not to follow the rules set forth in [Civil Code] Section 222.35 may be based on one or more of the following considerations:

(a) Request of the parent or parents.

(b) The extraordinary physical or emotional needs of the child.

(c) The child is legally free for adoption for a period exceeding 90 days during which a diligent search was conducted, and no family meeting the placement preference criteria is available for placement. Documentation shall be necessary in order to make a finding of good cause under this section.

(d) Application of these rules would not be in the best interests of the child.

Civ.Code, § 222.37

Every public or private agency shall maintain records for the placement of each child to show that a diligent search has been conducted for families meeting the criteria of [Civil Code] Section 222.35, and in accordance with diligent search rules which shall be adopted by the department. In conducting a diligent search, each agency shall use all appropriate resources, as necessary, in a directed effort to recruit a family meeting the placement preference criteria through (a) the use of all appropriate intra-agency and inter-agency, state, regional, and national exchanges and listing books, (b) child-specific recruitment in electronic and printed media coverage, and (c) the use of agency contacts with parents groups to advocate for specific waiting children.

Records of agencies maintained pursuant to this section may be reviewed upon request by the state department.

FIGURE 8–3 California Civil Code Sections 222.35, 222.36, and 222.37

A third area of current controversy involves the placement of adoptees with gay and lesbian adoptive parents. Some states, such as Florida and New Hampshire, have enacted statutes that explicitly prohibit such adoptions.[47] Where no statutes prevent them, they have been permitted, at least where the most difficult-to-place children are concerned.[48] However, the preference of agencies for married couples is sometimes used as a convenient justification for opposing placements that are really rejected because the adoptive parents are gays or lesbians.

Some courts have explicitly confronted the issue and have been reluctant to approve these placements. In 1986 an Arizona appellate court, in affirming the ruling of the trial court, commented that it would be inconsistent for the state to declare sodomy to be criminal conduct and yet permit a bisexual man to become an adoptive parent.[49] The stated reasons for rejecting gays and lesbians as adoptive parents are often based on the perceived incompatibility of the "'gay lifestyle' with social mores and on a fear that an adoptive child would be exposed to an increased risk of contracting AIDS."[50] Other courts have been more flexible, as evidenced in the following Massachusetts case in which the Supreme Judicial Court had to decide whether two lesbians could jointly become adoptive parents.[51]

Adoption of Tammy
619 N.E.2d 315
Supreme Judicial Court of Massachusetts
September 10, 1993

Greaney, Justice

In this case, two unmarried women, Susan and Helen, filed a joint petition in the Probate and Family Court Department . . . to adopt as their child Tammy, a minor, who is Susan's biological daughter. Following an evidentiary hearing, a judge of the Probate and Family Court entered a memorandum of decision containing findings of fact and conclusions of law. Based on her finding that Helen and Susan "are each functioning, separately and together, as the custodial and psychological parents of [Tammy]," and that "it is the best interest of said [Tammy] that she be adopted by both," the judge entered a decree allowing the adoption. Simultaneously, the judge reserved and reported to the Appeals Court the evidence and all ques-

tions of law. . . . We transferred the case to this court on our own motion. We conclude that the adoption was properly allowed under G. L. c. 210.

We summarize the relevant facts as found by the judge. Helen and Susan have lived together in a committed relationship, which they consider to be permanent, for more than ten years. In June, 1983, they jointly purchased a house in Cambridge. Both women are physicians specializing in surgery. At the time the petition was filed, Helen maintained a private practice in general surgery at Mount Auburn Hospital and Susan, a nationally recognized expert in the field of breast cancer, was director of the Faulkner Breast Center and a surgical oncologist at the Dana Farber Cancer Institute. Both women also held positions on the faculty of Harvard Medical School.

For several years prior to the birth of Tammy, Helen and Susan planned to have a child, biologically related to both of them, whom they would jointly parent. Helen first attempted to conceive a child through artificial insemination by Susan's brother. When those efforts failed, Susan successfully conceived a child through artificial insemination by Helen's biological cousin, Francis. The women attended childbirth classes together and Helen was present when Susan gave birth to Tammy on April 30, 1988. Although Tammy's birth certificate reflects Francis as her biological father, she was given a hyphenated surname using Susan and Helen's last names.

Since her birth, Tammy has lived with, and been raised and supported by, Helen and Susan. Tammy views both women as her parents, calling Helen "mama" and Susan "mommy." Tammy has strong emotional and psychological bonds with both Helen and Susan. Together, Helen and Susan have provided Tammy with a comfortable home, and have created a warm and stable environment which is supportive of Tammy's growth and over-all well being. Both women jointly and equally participate in parenting Tammy, and both have a strong financial commitment to her. During the work week, Helen usually has lunch at home with Tammy, and on weekends both women spend time together with Tammy at special events or running errands. When Helen and Susan are working, Tammy is cared for by a nanny. The three vacation together at least ten days every three to four months, frequently spending time with Helen's and Susan's respective extended families in California and Mexico. Francis does not participate in parenting Tammy and does not support her. His intention was to assist Helen and Susan in having a child, and he does not intend to be involved with Tammy, except as a distant relative. Francis signed an adoption surrender

and supports the joint adoption by both women.

Helen and Susan, recognizing that the laws of the Commonwealth do not permit them to enter into a legally cognizable marriage, believe that the best interests of Tammy require legal recognition of her identical emotional relationship to both women. Susan expressed her understanding that it may not be in her own long-term interest to permit Helen to adopt Tammy because, in the event that Helen and Susan separate, Helen would have equal rights to primary custody. Susan indicated, however, that she has no reservation about allowing Helen to adopt. Apart from the emotional security and current practical ramifications which legal recognition of the reality of her parental relationships will provide Tammy, Susan indicated that the adoption is important for Tammy in terms of potential inheritance from Helen. Helen and her living issue are the beneficiaries of three irrevocable family trusts. Unless Tammy is adopted, Helen's share of the trusts may pass to others. Although Susan and Helen have established a substantial trust fund for Tammy, it is comparatively small in relation to Tammy's potential inheritance under Helen's family trusts.

Over a dozen witnesses, including mental health professionals, teachers, colleagues, neighbors, blood relatives and a priest and nun, testified to the fact that Helen and Susan participate equally in raising Tammy, that Tammy relates to both women as her parents, and that the three form a healthy, happy, and stable family unit. Educators familiar with Tammy testified that she is an extremely well-adjusted, bright, creative, cheerful child who interacts well with other children and adults. A priest and nun from the parties' church testified that Helen and Susan are active parishioners, that they routinely take Tammy to church and church-related activities, and that they attend to the spiritual and moral development of Tammy in an exemplary fashion. Teachers from Tammy's school testified that Helen and Susan both actively participate as volunteers in the school community and communicate frequently with school officials. Neighbors testified that they would have no hesitation in leaving their own children in the care of Helen or Susan. Susan's father, brother, and maternal aunt, and Helen's cousin testified in favor of the joint adoption. Members of both women's extended families attested to the fact that they consider Helen and Susan to be equal parents of Tammy. Both families unreservedly endorsed the adoption petition.

The Department of Social Services (department) conducted a home study in connection with the adoption petition which recommended the adoption, concluding that "the petitioners and their home are suitable for the proper rearing of this child." Tammy's pediatrician reported to the department that Tammy receives regular pediatric care and that she "could not have more excellent parents than Helen and Susan." A court-appointed guardian ad litem, Dr. Steven Nickman, assistant clinical professor of psychiatry at Harvard Medical School, conducted a clinical assessment of Tammy and her family with a view toward determining whether or not it would be in Tammy's best interests to be adopted by Helen and Susan. Dr. Nickman considered the ramifications of the fact that Tammy will be brought up in a "non-standard" family. As part of his report, he reviewed and referenced literature on child psychiatry and child psychology which supports the conclusion that children raised by lesbian parents develop normally. In sum,

he stated that "the fact that this parent-child constellation came into being as a result of thoughtful planning and a strong desire on the part of these women to be parents to a child and to give that child the love, the wisdom and the knowledge that they possess . . . [needs to be taken into account]. . . . The maturity of these women, their status in the community, and their seriousness of purpose stands in contrast to the caretaking environments of a vast number of children who are born to heterosexual parents but who are variously abused, neglected and otherwise deprived of security and happiness." Dr. Nickman concluded that "there is every reason for [Helen] to become a legal parent to Tammy just as [Susan] is," and he recommended that the court so order. An attorney appointed to represent Tammy's interests also strongly recommended that the joint petition be granted.

Despite the overwhelming support for the joint adoption and the judge's conclusion that joint adoption is clearly in Tammy's best interests, the question remains whether there is anything in the law of the Commonwealth that would prevent this adoption. The law of adoption is purely statutory, . . . and the governing statute . . . is to be strictly followed in all its essential particulars. . . .

The primary purpose of the adoption statute, particularly with regard to children under the age of fourteen, is undoubtedly the advancement of the best interests of the subject child. . . .

With these considerations in mind, we examine the statute to determine whether adoption in the circumstances of this case is permitted.

1. The initial question is whether the Probate Court judge had jurisdiction under G. L. c. 210 to enter a judgment on a

joint petition for adoption brought by two unmarried cohabitants in the petitioners' circumstances. We answer this question in the affirmative.

There is nothing on the face of the statute which precludes the joint adoption of a child by two unmarried cohabitants such as the petitioners. . . .

In the context of adoption, where the legislative intent to promote the best interests of the child is evidenced throughout the governing statute, and the adoption of a child by two unmarried individuals accomplishes that goal, construing the term "person" as "persons" clearly enhances, rather than defeats, the purpose of the statute. Furthermore, it is apparent from the first sentence of G. L. c. 210, § 1, that the Legislature considered and defined those combinations of persons which would lead to adoptions in violation of public policy. Clearly absent is any prohibition of adoption by two unmarried individuals like the petitioners.

While the Legislature may not have envisioned adoption by same-sex partners, there is no indication that it attempted to define all possible categories of persons leading to adoptions in the best interests of children. . . .

The limitations on adoption that do exist derive from the written consent requirements contained in § 2, from specific conditions set forth in § 2A, which must be satisfied prior to the adoption of a child under the age of fourteen, and from several statutory and judicial directives which essentially restrict adoptions to those which have been found by a judge to be in the best interests of the subject child. . . .

In this case . . . [a]doption will not result in any tangible change in Tammy's daily life; it will, however, serve to provide her with a significant legal relationship which may be important to her future. At the most practical level, adoption will entitle Tammy to inherit from Helen's family trusts and from Helen and her family under the law of intestate succession . . . , to receive support from Helen, who will be legally obligated to provide such support . . . , to be eligible for coverage under Helen's health insurance policies, and to be eligible for social security benefits in the event of Helen's disability or death. . . .

Of equal, if not greater significance, adoption will enable Tammy to preserve her unique filial ties to Helen in the event that Helen and Susan separate, or Susan predeceases Helen.

Adoption serves to establish legal rights and responsibilities so that, in the event that problems arise in the future, issues of custody and visitation may be promptly resolved by reference to the best interests of the child within the recognized framework of the law. . . . There is no jurisdictional bar in the statute to the judge's consideration of this joint petition. The conclusion that the adoption is in the best interests of Tammy is also well warranted.

2. The judge also posed the question whether . . . Susan's legal relationship to Tammy must be terminated if Tammy is adopted. Section 6 provides that, on entry of an adoption decree, "all rights, duties and other legal consequences of the natural relation of child and parent shall . . . except as regards marriage, incest or cohabitation, terminate between the child so adopted and his natural parents and kindred." Although G. L. c. 210, § 2, clearly permits a child's natural parent to be an adoptive parent, § 6 does not contain any express exceptions to its termination provision. The Legislature obviously did not intend that a natural parent's legal

relationship to its child be terminated when the natural parent is a party to the adoption petition.

Section 6 clearly is directed to the more usual circumstances of adoption, where the child is adopted by persons who are not the child's natural parents (either because the natural parents have elected to relinquish the child for adoption or their parental rights have been involuntarily terminated). The purpose of the termination provision is to protect the security of the child's newly-created family unit by eliminating involvement with the child's natural parents. Although it is not uncommon for a natural parent to join in the adoption petition of a spouse who is not the child's natural parent, the statute has never been construed to require the termination of the natural parent's legal relationship to the child in these circumstances.

Reading the adoption statute as a whole, we conclude that the termination provision contained in § 6 was intended to apply only when the natural parents (or parent) are not parties to the adoption petition.

3. We conclude that the Probate Court has jurisdiction to enter a decree on a joint adoption petition brought by the two petitioners when the judge has found that joint adoption is in the subject child's best interests. We further conclude that, when a natural parent is a party to a joint adoption petition, that parent's legal relationship to the child does not terminate on entry of the adoption decree.

4. So much of the decree as allows the adoption of Tammy by both petitioners is affirmed. So much of the decree as provides in the alternative for the adoption of Tammy by Helen and the retention of rights of custody and visitation by Susan is vacated.

So ordered.

Case Questions

1. Why did the court rule that Tammy would significantly benefit from being jointly adopted by both Susan and Helen?
2. What role did the fact that the petitioners were persons of the same gender play in the court's decision? Can you construct an argument that would have led to a contradictory result if the court had been so inclined?

Voluntary/Involuntary Adoption

Adoptions may be classified as voluntary or involuntary. Involuntary adoptions occur after a court has formally terminated the parental rights of the birth parent(s) on grounds such as abuse, abandonment, or neglect. In such a situation an agency is generally responsible for placement. If the adoption is voluntary, the birth parent(s) consent to the termination of their parental rights and either surrender the child to an agency for placement or to adoptive parents of their choosing.

The Adoption Petition

The adoption process starts with the filing of a petition for adoption by the adoptive parents and the serving of a summons on all affected parties (the child, the agency, birth parents, guardian, etc.). In voluntary adoptions, care must be taken to account for all relevant parties, and obtaining the consent of necessary third parties is a major consideration. Where both birth parents have an intact marriage, they must jointly consent to a proposed adoption of their child. If the parents are not married to each other, and both the noncustodial and custodial parents have taken an active role in fulfilling parental obligations, each has the right to withhold or grant consent to the adoption of their child.

The following case discusses whether consent is required from a noncustodial parent who has only sporadically visited and supported his child and who has otherwise shown little or no interest in functioning as a parent. The biological father in the case filed a petition asking a state trial court to vacate its adoption order, claiming that his Fourteenth Amendment Equal Protection and Due Process rights had been violated. The trial court's denial of the motion was affirmed by two state appellate courts, and the matter was subsequently appealed to the U.S. Supreme Court.

Lehr v. Robertson
463 U.S. 248
U.S. Supreme Court
June 27, 1983

Justice Stevens delivered the opinion of the Court.

The question presented is whether New York has sufficiently protected an unmarried father's inchoate relationship with a child whom he has never supported and rarely seen in the two years since her birth. The appellant, Jonathan Lehr, claims that the Due Process and Equal Protection Clauses of the Fourteenth Amendment, . . . give him an absolute right to notice and an opportunity to be heard before the child may be adopted. We disagree.

Jessica M. was born out of wedlock on November 9, 1976. Her mother, Lorraine Robertson, married Richard Robertson eight months after Jessica's birth. On December 21, 1978, when Jessica was over two years old, the Robertsons filed an adoption petition in the Family Court of Ulster County, New York. The court heard their testimony and received a favorable report from the Ulster County Department of Social Services. On March 7, 1979, the court entered an order of adoption. In this proceeding, appellant contends that the adoption order is invalid because he, Jessica's putative father, was not given advance notice of the adoption proceeding.

The State of New York maintains a "putative father registry." A man who files with that registry demonstrates his intent to claim paternity of a child born out of wedlock and is therefore entitled to receive notice of any proceeding to adopt that child. Before entering Jessica's adoption order, the Ulster County Family Court had the putative father registry examined. Although appellant claims to be Jessica's natural father, he had not entered his name in the registry.

In addition to the persons whose names are listed on the putative father registry, New York law requires that notice of an adoption proceeding be given to several other classes of possible fathers of children born out of wedlock—those who have been adjudicated to be the father, those who have been identified as the father on the child's birth certificate, those who live openly with the child and the child's mother and who hold themselves out to be the father, those who have been identified as the father by the mother in a sworn written statement, and those who were married to the child's mother before the child was six months old. Appellant admittedly was not a member of any of those classes. He had lived with appellee prior to Jessica's birth and visited her in the hospital when Jessica was born, but his name does not appear on Jessica's birth certificate. He did not live with appellee or Jessica after Jessica's birth, he has never provided them with any financial support, and he has never offered to marry appellee. . . .

Appellant has now invoked our appellate jurisdiction. He offers two alternative grounds for holding the New York statutory scheme unconstitutional. First, he contends that a putative father's actual or potential relationship with a child born out of wedlock is an interest in liberty which may not be destroyed without due process of law; he argues therefore that he had a constitutional right to prior notice and an opportunity to be heard before he was deprived of that interest. Second, he contends that the gender-based classification in the statute, which both denied him the right to consent to Jessica's adoption and accorded him fewer procedural rights than her mother, violated the Equal Protection Clause.

The Due Process Claim

The Fourteenth Amendment provides that no State shall deprive any person of life, liberty, or property without due process of law. When that Clause is invoked in a novel context, it is our practice to begin the inquiry with a determination of the precise nature of the private interest that is threatened by the State. . . .

Only after that interest has been identified, can we properly evaluate the adequacy of the State's process. . . . We therefore first consider the nature of the interest in liberty for which appellant claims constitutional protection and then turn to a discussion of the adequacy of the procedure that New York has provided for its protection.

I

The intangible fibers that connect parent and child have infinite variety. They are woven throughout the fabric of our society, providing it with strength, beauty, and flexibility. It is self-evident that they are sufficiently vital to merit constitutional protection in appropriate cases. In deciding whether this is such a case, however, we must consider the broad framework that has traditionally been used to resolve the legal problems arising from the parent-child relationship.

In the vast majority of cases, state law determines the final outcome. . . . Rules governing the inheritance of property, adoption, and child custody are generally specified in statutory enactments that vary from State to State. Moveover, equally varied state laws governing marriage and divorce affect a multitude of parent-child relationships. The institution of marriage has played a critical role both in defining the legal entitlements of family members and in developing the decentralized structure of our democratic society. In recognition of that role, and as part of their general overarching concern for serving the best interests of children, state laws almost universally express an appropriate preference for the formal family.

In some cases, however, this Court has held that the Federal Constitution supersedes state law and provides even greater protection for certain formal family relationships. . . . In these cases the Court has found that the relationship of love and duty in a recognized family unit is an interest in liberty entitled to constitutional protection. . . .

There are also a few cases in which this Court has considered the extent to which the Constitution affords protection to the relationship between natural parents and children born out of wedlock.

In this case, however, it is a parent who claims that the State has improperly deprived him of a protected interest in liberty. This Court has examined the extent to which a natural father's biological relationship with his child receives protection under the Due Process Clause in precisely three cases: *Stanley v. Illinois,* 405 U.S. 645, . . . (1972), *Quilloin v. Walcott,* 434 U.S. 246, . . . (1978), and *Caban v. Mohammed,* 441 U.S. 380, . . . (1979).

Stanley involved the constitutionality of an Illinois statute that conclusively presumed every father of a child born out of wedlock to be an unfit person to have custody of his children. The father in that case had lived with his children all their lives and had lived with their mother for 18 years. There was nothing in the record to indicate that Stanley had been a neglectful father who had not cared for his children. . . .

Under the statute, however, the nature of the actual relationship between parent and child was completely irrelevant. Once the mother died, the children were automatically made wards of the State. . . .

[T]he Court held that the Due Process Clause was violated by the automatic destruction of the custodial relationship without giving the father any opportunity to present evidence regarding his fitness as a parent.

Quilloin involved the constitutionality of a Georgia statute that authorized the adoption, over the objection of the natural father, of a child born out of wedlock. The father in that case had never legitimated the child. It was only after the mother had remarried and her new husband had filed an adoption petition that the natural father sought visitation rights and filed a petition for legitimation. The trial court found adoption by the new husband to be in the child's best interests, and we unanimously held that action to be consistent with the Due Process Clause.

Caban involved the conflicting claims of two natural parents who had maintained joint custody of their children from the time of their birth until they were respectively two and four years old. The father challenged the validity of an order authorizing the mother's new husband to adopt the children; he relied on both the Equal Protection Clause and the Due Process Clause. Because this Court upheld his equal protection claim, the majority did not address his due process challenge. The comments on the latter claim by the four dissenting Justices are nevertheless instructive, because they identify the clear distinction between a mere biological relationship and an actual relationship of parental responsibility.

Justice Stewart correctly observed:

"Even if it be assumed that each married parent after divorce has some substantive due process right to maintain his or her parental relationship, . . . it by no means follows that each unwed parent has any such right. *Parental rights do not spring full-blown from the biological connection between parent and child. They require relationships more enduring."* . . .

When an unwed father demonstrates a full commitment to the responsibilities of parenthood by "com[ing] forward to participate in the rearing of his child," *Caban,* . . . , his interest in personal contact with his child acquires substantial protection under the Due Process Clause. At that point it may be said that he "act[s] as a father toward his children." . . . But the mere existence of a biological link does not merit equivalent constitutional protection. The actions of judges neither create nor sever genetic bonds. "[T]he importance of the familial relationship, to the individuals involved and to the society, stems from the emotional attachments that derive from the intimacy of daily association, and from the role it plays in 'promot[ing] a way of life' through the instruction of children . . . as well as from the fact of blood relationship." . . .

The significance of the biological connection is that it offers the natural father an opportunity that no other male possesses to develop a relationship with his offspring. If he grasps that opportunity and accepts some measure of responsibility for the child's future, he may enjoy the blessings of the parent-child relationship and make uniquely valuable contributions to the child's development. If he fails to do so, the Federal Constitution will not automatically compel a State to listen to his opinion of where the child's best interests lie.

In this case, we are not assessing the constitutional adequacy of New York's procedures for terminating a developed relationship. Appellant has never had any significant custodial, personal, or financial relationship with Jessica, and he did not seek to establish a legal tie until after she

was two years old. We are concerned only with whether New York has adequately protected his opportunity to form such a relationship.

II

. . . Appellant argues, however, that even if the putative father's opportunity to establish a relationship with an illegitimate child is adequately protected by the New York statutory scheme in the normal case, he was nevertheless entitled to special notice because the court and the mother knew that he had filed an affiliation proceeding in another court. This argument amounts to nothing more than an indirect attack on the notice provisions of the New York statute. The legitimate state interests in facilitating the adoption of young children and having the adoption proceeding completed expeditiously that underlie the entire statutory scheme also justify a trial judge's determination to require all interested parties to adhere precisely to the procedural requirements of the statute. The Constitution does not require either a trial judge or a litigant to give special notice to nonparties who are presumptively capable of asserting and protecting their own rights. Since the New York statutes adequately protected appellant's inchoate interest in establishing a relationship with Jessica, we find no merit in the claim that his constitutional rights were offended because the Family Court strictly complied with the notice provisions of the statute.

The Equal Protection Claim

The concept of equal justice under law requires the State to govern impartially. . . . The sovereign may not draw distinctions between individuals based solely on differences that are irrelevant to a legitimate governmental objective. . . . Specifically, it may not subject men and women to disparate treatment when there is no substantial relation between the disparity and an important state purpose. . . . The legislation at issue in this case . . . is intended to establish procedures for adoptions. Those procedures are designed to promote the best interests of the child, to protect the rights of interested third parties, and to ensure promptness and finality. To serve those ends, the legislation guarantees to certain people the right to veto an adoption and the right to prior notice of any adoption proceeding. The mother of an illegitimate child is always within that favored class, but only certain putative fathers are included. Appellant contends that the gender-based distinction is invidious.

As we have already explained, the existence or nonexistence of a substantial relationship between parent and child is a relevant criterion in evaluating both the rights of the parent and the best interests of the child. . . .

Because appellant, . . . has never established a substantial relationship with his daughter, . . . the New York statutes at issue in this case did not operate to deny appellant equal protection.

. . . Whereas appellee had a continuous custodial responsibility for Jessica, appellant never established any custodial, personal, or financial relationship with her. If one parent has an established custodial relationship with the child and the other parent has either abandoned or never established a relationship, the Equal Protection Clause does not prevent a state from according the two parents different legal rights.

The judgment of the New York Court of Appeals is

Affirmed.

Case Questions

1. What is the basis for the father's claim that his constitutionally protected liberty interest has been denied by the State of New York?
2. Why does the father claim that New York's adoption procedures violate the Equal Protection Clause of the Fourteenth Amendment? Does the Supreme Court agree with him?
3. What does the Supreme Court decide in this case?

The birth parents and adoptive parents are not the only individuals who have legal interests in adoptions. The adoptee and grandparents, for example, also may have legal rights. An adoptee, if over a specified age (often twelve or fourteen), has a right to refuse to be adopted. Even the grandparents of a child born out of wedlock may have legally enforceable visitation rights where the birth father's parental rights may have been terminated.

In addition to providing notice to affected individuals, the petition for adoption will also indicate whether the parental rights have been voluntarily or involuntarily terminated and will allege that the adoption is in the best interests of the child.

Interim Orders

After the adoption petition has been filed, the parties properly served, and all necessary consents obtained, the court will frequently issue interim orders. In voluntary adoptions the court will order the birth parents' rights terminated and grant the adoptive parents temporary legal custody of the child, pending issuance of the final decree. A hearing can then be scheduled to take testimony about whether the final decree of adoption should be approved by the court. State statutes usually require that the adoptive parents have temporary custody of the adopted child for a statutorily determined minimum period of time so that the court will have evidence that the adoptive parents and child are making a successful adjustment. This waiting period is usually waived in related adoptions. After the waiting time has passed, the court will enter a final decree declaring that the adopted person is now the child of the petitioner(s), and a new birth certificate will be issued to reflect this change.[52]

Whether or not the adopted child will be able to learn the identity of the birth parents varies from state to state. In recent years there has been some movement away from permanently sealing such information. Today, although many states maintain the confidentiality of adoption records, the trend is toward more openness.[53] Over thirty states have some type of registry system whereby consenting birth parents and their subsequently adopted children can mutually indicate a desire for contact.[54] Adoptees frequently wish to learn more about their birth parents, not only out of curiosity, but also to gain information about their parents' medical histories.

Foster Care

There are an estimated 462,000 children presently in foster care in the United States, of whom 47 percent are white and 31 percent black.[55] Although parents can voluntarily choose to place their child in foster care while efforts are made to remedy a serious family problem, most placements result from court intervention because of alleged child abuse or neglect.[56] Once a court determines that a child is abused or neglected, it can determine that foster care is the most appropriate disposition under the circumstances.

In many situations, foster care is intended to provide temporary care for children while the biological parents work to fulfill the requirements of a case plan. The objective in such situations is reunification of the family, once case workers have helped the family to work out its problems. If the birth parents address the problems that gave rise to the judicial intervention in the first place, the child will generally be returned to the parents. If the parents are uncooperative or fail to complete the intervention plan, the court may ultimately decide that it is in the best interests of the child to terminate the parental rights and place the child for adoption. It is reported that less than 8 percent of foster children are adopted and that over 66 percent are ordered returned to their families.[57] State governments license foster homes, and federal and state resources financially support foster children. The foster care system is criticized as being underfunded, overwhelmed with cases, and staffed by persons who are not trained as social workers.[58]

Children's rights attorneys maintain that the states are not meeting their responsibilities to foster care children and have initiated lawsuits based on the federal Adoption Assistance and Child Welfare Act of 1980. This statute requires that states make "reasonable efforts" to keep families together before placing children in foster care. The plaintiffs in these suits claim that many states are ignoring the Act unless sued.[59]

FAMILY RELATIONS IN ONGOING FAMILIES

Where families are intact, the law recognizes that spouses and children assume obligations to each other and are entitled to certain rights and benefits. Some of these rights, benefits, and obligations are economic and others are noneconomic.

Spousal Considerations

Although modern marriages are essentially partnerships, historically husbands and wives were legally considered to be a single unit, with husbands holding the preferred status as head of the household.[60]

Before the enactment of married women's property statutes in the 1800s, wives did not generally own property in their own names. Upon marriage, a wife's property was generally controlled by her husband. An exception was created by equitable courts that allowed fathers to establish trusts for their daughters. This device was used to keep family assets out of the control of sons-in-law, but few women from the lower and middle classes were the beneficiaries of such arrangements. A husband, while benefitting from the preferred status as head of the household, was also legally obligated to provide economic support for his wife. The term traditionally associated with this responsibility for support is "necessaries," usually defined to include food, clothing, shelter, and medical care.[61] In earlier times this obligation only applied to husbands; however, it is now shared by both spouses.

Courts were initially resistant to statutory reforms expanding women's property rights and often construed them very narrowly.[62] Today, in common law states, married women have essentially achieved legal equality. Both spouses retain title to property owned prior to marriage, have separate rights to their own earnings, and have title to property acquired separately during marriage.

In community property states (see Figure 8–4), each spouse is legally entitled to one-half of what the state defines as *community property*. Although

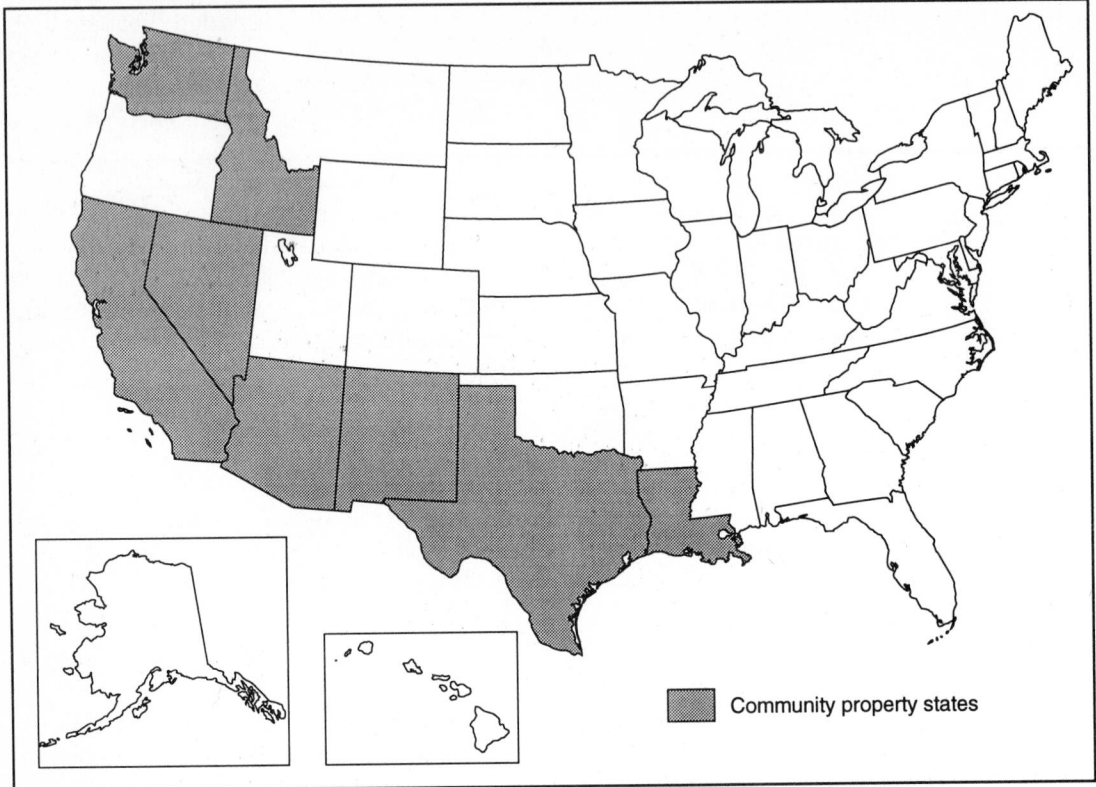

FIGURE 8–4 Community Property States

state differ, community property is usually defined as including the earnings of both spouses and property rights acquired with those earnings during the marriage. State statutes, however, usually exclude from community property any property rights acquired prior to marriage and spousal inheritances and gifts received during the marriage. These are classified as separate property. Community property states differ on whether the earnings from separate property should be treated as community property.

Decision Making Within Traditional Families

Spouses have great latitude in deciding how their household will operate. Decisions about who is responsible for particular household chores, about how recreational time is used, and about having children and child rearing are often jointly made. Of course, a woman's decision to obtain an abortion early in a pregnancy can be made unilaterally—without regard to the wishes of the putative father. A married woman also has the right to retain her own surname, if she chooses.

Evidentiary Privileges

The rules of evidence often contain privileges such that a spouse may refuse to testify against his or her spouse in a criminal trial and may also refuse to testify about confidential communications that occurred between spouses during their marriage.

The Parent–Child Relationship

Historically, parents have been legally responsible for the financial costs of providing their children with food, clothing, shelter, medical care, and education. This duty exists irrespective of whether the parents are married, divorced, separated, living together, or living apart. The breach of this duty is treated by most states as a criminal offense and can also result in civil actions for nonsupport and child neglect. The government is most eager to identify and locate "deadbeat parents" and to hold them financially accountable for their children so that the public doesn't have to bear these costs. The facts in the following case are admittedly unusual, but they illustrate the lengths to which society will go to impose liability on parents for the support of their offspring.

State ex rel. Hermesmann v. Seyer
847 P.2d 1273
Supreme Court of Kansas
March 5, 1993

Holmes, Chief Justice

Shane Seyer *et al.*, appeal from an order of the district court granting the Kansas Department of Social and Rehabilitation Services (SRS) judgment for amounts paid for the birth and support of Seyer's daughter and ordering Seyer to pay monthly child support reimbursement to SRS.

The facts, as best we can determine them from an inadequate record, do not appear to be seriously in dispute.

Colleen Hermesmann routinely provided care for Shane Seyer as a baby sitter or day care provider during 1987 and 1988. The two began a sexual relationship at a time when Colleen was 16 years old and Shane was only 12. The relationship continued over a period of several months and the parties engaged in sexual intercourse on an average of a couple of times a week. As a result, a daughter, Melanie, was born to Colleen on May 30, 1989. At the time of the conception of the child, Shane was 13 years old and Colleen was 17. Colleen applied for and received financial assistance through the Aid to Families with Dependent Children program (ADC) from SRS.

On January 15, 1991, the district attorney's office of Shawnee County filed a petition requesting that Colleen Hermesmann be adjudicated as a juvenile offender for engaging in the act of sexual intercourse with a child under the age of 16, Shanandoah (Shane) Seyer, to whom she was not married, in violation of K.S.A.

Thereafter, Colleen Hermesmann entered into a plea agreement with the district attorney's office, wherein she agreed to stipulate to the lesser offense of contributing to a child's misconduct, K.S.A. On September 11, 1991, the juvenile court accepted the stipulation, and adjudicated Colleen Hermesmann to be a juvenile offender.

On March 8, 1991, SRS filed a petition on behalf of Colleen Hermesmann, alleging that Shane Seyer was the father of Colleen's minor daughter, Melanie. The petition also alleged that SRS had provided benefits through the ADC program to Colleen on behalf of the child and that Colleen had assigned support rights due herself and her child to SRS. The petition requested that the court determine paternity and order Shane to reimburse SRS for all assistance expended by SRS on Melanie's behalf. On December 17, 1991, an administrative hearing officer found Shane was Melanie's biological father. The hearing officer further determined that Shane was not required to pay the birth expenses or any of the child support expenses up to the date of the hearing on December 17, 1991, but that Shane had a duty to support the child from the date of the hearing forward.

Shane requested judicial review of the decision of the hearing officer, contending that the hearing officer "should have found a failure of consent would terminate rights." SRS sought review, asserting that the hearing officer correctly ruled that the issue of consent was irrelevant, but erred in allowing Shane to present evidence pertaining to the defense of consent. SRS also alleged that the hearing officer's denial of reimbursement to the State for funds already paid was arbitrary and capricious and contrary to the mandates of K.S.A. 1992 Supp. 39–718b.

The district judge, upon judicial review of the hearing officer's order, determined that Shane was the father of Melanie Hermesmann and owed a duty to support his child.

The court found that the issue of Shane's consent was irrelevant and ordered Shane to pay child support of $50 per month. The court also granted SRS a joint and several judgment against Shane and Colleen in the amount of $7,068, for assistance provided by the ADC program on behalf of Melanie through February 1992. The judgment included medical and other birthing expenses as well as assistance paid after Melanie's birth. Shane appeals the judgment rendered and the order for continuing support but does not contest the trial court's paternity finding. SRS has not cross-appealed from any of the orders or judgment of the district court.

This case was transferred from the Court of Appeals by this court's own motion. K.S.A. 20–3018(c).

Shane has designated three issues on appeal which he states as follows:

> "I. Can a minor, who is a victim of the crime of indecent liberties with a child, be responsible for any children conceived of the criminal union?
>
> "II. Is it sound public policy for a court to order child support when the order creates a clash of one minor's right to protection from being the victim of a crime with another minor's right to parental support?
>
> "III. Can a judgment ordering joint and several liability for child support be an adequate remedy when it fails to account for the wrongdoing of Plaintiff-appellee Hermesmann?"

Shane's argument on appeal is based on three basic premises. (1) Shane Seyer, as a minor under the age of 16, was unable to consent to sexual intercourse. (2) Because he was unable to consent to sexual intercourse, he cannot be held responsible for the birth of his child. (3) Because he cannot be held responsible for the birth, he cannot be held jointly and severally liable for the child's support.

Shane asserts as his first issue that, because he was a minor under the age of 16 at the time of conception, he was legally incapable of consenting to sexual intercourse and therefore cannot be held legally responsible for the birth of his child. Shane cites no case law to directly support this proposition. Instead, he argues that Colleen Hermesmann sexually assaulted him, that he was the victim of the crime of statutory rape, and that the criminal statute of indecent liberties with a child should be applied to hold him incapable of consenting to the act.

Although the issue of whether an under-age alleged "victim" of a sex crime can be held liable for support of a child born as a result of such crime is one of first impression in Kansas, other jurisdictions have addressed the question.

In *In re Paternity of J.L.H.,* . . . 441 N.W.2d 273 (1989), J.J.G. appealed from a summary judgment in a paternity proceeding determining that he was the father of J.L.H. and ordering him to pay child support equal to 17 percent of his gross income. J.J.G. was 15 years old when the child was conceived. On appeal, he asserted that the child's mother, L.H., sexually assaulted him, and that, as a minor, he was incapable of consent under the sexual assault law. The court rejected this argument and stated:

> "If voluntary intercourse results in parenthood, then for purposes of child support, the parenthood is voluntary. This is true even if a fifteen-year old boy's parenthood resulted from a sexual assault upon him within the meaning of the criminal law." . . .

Although the question of whether the intercourse with Colleen was "voluntary," as the term is usually understood, is not specifically before us, it was brought out in oral argument before this court that the sexual relationship between Shane and his baby sitter, Colleen, started when he was only 12 years old and lasted over a period of several months. At no time did Shane register any complaint to his parents about the sexual liaison with Colleen.

In *Schierenbeck v. Minor,* 367 P.2d 333 (1961), Schierenbeck, a 16-year-old boy, appealed the adjudication in a dependency proceeding that he was the father of a child born to a 20-year-old woman. On appeal, Schierenbeck cited a Colorado criminal statute which defined rape in the third degree by a female of a male person under the age of 18 years. In discussing the relevance of the criminal statute, the court stated:

> "'The putative father may be liable in bastardy proceedings for the support and maintenance of his child, even though he is a minor. . . .' Bastards, 10 C.J.S. 152, § 53. If Schierenbeck is adjudged to be the father of [the child] after a proper hearing and upon sufficient evidence, he should support [the child] under this fundamental doctrine." 367 P.2d 333.

The trial court decision was reversed on other grounds not pertinent to the facts of our case and remanded for further proceedings.

The Kansas Parentage Act, K.S.A. 38–1110 *et seq.*, specifically contemplates minors as fathers and makes no exception for minor parents regarding their duty to support and educate their child. K.S.A. 38–1117 provides, in part:

> "If a man alleged or presumed to be the father is a minor, the court shall cause notice of the pendency of the proceedings and copies of the pleadings on file to be served upon the parents or guardian of the minor and shall appoint

a guardian ad litem who shall be an attorney to represent the minor in the proceedings."

K.S.A.1992 Supp. 38–1121(c) provides, in part:

"Upon adjudging that a party is the parent of a minor child, the court shall make provision for support and education of the child including the necessary medical expenses incident to the birth of the child. The court may order the support and education expenses to be paid by either or both parents for the minor child."

If the legislature had wanted to exclude minor parents from responsibility for support, it could easily have done so.

As previously stated, Shane does not contest that he is the biological father of the child. As a father, he has a common-law duty, as well as a statutory duty, to support his minor child.

We conclude that the issue of consent to sexual activity under the criminal statutes is irrelevant in a civil action to determine paternity and for support of the minor child of such activity. Consequently, Shane's reliance on the foregoing criminal case is misplaced.

For Shane's next issue, he asserts that it is not sound public policy for a court to order a youth to pay child support for a child conceived during the crime of indecent liberties with a child when the victim was unable to consent to the sexual intercourse. He claims that while the Kansas Parentage Act creates a State interest in the welfare of dependent relatives, the policy behind the Parentage Act is not to force a minor, who is unable to consent to sexual intercourse, to support a child born from the criminal act.

Shane provides no case law specifically on point, but once again relies upon the Kansas cases involving statutory rape.

Other jurisdictions have recognized the conflict between a State's interest in protecting juveniles and a State's interest in requiring parental support of children. In *In re Parentage of J.S.*, 550 N.E.2d 257 (1990), the trial court ordered a minor father to pay child support for his illegitimate son. The minor father appealed the order, but did not contest the trial court's paternity finding. In affirming the trial court's decision ordering support, the court stated:

"In the instant case, *we find that the public policy mandating parental support of children overrides any policy of protecting a minor from improvident acts.* We therefore hold that the trial court properly found that the respondent was financially responsible for his child." (Emphasis added.) 550 N.E.2d 257.

In *Commonwealth v. A Juvenile*, 442 N.E.2d 1155 (1982), a 16-year-old father was ordered to pay child support of $8 a week toward the support of his child born out of wedlock. The minor father admitted his paternity, but appealed the support order. On appeal, the court affirmed the judgment of the lower court and said:

"The defendant's claim rests on an assertion that a support order is inconsistent with the statutory purpose of treating a juvenile defendant as a child 'in need of aid, encouragement and guidance.' [Citation omitted.] Although we acknowledge that purpose, we see no basis, and certainly no statutory basis, for concluding that a juvenile should be free from any duty to support his or her illegitimate child. The illegitimate child has interests, as does the Commonwealth." 442 N.E.2d 1155.

This State's interest in requiring minor parents to support their children overrides the State's competing interest in protecting juveniles from improvident acts, even when such acts may include criminal activity on the part of the other parent. Considering the three persons directly involved, Shane, Colleen, and Melanie, the interests of Melanie are superior, as a matter of public policy, to those of either or both of her parents. This minor child, the only truly innocent party, is entitled to support from both her parents regardless of their ages.

As his third issue, Shane asserts that the district court erred in finding he and Colleen were jointly and severally liable for the child support. He argues that, as Colleen was the perpetrator of the crime of statutory rape, she alone should be held responsible for the consequences of the act, and he requests this court to remand the case to the district court with instructions to order Colleen solely responsible for the support pursuant to K.S.A. 39–718a. He states that K.S.A. 39–701 *et seq.* does not require a judgment ordering joint and several liability for child support.

Nowhere does the law in this state suggest that the mother's "wrongdoing" can operate as a setoff or bar to a father's liability for child support. Under the facts as presented to this court, the district court properly held that Shane owes a duty of support to Melanie and properly ordered that Shane and Colleen were jointly and severally liable for the monies previously paid by SRS.

Finally, we call attention to the fact that no issue was raised as to the propriety of the judgment against a youngster who was still a full-time student when these proceedings were commenced. When questioned in oral argument about the policy of SRS in seeking a judgment in excess of $7,000, counsel replied with the surprising statement that SRS had no intention of ever attempting to collect its judgment. Under such circumstances, the reason for seeking that portion of the judgment still eludes us.

The judgment of the district court is affirmed.

Case
Questions

1. What two state interests are in conflict in this case?
2. On what grounds did the Kansas Supreme Court reject Seyer's argument that a boy who was a thirteen-year-old victim at the time of his child's conception should not be held financially responsible for the birth of his child?
3. Do you believe this decision makes good public policy?

Child Support

The nature and extent of the parental support obligation varies and depends on the child's needs as well as on the parents' financial condition. Though all states require that parents fulfill support obligations, some have gone so far as to require stepparents[63] and grandparents[64] to provide child support. When marriages break up, a court will usually require the noncustodial parent to pay child support until the child attains the age of majority, marries, becomes emancipated, or dies. Even after a child reaches the age of majority, parents often have a continuing support obligation if their offspring are disabled, if their offspring are still in high school, or pursuant to the terms of a separation agreement.

One of the areas of recent conflict relates to a parent's duty to pay for a child's college education, an expense that usually isn't payable until after the child has passed the age of majority. Although parents in intact families have no legal duty to fund college educations for their children, as we see in the next case, some courts have ruled that a parent's support obligation can include funding their child's college education.

Nash v. Mulle
846 S.W.2d 803
Supreme Court of Tennessee
January 19, 1993

Daugherty, Justice

The essential facts in this case are not in dispute. What is contested is the extent of the child support obligation of Charles Mulle, who fathered Melissa Alice Matlock as the result of an extramarital affair with the appellant, Helen Nash, in 1981 but has since had nothing to do with mother or child. After an order was entered establishing his paternity in 1984, the Juvenile Court also ordered him to pay $200.00 each month in child support, in addition to other specified expenses. In 1990, Helen Nash filed this action seeking an increase in the amount of his payments because of Charles Mulle's dramatically increased income. The Juvenile Court then order Mulle to pay $3,092.62 per month, with $1,780.17 reserved for a trust fund established for Melissa's college education. The Court of Appeals reversed, limiting the award to $1,312.00 per month, or exactly 21 percent of $6,250.00, the top monthly income to which the child support guidelines explicitly apply. The Court of Appeals also disallowed the

trust, finding that it improperly extended the parental duty of support beyond the age of majority. Because the facts are not disputed, we review *de novo* the questions of law presented on appeal.

Child support in Tennessee is statutorily governed by T.C.A. § 36–5–101. Section 86–5–101(e)(I) provides that "[i]n making its determination concerning the amount of support of any minor child . . . of the parties, the court shall apply as a rebuttable presumption the child support guidelines as provided in this subsection." The General Assembly adopted the child support guidelines promulgated by the Tennessee Department of Human Services in order to maintain compliance with the Family Support Act of 1988, codified in various sections of 42 U.S.C.

I

The first issue presented concerns the proper measure of child support to be awarded in this case in view of the fact that Charles Mulle's monthly income exceeds $6,250.00. The guidelines apply in *all* cases awarding financial support to a custodial parent for the maintenance of a child, whether or not the child is a welfare recipient, and whether or not the child's parents are married. The guidelines are based, however, on several goals; they make many assumptions; and they permit deviation in circumstances that do not always comport with the assumptions. In studying the goals, premises, and criteria for deviation, we are convinced that the guidelines permit a monthly award greater than $1,312.00 without a specific showing of need by the custodial parent.

One major goal expressed in the guidelines is "[t]o ensure that when parents live separately, the economic impact on the child(ren) is minimized and to the extent that either parent enjoys a higher standard of living, the child(ren) share(s) in that higher standard." . . . This goal becomes significant when, as here, one parent has vastly greater financial resources than the other. It reminds us that Tennessee does not define a child's needs literally, but rather requires an award to reflect both parents' financial circumstances. This goal is consistent with our long-established common law rule, which requires that a parent must provide support "in a manner commensurate with his means and station in life."

The guidelines are currently structured to require payment by the non-custodial parent of a certain percentage of his or her net income, depending upon the number of children covered by the support order (21 percent for one child, 32 percent for two children, etc.). The statute promulgating the use of the guidelines creates a "rebuttable presumption" that the scheduled percentages will produce the appropriate amounts to be awarded as monthly child support. However, they are subject to deviation upward or downward when the assumptions on which they are based do not pertain to a particular situation. For example, one assumption on which the percentages are based is that

the "children are living primarily with one parent but stay overnight with the other parent as often as every other weekend . . . , two weeks in the summer and two weeks during holidays. . . ." The criteria for deviation provide that when this level of visitation does not occur, child support should be adjusted upward to provide for the additional support required of the custodial parent. Additionally, "[e]xtraordinary educational expenses and extraordinary medical expenses not covered by insurance" are given as reasons for deviation. The guidelines thus recognize that "unique case circumstances will require a court determination on a case-by-case basis."

Among the "unique cases" specifically anticipated in the guidelines are those cases in which the income of the parent paying support exceeds $6,250.00 per month. In the criteria for deviation the guidelines provide that among the "cases where guidelines are neither appropriate nor equitable" are those in which "the net income of the obligor exceeds $6,250 per month." In the present case, the Juvenile Court calculated Charles Mulle's net monthly income to be $14,726.98, a figure well above the $6,250.00 figure justifying deviation from the guidelines. Yet the total award of $3,092 ordered by the trial judge is exactly 21 percent of Mulle's monthly income.

Obviously, to treat the monthly income figure of $6,250.00 as a cap and automatically to limit the award to 21 percent of that amount for a child whose non-custodial parent makes over $6,250.00 may be "neither appropriate nor equitable." Such an automatic limit fails to take into consideration the extremely high standard of living of a parent such as Charles Mulle, and thus fails to reflect one of the primary goals of the guidelines, *i.e.*, to allow the child of a well-to-do parent to share in that very high standard of living. On the other hand, automatic application of the 21 percent multiplier to every dollar in excess of $6,250.00 would be equally unfair.

. . . [W]e conclude that the trial court should retain the discretion to determine —as the guidelines provide, "on a case-by-case basis"—the appropriate amount of child support to be paid when an obligor's net income exceeds $6,250.00 per month, balancing both the child's need and the parents' means.

II

As he did before the Court of Appeals, Charles Mulle contends that the establishment of an educational trust fund for his daughter unlawfully requires him to support her past her minority. Citing *Garey v. Garey*, 482 S.W.2d 133 (Tenn.1972), he argues that the trust fund is incompatible with Tennessee case law. In *Garey*, this Court held that "[b]y lowering the age of majority from 21 to 18 years of age the Legislature has completely emancipated the minor from the control of the parents and relieved the parents of their attendant legal duty to support the child." . . . Because the trust fund is intended for Melissa's college education, her father insists that it unlawfully requires post-minority support.

We conclude, to the contrary, that the establishment of the trust fund in this case does not conflict with the holding in *Garey*. Although child support payments may not extend beyond the child's minority (except in extraordinary circumstances involving physical or mental disability), the benefits from such payments can. Hence, it is consistent with established rules of Tennessee law to hold, as we do here, that funds ordered to be accumulated during a child's minority that are in

excess of the amount needed to supply basic support may be used to the child's advantage past the age of minority.

In reaching this conclusion, we must recognize the obvious fact that responsible parents earning high incomes set aside money for their children's future benefit and often create trusts for that purpose. They save for unforeseen emergencies; they accumulate savings for trips and other luxuries; and they may, and usually do, save for their children's college educations. Melissa's mother has expressed her intention to send her daughter to college. As all parents realize, however, the goal of sending a child to college often requires the wise management of money through savings. For a child of Melissa's age, assumed to begin college in the fall of 2000, it has been estimated that a parent must invest $457.00 per month for a public college education, or $964.00 per month for a private education, in order to save the $61,571.00 or $129,893.00, respectively, that will be required to fund a college education beginning that year. Lacking the resources to write a check for the full amount of college tuition, room, board, and other expenses when that time arrives, Helen Nash must accumulate these savings over the course of the child's minority, or be forced to borrow the money later on. Such savings in this case would inevitably deplete Melissa's child support award. While in many cases parents undergo serious financial sacrifices to make college possible for their children, in this case, as the Juvenile Court found, Charles Mulle's income can afford Melissa a high standard of living that also includes savings for college.

We believe that an approach that refuses to recognize the laudable goal of post-secondary education and instead provides only for the child's immediate needs, would not be a responsible approach. If the most concerned, caring parents do not operate in such a haphazard way, surely the courts cannot be expected to award child support in such a fashion. Thus, we conclude that establishing a program of savings for a college education is a proper element of child support when, as in this case, the resources of the non-custodial parent can provide the necessary funds without hardship to that parent.

Moreover, the use of a trust fund for just such a purpose is explicitly approved by the guidelines. In the section on criteria for deviation, . . . [t]here are . . . cases where guidelines are neither appropriate nor equitable when a court so finds. Guidelines are inappropriate in cases including but not limited to, the following: (a) In cases where the net income of the obligor . . . exceeds $6,250 per month. *These cases may require such things as the establishment of educational or other trust funds* for the benefit of the child(ren) or other provisions as may be determined by the court. . . . Thus, the guidelines specifically recommend a trust fund in cases in which a large cash award may be inappropriate. Moreover, the guidelines do not limit expenditures from such trusts to the child's minority. We defer to the policy judgment of the legislature in adopting the guidelines and uphold the use of the trust in this case.

In addition to adhering to the guidelines and providing a mechanism for this laudable use of savings, a trust fund for college education achieves several other goals. First, in a case such as this one involving a large difference in the parents' incomes, the trust allows for equitable contributions from each parent while avoiding an immediate cash windfall to one of them. When a large award given to a custodial parent with a much lower income would result in a windfall to the custodial parent, a trust fund helps to ensure that money earmarked for the child actually inures to the child's benefit. Thus, the trust fund is properly used to minimize unintended benefits to the custodial parent.

We also note the need for a trust as protection for the child of an uncaring noncustodial parent.

When a non-custodial parent has shown normal parental concern for a child, a trust fund may be unnecessary to ensure that his or her feelings are reflected in spending. However, when a non-custodial parent shows a lack of care, the court may step in and require the parent to support his or her child. The establishment of a trust is simply one discretionary mechanism used in the endeavor.

Thus, Charles Mulle's argument that the absence of a relationship with Melissa obviates the need to fund her college education is simply backwards. Child support is designed to prevent a non-custodial parent from shirking responsibility for the child he or she willingly conceived. It is precisely when natural feelings of care and concern are absent, and no parent-child relationship has been developed, that the court must award child support in a manner that best mirrors what an appropriate contribution from an interested parent would be. In fact, at least one court has gone beyond the acknowledgment of this lack of parental interest, and has spoken in terms of compensating the child for the parent's lack of concern.

While we do not adhere to this compensatory view of child support, we do believe that an appropriate child support award should reflect an amount that would normally be spent by a concerned parent of similar resources.

We thus find no merit to Charles Mulle's complaint that the order deprives him of the freedom to decide his daughter's educational fate, arguing that a requirement is being imposed upon him that does not exist for married parents. He contends in his brief that "some parents plan for the future education of their children and some do not"; he argues that "[s]urely a divorce decree or a paternity order should not give children rights that children who are living with their parents who are married do not have." This argument overlooks the obvious fact that divorced and unmarried parents face a substantial loss of parental autonomy whenever a court must step in to exercise responsibility for their children in the absence of parental cooperation. Married parents may choose to rear their children in an extravagant or miserly fashion; they may send their children to expensive private schools and universities; or they may require their children to make their ways in the world at age 18. Nevertheless, when children become the subject of litigation, courts must judge the children's needs. Long-standing Tennessee law requires the courts to evaluate children's needs not in terms of life's essentials, but in terms of the parents' "means and station in life."

The guidelines' requirement that child support allow a child to share in the higher standard of living of a high-income parent continues this objective. Thus, Mulle's complaint about the alleged unfairness of the court's judgment concerning the benefits his standard of living should afford Melissa is misplaced.

. . . Given the public policy favoring higher education in Tennessee, likewise evidenced by our many colleges and universities, it would be highly improper in this case to cast the burden of Melissa's higher education entirely on her mother, or on the "bounty of the state," when her father can provide for her education without unduly burdening himself.

In ruling the trust in this case illegal because it "has no relation to the support of the child during minority," the Court of Appeals relied for authority on prior Tennessee case law discussed earlier in this section, as well as cases from other jurisdictions, primarily Illinois and Hawaii. But, the Tennessee precedents predate the enactment of the Child Support Guidelines, which specifically authorize the use of trusts in cases involving non-custodial parents with high income, without limiting expenditures to the beneficiary's minority. Moreover the courts and legislatures of many other states have approved the funding of a college education by non-custodial parents who can afford such an expense. Indeed, several courts have done so without explicit statutory permission. In Pennsylvania, for example, the rule that a parent owes no duty of support for a child's college education is subject to an important exception. A parent may be ordered to provide such support if that parent has the "earning capacity or income to enable him to do so without undue hardship to himself." *See Commonwealth v. Thomas*, 364 A.2d 410, 411 (1976); *see also Brake v. Brake*, 413 A.2d 422 (1979). Therefore, in appropriate cases, the Pennsylvania courts require college support even though the age of majority in that jurisdiction is 18. An Alabama court, similarly, has required the establishment of a trust during a child's minority for educational expenses incurred after the age of majority. *See Armstrong v. Armstrong*, 391 So.2d 124, (1980). The Iowa Supreme Court decreed in *Hart v. Hart*, 30 N.W.2d 748 (1948), that a non-custodial parent should provide his sons with four-year college educations despite the fact that college funding would likely require support beyond the 21-year-old age of majority in existence at that time. New Hampshire courts also have the discretion to award college support past the age of majority. . . . These courts have used their equitable powers to require wealthy non-custodial parents to fund their children's college educations past the age of majority.

In yet other states, the authority of the courts to require non-custodial parents to fund a college education for their children is provided by statute. In Washington, after the child support statute was amended to include support for "dependents," the Washington Supreme Court declared that a college education could be included in the duty of support in cases where it "works the parent no significant hardship and . . . the child shows aptitude." . . . Oregon, similarly, allows courts to award support to children until the age of 21, three years past the age of majority, if they attend school. Or.Rev.Stat. § 107.108 (1991). . . . Indiana allows child support for college expenses if the parent has the financial ability and the child has the aptitude. Ind.Code § 31–1–11.5–12(b) (1991). . . .

Other legislatures have taken the lead from court decisions allowing college support and now statutorily provide for such support. For example, Illinois has codified prior case law that had established a parent's duty to provide for his or her child's education whether the child was of minority or majority age. . . .

. . . In addition, a New York statute permits an award for post-secondary educational expenses when the court determines that the award is appropriate in light of "the circumstances of the case and of the respective parties and the best interests of the child and as justice requires." . . . New York's statute replaces years of case law holding that a college education could be a "special circumstance" meriting support past minority.

. . . Thus, whether based on statute or rooted in the courts' equitable powers in family matters, the efforts of these states to provide for the college educations of children with wealthy parents persuade us that reason and public policy permit the use of a trust fund in this case.

In light of the guidelines' explicit provision for the use of trusts in cases involving high-income parents, the goals promoted by the use of a trust in this instance, and the reasoned support of other state courts and legislatures, we find the use of an educational trust in this case to be proper. As noted in Section I, however, there remains the question of the level at which the trust should be funded in this case. We therefore reverse the judgment of the Court of Appeals, and remand the case to the Juvenile Court for calculation of an award in accordance with this opinion.

Finally, we grant the appellant her attorney's fees and all other costs of the appeal, pursuant to T.C.A. § 36–5–101(i).

Case Questions

1. Based on the facts of this case, do you agree with the court's decision that a biological father has a financial obligation to pay for his child's college education by making contributions to a trust fund?
2. Because parents in intact families have no legal duty to financially fund college educations for their children, why should the law impose that

requirement in a case such as this? Should a child's aptitude for college be considered?

Noneconomic Obligations

Parents' noneconomic obligations include nurturing and controlling their children, seeing that they attend school, and protecting them from abuse and neglect. Authorities can intervene if parents fail to perform these duties. Although parents generally have the right to make decisions on their child's behalf about religious training and educational and medical needs, this right is limited. When a child's life is threatened, for example, and the parents' religious beliefs prevent them from seeking necessary medical care, the state will often intervene and ensure that the child receives treatment.

Children also have obligations, the single most important of which is to obey their parents. When children perpetually defy their parents, a judicial CHINS (child in need of supervision) proceeding may be instituted. Many states also statutorily require adult children to provide their parents with necessaries in the event that the parents become unable to provide for themselves.[65]

Parental Immunity from Suit by Child

As we will see in Chapter 11, parents have traditionally been protected from suit by their children for negligence and intentional torts by an immunity. Over the last thirty years, however, many states have created exceptions to this immunity and have permitted suits in cases of child abuse, neglect, serious batteries, and the negligent operation of automobiles. Today, most states have either abolished the immunity or severely limited its use.

ENDING SPOUSAL RELATIONSHIPS

Spousal relationships can be ended through the legal actions of annulment and divorce, and they can be judicially altered by legal separation.

Annulment

An action to *annul* is appropriate when a marriage partner seeks to prove that no valid marriage ever existed. Thus the plaintiff is not seeking to terminate a valid marriage but, rather, to have a court declare that no valid marriage ever occurred. Annulments were historically important, especially during periods when divorces were difficult to obtain. Obtaining an annulment of a marriage was very useful because it could end the spousal relationship without branding either party as being "divorced" and thus enable each to remarry. Today, with the advent of no-fault divorce, actions for annulment are much less popular, except among those who for religious reasons prefer to end a marriage legally without going through a divorce.

Although each state has its own grounds for annulments, common reasons include bigamy (where a person who is already married marries yet again), incest (where a person marries someone who is a close blood relative contrary to law), mental incompetence (such as where the parties were intoxicated at the time of the ceremony),[66] fraud (such as where one party misrepresents a willingness to engage in sexual relations and have children),[67] coercion, and one or both parties' being underage at the time of the marriage.

Because of the serious potential consequences of an annulment, particularly to property rights, many states have declared the children born to parents whose marriage has been annulled to be legitimate.[68] These states provide by statute that child support and custody matters will be determined in the same way as in divorce cases.[69] Many state courts award temporary alimony and some award permanent alimony to dependent spouses.[70] Each party to an annulment recovers the property held prior to the marriage and is considered a co-owner of property acquired during the marriage.

Legal Separations

Many states have statutorily recognized an action for *legal separation*, also called a *mensa et thoro* divorce (from pillow and table).[71] The so-called *mensa* divorce can be granted when lawfully married parties have actually separated and when adequate grounds for a legal separation have been shown. Although states differ on what constitutes sufficient grounds, common reasons include irreconcilable differences, adultery, desertion, cruelty, and nonsupport. If a court grants a legal separation, the parties remain married to each other but live apart. A criminal action can be brought if one spouse interferes with the other spouse's privacy. Unlike a final divorce, neither party to a legal separation is free to remarry. The court, after considering the financial conditions of each party, can require one spouse to support the other and can determine child custody. States differ about whether a property division should occur. During the legal separation, the possibility of reconciliation still exists, as does the option to proceed with a final divorce. The separation period allows the estranged parties to try to work out their difficulties while living apart.

Divorce/Dissolution

From the perspective of the 1990s, it is difficult to understand the degree to which contemporary expectations of marriage differ from those of our ancestors. Historically, absolute divorce under Anglo-American law was very difficult to obtain. In New York, for example, the legislature had to approve each divorce until 1787, when courts were statutorily authorized to grant divorces in cases of adultery, which was New York's only ground for a lawful divorce until 1966![72] In nineteenth-century America it was assumed that persons were married for life.[73] In 1900 women lived an average of only forty-eight years,[74] so people were married for shorter periods of time. The social, legal, and economic circumstances of that era encouraged husbands and wives to remain formally married despite the existence of dysfunctional relationships and irreparable differences between the parties.

Today, people live longer lives and have more choices.[75] There are fewer pressures on people to marry in the first place, and the miserably married are less likely to remain in intolerable relationships.[76] The availability of birth control permits people to be sexually active without conceiving children. Single parenting is common and is no longer considered unusual. Women have more economic opportunities than they did in 1950. The social stigma of being thirty and divorced or unmarried has greatly diminished. People who marry today do so primarily for companionship,[77] a need that can bring people together, but can also cause them to follow different paths as their lives evolve with time.

This social transformation has gradually produced legal changes as well. Although many states had liberalized their divorce laws more than New York by the early 1960s, divorces were generally limited—at least theoretically—to plaintiffs who proved that their spouses had engaged in adultery, cruelty (sometimes interpreted very liberally), and/or desertion.[78] The fact that a married couple had irreconcilable differences and were married in name only was not a sufficient basis under the law for a divorce. The fault-based approach was antidivorce and existed because of widely held fears about the social consequences to families and society that would result from what was feared might become divorce on demand. When states began to liberalize their laws to meet the increasing demand for divorce, they often required long waiting periods before a divorce became final. During the waiting period it was unlawful for people to remarry, start new families, and get on with their lives.[79] To get around such restrictions, people often went to Nevada to obtain what were called "quickie divorces," because that state required only a six-week waiting period.[80] Reformers pressed for change, urging lawmakers to focus on the marriage relationship itself and to recognize that the adversarial process of proving fault was making a bad situation worse. It was damaging the parties and making the process of ending a marriage more difficult and painful than it ought to be. It encouraged collusion and caused some parties to perjure themselves, "admitting" things they had not done, just in order to qualify for a divorce.[81] In California, proponents of reform carefully drafted and quietly pursued the legislative process[82] and were rewarded with enactment of the nation's first "no-fault" divorce law, which took effect on January 1, 1970.[83] Once that dam was broken, all states adopted some form of no-fault divorce; the last state acted in 1985. (see Figure 8–5)[84] Today, in many states, the plaintiff can choose to proceed either on a no-fault basis or on the traditional fault basis. Proving fault can sometimes be advantageous if it makes it possible to avoid the waiting period that some states require before

YEAR	MARRIAGES						DIVORCES AND ANNULMENTS		
	Number (1,000)	Rate per 1,000 population					Number (1,000)	Rate per 1,000 Population	
		Total	Men, 15 yrs. old and over	Women, 15 yrs. old and over	Unmarried Women			Total	Married Women, 15 yrs. old and over
					15 yrs. old and over	15 to 44 yrs. old			
1970	2,159	10.6	31.1	28.4	76.5	140.2	708	3.5	14.9
1975	2,153	10.0	27.9	25.6	66.9	118.5	1,036	4.8	20.3
1980	2,390	10.6	28.5	26.1	61.4	102.6	1,189	5.2	22.6
1981	2,422	10.6	28.4	26.1	61.7	103.1	1,213	5.3	22.6
1982	2,456	10.6	28.4	26.1	61.4	101.9	1,170	5.0	21.7
1983	2,446	10.5	28.0	25.7	59.9	99.3	1,158	4.9	21.3
1984	2,477	10.5	28.1	25.8	59.5	99.0	1,169	5.0	21.5
1985	2,413	10.1	26.9	24.8	57.0	94.9	1,190	5.0	21.7
1986	2,407	10.0	26.5	24.5	56.2	93.9	1,178	4.9	21.2
1987	2,403	9.9	26.2	24.2	55.7	92.4	1,166	4.8	20.8
1988	2,396	9.7	25.9	23.9	54.6	91.0	1,167	4.7	20.7

FIGURE 8–5 Marriages and Divorces: 1970–1988

Sources: U.S. National Center for Health Statistics, *Vital Statistics of the United States*, annual; *Monthly Vital Statistics Report*; and unpublished data.

a divorce becomes final. And in some jurisdictions, proving fault can affect alimony and child custody decisions.

Although state no-fault laws differ, a plaintiff usually has to prove marital breakdown and to prove that the parties have been living separately for a statutorily determined minimum period of time. In most states, a divorce can be granted despite the defendant's objection.[85] As a result of the philosophical changes that have occurred in recent years, the term *divorce* is increasingly being replaced with the more neutral term *dissolution*, which denotes the legal ending of the marital relationship.

Jurisdictional and Procedural Considerations

You will recall the discussions of *in personam* and *in rem* jurisdiction in Chapter 2 and of civil procedure in Chapter 3. Because terminating a marriage often involves some interesting jurisdictional problems and specialized procedures, it is important briefly to revisit these topics as they are related to divorce.

Jurisdiction

If it is determined that a court granted a divorce, awarded alimony, or determined custody of a child without having jurisdiction, the court's action is void and without effect. Furthermore, this jurisdictional deficiency would make the court's judgment ineligible for full faith and credit in other states. Although constitutional due process often permits the termination of a marriage on the basis of *in rem* jurisdiction, a court must have *in personam* jurisdiction over a person who is to be required to make alimony and child support payments. Thus a court has jurisdiction to grant a divorce decree where at least one marital party has lived within the forum state long enough to satisfy that state's residency requirement. The residency requirement demonstrates a substantial connection with the forum state and helps to establish the *in rem* notion that the marriage itself (the *res*) is physically located within the forum state.

If the plaintiff seeks to have a court decree alimony or order child support in addition to terminating the marriage, however, *in rem* jurisdiction is insufficient and the minimum contacts requirement of *in personam* jurisdiction must be satisfied.

Procedure

Many states statutorily permit a court to issue temporary support orders once a divorce action is initiated. This order may temporarily require one party to pay for an economically dependent spouse's necessaries, determines child custody and support, and determines who is responsible for paying which debts. This order is limited and is intended only to enable both parties to meet their living expenses while the action is pending. These issues are not permanently decided until the divorce and related claims have been acted on and a final judgment and order are entered in the case.

Although lay people generally use the term *divorce* to refer to the entire process of concluding and reordering a couple's marital, parental, and economic relationships, this is actually a misnomer. It is common in many states for each of the divorce-related claims to be decided in segments rather than in one long trial. This approach is called *bifurcation*, and it means that child custody, alimony, property division, and marriage dissolution are taken up separately by the court.

Procedural requirements in a divorce action generally vary with the type and complexity of the claims that must be resolved. Thus a contested divorce will generally be more procedurally cumbersome than an uncontested action, and a no-fault action will often be less procedurally complex than a fault-based action. In some states, cooperating parties can privately negotiate a separation agreement that reflects their mutual decision about how property should be divided, the amounts and types of support to be paid, and even proposals about child custody. If the terms of this contract are not unconscionable, the laws of the state can make this agreement binding on the court except as it relates to child custody provisions. Parties to no-fault divorces who have no children and no substantial assets can end their marriages in some states in a matter of minutes.

Allocation of Financial Obligations

When people divorce, in addition to terminating their marital relationship, there is a need to untangle their financial affairs so that each spouse can function independently. This involves determining whether alimony and child support will be paid and allocating the marital assets and liabilities. In some cases the parties are able to negotiate these matters successfully; in others a judge must ultimately make the decision.

Court-ordered Alimony

Virtually all states permit a court to require an economically strong spouse to pay financial support to an economically dependent spouse where it is necessary and appropriate. This payment, which is discretionary with the court, is often referred to as *alimony*, although it is also called spousal support.[86] Some jurisdictions deny it to any spouse whose marriage ended as a result of that person's marital fault.

One form of spousal support is called *permanent alimony* because it continues until the recipient dies or is remarried. This form of alimony is intended to compensate an economically dependent wife who was married in another era, when homemaking was commonly viewed as a career and when it was reasonable to expect that one's husband would provide support for life. Someone who invested many years taking care of her home and her family, rather than working outside the home, is granted alimony when her marriage is terminated so that she receives economic justice. This form of alimony is on the decline, because public policy today favors sexual equality and because women today generally have the skills and education necessary to get a job and to be self-supporting.

Another type of spousal support called *rehabilitative alimony* is awarded for a specified period of years and is intended to provide funds so that the recipient can obtain education or training that will strengthen the person's job prospects. In deciding whether to grant rehabilitative alimony, a court takes into consideration many factors, including the payor's earning capacity; the dependent spouse's health status, work history, and present and future prospects for employment; and the likelihood that the person will take advantage of training and educational opportunities.

A court can order that alimony be paid either in a lump sum or periodically, usually on a monthly basis. If conditions materially change over time, either party can petition for modification. The payor, for example, might seek a reduction because of ill health and unemployment and the fact that the recipient, though not remarried, is cohabiting and has less financial need. The recipient, for example, might argue for an increase to offset inflation's impact on purchasing power and the recipient's need to pay for necessary medical treatment.

Enforcing payment of alimony is very problematic, because courts are reluctant to incarcerate defaulters (how can they earn money while in jail?) and because it is often too expensive for recipients to use the normal remedies available for enforcing civil judgments (these remedies were discussed in Chapter 3).

Child Custody and Child Support

The general responsibility of parents to support their children was previously addressed in this chapter. The current discussion focuses on child custody and support in the context of a divorce, annulment, or temporary separation.

Although parents can negotiate an agreement and resolve many issues, they can only recommend whether the court should grant custody to both parents (*joint custody*) or grant custody to only one parent. Although the court has the responsibility to protect children, it usually will incorporate into the final judgment the custodial arrangements that have been agreed to by the parents if the arrangements are reasonable and appropriate. The court's decision is of great importance because of the custodial parent's right to make important decisions regarding a child's upbringing. Although judges historically have granted custody of young children to their mothers,[87] most states have discarded the *"tender years doctrine,"* at least as a rigid rule, in response to increasing challenges from fathers during the 1970s.[88] The "best interest of the child" rule, preferred custody statutes (that favor the primary caretaker), and joint custody have become the most widely accepted standards for determining custody.[89]

The *"best interest of the child"* rule requires judges to show no gender preference and to act in the best interest of each child. When making this decision, the courts consider such matters as each parent's ability to provide, and interest in providing, the child with love, a good home, food, clothing, medical care, and education. Inquiry will be made into the stability of each parent's employment and whether the employment is compatible with the child's needs. Courts also look for instances of parental misconduct (such as substance abuse and sexually and morally questionable behavior), continuity of care,[90] and a sound moral foundation for the child. The following case demonstrates the difficulty of applying the "best interest of the child" rule. Notice how issues of employment, educational and professional accomplishment, and parental bonding bear on the determination of custody.

In re Marriage of Riddle
500 N.W.2d 718
Court of Appeals of Iowa
March 30, 1993

Donielson, Judge

Dorothy Riddle appeals from the district court dissolution decree which awarded primary physical custody of the parties' minor child to Michael Riddle.

Dorothy and Michael Riddle were married in August 1986. They have one minor child, Lauren, who was born in January 1987.

Dorothy was born in 1966. At age sixteen, she married Pat Pepples. The marriage lasted only nine months and bore one child, Ashley, in June 1983. Dorothy has sole custody of Ashley. Dorothy married Michael just prior to her sophomore year at Iowa State University. While attending college, Dorothy held a number of part-time jobs. Dorothy has now graduated from Iowa State with a Bachelor of Science degree in nutrition. She is currently employed as the chief clinical dietician at Broadlawns Medical Center in Des Moines and earns a net monthly income of $1560.

Michael was born in 1964. He attends college at Iowa State University and intends to complete his degree in ele-

mentary education in about two years. Michael currently works several part-time jobs including assistant coaching duties, handyman work for the Ames School District, and sales for the Fuller Brush Company. His net monthly income is about $1102.

In July 1990, Dorothy filed a petition for dissolution of marriage. The petition was not served on Michael until November 1991. In January 1992, the district court awarded temporary physical custody of Lauren to Dorothy.

In August 1992, following a hearing, the district court issued its dissolution decree. The court determined, among other matters, primary physical custody of Lauren should be awarded to Michael. The court ordered Dorothy to pay $351 per month in child support.

Dorothy now appeals. Dorothy contends the district court erred in awarding primary physical custody to Michael. She specifically claims the district court erred in: (1) finding Lauren's long-term best interests were best served by awarding primary physical custody to Michael; [and] (2) separating Lauren from her half-sister, Ashley. . . .

In child custody cases, the best interests of the child is the first and governing consideration. . . .

The critical issue in determining the best interests of the child is which parent will do better in raising the child. . . . Gender is irrelevant, and neither parent should have a greater burden than the other in attempting to gain custody in a dissolution proceeding. . . .

We agree with the district court's finding that the issue of primary physical custody was a "close call." Both Michael and Dorothy care deeply for Lauren and her welfare. They both clearly offer Lauren a stable environment both emotionally and financially.

We admire Dorothy's diligence in completing her bachelor's degree while helping to raise two children. Dorothy has found a responsible and challenging job which provides her with considerable financial stability. In comparison, we recognize Michael's future plans are not as certain and that his income is less than that of Dorothy's. However, the fact Michael is employed only by several part-time jobs and the fact he has a lower income do not constitute evidence that Michael is unable to offer Lauren stability.

On our review, the record supports the finding that the long-term best interests of Lauren would be better served if Michael were the physical custodian. As Dorothy spent considerable time working and completing her degree, Michael became the primary caretaker for Lauren. Michael has done an excellent job as the primary caretaker to Lauren during the first five years of her life. As a coach, Michael takes Lauren to many of his practices and games. At trial, many witnesses testified to the close bond between Michael and Lauren.

Dorothy asserts she is being "punished" for having assumed the "traditional male duties" of being the family breadwinner. We do not agree. Our decision is based on an examination of which parent had been the child's primary psychological parent and with which parent the child had more closely bonded. . . . Here, the evidence suggests Lauren has consistently demonstrated a greater emotional attachment to her father.

In our decision, we recognize the preference for not separating siblings. . . . Admittedly, Lauren and her half sister, Ashley, are close. However, Michael is not the legal father of Ashley and he has no right to seek physical custody of Ashley in the dissolution. Michael therefore argues it would be unfair to give substantial weight to the preference for keeping siblings together because this gives Dorothy an unfair advantage in the contest for physical care of Lauren.

In *In re Marriage of Orte*, 389 N.W.2d 373, . . . (1986), the supreme court examined the issue of how much weight should be given to the preference for keeping siblings together in the case of half siblings. The court found the general principles governing the separation of siblings should govern, regardless of the advantage given to the parent of the half sibling. . . . The court found, in order to depart from the preference for keeping siblings together, "it must appear that separation 'may better promote the long-range interests of children.'" . . .

Here we find the district court did have a good and compelling reason to separate Lauren and Ashley. Lauren and Michael have a close relationship, and Michael has been the primary caretaker of Lauren throughout her life. There is no evidence that Lauren and Ashley will not be able to continue their close relationship despite the separation. On our review, we find granting Michael primary physical care will better promote the long-range best interests of Lauren.

We remind Michael that liberal visitation rights are in the best interests of the children. Iowa Code § 598.41(1) (1991); . . . Both parents, as joint custodians, are charged with maintaining those interests. Unless visitation with the noncustodial parent will in some way injure the child, it is not to be prohibited.

For the reasons stated, we affirm the judgment of the district court.

Affirmed.

Case
Questions

1. Are you satisfied with the Iowa Court of Appeals' explanation of the basis for its decision?
2. How should courts weigh the economic contributions of a parent who works outside the home and the contributions of a parent who provides child care and psychological support?
3. Do you agree with the trial and appellate courts that a compelling reason had been shown which justified rejecting the Iowa preference for not separating siblings in child custody disputes?

Preferred Custody Statutes

Preferred custody statutes were enacted because it was uncertain whether judges had sufficient reliable information to predict accurately what would be in a child's best interest.[91] Some states require that preference be given to a child's primary caretaker, where the primary caretaker can be established. Such an approach has the advantage of not favoring either gender, and it provides the child with continuity and stability in the parenting role.

When the statutory preference is for joint custody, the public policy provides that even though the marital relationship between the parents has ended, their parenting roles and responsibilities will continue as before. Both parents will share decision making in regard to their child's upbringing. Joint custody produces no winners and losers of a custody battle. The parents continue to share a family, but not a marriage.[92] When joint custody works, the child benefits from the active involvement of both a mother and a father. But it works only where divorcing parents are willing and able to separate their marital and parental relationships and act cooperatively to benefit their child.[93]

Once a court has determined that one parent should have custody, the noncustodial parent will normally be awarded visitation rights. It is important to encourage the noncustodial parent to continue to play an active role in the child's life. Sometimes the custodial parent wants to relocate, which would have the effect of curtailing the visitation opportunities of the noncustodial spouse. Courts are divided on what standard to apply when the parents disagree about making such a move.[94] Although the initial custody determination can be modified at a future date if material changes in the child's circumstances prove harmful, courts are reluctant to unsettle a child unless compelling reasons are shown.

Child Support

Earlier in this chapter we learned that although parents can formally and informally break up with one another, they cannot divorce their minor children. We also learned that the parental support generally continues until the child reaches the age of majority and, in some circumstances, even beyond. We focus now on the special circumstances that arise in conjunction with a divorce.

When a marriage that involves children is terminated, the court will examine the earning capacity of each parent and the needs of each child, will determine who has custody, and will determine each parent's support obligation. Every state has some guidelines to help judges make this determination. Generally, where custody has been awarded to one parent, the noncustodial parent will be ordered to make support payments. This parent is legally required to make the payments irrespective of side issues such as whether the custodial parent has violated the noncustodial parent's visitation rights or whether the custodial parent is spending the support payment money for other purposes than the children. Although child support is awarded to provide for the needs of the child, courts disagree about the exact meaning of that term. It certainly includes a child's necessaries, and there are cases in which noncustodial parents have been required to pay for their children's college educations.[95] Nevertheless, child support has a theoretically different purpose from that of alimony and property awards, which are intended to benefit a spouse.

When parents divorce, remarry, and establish second families, their support obligation to their first family continues, and many states require that the children from the first family receive priority over the children in the second family. Some states are moving away from this traditional approach and are structuring child support so that it benefits both families.[96] As was previously indicated, states differ about whether stepparents have a support liability for stepchildren.

As is the case with alimony, either party can petition for modification of the support order where there is a substantial change of circumstances.

Property Division

When people divorce, the property that they have accumulated during their marriage is apportioned between them. It is common for married people to concurrently own a house, cars, and other tangible personal property and to have joint accounts at the bank. If they have been married for a long time, they will probably have accumulated much property. States address the distribution problem differently, depending on whether they basically follow the common law/equitable distribution approach or the community property approach.

Common Law/Equitable Distribution Approach

In most states, what is known as equitable distribution has replaced the traditional common-law approach to determining property rights. Under the common law, the person who had title to property owned it, and generally this meant the husband. When lawmakers and judges began to look upon marriage as an economic partnership, property acquired during marriage was perceived in different terms. This new perspective produced reforms intended to result in the more equitable distribution of property to each of the divorcing parties. Though not all states that adopt equitable distribution classify property, many do. In those states, property is classified as separate property or as marital property. *Marital property* is nonseparate property acquired during the marriage and is subject to an equitable distribution by a judge. *Separate property*, that which was owned prior to the marriage or was received as a gift or inheritance, is not subject to distribution.

Obviously, the legal definition of property is crucial to any distribution scheme. Many states now treat pensions in which the ownership rights have matured (vested) and medical insurance benefits as also subject to distribution.

Though not all states agree with the holding in the following case, it is looked upon as a landmark decision. In the *O'Brien* case, the court declared that a spouse who has made significant contributions to her husband's medical education and licensing as a doctor was entitled to a property interest in his license at the time of their divorce.

O'Brien v. O'Brien
489 N.E.2d 712
Court of Appeals of New York
December 26, 1985

Simons, Judge

In this divorce action, the parties' only asset of any consequence is the husband's newly acquired license to practice medicine. The principal issue presented is whether that license, acquired during their marriage, is marital property subject to equitable distribution under Domestic Relations Law § 236(B)(5). Supreme Court held that it was and accordingly made a distributive award in defendant's favor. It also granted defendant maintenance arrears, expert witness fees and attorneys' fees. . . . On appeal to the Appellate Division, a majority of that court held that plaintiff's medical license is not marital property and that defendant was not entitled to an award for the expert witness fees. It modified the judgment and remitted the case to Supreme Court for further proceedings, specifically for a determination of maintenance and a rehabilitative award. . . . The matter is before us by leave of the Appellate Division.

We now hold that plaintiff's medical license constitutes "marital property" within the meaning of Domestic Relations Law § 236(B)(1)(c) and that it is therefore subject to equitable distribution pursuant to subdivision 5 of that part. . . .

I

Plaintiff and defendant married on April 3, 1971. At the time both were employed as teachers at the same private school. Defendant had a bachelor's degree and a temporary teaching certificate but required 18 months of postgraduate classes at an approximate cost of $3,000, excluding living expenses, to obtain permanent certification in New York. She claimed, and the trial court found, that she had relinquished the opportunity to obtain permanent certification while plaintiff pursued his education. At the time of the marriage, plaintiff had completed only three and one-half years of college but shortly afterward he returned to school at night to earn his bachelor's degree and to complete sufficient premedical courses and enter medical school. In September 1973 the parties moved to Guadalajara, Mexico, where plaintiff became a full-time medical student. While he pursued his studies defendant held several teaching and tutorial positions and contributed her earnings to their joint expenses. The parties returned to New York in December 1976 so that plaintiff could complete the last two semesters of medical school and internship training here. After they returned, defendant resumed her former teaching position and she remained in it at the time this action was commenced. Plaintiff was licensed to practice medicine in October 1980. He commenced this action for divorce two months later. At the time of trial, he was a resident in general surgery.

During the marriage both parties contributed to paying the living and educational expenses and they received additional help from both of their families. They disagreed on the amounts of their respective contributions but it is undisputed that in addition to performing household work and managing the family finances defendant was gainfully employed throughout the marriage, that she contributed all of her earnings to their living and educational expenses and that her financial contributions exceeded those of plaintiff. The trial court found that she had contributed 76% of the parties' income exclusive of a $10,000 student loan obtained by defendant. Finding that plaintiff's medical degree and license are marital property, the court received evidence of its value and ordered a distributive award to defendant.

Defendant presented expert testimony that the present value of plaintiff's medical license was $472,000. Her expert testified that he arrived at this figure by comparing the average income of a college graduate and that of a general surgeon between 1985, when plaintiff's residency would end, and 2012, when he would reach age 65. After considering Federal income taxes, an inflation rate of 10% and a real interest rate of 3% he capitalized the difference in average earnings and reduced the amount to present value. He also gave his opinion that the present value of defendant's contribution to plaintiff's medical education was $103,390. Plaintiff offered no expert testimony on the subject.

The court, after considering the lifestyle that plaintiff would enjoy from the enhanced earning potential his medical license would bring and defendant's contributions and efforts toward attainment of it, made a distributive award to her of $188,800, representing 40% of the value of the license, and ordered it paid in 11 annual installments of various amounts beginning November 1, 1982 and ending November 1, 1992. The court also directed plaintiff to maintain a life insurance policy on his life for defendant's benefit for the unpaid balance of the award and it ordered plaintiff to pay defendant's counsel fees of $7,000 and her expert witness fee of $1,000. It did not award defendant maintenance.

A divided Appellate Division . . . concluded that a professional license acquired during marriage is not marital property subject to distribution. It therefore modified the judgment by striking the trial court's determination that it is and by striking the provision ordering payment of the expert witness for evaluating the license and remitted the case for further proceedings. . . .

II

The Equitable Distribution Law contemplates only two classes of property: marital property and separate property (Domestic Relations Law § 236[B][1][c], [d]). The former, which is subject to equitable distribution, is defined broadly as *"all* property acquired by either or both spouses during the marriage and before the execution of a separation agreement or the commencement of a matrimonial action, *regardless of the form in which title is held"* (Domestic Relations Law § 236[B][1][c] [emphasis added]; *see* § 236 [B][5][b], [c]). Plaintiff does not contend that his license is excluded from distribution because it is separate property; rather, he claims that it is not property at all but represents a personal attainment in acquiring knowledge. He rests his argument on decisions in similar cases from other jurisdictions and on his view that a license does not satisfy common-law concepts of property. Neither contention is controlling because decisions in other States rely principally on their own statutes, and the legislative history underlying them, and because the New York Legislature deliberately went beyond traditional property concepts when it formulated the Equitable Distribution Law. . . . Instead, our statute recognizes that spouses have an equitable claim to things of value arising out of the marital relationship and classifies them as subject to distribution by focusing on the marital status of the parties at the time of acquisition. Those things acquired during marriage and subject to distribution have been classified as "marital property" although, as one commentator has observed, they hardly fall within the traditional property concepts because there is no common-law property interest remotely resembling marital property. "It is a statutory creature, is of no meaning whatsoever during the normal course of a marriage and arises full-grown, like Athena, upon the signing of a separation agreement or the commencement of a matrimonial action. [Thus] [i]t is hardly surprising, and not at all relevant, that traditional common law property concepts do not fit in parsing the meaning of 'marital property.' " . . . Having classified the "property" subject to distribution, the Legislature did not attempt to go further and define it but left it to the courts to determine what interests come within the terms of section 236(B)(1)(c).

We made such a determination in *Majauskas v. Majauskas,* . . . 463 N.E.2d 15, holding there that vested but unmatured pension rights are marital property subject to equitable distribution. Because pension benefits are not specifically identified as marital property in the statute, we looked to the express reference to pension rights contained in section

236(B)(5)(d)(4), which deals with equitable distribution of marital property, to other provisions of the equitable distribution statute and to the legislative intent behind its enactment to determine whether pension rights are marital property or separate property. A similar analysis is appropriate here and leads to the conclusion that marital property encompasses a license to practice medicine to the extent that the license is acquired during marriage.

Section 236 provides that in making an equitable distribution of marital property, "the court shall consider: . . . (6) any equitable claim to, interest in, or direct or indirect contribution made to the acquisition of such marital property by the party not having title, including joint efforts or expenditures and contributions and services as a spouse, parent, wage earner and homemaker, and *to the career or career potential* of the other party [and] . . . (9) the impossibility or difficulty of evaluating any component asset or any interest in a business, corporation or *profession*" (Domestic Relations Law § 236 [B][5][d][6], [9] [emphasis added]). Where equitable distribution of marital property is appropriate but "the distribution of an interest in a business, corporation or *profession* would be contrary to law" the court shall make a distributive award in lieu of an actual distribution of the property (Domestic Relations Law § 236[B][5][e] [emphasis added]). The words mean exactly what they say: that an interest in a profession or professional career potential is marital property which may be represented by direct or indirect contributions of the non-title-holding spouse, including financial contributions and nonfinancial contributions made by caring for the home and family.

The history which preceded enactment of the statute confirms this interpretation. Reform of section 236 was advocated because experience had proven that application of the traditional common-law title theory of property had caused inequities upon dissolution of a marriage. The Legislature replaced the existing system with equitable distribution of marital property, an entirely new theory which considered all the circumstances of the case and of the respective parties to the marriage. . . . Equitable distribution was based on the premise that a marriage is, among other things, an economic partnership to which both parties contribute as spouse, parent, wage earner or homemaker. . . . Consistent with this purpose, and implicit in the statutory scheme as a whole, is the view that upon dissolution of the marriage there should be a winding up of the parties' economic affairs and a severance of their economic ties by an equitable distribution of the marital assets. Thus, the concept of alimony, which often served as a means of lifetime support and dependence for one spouse upon the other long after the marriage was over, was replaced with the concept of maintenance which seeks to allow "the recipient spouse an opportunity to achieve [economic] independence." . . .

The determination that a professional license is marital property is also consistent with the conceptual base upon which the statute rests. As this case demonstrates, few undertakings during a marriage better qualify as the type of joint effort that the statute's economic partnership theory is intended to address than contributions toward one spouse's acquisition of a professional license. Working spouses are often required to contribute substantial income as wage earners, sacrifice their own educational or career goals and opportunities for child rearing, perform the bulk of household duties and responsibilities and forego the acquisition of marital assets that could have been accumulated if the professional spouse had been employed rather than occupied with the study and training necessary to acquire a professional license. In this case, nearly all of the parties' nine-year marriage was devoted to the acquisition of plaintiff's medical license and defendant played a major role in that project. She worked continuously during the marriage and contributed all of her earnings to their joint effort, she sacrificed her own educational and career opportunities, and she traveled with plaintiff to Mexico for three and one-half years while he attended medical school there. The Legislature has decided, by its explicit reference in the statute to the contributions of one spouse to the other's profession or career . . . that these contributions represent investments in the economic partnership of the marriage and that the product of the parties' joint efforts, the professional license, should be considered marital property.

The majority at the Appellate Division held that the cited statutory provisions do not refer to the license held by a professional who has yet to establish a practice but only to a going professional practice. . . . There is no reason in law or logic to restrict the plain language of the statute to existing practices, however, for it is of little consequence in making an award of marital property, except for the purpose of evaluation, whether the professional spouse has already established a practice or whether he or she has yet to do so. An established practice merely represents the exercise of the privileges conferred upon the professional spouse by the license and the income flowing from that practice represents the receipt of the enhanced earning capacity that licensure allows. That being so, it would be unfair not to consider the license a marital asset.

Plaintiff's principal argument, adopted by the majority below, is that a professional license is not marital property because it does not fit within the traditional view of property as something which has an exchange value on the open market and is capable of sale, assignment or transfer. The position does not withstand analysis for at least two reasons. First, as we have observed, it ignores the fact that whether a professional license constitutes marital property is to be judged by the language of the statute which created this new species of property previously unknown at common law or under prior statutes. Thus, whether the license fits within traditional property concepts is of no consequence. Second, it is an overstatement to assert that a professional license could not be considered property even outside the context of section 236(B). A professional license is a valuable property right, reflected in the money, effort and lost opportunity for employment expended in its acquisition, and also in the enhanced earning capacity it affords its holder, which may not be revoked without due process of law. . . . That a professional license has no market value is irrelevant. Obviously, a license may not be alienated as may other property and for that reason the working spouse's interest in it is limited. The Legislature has recognized that limitation, however, and has provided for an award in lieu of its actual distribution. . . .

Plaintiff also contends that alternative remedies should be employed, such as an award of rehabilitative maintenance or reimbursement for direct financial contributions. . . . The statute does not expressly authorize retrospective maintenance or rehabilitative awards and we have no occasion to decide in this case whether the authority to do so may ever be implied from its provisions. . . . It is sufficient to observe that normally a working spouse should not be restricted to that relief because to do so frustrates the purposes underlying the Equitable Distribution Law. Limiting a working spouse to a maintenance award, either general or rehabilitative, not only is contrary to the economic partnership concept underlying the statute but also retains the uncertain and inequitable economic ties of dependence that the Legislature sought to extinguish by equitable distribution. Maintenance is subject to termination upon the recipient's remarriage and a working spouse may never receive adequate consideration for his or her contribution and may even be penalized for the decision to remarry if that is the only method of compensating the contribution. As one court said so well, "[t]he function of equitable distribution is to recognize that when a marriage ends, each of the spouses, based on the totality of the contributions made to it, has a stake in and right to a share of the marital assets accumulated while it endured, not because that share is needed, but because those assets represent the capital product of what was essentially a partnership entity" (*Wood v. Wood*, . . . 465 N.Y. S.3d 475). The Legislature stated its intention to eliminate such inequities by providing that a supporting spouse's "direct or indirect contribution" be recognized, considered and rewarded (Domestic Relations Law § 236[B][5][d][6]).

Turning to the question of valuation, it has been suggested that even if a professional license is considered marital property, the working spouse is entitled only to reimbursement of his or her direct financial contributions. . . . If the license is marital property, then the working spouse is entitled to an equitable portion of it, not a return of funds advanced. Its value is the enhanced earning capacity it affords the holder and although fixing the present value of that enhanced earning capacity may present problems, the problems are not insurmountable. Certainly they are no more difficult than computing tort damages for wrongful death or diminished earning capacity resulting from injury and they differ only in degree from the problems presented when valuing a professional practice for purposes of a distributive award, something the courts have not hesitated to do. . . . The trial court retains the flexibility and discretion to structure the distributive award equitably, taking into consideration factors such as the working spouse's need for immediate payment, the licensed spouse's current ability to pay and the income tax consequences of prolonging the period of payment . . . and, once it has received evidence of the present value of the license and the working spouse's contributions toward its acquisition and considered the remaining factors mandated by the statute . . . , it may then make an appropriate distribution of the marital property including a distributive award for the professional license if such an award is warranted. When other marital assets are of sufficient value to provide for the supporting spouse's equitable portion of the marital property, including his or her contributions to the acquisition of the professional license, however, the court retains the discretion to distribute these other marital assets or to make a distributive award in lieu of an actual distribution of the value of the professional spouse's license. . . .

III

. . . Accordingly, in view of our holding that plaintiff's license to practice medicine is marital property, the order of the Appellate Division should be modified, with costs to defendant, by reinstating the judgment and the case remitted to the Appellate Division for determination of the facts, including the exercise of that court's discretion (CPLR 5613), and, as so modified, affirmed.

Case Questions

1. When Loretta O'Brien sued her husband Michael for divorce, what claim did she make with respect to the marital property of the couple?
2. What was the basis of her claim?
3. How does the court define marital property in this case? What social values does this approach reflect?

Determining Fairness

For a distribution to be fair, the court must identify, classify, and determine the value of each spouse's assets—or their detriment, in the case of debts. The court must also consider the circumstances and needs of the parties, the length of their marriage, their marital standard of living, their contributions to the marriage, and other similar factors.

Although it is possible to take such matters to trial and have them decided by a judge, it is often faster—and the parties have more control over the outcome—if they negotiate a property settlement in lieu of fighting it out in court. Property dispute battles can be very expensive. Appraisals and expensive expert witnesses are required to establish the value of assets. Litigation costs can also increase dramatically and diminish the assets ultimately available for distribution. Judges frequently incorporate a negotiated agreement that equitably allocates marital assets and debts into the final judgment.

Community Property Approach

The states of Louisiana, Texas, California, New Mexico, Arizona, Nevada, Washington, Idaho, and Wisconsin have statutorily decided to treat all property that is not separate property and that was acquired during the marriage as presumptively community property that belongs equally to both spouses. Under this approach, it doesn't matter who worked and earned the money for a purchase or who purchased the property. Both spouses have the right to make management decisions regarding community property (such as whether it is leased, loaned, invested, etc.).

If the parties wish to alter the community property presumption, they may do so by agreement, by gift, and by commingling separate and community assets so that separate property loses its character (such as the merger of a separate stamp collection with a community collection or the deposit of birthday money into the community checking account). In the event of a divorce, the court in a community property state makes an equitable division of all community property to each spouse.

Conclusion

Irrespective of whether the issues are negotiated or litigated, at the end of the process the court issues a judgment that dissolves the marriage, distributes the property, and determines claims for alimony, child custody, and child support. The attorneys for the parties then assist the former spouses to implement the orders. Property must be exchanged, ownership rights transferred, money transferred, debts paid, insurance policies obtained, pension rights transferred, and other details wrapped up.

Chapter Questions

1. Define the following terms:

adoption	legal separation
alimony	marital property
annulment	marriage
child support	natural parent
common-law marriage	necessaries
community property	noncustodial parent
custodial parent	open adoption
divorce	physical custody
family	separate property
foster parent	separation agreement
joint custody	

2. Andrea Moorehead was abandoned by her birth mother, a crack cocaine user who had tested positive for venereal disease, shortly after birth. Andrea was placed with foster parents when she was nine days old. The foster parents, Melva and Robert Dearth, sought to adopt Andrea when she was ten months old. The county's Children's Service Bureau (CSB) opposed this proposed adoption. The Dearths alleged that CSB's decision was predicated on the fact that they were white and Andrea was black. They proved that they lived in an interracial neighborhood, that they attended an interracial church, and that their two children attended an interracial school. They had a stable marriage and financial standing. The Dearths filed a motion for review of this administrative decision in the Common Pleas Court. They requested that CSB's custody be terminated and that permanent custody of Andrea be granted to them. The Court denied the Dearths'

motion. The Dearths appealed. The appeals court found that there was clear evidence that CSB had a documented policy of placing black children with white adoptive parents only when no black parents could be found. Under Ohio law, adoption placements are to be made in the "best interests of the child." To what extent can adoption agencies such as CSB consider factors such as race and culture in determining adoption placements? Under the law, can the racial factor outweigh all other considerations?

In re Moorehead, 600 N.E.2d 778 (1991)

3. Charles Collins and Bethany Guggenheim began living together in 1977. They were not married to each other. Bethany was recently divorced and had two children from the prior marriage. As part of the property settlement, she had received title to a 68-acre farm, and Charles, Bethany, and the children moved there in 1979. They intended to restore the farmhouse (circa 1740). Charles and Bethany jointly became liable for and made payments on a bank mortgage loan, insurance, and property taxes. They maintained a joint checking account to pay for joint expenses as well as individual checking accounts. They jointly purchased a tractor and other equipment, Charles paying two-thirds of the cost and Bethany one-third. Charles also invested $8,000 of his money in additional equipment and improvements for the farm. For several years they jointly operated a small business that made no profit. Despite Charles's contributions, the title to the farm remained at all times with Bethany. The parties experienced personal difficulties, and when they could not reconcile their differences, they permanently separated in 1986. During their cohabitation period, Charles contributed approximately $55,000 and Bethany $44,500 to the farm. Charles filed suit against Bethany. He claimed that fairness required either that Bethany and he should share title to the farm as tenants in common or that he should receive an equitable distribution of the property acquired during the period of cohabitation. Charles did not allege that Bethany had breached any contract or engaged in any type of misconduct. The trial court dismissed the complaint. What action should a court take in a situation such as this, where unmarried, cohabiting people go their separate ways?

Collins v. Guggenheim, N.E.2d (1994)

4. James Ellam filed suit for divorce against his wife, Ann, on the ground that they had been living separately and apart. Ann counterclaimed against James for desertion. The facts reveal that James moved out of the marital home on July 5, 1972, because of severe marital discord. He moved back to his mother's home in a nearby city, where he slept, kept his clothes, and ate some of his meals. For the next eighteen months, James had an unusual weekday routine. His mother would drive James early in the morning from her home to the marital home so that James could see his dog, check on the house, take his car out of the garage, and go to work, much as he had done before he and Ann "separated." At the end of the day, James would drive to the marital residence, put the car back in the garage, play with the dog, talk with his wife until she went to bed, and watch television until

12:30 A.M. when his mother would pick him up and take him "home." On weekends, James would do chores at the marital home and even socialize with his wife (although the parties had terminated their sexual relationship). James lived this way because he claimed to love his wife and especially the dog, he wanted to maintain the marital home properly, and he did not want the neighbors to know about his marital problems. New Jersey law provides that persons who have lived separate and apart for a statutory period of time may be granted a divorce. Should the trial court have granted a divorce on the grounds that James and Ann had satisfied the statutory requirements by living "separate and apart in different habitations" as permitted under New Jersey law?

Ellam v. Ellam, 333 A.2d 577 (1975)

5. The Washington Revised Code (Section 26.16.205) provides as follows:

> The expenses of the family . . . are chargeable upon the property of both husband and wife, or either of them, and in relation thereto they may be sued jointly or separately. . . .

Should a husband be financially obligated to pay the legal costs resulting from his wife's appeal of criminal convictions?

State v. Clark, 563 P.2d 1253 (1977)

6. Oregon law provides for "no-fault" divorces. Marie and Max Dunn had been married for twenty years when Marie filed for divorce. After Marie presented evidence of irremediable and irreconcilable differences between herself and her husband, the trial court entered a decree dissolving the marriage. The court also awarded Marie custody of their two minor children and set alimony at $200 per month. Max appealed to the Oregon Court of Appeals on the ground that the trial court's decree was premature and was not supported by adequate proof. Max argued that the court acted without considering the views of both parties to the marriage. The appellate court interpreted the Oregon statute to require only that the trial court determine whether the existing difference "reasonabl[y] appears to the court to be in the mind of the petitioner an irreconcilable one, and based on that difference . . . whether or not . . . the breakdown of that particular marriage is irremediable." What public policy arguments can you identify related to the facts in the above case that would favor "no-fault" divorces? What arguments could be brought to bear against them?

Dunn v. Dunn, 511 P.2d 427 (1973)

7. Two women brought suit against the Jefferson County (Kentucky) Clerk of Courts because the clerk refused to issue them a license to become married to each other. The women alleged that the clerk's refusal denied them various constitutionally protected rights, among these the right to become married, the right to freedom of association, and the right to freedom from cruel and unusual punishment. The trial court ruled that persons seeking to enter into a same-sex marriage were not entitled under the law to a marriage license. The women appealed to the Court of Appeals of Kentucky.

The Kentucky statutes do not define the term *marriage*. The appeals court disposed of the case without even reaching the appellants' constitutional claims. Can you surmise on what grounds the appeals court decided the case?

Jones v. Hallahan, 501 S.W.2d 588 (1973)

Notes

1. J. Demos, "A Little Commonwealth: Family Life in Plymouth," in *Family and State*, ed. L. Houlgate (Totowa, NJ: Rowman & Littlefield, 1988), pp. 30–31.

2. See U.S. Bureau of the Census, *Statistical Abstract of the United States: 1993* (113th Edition) (Washington, D.C., 1993), Figure 1.2, "Percent Distribution of Children by Presence of Parents: 1980 and 1992."

3. B. Yorburg, *The Changing Family* (New York: Columbia University Press, 1973), p. 194.

4. D. Castle, *Early Emancipation Statutes: Should They Protect Parents as Well as Children*, 20 Family Law Quarterly 3, 363 (Fall 1986).

5. H. Jacob, *Silent Revolution* (Chicago: University of Chicago Press, 1988), p. 1.

6. M. Grossberg, *Governing the Hearth* (Chapel Hill: University of North Carolina Press, 1985), p. 3.

7. L. Houlgate, *Family and State* (Totowa, NJ: Rowman & Littlefield, 1988).

8. E. Pound, *Individual Interests in Domestic Relations*, 14 Michigan Law Review 177, 179–81 (1916).

9. L. Wardle, C. Blakeseley, and J. Parker, *Contemporary Family Law*, Sec. 1:02 (Deerfield, IL: Clark Boardman Calaghan, 1988).

10. E. Jenks, *A Short History of English Law* (2nd Revised Edition) (Boston: Little, Brown & Co., 1922), note 24 at 20–22.

11. Wardle, Blakeseley, and Parker, Sec. 1:02.

12. Ibid., Sec. 1:03.

13. P.C. Hoffer, *Law & People in Colonial America* (Baltimore: Johns Hopkins University Press, 1982), pp. 19–24.

14. Grossberg, pp. 3–4.

15. Ibid., p. 5.

16. Ibid., p. 6.

17. *Griswold v. Connecticut*, 381 U.S. 479 (1965).

18. Some state legislatures are currently attempting to influence the decisions of AFDC mothers by financially penalizing them for giving birth to more than a legislatively determined number of children.

19. *Wisconsin v. Yoder*, 406 U.S. 205 (1972) 229–30.

20. R. Melton, *Evolving Definition of "Family,"* 29 Journal of Family Law 504 (1990–1991).

21. *Braschi v. Stahl Association*, 543 N.E.2d 49 (1989) 58.

22. *Braschi*, 543 N.E.2d at 53–54.

23. J. Collier, M. Rosaldo, and S. Yanagisako, "Is There a Family? New Anthropological Views," in *Rethinking the Family: Some Feminist Questions*, eds. B. Thorne and M. Yalon (New York: Longman, 1982), pp. 25–39.

24. M. Farmer, *The Family* (London: Longmans, Green and Co., 1970), p. 17.

25. H.D. Krause, *Family Law* (2nd Ed.) (St. Paul: West Publishing, 1986), pp. 31–32.

26. *Braschi v. Stahl Association*, 543 N.E.2d 49 (1989).

27. *Braschi*, 543 N.E.2d at 53–54.

28. New York City, San Francisco, Berkeley, West Hollywood, Santa Cruz, and Madison, Wisconsin are examples. See R. Melton, *Evolving Definition of a Family*, 29 Journal of Family Law 497, 504 (1990–1991). An administrative regulation of this type in Austin, Texas, however, was overturned by voters in 1994.

29. *Maynard v. Hill*, 125 U.S. 190 (1888).

30. Wardle, Blakeseley, and Parker, Sec. 3:02.

31. National Commission for Adoption, *Adoption Factbook 18* (1989).

32. J. Evall, *Sexual Orientation and Adoptive Matching*, 24 Family Law Quarterly 349 (1991).

33. Some states require that a petitioner be at least ten years older than the person to be adopted while others require that the adoptee not be related to the petitioner. Some states also refuse to allow an adult petitioner to adopt another adult who happens to be the petitioner's homosexual partner, where the parties may be trying to use the adoption law to circumvent the marriage, contract, and probate laws.

34. Krause, p. 163.

35. E. Bartholet, *Family Bonds* (Boston: Houghton Mifflin, 1993), p. 66.

36. Ibid., p. 71.

37. Ibid., pp. 70–72.

38. *Palmore v. Sidoti*, 466 U.S. 429 (1984).

39. *Compos v. McKeithen*, 341 F.Supp. 264 (E.D. La. 1972).

40. K. Forde-Mazrui, *Black Identity and Child Placement: The Best Interests of Black and Biracial Children*, 92 Michigan Law Review 939 (1994).

41. A. McCormick, *Transracial Adoption: A Critical View of the Courts' Present Standards*, 28 Journal of Family Law 314 (1989–1990); Forde-Mazrui, pp. 925, 929–930.

42. McCormick, pp. 303, 309; E. Bartholet, *Where Do Black Children Belong? The Politics of Race Matching in Adoption*, 139 U. Pa. Law Rev. 1163, 1183–1200 (1991).

43. L. Schwartz, *Religious Matching for Adoption: Unraveling the Interests Behind the "Best Interests" Standard*, 25 Family Law Quarterly 2 (Summer 1991).

44. Ibid., p. 179.

45. Ibid., p. 189.

46. Ibid.

47. Florida Statutes Annotated Sec. 63.042(3) (West 1985); and New Hampshire Revised Statutes Section 170-B:4 (Supp. 1989).

48. J. Evall, *Sexual Orientation and Adoptive Matching*, 24 Family Law Quarterly 3, 354–355 (1991).

49. *Appeal in Pima County Juvenile Action B-10489*, 727 P.2d 830 (Ariz. App. 1986).

50. Evall, pp. 356–357.

51. The child was the birth child of Susan as a result of artificial insemination, and Tammy was adopted jointly by the women, who have raised her from birth. A similar decision was made in Vermont [*Adoption of B.L.V.B.*, 628 A.2d 1271 (1993)].

52. Bartholet, p. 48.

53. Ibid., p. 55.

54. Ibid., p. 56.

55. American Public Welfare Association, as quoted in *Newsweek*, April 25, 1994, p. 55.

56. A. Hardin, ed., *Foster Children in the Courts*, Foster Care Project, National Legal Resource Center for Child Advocacy and Protection (Chicago: American Bar Association, 1983), p. 70.

57. American Public Welfare Association, *Newsweek*, p. 56.

58. Ibid., p. 55.

59. R. Sherman, *Suits Seek to Reform Foster Care*, The National Law Journal 1, 25 (June 27, 1994); see also T. Weidlich, *Children's HIV Tests*, The National Law Journal A4 (June 27, 1994). The Weidlich article discusses a threatened lawsuit that convinced New York State to test all foster care children for HIV.

60. Jacob, p. 1.

61. States differ as to exactly what level of support must be provided. Some states define necessaries to be essentially the most basic needs, whereas other states are more generous in their construction of the term.

62. C. Hused, *Married Woman's Property Law 1800–1850*, 71 Georgetown Law Journal 1359, note 4 at 1400 (1983). Also see *Thompson v. Thompson*, 218 U.S. 611 (1910).

63. See Kentucky Revised Statutes Sec. 205.310, South Dakota Codified Laws Annotated Sec. 25-7-8, and Washington Revised Code Sec. 26.16.205. See also *M.H.B. v. H.T.B.* 498 A.2d 775 (1985).

64. See Alaska Statute Section 47.25.250, Iowa Code Section 252.5, *Estate of Hines*, 573 P.2d 1260 (1978), and Wisconsin Statutes Annotated Section 940.27.

65. See Alaska Statute Sec. 25.20.030 and Oregon Revised Statute Sec. 109.010.

66. See *Mahan v. Mahan*, 88 So.2d 545 (1956).

67. See *Heup v. Heup*, 172 N.W.2d 334 (1969).

68. Maryland Annotated Code Article 16, Sec. 27.

69. New Hampshire Revised Statutes Annotated Sec. 458:17, Minnesota Statute Sec. 518.57, California Civil Code Sec. 4453.

70. 4 American Jurisprudence 2d, 513.

71. *Posner v. Posner*, 233 So.2d 381 (1970).

72. Jacob, p. 30.

73. Ibid., p. 4.

74. U.S. Bureau of the Census, *Historical Statistics of the United States, Colonial Times to 1957* (Washington, D.C., 1960), p. 25.

75. This is not to suggest that the amount of choice is equally distributed throughout society and is not impacted by considerations of race, gender, and socioeconomic status.

76. It is important to emphasize that in all eras, spouses and parents have deserted their partners and families without bothering with legal formalities. Note also that the primary victims have been women who devoted their lives to their families and homes and who were often left destitute and with children. This has contributed to what is often referred to as the feminization of poverty.

77. Jacob, p. 251.

78. Ibid., p. 47.

79. Ibid., pp. 46–47.

80. Ibid., p. 34.

81. Wadlington, *Divorce Without Fault Without Perjury*, 52 Virginia Law Revue 32, 40 (1966).

82. Jacob, pp. 60–61.

83. Ibid., p. 59.

84. Ibid., p. 80.

85. *Hagerty v. Hagerty*, 281 N.W.2d 386 (1979).

86. Freed and Walker, *Family Law in the Fifty States: An Overview*, 24 Family Law Quarterly 309, 355 (1991).

87. A. Schepard, *Taking Children Seriously: Promoting Cooperative Custody After Divorce*, 64 Texas Law Review 687 (1985).

88. S. Quinn, *Fathers Cry for Custody*, Juris Doctor 42 (May 1976).

89. R. Cochran, Jr., "Reconciling the Primary Caretaker Preference, and Joint Custody Preference and the Case-by-Case Rule," in *Joint Custody and Shared Parenting*, ed. Jay Folberg (New York: The Guilford Press, 1991), pp. 218–219.

90. J. Goldstein, A. Freud, and A. Solnit, *Beyond the Best Interests of the Child* (New York: The Free Press, 1979), pp. 107–109.

91. Cochran, p. 222.

92. M. Elkin, "Joint Custody: In the Best Interests of the Family," in *Joint Custody and Shared Parenting*, ed. Jay Folberg (New York: The Guilford Press, 1991), pp. 12–13.

93. Ibid., p. 13.

94. See *Gruber v. Gruber*, 583 A.2d 434 (1990), and *In re Miroballi*, 589 N.E.2d 565 (1992), for cases supporting parent's right to relocate. See *Plowman v. Plowman*, 597 A.2d 701 (1991), for a contrary opinion.

95. See *Fortenberry v. Fortenberry*, 338 S.E.2d 342 (1985), *Toomey v. Toomey*, 636 S.W.2d 313 (1982), and *Neudecker v. Neudecker*, 577 N.E.2d 960 (1991).

96. H. Krause, *Family Law in a Nutshell* (2nd Ed.) (St. Paul: West Publishing, 1986), p. 211.

IX

Contracts

A BRIEF HISTORY OF
AMERICAN CONTRACT LAW

The modern contract action can be traced to the English common law writs of debt, detinue, and covenant, which were created in the twelfth and thirteenth centuries.[1] The *debt* action was used to collect a specific sum of money owed. *Detinue* was used against one who had possessory rights to another's personal property but who refused to return it when requested by the true owner. *Covenant* was initially used to enforce agreements relating to land (especially leases).[2] Later it was employed to enforce written agreements under seal.[3] Gradually, these writs were supplemented by the common law *writ of trespass*, which included trespass to land, assaults, batteries, the taking of goods, and false imprisonment. Each of these acts involved a tortfeasor who directly caused injury to the victim by force and arms and thereby violated the King's peace.

In 1285, Parliament enacted the Statute of Westminster, which authorized the chancery to create a new writ, called *trespass on the case*, to address private wrongs that fell outside the traditional boundaries of trespass.[4] Case, as it came to be called, could remedy injuries that resulted from the defendant's failure to perform a professional duty that in turn resulted in harm to the plaintiff. Thus case would be appropriate where A's property was damaged while entrusted to B, as a result of B's failure to exercise proper skill or care.[5] These early writs were based on property rights and were not based on modern contractual notions such as offer, acceptance, and consideration.

In the fifteenth and sixteenth centuries, some breaches of duty (called undertakings), that had been included within the writ of trespass on the case evolved into a new writ called *assumpsit*.[6] For example, in one early case a ferry operator was sued in assumpsit for improperly loading his boat such that the plaintiff's mare drowned while crossing the Humber River.[7] By the early 1500s, a plaintiff could also sue in assumpsit for nonfeasance (failure to perform a promise).[8] During the 1560s, plaintiffs bringing assumpsit actions were generally required to allege that undertakings were supported by consideration.[9] Consideration grew in importance and in the 1700s, chancellors began refusing to order specific performance if they thought the consideration inadequate.[10] This development made the enforceability of contracts uncertain because judges could invalidate agreements reached by the parties and could prevent the parties from making their own bargains.

Assumpsit was the principal "contract" action until the early 1800s when economic changes and widespread dissatisfaction with the technical requirements and expense of common law pleading resulted in an erosion of the common law approach.[11] The 1800s brought a significant shift in thinking away from the old writs and toward the emerging new substantive action, called contract, which included all types of obligations. Contributing to the demise of assumpsit was the old-fashioned notion that courts had a responsibility to ensure that contracting parties received equivalent value from their bargains.[12] It became apparent that commercial prosperity required that courts protect their expectation damages (the return they had been promised in an agreement).[13] When the courts responded to these changes and demands, contract law rapidly developed. New York's replacement of the writ system in 1848 with its newly enacted Code of Civil Procedure established a trend toward modern code pleading that swept the nation.[14]

By 1850, American courts had accepted the notion that contracts are based on the reciprocal promises of the parties.[15] As courts became increasingly willing to enforce private agreements, they began to recognize the customs of each trade, profession, and business rather than general customs. The courts would often disregard existing legal requirements in favor of the rules created by the contract part. This fragmentation of law was bad for business. The absence of a widely accepted code of contract rules resulted in unpredictability and uncertainty in American society, the economy, and the courts. This caused business firms to press for uniform laws dealing with commercial transactions among states.

In the 1890s, the American Bar Association established the National Conference of Commissioners on Uniform State Laws to encourage states to enact uniform legislation. The Uniform Sales Act and the Negotiable Instruments Law were two products of this movement. During this era, Samuel Williston and Arthur Corbin wrote widely accepted treatises on the law of contracts. Then, in 1928 a legal think tank of lawyers and judges, called the American Law Institute, developed and published the Restatement of Contracts, a proposed code of contract rules that was grounded in the common law.

In 1942, the American Law Institute and the American Bar Association sponsored a project to develop a Uniform Commercial Code (UCC), which was completed in 1952. Pennsylvania was the first state to adopt the UCC in 1953. The code covers sales, commercial paper, bank collection processes, letters of credit, bulk transfers, warehouse receipts, bills of lading, other documents of title, investment securities, and secured transactions. The UCC governs only sales of (and contracts to sell) goods, defined as movables, or personal property having tangible form. It does not cover transactions involving realty, services, or the sale of intangibles. If a contract involves a mixed goods/services sale (for example, application of a hair product as part of a beauty treatment), the courts tend to apply the UCC only if the sale-of-goods aspect dominates the transaction. The UCC has been adopted at least partially in all fifty states, and has had the largest legislative impact on the law of contracts.

NATURE AND CLASSIFICATION OF CONTRACTS

A *contract* is a legally enforceable agreement containing one or more promises. Not every promise is a contract—only those promises enforceable by law. Although the word *contract* is often used when referring to a written document that contains the terms of the contract, in the legal sense, the word *contract* does not mean the tangible document, but the legally enforceable agreement itself.

In order to establish an enforceable contract, there must be (1) an agreement, (2) between competent parties, (3) based on genuine assent of the parties, (4) supported by consideration, (5) that does not contravene principles of law, and (6) that must be in writing in certain circumstances. Each of these requirements is discussed in detail in this chapter.

An *agreement* is an expression of the parties' willingness to be bound to the terms of the contract. Usually, one party offers a proposal, and the other agrees to the terms by accepting it. Both parties to the contract must be *competent*. Some people—because of age or mental disability—are not competent and thus do not have, from the legal standpoint, the capacity to bind themselves contractually. *Genuine assent* of both parties is also necessary. It is presumed to exist unless one of the parties is induced to agree because of misrepresentation, fraud, duress, undue influence, or mistake.

Consideration on the part of both parties is an essential element of a contract. One party's promise (or consideration) must be bargained for and given in exchange for the other's act or promise (his consideration). The bargain cannot involve something that is prohibited by law or that is against the best interests of society. And finally, certain contracts, to be enforceable, must be evidenced in writing.

Common law is the primary source of the law of contracts. Many statutes affect contracts, especially specific types of contracts, such as employment and insurance. But the overwhelming body of contractual principles is embodied in court decisions.

Valid, Void, Voidable, and Unenforceable Contracts

Contracts can be classified in terms of validity and enforceability. A *valid contract* is a binding and enforceable agreement which meets all the necessary contractual requirements. A contract is said to be valid and enforceable when a person is entitled to judicial relief in case of breach by the other party.

A *void contract* means no contract, because no legal obligation has been created. When an agreement lacks a necessary contractual element—such as consideration—the agreement is without legal effect, and therefore void.

A *voidable contract* exists when one or more persons can elect to avoid an obligation created by a contract because of the manner in which the contract was brought about. For example, someone who has been induced to make a contract by fraud or duress may be able to avoid the obligation created by the contract. Contracts made by those who are not of legal age are also voidable, at the option of the party lacking legal capacity. A voidable contract is not wholly lacking in legal effect, however, because not all the parties can legally avoid their duties under it.

A contract is *unenforceable* (not void or voidable) when a defense to the enforceability of the contract is present. For example, the right of action is lost in a situation in which a sufficient writing is required and cannot be produced. Also, when a party wanting to enforce a contract waits beyond the time period prescribed by law to bring the court action (statute of limitations), the contract is unenforceable.

Bilateral and Unilateral Contracts

All contracts involve at least two parties. *Bilateral contracts* consist simply of mutual promises to do some future act. The promises need not be express on both sides; one of the promises could be implied from the surrounding circumstances.

A *unilateral contract* results when one party makes a promise in exchange for another person performing an act or refraining from doing something. For example, assume that someone wants to buy an item owned by another for $100. If the buyer promises to pay the owner $100 for the item *if and when* the owner conveys legal title and possession to the buyer, a *uni*lateral contract is created. It is a promise of an act. The contract comes into existence when the act of conveying title and possession is performed. If, however, the buyer promises to pay $100 in exchange for the owner's promise to convey title and possession of the item, a bilateral contract results. A *bi*lateral contract comes into existence when mutual promises are made.

AGREEMENT

In order for a contract to be formed, there must be mutual *agreement* between two or more competent parties who must manifest their intent to be bound to definite terms. The agreement is usually reached by one party making an offer and the other—expressly or impliedly—accepting the terms of the offer.

The intention of the parties is the primary factor determining the nature of the contract. This is ascertained not just from the words used by the parties, but also from the entire situation, including the acts and conduct of the parties. In determining the intent of the parties, the courts generally use an objective rather than a subjective test. In an objective test, the question is "What would a reasonable person in the position of party A think was meant by the words, conduct, or both, of party B?" If a subjective test were used, the question would be "What did party A actually mean by certain expressions?" For example, suppose that one of the parties is not serious about creating a legal obligation, but the other party has no way of knowing this. Under the objective test, a contract would still be created.

In law, invitations to social events lack contractual intention, and, when accepted, do not give rise to a binding contract. For example, when two people agree to have dinner together or to go to a baseball game together, each usually feels a moral obligation to fulfill his or her promise. Neither, however, expects to be legally bound by the agreement. An agreement also lacks contractual intent when a party's assent to it is made in obvious anger, excitement, or jest. This is true even when the parties' expressions, if taken literally as stated, would amount to mutual assent. Sometimes it is not obvious that a proposal is made in anger, excitement, or jest. Under the objective test, the surrounding circumstances and context of the expressions would be examined to determine what a reasonably prudent person would believe.

Offer

An *offer* is a proposal to make a contract. It is a promise conditional on a return promise, act, or forbearance being given by the offeree. The return promise, act, or forbearance is acceptance of the offer.

A legally effective offer must be (1) a definite proposal (2) made with the intent to contract and (3) communicated to the offeree. The terms of the offer, on acceptance, become the terms of the contract. An offer must be definite and certain, so that when the offeree accepts, both parties understand the obligations they have created.

It is important to distinguish between a definite proposal, which is an offer, and a solicitation of an offer. A willingness to make or receive an offer is not itself an offer, but an invitation to negotiate. For example, the question "Would you be interested in buying my television set for $100?" is considered an invitation to negotiate. A "yes" response would not create a contract, since there was no definite proposal made (form of payment, when due, etc.).

For an offer to be effective, it need not be made to one specific named person. It can be made to the general public, in the form of an advertisement. These may be circulars, quotation sheets, displays, and announcements in publications. However, the publication of the fact that an item is for sale, and its price, is usually an invitation to negotiate, not an offer.

Termination of an Offer

The offeree can bind the offeror to his or her proposal for the duration of the offer—the time from the moment an offer is effectively communicated to the offeree until it is terminated. An offer can be terminated by (1) revocation by the offeror, (2) lapse of time, (3) subsequent illegality, (4) destruction of the subject matter, (5) death or lack of capacity, (6) rejection, (7) a counteroffer, and (8) acceptance.

An offeror has the power to terminate the offer by revocation at any time before it is accepted. Even when an offeror promises to hold an offer open for a certain period of time, the offeror can revoke the offer before that time, unless consideration is given to hold the offer open. For example, if a seller promises in an offer to give the offeree one week to accept the offer, the seller still retains the power to withdraw the offer at any time.

A contract whereby an offeror is bound to hold an offer open is called an *option*. In an option contract, consideration is necessary in return for the promise to hold the offer open. For example, if the offeree pays the offeror ten dollars to hold an offer open for ten days, the offeror does not have the power to withdraw the offer before the ten-day period is up.

If an offer stipulates how long it will remain open, it automatically terminates with the expiration of that period of time. When an offer does not stipulate a time period within which it may be accepted, it is then effective for a "reasonable" length of time.

An offer to enter into an agreement forbidden by law is ineffective and void, even if the offer was legal when made. If the subject matter of an offer is destroyed, the offer is automatically terminated because of impossibility.

An offer is terminated at the death of either the offeror or the offeree. Adjudication of insanity usually has the same effect as death in terminating an offer. The termination is effective automatically without any need to give notice. For example, if a person offers to sell an item at a stated price, but dies before the offer is accepted, there can be no contract, because one of the parties died before a meeting of the minds took place. If the offeree had accepted the offer before the death, however, there would have been a meeting of minds and the offeror's estate would be responsible under the contract.

An offer is also terminated by a rejection or a counteroffer. When an offeree does not intend to accept an offer and so informs the offeror, the offer is said to have been terminated by rejection. If the offeree responds to an offer by making another proposal, the proposal constitutes a counteroffer and terminates the original offer. For example, if an offer is made to sell merchandise for $300 and the offeree offers to buy this merchandise for $250, the offeree has rejected the original offer by making a counteroffer. However, an *inquiry*, or a request for additional terms by the offeree, is not a counteroffer and does not terminate the offer. Thus, if the offeree had asked whether the offeror would consider reducing the price to $250, this inquiry would not terminate the original offer.

Acceptance

An acceptance is the agreement of the offeree to be bound by the terms of the offer. There is no meeting of the minds until the offeree has consented to the proposition contained in the offer. In order for an acceptance to be effective in creating a contract, there must be (1) an unconditional consent, (2) to an open offer, (3) by the offeree only, and (4) communicated to the offeror. In addition, there must be some act of manifestation of the intention to contract. This can be in the form of (1) silence or inaction, (2) a promise, (3) an act or forbearance from an act, or (4) any other manner specifically stipulated in the offer.

In most situations, silence or inaction on the part of the offeree does not constitute acceptance. When a person receives goods or services expecting that they will have to be paid for, the act of receiving the goods or services constitutes acceptance of the offer. An offeror is usually not permitted to word the offer in such a way that silence or inaction of the offeree constitutes acceptance. However, silence or inaction *can* do so in situations in which this method of dealing has been established by agreement between the parties, or by prior dealings of the parties.

In an offer to enter into a bilateral contract, the offeree must communicate acceptance in the form of a promise to the offeror. The offeror must be made aware, by the express or implied promise, that a contract has been formed. An offer to enter into a unilateral contract requires an acceptance in the form of an act. A mere promise to perform the act is not an effective acceptance.

The offeror has the power to specify the means and methods of acceptance and the acceptance must comply with those requirements. For example, an oral acceptance of an offer that called for a written acceptance would be ineffective. If nothing is stated, a reasonable means or method of acceptance is effective. An offer can provide that the acceptance is effective only on the completion of specified formalities. In such a situation, all these formalities must be complied with in order to have an effective acceptance.

At common law, an acceptance must be a "mirror image" of the offer. If it changes the terms of an offer in any way it acts only as a counteroffer and has no effect as an acceptance. Under the UCC (2-207), an acceptance that adds some new or different terms to contracts involving the sale of goods does create a contract. The new terms are treated as proposals that must be accepted separately.

The plaintiffs in the following case lost their suit because their offer to purchase one hundred acres of land was not unconditionally accepted by the defendants.

Pluhacek v. Nebraska Lutheran Outdoor Ministries, Inc.
420 N.W.2d 286
Supreme Court of Nebraska
March 11, 1988

Boslaugh, Justice

This case arises out of a controversy concerning an alleged contract for the sale of land. The property involved is a 100-acre tract of land in Douglas County, Nebraska, located near west Q Street and the Elkhorn River.

The owner of the property, the defendant, Nebraska Lutheran Ministries, Inc., listed the property for sale in 1985. The original listing price was $210,000. On April 17, 1985, the listing price was reduced to $195,000; on July 22, 1985, it was reduced to $175,000. In January 1986, the listing price was reduced to $155,000.

The plaintiff Thomas J. Pluhacek is a licensed real estate agent. On March 2, 1986, the plaintiffs submitted an offer to purchase the property for $110,000, subject to their ability to obtain an $88,000 conventional mortgage.

In a conference call on March 5, 1986, the executive director and executive committee of the defendant considered the plaintiff's offer. The committee decided to submit a counterproposal subject to the following conditions: the offer must be a cash offer not contingent upon the buyers' obtaining a loan; the earnest deposit must be increased to $5,000; the seller was to retain the insurance proceeds resulting from a fire on February 7, 1986; the 1985 taxes were to be prorated; and "[a]cceptance [was] subject to full Board of Directors approval on March 17, 1986." The conditions were written on the uniform purchase agreement form on which the plaintiffs' offer had been submitted, in the following language:

> "Except offer to be CASH (No loan contingency); Earnest Deposit to be raised to $5,000; Sellers to retain any insurance proceeds as a result of the fire on or about February 7, 1986, 1985 taxes that are payable in 1986 are to be prorated and treated as though all are current taxes. This contract is subject to the full Board of Directors approval of the Nebraska Lutheran Outdoor Ministries on or before March 17, 1986."

The acceptance was then signed by the president of the defendant, and the document was returned to the plaintiffs.

On March 7, 1986, the plaintiffs added the following language to the agreement and signed their names: "We have read, understand and accept the terms and conditions of the above offer." The document was then returned to the defendant's real estate agent.

On March 10, 1986, the plaintiff Thomas Pluhacek delivered a $5,000 check to the office of the plaintiff's real estate agency for the earnest money.

On the following day, a news article appeared in the Omaha World-Herald stating that the defendant had signed a contract to sell the property. The article further stated that the board would act on the offer March 17. After seeing the article in the paper, the defendant's agent notified it that the article might stimulate interest in the property and generate additional offers.

On March 13, 1986, the Omaha/Council Bluffs Metropolitan YMCA submitted an offer to purchase the property for $135,000. On March 16, 1986, another offer to purchase the property, for $140,000, was submitted by Eric Petersen and Peter Bristol.

The defendant's board of directors met on March 17, 1986, considered the three offers to buy the property, and accepted the YMCA offer.

This action was commenced on March 18, 1986, to compel specific performance of the plaintiffs' alleged contract to purchase the property. The trial court found that approval of the contract by the full board of directors of the defendant was a condition precedent to the formation of a contract and that the defendant acted in good faith, and dismissed the petition. The plaintiffs have appealed. . . .

The threshold issue in a specific performance case is whether there was a contract. As we stated in *Rybin Investment Co., Inc. v. Wade,* . . . "Before a trial court may compel specific performance, there must be a showing that a valid, legally enforceable contract exists." . . . Furthermore, "[t]o establish an express contract, there must be shown what amounts to a definite proposal and an unconditional and absolute acceptance thereof. . . . The burden of proving the contract is on the party who seeks to compel specific performance." . . .

The plaintiffs' offer to purchase the defendant's property was not unconditionally accepted by the defendant. Although four of the conditions were capable of immediate acceptance by the plaintiffs, the final condition, that acceptance of the plaintiff's offer was subject to full board approval on March 17, 1986, was a contingency to which the plaintiffs could agree, but it prevented a contract from being made until the full board had accepted the offer.

As stated in *Rybin*, . . .

"[A]cceptance of the offer must be an unconditional acceptance of the offer as made, otherwise, no contract is formed. There must be no substantial variation between the offer and the acceptance. If the acceptance differs from the offer or is coupled with any condition that varies or adds to the offer, it is not an acceptance, but it is a counterproposition."

The plaintiffs' acceptance of the terms and conditions of the defendant's counterproposal on March 7, 1986, merely expressed their willingness to subject their offer to the five conditions specified.

A contract was not made on March 7, 1986. The condition that the sale was contingent on board approval postponed formation of a contract until March 17, 1986.

Before there could be a contract between the plaintiffs and the defendant for a sale of the property, the board of directors of the defendant had to approve the sale. Because this did not occur, there was no enforceable contract. The plaintiffs have failed to show by clear, satisfactory, and unequivocal evidence that they were entitled to specific performance. . . .

The judgment of the district court is affirmed.

Affirmed.

Case Questions

1. This case was an action brought by the plaintiff for specific performance. Exactly what does this mean?
2. According to the court, what must the plaintiff demonstrate in order to satisfy the threshold requirement for specific performance?
3. Why does the court rule that the plaintiff's offer to purchase the land was not accepted by the defendant?

REALITY OF CONSENT

Genuine assent to be bound by a contract is not present when one of the parties' consent is obtained through duress, undue influence, fraud, or innocent misrepresentation, or when either of the parties, or both, made a mistake concerning the contract. Such contracts are usually voidable, and the injured party has the right to elect to avoid or affirm the agreement. (These defenses against the enforceability of a contract can also be used against other legal documents, such as wills, trust agreements, and executed gifts.)

An injured party who wishes to avoid or rescind a contract should act promptly. Silence beyond a reasonable length of time may be deemed an implied ratification. An injured party who elects to rescind a contract is entitled to *restitution*—the return of any property or money given in performance of the contract. The injured party must also return any property or money received through the contract.

Duress

Freedom of will of both parties to a contract is absolutely necessary. When one of the parties' will is overcome because of duress, the agreement is voidable. *Duress* is any unlawful constraint exercised on people that forces their consent to an agreement that they would not otherwise have made. Unlike those situations in which people act as a result of fraud, innocent misrepresentation, or mistake, a person acting under duress does so knowingly. Three elements are necessary for duress to exist: (1) coercion, (2) causing a loss of free will, and (3) resulting in a consent to be bound by a contract.

Any form of constraint improperly exercised in order to get another's consent to contract is sufficient for coercion. Exercise of pressure to contract is not enough; it must be exercised wrongfully. Thus, advice, suggestion, or persuasion are not recognized as coercive. Likewise, causing a person to fear embarrassment or annoyance usually does not constitute duress. In order to amount to coercion, the constraint must entail threatened injury or force. For duress to exist, the person must enter into the agreement while under the influence of this threat.

The threat need not necessarily be to the person or the property of the contracting party. For example, a threat to injure the child of a contracting party could amount to duress. A threat of criminal prosecution gives rise to duress when fear overcomes judgment and deprives the person of the exercise of free will. Making a threat of civil action, however—with the honest belief that it may be successful—is not using duress. For example, assume that an employee embezzles an undetermined amount of money from an employer. The employer estimates that the theft amounts to about $5,000, and threatens to bring a civil suit for damages unless the employee pays $5,000. Even though the employee takes the threat seriously and pays the $5,000, no duress exists. If the employer were to threaten to bring criminal charges under the same circumstances, duress would take place.

Economic distress or business compulsion may be grounds for duress. The surrounding circumstances of the business setting and the relative bargaining positions of the contracting parties are examined in order to determine whether duress is present.

Undue Influence

Undue influence results when the will of a dominant person is substituted for that of the other party, and the substitution is done in an unlawful fashion, resulting in an unfair agreement. Usually, undue influence is found when there is (1) a confidential relationship that is used to create (2) an unfair bargain.

In determining whether a confidential relationship exists, all the surrounding circumstances are examined to find out whether one of the parties dominates the other to the extent that the other is dependent on him or her. Family relationships, such as husband-wife or parent-child, often give rise to confidential relationships. Some relationships involving a special trust—such as trustee-beneficiary or attorney-client—entail a confidential relationship. Sometimes confidential relationships are created between business associates, neighbors, or friends. A person who is mentally weak—because of sickness, old age, or distress—may not be capable of resisting the dominant party's influence.

Whenever there is dominance in a confidential relationship, the court must determine whether the contract was equitable and voluntary. A contract is not invalid simply because there is a confidential relationship. A contract is voidable if one abuses the confidence in a relationship in order to obtain personal gain by substituting one's own will or interest for that of another. Whether the weaker party has had the benefit of independent advice is an important factor in determining fairness in contractual dealings. A legitimate suggestion or persuasion may influence someone, but it is not undue influence; nor, usually, is an appeal to the affections. When methods go beyond mere persuasion and prevent a person from acting freely, undue influence is present.

Fraud

The term *fraud* covers all intentional acts of deception used by one individual to gain an advantage over another. The essential elements of actionable fraud are (1) the misstatement of a material fact, (2) made with knowledge of its falsity, or in reckless disregard of its truth or falsity, (3) with the intention to deceive, (4) inducing reliance by the other party, and (5) that results or will result in injury to the other party.

For fraud, misstatements must be of a fact, a *fact* being something that existed in the past or exists at present. The misstated fact must be material. The often-used definition of a *material fact* is that it is a fact without which the contract would not have been entered into. The speaker, when making the statement of fact, must know that it is false. The stating party must have the intention to deceive, and thereby induce the other party to enter into the contract.

The deceived party's reliance on the misstatement must be justified and reasonable. A party wishing to rescind a contract need not show actual damages resulting from the fraud. However, a party wishing to sue for damages in addition to rescission must prove that actual damage has been sustained. Assume, for example, that Carlotta purchases a dog from Enrique based on his statements that the dog is a purebred with a pedigree from the American Kennel Club. Carlotta can rescind the contract, return the dog, and recover the purchase price from Enrique if she later discovers that the dog actually is a crossbred. Carlotta may also be able to recover for the dog's medical care, food, and supplies, based on their value to Enrique.

Misrepresentation

When a party to a contract misrepresents a material fact, *even though unknowingly,* and the other party relies on and is misled by the falsehood, *misrepresentation* is present. If a contract is induced by misrepresentation, the deceived party has the right of rescission. Fraud and misrepresentation are quite similar. However, the *intent* to deceive is the primary distinction between fraudulent and nonfraudulent misrepresentation. Rescission and restitution are available for both, although damages are not obtainable in cases of misrepresentation.

Mistake

Sometimes one or both of the parties to a contract understand the facts to be other than what they are. If ignorance of a fact is material to the contract, a *mistake* exists and the contract may be voidable. Although a mistake of material fact related to the contract is sufficient for relief, a mistake of law is not. In addition, the mistake must refer to a past or present material fact, not to a future possibility.

When one enters into a plain and unambiguous contract, one cannot avoid the obligation created by proving that its terms were misunderstood. Lack of due diligence, poor judgment, lack of wisdom, or a mistake as to the true value of an item contracted for are not grounds for relief. Relief based on mistake may not be had simply because one party to a speculative contract expected it to turn out differently.

The court in the following case ordered rescission of an executed agreement and restitution because the parties to the contract made a mutual mistake.

Carter v. Matthews
701 S.W.2d 374
Supreme Court of Arkansas
January 13, 1986

Newbern, Justice

This is a real estate sale case in which the chancellor granted rescission in favor of the appellant on the ground of mutual mistake but did not award the money damages she claimed. The damages she sought were for her expenses in constructing improvements which subsequently had to be removed from the land. The

appellant claims it was error for the chancellor to have found she did not rely on misrepresentations made by the appellees through their real estate agent, and thus it was error to refuse her damages for fraud plus costs and an attorney fee. On cross-appeal, the appellees contend the only possible basis for the rescission was fraud, not mistake, and the chancellor erred in granting rescission once he had found there was no reliance by the appellant on any active or constructive misrepresentations of the appellees. We find the chancellor was correct on all counts, and thus we affirm on both appeal and cross-appeal.

1. Rescission

The chancellor found that conversations between the appellant and the appellees' agent showed that both parties were under the mistaken impression that the low, flat portion of land in question was suitable for building permanent structures such as a barn, horse corral and fencing. In fact, however, the area where the appellant attempted to build a barn and corral and which she wanted to use as pasture for horses was subject to severe and frequent flooding. The chancellor held there was thus a mutual mistake of fact making rescission proper. While there was evidence the appellees had known of one instance of severe flooding on the land, the evidence did not show they knew it was prone to the frequent and extensive flooding which turned out to be the case.

Other matters not known to the parties were that the low portion of the land, about two-thirds of the total acreage, is in the 100 year floodplain and that a Pulaski County ordinance . . . requires a seller of land lying in the floodplain to inform the buyer of that fact no later than ten days before closing the transaction. The county planning ordinance also requires that no structures be built in the floodplain. If the chancellor's decision had been to permit rescission because of the parties' lack of knowledge of these items, we would have had before us the question whether the mistake was one of law rather than fact and thus perhaps irremediable. . . .

While the chancellor mentions these items, his basis for rescission was the mutual lack of knowledge about the extent of the flooding, and misunderstanding of the suitability of the property, as a matter of fact, for the buyer's purposes which were known to both parties. We sustain his finding that there was a mutual mistake of fact. A mutual mistake of fact as to a material element of a contract is an appropriate basis for rescission. . . .

2. Damages for Fraud

The chancellor refused to allow the appellant any damages for the loss she sustained with respect to the improvements she had placed in the floodplain. He found the appellant had made an independent investigation of the propensity of the property to become flooded and had ascertained, erroneously, that the property was not in the floodplain. Thus, in spite of the legal duty on the part of the appellees to tell the appellant that the land was in the floodplain, and what might have been the resultant constructive fraud upon failure to inform her, he held that fraud may not be the basis of a damages award absent reliance on the misrepresentation. For the same reason the chancellor refused to base his decision on any alleged fraud resulting from the appellees' failure to tell the appellant what they may have known about the land's propensity to flood. He was correct. An essential element of an action for deceit is reliance by the plaintiff on the defendant's misrepresentation. . . . In view of the strong evidence, including her own testimony, that the appellant made her own investigation as to whether the land flooded, the extent to which a creek running through the land was in the floodplain and the feasibility of bridging the creek above the floodplain, we can hardly say the chancellor's factual determination that the appellant did not rely on the failure of the appellees to give her information known to them or which they had a duty to disclose to her under the ordinance was clearly erroneous. . . .

When rescission is based on mutual mistake rather than fraud, the recoveries of the parties are limited to their restitutionary interests. . . . As the appellant could show no benefit conferred on the appellees from her attempted improvements on the land, she was entitled to no recovery in excess of the return of the purchase price, which was awarded to her by the chancellor, as well as cancellation of her note and mortgage. . . .

Affirmed.

Case Questions

1. The plaintiff-appellant in this case went to court seeking rescission as well as damages. What exactly is the remedy called rescission?
2. Why did the chancellor agree to grant rescission? What was the rationale behind this ruling?
3. Why did the chancellor refuse to allow the appellant any damages for fraud?
4. What recovery was made by the appellant?

CONSIDERATION

Consideration is simply that which is bargained for and given in exchange for another's promise. Each party to a contract has a motive or price that induces the party to enter into the obligation. This cause or inducement is called *consideration*. Consideration usually consists of an act or a promise to do an act. Forbearance or a promise to forbear may also constitute consideration. Forbearance is refraining from doing an act, or giving up a right.

A person must bargain specifically for the promise, act, or forbearance in order for it to constitute consideration. A promise is usually binding only when consideration is given in exchange. If a person promises to give another $100, this is a promise to make a gift, and it is unenforceable since the promise lacked consideration. If, however, the promisee had promised to convey a television set in return for the promise to convey $100, the promise to give $100 would have been supported by consideration and therefore would be enforceable. Although a promise to make a gift is not enforceable, a person who has received a gift is not required to return it for lack of consideration.

Consideration must be legally sufficient, which means that the consideration for the promise must be either a detriment to the promisee or a legal benefit to the promisor. In most situations both exist. *Benefit* in the legal sense means the receipt by the promisor of some legal right that the person had not previously been entitled to. *Legal detriment* is the taking on of a legal obligation or the doing of something or giving up of a legal right by the promisee.

Assume that an uncle promises to pay a niece $1,000 if she enrolls in and graduates from an accredited college or university. If the niece graduates from an accredited college, she is entitled to the $1,000. The promisee-niece did something she was not legally obligated to do, so the promise was supported by legally sufficient consideration. The legal detriment of the niece certainly did not amount to actual detriment. It can hardly be said that the uncle received any actual benefit either.

Consideration should not be confused with a condition. A *condition* is an event the happening of which qualifies the duty to perform a promise. A promise to give a person $100 if the person comes to your home to pick it up is a promise to make a gift on the condition that the person picks up the money. A promisee who shows up is not legally entitled to the $100.

When one party to an agreement makes what appears at first glance to be a promise but when on examination no real promise is made, this situation is called an *illusory promise*. A contract is not entered into when one of the parties makes an illusory promise, because there is no consideration. For example, a promise to work for an employer at an agreed rate for as long as the promisor wishes to work is an illusory promise. The promisor is really promising nothing and cannot be bound to do anything.

A court will not concern itself with the terms of a contract as long as the parties have capacity and there has been genuine assent to the terms. Whether the bargain was a fair exchange is for the parties to decide when they enter into the agreement. Consideration need not have a pecuniary or money value. If a mother promises her son $100 if he does not drink or smoke until he reaches the age of eighteen, there is no pecuniary value to the abstinence; yet it is a valid consideration.

It is not necessary to state the consideration on the face of the document when an agreement is put in writing. It may be orally agreed on or implied. While the recital of consideration is not final proof that it exists, it is evidence of consideration that is *prima facie*, or sufficient on its face. Evidence that no consideration existed will overcome the presumption that the recital creates, however. And a statement of consideration in an instrument does not create consideration where it was really never intended or given.

If a promise is too vague or uncertain concerning time or subject matter, it will not amount to consideration. If a promise is obviously impossible to perform, it is not sufficient consideration for a return promise. When a promise is capable of being performed, even though improbable or absurd, it is consideration.

Consideration must be bargained for and given in exchange for a promise. Past consideration is not consideration. If a person performs a service for another without the other's knowledge, and later the recipient of the service promises to pay for it, the promise is not binding, since the promise to pay was not supported by consideration. A promise to do what one is already legally obligated to do cannot ordinarily constitute consideration. For example, a promise by a father to pay child support payments that are already an existing legal obligation determined by a court will not constitute consideration. Similarly, consideration is also lacking when a promise is made to refrain from doing what one has no legal right to do.

The court in the following case found that adequate consideration existed to support enforcement of a restrictive covenant clause in an employment contract.

**Modern Laundry and Dry Cleaning
v. Farrer**
536 A.2d 409
Superior Court of Pennsylvania
January 19, 1988

Popovich, Judge

This is an appeal from the Order entered April 16, 1987, in the Court of Common Pleas of Montgomery County, which dissolved appellant's temporary restraining order and dismissed his petition for a preliminary injunction. Appellant alleges the lower court erred in declaring that the restrictive employment covenant was invalid, and, consequently, it erred in denying the Motion for Preliminary Injunction. For the following reasons, we reverse and remand the case for determination of the remaining issue, i.e., whether the restrictive covenant is reasonably limited in time and territory.

On November 6, 1982, Modern Laundry and Dry Cleaning Company (Modern) hired William Farrer to work as a route salesman. For approximately one month, Farrer trained as a probationary employee under the supervision of an experienced route salesman on company Route Thirty-Six. During this probation period, Farrer worked without an employment contract. Under Modern's training program, Farrer was taught how to handle a particular route but was not given any responsibility for the route until Modern was satisfied with his performance. Once Modern became confident in Farrer's ability, he was offered full-time employment. In order to assume full-time status, Farrer was required to sign an employment contract.

Included in the employment contract was the following restrictive covenant:

"As an inducement to the execution of this agreement, and to any renewal or continuation thereof, it is agreed that in the event Employee shall leave the said employment, or be discharged by Employer, during, or at the expiration of this agreement, or any renewal or extension thereof, the said Employee agrees that he shall not, or will not, directly or indirectly, for the space of one year after ceasing in any manner to be in the employ of the Employer, engage in the laundry business in any form or manner on his own account, or as agent, employee, or in any other capacity, for any other person, firm, company, or corporation, in the route or routes, territory or territories assigned to, covered, or served by him, or within three full squares of any point in or on said territory; and that he will not, directly or indirectly, for himself on his own account, or as driver, canvasser, or in any other capacity, for any other person, persons, firm, company or corporation, or within the route or routes, territory or territories assigned to, covered, or served by him, or within three squares of any point in or on said route or routes, territory or territories, solicit for or do any laundry work, or furnish any laundry service whatsoever, to any customer or customers served by said Employer, whether said customer or customers originally belonged to the Employer or were secured by the Employee, or through his efforts, while in the employ of the Employer."

Once the contract was signed, Farrer assumed complete responsibility for Route Thirty-Six. Farrer continued to service

Route Thirty-Six for Modern until January 30, 1987, at which time he notified the company that he was terminating his employment effective immediately.

After Farrer's departure, Modern estimated that from January, 1987, to April, 1987, the company lost approximately 41% of its customers on Route Thirty-Six. In late March, 1987, Modern learned that Farrer had started his own laundry and dry cleaning business and that he was servicing his old route in violation of the restrictive covenant in his employment contract. Modern sought to prevent Farrer from operating his business within his old territory and to gain access to his business records so that the damages to Modern's business could be determined.

On April 7, 1987, Modern filed a Complaint in Equity and a Motion for Temporary Restraining Order and Preliminary Injunction. A temporary restraining order enjoining Farrer from soliciting or servicing any person within "three full squares" of his previous territory was issued. After hearings on April 13, 1987, and April 15, 1987, the lower court ordered the Temporary Restraining Order dissolved and denied the Motion for Preliminary Injunction. This appeal followed.

It is the law of the Commonwealth that for a covenant in restraint of trade to be enforceable, it must meet the following requirements: (1) the covenant must relate to (be ancillary to) a contract for the sale of the good will of a business or to a contract of employment; (2) the covenant must be supported by adequate consideration; (3) the covenant must be limited in both time and territory. . . . Our courts have consistently held that the taking of employment is sufficient consideration for a restrictive covenant. . . .

In the instant case, the lower court ruled that the employment contract between the parties was not ancillary to his taking of employment, and, therefore, it was invalid and unenforceable. However, the appellant cites cases and the record reveals facts which support appellant's contention that the contract was ancillary to the taking of employment. To be valid the restrictive covenant need not appear in the initial employment contract. . . . Therefore, the fact that Modern and Farrer did not enter into the contract containing the restrictive covenant at the beginning of Farrer's employment does not automatically invalidate the covenant. As long as the restrictive covenant is an auxiliary part of the taking of employment and not a later attempt to impose additional restrictions on an unsuspecting employee, a contract of employment containing such a covenant is supported by valid consideration and is therefore enforceable. . . .

In a case similar to the one *sub judice*, *Morgan's Home Equipment Corp. v. Martucci*, . . . the purchaser of a business retained certain employees on a provisional basis and, one month later, offered them regular employment upon the condition that they sign a covenant not to compete. Our Supreme Court held that because the parties entered into a "regular employment relationship in contradistinction to provisional employment" at the same time the employment contract was signed, the restrictive covenant was ancillary to the employment contract. . . . In the instant case, Farrer began his employment with Modern as a trainee on a strictly provisional basis. After his one month training period, Modern believed Farrer was capable of handling Route Thirty-Six, and, on December 7, 1972, Modern offered Farrer full-time employment, provided he signed an employment contract containing a covenant not to compete. Following the analysis in *Morgan's Home*, the requirement of adequate consideration for the contract is met by

Modern's offer of full-time employment coupled with Farrer's signing of the contract containing the covenant not to compete. Consequently, the restrictive covenant would be ancillary to the employment contract and supported by adequate consideration. Thus, the covenant would be valid.

Even if this court had determined that the covenant was not ancillary to the taking of employment, the covenant would still be valid. If an employment contract containing a restrictive covenant is entered into subsequent to employment, it must be supported by new consideration which could be in the form of a corresponding benefit to the employee or a beneficial change in his employment status. . . .

After signing the employment contract, Farrer experienced a significant change in his employment status. He was no longer a provisional employee under the charge of an experienced salesman. Farrer had become his own supervisor solely responsible for the operation of Route Thirty-Six. The case of *M.S. Jacobs & Associates, Inc. v. Duffley* . . . presents facts resembling the case before us. In *M.S. Jacobs*, prior to signing an employment contract, the employee was paid only a salary while working in support of an experienced salesman. But, after signing the employment contract containing the restrictive covenant, the employee was given his own territory and received a commission on his total sales. Our Supreme Court held that the employee had received a substantial beneficial change in his employment constituting sufficient

consideration to support an anticompetition clause in his employment contract. . . . Likewise, Farrer's employment status changed beneficially when the parties reduced their agreement to writing. Hence, the instant restrictive covenant is valid.

In addition to the beneficial change in employment status, Farrer was given the opportunity to increase his earnings substantially. Pursuant to his employment contract, Farrer received 17% of all the cash he collected and paid over to his employer. In addition, Farrer's earnings would increase in direct proportion to the new business he procured on his route. . . . [T]his court [has] ruled that the potential to realize monetary gains due to a change in employment status [is] adequate consideration to support a restrictive covenant entered into after initial employment. . . . Accordingly, Farrer's opportunity to increase his earnings due to his change in employment status is sufficient consideration to support the restrictive covenant in his employment contract.

In conclusion, we hold that the restrictive covenant was ancillary to Farrer's taking of employment and supported by adequate consideration. Therefore, the restrictive covenant is valid and, if the covenant is found to be reasonably limited in time and territory, enforceable. We reverse the lower court decision and remand this case for determination of whether the covenant is reasonably limited in time and territory.

Reversed and remanded. Jurisdiction relinquished.

Case Questions

1. Why did the lower court in this case rule that the restrictive covenant was unenforceable?

2. The Pennsylvania Superior Court ruled that the restrictive covenant was ancillary to the taking of employment. What is the court's rationale?
3. The superior court even goes so far as to say that the covenant would be valid if it had been contained in an employment contract entered into after employment. Why?
4. Why is the presence of consideration so essential to an enforceable agreement?

CAPACITY

In order to create a contract that is legally binding and enforceable, the parties must have the legal capacity to contract. All parties do not have the same legal capacity to enter into a contract, however. Full contractual capacity is met when a person is of legal age without mental disability or incapacity.

It is presumed that all parties to an agreement have full legal capacity to contract. Therefore any party seeking to base a claim or a defense on incapacity has the burden of alleging *and proving* the incapacity. The principal classes given some degree of special protection on their contracts because of their incapacity are (1) minors, (2) insane people, and (3) intoxicated people.

Minors

At common law, people remained minors until they reached the age of twenty-one. Generally, present legislation has reduced this age to eighteen. The law pertaining to minors entering into contracts formerly held that those contracts were void. Now that law has been almost universally changed and holds that such contracts are voidable. This law applies not only to contracts, but also to executed transactions such as a sale.

The law grants minors this right in order to protect them from their lack of judgment and experience, limited will power, and presumed immaturity. A contract between an adult and a minor is voidable only by the minor; the adult must fulfill the obligation, unless the minor decides to avoid the contract. Ordinarily, parents are not liable for contracts entered into by their minor children.

Adults contract with minors at their own peril. Thus an adult party frequently will refuse to contract with or sell to minors because minors are incapable of giving legal assurance that they will not avoid the contract.

Transactions a Minor Cannot Avoid

Through legislation, many states have limited minors' ability to avoid contracts. For instance, many states provide that a contract with a college or university is binding. A purchase of life insurance has also been held to bind a minor. Some statutes take away the right of minors to avoid contracts after they are married. Most states hold that a minor engaging in a business and operating in the same manner as a person having legal capacity will not be permitted to set aside contracts arising from that business or employment. Court decisions or statutes have established this law in order to prevent minors from using the shield of minority to avoid business contracts.

Minors are liable for the reasonable value (not the contract price) of any necessary they purchase, whether goods or services, if they accept and make use of it. The reasonable value of the necessaries, rather than their contract price, is specified to protect them against the possibility that the other party to the agreement has taken advantage of them by overcharging them. If the necessaries have not yet been accepted or received, the minor may disaffirm the contract without liability.

In general, the term *necessaries* includes whatever is needed for a minor's subsistence as measured by age, status, condition in life, and so on. These include food, lodging, education, clothing, and medical services. Objects used for pleasure and ordinary contracts relating to the property or business of the minor are not classified as necessaries.

Disaffirmance of Contract

Minors may avoid both *executed* (completed) and *executory* (incompleted) contracts at any time during their infancy. They may also disaffirm a contract for a reasonable period of time after they attain their majority. In this way, former minors have a reasonable time in which to evaluate transactions made during their infancy. What constitutes a reasonable time depends on the nature of the property involved and the surrounding circumstances. As long as minors do not disaffirm their contracts, they are bound by the terms. They cannot refuse to carry out their part of an agreement, while at the same time requiring the adult party to perform.

Disaffirmance of a contract by a minor may be made by any expression of an intention to repudiate the contract. Disaffirmance need not be verbal or written. If a minor performs an act inconsistent with the continuing validity of a contract, that is considered a disaffirmance. For example, if a minor sells property to Gaskins and later, on reaching majority, sells the same property to Ginger, the second sale to Ginger would be considered a disaffirmance of the contract with Gaskins.

Minors may disaffirm wholly executory contracts, that is, contracts that neither party has performed. In addition, if only the minors have performed, they may disaffirm and recover the money or property they have paid or transferred to an adult. A conflict arises, however, if the contract is wholly executed or if only the adult has performed and the minor has spent what he or she has received and, therefore, cannot make restitution. As a general rule, minors must return whatever they have in their possession of the consideration under the contract; if the consideration has been destroyed, they may nevertheless disaffirm the contract and recover the consideration they have given. For example, suppose Weldon, a minor, purchases an automobile and has an accident that demolishes the car. She may obtain a full refund by disaffirming the contract and also will not be liable for the damage to the car.

A few states, however, hold that if the contract is advantageous to the minor and if the adult has been fair in every respect, the contract cannot be disaffirmed unless the minor returns the consideration. In the preceding example, the minor would have to replace the reasonable value of the damaged automobile before she could disaffirm the contract and receive the consideration she gave for the automobile. These states also take into account the depreciation of the property while in the possession of the minor.

Although minors may disaffirm or avoid their contracts before reaching their majority, they cannot effectively ratify or approve their contracts until they have attained their majority. Ratification may consist of any expression or action that indicates an intention to be bound by the contract, and may come from the actions of the minor who has now reached majority. For example, if a minor acquired property under a contract and, after reaching majority, makes use of or sells the property, he or she will be deemed to have ratified the contract.

Some states have enacted statutes that prevent minors from disaffirming contracts if they have fraudulently misrepresented their age. Generally, however, the fact that minors have misrepresented their age in order to secure a contract that they could not have otherwise obtained will not later prevent them from disaffirming that contract on the basis of their minority. Most courts will hold minors liable for any resulting damage to, or deterioration of, property they received under the contract. Minors are also generally liable for their torts; consequently, in most states, the other party to the contract could recover in a tort action for deceit. In any case, the other party to the contract may avoid it because of the minor's fraud.

Insane People

People are said to be insane when they do not understand the nature and consequences of an act at the time of their entering into an agreement. In such cases, they lack capacity and their contracts are either void or voidable. The contracts of a person who has been judicially declared insane by a court are void. Such a person will have a judicially appointed guardian who is under a duty to transact all business for him or her.

The contracts of insane people who have not been judicially declared insane are generally voidable. Although such people may not ratify or disaffirm a contract during their temporary insanity, they may do so once they regain their sanity. However, if the contract is executed and the sane party to the contract acts in good faith, not knowing that the other party is temporarily insane, most courts refuse to allow the temporarily insane person the right to avoid the contract, unless the consideration that has been received can be returned. On the other hand, if the sane party knows that the other party is mentally incompetent, the contract is voidable at the option of the insane person.

As in the case of minors, the party possessing capacity to contract has no right to disaffirm a contract merely because the insane party has the right to do so. The rule in regard to necessaries purchased by temporarily insane persons is the same as in the case of minors.

If persons enter into a contract when they are so intoxicated that they do not know at the time they are executing a contract, the contract is voidable at their option. The position of the intoxicated person is, therefore, much the same as that of the temporarily insane person.

ILLEGALITY

An agreement is *illegal* when either its formation or performance is criminal, tortious, or opposed to public policy. When an agreement is illegal, courts will not allow either party to sue for performance of the contract. The court will literally "leave the parties where it finds them." Generally, if one of the parties has performed, that person cannot recover either the value of the performance or any property or goods transferred to the other party. There are three exceptions to this rule, however.

First, if the law that the agreement violates is intended for the protection of one of the parties, that party may seek relief. For example, both federal and state statutes require that a corporation follow certain procedures before stocks and bonds may be offered for sale to the public. It is illegal to sell such securities without having complied with the legal requirements. People who have purchased securities from a corporation that has not complied with the law may obtain a refund of the purchase price if they desire to do so.

Second, when the parties are not equally at fault, the one less at fault is granted relief when the public interest is advanced by doing so. This rule is applied to illegal agreements that are induced by undue influence, duress, or fraud. In such cases, the courts do not regard the defrauded or coerced party as being an actual participant in the wrong and will, therefore, allow restitution.

A third exception occurs within very strict limits. A person who repents before actually having performed any illegal part of an illegal contract may rescind it and obtain restitution. For example, suppose James and Richardo wager on the outcome of a baseball game. Each gives $500 to Smith, the stakeholder, who agrees to give $1,000 to the winner. Prior to the game, either James or Richardo could recover $500 from Smith through legal action, since the execution of the illegal agreement would not yet have occurred.

If the objectives of an agreement are illegal, the agreement is illegal and unenforceable, even though the parties were not aware, when they arrived at their agreement, that it was illegal.

On the other hand, as a general rule, even if one party to an agreement knows that the other party intends to use the subject matter of the contract for illegal purposes, this fact will not make the agreement illegal unless the illegal purpose involves a serious crime. For example, suppose Aiello lends money to Roja, at a legal interest rate, knowing Roja is going to use the money to gamble illegally. After Roja loses her money, she refuses to repay Aiello on the grounds the agreement was illegal. Aiello can recover her money through court action, even though she knew Roja was going to illegally gamble with the money she lent her.

Contracts Against Public Policy

A contract provision is contrary to public policy if it is injurious to the interest of the public, contradicts some established interests of society, violates a statute, or tends to interfere with the public health, safety, or general welfare. The term *public policy* is vague and variable; it changes as our social, economic, and political climates change. One example is the illegal lobbying agreement, an agreement by which one party uses bribery, threats of a loss of votes, or any other improper means to procure or prevent the adoption of particular legislation by a lawmaking body, such as Congress or a state legislature. Such agreements are clearly contrary to the public interest since they interfere with the workings of the democratic process. They are both illegal and void.

The court in the following case ruled that Iowa's public policy was not violated by an automobile liability insurance policy that excluded from coverage bodily injury to members of the insured owner's family.

Principal Casualty Insurance Company v. Blair
500 N.W.2d 67
Supreme Court of Iowa
May 19, 1993

Schultz, Justice

We must decide in this appeal whether a family exclusion provision contained in a homeowners insurance policy is effective to prevent coverage for personal liability and medical payments to others. The Principal Casualty Insurance Company (Principal) issued a homeowners policy to Stephen and Debbie Blair. Debbie Blair, individually and as mother and next best friend of Michael Blair, commenced an action for damages against her husband, Stephen Blair, for injuries their son Michael sustained when a wheel came off of his bicycle and caused him to fall. In her petition, Debbie alleged that Stephen had negligently assembled the bicycle.

Principal commenced this declaratory judgment action, claiming its policy did not provide liability coverage for Stephen and medical payments coverage for Michael because of its family exclusion clauses. The district court sustained Principal's motion for summary judgment, ruling that there was no insurance coverage. We affirm.

In this case the facts are not in dispute. Our review is to determine whether the district court correctly determined the legal consequences arising from the terms of the insurance policy. . . .

Principal's homeowners policy provides clauses for personal liability protection and for medical payment coverage. The "Personal Liability Coverage" for an insured excludes coverage for bodily injury to "your relatives residing in your household. . . ." The policy clause for "Medical Payment to Others Coverage" pays medical expenses for persons who sustain bodily injury caused by activities of an insured person;" however, the clause specifies that the insurer does not cover injury to an "insured person." One of the definitions of an "insured person" is "your relatives residing in your household." Michael Blair, a minor, resides with Stephen and Debbie Blair, the named insureds. Principal named all of the Blairs as defendants in this lawsuit. Hereinafter we shall refer to them as the Blairs.

Principal maintains the exclusion of "relatives residing in your household" (family exclusion), deprives the Blairs of liability coverage and medical payments coverage. The Blairs contend the "family exclusion" is void because it is contrary to public policy. . . .

I. Public Policy

The Blairs present affidavits to the effect that no other Iowa insurers offer coverage to insureds who negligently injure family members residing in the household. The Blairs urge that a significant population is irrationally excluded from insurance coverage contrary to public policy.

The Blairs cite us no case authority to support their position. We find no cases of our own involving the application of the "family exclusion" to a homeowners policy; however, many other jurisdictions have recognized the validity of the exclusion without discussing public policy.

We have stated that the term "public policy" is not susceptible of an exact definition, but "a court ought not enforce a contract which tends to be injurious to the public or contrary to the public good." *Walker v. American Family Mut. Ins. Co.,* 340 N.W.2d 599, 601 (Iowa 1983). Further, we have observed that when a court determines whether a contract is contrary to the public good it must be cautious and act only in cases free from doubt. We must harmonize public policy and the freedom of parties to contract. In *Walker,* we reviewed our statutes and case law and rejected an attempt to nullify a clause in an automobile insurance policy excluding liability coverage for bodily injury to an "insured or any member of the family of the insured residing in the same household as the insured." While *Walker* involved the named insured, we believe the same policy arguments are applicable to a member of the household.

No statutes or court cases have been cited that require a private citizen to obtain homeowners insurance that provides coverage for negligently injuring family members. We disagree with the Blairs' contention that the lack of insurers willing to provide the type of coverage they seek in this case should cause us to act. We believe that this is a policy decision for the legislature, not the judiciary. Further, we believe that we should follow the lead of the jurisdictions that have rejected similar public policy claims. . . .

We affirm the judgment entered by the district court.

Affirmed.

Case Questions

1. The trial and appellate courts were urged to invalidate a clause in a homeowner's insurance policy on public policy grounds. Explain the basis of the public policy argument.

2. What does the Supreme Court of Iowa decide? What is the basis for the decision?

Agreements to Commit Crimes

An agreement is illegal and therefore void when it calls for the commission of any act that constitutes a crime. Agreements to commit murder, robbery, arson, burglary, and assault are obvious examples, but less obvious violations are also subject to the rule.

Agreements to Commit Civil Wrongs

An agreement that calls for the commission of a civil wrong is also illegal and void. Examples are agreements to slander a third person, to defraud another, to damage another's goods, or to infringe upon another's trademark or patent.

A contract that calls for the performance of an act or the rendering of a service may be illegal for one of two reasons. (1) The act or service itself may be illegal (illegal *per se*), and thus any contract involving this act or service is illegal. Prostitution is a good example. (2) Certain other service contracts are not illegal *per se*, but may be illegal if the party performing or contracting to perform the service is not legally entitled to do so. This latter condition refers to the fact that a license is required before a person is entitled to perform certain functions for others. For example, doctors, dentists, lawyers, architects, surveyors, real estate brokers, and other rendering specialized professional services must be licensed by the appropriate body before entering into contracts with the general public.

All the states have enacted regulatory statutes concerning the practice of various professions and the performance of business and other activities. However, these statutes are not uniform in their working or in their scope. Many of the statutes specifically provide that all agreements that violate them shall be void and unenforceable. When such a provision is lacking, the court will look to the intent of the statute. If the court is of the opinion that a statute was enacted for the protection of the public, it will hold that agreements in violation of the statute are void. If, however, the court concludes that the particular statute was intended solely to raise revenue, then it will hold that contracts entered in violation of the statute are legal and enforceable.

A contract that has for its purpose the restraint of trade and nothing more is illegal and void. A contract to monopolize trade, to suppress competition, or not to compete in business, therefore, cannot be enforced because the sole purpose of the agreement would be to eliminate competition. A contract that aims at establishing a monopoly is not only unenforceable, but also renders the parties to the agreement liable to indictment for the commission of a crime.

When a business is sold, it is commonly stated in a contract that the seller shall not go into the same or similar business again within a certain geographical area, or for a certain period of time, or both. In early times, such agreements were held void since they deprived the public of the service of the person who agreed not to compete, reduced competition, and exposed the public to monopoly. Gradually, the law began to recognize the validity of such restrictive provisions. To the modern courts, the question is whether under the circumstances the restriction imposed upon one party is reasonable or whether the restriction is more extensive than is required to protect the other party. A similar situation arises when employees agree not to compete with their employers should they leave their jobs.

The plaintiff in the following case sought to invalidate a postemployment noncompetition agreement he had entered into with the defendant.

Diaz v. Indian Head, Inc.
402 F.Supp. 111
U.S. District Court, Northern District
of Illinois
March 12, 1975

Decker, District Judge

This is a diversity case in which a former employee seeks to have declared unenforceable a provision in his employment contract which precludes competition with his former employer for eighteen months subsequent to termination. Plaintiff Albert J. Diaz is a resident of Maryland. The defendant, Indian Head, Inc. (hereafter, "Indian Head"), is a Delaware corporation, also doing business as "Information Handling Services" in Colorado. . . . The employment agreement specifically provides that New York law shall govern. . . .

Indian Head is currently one in a growing field of over a hundred companies in the microform publishing business. These companies reproduce various publications on little plastic microfilm cards. Aside from gaining the ease of storing and preserving publications in this form, the buyer of these cards benefits when he desires esoteric, arcane, and hard to locate publications because the market demand may simply be too low to justify economically conventional printing or reprinting of an item in the quantity needed. Because of this benefit, the companies in this field have to develop expertise in selecting publications to replicate and in advertising those selections to likely customers. A company which is unable to develop this expertise would either have to rely solely on unsolicited orders, or else end up replicating those very items which by definition are not in demand, and hoping to find, by chance, some one or more customers who wanted them. Because of similar considerations, these companies must develop contacts with likely customers including libraries and universities, and they must develop marketing methods. These goals are partly accomplished through representation of the companies at booths in conventions of likely customers, such as librarians.

Plaintiff Diaz developed in himself that special expertise that is so important in this field. Indeed, there is agreement that he is one of the ten or fifteen best qualified persons in the country for selecting those subjects and titles which would be profitable to replicate in microform. Further, in working for Indian Head and other such companies, Diaz has had substantial contact with many actual and potential customers. Part of that contact arose through his attendance at various conventions and through being involved with orders actually placed. In addition, while with Indian Head and other companies, Diaz has been in a position to plan the selection and marketing of titles. There is no doubt that the services of Albert J. Diaz would be of great value to a company in this field. . . .

In February 1975, Diaz elected to terminate his employment with Indian Head and accepted an offer of employment with the Northern Engraving Company. . . . Diaz's position at Indian Head has since been filled. Commendably, Diaz, according to his testimony, has refrained from actually competing, pending this court's construction of the agreement.

New York law looks with disfavor upon agreements that prevent a talented person from engaging in his or her chosen profession. In the balance between the public interest in productivity, the employer's legitimate business interest, and the employee's interest, the first weighs more heavily. The method of enforcement of non-competition agreements is generally injunction. For these reasons, post-employment non-competition agreements have been held void unless they threatened irreparable injury to the employer's legitimate business interest. . . . This injury generally falls into one of three categories:

1. Trade secrets might be divulged. . . .
2. Particular customers might be swept away by the new competitor, or there might be a loss of "good will" which had been bargained for at the time of employment. . . .
3. The employee may have been special, unique, or extraordinary. . . .

What these categories of injury all have in common is the prospect that the employee will *affirmatively* harm the former employer other than through merely being productive for another employer. The employee may be *taking away* existing customers. . . . Where a trade secret is involved, what is at stake is a company asset which, like the business of a major customer, is not inextricably related to that special talent of the employee which New York law seeks to keep productive for the public benefit.

No issue of trade secrets is presented in this case. However, the question presented is whether, by virtue of his familiarity with the pool from which customers are drawn and with specific customers of Indian Head, competition from Diaz may amount to irreparable injury. The question must be answered in the negative. The customers, actual and potential, are already known or available to Indian Head's competitors. . . .

The names of libraries are not secret. Even if a list of known available customers was acquired at great expense over many years, a former employee would ordinarily be free to turn to it. . . . More importantly, Indian Head does not rely on a limited set of customers who supply most of its business, as might be the case of a medical practice in a small area, such as oral surgery. . . . Furthermore, the small-volume-per-customers nature of Indian Head's business renders insignificant the possibility that a few extremely important clients will follow Diaz rather than stay with their current microfilm supplier, or that a particular order will be pre-empted. . . .

The remaining major issue is whether Diaz was in some way unique or extraordinary in the sense that New York policy requires the enforcement of his agreement with Indian Head. To begin with, no New York case has been cited or discovered in which such an agreement has been enforced on this rationale in a comparable fact (managerial or sales) situation in the absence of customer solicitation or trade secrets. This qualification may of course be fulfilled where the individual is not merely very talented, but what he does is unique, such as the way he sings. . . . The fact that Diaz excels in his professed craft does not make his services "unique." More must, of course, be shown to establish such a quality than that the employee excels at his work or that his performance is of high value to his employer. . . .

The court is aware of *Bradford v. New York Times Company*, . . . which found a vice president with 16 years experience with a single newspaper to be unique enough to make a non-competition agreement enforceable. The Second Circuit relied in part on the employee's high administrative position in so finding. The employee, Bradford, was being compensated for his period of non-competition, as is Diaz. However, Diaz's one-year association with Indian Head is much less than Bradford's 16 years. Furthermore, *Bradford* paid little attention to New York's strong policy of keeping talented people productive. . . .

Accordingly, this court concludes that plaintiff is entitled to a declaratory judgment that the agreement between Albert J. Diaz and Indian Head, Inc., is void and unenforceable insofar as it restricts Diaz from entering into competition after his full-time employment with Indian Head terminates. . . .

Case Questions

1. List some specific employment examples where a postemployment noncompetition agreement would be enforceable.
2. The employment contract specifically provided that New York law should govern. Why would the parties put such a provision in their contract? Could the right to choose and agree on the state law that shall govern a contract be abused?

WRITING

Every state has statutes requiring that certain contracts be in writing to be enforceable. Called the *statutes of frauds*, these statutes are generally in agreement as to their material provisions and are based on "An Act for the Prevention of Frauds and Perjuries," passed by the English Parliament in 1677.

Six kinds of contracts are governed by the statute of frauds: (1) an agreement by an executor or administrator to answer for the debt of the decedent, (2) an agreement made in consideration of marriage, (3) an agreement to answer for the debt or default of another, (4) an agreement that cannot be performed in one year, (5) an agreement for the sale of an interest in real property, and (6) an agreement for the sale of goods above a certain dollar amount. Which of these contracts are included within the statute of frauds may differ from state to state.

The writing required by the statute need not be in any special form or use any special language. Usually, the terms that must be shown on the face of the writing include the names of the parties, the terms and conditions of the contract, the consideration, a reasonably certain description of the subject matter of the contract, and the signature of the party, or the party's agent, against whom enforcement is sought. These terms need not be on one piece of paper but may be on several pieces of paper, provided that their relation or connection with each other appears on their face by the physical attachment of the papers to each other or by reference from one writing to the other. At least one, if not all, of the papers must be signed by the party against whom enforcement is sought. (The requirements of memorandums involving the sale of goods differ.)

Agreement by Executor or Administrator

A promise by an executor or administrator to answer for the debt of the decedent is within the statute and must be in writing to be enforced. In order for the statute to operate, the executor's promise must be to pay out of the executor's own personal assets (pocket); a promise to pay a debt out of the assets of a decedent's estate is not required to be in writing.

Agreement in Consideration of Marriage

Agreements made in consideration of marriage are to be in writing. Mutual promises to marry are not within the statute, as the consideration is the exchanged promise, not the marriage itself. However, promises made to a prospective spouse or third party with marriage as the consideration are within the statute. For example, a promise by one prospective spouse to convey property to the other, provided the marriage is entered into, is required to be in writing. Similarly, if a third party, say a rich relative, promises to pay a certain sum of money to a prospective spouse if a marriage is entered into, the promise will be unenforceable unless in writing.

Agreement to Answer for the Debt of Another

Agreements to answer for the debt or default of another shall be unenforceable unless in writing. The rationale for this provision is that the guarantor or surety has received none of the benefits for which the debt was incurred and, therefore, should be bound only by the exact terms of the promise. For example, Bob desires to purchase a new law text on credit. The bookstore is unsure as to Bob's ability to pay, so Bob brings in his friend, Ellen, who says, "If Bob does not pay for the text, I will." In effect, the promise is that the bookstore must first try to collect from Bob, who is primarily liable. After it has exhausted all possibilities of collecting from him, then it may come to Ellen to receive payment. Ellen is therefore secondarily liable. Ellen has promised to answer for Bob's debt even though she will not receive the benefit of the new law text; therefore, her agreement must be in writing to be enforceable.

This situation must be distinguished from those in which the promise to answer for the debt of another is an original promise; that is, the promisor's objective is to be primarily liable. For example, Bob wants to purchase a new law text. When he takes the book to the cashier, his friend Ellen steps in and says, "Give him the book. I will pay for it." Ellen has made an original promise to the bookstore with the objective of becoming primarily liable. Such a promise need not be in writing to be enforceable.

Sometimes it is difficult to ascertain whether the purpose of the promisor is to become primarily liable or secondarily liable. In resolving the issue, courts will sometimes use the leading object rule. This rule looks not only to the promise itself, but also to the individual for whose benefit the promise was made. The logic of the rule is that if the leading object of the promise is the personal benefit of the promisor, then the promisor must have intended to become primarily liable. In such a case, the promise will be deemed to be original and need not be in writing to be enforced.

Agreements Not to Be Performed in One Year

Most statutes require contracts that cannot be performed within one year from the time the contract is formed to be in writing. This determination is made by referring to the intentions of the parties, to the nature of the performance, and to the terms of the contract itself. For example, if Jack agrees to build a house for Betty, the question is whether the contract is capable of being performed within one year. Houses can be built in one year. Therefore, this agreement need not be in writing even if Jack actually takes more than one year to build the house.

It is important to remember that the *possibility* that the contract can be performed within one year is enough to take it out of the operation of the statute regardless of how long performance actually took.

Agreement Conveying an Interest in Real Property

The statute of frauds generally renders unenforceable oral agreements conveying interests in real estate. Most problems center on what an interest in real estate is and whether the agreement contemplates the transfer of any title, ownership, or possession of real property. Both must be involved to bring the statute into effect. Real property has been held to commonly include land, leaseholds, easements, standing timber, and under certain conditions, improvements and fixtures attached to the land.

The landlord in the following case brought suit to enforce a written but unsigned two-year lease. The court ruled that there was no leasehold and that only a month-to-month tenancy existed because the requirements of the statute of frauds were not satisfied.

Mulford v. Borg-Warner Acceptance Corp.

495 N.Y.S.2d 493
Supreme Court of New York,
Appellate Division
November 21, 1985

Harvey, Justice

Appeal from an order and judgment of the Supreme Court at Special Term (Murphy, J.), entered April 19, 1985 in Madison County, which granted defendant's motion for summary judgment dismissing the complaint.

This is an action involving a written lease for certain office space in the Village of Canastota, Madison County, for a period of two years. The lease was never subscribed by anyone on behalf of defendant. Prior to the lease in issue, there were three written leases between these parties involving space in the same office building owned by plaintiff. Each lease expired on March 31, 1983. Prior to the expiration date, plaintiff proposed a new lease for a three-year period involving the same accommodations. Defendant informed plaintiff that it would not lease one of the office suites previously occupied by it and that, as to the remaining space, it would only be interested in a two-year lease. Thereafter, and on the expiration date of the original lease, plaintiff prepared a written two-year lease, subscribed it and delivered it to defendant. Although defendant retained possession of the property described in the document and paid rent at a rate in accordance with the provisions contained therein, it never signed the new lease. On August 2, 1983, defendant notified plaintiff that it was quitting the premises as of August 31, 1983, and paid the rent for that month.

Plaintiff commenced this action alleging that the unexecuted lease was a valid lease and demanded unpaid rent and other expenses alleged to have resulted from defendant's default. After issue was joined, defendant moved . . . for summary judgment dismissing the complaint, relying upon General Obligations Law § 5-703(2) as an absolute defense. Special Term granted the motion and this appeal ensued.

General Obligations Law § 5-703(2) provides:

> "A contract for the leasing for a longer period than one year, or for the sale, of any real property, or an interest therein, is void unless the contract or some note or memorandum, is in writing, subscribed by the party to be charged, or by his lawful agent thereunto authorized by writing."

Although plaintiff freely admits that the proposed lease was never subscribed by defendant, he contends that signed checks delivered to plaintiff for monthly rentals in the amounts as would have been required by the proposed lease constitute sufficient memoranda to satisfy the Statute of Frauds. We disagree. The law requires that the memoranda embody all the essential and material parts of the lease contemplated with such clarity and certainty as to show that the parties have agreed on all the material parts of the lease contemplated. . . . The only material factors which could be established by the checks were the fact of possession and the amount of monthly rental. Nothing contained in the checks or any memoranda attached thereto gave any clue as to the term of the lease. The notation on the memo portion of the first check stating "additional rent due for April (new lease)" is consistent with a month-to-month tenancy. This notation is insufficient to establish a tenancy involving all the provisions, including the term, of the proposed written but unsigned lease. We conclude, therefore, that defendant's occupancy of the premises from April 1, 1983 to August 31, 1983 was on the basis of a month-to-month tenancy. . . .

Order and judgment modified, on the law and the facts, without costs, by granting plaintiff judgment for one month's rent for September 1983 . . . and, as so modified, affirmed.

Case Questions

1. What is the rationale behind requiring that contracts for longer than one year satisfy the statute of frauds?
2. The plaintiff argued that the monthly rental checks paid by the defendant to the plaintiff should be held to satisfy the statute of frauds. Why does the appellate court disagree?

Sale of Goods

Generally, a contract for the sale of goods for the price of $500 or more is not enforceable unless there is some writing to serve as evidence that a contract has been entered into. An informal or incomplete writing will be sufficient to satisfy the UCC statute of frauds, providing that it (1) indicates that a contract between the parties was entered into, (2) is signed by the party against whom enforcement is sought, and (3) contains a statement of the quantity of goods sold. The price, time and place of delivery, quality of the goods, and warranties may be omitted without invalidating the writing, as the UCC permits these terms to be shown by outside evidence, custom and usage, and prior dealings between the parties. Thus, the provisions that must be included in a writing that will conform with the UCC statute of frauds are substantially less than those necessary in a writing that evidences one of the other types of contracts governed by the statute of frauds. Under the UCC, the contract will be enforced only as to the quantity of goods shown in the writing (UCC 2-201 [1]).

Parol Evidence Rule

After contracting parties have successfully negotiated a contract, they often sign a written document that contains what they intend to be a definitive and complete statement of the agreed upon terms. Courts will usually presume that such a writing is accurate. Therefore, under the *parol evidence rule*, evidence of alleged prior agreements or terms not contained in the written document will be inadmissible if offered to change the terms of the document.

The parol evidence rule would not apply, however, where the contracting parties have prepared only a partial memorandum or other incomplete writing. In that context the incomplete writing is only partially integrated (i.e., it is intended to be a final and complete statement of the terms adressed in the memorandum but not as to omitted terms which can be proven extrinsically). There are several exceptions to the parol evidence rule. For example, parol evidence can be used to prove fraud or the absence of consideration in the formation of a contract and to explain the meaning of ambiguous words.

The following case involves the sale of goods at a price in excess of $500 pursuant to an oral agreement. The court had to rule whether a signed check was a sufficient writing to satisfy the requirements of the UCC statute of frauds.

Jinright v. Russell
123 Ga. App. 766, 182 S.E.2d 328
Court of Appeals of Georgia
April 28, 1971

Whitman, Judge

This is an appeal by the defendants below from the denial of their motion for a summary judgment. The complaint alleges that the parties made an oral agreement whereby the defendants agreed: "[T]o purchase from the plaintiff all fixtures, stock, good will and name or trade name located in the establishment known as the Bottle Shop Liquor Store. . . . for a sum of $6500. Said money being payable $1500 down and the balance payable as soon as the license was transferred."

It is further alleged that the defendants gave the plaintiff a check in the amount of $1500 as partial payment of the contract price, but then stopped payment on the check. The defendants denied the material allegations of the complaint and set up several matters in defense.

One ground of the defendants' motion for summary judgment which is urged on appeal is that: "[T]he alleged agreement sued upon is oral and is void and unenforceable in that it is for the sale of goods at a price of more than $500 and that no memorandum in writing was executed pursuant to the Statute of Frauds and there has not been sufficient past per-

formance so as to removed said alleged agreement from the application of the Statute of Frauds."

Both defendants filed an affidavit in support of their motion. The affidavits admit that there were negotiations between the parties regarding the sale of the store. It is deposed that they were quoted a price of $5500, and further that they did give plaintiff a check for $1500. [B]ut when the plaintiff mentioned a balance remaining different from what they had understood, "rather than get into a hassle . . . over the purchase price, we stopped payment on the check and discontinued negotiations the same day it [the check] was given."

The check was before the lower court for consideration. It is for the amount of $1500 payable to the plaintiff, and is drawn on Mrs. Hurshell Jinright's account with the Fourth National Bank of Columbus, Columbus, Georgia, and is signed "Mrs. Hurshell Jinright." The check bears the notation "For Binder on Store." It is endorsed by the plaintiff. On its face the check is stamped "Payment Stopped."

The applicable statute . . . provides: ". . . Except as otherwise provided in this section a contract for the sale of goods for the price of $500 or more is not enforceable by way of action or defense unless there is some writing sufficient to indicate that a contract for sale has been made between the parties and signed by the party against whom enforcement is sought or by his authorized agent or broker. A writing is not insufficient because it omits or incorrectly states terms agreed upon but the contract is not enforceable under this paragraph beyond the quantity of goods shown in such writing."

The Comment to Section 2-201(1) of the 1962 official text of the UCC . . . states: "The required writing need not contain all the material terms of the contract and such material terms as are stated need not be precisely stated. All that is required is that the writing afford a basis for believing that the offered oral evidence rests on a real transaction. It may be written in lead pencil on a scratch pad. It need not indicate which party is the buyer and which the seller. The only term which must appear is the quantity term which need not be accurately stated but recovery is limited to the amount stated. The price, time and place of payment or delivery, the general quality of the goods, or any particular warranties may all be omitted. . . .

"Only three definite and invariable requirements as to the memorandum are made by this subsection. First, it must evidence a contract for the sale of goods; second, it must be 'signed,' a word which includes any authentication which identifies the party to be charged; and third, it must specify a quantity." . . .

In our view, the signed check in the present case, with its notation "For Binder on Store," meets all the requirements of a writing sufficient to indicate that contract for sale was made between the parties. The check does not prove a contract, but it would authorize the introduction of oral evidence toward that end. The party asserting the contract still must bear the burden of proving its existence and the terms. . . .

Judgment affirmed.

Case
Questions

1. What is the policy behind the decision of the court?
2. What constituted the writing in this case? What were the terms included?

ASPECTS OF CONTRACT PERFORMANCE

When parties enter into a contract, they generally expect that each side will fully perform in the manner called for in the agreement. Often, however, problems arise and full performance does not occur, as in the following examples.

Accord and Satisfaction

One party may agree to take something less than full performance to satisfy the agreement. For example, suppose that A asks B to pay a debt for services rendered and B states that he is too poor to pay the full amount. A may agree to accept payment for only half of the debt. In this situation, the parties have worked out an accord and satisfaction. An *accord* is the offer of something different from what was due under the original contract. The *satisfaction* is the agreement to take it. Since the law favors a compromise, courts try to uphold any good-faith modification agreement.

Anticipatory Repudiation

Suppose that A, who is one party to a contract, clearly manifests that she will not perform at the scheduled time. The other party, B, has a choice at common law. B may either sue immediately or ignore A's repudiation and wait for the day of performance. If B waits, A may change her mind and still perform according to the original contract. Under UCC section 2-610, the injured party may not wait until the day of performance. B may wait for a change of mind only for a commercially reasonable period of time after repudiation before taking action.

Warranties

A *warranty* is a contractual obligation that sets a standard by which performance of the contract is measured. If the warranties are created by the parties to the contract, they are *express*. Under UCC section 2-313, express warranties exist whenever a seller affirms facts or describes goods, makes a promise about the goods, or displays a sample model.

If warranties are imposed by law, they are *implied*. There are two types of implied warranties under UCC section 2-314 and section 2-315. (1) When a merchant sells goods that are reputed to be fit for the ordinary purpose for which they are intended and are of average quality and properly labeled and packaged, the merchant is bound by an *implied warranty of merchantability*. (2) When the seller has reason to know some particular (nonordinary) purpose for which the buyer has relied on the seller's skill or judgment in making a selection, the seller is bound by an *implied warranty of fitness* for a particular purpose.

Implied warranties may be disclaimed by a conspicuous disclaimer statement that the goods are being sold "as is." Once an express warranty is created, however, it cannot be disclaimed and any attempt to do so is void. The Magnuson-Moss Federal Warranty Act is an act requiring that written warranties for consumer products be categorized as "full" or "limited" so that consumers know what type of warranty protection they are getting. In addition, under this act, a consumer may sue under both the federal and state warranties to recover actual damages.

Originally, a warranty was enforceable only by purchasers, but the trend has been to extend the warranty to nonbuyers (such as recipients of gifts) who have been injured by the defective product.

Discharge, Rescission, and Novation

A *discharge* from a duty to perform occurs because of objective impossibility, by operation of law, or by agreement. Thus one party may die or become physically incapable of performing, a statute may be passed that prevents a party from performing, or a duty to perform may be discharged in bankruptcy. Parties can also agree to end their contractual relationship through a rescission. In a *rescission* each party gives up its right to performance from the other; this constitutes sufficient consideration for the discharge. A *novation* occurs when a promisee agrees to release the original promisor from a duty and enters into a new agreement with another party.

Transfers of Duties and Rights

Sometimes one of the original parties to a contract decides to transfer its rights or duties to some third person who was not originally a party to the agreement. The transfer of rights is called an *assignment*, and the transfer of duties is called a *delegation*. An assignor assigns his or her rights to an assignee. For example, a creditor (the assignor) may decide to transfer her right to collect money owed by a debtor to a finance company (the assignee).

In another example, Smith may contract with a builder to construct a garage next to her house using the turnkey method of construction (this means that the developer finances and builds the garage and receives payment when it is completed). The builder would negotiate a bank loan to finance the project, and the bank probably would negotiate a requirement that the contractor transfer his rights to payment to the bank as security for the loan. A right is not assignable if it significantly affects the corresponding duty associated with that right. Thus Smith probably would not be permitted to assign her right (to have the builder construct a garage) to her sister who lives twenty miles away, since the added distance would be a significant detriment to the building contractor.

A person contractually obligated to perform a duty may often delegate that duty to a third person. If Smith contracts with a painter to paint her new garage, the painter could delegate that duty to other painters. A party cannot delegate a duty if there is a personal component involved such that the duty can only be performed by the party to the original agreement. For example, the personal component exists when a person contracts with a famous photographer to take her portrait. The photographer in this situation would not be permitted to delegate the duty to just any other photographer.

An assignee is legally responsible for any claims that were originally available against the assignor. Thus the debtor would be entitled to raise his or her defenses (such as capacity, duress, illegality, or mistake) against the finance agency that were available against the creditor. The rules are similarly strict vis-à-vis the delegation of a duty. Smith's painter would be responsible if the painter to whom he delegated the painting duty (painter #2) performed inadequately. If Smith agrees to a novation, however, the original contracting painter could be relieved of his duty to perform and painter #2 could be substituted.

Statutory provisions generally require that some assignments be in writing. Statutes also prohibit contractual restrictions on most assignments of rights.

The following case illustrates what happens when one original contracting party assigns rights and delegates duties over the objection of the other contracting party.

Macke Company v. Pizza of Gaithersburg, Inc.

270 A.2d 645
Court of Appeals of Maryland
November 10, 1970

Singley, Judge

The appellees and defendants below, Pizza of Gaithersburg, Inc.; Pizzeria, Inc.; The Pizza Pie Corp., Inc. and Pizza Oven, Inc., four corporations under the common ownership of Sidney Ansell, Thomas S. Sherwood and Eugene Early and the same individuals as partners or proprietors (the Pizza Shops) operated at six locations in Montgomery and Prince George's Counties. The appellees had arranged to have installed in each of their locations cold drink vending machines owned by Virginia Coffee Service, Inc., and on 30 December 1966, this arrangement was formalized at five of the locations, by contracts for terms of one year, automatically renewable for a like term in the absence of 30 days' written notice. A similar contract for the sixth location, operated by Pizza of Gaithersburg, Inc., was entered into on 25 July 1967.

On 30 December 1967, Virginia's assets were purchased by The Macke Company (Macke) and the six contracts were assigned to Macke by Virginia. In January, 1968, the Pizza Shops attempted to terminate the five contracts having the December anniversary date, and in February, the contract which had the July anniversary date.

Macke brought suit in the Circuit Court for Montgomery County against each of the Pizza Shops for damages for breach of contract. From judgments for the defendants, Macke has appealed.

The lower court based the result which it reached on two grounds: first, that the Pizza Shops, when they contracted with Virginia, relied on its skill, judgment and reputation, which made impossible a delegation of Virginia's duties to Macke; and second, that the damages claimed could not be shown with reasonable certainty. These conclusions are challenged by Macke.

In the absence of a contrary provision —and there was none here—rights and duties under an executory bilateral contract may be assigned and delegated, subject to the exception that duties under a contract to provide personal services may never be delegated, nor rights be assigned under a contract where *delectus personae** was an ingredient of the bargain. . . .

The six machines were placed on the appellees' premises under a printed "Agreement-Contract" which identified the "customer," gave its place of business, described the vending machine, and then provided:

"TERMS

"1. The Company will install on the Customer's premises the above listed equipment in good operating order and stocked with merchandise.

"2. The location of this equipment will be such as to permit accessibility to persons desiring use of same. This equipment shall remain the property of the Company and shall not be moved

*Delectus personae means choice of person.—*Ed.*

from the location at which installed, except by the Company.

"3. For equipment requiring electricity and water, the Customer is responsible for electrical receptacle and water outlet within ten (10) feet of the equipment location. The Customer is also responsible to supply the Electrical Power and Water needed.

"4. The Customer will exercise every effort to protect this equipment from abuse or damage.

"5. The Company will be responsible for all licenses and taxes on the equipment and sale of products.

"6. This Agreement-Contract is for a term of one (1) year from the date indicated herein and will be automatically renewed for a like period, unless thirty (30) day written notice is given by either party to terminate service.

"7. Commission on monthly sales will be paid by the Company to the Customer at the following rate: . . . "

The rate provided in each of the agreements was "30% of Gross Receipts to $300.00 monthly[,] 35% over [$]300.00," except for the agreement with Pizza of Gaithersburg, Inc., which called for "40% of Gross Receipts."

. . . We cannot regard the agreements as contracts for personal services. They were either a license or concession granted Virginia by the appellees, or a lease of a portion of the appellees' premises, with Virginia agreeing to pay a percentage of gross sales as a license or concession fee or as rent, . . . and were assignable by Virginia unless they imposed on Virginia duties of a personal or unique character which could not be delegated. . . . [T]he agreements with Virginia were silent as to the details of the working arrangements and contained only a provision requiring Virginia to "install . . . the above listed equipment and . . . maintain the equipment in good operating order and stocked with merchandise." . . . Moreover, the difference between the service the Pizza Shops happened to be getting from Virginia and what they expected to get from Macke did not mount up to such a material change in the performance of obligations under the agreements as would justify the appellees' refusal to recognize the assignment. . . . Modern authorities . . . hold that, absent provision to the contrary, a duty may be delegated, as distinguished from a right which can be assigned, and that the promisee cannot rescind, if the quality of the performance remains materially the same.

Restatement, Contracts § 160(3) (1932) reads, in part:

"Performance or offer of performance by a person delegated has the same legal effect as performance or offer of performance by the person named in the contract, unless,

"(a) performance by the person delegated varies or would vary materially from performance by the person named in the contract as the one to perform, and there has been no . . . assent to the delegation. . . ."

In cases involving the sale of goods, the Restatement rule respecting delegation of duties has been amplified by Uniform Commercial Code § 2-210(5), Maryland Code (1957, 1964 Repl.Vol.) Art 95B § 2-210(5), which permits a promisee to demand assurances from the party to whom duties have been delegated. . . .

As we see it, the delegation of duty by Virginia to Macke was entirely permissible under the terms of the agreements. . . .

Judgment reversed as to liability; judgment entered for appellant for costs, on appeal and below; case remanded for a new trial on the question of damages.

| *Case*
Questions | 1. When the Virginia Coffee Service sold its assets to the Macke Company, what rights did it assign? |
| | 2. What duties were delegated? |

Contracts for the Benefit of Third Parties

In some situations, the parties contract with a clear understanding that the agreement is intended to benefit some other, noncontracting person. For example, a son and daughter might contract with a carpenter to repair the back stairs at their elderly mother's house. In another case, a woman might have accidentally damaged a neighbor's fence and agreed to have the fence repaired. The woman might want to discharge this obligation by contracting with a carpenter to repair the damage.

The third person in the first example (the mother) is classified as a *donee beneficiary*, and the third person in the second example (the neighbor) is classified as a *creditor beneficiary*. American law generally permits donee beneficiaries and creditor beneficiaries to sue for breach of contract. The third party's right to sue, however, only exists if that party's rights have "vested," that is, have matured to the point of being legally enforceable. Jurisdictions generally choose one of the following three rules to decide when rights vest: (1) rights vest when the contract is formed, (2) rights vest when the beneficiary acquires knowledge about the contract, or (3) rights vest when the beneficiary relies on the contract and changes his or her position.

The following case illustrates the difficulties encountered by one claiming status as a third-party beneficiary.

Castorino v. Unifast Bldg. Products
555 N.Y.S.2d 350
Supreme Court, Appellate Division,
First Department
May 17, 1990

Memorandum Decision

Order, Supreme Court, New York County (Eugene L. Nardelli, J.), entered November 30, 1988, denying, without prejudice to renewal following discovery, defendant Unifast Building Products Corp.'s motion for summary judgment dismissing plaintiff's amended complaint and all cross-claims against it, unanimously modified, on the law, to dismiss the amended complaint against said defendant, and, except as so modified, affirmed, without costs or disbursements.

In this wrongful death action it is alleged that plaintiff's decedent was assaulted and murdered in her apartment by someone who gained entry either through a window which did not have locking devices or which did not have locking devices in proper working condition. Liability against defendant appellant Unifast, which had contracted with defendant DCI Contracting Corp. to supply and install windows throughout the apartment building in which decedent resided, is predicated on a claim that the window locking mechanisms were defective and that the windows could not be properly closed or locked.

Unifast moved for summary judgment, arguing, *inter alia*, that plaintiff could not recover on a theory of contractual liability since it had no contract with plaintiff's decedent, nor was decedent an intended beneficiary of any contract between Unifast and the landlord. In addition, Unifast urged that there could be no recovery in tort since Unifast had not undertaken any duty to decedent in agreeing to supply windows to the building in which she resided. Finding a question as to whether Unifast owed a duty to the decedent, the [trial] court denied summary judgment, without prejudice to renewal following discovery, since it could not yet be determined whether the windows were manufactured and delivered in a defective condition.

In view of the broad "hold harmless [clause]" included in the contract between Unifast and DCI, the only party whose cross-claims appear in the record, we agree with the [trial] court insofar as it denied Unifast's motion for summary judgment dismissing the cross-claims against it. However, since we find no basis, under principles of either contract or tort law, for a finding of liability against Unifast, we modify to grant Unifast's motion and dismiss the complaint against it.

Plaintiff predicates Unifast's contractual liability on an assertion that the decedent was an intended beneficiary of the contract between Unifast and DCI, the landlord's general contractor. While the law is settled that an intended beneficiary may maintain an action as a third party for breach of contract, he must establish "(1) the existence of a valid and binding contract between the parties, (2) that the contract was intended for his benefit and (3) that the benefit to him is sufficiently immediate, rather than incidental, to indicate the assumption by the contracting parties of a duty to compensate him if the benefit is lost." . . . Since there is nothing in the subcontract between Unifast and DCI which "evince[s] a discernible intent to allow recovery for the specified damages to the third party that result[ed] from a breach thereof," no cause of action against Unifast can be maintained.

Einhorn v. Seeley, . . . 525 N.Y.S.2d 212, . . . also mandates the conclusion that this theory is unavailable here. *Einhorn* was a personal injury action in which plaintiff was allegedly assaulted and raped in an apartment building and sued, *inter alia*, a locksmith, on a theory that it had improperly installed or repaired the lock on the front door of the building, through which the assailant might have gained access to the premises. We held that the action was "not maintainable in contract on a third-party beneficiary theory since plaintiffs were, at most, incidental rather than intended beneficiaries of any agreement between the landlord and [the locksmith]."

Nor, under *Einhorn*, can defendant be held liable in tort. Rejecting plaintiff's claim against the locksmith for tort liability, the *Einhorn* court held that the locksmith did not undertake a duty to the injured plaintiff when it entered into its relationship with the landlord: "Here we are concerned with a possible liability for an injury to a mere guest of a tenant caused by an unlawful act of a third party. Under these circumstances, to hold a locksmith responsible for the alleged consequences of an allegedly defective lock would be to enlarge the obligations of such artisans far beyond the existing law and beyond sound public policy." . . .

Similarly, it would be an unacceptable extension of existing law to hold the supplier/installer of windows responsible for the alleged consequences of an allegedly defective window locking mechanism. It is "the responsibility of courts, in fixing the orbit of duty, 'to limit the legal consequences of wrongs to a controllable degree' [citations omitted], and to protect against crushing exposure to liability [citations omitted]. . . . The courts' definition of an orbit of duty based on public policy may at times result in the exclusion of some who might otherwise have recovered for losses or injuries if traditional tort principles had been applied."
. . .

The fact that in this case plaintiff's decedent was a resident of the building in which the attack occurred, while the injured plaintiff in *Einhorn* was merely a guest of a tenant—and was explicitly referred to as such . . . —does not warrant a contrary conclusion. The decision in *Einhorn* turned not on the fact that plaintiff was a guest but on the rule that "[t]here will ordinarily be no duty thrust on a defendant to prevent a third party from causing harm to another."[1] . . . It is clear that the result would have been no different if plaintiff had been a tenant.

[1]An exception to this rule "may occur in the case where a special relationship exists between the defendant and the third person so as to give rise to a duty to control, or alternatively, when a special relationship exists between the defendant and the victim which gives the latter the right to protection [citation omitted]" (*Einhorn, supra.* . . .). This exception is inapplicable here, however, since there is nothing in the record to support the claim in plaintiff's brief that the assailant "is believed to be an employee, contractor, or agent of [Unifast] or its agents."

Case Questions

1. Why did the appellate court reverse the trial court's grant of summary judgment in favor of the defendants?
2. Common law courts were historically opposed to recognizing any third-party rights. Based on your knowledge of contract fundamentals, why do you think there was such judicial resistance?

The Duty to Perform and Breach of Contract

Many agreements include conditions precedent and conditions subsequent that may affect a party's duty to perform. A *condition precedent* exists when some specified event must occur before a duty to perform becomes operative (i.e., obtain a mortgage at a specified rate of interest). A *condition subsequent* exists when a specified event occurs that discharges the parties from their duties.

A breach of contract occurs when a party fails to perform a duty, or inadequately performs what he or she has promised. A breach of contract is a material breach if the nonperforming party totally or substantially fails to perform. Thus a material breach has occurred if a homeowner contracts with a painter to paint a house with two coats of primer and one finish coat, and the painter quits after painting one coat of primer. The homeowner has not received the substantial benefit of his or her bargain.

In the next case an exterminating company breached its contract with a homeowner through inadequate performance of its duty.

Clarkson v. Orkin Exterminating Co., Inc.
761 F.2d 189
U.S. Court of Appeals, Fourth Circuit
May 9, 1985

Haynsworth, Senior Circuit Judge

A jury awarded the plaintiff damages on three separate claims. She claimed breach of a contract to inspect for termites and to treat again if necessary. There was a claim of fraud and of a violation of South Carolina's Unfair Trade Practices Act. § 39–0(a), Code of Laws of South Carolina, 1976.

There was adequate proof that Orkin broke its contract, though an improper measure of damages was applied. There is no evidence in the record, however, to support the finding of fraud or a violation of the Unfair Trade Practices Act. Hence, we reverse in part and affirm in part, but remand the contract claim for an appropriate assessment of damages.

I.

In 1976 Mrs. Clarkson purchased a house. Orkin had contracted with her predecessor in title to retreat the house in the event that a termite problem developed. Orkin also promised, for a fee, to inspect the house yearly and, if necessary, retreat it for termites before certifying that the house remained free of termites.

In early 1983, Mrs. Clarkson offered her home for sale. When prospective purchasers noticed evidence of termite infes-

tation, Mrs. Clarkson called Orkin and requested that they inspect the house. Orkin complied with her request and issued a report that the house was free of termites. The report also mentioned the presence of a moisture problem, which had been reported to Mrs. Clarkson on several earlier occasions but which remained uncorrected. For the moisture problem, Orkin had unsuccessfully attempted to sell a protective chemical treatment to Mrs. Clarkson.

The day after Orkin's 1983 inspection, Mrs. Clarkson had the house inspected by the representative of another exterminating company. He found two termite tunnels and damage from water. He attributed the water damage to a drainage problem and expressed the opinion that the water damage would progress unless there were alterations to a porch to prevent drainage of water into the basement.

After a contractor had made the necessary repairs and the recommended alterations, Mrs. Clarkson sought to have Orkin reimburse her for her entire cost of the reconstruction work. She also asked that Orkin reinspect the house and certify that the house was free of termite infestation. Orkin refused both requests.

A jury awarded Mrs. Clarkson $613.47 on the breach of contract claim, $551 on the Unfair Trade Practices Act Claim and $1,148 actual damages and $5,000 punitive damages on the fraud claim. The district judge concluded that the Unfair Trade Practices Act claim was a willful one and tripled the award on that claim and ordered Orkin to pay the plaintiff's attorneys' fees.

II.

As proof of a violation of the South Carolina Unfair Trade Practices Act, Mrs. Clarkson points (1) to the fact that Orkin certified in 1983 that the house was free of termites when significant infestation was visible, and (2) the fact that Orkin on several occasions had attempted, though unsuccessfully, to sell to Mrs. Clarkson a "moisture problem treatment package" that would not have been an adequate corrective of an improper drainage problem.

It is abundantly clear that in its 1983 inspection Orkin's representative failed to discover termite infestation which was present and visible. This, however, does not establish a violation of the South Carolina Unfair Trade Practices Act. It shows no more than that Orkin's representative was negligent or incompetent. Mrs. Clarkson had not directed his attention to the area where the infestation was present, though she did direct the attention of the other exterminator to that area.

. . .

III.

There is enough to support a finding of contract violation. Orkin failed to retreat the house when a termite infestation was present, and it refused Mrs. Clarkson's subsequent request that it reinspect and spray the house after the repairs had been made.

There is no claim that Mrs. Clarkson lost an opportunity to sell the house because of the termite problem. What she claimed was the cost of repairs and alterations. On the breach of contract claim, the jury assessed the damaged at $613.47, which was precisely the cost to Mrs. Clarkson of replacing the wood damaged by the termites. In effect, the jury converted Orkin's retreatment contract into a repair contract.

Orkin offers its customers alternatives. It will promise and guarantee to provide retreatment if there is a later termite infestation. For a higher fee, it will promise and guarantee to effect necessary repairs after a termite infestation has occurred. Mrs. Clarkson's predecessor in title, and she, elected to take the lower option. In Orkin's guarantee to Mrs. Clarkson, there is an express recital of her waiver and release of Orkin from any liability for damage to the structure occasioned by termites. Mrs. Clarkson cannot now claim the benefits of a repair guarantee she chose not to purchase.

Mrs. Clarkson was entitled to a proper performance by Orkin of its contract, which was to inspect and treat again if an infestation was found. That promise was not properly performed, and Mrs. Clarkson is entitled to any damage she suffered by reason of that non-performance. Since she knew of the termite infestation one day after Orkin failed to detect it, her damage would apparently be limited to the cost of inspection by the other exterminator plus the cost of any retreatment she may have procured.

While we agree that the evidence supports a finding of a breach of contract, we remand that claim for further proceedings on damages as may be consistent with this opinion. Judgment in the plaintiff's favor on the unfair trade practice and fraud claims is reversed.

Reversed in part; Affirmed in part, and remanded.

Case
Questions

1. In what way did Orkin breach its duty?
2. Why did the court remand the breach of contract claim for further proceedings?

REMEDIES FOR BREACH OF CONTRACT

An injured party who has established a breach of contract is entitled to turn to a court for legal or equitable relief, as discussed in Chapter 6.

Common Law Remedies

In most cases of breach, the injured party is awarded money damages which can be compensatory, nominal, or liquidated.

The following case involves breach of contract claims between homeowners and a building contractor. The homeowners discharged the contractor because of defective work. The contractor filed suit against the homeowners to recover the damages. The Maine Supreme Court vacated the trial court's judgment on the counterclaim because of errors in the jury instructions regarding damages.

Anuszewski v. Jurevic
566 A.2d 742
Supreme Judicial Court of Maine
November 28, 1989

Clifford, Justice

Defendants and counterclaim plaintiffs Richard and Judy Jurevic appeal from a judgment entered after a jury trial in Superior Court. . . . Because we conclude that the court improperly limited the jury's consideration of damages claimed by the Jurevics, we vacate the judgment on the counterclaim.

In early 1987, the Jurevics contracted with the plaintiff, Robert E. Anuszewski, a contractor doing business as Pine Tree Post & Beam, for Anuszewski to construct a home for the Jurevics in Kennebunkport. The home was to be completed by June 1, 1987, at a cost of $134,000, and the contract called for the Jurevics to make periodic progress payments. The home was only about fifty percent complete on June 1, 1987. In January, 1988, the Jurevics discharged Anuszewski. In March, 1988, Anuszewski brought an action against the Jurevics to recover $39,590.[2] The Jurevics filed a counterclaim.

At trial, the Jurevics presented evidence that the construction work was defective and testimony in the form of an expert opinion as to the total cost to correct the defects and to complete the house. The testimony indicated that this cost would include a general contractor markup of fifty percent added to the

---

[2] The $39,500 represented, alternatively, the unpaid part of the contract price, or the value of the labor and materials provided by Anuszewski for which he had not been paid.

actual cost of the work to be done for overhead and profit, and that this was a usual and customary practice of the industry. The Jurevics also claimed damages for rental and other incidental expenses caused by Anuszewski's delay in completing the house. The court, however, prohibited the Jurevics from presenting evidence of delay damages beyond January 5, 1988, the date the Jurevics terminated the contract with Anuszewski.

At the conclusion of the evidence, the court, in its jury instructions, precluded the jury from considering the general contractor's markup as follows:

"[I]f you find that the Jurevics are entitled to recover damages from Mr. Anuszewski for completion of the work not done or for repairing work not performed in a workmanlike manner, any amount of damages that you award must be the cost of doing that work by the various workmen without any markup to a general contractor, such as was testified to by [the Jurevics' expert witness]."

The jury returned a verdict awarding Anuszewski damages of $25,000 on his complaint and awarding $22,000 to the Jurevics on their counterclaim. This appeal by the Jurevics followed the denial of their motions for a mistrial, or in the alternative, for a new trial, and for additur.

We find merit in the Jurevics' contention that the court impermissibly restricted the jury's consideration of the full amount of damages that they were entitled to recover. The purpose of contract damages is to place the injured parties in the position they would have been in but for the breach, by awarding the value of the promised performance. . . . Those damages for breach of a construction contract are measured by either the difference in value between the per-

formance promised and the performance rendered, or the amount reasonably required to remedy the defect. . . . The amount reasonably required to remedy the defect may be measured by the *actual* cost of necessary repairs. . . . Those costs may be proven by the presentation of expert testimony, as the Jurevics did here. . . .

The court correctly instructed the jury that the Jurevics' measure of recovery for incomplete or defective work was "the amount reasonably required to remedy the defect" as specifically measured by the actual cost of repair. . . . The court went on, however, to instruct the jury that the cost of repair was to be considered "without any markup to a general contractor." This instruction was given despite testimony from an expert witness that the actual cost to remedy the incomplete and defective construction work of Anuszewski would include a general contractor markup for overhead and profit, and that such a markup was customary and usual in the construction business. Although Anuszewski defends the court's instruction, he did not argue at trial, nor does he now, that the Jurevics were not entitled to have the jury consider their claim that it was reasonable for them to hire a general contractor to supervise the repairs and completion of the house. If the jury concluded that it would be reasonable for the Jurevics to hire a substitute general contractor to supervise the repairs and completion, but was precluded by the court's instruction from considering the award of damages for the reasonable cost of the substitute contractor's overhead, for which the evidence suggests they would be charged as a matter of routine, then the Jurevics could be deprived of full recovery in their breach of contract claim. They would not be placed in the same position they would have been had Anuszewski performed the contract. . . .

In breach of contract cases we have upheld repair or replacement damage awards of the amount required to bring a home into compliance with the contract. . . . In addition, we have affirmed the computation of indebtedness owed a builder by a homeowner that included a contractor's overhead and profit. . . . We see no reason to exclude reasonable and customary profit and overhead of a contractor from the cost of repairs to remedy defects in a breach of contract case.

The entry is:

Judgment on the complaint affirmed. Judgment on the counterclaim vacated.

Remanded to the Superior Court for further proceedings consistent with the opinion herein.

Case Questions

1. According to the Jurevics, what error was committed by the trial judge?
2. What is a counterclaim?

Punitive Damages

You may recall from Chapter 6 that punitive damages are awarded in tort cases to punish defendants for their wanton, reckless, malicious, or oppressive conduct and to deter others from similar antisocial conduct. Traditionally, punitive damages have not been awarded in contract cases. A few courts will deviate from the traditional rule when certain types of contractual breaches have been proven:

1. Breaches that are accompanied by an independent tort (such as where an employee sues her employer for wrongful discharge from employment and slander).
2. Breaches where the conduct that establishes the breach independently establishes a common law tort (such as where a malicious or wanton breach of contract causes the plaintiff to suffer emotional distress).
3. Breaches of insurance contracts by insurance companies.
4. Breaches that involve fraud, malice, gross negligence, or oppression, where the public interest would be advanced by the deterrent effect resulting from the imposition of punitive damages (as in the following case).

Hibschman Pontiac, Inc. v. Batchelor
362 N.E.2d 845
Supreme Court of Indiana
May 13, 1977

Givan, Chief Justice

Batchelor brought an action for breach of contract and oppressive conduct by Hibschman Pontiac, Inc. and General Motors Corporation. A trial before a jury resulted in a verdict for Batchelor and against Hibschman Pontiac and General Motors Corporation in the amount of $1,500.00. Further, the jury assessed punitive damages against Hibschman Pontiac, Inc. in the amount of $15,000.00.

The Court of Appeals, Third District, reversed the grant of punitive damages. . . . Batchelor now petitions for transfer.

The record reveals the following evidence: Prior to buying the Pontiac GTO automobile involved in this case, Batchelor inquired of the salesman, the service manager and the vice president as to the quality of Hibschman Pontiac's service department, as it was important that any deficiencies in the car be corrected. The salesman and the service manager responded that the service department at Hibschman Pontiac was above average. Jim Hibschman, the vice president, assured him that he would personally see that any difficulties would be corrected. Batchelor stated that he relied on the statements of the three men and ordered a 1969 GTO Pontiac automobile.

When Batchelor picked up the new car he discovered several problems with it. As requested by the service manager of Hibschman Pontiac, Batchelor made a list of his complaints and brought the car in for repair a few days later. The service manager attached the list to a work order but did not list the deficiencies on the work order. Later the manager called Batchelor and said that the car was ready. When he picked up the car Batchelor noticed that several items on the list had not been touched. Batchelor testified that there were many occasions when he took the car to Hibschman Pontiac for repairs and the service manager told him that the defects had been fixed when in fact they were not fixed. Batchelor testified that the service manager knew the defects were not corrected, but represented to him that the defects were corrected. Batchelor

stated that he relied on the service manager's statements and took the car on several trips, only to have it break down. Some of the deficiencies resulted in abnormal wear of the car and breakdowns after the warranty period had expired.

Batchelor testified that he had taken the car in for repairs five times before he had owned it a month but that the defects had not been corrected. Batchelor had taken the car in 12 times during the warranty period for overnight repair and at least 20 times in all during the period. During the warranty period Batchelor lost use of the car approximately 45 days while it was at Hibschman Pontiac.

Batchelor had appealed to Jim Hibschman on several occasions to take care of his car. Hibschman replied that he realized the repairs were not effected properly but that Hibschman Pontiac would "do everything to get you happy." On another occasion Jim Hibschman responded they had done all they could with the car but that Batchelor was just a particular, habitual complainer whom they could not satisfy and "I would rather you would just leave and not come back. We are going to have to write you off as a bad customer."

On several occasions Batchelor attempted to see Dan Shaules, an area service representative from Pontiac Division, about the car but was kept waiting so long that he had to leave without seeing him. Batchelor did see Shaules in Buchanan, Michigan, when he took the car to an authorized Pontiac dealer there after the warranty had expired. Shaules inspected the car and told Batchelor to return the car to Hibschman Pontiac for repairs.

Hugh Haverstock, the owner of the garage where several of the deficiencies were corrected after the expiration of the warranty, testified that Batchelor was a good customer and paid his bills. He stated that an average transmission man could have corrected the problem with the transmission and that a problem with the timing was discovered and corrected when a tune-up lasted only 800 miles. Haverstock stated that the difference in value of the car without defects and with the defects it had was approximately $1,500.00. Haverstock testified that when a person complains about problems with cars that have not been fixed by dealerships, word gets out and others do not want to work on the cars.

Arnold Miexel, the service manager for Hibschman Pontiac during the time in question, testified that his representation to Batchelor regarding Hibschman Pontiac service department was based on the fact that the mechanics were factory trained and that he had received no complaints regarding their work. He further stated that he could not check the work of the mechanics. Miexel testified that if their work was unsatisfactory it was done over but no work order was written for it. He stated that it was possible that Batchelor made complaints about the car, but the defects were not corrected. The warranty expired and, as a consequence, later work was not considered under warranty.

Dan Shaules testified that Miexel was an average service manager. He testified that not all of the deficiencies in the car were corrected properly. He further stated that if any defects in the car were brought to their attention within the warranty period, items would be corrected if necessary after the warranty had expired.

Appellant first argues that there was insufficient evidence to permit the issue of punitive damages to go to the jury and that the court should have rendered a directed verdict on the issue of punitive damages on behalf of Hibschman Pontiac. This Court has recently dealt with the question of punitive damages in a con-tract action. In *Vernon Fire & Casualty Ins. Co. v. Sharp* (1976) . . . the majority restated the general provision that punitive damages are not recoverable in contract actions and went on to state exceptions to this rule. Where the conduct of a party, in breaching his contract, independently establishes the elements of a common law tort, punitive damages may be awarded for the tort.

Punitive damages may be awarded in addition to compensatory damages "whenever the elements of fraud, malice, gross negligence or oppression *mingle* in the controversy." (emphasis supplied.)

Further, where a separate tort accompanies the breach or the elements of tort mingle with the breach, it must appear that the public interest will be served by the deterrent effect of the punitive damages.

Appellant urges that the evidence presented does not indicate tortious conduct of any sort on its part. While a reasonable inference could be made from the evidence that appellant merely attempted to fulfill its contract and to do not more than that contract required, it is also reasonable to infer that Hibschman Pontiac acted tortiously and in willful disregard of the right of Batchelor. This Court has often stated the maxim that it will not reweigh the evidence nor determine the credibility of witnesses, but will sustain a verdict if there is any evidence of probative value to support it. . . .

A corporation can act only through its agents, and their acts, when done within the scope of their authority, are attributable to the corporation. . . .

Here, the jury could reasonably have found elements of fraud, malice, gross negligence or oppression mingled into the breach of warranty. The evidence showed that requested repairs were not satisfactorily completed although covered by the warranty and capable of correction. Some of these defects were clearly breaches of warranty. Paint was bubbled, the radio never worked properly, the hood and bumper were twisted and misaligned, the universal joints failed, the transmission linkage was improperly adjusted, the timing chain was defective causing improper tune-ups and the carburetor was defective, among other things. Batchelor took the car to the defendant with a list of defects on numerous occasions and picked up the car when told it was "all ready to go." It was reasonable to infer that the defendant's service manager represented repairs to have been made when he knew that the work had not been done and that in reliance on his representations, Batchelor drove the car on trips and had breakdowns. Before purchasing the car Batchelor was given special representations on the excellence of Hibschman's service department, and the jury could find that Batchelor relied on these in buying the car from the defendant. After having brought the car in on numerous occasions, Batchelor was told by Jim Hibschman, "I would rather you would just leave and not come back. We are going to have to write you off as a bad customer." And he was told by one of Hibschman's mechanics that, "If you don't get on them and get this fixed, they will screw you around and you will never get it done." From these statements the jury could infer that the defendant was attempting to avoid making certain repairs by concealing them during the period of the warranty. Batchelor gave the defendant numerous opportunities to repair the car and the defendant did not do so; instead he tried to convince Batchelor that the problems were not with the car, but rather with Batchelor. We are of the opinion that in this case the jury could have found there was cogent proof to establish malice, fraud, gross negligence and oppressive conduct.

Although fraudulent conduct was not alleged in the complaint, evidence on the subject was admitted. Any inconsistency between the pleadings and proof will be resolved in favor of the proof at trial. . . . Thus there was probative evidence supporting the claim for punitive damages. The trial court did not err in denying a directed verdict as to that issue. . . .

Case Questions

1. Under what conditions can punitive damages be allowed for breach of contract in Indiana?
2. Why do you think courts have been so resistant to the award of punitive damages for routine breaches of contract?

Equitable Remedies

If money damages are deemed to be an inadequate remedy, the court may be persuaded to grant equitable relief. The discussion in Chapter 6 addresses the most common forms of equitable relief in breach of contract cases (injunctions, restitution after the court has granted rescission, and specific performance).

UCC Remedies for Breach of Contract for the Sale of Goods

The Uniform Commercial Code provides special rules for breaches of contracts involving the sale of goods. For example, if a seller breaches his or her contract to deliver goods, the buyer is entitled to (1) rescind the contract, (2) sue for damages, and (3) obtain restitution for any payments made. If the goods are unique such as rare artwork, or custom-made, a court may order specific performance. Replevin also is permitted in some situations. If a buyer breaches a sales contract by not accepting delivery of goods, or wrongfully revokes a prior acceptance, the injured seller is entitled to (1) cancel the contract, (2) stop delivery of goods, and (3) recover money damages from the buyer.

Chapter Questions

1. Define the following terms:

acceptance	offer
accord	option
assignee	parol evidence rule
assignor	promisee
bilateral contract	promisor
breach of contract	rescission
capacity	satisfaction
condition precedent	statute of frauds
condition subsequent	unenforceable
consideration	Uniform Commercial Code
creditor beneficiary	undue influence
donee beneficiary	unilateral contract
discharge	void
duress	voidable
fraud	warranty
novation	

2. Mr. Lucy and Mr. Zehmer were talking at a restaurant. After a couple of drinks, Lucy asked Zehmer if he had sold the Ferguson farm. Zehmer replied that he had not, and did not want to sell it. Lucy said "I bet you wouldn't take $50,000 cash for that farm," and Zehmer replied, "You haven't got $50,000 cash." Lucy said, "I can get it." Zehmer said he might form a company and get it, "but you haven't got $50,00 to pay me to-night." Lucy asked him if he would put it in writing that he would sell him this farm. Zehmer then wrote on the back of a pad, "I agree to sell the Ferguson Place to W. O. Lucy for $50,000 cash." Lucy said, "All right, get your wife to sign it." Zehmer subsequently went to his wife and said, "You want to put your name to this?" She said no, but he said in an undertone,

"It is nothing but a joke," and she signed it. At that time, Zehmer was not too drunk to make a valid contract. The Zehmers refused to convey legal title to the property, and Lucy sued for specific performance. What defense would the Zehmers use in the suit? Who should win the suit?

Lucy v. Zehmer, 196 Va. 493, 84 S.E.2d 516 (1954)

3. National Beverages, Inc., offered to the public prizes to be awarded in a contest known as "Pepsi-Cola Streator-Chevrolet Sweepstakes." The first prize was a Chevrolet Corvair. No order of drawing was announced prior to the close of the contest. After the close of the contest, just prior to the drawing, a sign was displayed stating the order of drawing. The first tickets drawn would receive twelve cases of Pepsi-Cola and the last ticket drawn would receive the automobile. Walters' ticket was the first ticket to be drawn from the barrel. She claims that her number being the first qualified number drawn entitles her to the first prize, the Chevrolet Corvair. She bases her claim on the wording of the offer, which listed the automobile as the first prize. She accepted the offer by entering the contest. Is Walters entitled to the automobile?

Walters v. National Beverages, Inc., 18 Utah 2d 301, 422 P.2d 524 (1967)

4. Green signed a roofing contract with Clay Tile, agent for Ever-Tite Roofing Company, to have a new roof put on his house. The agreement stated that this contract was subject to Ever-Tite's approval and that the agreement would become binding upon written notice of acceptance or commencement of work. Nine days later, Clay Tile loaded up his truck and drove to Green's house, only to find that someone else was already doing the job. Ever-Tite wishes to sue on the contract for damages. Was Green's offer to Ever-Tite accepted before the offer was revoked?

Ever-Tite Roofing Corporation v. Green, 83 So.2d 449 (La.App. 1955)

5. Workers agreed to work aboard a canning ship during the salmon canning season. The contract, signed individually by each worker, was to last for the length of time it took to sail from San Francisco to Pyramid Harbor, Alaska, and back. Each worker was to receive a stated compensation. They arrived in Alaska at the height of the fishing and canning season. Knowing that every day's delay would be financially disastrous and that it would be impossible to find workers to replace them, the workers refused to work unless they were given substantial wage increases. The owner of the canning ship acceded to their demands. When the ship returned to San Francisco, the owner paid them in accordance with the original agreement. The workers now bring suit to recover the additional amounts due under the second agreement. Will the contract be upheld?

Alaska Packers Association v. Domenico, 117 F.99 (9th Cir. 1902)

6. A little girl found a pretty stone about the size of a canary bird's egg. She had no idea what it was, so she took it to a jeweler who eventually bought it from her for a dollar, although he too did not know what it was. The

stone turned out to be an uncut diamond worth $10,000. The girl tendered back the $1 purchase price and sued to have the sale voided on the basis of mutual mistake. Should mutual mistake be a basis for recovery?

Wood v. Boynton, 64 Wis. 265, 25 N.W. 42 (1885)

7. William E. Story agreed orally with his nephew that if he would refrain from drinking liquor, using tobacco, swearing, and playing cards or billiards for money until he became twenty-one years old, then he, Story, would pay his nephew $5,000 when the nephew reached age twenty-one. The nephew fully performed his part of the agreement. But when he reached age twenty-one, his uncle stated that he had earned the $5,000 and that he would keep it at interest for his nephew. Twelve years later, Story died, and his nephew brought an action to recover the $5,000 plus interest. Was there sufficient consideration to create a contract?

Hamer v. Sidway, 124 N.Y. 538, 27 N.E. 256 (1891)

8. The Kentucky Bankers Association provided a reward of $500 for the arrest and conviction of each bank robber. Three armed men robbed First State Bank. Later in the day, they were apprehended and placed under arrest by three policemen. Two of the policemen were from the county of the bank and the other was from a neighboring county and out of his jurisdiction. Four employees of the bank gave the officers the details of the crime and described the culprits. The information was used in capturing the robbers. After the conviction of the robbers, the employees of the bank and the policemen wanted to share in the reward. Who would be entitled to the reward?

Denney v. Reppert, 432 S.W. 647 (Ky. 1968)

9. Robert Rogers turned seventeen, quit high school, and married his hometown sweetheart. To provide her with the style of life with which she had become accustomed, Robert went out in search of employment. He signed an agreement with the Gastonia Personnel Corporation, agreeing to pay a commission of $293 to it if it was successful in procuring him a job. Gastonia found him a job, but Robert refuses to pay and denies liability on the grounds of minority. Can he avoid payment on this ground?

Gastonia Personnel Corporation v. Rogers, 276 N.C. 279, 172 S.E.2d 19 (1970)

10. Seventeen-year-old Robertson purchased a truck from Julian Pontiac Company for $1,743.85. He traded in his passenger car for which he was given a credit of $723.85, leaving a balance of $1,020 payable in twenty-four monthly installments. Robertson was unable to get insurance because of his young age. He returned the truck to the dealer for repair of defective wiring, but the condition was not remedied. The truck caught fire and was practically destroyed. Robertson lived at home with his parents, and he did not need the truck in connection with any work. Julian Pontiac Company disposed of the car it received in the trade and cannot restore it to Robert-

son. Can Robertson, who is still a minor, rescind the contract and, if so, what would be the remedy?

Robertson v. King, 225 Ark. 276, 280 S.W.2d 402 (1955)

11. Manual Tovar was employed as a resident physician by Paxton Community Memorial Hospital in Illinois. Tovar had never been licensed to practice medicine in that state. In order to assume the position, he had had to resign his position in Kansas and move to Illinois. After two weeks of employment, the hospital discharged him. The hospital was aware of his background, professional experience, and licensing when it hired him. Should Tovar recover for breach of his employment contract?

    Tovar v. Paxton Community Memorial Hospital, 29 Ill. App.3d 218, 330 N.E.2d 247 (1975)

12. In 1941, Liebman gave Rosenthal $28,000 worth of jewels so that Rosenthal, a good friend of the Portuguese consul in France, would obtain visas for Liebman and his family so they could get out of France and into Portugal. This transaction took place during World War II, when it was illegal to obtain such visas. Rosenthal absconded to America with the jewels without procuring the visas. Four years later, Liebman and Rosenthal met in New York, where Liebman demanded the return of the jewels. Rosenthal's defense is that the agreement is illegal and, therefore, unenforceable. Is he right?

    Liebman v. Rosenthal, 57 N.Y.S.2d 875 (1945)

13. Voss approached the law firm of Preval, Wilson and Matthews to represent him in a patent infringement suit filed by his company, V & S Ice Machine Company. Since V & S Ice Machine Company is a shell corporation, its only asset being an ice blade patent, the law firm sought personal assurances from Voss that their firm would be paid. Voss agreed to take care of the fee and said that he expected to pay between $10,000 and $20,000 for their legal services. The suit was unsuccessful, and Voss received a bill for $14,000. He refused payment, and suit is being brought for collection. Voss defends on the ground that the agreement was for him to answer for the debt of the corporation, and that it is unenforceable because it violates the statute of frauds, in that it was never reduced to writing. Is this a valid defense?

    Preval, Wilson and Matthews v. Voss, 471 F.2d 1186 (5th Cir. 1973)

14. Hedda Hopper, a famous radio and television personality, orally contracted with Lennen & Mitchell, advertising agents, to do weekly radio advertisements over a term of five years. This five-year period was divided into ten 26-week segments, and Lennen & Mitchell had the right to cancel the contract simply by giving written notice four weeks before the end of any 26-week segment. Hedda refused to perform under the contract, and Lennen & Mitchell sued for damages. Is enforcement of the contract barred by the statute of frauds?

    Hopper v. Lennen & Mitchell, 146 F.2d 364 (9th Cir. 1944)

Notes

1. W. Walsh, *A History of Anglo-American Law* (Indianapolis: Bobbs-Merrill Company, 1932), p. 339; A.W.B. Simpson, *A History of the Common Law of Contract* (Oxford: Clarendon Press, 1975), pp. 12, 53; A.K.R. Kiralfy, *Potter's Historical Introduction to English Law* (London: Sweet and Maxwell Ltd., 1962), pp. 452–457.

2. Kiralfy, p. 456.

3. Ibid., pp. 456–457.

4. Ibid., pp. 305–307; Walsh, p. 344.

5. Walsh, p. 342.

6. Simpson, p. 199; Walsh, p. 344.

7. Simpson, p. 210; Kiralfy, p. 461; Walsh, p. 341.

8. Walsh, p. 340; Simpson, p. 224; Plucknett, p. 639.

9. Walsh, pp. 345, 351; Simpson, p. 406; Plucknett, pp. 649–656.

10. Kiralfy, p. 626.

11. B. Schwartz, *The Law in America* (New York: McGraw-Hill, 1974), pp. 59–62; W.E. Nelson, *Americanization of the Common Law* (Cambridge: Harvard University Press, 1975), p. 86.

12. M. Horwitz, *The Transformation of American Law, 1780–1860* (Cambridge: Harvard University Press, 1977), pp. 164–180; Nelson, p. 154.

13. Horwitz, pp. 167, 173.

14. Schwartz, p. 72; Nelson, p. 86.

15. Horwitz, p. 185.

X

Property

Property refers to a person's ownership rights to things and to a person's interests in things owned by someone else. Property includes the rights to possess, use, and dispose of things. These may be tangible objects, such as a car, book, or item of clothing, or they may be intangible—the technology in a camera, a song, or the right of publicity. While many people refer to the objects themselves as property, "property" actually refers only to ownership rights and interests.

HISTORICAL DEVELOPMENT OF THE REGULATION OF REAL PROPERTY

When we discuss property law, we must remember that the English common law greatly influenced legal thinking in the prerevolutionary colonies and in the new American states.[1] Private property was thought to be essential to individual liberty, a proposition advanced by the English philosopher John Locke (1632–1704). Locke was a "natural law" philosopher who argued that before the creation of governments, people existed in a natural state in which they had total control over their life, liberty, and property. He reasoned that people who established governments retained these inalienable rights and were entitled to resist any government that failed to respect them. Locke's emphasis on the inviolability of private property was reflected in the decisions of colonial legislatures, judges, and political leaders.[2]

Although American law was significantly influenced by the common law, most colonies were willing to take a different path when solutions provided by common law seemed inappropriate. The Puritans in New England, for example, refused to follow a rule of English common law (which was accepted in southern colonies[3]) that prevented a husband from conveying land without his wife's consent. They believed this was a bad social policy, because it treated husbands and wives as individuals with separate legal interests rather than as a single, unified entity. They changed the law to allow husbands to make unilateral decisions for the family regarding the sale of real property.[4]

Before the industrial revolution, the economies of America and England were primarily based on agriculture. England's industrial revolution began with the rise of the textile industry in the 1700s. At this time most economic and political power was held by large landowners such as the church, monarchy, military, and landed gentry.[5] There, as in colonial America, the law recognized property owners as having absolute dominion over their land.[6] But no one could use his or her land in a manner that caused injury to any other landowner. For example, a landowner could not divert the natural flow of a navigable river or stream in order to establish a mill if it created a detriment to another landowner.[7] The fact that economic and social benefits would result from the operation of a new mill was of no consequence.[8]

Legal attitudes toward property began to change as America became industrialized in the 1800s and moved toward a market economy. After the Civil War, courts began to recognize that encouraging competition and economic development benefitted the public.[9] When one landowner's property use conflicted with another's, the courts balanced the nature of the infringement against its socially desirable economic benefits, and the developers usually prevailed.[10] This legal preference for development continued throughout the nineteenth and into the twentieth centuries. Although it produced new technology, new products, and an expanding economy, it also resulted in environmental pollution, the exploitation of workers, hazardous work environments, and labor-management conflict. These conditions resulted in legislative reform efforts throughout the century designed to protect society. Around 1900, the U.S. Supreme Court began to strike down state laws that interfered with employer-employee contracts with respect to wages, hours, and working conditions.[11] The Court concluded that these laws exceeded the state's legislative power because they infringed upon the individual's constitutionally protected due process liberty interest in freedom of contract.

Since the 1930s, the individual's property rights in land have declined as legislatures have acted to protect society from irresponsible and harmful uses of private property. Today, for example, zoning laws regulate land use and building codes regulate building construction. Environmental laws prohibit landowners from filling in wetlands and control the discharge of pollutants into the air, ground, and water.

As environmental regulations have increased in number, they have impacted an increasing number of landowners. A heated ongoing national debate has resulted between supporters and opponents of the legal status quo. Opponents have charged that the existing legislation and case law are excessively antidevelopment and that government agencies are overzealous in enforcing environmental protection regulations. Environmental protection, they conclude, is often achieved without regard for the legitimate rights of landowners.

Supporters of current environmental policies maintain that removing the regulations will produce a precipitous decline in habitat for endangered species and, in many instances, will ultimately lead to extinction. They also argue that backsliding from current standards will produce serious environmental hazards to the public's air, water, and land resources. In the 1990s, the Congress, many state legislatures, and federal and state courts have been rethinking whether our nation's environmental laws properly reflect society's dual interests of protecting both the environment and private property rights. We will examine this question in more detail later in this chapter when we discuss takings and eminent domain.

CLASSIFICATIONS OF PROPERTY

Property can be classified as real, personal (tangible or intangible), or fixtures. Property interests can also be classified as either contingent or vested.

Real property, or realty, includes land and things that are attached permanently to land. It is distinguishable from personal property in that real property is immovable.

Practically every person in the United States owns personal property. *Personal property*, or *personalty*, consists of physical objects that are not realty (or fixtures) and all intangible rights, duties, and obligations arising out of the ownership of physical objects. Personal property also includes intangible property, such as money, stocks, and bonds, that are paper substitutes for certain ownership rights. Thus personal property includes not only a physical or representative object, but also the right to own, use, sell, or dispose of it as regulated by law.

Tangible personal property consists of those physical objects that in themselves embody the rights of ownership. Intangible personal property is personal property that is not a physical object. Ownership of *intangible* property is usually evidenced by some type of legal document that sets forth the ownership rights. For example, a bank savings account is personal property. The passbook that the bank issues to the saver represents the savings account. The passbook, therefore, is evidence of the saver's right to title and right to possession of the funds contained in the account. Other examples of intangible personal property are patents, copyrights, and promissory notes.

An item of personal property can be the subject of both tangible and intangible property rights. For example, suppose that you buy a camera, the design of which is protected by a valid federal patent. Although you have acquired a piece of tangible personal property that you can use and dispose of in any legal manner, the law will recognize that you do not have all the rights vis-à-vis the camera. The patent holder, for example, has intangible property rights in the camera's technology that prevent a purchaser from selling duplicates of the product, or the technology, without permission. Thus both the patent holder and the purchaser have property rights to the same object.

A *fixture* is a category of property between realty and personalty. For example, a dishwasher is classified as personalty when it is purchased at an appliance store. When it is permanently built into the buyer's kitchen, however, it becomes a fixture.

Property rights are *contingent* when some future event must occur for the right to become *vested* (fully effective). For example, employers often require that employees work for a company for a specified number of years before their pension rights mature. Once pension rights vest, they belong to the employees even if they subsequently leave the company.

These distinctions are based on practical considerations; for example, tax rates may differ for realty, fixtures, and personalty. In addition, the common law of each state governs real property, whereas the Uniform Commercial Code often governs personalty.[12] The outcome of the next case depends on whether the property is classified as a fixture or as personal property.

Far West Modular Home Sales, Inc. v. Proaps
604 P.2d 452
Court of Appeals of Oregon
December 24, 1979

Campbell, Judge

In this replevin action[1] the plaintiff sought to recover the possession of a modular home. The parties waived a jury, and following trial to the court, judgment was entered for the plaintiff. The defendants have appealed, and we reverse.

In July 1977 the plaintiff contracted to sell a modular home to the defendants. In January 1978 the home was delivered in two sections from plaintiff's factory to the defendants' property. It was of wood construction, and was mounted and secured on a concrete foundation by bolts and nails. It was connected to sewer, water and electric outlets. When the modular home was in place it measured 60 feet by 24 feet and its accommodations included three bedrooms and two baths. The defendants and their family used it as a residence.

[1]An action to have personal property returned to the original possessor.—*Ed.*

A dispute arose over the price and the plaintiff filed this replevin action. The trial court found that the modular home was personal property. The defendants appealed and have assigned as the only error:

"The court erred in concluding that the modular home should be treated as personal property, thereby subject to replevin, and awarding same to Plaintiff."

The defendants contend that the modular home was so affixed to their real property that it lost its character as personalty and, therefore, was not subject to replevin.

The test for determining whether property retains its character as personal property, or loses its separate identity and becomes a fixture, is composed of three factors: annexation, adaptation and intention.

The plaintiff in its brief in this court concedes "the modular home was adaptable to the real property upon which it was placed." Therefore we will consider only the questions of annexation and intention.

The degree of annexation necessary to turn a chattel into a fixture depends upon the circumstances of the particular case.

Annexation of a chattel to real property may be either actual or constructive. . . .

The plaintiff in effect argues that the physical attachment of the modular home to the real property was so slight that the annexation factor was not satisfied. It points to the testimony of its witnesses that the home could be unbolted, the utilities unhooked, and the entire unit removed from defendants' property in less than an hour. The removal operation would require a crane and two trucks equipped with low-boys at a total cost of $2,500. It would cost an additional $2,200 to remove the concrete foundation and restore the defendants' land to its previous state.

Since there is no requirement that a chattel actually be attached to the real property to satisfy the annexation test, . . . testimony illustrating the ease with which the modular home could be removed is not controlling. Rather, the fact that this chattel is a home, coupled with evidence that it was bolted and nailed to a foundation and connected to all utilities, established that it was annexed to defendants' real property. This conclusion is further supported by the fact that it would cost $4,700 to remove the modular home and restore the land.

The paramount factor in the determination of whether a chattel has become a fixture is the objective intent of the annexor to make the item a permanent accession of the freehold. . . .

The annexor's intent can be inferred from "the nature of the article, the relation (to the realty) of the party annexing, the policy of law in relation thereto, the structure and mode of annexation, and the purpose and use" for which the item was annexed. . . . The annexor's objective, controlling intent, is determined from all the circumstances.

We begin with the presumption that a building or similar structure is a fixture and therefore a part of the real property. . . .

Also, when annexation is made by an owner of realty, an intent to affix may more readily be found. . . . The fact that here the vendor physically placed the unit on defendants' property does not detract from defendants' status as an annexing party. Moreover, the fact that the home was to be manufactured elsewhere in two large sections before being placed on the homesite does not detract from defendants' objective intent to affix the home to their land. . . .

The plaintiff argues "that no reasonable person would intend that a modular home lost its identity as personal property simply by dropping it on the foundation which had been prepared for it." Instead, plaintiff continues, "reasonable people would [intend] that the modular home would become a fixture contemporaneously with the payment of the purchase price." We find it relevant that plaintiff by implication admits that the installed home would become a fixture. However, plaintiff has not cited us a case, and we have been unable to find one, that holds payment of the purchase price is controlling as to the parties' intention.

A modular home has been defined as "a structure which is prefabricated in a factory and delivered to its intended site where it is installed on a foundation." *Prospecting Unlimited, Inc. v. Norberg*, 376 A.2d 702, 703 (Rhode Island 1977). The *Norberg* court went on to hold:

> "that once the modules were actually incorporated into completed houses, they became part of the real estate just as any other house usually does. When the houses were completed, the modules were not removable without damage to

themselves or the realty. Furthermore, they were permanently fastened to their foundations, were intended to remain so, and were adapted for use as housing, as was the realty to which they were attached."

. . . By way of comparison, the Washington Court of Appeals has held that certain mobile homes which had not lost their identity as mobile units remained personal property. In reaching its conclusion, the court noted that "[a]lthough the hitches and wheels were removed,

the axles were left on the units. They were placed on blocks rather than permanent foundations, and the utility connections . . . [were] not fixed pipes but flexible hoses which . . . [could] easily be disconnected." . . .

We are of the opinion that in this case the evidence is so clear that the only conclusion that can be drawn therefrom is that the modular home was a fixture of the real property and therefore not subject to an action of replevin.

Reversed.

Case Questions

1. What three factors do courts consider in determining whether personal property has become a fixture?
2. What difference does the classification of the mobile home as personalty or as a fixture make in this case?

Property Ownership

Property can be owned in several different forms, including severalty ownership, concurrent ownership, and community property. Severalty ownership exists when property is owned by one person. Concurrent ownership exists when property is held simultaneously by more than one person. This can occur in one of three ways—joint tenancy, tenancy in common, and tenancy by the entirety.[13] In joint tenancy, each joint tenant takes an equal, undivided interest in the ownership of property from the same source and at the same time. Each joint tenant also has an undivided right of survivorship. Thus in a joint tenancy involving three tenants, the entire tenancy passes to the two survivors upon the death of the third and by-passes the deceased person's will and heirs. Tenancy in common is similar to a joint tenancy; however, there is no automatic passing of the deceased's rights to the surviving tenants. Instead, the deceased's rights pass according to the will. Tenancies in common can be sold, inherited, and given as a gift. Tenancy by the entirety can exist only between legally married husbands and wives and can be ended only through death, divorce, or mutual consent. Upon the death of one of the tenants, title passes to the surviving spouse. If a divorce occurs, the tenancy is converted into a tenancy in common.

Community property is recognized in the states of Arizona, California, Idaho, Louisiana, Nevada, New Mexico, Texas, and Washington. Each spouse has an equal and undivided interest in property rights that either spouse acquires during the course of their marriage. Property that is acquired because of an inheritance or gift and property owned before the marriage are treated as exceptions. Each spouse has the right to control one-half of the community property in a will upon death. If there is a divorce, the spouses divide the community property.

Title

Title refers to ownership rights in property. For example, when a student purchases a textbook from a bookstore, he or she is purchasing the seller's *title* to the book. This means that the bookstore is selling all its rights in the book to the student. The bookstore will provide the purchaser with a receipt (bill of sale) to evidence the purchase of these rights and the transfer of ownership. If the student purchased the textbook from a thief, however, the student would not obtain title to the book. The larceny victim would still have the title, and the thief would be an unlawful possessor.[14]

A student who has purchased title to a textbook has many rights vis-à-vis that object. The student may decide to temporarily loan possessory rights to the book to another student. The student also has the right to decide whether to dispose of the book after completion of the course. For instance, the student might decide to make a gift or sell the rights in the book to another student or resell it back to the bookstore.

A bookstore does not have to produce a written document to establish its ownership when it sells a textbook to a student. However, the law does require the use of title documents to provide evidence of title for some property items. A seller of a motor vehicle, for example, must have a valid title document from the state to transfer ownership rights to the purchaser, and purchases of land require a title document called a deed.

GOVERNMENT'S RIGHT TO REGULATE AND TAKE PRIVATE PROPERTY

State government bears the primary responsibility for defining and limiting the exercise of private property rights through the police power. The police power refers to the authority of state legislatures to enact laws regulating and restraining private rights and occupations for the promotion of the public health, welfare, safety, and morals. The police power of the states is not a grant derived from a written constitution; the federal Constitution assumes the preexistence of the police power and the Tenth Amendment reserves to the states any power not delegated to the federal government in Article I. Limitations on the police power have never been drawn with precision or determined by a general formula. But the Fifth and Fourteenth amendments' due process clauses require that state actions based on the police power be exercised in the public interest, be reasonable, and be consistent with the rights implied or secured in the Constitution. Government uses of the police power with respect to property include zoning, eminent domain, taxation, and nuisance. See Figure 10–1 for an overview of the government's role in taking private property.

Zoning

State legislatures originally authorized local governments to enact zoning regulations to promote public health and safety by separating housing districts form incompatible commercial and industrial uses. Today, zoning ordinances also preserve a community's historically significant landmarks and neighborhoods and restrict adult entertainment. State and local environmental protection agencies often resort to zoning ordinances in deciding whether to grant licenses to land developers where a proposed land use threatens wetlands or natural habitat and increases air and water pollution. Zoning ordinances can be very controversial, such as where they prohibit trailer parks or require that structures and lots be large (and therefore often unaffordable to low income people). In the Family Law chapter (Chapter 8) you can see another example of restrictive zoning. In a 1977 case decided by the U.S. Supreme Court entitled *Moore v. City of East Cleveland*, governmental authorities unsuccessfully sought to use a zoning ordinance to prohibit a grandmother from living with her two grandchildren.

Eminent Domain

The government can take private property for a public purpose over the objection of a landowner pursuant to what is called the power of *eminent domain*. The Fifth Amendment provides that whenever the federal government takes property to benefit the public, it must pay just compensation. This constitutional control on government has been incorporated into the Fourteenth Amendment and is also binding on the states. The *Takings Clause* protects individual private property rights by ensuring that taxpayers, rather than targeted private individuals, pay for public benefits.

Government obtains title to private land through condemnation proceedings in which a court ensures that statutory and constitutional requirements are satisfied. In a related proceeding, a court will determine the fair market value of the land that will be paid to the property owner.

The U.S. Supreme Court has been unsuccessful to date in precisely establishing what constitutes a "taking." It has, however, recognized that takings can assume different forms. One obvious example is where the government takes title to land for the purpose of building a public highway. Other takings, however, are less obvious. The Supreme Court found in 1946 that a taking had occurred where low flying military aircraft created so much noise while flying over a chicken farm that the farm went out of business.[15] The Court ruled that under these circumstances the government had exploited and in effect taken airspace above it for a flight path (a public purpose), to the commercial detriment of the farmer. The farmer, said the Court, was entitled to compensation.

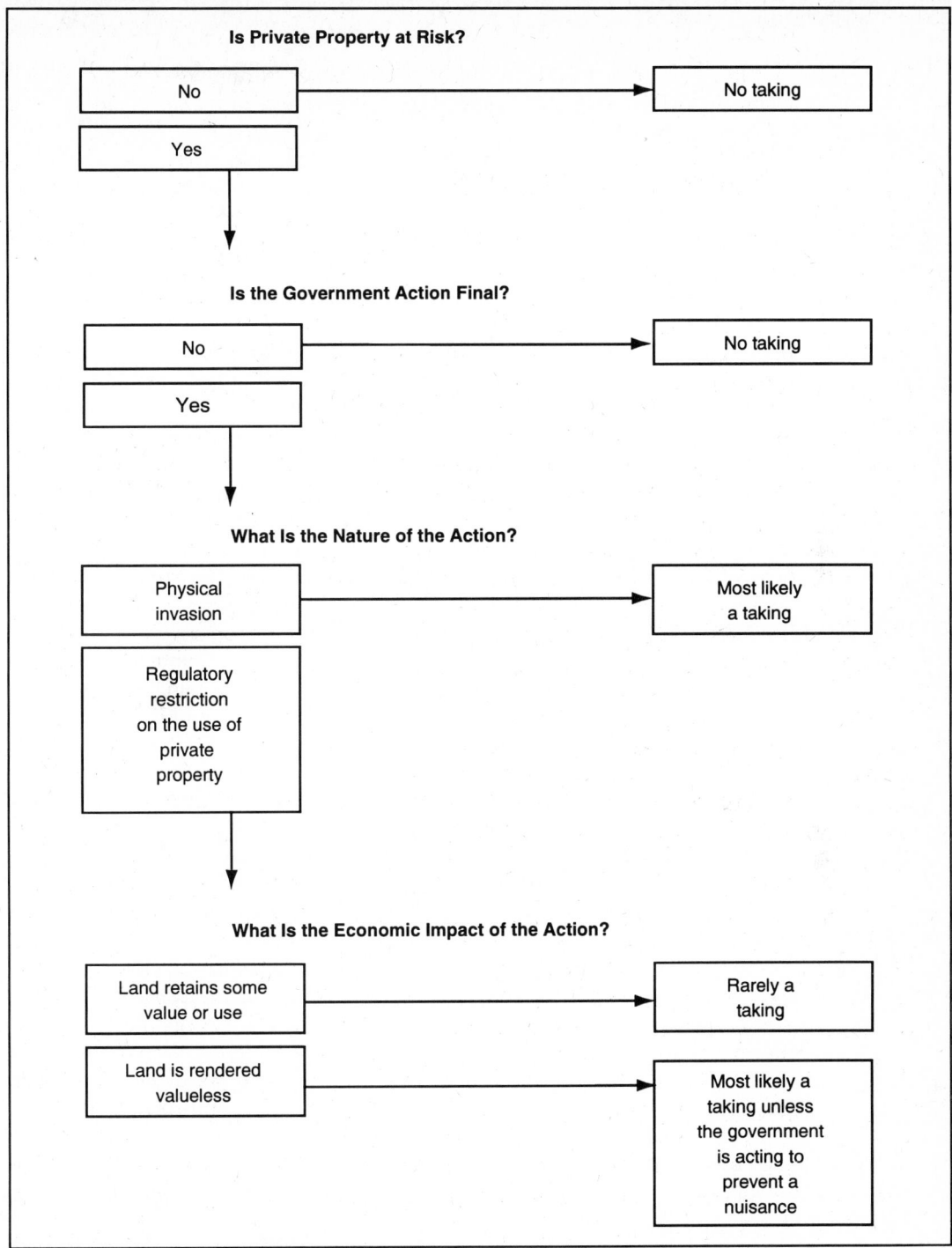

FIGURE 10–1 When Does Government Action Become a Taking of Private Property?

Source: Kathleen C. Zimmerman and David Abelson, "Takings Law: A Guide to Government, Property, and the Constitution," Copyright © 1993 by The Land & Water Fund of the Rockies, Inc.

In a 1978 case, the U.S. Supreme Court had to rule whether New York City, as part of a historic landmarks preservation program, could impose limitations on the development of historic buildings such as Grand Central Station. The City wanted to prevent the construction of a large office building above the Station. To the developer the restrictions imposed by the Landmark Preservation Law amounted to a taking of private property (the airspace above the Station) for a public purpose, for which compensation was due. The Court ruled in favor of the City, largely because the law served a public purpose (improving the quality of life for all New Yorkers) and provided the developer with a reasonable economic return on investment.

Since the ruling in the Grand Central Station case, the concerns of landowners have intensified. One aspect of the dispute that has evolved throughout the 1990s has focused on the point at which taxpayers should be required to compensate property owners whose property values have declined due to governmental environmental regulations.

One widely publicized example of this debate has been the conflict over environmental regulations intended to preserve the habitat of an endangered species called the northern spotted owl. Environmental legislation has been interpreted to prevent owners of land lying within the owl's habitat from commercially logging their own trees. Many landowners have argued that the law is unfairly denying them compensation when their property values fall as a result of governmental restrictions that prevent them from commercially developing their land and its natural resources. Defenders maintain that such regulations are necessary because the cumulative effect of the individual actions of private landowners would likely result in endangered species becoming extinct. Legislative initiatives designed to protect the environment, and preserve aesthetic and cultural landmarks, have generally been upheld by the Supreme Court. Whether this trend will continue is in doubt.

The next case was decided by the U.S. Supreme Court in 1994. It involved a dispute between a property owner/businesswoman and the City of Tigard, Oregon. The Supreme Court had to determine whether the City could require that the property owner dedicate 10 percent of her property for public uses—a public greenway, bike path, and contributions to an improved storm drainage system. In return, the City would grant her permission to replace the building housing her plumbing-supply business with a new and larger structure and to make other commercially valuable improvements to her parcel. The Court had to consider both the proper reach of the City's power to regulate businesses, and the reach of the Fifth Amendment's takings clause.

Dolan v. City of Tigard
114 S.Ct. 2309
U.S. Supreme Court
June 24, 1994

Chief Justice Rehnquist delivered the opinion of the Court.

I

The State of Oregon enacted a comprehensive land use management program in 1973. The program required all Oregon cities and counties to adopt new comprehensive land use plans that were consistent with the statewide planning goals. . . . Pursuant to the State's requirements, the city of Tigard, a community of some 30,000 residents on the southwest edge of Portland, developed a comprehensive plan and codified it in its Community Development Code (CDC). The CDC requires property owners in the area zoned Central Business District to comply with a 15% open space and landscaping requirement, which limits total site coverage, including all structures and paved parking, to 85% of the parcel. . . .

After the completion of a transportation study that identified congestion in the Central Business District as a particular problem, the city adopted a plan for a pedestrian/bicycle pathway intended to encourage alternatives to automobile transportation for short trips. The CDC requires that new development facilitate this plan by dedicating land for pedestrian pathways where provided for in the pedestrian/bicycle pathway plan.

The city also adopted a Master Drainage Plan (Drainage Plan). The Drainage Plan noted that flooding occurred in several areas along Fanno Creek, including areas near petitioner's property. . . . The Drainage Plan also established that the increase in impervious surfaces associated with continued urbanization would exacerbate these flooding problems. To combat these risks, the Drainage Plan suggested a series of improvements to the Fanno Creek Basin, including channel excavation in the area next to petitioner's property. . . . Other recommendations included ensuring that the floodplain remains free of structures and that it be preserved as greenways to minimize flood damage to structures. . . .

The Drainage Plan concluded that the cost of these improvements should be shared based on both direct and indirect benefits, with property owners along the waterways paying more due to the direct benefit that they would receive. . . . CDC Chapters 18.84, 18.86 and CDC § 18.164.100 and the Tigard Park Plan carry out these recommendations.

Petitioner Florence Dolan owns a plumbing and electric supply store located on Main Street in the Central Business District of the city. The store covers approximately 9,700 square feet on the eastern side of a 1.67-acre parcel, which includes a gravel parking lot. Fanno Creek flows through the southwestern corner of the lot and along its western boundary. The year-round flow of the creek renders the area within the creek's 100-year floodplain virtually unusable for commercial development. The city's comprehensive plan includes the Fanno Creek floodplain as part of the city's greenway system.

Petitioner applied to the city for a permit to redevelop the site. Her proposed plans called for nearly doubling the size of the store to 17,600 square feet, and paving a 39-space parking lot. The existing store, located on the opposite side of the parcel, would be razed in sections as construction progressed on the new building. In the second phase of the project, petitioner proposed to build an additional structure on the northeast side of the site for complementary businesses, and to provide more parking. The proposed expansion and intensified use are consistent with the city's zoning scheme in the Central Business District. . . .

The City Planning Commission granted petitioner's permit application subject to conditions imposed by the city's CDC. The CDC establishes the following standard for site development review approval:

"Where landfill and/or development is allowed within and adjacent to the 100-year floodplain, the city shall require the dedication of sufficient open land area for greenway adjoining and within the floodplain. This area shall include portions at a suitable elevation for the construction of a pedestrian/bicycle pathway within the floodplain in accordance with the adopted pedestrian/bicycle plan." . . .

Thus, the Commission required that petitioner dedicate the portion of her property lying within the 100-year floodplain for improvement of a storm drainage system along Fanno Creek and that she dedicate an additional 15-foot strip of land adjacent to the floodplain as a pedestrian/bicycle pathway. The dedication required by that condition encompasses approximately 7,000 square feet, or roughly 10% of the property. In accordance with city practice, petitioner could rely on the dedicated property to meet the 15% open space and landscaping requirement mandated by the city's zoning scheme.

The city would bear the cost of maintaining a landscaped buffer between the dedicated area and the new store.

Petitioner requested variances from the CDC standards. . . . The Commission denied the request.

The Commission made a series of findings concerning the relationship between the dedicated conditions and the projected impacts of petitioner's project. First, the Commission noted that "[i]t is reasonable to assume that customers and employees of the future uses of this site could utilize a pedestrian/bicycle pathway adjacent to this development for their transportation and recreational needs."

The Commission noted that the site plan has provided for bicycle parking in a rack in front of the proposed building and "[i]t is reasonable to expect that some of the users of the bicycle parking provided for by the site plan will use the pathway adjacent to Fanno Creek if it is constructed." . . . In addition, the Com-

mission found that creation of a convenient, safe pedestrian/bicycle pathway system as an alternative means of transportation "could offset some of the traffic demand on [nearby] streets and lessen the increase in traffic congestion." . . .

The Commission went on to note that the required floodplain dedication would be reasonably related to petitioner's request to intensify the use of the site given the increase in the impervious surface. The Commission stated that the "anticipated increased storm water flow from the subject property to an already strained creek and drainage basin can only add to the public need to manage the stream channel and floodplain for drainage purposes." . . . Based on this anticipated increased storm water flow, the Commission concluded that "the requirement of dedication of the floodplain area on the site is related to the applicant's plan to intensify development on the site." The Tigard City Council approved the Commission's final order. . . .

Petitioner appealed to the Land Use Board of Appeals (LUBA) on the ground that the city's dedication requirements were not related to the proposed development, and, therefore, those requirements constituted an uncompensated taking of their property under the Fifth Amendment. . . . Given the undisputed fact that the proposed larger building and paved parking area would increase the amount of impervious surfaces and the runoff into Fanno Creek, LUBA concluded that "there is a 'reasonable relationship' between the proposed development and the requirement to dedicate land along Fanno Creek for a greenway." . . .

With respect to the pedestrian/bicycle pathway, LUBA noted the Commission's finding that a significantly larger retail sales building and parking lot would attract larger numbers of customers and employees and their vehicles. It again found a "reasonable relationship" between alleviating the impacts of increased traffic from the development and facilitating the provision of a pedestrian/bicycle pathway as an alternative means of transportation. . . .

The Oregon Court of Appeals affirmed. . . .

We granted certiorari. . . .

II

The Takings Clause of the Fifth Amendment of the United States Constitution, made applicable to the States through the Fourteenth Amendment, . . . provides: "[N]or shall private property be taken for public use, without just compensation." One of the principal purposes of the Takings Clause is "to bar Government from forcing some people alone to bear public burdens which, in all fairness and justice, should be borne by the public as a whole." . . .

Without question, had the city simply required petitioner to dedicate a strip of land along Fanno Creek for public use, rather than conditioning the grant of her permit to redevelop her property on such a dedication, a taking would have occurred. . . . Such public access would deprive petitioner of the right to exclude others, "one of the most essential sticks in the bundle of rights that are commonly characterized as property."

. . . On the other side of the ledger, the authority of state and local governments to engage in land use planning has been sustained against constitutional challenge. . . .

. . . "Government hardly could go on if to some extent values incident to property could not be diminished without paying for every such change in the general law." *Pennsylvania Coal Co. v. Mahon,*

. . . (1992). A land use regulation does not effect a taking if it "substantially advance[s] legitimate state interests" and does not "den[y] an owner economically viable use of his land." *Agins v. Tiburon,* . . . (1980).

The sort of land use regulations discussed in the cases just cited, however, differ in two relevant particulars from the present case. First, they involved essentially legislative determinations classifying entire areas of the city, whereas here the city made an adjudicative decision to condition petitioner's application for a building permit on an individual parcel. Second, the conditions imposed were not simply a limitation on the use petitioner might make of her own parcel, but a requirement that she deed portions of the property to the city. In *Nollan v. California Coastal Comm'n,* we held the governmental authority to exact such a condition was circumscribed by the Fifth and Fourteenth Amendments. Under the well-settled doctrine of "unconstitutional conditions," the government may not require a person to give up a constitutional right—here the right to receive just compensation when property is taken for a public use—in exchange for a discretionary benefit conferred by the government where the property sought has little or no relationship to the benefit. . . .

Petitioner contends that the city has forced her to choose between the building permit and her right under the Fifth Amendment to just compensation for the public easements. Petitioner does not quarrel with the city's authority to exact some forms of dedication as a condition for the grant of a building permit, but challenges the showing made by the city to justify these exactions. She argues that the city has identified "no special benefits" conferred on her, and has not identified any "special quantifiable burdens"

created by her new store that would justify the particular dedications required
from her which are not required from the
public at large.

III

In evaluating petitioner's claim, we must
first determine whether the "essential
nexus" exists between the "legitimate
state interest" and the permit condition
exacted by the city. . . . If we find that a
nexus exists, we must then decide the
required degree of connection between
the exactions and the projected impact of
the proposed development. We were not
required to reach this question in *Nollan*,
because we concluded that the connection
did not meet even the loosest standard.
. . . Here, however, we must decide this
question.

A

We addressed the essential nexus question
in *Nollan*. The California Coastal Commission demanded a lateral public easement across the Nollan's beachfront lot in
exchange for a permit to demolish an
existing bungalow and replace it with a
three-bedroom house. . . . The public easement was designed to connect two public
beaches that were separated by the
Nollan's property. The Coastal Commission had asserted that the public easement
condition was imposed to promote the
legitimate state interest of diminishing the
"blockade of the view of the ocean" caused
by construction of the larger house.

We agreed that the Coastal Commission's concern with protecting visual access to the ocean constituted a legitimate
public interest. . . . We also agreed that
the permit condition would have been
constitutional "even if it consisted of the
requirement that the Nollans provide a

viewing spot on their property for pas-
sersby with whose sighting of the ocean
their new house would interfere." . . . We
resolved, however, that the Coastal Commission's regulatory authority was set
completely adrift from its constitutional
moorings when it claimed that a nexus
exited between visual access to the ocean
and a permit condition requiring lateral
public access along the Nollan's beachfront lot. . . . How enhancing the public's
ability to "traverse to and along the shore-
front" served the same governmental
purpose of "visual access to the ocean"
from the roadway was beyond our ability
to countenance. The absence of a nexus
left the Coastal Commission in the position of simply trying to obtain an easement through gimmickry, which converted a valid regulation of land use into
"an out-and-out plan of extortion." . . .

No such gimmicks are associated with
the permit conditions imposed by the city
in this case. Undoubtedly, the prevention
of flooding along Fanno Creek and the
reduction of traffic congestion in the Central Business District qualify as the type of
legitimate public purposes we have upheld. . . . It seems equally obvious that a
nexus exits between preventing flooding
along Fanno Creek and limiting development within the creek's 100-year floodplain. Petitioner proposes to double the
size of her retail store and to pave her
now-gravel parking lot, thereby expanding the impervious surface on the property and increasing the amount of storm-
water run-off into Fanno Creek.

The same may be said for the city's
attempt to reduce traffic congestion by
providing for alternative means of transportation. In theory, a pedestrian/bicycle
pathway provides a useful alternative
means of transportation for workers and
shoppers: "Pedestrians and bicyclists
occupying dedicated spaces for walking

and/or bicycling . . . remove potential vehicles from streets, resulting in an over-all improvement in total transportation system flow." . . .

B

The second part of our analysis requires us to determine whether the degree of the exactions demanded by the city's permit conditions bear the required relationship to the projected impact of petitioner's proposed development. . . .

The city required that petitioner dedicate "to the city as Greenway all portions of the site that fall within the existing 100-year floodplain [of Fanno Creek] . . . and all property 15 feet above [the floodplain] boundary. "In addition, the city demanded that the retail store be designed so as not to intrude into the greenway area. The city relies on the Commission's rather tentative findings that increased stormwater flow from petitioner's property "can only add to the public need to manage the [floodplain] for drainage purposes" to support its conclusion that the "requirement of dedication of the floodplain area on the site is related to the applicant's plan to intensify development on the site." . . .

The city made the following specific findings relevant to the pedestrian/bicycle pathway:

> "In addition, the proposed expanded use of this site is anticipated to generate additional vehicular traffic thereby increasing congestion on nearby collector and arterial streets. Creation of a convenient, safe pedestrian/bicycle pathway system as an alternative means of transportation could offset some of the traffic demand on these nearby streets and lessen the increase in traffic congestion."

. . .

The question for us is whether these findings are constitutionally sufficient to justify the conditions imposed by the city on petitioner's building permit. Since state courts have been dealing with this question a good deal longer than we have, we turn to representative decisions made by them. . . . Despite any semantical differences, general agreement exists among the courts "that the dedication should have some reasonable relationship to the needs created by the [development]."

We think the "reasonable relationship" test adopted by a majority of the state courts is closer to the federal constitutional norm than either of those previously discussed. But we do not adopt it as such, partly because the term "reasonable relationship" seems confusingly similar to the term "rational basis" which describes the minimal level of scrutiny under the Equal Protection Clause of the Fourteenth Amendment. We think a term such as "rough proportionality" best encapsulates what we hold to be the requirement of the Fifth Amendment. No precise mathematical calculation is required, but the city must make some sort of individualized determination that the required dedication is related both in nature and extent to the impact of the proposed development. . . . It is axiomatic that increasing the amount of impervious surface will increase the quantity and rate of storm-water flow from petitioner's property. . . . Therefore, keeping the floodplain open and free from development would likely confine the pressures on Fanno Creek created by petitioner's development. In fact, because petitioner's property lies within the Central Business District, the Community Development Code already required that petitioner leave 15% of it as open space and the undeveloped floodplain would have nearly satisfied that requirement. . . . But the city demanded more—it not only wanted petitioner not to build in the floodplain, but it also wanted petitioner's property along Fanno Creek for its Greenway system. The city has never said why a public greenway, as opposed to a private one, was required in the interest of flood control.

The difference to petitioner, of course, is the loss of her ability to exclude others. As we have noted, this right to exclude others is "one of the most essential sticks in the bundle of rights that are commonly characterized as property." It is difficult to see why recreational visitors trampling along petitioner's floodplain easement are sufficiently related to the city's legitimate interest in reducing flooding problems along Fanno Creek, and the city has not attempted to make any individualized determination to support this part of its request. . . .

Admittedly, petitioner wants to build a bigger store to attract members of the public to her property. She also wants, however, to be able to control the time and manner in which they enter.

. . . By contrast, the city wants to impose a permanent recreational easement upon petitioner's property that borders Fanno Creek. Petitioner would lose all rights to regulate the time in which the public entered onto the Greenway, regardless of any interference it might pose with her retail store. Her right to exclude would not be regulated, it would be eviscerated.

If petitioner's proposed development had somehow encroached on existing greenway space in the city, it would have been reasonable to require petitioner to provide some alternative greenway space for the public either on her property or elsewhere.

. . . We conclude that the findings upon which the city relies do not show the required reasonable relationship between the floodplain easement and the petitioner's proposed new building.

With respect to the pedestrian/bicycle pathway, we have no doubt that the city was correct in finding that the larger retail sales facility proposed by petitioner will increase traffic on the streets of the Central Business District. The city estimates that the proposed development would generate roughly 435 additional trips per day. Dedications for streets, sidewalks, and other public ways are generally reasonable exactions to avoid excessive congestion from a proposed property use. But on the record before us, the city has not met its burden of demonstrating that the additional number of vehicle and bicycle trips generated by the petitioner's development reasonably relate to the city's requirement for a dedication of the pedestrian/bicycle pathway easement. The city simply found that the creation of the pathway "could offset some of the traffic demand . . . and lessen the increase in traffic congestion." . . .

As Justice Peterson of the Supreme Court of Oregon explained in his dissenting opinion, however, "[t]he findings of fact that the bicycle pathway system *'could* offset some of the traffic demand' is a far cry from a finding that the bicycle pathway system *will*, or is *likely to*, offset some of the traffic demand." No precise mathematical calculation is required, but the city must make some effort to quantify its findings in support of the dedication for the pedestrian/bicycle pathway beyond the conclusory statement that it could offset some of the traffic demand generated.

Cities have long engaged in the commendable task of land use planning, made necessary by increasing urbanization particularly in metropolitan areas such as Portland. The city's goals of reducing flooding hazards and traffic congestion, and providing for public greenways, are laudable, but there are outer limits to how this may be done. "A strong public desire to improve the public condition [will not] warrant achieving the desire by a shorter cut than the constitutional way of paying for the change."

The judgment of the Supreme Court of Oregon is reversed, and the case is remanded for further proceedings consistent with this opinion.

It is so ordered.

Justice Stevens, with whom Justice Blackmun and Justice Ginsburg join, dissenting

The record does not tell us the dollar value of petitioner Florence Dolan's interest in excluding the public from the greenway adjacent to her hardware business. The mountain of briefs that the case has generated nevertheless makes it obvious that the pecuniary value of her victory is far less important than the rule of law that this case has been used to establish. It is unquestionably an important case.

Certain propositions are not in dispute. The enlargement of the Tigard unit in Dolan's chain of hardware stores will have an adverse impact on the city's legitimate and substantial interests in controlling drainage in Fanno Creek and minimizing traffic congestion in Tigard's business district. That impact is sufficient to justify an outright denial of her application for approval of the expansion. The city has nevertheless agreed to grant Dolan's application if she will comply with two conditions, each of which admittedly will mitigate the adverse effects of her proposed development. The disputed question is whether the city has violated the Fourteenth Amendment to the Federal Constitution by refusing to allow Dolan's planned construction to proceed unless those conditions are met.

The Court is correct in concluding that the city may not attach arbitrary conditions to a building permit or to a variance even when it can rightfully deny the application outright. I also agree that state court decisions dealing with ordinances that govern municipal development plans provide useful guidance in a case of this kind. Yet the Court's description of the doctrinal underpinnings of its decision, the phrasing of its fledgling test of "rough proportionality," and the application of that test to this case run contrary to the traditional treatment of these cases and break considerable and unpropitious new ground.

I

Candidly acknowledging the lack of federal precedent for its exercise in rulemaking, the Court purports to find guidance in . . . "representative" state court decisions. To do so is certainly appropriate. The state cases the Court consults, however, either fail to support or decidedly undermine the Court's conclusions in key respects. . . .

II

It is not merely state cases, but our own cases as well, that require the analysis to focus on the impact of the city's action on the entire parcel of private property. In *Penn Central Transportation Co. v. New York City,* . . . we stated that takings jurisprudence "does not divide a single parcel into discrete segments and attempt to determine whether rights in a particular segment have been entirely abrogated." . . . Instead, this Court focuses "both on the character of the action and on the nature and extent of the interference with rights in the parcel as a whole." *Andrus v. Allard* . . . reaffirmed the nondivisibility principle outlined in *Penn Central*, stating that "[a]t least where an owner possesses a full 'bundle' of property rights, the destruction of one 'strand' of the bundle is not a taking, because the aggregate must be viewed in its entirety."

Although limitation of the right to exclude others undoubtedly constitutes a significant infringement upon property ownership, restrictions on that right do not alone constitute a taking, and do not do so in any event unless they "unreasonably impair the value or use" of the property.

The Court's narrow focus on one strand in the property owner's bundle of rights is particularly misguided in a case involving the development of commercial property. As Professor Johnston has noted:

> "The subdivider is a manufacturer, processer, and marketer of a product; land is but one of his raw materials. In subdivision control disputes, the developer is not defending hearth and home against the king's intrusion, but simply attempting to maximize his profits from the sale of a finished product. As applied to him, subdivision control exactions are actually business regulations." Johnston, Constitutionality of Subdivision Control Exactions: The Quest for A Rationale, 52 Cornell L.Q. 871, 923 (1967).

The exactions associated with the development of a retail business are likewise a species of business regulation that heretofore warranted a strong presumption of constitutional validity.

In Johnston's view, "if the municipality can demonstrate that its assessment of financial burdens against subdividers is rational, impartial, and conducive to fulfillment of authorized planning objectives, its action need be invalidated only in those extreme and presumably rare cases where the burden of compliance is sufficiently great to deter the owner from proceeding with his planned development." . . . The city of Tigard has demonstrated that its plan is rational and impartial and that the conditions at issue are "conducive to fulfillment of authorized planning objectives." Dolan, on the other hand, has offered no evidence that her burden of compliance has any impact at all on the value or profitability of her planned development. Following the teaching of the cases on which it purports to rely, the Court should not isolate the burden associated with the loss of the power to exclude from an evaluation of the benefit to be derived from the permit to enlarge the store and the parking lot.

The Court's assurances that its "rough proportionality" test leaves ample room for cities to pursue the "commendable task of land use planning," . . . even twice avowing that "[n]o precise mathematical calculation is required," . . . are wanting given the result that test compels here. Under the Court's approach, a city must not only "quantify its findings," . . . and make "individualized determination[s]" with respect to the nature *and* the extent of the relationship between the conditions and the impact, . . . but also demonstrate "proportionality." The correct inquiry should instead concentrate on whether the required nexus is present and venture beyond considerations of a condition's nature or germaneness only if the developer establishes that a concededly germane condition is so grossly disproportionate to the proposed development's adverse effects that it manifests motives other than land use regulation on the part of the city.

III

Applying its new standard, the Court finds two defects in the city's case. First, while the record would adequately support a requirement that Dolan maintain the portion of the floodplain on her property as undeveloped open space, it does not support the additional requirement that the floodplain be dedicated to the city. . . . Second, while the city adequately established the traffic increase that the proposed development would generate, it failed to quantify the offsetting decrease in automobile traffic that the bike path will produce.

IV

The Court has made a serious error by abandoning the traditional presumption of constitutionality and imposing a novel burden of proof on a city implementing an admittedly valid comprehensive land use plan. Even more consequential than its incorrect disposition of this case, however, is the Court's resurrection of a species of substantive due process analysis that it firmly rejected decades ago. . . .

It applied the same kind of substantive due process analysis more frequently identified with a better known case that accorded similar substantive protection to a baker's liberty interest in working 60 hours a week and 10 hours a day. See *Lochner v. New York*, . . . (1905).

Later cases have interpreted the Fourteenth Amendment's substantive protection against uncompensated deprivations of private property by the States as though it incorporated the text of the Fifth Amendment's Takings Clause. . . . There was nothing problematic about that interpretation in cases enforcing the Fourteenth Amendment against state action that involved the actual physical invasion of private property. . . . Justice Holmes charted a significant new course, however, when he opined that a state law making it "commercially impracticable to mine certain coal" had "very nearly the same effect for constitutional purposes as appropriating or destroying it." *Pennsylvania Coal Co. v. Mahon*, . . . (1922). The so-called "regulatory takings" doctrine that the Holmes dictum kindled has an obvious kinship with the line of substantive due process cases that *Lochner* exemplified. Besides having similar ancestry, both doctrines are potentially open-ended sources of judicial power to invalidate state economic regulations that Members of this Court view as unwise or unfair.

This case inaugurates an even more recent judicial innovation than the regulatory takings doctrine: the application of the "unconstitutional conditions" label to a mutually beneficial transaction between a property owner and a city. The Court tells us that the city's refusal to grant Dolan a discretionary benefit infringes her right to receive just compensation for the property interests that she has refused to dedicate to the city "where the property sought has little or no relationship to the benefit." . . .

Dolan has no right to be compensated for a taking unless the city acquires the property interests that she has refused to surrender. Since no taking has yet occurred, there has not been any infringement of her constitutional right to compensation. . . .

The Court has decided to apply its heightened scrutiny to a single strand—the power to exclude—in the bundle of rights that enables a commercial enterprise to flourish in an urban environment. . . .

In its application of what is essentially the doctrine of substantive due process, the Court confuses the past with the present. On November 13, 1922, the village of Euclid, Ohio, adopted a zoning ordinance that effectively confiscated 75 percent of the value of property owned by the Ambler Realty Company. Despite its recognition that such an ordinance "would have been rejected as arbitrary and oppressive" at an earlier date, the Court (over the dissent of Justices Van Devanter, McReynolds and Butler) upheld the ordinance. Today's majority should heed the words of Justice Sutherland:

> "Such regulations are sustained, under the complex conditions of our day, for reasons analogous to those which justify traffic regulations, which, before the advent of automobiles and rapid transit street railways, would have been condemned as fatally arbitrary and unreasonable. And in this there is no inconsistency, for while the meaning of constitutional guaranties never varies, the scope of their application must expand or contract to meet the new and different conditions which are constantly coming within the field of their operation. In a changing world, it is impossible that it should be otherwise." *Euclid v. Ambler* . . . (1926).

In our changing world one thing is certain: uncertainty will characterize predictions about the impact of new urban developments on the risks of floods, earthquakes, traffic congestion, or environmental harms. When there is doubt concerning the magnitude of those impacts, the public interest in averting them must outweigh the private interest of the commercial entrepreneur. If the government can demonstrate that the conditions it has imposed in a land-use permit are rational, impartial and conducive to fulfilling the aims of a valid land-use plan, a strong presumption of validity should

attach to those conditions. The burden of demonstrating that those conditions have unreasonably impaired the economic value of the proposed improvement belongs squarely on the shoulders of the party challenging the state action's constitutionality. That allocation of burdens has served us well in the past. The Court has stumbled badly today by reversing it.

I respectfully dissent.

Justice Souter, dissenting

This case, like *Nollan v. California Coastal Comm'n,* . . . (1987), invites the Court to examine the relationship between conditions imposed by development permits, requiring landowners to dedicate portions of their land for use by the public, and governmental interests in mitigating the adverse effects of such development. *Nollan* declared the need for a nexus between the nature of an exaction of an interest in land (a beach easement) and the nature of governmental interests. . . .

I cannot agree that the application of *Nollan* is a sound one here, since it appears that the Court has placed the burden of producing evidence of relationship on the city, despite the usual rule in cases involving the police power that the government is presumed to have acted constitutionally. Having thus assigned the burden, the Court concludes that the City loses based on one word ("could" instead of "would"), and despite the fact that this record shows the connection the Court looks for. Dolan has put forward no evidence that the burden of granting a dedication for the bicycle path is unrelated in kind to the anticipated increase in traffic congestion, nor, if there exists a requirement that the relationship be related in degree, has Dolan shown that the exaction fails any such test. The city, by contrast, calculated the increased traffic flow that would result from Dolan's proposed development to be 435 trips per day, and its Comprehensive Plan, applied here, relied on studies showing the link between alternative modes of transportation, including bicycle paths, and reduced street traffic congestion. . . . *Nollan*, therefore, is satisfied, and on that assumption the city's conditions should not be held to fail a further rough proportionality test or any other that might be devised to give meaning to the constitutional limits. As Members of this Court have said before, "the common zoning regulations requiring subdividers to . . . dedicate certain areas to public streets, are in accord with our constitutional traditions because the proposed property use would otherwise be the cause of excessive congestion." . . .

. . . The bicycle path permit condition is fundamentally no different from these.

In any event, on my reading, the Court's conclusions about the city's vulnerability carry the Court no further than *Nollan* has gone already, and I do not view this case as a suitable vehicle for taking the law beyond that point. The right case for the enunciation of takings doctrine seems hard to spot.

Case Questions

1. What test did the Supreme Court adopt in deciding this case?
2. Can you see any consequences that might flow from this decision in the future?
3. The Court's decision in this case was supported by five of the justices. Why did four justices dissent?

Taxation

A property owner is usually required to pay taxes to the government based on the value and use of the property. Failure to pay these taxes can result in the filing of a lien and eventually in the public taking of the property to satisfy the taxes. Government frequently uses tax concessions to encourage property uses it favors.

Nuisance

A nuisance exists when an owner's use of his or her property unreasonably infringes on other persons' use and enjoyment of their property rights. Nuisances are classified as public, private, or both. A *public nuisance* exists when a given use of land poses a generalized threat to the public. It is redressed by criminal prosecution and injunctive relief. Examples of public nuisances include houses of prostitution, actions affecting the public health (such as water and air pollution), crack houses, and dance halls. A *private nuisance* is a tort that requires proof of an injury that is distinct from that suffered by the general public. (It differs from trespass because the offensive activity does not occur on the victim's property.) A party injured by a private nuisance can obtain both damages and injunctive relief.

The facts in the following public nuisance case would also be actionable as a private nuisance.

Feeley v. Borough of Ridley Park
551 A.2d 373
Commonwealth Court of Pennsylvania
December 9, 1988

Colins, Judge

Appellant, Veronica Feeley appeals an order of the Delaware County Court of Common Pleas which was entered on December 15, 1987. This order declared appellant's house a public nuisance and required appellant to *inter alia:* keep no more than four cats at one time; to have the cats in her possession neutered, vaccinated, and examined by a veterinarian and; have her home professionally cleaned and deodorized.

In July, 1985, the Borough of Ridley Park (Borough) filed an action in equity against appellant seeking a preliminary injunction contending that the conditions of appellant's home constituted a nuisance. The Borough's complaint alleged that appellant's home was in a deplorable state of disrepair, lacking proper plumbing, electricity, or water. In addition, the complaint alleged that appellant maintained approximately eighteen cats on her premises and, because of appellant's failure to adhere to proper animal husbandry, cat feces were present in every room, on every floor, and on the furniture; the odor of cat urine overpowered the premises; and that fleas, flies, and ants infest the entire house, all of which result in a terrible odor emanating from appellant's home.

A preliminary injunction was entered on August 6, 1985, which ordered the appellant to eliminate the odors coming from her home by having the premises fumigated no later than August 19, 1985. The order authorized the Borough to obtain a veterinarian for the purpose of examining the cats on appellant's premises and also authorized the Borough to enter appellant's premises for a general inspection.

While it appears that appellant initially acted upon the August 6, 1985 order, she again became lax in her housekeeping and, on August 9, 1987, the Borough petitioned the court to find appellant guilty of contempt. At the hearing, the Borough presented witnesses who testified that as a result of the noxious and overpowering odors emanating from appellant's home, they were forced to keep their windows closed. Thus, on August 25, 1987, the Chancellor issued an order requiring appellant to deodorize and clean her home within one week; submit her home to monthly inspections by the Borough's health officer; submit her cats to an inspection by an independent veterinarian; and not increase the number of cats in her possession beyond thirty. Following the inspection and subsequent report by Dr. Peter Herman, V.M.D., the court entered its final order on December 15, 1987, which appellant now appeals. . . .

We are limited in our review of this action to a determination of whether the Chancellor's findings of fact are supported by substantial evidence, whether an error of law has been made, or whether the Chancellor abused his discretion. . . . Moreover, the presence of evidence contrary to the Chancellor's findings does not make them unsupported since issues of credibility and evidentiary weight are within the exclusive province of the Chancellor.

. . . The issues presented by appellant for our determination are whether the Chancellor's decision that appellant's house constitutes a public nuisance is supported by substantial evidence and whether the Borough has authority to abate the nuisance in the manner ordered by the Chancellor.

This Court has noted:

"In legal phraseology, the term 'nuisance' is applied to that class of wrongs that arise from the unreasonable, unwarrantable, or unlawful use by a person of his own property, real or personal, or from his own improper, indecent, or unlawful personal conduct, working on [sic] obstruction or injury to a right of another, or of the public, and producing such material annoyance, inconvenience, discomfort or hurt that the law will presume a consequent damage. . . ."

Thus, to constitute a public nuisance, the conduct must be an inconvenience or troublesome offense that annoys the whole community in general, and not merely some particular person.

The evidence presented by the Borough in the instant matter certainly indicates appellant's home constitutes a public nuisance. For example, the general comments provided by Peter H. Herman, V.M.D., following a *prearranged* inspection of appellant's home on November 20, 1987, noted that there were not enough litter boxes for the number of cats in appellant's house; the litter boxes had not been cleaned for many days; litter, feces and urine were observed on the floors of multiple rooms; the environment of the house constituted a poor and unhealthy environment for cats as well as appellant; there were numerous flies in every room; and, a very strong ammonia odor was

smelled in every room. The doctor found that appellant's residence was a dirty, moldy, dark, and malodorous place. Dr. Herman concluded his report by opining that on the day of his inspection, the unsanitary condition of appellant's home rendered it unfit for both feline and human habitation.

In addition, evidence was presented to the Chancellor that neighbors who live not only next door to appellant but also those who live down the block and around the corner were bothered by the noxious odors emanating from appellant's home. Since 1985, the residents of Ridley Park have complained about the conditions at appellant's home. Still, despite the order of the trial court entered August 6, 1985, appellant has failed to maintain her cats and her house in such a manner as to not offend the neighbors in her community.

Accordingly, we find that appellant's use of her property is both unwarrantable and unreasonable. The Borough has demonstrated by substantial evidence the deplorable conditions of appellant's home, as well as the fact that appellant's home constitutes a public nuisance.

Having concluded that appellant's home does, in fact, constitute a public nuisance, we turn now to the determination of whether the Borough has the authority to abate the nuisance in the manner prescribed by the Chancellor. In the instant matter, the Chancellor specifically found: "The Borough plainly in this case has the authority to act." Yet, in her appeal, appellant asserts that because the Chancellor did not declare that her pets or number of pets creates a nuisance, the Borough lacks the authority to issue an order limiting the number of cats maintained on appellant's property.

Section 1202 of The Borough Code, enumerates the specific powers of

Boroughs. Included within those powers is Section 1202(5), which provides that the Borough may:

> "[P]rohibit and remove any nuisance, including but not limited to accumulations of garbage and rubbish and the storage of abandoned or junked automobiles and . . . prohibit and remove any dangerous structure on public or private grounds, or . . . require the removal of any such nuisance or dangerous structure by the owner or occupier of such grounds, in default of which the borough may cause the same to be done, and collect the cost thereof, together with a penalty of ten per cent [sic] of such cost, in the manner provided by law for the collection of municipal claims, or by action of assumpsit, or may seek relief by bill in equity."

We find appellant's argument, with respect to the Borough's authority to act in this matter, to be meritless. The low level of animal husbandry to which appellant adheres certainly contributes to the foul odors of which the neighbors complain. Moreover, the court afforded appellant the opportunity to keep as many animals as she desired in its 1985 order, but appellant was unable to properly care for the animals so as to not offend the community. The Borough merely seeks to abate the nuisance which appellant herself failed to abate. Thus, we conclude that the Chancellor's order is directed toward abating the nuisance and is neither unduly harsh nor capricious.

Accordingly, the order of the Chancellor is affirmed.

Case Questions

1. What is required to change a private nuisance into a public nuisance?
2. If the Borough of Ridley Park filed the original action and later petitioned the court to find Feeley in contempt, why is the case captioned *Feeley v. Borough of Ridley Park*?
3. Do you agree that a local government should be able to control the number of pets a citizen can possess?

REAL PROPERTY

The laws that govern real property in America have their origins in medieval England. Under feudal law all land was derived from the king; thus people could own estates in land but not the actual land itself. Estates were classified according to their duration, a practice that continues in American law today.

Estates in Land

The word *estate* is derived from the Latin word for status. An estate in land, therefore, is the amount of interest a person has in land. Some estates in land can be inherited. A person who holds an estate in what is known as fee simple can pass his or her interest on to heirs. This represents the maximum ownership right to land that is permissible by law. A person who has an estate in land for the duration of his or her life has a life estate in land. Life estates cannot be passed on to heirs. A person who leases real property has only a possessory interest in land called a leasehold. Leaseholds allow tenants to obtain possessory interests in real property for a month, a year, or even at will.

A landowner has the right to minerals that exist beneath the surface of the land. Landowners also have the right to control and use the airspace above their land. Governmental regulations regarding the height of buildings, as well as engineering limitations that are associated with a particular property, often limit the exercise of this right.

Easements

Easements and licenses are interests in land that do not amount to an estate, but affect the owner's use of land. An *easement* is a nonpossessory property right in land; it is one person's right to use another person's land. For example, B might grant A an easement that permits her to use a private road on B's property. Because B continues to own the land, B can grant similar easements to persons C and D. B can grant these additional easements without having to obtain permission from A, because A lacks possessory rights on B's land. Easements are often classified as affirmative or negative. An affirmative easement would exist where landowner A conveys to B the right to lay a pipeline across A's land. A negative easement would exist where A conveys part of her land to B and retains an easement that forbids B to burn trash or plant trees within five yards of A's property line.

An easement also may be created by eminent domain. In such a case, the landowner is constitutionally entitled to receive just compensation. Easements often are created by deed, and usually have to be in writing to be legally enforceable. They can be limited to a specific term or event or they can be of infinite duration. It is commonly said that easements "run with the land," meaning that the burden or benefit of the easement is transferred with the land to the subsequent owners.

Licenses

A *license* is a temporary grant of authority to do specified things on the land of another, for example, hunt or fish. A license can be oral because it is not an actual estate in land and therefore is not subject to the statute of frauds (see Chapter 9). Licenses can generally be revoked at will.

Covenants

To protect themselves from sellers who don't have title, purchasers of land often require the seller to make certain promises in the deed that are called *covenants*. The grantor's covenants ensure that he or she has possessory rights to the premises and that the title is good and is free and clear of encumbrances. The grantor will further promise to defend this title against the claims and demands of other people.

Other covenants that affect land use are those that run with the land. Historically, restrictive covenants have discriminated against people because of race, religion, and national origin. Today such covenants are illegal and contrary to public policy and would not be enforced in any court. Courts will, in appropriate cases, enforce nondiscriminatory covenants that run with the land and that create contractual rights in property. Although easements have traditionally been used to affect land use, lawyers began to resort to covenants to augment the kind of restrictions sellers could require of purchasers beyond the scope of easements. A baker, for example, might be willing to sell an adjacent lot that he owns; however, he might protect his business by requiring the purchaser to covenant that the premises conveyed will not be used for the operation or maintenance of a bakery, lunchroom, or restaurant.

Covenants that run with the land are regulated closely by courts because they restrict the use of property. For a covenant to run with the land and bind successive landowners, the original grantor and grantee must have intended that the restrictions on the covenant go with the land. In addition, a close, direct relationship known as *privity of estate* must exist between a grantor and a grantee. The privity requirement is satisfied, for example, when land developer A deeds part of her land to B, and B covenants not to put up a fence on B's land without A's written approval. Finally, covenants must "touch and concern" land; they may not be promises that are personal and unrelated to land. Successors in interest to the original grantor and grantee will be bound by the terms of a properly created covenant that runs with the land.

In the following case, a housing development home owners' association used a covenant to restrict a fellow landowner from building a "dog pen" on his property.

Sherwood Estates Homes Association, Inc. v. McConnell
714 S.W.2d 848
Missouri Court of Appeals, Western District
July 15, 1986

Per Curiam

This is a civil action involving the construction of a restrictive covenant. The judgment is affirmed. . . .

The parties agree that appellant became a landowner within the development known as Sherwood Estates and that appellants knew of the restrictions applic-able to the homesites therein. There is no dispute that respondent is the proper substitute for the original developing company. Appellants made various improvements to their residence, including the installation of a bay window and deck. They also erected a dog pen in their yard. None of these changes or additions were done with prior approval from respondent. The matter was brought to the attention of respondent. All of the changes and additions made by appellants, except one, were approved by respondent and that approval was retroactive. The one addition not approved was the erection of a dog pen in appellants' yard. Respondent's efforts to have appellants remove the dog pen being unsuccessful caused this action to be filed. Respondent contended that the dog pen violated the prohibition set forth in Restriction VII of its Declaration of Restrictions which reads as follows:

"VII: Approval of Plans
"No building, fence, wall or other structure shall be commenced, erected or maintained, nor shall any addition thereto or change or alterations therein be made, until plans and specifications, color scheme, plot plan and grading plan therefor, or other information satisfactory to the Company shall have been submitted to and approved in writing by the Company and a copy thereof as finally approved lodged with the Company. In so passing upon such plans, specifications and other requirements, the Company may take into consideration the suitability of the proposed building or other structure and the materials of which it is to be built, to the site upon which, it is proposed to erect same, the harmony thereof with the surroundings and the effect of the building or other structure as planned on the outlook from adjacent or neighboring property."

Respondent presented uncontroverted evidence that such a dog pen did not help property values and in fact lessened property values. The dog pen in question has concrete block flooring and is enclosed by fencing. The entire structure is housed inside the rear fenced yard of appellants'.

The trial court entered its Findings of Fact and Conclusions of Law and its judgment. In its findings, the court concluded that appellants' dog pen is a "structure" as that term is used in Restriction VII. The trial court then ordered appellants to remove their dog pen. This appeal followed. . . .

The question of enforcement of Restriction VII is not at issue in this case because this court has previously ruled that respondent may enforce restrictions. . . . Thus, as the parties have noted, the only real issue is whether appellants' dog pen is a structure within the meaning and contemplation of the term "other structure" as expressed in Restriction VII.

A reading of the Declaration of Restrictions discloses the intent and purpose thereof is to maintain a harmonious residential area. In addition, the Declaration of Restrictions is intended to safeguard against the effects of any structure upon the surrounding area and dwellings already upon the land. It is also obvious that the protection of the value of the various properties is one of the main purposes of the Declaration.

A structure has been defined as

"Any construction or any production or piece of work artificially built up or composed of parts joined together in some definite manner. That which is built or constructed; an edifice or building of any kind. A combination of material, to form a construction for occupancy, use or ornamentation, whether installed on, above or below the surface of a parcel of land." Black's Law Dictionary 1276 (rev. 5th ed. 1969).

The evidence herein revealed that appellants' dog pen has a concrete block flooring. In addition, it is a manufactured fence type structure which can be assembled by the owner. According to appellants, it is portable and can be moved by two or more persons.

There is no doubt that appellants' dog pen falls within the definition of structure as that term is defined by Black's, *supra*. In addition, our courts have held that the term "structure" is not synonymous with the term "building." . . .

A further matter which must be considered is that by appellants' own testimony, their dog pen is a fence construction. Restriction VII, *supra*, also limits the erection of any fence without prior approval by respondent. Thus, appellants' dog pen runs afoul of Restriction VII.

These modern times bear witness to the continual conflict between the unrestricted and free use of land so jealously guarded by our heritage, and the ever increasing closeness produced by residential expansion to serve the needs of our expanding population. The present case illustrates this conflict. One interest must prevail over the other when the two interests collide. In the present case, the evidence is uncontroverted that Sherwood Estates was developed for residential use and to further that use the developing company set forth certain restrictions. There is no dispute that respondent herein is the proper substituted party for the developing company. It is likewise not in dispute that appellants acquired their property with full knowledge and acceptance of the restrictions. Enforcement of the restrictions by respondent is also not in dispute.

This court holds, and thus rules, that appellants' dog pen falls within the definition of the term "structure", Black's, *supra*, and further, that their dog pen is a structure with the meaning and contemplation of the term "other structure" as that term is found and is made use of in Restriction VII. . . .

The judgment of the trial court is affirmed and appellants are hereby ordered to remove their dog pen from their property described as Lot 26, Block 10 Sherwood Estates, commonly known as 4931 N. Sherwood Drive, Kansas City, Missouri, forthwith.

Case Questions

1. How is the privity of estate requirement satisfied in this case?
2. Why should the home owners' association have any right to approve or disapprove of the way in which the McConnells want to use their land?

Adverse Possession

A person who has no lawful right of possession can obtain title to another's land by complying with the rules for *adverse possession*. The law requires property owners to ensure that no one else uses the land without permission, and a person who fails to use or protect his or her land for many years may one day lose title to an adverse possessor. In order to obtain title by adverse possession, the adverse possessor must take actual possession of the land, the possession must be hostile (without the consent of the owner), the possession must be adverse (against the owner's interest), the possession must be open and notorious (obvious and knowable to anyone who is interested), and the possession must be continuous for a statutorily determined period of time, often twenty years. A successful adverse possessor cannot sell the land because he or she does not have a marketable title (clear ownership of the land). The adverse possessor would have to file what is called a quiet title action and have the court determine who is entitled to title. If the court rules in favor of the adverse possessor, he or she will receive a marketable title.

The Recording System

The *recording system* gives purchasers of land notice of claims against real property. It also helps resolve questions of priority if, for example, a seller deeds land to one person and then deeds the same land to a second person. In every county there is a governmental office called the registry of deeds usually located in the county courthouse. There the registrar of deeds maintains an index of documents relating to all real property transactions. These include deeds, easements, options, and mortgages. The recording system permits buyers of real property to evaluate the quality of the seller's title. In addition, the purchaser's attorney or a bank's attorney may obtain a document called a title abstract or an insurance company's agreement to insure the title. The abstract is a report that summarizes all the recorded claims that affect the seller's title. If a dispute arises between competing claimants, the recording statutes help the courts resolve who the law will recognize as having title to the property.

PERSONAL PROPERTY

There are many ways by which title to personal property is acquired. These include purchase, creation, capture, accession, finding, confusion, gift, and inheritance. In addition, one person may acquire the personal property of another, though not the title to that property, through bailment.

Purchase

The purchase or sale of goods is the most common means of obtaining or conveying ownership rights to personal property. Most purchases involve an exchange of money for the ownership rights to goods. This is a contractual relationship and is governed by the Uniform Commercial Code.

Creation

A person who manufactures products out of raw materials through physical or mental labor has title to the items created. Thus a person who builds a boat, writes a song, makes a quilt, or develops a software program will have title to that item. A person who is employed to produce something, however, will not have title; ownership rights will belong to the employer.

Capture

A person who acquires previously unowned property has title to the items captured. For example, a person who catches fish on the high seas has title by way of *capture*. Such captures usually require the purchase of a fishing or hunting license. This license authorizes the holder to take title by way of capture according to established regulations that define the size of the daily catch and determine the season, for example.

Accession

A person can take title to additions that occur to his or her property because of natural increases. This means that the owner of animals has title to the offspring by way of *accession*. Similarly, the owner of a savings account has title to the interest that is earned on that account by way of accession.

Finding

A finder of lost property has title that is good against everyone except the true owner. Some states provide that a finder of a lost item above some designated dollar value has a duty to turn the item over to an agency (often the police) for a period of time. If the true owner fails to claim the item, the finder takes title and the true owner's ownership rights are severed. A finder has a duty to make reasonable efforts to locate the true owner, although no expenses must be incurred to satisfy this obligation. Lost property differs from mislaid and abandoned property. If you inadvertently leave your jacket in a classroom after a class, you have mislaid it. As we see in the next case, a finder who is a trespasser acquires neither possessory nor ownership rights.

Favorite v. Miller
407 A.2d 974
Supreme Court of Connecticut
December 12, 1978

Bogdanski, Associate Justice

On July 9, 1776, a band of patriots, hearing news of the Declaration of Independence, toppled the equestrian statue of King George III, which was located in Bowling Green Park in lower Manhattan, New York. The statue, of gilded lead, was then hacked apart and the pieces ferried over Long Island Sound and loaded onto wagons at Norwalk, Connecticut, to be hauled some fifty miles northward to Oliver Wolcott's bullet-molding foundry in Litchfield, there to be cast into bullets. On the journey to Litchfield, the wagoners halted at Wilton, Connecticut, and while the patriots were imbibing, the loyalists managed to steal back pieces of the statue. The wagonload of the pieces lifted by the Tories was scattered about in the area of the Davis Swamp in Wilton and fragments of the statue have continued to turn up in that area since that time.

Although the above events have been dramatized in the intervening years, the unquestioned historical facts are: (1) the destruction of the statue; (2) cartage of the pieces to the Wolcott Foundry; (3) the pause at Wilton where part of the load was scattered over the Wilton area by loyalists; and (4) repeated discoveries of fragments over the last century.

In 1972, the defendant, Louis Miller, determined that a part of the statue might be located within property owned by the plaintiffs. On October 16 he entered the area of the Davis Swamp owned by the plaintiffs although he knew it to be private property. With the aid of a metal detector, he discovered a statuary fragment fifteen inches square and weighing twenty pounds which was embedded ten inches below the soil. He dug up this fragment and removed it from the plaintiffs' property. The plaintiffs did not learn that a piece of the statue of King George III had been found on their property until they read about it in the newspaper, long after it had been removed.

In due course, the piece of the statue made its way back to New York City, where the defendant agreed to sell it to the Museum of the City of New York for $5500. The museum continues to hold it pending resolution of this controversy.

In March of 1973, the plaintiffs instituted this action to have the fragment returned to them and the case was submitted to the court on a stipulation of facts. The trial court found the issues for the plaintiffs, from which judgment the defendant appealed to this court. The sole issue presented on appeal is whether the claim of the defendant, as finder, is superior to that of the plaintiffs, as owners of the land upon which the historic fragment was discovered.

Traditionally, when questions have arisen concerning the rights of the finder as against the person upon whose land the property was found, the resolution has turned upon the characterization given the property. Typically, if the property was found to be "lost" or "abandoned,"

the finder would prevail, whereas if the property was characterized as "mislaid," the owner or occupier of the land would prevail.

Lost property has traditionally been defined as involving an involuntary parting, i.e., where there is no intent on the part of the loser to part with the ownership of the property.

Abandonment, in turn, has been defined as the voluntary relinquishment of ownership of property without reference to any particular person or purpose; i.e., a "throwing away" of the property concerned; . . . while mislaid property is defined as that which is intentionally placed by the owner where he can obtain custody of it, but afterwards forgotten.

It should be noted that the classification of property as "lost," "abandoned," or "mislaid" requires that a court determine the intent or mental state of the unknown party who at some time in the past parted with the ownership or control of the property.

The trial court in this case applied the traditional approach and ruled in favor of the landowners on the ground that the piece of the statue found by Miller was "mislaid." The factual basis for that conclusion is set out in the finding, where the court found that "the loyalists did not wish to have the pieces [in their possession] during the turmoil surrounding the Revolutionary War and hid them in a place where they could resort to them [after the war], but forgot where they put them."

The defendant contends that the finding was made without evidence and that the court's conclusion "is legally impossible now after 200 years with no living claimants to the fragment and the secret of its burial having died with them." While we cannot agree that the court's conclusion was legally impossible, we do agree that any conclusion as to the mental state of persons engaged in events which occurred over two hundred years ago would be of a conjectural nature and as such does not furnish an adequate basis for determining rights of twentieth century claimants.

The defendant argues further that his rights in the statue are superior to those of anyone except the true owner (i.e., the British government). He presses this claim on the ground that the law has traditionally favored the finder as against all but the true owner, and that because his efforts brought the statue to light, he should be allowed to reap the benefits of his discovery. In his brief, he asserts: "As with archeologists forever probing and unearthing the past, to guide man for the betterment of those to follow, explorers like Miller deserve encouragement, and reward, in their selfless pursuit of the hidden, the unknown."

There are, however, some difficulties with the defendant's position. The first concerns the defendant's characterization of himself as a selfless seeker after knowledge. The facts in the record do not support such a conclusion. The defendant admitted that he was in the business of selling metal detectors and that he has used his success in finding the statue as advertising to boost his sales of such metal detectors, and that the advertising has been financially rewarding. Further, there is the fact that he signed a contract with the City Museum of New York for the sale of the statuary piece and that he stands to profit thereby.

Moreover, even if we assume his motive to be that of historical research alone, that fact will not justify his entering upon the property of another without permission. It is unquestioned that in today's world even archeologists must obtain permission from owners of property and the government of the country involved before they can conduct their explorations. Similarly, mountaineers must apply for permits, sometimes years in advance of their proposed expeditions. On a more familiar level, backpackers and hikers must often obtain permits before being allowed access to certain of our national parks and forests, even though that land is public and not private. Similarly, hunters and fishermen wishing to enter upon private property must first obtain the permission of the owner before they embark upon their respective pursuits.

Although few cases are to be found in this area of the law, one line of cases which have dealt with this issue has held that except where the trespass is trivial or merely technical, the fact that the finder is trespassing is sufficient to deprive him of his normal preference over the owner of the place where the property was found. The presumption in such cases is that possession of the article found is in the owner of the land and that the finder acquires no rights to the article found.

The defendant, by his own admission, knew that he was trespassing when he entered upon the property of the plaintiffs. He admitted that he was told by Gertrude Merwyn, the librarian of the Wilton Historical Society, *before* he went into the Davis Swamp area, that the land was privately owned and that Mrs. Merwyn recommended that he call the owners, whom she named, and obtain permission before he began his explorations. He also admitted that when he later told Mrs. Merwyn about his discovery, she again suggested that he contact the owners of the property, but that he failed to do so.

In the stipulation of facts submitted to the court, the defendant admitted entering the Davis Swamp property "with the belief that part of the 'King George Statue' . . . might be located within said property and with the intention of removing [the] same if located." The defendant has also admitted that the piece of the statue which he found was embedded in the ground ten inches below the surface and that it was necessary for him to excavate in order to take possession of his find.

In light of those undisputed facts the defendant's trespass was neither technical nor trivial. We conclude that the fact that the property found was embedded in the earth and the fact that the defendant was a trespasser are sufficient to defeat any claim to the property which the defendant might otherwise have had as a finder.

Where the trial court reaches a correct decision but on mistaken grounds, this court has repeatedly sustained the trial court's action if proper grounds exist to support it. The present case falls within the ambit of that principle of law and we affirm the decision of the court below.

There is no error.

Case Questions

1. On what grounds did the trial court hold for the plaintiff?
2. Why did the Supreme Court of Connecticut disagree with the lower court's reasoning?
3. What fact was most important to the appellate court?

Confusion

Confusion involves the blending or intermingling of fungible goods—goods of a similar character that may be exchanged or substituted for one another; for example, wheat, corn, lima beans, and money. Once similar items are mingled, it is impossible to separate the original owner's money or crops from those of others. In such cases each depositor owns an equivalent tonnage or number of bushels of the crop in an elevator or an equivalent dollar amount on deposit with a bank.

Gift

A person who has title to an item can make a gift by voluntarily transferring all rights in the item to another. A person making a gift is called a donor and the recipient of the gift is called a donee. The donor has donative intent—he or she is parting with all property rights and expects nothing (except love or appreciation) in return. The law requires that a donor make an actual or constructive delivery of the item. This means that if the donor is making a gift of a car, for example, the donor must bring the car to the donee (actual delivery) or present the car keys to the donee (constructive delivery). The donee must accept for a valid gift to occur.

Inheritance

A person can acquire property from the estate of a deceased person. This is called an inheritance. When a person making a will (a testator or testatrix) makes a bequest of property, the title to the item will be transferred from a deceased's estate. If the person died without a will (intestate), property is transferred according to a statutory plan enacted by the state legislature (called a statute of descent).

BAILMENTS

A *bailment* relationship exists when one person (called the bailor) delivers personal property to another person (called the bailee) without conveying title. Although the possession of the object is transferred in a bailment, the bailor intends to recover possession of the bailed object, and thus does not part with the title. When a person borrows, loans, or rents a videotape or leaves one's lawn mower or car for repair, for example, a bailment is created.

Some bailments primarily benefit only one person, either the bailee or the bailor. These are called gratuitous bailments. For example, the bailee primarily benefits when he or she borrows a lawn mower from a neighbor. Other bailments primarily benefit the bailor, for example, when he or she asks to leave a motor vehicle in the bailee's garage for a month. Some bailments are mutually beneficial, such as when the bailor leaves shoes for repair at a shoe repair shop or takes clothes to the dry cleaners.

Some bailments are created by contract, such as when a person rents a car from a car rental company. Other bailments are created by a delivery and acceptance of the object, such as when one student loans a textbook to another student. Here there is no contract, because there is no consideration.

All types of bailments involve rights and obligations. In a mutual benefit bailment, the bailee has the duty to exercise reasonable care toward the bailed object. The bailee is not allowed to use the bailed object for his benefit, but may work on the object for the benefit of the bailor. The bailor's duties include paying the bailee and warning the bailee of any hidden dangers associated with the bailed object.

With a gratuitous bailment for the benefit of the bailor the bailee must exercise at least slight care and store the bailed object in the agreed-upon manner. There is no compensation or quid pro quo involved.

With respect to a bailment for the benefit of the bailee a bailee must exercise a high degree of care. Since the bailor is acting solely out of friendship and is not receiving any benefit and the bailee is allowed to use the bailed object without charge, the bailee must use the bailed object in the proper manner and return it in good condition when the bailment period ends. The bailee is responsible in negligence for any damages caused to the bailed object. As we see in the next case, the bailor can end the bailment period at any time and ask for the return of the bailed object.

York v. Jones
717 F.Supp. 421
U.S. District Court,
E.D. Virginia,
Norfolk Division
July 10, 1989

Memorandum Opinion and Order

Clarke, District Judge

. . . The plaintiffs' Complaint in this case raises an issue of first impression in the rapidly developing field of human reproductive technology. The plaintiffs, Steven York, M.D. and Risa Adler-York (the Yorks), are the progenitors of the cryopreserved human pre-zygote (the pre-zygote) at issue in this case. The plaintiffs seek the release and transfer of the pre-zygote from the defendant The Howard and Georgeanna Jones Institute For Reproductive Medicine (Jones Institute) in Norfolk, Virginia to the Institute for Reproductive Research at the Hospital of the Good Samaritan located in Los Angeles, California. The defendants have refused to consent to an inter-institutional transfer of the pre-zygote. . . . Because this matter is before the Court on defendants' Motion to Dismiss the Complaint for failure to state a claim upon which relief can be granted, the Court will construe the Complaint in a light most favorable to the plaintiffs.

Facts

The plaintiffs have made the following factual allegations in their Complaint. The plaintiffs were married in 1983 and have been attempting to achieve a pregnancy since 1984. Because of damage to Mrs. York's remaining Fallopian tube, the Yorks are unable to achieve a pregnancy through normal coital reproduction. The plaintiffs were advised that through *in vitro* fertilization, plaintiffs would be able to become the parents of their own genetic child. The *in vitro* fertilization process involves removing one or more oocytes or eggs from the woman's body, fertilizing those eggs *in vitro* (outside the womb) with the husband's sperm, and then depositing the developing masses into the woman's uterus up to the eight-cell stage. . . .

In the spring of 1986, plaintiffs consulted with Drs. Jones and Kreiner at the Jones Institute in Norfolk, Virginia in order to determine whether they were viable candidates for the *in vitro* fertilization (IVF) program, known as the Vital Initiation of Pregnancy (VIP) program. The Yorks were accepted into the IVF program and signed VIP Consent Form No. 6B.

Consent Form 6B stated, and Dr. Kreiner assured the Yorks, that the expectation of pregnancy is about 20 percent after the transfer of one fertilized mature egg, about 28 percent after the transfer of two fertilized mature eggs and about 38 percent after the transfer of three fertilized mature eggs. At the time the Yorks entered the IVF program in Norfolk, they were residents of New Jersey. During the course of treatment, the Yorks moved to California.

The Yorks returned to the Jones Institute on four separate occasions to undergo the *in vitro* fertilization process. None of these *in vitro* fertilization attempts resulted in pregnancy. Prior to the attempt in May 1987, the plaintiffs signed a form entitled "Informed Consent: Human Pre-Zygotes Cryopreservation". . . . The consent form outlined the procedure for cryopreservation or freezing of pre-zygotes and detailed the couple's rights in the frozen pre-zygote.

The Cryopreservation Agreement explained that the cryopreservation procedure is available in the event more than five pre-zygotes are retrieved during the IVF treatment. The Agreement further stated that the cryopreservation procedure is intended to reduce the risk of multiple births, while simultaneously "creating additional opportunities for the initiation of pregnancy with the transfer of concepti developed from frozen-thawed pre-zygotes." After signing the Agreement, the plaintiffs underwent the IVF process on May 17, 1987. On May 27, 1987, Dr. Kreiner removed six eggs from Mrs. York and fertilized those eggs with Dr. York's sperm, creating six embryos. On May 29, 1987, five embryos were transferred to Mrs. York's uterus. The remaining embryo, which is the subject of this litigation, was cryogenically preserved in accordance with the procedures outlined in the Cryopreservation Agreement.

In May of 1988, a year after the pre-zygote was frozen, the Yorks sought to have the pre-zygote transferred from the Jones Institute in Norfolk, Virginia to the Institute for Reproductive Research at the Hospital of the Good Samaritan in Los Angeles, California. At the Los Angeles clinic, Dr. Richard Marrs would thaw the embryo and insert it in Mrs. York through *in vitro* fertilization. The plaintiffs consulted two embryologists to arrange for proper cryogenic support in order to successfully transport the embryo. The plaintiffs planned to have Dr. York personally retrieve the embryo from Norfolk and transport it to California by commercial airliner. The pre-zygote would be housed in a biological dry shipper during the flight.

On May 28, 1988, the Yorks wrote Dr. Muasher and indicated their intent to retrieve and transfer the pre-zygote. By letter dated June 13, 1988, Dr. Muasher,

writing on behalf of the Jones Institute, refused to allow such a transfer. On June 18, 1988, Dr. Richard Marrs, on behalf of the Yorks, sought consent to transfer the pre-zygote from physicians at the Jones Institute. By letter dated August 9, 1988, Dr. Jones refused to approve the transfer of the frozen pre-zygote.

Breach of Contract

The plaintiffs allege that the defendants' continued dominion and control over the frozen pre-zygote is contrary to the language of the Cryopreservation Agreement. . . . The pertinent provision of the Cryopreservation Agreement provides:

> "We may withdraw our consent and discontinue participation at any time without prejudice and we understand our pre-zygotes will be stored only as long as we are active IVF patients at The Howard and Georgeanna Jones Institute For Reproductive Medicine or until the end of our normal reproductive years. We have the principle responsibility to decide the disposition of our pre-zygotes. Our frozen pre-zygotes will not be released from storage for the purpose of intrauterine transfer without the written consents of us both. In the event of divorce, we understand legal ownership of any stored pre-zygotes must be determined in a property settlement and will be released as directed by order of a court of competent jurisdiction. Should we for any reason no longer wish to attempt to initiate a pregnancy, we understand we may choose one of three fates for our pre-zygotes that remain in frozen storage. Our pre-zygotes may be: 1) donated to another infertile couple (who will remain unknown to us) 2) donated for approved research investigation 3) thawed but not allowed to undergo further development."

The defendants argue that plaintiffs' proprietary rights in the pre-zygote are limited to the "three fates" enumerated in this provision because there is no established protocol for the inter-institutional transfer of pre-zygotes.

The Court begins its analysis by noting that the Cryopreservation Agreement created a bailor-bailee relationship between the plaintiffs and defendants. While the parties in this case expressed no intent to create a bailment, under Virginia law, no formal contract or actual meeting of the minds is necessary. Rather, all that is needed "is the element of lawful possession however created, and duty to account for the thing as the property of another that creates the bailment. . . ." The essential nature of a bailment relationship imposes on the bailee, when the purpose of the bailment has terminated, an absolute obligation to return the subject matter of the bailment to the bailor. The obligation to return the property is implied from the fact of lawful possession of the personal property of another.

In the instant case, the requisite elements of a bailment relationship are present. It is undisputed that the Jones Institutes' possession of the pre-zygote was lawful pursuant to the Cryopreservation Agreement. The defendants also recognized their duty to account for the pre-zygote by virtue of a paragraph in the Cryopreservation Agreement purporting to disclaim liability for any injury to the pre-zygote. Finally, the defendants consistently refer to the pre-zygote as the "property" of the Yorks in the Cryopreservation Agreement. Although the Cryopreservation Agreements constitutes a bailment contract, the Agreement is nevertheless governed by the same principles as apply to other contracts.

The defendants have further defined the limits of their possessory interest by recognizing the plaintiffs' proprietary rights in the pre-zygote. The Agreement repeatedly refers to "our pre-zygote," and explicitly provides that in the event of a divorce, the legal ownership of the pre-zygote "must be determined in a property settlement" by a court of competent jurisdiction. The Agreement further provides that the plaintiffs have "the principal responsibility to decide the disposition" of the pre-zygote and that the pre-zygote will not be released from storage without the written consent of both plaintiffs. The Court finds that the inference to be drawn from these provisions of the Cryopreservation Agreement is that the defendants fully recognize plaintiffs' property rights in the pre-zygote and have limited their rights as bailee to exercise dominion and control over the pre-zygote.

The defendants take the position that the plain language of the Cryopreservation Agreement limits the plaintiffs' proprietary right to the pre-zygote to the "three fates" listed in the Agreement: (1) donation to another infertile couple; (2) donation for approved research; and (3) thawing. The Court finds, however, that the applicability of the three fates is limited by the following language, "Should we [the Yorks] for any reason no longer wish to initiate a pregnancy, we understand we may choose one of three fates for our pre-zygotes that remain in frozen storage." The allegations of plaintiffs' Complaint, and the entire thrust of this litigation, suggest that plaintiffs continue to desire to achieve pregnancy. The Agreement does not state that the attempt to initiate a pregnancy is restricted to procedures employed at the Jones Institute. The "three fates" are therefore inapplicable to the case at bar.

For the reasons stated herein, the Court finds that Count I of plaintiffs' Complaint states a claim upon which relief can be granted. Count II is pled in the alternative alleging an action based on quasi-contract. Accordingly, defendants' Motion to Dismiss Counts I and II are Denied.

Detinue

In Count III of the Complaint, plaintiffs allege a cause of action in detinue. The requisite elements of a detinue action in Virginia are as follows: (1) plaintiff must have a property interest in the thing sought to be recovered; (2) the right to immediate possession; (3) the property is capable of identification; (4) the property must be of some value; and (5) defendant must have had possession at some time prior to the institution of the act.

Moreover, if the property is in the possession of a bailee, an action in detinue accrues upon demand and refusal to return the property or upon a violation of the bailment contract by an act of conversion. . . .

After review of plaintiffs' Complaint, the Court finds that plaintiffs have properly alleged a cause of action in detinue. Accordingly, defendants' Motion to Dismiss Count III is Denied.

Case Questions

1. As a result of this court's decision, will the Yorks receive the pre-zygotes?
2. Why do you think the Jones Institute wants to keep the pre-zygotes?
3. When a bailor transfers property to a bailee, does the bailee obtain title?

Chapter Questions

1. Define the following terms:

accession	grantor
adverse possession	intangible
bailment	leasehold
bailor	license
capture	life estate
covenant	nuisance
creation	personalty
easement	police power
eminent domain	realty
estate	recording system
fee simple	tangible
fixture	vested
grantee	

2. Hiram Hoeltzer, a professional art restorer, sought declaratory relief to quiet title to a large mural that once was affixed to the walls of the Stamford High School. This mural had been painted as part of the Works

Progress Administration (WPA) in 1934. Workers removed the mural when the high school was renovated in the summer of 1970. They cut it into thirty pieces, and placed it on top of a heap of construction debris, adjacent to a dumpster. This was done despite oral and written requests from school officials that the mural be taken down and preserved. A 1970 graduate of Stamford High, recognizing the value of the mural, placed the mural pieces into his car and took them home. The student took the mural to Karel Yasko, a federal official responsible for supervising the restoration of WPA artwork. Yasko suggested that the mural be taken to Hiram Hoeltzer. In 1980, city officials and other interested people began contacting Hoeltzer about the mural. In 1986, the city formally wrote to Hoeltzer and claimed title. Hoeltzer, however, who had retained possession of the mural for ten years, claimed that he was the rightful owner of the mural. Who has legal title to the mural? Why?

Hoeltzer v. City of Stamford, Conn., 722 F.Supp. 1106 (1989)

3. Leonard and Bernard Kapiloff are stamp collectors. In 1976 they purchased two sets of stamps worth $150,400. Robert Ganter found the stamps in a dresser he had purchased for $30 in a used furniture store in 1979 or 1980. Ganter had taken the stamps to an auction house and they were listed for sale in a nationally distributed catalogue that was read by the Kapiloff brothers. The brothers contacted Ganter and demanded the return of the stamps. Ganter refused. The brothers then contacted the FBI which took physical possession of the stamps. The brothers then brought a replevin action against Ganter for the stamps, and asked the court for a declaratory judgment that they were the true owners of the stamps. The person who originally sold the brothers the stamps supported the brothers' allegations that the stamps Ganter found were the same stamps that had belonged to the Kapiloffs. Who is the owner of the stamps?

Ganter v. Kapiloff, 516 A.2d 611 (1986)

4. The case of *Clevenger v. Peterson Construction Company* turned on the question of whether forty-four mobile trailers should be classified as personal property or fixtures. The trailers had axles, although they were without hitches or wheels. They were positioned on concrete blocks and not on permanent foundations, and were connected to utilities with flexible hoses. Which classification is more appropriate?

Clevenger v. Peterson Construction Company, Inc., 542 P.2d 470 (1975)

5. The District of Columbia enacted an ordinance that made it unlawful for any hotel to exclude any licensed taxicab driver from picking up passengers at hotel taxicab stands. The Washington Hilton did not have to operate a taxicab stand on its property, but elected to do so for the convenience of its guests. The hotel was dissatisfied with the quality of service provided by some of the taxicab drivers and with the cleanliness of some of their vehicles. The hotel wanted to discriminate against some taxis in favor of others. It wanted to require cab drivers to obtain permits and pay an

annual fee to use the hotel's taxicab stand. The city's attorney was consulted about these plans and ruled that they violated the Taxicab Act. Does this ordinance constitute a taking of the hotel's property by the District?

Hilton Washington Corporation v. District of Columbia, 777 F.2d 47 (1985)

6. Terry Bohn presented Tommie Louise Lowe with a ring in 1974, when they became engaged to be married. Tommie had a continuing series of strokes over the next ten years and the marriage never took place. She still possessed the engagement ring at the time of her death in 1984. After her death, Terry brought suit against Tommie's estate to recover the engagement ring. Who has title to the ring?

Matter of Estate of Lowe, 379 N.W.2d 485 (1985)

7. Robert Lehman and Aki Eveline Lehman were married in 1964. They separated in 1971. They became divorced in 1976. At the time of the separation, Aki retained possession of forty-three art objects that were in the house. Robert and Aki each claimed ownership rights to these objects. Robert claimed that forty-two of the items were either purchased by him or given to him by his father. One item was given to him by Aki. Aki claimed ownership of the items as a result of her purchases made with joint funds, as well as a result of gifts from Robert and Robert's father. Aki took all forty-three items to Paris when she and their children moved there in 1972. Robert demanded that Aki return his property. When she refused, he filed suit against Aki for replevin, conversion, and breach of bailment. At the time the lawsuit was filed, only thirteen items were still in Aki's possession. Aki testified at trial that she didn't know what had happened to the thirty missing items. The court determined that Robert was the exclusive owner of forty of the forty-three items, and Robert and Aki jointly owned the remaining three items. What relief will the court order? Why?

Lehman v. Lehman, 591 F.Supp 1523 (1984)

8. Michael and Albina Kloss purchased a tract of land from John and Anne Molenda in 1950. No land survey was conducted to determine the precise boundary line between the two properties. Instead, John and Michael paced off the lot and placed stakes in the ground to mark the boundary. The Klosses built a house on their lot and installed a concrete sidewalk along the property which extended to the boundary stake. They also installed a concrete driveway that came within thirty inches of the boundary line separating their property from the Molendas'. They put topsoil in the thirty-inch strip of land between the driveway and the boundary line, and planted this area with grass. They continuously maintained this grassy strip for over thirty years. The Molendas planted a hedge on their side of the staked property line. John Molenda died in 1983 and a survey of the land was completed. The surveyor found that the thirty-inch grassy strip was actually on Molenda property. Anne Molenda

thereupon installed a fence along the edge of the Kloss driveway. The Klosses filed suit claiming ownership of the grassy strip. Who should own the strip of land? Why?

Kloss v. Molenda, 513 A.2d 490 (1986)

9. Toby and Rita Kahr were the owners of twenty-eight pieces of sterling silver that Rita's father had given them as a wedding present twenty-seven years previously. Each piece of silver was engraved with the letter "K." On April 5, 1983, the Kahrs brought used clothing to Goodwill Industries and told Goodwill personnel that they wanted to make a donation of clothing. Unknown to Toby and Rita, the sterling silver, along with a wallet containing their credit cards, were included in the sacks. The Kahrs called Goodwill two hours later, when they realized what had happened, and were told that the silver had been sold for $15 to Karen Markland. The Kahrs alleged that the silver had a value of $3,791. The Kahrs brought a replevin action against Goodwill and Markland to recover the silver. Markland claimed that she had purchased the silver from a merchant who deals in that kind of goods and that she was the lawful owner of the silver. Should the court order replevin? Was the silver abandoned by the Kahrs?

Kahr v. Markland, 543 N.E.2d 579 (1989)

10. Dennis Schaefer keeps a live, declawed tiger at his home in a residential neighborhood. The tiger is housed in a six-foot-high chain-link fence cage. The cage has a roof. Schaefer has been issued an "Exotic Wildlife Possession Permit" to possess the tiger by the state game commission. Fairview Township filed suit in equity requesting an order requiring Schaefer to remove the tiger from the township. The township contends that the presence of the tiger is a nuisance and threatens the public safety. Although the tiger weighs 225 pounds, it will grow to weigh approximately 600 pounds. The tiger has been able to push the chain-link fence so that it has bulges in some places. The cage is constructed such that the tiger can reach its paw outside of the cage. There is evidence that on one occasion, Schaefer let the tiger out of his cage and allowed it to sprawl on his car roof. Schaefer contends that he has complied with the specific requirements of the state Game and Wildlife Code and that he is entitled to retain the tiger at his home. Did the trial judge have sufficient evidence to find that the tiger is a nuisance?

Fairview Township v. Schaefer, 562 W.2d 989 (1989)

Notes

1. P.C. Hoffer, *Law and People in Colonial America* (Baltimore: Johns Hopkins University Press, 1982), pp. 19–24; D.H. Flaherty, *Essays in the History of Early American Law* (Chapel Hill: Institute of Early American History and Culture, 1969), pp. 272–273;

B. Schwartz, *The Law in America* (New York: McGraw-Hill Book Co., 1974), pp. 8–18; M. Horwitz, *The Transformation of American Law 1780–1860* (Cambridge: Harvard University Press, 1977), pp. 4–6.

2. Horwitz, pp. 7–9, 84.

3. L. Salmon, *Women and the Law of Property in Early America* (Chapel Hill: The University of North Carolina Press, 1986), pp. 18–22.

4. Ibid., pp. 14–15, 22–25.

5. W. Hurst, *Law and the Conditions of Freedom in the Nineteenth Century* (Madison: The University of Wisconsin Press, 1967), p. 8.

6. W.E. Nelson, *Americanization of the Common Law* (Cambridge: Harvard University Press, 1975), p. 47; Horwitz, p. 102.

7. Horwitz, p. 35.

8. Nelson, p. 159; Horwitz, p. 36.

9. Horwitz, p. 102; Hurst, pp. 28–29.

10. Hurst, pp. 24–25.

11. *Lochner v. New York*, 198 U.S. 45 (1905).

12. The Uniform Commercial Code is not uniformly adopted from state to state. Each state legislature decides whether to adopt the Uniform Commercial Code, and the extent to which they accept or modify its terms. Other differences can arise from judicial interpretations.

13. Many jurisdictions only recognize the tenancy by the entirety in conjunction with real property.

14. There are two exceptions to this general rule. A good faith purchaser of bearer bounds can take title from a thief and a buyer in the ordinary course of business who purchases goods from a merchant can take title even if the merchant obtained the items from a thief. Public policy reasons support these exceptions because it is very important to the economy that people who buy goods from merchants can rely on the seller's claims of title to the goods.

15. *U.S. v. Causby*, 328 U.S. 256 (1946).

XI

The Law of Torts

A tort is a civil wrong other than a breach of contract for which courts provide a remedy in the form of an action for damages. Tort law seeks to provide reimbursement to members of society who suffer losses because of the dangerous or unreasonable conduct of others. Each of the fifty states determines its own tort law which is divided into the following three categories: intentional torts, negligence, and strict liability.

HISTORICAL EVOLUTION OF AMERICAN TORT LAW

The word *tort* (meaning "wrong") is one of many Norman words that became a part of the English and American legal lexicon. American tort law evolved from the writs of trespass[1] and trespass on the case.[2] Trespass covered a variety of acts, which included trespass to land, assaults, batteries, the taking of goods, and false imprisonment. Each of the acts involved a tortfeasor directly causing injury to a victim. It was commonplace for plaintiffs to use trespass to recover money damages for personal injuries by the end of Henry III's reign.[3] In 1285, Parliament enacted the Statute of Westminster[4] which authorized the chancery to create new writs to address wrongs that fell outside the boundaries of trespass. Because the new writs were designed to remedy the factual circumstances of a particular case, they were called trespass actions on the case (also called "actions on the case"). From trespass on the case came our contemporary concept of negligence.

One of the major drawbacks of the writ system was that it lacked any comprehensive underlying theoretical base. In the 1800s, as the writ system was being replaced with more modern forms of pleading, American law

491

professors and judges began to develop a basic theory for tort law based on fault.

FUNCTIONS OF TORT LAW

Tort law establishes standards of conduct for all members of society. It defines as civil wrongs these antisocial behaviors: the failure to exercise reasonable care (negligence); intentional interference with one's person, reputation, or property (intentional torts); and in some circumstances, liability without fault (strict liability). Tort law deters people from engaging in behavior patterns that the law does not condone and compensates victims for their civil injuries. It is thus a vehicle by which an injured person can attempt to shift the costs of harm to another person.

Tort law is not static; courts can create new causes of action to remedy an injustice. Thus the argument that a claim is novel does not prevent a court from granting relief when it becomes clear that the law should protect the plaintiff's rights.

INTENTIONAL TORTS

Intentional torts are based on willful misconduct or intentional wrongs. A tortfeasor who intentionally invades a protected interest of another, under circumstances for which there is no lawful justification or excuse, is legally and morally "at fault." The intent is not necessarily a hostile intent or even a desire to do serious harm. A person acts intentionally if he or she has a conscious desire to produce consequences the law recognizes as tortious. A person who has no conscious desire to cause the consequences, but is aware that the consequences are highly likely to follow, can also act intentionally.

Assault

Civil liability for *assault* results from an act that makes another reasonably apprehensive of immediate and harmful contact. Even if the purpose of inflicting injury is abandoned, liability for assault results as long as the actor placed another in a state of apprehension. Mere words alone, however, usually will not constitute an assault, no matter how threatening or abusive they may be.

Battery

An unpermitted, unprivileged, intentional contact with another's person is defined as *battery*. This includes contact that is actually harmful or is merely offensive. The standard used to determine offensiveness is not whether a particular plaintiff is offended, but whether an ordinary person who is not unusually sensitive in the matter of dignity would be offended. It is not essential that the plaintiff be conscious of the contact at the time it occurs.

Assault or battery may occur without the other, but usually both result from the same occurrence. As a result of an assault and battery—as well as other intentional torts—the injured party may bring a civil suit for damages and have a criminal prosecution brought for the same act. The two actions are independent of each other; the outcome of one does not determine the result of the other.

The following case illustrates the intentional torts of assault, battery, and invasion of privacy (discussed on page 504).

Estate of Berthiaume v. Pratt, M.D.
365 A.2d 792
Supreme Judicial Court of Maine
November 10, 1976

Pomeroy, Justice

The appellant, as administratrix, based her claim of right to damages on an alleged invasion of her late husband's "right to privacy" and on an alleged assault and battery of him. At the close of the evidence produced at trial, a justice of the Superior Court granted defendant's motion for a directed verdict. Appellant's seasonable appeal brings the case to this court.

The appellee is a physician and surgeon practicing in Waterville, Maine. It was established at trial without contradiction that the deceased, Henry Berthiaume, was suffering from a cancer of his larynx. Appellee, an otolaryngologist, had treated him twice surgically. A laryngectomy was performed; and later, because of a tumor which had appeared in his neck, a radical neck dissection on one side was done. No complaint is made with respect to the surgical interventions.

During the period appellee was serving Mr. Berthiaume as a surgeon, many photographs of Berthiaume had been taken by appellee or under his direction. The jury was told that the sole use to which these photographs were to be put was to make the medical record for the appellee's use. . . .

Although at no time did the appellee receive any written consent for taking of photographs from Berthiaume or any members of his family, it was appellee's testimony that Berthiaume had always consented to having such photographs made.

At all times material hereto, Mr. Berthiaume was a patient of a physician other than the appellee. Such other physician had referred the patient to appellee for surgery. On September 2, 1970, appellee saw the patient for the last time for the purpose of treatment or diagnosis. The incident which gave rise to this lawsuit occurred on September 23, 1970. It was also on that day Mr. Berthiaume died.

Although appellee disputed the evidence appellant produced at trial in many material respects, the jury could have concluded from the evidence that shortly before Mr. Berthiaume died on the 23rd, the appellee and a nurse appeared in his hospital room. In the presence of Mrs. Berthiaume and a visitor of the patient in the next bed, either Dr. Pratt or the nurse, at his direction, raised the dying Mr. Berthiaume's head and placed some blue operating room toweling under his head and beside him on the bed. The appellee testified that this blue toweling was placed there for the purpose of obtaining a color contrast for the photographs which he proposed to take. He then proceeded to take several photographs of Mr. Berthiaume.

The jury could have concluded from the testimony that Mr. Berthiaume protested the taking of pictures by raising a clenched fist and moving his head in an attempt to remove his head from the camera's range. The appellee himself testified that before taking the pictures he had been told by Mrs. Berthiaume when he talked with her in the corridor before entering the room that she "didn't think that Henry wanted his picture taken."

It is the raising of the deceased's head in order to put the operating room towels under and around him that appellant claims was an assault and battery. It is the taking of the pictures of the dying Mr. Berthiaume that appellant claims constituted the actionable invasion of Mr. Berthiaume's right to privacy. . . .

The law of privacy addresses the invasion of four distinct interests of the individual. Each of the four different interests, taken as a whole, represent an individual's right "to be let alone." These four kinds of invasion are: (1) intrusion upon the plaintiff's physical and mental solitude or seclusion; (2) public disclosure of private facts; (3) publicity which places the plaintiff in a false light in the public eye; [and] (4) appropriation for the defendant's benefit or advantage of the plaintiff's name or likeness. . . .

"As it has appeared in the cases thus far decided, it is not one tort, but a complex of four. To date the law of privacy comprises four distinct kinds of invasion of four different interests of the plaintiff, which are tied together by the common name, but otherwise have almost nothing in common except that each represents an interference with the right of the plaintiff 'to be let alone.' . . .

"Taking them in order—intrusion, disclosure, false light, and appropriation —the first and second require the invasion of something secret, secluded or private pertaining to the plaintiff; the third and fourth do not. The second and third depend upon publicity, while the first does not, nor does the fourth, although it usually involves it. The third requires falsity or fiction; the other three do not. The fourth involves a use for the defendant's advantage, which is not true of the rest. . . . "

All cases so far decided on the point agree that the plaintiff need not plead or prove special damages. Punitive damages can be awarded on the same basis as in other torts where a wrongful motive or state of mind appears . . . , but not in cases where the defendant has acted innocently as, for example, in the mistaken but good faith belief that the plaintiff has given his consent. . . .

In this case we are concerned only with a claimed intrusion upon the plaintiff's intestate's physical and mental solitude or seclusion. The jury had a right to conclude from the evidence that plaintiff's intestate was dying. It could have concluded he desired not to be photographed in his hospital bed in such condition and that he manifested such desire by his physical motions. The jury should have been instructed, if it found these facts, that the taking of pictures without decedent's consent or over his objection was an invasion of his legally protected right to privacy, which invasion was an actionable tort for which money damages could be recovered.

Instead, a directed verdict for the defendant was entered, obviously premised on the presiding justice's announced incorrect conclusion that the taking of pictures without consent did not constitute an invasion of privacy and the further erroneous conclusion that no tort was committed in the absence of "proof they [the photographs] were published."

Another claimed basis for appellant's assertion that a right to recover damages was demonstrated by the evidence is the allegations in her complaint sounding in the tort of assault and battery. The presiding justice announced as his conclusion that consent to a battery is implied from the existence of a physician-patient relationship. . . .

There is nothing to suggest that the appellee's visit to plaintiff's intestate's room on the day of the alleged invasion of privacy was for any purpose relating to the *treatment* of the patient. Appellee acknowledges that his sole purpose in going to the Berthiaume hospital room and the taking of pictures was to conclude the making of a photographic record to complete appellee's record of the case. From the evidence, then, it is apparent that the jury had a right to conclude that the physician-patient relationship once existing between Dr. Pratt and Henry Berthiaume, the deceased, had terminated.

As to the claimed assault and battery, on the state of the evidence, the jury should have been permitted to consider the evidence and return a verdict in accordance with its fact-finding. It should have been instructed that consent to a touching of the body of a patient may be implied from the patient's consent to enter into a physician-patient relationship whenever such touching is reasonably necessary for the diagnosis and treatment of the patient's ailments while the physi-cian-patient relationship continues. Quite obviously also, there would be no actionable assault and battery if the touching was expressly consented to. Absent express consent by the patient or one authorized to give consent on the patient's behalf, or absent consent implied from the circumstances, including the physician-patient relationship, the touching of the patient in the manner described by the evidence in this case would constitute assault and battery if it was part of an undertaking which, in legal effect, was an invasion of the plaintiff's intestate's "right to be let alone." . . .

We recognize the benefit to the science of medicine which comes from the making of photographs of the treatment and of medical abnormalities found in patients. . . . "The court [also] recognizes that an individual has the right to decide whether that which is his shall be given to the public and not only to restrict and limit but also to withhold absolutely his talents, property, or other subjects of the right of privacy from all dissemination." . . .

Because there were unresolved, disputed questions of fact, which, if decided by the fact finder in favor of the plaintiff, would have justified a verdict for the plaintiff, it was reversible error to have directed a verdict for the defendant. . . .

New trial ordered.

Case
Questions

1. Battery is unpermitted, unprivileged, intentional contact with another's person. In a physician-patient relationship, how does a physician receive consent to touch the body of a patient?

2. Could there have been a battery if Dr. Pratt used rubber gloves in handling Mr. Berthiaume's head in preparation for the pictures? Could there have been a battery if Dr. Pratt raised Mr. Berthiaume's head by cranking the hospital bed?

3. Could there have been an assault if Mr. Berthiaume was unconscious at the time Dr. Pratt raised his head and placed the blue operating towel under his head?

4. Are plaintiffs able to recover anything in suits for battery if they are unable to prove any actual physical injury?

Conversion

Any unauthorized act that deprives an owner of possession of his or her tangible personal property is *conversion*. There may be liability for the intentional tort of conversion even when the defendant acted innocently. For example, D, an auctioneer, receives a valuable painting from X, reasonably believing that X owns it. D sells the painting for X, but it turns out that P owns the painting. D is liable to P for conversion, even though the mistake is honest and reasonable.

Conversion may be accomplished in a number of ways, for example, if a defendant refuses to return goods to the owner or destroys or alters the goods. Even the use of the chattel may suffice. If you lend your car to a dealer to sell and the dealer drives the car once on business for a few miles, it would probably not be conversion. But conversion would result if the dealer drives it for 2,000 miles.

Because conversion is considered a forced sale, the defendant must pay the full value, not merely the amount of the actual harm. However, courts consider several factors in determining whether defendant's interference with plaintiff's property is sufficient to require defendant to pay its entire value. These include dominion, good faith, harm, and inconvenience.

Trespass

The intentional tort of *trespass* includes the unauthorized entry on the land of another as well as any offense or transgression that damages another's personal property. Trespasses to land can occur through either a direct or an indirect entry. A direct entry would occur when one person walks on another person's land without permission. An indirect entry would occur when one person throws an object on another's land or causes it to flood with water.

The law's protection of the exclusive possession of land is not limited to the surface of real property. It extends below the surface as well as above it. Thus a public utility that runs a pipe below the surface of a landowner's property without obtaining an easement or consent can commit a trespass. Similarly, overhanging structures, telephone wires, and even shooting across land have been held to be violations of owners' right to the air space above their land. Although the extent of such rights are still in the process of determination, the legal trend is for landowners to have rights to as much of the air space that is immediately above their property as they can effectively occupy or use. Trespass may also occur to personal property, but most interference with the possession of personal property would be considered conversion.

The plaintiff in the following case brought suit in trespass after sustaining serious injury when an overhanging limb fell from the defendant's maple tree onto the plaintiff's driveway and struck the plaintiff.

Ivancic v. Olmstead
488 N.E.2d 72
Court of Appeals of New York
November 26, 1985

Jasen, Judge

At issue on this appeal is whether plaintiff, who seeks to recover for injuries sustained when an overhanging limb from a neighbor's maple tree fell and struck him, established a prima facie case of negligence and whether Trial Term erred, as a matter of law, in refusing to submit to the jury the cause of action sounding in common-law trespass.

Plaintiff was working on his truck in the driveway of his parents' home located in the Village of Fultonville, New York. Since 1970, defendant has owned and lived on the property adjoining to the west. A large maple tree stood on defendant's land near the border with plaintiff's parents' property. Branches from the tree had extended over the adjoining property. During a heavy windstorm on September 26, 1980, an overhanging limb from the tree fell and struck plaintiff, causing him serious injuries. As a result, plaintiff commenced this action, interposing causes of action in negligence and common-law trespass.

At trial, the court declined to charge the jury on the common-law trespass cause of action or on the doctrine of res ipsa loquitur, submitting the case solely on the theory of negligence. The jury rendered a verdict in favor of the plaintiff in the sum of $3,500. Both parties moved to set aside the verdict, the plaintiff upon the ground of inadequacy, and the defendant upon the ground that the verdict was against the weight of the evidence. The court ultimately . . . ordered a new trial on the issues of both liability and damages.

Upon cross appeals, the Appellate Division reversed, on the law, and dismissed the complaint. The court reasoned that no competent evidence was presented upon which it could properly be concluded that defendant had constructive notice of the alleged defective condition of the tree. The Appellate Division did not address the correctness of the trial court's ruling in declining to charge the jury on the common-law trespass cause of action.
. . .

Considering first the negligence cause of action, it is established that no liability attaches to a landowner whose tree falls outside of his premises and injures another unless there exists actual or constructive knowledge of the defective condition of the tree. . . .

Inasmuch as plaintiff makes no claim that defendant had actual knowledge of the defective nature of the tree, it is necessary to consider whether there was sufficient competent evidence for a jury to conclude that defendant had constructive notice. We conclude, as did the Appellate Division, that plaintiff offered no competent evidence from which it could be properly found that defendant had constructive notice of the alleged defective condition of the tree. Not one of the witnesses who had observed the tree prior to the fall of the limb testified as to observing so much as a withering or dead leaf, barren branch, discoloration, or any of the indicia of disease which would alert an observer to the possibility that the tree or one of its branches was decayed or defective.

At least as to adjoining landowners, the concept of constructive notice with respect to liability for falling trees is that there is no duty to consistently and constantly check all trees for nonvisible decay. Rather, the manifestation of said decay must be readily observable in order to require a landowner to take reasonable steps to prevent harm. . . . The testimony of plaintiff's expert provides no evidence from which the jury could conclude that defendant should reasonably have realized that a potentially dangerous condition existed. Plaintiff's expert never saw the tree until the morning of the trial when all that remained of the tree was an eight-foot stump. He surmised from this observation and from some photographs of the tree that water had invaded the tree through a "limb hole" in the tree, thus causing decay and a crack occurring below. However, the expert did indicate that the limb hole was about eight-feet high and located in the crotch of the tree which would have made it difficult, if not impossible, to see upon reasonable inspection. Although there may have been evidence that would have alerted an expert, upon close observation, that the tree was diseased, there is no evidence that would put a reasonable landowner on notice of any defective condition of the tree. Thus,

the fact that defendant landowner testified that she did not inspect the tree for over 10 years is irrelevant. On the evidence presented, even if she were to have inspected the tree, there were no indicia of decay or disease to put her on notice of a defective condition so as to trigger her duty as a landowner to take reasonable steps to prevent the potential harm.

Since the evidence adduced at trial failed to set forth any reasonable basis upon which notice of the tree's defective condition could be imputed to defendant, . . . we agree with the view of the Appellate Division that plaintiff failed to establish a prima facie case of negligence.

Turning to plaintiff's claim of error by the trial court in declining to submit to the jury the cause of action sounding in common-law trespass, we conclude that there was no error. The scope of the common-law tort has been delineated in *Phillips v. Sun Oil Co.*, . . . 121 N.E.2d 249, wherein this court held: "while the trespasser, to be liable, need not intend or expect the damaging consequences of his intrusion, he must intend the act which amounts to or produces the unlawful invasion, and the intrusion must at least be the immediate or inevitable consequence of what he willfully does, or which he does so negligently as to amount to willfulness." In this case, there is evidence that defendant did not plant the tree, and the mere fact that defendant allowed what appeared to be a healthy tree to grow naturally and cross over into plaintiff's parents' property airspace, cannot be viewed as an intentional act so as to constitute trespass. . . .

Accordingly, the order of the Appellate Division should be affirmed, with costs.

*Case
Questions*

1. The trial court and the appellate court concluded that the plaintiff was not entitled to an instruction with respect to common law trespass. Why was the instruction refused?
2. Why was the plaintiff's negligence claim rejected?
3. Why should a plaintiff be entitled to recover for a trespass under circumstances where no actual harm has been shown?

Malicious Prosecution

A civil suit for the tort of *malicious prosecution* may result from either a criminal prosecution or a civil suit if the proceeding was instituted maliciously, without probable cause, and with a decision favorable to the defendant. The threat of bringing suit is not enough to result in civil liability on the part of the would-be plaintiff.

In a criminal case, the prosecutor is absolutely immune from malicious prosecution suits, even if it is shown the prosecutor acted in bad faith. In addition, plea bargaining does not suffice to meet the favorable decision criterion.

False Imprisonment

The unlawful detention of persons, whereby they are deprived of their personal liberty against their will, and without authority, is *false imprisonment*. The detention need not be in a jail. It may take place in a mental institution, hospital, restaurant, hotel room, automobile, parking lot, office, and so forth. Most courts have held that plaintiffs must be aware of their confinement while suffering it, or if not, then they must suffer some type of actual harm.

The plaintiffs in the following case brought suit against a retail store for false imprisonment after they were acquitted in a criminal trial of shoplifting charges.

Hainz v. Shopko Stores, Inc.
359 N.W.2d 397
Court of Appeals of Wisconsin
October 3, 1984

Brown, Presiding Judge

This case interprets sec. 943.50(3), Stats., the statute immunizing merchants from such claims as false imprisonment for shoplifting detentions. Merchants are protected from liability as long as they have probable cause to detain and as long as they detain only for a reasonable manner and a reasonable time. The issue here is whether "reasonable manner" means that a merchant has a duty to fully investigate each charge including the alleged shoplifter's side of the story. . . .

On October 15, 1981, plaintiffs Hainz and Fremlin went into the Racine Shopko store to buy some hunting arrows and other items. While in the sporting goods department, a store employee allegedly saw Fremlin remove the price tags from arrows marked two for $1.29 and place the tags on higher priced arrows. Hainz and Fremlin then proceeded to the check-out counter and purchased the arrows. The two were stopped by Shopko security personnel and taken to a room. Hainz and Fremlin were asked to sign a confession. They refused, and the police were called. The total detention time was approximately fifteen minutes. Both Hainz and Fremlin were charged with shoplifting but were acquitted after court trials.

The plaintiffs then brought this action claiming they had been falsely imprisoned by the employees of Shopko. Shopko claimed immunity from civil liability for the actions of their employees under sec. 943.50(3), Stats. At the close of the plaintiffs' case, Shopko moved to dismiss on the ground that there was no credible evidence to support the claim that the plaintiffs were unreasonably detained. The trial court denied the motion. The jury found Hainz and Fremlin had been unreasonably detained and awarded compensatory damages in the amounts of $182.68 and $75.00, respectively. The jury further found the conduct of Shopko's employees was in wanton, willful or reckless disregard of the plaintiffs' rights and awarded each of them $6,250 in punitive damages.

Section 943.50(3), Stats., affords civil and criminal immunity to a shopkeeper for detaining a suspected shoplifter under certain circumstances. It reads:

"(3) A merchant or merchant's adult employee who has probable cause for believing that a person has violated this section in his or her presence *may detain the person in a reasonable manner* for a reasonable length of time to deliver the person to a peace officer, or to his or her parent or guardian in the case of a minor. The detained person must be promptly informed of the purpose for the detention and be permitted to make phone calls, but he or she shall not be interrogated or searched against his or her will before the arrival of a peace officer who may conduct a lawful interrogation of the accused person. Any merchant or merchant's adult employee who acts in good faith in any act authorized under this section is immune from civil or criminal liability for those acts." [Emphasis added.]

Shopko maintains their employees acted in accordance with the statutory directive and that they were improperly denied immunity from liability. Hainz and Fremlin, on the other hand, assert that they were not detained "in a reasonable manner," and, therefore, Shopko cannot take advantage of the immunity statute. They testified that after they were informed of the "ticket-switching" accusation, they were asked to sign a confession. They refused and vehemently denied their guilt. They then asked the Shopko employees to check the price tags in the sporting goods department to verify their innocence. This was not done.

Later that day, after they had been released from police custody, Hainz and Fremlin returned to the Racine Shopko store and purchased the same arrows they had previously purchased. They were charged at the lower price. The plaintiffs maintain that their detention was conducted in an unreasonable manner due to the unwillingness of the Shopko employees to return to the sporting goods portion of the store and check the price of the arrows in question.

Before addressing the merits, we must first explain the proper standard of review. The sole question here is whether the phrase "in a reasonable manner" includes the affirmative duty to investigate. . . . It is uncontroverted that there was a failure to investigate. Where there is no conflict in the evidence regarding the length of time and the circumstances under which the customer was held, the reasonableness of the detention is one for the court. . . . We conclude this issue is a question of law that we may review independent of the trial court's determination.

In interpreting a statute, we must first look to the plain meaning of the statute. . . . If the statute is still ambiguous after reading it for its plain meaning, we must then look to intrinsic and extrinsic aids in order to determine legislative intent. . . .

At common law, a merchant was without privilege to detain a shoplifter without a warrant, even if the misdemeanor was committed in his presence. . . . Suits such as false imprisonment, which is the unlawful restraint by one person of the physical liberty of another, predominated in those instances. . . .

The plain meaning of sec. 943.50(3), Stats., is to immunize the merchant from such suits as long as two prongs are satisfied. First, the merchant must have had probable cause to believe that a person committed the crime of shoplifting. Second, the qualified privilege of detention without fear of liability may be lost by the manner in which it is exercised. Although probable cause gives the merchant a right to detain, such person may only be detained in a reasonable manner and only for the reasonable length of time necessary. Therefore, we know from the plain meaning of the statute that probable cause will give the merchant the immunity desired but that the immunity can be lost if the detention is unreasonable in time or manner.

There is no dispute that the merchant had probable cause. The dispute is whether the immunity was lost by reason of the merchant's subsequent action. The plain meaning of the statute does not help us with this question, and we must turn to extrinsic aids for guidance.

An extrinsic aid which helps in analyzing statutes is the use of judicial interpretation of similar statutes in other states. . . . In examining case law of other jurisdictions where the reasonableness of a customer's detention is raised, we find that the inquiry focuses on two major components: (1) whether the merchant's behavior was rude to the point of public embarrassment, and (2) the physical environment of detention. Specifically, the inquiries include: whether the employee's manner was harsh, loud or abusive; whether the questioning took place in a public or private area; whether unreasonable force was used in detaining the suspect, and whether there was a general showing of ill treatment toward the suspect. As summarized by one court, "the qualified privilege under the statute does not give the merchant the right to embarrass or harass individuals suspected, in public view of every one, in a rude manner." . . . No case contains, as one of its elements, the affirmative duty of the merchant to investigate the customer's recitation of events. . . .

We conclude that "reasonable manner" means that the right to detain is no license to use unjustifiable force, physical detention in dark rooms or the like, or ill treatment. Neither is it a license to insult or abuse the customer by excessive vehemence.

Finally, we note that another aid to statutory interpretation is that statutes in derogation of the common law must be strictly construed. . . . We reiterate that the common law gave merchants no immunity from suits arising out of detention of a customer against that person's will. The statute is in derogation of the common law. It greatly limits the merchant's actions and provides guidelines to protect the individual. The statute provides that the merchant may detain the customer; it does not allow an arrest. At common law, investigation and arrest were the domain of law enforcement officials. In the absence of clear language in the statute, we must presume that this has not changed. Indeed, the statute specifically provides that it is the peace officer's job, upon arrival, to conduct a lawful interrogation of the accused person. The only fair reading is that it is also the officer's job to make an investigation and, possibly, an arrest. Investigation of the customer's account of the events is more properly undertaken by the police upon arrival, not by the merchant beforehand. Strictly construing the statute, the merchant has no affirmative duty to investigate the customer's account of the events because that duty would be inconsistent with common law.

An examination of all the evidence presented, when taken in a light most favorable to the plaintiffs, only permits us to conclude that the detention was reasonable. The record contains no evidence that the Shopko employees were abusive, that any force was used or that the questioning took place in a public environment subjecting the plaintiffs to humiliation and embarrassment. Further, there has been no evidence to indicate that the Shopko employees were not acting in good faith when they detained the plaintiffs. The plaintiffs have relied solely on the failure of the Shopko employees to investigate as constituting an unreasonable detention. As we have already held that investigation is not a proper element of a reasonable detention, no credible evidence exists to support the jury's verdict.

Therefore, we reverse this judgment and remand with directions to the trial court to grant the defendant's motion for a directed verdict.

Judgment reversed and cause remanded with directions.

Case Questions

1. What is the purpose of antishoplifting statutes such as the one in this case? What costs does it seek to reduce? What effect might such a statute have on would-be shoplifters?
2. What factors does the court look at in determining whether the detention of the plaintiff was reasonable?
3. What was the issue in this case? What did the Wisconsin Court of Appeals decide? Why?

Defamation

The intentional tort of *defamation* results from the act of injuring another's character, fame, or reputation by false and malicious statements. Defamation is based on the policy that people should be able to enjoy their good name free of malicious and defamatory attacks. A publication is defamatory if it tends to lower a person in others' esteem. Language that is merely annoying cannot be defamatory. Generally, the truth of the statement is a complete defense in a suit for defamation because true statements are not considered to be malicious.

Libel and slander are both forms of defamation. *Libel* is defamation expressed by print, writing, signs, pictures, and, in the absence of statutory provisions to the contrary, radio and television broadcasts. *Slander* involves spoken words that have been heard by someone other than the person slandered.

The law treats some defamatory expressions as slanderous per se. Examples of slander per se include falsely accusing another of committing a crime of moral turpitude (rape, murder, or selling narcotics), false accusations that another person has contracted a morally offensive communicable disease (such as leprosy, syphilis, or gonorrhea), or defamatory expressions that interfere with another person's trade, business, or profession (saying that a banker is dishonest or that a doctor is a "quack"). In defamation cases, the law requires that special damages such as loss of job, loss of customers or clients, or loss of credit be proven before the plaintiff can recover general damages, such as mental anguish and loss of reputation.[5] However, a plaintiff who proves slander per se is not required to prove special damages because such expressions are almost certain to harm the plaintiff's reputation and produce economic loss. Not having to prove special damages is very helpful to the plaintiff because they are difficult to prove. The defendant can usually lessen the amount of damages awarded by publishing a retraction.

Interference with Contract Relations

The intentional tort of *interference with contract relations* takes place when a noncontracting party or third person wrongfully interferes with the contract relations between two or more contracting parties. (See Chapter 9 for discussion of contracts.) The tort of interference includes all intentional invasions of contract relations, including any act injuring a person or destroying property that interferes with the performance of a contract. For example, an intentional tort occurs when someone wrongfully prevents an employee from working for an employer or prevents a tenant from paying rent to the landlord.

In order to maintain an action against a third person for interference, it must be proved that the defendant maliciously and substantially interfered with the performance of a valid and enforceable contract. The motive or purpose of the interfering party is an important factor in determining liability.

Infliction of Mental Distress

A person has a cause of action for infliction of mental distress when the conduct of the defendant is serious in nature and causes anguish in the plaintiff's mind. Because it is difficult to prove mental anguish and to place a dollar amount on that injury, early cases allowed recovery for mental distress only when it was accompanied by some other tort, such as assault, battery, or false imprisonment. Today, the infliction of mental distress is generally considered to be an intentional tort, standing alone.

Recovery for mental distress is allowed only in situations involving extreme misconduct, for example, telling a wife the made-up story that her husband shot himself in the head. Mental worry, distress, grief, and mortification are elements of mental suffering for which an injured person can recover. Recovery is not available for mere annoyance, disappointment, or hurt feelings. For example, the mere disappointment of a grandfather because his grandchildren were prevented from visiting him on account of delay in the transmission of a fax message would not amount to mental distress.

Invasion of Privacy

The law recognizes one's right to be free from unwarranted publicity and, in general, one's right to be let alone. If one person invades the right of another to withhold self and property from public scrutiny, the invading party can be held liable in tort for invasion of the right of privacy. A suit for invasion of privacy may involve unwarranted publicity that places the plaintiff in a false light, or intrudes into the plaintiff's private life, or discloses embarrassing private facts, or uses the plaintiff's name or likeness for the defendant's gain. Generally, the motives of the defendant are unimportant.

The standard used to measure any type of invasion of privacy is that the effect must be highly offensive to a reasonable person. For example, if a frustrated creditor puts up a notice in a store window stating that a named debtor owes money, this is an invasion of the debtor's privacy.

Technological developments in information storage and communications have subjected the intimacies of everyone's private lives to exploitation. The law protects individuals against this type of encroachment. A person who has become a public figure has less protection, however, because society has a right to information of legitimate public interest.

Although invasion of privacy and defamation are similar, they are distinct intentional torts, and both may be included in a plaintiff's complaint. The difference between a right of privacy and a right to freedom from defamation is that the former is concerned with one's peace of mind, while the latter is concerned with one's reputation or character. Truth is generally not a defense for invasion of privacy.

Johnny Carson brought suit in the following case alleging that the defendant had invaded his right of privacy and publicity by selling "Here's Johnny" portable toilets.

Carson v. Here's Johnny Portable Toilets, Inc.
698 F.2d 831 (1983)
U.S. Court of Appeals, Sixth Circuit
February 1, 1983

Brown, Senior Circuit Judge

This case involves claims of unfair competition and invasion of the right of privacy and the right of publicity arising from appellee's adoption of a phrase generally associated with a popular entertainer.

Appellant, John W. Carson (Carson), is the host and star of "The Tonight

Show," a well-known television program broadcast five nights a week by the National Broadcasting Company. Carson also appears as an entertainer in night clubs and theaters around the country. From the time he began hosting "The Tonight Show" in 1962, he has been introduced on the show each night with the phrase "Here's Johnny." This method of introduction was first used for Carson in 1957 when he hosted a daily television program for the American Broadcasting Company. The phrase "Here's Johnny" is generally associated with Carson by a substantial segment of the television viewing public. In 1967, Carson first authorized use of this phrase by an outside business venture, permitting it to be used by a chain of restaurants called "Here's Johnny Restaurants."

Appellant Johnny Carson Apparel, Inc. (Apparel), formed in 1970, manufactures and markets men's clothing to retail stores. Carson, the president of Apparel and owner of 20% of its stock, has licensed Apparel to use his name and picture, which appear on virtually all of Apparel's products and promotional material. Apparel has also used, with Carson's consent, the phrase "Here's Johnny" on labels for clothing and in advertising campaigns. In 1977, Apparel granted a license to Marcy Laboratories to use "Here's Johnny" as the name of a line of men's toiletries. The phrase "Here's Johnny" has never been registered by appellants as a trademark or service mark.

Appellee, Here's Johnny Portable Toilets, Inc., is a Michigan corporation engaged in the business of renting and selling "Here's Johnny" portable toilets. Appellee's founder was aware at the time he formed the corporation that "Here's Johnny" was the introductory slogan for Carson on "The Tonight Show." He indicated that he coupled the phrase with a second one, "The World's Foremost Commodian," to make "a good play on a phrase."

Shortly after appellee went into business in 1976, appellants brought this action alleging unfair competition, trademark infringement under federal and state law, and invasion of privacy and publicity rights. They sought damages and an injunction prohibiting appellee's further use of the phrase "Here's Johnny" as a corporate name or in connection with the sale or rental of its portable toilets.

After a bench trial, the district court issued a memorandum opinion and order . . . which served as its findings of fact and conclusions of law. The court ordered the dismissal of the appellants' complaint. On the unfair competition claim, the court concluded that the appellants had failed to satisfy the "likelihood of confusion" test. On the right of privacy and right of publicity theories, the court held that these rights extend only to a "name or likeness," and "Here's Johnny" did not qualify.

I

Appellants' first claim alleges unfair competition from appellee's business activities in violation of § 43(a) of the Lanham Act . . . and of Michigan common law. The district court correctly noted that the test for equitable relief under both § 43(a) and Michigan common law is the "likelihood of confusion" standard. . . . Although the appellee had intended to capitalize on the phrase popularized by Carson, the court concluded that appellee had not intended to deceive the public into believing Carson was connected with the product. . . . The court noted that there was little evidence of actual confusion and no evidence that appellee's use of the phrase had damaged appellants. For these reasons, the court determined that appellee's use of the phrase "Here's Johnny" did not present a likelihood of confusion, mistake, or deception. . . .

Our review of the record indicates that none of the district court's findings is clearly erroneous. Moreover, on the basis of these findings, we agree with the district court that the appellants have failed to establish a likelihood of confusion. The general concept underlying the likelihood of confusion is that the public believe that "the mark's owner *sponsored or otherwise approved* the use of the trademark." . . .

The facts as found by the district court do not implicate such likelihood of confusion, and we affirm the district court on this issue.

II

The appellants also claim that the appellee's use of the phrase "Here's Johnny" violates the common law right of privacy and right of publicity. The confusion in this area of the law requires a brief analysis of the relationship between these two rights.

In an influential article, Dean Prosser delineated four distinct types of the right of privacy: (1) intrusion upon one's seclusion or solitude, (2) public disclosure of embarrassing private facts, (3) publicity which places one in a false light, and (4) appropriation of one's name or likeness for the defendant's advantage. . . . This fourth type has become known as the "right of publicity." . . .

We do not believe that Carson's claim that his right of privacy has been invaded is supported by the law or the facts. Apparently, the gist of this claim is that Carson is embarrassed by and considers it odious to be associated with the appel-

lee's product. Clearly, the association does not appeal to Carson's sense of humor. But the facts here presented do not, it appears to us, amount to an invasion of any of the interests protected by the right of privacy. In any event, our disposition of the claim of an invasion of the right of publicity makes it unnecessary for us to accept or reject the claim of an invasion of the right of privacy.

The right of publicity has developed to protect the commercial interest of celebrities in their identities. The theory of the right is that a celebrity's identity can be valuable in the promotion of products, and the celebrity has an interest that may be protected from the unauthorized commercial exploitation of that identity. In *Memphis Development Foundation v. Factors Etc., Inc.,* . . . we stated: "The famous have an exclusive legal right during life to control and profit from the commercial use of their name and personality." . . .

The district court dismissed appellants' claim based on the right of publicity because appellee does not use Carson's name or likeness. . . . We believe that, on the contrary, the district court's conception of the right of publicity is too narrow. The right of publicity, as we have stated, is that a celebrity has a protected pecuniary interest in the commercial exploitation of his identity. If the celebrity's identity is commercially exploited, there has been an invasion of his right whether or not his "name or likeness" is used. Carson's identity may be exploited even if his name, John W. Carson, or his picture is not used. . . .

In this case, Earl Braxton, president and owner of Here's Johnny Portable Toilets, Inc., admitted that he knew that the phrase "Here's Johnny" had been used for years to introduce Carson. . . .

That the "Here's Johnny" name was selected by Braxton because of its identification with Carson was the clear inference from Braxton's testimony irrespective of such admission in the opening statement.

We therefore conclude that, applying the correct legal standards, appellants are entitled to judgment. The proof showed without question that appellee had appropriated Carson's identity in connection with its corporate name and its product.

. . .

It should be obvious from the majority opinion and the dissent that a celebrity's identity may be appropriated in various ways. It is our view that, under the existing authorities, a celebrity's legal right of publicity is invaded whenever his identity is intentionally appropriated for commercial purposes. . . . It is not fatal to appellant's claim that appellee did not use his "name." Indeed, there would have been no violation of his right of publicity even if appellee had used his name, such as "J. William Carson Portable Toilet" or the "John William Carson Portable Toilet" or the "J. W. Carson Portable Toilet." The reason is that, though literally using appellant's "name," the appellee would not have appropriated Carson's identity as a celebrity. Here there was an appropriation of Carson's identity without using his "name."

With respect to the dissent's general policy arguments, it seems to us that the policies there set out would more likely be vindicated by the majority view than by the dissent's view. Certainly appellant Carson's achievement had made him a celebrity which means that his identity has a pecuniary value which the right of publicity should vindicate. Vindication of the right will tend to encourage achievement in Carson's chosen field. Vindication of the right will also tend to prevent unjust enrichment by persons such as appellee who seek commercially to exploit the identity of celebrities without their consent.

The judgment of the district court is vacated and the case remanded for further proceedings consistent with this opinion.*

Kennedy, Circuit Judge, dissenting

I respectfully dissent from that part of the majority's opinion which holds that appellee's use of the phrase "Here's Johnny" violates appellant Johnny Carson's common law right of publicity. While I agree that an individual's identity may be impermissibly exploited, I do not believe that the common law right of publicity may be extended beyond an individual's name, likeness, achievements, identifying characteristics or actual performances, to include phrases or other things which are merely associated with the individual, as is the phrase "Here's Johnny." The majority's extension of the right of publicity to include phrases or other things which are merely associated with the individual permits a popular entertainer or public figure, by associating himself or herself with a common phrase, to remove those words from the public domain.

The phrase "Here's Johnny" is merely associated with Johnny Carson, the host and star of "The Tonight Show" broadcast by the National Broadcasting Company. Since 1962, the opening format of "The Tonight Show," after the theme music is played, is to introduce Johnny Carson with the phrase "Here's Johnny." The words

*On remand the district court issued an injunction preventing the defendant company from using the "Here's Johnny" phrase anywhere in the country. The district court also awarded Carson $31,661.96 in damages, measured by the defendant's profits plus costs. The defendant appealed again to the Sixth Circuit Court of Appeals, requesting that the injunction be limited to the boundaries of the state of Michigan. The court of appeals affirmed the district court judgment but ruled that the company could "seek future modification of the injunction in the event of changed conditions that might make modification appropriate." See *Carson v. Here's Johnny Portable Toilets, Inc.*, 810 F.2d 104 (6th Cir. 1987).—*Ed.*

are spoken by an announcer, generally Ed McMahon, in a drawn out and distinctive manner. Immediately after the phrase "Here's Johnny" is spoken, Johnny Carson appears to begin the program. This method of introduction was first used by Johnny Carson in 1957 when he hosted a daily television show for the American Broadcasting Company. This case is not transformed into a "name" case simply because the diminutive form of John W. Carson's given name and the first name of his full stage name, Johnny Carson, appears in it. The first name is so common, in light of the millions of persons named John, Johnny or Jonathan that no doubt inhabit this world, that, alone, it is meaningless or ambiguous at best in identifying Johnny Carson, the celebrity. In addition, the phrase containing Johnny Carson's first stage name was certainly selected for its value as a double entendre. Appellee manufactures portable toilets. The value of the phrase to appellee's product is in the risqué meaning of "john"

as a toilet or bathroom. For this reason, too, this is not a "name" case.

Appellee has stipulated that the phrase "Here's Johnny" is associated with Johnny Carson and that absent this association, he would not have chosen to use it for his product and corporation, Here's Johnny Portable Toilets, Inc. I do not consider it relevant that appellee intentionally chose to incorporate into the name of his corporation and product a phrase that is merely associated with Johnny Carson. What is not protected by law is not taken from public use. Research reveals no case in which the right of publicity has been extended to phrases or other things which are merely associated with an individual and are not part of his name, likeness, achievements, identifying characteristics or actual performances. Both the policies behind the right of publicity and countervailing interests and considerations indicate that such an extension should not be made. . . .

Case Questions

1. What are the four distinct types of privacy rights recognized by the court?
2. After a bench trial, why did the district court find against Johnny Carson with respect to his right-of-privacy claim?
3. Although the appellee did not appropriate Carson's name, likeness, achievements, identifying characteristics, or actual performances, the court of appeals ruled that Carson was entitled to judgment. Why?
4. Why did Judge Kennedy dissent?

NEGLIGENCE

The law recognizes a duty or obligation to conform to a certain standard of conduct for the protection of others against unreasonable risk of harm. If the person fails to conform to the required standard, and that failure causes damage or loss, the injured party has a cause of action for *negligence*. Negligence is the *unintentional* failure to live up to the community's ideal of reasonable care; it is not based on moral fault. The fact that defendants may have suffered losses of their own through their negligent acts does not render them any less liable for plaintiffs' injuries.

An infinite variety of possible situations makes the determination of an exact set of rules for negligent conduct impossible. Conduct that might be considered prudent in one situation may be deemed negligent in another, depending on such factors as the person's physical attributes, age, and knowledge, the person to whom the duty was owed, and the situation at the time. If the defendant could not reasonably foresee any injury as the result of a certain conduct, there is no negligence and no liability.

The elements necessary for a cause of action for the tort of negligence are (1) a duty or standard of care recognized by law, (2) a breach of the duty or failure to exercise the requisite care, and (3) the occurrence of harm proximately caused by the breach of duty. No cause of action in negligence is recognized if any of these elements is absent from the proof.

The plaintiff has the burden of proving, through the presentation of evidence, that the defendant was negligent. Unless the evidence is such that it can reasonably lead to but one conclusion, negligence is primarily a question of fact for the jury. A jury must decide whether the defendant acted as a reasonably prudent person would have under the circumstances—that is, a person having the same information, experience, physique, and professional skill. This standard makes no allowance for a person less intelligent than average.

Children are not held to the same standard as adults. A child must conform merely to the conduct of a reasonable person of like age, intelligence, and experience under like circumstances. This standard is subjective and holds a less intelligent child to what a similar child would do.

Malpractice

The term *malpractice* is a nonlegal term for negligence. Professional negligence takes different forms in different fields. Attorney negligence would include drafting a will but failing to see that it is properly attested; failing to file an answer in a timely manner on behalf of a client, with the result that the plaintiff wins by default; and failing to file suit prior to the running of the statute of limitation, thus barring the client's claim. Accountant negligence would occur if a client paid for an audit but the accountant failed to discover that the client's employees were engaging in embezzlement, exposing the client to postaudit losses that could have been prevented. The case of *Macomber v. Dillman* (Chapter 6) is an example of medical malpractice. In that case, a surgeon improperly performed a tubal ligation and the plaintiff subsequently gave birth to a child.

Plaintiffs in malpractice cases allege that the professional specifically breached a contractual duty (if the suit is in contract) or that the professional breached a duty of care imposed by law (if the suit is in tort). Professionals have a higher degree of knowledge, skills, or experience than a reasonable person and are required to use that capacity. They are generally required to act as would a reasonably skilled, prudent, competent, and experienced member of the profession in good standing within that state. Negligence in this area usually may be shown only by the use of expert testimony.

The plaintiff in the following case sued a supermarket, alleging that the store was negligent in the way it displayed and marketed its green peppers.

Gilhooley v. Star Market Co., Inc.
508 N.E.2d 609
Supreme Judicial Court of Massachusetts
June 8, 1987

O'Connor, Justice

In this tort action, the plaintiff alleges that, due to the defendant's negligence, he sustained personal injuries from slipping on a green pepper in the defendant's supermarket. By a special verdict, the jury found that the defendant had not been negligent. Accordingly, judgment [was] entered for the defendant. On appeal to the Appeals Court, the plaintiff claimed that the judge's instructions to the jury were erroneous because they focused exclusively on the question whether the defendant reasonably should have discovered and removed the pepper before the plaintiff fell. The plaintiff claimed that, as a result, the judge's instructions erroneously "did not permit the jury to find the defendant negligent for the way in which it displayed and marketed its produce." The Appeals Court affirmed the judgment. . . . and this court allowed the plaintiff's application for further appellate review. We, too, affirm the judgment for the defendant. The jury instructions were not erroneous.

We set forth the relevant portions of the jury instructions: "Under our law, the owner, occupant or lessee of premises is under a duty to exercise ordinary care in the management of such premises in order to avoid exposing persons who

come thereon, to an unreasonable risk of harm. . . . Negligence is the failure to observe due care, to take due care that someone is not placed in a condition of unreasonable risk of harm. So that for definition, I will tell you that the law says that negligence is the failure to use reasonable care. Reasonable care is that degree of care which a reasonably careful person would use under like circumstances, and negligence may consist of either doing something that a reasonably careful person would not do, or omitting to do something that a reasonably careful person would do. . . . Let me say to you this, that the mere unexplained presence of a foreign substance on the premises, and an accident occurring, does not, without more in and of itself establish negligence. If a substance is upon the floor of the defendant's premises, it is up to you to determine whether or not the defendant knew or should have known as to its presence. If he knew, the question is, did he make or did they make or take reasonable precaution to eliminate it. So if he could reasonably foresee its presence, did he take the necessary precautions, or did they take the necessary precautions to eliminate such an event."

At the conclusion of the instructions, the plaintiff objected to the failure of the judge to give certain instructions that the plaintiff had requested. The pertinent portions of the requested instructions are as follows: "You may find that the defendant was negligent for either or both of two grounds: (1) You may find that the defendant was negligent, if you find that the particular piece of produce on which the plaintiff slipped . . . had been on the floor of the defendant's store long enough before the plaintiff slipped on it for the defendant's employees, in the exercise of ordinary care and vigilance, to have noticed it and removed it. . . . (2) You may find that the defendant is negligent if you find that the presence of produce on the floor of the defendant's produce department was a usual, ordinary and foreseeable result of the way in which the defendant conducted its produce business. . . . The second ground does not depend on notice; it does not require that the defendant noticed or should have noticed the green pepper. If you find that the defendant's method of operating its produce department was such that it could be expected that produce would find its way to the floor, or was such that produce finding its way to the floor was an ordinary occurrence, then you may find the defendant negligent, even if it had no notice, actual or constructive, of the particular item on which the plaintiff slipped. . . .''

The requested instructions would have permitted the jury to find the defendant negligent on the basis of foreseeability of risk without the jury's addressing the question whether, despite foreseeable risk, the defendant's conduct met the standard set by an ordinarily prudent person in the same or similar circumstances. The plaintiff was not entitled to such instructions for two reasons: (1) To establish liability for negligence, the critical question is whether the defendant has failed to act as a reasonably prudent person would have acted in all the circumstances, "including the likelihood of injury to others, the seriousness of the injury, and the burden of avoiding the risk." . . . Foreseeability of risk is but one consideration. (2) Although there was evidence of foreseeability of risk, the evidence did not warrant a finding that the pepper had been on the floor as a result of the defendant's failure to display and market its produce according to the standard set by an ordinarily prudent person in the circumstances.

The evidence most favorable to the plaintiff showed that the produce section of the defendant's market was designed for self-service. The peppers were stacked on top of one another in a diagonal fashion in plastic bins on counters. The bins slanted down toward the aisle. Customers and employees sometimes dropped vegetables and fruit onto the floor, and sometimes vegetables and fruit rolled onto the floor when customers or employees touched them. Produce "constantly" had to be taken off the floor. Sweeping was a major concern of the defendant. It was not done according to any schedule, but it was done as often as necessary. It was done "every five minutes, or every minute," if necessary.

The plaintiff argues that self-service creates a risk of spillage, and that the risk may have been enhanced in this case by the peppers' being stacked in a "diagonal" display in bins tilted toward an aisle, the color of which tended to blend with the color of green peppers. We agree with the plaintiff that, in an appropriate case, the keeper of a grocery store may be liable to a customer who slips on produce that is on the floor because of the storekeeper's negligent marketing and display thereof. It is not always necessary for liability that the produce have been on the floor long enough for the storekeeper to have had a reasonable opportunity to have seen and removed it. But, here, there was no evidence of the defendant's failure to comply with industry practices, of inadequate monitoring, or of sloppy or precarious stacking of items. To establish liability, more must be shown than that produce was stacked at an unspecified angle in a self-service area of the defendant's store, and that, as a result of customer and employee activity, produce fell to the floor.

We conclude that, even if the jury instructions be construed to mean that the only theory on which the plaintiff could recover was that the pepper had been on the floor long enough for the defendant reasonably to have seen and removed it, the instructions were correct.

Judgment affirmed.

Case Questions

1. The plaintiff, Gilhooley, appealed because he believed the judges' instructions to the jury to be in error. What was the basis of his argument?
2. Why did the Massachusetts Supreme Judicial Court reject the plaintiff's argument?
3. If the plaintiff believed that a higher standard of care should have been applied to Star Market under the facts of this case, what should he have done to raise that issue?

Duty of Care

There can be no actionable negligence when there is no legal duty. Common law duty is found by courts where the kind of relationship that exists between the parties to a dispute requires the legal recognition of a duty of care. Legislative acts may also prescribe standards of conduct required of a reasonable person. It may be argued that a reasonable person would obey statutes such as traffic laws, ordinances, and regulations of administrative bodies.

In the case of legislative acts, plaintiffs must establish that they are within the limited class of individuals intended to be protected by the statute. In addition, the harm suffered must be of the kind that the statute was intended to prevent. Often the class of people intended to be protected may be very broad. For example, regulations requiring the labeling of certain poisons are for the protection of anyone who may come in contact with the bottle. Many traffic laws are meant to protect other people on the highway. Once it is decided that a statute is applicable, most courts hold that an unexcused violation is conclusive as to the issue of negligence. In other words, it is *negligence per se* and the issue of negligence does not go to the jury. However, some courts hold that the violation of such a statute is only *evidence* of negligence, which the jury may accept or reject as it sees fit.

Common law provides that one should guard against that which a reasonably prudent person would anticipate as likely to injure another. Damages for an injury are not recoverable if it was not foreseen or could not have been foreseen or anticipated. It is not necessary that one anticipate the precise injury sustained, however.

Courts do not ignore the common practices of society in determining the duty or whether due care was exercised in a particular situation. The scope of the duty of care that a person owes depends on the relationship of the parties. For example, those who lack mental capacity, the young, and the inexperienced are entitled to a degree of care proportionate to their incapacity to care for themselves.

As a general rule, the law does not impose the duty to aid or protect another. However, a duty *is* imposed where there is a special relationship between the parties—for example, parents must go to the aid of their children, and employers must render protection to their employees. In addition, if one puts another in peril, that person must render aid. A person can also assume a duty through contract where the duty would not otherwise exist. Although persons seeing another in distress have no obligation to be Good Samaritans, if they choose to do so they incur the duty of exercising ordinary care. Some states have changed this common law duty by passing Good Samaritan statutes that state that those administering emergency care are liable only if the acts performed constitute willful or wanton misconduct.

The plaintiff in the following case alleged that a radio station's giveaway contest created an unreasonable risk of harm to her husband and thus the station was liable in tort for his death.

Weirum v. RKO General, Inc.
123 Cal. Rpt. 468, 539 P.2d 36
Supreme Court of California
August 21, 1975

Mosk, Justice

A rock station with an extensive teen age audience conducted a contest which rewarded the first contestant to locate a peripatetic disk jockey. Two minors driving in separate automobiles attempted to follow the disc jockey's automobile to its next stop. In the course of their pursuit, one of the minors negligently forced a car off the highway, killing its sole occupant. In a suit filed by the surviving wife and children of the decedent, the jury rendered a verdict against the radio station. We now must determine whether the radio station owed decedent a duty of due care.

The facts are not disputed. Radio station KHJ is a successful Los Angeles broadcaster with a large teen age following. . . . In order to attract an even larger portion of the available audience and thus increase advertising revenue, KHJ inaugurated in July of 1970 a promotion entitled "The Super Summer Spectacular." . . . Among the programs included in the "spectacular" was a contest broadcast on July 16, 1970, the date of the accident.

On that day, Donald Steele Revert, known professionally as "The Real Don Steele," a KHJ disc jockey and television personality, traveled in a conspicuous red automobile to a number of locations in the Los Angeles metropolitan area. Periodically, he apprised KHJ of his whereabouts and his intended destination, and the station broadcast the information to its listeners. The first person to physically locate Steele and fulfill a specified condition received a cash prize. In addition, the winning contestant participated in a brief interview on the air with "The Real Don Steele." . . .

In Van Nuys, 17-year-old Robert Sentner was listening to KHJ in his car while searching for "The Real Don Steele." Upon hearing that "The Real Don Steele" was proceeding to Canoga Park, he immediately drove to that vicinity. Meanwhile in Northridge, 19-year-old Marsha Baime heard and responded to the same information. Both of them arrived at the Holiday Theater in Canoga Park to find that someone had already claimed the prize. Without knowledge of the other, each decided to follow the Steele vehicle to its next stop and thus be the first to arrive when the next contest question or condition was announced.

For the next few miles, the Sentner and Baime cars jockeyed for position closest to the Steele vehicle, reaching speeds up to 80 miles an hour. . . . The Steele vehicle left the freeway at the Westlake off ramp. Either Baime or Sentner, in attempting to follow, forced decedent's car onto the center divider, where it overturned. Baime stopped to report the accident. Sentner, after pausing momentarily to relate the tragedy to a passing peace officer, continued to pursue Steele, successfully located him, and collected a cash prize.

Decedent's wife and children brought an action for wrongful death against Sentner, Baime, RKO General, Inc. as owner of KHJ, and the maker of decedent's car. Sentner settled prior to the commencement of trial for the limits of his insurance policy. The jury returned a verdict against Baime and KHJ in the amount of $300,000 and found in favor of the manufacturer of decedent's car. KHJ

appeals from the . . . judgment. . . . Baime did not appeal.

The primary question for our determination is whether defendant owed a duty to decedent arising out of its broadcast of the giveaway contest. . . . Any number of considerations may justify the imposition of duty in particular circumstances, including the guidance of history, our continually refined concepts of morals and justice, the convenience of the rule, and social judgment as to where the loss should fall. . . . While the question whether one owes a duty to another must be decided on a case-by-case basis, every case is governed by the rule of general application that all persons are required to use ordinary care to prevent others from being injured as the result of their conduct. . . . [F]oreseeability of the risk is a primary consideration in establishing the element of duty. . . .

The verdict in plaintiffs' favor here necessarily embraced a finding that decedent was exposed to a foreseeable risk of harm. . . .

We conclude that the record amply supports the finding of foreseeability. These tragic events unfolded in the middle of a Los Angeles summer, a time when young people were free from the constraints of school and responsive to relief from vacation tedium. Seeking to attract new listeners, KHJ devised an "exciting" promotion. Money and a small measure of momentary notoriety awaited the swiftest response. It was foreseeable that defendant's youthful listeners, finding the prize had eluded them at one location, would race to arrive first at the next site and in their haste would disregard the demands of highway safety.

Indeed, "The Real Don Steele" testified that he had in the past noticed vehicles following him from location to location. He was further aware that the same contestants sometimes appeared at consecutive stops. This knowledge is not rendered irrelevant, as defendant suggests, by the absence of any prior injury. Such an argument confuses foreseeability with hindsight, and amounts to a contention that the injuries of the first victim are not compensable. "The mere fact that a particular kind of accident has not happened before does not . . . show that such accident is one which might not reasonably have been anticipated." . . . Thus, the fortuitous absence of prior injury does not justify relieving defendant from responsibility for the foreseeable consequences of its acts.

It is of no consequence that the harm to decedent was inflicted by third parties acting negligently. Defendant invokes the maxim that an actor is entitled to assume that others will not act negligently. . . . This concept is valid, however, only to the extent that the intervening conduct was not to be anticipated. . . . If the likelihood that a third person may react in a particular manner is a hazard which makes the actor negligent, such reaction whether innocent or negligent does not prevent the actor from being liable for the harm caused thereby. . . . Here, reckless conduct by youthful contestants, stimulated by defendant's broadcast, constituted the hazard to which decedent was exposed.

It is true, of course, that virtually every act involves some conceivable danger. Liability is imposed only if the risk of harm resulting from the act is deemed unreasonable—i.e., if the gravity and likelihood of the danger outweigh the utility of the conduct involved. . . .

We need not belabor the grave danger inherent in the contest broadcast by defendant. The risk of a high speed automobile chase is the risk of death or serious injury. Obviously, neither the entertainment afforded by the contest nor its commercial rewards can justify the creation of such a grave risk. Defendant could have accomplished its objectives of entertaining its listeners and increasing advertising revenues by adopting a contest format which would have avoided danger to the motoring public. . . .

We are not persuaded that the imposition of a duty here will lead to unwarranted extensions of liability. Defendant is fearful that entrepreneurs will henceforth be burdened with an avalanche of obligations: an athletic department will owe a duty to an ardent sports fan injured while hastening to purchase one of a limited number of tickets; a department store will be liable to injuries incurred in response to a "while-they-last" sale. This argument, however, suffers from a myopic view of the facts presented here. The giveaway contest was no common-place invitation to an attraction available on a limited basis. It was a competitive scramble in which the thrill of the chase to be the one and only victor was intensified by the live broadcasts which accompanied the pursuit. In the assertedly analogous situations described by defendant, any haste involved in the purchase of the commodity is an incidental and unavoidable result of the scarcity of the commodity itself. In such situations, there is no attempt, as here, to generate a competitive pursuit on public streets, accelerated by repeated importuning by radio to be the very first to arrive at a particular destination. Manifestly, the "spectacular" bears little resemblance to daily commercial activities.

Defendant . . . urges that it owed no duty of care to decedent . . . absent a special relationship, an actor is under no duty to control the conduct of third parties. . . . This doctrine is rooted in the common law distinction between action and inaction, or misfeasance and non-feasance. Misfeasance exists when the defendant is responsible for making the plaintiff's position worse, i.e., defendant has created a risk. Conversely, nonfeasance is found when the defendant has failed to aid plaintiff through beneficial intervention. . . [L]iability for nonfeasance is largely limited to those circumstances in which some special relationship can be established. If, on the other hand, the act complained of is one of misfeasance, the question of duty is governed by the standards of ordinary care discussed above. . . . [In this dispute,] [l]iability is not predicated on defendant's failure to intervene for the benefit of decedent but rather on its creation of an unreasonable risk of harm to him. . . .

Case
Questions

1. Was the exact injury, or result of the contest, foreseeable in this case?
2. Assume that a business entered a float in a commercial parade, and as the float traveled down the street, employees threw candy to the crowd. Children running to collect the candy injured a spectator. Would the injury be foreseeable on the part of the business?
3. Assume that a department store advertises portable television sets at a very low price. There is a limited number to be sold "while they last" after the doors open on a specified day. A customer interested in buying a television set runs over another customer. On the basis of *Weirum*, would the department store have a duty?

Liability Rules for Specialized Activities

The ordinary principles of negligence do not govern occupiers' liability to those entering their premises. For example, the duty the land occupier or possessor owes to a trespasser is less than the duty the possessor owes to the general public under the ordinary principles of negligence. The special rules regarding liability of the possessor of land stem from the English tradition of high regard for land and from the dominance and prestige of the English landowning class. In the eighteenth and nineteenth centuries, owners of land were considered sovereigns within their own boundaries and were privileged to do what they pleased within their domains. The unrestricted use of land was favored over human welfare. Visitors were classified as invitees, licensees, or trespassers. Although English law has since rejected these distinctions, they remain part of the U.S. common law.

An invitee is either a *public invitee* or a *business visitor*. A public invitee is a member of the public who enters land for the purpose for which the land is held open to the public, for example, a customer who enters a store. A business visitor enters land for a purpose directly or indirectly connected with business dealings with the possessor of the land. Thus plumbers, electricians, trash collectors, and letter carriers are classified as business invitees. Invitees are given the greatest protection by the courts. A landowner owes the invitee a duty to exercise ordinary care under the usual principles of negligence liability, and must exercise reasonable care to make the premises safe. This preferred status applies only to the area of invitation.

One who enters or remains on land by virtue of the possessor's implied or express consent is a *licensee*, for example, door-to-door salespeople or social guests. In addition, police officers and firefighters are usually classified as licensees because they often come on premises unexpectedly and it would not be fair to hold possessors to the standard of care applicable to invitees. Licensees must ordinarily accept the premises as they find them and look out for their own welfare. This is based on the principle that land occupiers cannot be expected to exercise a higher degree of care for licensees than they would for themselves. A possessor of land generally owes the licensee only the duty to refrain from willful or wanton misconduct; however, the courts have developed some exceptions to this rule. With respect to active operations, for example, the possessor of land is subject to liability to licensees for injury caused by failure to exercise reasonable care for their safety. What might constitute activities dangerous to licensees depends on the court's interpretation, and knowledge of the nature of the activities normally precludes recovery by the licensee. Generally, the possessor of land is under a duty to give warning of known dangers.

A *trespasser* is one who enters and remains on the land of another without the possessor's expressed or implied consent. Licensees or inviteees may become trespassers when they venture into an area where they are not invited or expected to venture, or if they remain on the premises for longer than necessary. Generally, possessors of land are not liable to trespassers for physical harm caused by their failure either to exercise reasonable care to make their land safe for their reception or to carry on their activities so as not to endanger them. The only duty that is owed to a trespasser by an occupier of land is to refrain from willful or wanton misconduct. However, a duty of reasonable care is owed to an adult trespasser whose presence has been discovered or who habitually intrudes on a limited area. Reasonable care is also owed to the child trespasser whose presence is foreseeable.

Some question the legal and moral justification of a rule that determines the legal protection of a person's life and limb according to this classification scheme. Although courts have been reluctant to abandon the land occupier's preferred position set forth by history and precedent, some courts have replaced the common law distinction with ordinary principles of negligence to govern occupiers' liability to those entering their premises.

The following case was brought by a victim of a criminal assault against the owner of a motel in whose parking lot the attack occurred. The Supreme Court of Virginia's position in this case represents the minority rule. The majority of states take the position that a business invitor has a duty to take positive action to protect a business invitee from assault by third parties while the invitee is on the business premises. The *Wright* case was selected to provoke class discussion.

Wright v. Webb
362 S.E.2d 919
Supreme Court of Virginia
November 25, 1987

Whiting, Justice

In this negligence case, we consider under what circumstances commercial property owners are liable for injuries to a business invitee caused by the criminal assault of a third party.

On October 23, 1980, Joann Webb (Webb) was criminally assaulted in the parking lot of a motel owned by John C. Wright and John R. Wright, partners, trading as Quality Inn–Lake Wright (the Wrights). Webb, claiming she was a business invitee, sought damages for personal injuries arising out of the Wrights' alleged negligence in failing to provide adequate exterior lighting on the parking lot, fencing, closed circuit television, perimeter patrols, and speed bumps to protect business invitees "against foreseeable criminal attack."

The trial court entered judgment on a jury's verdict for Webb. In conformity with well-established appellate principles, we consider the facts in the light most favorable to Webb, the prevailing party in the trial court.

The Wrights provided parking spaces on their property not only for the motel guests but also for patrons of an adjacent business owned by another party, known as the Lake Wright Dinner Theatre (the dinner theatre). At dusk on October 23, 1980, Webb, intending to attend a function at the dinner theatre, parked her car in the Wrights' parking lot. Webb entered the motel and asked for directions to the dinner theatre. After getting directions, Webb returned to her car to drive over to the theatre. It was dark by this time.

Just as Webb prepared to move the car, a man, later identified as Thomas Moore (Moore), opened the car door on the driver's side, put his hand over Webb's mouth and told Webb he "would blow [her] brains out" if she screamed. When Moore entered the car and started the engine, Webb tried to escape through the passenger's door. Webb was partially out of the car when she started to scream. Moore grabbed Webb by the hair and pulled her back into the car. Webb continued screaming during most of the ensuing five-minute struggle. Toward the end of the struggle, Moore bit off a portion of Webb's nose and left the car. Three male guests of the motel, who had heard Webb screaming, arrived shortly thereafter and offered assistance. Moore reappeared, and Webb identified him as her assailant. Moore was later arrested and convicted of the assault.

A Norfolk police officer testified concerning police reports of prior larcenies, which had occurred on an average of once or twice a month in either the motel rooms or in automobiles parked in the lot. Prior to this assault, the Wrights' motel manager knew about some of the prior larcenies which occurred in the parking lot, a physical assault upon a female guest in a motel room in November of 1979, and a double murder in the parking lot of an adjacent property, operated by the City of Norfolk as a golf course, in April of 1977.

There was evidence from which the jury could conclude that the parking lot was dimly lit. A security expert testified about other available precautions—such as fencing, closed circuit television, a patrol of the premises, and a speed bump —which might have deterred criminal activity in the parking lot.

We will assume, without deciding, that Webb was the Wrights' business invitee. Thus, the Wrights owed Webb the duty of ordinary care to maintain their parking lot in a reasonably safe condition. . . .

Ordinarily, the owner or possessor of land is under no duty to protect invitees from assaults by third parties while the invitee is upon the premises. Restatement (Second) of Torts § 314A (1965) recognizes exceptions to the rule of non-liability for the assaults of a third party where there is a special relationship between a possessor of land and his invitee giving rise to a duty to protect the invitee from such assaults. . . .

Webb urges us to adopt the Restatement rule by creating a duty of care requiring a business invitor to take positive action to protect his business invitee from assault by third parties while the invitee is on the business premises. We decline to do so for the reasons which follow.

A business invitor owes the same duty of reasonable care to his invitee that a landlord owes to his tenant. . . . [W]e [have] rejected the contention that the landlord-tenant relation imposed a duty upon the landlord to "act as policeman," . . . or "protect his tenant from a criminal act by a third person." . . .

As we said in *Gulf Reston*, in ordinary circumstances, acts of assaultive criminal behavior cannot reasonably be foreseen. . . .

"[I]n determining whether a duty exists, the likelihood of injury, the magnitude of the burden of guarding against it, and the consequences of placing that bur-

den on the defendant must be taken into account." In ordinary circumstances, it would be difficult to anticipate when, where, and how a criminal might attack a business invitee. Experience demonstrates that the most effective deterrent to criminal acts of violence is the posting of a security force in the area of potential assaults. In most cases, that cost would be prohibitive. Where invitor and invitee are both innocent victims of assaultive criminals, it is unfair to place that burden on the invitor.

Webb argues that the knowledge of frequent previous larcenies in the parking lot, some of which involved forcible entry, combined with knowledge of other criminal activity, should have alerted the Wrights to the likelihood of this assault. Courts in other jurisdictions have expressed conflicting views on this subject. We agree with those that hold that knowledge of prior crimes against property does not create a duty upon a business invitor to anticipate and guard against assaults upon its invitees, offenses involving a substantially different kind of criminal behavior.

Webb argues that even if we limit the special circumstances to prior crimes of violence against persons, her case meets the criteria of special circumstances requiring reasonable action by the Wrights to protect their invitees. In support of this argument, Webb cites evidence of one assault on a guest in a motel room almost a year before Webb was assaulted, as well as a double murder on an immediately adjoining property three and a half years before her assault. . . . We will not impose liability for negligence based solely upon such a background.

We hold that a business invitor, whose method of business does not attract or provide a climate for assaultive crimes, does not have a duty to take measures to protect an invitee against criminal assault unless he knows that criminal assaults against persons are occurring, or are about to occur, on the premises which indicate an imminent probability of harm to an invitee. In our opinion, two prior isolated acts of violence in this case would not lead a reasonable person in charge of a dinner theatre parking lot to conclude that there was an imminent danger of criminal assault, which required the invitor to take action to protect Webb.

Accordingly, we will reverse the judgment of the trial court and enter final judgment for the defendant.

Reversed and final judgment.

Case Questions

1. What argument did Webb make to the court about the duty of care that should be required of landowners? What evidence did she present to the jury to establish her contention that the landowner had been negligent in protecting her from attack?
2. What general duty of care did the landowner owe Joann Webb (a business invitee), given the facts of this case, according to the Virginia Supreme Court?
3. What arguments does the Virginia Supreme Court use to support its position?

Proximate Cause

For the plaintiff to support a negligence action there must be a reasonable connection between the negligent act of the defendant and the damage suffered by the plaintiff. For tort liability, however, proof of factual causation is not enough. Tort liability is predicated on the existence of *proximate cause*. Proximate cause means legal cause and consists of two elements: (1) causation in fact, and (2) foreseeability. A plaintiff must prove that his or her injuries were the actual or factual result of the defendant's actions. Causation in fact may be established directly or indirectly. Courts usually use a "but for" test to establish causation in fact: but for the defendant's negligence, the plaintiff's injuries would not have occurred. This test is an extremely broad one and could have far-reaching results.

Every event has many contributing causes, even though some may be very remote. The defendant is not relieved from liability merely because other causes have contributed to the result. In many situations, application of the "but-for" test will identify several persons who could be placed on a causation continuum. The question before the court in a negligence case is whether the conduct has been so significant and important a cause that the defendant should be legally responsible. For example, in a nighttime automobile accident, the fact that one of the drivers worked late at the office would be a factual cause of the collision. If she hadn't worked late, she wouldn't have been at the location of the accident. But this cause should not be recognized as a legal cause of the collision. Because demands that some boundary be set for the consequences of an act, proximate cause, rather than causation in fact, is used to determine liability.

An individual is only responsible for those consequences that are *reasonably foreseeable*, and will be relieved of liability for injuries that are not reasonably related to the negligent conduct. To illustrate, a driver drives his car carelessly and collides with another car causing it to explode. Four blocks away, a nurse carrying a baby is startled by the explosion and drops the infant. It is doubtful if any court would hold the driver liable to the infant, even though the driver was negligent and was the factual cause of the infant's injury. The baby's injury is so far removed from the driver that it would be unfair to hold the driver liable. The driver could not reasonably have foreseen the injury sustained by the infant. In other words, the driving would not be the proximate cause of the injury.

If there is more than one cause for a single injury, liability is possible if each alone would have been sufficient to cause the harm without the other. If there are joint tortfeasors of a single injury, each possible tortfeasor's actions must be examined to see if the acts were so closely related to the damage to have proximately caused the plaintiff's injury.

The plaintiff in the following case alleged that her injuries were proximately caused by the defendant's negligence in designing and maintaining a road and railroad tracks.

Anglin v. Florida Department of Transportation
472 So.2d 784
District Court of Appeal of Florida
July 2, 1985

Zehmer, Judge

In these consolidated personal injury cases, plaintiffs below appeal a final summary judgment, contending the trial court erred in ruling as a matter of law that appellees were insulated from liability by unforeseeable independent intervening causes. We reverse.*

On the night of September 3, 1979, Cleopatra Anglin, her husband, and her brother were traveling through drizzling

*This opinion also decides the consolidated case of *Anglin v. Seaboard Coast Line Railroad Company.*—Ed.

rain in a 1965 Chevrolet pickup truck. Upon crossing a Seaboard Coastline Railroad track on Alternate U.S. 27 in rural Polk County, they unexpectedly hit an accumulation of water that covered both lanes of travel and was approximately six inches deep. The truck motor was doused with water, sputtered for some distance after hitting the pool of water, and then died. The Anglins attempted to start the motor by pushing the truck down the road and then "popping" the clutch once the truck reached a moderate speed. Approximately fifteen minutes after their truck hit the water, during which time they attempted in vain to push-start the truck several times, a car driven by Edward DuBose passed the Anglin truck heading in the opposite direction. A short distance after passing the truck, which was still on the road and, according to some witnesses, still being pushed, Mr. DuBose turned his car around and headed back toward the truck to render assistance. Unfortunately, Mr. DuBose failed to timely see the truck, hit his brakes, slid into the rear of the truck, and pinned Mrs. Anglin between the two vehicles, causing injury resulting in the amputation of both legs. The distance between the pool of water and the accident scene was estimated by some witnesses as approximately 200 yards, by others up to three-tenths of a mile.

On February 16, 1981, Mrs. Anglin and her husband filed a complaint against the state Department of Transportation and Seaboard Coastline Railroad Company, alleging negligence in the design and maintenance of the road and railroad tracks by allowing the accumulation of water on the roadway immediately adjacent to the railroad tracks. Defendants filed a motion for summary judgment and, in addition to numerous depositions already taken, plaintiffs filed affidavits in opposition to the motion. A final summary judgment in favor of the defendants was entered on June 9, 1983, upon the trial judge's ruling as a matter of law that the actions of the plaintiffs in attempting to push-start their disabled pickup truck and the actions of Mr. DuBose in negligently losing control of his car and colliding with the plaintiff's truck were independent, efficient intervening causes of the accident that were unforeseeable by the defendants, thereby breaking the chain of causation between the purported negligence of the defendants and the injury.

As a general rule, a tortfeasor is liable for all damages proximately caused by his negligence. The term "proximate cause" (or "legal cause," in the language of the standard jury instructions) consists of two essential elements: (1) causation in fact, and (2) foreseeability. . . . Causation in fact is often characterized in terms of a "but for" test, i.e., *but for* the defendant's negligence, the resulting damage would not have occurred. In the present case, there is no question as to causation in fact because "but for" the defendants' alleged negligence in causing the pooling of water on the highway, there would have been no accidental stopping of plaintiff's truck and resulting injury.[1]

The second element of proximate cause, foreseeability, is, unlike causation in fact, a concept established through considerations of public policy and fairness whereby a defendant whose conduct factually "caused" damages may nevertheless be relieved of liability for those damages. Thus, proximate cause may be found lacking where the type of damage or injury that occurred is not within the scope of danger or risk created by the defendant's negligence and, thus, not a reasonably foreseeable result thereof. . . . It is not necessary, however, that the defendants "be able to foresee the exact nature and extent of the injuries or the precise manner in which the injuries occur;" all that is necessary to liability is that "the tort feasor be able to foresee that *some* injury will likely result in *some* manner as a consequence of his negligent acts." . . . In the instant case, it cannot be said as a matter of law that an injury to plaintiff was not within the scope of danger or risk arising out of the alleged negligence. In the field of human experience, one should expect that negligently permitting a pool of water on an open

---

[1] The defendants' negligence in permitting the pooling of water is not an issue on this appeal. The trial court did not find, nor have appellees argued to us, that there was a complete absence of any factual dispute warranting the entry of summary judgment for either side on this issue.

highway would likely pose a substantial hazard to motorists because a vehicle crashing unexpectedly into the water is likely to experience a stalled motor or other difficulty causing the vehicle to stop on the highway, thereby subjecting its occupants to the risk of injury from collision by other cars. . . .

Proximate cause may be found lacking, however, where an unforeseeable force or action occurring independently of the original negligence causes the injury or damage. This force or action is commonly referred to as an "independent, efficient intervening cause." . . . For the original negligent actor to be relieved of liability under this doctrine, however, the intervening cause must be "efficient," i.e., truly independent of and not "set in motion" by the original negligence. . . . The trial court's ruling that the conduct of the plaintiffs in pushing their truck down the road was an independent, efficient intervening cause of the accident was error because the existence of the pool of water set into motion the plaintiffs' subsequent actions in attempting to restart the motor that was stalled by driving through the water. These actions, having been "set in motion" by defendants' negligence, did not constitute an independent, efficient intervening cause. Whether the plaintiffs' conduct was negligent and caused the injury should be submitted to the jury under appropriate instructions on comparative negligence.

The trial court correctly characterized Mr. DuBose's negligent operation of his car as an independent intervening cause. The negligent pooling of water did not cause Mr. DuBose to negligently operate his vehicle into collision with the plaintiffs.[2]

---

[2] The result would be otherwise if, for example, Mr. DuBose had driven through the pool of water and failed to stop because his brakes became wet and ineffective.

The trial court erred, however, in ruling *as a matter of law* that such intervening cause warranted entry of summary judgment for defendants. If an intervening cause is reasonably foreseeable, the negligent defendants may be held liable. . . . Whether an intervening cause is foreseeable is ordinarily for the trier of fact to decide. . . . Only if reasonable persons could not differ as to the total absence of evidence to support any inference that the intervening cause was foreseeable may the court determine the issue as a matter of law. . . . In the circumstance of this case (the night was dark, it was raining, and the collision occurred in a rural area where traffic customarily moves rapidly), had DuBose come on the scene and collided with plaintiffs' stalled truck immediately after plaintiffs hit the pooled water, the question of foreseeability of that occurrence would most assuredly present a jury issue. The fact that plaintiffs attempted to push-start their stalled truck for approximately fifteen minutes and that Mr. DuBose collided with it while attempting to stop and provide assistance does not change this jury issue as to a question of law. The plaintiffs' exposure to danger was created by defendants' negligence, and the fact that a collision might occur while plaintiffs were extricating themselves from such danger up to fifteen minutes later presents a jury issue on foreseeability. . . . That is so because the defendants need not have notice of the particular manner in which an injury would occur; it is enough that the possibility of some accidental injury was foreseeable to the ordinarily prudent person. . . .

Reversed and remanded.

Booth, Chief Judge, dissenting

We should affirm the summary judgment entered below based on lack of proximate cause. The chain of events here between alleged negligent act and injury is too attenuated and is broken, in fact, by the independent, intervening actions of others.

For the purpose of this appeal, we assume that defendants were negligent in maintaining a depression on a rural roadway, a depression which, in the aftermath of Hurricane David, was filled with six inches of water. It would be foreseeable that a driver who unexpectedly traversed such a depression in the road could lose control of his vehicle, causing an accidental injury to himself or others. Stalling and the immediate consequences thereof are also not unforeseeable. Other results of the puddle could be termed as "foreseeable" in a philosophical, but not a legal, sense. For example, the disabled vehicle could have been struck by lightning, or the occupants could have been robbed or become ill but unable to seek medical care. In each instance, it could be said that, but for the stalling of their car caused by the defendant these subsequent events would not have occurred. Although there would be cause and effect relationship, such consequences would generally not be within the scope of the risk created by the negligent party who caused the vehicle to become immobile. The law does not impose liability because of the concept of "proximate cause," as stated in *Prosser and Keeton*.[1]

> "In a philosophical sense, the consequences of an act go forward to eternity, and the causes of an event go back to the dawn of human events, and beyond. But any attempt to impose responsibility upon such a basis would result in infinite liability for all wrongful acts, and would 'set society on edge and fill the courts with endless litigation.' As a practical matter, legal responsibility must be limited to those causes which

[1] Prosser and Keeton, *TORTS* 264 (5th ed.).

are so closely connected with the result and of such significance that the law is justified in imposing liability. Some boundary must be set to liability for the consequences of any act, upon the basis of some social idea of justice of policy."

Therefore, I would agree with the majority that there could be a jury question as to causation in fact. But, as to proximate cause, in this case at least, the principle is one of law. In the Prosser and Keeton treatise, it is stated:

> "Once it is established that the defendant's conduct has in fact been one of the causes of the plaintiff's injury, there remains the question whether defendant should be legally responsible for the injury. Unlike the fact of causation with which it is often hopelessly confused, this is primarily a problem of law. It is sometimes said to depend on whether the conduct has been so significant and important a cause that the defendant should be legally responsible. But both significance and importance turn upon conclusions in terms of legal policy, so that they depend essentially on whether the policy of the law will extend the responsibility for the conduct to the consequences which have in fact occurred. Quite often this has been stated, and properly so, as an issue of whether the defendant is under any duty to the plaintiff, or whether the duty includes protection against such consequences."

In the instant case, the Anglins testified that, after passing through the puddle of water, the engine sputtered and the vehicle was pulled to the side of the road as it came to a stop. At that point, the vehicle was off the road, and there were no injuries. The further events which occurred should not be charged to the act of defendants in allowing a rain-filled depression in the roadway. The Anglins testified that, after some minutes off the road, plaintiffs pushed the truck back onto the roadway and endeavored to push the vehicle down the road on that dark and rainy night.

At this point entered the next intervening force in the form of one Mr. DuBose, who passed, going in the opposite direction, and slowed to ask if plaintiffs would like help. DuBose then continued down the road some short distance and, as plaintiffs testified, "slammed on brakes, slid like and spun around," approached the plaintiffs' vehicle from the rear, and "with the engine roaring" and at a speed approaching 40 miles an hour, slammed into the back of the plaintiffs' truck, striking and seriously injuring Mrs. Anglin. The conduct of DuBose can only be considered gross negligence. . . .

The issue, then, is the scope of the legal duty to protect the plaintiff against intervening causes which are *possible but not probable*. As posed by Prosser and Keeton, *supra*, does defendant's duty include protecting plaintiff against these consequences? Plaintiff's injury occurred more than a quarter of an hour after, and three-tenths of a mile down the road from, the puddle. The accident occurred after, and as a result of, negligence of others, each acting independently of defendants.

The law does not impose unlimited liability for all consequences that may result from a puddle of water on the road. This case should illustrate that principle. The trial court correctly held that the injury occurring was not within the scope of danger attributable by law to defendants' conduct, and should be affirmed.

Case Questions

1. Proximate cause consists of two elements—what are they? What is important about each element?
2. What is an independent, efficient, intervening cause?
3. In this case, the trial judge ruled as a matter of law that an independent, efficient, intervening cause existed. According to the appellate court, when is such a decision justified?
4. What position does Chief Justice Booth take in dissent?

Contributory Negligence and Assumption of Risk Defenses

Even after a plaintiff has proved that a defendant was negligent, and that the negligence was the proximate cause of his or her injury, the defendant may counter by proving a defense. Contributory negligence and assumption of risk are two such defenses.

Contributory negligence is a defense that exists when the injured persons proximately contributed to their injuries by their own negligence. This is based on the theory that the plaintiff is held to the same standard of care as the defendant; that is, that of a reasonable person under like circumstances.

To illustrate, D-1 is driving his car and P is his passenger. Both are injured in a collision with D-2's car. If both cars were driven negligently, D-1 could not recover from D-2 because his own negligence contributed to his own injuries. Yet P could recover from both D-1 and D-2, because they were both joint tortfeasors in causing P's injuries.

The burden of proving contributory negligence is on the defendant.

The defense of *assumption of risk* exists when the plaintiffs had knowledge of the risk and made the free choice of exposing themselves to it. Assumption of risk may be express or implied. In an express assumption of risk, the plaintiff expressly agrees in advance that the defendant has no duty to care for him or her and is not liable for what would otherwise be negligent conduct. For example, parents often expressly assume the risk of personal injury to their children in conjunction with youth soccer, basketball, and baseball programs. Where the assumption of risk is implied, consent is manifested by the plaintiff's continued presence after he or she has become aware of the danger involved. The plaintiffs impliedly consent to take their chances concerning the defendant's negligence. For example, baseball fans who sit in unscreened seats at the ballpark know that balls and even bats may strike them; they implicitly agree to take a chance of being injured in this manner.

Comparative Negligence

When the defense of contributory negligence is used in a noncomparative negligence jurisdiction, the entire loss is placed on one party even when both are negligent. For this reason, most states now determine the amount of damage by comparing the negligence of the plaintiff with that of the defendant. Under this doctrine of *comparative negligence*, a negligent plaintiff may be able to recover a portion of the cost of an injury.

In negligence cases, comparative negligence divides the damages between the parties by reducing the plaintiff's damages in proportion to the extent of that person's contributory fault. The trier of fact in a case assigns a percentage of the total fault to the plaintiff and the plaintiff's total damages are usually reduced by that percentage. For example, a plaintiff who was considered to be 40 percent at fault by the trier of fact would recover $1,200 if the total damages were determined to be $2,000.

The plaintiff in the following case brought suit when his mechanically disabled truck, which was partially on a highway and partially on the shoulder, was struck in the rear by an automobile driven by the defendant.

Stein v. Langer

515 So.2d 507

Court of Appeal of Louisiana, First Circuit

October 14, 1987

LeBlanc, Judge

The issues presented in this personal injury case are the proper allocation of fault among the parties . . .

On the evening of September 5, 1982, plaintiff, David Stein, was driving his truck north on Louisiana Highway 1077, a two-lane rural road in St. Tammany Parish. Upon experiencing a mechanical breakdown, plaintiff steered his truck onto the highway shoulder as far as he could and parked. However, the shoulder was not wide enough for him to pull completely off the road. Although exactly how far the truck protruded onto the highway is disputed, it was at least six to eight inches.

Shortly thereafter, Everett Randall Cooper, one of the defendants, who was a friend of the plaintiff, passed in a southbound lane. Recognizing the plaintiff and noting that his truck appeared to be disabled, Cooper turned around and drove back to where plaintiff's truck was parked. Because he thought plaintiff's truck might need a jump-start, he parked his own truck facing south, with the front bumper of his truck several feet from the front bumper of plaintiff's truck. Cooper was unable to pull his truck as far on the shoulder as plaintiff had because of a traffic sign which prevented him from doing so. His truck protruded approximately a foot and a half onto the highway. In this position, one headlight was visible to traffic approaching in the northbound lane. The emergency flashers on Cooper's truck were also on. Once Cooper arrived plaintiff, who was concerned about running his battery down, turned off all the lights on his own truck, leaving it completely unlit.

Several northbound cars passed by the two trucks without incident by moving over partially into the southbound lane to pass. Approximately five minutes later, however, a car proceeding in the northbound lane and driven by defendant, Dianne Langer, struck the rear of plaintiff's truck. The force of the impact pushed plaintiff's truck into the front of Cooper's truck. Plaintiff was standing between the two trucks at the time and sustained injuries to his legs and knees.

Mrs. Langer testified that she saw the headlight of Cooper's truck five to ten seconds before impact, but did not see the plaintiff's black truck prior to hitting it. According to her testimony, she intended to avoid Cooper's vehicle, which appeared to be either a car or motorcycle approaching in her lane of traffic, by going around it on the right shoulder of the highway. She originally was driving approximately 35 mph, but had started to slow down upon seeing the headlight. She testified that her foot was on the brake when she struck plaintiff's truck.

Plaintiff filed suit against Mrs. Langer, [and] her husband, William Langer. . . . Following a jury trial, a verdict was rendered finding Diane Langer fifty-five percent (55%) at fault, plaintiff forty-five percent (45%) at fault and Everett Cooper guilty of no fault. The jury fixed plaintiff's damages at $3,100.00. Thereafter, on February 13, 1985, the trial court rendered judgment against the Langers and their insurer and in favor of plaintiff for $3,100, subject to a forty-five (45%) reduction. The judgment also dismissed all claims against Cooper. . . . Plaintiff has now appealed the judgment of February 13, 1985, arguing that the jury erred in assessing fault and in awarding him inadequate damages.

Specifically, plaintiff maintains the jury erred in not assessing Mrs. Langer with 100 percent of the fault or, in the alternative, in not finding Cooper guilty of any fault. The standard of review on appeal is that factual findings made by the trier-of-fact are entitled to great weight and will not be overturned unless manifestly erroneous. . . . Since a jury's findings as to percentage of fault are factual in nature, they will not be disturbed unless clearly wrong. . . .

After our thorough review of the record, we find no manifest error in the assessments of fault made by the jury in this case. The fact that plaintiff, as well as Mrs. Langer, was at fault is obvious upon review of the facts. By turning off all the lights on his truck, plaintiff made it much more difficult for motorists to observe the fact that his truck was partially obstructing the highway, thereby greatly increasing the danger of the situation.

Likewise, we find no error in the jury's conclusion that Cooper was not guilty of any fault. In order to give plaintiff's truck a jump-start, Cooper had no choice but to park as he did. Further, Cooper pulled over as far on the shoulder as he could and had both his headlights and emergency flashers turned on. Cooper's actions were reasonable under the circumstances present. In this regard, it is significant that several northbound cars had passed without difficulty before Mrs. Langer's car hit plaintiff's truck. For the above reasons, we affirm the assessments of fault made by the jury.

Case Questions

1. What are the advantages and disadvantages of comparative negligence in comparison with contributory negligence?
2. Under what circumstances will a court disturb a jury's allocation of the percentages of fault?
3. Assume that the jury found the plaintiff to be 51 percent at fault in this case and the defendant 49 percent at fault. If the plaintiff was more at fault than the defendant for this accident, why should the plaintiff recover any damages at all?

Negligence and Product Liability

Plaintiffs can recover in negligence by proving that a manufacturer's conduct violated the reasonable person standard and proximately caused injury. The manufacturer's allegedly tortious conduct could relate to any aspect of product design, manufacturing, quality control, packaging, and/or warnings.

In product liability suits it is often difficult to prove the defendant's act or omission that caused plaintiff's injury. Thus, in the interests of justice, courts developed the doctrine of *res ipsa loquitur* ("the thing speaks for itself"). This doctrine permits plaintiffs to circumstantially prove negligence if the following facts are proved: (1) the defendant had exclusive control over the the allegedly defective product during manufacture, (2) under normal circumstances, the plaintiff would not have been injured by the product if the defendant had exercised ordinary care, and (3) the plaintiff's conduct did not contribute significantly to the accident. From the proved facts, the law permits the jurors to infer a fact for which there is no direct, explicit proof—the defendant's negligent act or omission. The trial judge will instruct the jurors that the law permits them to consider the inferred fact as well as the proved facts in deciding whether the defendant was negligent.

The following case illustrates typical problems associated with a case involving negligent failure to warn. A manufacturer's duty to warn consumers depends on the nature of the product. Warnings are unnecessary for products that are obviously dangerous to everyone (knives, saws, and firearms). However, for products that may contain hazards that are not obvious, manufacturers have a duty to warn if the average person would not have known about a safety hazard. If the plaintiff is knowledgeable about the hazard that the warning would have addressed, the manufacturer's negligent failure to warn would not have proximately caused the plaintiff's injuries. Thus in such cases the extent of the plaintiff's actual knowledge and familiarity with the hazard and the product are relevant to the issue of causation.

Laaperi v. Sears Roebuck & Co., Inc.
787 F.2d 726
U.S. Court of Appeals for the First Circuit
March 31, 1986

Campbell, Chief Judge

This is an appeal from jury verdicts totalling $1.8 million entered in a product liability suit against defendants Sears, Roebuck & Co. and Pittway Corporation. The actions were brought by Albin Laaperi as administrator of the estates of his three sons, all of whom were killed in a fire in their home in December 1976, and as father and next friend of his daughter, Janet, who was injured in the fire. Plaintiff's theory of recovery was that defendants had a duty to warn plaintiff that a smoke detector powered by house current, manufactured by Pittway and sold to Laaperi by Sears, might not operate in the event of an electrical fire caused by a short circuit. Defendants contend on appeal that the district court erred in denying their motions for directed verdict and judgment notwithstanding the verdict; that the admission into evidence of purportedly undisclosed expert testimony violated Fed.R.Civ.P. 26(e); and that the award of $750,000 for injuries to Janet

Laaperi was excessive and improper. We affirm the judgments in favor of plaintiff in his capacity as administrator of the estates of his three sons, but vacate the judgment in favor of Janet Laaperi, and remand for a new trial limited to the issue of her damages.

I.

In March 1976, plaintiff Albin Laaperi purchased a smoke detector from Sears. The detector, manufactured by the Pittway Corporation, was designed to be powered by AC (electrical) current. Laaperi installed the detector himself in one of the two upstairs bedrooms in his home.

Early in the morning of December 27, 1976, a fire broke out in the Laaperi home. The three boys in one of the upstairs bedrooms were killed in the blaze. Laaperi's 13-year-old daughter, Janet, who was sleeping in the other upstairs bedroom, received burns over 12 percent of her body and was hospitalized for three weeks.

The uncontroverted testimony at trial was that the smoke detector did not sound an alarm on the night of the fire.

The cause of the fire was later found to be a short circuit in an electrical cord that was located in a cedar closet in the boys' bedroom. The Laaperi home had two separate electrical circuits in the upstairs bedrooms: one which provided electricity to the outlets and one which powered the lighting fixtures. The smoke detector had been connected to the outlet circuit, which was the circuit that shorted and cut off. Because the circuit was shorted, the AC-operated smoke detector received no power on the night of the fire. Therefore, although the detector itself was in no sense defective (indeed, after the fire the charred detector was tested and found to be operable), no alarm sounded.

Laaperi brought this diversity action against defendants Sears and Pittway, asserting negligent design, negligent manufacture, breach of warranty, and negligent failure to warn of inherent dangers. The parties agreed that the applicable law is that of Massachusetts. Before the claims went to the jury, verdicts were directed in favor of the defendants on all theories of liability other than failure to warn.

Laaperi's claim under the failure to warn theory was that he was unaware of the danger that the very short circuit which might ignite a fire in his home could, at the same time, incapacitate the smoke detector. He contended that had he been warned of this danger, he would have purchased a battery-powered smoke detector as a backup or taken some other precaution, such as wiring the detector to a circuit of its own, in order better to protect his family in the event of an electrical fire.

The jury returned verdicts in favor of Laaperi in all four actions on the failure to warn claim. The jury assessed damages in the amount of $350,000 in each of the three actions brought on behalf of the deceased sons, and $750,000 in the action

brought on behalf of Janet Laaperi. The defendants' motions for directed verdict and judgment notwithstanding the verdict were denied and defendants appealed.

II.

Defendants contend that the district court erred in denying their motions for directed verdict and judgment n.o.v. First, they claim that they had no duty to warn that the smoke detector might not work in the event of some electrical fires. Second, they maintain that even if they had such a duty, there was insufficient evidence on the record to show that the failure to warn proximately caused plaintiff's damages. We address these arguments in turn.

A. Duty to Warn

We must look, of course, to Massachusetts law. While we have found no cases with similar facts in Massachusetts (or elsewhere), we conclude that on this record a jury would be entitled to find that defendants had a duty to warn. In Massachusetts, a manufacturer[2] can be found liable to a user of the product if the user is injured due to the failure of the manufacturer to exercise reasonable care in warning potential users of hazards associated with use of the product. . . .

The manufacturer can be held liable even if the product does exactly what it is supposed to do, if it does not warn of the

---

[2] Defendants make no argument that the duty of Sears is any different from that of Pittway, the actual manufacturer. In the present case, Sears advertised the smoke detector as a "Sears Early One Fire Alarm." Pittway Corp. was not mentioned anywhere in these advertisements nor in the 12-page owner's manual packaged with the detector. Where a seller puts out a product manufactured by another as its own, the seller is subject to the same liability as though it were the manufacturer. . . .

potential dangers inherent in the way a product is designed. It is not necessary that the product be negligently designed or manufactured; the failure to warn of hazards associated with foreseeable uses of a product is itself negligence, and if that negligence proximately results in a plaintiff's injuries, the plaintiff may recover. . . .

The sole purpose of a smoke detector is to alert occupants of a building to the presence of fire. The failure to warn of inherent non-obvious limitations of a smoke detector, or of non-obvious circumstances in which a detector will not function, can, we believe, "create an unreasonable risk of harm in that the inhabitants of a structure may be lulled into an unjustified sense of safety and fail to be forewarned of the existence of a fire." . . . In the present case, the defendants failed to warn purchasers that a short circuit which causes an electrical fire may also render the smoke detector useless in the very situation in which it is expected to provide protection: in the early stages of a fire. We believe that whether such a failure to warn was negligent was a question for the jury.

To be sure, it was the fire, not the smoke detector per se, that actually killed and injured plaintiff's children. But as the Second Circuit recently held, the manufacturer of a smoke detector may be liable when, due to its negligence, the device fails to work:

> "Although a defect must be a substantial factor in causing a plaintiff's injuries, it is clear that a 'manufacturer's liability for injuries proximately caused by these defects should not be limited to [situations] in which the defect causes the accident, but should extend to situations in which the defect caused injuries over and above that which would have occurred from the accident, but for the defective design.'"

It is true that, unlike the above, there was no defect of design or manufacture in this case. But there was evidence from which it could be inferred that the absence of a warning enhanced the harm resulting from the fire. Plaintiff testified that if he had realized that a short circuit that caused an electrical fire might at the same time disable the smoke detector, he would have purchased a back-up battery-powered detector or wired the detector in question into an isolated circuit, thus minimizing the danger that a fire-causing short circuit would render the detector inoperative. We find, therefore, a sufficient connection between the children's deaths and injury and the absence of any warning.

Defendants contend that the district court nevertheless erred in denying their motions because, they claim, the danger that an electrical fire will incapacitate an electric-powered smoke detector is obvious. They point out that anyone purchasing a device powered by house electrical current will necessarily realize that if the current goes off for any reason, the device will not work.

In Massachusetts, as elsewhere, a failure to warn amounts to negligence only where the supplier of the good known to be dangerous for its intended use "has no reason to believe that those for whose use the chattel is supplied will realize its dangerous condition." . . .

Where the risks of the product are discernible by casual inspection, such as the danger that a knife can cut, or a stove burn, the consumer is in just as good a position as the manufacturer to gauge the dangers associated with the product, and nothing is gained by shifting to the manufacturer the duty to warn. Thus, a manufacturer is not required to warn that placing one's hand into the blades of a potato chopper will cause injury, . . . that

permitting a three-year-old child to ride on the running board of a moving tractor risks injury to the child, . . . or that firing a BB gun at another at close range can injure or kill. . . . If a manufacturer had to warn consumers against every such obvious danger inherent in a product, "[t]he list of obvious practices warned against would be so long, it would fill a volume."
. . .

Defendants ask us to declare that the risk that an electrical fire could incapacitate an AC-powered smoke detector is so obvious that the average consumer would not benefit from a warning. This is not a trivial argument; in earlier—some might say sounder—days, we might have accepted it. . . .

Our sense of the current state of the tort law in Massachusetts and most other jurisdictions, however, leads us to conclude that, today, the matter before us poses a jury question; that "obviousness" in a situation such as this would be treated by the Massachusetts courts as presenting a question of fact, not of law. To be sure, it would be obvious to anyone that an electrical outage would cause this smoke detector to fail. But the average purchaser might not comprehend the specific danger that a fire-causing electrical problem can simultaneously knock out the circuit into which a smoke detector is wired, causing the detector to fail at the very moment it is needed. Thus, while the failure of a detector to function as the result of an electrical malfunction due, say, to a broken power line or a neighborhood power outage would, we think, be obvious as a matter of law, the failure that occurred here, being associated with the very risk—fire—for which the device was purchased, was not, or so a jury could find.

. . . We think that the issue of obviousness to the average consumer of the danger of a fire-related power outage was one for the jury, not the court, to determine. In the present case, the jury was specifically instructed that if it found this danger to be obvious it should hold for the defendants. It failed to do so.

B. Causation

While, as just discussed, the danger the detector would fail in these circumstances was not so obvious as to eliminate, as a matter of law, any need to warn, we must also consider whether Laaperi's specialized electrical knowledge constituted a bar to his own recovery. . . . [P]laintiff's specialized knowledge is immaterial to whether defendants had a duty to warn, since that duty is defined by the knowledge of the average purchaser. But plaintiff's expertise *is* relevant to whether defendants' failure to warn caused plaintiff's damages. Even though defendants may have been required to provide a warning, plaintiff may not recover if it can be shown that because of his above-average knowledge, he already appreciated the very danger the warning would have described. In such event there would be no connection between the negligent failure to warn and plaintiff's damages.

Defendants here presented considerable evidence suggesting that Laaperi, who was something of an electrical handyman, knew of the danger and still took no precautions. Laaperi, however, offered evidence that he did not know of the danger, and that he would have guarded against it had he been warned. . . .

Self-serving as this testimony was, the jury was free to credit it. In reviewing the denial of a motion for directed verdict or judgment n.o.v., we are obliged to view the evidence in the light most favorable to the verdict winner. . . . In light of this standard, we cannot say that the district court erred in denying defendants' motions for directed verdict and judgment n.o.v., for the jury could have believed Laaperi's testimony in the colloquy quoted above, among other evidence, and concluded that had he been properly warned, Laaperi would have instituted different fire detection methods in his home to protect his family against the danger that his smoke detector would be rendered useless in the event of a fire-related power outage.

IV.

. . . Considering Janet's injuries alone, apart from the horrible nature of her brothers' deaths, we find the award of $750,000 was so grossly disproportionate to the injuries of Janet Laaperi as to be unconscionable. It is therefore vacated.

The judgments in favor of Albin Laaperi in his capacity as administrator of the estates of his three sons are affirmed. In the action on behalf of Janet Laaperi, the verdict of the jury is set aside, the judgment of the district court vacated, and the cause remanded to that court for a new trial limited to the issue of damages.

So ordered.

Case Questions

1. What warning should the defendants arguably have given the plaintiffs under the facts of this case?
2. Would the outcome in this case have been different if Albin Laaperi was a licensed electrician?
3. Why didn't the plaintiff proceed based on strict liability?

Imputed Negligence

Although people are always responsible for their own acts, one may be held liable for the negligence of another by reason of some relationship existing between two parties. This is termed *imputed negligence,* or vicarious liability.

Imputed negligence results when one person (the agent) acts for or represents another (the principal) by the latter's authority and to accomplish the latter's ends. A common example is the liability of employers for the torts that employees commit in the scope of their employment.

One should take a liberal view of the scope-of-employment concept, because the basis for vicarious liability is the desire to include in operational costs the inevitable losses to third persons incident to carrying on an enterprise, and thus distribute the burden among those benefited by the enterprise. Generally, an employee would not be within the scope of employment (1) if the employee is en route to or from home, (2) if the employee is on an undertaking of his own, (3) if the acts are prohibited by the employer, or (4) if the act is an unauthorized delegation by the employer.

One is not accountable for the negligent act of an independent contractor. *Independent contractors* are those who contract to do work according to their own methods and are not subject to the control of employers except with respect to the results. The right of control over the manner in which the work is done is the main consideration in determining whether one employed is an independent contractor or an agent. However, there are certain exceptions to this nonliability, for example, an employer who is negligent in hiring a contractor or who assigns a nondelegable duty may be liable.

The plaintiff in the following case attempted to establish an agency relationship between an employee (Shaefer) and the Norman Oil company so that the company could be made liable for Shaefer's allegedly negligent acts.

Dumas v. Lloyd
6 Ill. App. 3d 1026, 286 N.E.3d 566
Appellate Court of Illinois
June 9, 1972

English, Justice

This action was brought by plaintiff, William Dumas, to recover damages for personal injuries allegedly caused by the negligence of defendants, . . . Clarence Shaefer, Norman Oil Company, Inc., and William H. Frazier. . . . At the close of plaintiff's case at trial, verdicts were directed in favor of Norman Oil and Shaefer, and it is from the judgments entered thereon that plaintiff has appealed. It appears that the case as to defendant Frazier was abandoned in the trial court.

Defendant Norman Oil Company owns and supplies gasoline stations in the Chicago area, one of which is located at 143 S. California Avenue, Chicago. In September 1962, defendant Shaefer was hired by Dale Norman, an officer of Norman Oil Company, to operate the station or give Norman Oil money or security for the operation. Shaefer did not own anything at the station and was not permitted to sell any products other than those supplied by Norman Oil. He received a commission of four cents for each gallon of gasoline sold at the station, and each day he banked the receipts after deducting his commission, and sent copies of the deposit slips to Norman Oil.

Shaefer was empowered to hire other people to help him with work at the station but, in practice, did not hire anyone without telling Dale Norman. Defendant Frazier was one of those hired, and his employment continued at the times pertinent to the case. Each person hired by Shaefer was paid out of his own commissions.

The operating license for the service station was in the name of John Norman, president of Norman Oil Company. Each month, Norman Oil paid the rent on the property, the electric bills, and sales tax on all products sold at the station. All of the equipment, such as the gas pumps, air compressor, underground tanks, and signs, including one which said "Norman Oil Products," were owned by Norman Oil, and all products sold there were furnished and delivered to the station by the company, usually through Dale Norman. Either he or John Norman would visit the station once or twice a week and would instruct Shaefer as to keeping the station clean.

The company supplied all sales books and had its name on all books and records used at the station. Shaefer had no control over the price set for gasoline, that being determined by Norman Oil. Nor could Shaefer draw on the bank account which was in the name of the company.

On various occasions, Shaefer, in the presence of Dale Norman, accepted and held various items as security for products sold when the customer could not pay the full amount. On December 18 or 19, 1963, Shaefer took a revolver from a customer as security for a payment of $3.00 for gasoline. The gun had a belt wrapped around it which Shaefer did not remove, but he placed the gun with the belt in a desk drawer at the station. The desk had only one drawer and it was unlocked. He never unwrapped the belt and never looked to see if the gun was loaded.

The station was located in a rough neighborhood, and almost every day at 3:30 or 4:00 P.M., a small group of friends, including plaintiff, would meet at the station and sit in the room where the desk was located, to laugh and joke and have a good time. They usually stayed there until Frazier was off work at 9:00 or 9:30 P.M.

On December 19, 1963, Preston Evans, a friend of both plaintiff and Frazier, saw Frazier in the gas station with the gun which had been taken from the desk drawer. He was playing with the revolver by spinning it on his finger. Evans said to Frazier, "You are going to shoot someone if you don't quit playing," and Frazier replied, "There is no bullets in it." When he got through playing with the gun, Frazier put it back in the scabbard in the drawer.

The next day, plaintiff came to the gas station about 3:30 P.M. to visit Frazier and to have a grease job and oil change on his car, but it turned out to be too cold to do the grease job. He and Frazier had been pretty good friends for about five years and Frazier had been driving plaintiff's car all summer. About 5:30, while both

men were in the station, along with several others, a man entered and asked Frazier to help him charge the battery in his car. Frazier said he couldn't do it right away and when the man asked how long he would have to wait, Frazier refused to do it and talked to the man in rough language. Plaintiff said he would help, and left the station and got the car started.

When plaintiff returned, Frazier asked him how much the man had paid for plaintiff's help. Plaintiff replied that the man was his friend and he had charged him nothing.

Plaintiff, in a joking manner, "told Frazier if he talked to me like he did to that old man, I would cut his throat off, and I did like this with my keys [indicating], and I walked out the door." As he went out, Frazier, also laughing, turned to a friend and said, "Watch me scare Red" [plaintiff]. He opened the drawer, took out the gun, and said, "Red, I'm going to shoot you," and shot him. Whereupon, Frazier immediate said, "Damn, look what I done did," and ran to help plaintiff, saying, "Man, I am sorry." They brought plaintiff back into the station, where Frazier called the police and told them he had accidentally shot a man.

Plaintiff suffered severe and permanent injuries and brought an action to recover damages based on defendants' alleged negligence.

Plaintiff declared that, since he had proved a . . . case of agency between Norman Oil and Shaefer, the Trial Court erred in directing a verdict in favor of either Norman Oil or Shaefer because the latter's negligence is a question of fact for the jury.

Norman Oil makes three points: (1) that Shaefer was not its agent but an independent contractor; (2) that plaintiff's own misconduct bars recovery; and (3) that even if Shaefer were an agent and Frazier a sub-agent, Frazier's actions were outside the scope of his employment and do not subject Shaefer or Norman Oil to liability under the doctrine of *respondeat superior.*

Of primary consideration in the determination of whether a person is acting as an independent contractor or as an agent or employee is the degree and character of control exercised over the work being done. . . . When one undertakes to produce a given result without being in any way controlled as to the method used, he is considered an independent contractor and not an employee. . . . But the relationship of principal and agent exists if the principal has the right or the duty to supervise and control, and also the right to terminate the relationship at any time. . . . The test is in the right to control and is not dependent upon its exercise. . . . The general rule of liability is that a principal is liable for the negligent act of his agent, but not for those of an independent contractor. . . .

We believe that the evidence as introduced by plaintiff did establish that Shaefer was acting as Norman's agent in the operation of the service station and was not an independent contractor. Although the day-to-day operating procedures were managed by Shaefer, his authority was limited by the interest of the owner whose representative frequently visited the premises and laid down for Shaefer certain rules as to buying and distribution methods. Norman owned all of the equipment used by Shaefer and set the prices for all the products sold. Signs, records and accounts were in the name of Norman Oil and Shaefer was powerless to change them. Furthermore, on January 5, 1965, without prior notice to Shaefer, the owners closed the station and terminated their relationship with Shaefer effective at that time. We realize, of course, that at this point in the trial, Norman Oil had had no opportunity or need to introduce any countervailing evidence on this point in view of the court's directed verdict in its favor.

However, even though a principal-agent relationship between Shaefer and Norman Oil could have been found to exist, a principal cannot be made liable through the doctrine of *respondeat superior* when the actions of his agent in no way constitute negligence. Plaintiff contends that Frazier could not have discharged the gun were it not for the careless and negligent manner in which Shaefer permitted the loaded gun to remain at ready access in the desk drawer. Yet, the uncontroverted testimony of both Shaefer and Frazier discloses that Shaefer did not know if the gun was loaded, and Frazier definitely thought it was not. We believe Shaefer acted reasonably when he allowed the belt to remain wrapped around the pistol and its case and placed it in a drawer which, although unlocked, was out of sight from those persons who might enter the station. Under all the circumstances of this case, for a gas station attendant to keep a gun, whether loaded or not, in a desk of his service station, is, in our opinion, ordinary care as a matter of law. We also believe that the negligent or reckless act of Frazier was clearly not of a character which could be attributed to his employer. For both these reasons, therefore, we conclude that the trial judge acted properly in directing verdicts in favor of defendants Norman Oil and Shaefer. The judgments entered thereon are affirmed.

Affirmed.

Case
Questions

1. Do you agree with the result the court reached in this case? Was there a duty of ordinary care on the part of Shaefer to examine the gun to see whether it was loaded before placing it in the drawer?
2. The court says that a principal cannot be made liable through the doctrine of *respondeat superior* when the actions of his agent in no way constitute negligence. In light of your answer to Question 1, could it be argued that Norman Oil Company should be liable for the actions of agent Shaefer, despite the court's decision to the contrary?
3. In determining whether a relationship of principal and agent exists, would you consider the exercise of control by the principal to be the most important factor? Why or why not?

No-Fault Liability Statutes

The greatest number of civil cases in the United States are tort actions, and automobile collision suits account for most of these tort claims. Responding to widespread dissatisfaction with the delay and expense in the litigation of traffic accident cases, several states have passed no-fault liability statutes in an attempt to correct the injustices and inadequacies of the fault system in automobile accident cases. The first such statute was passed by Massachusetts and became effective on January 1, 1971.

Under a no-fault liability statute, parties sustaining damages from automobile accidents are compensated by their own insurance companies rather than by the parties whose negligence caused the accidents, or by those parties' insurers. The goal of the statutes is to reduce the cost of automobile insurance by saving litigation costs, including attorneys' fees, and by allowing little or no recovery for pain and suffering resulting from an automobile accident.

STRICT LIABILITY

In addition to intentional torts and negligence, there is a third type of tort called strict liability or absolute liability. This imposes liability on defendants without requiring any proof of lack of due care. Under the early common law, people were held strictly liable for trespass and trespass on the case without regard to their intentions and whether they exercised reasonable care. Although the breadth of strict liability diminished with the emergence of negligence and intentional torts, strict liability in tort is applied in cases involving what the common law recognized as abnormally dangerous activities and, more recently, in product liability cases.

Abnormally Dangerous Activities

One who is involved in abnormally dangerous activities is legally responsible for harmful consequences that are proximately caused. The possessor of a dangerous instrumentality is an insurer of the safety of others who are foreseeably within the danger zone. Because of jurisdictional differences, it is impossible to formulate a general definition or complete listing of all dangerous instrumentalities. However, poisons, toxic chemicals, explosives, and vicious animals are examples of items that have been found to fall into this category.

The plaintiff in the following case sustained personal injuries when she was bitten by the owner's dog while a guest of the defendant.

Westberry v. Blackwell
577 P.2d 75
Supreme Court of Oregon
April 18, 1978

Howell, Justice

Plaintiff filed this action to recover for personal injuries sustained when she was bitten by defendant's dog. The complaint alleged a cause of action for strict liability and another for negligence. The trial court granted a judgment of involuntary nonsuit on both causes of action. Plaintiff appeals. The evidence is viewed in the light most favorable to plaintiff.

On July 2, 1975, the plaintiff, accompanied by her young son and daughter, visited defendants' home. Plaintiff testified that as she went toward defendants' house from her car in the driveway the defendants' dog, a one-year-old St. Bernard named "Happy" gave her a superficial bite on her right hand. After plaintiff had been in the defendants' home for some time, her 12-year-old son ran into the house complaining that the dog had tried to bite him. The plaintiff further testified that after Mrs. Blackwell assured her of the dog's docility, Mrs. Westberry attempted to walk past the dog to her car in order to leave. As she did so, she was severely bitten two or three times by the dog, requiring stitches to be taken in her left hand.

The issue on this appeal is whether the evidence introduced by the plaintiff is sufficient to present a question of fact for the jury on either of the two charges, strict liability or negligence.

Plaintiff's first cause alleges that the defendants are strictly liable for the damages suffered by the plaintiff from the dog bite. The general rule is that the owner of a dog or other domestic animal is strictly liable for injuries caused by the animal only if the owner knows or has reason to know of the animal's dangerous propensities. . . . The Restatement (Second) of Torts states the rule in § 509:

> "(1) A possessor of a domestic animal that he knows or has reason to know has dangerous propensities abnormal to its class, is subject to liability for harm done by the animal to another, although he has exercised the utmost care to prevent it from doing the harm.
> "(2) This liability is limited to harm that results from the abnormally dangerous propensity of which the possessor knows or has reason to know." Restatement, supra at 15.

and goes on to apply it to licensees in § 513:

> "The possessor of a wild animal or an abnormally dangerous domestic animal who keeps it upon land in his possession, is subject to strict liability to persons coming upon the land in the exercise of a privilege whether derived from his consent to their entry or otherwise." . . .

Thus, in the present case, if a jury could reasonably conclude the defendants knew or had reason to know of their dog's tendency to bite, they would be liable. The knowledge necessary to constitute notice of the dog's dangerous propensity varies. Harper & James note that:

". . . Any knowledge of the animal's propensity to bite or attack, whether in anger or play, is sufficient. If the owner has seen or heard enough to convince a man of ordinary prudence of the animal's propensity to inflict the type of harm complained of, there is such notice or scienter as the law requires, the question being in each case whether the owner, as a fact, had the knowledge from which he might reasonably anticipate the general kind of harm which occurred." . . .

We have held on a previous occasion that a prior bite by a dog is not conclusive as to the existence of the dog's dangerous propensities nor as to the defendant's knowledge of the propensities. . . . [W]e held that the question of knowledge by the owner was a matter for the jury. We believe that the bite received by the plaintiff in the instant case as she went toward the house, coupled with her son's later statement, could reasonably lead a jury to believe that the dog had dangerous propensities, and that the defendants had knowledge of them.[1] Thus, the involun-

tary nonsuit on the strict liability cause was improperly granted.

Plaintiff's second cause of action alleged defendants were negligent in failing to confine the dog. Failure to confine or control such a domestic animal can give rise to a cause of action in negligence. The Restatement (Second) of Torts, § 518, states the rule as follows:

"Except for animal trespass, one who possesses or harbors a domestic animal that he does not know or have reason to know to be abnormally dangerous, is subject to liability for harm done by the animal if, but only if,

"(a) he intentionally causes the animal to do the harm or

"(b) he is negligent in failing to prevent the harm." Restatement, supra at 30.

Here, the evidence indicates that Mrs. Blackwell could have controlled or confined the dog when she knew plaintiff was leaving the premises. She knew the dog had bitten plaintiff on her way into the house. Whether a reasonable person in the exercise of ordinary care would have restrained the dog is properly a question for the jury.

The defendants' motion for a judgment of involuntary nonsuit should not have been granted. Viewing the evidence in the light most favorable to the plaintiff, a legitimate question of fact for the jury was presented, both as to the charge in strict liability and the charge in negligence.

Reversed and remanded.

---

[1] There was evidence that the dog had chased sheep on one occasion; that he once knocked a girl off her bicycle; and that he was usually chained in the back yard.

Case Questions   1. What is the general rule regarding an owner's strict liability for injuries caused by an animal?

2. Why was the trial court's judgment of involuntary nonsuit improperly granted?

Strict Liability and Product Liability

A purchaser of tangible, personal property may have a right to recover from the manufacturer for injuries caused by product defects. Product defects include defects in design, manufacturing defects, and warning defects. A person who has been injured by a product defect may be able to recover based on strict liability as well as on breach of warranty (see discussion in Chapter 9) and negligence (see earlier discussion in this chapter).

The use of strict liability in product liability cases occurred because of dissatisfaction with the negligence and warranty remedies. It was very difficult for average consumers to determine whether manufacturers, wholesalers, or retailers of defective goods were responsible for their injuries. Also the traditional requirement of privity limited the manufacturer's liability in tort and warranty actions to the person who purchased the defective product, often the wholesaler or retailer. Reformers argued that too often consumers assumed the full cost of the losses. They believed that it would be more just and economically wise to shift the cost of injuries to manufacturers, since manufacturers

---

§ 402A. Special Liability of Seller of Product for Physical Harm to User or Consumer

(1) One who sells any product in a defective condition unreasonably dangerous to the user or consumer or to his property is subject to liability for physical harm thereby caused to the ultimate user or consumer, or to his property, if

(a) the seller is engaged in the business of selling such a product, and

(b) it is expected to and does reach the user or consumer without substantial change in the condition in which it is sold.

(2) The rule stated in Subsection (1) applies although

(a) the seller has exercised all possible care in the preparation and sale of his product, and

(b) the user or consumer has not bought the product from or entered into any contractual relation with the seller.

FIGURE 11–1   Section 402A of the Restatement (Second) of Torts

Source: Copyright © 1965 by The American Law Institute. Reprinted with the permission of The American Law Institute.

could purchase insurance and could distribute the costs of the premiums among those who purchased their products.

In contrast to breach of warranty and negligence remedies, which focus on the manufacturer's conduct, modern strict liability focuses on the product itself. A plaintiff who relies on strict liability has to prove that the product was unreasonably dangerous and defective, and that the defect proximately caused the injury (although the unreasonably dangerous requirement is disregarded by some courts).

The following product liability case involves a Jeep CJ-7 that pitched over while being driven, killing two people and injuring two others. The plaintiffs brought suit claiming a design defect was responsible for their injuries. Notice how the Ohio Supreme Court refers to Section 402A of the Restatement of Torts and indicates that this section has been adopted as part of Ohio law. You can examine the text of Section 402A in Figure 11–1.

Leichtamer v. American Motors Corp.
424 N.E.2d 568
Supreme Court of Ohio
August 5, 1981

Brown, Justice

This litigation arises out of a motor vehicle accident which occurred on April 18, 1976. On that date, Paul Vance and his wife, Cynthia, invited Carl and Jeanne Leichtamer, brother and sister, to go for a ride in the Vance's Jeep Model CJ-7. The Vances and the Leichtamers drove together to the Hall of Fame Four-Wheel Club, of which the Vances were members. The Vances were seated in the front of the vehicle and the Leichtamers rode in the back. The club, located near Dundee, Ohio, was an "off-the-road" recreation facility. The course there consisted of hills and trails about an abandoned strip mine.

While the Vance vehicle was negotiating a double-terraced hill [proceeding *down* the hill], an accident occurred. The hill consisted of a 33-degree slope followed by a 70-foot-long terrace and then a 30-degree slope. Paul Vance drove over the brow of the first of these two slopes and over the first flat terrace without incident. As he drove over the brow of

the second hill, the rear of the vehicle raised up relative to the front and passed through the air in an arc of approximately 180 degrees. The vehicle landed upside down with its front pointing back up the hill. This movement of the vehicle is described as a pitch-over.

The speed that the Vance vehicle was travelling at the time of the pitch-over was an issue of dispute. The Leichtamers, who are the only surviving eyewitnesses to the accident, described the vehicle as travelling at a slow speed. Carl Leichtamer described the accident as occurring in this fashion:

> "Well, we turned there and went down this trail and got to the top of this first hill. . . . And Paul looked back and made sure that everybody had their seat belt fastened. That it was fastened down; and he pulled the automatic lever down in low and he put it in low wheel, four wheel, too. . . . And then he just let it coast like over the top of this hill and was using the brake on the way down, too. We came to the level-off part. He just coasted up to the top of the second hill, and then the next thing I remember is the back end of the Jeep going over.
> . . . When we got to the top of the second hill, the front end went down

like this (demonstrating) and the back end just started raising up like that (demonstrating)."

John L. Habberstad, an expert witness for American Motors Corporation, testified that the vehicle had to be travelling between 15 and 20 miles per hour. This conclusion was based on evidence adduced by American Motors that the vehicle landed approximately 10 feet from the bottom of the second slope, having traversed about 47 feet in the air and having fallen approximately 23.5 feet.

The pitch-over of the Jeep CJ-7, on April 18, 1976, killed the driver, Paul Vance, and his wife, Cynthia. Carl Leichtamer sustained a depressed skull fracture. The tail gate of the vehicle presumably struck Jeanne Leichtamer. Jeanne was trapped in the vehicle after the accident and her position was described by her brother as follows: "She was like laying on her stomach although her head was sticking out the jeep and the—she was laying on her stomach like and the tailgate of the jeep like, was laying lower, just a little bit lower or right almost on her shoulders and then the back seat of the jeep was laying on her lower part of her back. . . . [H]er legs were twisted through the front seat." Jeanne Leichtamer is a paraplegic as a result of the injury.

Carl and Jeanne Leichtamer, appellees, subsequently sued American Motors Corporation, American Motors Sales Corporation and Jeep Corporation, appellants, for "enhanced" injuries they sustained in the accident of April 18, 1976. The amended complaint averred that the permanent trauma to the body of Jeanne Leichtamer and the other injuries to her brother, Carl, were causally related to the displacement of the "roll bar" on the vehicle. Appellees claimed that Paul Vance's negligence caused the accident, but alleged that their injuries were "sub-stantially enhanced, intensified, aggravated, and prolonged" by the roll bar displacement.

Paul Vance purchased his Jeep CJ-7 four-wheel-drive motor vehicle from a duly licensed factory-authorized dealer, Petty's Jeep & Marine, Inc., owned and operated by Norman Petty. Vance purchased the vehicle on March 9, 1976. The vehicle came with a factory-installed roll bar. The entire vehicle was designed and manufactured by Jeep Corporation, a wholly owned subsidiary of American Motors. American Motors Sales Corporation is the selling agent for the manufacturer. Appellees did not claim that there was any defect in the way the vehicle was manufactured in the sense of departure by the manufacturer from design specifications. The vehicle was manufactured precisely in the manner in which it was designed to be manufactured. It reached Paul Vance in that condition and was not changed.

The focus of appellees' case was that the weakness of the sheet metal housing upon which the roll bar had been attached was causally related to the trauma to their bodies. Specifically, when the vehicle landed upside down, the flat sheet metal housing of the rear wheels upon which the roll bar tubing was attached by bolts gave way so that the single, side-to-side bar across the top of the vehicle was displaced to a position 12 inches forward of and 14½ inches lower than its original configuration relative to the chassis. The movement of the position of the intact roll bar resulting from the collapse of the sheet metal housing upon which it was bolted was, therefore, downward and forward. The roll bar tubing did not punch through the sheet metal housing, rather the housing collapsed, taking the intact tubing with it. That this displacement or movement of the intact roll bar is permitted by the thin nature of the sheet metal wheel housing to which it is attached and the propensity of the bar to do so when the vehicle lands upside down is central to appellees' case.

The appellants' position concerning the roll bar is that, from an engineering point of view, the roll bar was an optional device provided solely as protection for a side-roll.

The other principal element of appellees' case was that the advertised use of the vehicle involves great risk of forward pitch-overs. The accident occurred at the Hall of Fame Four-Wheel Club, which had been organized, among others, by Norman Petty, the vendor of the Vance vehicle. Petty allowed the club to meet at his Jeep dealership. He showed club members movies of the performance of the Jeep in hilly country. This activity was coupled with a national advertising program of American Motors Sales Corporation, which included a multimillion-dollar television campaign. The television advertising campaign was aimed at encouraging people to buy a Jeep, as follows: "Ever discover the rough, exciting world of mountains, forest, rugged terrain? The original Jeep can get you there, and Jeep guts will bring you back."

The campaign also stressed the ability of the Jeep to drive up and down steep hills. One Jeep CJ-7 television advertisement, for example, challenges a young man, accompanied by his girlfriend: "[Y]ou guys aren't yellow, are you? Is it a steep hill? Yeah, little lady, you could say it is a steep hill. Let's try it. The King of the Hill, is about to discover the new Jeep CJ-7." Moreover, the owner's manual for the Jeep CJ-5/CJ-7 provided instructions as to how "[a] four-wheel-drive vehicle can proceed in safety down a grade which could not be negotiated safely by a conventional two-wheel-drive vehicle." Both appellees testified that they had seen the commercials and that they thought the roll bar would protect them if the vehicle landed on its top.

Appellees offered the expert testimony of Dr. Gene H. Samuelson that all of the physical trauma to the body of Jeanne Leichtamer were causally related to the collapse of the roll bar support. These injuries—fractures of both arms, some ribs, fracture of the dorsal spine, and a relative dislocation of the cervical spine and injury to the spinal cord—were described by Samuelson as permanent. He also testified that the physical trauma to the body of Carl Leichtamer was causally related to the collapse of the roll bar.

Appellants' principal argument was that the roll bar was provided solely for a side-roll. Appellants' only testing of the roll bar was done on a 1969 Jeep CJ-5, a model with a wheel base 10 inches shorter than the Jeep CJ-7. Evidence of the test was offered in evidence and refused. With regard to tests for either side-rolls or pitch-overs on the Jeep CJ-7, appellants responded to interrogatories that no "proving ground," "vibration or shock," or "crash" tests were conducted.

The jury returned a verdict for both appellees. Damages were assessed for Carl Leichtamer at $10,000 compensatory and $100,000 punitive. Damages were assessed for Jeanne Leichtamer at $1 million compensatory and $1 million punitive. . . .

I(A)

Appellants' first three propositions of law raise essentially the same issue: that only negligence principles should be applied in a design defect case involving a so-called "second collision." In this case, appellees seek to hold appellants liable for injuries "enhanced" by a design defect of the vehicle in which appellees were riding when an accident occurred. This cause of action is to be contrasted with that where the alleged defect causes the accident itself. Here, the "second collision" is that between appellees and the vehicle in which they were riding.

Appellants assert that the instructions of law given to the jury by the trial court improperly submitted the doctrine of strict liability in tort as a basis for liability. The scope of this review is limited to the question of whether an instruction on strict liability in tort should have been given. For the reasons explained herein, we answer the question in the affirmative.

I(B)

The appropriate starting point in this analysis is our decision in *Temple v. Wean United, Inc.* (1977). In *Temple*, this court adopted Section 402A of the Restatement of Torts 2d, thus providing a cause of action in strict liability for injury from a product in Ohio.

. . . [T]he vast weight of authority is in support of allowing an action in strict liability in tort, as well as negligence, for design defects. We see no difficulty in also applying Section 402A to design defects. As pointed out by the California Supreme Court, "[a] defect may emerge from the mind of the designer as well as from the hand of the workman." A distinction between defects resulting from manufacturing processes and those resulting from design, and a resultant difference in the burden of proof on the injured party, would only provoke needless questions of defect classification, which would add little to the resolution of the underlying claims. A consumer injured by an unreasonably dangerous design should have the same benefit of freedom from proving fault provided by Section 402A as the consumer injured by a defectively manufactured product which proves unreasonably dangerous.

Strict liability in tort has been applied to design defect "second collision" cases. While a manufacturer is under no obligation to design a "crash-proof" vehicle, an instruction may be given on the issue of strict liability in tort if the plaintiff adduces sufficient evidence that an unreasonably dangerous product design proximately caused or enhanced plaintiff's injuries in the course of a foreseeable use. Here, appellants produced a vehicle which was capable of off-the-road use. It was advertised for such a use. The only protection provided the user in the case of roll-overs or pitch-overs proved wholly inadequate. A roll bar should be more than mere ornamentation. The interest of our society in product safety would best be served by allowing a cause in strict liability for such a roll bar device when it proves to be unreasonably dangerous and, as a result, enhances the injuries of the user.

I(C)

We turn to the question of what constitutes an unreasonably dangerous defective product.

Section 402A subjects to liability one who sells a product in a "defective condition, unreasonably dangerous" which causes physical harm to the ultimate user. Comment *g* defines defective condition as "a condition not contemplated by the ultimate consumer which will be unreasonably dangerous to him." Comment *i* states that for a product to be unreasonably dangerous, "[t]he article sold must be dangerous to an extent beyond that which would be contemplated by the ordinary consumer who purchases it, with the ordinary knowledge common to the community as to its characteristics."

With regard to design defects, the product is considered defective only because it causes or enhances an injury. "In such a case, the defect and the injury cannot be separated, yet clearly a product cannot be considered defective simply because it is capable of producing injury." Rather, in such a case the concept of "unreasonable danger" is essential to establish liability under strict liability in tort principles.

The concept of "unreasonable danger," as found in Section 402A, provides implicitly that a product may be found defective in design if it is more dangerous in use than the ordinary consumer would expect. Another way of phrasing this proposition is that "a product may be found defective in design if the plaintiff demonstrates that the product failed to perform as safely as an ordinary consumer would expect when used in an intended or reasonably foreseeable manner."

Thus, we hold a cause of action for damages for injuries "enhanced" by a design defect will lie in strict liability in tort. In order to recover, the plaintiff must prove by a preponderance of the evidence that the "enhancement" of the injuries was proximately caused by a defective product unreasonably dangerous to the plaintiff.

Affirmed.

Case Questions

1. According to the court, when should an instruction have been given on the issue of strict liability in tort?
2. What makes a defective product unreasonably dangerous in design?

Tort Reform

Although the current tort reform movement can be traced to the 1980s, efforts to replace the fault-based tort system with a less expensive, more equitable, and more efficient alternative can be traced to the 1920s.[6] At that time, public dissatisfaction with the tort system as a vehicle for compensating workplace injuries and encouraging accident prevention led to the enactment of worker's compensation laws. Forty-two states enacted this reform between 1910 and 1921. Worker's compensation laws replaced tort law with a no-fault-based administrative process so that laborers who were injured at work would receive compensation.[7]

Beginning in the 1960s, and continuing to the present, American courts have both broadened the scope of tort liability and shifted its costs toward insurers in third-party liability cases.[8] One consequence was that it became possible for plaintiffs to bring suit against defendants who were marginally at fault. The judicial shifts were intended to make it easier for injured plaintiffs to obtain compensation, while the cost of actually paying the bill was passed through insurance companies to premium-paying policy holders and ultimately to the customers of their products and services. Deserving plaintiffs would no longer be deprived of a recovery because those at fault for the injury were judgment proof or bankrupt and unable to pay.

During the 1980s the public again demanded reform when insurance companies began to raise premiums, increase deductibles, and lengthen the list of risks excluded from coverage. Insureds cried foul at the increased costs of insurance. The insurance companies claimed that they were facing dramatically increasing risks and pointed to very large jury awards and greedy lawyers as evidence of a tort system out of control. Plaintiffs' lawyers blamed insurance company greed, defective products, and malpractice by manufacturers, doctors, and other professionals for the problems. Legislatures frequently responded by enacting legislation intended to reduce a defendant's exposure to tort liability.

Joint and Several Liability

During the last ten years, thirty-three states have reformed or done away with the doctrine of joint and several liability.[9] Under the common law, if Sarah, Jose, and Soyinni commit a tort at the same time, liability for the entire harm is imposed on each of the tortfeasors jointly and individually. This means that the plaintiff could recover one-third from each defendant, or the entire judgment from one defendant (who could then seek contribution from the other two). The rule was created because limiting the plaintiff's recovery to a defendant's proportionate share would force the plaintiff to bear the loss of sums uncollectible from a bankrupt or judgment-proof defendant. This rule has been attacked because it permits collection of the total judgment from someone who was only minimally at fault. Thus a party who was only 3 percent at fault, but who was wealthy, could be made to pay 100 percent of the judgment. A person who was 97 percent at fault but who was indigent would escape liability.[10]

Caps on Noneconomic Damages

Many states have tried to lower jury awards by statutorily establishing ceilings on recoveries for noneconomic damages such as pain and suffering, loss of consortium, and loss of enjoyment of life (hedonic damages). The ceiling varies by state, but the range is generally from $250,000 to $1 million.[11]

Limiting Punitive Damages

Many states have abolished punitive damages unless such awards are permitted in specified types of cases by statute. Some states require that punitive damages be proven clearly and convincingly rather than by a preponderance of the evidence, and others require bifurcated trials for punitive damages.[12] It is common for state legislatures to impose dollar ceilings on punitive damage awards, and both houses of Congress have passed bills establishing ceilings on such recoveries in product liability cases. Although the U.S. Supreme Court has recently ruled that constitutional due process also imposes limits on punitive damage awards, it has not established a legal standard of what constitutes excessiveness.[13]

Statutes of Limitations

As we saw in the case of *Atkins v. Jiminy Peak, Inc.* (see page 192), legislatures often attempt to limit a potential defendant's exposure to tort liability by shortening the statute of limitations.

Court Annexed Alternative Dispute Resolution (ADR)

Legislatures have required that many tort claims be referred to alternative dispute resolution (ADR) before proceeding to a jury trial. See Chapter 14 for a discussion of ADR alternatives.

Collateral Source Rule

Many states have abandoned the common law rule and permitted, to varying extents, evidence of collateral source compensation.[14] The traditional rule prevents a defendant from informing jurors that the plaintiff has already recovered payment for economic damages such as disability, lost wages, and hospital and doctor bills, from Social Security, worker's compensation, or the plaintiff's own insurance company. Admitting collateral source evidence has the effect of shifting the cost of the injuries *from* the negligent party *to* the plaintiff's insurance company.

Efforts to find a generally acceptable alternative to the common law-based tort system have so far been unsuccessful. It is likely the tort reform battle will continue to rage for the foreseeable future, with much finger-pointing, and at great social cost.

Chapter Questions

1. Define the following terms:

agent	libel
assault	malicious prosecution
assumption of risk	negligence
battery	principal
contributory negligence	proximate cause
conversion	slander
defamation	vicarious liability
false arrest, imprisonment	wanton misconduct
independent contractor	warrant
invitee	

2. The plaintiff became ill in the defendant's store. The defendant undertook to render medical aid to the plaintiff, keeping the plaintiff in an infirmary for six hours without medical care. It was determined that when the plaintiff finally received proper medical care, the extended lapse of time had seriously aggravated the plaintiff's illness. Discuss what action, if any, the plaintiff has.

   Zelenka v. Gilbel Bros., Inc., 158 Misc. 904, 287 N.Y.S. 134 (1935)

3. Plaintiff came into defendant's grocery store and purchased some cigarettes. He then asked if the store had any empty boxes he could use. The defendant instructed the plaintiff that he could find some in the back room and told the plaintiff to help himself. Plaintiff entered the room, which was dark. While searching for a light switch, the plaintiff fell into an open stairwell and was injured. What is the status of the plaintiff (invitee, licensee, trespasser)? How will the status affect the plaintiff's ability to recover from the defendant, if at all? Do you think the fact that the defendant is operating a business should affect his duty?

   Whelan v. Van Natta Grocery, 382 S.W.2d 205 (Ky. 1964)

4. Plaintiff's intestate was killed when the roof of the defendant's foundry fell in on him. Plaintiff alleges that the defendant failed to make proper repairs to the roof, and that such neglect of the defendant caused the roof to collapse. The defendant claims, however, that the roof collapsed during a violent storm, and that, even though the roof was in disrepair, the high winds caused the roof to fall. What issue is raised, and how would you resolve it?

   Kimble v. Mackintosh Hemphill Co., 359 Pa. 461, 59 A.2d 68 (1948)

5. The plaintiff's intestate, who had been drinking, was crossing Broadway when he was negligently struck by one of defendant's cabs. As a result of the accident, the plaintiff's intestate was thrown about twenty feet, his thigh was broken, and his knee injured. He immediately became unconscious and was rushed to a hospital, where he died of delirium tremens (a disease characterized by violent shaking, often induced by excessive alcoholic consumption). Defendant argued that the deceased's alcoholism might have caused delirium tremens and death at a later date, even if defendant had not injured him. What is the main issue presented here? Who should prevail and why?

   McCahill v. N.Y. Transportation Co., 201 N.Y. 221, 94 N.E. 616 (1911)

6. Plaintiff, while a spectator at a professional hockey game, is struck in the face by a puck. The defendant shot the puck attempting to score a goal, but shot too high, causing the puck to go into the spectator area. Plaintiff brings suit, and defendant claims assumption of risk. Who prevails? Suppose the defendant had been angry at crowd reaction and intentionally shot the puck into the crowd. Would the outcome change?

7. Clay Fruit, a life insurance salesman, was required to attend a business convention conducted by his employer. The convention included social as well as business events, and Fruit was encouraged to mix freely with out-of-state agents in order to learn as much as possible about sales techniques. One evening, after all scheduled business and social events had concluded, Fruit drove to a nearby bar and restaurant, looking for some out-of-state colleagues. Finding none, he drove back toward his hotel. On the journey back, he negligently struck the automobile of the plaintiff, causing serious injuries to plaintiff's legs. Was Fruit in the course and scope of his employment at the time of the accident? From whom will the plaintiff be able to recover?

   Fruit v. Schreiner, 502 P.2d 133 (Alas. 1972)

8. John Prater was employed by Roy Goodman as a general handyman in Goodman's music store, particularly to work on piano cases, deliver pianos, and keep the delivery truck in repair. One evening, Goodman told Prater to take the truck home and work on the truck's body over the weekend. On the truck were a few of Goodman's trash cans, which Goodman had asked Prater to empty. The following morning, a Saturday, Prater loaded several of his own cans of garbage onto the truck. On his way back from the dump, Prater made a detour of a few blocks to pick up his daughter. On this detour, he had a collision with a car driven by W. M. Leuthold. Prater was later found to be negligent. Leuthold brought suit against Goodman for Prater's negligence. What issue does this raise, and how would you resolve it?

   Leuthold v. Goodman, 22 Wash.2d 583, 157 P.2d 326 (1945)

9. *Reader's Digest*, with a circulation in California alone of almost two million copies, published an article entitled "The Big Business of Hijacking." The purpose of the article was to describe various truck thefts and the efforts being made to stop such thefts. The plaintiff was mentioned by name in connection with a truck hijacking that had happened eleven years earlier in Danville, Kentucky. Nothing in the article indicated when the hijacking occurred. As a result of the publication, the plaintiff's daughter and friends learned of the incident for the first time. The plaintiff, a resident of California, filed suit against Reader's Digest Association for publishing the article, which disclosed truthful but embarrassing private facts about his past life. This case involved what intentional tort?

   Briscoe v. Reader's Digest Association, 93 Cal. Rptr. 866, 483 P.2d (1971)

10. Defendant was the owner and operator of the Argonne Apartments in the city of Seattle. Plaintiff had been a tenant in one of the apartments for approximately a year prior to April 29. On this day, the plaintiff had made arrangements to move to another apartment house. When the moving men came for her furniture, the defendant landlord appeared on the scene with a pistol in hand and threatened to shoot them full of holes if they moved

a single article belonging to the plaintiff. Soon thereafter, standing only a few feet from the plaintiff, the landlord pointed the pistol at her face and threatened to shoot her. What is the main question that the court must answer in deciding this case? How would you decide it?

Allen v. Hannaford, 138 Wash. 423, 244 P. 700 (1926)

11. During lunch, several employees were seated around a table. The defendant David, in an effort to tease the plaintiff Janet, whom he knew to be shy, put his arm around her and pulled her head toward him. Immediately after this "friendly unsolicited hug," the plaintiff suffered a sharp pain in the back of her neck and ear, and sharp pains in the base of her skull. As a result, she was paralyzed on the left side of her face and mouth. Was the "friendly unsolicited hug" an assault, battery, and / or negligence?

Spivey v. Battaglia, 258 So.2d 815 (Fla. 1972)

12. Plaintiff, a black person, was invited to a business convention at defendant's hotel, which included a buffet luncheon. As the plaintiff was standing in line with others, one of the defendant's employees snatched the tray from his hand and shouted that no Negro could be served in the hotel. Although the plaintiff was not actually touched, he was highly embarrassed by such conduct in the presence of his associates. What possible tort actions could be brought? Who is liable if the plaintiff succeeds in bringing suit?

Fisher v. Carrousel Motor Hotel, Inc., 424 S.W.2d 627 (Texas, 1967)

13. The defendant, while hunting ducks and other migratory birds, repeatedly discharged his rifle at fowl in flight over the plaintiff's land. Plaintiff brings a cause of action for trespass to land. Judgment for whom? Why?

Herrin v. Sutherland, 74 Mont. 587, 241 P. 328 (1925)

14. Anna Dorsey was a nurse in Joseph Larocque's employ at his home in Bernardsville, N.J. On September 26, Larocque's wife questioned Dorsey about the loss of certain jewelry. The following day, Dorsey was asked to go into a room where there were present other servants, Chief of Police Stryker, and a police officer named McGee. She was asked whether she was willing to "have your things searched." She consented. Her belongings were searched, and the lost property was not found. On October 4, Larocque subscribed and swore to an affidavit before the court recorder in Bernardsville. The affidavit accused Dorsey of stealing certain jewels. Stryker, the chief of police, later arrested Dorsey and, finding no proof of guilt on her part, released her. Dorsey later brought suit against Larocque for the intentional tort of malicious prosecution. Do you think she is entitled to recovery?

Larocque v. Dorsey, 299 F. 556 (2d Cir. 1924)

15. Plaintiff, who had an open account at defendant's shoe store, requested the cashier to cash her check. At the time, she explained to the cashier that

she had put a notation on the check so that the bank would recognize that it was her check and was not a forged check on her account. The cashier took the check to the credit manager who had received information of recent passing of checks bearing plaintiff's forged name. The credit manager called the police and then recognized the plaintiff as a regular customer at the shoe store. When the police arrived, the credit manager did not make a full disclosure to the police concerning plaintiff's identity. Plaintiff was arrested. She later brought suit against the store. What theory of tort law do you think she relied on? Explain the duty relationship between plaintiff and defendant.

Leon's Shoe Stores, Inc. v. Hornsby, 306 S.W.2d 402 (Tex. Civ. App. 1957)

16. While being treated at St. Joseph's Hospital, the plaintiff was given a blood transfusion. The hospital purchased the blood from Blood Services, Inc. Shortly after the transfusion, it was discovered that the plaintiff had contracted serum hepatitis, a highly contagious disease that can be transmitted by virus-infected transfused blood. Discuss the possible causes of action, parties, and theories of relief available to the plaintiff. Should strict liability be applied? Are there other products affecting your daily life that cannot be made entirely safe for use?

Hines v. St. Joseph's Hospital, 86 N.M. 763, 527 P.2d 1075 (1974)

Notes

1. T.F.F. Plucknett, *A Concise History of the Common Law* (Boston: Little, Brown and Co., 1956), p. 372.

2. A.K.R. Kiralfy, *Potter's Historical Introduction to English Law* (4th Ed.) (London: Sweet and Maxwell Ltd., 1962), pp. 376–377.

3. R. Walsh, *A History of Anglo-American Law* (Indianapolis: Bobbs-Merrill Co., 1932), p. 323.

4. Kiralfy, pp. 305–307; Walsh, p. 344.

5. More discussion about the different types of damages can be found in Chapter 6.

6. R.L. Rabin, *Some Reflections on the Process of Tort Reform*, San Diego Law Review 25, 13 (1988).

7. Ibid., p. 20.

8. Third-party liability policies involve an insured (A), who contracts with an insurance company (B), to defend a lawsuit brought by some other person (C—the third party) against A. In such a contract, B will be obligated to investigate any claims, defend A, and pay any judgment up to the maximum amount provided in the insurance contract.

9. L. Pressler and K.V. Schieffer, *Joint and Several Liability: A Case for Reform*, Denver University Law Review 64, 65 (1988).

10. W.P. Keeton et al., *Prosser and Keeton on the Law of Torts* (5th Ed.) (St. Paul: West Publishing Co., 1984), p. 351.

11. The National Law Journal, *The Tort Movement's Progress Across the Nation*, November 9, 1992, pp. 35–37.

12. Ibid.

13. *Honda Motor Company v. Oberg*, 114 S.Ct. 2331 (1994).

14. The National Law Journal, pp. 35–37.

XII

Administrative Law and Administrative Agencies

A discussion of the U.S. legal system would not be complete without an examination of the government's use of statutory law and administrative rules to regulate business practices. This chapter addresses administrative law and the role of administrative agencies.

THE RISE OF ADMINISTRATIVE AGENCIES

Administrative agencies have existed at the federal level since the early 1800s when Congress created the U.S. Patent Office (1802),[1] the Bureau of Indian Affairs (1824),[2] and the Army Corps of Engineers (1824).[3] The greatest growth occurred after 1900, however, when approximately two-thirds of current agencies were created.[4] Before President Franklin Roosevelt's New Deal, this country operated on the premise that the federal government should be kept relatively small. That model of government changed during the 1930s in response to the serious social and economic problems associated with the Great Depression. Newly created agencies included the Federal Deposit Insurance Corporation (1933), the Tennessee Valley Authority (1933), the Federal Communications Commission (1933), the Securities and Exchange Commission (1934), and the National Labor Relations Board (1935). More recently, Congress has created agencies to address important social and public welfare goals, such as the Equal Employment Opportunity Commission (1965), the Occupational Safety and Health Review Commission (1970), and the Environmental Protection Agency (1970). These and a multitude of other commissions, boards, authorities, and departments administer legislation that affect many aspects of daily life (see Figure 12–1).

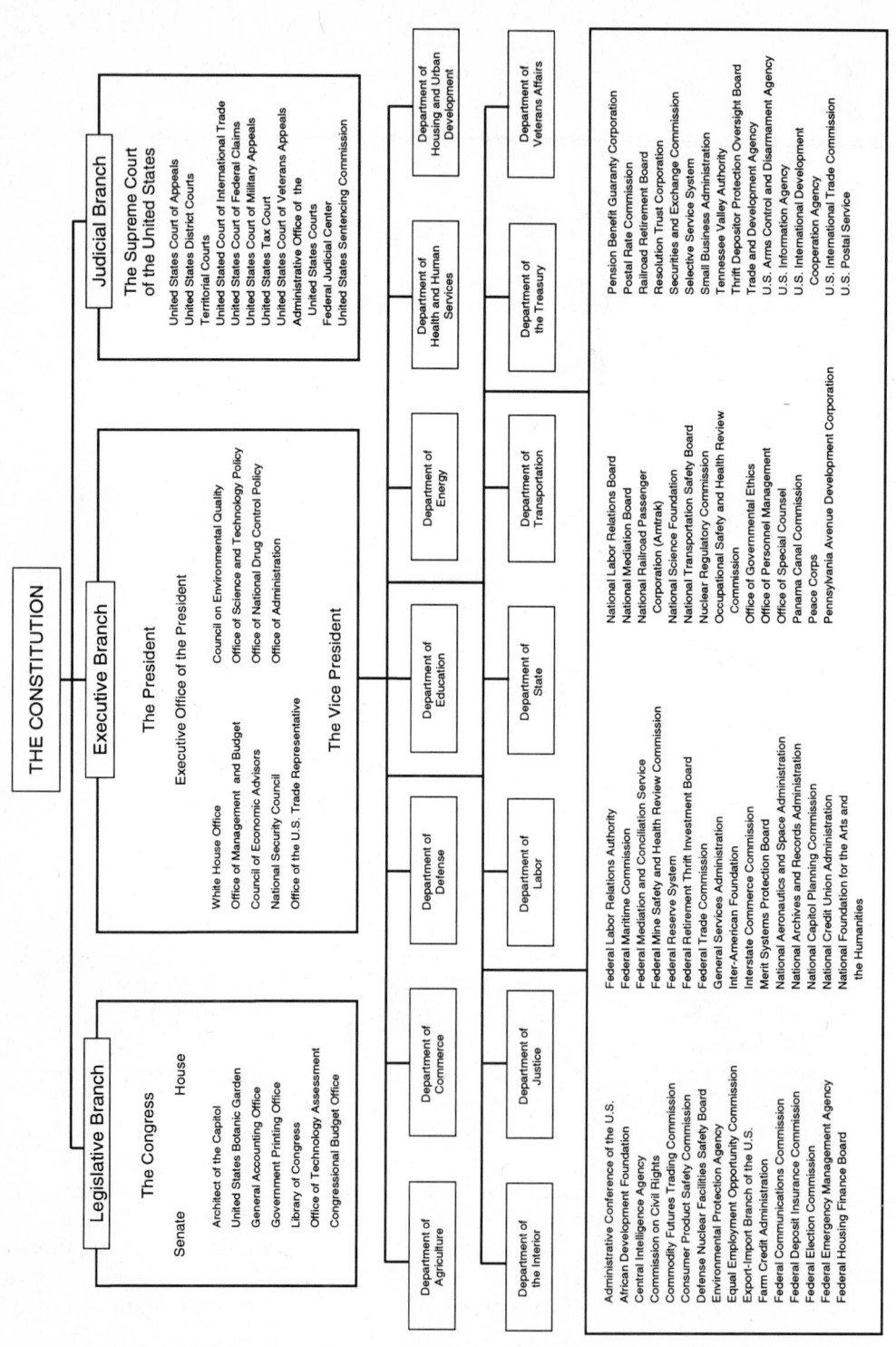

FIGURE 12-1   The Government of the United States

Source: Office of the Federal Register, National Archives and Records Administration, *U.S. Government Manual,* 1994–1995, p. 553.

Many regulatory bodies also exist at the state and local levels of government. State administrative agencies monitor environmental pollution, license drivers, determine automobile insurance rates, and oversee public utilities. They also regulate a wide range of professions and occupations including hairdressers, barbers, teachers, doctors, lawyers, and psychologists. At the local level, administrative agencies operate zoning boards, housing authorities, water and sewer commissions, and historical commissions.

This chapter is concerned with the legal framework for administrative law. It does not include political analyses of the role that ideology and resources play in agency decision making. Nor does this chapter focus on process questions, such as how administrative agencies decide which of competing policy alternatives will be adopted. These most interesting issues are often addressed in conjunction with political science courses.

ORGANIZATION AND CLASSIFICATION OF FEDERAL AGENCIES

Administrative agencies are commonly classified in terms of their organizational structure. Agencies that are organized into commissions and boards and directed by commissioners include the Federal Maritime Commission (FMC), Federal Reserve Board (FRB), Interstate Commerce Commission (ICC), National Labor Relations Board (NLRB), Nuclear Regulatory Commission (NRC), and the Securities and Exchange Commission (SEC). (See, for example, the SEC organizational chart in Figure 12–2.) Agencies that are structured as cabinet-level departments or administrations and are headed by secretaries or administrators include the Department of the Interior, Department of Agriculture, Department of Labor, and executive agencies such as the Environmental Protection Agency (EPA). (The EPA organizational chart can be seen in Figure 12–3.)

Commissioners, cabinet-level secretaries, and agency head administrators are nominated by the president and are subject to Senate confirmation. In general, commissions and boards are considered to be independent agencies because the commissioners do not serve at the pleasure of the president and can only be removed for cause, such as neglect of duty or inefficiency. In addition, Congress often requires that these agencies be bipartisan. The SEC, for example, has five members. The chairman is chosen by the president and normally is of the president's party. Because the SEC is a bipartisan agency, two Democrats and two Republicans will be chosen for the remaining four seats. Each commissioner serves a five-year staggered term; one term expires each June. Agencies headed by cabinet secretaries and head administrators are not independent, and their leaders serve at the pleasure of the president.

Functions of Administrative Agencies

Administrative agencies came into existence because legislative bodies recognized that they could not achieve desired economic and social goals within the existing governmental structure. Although legislatures could provide general

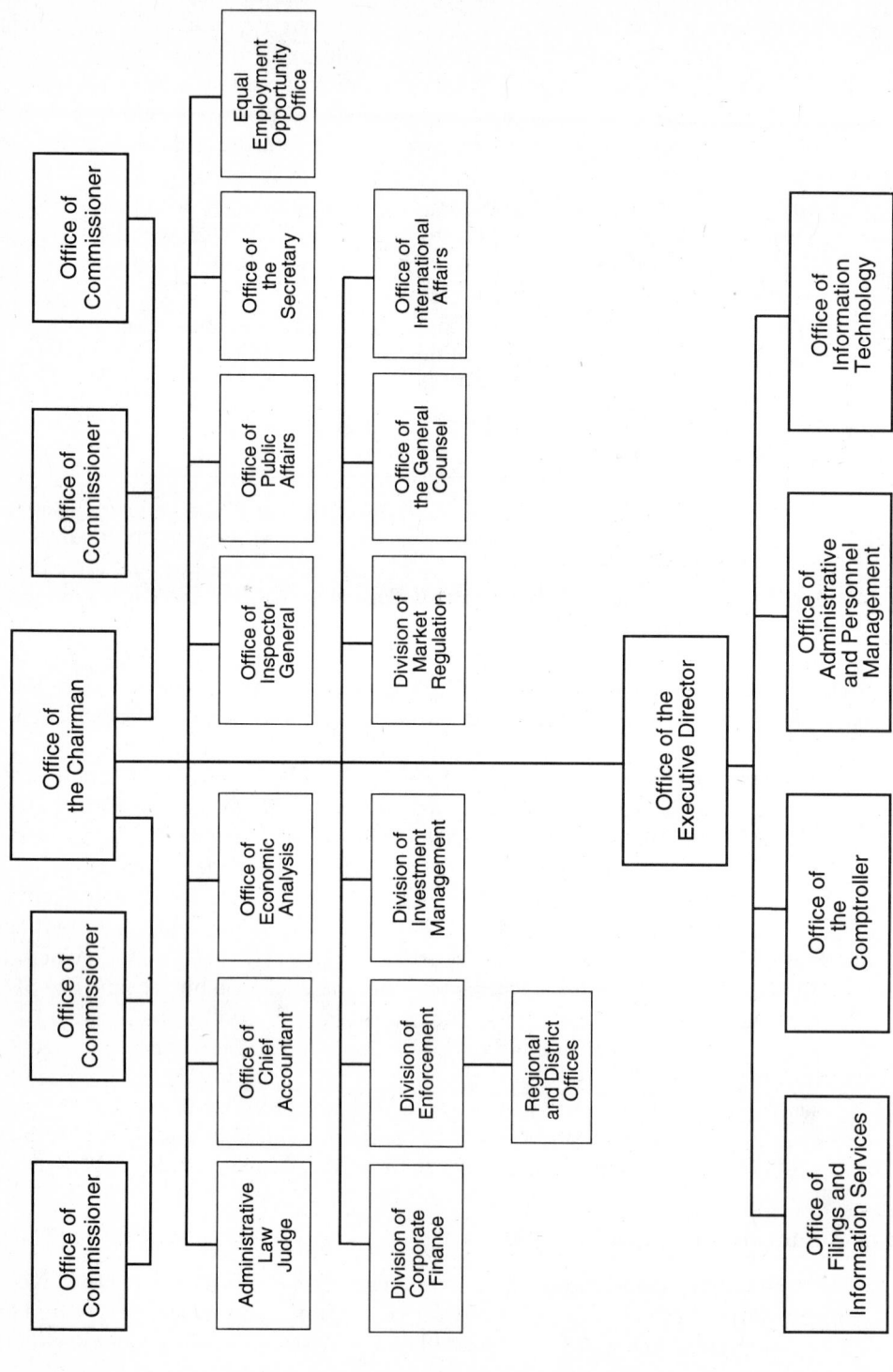

FIGURE 12–2 Securities and Exchange Commission

Source: Office of the Federal Register, National Archives and Records Administration, *U.S. Government Manual, 1994–1995,* p. 713.

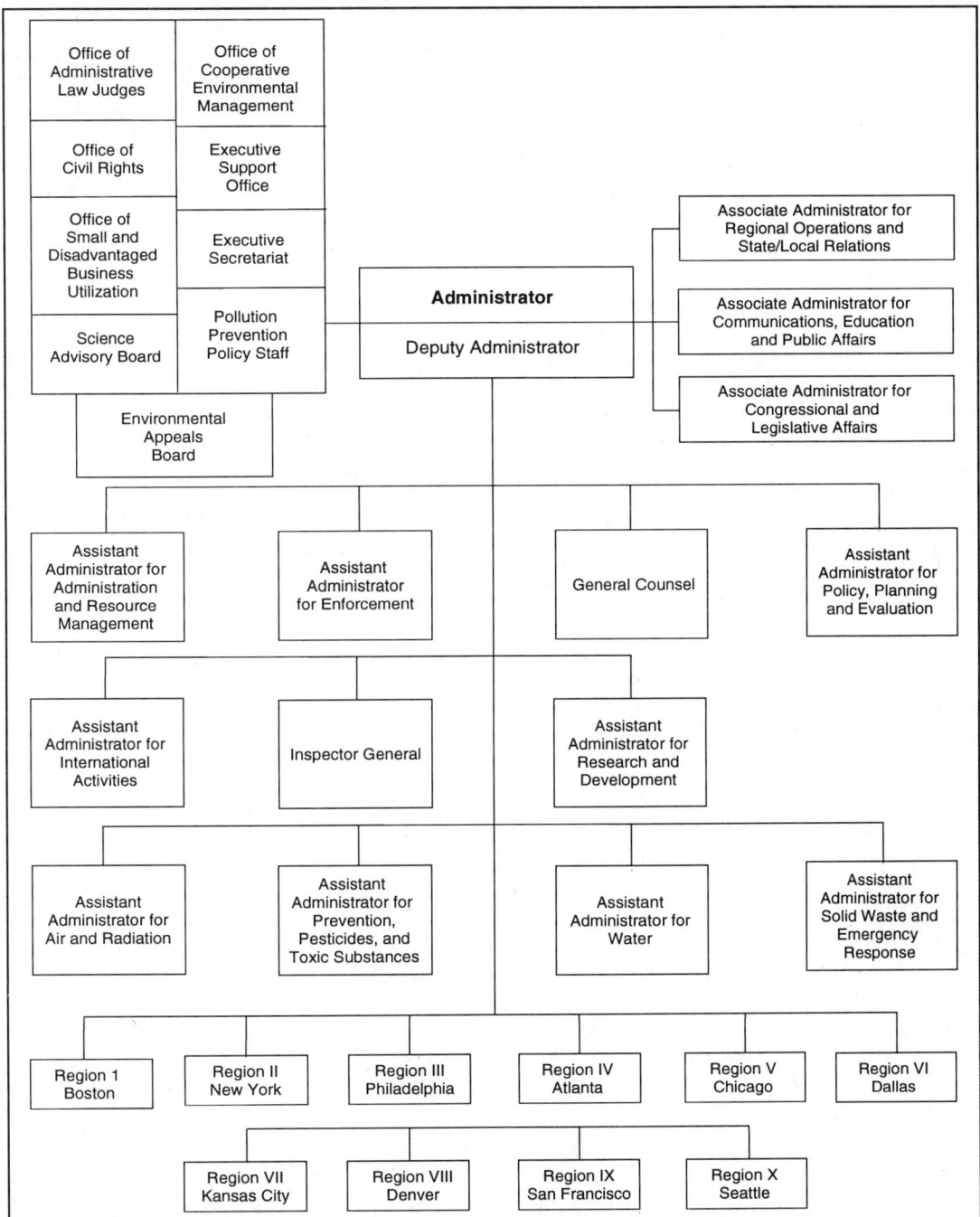

FIGURE 12-3 Environmental Protection Agency

Source: Office of the Federal Register, National Archives and Records Administration, *U.S. Government Manual,* 1994–1995, p. 553.

policy direction, they possessed limited subject matter expertise and could not devote continuing attention to the multitude of problems that confront our modern society. Agencies, on the other hand, can assemble experts who focus on one area and work toward achieving legislatively determined objectives.

Legislatures establish an administrative agency by enacting a statute called an *enabling act*. In addition to creating the agency, this act determines its organizational structure, defines its functions and powers, and establishes basic operational standards and guidelines. These standards and guidelines help reviewing courts control the abuse of discretion. Courts also use written directives to assess whether an agency is operating according to the legislature's intent. Administrative agencies can also be created by executive orders authorized by statute.

Agencies perform a variety of functions. For example, they monitor businesses and professions in order to prevent the use of unfair methods of competition and the use of deceptive practices; they help ensure that manufacturers produce pure medications and that food products are safe to consume; and they function to protect society from environmental pollution and insider stock-trading practices. Since the 1960s, several agencies have been created to protect citizens' rights in the work place and to ensure equal employment opportunity. Although there have been many notable achievements by administrative agencies, a lack of funding and political support, inadequate knowledge, and corruption have in some instances undermined agency effectiveness.

The plaintiff in the following case brought suit against the Commissioner of Public Safety for refusing to reinstate his driving privileges because of his non-driving-related use of alcohol.

Askildson v. Commissioner of Public Safety
403 N.W.2d 674
Court of Appeals of Minnesota
April 7, 1987

Leslie, Judge

Appellant's driving privileges were reinstated after revocation, conditioned upon his total abstinence from alcohol. Appellant was later found intoxicated in a restaurant, and the incident was reported to the Commissioner. His driving privileges were again revoked, and he petitioned to the trial court for reinstatement. The trial court denied all relief and dismissed the petition, and appellant brings an appeal from the order. We affirm.

Facts

Appellant Rick Marven Askildson's driving privileges were revoked at various times under the DWI and implied consent statutes as a result of violations occurring on August 30, 1975, April 24, 1976, January 6, 1984, and June 24, 1984. In addition, on July 26, 1984, all driving privileges were also cancelled and indefinitely denied as "inimical to public safety" pursuant to Minn.Stat. §§ 171.14 and 171.04(8), until such time as appellant submitted satisfactory evidence of successful rehabilitation.

Appellant submitted proof of rehabilitation and his driving privileges were reinstated effective December 18, 1985. As a part of his reinstatement, he signed a form agreeing to total abstinence as a condition for receipt of driving privileges and stating that any use of alcohol coming to the attention of the Commissioner would subject him to immediate cancellation and denial of driving privileges. He was issued a "B Card" with his driver's license which indicated that any use of alcohol or controlled substances invalidated the license.

On April 18, 1986, at 11:53 P.M., a police officer responded to a complaint of an intoxicated person at a restaurant. The officer found appellant "extremely intoxicated" and "passed out" inside one of the restaurant's booths. The officer took appellant to a detoxification center and sent a report of the incident to the Commissioner of Public Safety. The Commissioner, acting on that report, summarily cancelled and denied appellant's driving privileges effective May 2, 1986.

Appellant petitioned the trial court for reinstatement of his driving privileges. He did not challenge the fact that he was using alcohol, but claimed the Commissioner exceeded his authority in requiring abstention and in cancelling driving privileges when the reported use of alcohol was not directly related to driving a motor vehicle. Appellant also claimed there had been no findings that his use of alcohol made him "inimical to public safety," or that rehabilitation is required. The trial court dismissed appellant's petition for reinstatement, and denied the relief requested. The appellant brings an appeal from the trial court order.

Issues

1. Did the Commissioner exceed his authority and act in an arbitrary and capricious manner when he required appellant to abstain from the use of alcohol as a condition of reinstatement of driving privileges?

2. Was the Commissioner's cancellation and denial of appellant's driving privileges supported by adequate findings?

Analysis

1. The Commissioner cancelled appellant's driving privileges pursuant to Minn.Stat. §§ 171.04(8) and 171.14. Minn.Stat. § 171.04(8) (1986) states that the department shall not issue a driver's license "when the commissioner has good cause to believe that the operation of a motor vehicle on the highways by [a] person would be inimical to public safety or welfare." Minn.Stat. § 171.14 allows the commissioner to "cancel the driver's license of any person who, at the time of the cancellation, would not have been entitled to receive a license under the provisions of section 171.04."

Appellant petitioned for judicial review pursuant to Minn.Stat. § 171.19 (1984), seeking reinstatement of his driving privileges. In such proceedings, the petitioner has the burden of proving he is entitled to reinstatement. . . . The decision to cancel or deny driving privileges rests with the Commissioner of Public Safety. Minn.Stat. § 171.25 (1986). There is a presumption as to the regularity and correctness of these administrative acts. . . . In general, we will not reverse the decision of an administrative agency unless the decision is fraudulent, arbitrary, unreasonable, or not within the agency's jurisdiction and power. . . . These principles apply to review of driver's license proceedings. . . .

Appellant contests the Commissioner's authority to require total abstinence as a continuing condition for retaining a driver's license, and his authority to cancel and deny driving privileges for non-driving related use of alcohol. Appellant claims this is an attempt to control his private life. He asserts that without specific legislative authority, the Commissioner had no power to regulate non-driving use of alcohol; that the Commissioner's action here was arbitrary and capricious.

The legislature may delegate power to an administrative agency if the statute provides a reasonably clear policy to guide the administrative officers, so the law takes effect by its own terms, rather than according to the whim or caprice of the administrative officers. . . .

[I]n the present case, the Commissioner had the discretion to decide what conduct would render a driver "inimical to public safety." Administrative regulations promulgated by the Commissioner provide that he shall cancel and deny the driver's license of a person when there is sufficient cause to believe that he has consumed alcohol after completing rehabilitation. . . . It was not arbitrary or capricious for the Commissioner to regulate non-driving related alcohol consumption in this case.

We have upheld the Commissioner's authority to require total abstinence from alcohol as a condition of reinstatement or a period of abstinence from alcohol prior to reinstatement. . . .

In *Mechtel v. Commissioner of Public Safety*, . . . we explained that the Commissioner partially discharges his duty to minimize the risk to the public by drunken motorists "by requiring repeating offenders to prove abstinence and sobriety for a prescribed period of time." . . .

The abstinence requirement is not an attempt to control appellant's private life; instead, as the Commissioner states, it presented appellant with the choice of drinking or driving. Further, the fact that appellant was found intoxicated in a res-

taurant rather than a motor vehicle is irrelevant. It does not diminish the fact that appellant did not abide by the abstention requirement. . . . The Commissioner was within his discretion in requiring a driver with appellant's record to maintain abstinence from alcohol as a condition for retaining his driver's license. The determination that appellant was "inimical to public safety," justifying cancellation and denial of appellant's driver's license, was also within the Commissioner's discretion.

2. Appellant contends the Commissioner's decision to cancel driving privileges for non-driving related use of alcohol was arbitrary and capricious. He claims the Commissioner failed to make the necessary finding that appellant was "inimical to public safety" or in need of rehabilitation. However, under the circumstances of this case, the Commissioner's summary cancellation and denial of driving privileges was appropriate. Appellant signed a written agreement wherein he agreed to abstain from alcohol and controlled substances for so long as he lived. He did this as a condition of reinstatement of his driving privileges. Appellant fully understood that any use of alcohol that was brought to the attention of the Commissioner would be grounds for an immediate cancellation of his privilege to drive. No finding that appellant was inimical to public safety was required. A violation of a condition of reinstatement is sufficient to support cancellation and these facts were subsequently verified at the district court proceeding.

Minn.Stat. § 171.19 provides that the trial court is to "take testimony and examine into the facts of the case to determine whether the petitioner is entitled to a license or is subject to revocation, suspension, cancellation, or refusal of license, under the provisions of this chapter. . . ." The trial court made this determination, and the Commissioner's decision to cancel and deny appellant's driving privileges for his failure to abide by the abstinence requirement, was not arbitrary and capricious. The Commissioner's requirement of rehabilitation prior to license reinstatement is clearly based upon the appellant's

record and violation of the abstinence requirement, . . . and the Commissioner's rationale has been adequately explained. . . .

Decision

The order of the trial court is affirmed. Affirmed.

Case Questions

1. What factors did the court say an appellant must show in order to overcome the presumption of regularity and correctness of the commissioner's discretionary decisions regarding reinstatement?
2. Is an administrative agency a distinct branch of government?
3. According to the court, why must the legislature provide reasonably clear policy guidelines within the enabling act?

ADMINISTRATIVE AGENCY POWERS

Regulatory agencies interfere with individual and business decision making by exercising legislatively delegated rule-making, investigative, and adjudicative powers. Although the separation of powers doctrine states that the legislative, executive, and judicial functions of government should not exist in the same person or group of persons, the courts have ruled that combining such functions within a single agency does not conflict with the doctrine. Even though a wide range of powers may be delegated to an agency in its enabling act, there are checks on its activities. The creator of the agency, which is generally the legislature, retains the power to eliminate it or to alter the rules governing it. In addition, agency decisions are subject to judicial review, although this right in practice is very limited.

The 1946 Administrative Procedure Act (APA) was enacted to improve and strengthen the administrative process and to preserve the basic limits on judicial review. APA procedures address both the rule-making and adjudication functions. For example, the APA requires that rule-making follow notice and comment procedures. This means that agencies are required to publish notice of proposed rule making in the *Federal Register*. This notice gives interested parties a right to participate in the rule-making process by submitting written data or arguments. The opportunity for oral presentation may or may not be granted by the agency. In addition, publication of a substantive rule in the *Federal Register* is required not less than thirty days before its effective date.

The APA requires that agency adjudication processes include trial-type procedures such as the administration of oaths, the issuance of subpoenas, the taking of depositions, and the use of settlement conferences.

The APA applies to federal administrative agencies, unless Congress provides otherwise in each agency's enabling act. Most states have similar legislation.

Rule-making Power

Rule making is often referred to as the quasi-legislative function of administrative agencies. Agencies that have been granted rule-making powers are authorized to make, alter, or repeal rules and regulations to the extent permitted by the terms of their enabling statute. The statutes set the general standards, authorize the agencies to determine the content of the regulations, and provide general sanctions for noncompliance with the rules. The rule-making power of administrative agencies covers a vast range of business and governmental functions.

The plaintiffs in the following case challenged the validity of a U.S. Department of Agriculture regulation prohibiting the use of sorbates and sorbic acid in cooked sausage.

Chip Steak Company v. Hardin
332 F. Supp. 1084
U.S. District Court,
Northern District California
October 20, 1971

Sweigert, District Judge

This action, brought for declaratory and injunctive relief, is before the court on plaintiffs' and defendants' cross motions for summary judgment.

Plaintiffs Chip Steak Co. . . . [and] Western Meat Packers Association . . . bring this action against Clifford Hardin, Secretary of Agriculture. . . .

Plaintiffs allege in their first amended complaint that the Technical Services Division, Consumer and Marketing Service of U.S.D.A. prohibits the use of certain food preservatives, specifically, calcium sorbate, sodium sorbate, potassium sorbate and sorbic acid, in the manufacturing and processing of certain meat food products, by its practice of not approving

labels which declare the presence of said preservatives; that said practice is contrary to the provisions of the Wholesome Meat Act; that no scientific basis exists for prohibiting the use of these preservatives; that plaintiffs desire to use these chemical preservatives in their products and that continued enforcement of the above practice threatens great and irreparable damage to plaintiffs' property rights.

On the basis of the above allegations plaintiffs seek in their amended complaint a declaratory judgment "that an administrative practice of the United States Department of Agriculture is invalid in that it is contrary to the procedures of the Wholesome Meat Act of 1967"; an injunction against the enforcement of said administrative practice; and, an order directing U.S.D.A. to comply with statutory rule-making procedures.

Defendants deny the existence of the practice as alleged by plaintiffs but admit that U.S.D.A. is continuing to disapprove labels which declare that chemical preservatives are present such as to cause the product to be adulterated or misbranded. . . .

U.S.D.A. has . . . adopted a regulation pursuant to the Federal Meat Inspection Act of 1907, . . . as amended by the Wholesome Meat Act of 1967, . . . which provides as follows:

> "d. No substance may be used in or on any product if it conceals damage or inferiority or makes the product appear to be better or of greater value than it is.
> "Therefore: . . .
> "2. Sorbic acid, calcium sorbate, sodium sorbate, and other salts of sorbic acid may not be used in cooked sausage or any other product. . . ."

Plaintiffs allege that the prohibited additives have been safely used in the past; that plaintiffs desire to use these additives in their products; and that to prohibit these additives would cause plaintiffs irreparable harm. We will assume that, if plaintiffs endeavor to market products bearing or containing the additives prohibited by the regulation, the products will be deemed "adulterated" by the Secretary of Agriculture and that plaintiffs may be subject to adverse publicity, defense of condemnation charges and possible fines. . . .

Plaintiffs contend that they are entitled to a public oral hearing under the Administrative Procedure Act. . . . Plaintiffs are in error. [The act] . . . merely provides that, after having given notice of proposed rule-making, the agency must give "interested parties an opportunity to participate in the rule-making through submission of written data, views, or arguments with or without opportunity for oral presentation." . . . In the discretion of the Secretary of Agriculture, opportunity to submit written comments or materials sufficiently met the hearing requirement of the Act. . . . The administrative record of the rule-making proceedings here in question indicates that plaintiffs were given the opportunity to submit such written data and views as provided by the act and that they in fact did so. . . .

Plaintiffs next contend that the Secretary of Agriculture, in promulgating regulations on the use of food additives in meat products is bound by 21 C.F.R. 121.101, a regulation promulgated by the Secretary of Health, Education and Welfare pursuant to the Food, Drug and Cosmetic Act, 21 U.S.C. § 301 *et seq.*, permitting the use of certain food additives set forth in a list of substances characterized as "generally recognized as safe," among them calcium sorbate, potassium sorbate, sodium sorbate and sorbic acid. . . .

It is clear, however, that Congress, in amending the Federal Meat Inspection Act of 1907, 34 Stat. 1260 by enacting the Wholesome Meat Act of 1967, Pub. L. 90 n-201, 81 Stat. 584, 21 U.S.C. § 601 *et seq.* (Supp. 1971), intended to vest the Secretary of Agriculture with the power to pass regulations prohibiting or restricting the use of food additives *in meat products* notwithstanding the designation of such additives as "generally recognized as safe" in regulations promulgated by the Secretary of Health, Education and Welfare under the Food, Drug and Cosmetic Act. . . .

The legislative history of the Federal Meat Inspection Act . . . indicates that . . . Congress intended to "allow the Secretary of Agriculture to impose *more stringent* restrictions . . . for food additives . . . in or on meat products subject to the new act than are imposed by the Secretary of Health, Education and Welfare under the Federal Food, Drug and Cosmetic Act." [*U.S. Code Cong. & Admin. News,* 90th Cong., 1st Sess., vol. 2 at p. 2195 (1967).] . . .

Further, an Act of September 6, 1958, Pub. L. 85–929, 72 Stat. 1789, amending the Food, Drug and Cosmetic Act to empower the Secretary of Health, Education and Welfare to promulgate regulations on food additives, expressly provides in Section 7 as follows:

"Nothing in this Act (Federal Food, Drug and Cosmetic Act) shall be construed to exempt any meat or meat food product or any person from any requirement imposed by or pursuant to the . . . Meat Inspection Act of March 4, 1907, 34 Stat. 1260, as amended and extended (21 U.S.C. § 71 and the following)."

Plaintiffs finally contend that there exists no rational basis for . . . [the regulation]. . . . [The regulation] was promulgated by the Secretary of Agriculture pursuant to the authority granted in the proviso . . . which provides that products will be considered to be adulterated if they contain food additives which are prohibited by regulations of the Secretary of Agriculture and . . . [Federal Meat Inspection Act]. . . . [This act] provides that a meat product shall be considered "adulterated" if damage or inferiority has been concealed in any manner or if any substance has been added to it to make it appear better or of greater value than it actually is.

The prohibition of sorbates in the challenged regulation is expressly based on the ground that sorbates and sorbic acid are additives which conceal inferiority and damage and make the product appear better than it actually is.

The Secretary of Agriculture in promulgating . . . [the regulation] made a finding to that effect in the following stated "considerations:"

"Mold and bacterial slime develop on the surface of cooked sausages and similar products held for long periods under good refrigeration or for shorter periods at higher temperatures. The appearance of mold and other surface growth serves to alert consumers to the condition of the product. Sorbates are most effective moldicides and bactericides for products with high acidity, i.e., a pH of 5 or below. These chemicals are not effective in products such as cooked sausages since their pH ranges from 5.9 to 6.2. The presence of sorbates in subsurface sausage tissues results in changes in bacterial flora of the products. Sorbates have been demonstrated to inhibit selectively the development of aerobic bacteria and 'simultaneously permit the luxuriant growth of clostridium perfringes and clostridium botulinum, which are organisms associated with serious health hazards. The use of sorbates for such products therefore conceals damage and inferiority because of bacterial action, and makes the products appear better and of greater value than they are in view of their decomposing condition.'" . . .

On the basis of the . . . record and in view of the fact that the regulation in question presents questions of a technical nature which are properly within the expertise of the administrative agency, this court concludes that there was rational basis for the . . . [regulation]. . . .

From the affidavits of Vaughn and York, submitted by plaintiffs, and the affidavits of Johnston, submitted by defendants, as well as the documentary record of the rule-making proceedings, it appears that there is no genuine issue as to the following material fact, i.e., that sorbic acid and sorbates prevent the growth of mold and other surface growths in meat products, such as cooked sausages, while not inhibiting certain bacterial subsurface spoilage and thus make meat products appear better than they actually are, thereby misleading the consumer.

It follows, therefore, that, even assuming there could be dispute about the

Secretary's second ground for his regulation, the undisputed first ground would alone constitute a rational basis for 9 C.F.R. 318.7(d)(2).

Having found that [the] regulation . . . is both procedurally and substantively valid, this court is of the opinion that U.S.D.A. is authorized to disapprove labels which declare the presence of the prohibited additives because the use of the prohibited additives would render the product "adulterated" within the meaning of the Federal Meat Inspection Act. . . .

The Federal Meat Inspection Act . . . charges U.S.D.A. with the responsibility of ascertaining that products to which the official inspection legend is affixed are not "adulterated." The disapproval of labels bearing additives which would render the product "adulterated" is, therefore, a lawful exercise of the functions of U.S.D.A.

For the reasons above set forth it is ordered that plaintiffs' motion for summary judgment . . . is . . . denied; and defendants' motion for summary judgment . . . granted, insofar as it seeks a declaratory judgment that [the] regulation . . . is a valid and enforceable regulation of the Secretary of Agriculture and that the practice of disapproving labels as admitted by defendants is a lawful exercise of its functions under the Federal Meat Inspection Act. . . .

Case
Questions

1. What two agencies regulate meat products?
2. Administrative rule-making procedure has been described as "one of the greatest inventions of modern government." Why?

Investigative Power

Agencies cannot operate without access to facts for intelligent regulation and adjudication. Thus, the investigative power is conferred on practically all administrative agencies. As regulation has expanded and intensified, the agencies' quest for facts has gained momentum.

Statutes commonly grant an agency the power to use several methods to carry out its fact-finding functions such as requiring reports from regulated businesses, conducting inspections, and using judicially enforced subpoenas.

The power to investigate is one of the functions that distinguishes agencies from courts. This power is usually exercised in order to properly perform another primary function. However, some agencies are created primarily to perform the fact-finding or investigative function. Like any other power or function of the government, it must be exercised so as not to violate constitutionally protected rights.

The plaintiff in the following case challenged the Environmental Protection Agency's investigative use of a precision aerial mapping camera to photograph its plant.

Dow Chemical Company v. United States
476 U.S. 227
U.S. Supreme Court
May 19, 1986

Chief Justice Burger delivered the opinion of the Court.

We granted certiorari to review the holding of the Court of Appeals (a) that the Environmental Protection Agency's aerial observation of petitioner's plant complex did not exceed EPA's statutory investigatory authority, and (b) that EPA's aerial photography of petitioner's 2,000-acre plant complex without a warrant was not a search under the Fourth Amendment.

I

Petitioner Dow Chemical Co. operates a 2,000-acre facility manufacturing chemicals at Midland, Michigan. The facility consists of numerous covered buildings, with manufacturing equipment and piping conduits located between the various buildings exposed to visual observation from the air. At all times, Dow has maintained elaborate security around the perimeter of the complex barring ground-level public views of these areas. It also investigates any low-level flights by aircraft over the facility. Dow has not undertaken, however, to conceal all manufacturing equipment within the complex from aerial views. Dow maintains that the cost of covering its exposed equipment would be prohibitive.

In early 1978, enforcement officials of EPA, with Dow's consent, made an on-site inspection of two powerplants in this complex. A subsequent EPA request for a second inspection, however, was denied, and EPA did not thereafter seek an administrative search warrant. Instead, EPA employed a commercial aerial photographer, using a standard floor-mounted, precision aerial mapping camera, to take photographs of the facility from altitudes of 12,000, 3,000, and 1,200 feet. At all times the aircraft was lawfully within navigable airspace. . . .

EPA did not inform Dow of this aerial photography, but when Dow became aware of it, Dow brought suit in the District Court alleging that EPA's action violated the Fourth Amendment and was beyond EPA's statutory investigative authority. The District Court granted Dow's motion for summary judgment on the ground that EPA had no authority to take aerial photographs and that doing so was a search violating the Fourth Amendment. EPA was permanently enjoined from taking aerial photographs of Dow's premises and from disseminating, releasing, or copying the photographs already taken. . . .

The Court of Appeals reversed. . . .

II

. . .

Dow claims first that EPA has no authority to use aerial photography to implement its statutory authority for "site inspection" under . . . the Clean Air Act. . . . [S]econd, Dow claims EPA's use of aerial photography was a "search" of an area that, notwithstanding the large size of the plant, was within an "industrial curtilage" rather that an "open field," and that it had a reasonable expectation of privacy from such photography protected by the Fourth Amendment.

III

Congress has vested in EPA certain investigatory and enforcement authority, without spelling out precisely how this authority was to be exercised in all the myriad circumstances that might arise in monitoring matters relating to clean air and water standards. When Congress invests an agency with enforcement and investigatory authority, it is not necessary to identify explicitly each and every technique that may be used in the course of executing the statutory mission. Aerial observation authority, for example, is not usually expressly extended to police for traffic control, but it could hardly be thought necessary for a legislative body to tell police that aerial observation could be employed for traffic control of a metropolitan area, or to expressly authorize police to send messages to ground highway patrols that a particular over-the-road truck was traveling in excess of 55 miles per hour. Common sense and ordinary human experience teach that traffic violators are apprehended by observation.

Regulatory or enforcement authority generally carries with it all the modes of inquiry and investigation traditionally employed or useful to execute the authority granted. Environmental standards such as clean air and clean water cannot be enforced only in libraries and laboratories, helpful as those institutions may be.

Under § 114(a)(2), the Clean Air Act provides that "upon presentation of . . . credentials," EPA has a "right of entry to, upon, or through any premises." . . . Dow argues this limited grant of authority to enter does not authorize any aerial observation. In particular, Dow argues that unannounced aerial observation deprives Dow of its right to be informed that an inspection will be made or has occurred, and its right to claim confidentiality of the information contained in the places to be photographed. . . . It is not claimed that EPA has disclosed any of the photographs outside the agency.

Section 114(a), however, appears to expand, not restrict, EPA's general powers to investigate. Nor is there any suggestion in the statute that the powers conferred by this section are intended to be exclusive. There is no claim that EPA is prohibited from taking photographs from a ground-level location accessible to the general public. EPA, as a regulatory and enforcement agency, needs no explicit statutory provision to employ methods of observation commonly available to the public at large: we hold that the use of aerial observation and photography is within EPA's statutory authority.

IV

We turn now to Dow's contention that taking aerial photographs constituted a search without a warrant, thereby violating Dow's rights under the Fourth Amendment. In making this contention, however, Dow concedes that a simple flyover with naked-eye observation, or the taking of a photograph from a nearby hillside overlooking such a facility, would give rise to no Fourth Amendment problem.

In *California v. Ciraolo*, . . . decided today, we hold that naked-eye aerial observation from an altitude of 1,000 feet of a backyard within the curtilage of a home does not constitute a search under the Fourth Amendment.

In the instant case, two additional Fourth Amendment claims are presented: whether the common-law "curtilage" doctrine encompasses a large industrial complex such as Dow's, and whether photography employing an aerial mapping camera is permissible in this context. Dow argues that an industrial plant, even one occupying 2,000 acres, does not fall within the "open fields" doctrine of *Oliver v. United States* but rather is an "industrial curtilage" having constitutional protection equivalent to that of the curtilage of a private home. Dow further contends that any aerial photography of this "industrial curtilage" intrudes upon its reasonable expectations of privacy. Plainly a business establishment or an industrial or commercial facility enjoys certain protections under the Fourth Amendment. . . .

Two lines of cases are relevant to the inquiry: the curtilage doctrine and the "open fields" doctrine. The curtilage area immediately surrounding a private house has long been given protection as a place where the occupants have a reasonable and legitimate expectation of privacy that society is prepared to accept. . . .

As the curtilage doctrine evolved to protect much the same kind of privacy as that covering the interior of a structure, the contrasting "open fields" doctrine evolved as well. From *Hester v. United States*, . . . (1924), to *Oliver v. United States*, . . . (1984), the Court has drawn a line as to what expectations are reasonable in the open areas beyond the curtilage of a dwelling; "open fields do not provide the setting for those intimate activities that the [Fourth] Amendment is intended to shelter from governmental interference or surveillance." . . . In *Oliver*, we held that "an individual may not legitimately demand privacy for activities out of doors in fields, except in the area immediately surrounding the home." . . . To fall within the "open fields" doctrine the area "need be neither 'open' nor a 'field' as those terms are used in common speech." . . .

Dow plainly has a reasonable, legitimate, and objective expectation of privacy within the interior of its covered buildings, and it is equally clear that expectation is one society is prepared to observe. . . . Moreover, it could hardly be expected that Dow would erect a huge cover over a 2,000-acre tract. In contending that its entire enclosed plant complex is an "industrial curtilage," Dow argues that its exposed manufacturing facilities are analo-

gous to the curtilage surrounding a home because it has taken every possible step to bar access from ground level.

The Court of Appeals held that whatever the limits of an "industrial curtilage" barring *ground*-level intrusions into Dow's private areas, the open areas exposed here were more analogous to "open fields" than to a curtilage for purposes of aerial observation. . . . In *Oliver*, the Court described the curtilage of a dwelling as "the area to which extends the intimate activity associated with the 'sanctity of a man's home and the privacies of life.' " . . . The intimate activities associated with family privacy and the home and its curtilage simply do not reach the outdoor areas or spaces between structures and buildings of a manufacturing plant.

Admittedly, Dow's enclosed plant complex, like the area in *Oliver*, does not fall precisely within the "open fields" doctrine. The area at issue here can perhaps be seen as falling somewhere between "open fields" and curtilage, but lacking some of the critical characteristics of both. Dow's inner manufacturing areas are elaborately secured to ensure they are not open or exposed to the public from the ground. Any actual physical entry by EPA into any enclosed area would raise significantly different questions, because "[t]he businessman, like the occupant of a residence, has a constitutional right to go about his business free from unreasonable official entries upon his private commercial property." . . . The narrow issue raised by Dow's claim of search and seizure, however, concerns aerial observation of a 2,000-acre outdoor manufacturing facility *without* physical entry.

We pointed out in *Donovan v. Dewey*, . . . that the Government has "greater latitude to conduct warrantless inspections of commercial property" because "the expectation of privacy that the owner of commercial property enjoys in such property differs significantly from the sanctity accorded an individual's home." We emphasized that unlike a homeowner's interest in his dwelling, "[t]he interest of the owner of commercial property is not one in being free from any inspections." . . . And with regard to regulatory inspections, we have held that "[w]hat is observable by the public is observable without a warrant, by the Government inspector as well." . . .

Oliver recognized that in the open field context, "the public and police lawfully may survey lands from the air." . . . Here, EPA was not employing some unique sensory device that, for example, could penetrate the walls of buildings and record conversations in Dow's plants, offices, or laboratories, but rather a conventional, albeit precise, commercial camera commonly used in mapmaking. The Government asserts it has not yet enlarged the photographs to any significant degree, but Dow points out that simple magnification permits identification of objects such as wires as small as ½-inch diameter.

It may well be, as the Government concedes, that surveillance of private property by using highly sophisticated surveillance equipment not generally available to the public, such as satellite technology, might be constitutionally proscribed absent a warrant. But the photo-graphs here are not so revealing of intimate details as to raise constitutional concerns. Although they undoubtedly give EPA more detailed information than naked-eye views, they remain limited to an outline of the facility's buildings and equipment. The mere fact that human vision is enhanced somewhat, at least to the degree here, does not give rise to constitutional problems. An electronic device to penetrate walls or windows so as to hear and record confidential discussions of chemical formulae or other trade secrets would raise very different and far more serious questions; other protections such as trade secret laws are available to protect commercial activities from private surveillance by competitors.

We conclude that the open areas of an industrial plant complex with numerous plant structures spread over an area of 2,000 acres are not analogous to the "curtilage" of a dwelling for purposes of aerial surveillance; such an industrial complex is more comparable to an open field and as such it is open to the view and observation of persons in aircraft lawfully in the public airspace immediately above or sufficiently near the area for the reach of cameras.

We hold that the taking of aerial photographs of an industrial plant complex from navigable airspace is not a search prohibited by the Fourth Amendment.

Affirmed.

Case Questions

1. Why did the district court grant Dow's summary judgment motion?
2. What was the position of the U.S. Supreme Court with respect to the EPA's use of aerial photography as an investigative technique?
3. What is the U.S. Supreme Court's position with respect to Dow's contention that the aerial photography violated the company's Fourth Amendment rights?

Adjudicative Power

When an agency's action involves the rule-making function, it need not make use of judicial procedures. The *adjudicative function* of administrative agencies, however, involves a determination of legal rights, duties, and obligations, and adjudicatory hearings resemble a court's decision-making process. Thus, when an agency is intent on obtaining a binding determination or adjudication that affects the legal rights of an individual or individuals, it must use some of the procedures that have traditionally been associated with the judicial process.

Before sanctions can be imposed, an alleged violator is entitled to an administrative hearing that is conducted according to APA procedures (or the procedures specified in the enabling act) and that complies with the due process requirements of the Fifth and Fourteenth amendments. This means that the accused has to receive notice and a fair and open hearing before an impartial and competent tribunal. Parties affected by the agency action must be given the opportunity to confront any adverse witnesses and present oral and written evidence on their own behalf. (You might want to compare these requirements with those discussed in *Goss v. Lopez* in Chapter 1.) An agency may confine cross-examination to the essentials, thus avoiding the discursive and repetitive questioning common to courtroom cross-examinations.

Administrative agencies employ administrative law judges (ALJs) to conduct adjudicatory hearings. Like judges, ALJs decide both questions of fact and issues of law and they are limited to the evidence that is established on the record. ALJs are authorized to issue subpoenas, administer oaths, make evidentiary rulings, and conduct hearings. ALJs are not, however, members of the federal judiciary. They perceive their function as that of implementing and administering a legislative purpose rather than as judges impartially deciding between two litigants. In some agencies ALJs are quite active in questioning witnesses so that a thorough record of the proceedings is developed for the benefit of the agency's administrator or board.

However, administrative law judges *are* empowered to make findings of fact and to recommend a decision. The recommendation is sent to the board of final review in the administrative agency which retains the power to adopt, alter, or reverse it.

In theory, the decision of an administrative law judge is thoroughly reviewed before the agency's board of final review adopts it as its opinion. In reality, however, because of a board's heavy workload, the review may be delegated to members of its staff and board members may never even read the administrative law judge's opinion. Although this has been challenged as a lack of due process for the defendant, the courts often permit delegation of review to agency staff members. The courts require only that the board members make decisions and understand the positions taken by the agency.

JUDICIAL REVIEW

Judicial review is a relatively minor aspect of administrative law because the number of administrative adjudications is too great to allow court review in more than a small percentage of cases. In addition, the expense of obtaining judicial review is a barrier to many potential appellants.

Courts and administrative agencies are collaborators in the task of safe-guarding the public interest. Thus, unless exceptional circumstances exist, courts are reluctant to interfere with the operation of a program administered by an agency. As the courts' respect of the administrative process increases, judicial self-restraint also increases.

Timing of Review

Parties must address their complaints to administrative tribunals and explore every possibility for obtaining relief through administrative channels (*exhaust administrative remedies*) before appealing to the courts. The courts will generally not interrupt an agency's procedure until it has issued a final decision because where the administrative power has not been finally exercised, no irreparable harm has occurred—the controversy is not ripe.

The courts will hear a case before a final agency decision if the aggrieved party can prove that failure to interrupt the administrative process would be unfair. To determine the extent of fairness, the court will consider (1) the pos-sibility of injury if the case is not heard, (2) the degree of doubt of the agency's jurisdiction, and (3) the requirement of the agency's specialized knowledge.

The requirements of exhaustion of administrative remedies and ripeness are concerned with the timing of judicial review of administrative action, but the two requirements are not the same. Finality and exhaustion focus on whether the administrative position being challenged has crystallized and is, in fact, an institutional decision. Ripeness asks whether the issues presented are appropriate for judicial resolution. Although each doctrine has a separate and distinct aim, they frequently overlap.

Recognition of Administrative Competence and Scope of Review

In general, courts are willing to defer to an agency's competence. Courts will uphold administrative findings if they are satisfied that the agency examined the issues, reached its decision within the appropriate standards, and followed the required procedures.

It is impossible for a reviewing court to consider more than the highlights of the questions actually argued before an administrative agency since the fact situations are often complex and technical, and the time available for argument short. Instead, courts rely on an agency's expertise. Even when a court holds an original determination invalid, it usually remands the case for further con-sideration by the agency, rather than making its own final decision.

The courts have established standards as to the scope of judicial review. In general, questions of law are ultimately determined by courts and questions of fact are considered only to a very limited extent.

Questions of law must be reserved for the courts because the power of final decision on judicial matters involving private rights cannot constitutionally be taken from the judiciary. However, this does not mean that courts will review every issue of law involved in an administrative determination.

Courts will not reverse an agency's finding of fact unless (1) the action exceeded the agency's granted power, (2) procedural due process was lacking, or (3) there was lack of substantial evidence on the record as a whole to support the agency's finding.

The following case involved an appeal from the final decision of a state administrative agency. It illustrates the use of the state's Administrative Procedures Act, the exhaustion of administrative remedies, the limited grounds for judicial reversal of agency decisions, and the deference shown to the agency's competence.

Arndt v. Department of Licensing and Regulation
383 N.W.2d 136
Court of Appeals of Michigan
March 21, 1986

Per Curiam

Petitioner appeals as of right from a September 19, 1984, order and opinion of the Macomb County Circuit Court affirming a final order for the suspension of a license issued by respondent, the Department of Licensing and Regulation, Bureau of Realty and Environmental Services, Residential Builders and Maintenance and Alteration Contractors Board (board).

This action stems from a building contract entered into . . . by petitioner [and] Alfredo Puzzuoli to construct an addition onto Mr. Puzzuoli's residence. Petitioner has been a licensed builder since October 24, 1980. Apparently, there were problems with the work being done by petitioner. Mr. Puzzuoli was dissatisfied with the sewer installation, the concrete in the bathroom, the header supports, the aluminum trim, the vinyl siding, the doorwall, the roof construction, and ruts left in his yard by a cement truck. Mr. Puzzuoli filed a complaint with the Department of Licensing and Regulation on May 19, 1981.

An investigative hearing was begun on August 5, 1982, and concluded on September 28, 1982. The hearing examiner submitted a report on December 10, 1982, indicating that the addition to Mr. Puzzuoli's house was inspected by Michael Jozefiak, a Clinton Township building inspector. The building inspector reported that window leaks, the vinyl siding, tire ruts, and the failure to use Wolmanized (treated) lumber for the sole plates were main items of concern. He found that the doorwall was installed improperly, as was the aluminum trim, and that these items constituted poor workmanship. The building inspector also found that the new roof was installed with a dip and not only constituted poor workmanship but was a structural defect. Petitioner, aware of Mr. Puzzuoli's complaints, claimed that he did nothing to correct them because he believed he was not allowed on the property and also because Mr. Puzzuoli had refused to pay the remaining amount due on the contract.

The hearing examiner recommended that petitioner be fined $300 as a condition of continued licensure. However, the final order of suspension imposed an $1,800 fine and a license suspension for six months after payment of the fine.

On March 11, 1983, a petition for review was filed with the Macomb County Circuit Court. On September 18, 1984, the opinion and order affirming the final order of the Department of Licensing and Regulation was issued.

Petitioner's sole issue on appeal is that the circuit court erred in affirming the board's final suspension order. We disagree.

The proceedings in this case were conducted pursuant to the Administrative Procedures Act. Section 106 of the act provides:

"(1) Except when a statute or the constitution provides for a different scope of review, the court shall hold unlawful and set aside a decision or order of an agency if substantial rights of the petitioner have been prejudiced because the decision or order is any of the following:

"(a) In violation of the constitution or a statute.

"(b) In excess of the statutory authority or jurisdiction of the agency.

"(c) Made upon unlawful procedure resulting in material prejudice to a party.

"(d) Not supported by competent, material and substantial evidence on the whole record.

"(e) Arbitrary, capricious or clearly an abuse or unwarranted exercise of discretion.

"(f) Affected by other substantial and material error of law.

"(2) The court, as appropriate, may affirm, reverse or modify the decision or order or remand the case for further proceedings. M.C.L. § 24.306; M.S.A. § 3.560(206).

"Petitioner alleges violation of subdivisions (d) and (e)."

Substantial evidence is that evidence which a reasoning mind would accept as sufficient to support a conclusion. It consists of more than a scintilla of evidence but may be substantially less than a preponderance of the evidence. . . . This Court will affirm as long as the hearing examiner's findings are not contrary to law and are supported by competent, material, and substantial evidence, even if this Court might have reached a different result had it been making the initial decision. . . . It is not a reviewing court's function to resolve conflicts in the evidence or to pass on the credibility of witnesses. . . . Great deference is given to the findings of the hearing examiner because, as the trier of fact, he or she had the opportunity to hear the testimony and view the witnesses. . . .

The hearing examiner found that petitioner violated a rule of conduct of his occupation. . . . The rule violated is found in § 2411 of the Occupational Code and reads as follows:

"(2) A licensee or applicant who commits 1 of the following shall be subject to the penalties set forth in article 6: . . .

"(m) Poor workmanship or workmanship not meeting the standards of the custom or trade verified by a building code enforcement official." . . .

Petitioner does not argue with the fact that his work was an example of poor workmanship. He relies on the assertion that Mr. Puzzuoli prevented him from correcting the work. Petitioner's argument is without merit. First, he was under a duty to perform his work in a workmanlike manner from the beginning of the contract. Further, a letter sent by petitioner to the Department of Licensing and Regulation on July 20, 1981, belies the assertion that he felt he was prevented from correcting the work because he was not allowed on Mr. Puzzuoli's property. The letter reads in part as follows:

"A week after I had finished Mr. P. called and told me that there were some things that he was unhappy with. He said he had two complaints with the alum. siding and one with a header. I told him that I would come and take a look. I told him that I would have someone over right away to fix the siding but that I wouldn't do what he wanted to the header because it would be incorrect. He then sent me a registered letter telling me that unless I did what he wanted he wasn't going to pay me. I took the inspector over to look at Mr. P.'s request. The inspector told him that it was corrected as it is.

"After this I hired an attorney to help me collect my money. He advised me to stay completely away since I wasn't going to be paid anyway. The next thing I know is that I have 45 days to correct the stated things."

Petitioner received the building inspector's report on June 10, 1981. Mr. Puzzuoli testified that he did not prevent petitioner from correcting any of the defects. The hearing examiner was within his authority in believing Mr. Puzzuoli's testimony in this regard, especially since it was corroborated by petitioner's own letter to the Department of Licensing and Regulation. Thus, the evidence was clear that there were violations of the Occupational Code, verified by a building inspector. Petitioner chose not to make corrections in a timely manner. Accordingly, the findings of fact and conclusions of law were based on competent, material and substantial evidence and were properly affirmed by the circuit court.

Petitioner also argues that the sanctions imposed were arbitrary and an abuse of the board's discretion. Petitioner bases this assertion on the fact that the hearing examiner recommended a $300 fine and the board imposed an $1,800 fine and a six-month suspension of his license.

Section 602 of the Occupation Code provides:

"A person, school, or institution which violates a section of this act or a rule or order promulgated or issued under this act shall be assessed 1 or more of the following penalties:

"(a) Placement of a limitation on a license or certificate of registration for an occupation regulated under articles 8 to 25.

"(b) Suspension of a license or certificate of registration.

"(c) Denial of a license, certificate of registration, or renewal of a license or certificate of registration.

"(d) Revocation of a license or certificate of registration.

"(e) A civil fine to be paid to the department, not to exceed $10,000.00.

"(f) Censure.

"(g) Probation.

"(h) A requirement that restitution be made."

The recommended fine of $300 was just that, a recommendation. The hearing examiner had no authority to assess a penalty. The Residential Builders and Maintenance and Alteration Contractors Board is vested with total authority to assess penalties and exercised such authority in this case. One of the defects complained of by Mr. Puzzuoli, the roof dip, was more than just poor workmanship, but actually constituted a structural defect.

According to the circuit court, it is the policy of the board to require a builder who has violated the Occupational Code to pay some of the costs associated with the investigation and proceedings which resulted in that finding. In that light, the $1,800 fine is not excessive, nor an abuse of discretion.

Affirmed.

Case
Questions

1. What action of the Department of Licensing and Regulation is appealed in this case?
2. What is the position of Michael Arndt, the building contractor?
3. What does the court of appeals say about the duty of an appellate court in reviewing the orders of a hearing officer and administrative agency?
4. In reviewing an agency order, does the appellate court pass on the credibility of the witnesses or resolve conflicts in the evidence?

ADMINISTRATIVE AGENCIES AND THE REGULATION OF BUSINESSES

Congress has neither the time nor the expertise to regulate business. Congress has also decided that the judicial process is not well suited to the task. Instead it has entrusted the day-to-day responsibility for regulating business to administrative agencies. The following material focuses on three administrative agencies and how they perform this function.

Occupational Safety and Health Administration

Historically, the common law provided an employee injured on the job with little recourse against an employer who could use the assumption of risk and contributory negligence defenses or who invoked the fellow servant doctrine. With little incentive for employers to reduce employment-related injuries, the number of industrial injuries increased as manufacturing processes became more complex. Legislation was passed to improve job safety for coal miners during the late 1800s, and most states had enacted job safety legislation by 1920. Maryland and New York were the first states to establish workers' compensation laws, which have now been adopted in all fifty states. Although these laws modified the common law to enable injured employees to recover, they didn't change the practices that caused the dangerous conditions. Furthermore, state legislatures were reluctant to establish strict safety regulations, fearing that such actions would cause industry to move to other, less restrictive states.

In response to this problem, in 1970 Congress passed the Occupational Safety and Health Act to improve employees' safety and working conditions. The act established the National Institute of Occupational Safety and Health to conduct research in the area of employee health and safety. The act also created an administrative agency, called the Occupational Safety and Health Administration (OSHA), to set and enforce environmental standards within the work place.

An employee who suspects that there is a safety violation at his or her place of work can contact the local OSHA office. An OSHA inspector makes an unannounced visit to the premises and conducts an inspection. If the inspection reveals violations, appropriate citations—either civil or criminal—are issued.

For civil citations, OSHA may impose fines up to seventy thousand dollars for each willful and repeated violation and seven thousand dollars for less serious violations. An employer may contest the citation at a hearing before an administrative law judge. The ALJ's decision is appealable to the Occupational Health Review Commission, whose decision is appealable to the U.S. Court of Appeals.

Criminal cases are tried in federal court. Convicted offenders can be fined and imprisoned for willful violations of standards resulting in the death of an employee or for knowingly falsifying required documents. Sanctions may be doubled for repeat offenses. OSHA has rarely pursued criminal prosecutions.

In addition to sanctions, OSHA inspectors may post a job site as imminently dangerous and obtain an injunction in order to stop dangerous working conditions from continuing.

In the following case, the Supreme Court examined the question of whether employees can refuse work assignments that place them in jeopardy of death or serious bodily injury. The petitioner company challenged a regulation promulgated by the Secretary of Labor, which permitted employees in some circumstances to refuse to perform tasks that caused a reasonable apprehension of death or serious injury.

Whirlpool Corp. v. Marshall
445 U.S. 1
U.S. Supreme Court
February 26, 1980

Justice Stewart delivered the opinion of the Court.

The Occupational Safety and Health Act of 1970 (Act) prohibits an employer from discharging or discriminating against any employee who exercises "any right afforded by" the Act. The Secretary of Labor (Secretary) has promulgated a regulation providing that, among the rights that the Act so protects, is the right of an employee to choose not to perform his assigned task because of a reasonable apprehension of death or serious injury, coupled with a reasonable belief that no less drastic alternative is available. The question presented in the case before us is whether this regulation is consistent with the Act.

The petitioner company maintains a manufacturing plant in Marion, Ohio, for the production of household appliances. Overhead conveyors transport appliance components throughout the plant. To protect employees from objects that occasionally fall from these conveyors, the petitioner has installed a horizontal wire mesh guard screen approximately 20 feet above the plant floor. This mesh screen is welded to angle-iron frames suspended from the building's structural-steel skeleton.

Maintenance employees of the petitioner spend several hours each week removing objects from the screen, replacing paper spread on the screen to catch grease drippings from the material on the conveyors, and performing occasional maintenance work on the conveyors themselves. To perform these duties, maintenance employees usually are able to stand on the iron frames, but sometimes find it necessary to step onto the steel mesh screen itself.

In 1973, the company began to install heavier wire in the screen because its safety had been drawn into question. . . .

On June 28, 1974, a maintenance employee fell to his death through the guard screen in an area where the newer, stronger mesh had not yet been installed. Following this incident, the petitioner effectuated some repairs and issued an order strictly forbidding maintenance employees from stepping on either the screens or the angle-iron supporting structure. An alternative but somewhat more cumbersome and less satisfactory method was developed for removing objects from the screen. This procedure required employees to stand on power-raised mobile platforms and use hooks to recover the material.

On July 7, 1974, two of the petitioner's maintenance employees, Virgil Deemer and Thomas Cornwell, met with the plant maintenance superintendent to voice their concern about the safety of the screen. The superintendent disagreed with their view, but permitted the two men to inspect the screen with their foreman and to point out dangerous areas needing repair. Unsatisfied with the petitioner's response to the results of this inspection, Deemer and Cornwell met on July 9 with the plant safety director. At that meeting, they requested the name, address, and telephone number of a representative of the local office of the Occupational Safety and Health Administration (OSHA). . . . [T]he safety director . . . furnished the men with the information they requested. . . .

The next day, Deemer and Cornwell reported for the night shift at 10:45 P.M. Their foreman, after himself walking on some of the angle-iron frames, directed the two men to perform their usual maintenance duties on a section of the old screen. Claiming that the screen was unsafe, they refused to carry out this directive. The foreman then sent them to the personnel office, where they were ordered to punch out without working or being paid for the remaining six hours of the shift. The two men subsequently received written reprimands, which were placed in their employment files.

A little over a month later, the Secretary of Labor filed suit in the U.S. District Court . . . alleging that the petitioner's actions against Deemer and Cornwell constituted discrimination in violation of § 11(c)(1) of the Act.

. . . [T]he district court found that the regulation in question justified Deemer's and Cornwell's refusals to obey their foreman's order on July 10, 1974. . . . The District Court nevertheless denied relief, holding that the Secretary's regulation was inconsistent with the Act and therefore invalid. . . .

The Court of Appeals for the Sixth Circuit reversed the District Court's judgment. . . . Finding ample support in the record for the District Court's factual determination that the actions of Deemer and Cornwell had been justified under the Secretary's regulation, . . . the appellate court disagreed with the district court's conclusion that the regulation is invalid . . . because the decision of the Court of Appeals in this case conflicts with those of two other Courts of Appeals on the important question in issue. . . . That question, as stated at the outset of this opinion, is whether the Secretary's regulation authorizing employee "self-help" in some circumstances, 29 CFR § 1977.12(b)(2), is permissible under the Act.

The Act itself creates an express mechanism for protecting workers from employment conditions believed to pose an emergent threat of death or serious injury. Upon receipt of an employee inspection request stating reasonable grounds to believe that an imminent danger is present in a work place, OSHA must conduct an inspection. 29 U.S.C. § 657(f)(1). In the event this inspection reveals work place conditions or practices that "could reasonably be expected to cause death or serious physical harm immediately or before the imminence of such danger can be eliminated through the enforcement procedures otherwise provided by" the Act, 29 U.S.C. § 662(a), the OSHA inspector must inform the affected employees and the employer of the danger and notify them that he is recommending to the Secretary that injunctive relief be sought. § 662(c). At this juncture, the Secretary can petition a federal court to restrain the conditions or practices giving rise to the imminent danger. By means of a temporary restraining order or preliminary injunction, the court may then require the employer to avoid, correct, or remove the danger or to prohibit employees from working in the area. § 662(a).

To ensure that this process functions effectively, the Act expressly accords to every employee several rights, the exercise of which may not subject him to discharge or discrimination. An employee is given the right to inform OSHA of an imminently dangerous work place condition or practice and request that OSHA inspect that condition or practice. 29 U.S.C. § 657(f)(1). He is given a limited right to assist the OSHA inspector in inspecting the work place, §§ 657(a)(2), (e) and (f)(2), and the right to aid a court in determining whether or not a risk of imminent danger in fact exists. See § 660(c)(1). Finally, an affected employee is given the right to bring an action to compel the Secretary to seek injunctive relief if he believes the Secretary has wrongfully declined to do so. § 662(d).

In the light of this detailed statutory scheme, the Secretary is obviously correct when he acknowledges in his regulation that "as a general matter, there is no right afforded by the Act which would entitle employees to walk off the job because of potential unsafe conditions at the work place." . . .

As this case illustrates, however, circumstances may sometimes exist in which the employee justifiably believes that the express statutory arrangement does not sufficiently protect him from death or serious injury. Such circumstances will probably not often occur, but such a situation may arise when (1) the employee is ordered by his employer to work under conditions that the employee reasonably believes pose an imminent risk of death or serious bodily injury, and (2) the employee has reason to believe that there is not sufficient time or opportunity either to seek effective redress from his employer or to apprise OSHA of the danger.

Nothing in the Act suggests that those few employees who have to face this dilemma must rely exclusively on the remedies expressly set forth in the Act at the risk of their own safety. But nothing in the Act explicitly provides otherwise. Against this background of legislative silence, the Secretary has exercised his rule-making power under 29 U.S.C. § 657(g)(2) and has determined that, when an employee in good faith finds himself in such a predicament, he may refuse to expose himself to the dangerous condition without being subjected to "subsequent discrimination" by the employer.

. . . Our inquiry is informed by an awareness that the regulation is entitled to deference unless it can be said not to be a reasoned and supportable interpretation of the Act. . . .

The regulation clearly conforms to the fundamental objective of the Act—to prevent occupational deaths and serious injuries. The Act, in its preamble, declares that its purpose and policy is "to assure so far as possible every working man and woman in the Nation safe and healthful working conditions and to *preserve* our human resources . . ." 29 U.S.C. § 651(b). (Emphasis added.)

To accomplish this basic purpose, the legislation's remedial orientation is prophylactic in nature. . . . The Act does not wait for an employee to die or become injured. It authorizes the promulgation of health and safety standards and the issuance of citations in the hope that these will act to prevent deaths or injuries from ever occurring. It would seem anomalous to construe an Act so directed and constructed as prohibiting an employee, with no other reasonable alternative, the freedom to withdraw from a work place environment that he reasonably believes is highly dangerous.

Moreover, the Secretary's regulation can be viewed as an appropriate aid to the full effectuation of the Act's "general duty" clause. That clause provides that

"[e]ach employer . . . shall furnish to each of his employees employment and a place of employment which are free from recognized hazards that are causing or are likely to cause death or serious harm to his employees." 29 U.S.C. § 654(a)(1). As the legislative history of this provision reflects, it was intended itself to deter the occurrence of occupational deaths and serious injuries by placing on employers a mandatory obligation independent of the specific health and safety standards to be promulgated by the Secretary. Since OSHA inspectors cannot be present around the clock in every work place, the Secretary's regulation ensures that employees will in all circumstances enjoy the rights afforded them by the "general duty" clause. . . .

For these reasons we conclude that 29 CFR § 1977.12(b)(2) . . . was promulgated by the Secretary in the valid exercise of his authority under the Act. Accordingly, the judgment of the Court of Appeals is affirmed.

It is so ordered.

Case Questions

1. Why did the U.S. Supreme Court believe that the regulation was a reasoned and supportable interpretation of the Occupational Safety and Health Act?
2. Are there any constitutional problems that might arise because of a statute that authorizes surprise inspections of businesses?

Federal Trade Commission and Consumer Credit Protection

Although the first multi-use credit cards, Visa and MasterCard, came into existence only in 1959, consumer credit and loans presently exceed $790 billion per year. Initially, businesses that extended credit to consumers were subject to few regulations. They often imposed unduly high interest charges, failed to disclose their interest rates and associated credit charges, and mailed unsolicited credit cards to potential users. Because debt collection practices were unregulated, consumers were often harassed and threatened at home and at work. As a result, in 1968 Congress passed the Consumer Credit Protection Act (CCPA). Designed to promote the disclosure of credit terms and to establish the rights and responsibilities of both creditors and consumers, the CCPA is much more protective of the consumer than the existing common law. Although nine agencies share authority for enforcing and controlling the CCPA, the Federal Trade Commission bears primary responsibility for the CCPA's enforcement.

Under the CCPA, many early credit card and loan practices became illegal. Issuers of credit cards can no longer mail unsolicited cards. The question of which duties devolved on the merchant who accepts a credit card charge and which duties devolved on the card-issuing bank was also clarified. For example, under the CCPA, a bank may not withdraw funds from a cardholder's savings or checking accounts to cover a credit card charge without authorization from the cardholder. Also, under the CCPA a cardholder's liability for unauthorized charges is limited to fifty dollars in most cases.

One major problem not resolved by the CCPA is whether a cardholder may stop payment on a charge when the goods purchased have proved defective. Some states have passed legislation addressing this problem. At present, it appears that under federal law, a bank cardholder may refuse to pay off a card balance if the dispute involves a purchase over fifty dollars. Charges less than fifty dollars are treated as cash transactions that the cardholder must pay.

The CCPA is extremely lengthy and complex and is better known under its various subsections. Title I of the CCPA is known as the Truth in Lending Act. The Fair Credit Reporting Act was added in 1970, the Equal Credit Opportunity Act in 1974, and the Fair Debt Collection Practices Act in 1977.

The Truth in Lending Act is designed primarily to regulate the disclosure of terms and conditions of household purchases or purchases to be used for agricultural purposes that will be paid in five or more installments. The act also regulates common real estate transactions in the same way. The purpose of the act is to enable the consumer to do informed comparison shopping of credit terms. Before the passage of this act, many creditors did not disclose interest rates, finance charges, or other charges. Creditors who disclosed the rates did so in a variety of ways and the consumer had no measure for comparison. Under the Truth in Lending Act, creditors must disclose information about interest rates and other finance charges in a highly regulated and uniform manner. A knowing and willful violation of the disclosure requirements of the Truth in Lending Act may result in a criminal penalty of not more than five thousand dollars or imprisonment for not more than one year, or both. However, the most effective and most commonly used method of enforcing this act is through private suit. Violation of a disclosure requirement by a creditor results in a fine of one hundred dollars to one thousand dollars. This fine is in addition to attorney's fees and actual damages suffered by the individual consumer.

Because of the length and complexity of the Truth in Lending Act, the Truth in Lending Simplification and Reform Act was signed into law in 1980, effective in 1982. Extensions of credit primarily for agricultural purposes are now exempt from the Truth in Lending Act. Further, requirements for disclosure by creditors were simplified.

The Fair Credit Reporting Act of 1970, Title VI of the CCPA, is designed to ensure that consumers are treated fairly by credit-reporting agencies. Prior to its enactment, agencies that investigated individuals in order to provide companies with credit, insurance, employment, or other consumer reports were subject to few restraints. Individuals not only had no right to know the contents of the report, but businesses had no duty to disclose the fact that a report even existed. Hence many individuals were denied credit, employment, or other benefits without knowing that an investigation had been made. These reports also contained few guarantees of accuracy. Consumers now have the right to know the contents of any adverse report used by a business, and the name of the agency that compiled the report. Consumers may also correct the report or include their own explanation of facts contained in the report. Investigating agencies must follow "reasonable procedures" in compiling the report.

A consumer may recover actual damages from a business that violates this act and punitive damages where violations are willful. Criminal sanctions may be imposed by the appropriate federal agency against those who knowingly and willfully obtain information under false pretenses.

The Equal Credit Opportunity Act (ECOA) of 1974 is designed to eradicate discrimination in the granting of credit when the decision to grant it or refuse it is based on an individual's sex, marital status, race, color, age, religion, national origin, or receipt of public assistance. The major effect of this act has been to eliminate sex discrimination. Under the ECOA, a married woman can now obtain credit in her own name. A prospective creditor may not ask about an individual's marital status, childbearing plans, spouse or former spouse, or other similar criteria. Questions regarding alimony and child support are proper only if the applicant will rely on those sums to repay the obligation.

Because the ECOA is modeled after the Equal Employment Opportunity Act, it appears that facially neutral practices that have the effect of discriminating against a protected class are also prohibited.

The ECOA requires creditors to notify consumers of any decision about the extension or denial of credit, along with the creditor's reasons or a statement indicating that the individual is entitled to know the reasons. An individual may bring suit against a creditor for noncompliance with the ECOA to recover actual and punitive damages up to ten thousand dollars.

Environmental Protection Agency

The Environmental Protection Agency (EPA) was created by Congress in 1970 to replace the fifteen federal agencies that previously were responsible for enforcing the laws regulating environmental pollution. The EPA is charged with controlling water, air, noise, and radiation pollution; solid and hazardous waste treatment, storage, and disposal; and pesticides and toxic substances.

History of Pollution Control

Prior to the late 1960s, controlling pollution was a matter primarily governed by state legislation and the law of torts. Among the earliest examples of federal legislation is the Rivers and Harbors Act of 1886.[5] Although clean water legislation was enacted at the state level in the 1930s and 1940s,[6] Congress waited until the late 1940s to enact the Federal Insecticide, Fungicide, and Rodenticide Act (1947) and the Federal Water Pollution Control Act (1948). Although common law tort actions could be based on nuisance, trespass, negligence, and more recently, strict liability, common law remedies were inadequate to protect the public, because what was deemed tortious was decided by judges on a case-by-case basis in response to particular factual conditions.

In 1969, Congress recognized that the pollution problem was too large and complex to be adequately addressed by the states and enacted the National Environmental Policy Act (NEPA). NEPA, which took effect on January 1, 1979, required federal agencies to develop environmental impact statements (EIS) whenever their actions were likely to have significant consequences for the environment. In the 1970s Congress became very active in pollution control by amending previously existing legislation and by enacting new laws. Although political gridlock prevented most environmental legislation during the 1980s,[7] the passage of the Clean Air Act of 1990 was a major legislative attempt to protect the public health. A brief summary follows of some of the most important environmental statutes concerning air pollution, water pollution, pesticide control, and hazardous wastes control.

Air Pollution

The Clean Air Act of 1990 was intended to substantially reduce acid rain, urban smog, air pollution, and automobile exhaust emissions and to phase out the use of chemicals that harm the ozone layer. Air pollution was making people ill and contributing to an estimated 120,000 deaths per year,[8] as well as injuring crops, animals, wilderness areas, and historic buildings and monuments.[9] It required the EPA to develop detailed regulations that would make industrial plants reduce the amount of harmful toxins emitted into the air to the lowest achievable level given the limitations of existing technology. This legislation also introduced the use of market-based incentives to induce utility companies to reduce their sulfur dioxide emission allowances. A power plant that operates with clean fuel or purchases new technology accumulates unused sulfur dioxide allowances which can then be sold to other utilities that have exceeded their own allowances.[10] This "environmental dividend" can provide new capital to help companies pay for their investments in technology. The total amount of emissions permitted under the law in the year 2000 is over 1 million tons less than what was allowed in 1990. There is evidence that air quality in the United States has improved since 1975.[11]

Currently, local and state governments are being required to become active partners with the EPA in the control of air pollution. One example is the agency's insistence that states with severe pollution problems develop plans that have incentives to encourage car-pooling and public transportation.[12] Enormous controversy has surrounded the EPA's rule-making efforts based on economic and legal considerations.[13] The controversies have produced uncertainty, confusion, resistance, and delay in implementation.

Water Pollution

In 1972 Congress overrode President Nixon's veto and enacted the Clean Water Act.[14] Its goals included restoring water quality, so that it supports fish and wildlife and recreational uses, and eliminating the discharge of pollutants.[15] The act applies to publicly owned treatment works as well as private enterprises. When toxic chemicals, many originating from landfills and underground storage tanks, were found to have contaminated the drinking water, Congress responded by enacting the Safe Drinking Water Act in 1974. Pursuant to these acts, the EPA developed technical policies and effluent regulations for each industry.[16] These policies and regulations are enforced with a permit system. One of the conditions of obtaining a permit is that the EPA has the right to enter the premises of the discharger to inspect records and monitor compliance with federal law and EPA regulations. In 1987 Congress overrode President Reagan's veto and enacted a new Clean Water Act. Although this act required states to establish standards for removing harmful pollutants from fresh water by 1990, only thirty-five states had complied as of the end of 1991.[17]

The following case involves an alleged discharger who was accused of failing to obtain a required permit. Note that the EPA has power to take immediate administrative action without being subject to judicial review.

Southern Pines Associates v. United States
912 F.2d 713
U.S. Court of Appeals, Fourth Circuit
August 30, 1990

Ervin, Chief Judge

Southern Pines Associates ("Southern Pines") and VICO Construction Inc. ("VICO") appeal a district court order dismissing their complaint and petition for a temporary restraining order for lack of jurisdiction. For the reasons stated below, we affirm the district court order.

I

Southern Pines is a Virginia limited partnership which owns 293.41 acres of land located in Chesapeake, Virginia. VICO has a contract with Southern Pines and has been involved in clearing and building upon 40 acres of the property.

On May 23, 1989, the Environmental Protection Agency ("EPA") issued a" Findings of Violation and Order for Compliance" to Southern Pines, informing the company that it had violated section 301(a) of the Clean Water Act ("CWA" or the "Act"), 33 U.S.C. §§ 1251 *et seq.*, by discharging fill material into wetlands without a permit. The order instructed Southern Pines to (1) "cease and desist all filling activities in the wetlands" at the site; (2) "[c]ontact EPA within 5 working days" to discuss restoration of the areas; (3) implement a plan for restoration after

EPA approval; and (4) submit written notice of intent to comply with the order. In a cover letter accompanying the order, EPA asked Southern Pines to provide information about the site for it to review in order to make a "final determination of the boundaries of the wetlands that fall under the jurisdiction of the Clean Water Act."

Upon receiving EPA's order, Southern Pines and VICO discontinued all work except logging which does not require a permit. Southern Pines contacted EPA and scheduled a meeting in an effort to resolve the matter. However, the company later canceled the meeting and denied EPA access to the site.

On July 19, 1989, Southern Pines and VICO filed a complaint and a petition for a temporary restraining order. . . . They alleged that EPA's assertion of jurisdiction over the property created an actual controversy within the meaning of the Declaratory Judgment Act and argued that EPA lacks jurisdiction over the site because the wetlands on the property are not adjacent to any body of water.[1] The district court dismissed the case for lack of subject matter jurisdiction.

II

Southern Pines and VICO are asking this court (as they did the district court) to make a threshold determination of whether EPA has jurisdiction over the property. They argue that jurisdiction is proper under *Abbott Laboratories v. Gard-*

---

[1] The Act does not require Southern Pines to obtain a permit unless it is discharging fill materials into navigable waters. Navigable waters are "waters of the United States including the territorial seas." Waters of the United States include "wetlands adjacent to waters (other than waters that are themselves wetlands). . . ." 40 C.F.R. § 230.3(s)(7) (1988).

ner, . . . a case in which drug manufacturers challenged regulations promulgated by the Commissioner of Food and Drugs.

The Supreme Court held that judicial review was proper in *Abbott* because the Federal Food, Drug, and Cosmetic Act, . . . did not preclude review, and because the controversy was ripe for judicial resolution. However, the first question addressed by the Supreme Court in *Abbott* was whether "Congress by the Federal Food, Drug, and Cosmetic Act intended to forbid pre-enforcement review" of the regulation at issue in that case. The Court found that the statutory scheme did not preclude the action. The case before us today is distinguishable from Abbott because the statutory structure and history of the CWA provides clear and convincing evidence that Congress intended to exclude this type of action. . . . The language, structure, objectives, and history of the CWA, persuade us that Congress intended to preclude judicial review.

The objective of the CWA is "to restore and maintain the chemical, physical, and biological integrity of the Nation's waters." 33 U.S.C. § 1251. To achieve this goal, the Act prohibits any discharge of dredge or fill materials into waters of the United States unless authorized by a permit issued by the Corps of Engineers pursuant to section 404 of the Act. . . . Congress provided EPA with a choice of procedures for enforcing the Act. Section 309(a)(3) of the Act provides that when, on the basis of available information, the Administrator of EPA identifies a person in violation of the Act, the Administrator shall "either issue an order requiring such person to comply with [the Act], or he shall bring a civil action in accordance with subsection (b) of this section." . . . In 1987, Congress added section 309(g) to the Act which provides that EPA may also assess administrative penalties against those who violate the Act or a permit issued under the Act. . . . When EPA proceeds under section 309(g), the violator is entitled to a hearing before the agency, and the public is provided with an opportunity to comment. . . . Orders assessing administrative penalties are subject to judicial review. . . .

In this case, EPA issued a compliance order. A compliance order is a document served on the violator, setting forth the nature of the violation and specifying a time for compliance with the Act. . . . If a violator fails to abide by that order, EPA may seek to enforce the order by bringing a suit in federal district court under section 309(b) of the Act. . . . However, EPA need not issue a compliance order before bringing an action. The penalties for violating either the Act or a compliance order are the same. The court may issue an injunction to require compliance, and it may impose civil penalties of up to $25,000 per day for each violation of the Act, a permit, or a compliance order. . . . The violator is subject to the same injunction and penalties whether or not EPA has issued a compliance order.

The CWA is not the only environmental statute which allows EPA to issue pre-enforcement administrative orders. Both the Clean Air Act ("CAA"), . . . and the Comprehensive Environmental Response, Compensation, and Liability Act (CERCLA), . . . also provide for pre-enforcement agency action. The CAA, like the CWA, provides that EPA may issue a compliance order before bringing suit. Based upon the legislative history of the CAA, courts have found that Congress intended to preclude judicial review of compliance orders issued under the CAA. . . .

CERCLA allows the EPA to order that a site be cleaned up prior to bringing suit. . . . Prior to 1986 courts held that pre-enforcement remedial actions taken by the EPA under CERCLA were not subject to judicial review because litigation would interfere with CERCLA's policy of prompt agency response. . . . In 1986 Congress added a provision to CERCLA which specifically precludes federal jurisdiction over pre-enforcement remedial action. . . .

The structure of these environmental statutes indicates that Congress intended to allow EPA to act to address environmental problems quickly and without becoming immediately entangled in litigation. The CWA is not only similar in structure to the CAA and CERCLA, but its enforcement provisions were modeled after the enforcement provisions of the CAA. . . .

. . . Considering this legislative history, the structure of these statutes, the objectives of the CWA, and the nature of the administrative action involved, we are persuaded that Congress meant to preclude judicial review of compliance orders under the CWA just as it meant to preclude pre-enforcement review under the CAA and CERCLA.

III

Southern Pines and VICO argue that this case does not involve pre-enforcement review because the compliance order is an "enforcement procedure." . . .

Southern Pines' action seeks pre-enforcement review because EPA has not yet sought penalties for any violation of the Act or its order. . . . Allowing the parties to challenge the existence of EPA's jurisdiction would delay the agency's response in the same manner as litigation contesting the extent of EPA's jurisdiction. Southern Pines and VICO can contest the existence of EPA's jurisdiction if and when EPA seeks to enforce the penalties provided by the Act.

IV

Southern Pines and VICO argue that they have been denied due process, that under the fifth amendment, they are entitled to notice and an opportunity to be heard prior to the issuance of a compliance order. Contrary to their claim, appellants' fifth amendment rights are not violated because they are not subject to an injunction or penalties until EPA pursues an enforcement proceeding. Southern Pines and VICO will have an opportunity to make their constitutional arguments at any enforcement proceeding before they are subjected to any injunction or penalty.

V

Because we find that Congress intended to preclude, prior to enforcement action or imposition of penalties, judicial review of compliance orders issued under the Clean Water Act, we affirm the district court order dismissing this action.

Affirmed.

Case Questions

1. Why did Southern Pines Associates file suit against the Environmental Protection Agency?
2. Why did the district and appeals courts dismiss the plaintiff's complaint?

Pesticide Control

Congress enacted the Federal Insecticide, Fungicide, and Rodenticide Act (FIFRA) in 1947. This act was amended in 1972 and 1978 by the Federal Environmental Pesticide Control Act. These statutes provide that a pesticide cannot be distributed through interstate commerce unless its container displays cautionary warnings and the product has been registered with the EPA.[18] These acts also require pesticide manufacturers to undertake studies that demonstrate the effect their products have on humans.[19] The EPA is authorized to restrict public access to any product that is hazardous to humans. It may, for instance, require that certain products only be applied by certified applicators.[20] The EPA can also cancel registrations if a pesticide is found to unreasonably harm the environment. Civil and criminal fines and criminal jail sentences can be imposed on people who knowingly violate these acts.

Hazardous Wastes Disposal

The Resource Conservation and Recovery Act of 1976 (RCRA) was enacted to replace the Solid Wastes Disposal Act of 1965. Prior to RCRA, many producers of hazardous waste merely dumped their contaminated matter on their own property and in landfills. Despite the production of millions of tons of hazardous waste, the government could not determine what waste was being disposed, where it was disposed, and whether it was being disposed of properly. Under RCRA, dischargers are required to maintain detailed records regarding waste disposal. This information is vital to prevent the recurrence of situations such as Love Canal in New York.[21]

The act also requires operators of active hazardous waste disposal sites to operate their facilities in compliance with EPA regulations. EPA promulgates standards that regulate the generation, transportation, and disposal of hazardous wastes.[22] These standards require labeling, record maintenance, the use of environmentally appropriate receptacles, and reporting procedures.[23] The EPA relies on a permit system to track hazardous waste from its point of origin to its final destination. RCRA was amended in 1984 to regulate small quantities of hazardous waste and to prevent the land disposal of heavy metals such as lead, mercury, and nickel in amounts above EPA-approved concentrations.[24]

Although RCRA addressed active hazardous waste disposal sites, it did not confront the problem of inactive sites containing abandoned hazardous wastes.[25] Congress responded to this problem in 1980 when it enacted the Comprehensive Environmental Response, Compensation and Liability Act (CERCLA), also known as the Superfund law. This law, as amended, provides funds to be used by the EPA to clean up abandoned hazardous waste sites and spills. Amendments made to CERCLA in 1986 required users of hazardous wastes to report releases of regulated harmful substances into the environment, and they provided the public with a legally protected right to know the type and amount of toxic chemicals that are present in local communities.[26]

Enforcement of Environmental Laws

Those who violate the Clean Air Act, Clean Water Act, and RCRA are subject to administrative fines, civil fines, or criminal fines and imprisonment. Congress has also provided individual citizens with the right to sue, thereby creating pressure on business and the EPA to aggressively enforce the law.[27]

Chapter Questions

1. Define the following terms:

adjudication	hearing
Administrative Procedure Act	license
burden of proof	notice
delegate	record
discretion	ripe
exhaustion of administrative remedies	rule-making power
Federal Register	separation of powers
final decision	

2. Community antenna television (CATV) systems receive television broadcast signals, amplify them, and transmit them by wire to their subscribers' receivers. CATV did not exist when the Communications Act of 1934 was enacted. In the early stages of CATV development, the Federal Communications Commission, which derives its authority to regulate broadcasting from the Communications Act, took the position that it had no power to regulate CATV. The provisions of the act are explicitly applicable to "all interstate and foreign communications by wire or radio. . . ." The commission is required to endeavor to "make available to all the people of the United States a rapid, efficient, nationwide, and worldwide wire and radio communication service. . . ." In 1959 and 1966, the commission sought legislation from the Congress that would have explicitly authorized it to regulate CATV. Congress refused, stating that the question of whether or not the FCC had the authority to regulate CATV under the present law was for the courts to decide. Meanwhile, the CATV industry was growing rapidly. In 1960, the FCC gradually began to assert its authority to regulate, eventually issuing detailed rules. Pursuant to these rules, it issued an order restricting expansion of a particular CATV service. The U.S. Court of Appeals held that FCC lacked authority under the Communications Act of 1934 to issue such an order. Was the Court of Appeals correct? Why or why not?

   United States v. Southwestern Cable Co., 392 U.S. 157 (1968)

3. New York's Aid to Families with Dependent Children (AFDC) program, stressing "close contact" with beneficiaries, requires home visits by caseworkers as a condition for assistance "in order that any treatment or service tending to restore [beneficiaries] to a condition of self-support and to relieve their distress may be rendered and . . . that assistance or care may be given only in such amount and as long as necessary." Visitation with a beneficiary, who is the primary source of information to welfare authorities about eligibility for assistance, is not permitted outside working hours, and forcible entry and snooping are prohibited. The appellee was a beneficiary under the AFDC program. Although she had received several days' advance notice, she refused to permit a caseworker to visit her home. Following a hearing and advice that assistance would consequently be terminated, she brought suit for injunctive and declaratory relief, contending that home visitation is a search and, when not consented to or supported by a warrant based on probable cause, would violate her Fourth and Fourteenth amendment rights. The district upheld the appellee's constitutional claim. Was the district court correct? Why or why not?

   Wyman v. James, 400 U.S. 309 (1971)

4. Columbia East, Inc., the owner of 34.3 acres of farm land, wanted the zoning changed in order to develop a mobile home park. The board of zoning appeals granted a preliminary approval of the application for a special exception to develop a mobile home park in the area zoned as

agricultural. Final approval by the board of zoning appeals could only be granted after the plans and specifications for the development of the proposed trailer court had been completed and approved by the appropriate agencies. Neighboring landowners filed a suit in court challenging the board's preliminary approval, claiming the decision was made without adequate provision for sewage treatment. What should the court decide?

Downing v. Board of Zoning Appeals, 274 N.E.2d 542 (Ind. 1971)

5. The Occupational Safety and Health Act empowers agents of the Secretary of Labor to search the work area of any employment facility within the act's jurisdiction. No search warrant or other process is expressly required under the act. An OSHA inspector entered the customer service area of Barlow's, Inc., an electrical and plumbing installation business, and stated that he wished to conduct a search of the working areas of the business. Barlow, the president and general manager, asked the inspector whether he had received any complaints about the working conditions and whether he had a search warrant. The inspector answered both questions in the negative. The inspector was denied entry into the working areas. Marshall, Secretary of Labor, argued that warrantless inspections to enforce OSHA regulations are reasonable within the meaning of the Fourth Amendment, and relied on the act, which authorizes inspection of business premises without a warrant. Should the court accept Marshall's argument?

Marshall v. Barlow's, Inc., 436 U.S. 307 (1978)

6. The city of Denver was authorized by its charter to make local improvements and to assess the cost on the property specifically benefited. However, there first had to be notice by publication, and any interested person's comments were required to be heard. Then the city council had to approve. After completion of a project, the total cost of the improvement had to be published, and the share of the cost for each piece of land determined. Objections had to be heard by the city council before it could pass an ordinance assessing the cost of the improvement. Following this procedure, an improvement was made. The complainants filed objections, challenging the creation of the assessment district, the method of carrying out the improvement, and the final assessments against each piece of property. However, the city council adopted a resolution that "no complaint or objection had been filed or made against the apportionment of said assessment . . . but the complaints and objections filed deny wholly the right of the city to assess any district or portion of the assessable property of the city of Denver." Therefore, the council enacted an ordinance approving the proposed assessments. Was there a violation of complainants' rights of due process of law? Why or why not?

Londoner v. Denver, 210 U.S. 373 (1908)

7. The owner of some real estate in Denver brought a suit to enjoin the State Board of Equalization, the Colorado Tax Commission, and the assessor of Denver from effecting a 40 percent increase in the state tax valuation of all

taxable property in Denver. The plaintiff claimed that he had been given no opportunity to be heard, and that his property would therefore be taken without due process of law, contrary to the Fourteenth Amendment of the Constitution. The Supreme Court of Colorado sustained the order of the board and directed the suit to be dismissed. Compare the tax proposal with the subject matter of the procedure in Question 6. What are the differences? Was the Colorado Supreme Court correct?

Bi-Metallic Investment Co. v. State Board of Equalization, 239 U.S. 441 (1915)

8. Under the U.S. Community Health Centers Act, the Secretary of the Department of Health, Education, and Welfare was empowered to award monetary grants to health centers that complied with federal regulations. Temple University received funds under the act and was therefore required to meet the federal regulations. In addition, the Pennsylvania Department of Public Welfare and the County Mental Health and Retardation Board were charged with the responsibility of administering county health programs. In 1970, the Temple University Mental Health Center was required to cut back services and impose strict security measures because of campus riots. Members of the surrounding community brought suit against Temple University, charging that the center was not providing required services and that members of the community were deprived of access to the facility. What should the court's decision be?

North Philadelphia Community Board v. Temple University, 330 F.Supp. 1107 (1971)

9. In proceedings arising out of alleged violations of the price discrimination provisions of the Clayton Act, as amended by the Robinson-Patman Act, two courts of appeals reached opposite conclusions. The issue was whether it is within the authority of a court of appeals to postpone the operation of a valid cease-and-desist order of the Federal Trade Commission against a single firm until similar orders have been entered against that firm's competitors. The Eighth Circuit affirmed the commission's order against Moog Industries. Moog had moved to hold the entry of judgment in abeyance, on the ground that it would suffer serious financial loss if prohibited from engaging in pricing practices open to its competitors. In another case, C. E. Niehoff & Co. had requested the commission to hold the order in abeyance on the ground that it would have to go out of business if compelled to sell at a uniform price while its competitors were not under a similar restraint; the commission had denied this request. On review, the Seventh Circuit directed that the cease-and-desist order should take effect "at such time as the U.S. Court of Appeals for the Seventh Circuit may direct, *sua sponte*, or on motion of the Federal Trade Commission." What is involved in determining and correcting price discriminations? Is this an area requiring special agency expertise? Which court of appeals was correct?

Moog Industries, Inc. v. FTC, 355 U.S. 411 (1958)

10. A contractor, engaged in construction work for the Navy on the Island of Guam, maintained a recreation center for its employees. The center adjoined a channel that was so dangerous that swimming was forbidden, and signs to that effect were erected. One afternoon, an employee was drowned when he attempted to swim the channel in order to rescue two men in distress. Under the Longshoremen's and Harbor Worker's Compensation Act, extended to this employee by the Defense Bases Act, the deputy commissioner found as a "fact" that the employee's death arose out of, and was in the course of, his employment, and awarded a death benefit to his mother. A petition by the contractor to set aside the award was denied by the district court on the ground that "there is substantial evidence . . . to sustain the compensation order." On appeal, the court of appeals reversed, concluding: "The lethal currents were not a part of the recreational facilities supplied by the employer, and the swimming in them for the rescue of the unknown men was not recreation. It was an act entirely disconnected from any use for which the recreational camp was provided and not in the course of employment." Which court was correct? Why?

O'Leary v. Brown-Pacific-Maxon, Inc., 340 U.S. 504 (1951)

Notes

1. *Federal Regulatory Directory* (Washington, D.C.: Congressional Quarterly, Inc., 1990), p. 621.

2. Ibid., p. 687.

3. Ibid., p. 2.

4. Ibid., p. 3.

5. K.M. Mackenthun and J.I. Bregman, *Environmental Regulations Handbook* (Boca Raton: Lewis Publishers, 1991), p. 2.

6. Ibid.

7. G. Bryner, *Blue Skies, Green Politics: The Clean Air Act of 1990* (Washington, D.C.: 1993), pp. 90–93.

8. M. Freedman and B. Jaggi, *Air and Water Pollution Regulation* (Westport, CT: Quorum Books, 1993), p. 17.

9. Bryner, p. 6.

10. Freedman, p. 6.

11. Ibid., p. 16.

12. J.W. Waks and C.R. Brewster, *Clean Air Requires Commuting Options*, The National Law Journal 4, 18 (October 1993).

13. R.S. Frye and L.S. Ritts, *State Clean Air Act Programs Undefined*, The National Law Journal 21, 28 (June 1993).

14. Mackenthun, p. 9; Freedman, p. 21.

15. Mackenthun, p. 12.

16. Freedman, pp. 21–22.

17. Ibid.

18. Mackenthun, p. 17.

19. Ibid.

20. Ibid., p. 18.

21. Love Canal refers to an environmental and social tragedy that occurred during the late 1970s in a residential neighborhood in Niagara Falls, New York. The Love Canal neighborhood had been constructed on land that was heavily contaminated by toxic chemicals in the early 1950s. The chemical migrated below the surface of the land and allegedly caused community residents to suffer illnesses and even genetic damage. Over seven hundred families had to be moved from their homes and relocated at government expense because their properties had become unmarketable.

22. S.J. Buck, *Understanding Environmental Administration and Law* (Washington, D.C.: Island Press, 1991), p. 106.

23. Mackenthun, pp. 21–22.

24. Ibid., pp. 22, 175–176.

25. Ibid., p. 23.

26. Ibid., p. 24.

27. Ibid., pp. 217–228.

XIII

Employment and Discrimination

Employment is essential to a person's economic well-being, but it is also much more than that. Today, many employed people receive group health insurance, pensions, life insurance, and other economic fringe benefits that are often prohibitively expensive for an unemployed individual. Also of great importance is the status that comes from being employed. Employed people can provide for themselves and their families and can contribute to the well-being of their communities through the payment of taxes. For these reasons individuals and society as a whole have long valued employment, and the law has regulated the employment relationship since the Middle Ages.

THE CONCEPT OF EQUALITY

Equality is conceptually elusive because it has so many meanings, and it is emotionally charged because it purports to measure human worth. People often think that equality is synonymous with justice, but that isn't always the case. From another perspective, inequality and discrimination can be viewed as being not only good, but essential to achieving justice.[1] Because equality is such a powerful, emotion laden, and multifaceted concept, it is important to briefly consider some of its meanings as they relate to discrimination in the workplace.

People often question whether their employers are treating them fairly. Someone claiming to be a victim of discrimination will often explain in detail how one or more coworkers with equivalent qualifications received more favorable treatment than the complainant from their common employer. But to what degree preferential treatment, although perhaps discriminatory, is invidious, depends on what equality means in the workplace setting.[2]

Equality in the workplace, for example, might refer to an employee's right to advance in his or her field and to receive remuneration solely on the basis of the person's abilities, knowledge, and talents. Such a definition would refer to an equality of opportunity.[3]

Equality, however, might have a different meaning, such as where discrimination is advocated so that specified targeted results are achieved (equality of results). Equalizing results might be used to justify employment preferences based on such factors as gender, race, and status (a veteran or a person with a physical disability), rather than ability and achievement.[4] A third way to view equality might involve ignoring each person's individual attributes and focusing instead on the wants and needs that are common to all human beings. This form of equality is called the equality of consideration.[5] Equality, from this perspective, would prohibit consideration of an individual's sexual persuasion as a factor in employment decision making.

As you read the following discussion of American employment law, look for examples of arguments and decisions that reflect differing approaches to equality.

HISTORY OF EMPLOYMENT REGULATION

Beginning with an implied covenant in the Statute of Laborers (1562), the English common law prevented masters from discharging their servants except for just cause.[6] The courts presumed that employees were hired for one year unless an employment contract specified a longer term.[7] Until the end of the nineteenth century, American courts followed this rule.[8] The advent of the industrial revolution, however, brought about the demise of the face-to-face, personal relationship between masters and servants.[9] The rise of industry and the use of factories and power-driven machinery resulted in more impersonal relations between employers and employees. Commerce was king during this era, and freedom of contract and laissez-faire economic beliefs were widely held. America was very pro-business.[10]

The courts responded to the new economic order by replacing the English common law rules with the employment-at-will doctrine. This doctrine, which was originally stated in an 1877 legal treatise, permitted employers, in the absence of contractual obligations to the contrary, to fire employees "at will."[11] Employers could be discharged for good cause, bad cause, or no cause. Further, at the turn of the century, the U.S. Supreme Court interpreted the Constitution's due process clauses as protecting the freedom of contract from progressive legislation intended to benefit employees at the expense of employers (see Chapter 1). For example, the federal Erdman Act of 1898 prohibited the railroads from discharging employees for joining a labor union. When the railroads challenged this statute in the 1908 case of *Adair v. United States*,[12] the U.S. Supreme Court declared the statute unconstitutional and ruled that the interstate commerce clause did not give Congress the right to regulate labor relations in the railroad industry. The Court also ruled that the Fifth

Amendment's due process clause permitted the railroad to operate with a non-union work force.

Similarly, in the 1915 case of *Coppage v. Kansas*,[13] the Supreme Court reviewed a Kansas statute that prevented employers from requiring employees to contract not to join a labor union while in their employ. (This type of "agreement" was called a "Yellow Dog" contract.) The Court ruled that the statute violated the Fourteenth Amendment's due process clause. Justice Pitney wrote for the Court: "The Act . . . is intended to deprive employers of a part of their liberty of contract, to the corresponding advantage of the employed and the upbuilding of labor organizations." The Court's constitutionally based prohibition against legislation interfering with an employer's freedom of contract continued until 1937.

In 1935, Congress enacted the Wagner Act, a statute that guaranteed employees the right to join unions and collectively bargain with their employers regarding the terms of their employment. The constitutionality of this legislation was upheld by the Supreme Court in the 1937 case *National Labor Relations Board v. Jones & Laughlin Steel Corporation*.[14] In that case, the Supreme Court interpreted the Constitution's commerce clause to permit federal protection of eight steel company employees. The employees were members of the Amalgamated Association of Iron Workers, and their employer was attempting to discharge them because of their union activities. After *NLRB v. Jones & Laughlin*, the constitutional barrier against legislation favoring employees was removed and progressive legislation was enacted at the federal and state levels. These initiatives included statutes establishing minimum wages, maximum weekly work hours, and mandating extra compensation for overtime work. In addition, after 1937 the employer's right to discharge union members could be limited through job security clauses in collective bargaining agreements.

State Judicial Remedies

Although federal law addresses matters such as invidious discrimination, collective bargaining, occupational health and safety, and anti-reprisal statutes, the state also plays an important role in employment protection. For example, before the 1970s some at-will employees were fired because their employers wanted to deny them earned bonuses and commissions. These employees were unable to obtain significant common law remedies from the courts. However, state courts began responding to these abuses, most frequently by expanding the right of a wrongfully discharged employee to sue for breach of contract.[15] During the 1970s, courts began ruling that written employment contracts contained an implied covenant of good faith and fair dealing so that discharged at-will employees could recover for terminations that were intended to deprive them of earned bonuses or commissions. The contractual remedy, however, permits recovery only for money earned at the time of the discharge. There is usually no recovery for loss of fringe benefits or future compensation.[16]

Increasingly, at-will employees have asked courts to expand an employee's rights to sue in tort, particularly when employers discharge employees without good cause. Although the state courts have generally been unsympathetic to such requests, they have allowed wrongfully discharged employees to recover in tort on related theories such as the infliction of emotional distress, tortious interference with employment, and unlawful interference with an advantageous relationship.[17] Many state courts also have recognized a tort when a discharge occurs under circumstances that offend public policy. Each state decides for itself what constitutes a violation of public policy. Typically, a violation would exist where employees were discharged for (1) filing worker's compensation claims, (2) disobeying an employer and reporting for jury duty, or (3) violating consumer protection laws or regulatory statutes.[18]

State Wrongful Termination Legislation

State laws vary considerably in the protection provided to wrongfully discharged employees. Some states have severely curtailed the employment-at-will doctrine through a combination of statutes and case law. In Montana, for example, the Wrongful Discharge from Employment Act provides a statutory remedy for at-will employees who are not covered by collective bargaining agreements. An at-will employee who has satisfactorily completed the employer's probationary period can recover wages and fringe benefits for up to four years after the discharge date. Most states, however, do little to promote a good cause discharge rule.

TITLE VII OF THE CIVIL RIGHTS ACT OF 1964

In the 1940s and 1950s the federal government had moved by executive order against racial discrimination in governmental employment and against racial discrimination by companies that did business with the federal government. The Supreme Court also acted to prohibit some forms of racial discrimination by labor unions. However, it was the civil rights movement of the 1950s and 1960s that promoted the most important step against discrimination taken by Congress, the enactment of the 1964 Civil Rights Act.

This statute was the first comprehensive civil rights legislation passed since the 1870s. Title VII of the act addresses discrimination in employment and applies to both public and private sector employers of fifteen or more persons, employment agencies, and labor unions. This law recognizes race, religion, color, sex, and national origin as "protected classes." These protected classes are not equally broad in scope, however. An employer may not justify discrimination based on race or color for any reason. An employer may, in some circumstances, discriminate for or against someone because of that person's national origin, sex, or religion. The law permits some forms of discrimination if the particular protected class is a bona fide occupational qualification

(BFOQ) for the job. For example, ministers for Lutheran churches may be required to be Lutheran and a theater production might require a man rather than a woman for a particular role.

When Congress created Title VII, it clearly expressed its primary legislative purpose: to "open employment opportunities for Negroes in occupations that traditionally have been closed to them." Early decisions took the position that Asians, Hispanics, African-Americans, and Native Americans were the protected classes and several court decisions prior to 1976 held that the act did not protect whites. In 1976 the U.S. Supreme Court ruled that whites were also protected.[19]

Title VII Discrimination Theories

To be entitled to recover in a Title VII case, the aggrieved person must establish a *prima facie* case of discrimination. Some employers intend to discriminate against an employee or prospective employee. For example, in the past, many companies would only employ blacks and women in lower-skilled and lower-paying jobs. Similarly, women were denied certain jobs thought not to be "ladylike." This kind of discrimination is called *disparate treatment discrimination* and was outlawed by Title VII. A victim of disparate treatment discrimination must establish the following four factors to prevail at trial:

1. that he or she is included within a protected class;
2. that the employer was seeking applicants for employment or promotion, and the plaintiff was qualified for the job and submitted an application;
3. that the plaintiff, although qualified, was denied employment or promotion;
4. that the employer, after rejecting the applicant, continued to solicit applications from other people with similar qualifications as the plaintiff.

Subtler forms of discrimination also exist as when the employer's intention to discriminate is hidden behind an ostensibly neutral reason, such as a seniority system. Although following seniority is usually a lawful employment practice, an employer will not always be successful with this defense. The courts will reject it if the seniority system effectively perpetuates past discrimination against members of a protected class.

Sometimes an employer lacks discriminatory intent, even though the company's employment practices unnecessarily discriminate in fact. This is called *disparate impact discrimination*, because only the impact of an employer's discriminatory practices is examined. The employer's motives and intent are not at issue. To show disparate impact discrimination, the plaintiff must first identify specific policies or practices that are allegedly discriminatory. He or she must then prove that each has had a significantly disproportionate impact on employment opportunities. For example, a disparate impact victim will use statistical evidence to show that the racial make-up of the employer's work force does not reasonably match the relevant work force of the surrounding area.

Employer Defenses

At trial, after a plaintiff has established a *prima facie* case, an employer will generally present a defense to rebut the inference of discrimination. In a disparate impact case, an employer may defend by demonstrating that the policy or practice in question is *job related* or amounts to a *business necessity*. After the employer satisfies this burden, the plaintiff can only prevail by demonstrating the existence of some other reasonable, effective, and nondiscriminatory business alternative(s) to the challenged policy or practice.

An employer in a disparate treatment case can defend by producing a legitimate, nondiscriminatory reason for rejecting an employee. The employer may argue that an employee/complainant was rejected after the nondiscriminatory application of neutral policies, such as a seniority system or an ability test. If an employer relies on an ability test, it must be shown to be a reliable predictor of job performance. Employers also may use other explanations, such as the *bona fide occupational qualification* (BFOQ) defense; however, justifications based on stereotyped classifications of men and women are rarely considered valid. For example, several airlines tried to justify hiring only women for flight attendant positions by arguing (unsuccessfully) that women are better suited for the job.

Once the employer has produced evidence of a legitimate nondiscriminatory reason for the employee's rejection, the employee has the burden of demonstrating that the employer's reason is merely a pretext for discrimination. This will often require the plaintiff to show that the employer's true motivation was based on a prohibited ground, namely race, sex, color, etc.

The next case involves a disparate treatment issue and an unsuccessful attempt by an employer to rely on the BFOQ defense.

Sarni Original Dry Cleaners, Inc., v. Cooke

447 N.E.2d 1228
Supreme Judicial Court of Massachusetts
April 4, 1983

Hennessey, Chief Justice

On September 12, 1975, Ronnie Lee Cooke filed a complaint with the Massachusetts Commission Against Discrimination (commission) alleging that he had been terminated from his employment with Sarni Original Dry Cleaners, Inc., because of his race and color, in violation of G.L.c. 151B, § 4(1). A public hearing was held before a single member of the commission. The decision of the hearing Commissioner on October 25, 1978, found a violation of law on the part of Sarni Original Dry Cleaners, Inc., and ordered Sarni to reimburse Cooke for all lost wages since the termination, plus interest, minus all sums earned by Cooke since the termination. Sarni appealed to the full commission, which affirmed the decision of the hearing Commissioner on February 14, 1980.

Thereafter, Sarni filed a complaint in the Superior Court seeking reversal of the decision of the commission on matters of law. The matter was argued before a Superior Court judge on a motion for summary judgment filed jointly by the commission and Cooke. On May 6, 1982, the judge issued a memorandum of decision and order allowing the motion for summary judgment, and a judgment affirming the decision of the commission. Sarni appealed, and this court granted direct appellate review on the petition of the commission and Cooke. We affirm.

The facts as found by the hearing Commissioner are as follows. Sarni Original Dry Cleaners, Inc., is a Massachusetts corporation engaged in the dry cleaning business in Boston. Cooke, a black male, was employed by Sarni as a delivery truck driver from July to September, 1975. Sarni operated sixteen stores and three dry cleaning plants in the Boston area during the relevant period. As a normal part of his duties, Cooke made four deliveries a day to Sarni's store in South Boston. On one occasion early in September, 1975, during his third daily delivery to the South Boston store, a group of three or four youths, eight to ten years of age, threw rocks at the truck which Cooke was driving. There was no evidence that the truck or its contents were damaged, that the incident was racially motivated, or that the youths could see that the driver of the truck was black. The incident lasted only a few moments, did not interfere with Cooke's duties, did not injure him, and did not cause him to feel that he was in any danger.

Cooke reported the incident to Sarni upon returning to the plant. Cooke returned to the South Boston store once that afternoon, and four times each day for several days thereafter without further trouble. As a result of his personal observation during this period, Cooke believed that his job was in jeopardy. Three or four days after the incident, Cooke spoke to Sarni about switching routes with the driver of Sarni's other truck, or at least switching stores with the other driver. Cooke would then deliver to the Harbor Towers store instead of the South Boston

area. Sarni denied both requests without explanation. During this period, a white man named Mark regularly drove Sarni's second truck. Since Mark's attendance was sporadic, Rubin McRae, a black man, filled in for him on the second truck on those days when Mark was absent. When not driving the truck, McRae performed different tasks inside the plant.

At some point following the stone-throwing incident, Sarni discussed the incident with certain persons at a gasoline station in South Boston. An attendant there told Sarni that the incident had happened at the gasoline station, that the youths had attempted to tip the truck over, and that if Cooke came back there would be trouble. The actual incident took place more than a block away from the station. Sarni did not discuss the incident with Cooke. Approximately five days after the incident, Sarni offered Cooke one week's pay if he would resign. This offer was made after Sarni had denied Cooke's offer to switch either the routes or the stores on the routes. Cooke refused this offer and Sarni fired him. After Cooke's termination, a white man was hired to drive the route which included the South Boston store. Sarni admitted he would not have hired a black man to replace Cooke.

The Commissioner concluded that Cooke had established that he was the victim of overt racial discrimination by showing that a similarly-situated white driver would not have been fired.

In affirming the decision of the hearing Commissioner in all but one respect (the award for emotional distress), the full commission filed a twenty-four page decision in which it emphasized the importance of the case and described the issues as follows: ''[U]nder what circumstances, and according to what standard of review [may] an employer . . . restrict or deny the employment opportunities of a person of one race, because of perceived safety problems posed by anticipated racial attacks[?]" . . .

The burden of proof as to the unlawfulness of the challenged act or practice must be carried by the employee. . . . The employee is assigned the threshold burden of establishing a prima facie case, after which the burden of production shifts to the respondent to articulate a legitimate, nondiscriminatory reason for its action, and to "produce credible evidence to show that the reason or reasons advanced were the real reasons." . . .

Cooke has clearly established a prima facie case of racial discrimination. A member of a racial minority, he was qualified for, and worked successfully as, a delivery truck driver. He was discharged, and a white man was hired to drive his route. Sarni has, in fact, admitted that it would not have hired a black man to replace Cooke. The commission accepted Sarni's stated reasons (safety considerations) as real, and not a pretext. However, we disagree with Sarni's characterization of that reason as nondiscriminatory. Rather, we agree with the commission's conclusion and reasoning: "While [Sarni] argues that his reason was concern for the safety of the truck and driver, this safety concern was a general management objective, not a reason for the specific action in this case. In attempting to achieve that management objective, Sarni used a criterion for determining what type of driver was likely to be safe or unsafe. That criterion was the 'determinative cause,' . . . and was admittedly and exclusively racial. Unlike possible nondiscriminatory reasons (such as poor driving record, excessive absenteeism), Sarni's decisional criterion was facially improper. His reason was necessarily linked to [c]omplainant's race"; (footnote omitted). . . .

Sarni's argument, that it did not intend to discriminate, fails. It is true that the parties and the commission have treated this case as one of "disparate treatment," rather than "disparate impact," and in disparate treatment cases proof of discriminatory intent (motive) is critical. . . . Here, however, the commission has justifiably found that a prima facie case of overt discrimination has been established and no neutral reason has been offered, much less proved. . . . In such a case, intent is material only to show that the employer's actions were deliberate, rather than accidental.[5] In the instant case, it is shown that Sarni intentionally acted because of Cooke's race.

2. We turn now to the issue whether the commission was in error in deciding that Sarni had not established a defense of "bona fide occupational qualification" (BFOQ). Clearly such a defense is available to an employer charged with racial discrimination. General laws c. 151B § 4(1), inserted by St.1946, c. 368 § 4, states in relevant part: "It shall be an unlawful employment practice . . . because of the race, color, religious creed, national origin, age, sex, or ancestry of any individual, to refuse to hire or employ or to bar or to discharge . . . such individual . . . unless based upon a bona fide occupational qualification."

The commission opined, we think correctly, in its decision that the BFOQ exception is to be narrowly applied. . . . To qualify for this narrow exception an employer must show that "the essence of the business operation would be undermined by not hiring members of one [race]

---

[5] Nor, contrary to Sarni's argument, must it be proved in such a case that the employer acted with racial hostility or animosity. No such attitude on Sarni's part was established, or even alleged, in this case. Indeed, it was shown that Sarni employs a relatively high percentage of black persons.

exclusively" (emphasis omitted), *Diaz v. Pan American World Airways*, 442 F.2d 385. . . . The commission expressed doubt, but did not decide, whether external factors, such as the prejudices of third parties, could legitimize a BFOQ.[6] . . . We need not consider that issue, because we think the commission's conclusion that Sarni did not prove a BFOQ was warranted.

A BFOQ is an affirmative defense. The burden of proving the defense is on the employer. The standard is an objective one, and the subjective opinions of the employer, however sincere, are irrelevant if not shown, objectively, to be reasonable. In order to invoke the BFOQ successfully, the employer must show that it has "a *factual* basis for believing that all or substantially all [members of the excluded category] would be unable to perform safely and efficiently the duties of the job involved" (emphasis added). *Weeks v. Southern Bell Tel. & Tel. Co.*, 408 F.2d 228.

[6] The commission noted that commentators have used the example of the casting of actors for dramatic parts (e.g., a black actor to play Paul Robeson, or a white actor to play Robert E. Lee) to describe a valid BFOQ.

. . . This factual basis must be based upon objective evidence and not on "subjective doubts, which may themselves be based upon impermissible stereotypes." *Long v. Sapp*, 502 F.2d 34. . . .

As to the likelihood of damage to Sarni's property or personal injury to Cooke, Sarni failed in its burden. We think that the commission's analysis was fair and complete: "Apart from his own conclusory opinion, Sarni's only evidence on this issue was a hearsay conversation with some gasoline station employees who witnessed the incident from one block away. In contrast, as the [h]earing Commissioner found, there was no damage from the single incident, and the [c]omplainant drove the route four times a day for several days after the incident, without further trouble. We find that the [h]earing Commissioner's implicit adverse findings on this point [are] supported by substantial evidence. The record is clear that Sarni did not prove his defense."

We discern no error of law in the commission's decision, and we conclude that the decision is supported by substantial evidence.

Judgment affirmed.

Case Questions

1. What is the BFOQ defense?
2. What was Sarni's justification for firing Cooke?
3. What was the court's decision with respect to Sarni's defense?

Title VII Remedies

A victim of disparate impact discrimination is entitled to receive back pay (what he or she would have earned if hired or promoted at the appropriate time minus actual earnings) and attorney's fees. The employer also may be ordered to hire, reinstate, promote, or give advanced seniority to the victim. If an employer does not have any open positions to which the plaintiff can be hired, reinstated, or promoted at the time of the judgment, a court may also award "front pay" (the dollar value of the lost wages and benefits that the employee would be receiving if a position opening existed). Front pay is awarded until the victim fills the position.

A victim of disparate treatment discrimination is entitled to seek all of the above mentioned remedies and can additionally sue for compensatory and punitive damages. Prior to the Civil Rights Act of 1991, all Title VII cases were tried to the court because Congress did not provide any right to a jury trial. The 1991 act changed this policy at least with respect to disparate treatment (intentional discrimination) cases. Congress continued to deny plaintiffs in disparate impact cases access to a jury trial.

Although the act has not resulted in the eradication of all forms of discrimination, Title VII has enabled vast numbers of people to overturn discriminatory practices that had denied them equal opportunity in the work place.

Affirmative Action

In the context of employment, affirmative action involves the use of contracts, plans, goals, court orders, and consent agreements to expand the employment opportunities of minorities and women. Proponents argue that merely legislating equal opportunity for minorities and women will not undo the devastating economic and social consequences of the employment discrimination to which members of these groups have been historically subjected. Achieving a more balanced work force, they argue, requires the removal of artificial employment barriers such as racial and gender discrimination. It also requires that public and private employers be encouraged, and sometimes required, to take proactive steps to produce more equality of results.[20]

The term affirmative action was first used in a 1961 executive order issued by President John F. Kennedy. The order focused on encouraging federal contractors to promise that they would be more inclusive in their employment decisions and that they would not racially discriminate. President Lyndon Johnson went even further in 1965. He issued an executive order that required most contractors and subcontractors who do business with the federal government to develop affirmative action plans—complete with goals and timetables.[21] In 1972 Congress extended coverage to state and local governments.

Many employers have voluntarily established affirmative action programs. Reasons include support of affirmative action goals, the belief that such programs are good for business, or the desire to do business with the federal and state governments. Employers who voluntarily participate in affirmative action programs first undertake a study of their employees and their jobs to identify barriers to employment opportunities for women and minorities. If any substantial discrepancies are found, employers prepare affirmative action plans using goals and timetables. Employers must monitor their plans, collect and maintain records, and submit reports. Employers can satisfy affirmative action requirements by making sincere efforts to meet their goals and timetables.

Other employers develop affirmative action programs involuntarily. Title VII authorizes judges to "order such affirmative action as may be appropriate, which may include, but is not limited to, reinstatement or hiring of employees . . . or any other equitable relief as the court deems appropriate."[22] The use of court-ordered employment and promotional quotas is appropriate where intentional discrimination has been flagrant, egregious, and pervasive.[23] The U.S. Supreme Court currently permits the use of quotas only when they are intended to be temporary and when they are solely designed to remedy an employer's previous record of discrimination. It does not support the use of race-conscious quotas to maintain or achieve racial balance in employment. Frequently, employers enter into consent agreements and decrees requiring affirmative action in order to avoid or conclude Title VII litigation.

Affirmative action is controversial. Those favoring it maintain that although progress has been made over the last thirty years, it is premature to abolish the racial and gender preferences that have contributed so much to improving opportunities for minorities and women in our nation's work force.[24] Opponents argue that the law should be color-blind and gender-neutral and that it should not permit discrimination against innocent white males because of social policies established and maintained by earlier generations. In reality, they say, goals and timetables are quotas, and their use amounts to reverse discrimination.

Momentum is building in the Congress, the White House, and the states to reevaluate whether affirmative action programs are still necessary. Some suggest that it is time to shift the focus of affirmative action away from race and gender to economic status, rather than to abolish it altogether.

Support for affirmative action has also decreased in the Supreme Court in recent years, especially with respect to state programs. The Court has often deferred to Congress in the past and upheld federal programs containing racial preferences for remedial purposes. It has rejected reverse discrimination arguments where affirmative action plans were flexible, narrowly tailored to redress specifically identified forms of discrimination, and did not "unnecessarily trammel the interests of white employees."[25] While the Supreme Court has refused to totally prohibit the existence of affirmative action programs, it has continued to restrict their use.

The Supreme Court recently decided the case of *Adarand Constructors, Inc. v. Pena*. In this case, a federally funded Department of Transportation subcontract to install guardrails on a highway was awarded to an Hispanic-owned company despite the fact that a white-owned company had submitted a lower bid. The nonminority low bidder filed suit, alleging that the minority preference policy that financially encouraged general contractors to subcontract with minority firms denied him equal protection of the laws.

Adarand Constructors, Inc., v. Pena 132 L Ed 2d 158 U.S. Supreme Court June 12, 1995	Justice O'Connor announced the judgment of the Court and delivered an opinion with respect to Parts I, II, III-A, III-B, III-D, and IV, which is for the

Court except insofar as it might be inconsistent with the views expressed in Justice Scalia's concurrence, and an opinion with respect to Part III-C in which Justice Kennedy joins.

Petitioner Adarand Constructors, Inc., claims that the Federal Government's practice of giving general contractors on government projects a financial incentive to hire subcontractors controlled by "socially and economically disadvantaged individuals," and in particular, the Government's use of race-based presumptions in identifying such individuals, violates the equal protection component of the Fifth Amendment's Due Process Clause. The Court of Appeals rejected Adarand's claim. We conclude, however, that courts should analyze cases of this kind under a different standard of review than the one the Court of Appeals applied. We therefore vacate the Court of Appeals' judgment and remand the case for further proceedings.

I

In 1989, the Central Federal Lands Highway Division (CFLHD), which is part of the United States Department of Transportation (DOT), awarded the prime contract for a highway construction project in Colorado to Mountain Gravel & Construction Company. Mountain Gravel then solicited bids from subcontractors for the guardrail portion of the contract. Adarand, a Colorado-based highway construction company specializing in guardrail work, submitted the low bid. Gonzales Construction Company also submitted a bid.

The prime contract's terms provide that Mountain Gravel would receive additional compensation if it hired subcontractors certified as small businesses controlled by "socially and economically

disadvantaged individuals." . . . Gonzales is certified as such a business; Adarand is not. Mountain Gravel awarded the subcontract to Gonzales, despite Adarand's low bid, and Mountain Gravel's Chief Estimator has submitted an affidavit stating that Mountain Gravel would have accepted Adarand's bid, had it not been for the additional payment it received by hiring Gonzales instead. . . . Federal law requires that a subcontracting clause similar to the one used here must appear in most federal agency contracts, and it also requires the clause to state that "[t]he contractor shall presume that socially and economically disadvantaged individuals include Black Americans, Hispanic Americans, Native Americans, Asian Pacific Americans, and other minorities, or any other individual found to be disadvantaged by the [Small Business] Administration pursuant to section 8(a) of the Small Business Act." . . . Adarand claims that the presumption set forth in that statute discriminates on the basis of race in violation of the Federal Government's Fifth Amendment obligation not to deny anyone equal protection of the laws.

These fairly straightforward facts implicate a complex scheme of federal statutes and regulations, to which we now turn. The Small Business Act . . . declares it to be "the policy of the United States that small business concerns, [and] small business concerns owned and controlled by socially and economically disadvantaged individuals, . . . shall have the maximum practicable opportunity to participate in the performance of contracts let by any Federal agency." . . . The Act defines "socially disadvantaged individuals" as "those who have been subjected to racial or ethnic prejudice or cultural bias because of their identity as a member of a group without regard to their individual qualities," . . . and it defines "economically disadvantaged individuals" as "those socially disadvantaged individuals whose ability to compete in the free enterprise system has been impaired due to diminished capital and credit opportunities as compared to others in the same business area who are not socially disadvantaged." . . .

In furtherance of the policy stated in § 8(d)(1), the Act establishes "[t]he Government-wide goal for participation by small business concerns owned and controlled by socially and economically disadvantaged individuals" at "not less than 5 percent of the total value of all prime contract and subcontract awards for each fiscal year." . . . It also requires the head of each federal agency to set agency-specific goals for participation by businesses controlled by socially and economically disadvantaged individuals. . . .

The Small Business Administration (SBA) has implemented these statutory directives in a variety of ways, two of which are relevant here. One is the "8(a) program," which is available to small businesses controlled by socially and economically disadvantaged individuals as the SBA has defined those terms. The 8(a) program confers a wide range of benefits on participating businesses, . . . one of which is automatic eligibility for subcontractor compensation provisions of the kind at issue in this case. . . . The SBA presumes that Black, Hispanic, Asian Pacific, Subcontinent Asian, and Native American, as well as "members of other groups designated from time to time by SBA," are "socially disadvantaged." . . .

The other SBA program relevant to this case is the "8(d) subcontracting program," which unlike the 8(a) program is limited to eligibility for subcontracting provisions like the one at issue here. In determining eligibility, the SBA presumes social disadvantage based on membership in certain minority groups, just as in the 8(a) program, and again appears to require an individualized, although "less restrictive," showing of economic disadvantage. . . . A different set of regulations, however, says that members of minority groups wishing to participate in the 8(d) subcontracting program are entitled to a race-based presumption of social and economic disadvantage. . . .

The contract giving rise to the dispute in this case came about as a result of the Surface Transportation and Uniform Relocation Assistance Act of 1987 . . . (STURAA), a DOT appropriations measure. . . . STURAA provides that "not less than 10 percent" of the appropriated funds "shall be expended with small business concerns owned and controlled by socially and economically disadvantaged individuals." . . . STURAA also requires the Secretary of Transportation to establish "minimum uniform criteria for State governments to use in certifying whether a concern qualifies for purposes of this subsection." . . . Those regulations say that the certifying authority should presume both social and economic disadvantage (i.e., eligibility to participate) if the applicant belongs to certain racial groups, or is a woman.

The operative clause in the contract in this case reads as follows:

> "Subcontracting. This subsection is supplemented to include a Disadvantaged Business Enterprise (DBE) Development and Subcontracting Provision as follows:
>
> "Monetary compensation is offered for awarding subcontracts to small business concerns owned and controlled by socially and economically disadvantaged individuals. . . .
>
> "The Contractor will be paid an amount computed as follows:
>
> "1. If a subcontract is awarded to one DBE, 10 percent of the final amount

of the approved DBE subcontract, not to exceed 1.5 percent of the original contract amount.

"2. If subcontracts are awarded to two or more DBEs, 10 percent of the final amount of the approved DBE subcontracts, not to exceed 2 percent of the original contract amount." . . .

To benefit from this clause, Mountain Gravel had to hire a subcontractor who had been certified as a small disadvantaged business by the SBA, a state highway agency, or some other certifying authority acceptable to the Contracting Officer.

After losing the guardrail subcontract to Gonzales, Adarand filed suit against various federal officials in the United States Distinct Court for the District of Colorado, claiming that the race-based presumptions involved in the use of subcontracting compensation clauses violate Adarand's right to equal protection. The District Court granted the Government's motion for summary judgment. . . . The Court of Appeals for the Tenth Circuit affirmed. . . .

It understood our decision in *Fullilove v. Klutznick* . . . to have adopted "a lenient standard, resembling intermediate scrutiny, in assessing" the constitutionality of federal race-based action. . . . Applying that "lenient standard," . . . the Court of Appeals upheld the use of subcontractor compensation clauses. . . . We granted certiorari. . . .

III

The Government urges that "[t]he Subcontracting Compensation Clause program is . . . a program based on disadvantage, not on race," and thus that it is subject only to "the most relaxed judicial scrutiny." . . . To the extent that the statutes and regulations involved in this case are race neutral, we agree. The Government concedes,

however, that "the race-based rebuttable presumption used in some certification determinations under the Subcontracting Compensation Clause" is subject to some heightened level of scrutiny. The parties disagree as to what that level should be.

Adarand's claim arises under the Fifth Amendment to the Constitution, which provides that "No person shall . . . be deprived of life, liberty, or property, without due process of law." Although this Court has always understood that Clause to provide some measure of protection against arbitrary treatment by the Federal Government, it is not as explicit a guarantee of equal treatment as the Fourteenth Amendment, which provides that "No State shall . . . deny to any person within its jurisdiction the equal protection of the laws" (emphasis added). Our cases have accorded varying degrees of significance to the difference in the language of those two Clauses. We think it necessary to revisit the issue here.

B

Most of the cases [prior to 1978] . . . involved classifications burdening groups that have suffered discrimination in our society. In 1978, the Court confronted the question of whether race-based governmental action designed to benefit such groups should also be subject to "the most rigid scrutiny." *Regents of Univ. of California v. Bakke* . . . involved an equal protection challenge to a state-run medical school's practice of reserving a number of spaces in its entering class for minority students. The petitioners argued that "strict scrutiny" should apply only to "classifications that disadvantage 'discrete and insular minorities.'" . . .

Bakke did not produce an opinion for the Court, but Justice Powell's opinion announcing the Court's judgment rejected the argument. In a passage joined by Justice White, Justice Powell wrote that "[t]he guarantee of equal protection cannot mean one thing when applied to one individual and something else when applied to a person of another color." . . . He concluded that "[r]acial and ethnic distinctions of any sort are inherently suspect and thus call for the most exacting judicial examination." . . . On the other hand, four Justices in *Bakke* would have applied a less stringent standard of review to racial classifications "designed to further remedial purposes."

Two years after *Bakke*, the Court faced another challenge to remedial race-based action, this time involving action undertaken by the Federal Government. In *Fullilove v. Klutznick* . . . (1980), the Court upheld Congress' inclusion of a 10% set-aside for minority-owned businesses in the Public Works Employment Act of 1977. As in *Bakke*, there was no opinion for the Court.

In *Wygant v. Jackson Board of Education* . . . (1986), the Court considered a Fourteenth Amendment challenge to another form of remedial racial classification. The issue in *Wygant* was whether a school board could adopt race-based preferences in determining which teachers to lay off. Justice Powell's plurality opinion observed that "the level of scrutiny does not change merely because the challenged classification operates against a group that historically has not been subject to governmental discrimination," . . . and stated the two-part inquiry as "whether the layoff provision is supported by a compelling state purpose and whether the means chosen to accomplish that purpose are narrowly tailored." . . . In other words, "racial classifications of any sort must be subjected to 'strict scrutiny.'" . . .

The Court's failure to produce a majority opinion in *Bakke*, *Fullilove*, and

Wygant left unresolved the proper analysis for remedial race-based governmental action. . . .

The Court resolved the issue, at least in part, in 1989. *Richmond v. J.A. Croson Co.* . . . concerned a city's determination that 30% of its contracting work should go to minority-owned businesses. A majority of the Court in *Croson* held that "the standard of review under the Equal Protection Clause is not dependent on the race of those burdened or benefited by a particular classification," and that the single standard of review for racial classifications should be "strict scrutiny."

With *Croson*, the Court finally agreed that the Fourteenth Amendment requires strict scrutiny of all race-based action by state and local governments. But *Croson* of course had no occasion to declare what standard of review the Fifth Amendment requires for such action taken by the Federal Government. *Croson* observed simply that the Court's "treatment of an exercise of congressional power in *Fullilove* cannot be dispositive here," because *Croson*'s facts did not implicate Congress' broad power under § 5 of the Fourteenth Amendment.

A year later, however, the Court took a surprising turn. *Metro Broadcasting, Inc. v. FCC* . . . (1990), involved a Fifth Amendment challenge to two race-based policies of the Federal Communications Commission. In *Metro Broadcasting*, the Court repudiated the long-held notion that "it would be unthinkable that the same Constitution would impose a lesser duty on the Federal Government" than it does on a State to afford equal protection of the laws. . . . It did so by holding that "benign" federal racial classifications need only satisfy intermediate scrutiny, even though *Croson* had recently concluded that such classifications enacted by a State must satisfy strict scrutiny. . . .

Under *Metro Broadcasting*, certain racial classifications ("benign" ones enacted by the Federal Government) should be treated less skeptically than others; and the race of the benefited group is critical to the determination of which standard of review to apply. *Metro Broadcasting* was thus a significant departure from much of what had come before it.

The three propositions undermined by *Metro Broadcasting* all derive from the basic principle that the Fifth and Fourteenth Amendments to the Constitution protect persons, not groups. It follows from that principle that all governmental action based on race—a group classification long recognized as "in most circumstances irrelevant and therefore prohibited" . . .—should be subjected to detailed judicial inquiry to ensure that the personal right to equal protection of the laws has not been infringed. These ideas have long been central to this Court's understanding of equal protection, and holding "benign" state and federal racial classifications to different standards does not square with them. "[A] free people whose institutions are founded upon the doctrine of equality," . . . should tolerate no retreat from the principle that government may treat people differently because of their race only for the most compelling reasons. Accordingly, we hold today that all racial classifications, imposed by whatever federal, state, or local governmental actor, must be analyzed by a reviewing court under strict scrutiny. In other words, such classifications are constitutional only if they are narrowly tailored measures that further compelling governmental interests. To the extent that *Metro Broadcasting* is inconsistent with that holding, it is overruled.

C

As we have explained, *Metro Broadcasting* undermined important principles of this Court's equal protection jurisprudence, established in a line of cases stretching back over fifty years. . . . Those principles together stood for an "embracing" and "intrinsically soun[d]" understanding of equal protection "verified by experience," namely, that the Constitution imposes upon federal, state, and local governmental actors the same obligation to respect the personal right to equal protection of the laws. . . . By refusing to follow *Metro Broadcasting*, then, we do not depart from the fabric of the law; we restore it. . . . *Metro Broadcasting*'s untenable distinction between state and federal racial classifications lacks support in our precedent, and undermines the fundamental principle of equal protection as a personal right. In this case, as between that principle and "its later misapplications," the principle must prevail.

D

Our action today makes explicit what Justice Powell thought implicit in the *Fullilove* lead opinion: federal racial classifications, like those of a State, must serve a compelling governmental interest, and must be narrowly tailored to further that interest. . . .

Finally, we wish to dispel the notion that strict scrutiny is "strict in theory, but fatal in fact." . . . The unhappy persistence of both the practice and the lingering effects of racial discrimination against minority groups in this country is an unfortunate reality, and government is not disqualified from acting in response to it. As recently as 1987, for example, every Justice of this Court agreed that the Alabama Department of Public Safety's "pervasive, systematic, and obstinate discriminatory conduct" justified a narrowly tailored race-based remedy. . . . When race-based action is necessary to further a compelling interest, such action is within constitutional constraints if it satisfies the "narrow tailoring" test this Court has set out in previous cases.

IV

Because our decision today alters the playing field in some important respects, we think it best to remand the case to the lower courts for further consideration in light of the principles we have announced. The Court of Appeals, following *Metro Broadcasting* and *Fullilove*, analyzed the case in terms of intermediate scrutiny. It upheld the challenged statutes and regulations because it found them to be "narrowly tailored to achieve [their] significant governmental purpose of providing subcontracting opportunities for small disadvantaged business enterprises." . . . The Court of Appeals did not decide the question whether the interests served by the use of subcontractor compensation clauses are properly described as "compelling." It also did not address the question of narrow tailoring in terms of our strict scrutiny cases, by asking, for example, whether there was "any consideration of the use of race-neutral means to increase minority business participation" in government contracting, . . . or whether the program was appropriately limited such that it "will not last longer than the discriminatory effects it is designed to eliminate." . . .

Moreover, unresolved questions remain concerning the details of the complex regulatory regimes implicated by the use of subcontractor compensation clauses. . . . The question whether any of the ways in which the Government uses subcontractor compensation clauses can survive strict scrutiny, and any relevance distinctions such as these may have to that question, should be addressed in the first instance by the lower courts.

Accordingly, the judgment of the Court of Appeals is vacated, and the case is remanded for further proceedings consistent with this opinion.

It is so ordered.

Justice Stevens, with whom Justice Ginsburg joins, dissenting

III

This is the third time in the Court's entire history that it has considered the constitutionality of a federal affirmative-action program. On each of the two prior occasions, the first in 1980, *Fullilove v. Klutznick*, . . . and the second in 1990, *Metro Broadcasting, Inc. v. FCC*, . . . the Court upheld the program. Today the Court explicitly overrules *Metro Broadcasting* (at least in part), . . . and undermines *Fullilove* by recasting the standard on which it rested and by calling even its holding into question. . . . By way of explanation, Justice O'Connor advises the federal agencies and private parties that have made countless decisions in reliance on those cases that "we do not depart from the fabric of the law; we restore it." . . . A skeptical observer might ask whether this pronouncement is a faithful application of the doctrine of stare decisis. . . .

Ironically, after all of the time, effort, and paper this Court has expended in differentiating between federal and state affirmative action, the majority today virtually ignores the issue. . . . It provides not a word of direct explanation for its sudden and enormous departure from the reasoning in past cases. Such silence, however, cannot erase the difference between Congress' institutional competence and constitutional authority to overcome historic racial subjugation and the States' lesser power to do so.

Presumably, the majority is now satisfied that its theory of "congruence" between the substantive rights provided by the Fifth and Fourteenth Amendments disposes of the objection based upon divided constitutional powers. But it is one thing to say (as no one seems to dispute) that the Fifth Amendment encompasses a general guarantee of equal protection as broad as that contained within the Fourteenth Amendment. It is another thing entirely to say that Congress' institutional competence and constitutional authority entitles it to no greater deference when it enacts a program designed to foster equality than the deference due to a State legislature. . . . The latter is an extraordinary proposition; and, as the foregoing discussion demonstrates, our precedents have rejected it explicitly and repeatedly. . . .

Our opinion in *Metro Broadcasting* relied on several constitutional provisions to justify the greater deference we owe to Congress when it acts with respect to private individuals. . . . In the programs challenged in this case, Congress has acted both with respect to private individuals and, as in *Fullilove*, with respect to the States themselves. . . . When Congress does this, it draws its power directly from § 5 of the Fourteenth Amendment. . . . That section reads: "The Congress shall have power to enforce, by appropriate legislation, the provisions of this article." One of the "provisions of this article" that Congress is thus empowered to enforce reads: "No State shall make or enforce any law which shall abridge the privileges or immunities of citizens of the United States; nor shall any State deprive any person of life, liberty, or property, without due process of law; nor deny to any person within its jurisdiction the equal protection of the laws."
. . . The Fourteenth Amendment directly empowers Congress at the same time it expressly limits the States. . . . This

is no accident. It represents our Nation's consensus, achieved after hard experience throughout our sorry history of race relations, that the Federal Government must be the primary defender of racial minorities against the States, some of which may be inclined to oppress such minorities. A rule of "congruence" that ignores a purposeful "incongruity" so fundamental to our system of government is unacceptable.

In my judgment, the Court's novel doctrine of "congruence" is seriously misguided. Congressional deliberations about a matter as important as affirmative action should be accorded far greater deference than those of a State or municipality.

IV

. . . In the Court's view, our decision in *Metro Broadcasting* was inconsistent with the rule announced in *Richmond v. J.A. Croson Co.* . . . (1989). . . . But . . . *Metro Broadcasting* involved a federal program, whereas *Croson* involved a city ordinance. *Metro Broadcasting* thus drew primary support from *Fullilove*, which predated *Croson*, and which *Croson* distinguished on the grounds of the federal-state dichotomy that the majority today discredits. Although members of today's majority trumpeted the importance of that distinction in *Croson*, they now reject it in the name of "congruence." It is therefore quite wrong for the Court to suggest today that overruling *Metro Broadcasting* merely restores the status quo ante, for the law at the time of that decision was entirely open to the result the Court reached. Today's decision is an unjustified departure from settled law. . . .

VI

My skeptical scrutiny of the Court's opinion leaves me in dissent. The majority's concept of "consistency" ignores a difference, fundamental to the idea of equal protection, between oppression and assistance. The majority's concept of "congruence" ignores a difference, fundamental to our constitutional system, between the Federal Government and the States. And the majority's concept of stare decisis ignores the force of binding precedent. I would affirm the judgment of the Court of Appeals.

Case Questions

1. What exactly did the Supreme Court decide in this case?
2. Why was the case remanded by the Supreme Court?
3. The Court's *Adarand* ruling is grounded in philosophical notions of racial equality. Does its decision accord with your views of social and economic justice in the United States?
4. Do you see any role for affirmative action policies in the 1990s?

The Equal Employment Opportunity Commission

The Civil Rights Act of 1964 also created the Equal Employment Opportunity Commission (EEOC). This agency and similar state antidiscrimination agencies have enforcement responsibilities under Title VII. Aggrieved people must report their problems to both the EEOC and their state agency and usually wait six months before they can directly sue an employer. The EEOC and the state agencies may help negotiate a conciliatory agreement between the parties, dismiss the complaint, or find that the employer illegally discriminated against an employee. Any EEOC decision may be contested and tried *de novo* in a U.S. District Court. (This means that the action is tried without regard to the EEOC's findings of discrimination or lack of it). The EEOC also is empowered to investigate employment situations on its own initiative, to issue extensive guidelines for employment practices, and to require that affirmative action programs are implemented.

In the following case, the plaintiff successfully used Title VII to prevent his employer from discharging him because of his race.

Jones v. Western Geophysical Co.
761 F.2d 1158
U.S. Court of Appeals, Fifth Circuit
June 3, 1985

Garza, Circuit Judge

Cecil Jones, a black male, has maintained that his 1978 termination from the Western Geophysical Company's Galveston, Texas, plant was racially motivated and therefore in violation of Title VII of the Civil Rights Act of 1964, 42 U.S.C. Section 2000e *et seq.*, as well as the Civil Rights Act of 1866, 42 U.S.C. Section 1981. . . .

At the trial, the court, sitting without a jury, found that Jones's discharge had violated both Title VII and Section 1981 and entered judgment in his favor. . . . Western Geophysical appeals from the district court's judgment against it. . . . For the reasons stated below . . . we affirm the judgment of the district court.

I

Jones was employed by Western Geophysical from December 26, 1973, until his termination on November 2, 1978. During his tenure, Jones received numerous pay raises. Western Geophysical maintained at trial and still maintains that those raises were "across-the-board" and that Jones had always been a very slow worker. Nonetheless, on the basis of ample evidence, the district court found that some of the raises were, in fact, selective as to Jones. From this evidence, the court below properly concluded that Jones had performed satisfactorily during his employment at Western Geophysical.

During mid-1978, the period just prior to Jones's termination, race relations at the Galveston plant, which were never good, deteriorated. Racist graffiti appeared on the restroom walls with greater frequency. In the summer of that year, while attending a company-sponsored cardiopulmonary resuscitation (CPR) training session, an unidentified mid-level supervisor stated in very offensive terms that he would not perform CPR on a black employee. This remark was reported rapidly throughout the plant and upset black employees greatly.

In view of the increased racial tension at the plant, a group of black employees requested a meeting with Western Geophysical management. The company agreed, and in July or August of 1978, a meeting was held between Western Geophysical management and eight black employees, including Jones. Although one positive result of the meeting was visible when plant restroom walls were painted to cover the racist graffiti, Western Geophysical's other subsequent actions were not so worthy of praise. Five of the eight employees who attended the meeting soon received notices of criticism, typically the first step in the termination process. In the case of Jones, his notice of criticism dated September 28, 1978, was the first such notice of his four and one-half year tenure at Western Geophysical.

Jones's September notice of criticism alleged that he was the "slowest of the 257 company employees." Jones's supervisor, Sid Johnson, set out to verify Jones's slow work pace. Johnson asked three other employees how much time should be necessary to clean column guides on vibrator trucks. These employees' responses varied from 45 minutes to one and a half hours. Johnson then assigned the task to Jones. When Johnson reviewed Jones's time sheets for the task, he found that Jones had taken too long to perform the job, although how much time Jones actually required was never credibly established. In any event, Jones was immediately terminated.

II

From the facts as outlined above, the district court made the ultimate finding that Jones had been terminated on account of his race. Western Geophysical maintains that the district court based this determination on two interrelated misunderstandings of the law. Specifically, Western Geophysical maintains that the district court improperly ignored subjective evaluations by Jones's supervisors of his work habits. Moreover, Western Geophysical contends that the district court erroneously placed the burden on the company to *prove* a legitimate, nondiscriminatory reason for Jones's termination. . . . Since Western Geophysical articulated such a legitimate reason, it argues, the burden shifted to Jones to show that the proffered reason was pretextual. As Jones did not come forward with any such evidence, Western Geophysical argues that Jones failed to carry his burden of proof.

Western Geophysical's argument is flawed in two respects. First, it makes inaccurate suppositions as to what the district court actually did. The district court did not ignore subjective evidence of Jones's job performance; it merely completely discredited it in view of other, more tangible evidence that Jones was a good employee. Nor was this a case in which the district court held that, once the plaintiff had made a prima facie case, the burden of proof shifted to the defendant to show a legitimate, nondiscriminatory reason. . . . Indeed, in Conclusion of Law Six, the district court explicitly states that the "burden of persuasion does not shift to the defendant at any time." Read in context, Conclusion of Law Six states only that the district court believed Jones's characterization of his termination rather than Western Geophysical's.

Second, Western Geophysical's argument is flawed in that it misunderstands the proper role of the . . . three-step analysis. Once a plaintiff presents his prima facie case and the defendant responds with some evidence of a legitimate, nondiscriminatory reason, the . . . proper inquiry then becomes whether the defendant intentionally discriminated against the plaintiff. . . . In determining whether the plaintiff has carried his burden, the district court is to look at all the plaintiff's evidence, whether introduced as part of the prima facie case or as part of an attempt to show that the defendant's proffered reason is unworthy of belief. . . .

In the case of Jones, the court below examined all the evidence and determined that Jones was discharged because he is black. That finding cannot be disturbed unless it is clearly erroneous. The evidence here clearly supports the district court's finding of racial discrimination. . . .

V

The district court failed in its judgment to award post-judgment interest on the attorney's fee award that it granted Jones. Western Geophysical now concedes that this was error. Accordingly, the judgment of the district court is hereby modified to provide for interest at the lawful rate on the attorney's fee award from the date of the judgment until paid. In all other respects, the judgment of the district court is affirmed.

Case Questions

1. Explain the three-step analysis undertaking by this court to determine whether or not Jones was the victim of discrimination by Western Geophysical.
2. On what grounds did Western Geophysical appeal?

Gender-based Discrimination

Women were accidental beneficiaries of Title VII. When introduced, the act was intended to redress employment discrimination based on race, religion, and national origin. Civil rights opponents added gender-based discrimination at the last minute in the hope that sexism would ultimately prevail and cause the defeat of the entire bill.[26] This gambit was unsuccessful and Title VII included sex as a protected class. Women have used this law to challenge sexual harassment, pregnancy discrimination, and the sexual stereotypes that traditionally barred females from equal opportunity in the work place. In 1978, in response to a Supreme Court decision denying sick leave pay to pregnant employees, Congress amended Title VII by enacting the Pregnancy Discrimination Act (PDA). In 1980, the U.S. Supreme Court recognized sexual harassment as a form of sex discrimination under Title VII.

Sexual harassment includes linking employment benefits and opportunities to sexual favors. It also includes creating a hostile or offensive working environment.[27] A hostile environment exists where pervasive, "unwelcome sexual advances, requests for sexual favors, and other verbal or physical conduct of a sexual nature" occur in the work place and interfere with an employee's work performance.[28]

A review of Title VII gender-based discrimination cases illustrates various types of employment discrimination encountered by women. Employers have discriminated against women because they were the mothers of pre-school-age children, because they were married, or because they were unwed and pregnant. Some women have brought lawsuits because their employer required females to wear sexually revealing uniforms.

Women have also had to overcome state "protective" laws, enacted in the early 1900s, that treat women "more favorably" than men. For example, they require that women have frequent rest breaks, or they exclude women from jobs involving the lifting of heavy objects. Such laws have often had the effect of arbitrarily restricting women to employment in "female jobs," usually characterized by low wages, low status, and limited promotional opportunities. Such provisions in union contracts that discriminate are also unenforceable where they conflict with Title VII. Employers have even attempted to justify gender-based discrimination because of "protective" motives. One recent example involved an attempt to protect women and their offspring (but not men) from exposure to hazardous chemicals and radiation.[29]

The next case, involving two discharged restaurant employees, is an example of sexual discrimination based on pregnancy. These employees brought suit to obtain injunctive relief and back pay pursuant to Title VII.

EEOC v. Red Baron Steak Houses
47 FEP Cases 49
U.S. District Court,
Northern District of California
June 2, 1988

Legge, District Judge

1. This is an action brought by the Equal Employment Opportunity Commission ("Commission") under Title VII of the

Civil Rights Act of 1964, 42 U.S.C. §2000e *et seq.*, on behalf of Deborah Amick and Sandra Billia Spencer, two former female employees of the defendant. The Commission alleges that the defendant discriminated against Deborah Amick by cutting her hours and subsequently discharging her on account of her pregnancy. The Commission further alleges that the defendant discriminated against Sandra Spencer by discharging her when she protested the termination of Ms. Amick.

2. All jurisdictional prerequisites to suit have been satisfied, and the defendant is an employer within the meaning of Section 701(b) of Title VII of the Civil Rights Act of 1964, as amended, 42 U.S.C. §2000e (b).

3. The Commission has moved this Court for summary judgment as to all issues of liability and relief. Throughout this litigation the defendant, through its president Mark Rickert, has failed to retain counsel, failed to file necessary pleadings, and failed to appear for many of the hearings noticed herein, including these summary judgment proceedings. . . .

Deborah Amick

5. Deborah Amick went to work for defendant Red Baron Steak House at its Livermore, California location in 1980 as a hostess and cashier. In 1982, Ms. Amick was made a waitress as well as part-time bookkeeper, jobs that she continued to do when she became pregnant at the end of 1984.

6. In March, 1985 the defendant hired a new manager, Gillian Hauser, at its Livermore restaurant. After being told by Ms. Amick of her pregnancy, Ms. Hauser proceeded to reduce the number of hours that Ms. Amick was allowed to work as a waitress, at one point telling her that "it doesn't look right" to have someone pregnant waiting on tables. . . .

7. During the Commission's administrative investigation of Ms. Amick's allegations of discrimination, the defendant admitted that "[i]t is our policy to find other positions for pregnant employees when their [pregnancies] become visually obvious because of the possibility that the pregnancy my [sic] suffer from doing her waitress duties." . . .

8. Ms. Amick's payroll records indicate a 50% drop in hours from March to April 1985, the periods of time immediately following Ms. Hauser's being hired and being made aware of Ms. Amick's pregnancy. . . . The defendant during the Commission's pre-suit investigation admitted the reduction in hours stating that "Ms. Hauser felt that due to the already busy schedule that Ms. Amick had, it was in the best interest of the health of the mother and child to limit the extra shifts that Ms. Amick wanted to work." . . .

9. In May 1985, [Ms.] Amick was told by one of the other assistant managers, Dave Robinson, that another person had been hired to replace her and that she was terminated. . . .

10. Title VII of the Civil Rights Act of 1964, as amended, provides in relevant part that "it shall be unlawful employment practice for an employer . . . (2) to limit, segregate, or classify his employees in any way which would deprive or tend to deprive any individual of employment opportunities . . . because of such individual's sex. . . ." 42 U.S.C. §2000e-2(a).

11. The defendant's reduction of Ms. Amick's hours and her subsequent termination are *per se* violations of Title VII in view of the defendants's admission concerning the restrictions it put on the employment opportunities of Ms. Amick after becoming aware of her pregnancy. . . . The defendant has admitted that it reduced Ms. Amick's hours "in the best interest of the health of the mother and

the child," even though there is no evidence to suggest that she was not fully capable of performing her duties.

Further, in his deposition, Mark Richert, owner of the defendant, admitted that the defendant had no policy regarding pregnant employees being able to continue to work, stating that "we never had a problem before with a pregnant woman wanting to work . . . they always voluntarily quit."

12. Even if a *per se* violation were not established on the basis of the undisputed material facts, the evidence is clearly sufficient to establish a prima facie case of employment discrimination in the terms and conditions of Ms. Amick's employment. . . . There is no dispute that Ms. Amick's hours were substantially reduced against her wishes after she advised Ms. Hauser of her pregnancy, and thereafter her employment was altogether ended. The defendant's suggestion that Ms. Amick's termination was voluntary is unworthy of credence in view of the unrebutted evidence put forth by the plaintiff showing that Mrs. Spencer was terminated after she was ordered to fire Ms. Amick, an order subsequently carried out by Mr. Robinson. Consequently, the defendant's explanation for Ms. Amick's departure from employment is clearly pretextual. . . .

Sandra (Billia) Spencer

13. Mrs. Spencer started working for the defendant in 1980 and was made an assistant manager in January 1984. As mentioned above, shortly after she was hired, Ms. Hauser told Mrs. Spencer regarding Deborah Amick that "it is not right for a pregnant woman to wait on tables" as it "looks tacky." . . .

14. According to Mrs. Spencer, in late April or early May 1985, she was told by defendant's manager, Gillian Hauser, that Deborah Amick should be told that her waitress duties were being eliminated and that Ms. Amick was to be given to understand that she would have to agree to this or be fired. Mrs. Spencer states that she told Ms. Hauser that she did not think that there was any reason for Debbie Amick not to wait on tables even if she was pregnant. . . .

15. In early May 1985, Ms. Hauser instructed Mrs. Spencer that either she or one of the other assistant managers were to call Ms. Amick and tell her she was fired. . . . Mrs. Spencer refused and later that day was fired herself by Ms. Hauser, according to the defendant because "she refused to follow an order from her superior . . . [i]t is not for her to determine weather (sic) or not an employee should or should not be terminated. Ms. Hauser, the manager, acted in good faith and with the best interest of the company and the employee (Ms. Amick) in having Ms. D. Amick relieved of her waitress duties."
. . .

16. The defendant is liable for its retaliatory discharge of Mrs. Spencer after she complained about the defendant's discriminatory treatment of Ms. Amick. Reasonable opposition to practices made unlawful by Title VII is protected. . . . A prima facie case of retaliatory discharge is proven where the discharge follows opposition to such unlawful practices of which the employer was made known. . . . Indeed, given the defendant's admission that Mrs. Spencer was dismissed for refusing to follow orders, and in view of what the order was, a *per se* violation is again established. . . .

18. Even if a *per se* violation were not established, on the basis of the undisputed material facts, it is clear that a prima facie violation of Title VII has been established in that Mrs. Spencer's discharge followed

her opposition to the discrimination on account of her pregnancy that Ms. Amick was suffering by the defendant. . . . Further, by effectively admitting that Mrs. Spencer was fired for refusing to terminate Ms. Amick, the defendant has failed to articulate any non-discriminatory explanation for its treatment of Mrs. Spencer and the Title VII violation by her discharge is thereby unrebutted. . . .

Damages

19. Section 706(g) of Title VII, 42 U.S.C. §2000e-5(g) provides for both injunctive and affirmative relief, including the award of back pay, as appropriate. Back pay is to be awarded in Title VII actions following a finding of discrimination, unless there is some compelling reason to do otherwise, provided the claimant has fulfilled her duty to mitigate damages. Where backpay amounts are easily calculated, as here, prejudgment interest is appropriate. . . .

20. Deborah Amick's actual mitigated damages through March 31, 1988 are $21,756.62, exclusive of interest. This amount includes $557.39 for the loss in wages which she suffered from her reduced hours prior to her termination. It also includes $7,895 for that period during which Ms. Amick was unemployed, exclusive of the time she would not have worked at and following the birth of her child, and $13,304.23 of mitigated damages following her re-employment in February 1986 and thereafter to the present. Ms. Amick's damages have been calculated using an average monthly wage, including tips, of $1,547 based on her monthly income from the defendant immediately prior to her reduction in hours.

21. Plaintiff has requested prejudgment and post-judgment interest at 6.71% based on 28 U.S.C. Section 1961. . . . Applying this rate of interest on those amounts owing at year's end, the defendant owes Ms. Amick $25,056.66 through March 31, 1988. . . .

22. The Commission has requested that this Court order "front pay" for Ms. Amick for a period of time in order to compensate her for the fact that to the present she is still not making as much money as she did previously with the defendant. Title VII claimants are presumptively entitled to reinstatement at their former jobs. . . . However, front pay is an alternative to reinstatement, . . . particularly where there may be great antagonism between the employer and employee. . . . There seems little doubt that given the small size of the defendant, it would be impossible to reinstate Ms. Amick to her former position without substantial distress to her and to the defendant. . . . Further there is no doubt regarding Ms. Amick's considerable efforts to maintain employment since her discriminatory discharge by the defendant, thereby substantially mitigating the defendant's liability towards her. The fact that Ms. Amick is the sole support of her child has further heightened the impact of her not being able to work for the same wages as what she was making at the defendant. . . .

23. Ms. Amick worked for the defendant for five years and two months prior to her dismissal. She has indicated in her Declaration that she would have continued to work for the defendant into the foreseeable future. . . . Therefore, in order to put some bounds on what must obviously be speculation as to how long she would have worked for the defendant had she not been discharged, this Court will constructively continue Ms. Amick's employment with the defendant for another five years and two months beyond the date of her discharge, that is, until July 1990. Consequently, the defendant's front

pay obligation is for the difference between what Ms. Amick is now earning (which will presumably continue) deducted from what she would earn from April 1, 1988 to the end of the front pay period, discounted by the present value of that front pay obligation. At a difference in wages of $511 per month, from April 1, 1988 to July 1990, this would amount to front pay of $13,797. The present value of this amount based on the 6.71% interest rate requested by the plaintiff, is $12,113.76. . . . This amount will be added to the $25,056.66 previously found owing, for a judgment of $37,160.42 in favor of Ms. Amick against the defendant, interest to be applied thereafter until paid at 6.71% or such another rate as used by this Clerk's office. . . .

24. Sandra Spencer's backpay damages are $9,275, exclusive of interest. This amount is based on her monthly salary of $1,250 with the defendant at the time of her discharge and includes $625 for the period of her unemployment immediately following her termination, a $1,775 difference in wages owed during her employment thereafter, and $6,875 in damages from the date of her being laid off from this subsequent employment until she took herself out of the job market four months thereafter due to the impending birth of her child.

25. Applying a prejudgment interest rate of 6.71% on the total amount owed by the defendant as of the time that Mrs. Spencer left the job market, compounded annually, as before, through March 31, 1988 the defendant owes Mrs. Spencer $10,738.65. Because Mrs. Spencer has now voluntarily taken herself out of the job market, front pay is not appropriate in her case. Postjudgment interest shall be applied on this amount until paid at 6.71% or such other rate as used by this Clerk's office. . . .

Injunctive Relief

26. The Commission is requesting that this Court enter a permanent injunction forbidding the defendant from any future violations of Title VII, including retaliation against employees who oppose practices made unlawful by the Act. Such an injunction is appropriate as it will deter the defendant from future unlawful discrimination and protect employees from retaliation for exercising their rights under the Act. . . . This permanent injunction will "instruct (the defendant) that it must comply with federal law . . . subject it to the contempt power of the federal courts if it commits future violations, and . . . reduce the chilling effect of its alleged retaliation on its employees' exercise of their Title VII rights." . . . Such a permanent injunction is clearly necessary in this case.

Judgment

It is therefore ordered and adjudged that the defendant is hereby enjoined from future violations of Title VII of the Civil Rights Act of 1964, as amended, 42 U.S.C. §2000e et seq. Defendant is further ordered to pay, through the Clerk of Court's office, Deborah Amick $37,170.42 and Sandra Spencer $10,738.65, post-judgment interest on both amounts to accrue as set forth herein.

Case Questions

1. Do you believe an employer should be permitted to determine what is "in the best interest" of an employee?

2. Should a woman who is seven months pregnant be permitted to continue working as a cocktail waitress in a popular singles' bar?

3. What does it mean when the court says, "the claimant has fulfilled her duty to mitigate damages"?

Religion

Title VII is intended to prevent employers from discriminating against employees because of their religion. The law requires employers to attempt to accommodate their employees' religious practices and beliefs, "unless an employer demonstrates that he is unable to reasonably accommodate to an employee's or prospective employee's religious observance or practice without undue hardship on the conduct of the employer's business." For example, an employer must give an employee days off to observe religious holidays if the employee can reasonably make up the time without unfairly affecting other employees' work schedules. Title VII does permit religious organizations to discriminate on the basis of religion in church administration, the appointment of clergy, and the operation of churches. In the following case the employer engaged in an unlawful employment practice; it made no effort to accommodate the employee's religious beliefs.

E.E.O.C. v. Ithaca Industries, Inc.
849 F.2d 116
U.S. Court of Appeals, Fourth Circuit
June 8, 1988

Hall, Circuit Judge

Dannel Dean, the charging party in a civil action alleging religious discrimination in employment in violation of Title VII of the Civil Rights Act of 1964, appeals a decision of the district court granting judgment for his former employer, Ithaca Industries. . . .

I.

Dean began working for Ithaca at Gastonia, North Carolina, on July 23, 1979, on the second shift as a turning operator. Ithaca produced cloth for J.C. Penney, Nike, and Ocean Pacific at its Gastonia plant. On April 11, 1983, Dean was transferred to the first shift as a Morrison Machine Operator. From July 18, 1983, to January 16, 1984, he was on extended leave of absence due to a serious brain tumor. Upon his return, he was assigned to work as a dryer helper on the first shift.

Dean has been a member of the Church of God since 1977 and believes that he cannot work on Sunday because it would violate his religious beliefs. Dean made this belief clear to his supervisors and other Ithaca officials at the time of his initial employment and was told that Sunday work was strictly voluntary. During the first four years of his employment, Sunday work was not required.

In January, 1984, the plant's production demands became abnormally high which forced the plant to operate on eight

Sundays that year. When Sunday work was necessary, the plant operated on a reduced staffing basis in order to allow as many people as possible to have Sunday off. The normal daily complement of workers on the first shift was approximately 25 people. On Sundays the shift was manned by a skeleton crew of 12 to 15 people.

Dean was asked by his supervisor, Andrew Cain, to work the first two operating Sundays in 1984, January 23 and February 19. He refused, but received no reprimand or criticism of any kind. On March 17, Cain ordered Dean to work the following day, which was a Sunday. Dean informed Cain that he could not work because of his religious beliefs. Dean was not told that his absence would be considered unexcused.

On March 19, Cain gave Dean a written warning identifying his failure to work the preceding day as an unexcused absence and stating that "[a]nother unexcused absence will result in termination." This was the first time Dean was made aware that Cain considered his inability to work on Sundays, because of his religious beliefs, an inappropriate reason for not working.

The next Sunday on which work was required was April 1. On Saturday, March 31, Cain approached Dean and instructed him to work the next day. Dean again informed Cain that he could not work because of his religious beliefs. Cain responded that, if Dean did not report for work, he should not return on Monday because he would be terminated. Dean did not report to work that Sunday; Cain worked in Dean's stead. Cain discharged Dean on April 2.

. . . A civil action was filed by the Equal Employment Opportunity Commission ("EEOC") on December 16, 1985, alleging that Ithaca had violated . . . Title

VII of the Civil Rights Act of 1964 by discharging Dean because he refused to work on his Sabbath. A bench trial was conducted on November 18 and 19, 1986. At the trial, several employees testified that they would have been available to work on March 18 and April 1 in Dean's place if they had been asked. However, Cain did not contact any of those employees to see if they would work for Dean. On December 3, 1986, the district court entered judgment in favor of the company, concluding that Ithaca had made no effort to accommodate Dean but that an absolute refusal to work on Sunday was so unreasonable on its face that no reasonable accommodation was possible. This appeal followed.

II.

. . . Section 703(a)(1) of the Civil Rights Act of 1964, Title VII, 42 U.S.C. § 2000e-2(a)(1), makes it an unlawful employment practice for an employer to discriminate against an employee on the basis of his or her religion. In 1972, an amendment to Title VII, § 701(j), was enacted with the stated purpose to protect Sabbath observers whose employers fail to adjust work schedules to fit their needs. The Act thus requires that an employer, short of undue hardship, make reasonable accommodations to the religious needs of its employees. It is also clear that the burden is on the employer to offer this accommodation.

The district court's conclusion that unless Dean was willing to compromise his religious belief by agreeing to work Sundays on some occasions, Ithaca had no duty to attempt to accommodate the belief turns the statute on its head. It improperly places the burden on the employee to be reasonable rather than on the employer to attempt accommodation. Section 701(j) clearly anticipates that some employees will absolutely refuse to work on their Sabbath and this firmly held religious belief requires some offer of accommodation by employers.

The district court found, as a matter of fact, that Ithaca had made no specific effort to accommodate Dean. This absolute lack of effort at accommodation by the employer distinguishes this case from our previous case of *Jordan v. North Carolina Nat'l Bank*, 565 F.2d 72 (4th Cir.1977), and the Supreme Court's decision in *TWA v. Hardison*, 432 U.S. 63 . . . (1977). Appellee's continued reliance on these decisions is therefore misplaced.

In *Jordan*, a prospective employee demanded that she be guaranteed that she would never have to work on her Sabbath if she were to accept employment. There was evidence presented that the employer made some offers of accommodation to Jordan which she refused. This Court subsequently ruled that any further accommodations would constitute an undue hardship.

The Supreme Court in *Hardison* held that the employer, TWA, could not reasonably accommodate the employee's refusal to work on his Sabbath without undue hardship. TWA, however, made several efforts to accommodate the employee. Job swaps, change of days off, and shift transfers were all attempted before TWA concluded that any further accommodation would create an undue hardship.

It is true that in this case Ithaca did demonstrate an effort to accommodate *all* their employees when Sunday work was assigned. These accommodations, however, were clearly not for reasons of religion, nor were they specifically aimed at addressing Dean's beliefs. In addition, Ithaca made no effort to accommodate Dean by any of the methods suggested by the guidelines in the regulations. 20 C.F.R. 1605.2(d)(1)(i). We therefore conclude that Ithaca did violate the Civil Rights Act by discriminating against Dean.

III.

Ithaca contends that the religious accommodation provisions of Title VII violate the First Amendment of the Constitution. The district court declined to reach this issue since it decided the case on other grounds. Assuming that the question is before us, we find no merit in Ithaca's constitutional challenge. Ithaca concedes that its argument has been rejected by other courts but argues that if this issue reached the Supreme Court, it would find § 701(j) unconstitutional. We disagree. Every court of appeals that has addressed this issue has held that § 701(j) does not violate the First Amendment. . . .

We now join these circuits in holding that § 701(j) passes muster under the Supreme Court's three-prong test for constitutionality. . . . We are convinced that: (1) § 701(j) clearly has a secular purpose—the elimination of discrimination in the workplace; (2) it has the primary secular effect of preserving the equal employment opportunities of those employees whose moral scruples conflict with work rules; and (3) there is no excessive government entanglement. For these reasons, we conclude that § 701(j) does not violate the First Amendment.

IV.

For the foregoing reasons, we reverse the judgment of the district court and remand for determination of appropriate relief.

Reversed and remanded.

Case
Questions

1. What error was made by the district court at trial that resulted in reversal by the appeals court?
2. How can the *Ithaca* case be distinguished from the case relied upon by the appellee (the *Jordan* case)?

ADDITIONAL PROTECTION AGAINST DISCRIMINATION

Congress passed two major civil rights acts during the Reconstruction era following the Civil War. Enacted to implement the Thirteenth, Fourteenth, and Fifteenth amendments, these were the Civil Rights Act of 1866 (Sec. 1981 and 1982) and the Civil Rights Act of 1871 (Sec. 1983).

Section 1981 prohibits both public and private employers from discriminating in the making and enforcement of employment contracts. Section 1982 provides that people of all races have the same right "to inherit, purchase, . . . hold and convey . . . property." Civil rights advocates used these statutes during the 1950s and 1960s to challenge state and local laws that interfered with blacks' contractual and business rights.

Although section 1983 provides no substantive rights, it does provide public, nonfederal employees with a remedy against their public employers. This section benefits police officers, firefighters, and teachers, who have suffered violations of constitutional rights (such as violations of the Fourteenth Amendment and Sections 1981 and 1982). Plaintiffs are entitled to a jury trial and to sue for back pay, compensatory, and punitive damages.

Discrimination Against Disabled People

The Rehabilitation Act of 1973 provides remedies to disabled people who suffered employment discrimination by federal employers, federal contractors, or employers receiving federal funds. A much more comprehensive act, the Americans with Disabilities Act (ADA), was enacted in 1990. Title I of the ADA, the employment section, applies to most public employers (except the federal government), labor unions, and to private employers who have fifteen or more employees.

The ADA prohibits employment discrimination due to a person's qualifying disability in application procedures, hiring, discharge, compensation, advancement, job training, and other aspects of employment. The act defines a disability as "a physical or mental impairment that substantially limits one or more of the major life activities."[30] EEOC regulations have interpreted major life activities to mean the type of activities performed by "the average person in the general population."[31] Being able to work is certainly such an activity. Examples of ADA-protected physical or mental impairments include HIV, epilepsy, MS, MD, speech and hearing impairments, and learning disabilities.

Conditions that do not qualify for statutory protection include gambling addictions, being homosexual, and being homeless.[32]

Disabled plaintiffs who prove disparate impact discrimination by their employers are entitled to recover front pay, back pay, and injunctive relief. Plaintiffs proving intentional discrimination are also entitled to recover money damages and to try their cases to a jury.

The ADA requires employers to make reasonable efforts to accommodate the disabilities of qualified employees or job applicants. However, employers can deny employment to disabled people where employment of a disabled person would pose a direct threat to the health or safety of other people or where an "undue hardship" would result—for example, when the financial burdens incurred by the employer in accommodating the disabled person would be excessive, or when such employment would fundamentally alter the nature of the business or program.

In the next case, a government employer, the Tennessee Valley Authority, discriminated against a dyslexic person who sought admittance to an apprenticeship program which would have trained him to become a heavy equipment operator. The employer denied him entry to the program because his scores on a written aptitude test were too low. This action violated the Rehabilitation Act.

Stutts v. Freeman
694 F.2d 666
U.S. Court of Appeals, Eleventh Circuit
January 3, 1983

Fay, Circuit Judge

This is an appeal from the denial of a . . . motion to alter or amend a judgment. That motion was made challenging the granting of a motion for summary judgment in favor of the defendant in a suit brought under the Rehabilitation Act of 1973, *as amended*, 29 U.S.C. § 701 et seq. (1978). . . . [T]he appellant, Mr. Stutts, contends that the defendant, Tennessee Valley Authority (TVA), violated 29 U.S.C. § 794 in refusing to allow him, as a TVA employee, to enter an apprenticeship program for the position of heavy equipment operator. Mr. Stutts argues that he is an "otherwise qualified handicapped individual" under the statute and that summary judgment was improper. While we do not decide the question whether Mr. Stutts was an "otherwise qualified handicapped individual," we agree that summary judgment should not have been granted in TVA's favor and reverse. . . .

Facts

The uncontroverted facts show that in 1971, Mr. Stutts was hired by TVA as a laborer at TVA's Colbert Steam Plant in Colbert County, Alabama where he worked temporarily until 1973 when he was hired on a permanent basis. In 1979, Mr. Stutts applied for an opening with TVA in an apprenticeship training program to become a heavy equipment operator. His application was denied on the basis of a "low" score on the General

Aptitude Test Battery (GATB), a test used by TVA to predict the probability of success of an applicant in the training program.

Mr. Stutts has been diagnosed as having the condition of dyslexia, which impairs his ability to read. The record indicates that this disability renders Mr. Stutts incapable of reading beyond the most elementary level, and leads to an inability to perform well on written tests such as the GATB. There is evidence that Mr. Stutts was evaluated by doctors and tested with non-written tests after receiving results of his GATB test and was judged to have above average intelligence, coordination and aptitude for a position as a heavy equipment operator. TVA tried to obtain the results of these non-verbal tests in connection with Mr. Stutts' application for the apprenticeship training program, but was unable to do so. Attempts to persuade the testing service to give Mr. Stutts an oral GATB were unsuccessful because scoring on the written GATB is based on standardized and uniform testing conditions and cannot be accurately translated from an oral test. Despite TVA's knowledge of and unsuccessful efforts to obtain alternate forms of evaluation, Mr. Stutts' nonselection was based solely on his low score on the written GATB test.

Discussion

The controlling section of the Rehabilitation Act of 1973 reads in part as follows:

> "No otherwise qualified handicapped individual in the United States, . . . shall solely by reason of his handicap, be excluded from the participation in, be denied the benefits of, or be subjected to discrimination under any program or activity receiving Federal financial assis-

tance or under any program or activity conducted by any Executive agency. . . ."

29 U.S.C. § 794.

"Handicapped individual" is defined as follows:

> "[A]ny individual who (i) has a physical or mental disability which for such individual constitutes or results in a substantial handicap to employment and (ii) can reasonably be expected to benefit in terms of employability from vocational rehabilitation services. . . . (B) . . . [A]ny person who (i) has a physical or mental impairment which substantially limits one or more of such person's major life activities; (ii) has a record of such an impairment, or (iii) is regarded as having such an impairment."

29 U.S.C. § 706(7)(A), (B).

The policy underlying the Rehabilitation Act of 1973 is clear—"to promote and expand employment opportunities in the public and private sectors for handicapped individuals." 298 U.S.C. § 701(8). Both parties agree that Mr. Stutts is a handicapped individual and that the main hiring criteria—the GATB test—could not accurately reflect Mr. Stutts' abilities. There is considerable evidence supporting Mr. Stutts' contention that he is fully capable of performing well as a heavy equipment operator and we find a genuine issue as to whether or not he could successfully complete the training program, either with the help of a reader or by other means. Congress has clearly directed entities in its sphere of control to make efforts to expand employment opportunities for handicapped persons. TVA has not satisfied its obligation under the statute by merely asking for results of alternate testing methods and accepting a rejection.

We do not hold that Mr. Stutts must be given a position as a heavy equipment operator, nor do we hold that he must be admitted into the training program. We do hold that when TVA uses a test which cannot and does not accurately reflect the abilities of a handicapped person, as a matter of law they must do more to accommodate that individual than TVA has done in regard to Mr. Stutts. TVA argues that their efforts on behalf of Mr. Stutts showed that he received better treatment than a non-handicapped applicant. TVA sought to have a non-written GATB test given to Mr. Stutts. They tried to obtain the results of other examinations and tests given Mr. Stutts after his dyslexic condition was discerned. But the fact remains that these efforts were not successful. In the final analysis TVA made its decision based on the GATB test. TVA's unsuccessful efforts do not amount to "reasonable accommodation" of the handicapped as required by 45 C.F.R. § 84.12 (1981).

The district court granted TVA's motion for summary judgment on the ground that Mr. Stutts had failed to show that he had similar qualifications to non-handicapped individuals who were hired for the position. . . . To the extent that the district court based this finding on the GATB test results, it was in error. . . . Such abuse is present here. When an employer like TVA chooses a test that discriminates against handicapped persons as its sole hiring criterion, and makes no meaningful accommodation for a handicapped applicant, it violates the Rehabilitation Act of 1973.

The summary judgment is set aside and the case remanded for further proceedings consistent with this opinion.

Case Questions

1. Why did the appeals court find that the TVA had not made a reasonable effort to accommodate Stutts?
2. Under the Rehabilitation Act of 1973 (cited in the *Stutts* case), would companies like McDonald's, Nike, or Disney be required to similarly accommodate dyslexic job applicants?

Age Discrimination in Employment Act

In 1967, Congress enacted the Age Discrimination in Employment Act (ADEA). As amended, this act protects people aged forty and older from age-based discrimination in employment. Seeking to "promote employment of older persons based on their ability rather than age," the Act provides that employers may not "discriminate against any individual with respect to his compensation, terms, conditions, or privileges of employment, because of such individual's age." The ADEA applies to public and private employers, employment agencies, and labor organizations. It does not apply to elected officials and their appointees who work on a policy-making level. Like Title VII, the ADEA classifies discrimination as disparate impact and disparate treatment.

The ADEA prohibits employers from requiring that employees retire at a specified age with two exceptions:

1. Business executives who have pension benefits of at least $44,000 per year can be forced to retire at age sixty-five.
2. Collective bargaining agreements that provide for a retirement age can still be enforced.

A person claiming protection under this act may simultaneously file with the EEOC and the state antidiscrimination agency. Claimants other than federal employees are entitled to try their cases to a jury.[33]

Plaintiffs rely heavily on statistical evidence in disparate impact cases that allege age discrimination. The defendant can rebut the statistics or prove that a legitimate business necessity justifies the employment practice.

In a disparate treatment (intentional discrimination) case, the plaintiff has to prove the employer intended to discriminate and that age was a factor and "played a determining influence on the outcome."[34] The plaintiff must show that he or she is protected by the ADEA, is qualified for a particular job, was unfavorably treated by the employer, and that people not protected by the ADEA were more favorably treated. The employer can defend by proving that a "reasonable factor other than age" was the cause for the employee's treatment (the RFOA defense) or by establishing a BFOQ. Although the BFOQ defense allows the employer to admit that age was a factor in the employment decision, the employer must prove that age is a legitimate occupational qualification and is reasonably necessary to the particular business.

Finally, the employee has the burden of convincing the trier of fact that the employer's defense was a mere pretext for the discrimination and that age had a "determinative influence on the employment decision."[35]

In a disparate impact case, the employee must prove that a particular unlawful employment practice caused a disparate impact based on employees over forty years of age when compared to employees under forty. The employer can then rebut this evidence with proof that the employment practice is job related and is consistent with a business necessity. Lastly, the employee can win the suit by demonstrating that a nondiscriminatory alternative practice exists that is both job related and compatible with a business necessity.

Applying the ADEA is sometimes difficult, as, for example, when companies are engaging in reductions in force (RIFs) due to business necessities. Although courts have used the ADEA to prevent employers from laying off highly paid, experienced (and older) employees to save money, they have also used it to review business decisions.

The ADEA provides that courts have equitable and legal powers to grant relief. They may render judgments "compelling employment, reinstatement, or promotions or enforcing the liability for amounts deemed to be unpaid minimum wages or unpaid time compensation."

The following case was brought by corporate airline pilots. They contended that their employer was violating the ADEA by requiring them to retire at age sixty. The defendants responded by raising the BFOQ defense.

E.E.O.C. v. El Paso Natural Gas Co.

626 F.Supp.182
U.S. District Court, W.D. Texas,
El Paso Division
December 31, 1985

Memorandum Opinion and Order

Hudspeth, District Judge

This is an action pursuant to the Age Discrimination in Employment Act, 29 U.S.C. § 623 et seq. The issue presented is whether a company policy requiring the pilots of corporate aircraft to cease flying operations at age 60 is a violation of the Age Discrimination in Employment Act, or, whether it is, as the Defendants contend, a bona fide occupational qualification. The trial was bifurcated, and the issue of liability alone was tried to the Court without a jury. The Court's findings of fact and conclusions of law with respect to the issue of liability are included in this opinion.

A. Factual Background

Defendant El Paso Natural Gas Company is a Delaware corporation doing business in the State of Texas and in the Western District of Texas. Its principal office is engaged in the business of operating natural gas pipelines in interstate commerce, and at all times relevant to this lawsuit it has employed more than 20 employees. Defendant, The El Paso Company, is the parent company of El Paso Natural Gas Company and it maintains its principal office in El Paso, Texas. It is engaged in the production and distribution of petrochemical products, fibers, textiles and other products and services in interstate commerce, and at all times relevant to this lawsuit it has employed more than 20 employees. Defendant El Paso

Products Company was at all times prior to January 1, 1984 a subsidiary of The El Paso Company. It is a Texas corporation with its principal office located in Odessa, Texas. It is engaged in the production and distribution of petrochemicals and agricultural chemicals in interstate commerce, and at all times relevant to this lawsuit it has employed more than 20 employees. Plaintiff Equal Employment Opportunity Commission is an agency of the United States Government charged with the enforcement of the Age Discrimination in Employment Act. It is authorized to bring the present action by 29 U.S.C. § 626(b) as amended by Section 2 of Reorganization Plan No. 1 of 1978, 92 Stat. 3781.

The Defendants maintain a fleet of corporate aircraft for the purpose of providing air transportation to the executives, personnel and business guests of the El Paso Natural Gas Company and its affiliated companies. . . . At the time of the trial, the Defendants employed 19 pilots to operate the corporate aircraft fleet. . . .

The Defendants require their pilots to hold Class I medical certificates, meaning that the pilots must undergo a physical examination every six months. Those pilots who operate . . . jet aircraft are additionally required to undergo simulator training twice a year, and the twin-engine turboprop pilots are required to undergo simulator training annually. The duties of the companies' pilots include flying days and nights, visual and instrument, doing their own weather checking and fuel computation, and frequently landing at airports with which the pilot is not familiar.

Since they began their flying operations, the Defendants have followed a policy of requiring their corporate pilots to cease flying operations upon reaching the age of 60. If a nonflying position for which the pilot is qualified is available within the company organization at the time he reaches his sixtieth birthday, the pilot is given the opportunity to transfer to the nonflying position. If he declines to accept the transfer, or if no position is available for which the pilot is qualified, he is retired. Since the institution of this policy, a total of seven corporate pilots have reached the age of 60 and have been required to cease flying operations.

B. Is Defendants' Age 60 Rule a Bona Fide Occupational Qualification?

The Age Discrimination in Employment Act, 29 U.S.C. § 623 et seq., protects workers between the ages of 40 and 70 from discrimination on the basis of age. It is undisputed that the Plaintiff has shown a prima facie case of violation of the Age Discrimination in Employment Act by showing that Defendants require their corporate pilots to retire from flying status when they reach their sixtieth birthday. The burden shifted to the Defendants to establish by a preponderance of the evidence that their policy constituted a bona fide occupation qualification.

Title 29, United States Code, Section 623(f) provides in pertinent part as follows:

"It shall not be unlawful for an employer, employment agency, or labor organization—
"(1) to take any action otherwise prohibited . . . where age is a bona fide occupational qualification reasonably necessary to the normal operation of the particular business. . . ."

The "particular business" involved in this case is not the entire spectrum of corporate business, but rather the specific "business" of the operation of corporate aircraft by the Defendants' corporate pilots. In other words, "particular business"

means the specific job or position from which the protected individual is excluded by virtue of his or her age. . . . The regulations promulgated by the Equal Employment Opportunity Commission under the Age Discrimination in Employment Act correctly state the burden of proof when an employer relies upon the bona fide occupational qualification (BFOQ) exception to the Act. Title 29, CFR § 1625.6(b) provides as follows:

"An employer asserting a BFOQ defense has the burden of proving that (1) the age limit is reasonably necessary to the essence of the business, and either (2) that all or substantially all individuals excluded from the job involved are in fact disqualified, or (3) that some of the individuals so excluded possess a disqualifying trait that cannot be ascertained except by reference to age. If the employer's objective in asserting a BFOQ is the goal of public safety, the employer must prove that the challenged practice does indeed effectuate that goal and that there is no acceptable alternative which would better advance it or equally advance it with less discriminatory impact."

In the instant case, the Defendants contend that the age limit on pilots is reasonably necessary to the safe operation of its corporate aircraft, and that it is impossible or highly impractical to deal with pilots over the age of 60 on an individual or case-by-case basis. The proof offered by Defendants in an effort to sustain their burden proceeded along two distinct but parallel lines. First, the Defendants contend that they are entitled to rely upon the determination by the Federal Aviation Administration that pilots of commercial aircraft not be permitted to fly after attaining the age of 60. Second, the Defendants offered expert witnesses of their own in an effort to prove that it is "impossible or highly impractical" to deal with older pilots on an individualized basis.

1. The Federal Aviation Administration's Age 60 Rule for Commercial Airline Pilots.

In 1959, the Federal Aviation Administration adopted the predecessor to the rule now codified at 14 CFR § 121.383(c), which provides in pertinent part as follows:

> "No person may serve as a pilot on an airplane engaged in operations under this part if that person has reached his 60th birthday."

The genesis of the age 60 rule lay in the Administration's concern about two primary factors: The introduction of jet aircraft into commercial aviation, with the increased speeds at which these anticipated aircraft would operate, and the aging of the overall commercial pilot population. Pursuant to the recommendation of a committee appointed by the Administrator to study the matter, the so-called "age 60" rule was adopted. The rule has remained intact for over 25 years, and remains in force today, despite frequent reconsideration and review. For example, in 1979 Congress enacted Public law 96–171, 93 Stat. 1285, which directed the National Institutes of Health in consultation with the Secretary of Transportation to conduct a special study to determine whether the age 60 rule was medically warranted. In response to this legislation, the Director of the National Institutes of Health assigned primary responsibility to the National Institute on Aging, which assembled a panel of experts to study the matter. In 1981, the Panel issued its report, which contained the following conclusions and recommendations:

> "The Panel attaches no special medical significance to age 60 as a mandatory age for retirement of airline pilots. It finds, however, that age-related changes in health and performance influence adversely the ability of increasing numbers of individuals to perform as pilots with the highest level of safety and, consequently, endanger the safety of the aviation system as a whole. Moreover, the Panel could not identify the existence of a medical or performance appraisal system that can single out those pilots who would pose the greatest hazard because of early, or impending, deterioration in health or performance.
>
> "The panel therefore recommends: (1) that the present age limit for air carrier pilots in command and first officers be retained." . . .

The FAA rule requiring retirement of commercial airline pilots at age 60 is, of course, relevant evidence in support of the Defendants' BFOQ defense in the instant case. . . . The extent to which the rule is probative turns upon the congruity between the occupations of commercial airline pilot and corporate pilot. . . . In this case, the Defendants argue that there is complete and utter congruity between the two occupations. The Court agrees. There is no substantial difference between the work performed by commercial airline pilots and the corporate pilots employed by the Defendants in this case. The Defendants' pilots transport significant numbers of passengers over long distances in various kinds of aircraft including jet aircraft. If anything, the duties imposed upon the Defendants' corporate pilots are more onerous than those undertaken by airline pilots. For example, the Defendants' pilots are expected to be ready to fly at any time of the day or night with little advance warning. They are frequently asked to fly into and out of unfamiliar airports, and, unlike airline pilots, they are required to handle their own weather checking and fuel computations. Under the circumstances, the Defendants are entitled to rely upon the expertise of the Federal Aviation Administration and apply the age 60 rule to their own pilots as a bona fide occupation qualification.

2. *The Expert Testimony.*

. . . The Fifth Circuit adopted a two-pronged test for determining the validity of a BFOQ defense in cases in which the duties of the employees concerned involved the safe transportation of passengers. First, the job qualification established by the employer must be reasonably necessary to the safe transportation of passengers. . . . Second, the employer must establish either that all or substantially all persons over the age limit would be unable to perform safely and efficiently the duties of the job involved, or that it is impossible or highly impractical to deal with the older employees on an individualized basis. . . . The two-pronged test adopted by the Fifth Circuit has recently been specifically approved by the Supreme Court. . . . In the instant case, the Court finds that the Defendants have sustained their burden of proving by a preponderance of the evidence that the age limit they have imposed upon corporate pilots is reasonably necessary to the safe operation of corporate aircraft, and that it is impossible or highly impractical to deal with pilots over the age of 60 on an individual basis.

In their case in chief, the Defendants presented the testimony of four expert witnesses with outstanding credentials. Three of the experts were medical doctors, the remaining expert was a psychologist. These experts all testified that aging pilots, in common with all other human beings, experience physiological and psychological deterioration that at some point will affect their ability to fly safely. Furthermore, these experts were unanimous in testifying that a medical and/or psychological appraisal system does not yet exist that would be capable of singling out those individual pilots who would pose a safety hazard because of deterioration in health or overall ability to perform.

. . . Having weighed the testimony and judged its credibility, the Court finds that the Defendants have carried their burden of establishing by a preponderance of the evidence that it is impossible or at least highly impractical to deal with pilots over 60 years of age on an individualized basis. In reaching this conclusion, the Court is mindful of the statement of the Supreme Court in its opinion in *Western Airlines v. Criswell, supra,* 105 S.Ct. at 2754:

> "When an employer establishes that a job qualification has been carefully formulated to respond to documented concerns for public safety, it will not be overly burdensome to persuade a trier of fact that the qualification is 'reasonably necessary' to safe operation of the business. The uncertainty implicit in the concept of managing safety risks always makes it 'reasonably necessary' to err on the side of caution in a close case. The employer cannot be expected to establish the risk of an airline accident 'to a certainty, for certainty would require running the risk until a tragic accident would prove that the judgment was sound.'"

Having concluded that the Defendants have carried their burden of showing that their age 60 rule for corporate pilots is a bona fide occupational qualification, the Court finds that judgment should be entered in favor of the Defendants with respect to the issue of liability. In view of this decision, the bifurcated trial comes to an end, and a hearing on the merits will not be necessary with respect to remedies.

It is therefore ordered that judgment be, and it is hereby, entered in favor of the Defendants, and that the Plaintiff take nothing by its suit.

It is further ordered that the Plaintiff pay the costs of suit herein incurred.

Case Questions

1. The defendants claimed that age was a bona fide occupational qualification. What was the basis for their argument?
2. How is the burden of proof allocated when a defendant raises age as a bona fide occupational qualification?
3. What evidence did the employer offer to satisfy its burden of proof?

Employment Discrimination and Sexual Preference

Although federal employees who are homosexual have found some protection from employment discrimination in the federal sector, sexual preference discrimination in public sector employment is common. The federal courts have ruled that Congress did not intend Title VII to protect homosexuals, bisexuals, or transsexuals; however, some federal courts have recognized that the Fourteenth Amendment protects homosexuals from discharge because of sexual preference under some circumstances based on equal protection grounds.[36]

At the state level, Wisconsin, Massachusetts, Hawaii, Connecticut, New Jersey, California, Minnesota, and Vermont have enacted fair employment laws that protect homosexuals from public and private sector discrimination. Other states have issued executive orders that prevent state governmental employers from discriminating on the basis of sexual preference. Many city, town, and county governments have similarly prohibited such discrimination via executive orders and ordinances. In the private sector, some corporate employers have voluntarily developed and implemented nondiscriminatory policies.

The next case is a consolidated appeal by six homosexual appellants. The appellants brought their cases to the Court of Appeals because they hoped to convince it to rule that Title VII prohibits employment discrimination based on sexual preference.

DeSantis v. Pacific Tel. & Tel. Co., Inc.
608 F.2d 327
U.S. Court of Appeals, Ninth Circuit
May 31, 1979
Choy, Circuit Judge

Male and female homosexuals brought three separate federal district court actions claiming that their employers or former employers discriminated against them in employment decisions because of their homosexuality. They alleged that such discrimination violated Title VII of the Civil Rights Act of 1964, 42 U.S.C. § 2000e et seq. . . . The district courts dismissed the complaints as failing to state claims under either statute. Plaintiffs below appealed. Because of the similarity of issues involved, this court consolidated the appeals at the request of counsel for appellants. We affirm.

I. Statement of the Case

A. Strailey v. Happy Times Nursery School, Inc.

Appellant Strailey, a male, was fired by the Happy Times Nursery School after two years service as a teacher. He alleged that he was fired because he wore a small gold ear-loop to school prior to the commencement of the school year. He filed a charge with the Equal Employment Opportunity Commission (EEOC) which the EEOC rejected because of an alleged lack of jurisdiction over claims of discrimination based on sexual orientation. He then filed suit on behalf of himself and all others similarly situated, seeking declaratory, injunctive, and monetary relief. The district court dismissed the complaint as failing to state a claim under either Title VII or § 1985(3).

B. DeSantis v. Pacific Telephone & Telegraph Co.

DeSantis, Boyle, and Simard, all males, claimed that Pacific Telephone & Telegraph Co. (PT&T) impermissibly discriminated against them because of their homosexuality. DeSantis alleged that he was not hired when a PT&T supervisor concluded that he was a homosexual. According to appellants' brief, "BOYLE was

continually harassed by his co-workers and had to quit to preserve his health after only three months because his supervisors did nothing to alleviate this condition." Finally, "SIMARD was forced to quit under similar conditions after almost four years of employment with PT&T, but he was harassed by his supervisors [as well]. . . . In addition, his personnel file has been marked as not eligible for rehire, and his applications for employment were rejected by PT&T in 1974 and 1976." Appellants DeSantis, Boyle, and Simard also alleged that PT&T officials have publicly stated that they would not hire homosexuals.

These plaintiffs also filed charges with the EEOC, also rejected by the EEOC for lack of jurisdiction. They then filed suit on behalf of themselves and all others similarly situated seeking declaratory, injunctive, and monetary relief under Title VII and § 1985(3). They also prayed that the district court issue mandamus commanding the EEOC to process charges based on sexual orientation. The district court dismissed their complaint. It held that the court lacked jurisdiction to compel the EEOC to alter its interpretation of Title VII. It also held that appellants had not stated viable claims under either Title VII or § 1985(3).

C. Lundin v. Pacific Telephone & Telegraph

Lundin and Buckley, both females, were operators with PT&T. They filed suit in federal court alleging that PT&T discriminated against them because of their known lesbian relationship and eventually fired them. They also alleged that they endured numerous insults by PT&T employees because of their relationship. Finally, Lundin alleged that the union that represented her as a PT&T operator failed adequately to represent her interests and failed adequately to present her grievance regarding her treatment. Appellants sought monetary and injunctive relief. The district court dismissed their suit as not stating a claim upon which relief could be granted. It also refused leave to amend their complaint to add a claim under § 1985(3).

II. Title VII Claim

Appellants argue first that the district courts erred in holding that Title VII does not prohibit discrimination on the basis of sexual preference. They claim that in prohibiting certain employment discrimination on the basis of "sex," Congress meant to include discrimination on the basis of sexual orientation. They add that in a trial they could establish that discrimination against homosexuals disproportionately [a]ffects men and that this disproportionate impact and correlation between discrimination on the basis of sexual preference and discrimination on the basis of "sex" requires that sexual preference be considered a subcategory of the "sex" category of Title VII.

A. Congressional Intent in Prohibiting "Sex" Discrimination

In *Holloway v. Arthur Andersen & Co.*, 566 F.2d 659 (9th Cir. 1977), . . . [t]his court rejected that claim writing:

> "The cases interpreting Title VII sex discrimination provisions agree that they were intended to place women on an equal footing with men. [Citations omitted.]
> "Giving the statute its plain meaning, this court concluded that Congress had only the traditional notions of 'sex' in mind. Later legislative activity makes

this narrow definition even more evident. Several bills have been introduced to *amend* the Civil Rights Act to prohibit discrimination against 'sexual preference.' None have [*sic*] been enacted into law.

> "Congress has not shown any intent other than to restrict the term 'sex' to its traditional meaning. Therefore, this court will not expand Title VII's applica-tion in the absence of Congressional mandate. The manifest purpose of Title VII's prohibition against sex discrimination in employment is to ensure that men and women are treated equally, absent a bona fide relationship between the qualifications for the job and the person's sex. . . ."

Following *Holloway*, we conclude that Title VII's prohibition of "sex" discrimination applies only to discrimination on the basis of gender and should not be judicially extended to include sexual preference such as homosexuality. . . .

E. Effeminacy

Appellant Strailey contends that he was terminated by the Happy Times Nursery School because that school felt that it was inappropriate for a male teacher to wear an earring to school. He claims that the school's reliance on a stereotype—that a male should have a virile rather than an effeminate appearance—violates Title VII.

In *Holloway* this court noted that Congress intended Title VII's ban on sex discrimination in employment to prevent discrimination because of gender, not because of sexual orientation or preference. . . . Recently the Fifth Circuit similarly read the legislative history of Title VII and concluded that Title VII thus does not protect against discrimination because of effeminacy. . . . We agree and hold that discrimination because of effeminacy, like discrimination because of homosexuality

. . . or transsexualism . . . does not fall within the purview of Title VII.

Having determined that appellants' allegations do not implicate Title VII's prohibition on sex discrimination, we affirm the district court's dismissals of the Title VII claims.

Case Questions

1. Because the appellants could not rely on any specific law that prohibits discrimination based on sexual preference, what did they hope to achieve by this lawsuit?
2. The trial and appellate courts agreed that Title VII provides no protection against employment discrimination based on sexual preference. What rationale did these courts use to reach this conclusion?

EMPLOYMENT DISCRIMINATION AND THE UNION MOVEMENT

Prior to the passage of the National Labor Relations Act (the Wagner Act) in 1935, employers were allowed to pursue almost any business tactic that served to inhibit or destroy the collective bargaining power of employees. In their struggle against the union movement, companies used discharges, blacklisting, lockouts (withholding work from employees), injunctions that prohibited employees from picketing, and violence. Although some legislation had been passed to protect the rights of employees, the first act that dealt comprehensively with employer-employee relations was the Wagner Act. This act stated the right of a union to exist and the rights of employees to associate with and bargain collectively through a union without interference from the employer. The law gave employees the power to legally engage in group activities, and it helped equalize the bargaining positions of companies and laborers by outlawing employers' practices that constituted "unfair labor practices." In the following case, the Textile Workers accused an employer of an unfair labor practice.

Textile Workers v. Darlington Manufacturing Company
380 U.S. 263
U.S. Supreme Court
March 25, 1965

Mr. Justice Harlan delivered the opinion of the Court.

We here review judgments of the Court of Appeals setting aside and refusing to enforce an order of the National Labor Relations Board which found respondent Darlington guilty of an unfair labor practice by reason of having permanently closed its plant following petitioner union's election as the bargaining representative of Darlington's employees.

Darlington Manufacturing Company was a South Carolina corporation operating one textile mill. A majority of

Darlington's stock was held by Deering Milliken, a New York "selling house" marketing textiles produced by others. Deering Milliken in turn was controlled by Roger Milliken, president of Darlington, and by other members of the Milliken family. The National Labor Relations Board found that the Milliken family, through Deering Milliken, operated 17 textile manufacturers, including Darlington, whose products, manufactured in 27 different mills, were marketed through Deering Milliken.

In March 1956 petitioner Textile Workers Union initiated an organizational campaign at Darlington which the company resisted vigorously in various ways, including threats to close the mill if the union won a representation election. On September 6, 1956, the union won an election by a narrow margin. When Roger Milliken was advised of the union victory, he decided to call a meeting of the Darlington board of directors to consider closing the mill. . . .

The board of directors met on September 12 and voted to liquidate the corporation, action which was approved by the stockholders on October 17. The plant ceased operations entirely in November, and all plant machinery and equipment were sold piecemeal at auction in December.

The union filed charges with the Labor Board claiming that Darlington had violated §§ 8(a)(1) and (3) of the National Labor Relations Act by closing its plant, and § 8(a)(5) by refusing to bargain with the union after the election. The Board, by a divided vote, found that Darlington had been closed because of the antiunion animus of Roger Milliken, and held that to be a violation of § 8(a)(3). The Board also found Darlington to be part of a single integrated employer group controlled by the Milliken family through Deering Milliken; therefore Deering Milliken could be held liable for the unfair labor practices of Darlington. Alternatively, since Darlington was a part of the Deering Milliken enterprise, Deering Milliken had violated the Act by closing part of its business for a discriminatory purpose. The Board ordered back pay for all Darlington employees until they obtained substantially equivalent work or were put on preferential hiring lists at other Deering Milliken mills. Respondent Deering Milliken was ordered to bargain with the union in regard to details of compliance with the Board order. . . .

On review, the Court of Appeals, sitting *en banc*, set aside the order and denied enforcement by a divided vote. . . . We granted certiorari . . . to consider the important questions involved. We hold that so far as the Labor Relations Act is concerned, an employer has the absolute right to terminate his entire business for any reason he pleases, but disagree with the Court of Appeals that such right includes the ability to close part of a business no matter what the reason. We conclude that the cause must be remanded to the Board for further proceedings. . . .

I.

We consider first the argument, advanced by the petitioner union but not by the Board, and rejected by the Court of Appeals, that an employer may not go completely out of business without running afoul of the Labor Relations Act if such action is prompted by a desire to avoid unionization. . . . A proposition that a single businessman cannot choose to go out of business if he wants to would represent such a startling innovation that it should not be entertained without the clearest manifestation of legislative intent or unequivocal judicial precedent so construing the Labor Relations Act. We find neither.

So far as legislative manifestation is concerned, it is sufficient to say that there is not the slightest indication in the history of the Wagner Act or of the Taft-Hartley Act that Congress envisaged any such result under either statute. . . .

The courts of appeals have generally assumed that a complete cessation of business will remove an employer from future coverage by the Act. . . .

The AFL–CIO suggests in its *amicus* brief that Darlington's action was similar to a discriminatory lockout, which is prohibited " 'because designed to frustrate organizational efforts, to destroy or undermine bargaining representation, or to evade the duty to bargain.' " One of the purposes of the Labor Relations Act is to prohibit the discriminatory use of economic weapons in an effort to obtain future benefits. The discriminatory lockout designed to destroy a union, like a "runaway shop," is a lever which has been used to discourage collective employee activities in the future. But a complete liquidation of a business yields no such future benefit for the employer, if the termination is bona fide. It may be motivated more by spite against the union than by business reasons, but it is not the type of discrimination which is prohibited by the Act. The personal satisfaction that such an employer may derive from standing on his beliefs and the mere possibility that other employers will follow his example are surely too remote to be considered dangers at which the labor statutes were aimed. Although employees may be prohibited from engaging in a strike under certain conditions, no one would consider it a violation of the Act for the same employees to quit their employment *en masse*, even if motivated by a desire to ruin the employer. The very permanence of such action would negate any future economic benefit to the employees. The employer's right to go out of business is no different.

We are not presented here with the case of a "runaway shop," whereby Darlington would transfer its work to another plant or open a new plant in another locality to replace its closed plant. Nor are we concerned with a shutdown where the employees, by renouncing the union, could cause the plant to reopen. Such cases would involve discriminatory employer action for the purpose of obtaining some benefit from the employees in the future. We hold here only that when an employer closes his entire business, even if the liquidation is motivated by vindictiveness toward the union, such action is not an unfair labor practice.[20]

---

[20] Nothing we have said in this opinion would justify an employer's interfering with employee organizational activities by threatening to close his plant, as distinguished from announcing a decision to close already reached by the board of directors or other management authority empowered to make such a decision. We recognize that this safeguard does not wholly remove the possibility that our holding may result in some deterrent effect on organizational activities independent of that arising from the closing itself. An employer may be encouraged to make a definitive decision to close on the theory that its mere announcement before a representation election will discourage the employees from voting for the union, and thus his decision may not have to be implemented. Such a possibility is not likely to occur, however, except in a marginal business; a solidly successful employer is not apt to hazard the possibility that the employees will call his bluff by voting to organize. We see no practical way of eliminating this possible consequence of our holding short of allowing the Board to order an employer who chooses so to gamble with his employees not to carry out his announced intention to close. We do not consider the matter of sufficient significance in the overall labor-management relations picture to require or justify a decision different from the one we have made.

II.

While we thus agree with the Court of Appeals that viewing Darlington as an independent employer the liquidation of its business was not an unfair labor practice, we cannot accept the lower court's view that the same conclusion necessarily follows if Darlington is regarded as an integral part of the Deering Milliken enterprise.

The closing of an entire business, even though discriminatory, ends the employer-employee relationship; the force of such a closing is entirely spent as to that business when termination of the enterprise takes place. On the other hand, a discriminatory partial closing may have repercussions on what remains of the business, affording employer leverage for discouraging the free exercise of § 7 rights among remaining employees of much the same kind as that found to exist in the "runaway shop" and "temporary closing" cases. . . . Moreover, a possible remedy open to the Board in such a case, like the remedies available in the "runaway shop" and "temporary closing" cases, is to order reinstatement of the discharged employees in the other parts of the business. No such remedy is available when an entire business has been terminated. By analogy to those cases involving a continuing enterprise we are constrained to hold, in disagreement with the Court of Appeals, that a partial closing is an unfair labor practice under § 8 (a) (3) if motivated by a purpose to chill unionism in any of the remaining plants of the single employer and if the employer may reasonably have foreseen that such closing would likely have that effect.

While we have spoken in terms of a "partial closing" in the context of the Board's finding that Darlington was part of a larger single enterprise controlled by the Milliken family, we do not mean to suggest that an organizational integration of plants or corporations is a necessary prerequisite to the establishment of such a violation of § 8 (a) (3). If the persons exercising control over a plant that is being closed for antiunion reasons (1) have an interest in another business, whether or not affiliated with or engaged in the same line of commercial activity as the closed plant, of sufficient substantiality to give promise of their reaping a benefit from the discouragement of unionization in that business; (2) act to close their plant with the purpose of producing such a result; and (3) occupy a relationship to the other business which makes it realistically foreseeable that its employees will fear that such business will also be closed down if they persist in organizational activities, we think that an unfair labor practice has been made out.

Although the Board's single employer finding necessarily embraced findings as to Roger Milliken and the Milliken family which, if sustained by the Court of Appeals, would satisfy the elements of "interest" and "relationship" with respect to other parts of the Deering Milliken enterprise, that and the other Board findings fall short of establishing the factors of "purpose" and "effect" which are vital requisites of the general principles that govern a case of this kind.

Thus, the Board's findings as to the purpose and foreseeable effect of the Darlington closing pertained *only* to its impact on the Darlington Employees. No findings were made as to the purpose and effect of the closing with respect to the employees in the other plants comprising the Deering Milliken group. It does not suffice to establish the unfair labor practice charged here to argue that the Darlington closing necessarily had an adverse impact upon unionization in such other plants. We have heretofore observed that employer action which has a foreseeable consequence of discouraging concerted activities generally does not amount to a violation of § 8 (a) (3) in the absence of a showing of motivation which is aimed at achieving the prohibited effect. . . . In an area which trenches so closely upon otherwise legitimate employer prerogatives, we consider the absence of Board findings on this score a fatal defect in its decision. The Court of Appeals for its part did not deal with the question of purpose and effect at all, since it concluded that an employer's right to close down his entire business because of distaste for unionism, also embraced a partial closing so motivated.

Apart from this, the Board's holding should not be accepted or rejected without court review of its single employer finding, judged, however, in accordance with the general principles set forth above. Review of that finding, which the lower court found unnecessary on its view of the cause, now becomes necessary in light of our holding in this part of our opinion, and is a task that devolves upon the Court of Appeals in the first instance. . . .

In these circumstances, we think the proper disposition of this cause is to require that it be remanded to the Board so as to afford the Board the opportunity to make further findings on the issue of purpose and effect. . . . This is particularly appropriate here since the cases involve issues of first impression. If such findings are made, the cases will then be in a posture for further review by the Court of Appeals on all issues. Accordingly, without intimating any view as to how any of these matters should eventuate, we vacate the judgments of the Court of Appeals and remand the cases to that court with instructions to remand them to the Board for further proceedings consistent with this opinion.

It is so ordered.

Case Questions

1. According to the Supreme Court, is it an unfair labor practice for an employer to close his entire business to prevent the unionization of his former employees?
2. Does it make any difference if an employer closes only one of several plants for the purpose of discouraging unionism in the employer's remaining plants?

National Labor Relations Board

The Wagner Act also established the National Labor Relations Board (NLRB). The NLRB has two major functions. First, it oversees union elections and certifies the union that is elected to represent employees. Second, it hears and settles charges of unfair labor practices committed by either employers or unions.

The NLRB has broad discretionary powers to remedy any unfair labor practice. It may order reinstatement of an employee who was wrongfully fired and award back pay and commensurate seniority for that employee. It may issue a cease-and-desist order to an employer who engages in unfair labor practices. Finally, it may order a union and employer to bargain.

Following the passage of the Wagner Act, union activity flourished, particularly since the Wagner Act delineated illegal employer practices, but no illegal union activities. The Labor-Management Relations Act of 1947 (the Taft-Hartley Act) was enacted to further balance the power between unions and employers. Union activities such as coercion of employees to get them to join a union, forcing an employer to pay for work that is not performed (feather-bedding), and secondary boycotts (when coercive pressure is exerted on customers to make them refrain from patronizing an unfavored business) became illegal. Employees were given the right to refuse to join a union. The First Amendment rights of free speech of employers were protected, allowing them to disseminate probusiness literature. (This was illegal under the Wagner Act.) The Taft-Hartley Act also established a general counsel to the NLRB. The general counsel has final authority to oversee the investigation of charges and prosecution of complaints regarding unfair labor practices. In addition, the general counsel has the power to obtain court orders to enforce decisions. Although the board retains the power to adjudicate disputes, decisions of the NLRB can be appealed to the U.S. Court of Appeals.

For practical reasons, the NLRB does not investigate every charge brought before it, but limits its own jurisdiction to the larger disputes and disputes in certain settings, such as those of nonprofit hospitals and private universities. Other disputes are overseen by appropriate state agencies and are decided in state courts.

The general contractor in the following case charged Teamsters, Local 456 with featherbedding, in violation of the Taft-Hartley Act.

**Teamsters, Local 456 and
  J. R. Stevenson Corporation**
212 NLRB 1452
National Labor Relations Board
August 22, 1974

Before Miller, Chairman; Kennedy and Penello, Members

. . . Stevenson is a general contractor engaged in the construction of a $21 million county courthouse complex in White Plains, New York. Work on the project began in March 1970 with an expected completion date of December 31, 1973. On May 21, 1970, Stevenson signed a contract with Respondent which, by its terms, expired on June 30, 1970. Thereafter, the parties entered into another agreement extending from July 1, 1970, to June 30, 1973. Each of these contracts contained a recognition clause covering employees engaged in a variety of intrasite and intersite driving duties. In addition, article XIX provided, in relevant part:

> "2. On outside construction job sites, the employer shall provide a heated trailer with telephone for employees covered hereby.

"3. A shop steward shall be assigned to each supply yard and each road-and-building-construction job site at all times, and shall be furnished with a vehicle for means of transportation. If an employer has more than one such job site in operation, a shop steward may cover all of such job sites."

Pursuant to its first collective bargaining agreement with Respondent, Stevenson hired Victor Toran, a member of Respondent, in May 1970 and, under the contract's terms, paid him about $20,000 per year and furnished him a heated trailer with telephone. According to credited testimony, Toran spent his working time in the heated trailer or, when outside, checking incoming trucks to see if the drivers carried Teamsters cards. Otherwise, he performed virtually no services for Stevenson. Once during his employment, he was asked by Stevenson to drive a truck. He refused to do so, and suggested that if Stevenson needed a driver, it should hire another teamster to perform that service. The matter was not pursued further. Toran continued in Stevenson's employ until January 1972 when he retired. He was then replaced by Arpad Korchma who assumed his duties as shop steward, and enjoyed the same privileges of a heated trailer and telephone as had Toran. Stevenson presented evidence indicating that, in addition to the salary it paid Korchma, it paid approximately $100 per month for Korchma's use of the trailer telephone.

In April 1973, Respondent notified Stevenson of its desire to negotiate a new agreement to succeed the one expiring on June 30. By letter, dated June 27, Stevenson replied that it did not employ teamsters in its operation and that it therefore had no need to enter into another agreement. On June 29, Stevenson notified Arpad Korchma, the Teamsters shop steward then in its employ, that he would be terminated on June 30.

On July 3, Korchma and others appeared at the jobsite with picket signs. Respondent picketed Stevenson on July 3, 5, 6, and 9. On July 9, the same date on which it filed the instant charge, Stevenson agreed to sign a new agreement with Respondent and, upon signing such an agreement, Stevenson rehired Korchma on July 10. Since July 10, Korchma has performed no services for Stevenson which could be termed relevant or productive. Instead, he has devoted his time to checking drivers entering the jobsite to see if they carried Teamsters cards. Pursuant to the new agreement, which expires June 30, 1976, Korchma's earnings are at least $65 per day, with 50-cent-an-hour increases effective July 1, 1974 and July 1, 1975. In addition, Korchma continues to have use of the heated trailer and telephone.

The Administrative Law Judge's Decision

The Administrative Law Judge found that Respondent violated Section 8(b)(6) of the Act by forcing Stevenson to hire, and pay money to, Arpad Korchma, one of its members, at a time when Respondent knew that Stevenson had no need or use for Korchma's services. The Administrative Law Judge further found that Korchma did not perform or make a bona fide offer to perform, relevant services for Stevenson and recommended that Respondent be ordered to reimburse Stevenson for all wages paid to Korchma for services not performed and not to be performed by Korchma for the period not barred by Section 10(b) of the Act. . . .

Discussion

The record . . . is clear that on June 27 Stevenson notified Respondent that it did not need the services of a teamster and that it therefore considered it unnecessary to negotiate a new contract with Respondent. And, upon expiration of its then current agreement with Respondent on June 30, Stevenson terminated Korchma's employment. There is no allegation that the discharge of Korchma violated Section 8(a)(3) of the Act. Rather, the record as a whole supports Respondent's assertion that, as of June 30, Stevenson had no need for Korchma's services and, indeed, there is no evidence whatever in the record that Korchma thereafter offered to perform or performed relevant services for Stevenson.

Section 8(b)(6) of the Act forbids a labor organization "to cause or attempt to cause an employer to pay or deliver or agree to pay or deliver any money or other thing of value, in the nature of an exaction, for services which are not performed or not to be performed." The Supreme Court narrowly construed the provisions of Section 8(b)(6) in *American Newspaper Publishers Association* and *Gamble.*

In *American Newspaper Publishers Association*, the Supreme Court . . . observed that:

> "The Act now limits its condemnation to instances where a labor organization or its agents exact pay from an employer in return for services not performed or not to be performed. Thus, where work is done by an employee, with the employer's consent, a labor organization's demand that the employee be compensated for time spent in doing the disputed work does not become an unfair labor practice. The transaction simply does not fall within the kind of featherbedding defined in the statute. In the absence of proof to the contrary, the employee's compensation reflects his entire relationship with his employer."

The Court so concluded by examining the legislative history behind Section 8(b)(6) and in particular Senator Taft's observation that the clause, substituted by the Conference Committee for the extensive provisions in the House Bill concerning "featherbedding," which became the present Section 8(b)(6), "makes it an unlawful-labor practice for a union to accept money for people who do not work." The Court found that Section 8(b)(6) left to collective bargaining "the determination of what, if any, work, including bona fide 'made work,' shall be included as compensable services and what rate of compensation shall be paid for it."

In *Gamble* the issue presented to the Court was whether a union violated Section 8(b)(6) when it insisted that a theater, which was part of an interstate chain, employ a local orchestra to play in connection with certain programs, although the theater did not need or want to employ the local orchestra. The union demanded that the local orchestra be hired to play "overtures, intermissions and chasers." Again the Board had dismissed the 8(b)(6) complaint but the Sixth Circuit set aside the Board's dismissal. The Supreme Court reversed the judgment of the Sixth Circuit and accepted the Board's finding that the union sought actual employment for its members as opposed to mere standby pay. Because the Court agreed with the Board's treatment of the union's proposals as made "in good faith contemplating the performance of actual services," the Court concluded that the union had not violated Section 8(b)(6). The Court observed:

> "We are not dealing here with offers of mere 'token' or nominal services. The proposals before us were appropriately treated by the Board as offers in good faith of substantial performances by competent musicians. There is no reason to think that sham can be substituted for substance under § 8(b)(6) any more than under any other statute. Payments for

'standing-by,' or for the substantial equivalent of 'standing-by,' are not payments for services performed, but when an employer receives a bona fide offer of competent performance of relevant services, it remains for the employer, through free and fair negotiation, to determine whether such offer shall be accepted and what compensation shall be paid for the work done."

It cannot be gainsaid that in both cases the Supreme Court used as a touchstone for its construction of Section 8(b)(6) the fact that work was performed. In both cases before the Court, work had been done even though the employer in each case had no use for the work. . . .

We believe the facts and the holdings in *Gamble* and *American Newspaper Publishers Association* to be distinguishable from the facts and the issue before us. Stevenson indicated it had no use for the services of a teamster. The uncontradicted testimony reveals that since July 1, 1973, Korchma has not performed any teamster duties and Stevenson has had neither a need nor a desire for him to perform any. Respondent, well knowing that these were the facts, nevertheless demanded that Stevenson pay for Korchma's unwanted and unneeded daily presence when there was no contemplation of his performing any bona fide relevant services. As of July 1, 1973, Stevenson did not have "even a prospective need for the specialized services" of a teamster. Respondent's demand for a new contract calling for payments for the presence of one of its members at the jobsite when no teamster work was being performed and where the Employer indicated it had no need for teamster labor, coupled with a strike to make the Employer respond to such a demand, is an exaction within the meaning of Section 8(b)(6). Respondent's demand falls considerably short of being a bona fide offer of the competent performance of relevant services. Both *American Newspaper Publishers Association* and *Gamble* make it clear that "relevant services" must be contemplated for a labor organization's demand for pay to its members to escape the sanctions of Section 8(b)(6). Here all parties—including Respondent—knew perfectly well that Korchma simply performed no work—made work or otherwise—for Stevenson. Although he may have checked union cards in his capacity as shop steward, such work was done solely as an agent of Respondent and was for Respondent's benefit; it surely was not even remotely related to Stevenson's work requirements. Accordingly, we agree with the Administrative Law Judge's determination that Respondent violated Section 8(b)(6) of the Act.

Having found that Respondent violated Section 8(b)(6) of the Act as of July 1, 1973, we shall order Respondent to reimburse Stevenson for wages paid as of that date and thereafter. . . . [B]ecause of the nature of Respondent's violation we find merit in Charging Party's contention that, in order to restore the status quo and thus provide a full remedy herein, it should be reimbursed for all reasonable expenditures directly incurred in its employment of Arpad Korchma. We shall, however, leave to the compliance stage of the proceeding herein the determination of the amounts due Stevenson for these expenses. Accordingly, we shall amend the recommended Order to reflect these changes.

Order: Cease and desist from coercing employer to pay for unneeded services. Post notice: reimburse employer for wages paid to, and reasonable expenses directly incurred in employment of, unneeded worker.

Case	1. What is featherbedding?
Questions	2. What distinction did the NLRB make between featherbedding and situations where a union member performed work but the work was of no use to the employer?

Labor-Management Reporting and Disclosure Act

The Wagner Act and the Taft-Hartley Act were followed by the Labor-Management Reporting and Disclosure Act of 1959 (the Landrum-Griffin Act). Smaller in scope than the Wagner and Taft-Hartley acts, it was enacted primarily to eliminate widespread union corruption and to set out the rights of individual employees. It more completely eliminated the practice of some types of secondary boycotts that were allowed under the Taft-Hartley Act. It also set forth in detail the governance of unions.

Taken together, these three major acts attempt to equalize the bargaining positions of unions and employers and to outlaw activities of a coercive or violent nature, while preserving the peaceful but effective activities engaged in by unions and employers.

Chapter Questions

1. Define the following terms:

affirmative action	Equal Employment Opportunity
ADA	Commission (EEOC)
ADEA	offense against public policy
BFOQ defense	*prima facie* case
consent agreement	protected classes
disparate impact	RFOA defense
disparate treatment	reverse discrimination
employment-at-will	Title VII (Civil Rights Act of 1964)

2. Jeri Platner worked as a flag-person for Cash & Thomas Contractors, Inc., as general contracting and pipe-laying firm. The firm was owned by Jack Thomas. Jack's daughter-in-law, Savonda, was jealous of Jeri and believed that Jeri was involved with her husband, Steve, who worked on the same crew as Jeri. Jack dismissed Jeri to end the discord. Jeri filed suit against the firm, Jack, and Savonda. She maintained that she was fired because of her alleged involvement in an office romance. Jack's son, Steve, who was also allegedly involved, was not fired. Was Jeri the victim of sex discrimination?

   Planter v. Cash & Thomas Contractors, Inc. 908 F.2d 902 (1990)

3. The Constitution of Vermont provides that all state justices and judges have to retire at age seventy. On December 24, 1988, Vermont Supreme Court Justice Louis P. Peck celebrated his seventieth birthday and was scheduled for retirement on June 30, 1989, solely because of the constitutional requirement. Justice Peck filed a complaint with the EEOC against the State of Vermont, the Court Administrator and the Department of Finance and Management. He claimed that the Vermont Constitution's mandatory retirement provisions violated the Age Discrimination in Employment Act. The EEOC brought suit on Peck's behalf. The commission sought injunctive relief to prevent his involuntary retirement, and monetary relief. Does the ADEA cover Vermont judges?

   E.E.O.C. v. State of Vermont, 904 F.2d 794 (1990)

4. Susan Long Little was employed as a tenured teacher by the St. Mary Magdalene Parish, despite the fact that she wasn't Catholic. Her annual contract contained a clause that permitted the parish to terminate her employment for "public rejection of the official doctrine or laws of the Roman Catholic Church." Little requested a leave of absence for the 1986–87 school year, which was approved by the parish. During her leave, Little, who was divorced in 1979, married a Roman Catholic without obtaining an annulment of her prior marriage. Little's request for an employment contract for the 1987–88 school year was denied by the parish which believed that Little's failure to obtain an annulment was a public rejection of the Church's teachings and laws. Does a religious organization, which is exempt from claims of religious discrimination under Title VII, waive the exemption when it employs a person who is not a member of the church organization?

   Little v. St. Mary Magdalene Parish, 739 F.Supp 1003 (W.D.Pa. 1990)

5. Ralph Minker was a sixty-three-year-old Methodist minister. He was employed by the Baltimore Annual Conference of the United Methodist Church. After serving for ten years he asked to be reassigned, and he became a temporary, emergency pastor of the Mount Ranier Methodist Church. This pastorate did not pay him as much as a person of his experience and background would usually receive. Despite verbal promises from the district superintendent of a more appropriate assignment, four years passed without any reassignment. In July 1987, Minker filed suit in district court alleging that he had been discriminated against and denied a promotion because of his age. He claimed that people younger than himself had been selected for open positions and that this violated the federal Age Discrimination in Employment Act. He also claimed that the church bishop responsible for pastoral appointments had indicated that pastors in their fifties should not expect more lucrative appointments. Should courts apply the ADEA in this church context?

   Minker v. Baltimore Annual Conference of United Methodist Church, 894 F.2d 1354 (D.C. Cir. 1990)

6. Carl Malinga was elected prosecuting attorney for Macomb County, Michigan. Malinga decided to fire five assistant prosecutors who had been

appointed by his predecessor. The five discharged assistants filed suit, claiming that they were wrongfully terminated in part because of their political affiliation. Under Michigan law an assistant prosecutor performs "any and all duties pertaining to the office of prosecuting attorney at such time or times as he may be required so to do by the prosecuting attorney and during the absence or disability of the prosecuting attorney" (Mich. Comp. Laws Sec. 49.42, 49.52). Is political affiliation a pertinent requirement for the effective performance of an assistant prosecutor?

Monks v. Malinga, 732 F.Supp 749 (E.D.Mich. 1990)

7. Plaintiff John Doe was a member of the naval reserve. On July 13, 1985, he was accepted as an active duty officer in a program that trained him to be a naval reserve recruiter. His work was excellent, and his work as a recruiter was extended from May 31, 1986 until September 30, 1986. The navy tentatively approved another extension on July 8, 1986 that would have maintained him as a recruiter until September 30, 1987. Doe was admitted to a navy hospital on July 20, 1986 after he was found to have tested positive for the AIDS virus. He did not show any AIDS symptoms. On September 30, 1986 the navy released Doe from active duty and returned him to inactive status as a member of the naval reserve. In September 1986, Doe filed suit against the secretary of the navy. He claimed that the navy had violated the Rehabilitation Act when it excluded him from continuing as an active duty officer in the recruitment program. Should the Rehabilitation Act be interpreted so as to permit uniformed personnel to bring suit against the military, based on handicap, when statutory claims based on sex, race, religion, or national origin are barred?

Doe v. Garrett, 903 F.2d 1455 (11th Cir. 1990)

8. Gerald Moore is a member of the Seventh-day Adventist Church. Adventists observe the Sabbath from sundown on Friday until sundown on Saturday, and refrain from working during this period. Moore had worked on Saturdays from 1976 until the middle of 1985. At that time he gave notice to his employer, the A.E. Staley Co., and his union that he no longer was willing to work on his Sabbath. Staley and the union had negotiated a clause in three successive collective bargaining agreements by which job and shift preferences were determined by a plant-wide bidding process based on seniority. Staley attempted to avoid scheduling Moore, but he could not be transferred to another shift without violating the job-bidding procedures in the collective bargaining agreement. The union membership rejected proposals to schedule contrary to the collective bargaining agreement. All employees would have been denied an equal share of free Saturdays if Moore had been given preferential scheduling. Staley and the union collaborated to solicit voluntary swaps from Moore's coworkers. Various other alternatives were discussed by the parties, but were rejected.

Moore filed a complaint with the EEOC and received a right to sue letter. He then filed suit in federal district court, claiming that his employer and union failed to reasonably accommodate his religious beliefs, contrary to Title VII. The union and employer argued to the court that their joint program of supporting and soliciting voluntary swaps should satisfy Title VII. They maintained that they had met their obligation to attempt to accommodate Moore's religious practices without creating undue hardship on the employer. Do you agree with their assertions? Should the union and employer have to breach their collective bargaining agreement in order to accommodate Moore?

Moore v. A.E. Staley Mfg. Co., 727 F.Supp 1156 (N.D.Ill. 1989)

9. Gerald Schafer was employed as a teacher by the Pittsburgh Board of Education. In late August or early September of 1981, Schafer requested a one-year, unpaid child-rearing leave. This request was made pursuant to a provision in the collective bargaining agreement negotiated between the teacher's union and the school board. This agreement provided child-rearing leaves for female, but not male, employees. The board of education denied Schafer's application for the child-rearing leave on November 20, 1981. Schafer subsequently resigned, claiming that he could not find appropriate child care for his son. His request for reinstatement, after he found child care, was denied. Schafer filed suit against the school board. Does the Pregnancy Discrimination Act permit employers to offer up to one-year child-rearing leaves only to female employees?

Schafer v. Board of Public Education of the School District of Pittsburgh, Pa. 903 F.2d 243 (3rd Cir. 1990)

10. Lynn Rannels brought suit against Sarah Hargrove, the state banking secretary, because the Meridian Bancorp allegedly violated the Age Discrimination in Employment Act. Rannels maintained that the secretary harmed her by encouraging and failing to bar illegal practices. Rannels complained in particular about Meridian's practice of giving certificate of deposit customers who were over age fifty an extra one-quarter of one percent interest on their certificate. Meridian refused to extend this offer to Rannels because she was under fifty years of age. Is reverse age discrimination, where older citizens are benefited at the expense of younger citizens, a violation of the ADEA?

Rannels v. Hargrove, 731 F.Supp. 1214 (E.D.Pa.1990)

Notes

1. M. Rosenfelt, *Affirmative Action and Justice* (New Haven: Yale University Press, 1991), p. 3.
2. Ibid., pp. 22–42.
3. S. Verba and G.R. Orren, *Equality in America: The View from the Top* (Cambridge: Harvard University Press, 1988), p. 5.
4. D. Bell, *Meritocracy and Equality*, The Public Interest 40 (Fall 1972); Verba, pp. 5–7.

5. H.P. Brown, *Egalitarianism and the Generation of Inequality* (New York: Oxford University Press, 1988), p. 485.

6. G. Murg and C. Scharman, *Employment at Will: Do the Exceptions Overwhelm the Rule?* Boston College Law Review 23, 329 (1982).

7. A.D. Hill, *"Wrongful Discharge" and the Derogation of the At-Will Employment Doctrine* (Philadelphia: The Wharton School, University of Pennsylvania, 1987), pp. 1–3.

8. Ibid., p. 1.

9. Ibid., p. 4.

10. L. Friedman, *History of American Law* (New York: Simon & Schuster, 1973), pp. 484–494.

11. M. Linder, *The Employment Relationship in Anglo-American Law* (New York: Greenwood Press, 1989), p. 144; Hill, p. 5.

12. 208 U.S. 161 (1908).

13. 236 U.S. 1 (1915).

14. 301 U.S. 1 (1937).

15. I. Shepard, P. Heyman, and R. Duston, *Without Just Cause* (Washington, D.C.: Bureau of National Affairs, 1989), pp. 38–39.

16. Hill, pp. 19–25.

17. *Agis v. Howard Johnson Co.*, 371 Mass. 140 (1976); *Tosti v. Ayik*, 386 Mass. 721 (1982); *Comey v. Hill*, 387 Mass. 11 (1982).

18. *Nees v. Hocks*, 536 P.2d 512 (1975); *Frampton v. Central Indiana Gas Co.*, 297 N.E.2d 425 (1973); *Harless v. First National Bank*, 246 S.E.2d 270 (1978).

19. *McDonald v. Sante Fe Trail Transportation Co.*, 427 U.S. 273 (1976).

20. D.C. Maguire, *A Case for Affirmative Action* (Dubuque: Shepherd, Inc., 1991), pp. 141–167.

21. Ibid., p. 31.

22. Section 706(g), 42 U.S.C. Sec. 2000e-5(g) (1982).

23. *Local 28, Sheet Metal Workers International Association v. EEOC*, 478 U.S. 421 (1986).

24. Maguire, p. 29.

25. *Sheet Metal Workers International Association v. EEOC*, 478 U.S. 421 (1986); *United States v. Paradise*, 480 U.S. 149 (1987).

26. L. Kanowitz, *Sex-Based Discrimination in American Law: Title VII of the 1964 Civil Rights Act and Equal Pay Act of 1963*, 20 Hastings Law Journal 305, 310–312 (1968–1969); M.A. Player, *Federal Law of Employment Discrimination in a Nutshell* (St. Paul, MN: West, 1981), p. 125.

27. *Meritor Savings Bank v. Vinson*, 477 U.S. 57 (1986).

28. 29 C.F.R. Sec. 1604.11(a).

29. In the 1991 case of *International Union, UAW v. Johnson Controls, Inc.* (111 S.Ct. 1196), the U.S. Supreme Court ruled that Title VII, as amended by the PDA, forbids gender-specified fetal-protection policies. The Court noted that the company permitted fertile men to decide whether to risk their reproductive health and that discrimination against fertile women amounted to a facially discriminatory classification based on gender. Justice Blackmun wrote for the majority: "Decisions about the welfare of future children must be left to the parents who conceive, bear, support, and raise them rather than to employers who hire those parents."

30. I.D. Schneid, *The Americans with Disabilities Act* (New York: Van Nostrand Reinhold, 1992), p. 25.

31. 29 C.F.R. Sec. 1630, 2(j) (i)–(ii).

32. Schneid, p. 29; 42 U.S.C. Sec. 12211.

33. In a 1981 case, the Supreme Court ruled that Congress did not intend to provide federal employees with the right to a jury trial.

34. *Hazen Paper Co. v. Biggins,* 113 S.Ct. 1701 (1993).

35. Ibid.

36. A recent example involves the case of *Meinhold v. Department of Defense,* 34 F.3d 1469 (9th Cir. 1994). In that case, the Court of Appeals affirmed a lower court injunction prohibiting the navy from dismissing Petty Officer Volker Keith Meinhold from the navy for having admitted on ABC's "World News Tonight" that he is gay. Navy regulations provide for dismissing any person "who engages in, desires to engage in, or intends to engage in homosexual acts." The 9th Circuit ruled that because neither Meinhold's conduct nor his statement referred in any way to homosexual acts or an intent or desire to engage in such acts, there had been no violation of the navy regulation.

XIV

Alternative Dispute Resolution

Litigation is not the only mechanism available for the resolution of a dispute. Disputants who are unable to negotiate a solution to a pending conflict, but who wish to avoid a public court trial, can choose what is currently called alternative dispute resolution (ADR). ADR has gained in popularity largely because many people are dissatisfied with the workings of the traditional legal system.

People's dissatisfaction with the legal system has many origins. The tremendous volume of cases filed, for example, is overwhelming the court system and producing gridlock.[1] Almost 20 million civil cases were filed in American courts in 1992, representing an increase of 3 percent over the previous year.[2] During fiscal 1993, the Equal Employment Opportunity Commission reported that some 88,000 employees filed charges with that agency against their employers, an increase of 22 percent over 1992.[3]

Despite evidence that most litigants settle their cases out of court, lawyers prepare each case as if it will be tried and charge their clients for the costs. They over-prepare for a variety of professional and strategic reasons. Because litigation is an adversarial process, lawyers assume that opponents will resort to every legal device to win. Attorneys anticipate a continuing series of battles with the opponent at the pretrial, trial, and appellate stages of a process that can take years to determine an ultimate winner. They know that there are many ways to lose a case, and they worry about malpractice claims. Trial victories require more than good facts and sound legal arguments; they result from careful preparation and thorough discovery.

Dissatisfaction also results when lawyers adopt a strategy of winning by exhausting an opponent's financial resources. Although case preparation generally will not compensate for a weak case, sometimes a weak case can be won if the client has vastly superior resources. An attorney may take such a case to trial in order to drag out the proceedings, dramatically increase the opponent's litigation expenses, and force the opponent to settle the case on unfavorable terms.

The fact that lawyers become heavily involved in preparing attacks upon their client's opponent often means that they avoid looking at possible weaknesses in their own cases until just before trial. Lawyers often view themselves as their client's champion, and they frequently engage in posturing and puffery. Some refuse to initiate settlement discussions with the opponents, because they fear that this might be interpreted by their clients as well as their client's opponents as a sign of weakness. If settlement discussions do occur, neither side is likely to be candid and reveal the amount that would be accepted in settlement of the case. Further, a tactical advantage can be gained by responding to an opponent's proposal, rather than being the first to suggest a settlement figure. This game-like approach to litigation only compounds costs in money and time as the parties prepare for a trial that statistically is unlikely to occur.

Many litigants often find the judicial system's traditional "winner-take-all" approach unsatisfactory because it produces a pyrrhic victory.[4] Both parties can lose when the disputants have an ongoing relationship, as in business, labor-management, or child custody cases, and one party thoroughly clobbers the other in court. Because ADR methods can often resolve disputes more satisfactorily than trials—at less expense and in less time—some lawyers are required to explain the existence of options to litigation to their clients.[5]

Businesses have been looking for ways to resolve disputes that avoid class action lawsuits and jury trials, which expose them to the possibility of high damage awards.[6] Congress' enactment of the Civil Justice Reform Act (CJRA) of 1990[7] increased judicial interest in ADR. The CJRA required federal courts to develop plans for reducing the costs and delays associated with litigation. State courts also have been looking for cost-efficient ways to reduce the length of their burgeoning dockets, given the fact that only 3–4 percent of their civil cases actually are tried.[8] Some jurisdictions offer a menu of ADR options; others focus on a preferred procedure, such as mediation.[9]

Disputants become participants in ADR either because they choose to do so or because they have been required to do so by legislation or court rule (court-annexed ADR).

VOLUNTARY ADR

When parties to a dispute decide to avoid the negative aspects of a court trial, they may voluntarily choose to resort to ADR, because it can often produce a fair result faster and at less cost than a public court trial. In fact, several major corporations will contract only with vendors who agree to participate in ADR. Disputants often prefer ADR because they can choose the procedure that seems most appropriate to their needs. They may also like having their dispute resolved by a person or persons who have particular expertise in that subject area.

When parties voluntarily participate in ADR, they negotiate a contract that sets forth the rules that will govern the proceedings. There are several agencies to which they can turn for model ADR rules and procedures. This is helpful because attorneys who are inexperienced with ADR are sometimes reluctant to negotiate an ADR agreement with a more seasoned opponent. Model rules are even-handed, and their terms provide neither side with an advantage. They establish reasonable and simplified discovery rules, and simplified rules of evidence, which allow the parties to introduce documents that might otherwise be inadmissible hearsay. The rules also can provide for confidentiality: businesses and individuals often would prefer to deny competitors, the general public, and the news media access to private and potentially embarrassing information that would be revealed in conjunction with public court litigation.[10]

ADR practitioners and firms often advertise in trade publications and list themselves in many metropolitan area telephone directories under "arbitration." To attract customers, increasing numbers of automobile manufacturers, local home contractors, businesses, and professionals advertise that they participate in ADR. The Center for Public Resources, the American Arbitration Association, and the Federal Conciliation and Mediation Service maintain panels of arbitrators and impartial third parties (called neutrals) who can be engaged to provide ADR services. National dispute resolution firms have offices in major cities, have employed hundreds of retired judges (even state supreme court justices), and have annual revenues exceeding $40 million.[11]

COURT-ANNEXED ADR

Participation in ADR is legislatively or judicially authorized in many jurisdictions. Rule 16(a) of the Federal Rules of Civil Procedure, for example, permits the use of ADR, but it doesn't explicitly authorize judicial compulsion to force participation in such proceedings. Federal circuit courts of appeals are currently divided as to whether federal district judges can compel litigants to participate in ADR.

Where federal and state judges claim authority to compel ADR participation, they usually promulgate local court rules. Such rules, the judges claim, are an appropriate exercise of a court's inherent power to manage its docket. These rules require parties to participate in nonbinding, court-annexed ADR programs before they are permitted access to a jury trial. Such programs encourage settlements, reduce court dockets, and lessen the financial burdens on taxpayers who pay for the operation of the judicial system.

Some would relieve court overcrowding by limiting access to jury trials. They argue that jury trials are expensive and time consuming and result in unqualified lay jurors deciding complex disputes. The Seventh Amendment to the U.S. Constitution, which guarantees most civil litigants in federal courts the right to a jury trial, has prevented the implementation of such proposals. Many state constitutions contain similar protection for litigants in state courts.

The scope of the Seventh Amendment's jury trial right is deeply rooted in our history. Under our law, the right to a jury trial is recognized for all actions that were tried by English juries at the time of the Constitution's ratification and for other actions that are closely related to common law claims. There is no jury trial right for litigants who seek equitable relief or for actions that were unknown to the common law. Compulsory ADR has been structured so that there is no infringement of the right to a jury trial. Litigants are required to participate in pretrial ADR, but they can reject ADR solutions and then proceed to a trial by jury.

In the following case, the petitioner challenged the authority of the Court of Common Pleas of Philadelphia to enforce a local court rule that denied litigants a jury trial in asbestos canes unless the party had first participated in a bench trial. Either party could insist on a jury trial if it was dissatisfied with the suggested judgment. Note the court's rationale for resorting to the ADR approach.

Pittsburgh Corning Corp. v. Bradley
453 A.2d 314
Supreme Court of Pennsylvania
December 14, 1982

Roberts, Justice

Petitioner, Pittsburgh Corning Corporation, a defendant in asbestos litigation, has requested this Court to exercise its plenary jurisdiction and to issue a writ of prohibition barring the implementation of Philadelphia General Court Regulation 82–5, which establishes a program of non-jury trials, with a right of jury trial de novo, for asbestos litigation in the Court of Common Pleas of Philadelphia. For the reasons set forth, we grant the petition to assume plenary jurisdiction and deny the petition for a writ of prohibition.

I

The past ten years have witnessed both the emergence and the explosion of asbestos-related litigation throughout the country, with over 16,000 cases having been filed nationwide. As a center for industries such as shipyards which have used large amounts of asbestos, Philadelphia has experienced the third largest number of asbestos-related case filings of any jurisdiction in the nation, with over 1,850 cases pending and new cases currently being filed at the rate of approximately seventy-five per month. Because the latency period between initial exposure to asbestos and the development of disease symptoms can be as long as twenty to thirty years, it is reasonable to assume that asbestos cases will continue to be filed in substantial numbers for years to come.

In an attempt to deal with the problems created by the influx of asbestos litigation, the Court of Common Pleas of Philadelphia created a separate asbestos docket in 1976, and an asbestos calendar judge was appointed. Subsequently, several judges—currently six—were assigned to hear asbestos cases. Thus far, however, fewer than twenty-five cases have been tried to verdict, all by jury, with each case lasting an average of two to three weeks. Attempts to achieve settlements have been hampered by the presence of fifteen to thirty defendant companies in each asbestos suit, and in recent years virtually no asbestos cases have been settled.

In the face of this steadily increasing caseload, the Court of Common Pleas of Philadelphia promulgated Philadelphia General Court Regulation 82–5, effective July 12, 1982. The regulation authorizes the asbestos calendar judge to assign any case on the Philadelphia docket to a judge for a non-jury trial, following the completion of which any party may demand a de novo trial by jury.

The present petition was promptly filed, as well as an application for an injunction staying the operation of the regulation pending this Court's decision on whether to issue the requested writ. The injunction was granted on July 13, 1982.

II

. . . Petitioner asserts that the requirement of an initial non-jury trial in asbestos cases unconstitutionally burdens its right to a jury trial, as provided by Article I, section 6 of the Pennsylvania Constitution. It is settled by our case law, however, that where, as here, a jury trial de novo is available to litigants prior to a final determination of their rights, the requirement that the litigants proceed first in another forum does not offend the Constitution.

Here, it is precisely the "practical unavailability" of a jury trial in asbestos cases that led to the creation of the non-jury program. As has been noted, the court of common pleas faces a steadily increasing backlog of asbestos cases, with a current inventory of over 1,850 cases. If the six judges currently assigned to hear asbestos cases were to try all of these

cases before juries, at the present average length of two and one-half weeks per jury trial they could hear only 125 cases a year. If asbestos cases continue to be filed at the present rate of 75 per month, or 900 a year, the number of pending cases would nearly double within two years. Even if no new asbestos cases were to be filed, it would take nearly fifteen years to dispose of the current inventory. If the twenty judges currently trying other civil cases in the Court of Common Pleas of Philadelphia were to be assigned to hear only asbestos jury trials, the number of cases pending would still increase by approximately 350 a year, if the present rate of filing continues; even if all fifty-seven judges in the trial division in the court of common pleas were to do nothing but preside over asbestos jury trials, it would take nearly two years to dispose of the present case inventory, by which time another 1,500 asbestos cases would have been filed.

Manifestly, the most onerous burden on asbestos litigants' right to a jury trial is the effect of the sheer volume of asbestos cases pending and yet to be filed. The requirement that the parties proceed initially before a judge is intended to alleviate, not increase this burden. Because non-jury trials invariably take less time than jury trials, the non-jury trials will provide asbestos litigants with a more prompt adjudication of their rights than they would otherwise receive. Although either party may challenge the court's decision by way of a jury trial de novo, it is reasonable to conclude, on the basis of the success of past and present non-jury programs such as arbitration, that many litigants will find the initial decision fair and equitable and will choose not to seek de novo review. Thus, many of those who do demand a subsequent jury trial may have that trial sooner than would be possible if all cases were tried by jury in the first instance.

. . . As we conclude that a program of initial non-jury trials for asbestos litigation in the Court of Common Pleas of Philadelphia does not unduly burden the parties' right to a trial by jury, but rather may serve to avoid intolerable delay in the vast majority of asbestos cases, petitioner's challenge on this ground must be rejected. So, too, we must reject petitioner's contention that, by applying only to asbestos cases, the program of initial non-jury trials is violative of the Equal Protection Clause of the Fourteenth Amendment to the United States Constitution and Article III, section 32 of the Pennsylvania Constitution. There is a manifest need for an effective procedure to facilitate the prompt disposition of the growing backlog of asbestos cases in the Court of Common Pleas of Philadelphia, and the procedure chosen is clearly related to the paramount goal of achieving timely justice.

III

. . . Petitioner's final contention is that the court of common pleas lacked authority to promulgate Regulation 82–5. We do not reach this contention, for we conclude that the critical nature of the problem created by the avalanche of asbestos litigation requires that we exercise the "general supervisory and administrative authority over all the courts . . ." conferred upon this Court by Article V, section 10 of the Pennsylvania Constitution. In the interest of the fair and speedy resolution of asbestos cases, we direct that all asbestos-related litigation in the Court of Common Pleas of Philadelphia proceed initially to a non-jury trial, with a right of a jury trial de novo. The Court of Common Pleas of Philadelphia may, of course, adopt such procedures as are necessary to implement our mandate.

Our overriding concern in mandating this non-jury trial program is to achieve the efficient disposition of asbestos cases without unfairly depriving any litigant of an opportunity to obtain a full and fair adjudication of his rights. As this Court has observed,

> "[i]t is the constitutional right of every person who finds it necessary or desirable to repair to the courts for the protection of his legally recognized interests to have justice administered without sale, denial or delay."

. . . Having assumed plenary jurisdiction over petitioner's challenge to Philadelphia General Court Regulation 82–5 and having exercised our constitutional authority to direct that there be a non-jury trial with a right of a jury trial de novo in all asbestos-related litigation in the Court of Common Pleas of Philadelphia, this Court will closely monitor the course of that litigation to ensure that the program is meeting its objectives.

Writ of prohibition denied. Plenary jurisdiction assumed, and record remanded for proceedings consistent with this opinion.

Case Questions

1. Should a court have the power to compel litigants to participate in (and pay for) a bench trial before permitting a jury trial? Isn't this a waste of time and money?

2. Why does the court conclude that the constitutionally protected right to a jury trial has not been offended?
3. What is a writ of prohibition?

ADR TECHNIQUES

The demand for trial-avoidance methods to resolve disputes has resulted in increasing reliance on settlement conferences, arbitration, and mediation—three of the oldest and the most popular ADR options—as well as the development of newer techniques such as private trials, mini-trials, and summary jury trials.

Settlement Conferences

Rule 1 of the Federal Rules of Civil Procedure states that judges are expected to promote "the just, speedy, and inexpensive determination of every action." This very general charge gives judges considerable flexibility in determining how they will achieve this goal. Many judges use settlement conferences, which are a traditional step in the litigation process, as an informal method for resolving a dispute without a trial.[12]

A judge who is willing to be assertive can help parties explore a lawsuit's settlement potential. The judge can initiate the process or respond to a request for assistance from one or more of the parties. This intervention can be helpful when neither of the opposing attorneys is willing to make the first move toward a settlement. The parties, however, often leap at an opportunity to discuss settlement if the judge broaches the subject. An assertive judge may personally convene a settlement conference, carefully review the case, and emphasize each side's weaknesses and strengths. This is important because the evidence is frequently inconclusive. A judge who is knowledgeable about the relevant law can be very influential. He or she can point out the costs of going to trial and emphasize the risks each side incurs by trying the matter to an unpredictable jury.[13] The judge may know about recent verdicts in similar cases that went to trial and may suggest ADR options that could help each side avoid the necessity of a trial. Some judges, if requested by the parties, will propose a settlement figure. Judges who have the time, skill, and interest to function as mediators may meet privately with each side, or with only the clients. They may even request that the clients meet without their attorneys being present. The judge's participation is the key ingredient. It is one thing for an attorney to engage in puffery with a client or an opponent. It is another matter to refuse to acknowledge the weaknesses of one's case to an experienced trial judge. Many judges, however, don't define their role in this way, believing that settlement is a matter to be decided solely by the parties without judicial involvement.

Serious issues arise regarding the judge's proper role in the settlement conference. Many lawyers are concerned that a party who refuses to settle may encounter bias if the matter is subsequently set for trial before the settlement judge. They fear that the judge might rule against the "uncooperative" party on motions and evidence admissibility at trial. One solution to this problem is to make sure that the judge conducting the settlement conference does not sit as the trial judge. Another is to use a lawyer-mediator instead of the judge at the settlement conference. The next case illustrates what can happen when a judge coerces the parties into a settlement.

Kothe v. Smith
771 F.2d 667
U.S. Court of Appeals, Second Circuit
September 4, 1985

Van Graafeiland, Circuit Judge

Dr. James Smith appeals from a judgment of the United States District Court for the Southern District of New York (Sweet, J.), which directed him to pay $1,000 to plaintiff-appellee's attorney, $1,000 to plaintiff-appellee's medical witness, and $480 to the Clerk of the Court. For the reasons hereinafter discussed, we direct that the judgment be vacated.

Patricia Kothe brought this suit for medical malpractice against four defendants, Dr. Smith, Dr. Andrew Kerr, Dr. Kerr's professional corporation, and Doctors Hospital, seeking $2 million in damages. She discontinued her action against the hospital four months prior to trial. She discontinued against Dr. Kerr and his corporation on the opening day of the trial.

Three weeks prior thereto, Judge Sweet held a pretrial conference, during which he directed counsel for the parties to conduct settlement negotiations. Although it is not clear from the record, it appears that Judge Sweet recommended that the case be settled for between $20,000 and $30,000. He also warned the parties that, if they settled for a comparable figure after trial had begun, he would impose sanctions against the dilatory party. Smith, whose defense has been conducted throughout this litigation by his malpractice insurer, offered $5,000 on the day before the trial, but it was rejected.

Although Kothe's attorney had indicated to Judge Sweet that his client would settle for $20,000, he had requested that the figure not be disclosed to Smith. Kothe's counsel conceded at oral argument that the lowest pretrial settlement demand communicated to Smith was $50,000. Nevertheless, when the case was settled for $20,000 after one day of trial, the district court proceeded to penalize Smith alone. In imposing the penalty, the court stated that it was "determined to get the attention of the carrier" and that "the carriers are going to have to wake up when a judge tells them that they want [sic] to settle a case and they don't want to settle it." Under the circumstances of this case, we believe that the district court's imposition of a penalty against Smith was an abuse of the sanction power given it by Fed.R.Civ.P. 16(f).

Although the law favors the voluntary settlement of civil suits, . . . it does not sanction efforts by trial judges to effect settlements through coercion. . . . *Wolff v. Laverne, Inc.*, 17 A.D.2d 213 . . . (1962). . . . In the *Wolff* case . . . the Court said:

> "We view with disfavor all pressure tactics whether directly or obliquely, to coerce settlement by litigants and their counsel. Failure to concur in what the Justice presiding may consider an

adequate settlement should not result in an imposition upon a litigant or his counsel, who reject it, of any retributive sanctions not specifically authorized by law."

. . . In short, pressure tactics to coerce settlement simply are not permissible. . . . "The judge must not compel agreement by arbitrary use of his power and the attorney must not meekly submit to a judge's suggestion, though it be strongly urged." *Brooks v. Great Atlantic & Pacific Tea Co.*, 92 F.2d 794, 796 (9th Cir.1937).

Rule 16 of the Fed.R.Civ.P. was not designed as a means for clubbing the parties—or one of them—into an involuntary compromise. . . . Although subsection (c)(7) of Rule 16, added in the 1983 amendments of the Rule, was designed to encourage pretrial settlement discussions, it was not its purpose to "impose settlement negotiations on unwilling litigants." . . .

We find the coercion in the instant case especially troublesome because the district court imposed sanctions on Smith alone. Offers to settle a claim are not made in a vacuum. They are part of a more complex process which includes "conferences, informal discussions, offers, counterdemands, more discussions, more haggling, and finally, in the great majority of cases, a compromise." . . . In other words, the process of settlement is a two-way street, and a defendant should not be expected to bid against himself. In the instant case, Smith never received a demand of less than $50,000. Having received no indication from Kothe that an offer somewhere in the vicinity of $20,000 would at least be given careful consideration, Smith should not have been required to make an offer in this amount simply because the court wanted him to.

Smith's attorney should not be condemned for changing his evaluation of the case after listening to Kothe's testimony during the first day of trial. As every experienced trial lawyer knows, the personalities of the parties and their witnesses play an important role in litigation. It is one thing to have a valid claim; it is quite another to convince a jury of this fact. It is not at all unusual, therefore, for a defendant to change his perception of a case based on the plaintiff's performance on the witness stand. We see nothing about that occurrence in the instant case that warranted the imposition of sanctions against the defendant alone.

Although we commend Judge Sweet for his efforts to encourage settlement negotiations, his excessive zeal leaves us no recourse but to remand the matter with instructions to vacate the judgment.

Case Questions

1. What are the pros and cons of a judge playing an active role in the settlement process?
2. The judge in this case recommended that the case be settled for between twenty and thirty thousand dollars. The judge further threatened to impose sanctions against any dilatory party. At whom was this threat really directed?

Arbitration

Arbitration is the most used form of ADR[14] and was in existence long before the emergence of the English common law.[15] It was well known in the eighteenth century, and George Washington's will even contained an arbitration clause in the event that disputes arose between his heirs.[16] American courts were traditionally opposed to arbitration awards because the parties had rejected the judicial system and had chosen to settle their disputes privately. Many judges believed that people who chose arbitration over the judicial system should not be entitled to come to the judiciary for enforcement of nonjudicial decisions. In the 1925 Federal Arbitration Act, however, Congress established a national policy favoring the arbitration of commercial transactions. In the act, Congress provided that arbitration contracts "shall be valid, irrevocable, and enforceable save upon such grounds as exist at law or in equity for the revocation of any contract," and required that courts enforce most arbitration awards.[17] The Labor Management Relations Act of 1947 extended the use of arbitration to disputes arising out of collective bargaining, and in 1960 the U.S. Supreme Court decided three cases that further strengthened the roles of arbitrators and emphasized the enforceability of arbitration awards.[18]

Some disputants end up in arbitration because it is required by a court-annexed program or as a condition of being employed. In other instances, parties voluntarily submit their disputes to an arbitrator for resolution. In the following case before the United States Supreme Court, an employee sued his employer for allegedly engaging in age discrimination. The employer brought a motion to compel the employee to submit his claim to arbitration, claiming that the employee had contracted to arbitrate dismissal claims.

Gilmer v. Interstate/Johnson Lane Corp.
111 S.Ct. 1647
U.S. Supreme Court
May 13, 1991

Justice White delivered the opinion of the Court.

The question presented in this case is whether a claim under the Age Discrimination in Employment Act of 1967 (ADEA) . . . can be subjected to compulsory arbitration pursuant to an arbitration agreement in a securities registration application. The Court of Appeals held that it could, . . . and we affirm.

I

Respondent Interstate/Johnson Lane Corporation (Interstate) hired petitioner

Robert Gilmer as a Manager of Financial Services in May 1981. As required by his employment, Gilmer registered as a securities representative with several stock exchanges, including the New York Stock Exchange (NYSE). . . . His registration application, entitled "Uniform Application for Securities Industry Registration or Transfer," provided, among other things, that Gilmer "agree[d] to arbitrate any dispute, claim or controversy" arising between him and Interstate "that is required to be arbitrated under the rules, constitutions or by-laws of the organizations with which I register." . . . Of relevance to this case, NYSE Rule 347 provides for arbitration of "[a]ny controversy between a registered representative and any member or member organization arising out of

the employment or termination of employment of such registered representative."
. . .

Interstate terminated Gilmer's employment in 1987, at which time Gilmer was 62 years of age. After first filing an age discrimination charge with the Equal Employment Opportunity Commission (EEOC), Gilmer subsequently brought suit in the United States District Court for the Western District of North Carolina, alleging that Interstate had discharged him because of his age, in violation of the ADEA. In response to Gilmer's complaint, Interstate filed in the District Court a motion to compel arbitration of the ADEA claim. In its motion, Interstate relied upon the arbitration agreement in Gilmer's registration application, as well as the Federal Arbitration Act (FAA), . . . The District Court denied Interstate's motion, . . . because it concluded that "Congress intended to protect ADEA claimants from the waiver of a judicial forum." . . . The United States Court of Appeals for the Fourth Circuit reversed, finding "nothing in the text, legislative history, or underlying purposes of the ADEA indicating a congressional intent to preclude enforcement of arbitration agreements." . . .

. . . We granted certiorari . . . to resolve a conflict among the . . . Courts of Appeals regarding the arbitrability of ADEA claims.

II

The FAA was originally enacted in 1925, . . . and then reenacted and codified in 1947 as Title 9 of the United States Code. Its purpose was to reverse the longstanding judicial hostility to arbitration agreements that had existed at English common law and had been adopted by American courts, and to place arbitration agreements upon the same footing as other contracts.

The FAA also provides for stays of proceedings in federal district courts when an issue in the proceeding is referable to arbitration, § 3, and for orders compelling arbitration when one party has failed, neglected, or refused to comply with an arbitration agreement, § 4. These provisions manifest a "liberal federal policy favoring arbitration agreements."
. . . "[B]y agreeing to arbitrate a statutory claim, a party does not forgo the substantive rights afforded by the statute; it only submits to their resolution in an arbitral, rather than a judicial, forum." . . .

It is by now clear that statutory claims may be the subject of an arbitration agreement, enforceable pursuant to the FAA.
. . .

Although all statutory claims may not be appropriate for arbitration, "[h]aving made the bargain to arbitrate, the party should be held to it unless Congress itself has evinced an intention to preclude a waiver of judicial remedies for the statutory rights at issue." . . . In this regard, we note that the burden is on Gilmer to show that Congress intended to preclude a waiver of a judicial forum for ADEA claims.

. . . If such an intention exists, it will be discoverable in the text of the ADEA, its legislative history, or an "inherent conflict" between arbitration and the ADEA's underlying purposes. . . . Throughout such an inquiry, it should be kept in mind that "questions of arbitrability must be addressed with a healthy regard for the federal policy favoring arbitration." . . .

III

Gilmer concedes that nothing in the text of the ADEA or its legislative history explicitly precludes arbitration. He argues, however, that compulsory arbitration of ADEA claims pursuant to arbitration agreements would be inconsistent with the statutory framework and purposes of the ADEA. Like the Court of Appeals, we disagree. . . .

A

Congress enacted the ADEA in 1967 "to promote employment of older persons based on their ability rather than age; to prohibit arbitrary age discrimination in employment; [and] to help employers and workers find ways of meeting problems arising from the impact of age on employment." . . . To achieve those goals, the ADEA, among other things, makes it unlawful for an employer "to fail or refuse to hire or to discharge any individual or otherwise discriminate against any individual with respect to his compensation, terms, conditions, or privileges of employment, because of such individual's age."

. . .

B

In arguing that arbitration is inconsistent with the ADEA, Gilmer also raises a host of challenges to the adequacy of arbitration procedures. Initially, we note that in our recent arbitration cases we have already rejected most of these arguments as insufficient to preclude arbitration of statutory claims. Such generalized attacks on arbitration "res[t] on suspicion of arbitration as a method of weakening the protections afforded in the substantive law to would-be complainants," and as such, they are "far out of step with our current strong endorsement of the federal statutes favoring this method of resolving disputes." . . .

Gilmer first speculates that arbitration panels will be biased. However, "[w]e decline to indulge the presumption that

the parties and arbitral body conducting a proceeding will be unable or unwilling to retain competent, conscientious and impartial arbitrators." . . .

. . . In any event, we note that the NYSE arbitration rules, which are applicable to the dispute in this case, provide protections against biased panels.

. . . The FAA also protects against bias, by providing that courts may overturn arbitration decisions "[w]here there was evident partiality or corruption in the arbitrators." . . . There has been no showing in this case that those provisions are inadequate to guard against potential bias. . . .

Gilmer also complains that the discovery allowed in arbitration is more limited than in the federal courts, which he contends will make it difficult to prove discrimination. It is unlikely, however, that age discrimination claims require more extensive discovery than other claims that we have found to be arbitrable, such as RICO and antitrust claims. . . .

A further alleged deficiency of arbitration is that arbitrators often will not issue written opinions, resulting, Gilmer contends, in a lack of public knowledge of employers' discriminatory policies, an inability to obtain effective appellate review, and a stifling of the development of the law. The NYSE rules, however, do require that all arbitration awards be in writing, and that the awards contain the names of the parties, a summary of the issues in controversy, and a description of the award issued. . . . In addition, the award decisions are made available to the public. . . . Furthermore, judicial decisions addressing ADEA claims will continue to be issued because it is unlikely that all or even most ADEA claimants will be subject to arbitration agreements. . . .

It is also argued that arbitration procedures cannot adequately further the purposes of the ADEA because they do not provide for broad equitable relief and class actions. As the court below noted, however, arbitrators do have the power to fashion equitable relief. . . . Indeed, the NYSE rules applicable here do not restrict the types of relief an arbitrator may award, but merely refer to "damages and/or other relief."

. . . Finally, it should be remembered that arbitration agreements will not preclude the *EEOC* from bringing actions seeking class-wide and equitable relief.

C

An additional reason advanced by Gilmer for refusing to enforce arbitration agreements relating to ADEA claims is his contention that there often will be unequal bargaining power between employers and employees. Mere inequality in bargaining power, however, is not a sufficient reason to hold that arbitration agreements are never enforceable in the employment context. Relationships between securities dealers and investors, for example, may involve unequal bargaining power, but we nevertheless held in *Rodriguez de Quijas* . . . that agreements to arbitrate in that context are enforceable. . . .

. . . There is no indication in this case, however, that Gilmer, an experienced businessman, was coerced or defrauded into agreeing to the arbitration clause in his registration application. As with the claimed procedural inadequacies discussed above, this claim of unequal bargaining power is best left for resolution in specific cases. . . .

IV

In addition to the arguments discussed above, Gilmer vigorously asserts that our decision in *Alexander v. Gardner-Denver* . . .

precludes arbitration of employment discrimination claims. Gilmer's reliance on these cases, however, is misplaced.

In *Gardner-Denver*, the issue was whether a discharged employee whose grievance had been arbitrated pursuant to an arbitration clause in a collective-bargaining agreement was precluded from subsequently bringing a Title VII action based upon the conduct that was the subject of the grievance. In holding that the employee was not foreclosed from bringing the Title VII claim, we stressed that an employee's contractual rights under a collective-bargaining agreement are distinct from the employee's statutory Title VII rights:

> "In submitting his grievance to arbitration, an employee seeks to vindicate his contractual right under a collective-bargaining agreement. By contrast, in filing a lawsuit under Title VII, an employee asserts independent statutory rights accorded by Congress. The distinctly separate nature of these contractual and statutory rights is not vitiated merely because both were violated as a result of the same factual occurrence." . . .

We also noted that a labor arbitrator has authority only to resolve questions of contractual rights. . . . The arbitrator's "task is to effectuate the intent of the parties" and he or she does not have the "general authority to invoke public laws that conflict with the bargain between the parties." . . . By contrast, "in instituting an action under Title VII, the employee is not seeking review of the arbitrator's decision. Rather, he is asserting a statutory right independent of the arbitration process."

There are several important distinctions between the *Gardner-Denver* line of cases and the case before us. First, those cases did not involve the issue of the enforceability of an agreement to arbitrate statutory claims. Rather, they involved the quite different issue whether arbitration of contract-based claims precluded subsequent judicial resolution of statutory claims. Since the employees there had not agreed to arbitrate their statutory claims, and the labor arbitrators were not authorized to resolve such claims, the arbitration in those cases understandably was held not to preclude subsequent statutory actions. Second, because the arbitration in those cases occurred in the context of a collective-bargaining agreement, the claimants there were represented by their unions in the arbitration proceedings. An important concern therefore was the tension between collective representation and individual statutory rights, a concern not applicable to the present case. Finally, those cases were not decided under the FAA, which, as discussed above, reflects a "liberal federal policy favoring arbitration agreements." . . . Therefore, those cases provide no basis for refusing to enforce Gilmer's agreement to arbitrate his ADEA claim.

V

We conclude that Gilmer has not met his burden of showing that Congress, in enacting the ADEA, intended to preclude arbitration of claims under that Act. Accordingly, the judgment of the Court of Appeals is
Affirmed.

Justice Stevens, with whom Justice Marshall joins, dissenting

Section 1 of the Federal Arbitration Act (FAA) states:

> "[N]othing herein contained shall apply to contracts of employment of seamen, railroad employees, or any other class of workers engaged in foreign or interstate commerce." 9 U.S.C. § 1.

The Court today, in holding that the FAA compels enforcement of arbitration clauses even when claims of age discrimination are at issue, skirts the antecedent question of whether the coverage of the Act even extends to arbitration clauses contained in employment contracts, regardless of the subject matter of the claim at issue. In my opinion, arbitration clauses contained in employment agreements are specifically exempt from coverage of the FAA, and for that reason respondent Interstate/Johnson Lane Corporation cannot, pursuant to the FAA, compel petitioner to submit his claims arising under the Age Discrimination in Employment Act of 1967 (ADEA), 29 U.S.C. § 621 *et seq.*, to binding arbitration.

II

In my opinion the Court too narrowly construed the scope of the exclusion contained in § 1 of the FAA.

There is little dispute that the primary concern animating the FAA was the perceived need by the business community to overturn the common-law rule that denied specific enforcement of agreements to arbitrate in contracts between business entities. The Act was drafted by a committee of the American Bar Association (ABA), acting upon instructions from the ABA to consider and report upon "the further extension of the principle of commercial arbitration." . . . At the Senate Judiciary Subcommittee hearings on the proposed bill, the chairman of the ABA committee responsible for drafting the bill assured the Senators that the bill "is not intended [to] be an act referring to labor disputes, at all. It is purely an act to give the merchants the right or the privilege of sitting down and agreeing with each other as to what their damages are, if they want to do it. Now that is all there is in this."

... At the same hearing, Senator Walsh stated:

> "The trouble about the matter is that a great many of these contracts that are entered into are really not [voluntary] things at all. Take an insurance policy; there is a blank in it. You can take that or you can leave it. The agent has no power at all to decide it. Either you can make that contract or you can not make any contract. It is the same with a good many contracts of employment. A man says, 'These are our terms. All right, take it or leave it.' Well, there is nothing for the man to do except to sign it; and then he surrenders his right to have his case tried by the court, and has to have it tried before a tribunal in which he has no confidence at all."

Given that the FAA specifically was intended to exclude arbitration agreements between employees and employers, I see no reason to limit this exclusion from the coverage to arbitration clauses contained in agreements entitled "Contract of Employment." In this case, the parties conceded at oral argument that Gilmer had no "contract of employment" as such with respondent. Gilmer was, however, required as a condition of his employment to become a registered representative of several stock exchanges, including the New York Stock Exchange (NYSE). Just because his agreement to arbitrate any "dispute, claim or controversy" with his employer that arose out of the employment relationship was contained in his application for registration before the NYSE rather than in a specific contract of employment with his employer, I do not think that Gilmer can be compelled pursuant to the FAA to arbitrate his employment-related dispute. Rather, in my opinion the exclusion in § 1 should be interpreted to cover any agreements by the employee to arbitrate disputes with the employer arising out of the employment relationship, particularly where such agreements to arbitrate are conditions of employment. ...

IV

When the FAA was passed in 1925, I doubt that any legislator who voted for it expected it to apply to statutory claims, to form contracts between parties of unequal bargaining power, or to the arbitration of disputes arising out of the employment relationship. In recent years, however, the Court "has effectively rewritten the statute," and abandoned its earlier view that statutory claims were not appropriate subjects for arbitration.

... Although I remain persuaded that it erred in doing so, the Court has also put to one side any concern about the inequality of bargaining power between an entire industry, on the one hand, and an individual customer or employee, on the other. ... Until today, however, the Court has not read § 2 of the FAA as broadly encompassing disputes arising out of the employment relationship. I believe this additional extension of the FAA is erroneous. Accordingly, I respectfully dissent.

Case Questions

1. Why did the trial court deny Interstate's motion?
2. What does the Supreme Court decide and what rationale do the justices use to support their decision?

3. Why do Justices Stevens and Marshall dissent?

4. Who do you think is right? Why?

Voluntary Arbitration

Voluntary arbitration is increasingly used to resolve business disputes, because it provides prompt decisions at a reasonable cost. The voluntary arbitration process is very different from the judicial process. In voluntary arbitrations, for example, the arbitrator makes a binding decision on the merits of the dispute and can base his or her decision on a lay or business sense of justice rather than on the rules of law that would be applied in court. A private arbitration proceeds pursuant to a contract in which the parties promise to bind themselves to arbitrate their controversy and abide by the arbitrator's decision (which is called an *award*). Because a person who chooses to arbitrate waives the right to a jury trial, arbitration agreements must be in writing to be enforceable in court. Some parties agree to arbitrate their agreements prior to the existence of any dispute.[19] Contracts between unions and management, investors and stock brokers,[20] and banks and their customers,[21] often include arbitration clauses. Many major corporations routinely include arbitration clauses in contracts they make with their suppliers. Arbitration agreements can also be negotiated after a controversy has arisen.

Arbitrators are selected by agreement of the parties. The nonprofit American Arbitration Association has been a supplier of arbitrators since 1926.[22] Arbitrators in business disputes are often chosen because of their expertise in a specific field. This better enables them to render a reasonable and proper decision. This should be contrasted with the trial decisions that are made by a randomly selected judge and jury. The parties can choose a person whom they believe will conduct the proceedings fairly and with integrity. However, the legal continuity of the judicial system is not necessarily present in a voluntary arbitration. Arbitrators, for example, do not have to follow precedent in their decision-making process, nor do they have to prepare written explanations for their award (although they often do both).

Each arbitration hearing is convened for the sole purpose of deciding a particular dispute. Arbitration hearings are often conducted in hotels, motels, and offices, and, unlike court trials, are generally not open to the public. Although the formalities of a court proceeding need not be followed, arbitration hearings usually follow the sequence of opening statements by the opposing parties, direct and cross-examination of the witnesses, introduction of exhibits, and closing arguments. Arbitrators base their decisions on the evidence and the arguments made before them. However, they are generally not bound by the rules of evidence used in litigation.

Although the parties to an arbitration usually comply with the terms of the arbitrator's award, judicial enforcement action can be taken against a party who reneges.

Judicial Enforcement of Arbitration Awards

Either party to an arbitration may institute a court action seeking *confirmation* (judicial enforcement) or modification of the award. Federal and state laws provide for jurisdiction in specified courts to (1) recognize and enforce arbitration, (2) provide standards of conduct for arbitration hearings, (3) make arbitration agreements irrevocable, and (4) provide that court action cannot be initiated until the arbitration has concluded.

Courts have limited powers when reviewing an arbitration award. They will usually confirm the award unless the arbitrator violated the terms of the arbitration contract, the arbitration offended fundamental due process, or the award violated public policy. The reviewing court will not review the arbitrator's findings of fact.

The Supreme Court granted *certiorari* in *Mastrobuono v. Shearson Lehman Hutton, Inc.* to review whether an arbitrator's punitive damage award was consistent with the terms of the Federal Arbitration Act and the arbitration agreement. Prior to reading this case, you may want to review the choice-of-law discussion as it relates to contracts in Chapter 4. In reading the case, notice how artfully the investment firm drafted the terms in its agreement with its clients. This agreement contained a clause requiring the arbitration of disputes in lieu of litigation and a choice-of-law clause specifying that New York law would govern its terms. In this way, the firm could avoid the risks of a jury trial and the possibility of punitive damage awards in either a judicial or arbitral forum.[23] In recent years, various federal appeals courts have disagreed about whether the Federal Arbitration Act takes precedence over New York's public policy and permits punitive damage awards. The Supreme Court granted *certiorari* to resolve the conflict between the circuits.

Mastrobuono v. Shearson Lehman Hutton, Inc.
115 S.Ct. 1212
U.S. Supreme Court
March 6, 1995

Justice Stevens delivered the opinion of the Court.

New York law allows courts, but not arbitrators, to award punitive damages. In a dispute arising out of a standard-form contract that expressly provides that it "shall be governed by the laws of the State of New York," a panel of arbitrators awarded punitive damages. The District Court and Court of Appeals disallowed that award. The question presented is whether the arbitrator's award is consistent with the central purpose of the Federal Arbitration Act to ensure "that private agreements to arbitrate are enforced according to their terms." . . .

I

In 1985 petitioners, Antonio Mastrobuono, then an assistant professor of medieval literature, and his wife Diana Mastrobuono, an artist, opened a securities trading account with respondent Shearson Lehman Hutton, Inc. (Shearson), by executing Shearson's standard-form Client's Agreement. Respondent Nick DiMinico, a vice president of Shearson, managed the

Mastrobuonos' account until they closed it in 1987. In 1989, petitioners filed this action in the United States District Court for the Northern District of Illinois, alleging that respondents had mishandled their account and claiming damages on a variety of state and federal law theories.

Paragraph 13 of the parties' agreement contains an arbitration provision and a choice-of-law provision. Relying on the arbitration provision and on §§ 3 and 4 of the Federal Arbitration Act (FAA), 9 U.S.C. §§ 3, 4, respondents filed a motion to stay the court proceedings and to compel arbitration pursuant to the rules of the National Association of Securities Dealers. The District Court granted that motion, and a panel of three arbitrators was convened. After conducting hearings in Illinois, the panel ruled in favor of petitioners.

In the arbitration proceedings, respondents argued that the arbitrators had no authority to award punitive damages. Nevertheless, the panel's award included punitive damages of $400,000, in addition to compensatory damages of $159,327. Respondents paid the compensatory portion of the award but filed a motion in the District Court to vacate the award of punitive damages. The District Court granted the motion, . . . and the Court of Appeals for the Seventh Circuit affirmed. . . . Both courts relied on the choice-of-law provision in Paragraph 13 of the parties' agreement, which specifies that the contract shall be governed by New York law. Because the New York Court of Appeals has decided that in New York the power to award punitive damages is limited to judicial tribunals and may not be exercised by arbitrators, *Garrity v. Lyle Stuart, Inc.*, . . . 353 N.E.2d 793 (1976), the District Court and the Seventh Circuit held that the panel of arbitrators had no power to award punitive damages in this case.

We granted certiorari . . . because the Courts of Appeals have expressed differing views on whether a contractual choice-of-law provision may preclude an arbitral award of punitive damages that otherwise would be proper. . . .

II

. . . [T]he Seventh Circuit interpreted the contract to incorporate New York law, including the *Garrity* rule that arbitrators may not award punitive damages. Petitioners ask us to hold that the FAA preempts New York's prohibition against arbitral awards of punitive damages because this state law is a vestige of the """"ancient"""" judicial hostility to arbitration. . . . Petitioners rely on *Southland Corp. v. Keating*, 465 U.S. 1, . . . (1984), and *Perry v. Thomas*, 482 U.S. 483, . . . (1987), in which we held that the FAA pre-empted two California statutes that purported to require judicial resolution of certain disputes. In *Southland*, we explained that the FAA not only "declared a national policy favoring arbitration," but actually "withdrew the power of the states to require a judicial forum for the resolution of claims which the contracting parties agreed to resolve by arbitration." . . .

Respondents answer that the choice-of-law provision in their contract evidences the parties' express agreement that punitive damages should not be awarded in the arbitration of any dispute arising under their contract.

. . . They argue that the parties may themselves agree to be bound by *Garrity*, just as they may agree to forgo arbitration altogether. In other words, if the contract says "no punitive damages," that is the end of the matter, for courts are bound to interpret contracts in accordance with the expressed intentions of the parties—even if the effect of those intentions is to limit arbitration.

We have previously held that the FAA's pro-arbitration policy does not operate without regard to the wishes of the contracting parties. . . .

. . . [R]espondents . . . argue that the parties to a contract may lawfully agree to limit the issues to be arbitrated by waiving any claim for punitive damages. On the other hand, we think our decisions in . . . *Southland,* and *Perry* make clear that if contracting parties agree to *include* claims for punitive damages within the issues to be arbitrated, the FAA ensures that their agreement will be enforced according to its terms even if a rule of state law would otherwise exclude such claims from arbitration. Thus, the case before us comes down to what the contract has to say about the arbitrability of petitioners' claim for punitive damages.

III

Shearson's standard-form "Client Agreement," which petitioners executed, contains 18 paragraphs. The two relevant provisions of the agreement are found in Paragraph 13. The first sentence of that paragraph provides, in part, that the entire agreement "shall be governed by the laws of the State of New York." . . . The second sentence provides that "any controversy" arising out of the transactions between the parties "shall be settled by arbitration" in accordance with the rules of the National Association of Securities Dealers (NASD), or the Boards of Directors of the New York Stock Exchange and/or the American Stock Exchange. . . . The agreement contains no express reference to claims for punitive damages.

. . . Respondents' argument is persuasive only if "New York law" means "New York decisional law, including that State's

allocation of power between courts and arbitrators, notwithstanding otherwise-applicable federal law." But . . . the provision need not be read so broadly. It is not, in itself, an unequivocal exclusion of punitive damages claims. . . . .

Although neither the choice-of-law clause nor the arbitration clause, separately considered, expresses an intent to preclude an award of punitive damages, respondents argue that a fair reading of the entire Paragraph 13 leads to that conclusion. On this theory, even if "New York law" is ambiguous, and even if "arbitration in accordance with NASD rules" indicates that punitive damages are permissible, the juxtaposition of the two clauses suggests that the contract incorporates "New York law relating to arbitration." We disagree. At most, the choice-of-law clause introduces an ambiguity into an arbitration agreement that would otherwise allow punitive damages awards. . . . [W]hen a court interprets such provisions in an agreement covered by the FAA, "due regard must be given to the federal policy favoring arbitration, and ambiguities as to the scope of the arbitration clause itself resolved in favor of arbitration."

Moreover, respondents cannot overcome the common-law rule of contract interpretation that a court should construe ambiguous language against the interest of the party that drafted it. . . . Respondents drafted an ambiguous document, and they cannot now claim the benefit of the doubt. The reason for this rule is to protect the party who did not choose the language from an unintended or unfair result. That rationale is well-suited to the facts of this case. As a practical matter, it seems unlikely that petitioners were actually aware of New York's . . . approach to punitive damages, or that they had any idea that by signing a standard-form agreement to arbitrate disputes they might be giving up an important substantive right. In the face of such doubt, we are unwilling to impute this intent to petitioners.

Finally the respondents' reading of the two clauses violates another cardinal principle of contract construction: that a document should be read to give effect to all its provisions and to render them consistent with each other.

. . . We think the best way to harmonize the choice-of-law provision with the arbitration provision is to read "the laws of the State of New York" to encompass substantive principles that New York courts would apply, but not to include special rules limiting the authority of arbitrators. Thus, the choice-of-law provision covers the rights and duties of the parties, while the arbitration clause covers arbitration; neither sentence intrudes upon the other. In contrast, respondents' reading sets up the two clauses in conflict with one another: one foreclosing punitive damages, the other allowing them. This interpretation is untenable.

We hold that the Court of Appeals misinterpreted the parties' agreement. The arbitral award should have been enforced as within the scope of the contract. The judgment of the Court of Appeals is, therefore, reversed.

It is so ordered.

Case Questions

1. Do you think that the Supreme Court actually resolved the major question raised by this case? How might investment firms react?
2. Why did the Supreme Court resolve the ambiguity against the investment firm?

Court-Annexed Arbitration

Court-annexed arbitration includes both voluntary and mandatory procedures. Mandatory arbitrations, however, for reasons founded in the Seventh Amendment, can only produce nonbiding decisions.[24] The court determines the types of cases that must be arbitrated, which commonly include personal injury, property damage, and commercial cases in which the amount claimed does not exceed a designated sum. That sum, called the jurisdictional amount, varies among jurisdictions. Some jurisdictions limit arbitrations to small claims cases, medical malpractice, or motor vehicle cases with damages under a specified amount.

The court's arbitration rules usually provide for limited discovery and modified rules of evidence. In brief trial-like hearings lasting about three hours, attorneys offer documentary evidence, present witness testimony, and cross-examine opposing witnesses. Arbitrators, usually retired judges and local lawyers, are selected in various ways. In some courts, the clerk of court randomly assigns arbitrators. In other jurisdictions the parties participate in the selection process.

Arbitrators listen to the presentations, ask questions of the presenters, and determine the liability and damages issues. They do not make findings of fact or conclusions of law or attempt to mediate the dispute, critique the parties, or propose settlement terms. The award becomes a final judgment unless the parties reject it and demand a traditional jury trial (called a *trial de novo*). Unless the trial judgment exceeds the arbitration award, a party demanding a trial *de novo* often will be penalized and required to pay the arbitration costs.

The following case demonstrates the results of an attorney's failure to "meaningfully" participate in a court-mandated arbitration.

Gilling v. Eastern Airlines, Inc.
680 F.Supp. 169
U.S. District Court, D. New Jersey
March 2, 1988

Sarokin, District Judge

I. Introduction

In order for the compulsory arbitration program to function properly, it is essential that the parties participate in a meaningful manner. This is particularly so in a case such as this in which one of the parties is a substantial corporation and the other party is one or more individuals. The purposes of the arbitration program are to provide the parties with a quick and inexpensive means of resolving their dispute while, at the same time, reducing the court's caseload.

These purposes are thwarted when a party to the arbitration enters into it with the intention from the outset of rejecting its outcome and demanding a trial de novo. Rather than reducing the cost and promoting efficiency in the system, such an attitude increases the costs and reduces the efficiency. Furthermore, such conduct can serve to discourage the poorer litigant and diminish his or her resolve to proceed to final judgment. Explicit in this court's

arbitration program is the need for the parties to participate in good faith. Failure to do so warrants appropriate sanctions by the court.

Here, defendants move for trial de novo after the entry of an adverse arbitration award. The court grants the motion, but imposes sanctions on defendants for failure to participate in the arbitration meaningfully.

II. Background

Plaintiffs were passengers aboard a flight of defendant Eastern Air Lines from Miami to Martinique on November 27, 1983. They allege that they were wrongfully ejected from their flight during a stopover in St. Croix after two incidents on board involving knives. Their complaint states claims for breach of contract, negligence, false imprisonment, battery, assault, slander, invasion of privacy, infliction of emotional distress and conversion.

The court referred the matter to compulsory arbitration, as General Rule 47 requires. The arbitrator heard the case on May 20, 1987. The defendants did not attend the arbitration; their appearance was through counsel. Although the parties dispute the extent of defense counsel's presentation at the arbitration, they agree that she presented summaries of the defendants' position and read at least a few passages from deposition testimony and answers to interrogatories. The arbitrator found for each of the plaintiffs.

Within the thirty days allotted by General Rule 47(G)(1), defendants moved for a trial de novo. Plaintiffs opposed the motion, contending that defendants' failure to participate meaningfully in the arbitration as General Rule 47(E)(3) requires deprived them of their right to demand a trial de novo. As the court was unable to evaluate the meaningfulness of the defendants' participation in the arbitration, the court remanded the case to the arbitrator for a factual finding on that question.

On November 12, 1987, the arbitrator made the requested factual findings. Letter of Daniel E. Isles, Esq., Arbitrator (November 12, 1987). He found as a fact that defendants' attorney did not participate in the arbitration proceeding in a meaningful manner:

> "I find as a fact that she merely 'went through the motions.' I find as a fact that the foregoing was a predetermined position taken by her office, even though that position remains obscure to me. I find as a fact that her 'participation' in the arbitration proceeding rendered it a sham. . . .
>
> "I was . . . flabbergasted when [defendants' counsel] arrived with no witnesses. She stated . . . that all Eastern personnel were on assignment, and that she would render fact summaries and position summaries. While she may have read a few interrogatories and answers [sic] a few lines from one or more deposition transcripts, ninety five percent (95%) of her participation was in fact stating position summaries on behalf of Eastern, and stating fact summaries as to

what Eastern's personnel may have said in their own depositions. . . .

> "I recall another event that occurred at the arbitration proceeding which further buttresses my within findings of fact. At the end of the hearing I asked [defendants' counsel] as to whether she wanted damage awards broken down into compensatory damages and punitive damages, if I should determine to make such damage awards. Her reply to me as best I can paraphrase it now was 'Do what you want, or, we don't care what you do, we won't pay it anyway.'"

After the arbitrator filed his fact findings with the court, the defendants renewed their motion for a trial de novo. Defendants couple their request for a de novo trial with a request that the court vacate the arbitrator's findings.

III. Discussion

> "General Rule 47(E)(3) provides that the arbitration hearing may proceed in the absence of any party who, after notice, fails to be present. In the event that a party fails to participate in the arbitration process in a meaningful manner, as determined by the arbitrator, the Court may impose appropriate sanctions, including, but not limited to, the striking of any demand for a trial de novo filed by that party."

Defendants ask the court to vacate the arbitrator's finding that they did not participate in the arbitration in a meaningful manner. After examining General Rule 47, the court is unable to discover any standard of review of an arbitrator's findings. The rule simply authorizes the court to devise a sanction "in the event that a party fails to participate in the arbitration process in a meaningful manner, *as determined by the arbitrator*." General Rule 47(E)(3) (emphasis added). The rule thus appears to place the determination of meaningfulness entirely in the hands and discretion of the arbitrator, without being subject to district court review.

However, even if the court does have the authority to disturb an arbitrator's finding of no meaningful participation, it declines to do so in this case. The arbitrator had ample opportunity to observe the conduct of counsel at the arbitration. He had the opportunity to measure the earnestness of the defendants' presentation against the gravity of the plaintiff's allegations and the defendant's potentially sizeable exposure to liability. Although the defendants are correct that General Rule 47 did not require them to present live testimony, the arbitrator was certainly entitled to factor their decision not to call witnesses into his overall assessment of the meaningfulness of their participation. The arbitrator, examining the totality of the defendants' participation at the arbitration, concluded that the reading of brief position summaries and deposition and interrogatory excerpts did not amount to meaningful participation in the context of this case. The court concludes that this finding was supported by substantial evidence and was not clearly erroneous.

Defendants argue that the enforcement of General Rule 47(E)(3) against them would deprive them of their constitutional right to a jury trial and conflict with the Federal Rules of Civil Procedure. The court notes that compulsory pre-trial arbitration procedures like the one at issue in this case have withstood constitutional attack.

The court, however, need not reach the defendants' constitutional claim, for the rule does not require the court to deny the application for trial de novo. Rather, it allows the court to choose an "appropriate sanction," only one of which is the rather draconian striking of a demand for trial de novo. While such an extreme sanction may be appropriate where a party absolutely refuses to participate in or even attend arbitration, . . . the court declines to deprive defendants of their day in court because of their limited performance at arbitration, without in any way condoning it.

General Rule 47(E)(3) allows the court to devise an "appropriate sanction." In this case, where the defendants demonstrated such contempt for the arbitration proceeding, it is only fair that they should have to pay for it. The court therefore orders that defendants reimburse plaintiffs for all costs and fees which they incurred in preparing for and participating in the arbitration, as well as costs and fees incurred in opposing defendants' demand for a trial de novo.

The court has determined to impose this more limited sanction, although denial of the trial de novo would have been warranted, because of the lack of clear guidelines as to what participation is "meaningful." However, counsel should be on notice that a trial de novo will not be automatically permitted in those cases in which the party seeking it views the arbitration proceeding merely as a meaningless interlude in the judicial process.

Case Questions

1. In this case, the judge deferred to the arbitrator's determination that the defendants' attorney failed to "meaningfully" participate in a compulsory arbitration. The arbitrator's conclusion was heavily influenced by the failure

of the defense to present witness testimony. Should arbitrators be entitled to second-guess an attorney's litigation strategy, where such a decision can result in the imposition of financial sanctions?

2. Why did the court refuse to enforce General Rule 47(E)(3) and deprive the defendants of a trial de novo?

JOINTLY USED ADR METHODS

Mediation, mini-trials, and arbitration are used with both court-annexed and voluntary ADR. The following discussion briefly examines each of these methods.

Mediation

Mediation is a technique in which one or more neutral parties, called mediators, help disputants to find ways to settle their dispute.[25] Parties often attempt to resolve their disagreements by mediation before participating in binding arbitration or litigation. Informal, unstructured, and inexpensive, mediation focuses on settlement, not on victory at trial. Mediators have no formal power to make a decision: their role is that of facilitator, and different mediators use different styles and techniques to help parties come to an agreement. There is no formal hearing in a mediation. Instead, using joint meetings and private caucuses, mediators (1) help the parties identify their real goals, (2) narrow the issues, (3) look for alternatives and options as well as areas of common interest, and (4) prevent the parties from focusing on only one solution.

Court-annexed mediation often involves using trial attorneys as mediators. Mediators in some jurisdictions are paid and in others are volunteers. The theory is that neutral, experienced trial attorneys will be able to persuade litigants to look at their cases realistically and moderate their monetary demands. These are important hurdles that often stand in the way of a settlement.

Court-annexed mediation procedures vary. Lawyer-mediators are used in some jurisdictions and three-person panels in others. In complex cases, the court may appoint a person called a special master to serve as a mediator. Mediators vary in their approaches, but they tend to evaluate each case and predict what would happen if the case went to trial. They also indicate what they believe to be the settlement value of the case. These two determinations serve as a catalyst in starting settlement discussions between the parties.

In some jurisdictions the court refers most cases to mediation. In other jurisdictions mediation occurs pursuant to stipulation or a suggestion from the court. Mediation is nonbinding, and parties retain their rights to attempt other ADR methods and to go to trial.

There is a big difference in the focus of a trial and mediation. Trials exist to produce a winner and a loser. Mediation exists to help the parties settle their dispute in an amicable and expeditious manner. The objective is to find a solution to the dispute that is more acceptable to each party than going to trial. Mediation is more flexible than a trial and can produce a result that is more attuned to the underlying facts. Another advantage to mediation is that there are fewer enforcement problems. Because mediation produces an agreement between the parties, many problems that result when a judgment creditor attempts to enforce a judgment are avoided.

Parties who voluntarily choose mediation employ a person to function as a neutral and help them settle their dispute. In the following case, the mediator penalized the appellant for failing to accept the proposed award. Note how the court treated the appellant's Seventh Amendment claim.

Rhea v. Massey-Ferguson, Inc.
767 F.2d 266
U.S. Court of Appeals, Sixth Circuit
July 3, 1985

Per Curiam

Defendant-Appellant Massey-Ferguson, Inc. appeals from a jury verdict in favor of the plaintiff-appellee Wesley Rhea in this diversity personal injury suit. On appeal, Massey-Ferguson challenges the district court's submission of this case to mediation. . . . After considering these issues, we affirm the jury verdict.

Rhea was injured when he inadvertently shifted a Massey-Ferguson 245 tractor into gear as he stood beside it. The tractor began moving forward, although no one had depressed the clutch lever. The tractor's right rear wheel first rolled over Rhea's leg, forcing him under the machine before it rolled over his shoulder and chest. Rhea suffered numerous fractures and lost part of one ear in the accident. Rhea filed this action in state court alleging that Massey-Ferguson was liable for negligent design and breach of implied warranty. Massey-Ferguson removed the action to federal district court. A jury found damages of $300,000, but it also found Rhea 24% negligent. Under

Michigan's comparative negligence doctrine, the resulting verdict was $228,000.

First, Massey-Ferguson challenges the district court's referral of this case to mediation under the Eastern District of Michigan's Local Rule 32, which provides that a diversity case involving only monetary damages may be referred to mediation before trial. Massey-Ferguson rejected and Rhea accepted the resulting $100,000 proposed award. Therefore, under Local Rule 32.10(d), Massey-Ferguson was liable for actual costs unless the verdict at trial was more than ten percent below the evaluation. The jury returned a verdict that was more than twice the mediation evaluation and the district court awarded $5,400 in actual costs to Rhea.

Massey-Ferguson contends that this procedure violates its Seventh Amendment right to a jury trial and is inconsistent with various of the Federal Rules of Civil Procedure. The Seventh Amendment "was designed to preserve the basic institution of jury trial in only its most fundamental elements, not the great mass of procedural forms and details."

At the core of these fundamental elements is the right to have a "'jury *ultimately* determine the issues of fact if they cannot be settled by the parties or determined as a matter of law.'" . . .

Federal courts have repeatedly upheld mandatory arbitration procedures in the face of challenges based on the right to a jury trial. . . . In keeping with the Seventh Amendment's requirements Massey-Ferguson received the jury's determination of the disputed facts in the present action.

Massey-Ferguson also characterizes Local Rule 32 as violating numerous Federal Rules of Civil Procedure. Federal Rule of Civil Procedure 83 authorizes district courts to "regulate their practice in any manner not inconsistent with these rules." The challenged local rule is not inconsistent with Rule 38(b) merely because it interposes an additional step between the jury demand and trial. Nor does the Local Rule require two demands for a jury trial in violation of Rule 39(a). Nor is Local Rule 32 inconsistent with Rule 53 or 72–75, governing referral to masters or magistrates. The mediation panel merely issues a settlement evaluation that has no force unless accepted by the parties. In sum, no flaw requiring this Court to intervene in the district court's practice under Local Rule 32 has been raised in the present suit. . . .

For the foregoing reasons, we affirm the jury verdict and the district court's assessment of interest and attorney fees.

Case Questions

1. Should a litigant who is forced to participate in mediation be subject to a penalty for insisting on a trial where the verdict at trial was more than twice the mediator's recommended sum?
2. Is it fair for courts in one jurisdiction to require mediation when courts in other jurisdictions permit direct access to jury trials?

MINI-TRIALS

The mini-trial, used primarily to resolve business disputes, actually isn't a trial at all. It is a process in which each party makes an abbreviated presentation to a panel, generally consisting of a senior manager or decision maker from each side and a judge (in the case of a court-ordered mini-trial) or jointly selected neutral (in the case of a voluntary mini-trial). The theory behind this process is that the presenters for each side will educate the managers about the dispute.[26] The strength of this process is that the business managers, rather than lawyers, judges, and juries, make the decisions. The managers can often design creative solutions that make it possible to resolve the dispute. They are not restricted to the types of relief that courts can award after a trial. If the managers fail to agree, mini-trial rules often require a judge or neutral to forecast what he or she believes would happen if the case were to go to trial and indicate what he or she believes to be a reasonable settlement proposal. The parties in a court-annexed mini-trial can reject the judge's proposal but may incur a penalty. A party who insists on a trial but fails to recover a judgment more favorable than the judge's proposal may be assessed a substantial fine for each day that it takes to try the case.[27] The parties in a voluntary mini-trial can reject the neutral's proposal without a penalty.

Some courts schedule mini-trials only after the parties agree to participate. Other courts require parties to take part. Mini-trials are primarily used in complex, time-consuming cases where the substantial savings of money and time realized by limiting discovery and presentations are strong incentives. Mini-trials are most likely to succeed when both parties are serious about resolving the underlying issues with a minimum of acrimony.

The parties in a mini-trial have control over the procedures and can disregard the formal rules of civil procedure and evidence that apply in litigation. For example, they can set their own rules regarding the nature and scope of discovery and determine whether position papers will be exchanged prior to the hearing. They can also determine the procedures to be utilized at the hearing. For example, they can decide whether written summaries will be submitted in lieu of witness testimony, how many hours each side will have to present its case, how long opening statements will be, and whether cross-examination will be allowed.

The typical procedures for a mini-trial include an abbreviated presentation of each side's case to a panel of decision makers selected by the parties and the neutral. The decision makers then meet privately after the presentations have concluded and work to negotiate a solution to the dispute.

Summary Jury Trials

An Ohio federal district court judge developed the summary jury trial (SJT) process in 1980 as a court-annexed, mandatory procedure. It operates pursuant to local court rules and is used in cases that have proved difficult to settle—primarily damage cases. The key elements in the typical SJT are an advisory jury, an abbreviated, two-hour hearing, and a nonbinding verdict. The SJT procedure can be helpful where parties agree on the defendant's liability, but disagree about the damages. In such cases, the plaintiff's attorney doesn't want to settle for less than what he or she estimates a jury will award. Similarly, the defendant's lawyer will not want to settle for more than what a jury would probably require.

SJT procedures are similar to those at trial.[28] A judge presides, and each side has one or two hours to present its case. Case presentations include oral summaries of the evidence and the reading of witness depositions. Each side also has an opportunity to argue the case to the jury, which consists of five or six jurors. The judge gives the jury abbreviated oral instructions. The SJT juries are composed of persons summoned to court, but not chosen to sit on a regular trial jury that day.

After the judge's instructions, the SJT jurors retire and deliberate on both liability and damages. The jurors often are asked to discuss the case with the attorneys and clients after they return with a nonbinding verdict. The process works best when the client or some person with settlement authority attends the SJT and participates in this settlement conference.

The SJT process allows the attorneys to have a practice trial and the opportunity to see how a group of regular jurors reacted to each side's presentation. It also gives the parties "a day in court," which helps to satisfy some litigants' emotional needs. The fact that neutral jurors establish a damage figure is an additional plus. The SJT has had an impact on insurance companies as well as the attorneys and parties. Insurance companies are often more willing to settle after they have seen an SJT jury's verdict because they then have a dollar figure that can serve as a basis for settlement negotiations. If the parties are unable to settle the dispute, the case remains on the calendar for a regular trial.

One criticism of summary jury trials is that SJT presentations compress cases to such an extent that the jurors can't absorb the evidence and argument. In response, a few judges now allow one-week summary "trials." Others permit the use of live witness testimony.

The petitioner in the following case asked to be excused by the court from participation in a summary jury trial so that the matter could proceed directly to trial.

Arabian American Oil Co. v. Scarfone
119 F.R.D. 448
U.S. District Court,
M.D. Florida, Tampa Division
April 4, 1988

Order on motion to be excused from participation in summary trial

Kovachevich, District Judge

This cause is before the Court on Defendants', Robert Work and Jerry Konidaris, motions to excuse participation in summary trial. Mr. Work's motion was filed March 22, 1988, alleging that there is no possibility of settlement in the case, that even if settlement were possible the settlement must occur between Plaintiff and Defendant Scarfone, and that he desires to avoid the expenditure of time and money that participation in the summary trial would require. In support of the motion Defendant Work cites the recent Seventh Circuit Court of Appeals decision in *Strandell v. Jackson County, Illinois*, 838 F.2d 884 (7th Cir.1987).

On March 30, 1988, Defendant Konidaris filed his motion. Basically Konidaris joins the motion of Defendant Work, adding the factor that he is an individual with limited financial resources who lives and works in Greece and that it would be "absolutely meaningless and highly expensive for Konidaris to have to attend a Summary Jury Trial through himself or through his counsel."

In *Strandell*, the Seventh Circuit reversed the decision of the District Court for the Southern District of Illinois holding an attorney in criminal contempt for refusing to participate in a nonbinding summary jury trial. The court concluded that the parameters of Rule 16, Fed.R. Civ.P. do not permit courts to *compel* parties to participate in summary trials.

Rule 16(a)(1) and (5) and (c)(11) has been cited as a basis for the utilization of summary trial procedures. That rule gives the court the power to direct parties to appear before it for various purposes, including expediting the disposition of the action; facilitating the settlement of the case; and taking action in regard to matters which may aid in the disposition of the action. Rule 16 calls these procedures conferences but what is in a name. The obvious purpose and aim of Rule 16 is to allow courts the discretion and processes necessary for intelligent and effective case management and disposition. Whatever name the judge may give to these proceedings their purposes are the same and are sanctioned by Rule 16.

Statistically, the Middle District of Florida has the worst record in the nation for protracted trials; an accumulation of lengthy, untried causes, literally awaiting decades for trial disposition, are delayed because of their extraordinarily projected trial time. This Court has effectively utilized summary trials since 1985; without it, opportunity for resolution is delayed, and, justice is denied. The parties herein have had ample notice of this procedure; in fact, the January 1988 summary trial setting would have been held, but for courtroom space limitations. Defendants, for the first time, now raise objections on the eve of the April 12 and 13 summary trial; this constitutes a two-day investment in a *real* trial projected by the parties to consume 210 courtroom hours, or, seven courtroom weeks. Litigants are entitled to their day in court, but not to somebody else's day.

Under Article Three of the U.S. Constitution, definite work is assigned to, or expected of, the trial court; that is our duty. The inherent jurisdiction of the trial court to determine, set, and use management policies should not be abrogated; it is in the best position to identify, separate, process, and complete *all* of the cases for which it is held responsible, accountable, and exists to perform. Without the authority to perform the task, the ultimate mission of the courts of the United States—to properly administer justice in all matters properly before the court—is adversely affected.

The summary trial represents one alternative dispute resolution process which courts are employing in an effort to secure to civil litigants just, speedy, and inexpensive determination of their claims (Rule 1, Fed.R.Civ.P.) of which litigants may be otherwise deprived because of the overwhelming and overburdening caseloads which befall many district courts. The summary trial does not abolish any substantive rights of the parties; they are still entitled to a binding trial, if the summary proceedings do not lead to ultimate settlement of the cause of action.

Even if the summary procedures do not culminate in settlement of the case, the value of the summary trial in crystallizing the issues and the proof is immeasurable to the later binding trial, to which all parties come more fully prepared and rehearsed in their roles and the trial procedure. All attorneys and parties must be treated equally. Many attorneys come to trial prepared; *others do not*. After the jury is sworn in an involved case, it is an embarrassing professional exercise before the court and jury to see lawyers floundering in their presentations due to inadequate preparation, whether it be the facts from witnesses, or the law in proposed jury instructions and verdict interrogatories. The reality is that too many will *not* get ready until the day of a trial; a summary trial *forces* that day and that preparation!

This Court finds the summary trial to be a legitimate device to be used to implement the policy of this Court to provide litigants with the most expeditious and just case resolution. The Court does not find the *Strandell* case from the Seventh Circuit persuasive or binding precedent to this court. Accordingly, it is

Ordered that the motions to be excused from participation in the summary jury trial of Defendants Work and Konidaris are denied as far as the motions are based upon a suggestion that the

Court cannot require parties to participate in summary trial proceedings. Any
contention that individual defendants
should be excused from participation
based on reasons, such as inability to appear for financial reasons, should be addressed by the magistrate before whom
the summary trial is scheduled.

Case
Questions
1. Why does the judge reject the reasoning of the *Strandell* case?
2. Why isn't the court bound by the precedent established in *Strandell*?
3. What are the advantages of summary jury trials? Disadvantages?

Private Trials

Parties that have failed to resolve their dispute with mediation and/or arbitration may choose to litigate in a private court system. Provided by commercial
firms that employ retired federal, state, and local judges, such trials are held
in hotels, law schools, and even office buildings in which courtrooms that
replicate public courtrooms have been constructed. These firms exist to
provide timely, confidential, and affordable trials. In thirteen states the parties
can employ jurors selected from the public jury rolls to hear the case. The private trial system allows the parties to select a judge who has experience appropriate to the case. It also allows the parties to conduct their trial in private, an
important advantage in many contract, employment rights, professional liability, and divorce actions. The parties to a private trial often contract to use
simplified evidentiary and procedural rules, and to cooperate with discovery,
saving time and money for both parties. The parties also decide whether the
decision of the private judge/jury will be final or appealable, and some private
court systems even provide for private appeals.

Critics of the private court system maintain that it allows the wealthy to
avoid the delays and conditions that others must endure in the public court
system. They also express concern that the higher compensation that is paid
to private judges could result in a two-tier system of justice. The best judges
would handle the litigation of the wealthy in the private sector, while others
would litigate before less able judges in underfunded, overworked, public
sector courts.

Chapter Questions

1. Define the following terms:

alternative dispute resolution
arbitration
arbitration agreements

arbitration award
court-annexed
mediation

mini-trial	Seventh Amendment
private trial	summary jury trial
settlement conference	trial *de novo*

2. Frances J. Vukasin was employed by D. A. Davidson & Co. in August 1979. The company implemented an annual performance review in 1985 which rated her performance in each of six areas, gave her an overall rating, and indicated a recommended salary increase. Included in Vukasin's 1986 and 1987 performance reviews, directly above the employee's signature line, was a provision that read "Employment with D. A. Davidson & Co. is subject to arbitration." The review also provided that she or her employer could terminate employment at any time for any reason. There was also a statement that "I [the employee] . . . acknowledge and agree that any controversy between myself and the Company arising out of my employment or the termination of my employment with the Company for any reasons whatsoever shall be determined by arbitration." On December 12, 1988 Vukasin filed a complaint in a state court against the company. She alleged in the complaint that another employee had assaulted and battered her at the company's offices on April 30, 1988. She claimed damages for mental and emotional distress, pain and suffering, loss of wages, and various medical and therapy expenses. Is the allegation of assault and battery outside the scope of the arbitration clause and appropriate for litigation?
Vukasin v. D. A. Davidson & Co., 785 P.2d 713 (Mont. 1990)

3. James Clawson contracted with Habitat, Inc., to build a retaining wall and driveway at his home. The contract contained an arbitration clause. A dispute arose regarding the construction, and the matter was submitted to binding arbitration. The parties continued negotiation throughout the arbitration process. When it appeared that they were close to a settlement, they entered into a new agreement. The new agreement provided that the parties would retract the arbitration if they could negotiate a settlement by 3:00 P.M. on October 21, 1988. Clawson and Habitat disagreed about whether an agreement had been reached by that date. The arbitrator's decision was released on November 1, 1988. Both parties filed motions in the circuit court, Habitat to confirm the award, and Clawson to vacate the award. Should the circuit court confirm the award?
Clawson v. Habitat, Inc., 783 P.2d 1230 (Hawaii 1989)

4. The Medford (Oregon) Firefighters Association and the City of Medford reached a stalemate while negotiating a collective bargaining agreement. They unsuccessfully tried to mediate their dispute. Pursuant to state law, the Oregon Employment Relations Board appointed an arbitrator who held a hearing, prepared an agreement, and submitted it to the parties. The firefighters petitioned the circuit court for a writ of *mandamus* when the city refused to sign the agreement. The city claimed that the state law providing for binding arbitration was unconstitutional. Can the state

legislature constitutionally delegate legislative power to a private person as an arbitrator?

Medford Firefighters Association v. City of Medford, 595 P.2d 1268 (1979)

5. Roger Lockhart, a teen-ager, lost the sight in one of his eyes. He alleged that this was due to the negligence of Dr. Ramon Patel. A summary jury trial was conducted and the advisory jury awarded the plaintiff $200,000. The court held several formal and informal settlement conferences following the SJT. The court directed that the defense attorney attend a settlement conference on November 3, 1986, and that he bring with him a representative of Dr. Patel's liability insurance carrier who possessed authority to settle the case. The defense attorney appeared on November 3, but the insurance representative with settlement authority did not. The insurance carrier sent an adjuster instead. The court responded by (1) striking the defendant's pleadings, (2) declaring the defendant in default, (3) setting the trial for the following day, limited to the question of damages, and (4) set a hearing to show cause why the insurance carrier should not be punished for criminal contempt of the court. Does the court have the right to strike the defendant's pleadings because of the insurance carrier's failure to send a representative to attend the settlement conference?

Lockhart v. Patel, 115 F.R.D. 44 (E.D.Ky. 1987)

6. Elizabeth Garfield brought suit against her former employer, Thomas McKinnon Securities, Inc., claiming that McKinnon had discharged her on account of her age in violation of the Age Discrimination in Employment Act. McKinnon moved to dismiss the complaint and compel arbitration because Garfield had agreed to arbitrate any controversy arising out of her employment. Garfield responded that she and all registered brokers are required to execute arbitration agreements as a condition of employment. She maintained that Congress did not intend to permit persons to waive their statutory right to sue for ADEA violations in federal court via the execution of an arbitration agreement. Should the court dismiss the complaint and compel arbitration?

Garfield v. Thomas McKinnon Securities, Inc., 731 F.Supp. 841 (N.D.Ill. 1988)

7. Innis Achong was hired as a nursing attendant by the Cabrini Medical Center. He became a member of Local 1199 of the Drug, Hospital and Health Care Employees Union which was party to a collective bargaining agreement. On November 4, 1986, a disoriented and distraught patient kicked Achong as he walked by her stretcher. Cabrini claimed that Achong, who had a perfect performance record at the time, responded by cursing the patient and striking her on the leg. Cabrini discharged Achong for abusing the patient. The collective bargaining agreement provided for binding arbitration whenever the union and Cabrini disagreed upon whether an employee was discharged for just cause. Achong's dismissal was submitted to arbitration. The arbitrator made careful and detailed findings and conclusions. He ruled that just cause did not exist for

Achong's discharge, because Cabrini failed to establish how hard Achong touched the patient. He believed that summary discharge was too harsh a penalty under the circumstances and based on the limited evidence. He ruled that Achong should be reinstated without back pay (thereby imposing a forfeiture of nine months' pay) and given a warning against future conduct. Cabrini brought an action in federal court to set aside the award, and the union brought an action in state court to confirm. Cabrini removed the state action to federal court, where the two actions were consolidated. Cabrini argued that the award violated public policy based on a statutory provision that patients "shall be free from mental and physical abuse." Should the award be confirmed?

Cabrini Medical Center v. Local 1199 Drug, Hospital and Health Care Employees Union, 731 F.Supp. 612 (S.D.N.Y. 1990)

Notes

1. R. Samborn, *In Courts: Caseloads Still Rise*, The National Law Journal (July 5, 1993). A study conducted by the National Center for State Courts shows the likelihood that dockets will double by the year 2000.

2. R. Samborn, *Accelerating Caseloads Threaten to Swamp Courts*, The National Law Journal, A11 (May 9, 1994).

3. P.S. McDonough, *ADR for Labor Disputes: An Idea Whose Time Has Come*, Corporate Legal Times, 25 (September 1994).

4. *ADR Is More Than a Means of Resolving Disputes*, Corporate Legal Times, 36–44 (May 1994).

5. In 1991, for example, Colorado amended its Code of Professional Responsibility and required lawyers to advise their clients of this option.

6. R.C. Reuben, *Decision Gives Banking ADR a Boost*, American Bar Association Journal, 32 (December 1994).

7. 28 U.S.C. 471.

8. L. Shaw, *Courts Point Justice in a New Direction*, The National Law Journal, C1 (April 11, 1994).

9. Ibid., pp. C1, 16.

10. W.H. Schroder, Jr., *Private ADR May Offer Increased Confidentiality*, The National Law Journal, C14–16 (July 25, 1995).

11. J.H. Kennedy, "Merger Aimed at Settling Out of Court," Boston Globe, May 16, 1994, pp. 18–19.

12. D.M. Provine, *Settlement Strategies for Federal District Judges* (Federal Judicial Center, 1986).

13. H.N. Mazadoorian, *Widespread Disgust with Civil Justice Is Boon to ADR*, Corporate Legal Times, 17 (April 1994). Mazadoorian refers to a recent Deloitte & Touche report indicating that ADR costs are between 11 and 50 percent of litigation costs.

14. Ibid.

15. J.W. Keltner, *The Management of Struggle* (Cresskill, N.J.: Hampton Press, Inc., 1994), p. 152.

16. J.W. Cooley, *Arbitration vs. Mediation—Explaining the Differences*, Judicature, 69, 264 (1986).

17. Federal Arbitration Act, 9 U.S.C. Sec. 1.

18. Keltner, p. 151.

19. Some states, such as Alabama, have refused to enforce arbitration agreements entered into prior to the existence of any dispute. The U.S. Supreme Court is expected to decide whether such state decisions are preempted by the Federal Arbitration Act. Also, Reuben, p. 33.

20. *Shearson Lehman Hutton v. McMahon*, 482 U.S. 220 (1987).

21. Reuben, pp. 32–33.

22. Mazadoorian, p. 17.

23. K. Donovan, *The Arbitration Question: Why No Punitive Awards?* The National Law Journal, B1–2, (January 23, 1995); M.C. Collyer, *Punitive Damages in Arbitrations: The Second Circuit on a Collision Course with the U.S. Supreme Court*, Ohio State Journal on Dispute Resolution, 8, 385–399 (1993).

24. D. Hensler, "Court-Annexed ADR-Court Administered Arbitration," excerpt from *Wilkinson, Donovan, Leisure, Newton & Irvine ADR Practice Book* (New York: John Wiley & Sons, 1990), p. 53.

25. Cooley, p. 266.

26. J. Davis and L. Omlie, *Mini-trials: The Courtroom in the Boardroom*, Willamette Law Review, 21, 531 (1985).

27. The extent to which federal judges can order parties to participate in mini-trials and summary jury trials is a hotly contested issue. The United States Court of Appeals for the Sixth Circuit issued a writ of mandamus to stop a mandatory summary jury trial. See *In re NLO, Inc.*, 5 F.3d 154 (1993).

28. *Mandatory and Summary Jury Trial Guidelines for Ensuring Fair and Effective Process*, Harvard Law Review, 103, 1086 (1990).

The Constitution of the United States

We the people of the United States, in order to form a more perfect union, establish justice, insure domestic tranquility, provide for the common defense, promote the general welfare, and secure the blessings of liberty to ourselves and our posterity, do ordain and establish this Constitution for the United States of America.

ARTICLE I

Section 1.
All legislative powers herein granted shall be vested in a Congress of the United States, which shall consist of a Senate and House of Representatives.

Section 2.
1. The House of Representatives shall be composed of members chosen every second year by the people of the several States, and the electors in each State shall have the qualifications requisite for electors of the most numerous branch of the State Legislature.

2. No person shall be a representative who shall not have attained to the age of twenty-five years, and been seven years a citizen of the United States, and who shall not, when elected, be an inhabitant of that State in which he shall be chosen.

3. Representatives and direct taxes[1] shall be apportioned among the several States which may be included within this Union, according to their respective numbers, which shall be determined by adding to the whole number of free persons, including those bound to service for a term of years, and excluding Indians not taxed, three fifths of all other persons.[2] The actual enumeration shall be made within three years after the first meeting of the Congress of the United States, and within every subsequent term of ten years, in such manner

[1] Altered by the 16th Amendment.
[2] Altered by the 14th Amendment.

as they shall by law direct. The number of representatives shall not exceed one for every thirty thousand, but each State shall have at least one representative; and until such enumeration shall be made, the State of New Hampshire shall be entitled to choose three, Massachusetts eight, Rhode Island and Providence Plantations one, Connecticut five, New York six, New Jersey four, Pennsylvania eight, Delaware one, Maryland six, Virginia ten, North Carolina five, South Carolina five, and Georgia three.

4. When vacancies happen in the representation from any State, the executive authority thereof shall issue writs of election to fill such vacancies.

5. The House of Representatives shall choose their speaker and other officers; and shall have the sole power of impeachment.

Section 3.

1. The Senate of the United States shall be composed of two senators from each State, chosen by the legislature thereof,[3] for six years; and each senator shall have one vote.

2. Immediately after they shall be assembled in consequence of the first election, they shall be divided as equally as may be into three classes. The seats of the senators of the first class shall be vacated at the expiration of the second year, of the second class at the expiration of the fourth year and of the third class at the expiration of the sixth year, so that one third may be chosen every second year; and if vacancies happen by resignation, or otherwise, during the recess of the legislature of any State, the executive thereof may make temporary appointments until the next meeting of the legislature, which shall then fill such vacancies.[4]

3. No person shall be a senator who shall not have attained to the age of thirty years, and been nine years a citizen of the United States, and who shall not, when elected, be an inhabitant of that State for which he shall be chosen.

4. The Vice President of the United States shall be President of the Senate, but shall have no vote, unless they be equally divided.

5. The Senate shall choose their other officers, and also a president pro tempore, in the absence of the Vice President, or when he shall exercise the office of the President of the United States.

6. The Senate shall have the sole power to try all impeachments. When sitting for that purpose, they shall be on oath or affirmation. When the President of the United States is tried, the chief justice shall preside: And no person shall be convicted without the concurrence of two thirds of the members present.

7. Judgment in cases of impeachment shall not extend further than to removal from office, and disqualifications to hold and enjoy any office of honor, trust or profit under the United States: But the party convicted shall nevertheless be liable and subject to indictment, trial, judgment and punishment, according to law.

[3] Superseded by the 17th Amendment.

[4] Altered by the 17th Amendment.

Section 4.

1. The times, places, and manner of holding elections for senators and representatives, shall be prescribed in each State by the legislature thereof: But the Congress may at any time by law make or alter such regulations, except as to the places of choosing senators.

2. The Congress shall assemble at least once in every year, and such meeting shall be on the first Monday in December, unless they shall by law appoint a different day.

Section 5.

1. Each House shall be the judge of the elections, returns and qualifications of its own members, and a majority of each shall constitute a quorum to do business; but a smaller number may adjourn from day to day, and may be authorized to compel the attendance of absent members, in such manner, and under such penalties as each House may provide.

2. Each House may determine the rules of its proceedings, punish its members for disorderly behavior, and, with the concurrence of two thirds, expel a member.

3. Each House shall keep a journal of its proceedings, and from time to time publish the same, excepting such parts as may in their judgment require secrecy; and the yeas and nays of the members of either House on any question shall, at the desire of one fifth of those present, be entered on the journal.

4. Neither House, during the session of Congress, shall, without the consent of the other, adjourn for more than three days, nor to any other place than that in which the two Houses shall be sitting.

Section 6.

1. The senators and representatives shall receive a compensation for their services, to be ascertained by law, and paid out of the Treasury of the United States. They shall in all cases, except treason, felony, and breach of the peace, be privileged from arrest during their attendance at the session of their respective Houses, and in going to and returning from the same; and for any speech or debate in either House, they shall not be questioned in any other place.

2. No senator or representative shall, during the time for which he was elected, be appointed to any civil office under the authority of the United States, which shall have been created, or the emoluments whereof shall have been increased, during such time; and no person holding any office under the United States shall be a member of either House during his continuance in office.

Section 7.

1. All bills for raising revenue shall originate in the House of Representatives; but the Senate may propose or concur with amendments as on other bills.

2. Every bill which shall have passed the House of Representatives and the Senate, shall, before it become a law, be presented to the President of the United States; If he approves he shall sign it, but it not he shall return it, with his objections, to that House in which it shall have originated, who shall

enter the objections at large on their journal, and proceed to reconsider it. If after such reconsideration two thirds of that House shall agree to pass the bill, it shall be sent, together with the objections, to the other House, by which it shall likewise be reconsidered, and if approved by two thirds of that House, it shall become a law. But in all such cases the votes of both Houses shall be determined by yeas and nays, and the names of the persons voting for and against the bill shall be entered on the journal of each House respectively. If any bill shall not be returned by the President within ten days (Sundays excepted) after it shall have been presented to him, the same shall be a law, in like manner as if he had signed it, unless the Congress by their adjournment prevent its return, in which case it shall not be a law.

3. Every order, resolution, or vote to which the concurrence of the Senate and the House of Representatives may be necessary (except on a question of adjournment) shall be presented to the President of the United States; and before the same shall take effect, shall be approved by him, or being disapproved by him, shall be repassed by two thirds of the Senate and House of Representatives, according to the rules and limitations prescribed in the case of a bill.

Section 8.
The Congress shall have the power

1. To lay and collect taxes, duties, imposts, and excises, to pay the debts and provide for the common defense and general welfare of the United States; but all duties, imposts, and excises shall be uniform throughout the United States;

2. To borrow money on the credit of the United States;

3. To regulate commerce with foreign nations, and among the several States, and with the Indian tribes;

4. To establish an uniform rule of naturalization, and uniform laws on the subject of bankruptcies throughout the United States;

5. To coin money, regulate the value thereof, and of foreign coin, and fix the standard of weights and measures;

6. To provide for the punishment of counterfeiting the securities and current coin of the United States;

7. To establish post offices and post roads;

8. To promote the progress of science and useful arts, by securing for limited times to authors and inventors the exclusive right to their respective writings and discoveries;

9. To constitute tribunals inferior to the Supreme Court;

10. To define and punish piracies and felonies committed on the high seas, and offenses against the law of nations;

11. To declare war, grant letters of marque and reprisal, and make rules concerning captures on land and water;

12. To raise and support armies, but no appropriations of money to that use shall be for a longer term than two years;

13. To provide and maintain a navy;

14. To make rules for the government and regulation of the land and naval forces;

15. To provide for calling forth the militia to execute the laws of the Union, suppress insurrections and repel invasions;

16. To provide for organizing, arming, and disciplining the militia, and for governing such part of them as may be employed in the service of the United States, reserving to the States respectively, the appointment of the officers, and the authority of training the militia according to the discipline prescribed by Congress.

17. To exercise exclusive legislation in all cases whatsoever, over such district (not exceeding ten miles square) as may, by cession of particular States and the acceptance of Congress, become the seat of the government of the United States, and to exercise like authority over all places purchased by the consent of the legislature of the State in which the same shall be, for the erection of forts, magazines, arsenals, dockyards, and other needful buildings; and

18. To make all laws which shall be necessary and proper for carrying into execution the foregoing powers, and all other powers vested by the Constitution in the government of the United States, or any department or officer thereof.

Section 9.

1. The migration or importation of such persons as any of the States now existing shall think proper to admit, shall not be prohibited by the Congress prior to the year one thousand eight hundred and eight, but a tax or duty may be imposed on such importation, not exceeding ten dollars for each person.

2. The privilege of the writ of habeas corpus shall not be suspended unless when in cases of rebellion or invasion the public safety may require it.

3. No bill of attainder or ex post facto law shall be passed.

4. No capitation, or other direct, tax shall be laid, unless in proportion to the census or enumeration hereinbefore directed to be taken.[5]

5. No tax or duty shall be laid on articles exported from any State.

6. No preference shall be given by any regulation of commerce or revenue to the ports of one State over those of another: Nor shall vessels bound to, or from, one State be obliged to enter, clear, or pay duties in another.

7. No money shall be drawn from the treasury, but in consequence of appropriations made by law; and a regular statement and account of the receipts and expenditures of all public money shall be published from time to time.

8. No title of nobility shall be granted by the United States: And no person holding any office of profit or trust under them, shall, without the consent of

---

[5] Superseded by the 16th Amendment.

the Congress, accept of any present, emolument, office, or title, of any kind whatever, from any king, prince, or foreign State.

Section 10.

1. No State shall enter into any treaty, alliance, or confederation; grant letters of marque and reprisal; coin money; emit bills of credit; make any thing but gold and silver coin a tender in payment of debts; pass any bill of attainder, ex post facto law, or law impairing the obligation of contracts, or grant any title of nobility.

2. No State shall, without the consent of the Congress, lay any imposts or duties on imports or exports, except what may be absolutely necessary for executing its inspection laws: And the net produce of all duties and imposts laid by any State on imports or exports, shall be for the use of the treasury of the United States; and all such laws shall be subject to the revision and control of the Congress.

3. No State shall, without the consent of the Congress, lay any duty of tonnage, keep troops, or ships of war in time of peace, enter into any agreement or compact with another State, or with a foreign power, or engage in war, unless actually invaded, or in such imminent danger as will not admit of delay.

ARTICLE II

Section I.

1. The executive power shall be vested in a President of the United States of America. He shall hold his office during the term of four years, and, together with the Vice President, chosen for the same term, be elected as follows:

2. Each State shall appoint, in such manner as the legislature thereof may direct, a number of electors, equal to the whole number of senators and representatives to which the State may be entitled in the Congress: But no senator or representative, or person holding an office of trust or profit under the United States, shall be appointed an elector.

   The electors shall meet in their respective States, and vote by ballot for two persons, of whom one at least shall not be an inhabitant of the same State with themselves. And they shall make a list of all the persons voted for, and of the number of votes for each; which list they shall sign and certify, and transmit sealed to the seat of the government of the United States, directed to the president of the Senate. The president of the Senate shall, in the presence of the Senate and House of Representatives, open all the certificates, and the votes shall then be counted. The person having the greatest number of votes shall be President, if such number be a majority of the whole number of electors appointed; and if there be more than one who have such majority, and have an equal number of votes, then the House of Representatives shall immediately choose by ballot one of them for President; and if no person have a majority, then from the five highest on the list the said House shall in like manner choose the President. But in choosing the President, the votes shall be taken by States, the representation from each State having one vote; a quorum for this purpose shall consist of a member or members from two thirds of the States, and a majority of all the States shall be necessary to a choice. In every case, after the choice of the President, the person having the greatest number of votes of the electors shall be the Vice President. But if there should remain two or more who have equal votes, the Senate shall choose from them by ballot the Vice President.[6]

3. The Congress may determine the time of choosing the electors, and the day on which they shall give their votes; which day shall be the same throughout the United States.

4. No person except a natural born citizen, or a citizen of the United States, at the time of the adoption of this Constitution, shall be eligible to the office of President; neither shall any person be eligible to that office who shall not have attained to the age of thirty-five years, and been fourteen years a resident within the United States.

5. In case of the removal of the President from office, or of his death, resignation, or inability to discharge the powers and duties of the said office, the same shall devolve on the Vice President, and the Congress may by law provide for the case of removal, death, resignation or inability, both of the President and Vice President, declaring what officer shall then act as President, and such officer shall act accordingly, until the disability be removed, or a President shall be elected.

6. The President shall, at stated times, receive for his services a compensation, which shall neither be increased nor diminished during the period for which he shall have been elected, and he shall not receive within that period any other emolument from the United States, or any of them.

7. Before he enter on the execution of his office, he shall take the following oath or affirmation: "I do solemnly swear (or affirm) that I will faithfully execute the office of President of the United States, and will to the best of my ability, preserve, protect, and defend the Constitution of the United States."

Section 2.

1. The President shall be commander in chief of the army and navy of the United States, and of the militia of the several States, when called into the actual service of the United States; he may require the opinion, in writing, of the principal officer in each of the executive departments, upon any subject relating to the duties of their respective offices, and he shall have power to grant reprieves and pardons for offenses against the United States, except in cases of impeachment.

2. He shall have power, by and with the advice and consent of the Senate, to make treaties, provided two thirds of the senators present concur; and he shall nominate, and by and with the advice and consent of the Senate, shall appoint ambassadors, other public ministers and consuls, judges of the Supreme Court, and all other officers of the United States, whose appointment are not herein otherwise provided for, and which shall be established by law: But the Congress may by law vest the appointment of such inferior officers, as they think proper, in the President alone, in the courts of law, or in the heads of departments.

---

[6] Superseded by the 12th Amendment.

3. The President shall have power to fill up all vacancies that may happen during the recess of the Senate, by granting commissions which shall expire at the end of their next session.

Section 3.

He shall from time to time give to the Congress information of the state of the Union, and recommend to their considerations such measures as he shall judge necessary and expedient; he may, on extraordinary occasions, convene both Houses, or either of them, and in case of disagreement between them with respect to the time of adjournment, he may adjourn them to such time as he shall think proper; he shall receive ambassadors and other public ministers; he shall take care that the laws be faithfully executed, and shall commission all the officers of the United States.

Section 4.

The President, Vice President, and all civil officers of the United States, shall be removed from office on impeachment for, and conviction of, treason, bribery, or other high crimes and misdemeanors.

ARTICLE III

Section 1.

The judicial power of the United States shall be vested in one Supreme Court, and in such inferior courts as the Congress may from time to time ordain and establish. The judges, both of the Supreme and inferior courts, shall hold their offices during good behavior, and shall, at stated times, receive for their services, a compensation, which shall not be diminished during their continuance in office.

Section 2.

1. The judicial power shall extend to all cases, in law and equity, arising under this Constitution, the laws of the United States, and treaties made, or which shall be made, under their authority; — to all cases affecting ambassadors, other public ministers and consuls; — to all cases of admiralty and maritime jurisdiction; — to controversies to which the United States shall be a party;[7] — to controversies between two or more States; — between a State and citizens of another State; — between citizens of different States; — between citizens of the same State claiming lands under grants of different States, and between a State, or the citizens thereof, and foreign States, citizens or subjects.

2. In all cases affecting ambassadors, other public ministers and consuls, and those in which a State shall be party, the Supreme Court shall have original jurisdiction. In all the other cases before mentioned, the Supreme Court shall have appellate jurisdiction, both as to law and fact, with such exceptions, and under such regulations as the Congress shall make.

3. The trial of all crimes, except in cases of impeachment, shall be by jury; and such trial shall be held in the State where the said crimes shall have been committed; but when not committed within any State, the trial shall be at such place or places as the Congress may by law have directed.

[7] Cf. the 11th Amendment.

Section 3.

1. Treason against the United States shall consist only in levying war against them, or in adhering to their enemies, giving them aid and comfort. No person shall be convicted of treason unless on the testimony of two witnesses to the same overt act, or on confession in open court.

2. The Congress shall have power to declare the punishment of treason, but no attainder of treason shall work corruption of blood, or forfeiture except during the life of the person attained.

ARTICLE IV

Section 1.

Full faith and credit shall be given in each State to the public acts, records, and judicial proceedings of every other State. And the Congress may by general laws prescribe the manner in which such acts, records and proceedings shall be proved, and the effect thereof.

Section 2.

1. The citizens of each State shall be entitled to all privileges and immunities of citizens in the several States.[8]

2. A person charged in any State with treason, felony, or other crime, who shall flee from justice, and be found in another State, shall on demand of the executive authority of the State from which he fled, be delivered up to be removed to the State having jurisdiction of the crime.

3. No person held to service or labor in one State under the laws thereof, escaping into another, shall in consequence of any law or regulation therein, be discharged from such service or labor, but shall be delivered up on claim of the party to whom such service or labor may be due.[9]

Section 3.

1. New States may be admitted by the Congress into this Union; but no new State shall be formed or erected within the jurisdiction of any other State; nor any State be formed by the junction of two or more States, or parts of States, without the consent of the legislatures of the States concerned as well as the Congress.

2. The Congress shall have power to dispose of and make all needful rules and regulations respecting the territory or other property belonging to the United States; and nothing in this Constitution shall be so construed as to prejudice any claims of the United States, or of any particular State.

Section 4.

The United States shall guarantee to every State in this Union a republican form of government, and shall protect each of them against invasion; and on application of the legislature, or of the executive (when the legislature cannot be convened) against domestic violence.

[8] Superseded by the 14th Amendment, Sec. 1.

[9] Voided by the 13th Amendment.

ARTICLE V

The Congress, whenever two thirds of both Houses shall deem it necessary, shall propose amendments to this Constitution, or, on the application of the legislatures of two thirds of the several States, shall call a convention for proposing amendments, which in either case shall be valid to all intents and purposes, as part of this Constitution, when ratified by the legislatures of three fourths of the several States, or by conventions in three fourths thereof, as the one or the other mode of ratification may be proposed by the Congress; Provided that no amendment which may be made prior to the year one thousand eight hundred and eight shall in any manner affect the first and fourth clauses in the ninth section of the first article; and that no State, without its consent, shall be deprived of its equal suffrage in the Senate.

ARTICLE VI

1. All debts contracted and engagements entered into, before the adoption of this Constitution, shall be as valid against the United States under this Constitution, as under the Confederation.

2. This Constitution, and the laws of the United States which shall be made in pursuance thereof; and all treaties made, or which shall be made, under the authority of the United States, shall be supreme law of the land; and the Judges in every State shall be bound thereby, any thing in the Constitution or laws of any State to the contrary notwithstanding.

3. The senators and representatives before mentioned, and the members of the several State legislatures, and all executives and judicial officers, both of the United States and of the several States, shall be bound by oath or affirmation to support this Constitution; but no religious test shall ever be required as a qualification to any office or public trust under the United States.

ARTICLE VII

The ratification of the conventions of nine States shall be sufficient for the establishment of this Constitution between the States so ratifying the same.

Done in Convention by the unanimous consent of the States present the seventeenth day of September in the year of our Lord one thousand seven hundred and eighty-seven, and of the independence of the United States of America the twelfth. In witness thereof we have hereunto subscribed our names. [Names omitted.]

•   •   •

Articles in addition to, and amendment of, the Constitution of the United States of America, proposed by Congress, and ratified by the legislatures of the several States, pursuant to the fifth article of the original Constitution.

AMENDMENT I [First ten amendments ratified December 15, 1791]

Congress shall make no law respecting an establishment of religion, or prohibiting the free exercise thereof; or abridging the freedom of speech, or of the press; or the right of the people peaceably to assemble, and to petition the government for a redress of grievances.

AMENDMENT II

A well regulated militia, being necessary to the security of a free State, the right of the people to keep and bear arms, shall not be infringed.

AMENDMENT III

No soldier shall, in the time of peace be quartered in any house, without the consent of the owner, nor in time of war, but in a manner to be prescribed by law.

AMENDMENT IV

The right of the people to secure in their persons, houses, papers, and effects, against unreasonable searches and seizures, shall not be violated, and no warrants shall issue, but upon probable cause, supported by oath or affirmation, and particularly describing the place to be searched, and the persons or things to be seized.

AMENDMENT V

No person shall be held to answer for a capital, or otherwise infamous crime, unless on a presentment or indictment of a grand jury, except in cases arising in the land or naval forces, or in the militia, when in actual service in time of war or public danger; nor shall any person be subject for the same offense to be twice put in jeopardy of life or limb; nor shall be compelled in any criminal case to be a witness against himself; nor be deprived of life, liberty, or property, without due process of law; nor shall private property be taken for public use, without just compensation.

AMENDMENT VI

In all criminal prosecutions, the accused shall enjoy the right to a speedy and public trial, by an impartial jury of the State and district wherein the crime shall have been committed, which district shall have been previously ascertained by law, and to be informed of the nature and cause of the accusation; to be confronted with the witnesses against him; to have compulsory process for obtaining witnesses in his favor, and to have the assistance of the counsel for his defense.

AMENDMENT VII

In suits at common law, where the value in controversy shall exceed twenty dollars, the right of trial by jury shall be preserved, and no fact tried by a jury shall be otherwise reexamined in any court of the United States, than according to the rules of the common law.

AMENDMENT VIII

Excessive bail shall not be required, nor excessive fines imposed, nor cruel and unusual punishments inflicted.

AMENDMENT IX

The enumeration in the Constitution of certain rights shall not be construed to deny or disparage others retained by the people.

AMENDMENT X

The powers not delegated to the United States by the Constitution, nor prohibited by it to the States, are reserved to the States respectively, or to the people.

AMENDMENT XI [Ratified January 8, 1798]

The judicial power of the United States shall not be construed to extend to any suit in law or equity, commenced or prosecuted against one of the United States by citizens of another State, or by citizens or subjects of any foreign State.

AMENDMENT XII [Ratified September 25, 1804]

The electors shall meet in their respective States, and vote by ballot for President and Vice President, one of whom, at least, shall not be an inhabitant of the same State with themselves; they shall name in their ballots the person voted for as President, and in distinct ballots, the person voted for as Vice President, and they shall make distinct lists of all persons voted for as President and of all persons voted for as Vice President, and of the number of votes for each, which lists they shall sign and certify, and transmit sealed to the seat of the government of the United States, directed to the President of the Senate;—The President of the Senate shall, in the presence of the Senate and House of Representatives, open all the certificates and the votes shall then be counted;—The person having the greatest number of votes for President, shall be the President, if such number be a majority of the whole number of electors appointed; and if no person have such majority, then from the persons having the highest numbers not exceeding three on the list of those voted for as President, the House of Representatives shall choose immediately, by ballot, the President. But in choosing the President, the votes shall be taken by States, the representation from each State having one vote; a quorum for this purpose shall consist of a member or members from two thirds of the States, and a majority of all the States shall be necessary to a choice. And if the House of Representatives shall not choose a President whenever the right of choice shall devolve upon them, before the fourth day of March next following, then the Vice President shall act as President, as in the case of the death or other constitutional disability of the President. The person having the greatest number of votes as Vice President shall be the Vice President, if such number be a majority of the whole number of electors appointed, and if no person have a majority, then from the two highest numbers on the list, the Senate shall choose the Vice President; a quorum for the purpose shall consist of two thirds of the whole number of Senators, and a majority of the whole number shall be necessary to a choice. But no person constitutionally ineligible to the office of President shall be eligible to that of Vice President of the United States.

AMENDMENT XIII [Ratified December 18, 1865]

Section 1.
Neither slavery nor involuntary servitude, except as punishment for crime whereof the party shall have been duly convicted, shall exist within the United States, or any place subject to their jurisdiction.

Section 2.
Congress shall have power to enforce this article by appropriate legislation.

AMENDMENT XIV [Ratified July 28, 1868]

Section 1.
All persons born or naturalized in the United States, and subject to the jurisdiction thereof, are citizens of the United States and of the State wherein they reside. No State shall make or enforce any law which shall abridge the privileges or immunities of citizens of the United States; nor shall any State deprive any person of life, liberty, or property, without due process of law; nor deny to any person within its jurisdiction the equal protection of the laws.

Section 2.
Representatives shall be apportioned among the several States according to their respective numbers, counting the whole number of persons in each State, excluding Indians not taxed. But when the right to vote at any election for the choice of electors for President and Vice President of the United States, representatives in Congress, the executive and judicial officers of a State, or the members of the legislature thereof, is denied to any of the male inhabitants of such State, being twenty-one years of age, and citizens of the United States, or in any way abridged, except for participating in rebellion, or other crime, the basis of representation therein shall be reduced in the proportion which the number of such male citizens shall bear to the whole number of male citizens twenty-one years of age in such State.

Section 3.
No person shall be a senator or representative in Congress, or elector of President and Vice President, or hold any office, civil or military, under the United States, or under any State, who having previously taken an oath as a member of Congress, or as an officer of the United States, or as a member of any State legislature, or as an executive or judicial officer of any State, to support the Constitution of the United States, shall have engaged in insurrection or rebellion against the same, or given aid or comfort to the enemies thereof. But Congress may by a vote of two thirds of each House, remove such disability.

Section 4.
The validity of the public debt of the United States, authorized by law, including the debts incurred for payment of pensions and bounties for services in suppressing insurrection or rebellion, shall not be questioned. But neither the United States nor any State shall assume or pay any debt or obligation incurred in aid of insurrection or rebellion against the United States, or any claim for the loss or emancipation of any slave; but all such debts, obligations, and claims shall be held illegal and void.

Section 5.
Congress shall have power to enforce, by appropriate legislation, the provisions of this article.

AMENDMENT XV [Ratified March 30, 1870]

Section 1.
The right of citizens of the United States to vote shall not be denied or abridged by the United States or by any State on account of race, color, or previous condition of servitude.

Section 2.
The Congress shall have power to enforce this article by appropriate legislation.

AMENDMENT XVI [Ratified February 25, 1913]

The Congress shall have power to lay and collect taxes on incomes, from whatever source derived, without apportionment among the several States, and without regard to any census or enumeration.

AMENDMENT XVII [Ratified May 31, 1913]

The Senate of the United States shall be composed of two senators from each State, elected by the people thereof, for six years; and each senator shall have one vote. The electors in each State shall have the qualifications requisite for electors of the most numerous branch of the State legislature.

When vacancies happen in the representation of any State in the Senate, the executive authority of such State shall issue writs of election to fill such vacancies: *Provided,* That the legislature of any State may empower the executive thereof to make temporary appointments until the people fill the vacancies by election as the legislature may direct.

This amendment shall not be so construed as to affect the election or term of any senator chosen before it becomes valid as part of the Constitution.

AMENDMENT XVIII[10] [Ratified January 29, 1919]

After one year from the ratification of this article, the manufacture, sale, or transportation of intoxicating liquors within, the importation thereof into, or the exportation thereof from the United States and all territory subject to the jurisdiction thereof for beverage purposes is thereby prohibited.

The Congress and the several States shall have concurrent power to enforce this article by appropriate legislation.

This article shall be inoperative unless it shall have been ratified as an amendment to the Constitution by the legislature of the several States, as provided in the Constitution, within seven years from the date of the submission hereof to the States by Congress.

AMENDMENT XIX [Ratified August 26, 1920]

The right of citizens of the United States to vote shall not be denied or abridged by the United States or by any State on account of sex.

Congress shall have the power to enforce this article by appropriate legislation.

AMENDMENT XX [Ratified January 23, 1933]

Section 1.
The terms of the President and Vice President shall end at noon on the 20th day of January, and the terms of Senators and Representatives at noon on the 3d day of January, of the year in which such terms would have ended if this article had not been ratified; and the terms of their successors shall then begin.

---

[10] Repealed by the 21st Amendment.

Section 2.

The Congress shall assemble at least once in every year, and such meeting shall begin at noon on the 3d day of January, unless they shall by law appoint a different day.

Section 3.

If, at the time fixed for the beginning of the term of President, the President-elect shall have died, the Vice President-elect shall become President. If a President shall not have been chosen before the time fixed for the beginning of his term, or if the President-elect shall have failed to qualify, then the Vice President-elect shall act as President until a President shall have qualified; and the Congress may by law provide for the case wherein neither a President-elect nor a Vice President-elect shall have qualified, declaring who shall then act as President, or the manner in which one who is to act shall be selected, and such person shall act accordingly until a President or Vice President shall have qualified.

Section 4.

The Congress may by law provide for the case of the death of any of the persons from whom the House of Representatives may choose a President whenever the right of choice shall have devolved upon them, and for the case of the death of any of the persons from whom the Senate may choose a Vice President whenever the right of choice shall have devolved upon them.

Section 5.

Sections 1 and 2 shall take effect on the 15th day of October following the ratification of this article.

Section 6.

This article shall be inoperative unless it shall have been ratified as an amendment to the Constitution by the legislatures of three-fourths of the several States within seven years from the date of its submission.

AMENDMENT XXI [Ratified December 5, 1933]

Section 1.

The Eighteenth Article of amendment to the Constitution of the United States is hereby repealed.

Section 2.

The transportation or importation into any State, Territory, or possession of the United States for delivery or use therein of intoxicating liquors in violation of the laws thereof, is hereby prohibited.

Section 3.

This article shall be inoperative unless it shall have been ratified as an amendment to the Constitution by conventions in the several States as provided in the Constitution, within seven years from the date of the submission thereof to the States by the Congress.

AMENDMENT XXII [Ratified March 1, 1951]

No person shall be elected to the office of the President more than twice, and no person who has held the office of President, or acted as President, for more than two years of a term to which some other person was elected President shall be elected to the office of President more than once.

But this article shall not apply to any person holding the office of President when this article was proposed by the Congress, and shall not prevent any person who may be holding the office of President, or acting as President, during the term within which this article becomes operative from holding the office of President or acting as President during the remainder of such term.

This article shall be inoperative unless it shall have been ratified as an amendment to the Constitution by the legislature of three-fourths of the several States within seven years from the date of its submission to the States by the Congress.

AMENDMENT XXIII [Ratified March 29, 1961]

Section 1.

The District constituting the seat of Government of the United States shall appoint in such manner as the Congress may direct:

A number of electors of President and Vice President equal to the whole number of Senators and Representatives in Congress to which the District would be entitled if it were a State, but in no event more than the least populous State; they shall be in addition to those appointed by the States, but they shall be considered, for the purposes of the election of President and Vice President, to be electors appointed by a State; and they shall meet in the District and perform such duties as provided by the twelfth article of amendment.

Section 2.

The Congress shall have power to enforce this article by appropriate legislation.

AMENDMENT XXIV [Ratified January 24, 1964]

Section 1.

The right of citizens of the United States to vote in any primary or other election for President or Vice President, for electors for President or Vice President, or for Senator or Representative in Congress, shall not be denied or abridged by the United States or any State by reason of failure to pay any poll tax or other tax.

Section 2.

The Congress shall have power to enforce this article by appropriate legislation.

AMENDMENT XXV [Ratified February 10, 1967]

Section 1.

In case of the removal of the President from office or of his death or resignation, the Vice President shall become President.

Section 2.

Whenever there is a vacancy in the office of the Vice President, the President shall nominate a Vice President who shall take office upon confirmation by a majority vote of both Houses of Congress.

Section 3.

Whenever the President transmits to the President pro tempore of the Senate and the Speaker of the House of Representatives his written declaration that he is unable to discharge the powers and duties of his office, and until he transmits to them a written declaration to the contrary, such powers and duties shall be discharged by the Vice President as Acting President.

Section 4.
Whenever the Vice President and a majority of either the principal officers of the executive departments or of such other body as Congress may by law provide, transmit to the President pro tempore of the Senate and the Speaker of the House of Representatives their written declaration that the President is unable to discharge the powers and duties of his office, the Vice President shall immediately assume the powers and duties of the office as Acting President.

Thereafter, when the President transmits to the President pro tempore of the Senate and the Speaker of the House of Representatives his written declaration that no inability exists, he shall resume the powers and duties of his office unless the Vice President and a majority of either the principal officers of the executive departments or of such body as Congress may by law provide, transmit within four days to the President pro tempore of the Senate and the Speaker of the House of Representative their written declaration that the President is unable to discharge the powers and duties of his office. Thereupon Congress shall decide the issue, assembling within forty-eight hours for that purpose if not in session. If the Congress, within twenty-one days after receipt of the latter written declaration, or, if Congress is not is session, within twenty-one days after Congress is required to assemble, determines by two-thirds vote of both Houses that the President is unable to discharge the powers and duties of his office, the Vice President shall continue to discharge the same as Acting President; otherwise, the President shall resume the powers and duties of his office.

AMENDMENT XXVI [Ratified July 1, 1971]

Section 1.
The right of citizens of the United States, who are eighteen years of age or older, to vote shall not be denied or abridged by the United States or by any State on account of age.

AMENDMENT XXVII [Ratified May 7, 1992]

No law varying the compensation for the services of the senators and representatives shall take effect until an election or representatives shall have intervened.

Glossary of Selected Terms from The Law Dictionary*

ACCORD An agreement between two (or more) persons, one of whom has a right of action against the other that the latter should do or give, and the former accept, something in satisfaction of the right of action. When the agreement is executed, and satisfaction has been made, it is called accord and satisfaction, and operates as a bar to the right of action. Accord, Restatement (Second) of Contracts § 281(1).

ACT OF STATE DOCTRINE The principle that the courts will not examine the validity of a taking of property by a foreign government within its own territory, if the foreign government is extant and recognized by the United States at the time of the suit, in the absence of a treaty or other unambiguous agreement regarding controlling legal principles, even if the complaint alleges that the taking violates customary international law. The act in question must be public, and not commercial in nature. Expropriation claims may be heard as set-offs in some circumstances, however.

ADJUDICATION A judgment or decision. (2) Of bankruptcy, the declaring a debtor bankrupt.

ADMINISTRATIVE PROCEDURE ACT An act to establish a uniform system of administering laws by and among the agencies of the United States government, and to provide for administrative and judicial review of the decisions of those agencies. 5 U.S.C. §§ 1001 *et seq.;* 60 Stat. 237 (1946).

ADVISORY OPINION In some jurisdictions, the formal opinion of a higher court concerning a point at issue in a lower court. (2) The formal opinion of a legal officer, e.g., Attorney General, concerning a question of law submitted by a public official. (3) In some jurisdictions, the opinion of a court concerning a question submitted by a legislative body.

AFFIDAVIT A written statement of fact, signed and sworn to before a person having authority to administer an oath.

*The Law Dictionary (Cochran's Law Lexicon, 6/e), revised by Wesley Gilmer, Jr.. Anderson Publishing Co., Cincinnati. Reprinted by permission.

AFFIRM   To make firm; to establish. (1) To ratify or confirm the judgment of a lower court. (2) To ratify or confirm a voidable contract. (3) To declare or verify as a substitute for an oath.

AGE DISCRIMINATION IN EMPLOYMENT ACT OF 1967   An act to prohibit age discrimination in employment. 29 U.S.C. §§ 3322, 8335, 8339, 92 Stat. 189 (1978).

AGENT   A person authorized by another (the principal), to do an act or transact business for him, and to bind the principal within the limits of that authority. An agent may be general, to do all business of a particular kind; or special, to do one particular act. The agent's power to bind the principal is according to the scope of his authority.

ANSWER   In pleading, a statement of the defenses on which a party defending a lawsuit intends to rely. (2) A statement under oath, in response to written interrogatories, i.e., questions, or oral questions.

ANTI-TRUST ACTS or ANTITRUST ACTS   Various federal and state statutes intended to protect trade and commerce from unlawful restraints and monopolies.

APPELLANT   A person who initiates an appeal from one court to another.

APPELLATE JURISDICTION   The authority of a superior court to review and modify the decision of an inferior court.

APPELLEE   The party in a lawsuit against whom an appeal has been taken.

ARBITRATION   The voluntary submission of a matter in dispute to the nonjudicial judgment of one, two, or more disinterested persons, called arbitrators, whose decision is binding on the parties.

ARBITRATION AND AWARD   The voluntary settlement of a controversy by mutually agreeing to submit the controversy to arbitration, so that the decision in the arbitration is binding on the parties. (2) An affirmative defense which seeks to avoid a claim because it was previously submitted to arbitration and an award was established.

ARRAIGN   To bring an accused person to court for the purpose of having him answer the charge against him.

ARREST   The seizing of a person and detaining him in custody by lawful authority. (2) Taking of another into the custody of the actor for the actual or purported purpose of bringing the other before a court, or of otherwise securing the administration of the law. Restatement (Second) of Torts § 112. (3) The seizure and detention of personal chattels, especially ships and vessels libeled in a court of admiralty.

ASSAULT   Strictly speaking, threatening to strike or harm. (2) A threatening gesture, with or without verbal communication. If a blow is struck, it is battery (*q.v.*). (3) Attempting to cause or purposely, knowingly, or recklessly causing bodily injury to another, or negligently causing bodily injury to another with a deadly weapon, or attempting by physical menace to put another in fear of imminent serious bodily injury; also called simple assault. Model Penal Code § 211.1(1).

ASSUMPTION OF RISK   A defense to a claim for negligent injury to a person or property, i.e., a person who voluntarily exposes himself or his property to a known danger may not recover for injuries thereby sustained. Accord, Restatement (Second) of Torts § 496A.

BAIL To set at liberty a person arrested or imprisoned, on written security taken for his appearance on a day, and at a place named. The term is applied, as a noun, to the persons who become security for the defendant's appearance; to the act of delivering such defendant to his bondsmen; and also to the bond given by the sureties to secure his release. A person who becomes someone's bail is regarded as his jailer, to whose custody he is committed. The word "bail" is never used with a plural termination.

BAILEE A person to whom personal property (*q.v.*) is entrusted for a specific purpose. See also *Bailment.*

BAILMENT A broad expression which describes the agreement, undertaking, or relationship which is created by the delivery of personal property by the owner, i.e., the bailor, to someone who is not an owner of it, i.e., the bailee, for a specific purpose, which includes the return of the personal property to the person who delivered it, after the purpose is otherwise accomplished. In a bailment, dominion and control over the personal property usually pass to the bailee. The term is often used to describe, e.g.: (1) The gratis loaning of an automobile for the borrower's use. (2) The commercial leasing of an automobile for a fee. (3) The delivery of an automobile to a repairman for the purpose of having it repaired. (4) The delivery of an automobile to a parking attendant for storage, when the keys are left with the attendant.

BAILOR A person who commits goods to another person (the bailee) in trust for a specific purpose.

BATTERY An unlawful touching, beating, wounding or laying hold, however, trifling, of another's person or clothes without his consent.

BILATERAL CONTRACT An agreement in which two parties mutually promise to fulfill obligations reciprocally toward each other, e.g., one party promises to convey a house and lot and the other party promises to pay the agreed price for it.

BREACH OF CONTRACT A flexible term for the wrongful failure to perform one or more of the promises which a person previously undertook when he made a contract, e.g., failure to deliver goods.

BURDEN OF PROOF (ONUS PROBANDI) The duty of proving facts disputed on the trial of a case. It commonly lies on the person who asserts the affirmative of an issue, and is sometimes said to shift when sufficient evidence is furnished to raise a presumption that what is alleged is true. The shifting of the burden of proof is better characterized as the creation of a burden of going forward with the evidence; however, because the total burden of proof is not thereby changed, the burden of going forward with the evidence is apt to revert to the other party and change from time to time.

CASE LAW Judicial precedent generated as a by-product of the decisions which courts have made in resolving unique disputes, as distinguished from statutes and constitutions. Case law concerns concrete facts. Statutes and constitutions are written in the abstract.

CASES AND CONTROVERSIES A generic phrase denoting bona fide disputes or lawsuits in which something is decided either affirmatively or negatively. Controversy is usually descriptive of civil proceedings and cases usually include both criminal prosecutions and civil proceedings. Article III of the United States Constitution uses the terms, cases and controversies, to define the judicial power of the United States. (2) The difference between an abstract question and a case or controversy is one of degree and is not discernible by any precise test. The basic inquiry is whether the conflicting contentions of the parties present a real, substantial controversy between parties having adverse legal interests, a dispute definite and concrete, not hypothetical or abstract.

CAUSE OF ACTION A flexible term, the definition of which is occasionally controversial. (1) An aggregation of facts which will cause a court to grant relief, and therefore entitles a person to initiate and prosecute a lawsuit. (2) The concurrence of a right belonging to a plaintiff, and a wrong committed by a defendant, which breaches the right and results in damage. Under modern rules of civil procedure, the term has been partly superseded by claim for relief.

CERTIORARI Lat., "to be more fully informed," an original writ or action whereby a cause is removed from an inferior to a superior court for review. The record of the proceedings is then transmitted to the superior court. (2) A discretionary appellate jurisdiction that is invoked by a petition for certiorari, which the appellate court may grant or deny in its discretion. A dominant avenue to the United States Supreme Court. 28 U.S.C. §§ 1257(3), 2103.

CIVIL ACTION A lawsuit which has for its object the protection of private or civil rights or compensation for their infraction.

CIVIL LAW The law compiled by the Roman jurists under the auspices of the Emperor Justinian, which is still in force in many of the nations in Europe.

CLAYTON ACT An act to supplement earlier laws, including the Sherman Act, against unlawful restraints and monopolies. 15 U.S.C. §§ 12 *et seq.*, 18 U.S.C. §§ 402 *et seq.*, 29 U.S.C. §§ 52, 53; 38 Stat, 730 (1914).

COLLUSION A secret agreement between persons apparently hostile, to do some act in order to defraud or prejudice a third person, or for some improper purpose.

COMITY The practice by which one court follows the decisions of another court on a like question, though not bound by the law of precedents to do so.

COMMON LAW An ambiguous term. (1) A system of jurisprudence founded on principles of justice which are determined by reasoning and administration consistent with the usage, customs and institutions of the people and which are suitable to the genius of the people and their social, political and economic condition. The rules deduced from this system continually change and expand with the progress of society. (2) That system of law which does not rest for its authority upon any express statutes, but derives its force and authority from universal consent and immemorial usage, and which is evidenced by the decisions of the courts of law, technically so called, in contra-distinction to those of equity and the ecclesiastical courts.

COMPENSATORY DAMAGES Such as measure the actual loss; not exemplary or punitive.

COMPLAINT The charge made before a proper officer that an offense has been committed by a person named or described. (2) Under modern rules of civil procedure, a pleading which must be filed to commence an action.

CONDITION PRECEDENT   A qualification, restriction, or limitation, which suspends or delays the vesting or enlargement of an estate in property, or a right until a specified event has occurred. This terminology is not used in the Restatement (Second) of Contracts.

CONDITION SUBSEQUENT   A condition which, if not performed, defeats or diverts a right or estate existing or vested; this terminology is not used in the Restatement (Second) of Contracts.

CONFLICT OF LAWS   The variance between the laws of two states or countries relating to the subject matter of a suit brought in one of them, when the parties to the suit, or some of them, or the subject matter, belong to the other. See also *lex loci*.

CONSENT AGREEMENT   The meeting of minds. It presupposes mental capacity to act. It may be express, i.e., by word of mouth or in writing, or implied from acts, inaction, or silence which are consistent only with assent. If obtained by fraud or duress, it is not binding.

CONSIDERATION   The price, motive or matter of inducement of a contract, which must be lawful in itself. The term is flexible and includes that which is bargained for and paid in return for a promise, the benefits to the party making the promise and the loss or detriment to the party to whom the promise is made. A contract derives its binding force from the existence of a valuable consideration between the parties. Consideration may be *executed*, i.e., past or performed; *executory*, i.e., to be performed; or *continuing*, i.e., partly both. Good or meritorious consideration is that originating in relationship and natural affection. Valuable consideration is that which has a money value. A performance or a return promise which is bargained for. Restatement (Second) of Contracts § 71(1).

CONSTITUTION   The fundamental and basic law of a state or nation which establishes the form and limitation of government and secures the rights of the citizens. The constitution of the United States was adopted in a convention of representatives of the people, at Philadelphia, September 17, 1787, and became the law of the land on the first Wednesday in March, 1789. Each of the states composing the United States has a constitution of its own. Constitutions usually prescribe the manner in which they may be amended.

CONTEMPT   A willful disregard or disobedience of public authority. Courts may punish one who disobeys the rules, orders or process, or willfully offends against the dignity and good order of the court, by fine or imprisonment. Similar authority is exercised by each house of the Congress of the United States, by state legislatures and in some instances by administrative agencies. The contempt power is usually subject to judicial review.

CONTRACT   An agreement between competent parties, upon a legal consideration, to do or to abstain from doing some act. It is usually applied to simple or parol contracts, including written as well as verbal ones. Contracts may be *express*, in which the terms are stated in words; or *implied*, i.e., presumed by law to have been made from the circumstances and the relations of the parties; *mutual* and *dependent*, in which the performance by one is dependent upon the performance by the other; *independent*, when either promise may be performed without reference to the other; *entire*, in which the complete performance by one is a condition precedent to demanding performance of the other; *severable*, in which the things to be performed are capable of separation, so that on performance of part the party performing may demand a proportionate part of the consideration from the other; *executed,* in which the things each agrees to perform are done at the time the contract is made; *executory,* in which some act remains to be done by one or both of the parties; *personal,* i.e., depending on the skill or qualities of one of the parties; *contracts of beneficence,* by which only one of the contracting parties is to be benefited, e.g., loans and deposits. (2) The total legal obligation which results from the parties' agreement as affected by the U.C.C. and any other applicable rules of law. U.C.C. § 1–201(11). (3) A promise or a set of promises for the breach of which the law gives a remedy, or the performance of which the law in some way recognizes as a duty. Restatement (Second) of Contracts § 1.

CONTRIBUTORY NEGLIGENCE   The failure to exercise care by a plaintiff, which contributed to the plaintiff's injury. Even though a defendant may have been negligent, in the majority of jurisdictions, contributory negligence will bar a recovery by the plaintiff. (2) Conduct on the part of a plaintiff which falls below the standard to which he should conform for his own protection, and which is a legally contributing cause cooperating with the negligence of the defendant in bringing about the plaintiff's harm. Restatement (Second) of Torts § 463.

CONVERSIONS   A flexible term. (1) The wrongful appropriation of the goods of another. (2) An intentional exercise of dominion or control over a chattel which so seriously interferes with the right of another to control it that the actor may justly be required to pay the other the full value of the chattel. Restatement (Second) of Torts § 22A(1).

COUNTERCLAIM   The defendant's claim against the plaintiff, which most courts permit him to set up in his response to the complaint.

COURT   An institution for the resolving of disputes. (2) A place where justice is administered. (3) The judge or judges when performing their official duties. Courts may be classified as courts of record, those in which a final record of the proceedings is made, which imports verity and cannot be collaterally impeached, and courts not of record, in which no final record is made, though it may keep a docket and enter in it notes of the various proceedings; courts of original jurisdiction, in which suits are initiated, and which have power to hear and determine in the first instance, and appellate courts, which take cognizance of causes removed from other courts; courts of equity or chancery, which administer justice according to the principles of equity; and courts of law, which administer justice according to the principles of the common law; civil courts which give remedies for private wrongs; criminal courts, in which public offenders are tried, acquitted or convicted and sentenced; ecclesiastical courts, which formerly had jurisdiction over testamentary and matrimonial causes; courts of admiralty, which have jurisdiction over maritime causes, civil and criminal; courts-martial, which have jurisdiction of offenses against the military or naval laws, committed by persons in that service. In numerous instances, the various classifications of courts have been consolidated. The same court may serve as a court of equity, a court of law, a civil court, a criminal court and a court of admiralty. It may qualify as a court of record and be a court of original jurisdiction.

COVENANT   An agreement or unilateral contract such as is contained in a deed. See also *Contract.* The principal covenants in a deed conveying land are seisin, right to convey, for quiet enjoyment, against encumbrances, and for further assurances. A covenant is said to run with the land (or the reversion) when the benefit or burden of it passes to the assignee of the land. (2) Formerly one of the forms of action.

CRIMINAL LAW Jurisprudence concerning crimes and their punishment.

CROSS-EXAMINATION The questioning of a witness by the party opposed to the party which called the witness for direct examination. This usually occurs after the direct examination but on occasion may be otherwise allowed. The form of the questions on cross-examination is designed for the purpose of eliciting evidence from a hostile witness. (2) Cross-examination should be limited to the subject matter of the direct examination and matters affecting the credibility of the witness. The court may, in the exercise of discretion, permit inquiry into additional matters as if on direct examination. Fed. R. Evid. 611(b).

DAMAGES A flexible term for the reparation in money which is allowed by law on account of damage. They may be general, such as necessarily and by implication of law arise from the act complained of; or special, such as under the peculiar circumstances of the case arise from the act complained of, but are not implied by law; compensatory, sufficient in amount to cover the loss actually sustained; exemplary, punitive, or vindictive, when in excess of the loss sustained and allowed as a punishment for torts committed with fraud, actual malice, or violence; nominal, when the act was wrong, but the loss sustained was trifling; substantial, when the loss was serious; liquidated, fixed by agreement of the parties, as when it is agreed beforehand what amount one shall receive in case of a breach of contract by the other.

DE NOVO Lat., "anew; afresh." A trial de novo is a trial which is held for a second time, as if there had been no former decision.

DECLARATORY JUDGMENT, or DECLARATORY DECREE A determination or decision by a court, which states the rights of the parties to a dispute, but does not order or coerce any performance relative to those rights. The procedural and substantive conditions of the usual action must be present. The relief which the court grants is the distinguishing characteristic.

DEFAMATION A flexible term for the uttering of spoken or written words concerning someone, which tend to injure that person's reputation and for which an action for damages may be brought. (2) To create liability for defamation there must be (a) a false and defamatory statement concerning another, (b) an unprivileged publication to a third party, (c) fault amounting at least to negligence on the part of the publisher, and (d) either actionability of the statement irrespective of special harm or the existence of special harm caused by the publication. Restatement (Second) of Torts § 558. See also *Libel; Slander.*

DEFAULT A flexible term for the omission of that which a person ought to do. (2) The failure to plead or otherwise defend an action, by a party against whom a judgment for affirmative relief is sought.

DEFENDANT A person against whom an action is brought, a warrant is issued or an indictment is found.

DELEGATE A person authorized to act for another. (2) A person elected to represent others in a deliberative assembly, such as a political convention.

DEPOSITION A written record of oral testimony, in the form of questions and answers, made before a public officer, for use in a lawsuit. They are used for the purpose of discovery of information, or for the purpose of being read as evidence at a trial, or for both purposes.

DICTUM, or OBITER DICTUM   Lat., a statement by a judge concerning a point of law which is not necessary for the decision of the case in which it is stated. Usually, dictum is not as persuasive as its opposite, i.e., holding (*q.v.*).

DIRECT EXAMINATION   The initial questioning of a witness by the party who calls him.

DIRECTED VERDICT   A determination by a jury made at the direction of the court, in cases where there has been a failure of evidence, an overwhelming weight of the evidence, or where the law, as applied to the facts, is for one of the parties.

DISCHARGE   A flexible term that connotes finality, e.g., cancellation, rescission, or nullification. (2) The court order by which a person held to answer a criminal charge is set free. (3) The court order by which a jury is relieved from further consideration of a case.

DISCOVERY   A pliant method by which the opposing parties to a lawsuit may obtain full and exact factual information concerning the entire area of their controversy, via pretrial depositions, interrogations, requests for admissions, inspection of books and documents, physical and mental examinations and inspection of land or other property. The purpose of these pretrial procedures is to disclose the genuine points of factual dispute and facilitate adequate preparation for trial. Either party may compel the other party to disclose the relevant facts that are in his possession, prior to the trial. Fed. R. Civ. P. 26–37.

DISCRETION   The use of private independent judgment; the authority of a trial court which is not controlled by inflexible rules, but can be exercised one way or the other as the trial judge believes to be best in the circumstances. It is subject to review, however, if it is abused. (2) Ability to distinguish between good and evil.

DOCTRINE   A principle of law, often developed through court decisions; a precept or rule.

DONEE BENEFICIARY   A person to whom a gift is made or a power of appointment is given.

DURESS   Imprisonment; compulsion; coercion. (2) Threats of injury or imprisonment.

EASEMENT   A privilege or intangible right, which the owner of one parcel of real property, called the dominant tenement, has concerning another parcel of real property, called the servient estate, by which the owner of the latter is obligated not to interfere with the privilege. The most common easements are in the nature of passageways, e.g., road, walkway, railroad, pole line or pipeline. It is technically classified as an incorporeal hereditament.

EJECTMENT   Formerly a mixed action at common law, which depended on fictions in order to escape the inconveniences in the ancient forms of action. It was a mixed action, because it sought to recover both possession of land (a real property claim), and also damages (a personal property claim). Various statutory proceedings for the recovery of land, some of which bear the same name, have taken place in most of the United States.

EQUITY   Fairness. A type of justice that developed separately from the common law, and which tends to complement it. The current meaning is to classify disputes and remedies according to their historical relationship and development. Under modern rules of civil procedure, law and equity have been unified. Fed. R. Civ. P. 2. Historically, the courts of equity had a power of framing and adapting new remedies to particular cases, which the common law courts did not possess. In doing so, they allowed themselves latitude of construction and assumed, in certain matters such as trusts, a power of enforcing moral obligations which the courts of law did not admit or recognize. (2) A right or obligation attaching to property or a contract. In this sense, one person is said to have a better equity than another.

ESTATE   The condition and circumstance in which a person stands with regard to those around him and his property. (2) The quantum or quality of the interest which a person has in property. Estates in property may be: legal or equitable; real or personal; vested or contingent; in possession or in expectancy; absolute, determinable, or conditional; sole, joint, or in common; of freehold or less than freehold. (3) Includes the property of a decedent, trust, or person whose affairs are subject to the Uniform Probate Code, as originally constituted and as it exists from time to time during administration. Uniform Probate Code § 1–201(11).

EX PARTE   Lat., "of the one part"; an action which is not an adverse proceeding against someone else.

EXECUTION   The writ, order or process issued to a sheriff, directing him to carry out the judgment of a court, e.g., to make the money due on the judgment out of the property of the defendant.

EXEMPLARY, or PUNITIVE, or VINDICTIVE DAMAGES   An award of money given because of torts committed through malice or with circumstances of aggravation, which is in addition to compensation for the injury inflicted.

EXPRESS   Something which is stated in direct words, and not left to implications, e.g., an express promise, express trust.

FALSE ARREST, or FALSE IMPRISONMENT   A tort consisting of restraint imposed on a person's liberty, without proper legal authority. (2) False imprisonment is a misdemeanor consisting of knowingly restraining another unlawfully so as to interfere substantially with his liberty. Model Penal Code § 212.3.

FEDERAL QUESTION   An issue of law or controversy cognizable by the United States courts because it involves the construction of the Constitution, a federal law, or treaty.

FEE SIMPLE   A freehold estate of inheritance, absolute and unqualified. This is the highest and most ample estate known to the law, out of which all others are carved. An owner in fee has absolute power of disposition.

FELONY   A type of crime which is of a relatively serious nature, usually various offenses in various jurisdictions, for which the maximum penalty can be death or imprisonment in the state penitentiary, regardless of such lesser penalty as may in fact be imposed. Occasionally defined by various state statutes. (2) Formerly, every offense at common law which caused a forfeiture of lands or goods, besides being punishable by death, imprisonment or other severe penalty.

FINAL DECISION, or FINAL ORDER   A decree or judgment of a court, which terminates the litigation in the court which renders it. Cf. *Interlocutory*. (2) The United States Courts of Appeals have jurisdiction of appeals from certain final decisions of

United States District Courts (28 U.S.C. § 1291), but the courts have had difficulty defining final decision in that context. A decision may be final, even if it does not terminate the litigation, if the issue which is decided is fundamental to the further conduct of the case. (3) An order is a final judgment for purposes of United States Supreme Court jurisdiction if it involves a right separable from, and collateral to, the merits.

FIXTURE Formerly, an article which was a personal chattel, but which, by being physically annexed to a building or land, became accessory to it and part and parcel of it. It was treated as belonging to the owner of the freehold, and passed with it to a vendee, and, though annexed by a tenant for his own convenience in the occupation of the premises, could not be removed by him. The rule has been modified by statute in many of the states, and is significantly relaxed in practice, especially as between landlord and tenant. Trade fixtures and ornamental fixtures may usually be removed by the tenant at the end of his term, provided he does no material injury to the freehold. Written leases often make specific provisions concerning the matter.

FOREIGN LAWS Those enacted and in force in a foreign state, or country.

FORUM Lat., a court of justice; the place where justice must be sought. (2) Formerly, an open space in Roman cities, where the people assembled, markets were held, and the magistrates sat to transact their business.

FORUM NON CONVENIENS Lat., an inconvenient court.

FULL FAITH AND CREDIT The requirement that the public acts, records and judicial proceedings of every state shall be given the same effect by the courts of another state that they have by law and usage in the state of origin. U.S. Const., Art. IV, Sec. I. Congress has prescribed the manner in which they may be proven. Cf. *Comity*.

GENERAL VERDICT The decision of the jury, when they simply find for the plaintiff or defendant, without specifying the particular facts which they found from the evidence.

GRAND JURY A body of persons, not less than twelve, nor more than twenty-four, freeholders of a county, whose duty it is, on hearing the evidence for the prosecution in each proposed bill of indictment, to decide whether a sufficient case is made out, on which to hold the accused for trial. It is a body which is convened by authority of a court and serves as an instrumentality of the court. It has authority to investigate and to accuse, but it is not authorized to try cases. It is a creature of the common law which was instituted to protect the people from governmental oppression. In a few states, it has been partially abolished, but in others it exists by constitutional mandate. No person shall be held to answer for a capital or otherwise infamous federal crime, unless on a presentment or indictment of a grand jury, except in cases arising in the land or naval forces, or in the militia, when in actual service in time of war or public danger; U.S. Const., Amendment V.

GUARDIAN A person appointed by a court, to have the control or management of the person or property, or both, of another who is incapable of acting on his own behalf, e.g., an infant or a person of unsound mind. (2) Guardians ad litem are appointed by the court to represent such persons, who are parties to a pending action. (3) A person who has qualified as guardian of a minor or incapacitated person pursuant to testamentary or court appointment, but excludes one who is merely a guardian ad litem. Uniform Probate Code § 1–201(16). (4) A person who has qualified as a guardian of a minor or incapacitated person pursuant to parental or spousal nomination or court appointment, and includes a limited guardian, but excludes one who is merely a guardian ad litem. Uniform Probate Code § 5–103(6).

HABEAS CORPUS Lat., "that you have the body," words used in various writs, commanding one who detains another to have, or bring, him before the court issuing the same.

HEARING A flexible term for a court proceeding or the trial of a suit. (2) The examination of witnesses incident to the making of a judicial determination as to whether an accused person shall be held for trial.

HEARSAY EVIDENCE Statements offered by a witness, based upon what someone else has told him, and not upon personal knowledge or observation. Usually, such evidence is inadmissible, but exceptions are made, e.g., in questions of pedigree, custom, reputation, dying declarations, and statements made against the interest of the declarant. (2) A statement other than one made by the declarant while testifying at the trial or hearing, offered in evidence to prove the truth of the matter asserted. Fed. R. Evid. 801(c).

HOLDING The principle which reasonably may be drawn from the decision which a court or judge actually makes in a case; the opposite of dictum (*q.v.*). (2) The resolution of the unique dispute which is before a judge or court in a specific case. (3) A broad term for something which a person owns or possesses.

IMPEACH To charge a public official with crime or misdemeanor, or with misconduct in office. (2) To prove that a witness has a bad reputation for truth and veracity, and is therefore unworthy of belief.

IMPLIED CONTRACT Contract presumed by law to have been made from the circumstances and the relations of the parties.

IN PERSONAM Lat., against the person.

IN REM Lat., against the thing; opposed to *in personam.*

INDEPENDENT CONTRACTOR A person who agrees with another to do something for him, in the course of his occupation, but who is not controlled by the other, nor subject to the other's right to control, with respect to his performance of the undertaking, and is thereby distinguished from an employee.

INDICTMENT (DIT) A written accusation that one or more persons have committed a crime, presented upon oath, by a grand jury. The person against whom the indictment is found is said to be indicted.

INJUNCTION A flexible, discretionary process of preventive and remedial justice, which is exercised by courts that have equity powers. Courts issue injunctions when it appears that the ordinary remedy usually provided by law is not a full, adequate and complete one. Injunctions are preventive, if they restrain a person from doing something, or mandatory, if they command something to be done. They are preliminary, provisional or interlocutory, if they are granted on the filing of a bill, or while the suit is pending, to restrain the party enjoined from doing or continuing to do the acts complained of, until final hearing or the further order of the court. They are final, perpetual or permanent, if they are awarded after full hearing on the merits, and as a final determination of the rights of the parties.

INSURANCE   The act of providing against a possible loss, by entering into a contract with a licensed corporation that is willing to bind itself to make good such loss, should it occur. The instrument by which the contract is made is called a policy; the consideration paid to the insurer, who is sometimes called an underwriter, is called a premium. Fire and marine insurance is usually by way of indemnity, i.e., only such sum is paid by the insurer as is actually lost, and, on making such payment, he is entitled to stand in the place of the assured. (2) In the case of life or accident insurance, the insurer undertakes, in consideration of a premium, to pay a certain sum to the insured, or his legal representatives, on his death or injury by an accident. (3) There are many various types of insurance, each of which is defined by the respective policies which evidence the agreements between the parties, e.g., automobile insurance, creditor life insurance, homeowner insurance, owner, landlord, and tenant insurance, and workmen's compensation insurance.

INTANGIBLES   A kind of property which is nonphysical and not subject to being sensed, e.g., touched or felt, but which exists as a concept of people's minds. E.g., promissory notes, bank accounts and corporate stock.

INTERROGATORIES   Written questions propounded on behalf of one party in an action to another party, or to someone who is not a party, before the trial thereof. The person interrogated must give his answers in writing, and upon oath. Fed. R. Civ. P. 26, 33. (2) Verbal questions put to a witness before an examiner, and answered on oath. (3) Questions in writing, annexed to a commission to take the deposition of a witness, to be put to and answered by the witness under oath, whose answers are to be reduced to writing by the commissioner.

INVITEE   A person who goes upon land or premises of another by invitation, express or implied. (2) Either a public invitee or a business visitor: (a) Public invitee is a person who is invited to enter or remain on land as a member of the public for a purpose for which the land is held open to the public. (b) Business visitor is a person who is invited to enter or remain on land for a purpose directly or indirectly connected with business dealings with the possessor of the land. Restatement (Second) of Torts § 332.

ISSUE   A flexible term for offspring or lineal descendants. (2) All of a person's lineal descendants of all generations, with the relationship of parent and child at each generation being determined by the definitions of child and parent. Uniform Probate Code § 1–201(21). (3) The point or points which are left to be resolved by the jury or the court, at the conclusion of the pleadings. Issues may be of fact or of law. To join issue, is a technical phrase for closing the pleadings. To issue a writ or process, is for the proper officer to deliver it to the party suing it out, or to the officer to whom it is directed.

JUDGE   A public official with authority to determine a cause or question in a court of justice and to preside over the proceedings therein.

JURISDICTION   The authority of a court to hear and decide an action or lawsuit. (2) The geographical district over which the power of a court extends. Jurisdiction is limited when the court has power to act only in certain specified cases; general, or residual, when it may act in all cases in which the parties are before it, except for those cases which are within the exclusive jurisdiction of another court; concurrent, when the same cause may be entertained by one court or another; original, when the court has power to try to case in the first instance; appellate, when the court hears cases only on appeal, certiorari, or writ of error from another court; exclusive, when no other court has power to hear and decide the same matter. (3) Subject-matter jurisdiction defines the court's authority to hear a given type of case. (4) Personal jurisdiction requires that the court personally summon the defendant within its geographical district, or that it summon the defendant under the authority of a long-arm statute. This protects the individual interest that is implicated when a nonresident defendant is haled into a distant and possibly inconvenient court.

JURISPRUDENCE Law. (2) A body of law. (3) Philosophy of law.

JURY A body of citizens sworn to deliver a true verdict upon evidence submitted to them in a judicial proceeding. They are respectively called, jurymen or jurors. A grand jury is one summoned to consider whether the evidence presented by the state against a person accused of crime, warrants his indictment. A petty or petit jury is the jury for the trial of cases, either civil or criminal. It usually consists of twelve persons, but by various statutes in many of the states, and in England, a lesser number may constitute a jury in some courts. A special or struck jury is one selected especially for the trial of a given cause, usually by the assistance of the parties.

KNOWINGLY In criminal prosecutions, knowledge that one is acting in violation of some law or regulation; knowledge that the act done is illegal.

LACHES Negligence, or unreasonable delay, in pursuing a legal remedy, concurrent with a resultant prejudice to the opposing party, whereby a person forfeits his right.

LARCENY The unlawful taking and carrying away of personal property without color of right, and with intent to deprive the rightful owner of the same. Larceny is commonly classified as grand or petty, according to the value of the thing taken. Usually defined and classified by various state statutes.

LEASEHOLD Land held under a lease.

LEX FORI Lat., the law of the country where an action is brought. This regulates the forms of procedure and the nature of the remedy to be obtained.

LEX LOCI Lat., the law of the place where a contract is made, i.e., Lex loci contractus; or thing is done, i.e., Lex loci actus; tort is committed, i.e., Lex loci delicti; or where the thing, i.e., real estate, is situated, i.e., Lex loci rei sitae. It is usually applied in suits relating to such contracts, transactions, torts, and real estate.

LIBEL Defamatory writing; any published matter which tends to degrade a person in the eyes of his neighbors, or to render him ridiculous, or to injure his property or business. It may be published by writing, effigy, picture, or the like. Cf. *Slander*. (2) Broadcasting of defamatory matter by means of radio or television, whether or not it is read from a manuscript. Id. § 568A.

LICENSE Permission or authority to do something, which would be wrongful or illegal to do, if the permission or authority were not granted. The permission or authority may pertain to a public matter, e.g., the privilege of driving a motor vehicle on the public highways, or to a private matter, e.g., the privilege of manufacturing a patented article. In public matters, licenses are often required in order to regulate the activity.

LIEN A security device, by which there is created a right (1) to retain that which is in a person's possession, belonging to another, until certain demands of the person in possession are satisfied; or (2) to charge property in another's possession with payment of a debt, e.g., a vendor's lien. It may be either (a) particular, arising out of some charge or claim connected with the identical thing; (b) general, in respect of all dealings of a similar nature between the parties; or (c) conventional, by agreement, express or implied, between the parties, e.g., a mortgage; or (d) by operation of law, e.g., a lien for taxes or an attorney's lien.

LIFE ESTATE   An interest in property which has a termination date concurrent with someone's death. The interest may be measured by the lifetime of the owner, who is called a life tenant, or by someone else's lifetime.

LIQUIDATED DAMAGES   The exact amount, which the parties to a contract expressly agree must be paid, or may be collected, in the event of a future default or breach of contract.

MALICIOUS ARREST   Imprisonment or prosecution, a malicious setting in motion of the law, without probable cause, whereby someone is wrongfully and maliciously accused of a criminal offense or a civil wrong, and by reason of which that person sustains damage.

MAXIM   An axiom; a general or leading principle.

MEDIATION   The settlement of disputes by the amicable intervention of an outside party who is a stranger to the controversy.

MENS REA   Criminal intent; evil intent; guilty intent.

MERGER   In real property, an absorption by operation of law, of a lesser right or estate in a greater right or estate, upon the union of their ownership in the same person. It takes place independently of the will of the party. (2) A consolidation of corporations, in which only one of two or more former corporations survives the consolidation, or which brings into existence a new corporation and destroys the former corporations.

MISDEMEANOR   Any crime or offense not amounting to a felony (*q.v.*).

MONOPOLY   An exclusive privilege of buying, selling, making, working, or using a particular thing. (2) The absolute and exclusive control by a person, or combination of persons, of the sale of a particular commodity. (3) A combination of producers or dealers to raise commodity prices via the more or less exclusive control of the supply or the purchasing power.

MOOT   Descriptive of something which is not genuine or concrete, something which is pretended. (2) A meeting, especially for the purpose of arguing points of law by way of exercise.

NEGLIGENCE   A flexible term for the failure to use ordinary care, under the particular factual circumstances revealed by the evidence in a lawsuit. (2) Conduct which falls below the standard established by law for the protection of others against unreasonable risk of harm. It does not include conduct recklessly disregardful of an interest of others. Restatement (Second) of Torts § 282.

NOLO CONTENDERE   Lat., no contest; a plea in criminal cases whereby the defendant tacitly admits his guilt by throwing himself on the mercy of the court.

NOMINAL DAMAGES   A token sum awarded, where a breach of duty or an infraction of plaintiffs' rights is shown, but no substantial injury is proven to have been sustained.

NOTICE Information given to a person of some act done, or about to be done; knowledge. Notice may be actual, when knowledge is brought home to the party to be affected by it; or constructive, when certain acts are done in accordance with law, from which, on grounds of public policy, the party interested is presumed to have knowledge. It may be written, or oral, but written notice is preferable as avoiding disputes as to its terms. (2) A person has notice of a fact when he has actual knowledge of it, or he has received a notice or notification of it, or from all the facts and circumstances known to him at the time in question, he has reason to know that it exists. U.C.C. § 1–201(25).

NOVATION The substitution of a new obligor or obligation for an old one, which is thereby extinguished, e.g., the acceptance of a note of a third party in payment of the original promisor's obligation, or the note of an individual in lieu of that of a corporation. Accord, Restatement (Second) of Contracts § 280.

NUISANCE A flexible and imprecise term for various activities which annoy, harm, inconvenience or damage other persons, under the particular facts and circumstances proven in a lawsuit or criminal prosecution. It may be (a) private, as where one uses his property so as to damage another's or to disturb his quiet enjoyment of it; or (b) public, or common, where the whole community is annoyed or inconvenienced by the offensive acts, e.g., where a person obstructs a highway, or carries on a business that fills the air with noxious and offensive fumes.

PARDON the remission, by the chief executive of a state or nation, of a punishment which a person convicted of crime has been sentences to undergo.

PAROL EVIDENCE RULE A significant provision in American law, that when dealings between parties are reduced to an unambiguous written instrument, e.g., a deed, contract or lease, the instrument cannot be contradicted or modified by oral evidence. The rule is subject to various limitations and exceptions, however.

PAROLE Supervised suspension of the execution of a convict's sentence, and release from prison, conditional upon his continued compliance with the terms of parole. (2) A regular part of the rehabilitation process. Assuming good behavior, it is the normal expectation in the vast majority of cases. Statutes generally specify when a prisoner will be eligible to be considered for parole and detail the standards and procedures applicable.

PER SE Lat., by itself; alone.

PERSONALTY Personal property.

PETITION A request made to a public official or public body that has authority to act concerning it. The right to petition the government for a redress of grievances is secured to the people by the U.S. Const., Amendment I. (2) Under some codes of civil procedure, the written statement of the plaintiff's case which initiates a lawsuit. (3) A written request to the court for an order after notice. Uniform Probate Code § 5–103(15).

PLAINTIFF A person who initiates a lawsuit.

PLEADINGS The alternate and opposing written statements of the parties to a lawsuit. Under the Federal Rules of Civil Procedure, and analogous state rules of civil procedure, the pleadings consist of a Complaint and an Answer; a Reply to a Counterclaim denominated as such; an Answer to a Cross-claim, if the Answer contains a

Cross-claim; a Third-party Complaint, if a person who was not an original party is summoned; and a Third-party Answer, if a Third-party Complaint is served. No other pleadings shall be allowed, except that the court may order a Reply to an Answer or a Third-party Answer. Fed. R. Civ. P. 7(a). Pleadings consist of simple, concise and direct averments of claims for relief, defenses and denials. Matters which constitute an avoidance or affirmative defense must be set forth affirmatively. Id. 8.

POLICE POWER A flexible term for the authority of federal and state legislatures to enact laws regulating and restraining private rights and occupations for the promotions of public health, safety, welfare and order.

PRE-TRIAL CONFERENCE, or PRE-TRIAL HEARING A meeting between the judge and counsel for the parties, preliminary to the trial of a lawsuit. Under modern rules of civil procedure, in any lawsuit, the court may in its discretion direct the attorneys for the parties to appear before it for a conference, to consider any matters that may aid in the disposition of the lawsuit. Fed. R. Civ. P. 16.

PRICE DISCRIMINATION As prohibited by the Robinson-Patman Act (*q.v.*), the making of a distinction in price between customers, for reasons which do not reflect differences in cost of manufacture, transportation or sale.

PRIMA FACIE At first view; on the first aspect.

PRIMA FACIE EVIDENCE Proof of a fact or collection of facts, which creates a presumption of the existence of other facts, or from which some conclusion may be legally drawn, but which presumption or conclusion may be discredited or overcome by other relevant proof.

PRINCIPAL The leading, or most important; the original; a person, firm or corporation from whom an agent derives his authority; a person who is first responsible, and for whose fulfillment of an obligation a surety becomes bound; the chief, or actual, perpetrator of a crime, as distinguished from the accessory, who may assist him; the important part of an estate, as distinguished from incidents, or accessories; a sum of money loaned, as distinguished from the interest paid for its use.

PRIVILEGE An exceptional right, or exemption, It is either (a) personal, attached to a person or office; or (b) attached to a thing, sometimes called real. The exemption of ambassadors and members of Congress from arrest, while going to, returning from, or attending to the discharge of their public duties, is an example of the first. (2) The fact that conduct which, under ordinary circumstances, would subject an actor to liability, under particular circumstances does not subject him to liability. A privilege may be based upon (a) the consent of the other affected by the actor's conduct, or (b) the fact that its exercise is necessary for the protection of some interest of the actor or of the public which is of such importance as to justify the harm caused or threatened by its exercise, or (c) the fact that the actor is performing a function for the proper performance of which freedom of action is essential. Restatement (Second) of Torts § 10.

PRIVITY Participation in knowledge or interest. Persons who so participate are called privies. Privity in deed, i.e., by consent of the parties, is opposed to privity in law, e.g., tenant by curtesy.

PROBABLE CAUSE A reasonable ground for suspicion, supported by circumstances sufficiently strong to warrant a cautious man to believe that an accused person is guilty of the offense with which he is charged. (2) Concerning a search, probable cause is a flexible, common-sense standard. It merely requires that the facts available to the officer would warrant a person of reasonable caution in the belief that certain items may be contraband or stolen property or useful as evidence of a crime; it does not demand any showing that the belief is correct or more likely true than false. A practical, nontechnical probability that incriminating evidence is involved is all that is required.

PROCESS   The means whereby a court enforces obedience to its orders. Process is termed (a) original, when it is intended to compel the appearance of the defendant; (b) mesne, when issued pending suit to secure the attendance of jurors and witnesses; and (c) final, when issued to enforce execution of a judgment. (2) In patent law, the art or method by which any particular result is produced, e.g., the smelting of ores or the vulcanizing of rubber.

PROMISEE   A person to whom a promise is made. Accord, Restatement (Second) of Contracts § 2(3).

PROMISOR   A person who makes or gives a promise. Accord, Restatement (Second) of Contracts §2(2).

PROSECUTOR   A person who brings an action against another, in the name of the government. A public prosecutor is an officer appointed or elected to conduct all prosecutions in behalf of the government. A private prosecutor is an individual who, not holding office, conducts an accusation against another. Occasionally, an aggrieved person will employ a private attorney to serve as such a prosecutor.

PROXIMATE CAUSE   Something which produces a result, and without which, the result could not have occurred. (2) Any original event, which in natural unbroken sequence, produces a particular foreseeable result, without which the result would not have occurred.

PUBLIC POLICY   A highly flexible term of imprecise definition, for the consideration of what is expedient for the community concerned. (2) The principle of law which holds that no person can do that which has a tendency to be injurious to the public, or against the public good. (3) The statutes and precedents, and not the general considerations of public interest.

PUNITIVE DAMAGES   Damages in excess of the loss sustained and allowed as a punishment for torts committed with fraud, actual malice, or violence.

QUASH   To annul or suppress, e.g., an indictment, a conviction, or an order.

QUASI   Lat., as if; almost. Often used to indicate significant similarity or likeness to the word that follows, while denoting that the word that follows must be considered in a flexible sense.

QUASI-CONTRACT   An obligation which arises without express agreement between the parties; an implied contract.

REAL PROPERTY, REAL ESTATE, or REALTY   All land and buildings, including estates and interests in land and buildings which are held for life, but not for years, or some greater estate therein. (2) Real property includes land and any interest or estate in land. Uniform Partnership Act § 2.

RECOGNIZANCE, or RECOGNIZANCE BOND   An obligation, or acknowledgment of a debt, in a court of law, with a condition that the debt shall be void on the performance of a stipulated undertaking, e.g., to appear before the proper court, to keep the peace, or to pay the debt, interest and costs that the plaintiff may recover.

RECORD A written memorial of the actions of a legislature or of a court. (2) The copy of a deed or other instrument relating to real property, officially preserved in a public office.

REFORMATION, or RECTIFICATION The correction of a written instrument, via a lawsuit, so as to make it express the true agreement or intention of the parties.

REMAND To recommit a person to jail or prison. (2) To send a lawsuit back to the same court from which it came, for trial or other action.

REMEDY The legal means to declare or enforce a right or to redress a wrong. (2) Any remedial right, to which an aggrieved party is entitled, with or without resort to a tribunal. U.C.C. § 1–201(34).

REPLEVIN A form of lawsuit which is used to recover possession of specific chattels, which have been unlawfully taken from, or withheld from, the plaintiff. It may be brought by a general owner, who has the right to immediate possession, or by someone who has a special property in the chattel, e.g., a creditor whose claim is secured by the chattel. Usually defined by various state statutes. Occasionally called claim and delivery or order of delivery.

RES JUDICATA Lat., a controversy already judicially decided. The decision is conclusive until the judgment is reversed. In litigation, the judgment of a court of competent jurisdiction on the merits of a case is a bar to a new lawsuit involving the same cause of action (q.v.) between the same parties, before the same court or any other court, because it is in the interest of the state and individuals that there should be some end to litigation.

RESCISSION The cancellation of, or putting an end to, a contract by the parties, or one of them, e.g., for any reason mutually acceptable to the parties, or on the ground of fraud.

RESPONDENT A party against whom a motion is filed in the course of a lawsuit; analogous to a defendant or an appellee.

RESTITUTION The restoring of property, or a right, to a person who has been unjustly deprived of it. A writ of restitution is the process by which a successful appellant may recover something of which he has been deprived under a prior judgment.

ROBINSON-PATMAN ACT An act to amend the Clayton Antitrust Act, to prevent price discrimination (q.v.) and other discriminatory practices, 15 U.S.C. §§ 13 et seq.; 49 Stat. 1526 (1936).

SANCTION The power of enforcing a statute, or inflicting a penalty for its violation. (2) Consent.

SATISFACTION The payment of money owing.

SECONDARY BOYCOTT Variously, a combination to refrain from dealing with a person, or to advise or by peaceful means persuade his customers so to refrain, or to exercise coercive pressure upon such customers, actual or prospective, in order to cause them to withhold or withdraw patronage.

SERVICE The act of bringing a judicial proceeding to the notice of the person affected by it, e.g., by delivering to him a copy of a written summons or notice. (2) The relationship of an employee, or servant, to his employer, or master. (3) Formerly, the duty which an English tenant owed to his lord by reason of his estate, e.g., rent.

SHERMAN ACT, or SHERMAN ANTI-TRUST ACT. An act to protect trade and commerce against unlawful restraints and monopolies. 15 U.S.C. §§ 1 *et seq.*; 26 Stat. 209 (1890).

SLANDER The malicious defamation of a person, in his reputation, profession, or business, by spoken words. To impute a criminal offense, or misconduct in business, is actionable without proof of special damage, but in any case, proof of special damage arising from the false and malicious statements of another is a sufficient ground of action. Usually, the truth of the words spoken is a defense. Occasionally defined by various state statutes. Cf. *Libel (1)*. (2) Publication of defamatory matter by spoken words, transitory gestures, or any form of communication other than written words or embodiment in physical form or any other form of communication that has the potentially harmful qualities characteristic of written or printed words. Restatement (Second) of Torts § 568(2).

SOVEREIGN IMMUNITY A rule of law holding that a nation or state, or its political subdivisions, is exempt from being sued, without its consent, in its own courts or elsewhere. Often criticized as being erroneously conceived, anachronistic and unjust. Occasionally modified by court decisions, and various state and federal statutes, e.g., Tort Claims Act.

SOVEREIGNTY The supreme authority of an independent nation or state. It is characterized by equality of the nation or state among other nations or states, exclusive and absolute jurisdiction and self-government within its own territorial limits, and jurisdiction over its citizens beyond its territorial limits.

SPECIAL DAMAGES Reparation in money awarded for any peculiar injury sustained by the party complaining, beyond the general damages presumed by law.

SPECIFIC PERFORMANCE The actual carrying out of a contract in the particular manner agreed upon. Courts of equity will compel and coerce specific performance of a contract in many cases, where damages payable in money, the usual remedy at law, would not adequately compensate for its nonperformance, e.g., in the case of contracts concerning land, or for the sale of a unique chattel.

STARE DECISIS Lat., to stand by decided cases; to follow precedent. A flexible doctrine of Anglo-American law that when a court expressly decides an issue of law, which is generated by the facts of a unique dispute, that decision shall constitute a precedent which should be followed by that court and by courts inferior to it, when deciding future disputes, except when the precedent's application to a particular problem case is unsuitable to the character or spirit of the people of the state or nation, and their current social, political and economic conditions.

STATUTE OF FRAUDS Various state legislative acts, patterned after a 1677 English act, known by the same name. E.g., U.C.C. § 2–201. Because of the variations in each state, reference must be made to the specific state statutes. The main object was to take away the facilities for fraud, and the temptation to perjury, which arose in verbal obligations, the proof of which depended upon oral evidence. Its most common provisions are these: (a) all leases, excepting those for less than three years, shall have the force of leases at will only, unless they are in writing and signed by the parties or their agents; (b) assignments and surrenders of leases and interests in land must be in writing; (c) all declarations and assignments of trusts must be in writing, signed by the party (trusts arising by implication of law are, however, excepted); (d) no action shall be brought upon a guarantee, or upon any contract for sale of lands, or any interest in or concerning them, or upon any agreement which is not to be performed within a year, unless the agreement is in writing and signed by the party to be charged or his agent; (e) no contract for the sale of goods for a certain price or more, e.g., $500,000, U.C.C. § 2-201, shall be good, unless the buyer accept part, or give something in part payment, or some memorandum thereof be signed by the parties to be charged or their agents.

STATUTE OF LIMITATIONS Various periods of time, fixed by different state and federal statutes, called statutes of limitations, within which a lawsuit must be commenced, and after the expiration of which, the claimant will be forever barred from the right to bring the action. Generally, a statute of limitations is a procedural bar to a plaintiff's action which does not begin to run until after the cause of action has accrued and the plaintiff has a right to maintain a lawsuit.

SUBSTANTIVE LAW The positive law of duties and rights.

TAFT-HARTLEY ACT, or LABOR MANAGEMENT RELATIONS ACT OF 1947 An act to amend the National Labor Relations Act, to provide additional facilities for the mediation of labor disputes affecting commerce, and to equalize legal responsibilities of labor organizations and employers. 29 U.S.C. §§ 141 *et seq.*; 61 Stat. 136 1947.

TANGIBLE Descriptive of something which may be felt or touched; corporeal.

TITLE VII (CIVIL RIGHTS ACT OF 1964) An act to enforce the constitutional right to vote, to confer jurisdiction upon the district courts of the United States to provide injunctive relief against discrimination in public accommodations, to authorize the Attorney General to institute suits to protect constitutional rights in public facilities and public education, to extend the Commission on Civil Rights, to prevent discrimination in federally assisted programs, to establish a commission on Equal Employment Opportunity, and for other purposes. 28 U.S.C. § 1447; 42 U.S.C. §§ 1971, 1975–d, 2000a–200h–6; 78 Stat. 241 (1964).

TORT Any one of various, legally recognized, private injuries or wrongs, which do not arise as the result of a breach of contract.

TRADE SECRET A plan, process, tool, mechanism, or compound, known only to its owner, and those of his employees to whom it is necessary to confide it, in order to apply it to the uses intended. It is distinguishable from a patent, in that it may be used by anyone who is able to discover its nature.

TRESPASS Any transgression of the law, less than treason, felony, or misprision of either. (2) Especially, trespass quare clausum fregit, i.e., entry on another's close, or land without lawful authority. (3) Trespass on the case, or Case, is a general name for torts which formerly had no special writ or remedy. (4) Criminal trespass is entering or surreptitiously remaining in a building or occupied structure, or separately secured or occupied portion thereof, knowing that he is not licensed or privileged to do so. Model Penal Code § 221.2(1). (5) Defiant trespass is entering or remaining in any place as to which notice against trespass is given, knowing that he is not licensed or privileged to do so. The notice against trespass must be given by actual communication to the actor, posting in a manner prescribed by law or reasonably likely to come to the attention of intruders, or fending or other enclosure manifestly designed to exclude intruders. Model Penal Code § 221.2(2).

UNENFORCEABLE CONTRACT A contract (*q.v.*) for the breach of which neither the remedy of damages nor the remedy of specific performance is available, but which is recognized in some other way as creating a duty of performance, though there has been no ratification. Restatement (Second) of Contracts § 8.

UNIFORM COMMERCIAL CODE A proposal by the American Law Institute, and the National Conference of Commissioners on Uniform State Laws, for comprehensive legislation relating to commercial transactions, i.e., sales, commercial paper, bank deposits and collections, letters of credit, bulk transfers, warehouse receipts, bills of lading, other documents of title, investment securities, and secured transactions. It has been adopted in each of the states of the United States, except Louisiana, and in the District of Columbia and the Virgin Islands.

UNILATERAL CONTRACT A one-sided contract (*q.v.*); an agreement in which only one party makes a promise and on the other side of which the consideration has been fully performed, e.g., a promise to repay a loan of money. (2) Occasionally, an agreement which is void because only one party is bound by it and it therefore lacks mutuality of obligation.

UNJUST ENRICHMENT The doctrine which places a legal duty of restitution upon a defendant who has acquired something of value at the expense of the plaintiff.

VENUE (*ven'u*) or VISNE (*ven*) The neighborhood; the county in which a particular lawsuit should be tried; the county from which the jury is taken for the trial of a lawsuit. Often regulated by various state and federal statutes. A change of venue is the sending of a lawsuit to be tried before a jury of another county, e.g., when circumstances render it impossible to have an impartial trial in the county where the cause of action arose.

VICARIOUS LIABILITY Substituted or indirect responsibility, e.g., the responsibility of an employer for the torts committed by his employee within the scope of his employment.

VOID Of no force or effect; absolutely null.

VOIDABLE Descriptive of an imperfect obligation, which may be legally annulled or cured or confirmed, at the option of one of the parties, e.g., the contract of an infant with an adult.

WAIVER A positive act by which a legal right is relinquished.

WANTON MISCONDUCT Such behavior as manifests a disposition to perversity. It must be under such circumstances and conditions that the party doing the act, or failing to act, is conscious that his conduct will, in all common probability, result in injury.

WARRANT Written authority. (2) An order from a court, to an officer, directing the officer to arrest a person.

WARRANTY A guaranty concerning goods or land, which is expressly or impliedly made to a purchaser by the vendor.

WITHOUT PREJUDICE Free of any prejudgment, or bias which interferes with a person's impartiality and sense of justice.

WRIT A written court order, or a judicial process. It is issued by authority of a court, and directed to the sheriff, or other officer authorized by law to execute the same. He must return it, with a brief statement of what he has done in pursuance of it, to the court or officer who issued it. Writs are either (a) prerogative, when the granting of them is in the discretion of the court, as in the case of habeas corpus; or (b) of right, when the applicant is entitled as of course. The latter class includes original writs, by which an action is commenced, e.g., a summons, and judicial writs; under which head almost all writs at present fall, e.g., writs in aid, and writs of execution. (3) An action, e.g., the writs of waste and partition.

ZONING The division of a city or county into separate areas, and the application to each area of regulations which limit the various purposes to which the land and buildings therein may be devoted.

Case Index

Adams v. Williams, 288–292
Adarand Constructors, Inc., v. Pena, 603–611
Adkins v. Sky Blue, Inc., 155–160
Adoption of Tammy, 346–350
Alexander v. Chapman, 121–125
American Postal Workers Union v. Frank, 179–182
Anglin v. Florida Department of Transportation,
    521–525
Anuszewski v. Jurevic, 438–440
Arabian American Oil Co. v. Scarfone, 676–678
Arndt v. Department of Licensing and Regulation,
    572–575
Askildson v. Commissioner of Public Safety,
    558–561
Marybeth Atkins v. Jiminy Peak, Inc., 192–195, 547

Belk v. United States, 186–189
Estate of Berthiaume v. Pratt, M.D., 493–496
Bloch v. Hillel Torah North Suburban Day School,
    244–245

Calder v. Jones, 66, 69–72, 107, 166
Campbell Soup Company v. Wentz, 226, 237–239,
    243
Caporino v. Lacasse, 196–198
Carson v. Here's Johnny Portable Toilets, Inc.,
    504–508
Carson v. National Bank, 86–88
Carter v. Matthews, 232, 406–408
Castorino v. Unifast Bldg. Products, 433–435
Chip Steak Company v. Hardin, 562–565
Clarkson v. Orkin Exterminating Co., Inc., 436–438
Cline v. William H. Friedman & Assoc., 127–129

Cody v. Atkins, 130–133
Commonwealth v. Berggren, 274–276
Cruzan v. Director, Missouri Dept. of Health, 23–30

DeFunis v. Odegaard, 183–186
Department of Transportation v. Ronlee, Inc.,
    233–236
DeSantis v. Pacific Tel. & Tel. Co., Inc., 631–634
Diaz v. Indian Head, Inc., 420–422
Dolan v. City of Tigard, 458–469
Dorsey v. Gregg, 109–110
Dow Chemical Company v. United States, 566–569
Downey v. Dixon, 115–117
Draper v. United States, 283, 286–288
Dumas v. Lloyd, 534–537

E.E.O.C. v. El Paso Natural Gas Co., 627–631
E.E.O.C. v. Ithaca Industries, Inc., 619–622
E.E.O.C. v. Red Baron Steak Houses, 614–619
E.I. DuPont de Nemours & Co., Inc. v. Christopher,
    15–19

Far West Modular Home Sales, Inc. v. Proaps,
    452–454
Favorite v. Miller, 478–481
Feeley v. Borough of Ridley Park, 470–472
Forrester v. White, 200–203
Fracasse v. Brent, 100–104

Gano v. School District No. 411 of Twin Falls
    County, Idaho, 230–232
Gatch v. Hennepin Broadcasting Associates, Inc.,
    84–85

Gilhooley v. Star Market Co., Inc., 510–512

Gilling v. Eastern Airlines, Inc., 669–672

Gilmer v. Interstate/Johnson Lane Corp., 658–664

Gimpel v. Host Enterprises, Inc., 208–210

GNLV Corporation v. Jackson, 170–171

Goss v. Lopez, 38–42, 570

Hainz v. Shopko Stores, Inc., 499–502

Hibschman Pontiac, Inc. v. Batchelor, 440–443

Hubbard Manufacturing Co., Inc., v. Greeson, 166–168

Hurst v. Capitell, 206–207

Iacomini v. Liberty Mutual Insurance Company, 246–248

Ivancic v. Olmstead, 497–499

Jinright v. Russell, 427–428

Jones v. Western Geophysical Co., 611–613

Katko v. Briney, 44–48, 49

Kolender, Chief of Police of San Diego, v. Lawson, 33–37

Kothe v. Smith, 656–657

Laaperi v. Sears Roebuck & Co., Inc., 529–533

Lakewood Creative Costumers v. Sharp, 227–228

Lehr v. Robertson, 351–355

Leichtamer v. American Motors Corp., 541–545

Loving v. Commonwealth of Virginia, 259–263, 337–338

Macke Company v. Pizza of Gaithersburg, Inc., 431–433

Macomber v. Dillman, 217–222, 509

In re Marriage of Riddle, 377–379

Mastrobuono v. Shearson Lehman Hutton, Inc., 665–668

Meyers v. Ramada Hotel and Operating Co., Inc., 111–114

Modern Laundry and Dry Cleaning v. Farrer, 410–413

Moore v. City of East Cleveland, Ohio, 331–336

Mulford v. Borg-Warner Acceptance Corp., 425–426

Nash v. Mulle, 364–370

Newhouse v. Farmers National Bank, 134–136

New Jersey v. T.L.O., 293–298

New York Football Giants v. Los Angeles Chargers Football Club, 240–242

O'Brien v. O'Brien, 381–387

People v. Shaughnessy, 264–266

Pittsburgh Corning Corp. v. Bradley, 652–655

Pluhacek v. Nebraska Lutheran Outdoor Ministries, Inc., 401–403

Principal Casualty Insurance Company v. Blair, 417–419

Ramírez de Arellano v. Eastern Airlines, Inc., 79, 81–83

Rhea v. Massey-Ferguson, Inc., 673–674

In the Matter of the Application of Arthur Hyde RICE to Register and Confirm Title to Land Situate in Kailua, District of Koolaupoko, Oahu, City and County of Honolulu, State of Hawaii, 64–65

Sarni Original Dry Cleaners, Inc., v. Cooke, 598–601

Sherwood Estates Homes Association, Inc. v. McConnell, 474–476

Somportex Limited v. Philadelphia Chewing Gum Corporation, 171–174

Southern Pines Associates v. United States, 583–586

State v. Butler, 151, 152–154

State v. Gordon, 268–271

State ex rel. Hermesmann v. Seyer, 359–363

State v. Yelsen Land Company, 249–251

Stein v. Langer, 526–528

Strunk v. Strunk, 161–165

Stutts v. Freeman, 623–625

Suggs v. Norris, 50–53

Sullivan v. Louisiana, 308, 309–311

Teamsters, Local 456 and J.R. Stevenson Corporation, 639–643

Textile Workers v. Darlington Manufacturing Company, 634–638

Thompson v. Mercy Hospital, 204–205

In re Union Carbide Corporation Gas Plant Disaster at Bhopal, India, in December 1984, 73–76

United States v. Salerno, 299–304

United States v. Scott, 278–281

Volz v. Coleman Co., Inc., 223–226

Weirum v. RKO General, Inc., 413–516

Westberry v. Blackwell, 538–540

Whirlpool Corp. v. Marshall, 576–579

Wisconsin v. Yoder, 321–329, 344

Wright v. Webb, 518–520

York v. Jones, 483–486

Zablocki v. Redhail, 338–342

Subject Index

Abnormally dangerous activities, strict liability and, 537–540
Absolute liability. *See* Strict liability
Acceptance, 50
  of offer, 400–403
Accession, personal property and, 478
Accord, contract performance and, 428–429
Act of State doctrine, 189
Actus reus, 263–266, 267–268
Adair v. United States, 594–595
Adaptability, of law, 7
Adequacy, 14
Adjudicative power, of administrative agencies, 570
Administrative agencies, 553–592
  adjudicative powers of, 561, 570
  classification of, 555
  functions of, 558–561. *See also* Administrative agencies, business regulation by
  investigative power of, 561, 565–569
  judicial review by, 570–575
  organization of, 555, 556, 557
  powers of, 561–570
  rule-making power of, 561, 562–565
  as source of United States law, 149
Administrative agencies, business regulation by, 558, 575–587
  Environmental Protection Agency, 555, 557, 581–587
  Federal Trade Commission, 579–581
  Occupational Safety and Health Administration, 575–579
Administrative law judge (ALJ), 570
Administrative laws. *See* Administrative agencies
Administrative Procedure Act (APA), 561, 562
Administrator, statutes of frauds requirement for, 423
Admission, 107–108
Adoption, 342–356
  agency, 343
  gays and lesbians and, 346–350
  independent, 343
  interim orders and, 356
  interracial, 344, 345
  involuntary, 350
  matching and, 343–350
  open, 356
  petition for, 351–356
  religion and, 344
  voluntary, 350
Adoption Assistance and Child Welfare Act of 1980, 357
ADR. *See* Alternative dispute resolution
Adversary system, 282
Adverse possession, 476–477
Advisory opinion, 179
Affidavit, motion for summary judgment and, 111
Affirmance, 20
Affirmative action, 602–611
Age, employment discrimination and, 625–631
Age Discrimination in Employment Act (ADEA), 625–631

Agreement, contract law and, 397, 398–399
Air pollution, statutes on, 582–583
Alimony, 375–376
Alternative dispute resolution (ADR), 97, 99,
    547, 649–682
  arbitration, 99, 658–664
  arbitration awards, 658, 665–668
  court-annexed, 650, 651–655
  court-annexed arbitration, 668–672
  mediation, 99, 672–674
  mini-trials, 99, 674–675
  private trials, 678
  reasons for, 649–650
  settlement conference, 655–657
  summary jury trials, 99, 675–678
  voluntary, 650–651
  voluntary arbitration, 664
Alternative service, 107
Amendments, 145. *See also specific amendments*
American Arbitration Association, 664
American Bar Association, 396
American Law Institute, 396
Americans with Disabilities Act (ADA), 622–623
Analytical positivism, 4
Annulment, 370–371
Answer, 97, 105, 107, 108
  motion to dismiss and, 111
Anticipatory repudiation of contract, 429
Appeal, 134, 195. *See also* Appellate courts
  of criminal case, 313
  definition, 20
  discretionary, 313
  failure to object waives right to, 61
  notice of, 88
  Occupational Health Review Commission
    and, 576
Appellant, 19
Appellate courts, 3, 61–62. *See also* Appeal; U.S.
    Supreme Court
  state's judicial system and, 62
  U.S. courts of appeals, 77, 88–89, 90
Appellee, 19
Arbitration, 99, 658–664
  court-annexed, 668–672
  voluntary, 664
Arbitration awards, 658, 665–668
Arbitrators, 664
Arraignment, 306
Arrest, 283, 286–288
  custodial, 292
Arrest warrant, 283
Assault, 492

Assignee, 430
Assignment of contract rights, 430–433
Assignor, 430
Assumpsit, writ of, 395–396
Assumption of risk, 525, 526
Attempt, as inchoate crime, 276
Attorney
  appointment by court, 304–305
  fees, 100–101
  hiring, 100–105
  as mediator in settlement conference, 656
  right to, 304–305
Avoidable harm doctrine, 216

Bail, 298–304
Bailment, 482–486
Bailor, 482
Bankruptcy, Federal Bankruptcy Court and, 77
Bar and merger, principle of, 195, 196–198
Barbaric punishment, 263
Battery, 217, 264, 274, 492–496
Bench trial, 60, 99, 117
Beneficiary, third-party, 433–435
Benefit, 408
Benefit rule, 216, 217–222
Best evidence rule, 126
"Best interest of the child," 376–379
BFOQ defense, 598–601
Bifurcation, 375
Bilateral contract, 398
Bill of attainder, 148
Bill of information, 306
Bill of Rights, 3, 256. *See also specific amendments*
Bills of attainder, 258
Black, Donald, 5, 6
Blackstone, William, 12, 256
Bona fide occupational qualification (BFOQ),
    596–597, 598–601
Bracton, Henry, 12
Breach of contract, 50, 435–444
  common law remedies for, 438–440
  equitable remedies for, 443
  exemplary damages and, 223
  material, 435–438
  punitive damages, 440–443
  Uniform Commercial Code remedies, 444
Briefs, 20–21
  sample, 21–23
Business regulation. *See* Administrative
    agencies, business regulation by
Business visitor, 516–520
"But-for" test, of proximate cause, 520–521

Cabinet-level departments, 555
Cage v. Louisiana, 308
Canon law, 10, 13
Capacity to contract, 398, 409, 413–416
Capital offenses, 298
Capital punishment, 263
Capture, personal property and, 478
Case or controversy, 178–182
Case requirement, 178–182
Cases. *See also E.I. DuPont de Nemours & Co., Inc. v. Christopher*
    analysis of, 19–21
    reading, 15
Case (trespass on the case), 395
Causation
    of criminal offense, 274–276
    proximate cause and, 520–521
Cause of action, statutes of limitations and, 191–192
Certiorari
    petition for, 308–311, 313
    writ of, 89, 91
Chancellor, 13–14
Chapman v. Mitchell, 322
Charitable institutions, immunity from legal action, 178, 203–205
Child custody, divorce and, 375, 376–380
Children. *See* Child custody; Child support; Family law
Child support
    divorce and, 364, 376–379, 380
    marriage and, 338–342
    nature and extent of, 363–370
CHINS (child in need of supervision) proceeding, 370
Citizenship, diversity of citizenship jurisdiction and, 78–79, 81–83
Civil Justice Reform Act (CJRA), 650
Civil law, 141–142
    contracts, 49–50
    criminal law versus, 42–49
    due process and, 37
    torts, 49
Civil procedure, 96–140. *See also* Rules of evidence
    informal discovery, 100
    overview of, 97–100
    pretrial procedure. *See* Civil trial, pretrial procedure
    settlement conference, 101
    trial. *See* Civil trial
Civil rights, natural law and, 2

Civil Rights Act of 1964, 596
    Title VII of, 596–619
    affirmative action, 602–611
    BFOQ defense, 598–601
    discrimination theories, 597
    disparate impact discrimination, 597, 598, 601–602
    disparate treatment discrimination, 597, 598–601, 602
    employer defenses, 598–601
    Equal Employment Opportunity Commission, 611
    gender-based discrimination, 614–619
    protected classes and, 596–597
    religion, 619–622
    remedies, 601–602
Civil Rights Acts of 1866 and 1871, 622
Civil suit, 42
Civil trial, 117–125
    appeals and, 61
    definition, 117
    examination of witnesses, 121–125
    execution, 134–136
    judgment, 134
    jury selection, 117–119
    jury verdict, 60, 130
    motions, 129–130
    opening statements, 119–120
    posttrial motions, 130–134
    proceedings during, 118–119
    production of evidence, 120–121
Civil trial, pretrial procedure, 100–117
    discovery, 97, 114–117
    filing of complaint, 97, 105, 106
    hiring of lawyer, 100–105
    informal discovery, 100
    pleadings, 105–107
    pretrial conference, 99, 115
    pretrial motions, 110–114
    service of process, 105–110
    summons, 97, 105, 107
Civil wrongs, agreements to commit, 419–422
Clean Air Act, 582, 587
Clean hands, 14
Clean Water Act, 583, 587
Code Napoleon, 142
Code of Civil Procedure, 105, 396
Coercion, as defense to criminal offense, 278–281
Coke, Edward, 12
Collateral source rule, 547
Collective bargaining, 634

Collusion, 178
Comity, 171–174
"Commentaries on American Law" (Kent), 12
"Commentaries on the Laws of England" (Blackstone), 12, 256
Common law, 141. *See also* Common law remedies; Precedent
  contracts and, 395–396
  criminal law and, 257
  development of, 11–13
  employment law, 594
  equity court and, 13–14
  mens rea and, 267
  Norman invasion and, 10–11
  origins of, 9–10
  pleadings and, 105
  private property and, 449
  property and, 381
  stare decisis, 150–151, 155
  trespass, 491
Common law lien, 245
Common law marriage, 342
Common law remedies, 214–229
  for breach of contract, 438–440
  compensatory damages, 216–222
  ejectment, 214
  exemplary damages, 222–223
  liquidated damages, 226–229
  money damages, 14
  nominal damages, 226
  punitive damages, 222–226
  replevin, 214
  restitution and, 246–248
Community property, 357–358, 387–388, 454–455
Comparative negligence, 526–528
Compensatory damages, 216–222
Competency, contract and, 397
Competency of evidence, 125–126
Complaint
  civil, 97, 105, 106
  criminal, 96
Comprehensive Environmental Response, Compensation and Liability Act (CERCLA), 587
Concurrence, 267
Concurrent ownership, 454
Condition, 409
Condition precedent, 435
Condition subsequent, 435
Conflict of laws, 165–169
  contracts, 168–169
  torts, 166–168

Confusion, personal property and, 481
Conscience, court of, equity court and, 236–239
Consent agreements, 603
Consent to contract, 403–408
  duress, 404
  fraud, 405–406
  misrepresentation, 406
  mistake, 406–408
  undue influence, 404–405
Consideration, 50, 396, 397, 408–413
Conspiracy, 276
Constitution, 3, 142, 144
  amendments to, 145. *See also specific amendments*
  policymaking and, 23–30
  supremacy of, 146–147
Constitutional law. *See also* Due process
  basis of federal court system, 77
  case or controversy requirement, 178–172
  courts and, 59
  full faith and credit, 66
  limitations on criminalization, 258–263, 282
  privacy right, 258–259
  trial right, 306–307
Constitutions, as sources of United States law, 142
Constructive service, 107
Consumer Credit Protection Act (CCPA), 580
Contingent fee, 100
Continuity, of law, 6–7
Contract, 49–53. *See also* Breach of contract; Contract law; Contract performance
  against public policy, 417–419
  bilateral, 398
  to commit civil wrongs, 419–422
  to commit crimes, 419
  consideration, 50, 396, 397, 408–413
  definition, 397
  duration exceeding one year, 424
  illegal, 416–422
  immunity from legal action through, 208–210
  interference with contract relations and, 503
  parol evidence rule and, 426–428
  statutes of frauds, 422–428
  third-party beneficiary, 433–435
  unenforceable, 398
  unilateral, 398
  validity, 397–398
  void or voidable, 398, 405
  written, 422–428

Contract law, 3, 49–53. *See also* Breach of
      contract; Consent to contract; Contract;
      Contract performance
   acceptance, 50, 400–403
   agreement and, 397, 398–399
   capacity to contract, 398, 409, 413–416
   common law and, 13
   conflict of laws, 168–169, 395
   consent. *See* Consent to contract
   consideration, 50, 396, 397, 408–413
   counteroffer, 400
   definition, 396
   due process and, 32
   history of, 395–397
   illegal contract, 416–422
   intention of parties, 398–399
   offer, 50, 399–400
   option, 400
   rescission, 232–236, 406–408, 430
   restitution, 404, 406–408
   statutes of frauds, 422–428
   third-party beneficiary, 433–435
Contract performance, 428–435. *See also* Breach
      of contract
   accord, 428–429
   anticipatory repudiation, 429
   assignment of rights, 430–433
   delegation of duties, 430–433
   discharge, 429–430
   novation, 430
   recission, 232–236, 406–408, 430
   satisfaction, 428, 429
   third-party beneficiary and, 433–438
   warranties, 429
Contributory negligence, 525–526
Controversy requirement, 178–182
Conversion, 496
Coppage v. Kansas, 595
Corbin, Arthur, 396
Corporation
   citizenship rules for, 79
   in personam jurisdiction over, 67–69
   substituted service on designated agent, 107
   vicarious liability of, 273
Corpus Juris Civilis, 142
Counterclaim, 108–109
Counteroffer, 400
Court-annexed ADR, 650, 651–655
Court-annexed arbitration, 668–672
Court of Appeals for the Federal Circuit, 88
Court of conscience, equity court as, 236–239
Court of Military Appeals, 77, 91

Courts, 59–60. *See also* Appellate courts; Federal
      court system; State court system
   constitutionality of statutes and, 146–147
   decision making by, 149–165. *See also* Foreign
      law, recognition of; Precedent
   of limited jurisdiction, 62
   as source of United States law, 148
   statutory construction and, 148–149
   trial, 60–61
Covenant, 395
Covenants, 473–476
Creation, personal property and, 477
Creditor beneficiary, 433
Credit protection, Federal Trade Commission
      and, 579–581
Crimes. *See also* Criminal offense
   agreements to commit, 419
   classification of, 257–258, 273
   definition, 256
   felony, 42, 257–258
   misdemeanor, 42, 258
   treason, 42
Criminal action, 42
Criminal justice, 282, 284–285
Criminal law, 256–263. *See also* Criminal offense;
      Model Penal Code
   civil law versus, 42–49
   classification of crimes, 257–258, 267
   constitutional limits on criminalization and,
      258–263, 282
   due process and, 37
   Equal Protection Clause and, 259–263
   imposition of punishment and, 263
   sources of, 257
Criminal negligence, 268, 272, 273
Criminal offense, 263. *See also* Crimes
   causation, 274–276
   criminal state of mind (*mens rea*), 267–273
   defenses, 277–281
   failure to act, 266
   inchoate crime, 276
   intent requirements and, 271–273
   possession offenses, 266–267
   Racketeer Influenced and Corrupt
      Organization Act and, 277
   status crimes, 267
   strict liability, 273
   vicarious liability, 273
   wrongful act (*actus reus*), 263–266
Criminal procedure, 288. *See also* Criminal trial;
      Criminal trial, pretrial procedure
Criminal state of mind, 267–273

Criminal statutes, 148
Criminal trial, 306–314
  appeal, 61, 313
  district courts and, 77
  fair and public trial, 312
  habeas corpus, 313–314
  harmless-error doctrine and, 308–311
  jury trial, 311–312
  prosecution, 312
  right to, 306–307
  sentencing, 312–313
  speedy trial, 312
Criminal trial, pretrial procedure, 282–306
  arraignment, 306
  arrest, 283, 286–288
  bail, 298–304
  custodial interrogation, 291–292
  grand jury, 305–306, 307
  investigatory detentions (stop and frisk),
    288–291
  line-ups, 305
  preliminary hearing, 305
  right to attorney and, 304–305
  searches and seizures, 292–297
Cross examination, of witnesses, 121
Cruel and unusual punishment, 263
Curia Regis, 11
Custodial arrest, 292
Custodial interrogation, 291–292
Custodial parent, 351
Custom. *See* Historical jurisprudence

Damages, 20, 216. *See also* Common law
    remedies; Equitable remedies
  noneconomic, 546
  punitive, 546–547
Death penalty, 263
Debt, 395
Debt collection, 580
Debt of another, agreement to answer for,
    423–424
Declaratory judgment, 14, 248–249
Defamation, 502–503
Default, 109
Defendant, 19
  criminal, 307
  definition, 19
  jurisdiction over, 65–67
Defense, 108
Defenses, for criminal offenses, 277–281
Delegation, administrative agencies and, 570
Delegation of duties, 430–433

Demurrer, 111
Denial, 108
Departments, cabinet-level, 555
Depositions, 114–115
  motion for summary judgment and, 111
  oral, 114–115
  written, 115
Detention, investigatory, 288–292
Detinue, 395
Dictum, 20, 151
Direct examination, of witnesses, 121
Directed verdict, 130
Disabled people, employment discrimination
    against, 622–625
Discharge from a duty to perform contract,
    429–430
Discovery, 97, 114–117
  informal, 100
  reforms in, 96–97
Discretionary appeal, 313
Discrimination. *See* Employment discrimination
Dismiss, motion to, 111
Disparate impact discrimination, 597, 598,
    601–602
Disparate treatment discrimination, 597,
    598–601, 602
District courts. *See* U.S. district courts
Diversity of citizenship jurisdiction, 78–79, 81–83
Divorce, 371–388
  alimony and, 375–376
  child custody and, 376–380
  child support and, 364, 380
  conclusion of, 388
  jurisdiction and, 374
  mensa et thoro (legal separation) and, 371
  no-fault, 371, 372–374, 375
  procedural requirements for, 374–375
  property division and, 375, 380–388
  separation agreement and, 375
Domestic relations law. *See* Family law
Domicile, 66
Donee, 481
Donee beneficiary, 433
Donor, 481
Dred Scott case, 31
Due process, 30–42
  exclusionary rule, 292
  guilt beyond a reasonable doubt and, 307–308
  privacy right and, 258–259
  procedural, 37–42, 69
  state's right to criminalize conduct and,
    259–263

Due process (*continued*)
  substantive, 31–37
  summons and, 107
Duress
  contract law and, 404
  as defense to criminal offense, 278–281
Duties, delegation of, 430–433
Duty of care, 512–516

Easement, 473
Economic regulation, due process and, 32
Economy, law and, 7–8
E.I. DuPont de Nemours & Co., Inc. v. Christopher,
    15–19
  absence of precedent and, 161
  analysis of, 19–21
  brief for, 21–23
  Erie doctrine and, 86
  limited interlocutory appeal, 61
  motion to dismiss in, 111
Eighth Amendment
  bail and, 298
  cruel and unusual punishment and, 263
Ejectment, 214
Eminent domain, 456, 458–469
Employment-at-will doctrine, 594, 595
Employment discrimination, 596–645. *See also*
    Civil Rights Act of 1964, Title VII of
  affirmative action, 602–611
  age, 625–631
  disabled people, 622–625
  equality and, 593–594
  gender-based, 614
  religion, 619–622
  sexual preference, 631–634
  union movement and, 596, 635–643
Employment regulation. *See also* Civil Rights Act
    of 1964, Title VII of
  history of, 594–595
  state judicial remedies, 595–596
  state wrongful termination legislation, 596
  unions and, 634–643
Enabling act, 558
English Bill of Rights, 263
English common law. *See* Common law
Entrapment, as defense, 278
Environmental law, 458
  air pollution, 582–583
  Environmental Protection Agency and, 555,
    557, 581–587
  hazardous wastes disposal, 586–587
  pesticide control, 586

real property and, 450–451
  water pollution, 583–586
Environmental Protection Agency (EPA), 555,
    557, 581–587
Equal Credit Opportunity Act (ECOA), 580, 581
Equal Employment Opportunity Commission
    (EEOC), 611
Equality, employment discrimination and,
    593–594
Equal Protection Clause, 259–263
  of Fourteenth Amendment, 259
  state's right to criminalize conduct and,
    259–263
Equitable court, 13–14
Equitable distribution, of property, 381–387
Equitable maxims, 239–242
Equitable precedent, 14
Equitable remedies, 215, 229–251
  breach of contract, 443
  court of conscience and, 236–239
  declaratory judgement, 14, 248–249
  equitable maxims and, 239–242
  injunction, 14, 229–232
  jury trial and, 249–251
  recission, 232–236
  reformation, 232–236
  restitution, 245–248
  specific performance, 242–245
Equity. *See also* Equitable remedies
  court of conscience, 236–239
  equitable courts, 13–14
  equitable maxims, 239–242
  jury trial, 249
Erie doctrine, 85–88, 166
Erie Railroad Company v. Tompkins, 85
Estate, 472
Estate in land, 472–473
Evidence
  admissibility of. *See* Rules of evidence
  production of, 120–121
  search and seizure, 292–298
Exclusionary rule, 292–298
Exculpatory clause, 208–210
Execution, 134–136
Executor, statutes of frauds requirement for, 423
Exemplary damages, 222–223. *See also* Punitive
    damages
Exhaustion of remedies, administrative agencies
    and, 571
Ex parte injunction, 229
Expert witness, 126
Exploratory conversation, 100

Ex post facto laws 147–148, 258
Express contract, 50
Express warranties, 429

Fact, fraud and, 405
Factual issue, 60
Failure to act, as criminal act, 266
Fair Credit Reporting Act, 580, 581
Fair Debt Collection Practices Act, 580
Fair trial, right to, 312
False imprisonment, 499–502
Family. *See also* Family law
   changes in, 320
   definition of, 330–337
   immunity from legal action of members of,
    178, 205–207, 359, 370
Family autonomy, 320–329
Family law, 320–394. *See also* Adoption; Divorce;
   Foster care; Marriage
   annulment, 370–371
   child-parent relationship and, 359–363
   child support and, 363–370
   decision making in families and, 358–359
   definition of family and, 330–337
   evidentiary privilege and, 178, 205–207, 359,
    370
   family autonomy and, 320–329
   father's rights and, 321, 322
   legal separation and, 371
   noneconomic obligations and, 370
   spousal economic considerations and, 357–358
Father, role of, 321, 322. *See also* Family law
Featherbedding, 639–643
Federal Arbitration Act, 658, 665
Federal Bail Act of 1984, 299
Federal Bankruptcy Court, 77
Federal court system, 77–91. *See also* U.S. district
   courts; U.S. Supreme Court
   civil procedure and, 96
   Erie doctrine and, 85–88
   removal from state to, 83–85
   U.S. courts of appeals, 77, 88–89, 90
   venue and, 79, 83
Federal Environmental Pesticide Control Act,
   586
Federal government
   legislative power and, 144–145
   supremacy of, 145–146
Federal Insecticide, Fungicide, and Rodenticide
   Act (FIFRA), 582, 586
Federal question jurisdiction, 77–78

Federal Register, 561–562
Federal Reporter, 19
Federal Rules of Civil Procedure, 86, 96, 105,
   107, 651, 655
Federal Rules of Evidence, 125
Federal Tort Claims Act, 198
Federal Trade Commission, consumer credit
   protection and, 579–581
Federal Water Pollution Control Act, 582
Fee simple, 472
Felony, 42, 257–258
Feudalism, 10
Fifth Amendment
   due process and, 30, 31, 32, 33
   privacy right and, 259
   self-incrimination and, 291
   Takings Clause, 456, 458–469
Final decision, administrative agencies and, 571,
   572
Finding, personal property and, 478–481
First Amendment, privacy right and, 259
First impression, case of, 20
Fixture, 451–454
Foreign law, recognition of, 165–174. *See also*
   Conflict of laws
   comity, 171–174
   full faith and credit, 169–171
Foreseeability, proximate cause and, 520,
   521
Forum non conveniens, doctrine of, 72–73
Forum state, 65–66
   precedent in, 161
Foster care, 356–357
Fourteenth Amendment, 256
   due process and, 30, 31, 32, 33, 37, 292
   Equal Protection Clause, 259
   privacy right and, 259
   rights of accused, 311
Fourth Amendment
   investigatory detention and, 288
   privacy right and, 259
   searches and seizures and, 292
Fraud
   contract law and, 405–406
   statute of frauds and, 422–428
French legacy, in law, 10
Frisk, 288
   stop and, 288–292
Front pay, 602
Full faith and credit, 66, 169–171
Fundamental liberties, 259
Fundamental rights, 33

Gays, adoption and, 343, 346–350
Gender-based employment discrimination, 614–619
General appearance, 66
General damages, 217
General intent crimes, 267
General jurisdiction, courts of, 64
Genuine assent, contract and, 397
Gift, personal property and, 481
Good Samaritans, 513
Goss v. Lopez, 8
Government. *See* Property, government regulation of
Government officials, immunity from legal action, 178, 199–203
Governments. *See also under* Sovereigns
Grand jury, 305–306, 307
Gratuitous bailments, 482
Gross negligence, 440
Guilty plea, 306, 312

Habeas corpus, 313–314
Hardship, 14, 243
Harmless-error doctrine, 291, 308–311
Harold II of England, 10
Hazardous wastes disposal, statutes on, 586–587
Hearing, administrative agencies and, 570
Hearsay rule, 126
Henry I of England, 11
Henry II of England, 11–12
Henry III of England, 12
Henry VIII of England, 14
Hiss v. Hampton, 258
Historical jurisprudence, 2–3
Holding, 20, 151
Homicide, 274
Homosexuals
    adoption and, 343, 346–350
    employment discrimination and, 631
Hung jury, 311

Identity of claims, *res judicata* and, 196
Identity of parties, *res judicata* and, 195–196
Illegal contracts, 416–422
Illusory promise, 409
Immunity from legal action, 178, 198–207
    charitable institutions, 178, 203–205
    contract and, 208–210
    family members, 178, 205–207, 359, 370
    government officials, 178, 199–203
    sovereign immunity, 178, 198–199
Impeachment of testimony, 151

Implied-in-face contract, 50
Implied-in-law contract, 50
Implied warranties, 429
Imputed negligence (vicarious liability), 273, 533–537
Inchoate crime, 276
Independent contractor, negligence and, 534
Indictment, 306, 307
Infamous crimes, 306
Infliction of mental distress, 503–504
Informal discovery, 100
Inheritance, personal property and, 482
Injunction, 14, 20, 229–232
Injunctive relief, 230–232
In personam jurisdiction, 65–66
    long-arm statutes and, 66, 68
    over corporations, 67–69
    summons and, 66, 67
Inquiry, 400
In rem jurisdiction
    district courts and, 83
    over property, 69
    state courts and, 69
Insanity
    capacity to contract and, 415–416
    as defense, 277
In specie, 245
Intangible personal property, 451
Intent, as requirement of criminal offense, 271–273
Intentional tort, 49, 492–508
    assault, 492, 493–496
    battery, 264, 274, 492–496
    conversion, 496
    defamation, 502–503, 504
    definition, 492
    false imprisonment, 499–502
    infliction of mental distress, 503–504
    interference with contract relations, 503
    invasion of privacy, 493–496, 504–508
    malicious prosecution, 499
    punitive damages and, 222
    trespass, 496–499
Intention of the parties, 398–399
Interference with contract relations, 503
Interlocutory injunction, 229
Interracial adoption, 344, 345
Interrogation, custodial, 291–292
Interrogatories, 115
Intoxication
    capacity to contract and, 416
    as defense, 277–278

Investigative power, of administrative agencies, 561, 565–569
Investigatory detentions, 288–292
Invitee, 516–517
Involuntary adoption, 350
Irresistible impulse test, 277
Issue, 20

J.N.O.V. *See* Judgment notwithstanding the verdict
John, King of England, 30
Joint and several liability, 546
Joint custody, 376, 379
Joint tenancy, 454
Judge
  bench trial and, 60
  civil trial and, 117
  immunity of, 199–203
  jury trial and, 60
  sentencing and, 312–313
  settlement conference and, 655–656
  special verdict and, 60
Judge-made law, 149–150. *See also* Precedent
Judgment, 134
  appeal of, 134
  notwithstanding the verdict, 130–133
Judgment creditor, 65, 134
Judgment debtor, 65, 134
Judgment notwithstanding the verdict (j.n.o.v.), 130–133
Judicature Acts of 1873 and 1875, 14
Judicial decision making, 149–165. *See also* Foreign law, recognition of; Precedent
Judicial remedies. *See* Common law remedies; Equitable remedies
Judicial review, by administrative agencies, 570–575
Judiciary, policymaking role of, 23–30
Jurisdiction, 62–77. *See also In personam* jurisdiction; *In rem* jurisdiction; Subject matter jurisdiction; Venue
  diversity of citizenship, 78–79, 81–83
  divorce and, 374
  federal question, 77–78
  limited, 62
  long-arm statute, 66, 68
  minimum contacts rule for, 65–66
  original, 62, 89, 91
  over corporations, 67–69
  procedural due process requirements, 69
  removal, 83–85
  of U.S. Supreme Court, 89, 91

Jurisdictional amount, 79, 668
Jurisprudence, 1
  historical, 2–3
  sociological, 5
Jury, selection of, 117–119
Jury trial, 60–61
  in civil trial, 60
  court-annexed ADR and, 650, 651–655
  criminal, 311–312
  in equity cases, 249–251
  procedures for. *See* Civil procedure
  right to, 60, 61, 117, 249, 311–312
  selection of jury and, 117–119
  special verdict and, 60
  summary, 99
Jury verdict, 130
Justice, 7–8

Kent, James, 12
Knowingly, as category of intent, 271, 272, 273
Kolender v. Lawson, 258

Labor-Management Relations Act of 1947. *See* Taft-Hartley Act
Labor-Management Reporting and Disclosure Act of 1959, 643
Laches, 240, 243
Landmarks preservation programs, 458
Landrum-Griffin Act. *See* Labor-Management Reporting and Disclosure Act
Land use. *See* Real property
Larceny, 257, 263–264
Latin legacy, in law, 10–11
Law
  adaptability of, 7
  analytical positivism and, 4
  continuity and stability of, 6–7
  definition, 1–6
  economy of, 8
  historical jurisprudence and, 2–3
  justice and, 7–8
  legal realism, 5
  natural, 2
  objectives of, 6–8
  origin of in United States. *See* Common law
  as power, 1
  private, 6
  procedural, 31
  public, 6
  public policy and, 8
  sociology and, 5–6
  speed and, 7–8

Law (*continued*)
  substantive, 31
  utilitarian, 3–4
Leading questions, of witnesses, 121–125
Leasehold, 473
Legal detriment, 408–409
Legal literature, common law and, 12
Legal realism, 5
Legal separations, 371
Legal sociology, 5–6
Legislation, as source of United States law, 142–148
Lesbians, adoption and, 343, 346–350
Lex fori, 168
Lex loci contractus, 169
Lex loci delicti commissi, 166–168
Lex loci solutionis, 168
Liability. *See also* Negligence; Strict liability
  joint and several, 546
  vicarious, 273, 533–537
Libel, 503
Liberty, due process and, 31
License, 473
Licensee, 517
Lien, 134, 245
Life, due process and, 31
Life estate, 473
Limitations in seeking relief, 178–198. *See also* Immunity from legal action
  Act of State doctrine, 189
  case or controversy, 178–182
  mootness, 182–186
  political questions, 186–189
  res judicata, 195–198
  statute of limitations, 189–195
Limited jurisdiction, 62
Limiting construction, 146
Line-up, 305
Liquidated damages, 226–229
Litigation, dissatisfaction with, 649–650. *See also* Alternative dispute resolution
Locke, John, 31, 449
Long-arm statute, 66, 68

Magna Charta, 11, 30–31, 263
Magnuson-Moss Federal Warranty Act, 429
Mala in se crime, 257, 267
Mala prohibita crime, 257, 267, 273
Malicious prosecution, 499
Malpractice, 509–512

Mandatory injunction, 229
Mapp v. Ohio, 292
Marbury v. Madison, 146–147
Marital property, 381
Marriage, 337–342. *See also* Divorce; Family law
  agreement in consideration of, 423
  annulment of, 370–371
  child support and, 338–342
  common law, 342
  legal separation and, 371
  solemnization ceremony for, 342
Marshall, John, 146–147
Material breach of contract, 435–438
Material fact, 405
Materiality of evidence, 125
Maxims, equitable, 239–242
Mediation, 99, 672–674
Mensa et thoro divorce, 371
Mens rea (criminal state of mind), 267–273
Mental distress, infliction of, 503–504
Michigan Rules of Civil Procedure, 96
Military Justice Act, 91
Minimum contacts rule, for jurisdiction, 65–66
Mini-trial, 99, 674–675
Minor, capacity to contract and, 413–415
Miranda v. Arizona, 151, 291–292
Miranda warnings, 151, 291–292
Misdemeanor, 42, 258
Misrepresentation, 406
Missouri Compromise, 31
Mistake, in contract law, 406–408
Mistrial, 125
M'Naghten Rule, 277
Model Penal Code, 257, 264, 265, 267, 271–273, 277
Money damages, 14
Moore v. City of East Cleveland, 456
Moot cases, 182–186
More, Thomas, Sir, 14
Motion(s)
  to dismiss, 111
  for judgment notwithstanding the verdict, 130–133
  for new trial, 130–133
  for nonsuit, 129–130
  postrial, 130–134
  pretrial, 110–114
  for relief from judgment, 130
  summary judgment, 60, 99, 111–114
  trial, 129–130
Multiethnic Placement Act of 1994, 344
Mutual benefit bailment, 482

National Conference of Commissioners on Uniform State Laws, 396
National Environmental Policy Act (NEPA), 582
National Labor Relations Act. *See* Wagner Act
National Labor Relations Board (NLRB), 638–643
National Labor Relations Board v. Jones & Laughlin Steel Corporation, 595
Natural law, 2
Necessaries, 357, 370
  minors and, 414
Negligence, 491, 508–537
  assumption of risk, 525, 526
  business visitor, 516–520
  comparative, 526–528
  contributory, 525–526
  criminal, 268, 272, 273
  definition, 508–509
  duty of care, 512–516
  imputed, 533–537
  invitees, 516–517
  licensee, 517
  malpractice, 509–512
  no-fault liability statutes, 537
  product liability, 528–533
  proximate cause, 520–525
  public invitee, 516
  strict liability, 273
  trespasser, 517
Negotiable Instruments Law, 396
Neutrals, 651
New trial, motion for, 130–133
Ninth Amendment, privacy right and, 259
No-fault divorce, 372–374, 375
No-fault liability statutes, 537
Nolo contendere, 306
Nominal damages, 226
Noncustodial parent, 351–356
Noneconomic damages, 546
Nonfeasance, 396
Nonjury trial. *See* Bench trial
Nonsuit, motion for, 129–130
Norman invasion, common law and, 10–11
Not guilty plea, 306
Notice, administrative agencies and, 570
Notice of appeal, 90
Novation, 430
Nuisance, 469–472

Objection, failure as waiver of right to appeal, 61
Occupational Health Review Commission, 576

Occupational Safety and Health Act, 575
Occupational Safety and Health Administration (OSHA), 575–579
Offer, 50, 399–400
Open adoption, 356
Opening statements, 119–120
Option, 400
Oral contract, 50
Oral deposition, 114–115
Organized crime, 277
Original jurisdiction, 62, 89, 91
Ownership, of property, 454–455

Parental immunity, 205–207
Parents. *See* Family law
Parole, 263
Parol evidence rule, 426–428
Penal statutes, 148–149
Permanent alimony, 375–376
Permanent injunction, 229
Person, defense of as defense to criminal offense, 278
Personal jurisdiction. See *In personam* jurisdiction
Personal property, 477–482
  accession, 478
  bailment and, 482–486
  capture, 478
  confusion, 481
  creation, 477
  definition, 451
  finding, 478–481
  fixture versus, 452–454
  gift, 481
  inheritance, 482
  intangible, 451
  purchase, 477
  tangible, 451
Personal service, 107
Personalty. *See* Personal property
Pesticide control, statutes on, 582, 586
Petition, for adoption, 351–356
Plaintiff, 19, 307
Plea, 306
Plea bargaining, 306
Pleadings, 105–107
Police power, 145, 455–456. *See also* Property, government regulation of
Policymaking, judiciary and, 23–30
Political questions doctrine, 186–189
Pollution. *See* Environmental law
Possession offenses, as criminal act, 266–267

Posttrial motions, 130–134
Power, law as, 1
Practicality, 14
Precedent, 149–160, 150
  absence of, 160–165
  common law and, 12
  equitable, 14
  following, 150
  requirements for, 155
  retroactive vs. prospective effect of, 155–160
  rule of the case and, 151–154
Preferred custody statutes and, 376, 379–380
Pregnancy Discrimination Act (PDA), 614
Preliminary hearing, 305
Preliminary injunction, 229
Pretrial conference, 99, 115
Pretrial motions, 110–114
Pretrial order, 99
Preventive detention, 299–304
Prima facie, 409
  discrimination and, 597
Principle of bar and merger, 195, 196–198
Privacy
  constitutional right to, 258–259
  invasion of, 493–496, 504–508
Private law, 6
Private nuisance, 470–472
Private trials, 678
Privilege, 126–129
Privity, *res judicata* and, 196
Privity of estate, 474
Probable cause, 283, 286–288
Procedural due process, 37–42
  for jurisdiction, 69
Procedural law, 31
Procedure. *See* Civil procedure; Criminal
  procedure
Process, 96, 107. *See* Service of process;
  Summons
Production of documents, 115
Product liability
  negligence and, 528–533
  strict liability and, 540–545
Prohibitory injunction, 229
Promise, consideration and, 408–409
Promisee, 408, 409
Promisor, 409, 424
Property, 3. *See also* Personal property; Real
  property
  annulment and, 371
  bailment, 482–486
  classifications of, 451–454

common law and, 381
community, 357–358, 387–388
defense of as defense to criminal offense, 278
divorce and, 375, 380–388
due process and, 31
equitable distribution of, 381–387
jurisdiction over. *See In rem* jurisdiction
marital, 381
ownership, 454–455
political questions on rights to, 186–189
regulation of. *See* Property, government
  regulation of
separate, 358, 381
title, 455
women's rights on, 357
Property, government regulation of, 455–472
  eminent domain, 456, 458–469
  environmental laws, 450–451, 458
  nuisance, 469–472
  police power, 455–456
  taxation, 469
  zoning, 450, 456
Proprietary functions, 199
Prosecution, of criminal case, 312
Prosecutor, 312
Prospective decision, 155–160
Protected classes, Title VII of Civil Rights Act of
  1964 and, 596–597
Proximate cause, 274–276, 520–525
Public invitee, 516
Public law, 6
Public nuisance, 470–472
Public policy, 208
  contracts against, 417–419
  law and, 8
Public trial, right to, 312
Punishment, imposition of, 263
Punitive damages, 222–226, 546–547
  for breach of contract, 440–443
Purchase, of personal property, 477
Purposely, as category of intent, 271, 272

Questions of fact, 60
Questions of law, 60
Quiet title action, 477

Race, adoption and, 343–344, 345
Racketeer Influenced and Corrupt Organization
  Act (RICO), 277
Real property, 3, 472–477
  adverse possession, 476–477
  agreement conveying interest in, 424–426

Real property (*continued*)
  covenants, 473–476
  definition, 451
  easements, 473
  estates in land, 472–473
  history, 472
  history of regulation of, 449–451
  licenses, 473
  recording system, 477
Realty. *See* Real property
Reasonable doubt
  causation beyond, 274
  harmless-error doctrine and, 308–311
Reasonable force, 278
Recklessly, as category of intent, 272,
  273
Recognizance, 299
Recording system, for real property, 477
Redirect examination, of witnesses, 121
Reformation, 232–236
Rehabilitation Act of 1973, 622
Rehabilitative alimony, 376
Relevancy of evidence, 125
Relief from judgment, motion for, 130
Religion, employment discrimination based on,
  619–622
Remanding a case, 20
Remedies. *See* Breach of contract; Common law
  remedies; Equitable remedies
Removal jurisdiction, 83–85
Replevin, 214, 444
Reply, motion to dismiss and, 111
Request for admissions, 115
Request for waiver of service, 107
Rescission, 232–236, 406–408, 430
Res gestae, 126
Res ipsa loquitur, 528–529
Res judicata, 155, 195–198
  full faith and credit and, 169
Resource Conservation and Recovery Act,
  586–587
Restatement of Contracts, 396
Restitution, 232, 245–248, 404, 406–408
Retroactive decision, 155–160
Reversal, judgment of, 20
Reverse discrimination, 603
RFOA defense, 626
RICO. *See* Racketeer Influenced and Corrupt
  Organization Act
Riders, 143
Rights, fundamental, 33
Rights, assignment of, 430–433

Ripeness
  administrative agencies and, 571
  for judicial determination, 179
Rivers and Harbors Act, 582
Rule-making power, of administrative agencies,
  561, 562–565
Rule of the case, 151–154
Rules Enabling Act, 105
Rules of evidence, 125–129
  best evidence rule, 126
  competency, 125–126
  hearsay rule, 126
  materiality, 125
  mistrial and, 125
  privilege, 126–129
  relevancy, 125

Safe Drinking Water Act, 583
Sale of goods
  statute of frauds and, 426–428
  UCC Remedies for Breach of Contract for, 444
Satisfaction, contract performance and, 428, 429
Saving clause, statutes of limitation and, 192
Scope of employment, imputed negligence and,
  533
Search and seizure, 292–298
Securities and Exchange Commission (SEC), 555,
  556
Selective incorporation approach, due process
  and, 33
Self-incrimination, 291
Sentencing, 312–313
Separate property, 358, 381
Separation, legal, 371
Separation agreement, 375
Separation of powers, 561
Service of process, 107–110
  constructive, 107
  substituted or alternative, 107
  summons, 66, 67
Settlement conferences, 101, 655–657
Seventh Amendment, 249, 668
  alternative dispute resolution and, 651–652
  jury trial and, 117
Severalty ownership, 454
Sex discrimination, in employment, 631–634
Sexual harassment, 614
Significant relationship rule, 166–168, 169
Sixth Amendment, rights of accused and, 305,
  306, 311
Slander, 503
Slander per se, 503

Social regulation, due process and, 32
Sociological jurisprudence, 5
Solicitation, 276
Solid Wastes Disposal Act, 586
Sources of United States law, 141–149
  administrative agencies, 149
  constitutions, 142
  courts, 148
  criminal law, 257
  legislation, 142–148
Sovereigns
  Act of State doctrine and, 189
  immunity of, 178, 198–199
Sovereignty, 169
Special appearance, 66
Special damages, 217
Special verdict, 60
Specific intent crime, 268
Specific performance, 242–245
Speed, of law, 7–8
Speedy trial, right to, 312
Spousal support. *See* Alimony
Stability, of law, 6–7
Standing, 179–182
Stare decisis, 150–151, 155
State court system, 62, 63
  civil procedure and, 96
  Erie doctrine and, 85–88
  removal from to federal courts, 83–85
  subject matter jurisdiction in, 63–65
  venue, 79
State law. *See also* Foreign law, recognition of
  constitutions of, 142
  police power of, 145
  powers of, 144, 145–146
  Uniform Commercial Code and, 143–144
State procedural due process, 37
Status crimes, 267
Statute of Laborers, 594
Statute of limitations, 189–195, 398, 547
Statute of Westminster, 263, 395, 491
Statutes, 142–143
  constitutionality of, 146–147
  criminal, 148, 257
  penal, 148–149
  statutory construction and, 148–149
Statutes of frauds, 422–428
Statutory construction, 148–149
Statutory lien, 245
Stop and frisk (investigatory detentions), 288–292
Strict construction, 148–149

Strict liability, 273, 537–545
  abnormally dangerous activities and, 537–540
  product liability and, 540–545
Subject matter jurisdiction
  of state courts, 63–65
  of U.S. district courts, 77–83
Subpoena, 13, 120, 306
Subpoena duces tecum, 120
Substantive due process, 31–37
Substantive law, 31
Substituted service, 107
Summary judgment, motion for, 99, 111–114
Summary jury trial (SJT), 99, 675–678
Summons, 97, 105. *See also* Service of process
  in personam jurisdiction and, 66, 67
  substituted or alternative service, 107
Superfund law, 587
Supremacy clause, 145–146
Supreme Court. *See* U.S. Supreme Court
Suspect classification, 259

Taft-Hartley Act, 639–643, 658
Takings Clause, 456, 458–469
Tangible personal property, 451
Taxation, of property, 469
Temporary restraining order (TRO), 229
Tenancy by the entirety, 454
Tenancy in common, 454
Tenth Amendment, 145
Termination of offer, 399–400
Terry v. Ohio, 288
Third-party beneficiary, 433–435
Title, 455
Title VII, of Civil Rights Act of 1964. *See* Civil
  Rights Act of 1964, Title VII of
Toll, statute of limitations and, 192
Tort liability, immunity from. *See* Immunity
  from legal action
Torts, 49. *See also* Intentional tort; Negligence;
  Strict liability
  conflict of laws, 166–168
  definition, 491
  function, 492
  historical evolution, 491–492
  natural law philosophy of, 2
  reform, 545–547
  significant relationship rule, 166–168
  unintentional, 49
  wrongful discharge of employee, 595–596
Treason, 42
Trespass, 395, 496–499
  common law and, 491

Trespasser, 517
Trespass on the case, 395
Trial. *See also* Jury trial
  bench, 60, 99, 117
Trial court(s), 60–61
  in state court system, 62
  U.S. Supreme Court as, 91
Trial *de novo*, 669
Trial motions, 129–130
TRO. *See* Temporary restraining order
Truth in Lending Act, 580, 581
Truth in Lending Simplification and Reform
  Act, 580–581
Tucker Act, 198
"12 motion," 111

Unclean hands, 243
Undertakings, 395, 396
Undue influence, contract law and,
  404–405
Unenforceable contract, 398
Uniform Commercial Code (UCC), 452
  anticipatory repudiation of contract, 429
  breach of contract and, 444
  conflicts of law and, 169
  development and adoption of, 143–144
  purchase or sale of goods, 396–397, 477
  specific performance, 243
  statute of frauds, 426
Uniform Sales Act, 396
Unilateral contract, 398
Unintentional tort, 49
Unions, 595
  employment discrimination and, 596, 634–643
  National Labor Relations Board and, 638–643
U.S. Claims Court, 77, 88
U.S. Court of International Trade, 77, 88
U.S. courts of appeals, 77, 88–89, 90
U.S. district courts
  civil procedure and, 96
  Erie doctrine and, 85–88
  removal jurisdiction and, 83–85
  subject matter jurisdiction of, 77–83
U.S. Supreme Court, 3, 77, 89, 91, 92
  petition for *certiorari*, 308–311, 313
U.S. Tax Court, 77
United States v. Brown, 148, 258
Unjust enrichment, 246–248
Utilitarian law, 3–4

Valid contract, 397–398
Venue, 72–77, 79, 83

Verdict
  directed, 130
  jury, 130
Vested
  property rights as, 452
  rights as, 433
Vicarious liability. *See* Imputed negligence
Victimless crimes, 258
Virginia Declaration of Rights, 263
Void or voidable contract, 398, 405
Voir dire, 118
Voluntary adoption, 350
Voluntary alternative dispute resolution,
  650–651
Voluntary arbitration, 664

Wagner Act, 595, 634, 639, 643
Walder v. United States, 151
Wanton misconduct, 517
Warrant
  for arrest, 283
  for searches and seizures, 292, 293
Warranties, 429
Water pollution, statutes on, 582, 583–586
White-collar crime, 258
William I of England, 10–11
Williston, Samuel, 396
Witnesses
  examination of, 121–125
  expert, 126
  leading questions and, 121–125
  subpoena and, 13, 120, 306
Women
  employment discrimination and, 631–634
  sexual harassment and, 614
Work product, 97, 114, 126–127
Writ, 12, 491
  of *certiorari*, 89, 91
  of *habeas corpus*, 313–314
  pleadings and, 105
  of right, 12
  of subpoena, 13, 120, 306
  of summons, 13, 97, 105, 107
Written contracts, 422–428
Written deposition, 115
Written interrogatories, 115
Wrongful act. *See Actus reus*
Wrongful Discharge from Employment Act, 596

Year Books, 12
Yellow Dog contract, 595

Zoning laws, 450–451, 456